Age of Chivalry

DATES OF THE EXHIBITION

6 November 1987 – 6 March 1988

The exhibition is sponsored by

Age of Chivalry

Art in

Plantagenet England

1200–1400

edited by
JONATHAN ALEXANDER
&
PAUL BINSKI

Royal Academy of Arts, London, 1987

Catalogue published in association with

Weidenfeld and Nicolson, London

House editor Johanna Awdry
Designed by Harry Green for
Weidenfeld and Nicolson Limited
91 Clapham High Street, London SW4 7TA

Phototypeset by Keyspools Limited, Golborne, Lancs
Printed and bound by L.E.G.O., Vicenza, Italy
Colour separations by Newsele Litho

Contents

PATRONS

Her Majesty The Queen

The Most Revd and Rt Hon.
The Lord Archbishop of Canterbury Dr Robert Runcie

His Eminence Cardinal Basil Hume
The Archbishop of Westminster

The Most Revd and Rt Hon.
The Lord Archbishop of York John Habgood

SELECTION COMMITTEE

Dr Jonathan Alexander (Chairman)	Dr Phillip Lindley
Janet Backhouse	Dr John Maddison
Dr Paul Binski	Dr Richard Marks
Claude Blair	Nigel J. Morgan
Marian Campbell	David O'Connor
John Cherry	David Park
Ranald Clouston	Ann Payne
Dr Nicola Coldstream	Dr Nigel Ramsay
Dr Thomas Cocke	Professor Lucy Freeman Sandler
Dr Barrie Cook	Veronica Sekules
Dr Paul Crossley	Brian Spencer
Nicholas Dawton	Neil Stratford
Peter Draper	Dr Charles Tracy
Dr Jane Geddes	Dr Pamela Tudor-Craig
Dr Christa Grössinger	Paul Williamson
T. A. Heslop	Dr Christopher Wilson
Donald King	

EXECUTIVE COMMITTEE

Piers Rodgers, Secretary of the Royal Academy (Chairman)

Roger de Grey, President of the Royal Academy

Frederick Gore RA, Chairman of the Exhibitions Committee of the Royal Academy

Sir Philip Powell RA, Treasurer of the Royal Academy

Norman Rosenthal, Exhibitions Secretary. Royal Academy

Kenneth Tanner, Comptroller. Royal Academy

Iain Tweedie, Deputy Head Corporate Communications, Lloyds Bank

Secretary of the Committee: Annette Bradshaw

EXHIBITION ASSISTANT: Henrietta Harris
Assistant: Julie Summers
CATALOGUE CO-ORDINATOR: MaryAnne Stevens
EXHIBITION DESIGN: Paul Williams and Alan Stanton
EXHIBITION INSTALLATION: Plowden and Smith Ltd
CONSERVATION CONSULTANTS: Anna Plowden and Peter Smith
EXHIBITION PACKING AND TRANSPORT CONTRACTOR: Momart Ltd
EXHIBITION GRAPHIC DESIGN: John and Orna Designs
PUBLICITY GRAPHIC DESIGN: Minale, Tattersfield & Partners

Sponsor's Preface

I am delighted that Lloyds Bank is sponsoring this great exhibition of the treasures of the Age of Chivalry. No British bank goes back to that time, but our forerunners in the Plantagenet period were the Lombards, who have left their name to Lombard Street.

Lloyds Bank began in Birmingham in 1765, and over the subsequent two centuries gradually spread its network across the country. We were particularly attracted to this exhibition because it brings together in a central place exhibits from towns and cities throughout the country. And its benefits will radiate back from London, through the stimulation of local exhibitions and events and the supply of education packs to schools. These education packs of Royal Academy exhibitions are already part of our sponsorship programme for youth, which also includes the National Youth Orchestra, the Young National Trust Theatre and the Royal Society of Arts Design Bursaries.

In many ways the past is still part of this country's present. Medieval churches, cathedrals and castles punctuate the landscape; many institutions have their beginnings in the Plantagenet era. If the intervening years have set us apart from the men and women of those days, this exhibition can bring them closer to us. The vitality of their art gives us an insight into the life and fabric of a society remarkable in the quality and range of its creative work. And if they did not have bank branches, at least the black horse was a familiar symbol of strength and service then as now.

Jeremy Morse

SIR JEREMY MORSE, KCMG
Chairman, Lloyds Bank

Foreword

'Age of Chivalry: Art in Plantagenet England 1200–1400' is the successor to two other exhibitions, 'The Golden Age of Anglo-Saxon Art 966–1066' held by the British Museum and the British Library in 1984–5 and 'English Romanesque Art 1066–1200' held by the Arts Council at the Hayward Gallery in 1984. Between them these three exhibitions will have made accessible to the British public nearly five centuries of their art inheritance. The exhibition starts with the accession of King Henry III in 1216 and ends with the deposition and death of the last Plantagenet King, Richard II, in 1399. These two centuries see the introduction of the Gothic style into England from France, first in architecture, later in painting and sculpture. The last loan exhibition of English Gothic art, entitled 'English Medieval Art 700–1500', was held over fifty years ago in 1930 at the Victoria and Albert Museum. It was, therefore, high time a comprehensive major exhibition devoted to English Gothic Art should take place.

The committee responsible for choosing and cataloguing the works of art has been drawn from specialists working in Museums and Universities and was co-ordinated by Dr Jonathan Alexander, Reader in the History of Art at the University of Manchester. The circle of those involved in the exhibition has extended in numerous directions and we have drawn on the expertise and advice of curators, conservators, librarians and archivists from a wide variety of institutions. All have been most generous in sharing their time and their knowledge: in many ways this has been a typically medieval collaborative venture. To those involved at the centre it has often seemed not unlike the awesome task of building a great cathedral!

The complexity of the operation, and the difficulties surrounding the transport and display of such delicate and precious objects, have not been without their cost. The Royal Academy has been fortunate indeed that Lloyds Bank, as sponsors, should have agreed to bear the risk which such a a venture necessarily entails – a risk which the Academy alone could never sustain. Not only are the guarantees that they have afforded us the largest that this institution has ever received from a single source, but their involvement in all stages of the preparation of 'Age of Chivalry' has been a great source of strength and encouragement to us. Additional but nonetheless substantial support has been received from the J. Paul Getty Junior Charitable Trust. To both we are deeply grateful.

A very positive aspect of such exhibitions is the impetus they can give to the conservation of works of art. We are also most grateful, therefore, to the City Companies who have made very generous grants by means of which a number of important exhibits have been cleaned and conserved.

It has been very encouraging from the start to receive such a positive welcome to our project. We have been exceptionally fortunate in the way in which the lending institutions have greeted our requests to borrow their greatest treasures. The National Museums, especially the British Museum, the Victoria and Albert Museum and the British Library, have each contributed with an outstanding list of their most exceptional objects. The Oxford and Cambridge colleges and the two University libraries have been equally supportive. Perhaps the greatest lender, however, has been the Church of England. From the great cathedrals to the smallest parish churches we have received nothing but collaboration and kindness, and it is due to them perhaps above all that the contents of the exhibition is as glorious and various as it is. The stained glass from churches up and down the country, for instance, will surely be one of the most memorable aspects of the exhibition.

Finally, though the loans from other countries are a comparatively small part of the whole, they include many essential objects. We are particularly aware of the support which our colleagues in Norway have afforded us in lending us certain very fragile wooden objects of a kind which must once have been common in England but which have not survived here. But when all have been so generous, it is invidious to single out names, and I must conclude by expressing our gratitude to all.

ROGER DE GREY
President, Royal Academy of Arts

Introduction

The two-hundred-year period during which the Plantagenet kings ruled England and during which the works of art in this exhibition were made was so very different from our own in so many ways: in its social structures, its religious beliefs, its moral codes, its economic organisation and also in its art and architecture. This is true even though some of our most important institutions today, such as parliament and trial by jury, have their origins in that period. The works of art in this exhibition are therefore arranged thematically or in chronological order, not according to the materials from which they were made, so as to draw attention wherever possible to the specific historical conditions within which they were produced. A knowledge of those conditions will give the viewer a greater insight into the reasons why time and skill and expense were lavished on particular works of art, and into the meanings they held for contemporaries.

An example is the censer from Ramsey Abbey (Cat. 121). We are surely helped to appreciate it as a work of art if we know that it was used at the Mass to burn incense, which was thought of even from pre-Christian times as a symbol of prayer ascending to God. The censer was designed to be swung on a chain so that the air would penetrate its perforated lid and help the incense inside it to burn. Its design also incorporates symbolic meanings: its architectural forms refer not just simply to contemporary styles of canopies and tracery, but to the fact that Gothic church architecture and its decoration was thought of as an earthly symbol of a heavenly reality. The censer becomes itself a small-scale image of the Church at prayer. The Ramsey censer is grouped in the exhibition with other objects used in the Mass at the altar. All are in precious materials, even if less wealthy institutions than the great Benedictine abbey of Ramsey had to be content with simpler materials and craftsmanship. The punning reference to the abbey's name in the ram's head at either end of the incense boat which accompanies the censer reflects pride of ownership and a sense of institutional identity: such plays on words were themselves also thought in the Middle Ages to draw attention to higher truths. In the Ramsey Abbey Psalter (Cat. 565) the abbey's first abbot, Oswald, is represented enthroned with his feet on a ram. The psalter's rich pictorial imagery contains other references to the abbey's history and to John of Sawtry, the abbot under whom it was made. Elsewhere in the exhibition is a stone effigy of the early thirteenth century from Ramsey (Cat. 22), which may commemorate the lay founder, Ailwyn, who gave the land for the abbey in 969. This shows how the secular and religious spheres were interdependent. These three objects are specific instances of the abbey's patronage produced at particular junctures and embodying identifiable aims and attitudes. They are placed in the exhibition in particular sections to make such points in the context of other works of art.

Since royal government with the king at its centre is the fundamental political fact of these two centuries, the first section of the exhibition contains images of royalty and objects symbolic of it such as the crown and sceptre. The second section concentrates on pilgrimage as a vital expression of Christian belief in the power of the saints to help mankind, which affected all sections of society in the period. The four following sections concentrate on the social structure of church and state, and incorporate images of priests, the feudal nobility and their ladies, the merchants and, lastly, the peasants. Also shown are some of the possessions of the wealthier classes which contributed to their sense of identity and reflected their self-image – the knight's sword, for instance, symbolic of the values of chivalry, or the merchant's silver spoon.

The main historical sequence of the exhibition (Sections I–XVIII) then follows, running through the reigns of the five kings, Henry III, Edward I, Edward II, Edward III and Richard II. With the significant exception of Edward II, the personal patronage of particular works of art and architecture of each king can be demonstrated. The patronage widens out as the period progresses, extending beyond the great churchmen and the magnates lower down the social scale. The interconnections between the various arts of the period are stressed in this main chronological sequence with architecture always playing a central role. The photographs of important buildings, therefore, both suggest the physical setting of the works of art, particularly the sculpture, of course, and stress these interconnections.

Two other smaller sections complete the exhibition. The first, section XI, shows that the ways in which Gothic art has been described and defined, and that the reasons for which it has been valued, have varied over the centuries, and that this in turn has had an effect on what has been preserved. The second, section XII, concentrates on the artists and the processes of making the works of art. The artists were individual men and, less commonly, women (Cat. 442) who faced particular problems with particular commissions, using particular tools and materials. They had to earn their living from their work since in this period most were laypeople, and very few were monks (Cat. 438). Even if their relatively low social status meant that they seldom signed their works, at least contemporary accounts and contracts record their names (Cat. 443–6). Artistic ideas were disseminated in various ways. Works of art passed to different owners in different countries, the Peterborough Psalter being one of the most striking examples (Cat. 567). Artists used pattern-books to record motifs, and of course they travelled, some, such as Guillaume de Nourriche (Cat. 501), even working abroad.

In a Europe which was united in Christian belief and had so many political, social and cultural links, and which shared two languages, Latin, the language of learning, and French, the language of nobility and chivalric literature, it is not surprising that there were many similarities also in artistic styles and techniques as well as in subject-matter. What should be stressed, however, and what are most fascinating to observe, are the regional variations and divergencies. It is no longer the case that scholars see English Gothic art as some sort of provincial offshoot under the shadow of French Gothic art. It is precisely the differences within the European styles of Gothic which are creative and vital. It is to be hoped that this exhibition of English Gothic art, the first for over fifty years, will facilitate a re-evaluation of the specific characteristics and achievements of that art and the artists responsible for it.

JONATHAN ALEXANDER

Acknowledgements

We would like to thank the following who have contributed in many different ways to the organisation of the exhibition and the preparation of the catalogue.

François Avril

Keith Barley, Barley Studio

A. D. Baynes-Cope

Martin Blindheim

P. G. Brown, Rattee and Kett

Sarah Brown

Peter Burman

John Champness

Francis Cheetham

Canon John de Sausmarez

Peta Evelyn

Alfred Fisher, Chapel Studio

Geoffrey Fisher

Peter Foster

Margaret Freel

Richard Gem

Peter Gibson, The York Glaziers Trust

Paul Giudici, Giudici-Martin

Helen Glanville

Barbara Green

Ruth Hamran

John Hardacre

H. M. J. Harrison, Herbert Read Ltd

Paul Harrison, Harrison Hill Limited

Canon John Harvey

Erla Hohler

Eva Irblick

Katherine Jarvis

Thea Jirat-Wasiutynski

Shelley Jones

Martin Kay

Dennis King, G. King & Son (Lead Glaziers) Ltd

Harald Langberg

June Lennox, Stained Glass Studio Canterbury Cathedral

Neils-Knud Liebgott

Clare Lilley

Michael Liversidge

Richard Marsh, Wells Conservation Centre

Andrew Martindale

Ian McClure, Hamilton Kerr Institute

Penelope Morgan

Catherine Moriarty

Carole Morris

Richard Mortimer

Sir Roger Mynors

Enid Nixon

Malcolm Norris

Christopher Norton

Myra Orth

John Page-Phillips

Amanda Paulley

Joanna Payne

John Plummer

Trevor Proudfoot

Jane Reddish

Catherine Rickman

Andrew Saunders

David Saunders

Nick Savage

Martin Snape

Patricia Stirnemann

Torgeir Suul

Fran Terpack

Canon John Toy

Jeffrey West

Julia Willcock

List of Lenders

Photographic Acknowledgements

The exhibition organisers would like to thank the following for making photographs available. All other photographs were provided by the owners of the objects.

Reproduced by gracious permission of H.M. The Queen, *fig. 123*
Aerofilms Ltd, *Cat. 133; figs 32, 36*
Dr J. Agate, *fig. 121*
Warden and Fellows of All Souls College, Oxford, *fig. 74*
James Austin, Cambridge, *Cat. 22, 230, 559, 740*
Keith Barley, Barley Studio, *Cat. 561*
B. T. Batsford Ltd, *Cat. 134, 189, 327; fig. 122*
E. M. Beloe, *Monumental Brasses in Norfolk*, Kings Lynn, 1890–1, *Cat. 678*
Bibliothèque Royale Albert Ier, Brussels, *fig. 14*
Bildarchiv Foto Marburg, *Cat. 688*
Dr Paul Binski, *Cat. 236*
Claude Blair, *Cat. 172*
Bridgeman Art Library Ltd, London, *Cat. 406*
City of Bristol, Museum and Art Gallery, *Cat. 126, 517*
The British Library Board, *Cat. 38, 379; figs 6–7, 11–12, 15, 18, 26–7, 29, 88, 107–8, 112, 130*
Trustees of the British Museum, *Cat. 635–6; figs 2, 22, 73, 75*
Bodleian Library, Oxford, *Cat. 318, 682, 717, 720; figs 19, 23–4*
C.N.B. & C, Bologna, *Cat. 576*
Syndics of Cambridge University Library, *Cat. 40, 42, 312–13, 319, 353–4, 684; figs 10, 125*
Dean and Chapter of Carlisle Cathedral, *Cat. 124*
S. Cather, *Cat. 345*
Central Photographic Services, Cheltenham, *Cat. 131*
Jean-Loup Charmet, Paris, *Cat. 360*
Colchester and Essex Museum, *fig. 102*
A. C. Cooper Ltd, London, *Cat. 98, 138–40, 407, 697*
Conway Library, Courtauld Institute of Art, *Cat. 23–4, 101, 244 (upper photograph), 247, 287–8, 297, 490, 511, 530, 564, black and white), 602–5; figs 8, 16, 40, 60–1, 63, 67, 103;* © Fred H. Crossley and Maurice H. Ridgway, *Cat. 19, 224, 369, 470, 488, 512, 515, 537–8; figs 62, 83*
Corporation of London Records Office, *fig. 28*
Country Life, *Cat. 692*
Crown Copyright, reproduced with the permission of Her Majesty's Stationery Office, *Cat. 708–9*
Malcolm Crowthers, *Cat. 292–4, 329 (courtesy of the Dean and Chapter of Westminster), 713*
Murray R. Davison, *fig. 84*
Nicholas Dawton, *Cat. 340, 516*
The Danish National Museum, Second Department, Copenhagen, *fig. 76*
The School of Art History and Music, University of East Anglia, *Cat. 541 (black and white), 731*
East Midland Photographic Services, Derby, *Cat. 214*
English Heritage, *Cat. 137*
Exeter City Council Museums Service, *Cat. 210*
University of Exeter, *Cat. 638*
Alfred Fisher, Chapel Studio, *Cat. 734, 746*
Syndics of the Fitzwilliam Museum Cambridge, *Cat. 127, 467*
Foto Lintschnig, Austria, *Cat. 565*

Per E. Frederiksen, Norway, *Cat. 290*
Clive Friend (Woodmansterne Ltd), *Cat. 36*
G. G. S. Photography, Norwich, *Cat. 234–5, 237, 711*
P. J. Gates (Photography) Ltd, London, *Cat. 216*
Jane Geddes, *figs 118–20*
Paul Giudici, Giudici-Martin, *Cat. 509–10*
Douglas Gowen, Bangor, *Cat. 109*
Green Studio Ltd, Dublin, *Cat. 730; fig. 111 (courtesy of the Board of Trinity College, Dublin)*
David Griffiths, *Cat. 187–8; fig. 35*
Dr Christa Grössinger, *figs 86–7*
Sonia Halliday and Laura Lushington, *Cat. 739, 742*
John Hardacre, *Cat. 114*
B. J. Harris, *Cat. 546*
T. A. Heslop, *Cat. 141, 277, 282*
Historisk Museum, Bergen, Norway, *fig. 101*
Angelo Hornak, *frontispiece, pp. 192–3*
Borough of Ipswich, *Cat. 712*
Eirik Irgens Johnsen, Norway, *Cat. 311*
K. & S. Photos Ltd, London, *Cat. 233; fig. 117*
Karin Keimer, Hamburg, *Cat. 248*
Jim Kershaw, *Cat. 112*
A. F. Kersting, *Cat. 91, 238–9, 242, 262, 321, 323, 377, 487, 489, 494, 496, 589, 693; figs 30, 33–4, 39*
G. King & Son (Lead Glaziers) Ltd, *Cat. 28, 34, 612–13, 743; figs 106, 109*
The Trustees of Lambeth Palace Library, *fig. 65*
Alfred Lammer, *Cat. 735–6, 744*
Lennart Larsen, Denmark, *Cat. 307–9*
Layland-Ross Ltd, Nottingham, *Cat. 26, 180, 555, 699–701*
Dr Phillip Lindley, *Cat. 506, 508*
Mike Loveridge, London, *Cat. 161*
Robin Lubbock, Shoots, London, *Cat. 462*
President and Fellows, Magdalen College, Oxford, *fig. 81*
Master and Fellows, Magdalene College, Cambridge, *Cat. 466; fig. 20*
Manchester City Art Gallery, *fig. 116*
Manor, Kay and Foley, *Cat. 392*
Museum of London, *Cat. 47, 51, 55, 60–1, 66, 71, 73, 75, 79, 81–3, 85, 427*
The National Gallery, London, *fig. 104*
National Museum of Wales, Cardiff, *Cat. 258*
Godfrey New Photographics, London, *Cat. 386, 405*
Geoff Newman, Ely, *Cat. 399*
Ken Nicholls, Street, *Cat. 296*
Northern Counties Photographers, *Cat. 211*
David O'Connor, *Cat. 6, 32, 231, 562, 737*
Ann-Mazi Olsen, Norway, *Cat. 99*
Drawn by Oxford Illustrators, *Cat. 322, 368; figs 124, 126–9*
Pierpont Morgan Library, New York, *fig. 9*
Eric Purchase, Wells, *Cat. 244 (lower photograph), 257, 260, 500, 634*
Photogenic, Wantage, *Cat. 679*
Plowden and Smith Ltd, *Cat. 35*
Philip Pocock, USA, *Cat. 568*

Public Record Office, London, *fig. 79* (Crown Copyright material in the Public Record Office is reproduced by permission of the Controller of Her Majesty's Stationery Office)
Q. F. T. Photography Ltd, *Cat. 215*
Edward Reeves, Lewes, *Cat. 183*
Rheinisches Bildarchiv, Cologne, *Cat. 587; fig. 5*
David Robson, Salisbury, *Cat. 160, 164, 181, 295*
Royal Commission on the Historical Monuments of England, *Cat. 2–5, 17–18, 20–1, 29–31, 33, 89, 92–3, 103, 106, 135–6, 149, 190–2, 218–20, 227, 232, 240–1, 251, 263, 289, 326, 328–9, 344, 365, 419, 441, 468–9, 472–3, 475, 477–8, 491–3, 495, 497–9, 528–9, 531, 534–6, 539, 557, 560, 563, 564 (colour), 599, 601, 694–6, 732–3, 741, 748; figs 4, 31, 37–8, 43, 45, 59, 64, 71–2, 82, 90–100, 105, 110*
Yogish Sahota, *Cat. 324*
St Peter Hungate Museum, Norwich (Norfolk Museums Service), *Cat. 448*
By permission of the Marquess of Salisbury, *fig. 1*
Jerry Sampson, *Cat. 502–5*
Walter Scott (Bradford) Ltd, *Cat. 261; fig. 51*
Veronica Sekules, *Cat. 507; figs 13, 17*
Service photographique de la Réunion des musées nationaux, Paris, *Cat. 12, 43, 501, 595; figs 131–2*
L. Smestad, Norway, *Cat. 250*
J. C. D. Smith, *fig. 89*
Society of Antiquaries of London, *figs 78, 80*
Brian Spencer, *Cat. 54*
Neil Stratford, *Cat. 299–306; fig. 77*
Jenny Streeter, Selborne, *Cat. 246*
Drawn by Taurus Graphics, *figs 50, 54–8*
Gordon W. Taylor, *Cat. 86*
Rodney Todd-White & Son, London, *Cat. 314, 401, 403, 606–9, 640*
Thomas-Photos, Oxford, *Cat. 738*
Dr Charles Tracy, *Cat. 102, 104–5, 471, 522, 524, 532; fig. 85*
Verulamium Museum, Photographic Services, *Cat. 168*
The Board of Trustees of the Victoria and Albert Museum, London, *Cat. 113, 115, 123, 155–6, 245, 341–2, 374, 526–7, 540, 542, 585, 598; figs 3, 21, 25, 66, 68, 114–15*
The Warburg Institute, *fig. 70*
Canon David Welander, *Cat. 291*
Paul Williamson, *fig. 69*
Dr Christopher Wilson, *Cat. 90, 513–14; figs 41–2, 44, 46–9, 53*
Wiltshire Archaeological and Natural History Society, *Cat. 162*
Dennis Wompra Studios, Hartlepool, *Cat. 452*
David Wiltshire Photography, Warminster, *Cat. 440*
Courtesy of the Dean and Chapter of Westminster, *fig. 113*
The Warden and Scholars of Winchester College, *Cat. 600*
Gerry Yardy, Norwich, *Cat. 366, 541 (colour)*

Editorial Note

The introductions to each section of the catalogue have been written by Jeffrey Denton and Jonathan Alexander, with contributions by Neil Stratford (on Bishop John Grandisson) and Richard Davies (on William of Wykeham).

The editors wish to thank the publisher's editor, Johanna Awdry, for seeing the work through to publication. They are also indebted to Nicholas Savage and Margaret Freel for their work on the Bibliography, and to Nicholas J. Rogers for compiling the Index.

Unless otherwise stated, objects in the Catalogue are known or understood to be English in origin; a question mark indicates uncertainty.

Dimensions are metric: h. = height, l. = length, w. = width; d. = depth; diam. = diameter. Other abbreviations used are as follows:

beq.	bequeathed	LIT.	literature	PROV.	provenance
bt.	bought	n.	note	repr.	reproduction
Coll.	collection	no.	number	rev.	reverse
f./ff.	folio(s)	obv.	obverse	v.	verso
ill.	illustration	p.	page	wt	weight
inv.	inventory	pl.	plate		

Inscriptions in Lombardic lettering are given in capitals; those in black letter are given in upper and lower case italic.

The loan line gives details of shelfmarks and inventory or retrieval numbers where applicable. In entries on manuscripts the exhibited or illustrated pages are indicated by the folio number, e.g. f.20. Folio numbers refer to the recto of a page unless followed by v. (verso).

References to other entries in the Catalogue are indicated thus: Cat. 47.

Catalogue entries are initialled by the author, as follows:

JA	Dr Jonathan Alexander	ND	Nicholas Dawton	DO'C	David O'Connor
MA	Mary Ambrose	JD	Dr Jeffrey Denton	DP	David Park
JB	Janet Backhouse	PD	Peter Draper	AP	Ann Payne
PB	Dr Paul Binski	BE	Blanche Ellis	NLR	Dr Nigel Ramsay
CB	Claude Blair	JG	Dr Jane Geddes	LFS	Professor Lucy Freeman Sandler
MC	Michael Camille	CG	Dr Christa Grössinger	VS	Veronica Sekules
MLC	Marian Campbell	TAH	T. A. Heslop	BS	Brian Spencer
JC	John Cherry	DK	Donald King	NS	Neil Stratford
JAC	John Clark	GL	Graeme Lawson	JS	Julie Summers
RC	Ranald Clouston	PL	Dr Phillip Lindley	CT	Dr Charles Tracy
NC	Dr Nicola Coldstream	JMM	Dr John Maddison	PT-C	Dr Pamela Tudor-Craig
TC	Dr Thomas Cocke	RM	Dr Richard Marks	PW	Paul Williamson
BC	Dr Barrie Cook	NJM	Nigel J. Morgan	CW	Dr Christopher Wilson
PC	Dr Paul Crossley	AN	A. R. E. North		

The full history of an exhibit is given under PROV., unless it is either unknown or self-evident (as in the case of objects which have remained *in situ*).

Bibliographical references are given in chronological order under LIT., abbreviated to the name of the author and date of publication, e.g. Smith 1980. Exhibition catalogues are referred to by place and date of exhibition, e.g. London 1984. If exhibitions occurred in the same city in the same year, but in different institutions, they are arranged in alphabetical order of name of institution, e.g. London 1984a = Great Britain, Arts Council: London, Hayward Gallery, *English Romanesque Art 1066–1200*, 1984; London 1984b = London, British Museum, *The Golden Age of Anglo-Saxon Art 966–1066*, 1984.

Full bibliographical details of published and unpublished works cited in the Catalogue entries are given in the Bibliography on pp. 545–65.

Technical terms are defined in the Glossary on pp. 541–4.

Jeffrey Denton Image and History

What are the roots that clutch, what branches grow
Out of the stony rubbish? Son of man,
You cannot say, or guess, for you know only
A heap of broken images, where the sun beats,
And the dead tree gives no shelter, the cricket no relief,
And the dry stone no sound of water.

T.S. Eliot, *The Waste Land*

liot showed despondency in the face of present realities. But he was also speculating about a renewal of 'broken images'. Recapturing the past is a kind of pilgrimage; and surviving objects from the past form a kind of shrine. In the Middle Ages pilgrimage was more than a physical journeying, for the idea of pilgrimage was a metaphor for spiritual growth, reaching its highest expression in the Arthurian romances. A quest was a knightly ideal, and also an act of piety and a reflection of inner development towards God. The object of a pilgrimage was the shrine of a saint, which was a place of contact with another world – a world which, like the past for us, was distant and mysterious but, at the same time, intensely and incontrovertibly real. Miracles at the shrine were public manifestations of the linking of this world with the other, made possible through sanctity. They demonstrated that the man or woman being venerated was indeed a saint. The barriers separating the finite from the infinite were broken. For us, in the post-Darwinian age, there is a sense in which the infinite has been brought down to earth: an understanding of the past has been raised to an eminent, if not a pre-eminent, position for a comprehension of hidden realities.

Often associated with the pilgrimage in the Middle Ages were sacred symbols, pictorial representations of the life of a given saint, linked with images of the life of Jesus, as infant, as child, as preacher, on the Cross, and resurrected as God-man.[1] To these sacred images of Christ and of the founding saint the pilgrims brought images of their own, for the ancient and widespread practice at the shrine was to make offerings, which were commonly representations or replicas, perhaps of the part of the body cured or of an object associated with a miracle. Shrines had suspended above them 'countless miniature men, women, children, eyes, arms, hands, legs, hearts, breasts, heads'.[2] Many images presented at the shrine were of wax – wax eyes and wax teeth – and it was a common practice to measure a sick person with a piece of string and have a candle made of the same length to burn at the tomb. Often, too, images were of gold or of silver.

The powers of saints were closely associated with their tombs, or with parts of their bodies kept as relics, or with ampoules of their blood. But representations of saints in frescoes, in wooden or stone statues, or in stained glass, enabled their cult to spread widely.[3] Within a few decades of Becket's martyrdom, for example, an effigy of him was painted on the walls of a chapel in the crypt of the cathedral of Anagni. The thirteenth and fourteenth centuries saw a greatly increased spread of the cults of saints throughout Europe, promoted especially by the Franciscans and the Dominicans. Painted images were one of the main vehicles for this diffusion. There were no ecclesiastical regulations controlling religious devotion through iconography, for it was regarded by the Church as an aspect of private worship, permissible as long as it was not accompanied by undue signs of veneration. Images of saints flourished, often of local ones who were never officially canonised. There were effigies, for example, of the child martyr William of Norwich (cf. Cat. 447), who died in 1144, one of which was painted on a retable in the church of St John Maddermarket, Norwich, now in the Victoria and Albert Museum. Comparatively few, however, survive in England, because of the destruction caused by the Reformation. Images, although being in the first place votive offerings, thus came to be a means of communicating widely the characteristic traits of a particular saint, often a contemporary or near-contemporary figure, and in religious devotion they came to play a similar role to relics. Visual representations served to call up and to demonstrate powerful realities: the spiritual world and the natural world were brought together.

Is it possible – in like measure – for the surviving images of the thirteenth and fourteenth centuries to call up and to demonstrate the realities of the past? They have the potential to do so, though not perhaps as dramatically as the cures at the tomb or cures before the effigy. Indeed, in this quest modern pilgrims must be on their guard. Religious images at shrines or in churches were brought together by a more or less significant kind of cultural selection. Not so the selections now made, seven to eight hundred years later. First, we must recognise the extent of the destruction wrought by succeeding ages, whether by accident or by design. Destruction has affected the most imposing images of all: some of the greatest architectural achievements of the Middle Ages have been completely lost.

The Gothic achievement itself developed to some extent out of the ashes of the past. On 5 September 1174, less than four years after Becket's martyrdom, the east end of Canterbury Cathedral was destroyed by fire.[4] The great choir of the cathedral had been dedicated only thirty-four years previously. Sparks were carried to the roof of the choir by a southerly wind from the burning thatch of three cottages in Burgate Street. The Canterbury monk and chronicler, Gervase, was an eye-witness: 'The house of God, hitherto delightful as a paradise of pleasures, was now made a despicable heap of ashes, reduced to a dreary wilderness and laid open to all the injuries of the weather.' The prior and chapter of Canterbury chose the Frenchman William of Sens to undertake the supervision of the new work, and he decided upon a complete reconstruction of the choir, planned as an impressive building for the shrine of Becket. The shrine was placed behind and above the high altar, within its own round chapel or corona. Thus through the accident of fire a new style, light and elegant, showing distinct French influence, rapidly replaced the old Norman one.

No physical trace survives of some of the major achievements of the next two centuries, notably the grand royal fortification at Queenborough in Kent.[5] The building of Edward III's completely new castle in the Isle of Sheppey, for the defence of the Thames Estuary, began in 1361. A year or two later building also began on an adjoining town, named Queenborough in honour of Queen Philippa. Expenditure on the castle was from the first very high; already in 1363 two newly purchased images of the Assumption of the Blessed Mary were set up in the castle's chapel. The first part to be completed was the central round block containing the main residential apartments, followed by the six high towers of the inner wall. Work on the vast outer wall continued at least until 1371 and the whole was completed, it seems, by 1375. Already it had become one of the king's most favoured residences, and among its most noteworthy features was one of the first English mechanical striking clocks for which there is recorded evidence. Queenborough, one of the foremost royal castles of the later Middle Ages, was condemned to total destruction in 1650 by the Parliamentary Commissioners; and we have details of its great dimensions and of its remarkable concentric symmetry only from the building accounts and from a surviving plan and a drawing by Hollar (see figs 1, 2).

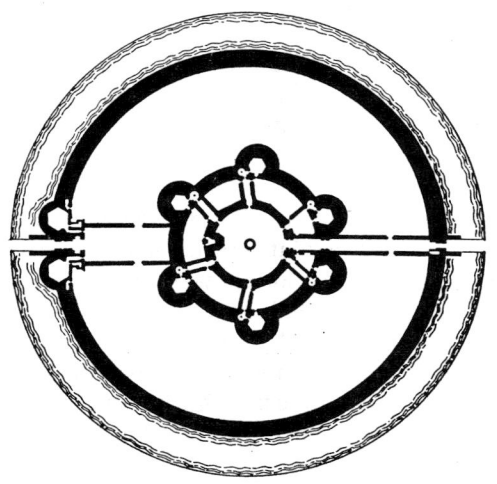

Fig. 1 Queenborough Castle, Kent, from an Elizabethan plan at Hatfield House

Fig. 2 Wenceslaus Hollar, *Queenborough Castle, Kent, looking north-east, c. 1643–77* (London, British Museum, 1859–8–6–387)

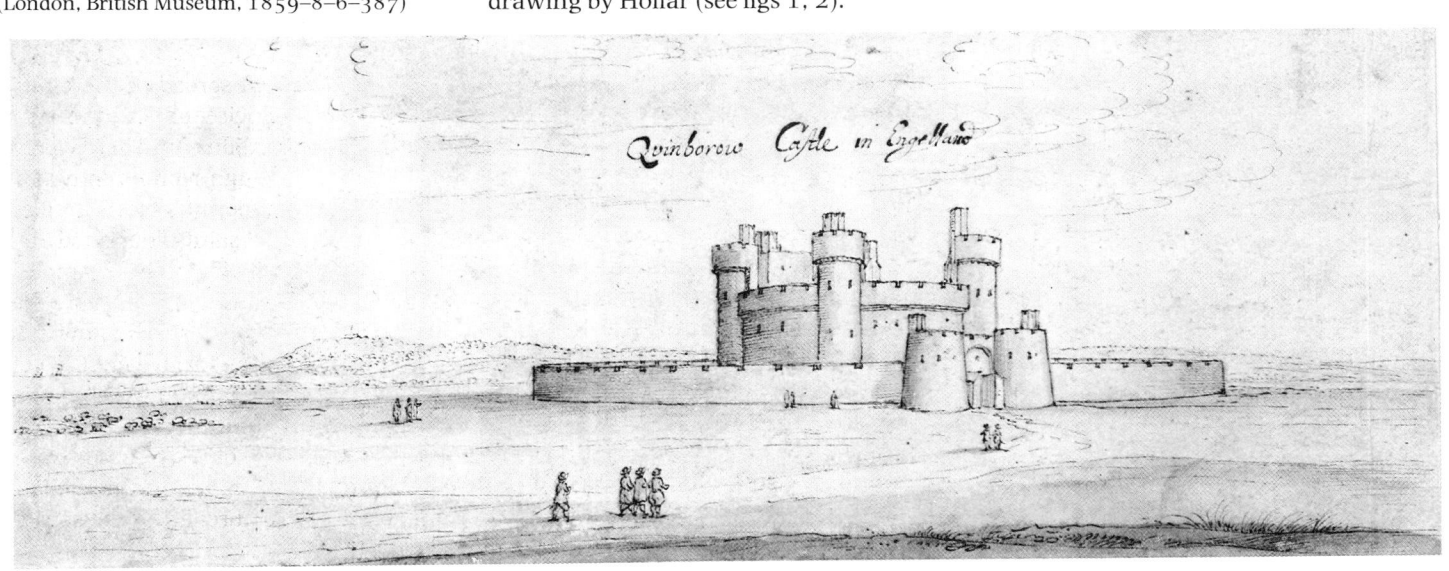

The demolition of so impressive a fortification and royal residence seems wilful enough. But it is insignificant when compared with the wide-ranging destruction in the sixteenth and seventeenth centuries of the manifestations of the medieval English Church. The attack on 'popery' was an attack on England's past. To understand the extent and the ferocity of this attack we must understand the nature of the linked achievements of art and religion up to the fifteenth century. The West was greatly influenced from the fourth century onwards by the Greek and Roman tradition of symbolic art, so that, despite the Judaic prohibition of the making and the worshipping of graven images, representations of the saints and of Christ became common features of religious devotion.[6] The West suffered no controversy concerning the role of the icon comparable with the divisions suffered by the Eastern Church in the eighth and ninth centuries. Indeed, religious practices and representational art developed in close partnership in the Western Church, one of the main reasons being the significance attached to intercessory prayers. The importance of art in religion was never greater than in the thirteenth and fourteenth centuries.

Throughout the Middle Ages a balance was in general maintained between the extremes of idolatry on the one hand and iconoclasm on the other. One aspect of the combating of paganism was always the condemnation of idol worship, and there was never in the West a strong propensity to sanctify the icon in any distinctive or formalised way. The tradition of representation, strong as it became, was predominantly one for the telling of a story or for the communication of the doctrine of the Church: it was understood as primarily narrative and didactic art. Letters of Gregory I (Pope from 590 to 604), sent to Serenus, Bishop of Marseilles, became much-quoted authorities. The Bishop of Marseilles had ordered the removal of sacred pictures from the churches of his diocese. Pope Gregory was eager to define the correct devotional use of images:

> . . . it has come to our notice that you, brother, seeing certain worshippers of images, broke up and threw away these same images. We commend you, indeed, for your zeal, lest anything made with human hands be worshipped; but we suggest that you ought not to have broken these images. For a picture is introduced into a church so that those who are ignorant of letters may at least read by looking at the walls what they cannot read in books. You, brother, should therefore have both preserved the images and prohibited the people from worshipping them, so that those who are ignorant of letters might have the means of gathering a knowledge of past events and so that the people might in no way sin by worshipping a picture.[7]

The fear of image worship was never far below the surface of Christian thinking. Nevertheless, the voices of those for whom the fear was strong were rarely heeded. Churches were filled with sacred art: reliquaries, rood screens, statues, crucifixes, wall paintings and stained glass. Popular piety was allowed full rein, and the combined historical and spiritual elements of Christianity were fully commemorated in art. The development had reached a peak by the fourteenth century, stimulated by the rising fortunes of towns, the continued growth of a money economy and the greater capacity of laymen to endow the devotional work of their parish churches. Within churches separate chapels and altars, often in the form of endowed chantries, proliferated, and along with them all the elaborate trappings of communal and family piety. Prayers, vigils, processions and the illumination of images were multiplied. Local guilds, with their close religious associations, gave added stimulus to the cult of saints. Several of the English guilds originated in the acquisition of a cross or an image or even an altar by a group of parishioners. At Spalding, for instance, the Guild of the Holy Trinity began with the presentation of a fully-furnished altar in 1370. Already a fraternity had come into existence in the parish church at Spalding after one John de Rughton had painted an image of St John the Baptist in 1358.[8]

All sections of society from the nobility downwards had thus become tied to the devotional work of the Church. Prayers and the saying of masses were central elements in the charitable work of the Church. The art of the Middle Ages in many of its aspects demonstrates this association of Church and people. However much the clergy defended their separate status in society and their separate rights, the Church was not a private corporation. Images in churches and chapels had a material aspect quite distinct from the materials from which they were fashioned: they were linked to the economic and family interests of the community which had created them. To attack sacred art was not just to attack the Church. Traditional beliefs and practices were the investments of all; an attack on these investments required a revolution in ideas of major and long-lasting proportions.

The assault came stage by stage. It was an assault upon a culture devoted to the visual. The very success of this culture had begun by the end of the fourteenth century to expose it to criticism.[9] Religion had attracted an abundance of elaborate decoration. Figures were brightly painted and gilded, and in addition they were then often festooned with gifts and bequests of jewels and vestments of all kinds. For example, on the apron of St Cuthburga in the church of Wimborne Minster, Dorset, in 1530 there hung 130 rings, three silver spoons and four large buckles of silver and gold.[10] Such exuberance of display allows us to understand the reaction of some Lollards in the late fourteenth century and after. It is clear, however, that John Wyclif himself had quite a moderate view of images: he wrote that 'It was after the establishment of the faith that images were introduced to be both books for the laity and commemorative signs for Christians in their proper worship of God's saints.' There must, of course, be no implication that divine qualities pertained to the image itself or that the Father or the Holy Spirit or the angels were corporeal. As Wyclif stressed in his *De Mandatis Divinis*, images were not well made if they were unduly delighted in for their 'beauty, costliness, or attachment to irrelevant circumstances'. Decoration could indulge the senses and be the work of the Devil. Despite these dangers, Wyclif believed that images could be well made. Even so, opposition to images distinguished the adherents of Lollard heresy from the beginning, with some Lollards certainly calling for their destruction.

In 1395 Thomas Arundel, Archbishop of Canterbury, imposed an oath on four men from Nottingham who were suspected of heresy. They were made to swear among other things that 'Fro this day forthward, I shall worship images, with praying and offeryng unto them in the worschop of the saintes, that they be made after: and also I shall never more despise pylgremage, ne states of holy chyrche in no degre.'[11]

For some Lollards ecclesiastical decoration represented the riches of the clergy and the despoiling of the poor. Images of the Trinity were considered to be particularly objectionable. The Trinity (Cat. 519) was shown often as Christ on the Cross, with the Holy Spirit above, descending as a dove, and the whole supported by the background figure of God. (See fig. 3, where the representation of the Holy Spirit was, we must assume, deliberately destroyed.) In the images of the Trinity the central spiritual elements of the Christian faith were given material form. Thereby, in the view of some Lollard preachers, the word of God was devalued. One of the earliest preachers put the matter succinctly: 'When the faith of God is published in Christendom, the word of God sufficeth to men's salvation, without ... miracles; and thus the word of God sufficeth to all faithful men and women without such images.'

The individual views of the Lollards caused some localised destruction, and the attacks were especially upon sculpture and upon the work of the painters and the gilders. One of the best known incidents took place in the 1380s, when a smith of Leicester, one William Smith, decided to put the sanctity of St Catherine to the test. Would the painted wooden image of the saint, if vandalised, show signs of life? William together with an associate needed the wood as fuel to cook their cabbage. The head of St Catherine was cut off, and since there was no bleeding the image was burnt. The figure was shown, to their satisfaction, to be a sham.

The assault had begun, but was sporadic. The iconoclasm of individuals, based on a reaction to the wealth of the Church and some of the clergy and on a fundamentalist belief in the commandment 'Thou shalt not make unto thee any graven image', was a minor matter when compared with the mass spoliation by government decree which began in the reign of Henry VIII.[12] Through to the early sixteenth century sacred figures were still being paid for, erected and beautified; roods and image-bearing lofts were still being constructed. Few of the 'books of the unlearned' would be cast into the flames at the instigation of the people themselves. The commands came from above. Henry VIII had evidently felt early in his life a reverence for the shrine of Our Lady at

Fig. 3 Alabaster of the Trinity, *c.* 1400 (London, Victoria and Albert Museum, A53–1946)

Walsingham. He had made offerings there and had ordered that a candle should burn continually at the shrine, which had become the most famous of the Marian shrines in England. Located in a small chapel built on a wooden platform, it was described by Erasmus, who had visited it in 1512 and perhaps again in 1514: 'Visitors are admitted through a narrow room on each side. There's very little light: only what comes from tapers, which have a most pleasing scent .... There was a dim religious light and the Virgin stood in the shadows to the right of the altar.'[13] A royal inquiry was made into the Walsingham shrine in 1535, with questions asked concerning the relics, including Our Lady's milk, and the offerings, and the miracles. The confiscation of the shrine, along with many others, came the following year.

Erasmus had also written about the shrine of Becket at Canterbury, fearing that the great riches of this tomb would not go to the poor.[14] An anonymous description of the tomb by an Italian gives a clear idea of the wealth of ornamentation that was about to be seized by the agents of the Crown.[15] After the raid on the Becket shrine it was reported that eight men had been needed to carry the gold out of the cathedral. The suppression of the monasteries, the destruction of their shrines and the confiscation of their treasures began in 1536 and proceeded rapidly and unscrupulously in the years which followed. The last monastic houses surrendered in the spring of 1540. Royal injunctions in 1536 forbade the clergy to 'set forth or extol any images, relics or miracles for any superstition or lucre' or to 'allure the people by enticements to the pilgrimage of any saint'. The injunction of 1538, drawn up by Thomas Cromwell and published in October of that year, was specific about images:

> That such feigned images as ye know of in any of your cures to be so abused with pilgrimages or offerings of anything made thereunto, ye shall, for avoiding of that most detestable sin of idolatry, forthwith take down and delay, and shall suffer from henceforth no candles, tapers, or images of wax to be set afore any image or picture, but only the light that commonly goeth across the church by the rood loft, the light afore the sacrament of the altar, and the light about the sepulchre; which for the adorning of the church and divine service ye shall suffer to remain; still admonishing your parishioners that images serve for no other purpose but as to be books of unlearned men, that can no letters, whereby they might be otherwise admonished of the lives and conversation of them that the said images do represent; which images, if they abuse for any other intent than for such remembrances, they commit idolatry in the same, to the great danger of their souls; and therefore the king's highness, graciously tendering the weal of his subjects' souls, hath in part already, and more will hereafter, travail for the abolishing of such images as might be an occasion of so great an offence to God, and so great danger to the souls of his loving subjects.[16]

The first stage of the English Reformation was thus made effective through destruction. It was not immediate wholesale destruction: for example, some abbey churches, such as St Albans and Great Malvern, were bought back from the Crown by local townsmen. But it was, from the start, extensive and dramatic enough to ensure that recovery could under any circumstances only be partial. In the event it was the beginning of long-term changes which meant a break with the religion and the art of the past. By 1553 parish churches had been largely stripped of both ornaments and vestments, so that only a minimum remained for the simplified Communion service. Jewels, gilding and silver clasps were being cut away from missals, statues were being broken, walls were being whitewashed and rood screens were being painted over (see fig. 4).

The modern pilgrim at the shrine of the thirteenth and fourteenth centuries thus has only a few images, often broken, to provide instruction and inspiration. The extent of the damage and destruction is, however, only one obstacle to comprehension. Another obstacle is the difficulty of grasping the significance at the time of the images created. To give them new life we must understand the climate of thought and belief within which they were fashioned. Notions of reality were then quite different from ours and were inseparable from the importance accorded to symbols and signs.[17] Scripture, for example, was understood in allegorical terms, so that unexpected events were signs of something beyond the realm of sensory experience. In all areas of

Fig. 4 St Mary's Priory, Binham, Norfolk. The rood screen was reused in the choir stalls; the medieval figures were painted over with texts from Tyndale's translation of the New Testament

NOTES

1. See Turner & Turner 1978, pp. 10–11.
2. Finucane 1977, p. 97.
3. Vauchez 1981, pp. 524–8.
4. Woodruff & Danks 1912, pp. 89–102.
5. Colvin 1963, II, pp. 793–804.
6. A useful survey is Jones 1977, pp. 75–105.
7. Migne 1862, cols 1027–8.
8. Westlake 1919, pp. 29–30.
9. For what follows see Aston 1984, pp. 135–92, esp. pp. 138, 143, 166, 168.
10. Cox 1913, p. 147.
11. Wilkins 1737, III, p. 225.
12. See Phillips 1973; Whiting 1982, pp. 30–47; Scarisbrick 1984, pp. 85–108.
13. Phillips 1973, pp. 74–5; Erasmus 1965 edn, pp. 292, 297.
14. Phillips 1973, pp. 71–2.
15. See p. 162.
16. Williams 1967, p. 812.
17. See Ladner 1979, pp. 223–56.
18. For the medieval world-view see Hamilton 1986, pp. 87–95.
19. Lewis 1964, p. 5; see also pp. 33–40.

knowledge, of God as of the natural world, symbols and signs were a bridge between things visible and things invisible. Everything tended by analogy towards unity, the oneness of God being the central feature of the universe. Images, whether in nature or in language or in art, were thus not just instruments aiding comprehension: they were essential elements in comprehension, real links in the chain of realities which stretched from forms of life on earth through man and the angels to God. Not all art was fashioned with this world-view in mind, but most art was influenced by it.[18] Spiritual powers were understood through representation since, as history was thought to demonstrate, the world was itself the battleground in the war between good and evil. Earthly powers too had their own essential insignia: the temporal signs of rulership were crowns, sceptres and orbs, the ecclesiastical signs mitres, staffs and rings.

As we have seen, the visual images were often described as 'books of the unlearned'. While popular devotion became closely involved in the visual, indeed in the elaborate and the ornate, medieval culture never in fact lost its reverence for the word. The authorities to which all turned were the writings from the Graeco-Roman world or from the Christian apologists of the early Church. 'In our society most knowledge depends, in the last resort, on observation. But the Middle Ages depended predominantly on books. Though literacy was of course far rarer then than now, reading was in one way a more important ingredient of total culture.'[19] As most realised in the Middle Ages, pictorial representations could be misused. There was no misuse when the visual was understood as a reflection of the importance of the word. Similarly, the biggest danger of all for the modern pilgrim is the unavoidably strong temptation to take the images of the past out of their own context. The visual images can directly and powerfully aid our comprehension; at the same time, we should perhaps heed the warnings of John Wyclif and not unduly delight in them for their 'beauty, costliness or attachment to irrelevant circumstances'. Throughout the Middle Ages both idolatry (veneration of the image) and iconoclasm (veneration of the word) were excesses. The image and the word were closely linked. So, too, ideally, are the study of art and the study of history.

Attitudes to the Visual Arts:

T. A. Heslop The Evidence from Written Sources

In August of 1306 Ralph Baldock, Bishop of London, gave judgement in a dispute concerning a carved wooden crucifix, which had been confiscated because of its unorthodox form.[1] It was to be 'borne forth ... to some place without our diocese, either at early dawn or late in the evening, when it can be done most secretly and with least scandal'. The origin of this curious case, in so far as we can trace it, is found in the previous year when the Annals of London record that 'on 15 April 1305 a certain terrifying cross [*crux horribilis*] was placed in the chapel at Coneyhoop [in the parish of St Mildred, Poultry, London], and on the following day [Good Friday] ... was adored [*adorabatur*] by many people ... on account of which Geoffrey of Wycombe, rector of the said church, incurred much harm at the instigation of the canons of St Paul's ... On 1 May the aforesaid cross was taken away during the night to the House of the canons of Holy Trinity [Aldgate].'[2]

Apart from its seeming 'horrible' there are two other significant facts that emerge about this crucifix: firstly that the horizontal cross arm was not of the accustomed shape (the bishop states this three times!) and secondly that it was made and sold by a German craftsman called Thydemann. The circumstantial evidence points overwhelmingly in one direction: this crucifix was of the type known as a *Gabelkreuz*. With their fork-shaped, branching arms and expressionistically distorted figure of the tortured Christ, these images were a recent invention that had gained currency in Italy as well as in Germany, where they were most popular and where they seem to have originated (fig. 5). Probably Thydemann's was the first of the type that Londoners had seen. The instant attention which it attracted suggests that it was a real novelty and that rumour was circulating about it before it was 'unveiled'. It cost the very considerable sum of £23, and is thus likely to have been large and well-carved and painted. But although the populace seem to have been moved to devotion by it, the authorities clearly found it unacceptable. The bishop claimed to be worried that the souls of his flock might be imperilled by their worshipping before it, and, though the remark in the Annals about the 'malice' of the canons of St Paul's might suggest something more directly political, two factors suggest that it really was the form of the object itself that caused the furore. Once in the hands of the authorities it could travel only under cover of darkness so that no one could see it, and Thydemann is made to promise that he will not make or display for sale another such cross.

The Crucifix was, of course, treated as the central image of Christianity. It was visible at a focal point at the entrance to the chancel or above the choir screen of every individual church (whether a great cathedral or monastery or a small parish church). For these reasons much medieval debate about imagery concentrates on the Cross. However, it is not usually its form that causes comment, but rather its proper function, and the condemnation of the various abuses it might give rise to.

Those early Fathers of both the Eastern and Western Churches who approved of paintings or sculptures of holy figures had a largely consistent view of their purpose.[3] They were visual reminders which should stir devotion and act as channels for it. Thus it was always stressed that although kneeling in prayer before an image one should not be revering the object itself – its material, its craftsmanship or any magical properties it might be thought to have – but one's mind should be fixed on the prototype of which it was a mere imitation wrought by human hand. This remained orthodox opinion throughout the Middle Ages among those churchmen, and they were always in the majority, who approved of visual aids to worship. However, as the Old Testament made clear, the creation of cult statues, whether the Golden Calf

Fig. 5 Gabelkreuz, 1304 (Cologne, Church of S. Maria im Kapitol)

(*Exodus* XXII) or Nebuchadnezzar's golden image (*Daniel* III), usually led to misdirected devotional excesses; idolatry and profligacy being the two most obvious. Christians too were prone to such abuses, and it often had to be stressed that there were correct and incorrect ways of behaving and thinking in front of images:

> When we come into any church we should kneel upon the ground, and when you see the Cross think with great sorrow and compunction of heart what death He suffered for mankind, and so before the Cross that moveth thee to devotion worship thou Christ with all thy might. And thus by images and paintings made by man's hand you may see and know how holy saints of Heaven loved Almighty God and how great and diverse were the passions that they suffered for the love they had for Him.[4]

But despite such guidance, no matter what a painting, or more usually a sculpture, looked like, its very existence could encourage idolatry. It was all too easy for the reverence proper to Christ and the saints to be diverted to the inanimate representation of them. 'Some simple people believe that the images themselves perform the miracles, and that this image of the Crucifix be Christ himself, or the saint that the image is representing . . . thus they say "the sweet Rood of Bromholm" . . . "Our dear Lady of Walsingham" but not "Our Lady of Heaven" nor "Our Lord Jesus Christ of Heaven".' Another consequence was the sight of pilgrims 'sadly stroking and kissing these old stones . . . and making vows . . . to come next year again, as if they *were* Christ and our Lady'.[5]

There are countless stories, particularly from the later Middle Ages, from all over Europe which show the extent of this problem. Some are intended to ridicule the simple-minded, such as the rustic whose arm had been broken by the fall of the crucifix in his local church. After a year refusing to go there again, his neighbours persuaded him as far as the door where, peeping in, he commented to the crucifix, 'I shall be able to bend my knee bow my head and worship you . . . but there will never again be love and faithful friendship between us.'[6] But such parables pointing out the folly of the unlearned were not strictly fair, since the clergy themselves circulated stories which either lent credence to the 'reality' of images in an attempt to instil awe and reverence into just such people, or recorded instances where people who treated an image as though it were real gained marks of divine favour. An English Franciscan of the later thirteenth century treasured up this story in his book of *Exempla* to be used in sermons. 'A certain poor woman loved the blessed Virgin, decking her image with roses and lilies and such ornaments as she could find. It befell that her son was taken and hanged. The woman . . . went to the image of the Blessed Virgin and besought her to restore her son.' But when her son did not return she said, ' "Is this the price of service to thee . . . If thou restore not my son, I will take away thy Son." And as she reached out her hand impetuously to bear away the image of the little Babe, behold her son stood by her. . . . "What dost thou, mother? . . . behold, the Mother of God has restored me to thee." The mother rejoiced to recover her son.' Similar tales were current throughout Europe in popular texts such as the Miracles of the Virgin and The Golden Legend: it became in its own right a subject for visual representation (figs 6,7).[7]

Another reason that such stories circulated among the clergy was that they too were susceptible to what we would now regard as pure superstition. It was believed that the crucifix at Meaux (see below) worked miracles partly because it had been carved on Fridays only. This was presumably done at the behest of, or at least with the support of, the monastic community, and while it is conceivable that this gesture was merely commemorative (Friday being the day of the Crucifixion), the chronicler has no doubt that this is a reason for its special power. There is an analogous case at St Albans, also in the mid-fourteenth century, of a cross carved on Fridays which worked miracles, so that it seems that the prescription of this was part of a recognised magical recipe.[8]

A symptom of the supernatural power attributed to free-standing sculpture in particular is more clearly seen in medieval attitudes to the works of classical antiquity. An English traveller to Rome soon after 1200 described in some detail several of the marbles and bronzes he saw there. He appreciated the huge cast bronze head,

Fig. 6, 7 'The image of the Christchild taken hostage': two scenes from an English psalter, *c.* 1320–30 (London, British Library, Royal MS 2 B. vii, ff. 229v., 230)

probably of Constantius II, now in the Palazzo dei Conservatori, for the artifice by which the metal was made to simulate the softness of hair, but he reserved his highest praise for a statue of Venus which he felt compelled to visit on three occasions: 'on account of some unknown magic power [*magicam persuasionem*]'. In the previous century William of Malmesbury had recounted stories of magical ancient statues in Rome, one of which was also of Venus.[9]

Fear of the continuing potency of such images may have been encouraged by the survival of pagan practices throughout the Middle Ages. A chronicle from Carlisle records as late as 1268 instances of Priapic worship, involving setting up an image (*simulacrum Priapi statuere*) in the hope of curing cattle disease. It can have done nothing to help Christian justification of free-standing sculptured figures that such things were still associated with active paganism.[10]

Quite apart from the dangers of idolatry, critics despaired at the resources lavished on imagery. 'Since Christ was made man, it is permitted for lay folk to have a poor crucifix ... and yet men err in crucifix making, for they paint it at great cost and hang much silver, gold, precious textiles and gems on and about it and suffer the poor, bought with Christ's precious blood, to go naked, hungry and thirsty ... who should be helped ... by this very treasure that is vainly wasted on these dead images.'[11] Perhaps it was as bad that such expenditure conveyed completely the wrong impression about His wealth and social status: ...' They deserve to be burnt or thrown out, as books would be if they suggested and taught that Christ was nailed on the cross with so much gold and silver and precious cloth, and a loincloth of gold decorated with jewels, and shoes of silver and a crown studded all over with precious gems ...' (ibid.). It was not only an error to show saints who had lived in poverty 'as though they had lived in wealth of this world and lusts of their flesh', but it was also hinted that there was a disreputable ulterior motive, for 'to the gayest and most richly-arrayed image will people offer most readily and not to some poor image standing in a simple church or chapel'.[12] St Bernard of Clairvaux had pointed out over two centuries earlier that such displays of wealth encouraged donations of money,[13] and clearly investment in 'art' was still yielding worthwhile returns in the fourteenth century by attracting the pilgrims who were the source of so much revenue.

This observation could be countered by the rather more nebulous, but none the less persuasive one that 'simple folk, when they see a fair image artificially painted and lavishly adorned ... by a certain carnal reverence their mind is stirred to adore with bodily humiliation that image rather than any other. Yet the intention is habitually directed towards God, in whose name they do worship such an image.... They judge of divine things from the analogy of corporeal things.'[14] But a consequence of this was that sanctity, and more so divinity, tended to be represented by the most precious materials, and in the most self-evidently beautiful and stylish manner. For as Robert Grosseteste, Bishop of Lincoln, put it, 'God is the most perfect perfection, the fullest completeness, the most beautiful form [*forma formosissima*] and the most splendid beauty [*species speciosissima*].'[15] Such concepts are crucial to understanding the richness and elegance of much high medieval art, for it was only with reference to all that was considered visually most perfect, and to some extent therefore fashionable, that one could hope to convey the ineffable majesty of the Godhead. An image such as the Coneyhoop *crux horribilis* was probably condemned in part because it showed Christ as a twisted and distorted figure, rather than as the epitome of beauty. There was clearly a danger that people would come to despise what was shown as ugly. Indeed, Christ's tormentors at the Mocking and on the Road to Calvary were often shown as twisted and grimacing precisely to stimulate in the spectator just such an attitude of loathing. As a result, care was usually taken to ensure beauty of bodily form when depicting holy personages. The carver who made the crucifix for the Cistercian abbey of Meaux 'had a naked man before him to look at, so that he might learn from his shapely form and carve the crucifix all the fairer [*secundam cuius formosam imaginem crucifixum ipsum aptius decoraret*]'.[16]

Not only in the historical record but in miracle literature too, there are references to the importance of physical beauty. In one such story a monk who was both a scribe and a painter had once been saved from death by the Virgin Mary. Later, while on a pilgrimage to Jerusalem, he fell into conversation with a Jew who was interested to know what Mary looked like and persuaded the monk to depict her. 'And so he portrayed a wonderously fair image of Our Lady, and her child on her arm ... And the Jew gazed fixedly upon her and thought her full fair. And so he asked the monk whether she was as fair as he had made her; and the monk said yes, and twenty times fairer than any man could make her.'[17]

A consequence of the propensity for carving and painting sacred figures as handsome forms, richly arrayed, must have been that they looked more like aristocratic people than like the peasantry. Thus the authority of divinity on the one hand and the power of the already wealthy sections of contemporary society reinforced each other's dominance through the assimilation of their visual appearances. No writer I have encountered states this as a reason for producing beautiful images, but it is hard to doubt that a consequence of representing Christ and the Apostles as poor would have been to give more confidence to the contemporary poor and thus weaken what seemed to be a divinely ordained social stratification. It certainly seems to be the case that conservative forces desired elegant and lavish display in churches, whereas those radicals who countenanced the use of 'art' at all wished for simplicity.

Given the difficulties attendant on the use of images for religious purposes, and the ambivalent attitudes to them that resulted, it might have been easier to dispense with their use altogether. But the Church would not dispense with them. The official justification, made famous by Pope Gregory the Great and widely repeated, was that 'pictures should be had in churches, in order that those who are ignorant of letters should at least read with their eyes upon the walls what they were not able to read in books'.[18] As John Mirk wrote, 'I say boldly that there are many thousands of people that could not imagine in their hearts how Christ was crucified if they did not learn it by looking at sculpture and painting.'[19] 'Painting, if it be truthful, without any element of misrepresentation, and not too curious, too much feeding men's wits, and not occasion of idolatry ... is as naked letters to a clerk to read the truth.'[20]

But painting frequently was 'curious'. A well-known treatise composed in the early thirteenth century begins with the words 'Struck with grief that in the sanctuary of God there should be foolish pictures, and what are rather misshapen monstrosities than ornaments ...' and goes on to decry representation of the 'double-headed eagle, ... centaurs with quivers, ... the fabled intrigues of the cock and fox, monkeys playing the pipe, and Boethius's ass and lyre'.[21] The presence of these 'sports of Fancy' (*fantasmatum ludibria*) is attributed to the criminal presumption of painters (*pictorum nefanda presumptio*); they are dismissed as meaningless (*inanes*). The author then points out those things which were proper subjects for churches, listing biblical narrative subjects, in each case giving an episode from the Life of Christ and then a short series of Old Testament subjects which were regarded as its prefigurations. The verse inscriptions which were supplied to accompany these paintings have led to the tract being called *Pictor in carmine* (literally The painter in poetry).

It might be thought that his declaiming against the licence of painters (*pictorum licentiam*) was no more than an excuse and justification for the treatise that followed. However, the subjects he censured survive in large numbers in painting and in sculpture, in churches and in sacred manuscripts; so there was some cause for complaint. Their obvious popularity he accounts for by stating that 'the eyes of our contemporaries are apt to be caught by a pleasure that is not only vain, but even profane'. No doubt if more secular schemes of decoration had survived from the Middle Ages, we would see that these profanities were as common in the secular as in the supposedly sacred environment. But even so, we would need to explain why they were permitted in churches at all.

As well as the shortcomings of unseemly elaboration, the decoration of churches tempted people to the sin of pride through the public exhibition of supposed generosity. The 'frere' in Piers Plowman hears Lady Mede's confession in return for a donation: 'We have a window under construction that will cost much money, would you glaze it and therein inscribe your name? Your soul would certainly go to Heaven.' In return for his overlooking her 'frailty' Mede agrees to 'roof your church, build your cloister, whiten the walls and glaze the windows, and have painted and portrayed the patroness of these works that everyone shall see I am a sister to your monastery'. As the poet goes on to comment, 'God prevents good people from such display as "writing" in windows of their good deeds lest pride be painted there, and worldly glory; for God knows your inner mind.'[22] Despite attempts to prevent boasting and false charity of this kind, hundreds of windows survive or are recorded which contain donor portraits and inscriptions. Failing that, there was also the attractive alternative of heraldry. The Tale of Beryn tells how the pilgrims (the Pardoner and the Miller) visiting Canterbury Cathedral 'peered fast and pored high upon the glass, counterfeiting gentlemen, the arms for to blaze', before struggling in vain to interpret the narratives.[23]

But perhaps the area where pomp most advertised itself was on tombs. Preachers were critical of sinful people who had the temerity to be buried in church and to disguise the truth of their rotting corpse with a painted image of their appearance while alive.[24] A cautionary tale in Handlyng Synne tells of a sinner pulled from his grave in a church by demons, and comments, 'His soul has greater pain for his pomp and pride in lying there.' The author even suggests that those lords 'busy about acquiring proud stones, lying on high on their graves, may be damned for that pride, even though they had no sin before'.[25] The issuing of such cautions may well have been one of the reasons for the invention of cadaver tombs and shroud brasses. For, from the late fourteenth century onwards, the bodily decay within the tomb might be chosen for depiction instead of, or as well as, the idealised image of former earthly status which had been ubiquitous before.

What we might regard as the secularity of much medieval church art is manifest in many ways. In inventories and in the lengthier descriptions included in some historical writings the material value of objects is frequently stressed. The list of precious chalices and vases belonging to Exeter Cathedral in 1327 begins with two gold vessels: 'of which that of purer gold weighs 79s.4d and the other 49s.6d'. The list of silver begins with ten gilt chalices 'one of which is large, weighing 67s.6d, another with pearls around the base weighs 25s.10d and a third with an enamelled knop weighs 27s', and so on.[26] Doubtless the weights given would help identify the objects if they should be stolen or misplaced, but there are other ways to describe things for such purposes than by material and quantity. It is obvious anyway from the numbers of cases of ecclesiastical treasures being pawned or melted down, that they had an acknowledged value as realisable assets. On the other hand, no weight is given for 'two small crosses of copper ornamented with glass, of no special value [*modici valoris*]'.

Even when objects are being described outside the context of an inventory the quality and quantity of their material tends to dominate. Matthew Paris, a writer and also an artist of considerable ability, was a monk at the Abbey of St Albans. In his *Gesta Abbatum* (Deeds of the Abbots) he gives quite lengthy accounts of the works commissioned for the monastery. In particular he dwells on metalwork and building. Abbot Simon commissioned from Master Baldwin, the pre-eminent goldsmith, 'a great golden chalice than which we have seen none nobler in the kingdom of England. It is of the best and purest gold, encircled by precious stones, appropriate to work in such a material, made most subtle with a delicate composition of intricate little flowers.' The purpose of Matthew's *Gesta* was partly to record, partly to encourage present and future abbots to behave in a way that would bear favourable comparison with noteworthy predecessors, but also to boast of the riches of his monastery. Such fame, as we have seen, was liable to attract new donations. The same metalworker, Baldwin, had made 'a small container [for the Eucharist], worthy of special admiration, of standard yellow gold, with jewels of divers priceless kinds fitted and properly placed on it, in which the "workmanship surpasses the material" '. When the king, Henry 11, heard of this he sent 'a most splendid and precious vessel' in which to place the one which Baldwin had made![27]

The interest which all such descriptions manifest in valuable materials, of pure colour and with strong light-reflecting properties, is also found in much poetic and visionary literature.

> Towards a forest I set my face,
> Where rich-hued crags came into sight.
> No mortal would believe their light,
> A gleaming glory glinting out . . .
> Adorned were all the hillsides there
> With crystal cliffs, while down below
> Brilliant woodlands were everywhere.
> Their branches blue as indigo;
> Like burnished silver the leaves swayed,
> Quivering close on the branches spread;
> They shimmered in splendour, glanced and played,
> When glinting gleams from the sky were shed . . .
> The adornment of those uplands fair
> Made my spirit forget to grieve.[28]

There is no hint in such a description that it was the monetary value of silver, crystal or indigo which brought joy to the soul. Rather it was flickering brightness and purity of hue for their own sakes. Doubtless connotations of wealth were an element in this appreciation, but it was also acknowledged that there were qualities within, for example light, which were deeply affecting in themselves. Robert Grosseteste attempted to define it thus: 'Light is beautiful in itself because its nature is simple . . . it is most uniform and, because of its equality, stands in most harmonious proportion to itself; and the harmony of proportions is beautiful'.[29] In other words he was trying to define one element of beauty by recourse to another, numerical ratio.

It is disconcerting, to people in the twentieth century who admire medieval art, that scholars in the Middle Ages who had the analytical powers and an adequate vocabulary never seriously wrote on applied aesthetics. Theoretical statements, like that of Grosseteste's just cited, exist in some quantity. Usually quite independent of this category are descriptions, whether factual, admiring or condemnatory, of actual 'works of art'. But while 'workmanship' and quality of materials may be slighted or praised, this tends to be in the most general terms. We are told that the first seal of the Mayors of London (Cat. 194–5) was replaced because it was 'crude, old and ugly', but looking at it now the first and last adjectives seem entirely inappropriate, and age is, in itself, of doubtful relevance: many seal matrices were used for centuries. In short, the terms of abuse levelled at it are far from being self-explanatory and we may regard them as little more than an excuse for its destruction, which had been decided on for quite other reasons. Of course the destruction of things for reasons of political or economic expediency is not unique to the Middle Ages. It was, none the less, sufficiently common then to cause us some doubts when we try to interpret the written records, for example as they relate to the Coneyhoop crucifix. As likely as not some underlying religious or political stance will lead to the open acceptance or rejection of a painting, object or building. The words chosen to justify the decision will merely be commonplace.

The ambivalence and the contradictions inherent in medieval attitudes can be illustrated with one final example. Richard of Bury, Bishop of Durham, wrote an entertaining treatise on the love of books, the Philobiblon, in which books themselves have a voice. One of the complaints they make is that 'in us the natural use is changed to that which is against nature . . . we who are a light unto faithful souls everywhere fall prey to painters knowing nought of letters, and are entrusted to goldsmiths to become, as though we were not sacred vessels of wisdom, repositories of gold leaf.' And yet, within a few chapters, the bishop can claim boastfully 'we had always in our different manors no small multitude of copyists and scribes, of binders, correctors and *illuminators*, and generally all who could labour *usefully* in the service of books' [author's italics].[30]

An exhibition such as this will, by its display, necessarily encourage the view that people in the Middle Ages loved embellishing things, whether for the glory of God, or to enhance their own reputation, or simply for visual pleasure. But it is equally the case that many texts, of which this essay contains just a sample, contradict this easy assumption. Pride and Luxury were vices which artifice could easily encourage. On the more positive side, displays of wealth encouraged awe and reverence, and religious imagery could be educational if it were adequately explained.[31] It is impossible for us to know in detail where, between these poles, the consensus lay at any particular time. While it is probably correct that actions (as manifest in the objects before us) speak louder than words, it would surely be a mistake to lose sight of the fact that 'art' was a subject of debate. But even if it surfaces only sporadically in the written record, the discussion will have had its effect on what was and what was not made.

NOTES

1. Baldock 1911 edn, p. 19; Lehmann-Brockhaus 1955–60, II, no. 2984; trans. in Coulton 1918, pp. 473–4.
2. *Annales Londonienses* 1882 edn, p. 136; Lehmann-Brockhaus 1955–60, II, no. 2979.
3. Mango 1972, p. 33; Davis-Weyer 1971, pp. 47–9.
4. Owst 1961, p. 142.
5. Ibid., p. 142.
6. Ibid., p. 146.
7. Little 1908, p. 30; trans. in Coulton 1967, I, no. 90; and cf. *Golden Legend* 1969 edn, pp. 527 (under Nativity of the Virgin Mary, 8 September); *Miracles of the Virgin* 1928 edn, no. 14; Warner 1912, p. 46, pl. 237b.
8. Meaux 1868, III, p. 35; *Gesta Abbatum* 1867, II, p. 335; both trans. in Coulton 1967, nos 102, 101 respectively.
9. Rushforth 1919, p. 51; trans. in Parks 1954, I, p. 261; Malmesbury 1887 edn, I, pp. 256–8; trans. in Giles 1847, pp. 232–4.
10. Stevenson 1839, p. 85; trans. in Coulton 1967, IV, no. 71.
11. Owst 1961, p. 144; Hudson 1978, no. 16.
12. Hudson, op. cit.
13. Bernardus Claraevellensis, 1963 edn, III, p. 105; trans. in Coulton 1967, IV, no. 55.
14. Owst 1961, p. 139.
15. Robert Grosseteste, *De Unica Forma Omnium*; cited by Tartarkiewicz 1970, II, p. 231.
16. Meaux 1868, III, p. 35; trans. Coulton 1967, no. 102.
17. Mirk 1905 edn, p. 302.
18. Owst 1961, p. 140
19. Mirk 1905 edn, p. 171; Owst 1961, p. 146.
20. Coulton 1967, no. 110; Hudson 1978, no. 19.
21. James 1951, pp. 141–2.
22. *Piers Plowman* 1978 edn, Passus III, ll. 48–72.
23. Beryn 1887 edn, ll. 147–58.
24. Owst 1926, p. 158 n. 3; Owst 1961, pp. 49, 313, 396.
25. *Handlyng Synne* 1901 edn, ll. 8777–82.
26. Oliver 1861, pp. 310–11.
27. *Gesta Abbatum* 1867 edn, I, 190; Lehmann-Brockhaus 1955–60, II, no. 3867; Oman 1932, esp. pp. 225–6; trans. in Frisch 1971.
28. *Pearl* 1978 edn, ll. 67–70, 73–80, 85–6, and see notes to ll. 77–80; trans. Stone 1964, pp. 144–5.
29. Robert Grosseteste, *Hexameron*; cited by Tartarkiewicz, 1970, II, p. 230.
30. *Philobiblon* 1970 edn, pp. 50–1, 94–5.
31. Mirk 1905 edn, p. 261.

The Language of Images

Michael Camille in Medieval England, 1200–1400

ow shulde I rede in the book of peynture and of ymagerie?' This question, put by Dives the rich layman, to Pauper the poor mendicant preacher in the Middle English prose dialogue, Dives and Pauper, might also be asked by today's visitor to an exhibition of English Gothic art. Many of these objects were far too important to their original spectators to be called 'art', for as Pauper explains, they function as 'a tokene and a book to the lewyd peple, that they moun redyn in ymagerye and peynture that clerkys redyn in boke'.[1]

This notion of visual art as a universal medium of communication, formulated most influentially by Pope Gregory the Great (reigned 590–604), is a commonplace in our perception of medieval art which requires some rethinking. Reading and writing are taken for granted in our society, as indeed are images. We probably see more of these in one day than a medieval person might see in a whole lifetime. That makes it difficult for us to appreciate the pervasive power of the visual for a culture in which very few people could read, and those who could did so very differently from ourselves. We read books and computer screens in the same way as we look at images; alone, silently scanning each framed unit in an internalised process of rapid reception. Medieval readers also used books in the ways they used images; in groups, speaking the words out loud, referring back and forth, repeating, returning, even adding to or correcting the unframed continuity of the work. Perception was a performance. As reading meant speaking aloud, it was easier for the illiterate to share in the experience.

The capacious medieval memory was also trained to store texts and images, since writing skills and materials were in such short supply. Images might not only be text substitutes, 'telling stories', but might actually contain words in the form of inscriptions, or might be part of a text in manuscript illuminations. In this sense we really do have to 'read' medieval representations. The visual arts functioned as a social language in medieval England, as I hope to show, not in any universal way, but as a means of addressing and distinguishing different and even competing groups in a society where three tongues were spoken, written and read.

It may also come as a suprise to find that, in an extensive display of English medieval art from 1200 to 1400, it is not until we arrive at the very latest works, such as the 'resemblaunce' of the poet Chaucer pointing to the truth of his 'lyknesse' (Cat. 721), that we can see and read in English. This is because after the Norman Conquest, the English language was demoted to a low and non-official status. It was not until the mid-fourteenth century that it was permitted in petitions to Parliament and in wills and deeds. If English was associated with plebeian slang, French or Anglo-Norman was throughout this period the *langue* used in polite society. Above both of these was Latin, the discourse of divinity and the language of lordship since it served both for the rituals of the Church and for the transactions of law.[2] As instruments of power and control Latin and French dominate the ideological strategies of the visual arts. Yet it would be simplistic to divide people in medieval England into three distinct speaking orders; in practice these boundaries were constantly being broken. During the thirteenth century a noble might be brought up with the proverbial prattle of his wet nurse, be taught the niceties of French by his mother, and learn Latin declensions under the tutor's birch; he would use English to address servants and tenants, Anglo-Norman within the family and for devotional and recreational reading, and reserve Latin for talking to God and for written records.

This trilingual hierarchy is nicely conveyed in the lavish pages of the Oscott Psalter which contain, as well as the Latin text of the Psalms, a 'parallel text' in French in the

Fig. 8 Cock preaching to a fox: marginal scene at Psalm XCVII in the Oscott Psalter (London, British Library, Add. MS 50000, f. 146v.; Cat. 352)

right column. We might see 'English' here too, not in text but in image: in the marginal scenes, which reflect proverbs and fables that were also told in the 'lewd' language. One of these (fig. 8) parodies Psalm XCVII, 'Sing unto the Lord a new song', by showing a clerical cock singing from an open book unaware that his audience, the fox, has him in mind for dinner. The way in which words interact thus with pictures is an important issue in the development of Gothic art in England, since language not only provides a matrix for social experience but also defines national identity and consciousness. How does the common tongue, moving as it does to centre stage from its previous marginality by the mid-fourteenth century, affect the visual arts? Reading the Gothic image, can we associate particular pictorial styles with certain languages? Is there, as has been suggested, a close relationship between the growth of vernacular reading and writing and the increasing naturalism of Gothic art?[3]

Just as some view English today, Latin in the Middle Ages was an international medium of communication for the élite, a prerogative of those in power which permeated all levels of society, secular as well as sacred. It was the *Logos*, the word of God enshrined in illuminated letters and waiting to be vocalised in the missals of the Mass itself (Cat. 714). Its magical aura would have been recognisable, even if not understandable, to all Christians who heard it recited and sung for their salvation. Spoken by the annunciating angel in the Hours of Alice de Reydon (Cat. 570) and introducing, with the ubiquitous *hic*, the subject taking place right before your eyes in the coronation scene of the Glazier Psalter (Cat. 8), Latin was the language of inscriptions precisely because it carried the authority of truth. Even secular subjects, such as the Chertsey tiles series depicting Richard the Lionheart's victory over Saladin, had elaborate Latin inscriptions, in this case in the circular borders (Cat. 16).

Most inscriptions in stained-glass windows from the great narrative scenes at Canterbury (Cat. 27) to the winding words of Magister Henricus de Mamesfield of Merton College, Oxford (Cat. 738) are labelling titles or *tituli*. For this Oxford scholar disputing and lecturing on books such as the 'new' translations of Aristotle in his college library (Cat. 318), Latin was the only medium of true knowledge. Those renowned for their learning as *litterati* included the influential new orders, like the barefooted friar who follows St Francis on the road in a thirteenth-century drawing, book in hand (Cat. 107). More than the regular clergy, the preaching friars were experts at explicating for their audiences not only God's word, but His images as well. For it is a puzzle how those without any formal Latin training who flocked to the large pilgrim churches such as Canterbury could have understood the writing on the windows (Cat. 27), which anyway is often too small to be clearly made out from the beholder's viewpoint. It is possible that these *tituli* were not meant to be read at all, but served only to authenticate the image. Speech scrolls held in the hands of dramatic interlocutors in so many Gothic pictures seem to serve aesthetic rather than functional purposes, as in the textless talking which fills the Tickhill Psalter (Cat. 568).

The power and prestige of Latin rested not only upon its efficacy in the salvation of one's soul but also on its uses in the political here and now. As Michael Clanchy has shown, the thirteenth century witnessed a communications revolution which had its initial impact on the use of writing in government legislation.[4] The written constitution, the Magna Carta (Cat. 1), is one of the earliest and most eloquent symbols of this transformation. Although as a document it was copied and recopied, even into French, its dissemination throughout the realm indicates the power of Latin as a living language of government. It was proclaimed aloud on numerous occasions after 1215, and in 1279 Archbishop Pecham ordered a copy of it to be posted at every cathedral and collegiate church 'so that it can be clearly seen by the eyes of everyone entering'. This shows the close association at this time not only between seeing and reading but also between the image-complexes of the Church and government propaganda.

The urge to witness as well as read writing is eloquently displayed in a scene from the Guthlac Roll (Cat. 37). The donations of land to Guthlac's abbey of Crowland are represented by Latin scrolls held by Ethelbald and twelve other benefactors. Each begins his oath with his *ego*: 'I Alan de Croun give you, Father Guthlac, the priory of Feinston, with appurtenances.' I see this device not only as an indication of the increasing place of written documents in legal proceedings of the period but also as a reference to the traditional use of scrolls in twelfth- and thirteenth-century art to represent speech, visible for example in the courteous French welcome spoken by Vegetius to the young Prince Edward in a later secular treatise. The scrolls on the Guthlac Roll are then both speech and script, stressing that this is a legal act ratified both in writing and in oral witness. Another class of objects on display, which are documents as well as symbols of authentication, are the seals which served cities, ecclesiastics, knights, and also the new merchant classes, people such as Henry le Callere (Cat. 200). These sometimes highly personalised objects are a carry-over from the use of swords and notched sticks in legal contracts and show once more the need for immediately recognisable proof, in that one signed not only with one's name but also with one's image.

This radical change in the role writing played in people's lives also had its impact on the content of visual imagery. The legend of Theophilus, who signed away his soul to the Devil in a legal document, was popular in manuscript illustrations (fig. 65) and stained glass. The new bureaucracy controlled the illiterate population in images like that of the scribe-demon Tutivillus who is painted and carved in parish churches to make written record of sinful gossip (Cat. 557, 561). Literacy might be a useful weapon indeed; one chronicle relates how the king's tax collectors were so frightened by some Latin phrases shouted at them by a group of clerics that they fled in terror.

Another important locus for Latinity was the private prayer book. Despite Walter Map's contention that to put the word of God before a layman was to cast pearls before swine, many wealthy lay people commissioned Latin psalters and later Books of Hours for their own use. The psalter was also the children's primer of the Middle Ages. On the Museé de Cluny panel in Paris, St Anne teaches the Virgin to read by pointing to the letters of Psalm XLV, 10, 'Hear, O Daughter, consider, and incline your ear.' This subject, which appears in monumental media and in manuscripts such as the Fitzwarin Psalter (Cat. 685), seems to have been especially popular in England. Perhaps here it provided the role-models for mothers and daughters of aristocratic households, who seem to have been at the forefront of new literacy patterns not only in Latin but, as we shall see, in the vernacular too (see also pp. 43–4). Another important literate lady, Dame Julian of Norwich, speaks of learning of God's greatness 'as if it were an ABC', just as Piers the Plowman tells an incredulous priest, amazed at his literacy, that 'Abstinence the Abbess taught me my ABC.'[5] One wonders whether the inscribed alphabet on the Studley bowl (Cat. 728) served a similarly didactic as well as decorative purpose.

Comparing two contemporary books, the Amesbury Psalter (Cat. 316), made for a nun of the richest nunnery in England, and the Cuerden Psalter (Cat. 355), made for an unknown lay couple, reveals what the 'quasi-literate' lay reader saw and read as opposed to the monastic literate. Both manuscripts have full-page prefatory pictures with the donors kneeling before the enthroned *Virgo Lactans*, an intimate subject of the Virgin suckling her Child, rare in Gothic art, which shows that devotional fashions

Fig. 9 Initial to Psalm XV from the Cuerden Psalter illustrating v.5, *Dominus pars haereditatis meae* (The Lord is the portion of my inheritance) (New York, Pierpont Morgan Library, M756, f. 24v.; Cat. 355)

Fig. 10 Opening rubric to Walter of Bibbesworth's 'How to speak French' written in the late thirteenth century for Lady Denise de Montchesny. Note the English interlineations 'to be littre' and 'midwis' (midwife) in this fine fourteenth-century copy (Cambridge University Library, MS Gg.I.I, f. 279v.)

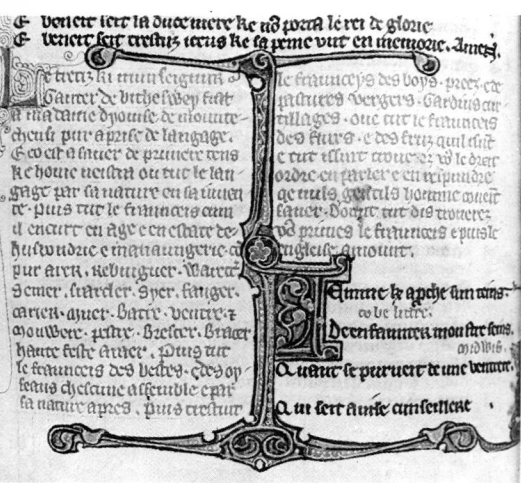

were already crossing the boundaries between cloistered and lay audiences. Looking at the Psalm text, however, we can see that the commissioners of the Cuerden Psalter had recourse to a more systematic series of visual aids in helping them to remember the Psalms. Whereas the nun of Amesbury has historiated initials at only the normal eight divisions of her text, this example has, in addition to these, 176 small initials which illustrate key phrases in each psalm. Sometimes these are very worldly indeed, perhaps suited to the material interests of the richly dressed donors. The initial to Psalm XV on fol. 24v. illustrates v. 5, 'The Lord is the portion of my inheritance', by a man counting out his money into three piles, the centre one being reserved for God who looks down from above (fig. 9). Giving part of one's wealth to the Church was a prescribed means of avoiding the sin of usury, into which the rising merchant class would be most apt to fall. Imbuing the Psalm with such a 'contemporary' reference makes it at once more relevant and memorable to these readers. The Franciscan Hugh of Digne complained that a friend read in the way 'a woman reads the Psalter, who by the time she gets to the end, can't remember what she read at the beginning'.

It would be wrong to equate Latin with schematic, hierarchical modes of representation, and vernaculars with a more naturalistic art, since it was precisely this necessity of making the Latin text more immediate that resulted in such vivid images. It could be a matter of life and death for this psalm to be memorised by the layperson, as it was one of the prescribed passages of the Bible which theoretically allowed an accused felon benefit of clergy. As Imagination tells the dreamer in Piers Plowman,

> And well may a child who is taught to read be grateful to those who sent him to school, for if he lives by the written word he may save his soul. '*Dominus pars haereditatis meae*' is indeed a cheerful verse to read, for it has saved dozens of mighty robbers from Tyburn! So where the illiterate thieves must swing for it, see how learning saves those who can read![6]

Though English was their 'mother tongue', in the thirteenth and fourteenth centuries most gentlemen wanted to learn polite French. After all, it was the 'language of love'. The high status of French and the importance of women in its diffusion is evidenced in a treatise by Walter of Bibbesworth, written for a Lady Denise de Montchesny of Hemingfield, near Chelmsford, that her children might 'learn French in few words' (*apryse de fraunceys en breves paroles*).[7] Set out with the English vocabulary in red above the French verse (fig. 10), it was designed especially for the mother of the household to teach her children not the word of God but words for parts of the body, knights, armour, and practical things like weights and measures; an indication of how different languages describe different worlds for different audiences. How different then was the art seen and read in this French ambiance?

The thirteenth-century monk of St Albans, Matthew Paris, circulated his French translations of saint's lives among a clientele of eminent noblewomen ('laypeople who letters know not') and hit upon a marketable medium for his talents as scribe and illustrator (see Cat. 39). In these works the narrative can be read with the pictures alone, with the red rubricated captions, or with the whole French text if need be, and Matthew even threw in some Latin *tituli* for good measure. The audience for whom Matthew catered would not have wasted their voices, but would have had clerks or ladies-in-waiting to read to them. Thus they were free to peruse the left-to-right thrust of the narrative scenes in these manuscripts in an experience mingling sight and sound, approaching our idea of the cinematic. This group perception of the picture book is also relevant to the other 'best-seller' of the period, the illustrated Apocalypse (see Cat. 347). In the case of the Trinity College Apocalypse (Cat. 349), we can imagine the rapt, perhaps royal reader of each revealed 'opening' simultaneously listening to the words of the visionary narrative which echo her own multi-sensory experience; 'And I John saw these things and heard them' (*Revelation* XXII, 8).

It is a pity that so much of the secular art of the Middle Ages has been lost. Documents tell us that rooms of Henry III's palaces depicted texts, not of the Bible, but of French romances. Nostalgia for the Middle Ages began during the Middle Ages itself, and the myth of an earlier, Arthurian, English golden age was an attractive ideology of royal charisma, especially for Henry III. The Chertsey tiles told the tale of

Tristram and Isolde, though how these fitted together to form a pavement in the hall, private chamber, or perhaps, as has been suggested, even the king's chapel at Clarendon itself, is not clear (Cat. 320). Fragments of inscriptions survive in the form of single stamped Lombardic letters which could be assembled, as were later monumental brass inscriptions, like typesetting. From these, S.R. Loomis pinpointed the literary source for the tiles in the lost French version by Thomas, written at the Court of Henry III's grandfather Henry II.[8] The tiles register moments of emotional surprise and personal anguish in the text, such as the angry Gormon clutching his cloak or the distressed fathers of Cornwall in another tile. Though such subjectivity is typical of 'romance' as opposed to earlier 'epic' narrative, the emotional codes of gesture and facial expression are the same as those used in contemporary Bible illustrations. Only two of the thirty-six extant tiles actually show Tristram and Isolde together; in one the young girl tentatively holds the harp during her first lesson in love. More emphasis is placed upon earlier scenes of quest and adventure, playing down the adulterous affair which would be inappropriate for a royal pavement. But the tale was so well known that, using the inscriptions, one could perhaps 'read between the tiles'.

These superb objects, like the Harbledown bowl illustrating a scene from the popular Romance of Guy of Warwick (Cat. 155), are rare reminders of a sophisticated secular language of images. It is remarkable that so few illuminated manuscripts of secular romances have survived, since we know from inventories that these were a treasured genre: Edward I took with him to the Holy Land in 1270 a 'Romance of Tristram'. The lively pen-drawn illustrations of the *Roman de toute chevalerie*, an Anglo-Norman poem about another favourite hero, Alexander (Cat. 313, 361), and the satirical Romance of Fauvain (Cat. 205) brought to life books that were for pleasure rather than preaching.

It would be wrong to see Anglo-Norman French as a highbrow language used only in courtly literature for, like Latin, it served widely divergent needs. The fundamental transformation in religious life instigated by the Fourth Lateran Council of 1215 was a requirement that the laity should be educated in the basic tenets of the Faith. A whole tradition of Anglo-French literature provides this in the form of biblical paraphrases and works of spiritual guidance in the vernacular. We can see the incursion of French prayers into the Latin structures of private devotion, especially in Books of Hours such as Egerton MS 1151 (Cat. 41). French could also function autonomously in newly intimate instruments of devotion like the sequence of Passion pictures, each introduced by an *ici* rather than a *hic*, in a St John's College manuscript (Cat. 42) or the little-known work, illustrated by the artist of the famous Queen Mary Psalter, which is a kind of layman's 'how to do it' manual for the Mass (Cat. 110). Pictures predominate over text and show the reader not only 'that which you should do' but also 'that which you should think' at each stage in the ritual (*Ceo qe vous devez fere & penser a chascun point de la messe*). For example, on f. 45v. three such 'mental' images, Virgin and Child, Resurrection and Crucifixion, are illustrated. A fourteenth-century preacher (this time in English) makes much of the relationship between the words 'image' and 'imagination', saying that many people could not 'ymagen in their hearts' how 'Christ was don on the rood' without the 'siʒt of ymages' of the same.[9]

If anything exemplifies the image-explosion of the later Middle Ages, the voracious visual appetite for 'ymagening' every moment of Christ's life in the multiplication of pseudo-apocryphal legends, it is the 231 pictures of the Holkham Bible Picture Book of *c.* 1320–30 (Cat. 221). Here 'ymages' are more important than the text, unlike a similar Bible picture book produced in France with the same half-page picture format where the captions still have priority (Paris, Bibliothèque nationale MS fr. 1753). The artist, under instruction from a Dominican who tells him in the first picture that this a book to be shown to 'riche gent' (rich people), put together his picture cycle from both English and French vernacular traditions as well as from Latin sources. The miracles of Christ's childhood (ff. 10–18v.) occur in Latin texts such as Petrus Comestor's *Historia Scholastica* (a Dominican's 'set text'), but these were also illustrated in an Anglo-Norman version (Cat. 203). The artist might not only have been dependent on this but also could have used oral accounts of the childhood miracles; an 'English' vernacular context which is surely suggested by their appearance in the more popular

Fig. 11 The Annunciation to the Shepherds and the miraculous gift of tongues from the Holkham Bible Picture Book (London, British Library, Add. MS 47682, f. 13; Cat. 221)

context of the Tring floor tiles (Cat. 217). It has also been suggested that the gruesome narrative details of the Passion in the Picture Book are related to a poem written in northern English dialect around 1300, and known as The Northern Passion.[10] Another source for representations was the 'living speech' of the Mystery Plays.

The scenes of the Annunciation to the Shepherds and their Adoration of the Christ Child on f. 13r. focus, like the Mystery Plays, on dramatic moments when languages collide (fig. 11). The first collision can be seen and read at the top of the page, in the sacred script of Latin spoken by the angel and the startled response of the shepherd. The angel's conventional *Gloria in excelsis* announcing the glad tidings (which today's viewer knows from the oral recitation of carols) is not understood by the rustic shepherd who replies in gobbledegook: '*Gum glo ceo ne est rien. Allums la, nous le saverums been.*' This joke at the expense of the dim-witted yokel occurs too in the Coventry Shepherds' Play at this point, and reminds us of the angel in Piers Plowman swooping down to the 'plain full of folk', who 'spoke something in Latin, for the ignorant folk could not speak for themselves'. Our 'ignorant' shepherd's reply to the Latin of the angel might not even be a parody of that language (like the contemporary *Missa Potatorum*, the Drunkard's Mass) but, in its very French-sounding words, a struggle on the part of the shepherd, mistaking Latin for French perhaps, to respond at one level higher on the linguistic hierarchy.[11]

In the next picture linguistic embarrassment is exploded in a miracle, for as the three shepherds approach the Holy Family, out of their mouths spurt speech scrolls in Latin: 'Gloria in excelsis Deo'! Given the gift of tongues by proximity to the holy, these men have climbed two rungs on the linguistic and social ladder. But the greatest surprise comes in another bifurcation of language in the caption above. As if to stress their transformation to the reader, this describes the peasants' miraculous leap into literacy in their own language – English:

> En le chant qe le angel ont chante
> En le honour de la nativite
> *Songen alle wid one stevene*
> *Also the angel song that cam from hevene.*
> Te Deum et Gloria.

English was accessible. Like the inscription on a royal jug which says 'lat on lust come nere' – 'let anyone who pleases come near' – (Cat. 727) it crossed all social classes. Although it seems to surface only late, in the manuscript copies of works by Chaucer, Gower and others, its presence can be felt, as I have suggested, in works written in French and even Latin much earlier. In the thirteenth-century Oscott Psalter (fig. 8), the parodic play of the marginal pictures admits the chatter of marketplace and plebeian laughter into the sacred text. They are not mere doodles, but refer to a rich though rarely recorded content. Folklorists are learning this language as it survives in living oral tradition, which is why we know the riddle of the Clever Daughter told in a Worcester misericord (Cat. 536); it is told all over the world, transcending linguistic and national boundaries.

The section of the exhibition devoted to these vivid images, in the margins of Latin prayer books, in the borders of stained glass and the 'underworld' of misericords, might seem the most natural and easy for us to 'read'. But we must guard against seeing the grotesque humour, or the scenes of peasants working in the margins of the Luttrell Psalter (Cat. 575; figs 15, 88) as somehow closer to an 'image of the people'. While these images are certainly expressive of the artist's freedom of expression, their function is not so much to expose the social conditions of the masses but to keep them in place, or rather displaced, at the edges of the Latin word – literally under the law which rules them in the case of the Smithfield Decretals (fig. 130). Degrees of naturalism correspond to degrees in the social order in English Gothic art as much as they do in subsequent centuries.

English was not one language in this period but many, spoken and written in different forms throughout the country and described by John of Trevisa in 1385 as 'straunge wlafferying, chiterynge, harrynge and garrynge grisbayting'. There is some evidence to suggest that English of diverse dialects was being incorporated into the language of images at an early date, in the form of inscriptions. The church at Wensley in Yorkshire (see p. 129) has one of the earliest recorded inscriptions in English – in fact in fourteenth-century broad Yorkshire – in a wall painting of the Three Living and the Three Dead, a moralising subject warning against the vanities of the flesh, and which is also found expressed in English terms in the contemporary De Lisle Psalter (Cat. 569). In the latter, although illustrating a French poem (the language used by Robert de Lisle in his bequest of the book) the words above the framed scene which are 'spoken' by the three young kings, as they confront their skeletal doubles, jump out of the page at the modern viewer: 'Ich am afert. Lo whet ich se.'[12] English could hardly have been the language solely of peasants, since here it is spoken by kings!

The resonance of English as a language of personal expression is suggested by a story in the Lanercost Chronicle under the year 1244, of a Norfolk son of a poor family who sets out to make his fortune in France with only a pig as inheritance. He becomes a rich man, and as a memorial to his 'roots' has his private room painted with a picture showing a boy leading a pig with an inscription in English reading: 'Wille Gris, Wille Gris, Thinche wat you was, and qwat you es.'[13] This is a fascinating account, since it links English with the growth of the subjective self-consciousness of autobiography, and nationality with personal identity. It is like the linguistic nationalism of the author of the early fourteenth-century treatise *Cursor Mundi*, who translates, he tells us, 'for the love of Englis'.

Elizabeth Salter suggested an equivalence between the 'Englishness' of thirteenth-century architecture as a 'national version of European Gothic' and literary masterpieces such as the English Owl and the Nightingale (*c.* 1200) which brilliantly blends earlier Anglo-Saxon with newer French as well as Latin forms.[14] It is therefore surprising that when we reach what has been called the 'Ricardian Renaissance', the period when Chaucer writes his Canterbury Tales (Cat. 719), English art seems in decline. That should make us wary of trying to weld all artistic expressions into one; it emphasises the fact that painters and sculptors are more dependent upon economics and trade, which suffered greatly during and after the Black Death of 1348–9. Also, while Latin manuscripts continued to be luxuriously illustrated, such as those made for the Bohuns (Cat. 686–91), books written in English served a much wider readership which lacked the money for expensive illustrations. This is most evident in the scribbles which illustrate the unique manuscript of the masterpiece of alliterative verse, Sir Gawain and the Green Knight (Cat. 718). These are the 'ymagenings' of a reader rather than a professional artist, and the same is true of the marginal depictions of characters in the Bodleian manuscript of Langland's poem which are more like *N.B.* marks than evocations of the text (Cat. 223). Another significant change in the later Middle Ages is the growth of the modern concept of private and silent reading, which makes the book less of a public image in performance and more of a personal tool. We can see this even in the 'portrait' of Chaucer (Cat. 721), who points the eye of the individual reader to the text and does not, like previous pointing figures in the exhibition, speak it aloud. By the time of this manuscript Continental French products define what is 'chic' in courtly circles.

A wooden chest (Cat. 710), usually described as carved with scenes from Chaucer's Pardoner's Tale,[15] really only depicts the *exemplum* at its source, 'the love of money is the root of all evil'. Text and image are here no longer interdependent in the subtle ways we witnessed in Latin manuscripts or the French poem 'told' in the Chertsey tiles. In fact they came into direct conflict. Langland condemns inscriptions in pictures as manifestations of worldly pride, and attacks those who have themselves portrayed in stained glass (Cat. 226–7, 231–2), for 'to wryten in wyndowes' is dangerous, 'leste prude be peyntid there and pompe of the worlde'.[16] It is also surely significant that those who pressed hardest for the adoption of English in religious practice, the Lollards, should also be the very iconoclasts who sought to break and destroy Gothic images. For them the image-complexes of the late medieval Church, the painted statues of the Virgin and the saints (fig. 130), were the idols of a corrupt and decadent Latinity, of which Dives in Dives and Pauper says 'I would they were brent every one.' The Lollards, and especially Wyclif, who committed the heresy of translating the Bible into English, represent a first and failed attempt – later to succeed in the Reformation proper – to alter the balance of power between word and image which had held for centuries; to make language the only means of spiritual communication with God.[17]

If I have presented English Gothic art as a talking picture, it is one that still today requires many subtitles. It needs to be activated in explanation and performance now, just as it did when the preacher pointed from his pulpit to the wall painting of the Last Judgement and asked his audience to 'thenk on this dome'.[18] Reading this 'boke of ymagerie' depends on our understanding of the society of readers who used it. Yet there are some forms of expression which are irreducible to words and do not depend upon specific languages; like the cross which Pauper calls a 'tokene' or sign of salvation to all Christians or at the other extreme the sound of the unfortunate duck whose 'queck' explodes amongst the words and images of the early fourteenth-century Gorleston Psalter (fig. 12)

Fig. 12 'Duck discourse' from the Gorleston Psalter (London, British Library, Add. MS 49622, f. 190v.; Cat. 574)

NOTES

1.	Barnum 1976, p. 82.	10.	Roberts 1973, p. 364.
2.	Clanchy 1979; Wilson 1943; Salter 1983.	11.	Camille 1985c, p. 145.
3.	Bäuml 1980; Camille 1985a.	12.	Sandler 1983, p. 5.
4.	Clanchy 1979.	13.	Wilson 1943, p. 51.
5.	Piers Plowman 1959 edn, p. 95.	14.	Salter 1983, p. 26.
6.	Piers Plowman 1959 edn, p. 147.	15.	Kolve 1984, p. 65.
7.	Clanchy 1979, pp. 151–2.	16.	Cited in Aston 1984, p. 112.
8.	Loomis 1938, p. 44.	17.	Aston 1984.
9.	Cited in Salter 1983, p. 5.	18.	Owst 1961, p. 516.

Women and Art in England in the Thirteenth and Fourteenth Centuries

Veronica Sekules

The Dominican friar Robert Holcot recorded in a book of anecdotes for preachers in the early fourteenth century that women talked more than men because they had more superfluous humidity, which enabled their tongues to move more quickly and easily in their mouths.[1] In asserting this he was giving a dubious biological justification for a prejudice against women long held by clerical misogynists. He and his ilk often pointed out that the uncontrolled chattering and wandering about of women disrupted the solemnity of religious observance. A fable was put about in order to draw attention to the likely consequences of this feminine weakness, which was much illustrated on capitals, corbels and stained-glass windows in churches (fig. 13; Cat. 557, 561). It was of the devil Tutivillus, who sat on the shoulders of the women who gossiped during the sermon and wrote down their words, which of course, because they were ignorant, they could not read.[2]

Chaucer's Wife of Bath exemplified the common medieval stereotype of the noisy woman. She was one of those who roamed the streets with her gossips and went to sermons to laugh at the preacher. She was also a lecherous, bullying wife who had seen five husbands to early graves.[3] Female attempts at supremacy over men were much lampooned in literature and in art. Although she is more likely to have been the victim rather than the antagonist, the wife beating her husband was a subject frequently depicted in misericords or manuscript marginalia, places where popular satires are to be found (see Cat. 538). However, it was universally acknowledged by both sexes that men were superior to women in the physical strength of their body and soul and that therefore they had a right to rule society. Even Christine de Pisan, the French writer who in the early fifteenth century espoused the cause of women, accepted that women were subservient to men and that only exceptionally, usually in widowhood, were they allowed to take power.[4] It is clear, however, that male supremacy was uneasily maintained, especially among the lower classes. It is probably for this reason that threats to it are only ever represented in burlesque fashion and the quarrelsome woman is never represented as of the refined upper classes. As an English homilist wrote in the thirteenth century, 'There are two kinds of dogs, for some are well-bred, others low-bred. The well-bred indeed are silent and free from guile; the low-bred are ill-tempered and fond of barking. So it is with women. The daughters of the nobles are restrained, silent and lovers of solitude; the ignoble to be sure are loud and roamers in the streets.'[5]

Attitudes towards women in the Middle Ages are often presented in the light of opposites, good and bad being represented as respectively socially superior and inferior. Medieval Catholicism was responsible for the fundamental polarisation of attitudes towards women, in setting up two opposing exemplars from the Bible. Eve, by submitting to temptation, was responsible for unleashing sinful forces on the whole of mankind. But the Blessed Virgin Mary was an agent of redemption in that she bore Jesus Christ.[6] It had no small bearing on the characteristics which were subsequently attributed to women, that Eve had condemned mankind with her foolish tongue, whereas Mary was recorded as having spoken only three times in her life.[7]

In the eyes of the church establishment all mortal women were the inheritors of Eve's untrustworthy nature. That women were destined to bear the brunt of the guilt, as a result of her succumbing to temptation, is often doubly stressed in visual representations, where the serpent is itself portrayed as a woman. In one particularly vivid instance it is wearing the kind of fashionable headdress that would have been worn by a bourgeois lady (Cat. 353). Women were feared by the Church as a

Fig. 13 Nave arcade corbel showing Tutivillus and the gossips (Sleaford, Lincolnshire, Church of St Denys)

potentially unruly and unsettling force. An English homilist wrote in the thirteenth century: 'Woman ... is the confusion of Man, an insatiable beast, a continuous anxiety, an incessant warfare, a daily ruin, a house of tempest, a hindrance to devotion.'[8] Manuscripts commissioned by the clergy abound with images of women as temptresses. In the Brussels Peterborough Psalter, the initial C of *Cantate Domino*, the first phrase of Psalm XCVII, is appropriately illustrated by a group of tonsured clerics singing (fig. 14; Cat. 567). Their eyes are raised, however, not to Heaven but to a figure of a woman depicted in the opposite border, dangling two songbirds in a cage before them as if taunting them for their life of enclosure. In the closely related Ramsey Psalter (Cat. 566), the initial D for *Domine exaudi orationem meam*, showing monks praying to God, is supported by a fashionable lady whose hips sway towards them, and whose eyes look flirtatiously askance (f. 107v.). Presumably such provocative behaviour was extremely unlikely in reality, but is invoked here as a warning against the temptations of the flesh.[9]

Fig. 14 Initial to Psalm XCVII from the Peterborough Psalter (Brussels, Bibliothèque Royale, MS 9961–62, f. 66; Cat. 567)

Nudity had little allure in English medieval art. It could represent innocence, as in the case of Adam and Eve before the Fall, or the lewdness of Luxuria, or the preparedness for the afterlife of a naked soul. As a device for demonstrating appreciation of the body it had absolutely no currency, though much pleasure seems to have been gained in general from the shape of the female form. Throughout the period, conventional representations show and describe the ideal as slender of body with narrow shoulders and hips, rounded breasts, 'long smal armys' (long slim arms) and graceful hands. In order to be considered beautiful, features had to be regular and small. A tiny nose was particularly admired, as we know indeed from Chaucer's vain Prioress.[10] A gentle inclination of the torso was evidently considered to be an elegant attitude for both men and women from the end of the thirteenth century and well into the fourteenth. The French Knight of La Tour Landry, in a book of manners written in the late fourteenth century for the moral instruction of his three daughters, declares repeatedly that it is unbecoming for a genteel woman to twist her head hither and thither or to crane her neck, but she must instead look straight ahead, or turn her whole body. Upper-class and holy women are nearly always so represented, both in England and in France.[11]

Throughout the fourteenth century in England, dresses became more revealing of the shape of the body, much to the scorn of the religious homilists. John Bromyard wrote predictably of the sideless overdress, fashionable from the mid-century: 'Christ opened his side for the redemption and salvation of many and these others open their sides for lascivious and carnal provocation, and for the perdition of those who behold them.'[12] Both figure-hugging clothing and make-up were mocked by John Waldeby as encouraging women to deny the rightness of God's natural creation:

If a noble painter, in the execution of some figure sculptures it well and artistically and also puts suitable colours upon it, would not the pupil or the owner of the figure do insult to such an artist, if he altered the form and colour of that same figure? So when women set about adorning their own persons by constricting themselves in tight clothing they wish to appear slender, and with artificial colours they desire to seem beautiful, thereby expressly insulting their Creator.[13]

Excessive finery was as much mocked. St Jerome himself recounted a story similar to that of Tutivillus, as a warning against the sins of vanity and pride, of a devil who settled on the trailing train of an overdressed woman; and there were many others who criticised extravagant female fashions.[14] The taste for fine clothes was condemned by the Knight of La Tour Landry, who advised his daughters not to be tempted to flaunt their wealth in this way and certainly not to be the first to introduce a new fashion, but instead to follow those favoured by the majority.[15]

Nevertheless, as the critics indicate by the very fact that the subject is given such prominence, rich clothing was greatly admired and was popularly believed to make women even more beautiful. According to Chaucer's version of the story of Patient Griselda in the Clerk's Tale, Griselda's elevation in social status from a simple peasant to a noble countess was signalled by her transformation from a natural beauty to an astonishing vision of loveliness as she was arrayed in her bridal garments.[16] Griselda perfectly exemplifies the association of beauty, wealth and goodness that character-ised the noblest of the female stereotypes in the Middle Ages. Despite opinions to the contrary from the more ascetic commentators already quoted, it is noticeable in religious images that a rich and beautiful appearance designates a corresponding level of sanctity. The point has been made elsewhere (see p. 29) that there was often little distinction made between the appearance of rich ladies as shown on tombs, and the images of saints and biblical women in image niches or in manuscripts, who could equally be shown dressed according to the latest fashion (Cat. 685). This served not only to reinforce the religious pretensions of the social élite but, by presenting their status in terms which vain mortals could readily understand, it was the clearest way of conveying an idea of the power of the saints in Heaven to a rigidly class-bound culture on earth.

The Queen of Heaven was the Blessed Virgin Mary. Pictures and statues of her, even more in the fourteenth than in the thirteenth century, show her as possessing an unmistakably regal appearance (see Cat. 699). Although she clearly conforms to the ideal of courtly beauty, with a well-proportioned and slender body and small, regular features, she is never made to look quite like other women. Her head is always more modestly inclined and her body more gracefully draped. By subtle means she is made to look even more gracious than any earthly queen (Cat. 682, f. 4v.).

Devotion to Mary took different forms for different sections of society. Devout men, particularly religious, went to some pains to assign her to a high plane of devotion which has been compared to the cult of courtly love.[17] So as not to taint her pure reputation, she had to be notionally divorced from any relationship with mortal women: 'Name hir to no woman, to mayden nor to wyfe/For thou knowist, nor I ne kan, non so trwe of life' (mention her to no woman, to virgin nor to wife as neither you nor I know any woman who is so virtuous), sang the nightingale to the clerk in a fourteenth-century poem.[18] To Henry of Chichester, Mary was directly accessible, as represented by a portrait in his missal (Cat. 108, f. 150).[19] He is in close communion with her through his prayers, and she and Christ lean attentively towards him. To the nun of Amesbury, in a similar portrait in another mid-thirteenth-century manuscript (Cat. 316), the Virgin and Child are a pair absorbed in each other to be adored by her from afar.[20]

The Virgin was regarded as a model of virtue to which ladies could aspire. The Knight of La Tour Landry encouraged his daughters to look to her as an example for her humility and courtesy.[21] A new illustration of the Virgin's life appears in England in the early fourteenth century in the Alphonso Psalter, the education of the Virgin by her mother, St Anne (Cat. 357, f. 3). In the fourteenth-century Fitzwarin Psalter (Cat. 685), the female donor of the manuscript is included in the scene kneeling before St Anne as she teaches the Virgin to read, as if she too is anxious to benefit from her instruction (cf. fig. 131).

There were differences of opinion among certain male authorities as to whether it was a good idea for women to be able to read. Philippe de Navarre, who wrote an instruction manual for ladies in French which had widespread currency, thought that, with the exception of nuns, the ability to read was unnecessary.[22] On the other hand, Humbert de Romans, general of the Dominicans, wrote that learning was particularly important for the daughters of the rich in case they wished to join the religious life or to devote themselves to the study of sacred texts. He recommended knowledge of the psalter, Hours of Our Lady, the Office of the Dead and other prayers.[23] Clearly his opinion prevailed. Few daughters of the rich are known to have written much during this period, but many owned fine books and were certainly able to read French, though anything more than limited comprehension of Latin was apparently rare even among nuns.[24]

The De Lisle Psalter (Cat. 569) was bequeathed to his daughters by Baron de Lisle in the 1330s. It would be interesting to know if he ordered for their use the unusually large number of learned schematic diagrams for the preface, which included the Tower of Theology of Master John of Metz, the Sphera of John Pecham, and the Tree of Salvation of St Bonaventure, among others. If so, then we can assume that some women were given the benefit of quite a superior education. Women who could afford them usually owned small devotional books for their own use and perhaps also for instructing their children. In one of the Bohun manuscripts (cf. Cat. 690) is a dedication picture (f. 181v.) in similar vein to that in the Fitzwarin Psalter, but here the patroness is introducing her child to the Virgin, perhaps in order to register her intention to teach her with the Virgin's guidance. Sometimes devotional books were exchanged as gifts, for example, Marie de St Pol, Countess of Pembroke, records in her will a little breviary given to her by the Queen.[25] Who commissioned one of the most lavishly decorated manuscripts of the period, the Queen Mary Psalter (London, British Library, Royal MS 2 B. VII) is not recorded, but the choice of illustrations, where women, particularly biblical queens and noblewomen, feature prominently, suggests that it is likely to have been made for a very high-born woman, perhaps in commemoration of the birth of a child. It has been suggested that it was made for Edward II's queen, Isabella, who also owned another more ordinary psalter which may have been made to mark the occasion of her wedding in 1308, as well as three missals, a breviary, two graduals and a martyrology, which were kept in her chapel.[26]

Unlike married women, or even men, widows were free to dispose of their property as they wished upon their death and as we know for certain from monastic records and wills, rich and pious widows tended to be generous benefactors to the Church, giving money, plate and jewels, vestments and books. Isabella Marshall, Countess of Clare and co-heiress of the Earl of Pembroke, gave, just before her death in 1240, an enormous quantity of chalices, reliquaries, vestments and books to Tewkesbury Abbey.[27] Her granddaughter Margaret probably commissioned the Clare Chasuble and two of her great-granddaughters, Eleanor de Clare and Elisabeth de Burgh, continued the family tradition of spectacular benefactions. Eleanor probably paid for much of the rebuilding of the east end of Tewkesbury Abbey in the 1320s and 1330s.[28] Elisabeth de Burgh employed four goldsmiths to take care of her jewellery and plate. She founded Clare College, Cambridge, and generously endowed the Augustinian priory at Clare, Suffolk.[29]

More often than not, the only means by which a benefaction is identifiable is through heraldry, which creates problems in the case of women, as they did not bear arms in their own right. Because they were beholden for their status to their fathers and husbands they were rarely, unless they were heiresses, manifest heraldically as separate personalities. There were cases when the arms they bore could be confused with those of male members of their family, as in the case of Joanna de Stuteville, who in her widowhood adopted her father's arms unimpaled (see Cat. 142). With more work on the complex customs for female heraldry it may be possible to shed far more light on the subject of women's patronage of the arts.[30]

Some clients must have played an active part in determining the appearance of the objects or buildings they commissioned, but we rarely have the information to be precise about this. A spandrel relief in the chapter house at Worcester Cathedral shows a woman instructing a mason[31] and in a few French manuscripts women are shown in conference with masons who are carving incised tomb slabs.[32] Tomb contracts between patrons and masons are rare and tend to be for later periods, but from other circumstantial evidence it is clear that widows were often responsible for commissioning their husbands' tombs, or at least for executing their husbands' instructions if they left any before their death. For example, two of the most famous tombs of knights of the period, William Longespée at Salisbury and Aymer de Valence at Westminster, were probably commissioned by their widows, both of whom, Countess Ela of Salisbury and Marie de St Pol, were powerful and wealthy in their own right.[33]

Tombs of women are very uniform in design, even more so than the tombs of men. There are no female equivalents of the active knights of the end of the thirteenth and early fourteenth century, lying cross-legged or half rising as if ready for battle. Women are normally shown, whether alone or beside their husbands, as if they were standing still, looking youthful and slender, their feet often resting on an image of a cherished pet dog (see Cat. 224) They are represented with eyes open, either engrossed in prayer with their hands folded, or holding a heart, a heraldic shield or a cloak strap. For most of the period there is little variation in fashion, clothes tending to be all-enveloping and voluminously draped, but towards the end of the fourteenth century (see p. 104) a shift in attitude is heralded by the tomb of Edward III's queen, Philippa of Hainault, at Westminster Abbey, showing her, presumably as she chose to be represented, as a middle-aged and portly figure in a fashionably close-fitting dress.[34]

Women were able to exercise influence over taste in artistic matters much more as patrons than they were as practitioners in this period. The fact that women were expected to bear the brunt of domestic responsiblity would have militated against many of them being able to undertake the same sort of professional artistic careers as were open to men. Nevertheless, women clearly were able to acquire the necessary skills, and a few, especially embroiderers, like Mabel of Bury St Edmunds, who worked extensively for the royal Court between 1239 and 1244, rose to quite a prominent status.[35] It seems to have been quite customary for craftswomen to supplement their incomes with commercial undertakings. In mid-fourteenth-century London, Dyonisia La Longe, gilder, and Matilda Weston, weaver, also ran alehouses, as did Matilda Myms, widow of John the 'imaginour', who bequeathed all her own materials for making pictures to her apprentice, William.[36] The roles played by women were normally governed by, or related to, the trade or skill of their husbands or families. Depending on their social status, they seem either to have worked as servants – hod carriers and plasterers' assistants in the mason's trade – or to have been entrusted with the managerial side of their operations. [37] London records are full of references to the daughters and widows of weavers and goldsmiths who were left in charge of shops, tools and apprentices.[38] Agnes Ramsey, daughter of the master mason William, evidently ran the workshop for many years after her father's death.[39] An entrepreneurial role seems to have been quite acceptable and it may have been her success as a builders' merchant that endeared Katherine Lyghtefote to master mason Henry Yevele, and they married shortly after they were both employed supplying the king's palace at Sheen in the 1380s.[40]

Despite their range of occupations, women, and for that matter men as well, are

Fig. 15   Women harvesting, from the Luttrell Psalter (London, British Library, Add. MS 42130, f. 172v.; Cat. 575)

Fig. 16   Praying woman and monkey, from the Gorleston Psalter (London, British Library, Add. MS 49622, f. 94; Cat. 574)

Fig. 17   Sedilia corbel showing a woman feeding nuts to a squirrel (Heckington, Lincolnshire, Church of St Andrew)

hardly ever depicted at work in any English source in the thirteenth and fourteenth centuries. The Luttrell Psalter (fig. 15) incorporates in its border illuminations practically the only series of scenes of everyday rural life. Among them are a few showing women labouring alongside men in fields, feeding chickens, carding and spinning wool and helping to bring in the corn under the stern eye of the reeve. In the context of a religious manuscript commissioned by a rich Lincolnshire landowner, it is not at all clear whether these pictures were intended to be taken at face value as records of his manorial duties, or whether they were pastoral conceits included for his amusement.

Images of women in medieval art were often used not to portray specific aspects of womanhood, but principally to convey messages about the fallibility of human virtue and the dangers inherent in too deep an admiration for earthly pleasures. The framework for the visual expression of the abstract notion of virtue was provided by a tremendously influential work written in the fifth century by Prudentius, the *Psychomachia*, an allegory of the virtues and vices.[41] In this book the conquest of vices such as anger, lust, discord and avarice was symbolised by mortal combat with the virtues such as fortitude, temperance, justice, charity, prudence, chastity, obedience, faith and hope. All the virtues, but only some of the vices, were represented as females. The conquest of vice by virtue, personified exactly as in the *Psychomachia* as a series of armed struggles, was a favourite subject, depicted in all media from the walls of Henry III's Painted Chamber at Westminster Palace, where eight virtues were depicted, to the copper figure now in the Victoria and Albert Museum (Cat. 331–2, 588) where an isolated episode represents the cycle.[42] There are also an enormous number of variations on the theme of the battle over vice, represented widely in medieval art, for example, as a fight between armed knights, or between men or women and various forms of devil incarnate. The most subtle of the variations are those which concern women, reflecting the belief that in them were embodied not virtue alone, but the polarising forces of virtue and vice. Burlesque images of women could turn the allegory on its head as a warning against false virtue and misplaced trust. Thus women who were depicted as triumphant in combat could echo the action of the personified virtue, but actually represent vice. The very notion of virtue for women was under attack, and those virtues which were deemed particularly desirable for women, obedience, chastity, temperance or prudence, were precisely those which were most often ridiculed or mocked.

Many of the images of women which inhabit the borders of manuscripts or the equivalent edges and semi-hidden places of buildings and furnishings, such as roof and buttress corbels and misericords, satirise the convention of female virtues. Among an extensive series of decorative corbels supporting liturgical furnishings and exterior buttresses at Sleaford, Ewerby, Heckington and Anwick, a group of parish churches in Lincolnshire, are many which are critical of female behaviour. There are women wearing ridiculous and excessive headdresses, women fighting men, women indulgently feeding their pets or being carried off by a variety of unpleasant creatures. They not only demonstrate the sins of pride and vanity, the vices of anger and discord, but also they satirise the virtues. Obedience is lampooned by the familiar image of the belligerent wife. False charity is shown by the woman feeding nuts to a squirrel but it would have been equally obvious to contemporaries that she was also a sly reference to licentiousness (fig. 17).[43]

Manuscript borders are well endowed with similar moralising or humorous images of women. The sources of some of these, it has long been recognised, are fables of the kind told in popular sermons to instruct the ignorant in the basic tenets of faith or moral issues.[44] These might be scenes from Aesop, or episodes from the story of Reynard the Fox and Chanticleer such as occur in the Ormesby and Gorleston Psalters (Cat. 573–4). Often the images are satirical. In this class are the numerous examples of a genre that was thought to be hugely funny, collectively known as 'the world turned upside-down', where for example, monkeys take the place of men. In the Gorleston Psalter (Cat. 574) such an image satirises the virtue of faith by poking fun at a pious woman who prays before a monkey masquerading as a priest. He is wearing a cowl and simultaneously holding aloft an anointing vessel and balancing a ball on his nose (fig. 16).

Allusions to sexual relationships between men and women are plentiful, especially in the borders of manuscripts, and they appear in a variety of disguises. The same range of images is common to religious and secular sources, but not necessarily for the same reasons. The storming of the Castle of Love, a scene possibly inspired by or related to a romance such as the Romance of the Rose, occurs in numerous contexts, for instance in the borders of the Brussels Peterborough Psalter (Cat. 567) and the Luttrell Psalter (Cat. 575). In the religious manuscripts the illustration could have reminded the readers both of the virtues of feminine chastity and of the half-hearted way in which it was maintained, thus reflecting the moral and misogynistic tendencies of the Romance of the Rose. On the other hand, the same illustration is frequently carved on French ivory caskets and mirrors, and it is hard to believe that it was there as anything more than an enjoyable decorative caprice celebrating love and valour.[45]

A series of romances is depicted in the little book known as the Taymouth Hours (London, British Library, Yates Thompson MS 13), made in the early fourteenth century for an unknown noblewoman. They are all of the 'brave knight overcomes adversary' or 'rescues damsel in distress' variety, and are illustrated as a series of *bas-de-page* scenes completely unrelated to the text of the Hours of the Virgin which they accompany, as if the lady who owned the book was in the habit of dreaming of Guy of Warwick (Cat. 155) or Bevis of Hampton in the middle of her prayers to the Virgin. They are followed by some twenty pictures of women hunting, and the book ends with an Office for the Dead illustrated, this time appropriately, with hideous torments of Hell. Scenes of women hunting are quite common and occur also in the Queen Mary Psalter and the Smithfield Decretals, but they do not always document known practice. In the Taymouth Hours, the series is prefaced by the inscription *Cy comence jeu de dames* (Here begins the sport of ladies) and includes pictures of genteel ladies trapping on foot, shooting rabbits with blunt arrows and carrying home their prey, slung over their shoulders (fig. 18).[46] The pictures may have been intended to be funny, in the 'world turned upside-down' tradition. More likely, however, they are allegorical, and allude to another kind of hunting altogether, that of men by women and vice versa. Female hunters call to mind the classical story of Diana the huntress, which was well known in the Middle Ages from Ovid's *Metamorphoses*; and these illustrations may well have been alluding to the ideas about chastity that this story would conjure up.[47] On the King's Lynn cup, however, where female hunters appear alongside men, the connotations, considering that this was probably a cup for wine, are rather different. Here a huntress is revealed as the cup is drained, which suggests that she has been caught or is about to catch the drinker. It is not an image of chastity but of conquest (see Cat. 541).

The image of the hunt often does refer quite evidently to lustful relationships between men and women. This has its parallel in medieval literature, where the stag chase is frequently of erotic significance.[48] In illustrations the subject tends to be treated with a certain levity. Stags being pursued by hounds, the stags looking suspiciously gleeful, are often illustrated on the same pages as seductive females. In an early fourteenth-century psalter in Oxford, a stag hunt is paired with a comic scene showing a woman chasing and embracing a man while he tries to mount his horse (fig. 19). Lucy Freeman Sandler has drawn attention to an episode in the margins of the Ormesby Psalter when animal pursuits of various kinds accompany a betrothal between a man and woman which is full of visual puns of an extremely bawdy kind.[49] Particularly in manuscripts commissioned by secular patrons, sexual innuendo was very close to the surface, as indeed it was in secular literature. The analogy of the animal chase with human seduction is again in the classical tradition: 'Well knows the hunter where to spread his nets for the stag, well knows he in what glen the boar with gnashing teeth abides; familiar are the copses to fowlers ... you too who seek the object of a lasting passion, learn first what places the maidens haunt.' Ovid wrote this in his poem *Ars Amatoria*, which was the inspiration behind many medieval treatises on the subject.[50] Ostensibly it was intended to warn men of the deceptive wiles of women, but really it was a guide to methods of seduction: 'Of safe love making do I sing, and permitted secrecy....'[51] It was perhaps 'permitted secrecy' that the hunt in the borders of medieval religious manuscripts could allude to the pleasures of the

Fig. 18 Woman shooting a rabbit, from the Taymouth Hours (London, British Library, Yates Thompson MS 13, f. 68v.)

Fig. 19 Marginal decoration from a fourteenth-century psalter (Oxford, Jesus College, MS 40, f. 80)

sexual chase while at the same time attacking its female inspiration. It was at this point that the secular and the religious attitudes to women converged and women were depicted as being forever forbidden but eternally desirable.

The range of illustrations of women in the visual arts from this period of the Middle Ages is remarkably limited, but perhaps that is not so surprising when one reflects on the context within which the images were seen, and the didactic purposes that they were required to serve. What come across very strongly are the conventions, largely established by the Church, by which attitudes to women were bound. These are expressed by pictorial equivalents which are equally limited within their own traditions. Women are alternately or even simultaneously oppressed and worshipped, insulted and adored, ridiculed and desired, depending on which facet of womanhood is being observed or which point of view is dominant. Women exist in medieval art as a series of stereotypes, or to use the medieval term, counterfeits. There is no interest in depicting individuals. We would look in vain for pictures about what women really did, or how they felt, or even what they really looked like.

NOTES

I am grateful for the advice and assistance of the following people: Caroline Barron, Susan Haskins, Sandy Heslop, Christopher Hohler, Andrew and Jane Martindale, Anna and Rex Mather, John Onians, Nicholas Pickwoad, Kate Sekules, Tony Sims, David Stocker.

1. Jarrett 1926, p. 84, from Holcot 1510, lect. 5, f. xi.
2. Owst 1926, pp. 176–7; Owst 1961, p. 387; Camille 1985a, p. 40.
3. Chaucer 1985 edn, The Wife of Bath's Prologue, pp. 76–84.
4. Christine de Pisan 1983 edn, pp. 31–2.
5. Owst 1961, p. 386, from Welter 1914 edn, fasc. v, p. 33.
6. Robbins 1960, pp. 172–6; Kraus 1967.
7. Owst 1961, p. 387; *Ancrene Wisse* 1962 edn, pp. 40–2.
8. Owst 1961, pp. 77–8, from *Speculum Laicorum* 1914, fasc. v, p. 77.
9. Repr. Sandler 1974, pl. 88, p. 45.
10. Chaucer 1985 edn, General prologue, p. 18.
11. *La Tour Landry* 1868 edn, pp. 15, 16–17.
12. Owst 1961, p. 397.
13. Owst 1961, p. 392.
14. Handlyng Synne 1901 edn, pp. 112, 116–17, 118–19.
15. La Tour Landry 1868 edn, pp. 29–31.
16. Chaucer 1985 edn, The Clerk's Tale, p. 105.
17. Warner 1978; Brooke 1978, p. 7; Stone 1964, pp. 42–59.
18. Robbins 1960, p. 31.
19. Repr. Rickert 1965, pl. 108.
20. Repr. Brieger 1957, pl. 64.
21. La Tour Landry 1868 edn, pp. 146–52.
22. Labarge 1986, p. 38.
23. Jarrett 1926, pp. 87–8.
24. Power 1922, pp. 246–55.
25. Jenkinson 1915, p. 433.
26. Evans 1915, p. 15; Alexander 1983, pp. 156–7.
27. Lehmann-Brockhaus 1955–60, II, no. 4369.
28. Verey 1970, pp. 369–70; Morris 1974, pp. 146–7; Altschul 1965, pp. 34, 40–2; Morris 1985, p. 93.
29. Labarge 1986, pp. 89–92.
30. Blair 1943, pp. 19–26.
31. Repr. Prior & Gardner 1912, fig. 271.
32. British Library, Add. MS 10292, f. 55b; MS Royal 14 E. III, f. 66.
33. Labarge 1986, pp. 92–4, 108; Jenkinson 1915.
34. Wilson, Tudor-Craig, Physick & Gem 1986, pp. 123–4; Evans 1915, pp. 154–5; Scott 1986, pp. 38–9.
35. Lancaster 1972, pp. 83–5; Parker 1984, pp. 48–9.
36. Sharpe 1889, pt I, pp. 575, 576, 621.
37. Knoop & Jones 1933, pp. 70, 71.
38. Sharpe 1889, pt I, pp. 194, 475, 664.
39. Cat. 135; Harvey 1984, pp. 243–4.
40. Harvey 1984, p. 363.
41. Katzenellenbogen 1968; Warner 1985, pp. 146–54.
42. Binski 1986, pp. 41–5.
43. Sandler 1985.
44. Randall 1966a.
45. Paris 1981–2, no. 127; Victoria and Albert Museum 1986a, pp. 214–15; Sandler 1974, p. 31, pl. 57.
46. British Library Yates Thompson MS 13, ff. 68a–83v; Klingender 1971, pp. 415–16; Thiébaux 1967, p. 260; Shahar 1983, p. 249.
47. Ovid 1916 edn; Thiébaux 1974, pp. 96–7.
48. Thiébaux 1974.
49. Sandler 1985.
50. Power 1926, p. 406; Thiébaux 1974, pp. 97–102; Ovid 1969 edn, pp. 36–7.
51. Ovid 1969 edn, p. 15.

Artists, Craftsmen and Design in England, 1200–1400

Nigel Ramsay

> With Poules wyndow corved on his shoos,
> In hoses rede he wente fetisly,

So wrote Chaucer of Absalon, the elegant parish clerk in the Miller's Tale:[1] he meant that the fashionable young man's shoes were cut with a pattern taken from tracery in Old St Paul's Cathedral (see Cat. 681). The way in which the Gothic style spread from architecture to other media is one theme of this essay, but so too must be the question of how this was possible. How did artists learn of new designs, and how were they in a position to disseminate them? What changes were there in the organisation of the artistic world so that in the thirteenth and fourteenth centuries the Gothic style came to be found in almost all media, whereas the Romanesque style can hardly be said to have spread from architecture to any other art form?

Gervase of Canterbury, comparing the capitals of the Romanesque work at Canterbury Cathedral with those carved under the direction of the French master mason William of Sens (the bringer of the Gothic style to Canterbury, *c.* 1174–8, and thus to England), thought that the Romanesque work seemed hewn by axes and the Gothic carved with chisels.[2] This, however, was merely his perception of a change in artistic style: there were very few additions to the range of available tools or materials from the twelfth to the fifteenth centuries, and almost every technical process practised in the Gothic period was known to Theophilus, writer of a craftsman's manual in the early twelfth century.[3] What formed an artist's style was rather his training, the designs that he encountered where he worked or travelled, and the patrons who employed him – influences that are virtually unquantifiable.

Various literary works describing artistic or architectural techniques were available in the thirteenth century, Theophilus's treatise for craftsmen and Vitruvius's antique work on architecture being the best known today, but there is no evidence that any English artist used either of these; sketchbooks and model books with specific designs undoubtedly circulated, as will be seen, but the prime influence on a master mason or artist must have been the master under whom he trained;[4] a man's style was likely to be spread most widely by his former apprentices. But this is only likely to be visible today in architectural works, where adaptations of moulding profiles may be discernible, or in documentary references, such as the bequest in 1417 by the master mason Stephen Lote of all the patterns in his chamber at Sheen Palace to Thomas Mapilton.[5]

More forcibly, and especially after the shortage of craftsmen resulting from the Black Death around 1349, the Crown sometimes impressed men into its service and thus put them under the control of its own master craftsmen: for royal palaces and castles as well as for military expeditions, men might be despatched from any part of England, although inevitably the craftsmen who were given the task of finding suitable men for the king's needs tended to draw them from one part of England.[6] Equally, craftsmen were attracted to the Crown by virtue of the lavish expenditure in which it so often indulged. The royal Court did not offer permanent posts to more than a handful of artists and masons, and these posts might be no better than that of a fairly low-paid sinecure such as a serjeantcy-at-arms,[7] but it offered a chance to meet other patrons and – no less important – other artists and their designs. The impermanency of most Crown employment speeded the spread of fashionable designs around the country as former employees of the King's Works returned to their own part of the country or went west to fresh patrons.

The Court was itself itinerant, and so were the nobility and bishops: their artists probably did not travel with them, not being part of their households, but their properties were scattered throughout England, and much decorative work as well as most architectural work could only be done on the spot. Only religious houses were limited to one place or area (although they used major towns, and especially London, as bases from which to buy luxuries or necessities that were not obtainable locally), and to these too the artist had to travel. For instance, Master John Bernetby, who was paid £15 for painting the table and tabernacle of the high altar of Thornton Abbey, Lincolnshire, in 1341,[8] is probably identifiable with the John Barneby who worked at St Stephen's Chapel, Westminster,[9] and William Burdon who in 1363–5 was paid £4 for painting a table in the king's chapel at Windsor and £40 in 1368 for painting a table in the canons' chapel there, as well as a reredos,[10] is possibly identifiable with the man of this name to whom Eynsham Abbey, Oxfordshire, paid 6s.8d in 1389–90 for painting the table on their high altar.[11]

Successful artists have doubtless always been collectors of works, and one chance bequest reveals a medieval English painter as the owner of an Italian panel painting: Master Hugh of St Albans in 1362 left a Lombard painting of six pieces, which he said had cost him £20.[12] Ten years earlier Hugh had been paid for designing the wall painting of St Stephen's Chapel, Westminster, and these have been noted for their Italianate features.[13] Equally, it must sometimes have been the case that English artists would seek to copy foreign works – a fourteenth-century bone writing tablet found in Southampton (Cat. 428) is a clear instance of an unskilful craftsman's attempt to reproduce a fashionable Parisian ivory – and straightforward copies are almost certain to be less successful than works that merely reflect the influence or inspiration of others.

The early twelfth-century treatise by the monk Theophilus provides accounts of how to make virtually any kind of artefact, whereas fourteenth- and fifteenth-century English artists' recipes cover a far more limited range of media.[14] Can this change be said to encapsulate a broader one, of the decline of the monastic craftsman and his replacement by secular specialists? Leaving aside architecture, which Theophilus did not seek to cover, it may first of all be said that monks certainly did increasingly employ laymen to write and decorate their books for them, although this change was a gradual one, beginning in the twelfth century and never complete. It is, besides, probably a mistake to draw too sharp a distinction between monastic and lay scribes and illuminators, for much writing, even in the Romanesque period, was done by clerks who had taken at least the first steps towards ordination to major holy orders and were perhaps hoping for an ecclesiastical benefice or office: such clerks formed part of a highly populated but shadowy world between the lay and the religious.[15]

How far monks had themselves ever been craftsmen working in wood, stone, metal or glass is doubtful. There were a few polymaths, of whom Matthew Paris of St Albans Abbey is the most celebrated, and a few men who had learnt a particular craft before entering the monastic life,[16] but such men were exceptional. It is more fruitful to look instead at what was unquestionably one of the greatest developments in the Gothic period – and one that coincided in its rise with that of Gothic art – the rise of the universities.

The secular clerks studying at Oxford and Cambridge needed a whole range of texts, many of them of a recent date of composition, and a book trade rapidly developed to meet this need, with bookbinders, 'stationers', *exemplarii* (copyists of certain prescribed texts, working in a particular, standardised way, cf. Cat. 429) and parchment-makers all being found in Oxford before 1240.[17] But what is intriguing is that the very first recorded book-trade member in Oxford was Roger the Illuminator, *c.* 1190, and that before 1300 the names of a further eighteen illuminators are known, and that these men were the most numerous section of the book trade, being especially prominent until *c.* 1250. The university students and masters did not need to have their texts illuminated, so these illuminators must have worked for other patrons and have settled in Oxford simply because it was a convenient base from the point of view of raw materials (such as parchment) and of the packaging of their produce (by the bookbinders). One mid-thirteenth-century illuminator, W. de Brailles, who signed two manuscripts and whose style is detectable in another five, is surely identifiable with William de Brailes who is recorded as an illuminator in Oxford at that date; two self-portraits show him as tonsured, indicating that he had received at least the lowest form of holy orders, the first tonsure.[18] Puzzlingly, de Brailes's manuscripts

Fig. 20 Drawing of window tracery
(Cambridge, Magdalene College, MS 1916,
f. 17v.; Cat. 466)

are almost the only ones that have been linked convincingly with Oxford; Eleanor, Countess of Leicester, in 1265 paid 14s for a breviary written there,[19] but otherwise there is little evidence of the Oxford book trade from non-Oxford sources. Equally, however, remarkably little evidence has yet been found for the writing or decoration of books in the thirteenth century in London and York, although this certainly took place in both, as well as in Norwich and other large towns.

In the fourteenth century documentation for the book trade in London multiplies; by early in the century the City must have surpassed Oxford as a centre for the production of illuminated books. It may be symptomatic of this change that in 1331 Queen Philippa at Westminster paid Richard of Oxford for illuminating two small Books of Hours of the Virgin for her:[20] his name suggests that he had come from Oxford and settled in Westminster, close to the Court.

The move of the book trade to London, or at least the burgeoning of the book trade within London, seems to have been matched in other crafts; and although our knowledge of this is still slight, it appears that London by the later fourteenth century had become such a centre for both the making of goods and the sale of imported luxury items that the provinces had generally either to go to London for their luxuries, or wait for one of the great regional fairs to bring such goods to them. The most powerful London guilds, such as the goldsmiths, sought to control not merely their own members but also the making of their speciality in the rest of England. The existence of several dozen London-based craft guilds resulted from the presence in the capital of so many specialised craftsmen, and while these were often working in such close collaboration as to be participants in what seem to us as workshops, the guilds saw it as their duty to make the individual craftsman responsible for his product. Craftsmen's marks were one outcome of this: the goldsmiths' are the best known (from 1363 onwards) but others pre-dated them, such as those of the turners (1347).[21] What may be maker's (or possibly engraver's) marks have been identified on monumental brasses of about the 1330s and of the late fourteenth century:[22] the marblers who made such brasses (see p. 171) – and who incidentally furnish a very clear-cut example of a craft activity that became based in London in the fourteenth century[23] – were not so numerous as to need marks to identify their products (and nor was the reliability of these in question), but their occasional use of marks may show the pride they took in their handiwork, like the sporadically-found signatures of scribes and illuminators.

Craft guilds were far from being limited to London, although they were most numerous there: before the close of the fourteenth century such large towns as York had many guilds of their craftsmen, even for such specialists as scribes,[24] although York's painters, stainers and goldbeaters were combined into one guild.[25] But the concentration of craftsmen into a few centres did take place, to the craftsmen's benefit. In an indeterminate or at least unquantifiable way again, it appears that in the course of the thirteenth and fourteenth centuries artists and even architects became much more settled in their place of work, so that their patrons came to them, rather than they to their patrons. This partly reflected the changes that have already been indicated, but it was also made possible by the increasing separation of design from execution, which made good designs more readily identifiable and thus more marketable.

The Gothic style was easily adapted from architecture to other media, and especially to the decorative arts: traceried designs, perhaps with the characteristically English feature of battlementing,[26] lent themselves to goldsmiths' work (Cat. 121), to the memorial brasses made by marblers (Cat. 678), to woodwork and even to such apparently intractable materials as leather, as well, of course, as to free-standing sculpture. What enabled the style to spread so successfully was the ease with which it could be drawn in two dimensions, as outline tracery, and therefore with which the design of a work could be separated from its execution. Designs could have a life of their own because they could be set out on parchment, or on metal or wood as architect's templates, and be carried around or even out of the country (fig. 20).

Inexpensive works of art were doubtless generally both designed and made by the one man, but exacting patrons could ensure that their wishes were met by providing the craftsman with a 'patron' or model to follow. Thus in 1331 Queen Philippa is

Fig. 21 Detail from the border of the Pienza embroidered cope, *c.* 1315–35 (Capitolo della Cattedrale di Pienza)

found paying the London goldsmith Simon de Berking 2s for the drawing of a ship in parchment, to have a model by which a ship for alms (or *nef*) could be made.[27] For large-scale works there was the further attraction that the limiting of a design to one or two men would ensure greater overall unity: for example, for the chapter house at St George's, Windsor, two craftsmen, Masters John Lyncoln and John Athelard, were paid for three days, at 1s a day each, for drawing out a design for the windows,[28] which five glaziers then painted on to glass (at 7d a day each) and which ten other glaziers then put into place (at 6d a day each). John Athelard was himself not a glazier, but a painter: in 1350 he was appointed to obtain painters for Edward III's other major current work, the decoration of St Stephen's Chapel, Westminster, and he resumed working there as a painter after he had finished his designing work at Windsor.[29]

The separation of design from execution can equally be demonstrated in the case of embroidered clothing,[30] and it was necessarily the case in architecture. A master mason would most likely carry designs around with him in the form of drawings, but once on site he would transfer these designs on to 'moulds' or templates. This was so even in the twelfth century, when William of Sens at Canterbury Cathedral is stated to have handed over to the masons moulds for cutting the stones:[31] his role was as a designer and supervisor, and he may not have carved any of the stones himself.[32] A busy master mason might not be expected even to supervise the execution of his plans: the celebrated Henry Yevele in the late fourteenth century may well have designed the metal effigies for the tomb of Richard II and Anne of Bohemia (see Cat. 446), and he certainly designed but did not erect (and was not contractually bound to supervise) the addition to Westminster Hall's walls of an extra 60 cm in height and a cornice that was to bear the country's largest and first ever hammerbeam roof (Cat. 445).

Many ecclesiastical patrons in the late twelfth and early thirteenth centuries must have had treatises providing them with suitable collections of, say, types and antitypes: the treatise *Pictor in Carmine* is known to have belonged to at least five English cathedrals or religious houses.[33] If lay patrons wanted to dictate to an artist a particular scheme of decoration, then they too would have been expected to provide him with some guide or model, literary or artistic. A fussy patron such as Henry III undoubtedly furnished the painters (or designers) of the Painted Chamber in Westminster Palace with literary models,[34] and once secular iconography had developed, it is likely that the nobility would have handed over such books as the bestiary (a combination of the literary and the artistic) as models for artists in their employ, as has been suggested in the case of the early fourteenth-century work at Longthorpe Tower, Northamptonshire.[35] Even the birds and animals that are such a feature of early fourteenth-century manuscripts are unlikely to have been drawn from nature, being taken instead from pattern books. The Sketch Book in Samuel Pepys's Library at Magdalene College, Cambridge, has a number of drawings of birds and animals (Cat. 466), some of which are similar to embroidered representations in *opus anglicanum*; such similarity does not, however, show that the Pepysian Sketch Book was itself the model for, say, the Pienza cope (fig. 21), but rather that there was a repertoire of designs current in England at that time.[36] The motif of, say, a rabbit disappearing down a burrow was doubtless to be found in dozens of pattern books.

Some designs circulated far and wide: the Swan mazer at Corpus Christi College, Cambridge (Cat. 543) is a *jeu d'esprit* in the form of a bird that appears to drink when any liquid is poured into the mazer bowl: this is of fourteenth-century workmanship, but the design is to be found in the Frenchman Villard de Honnecourt's sketchbook of the mid-thirteenth century.[37]

What may be called the cross-fertilisation of designs from one medium to another must have been dependent on the borrowing of pattern books, if not of a designer. A rare instance of the survival of both the finished product and what might even be its direct design source is the Tring tiles, representing episodes from the Infancy of Christ (fig. 22) and a French-language version of these miraculous occurrences (Oxford, Bodleian Library, MS Selden supra 38; figs 23–4).[38] Comparable, too, is the representation of the Nativity engraved (and once enamelled) on the Swinburne pyx (fig. 25), which appears to have been taken from a picture of the Virgin in Alice de Reydon's Book of Hours (Cat. 570). In this instance, the borrowing can be explained

Fig. 22 Miraculous scenes from the Infancy of Christ: the gathering in of corn, and Jesus being told that the pigs have been locked in an oven. Tile from Tring, Hertfordshire (London, British Museum, 1922, 4–12, 1–8; Cat. 217)

Fig. 23 Jesus sowing corn and an abundant harvest being gathered (Oxford, Bodleian Library, MS Selden supra 38, f. 21v.; Cat. 203)

Fig. 24 Jesus being told that the pigs have been locked in an oven (Oxford, Bodleian Library, MS Selden supra 38, f. 22v.; Cat. 203)

Fig. 25 Nativity scene from the Swinburne pyx, *c.* 1310–25 (London, Victoria and Albert Museum, M.15–1950; Cat. 571)

by the fact that the pyx came to the Swinburne family through marriage to a Reymes heiress and Alice de Reydon was herself born Reymes: it is likely that the pyx was commissioned by or in memory of Alice.[39]

Less direct means of transmission from one medium to another were more likely, especially at centres of artistic activity, as Westminster was for much of the second half of the thirteenth century: the architecture painted in the Old Testament scenes in the Painted Chamber there (cf. Cat. 330–9) perhaps shows a borrowing of designs from the adjacent masons' lodge, while the painted Retable in Westminster Abbey (see Cat. 329) is closely related to contemporary metalwork, and the highly 'architectural' Coronation Chair in the Abbey was initially planned to be made of bronze and was made in wood as an example for the bronze version to be based on.[40] What was done at Westminster was also copied elsewhere: the imitation of architectural tracery became a fashion and proliferated to an extent that makes it unlikely that any particular piece of, say, metalwork – such as the Ramsey Abbey censer (Cat. 121) – can be traced to any particular piece of architecture.

We tend to find attractive the cross-over of designs or motifs from one medium to another, and to look down on the repeated use of the same design within the one art or craft, but it was for repeated use that patterns were copied. Stained-glass windows might be made up of a series of cartoons that were reused in whole or in part, the same way round or back to front, in different colours and with different surrounds, so that a repeated figure was unlikely to be recognised; and the repetition had the advantage of giving balance to the design.[41] Such a direct reworking of designs could fall back into being an inadequate substitute for a fresh design: Knowles thought that one reason for the decline in the quality of later medieval English stained glass was the abandonment of the services of a specialist designer or draughtsman in favour of the repetition of figures, poses and gestures from the stock of cartoons in the glazier's workshop.[42] On the other hand, mass-produced objects are particularly dependent on market forces and will cease to sell if their standard is thought to be too low for their price. The English speciality of alabaster carvings would have lost their Continental and English markets if they had not continued to be seen as of a satisfactorily high standard.[43]

One explanation of the success of medieval mass-produced items is the high reputation that objects of a particular place might gain: mass production could bring renown, and objects might even become so identified with the place of their manufacture – such as baselards from Basle – as to lose their original name in favour of one derived from the leading centre for their production. Consequently, the thirteenth-century craftsman who wanted to do enamelling did well to go and work in Limoges (see Cat. 126), as did the tapestry weaver in Paris or the scribe in, say, Bologna or Oxford; fiscal records or inscriptions on surviving objects show that many English craftsmen went to work abroad, perhaps on a permanent basis. Even in the fourteenth century, when the wool trade was making her rich, England could not offer such a ready market for luxury goods (such as tapestries, the costliest of all works of art save jewel-encrusted goldsmithery) as could France or Italy. The English alabaster industry, a small-scale, low-price enterprise based near the alabaster quarries in the north Midlands (although the stone's exploitation had begun in London, in the second quarter of the fourteenth century),[44] cannot really be compared in importance with the leading luxury-goods industries of the Continent. One way forward for the English craftsman was to become an entrepreneur, selling imported goods.[45] Only the increasing nationalism of the fifteenth century was to stand in his way.

NOTES

1. Chaucer 1966 edn, p. 49, ll. 3318–9. *Fetisly*: gracefully, elegantly.
2. Stubbs 1879–80, I, p. 27.
3. Theophilus's treatise has been edited by Dodwell 1961, and by Hawthorne & Smith 1963.
4. Harvey 1975, ch. 3.
5. Harvey 1984, p. 188.
6. For impressed labour see Colvin 1963, I, pp. 180–5; a list of 29 masons despatched from Yorkshire to Windsor Castle, 1363, is printed by Knoop 1934, pp. 226–8.
7. For example, Nigel the Goldsmith was made serjeant-at-arms: British Library, Add. MS 60313, m. 3.
8. Major 1946, p. 175.
9. Smith 1807, p. 215.
10. Hope 1913, pt I, pp. 209, 211.
11. Salter 1907, 1908, II. p. lxxviii.
12. Harvey 1947, p. 305.
13. Binski & Park 1986, pp. 31ff.
14. Thompson 1935, pp. 410–30.
15. Knowles 1941, p. 520.
16. Swartout 1932, ch. 3.
17. Pollard 1964, pp. 336–44.

18. Pollard 1954–6, pp. 202–9.
19. Turner 1841, p. 24.
20. Manchester, John Rylands University Library, MS lat. 235, f. 11.
21. Sharpe 1904, pp. 160–1; cf. ibid., p. 307.
22. Norris 1978a, p. 86.
23. Blair 1981, pp. 256–7.
24. Sellers 1912, pp. 56–7. Prof. R.B. Dobson suggests a date in the late 1390s for these ordinances.
25. Ibid., pp. 164–6.
26. For this feature cf. Salzman 1967, p. 262.
27. *Pro purtractura cuiusdam navis in pergameno pro exemplari inde habendo pro quadam navis argentea pro elemosina iuxta exemplar predictum facienda*, Manchester, John Rylands University Library, MS lat. 235, f. 10.
28. *Protractacionem et ordinacionem vitri pro fenestris*, Hope 1913, I, p. 163.
29. Salzman 1926, p. 16.
30. See Staniland 1986, pp. 244, 245.
31. Willis 1845, p. 36.
32. See Shelby 1964.
33. James 1951.
34. See Binski 1986, p. 156 n. 57.
35. Yapp 1978.

36. Christie 1938, p. 11. In 1380–1 Durham Cathedral Priory paid 12d to a painter of Newcastle *pro pictura unius volucris sancti Cuthberti pro exemplare pro le Rerdos*, that is, for the Neville screen: Fowler 1898, 1901, III, p. 591.
37. Conveniently illustrated by Martindale 1972, p. 51.
38. James 1923.
39. Oman 1950.
40. Binski 1986, p. 74; I interpret *ad exemplar* as meaning that the bronze was to follow the wood, and not vice versa as indicated by Binski.
41. Knowles 1927a; a variant was printed in *Jnl. of the British Society of Master Glass-Painters*, I, no. 3, Oct. 1925, pp. 35–44.
42. Knowles 1927b, pp. 94–6.
43. See Randall 1966b.
44. For an account of the alabaster industry, see Ramsay in Blair & Ramsay (forthcoming).
45. The rarity with which men in York combined the role of craftsman with that of merchant (until the later fifteenth century) is discussed by Swanson 1980–1, pp. 333–97.

Medieval Heraldry

eraldry [is] a study which loads the memory without improving the understanding,' wrote the Norfolk antiquary and herald Peter Le Neve in 1696.[1] This view is one which is not entirely unknown today. But in the last generation much has been done to show how the study of heraldic art can not only be enjoyed for itself, but can be of value to the student of medieval society. This must surely be true above all for the thirteenth and fourteenth centuries, the richest and most vital period for the system of medieval heraldry. Heraldry was then a part of daily life. Almost every section of the exhibition bears witness to this. Coats of arms made their appearance, at least from the middle years of the thirteenth century, not just on the accoutrements of the mounted knight, but displayed in ways in which they could be seen by all. Heraldic devices came to adorn the vestments and liturgical vessels used in churches and monasteries; they appear on domestic plate and household objects; they are prominent in architecture, both ecclesiastic and secular – on gateways, gables, roof bosses and arcades, in wall paintings and stained glass. From the end of the thirteenth century they occur on the public monuments of the dead as well as the private possessions of the living. For a less literate, more visual age, these 'cognisances' on shields held a significance that may be hard for us now to comprehend.

The evolution of heraldry, defined as 'the systematic use of hereditary devices centred on the shield',[2] has been traced back to the second quarter of the twelfth century. Much that is known of this early period comes from the evidence of seals. Since armory began as a matter of convenience for recognition on the field of battle or during a tournament, the images on equestrian seals show arms first appearing on the shields, lance flags, horse trappings and surcoats of the mounted knight. Heraldry was centred on the shield, but seals show that other forms of display have always played their part. Indeed, it was the practice of painting arms on the linen surcoats worn by knights over their mail which gave rise to the term 'cote armure', or coat of arms. Increasingly the personal seals of the nobility show a hereditary tendency in the use of armorial devices. They show too how rapidly such devices were adopted by the whole military aristocracy of Europe.

By the early thirteenth century the forms and usages of heraldry had become subject to certain broadly clear conventions. They were intended to be seen at a distance, so the designs were mostly bold and uncomplicated. Many charges (i.e. devices) placed on shields consisted of simple geometric shapes (see fig. 26), while the colours used and the combinations in which they occurred were similarly restricted. The range of pictorial images was not large; but subjects like the symbolic lion, the eagle and the cross were popular. Punning or canting arms, seen to such effect in the seven winnowing fans or vanes of the family of Setvans (Cat. 234), were chosen from an early date. The shape of the shield, particularly the so-called heater shield – almost triangular with a straight top and slightly curving sides – had due effect on the placing of charges and the balance of the design.

At the beginning of the Gothic period arms were still largely confined to the great feudal families. In the course of the thirteenth century their use spread through a wider spectrum of society, and the increasing popularity of seals helped promote this advance (see pp. 114–17). As the personal, authenticating marks of their owners, seals lent themselves to the introduction of armorial devices which were well fitted to express a form of 'signature'. Shields began to appear as subject-matter for seals, not only as part of the equipment of the armed knight pictured there, but on the reverse of equestrian seals and alone upon smaller ones. From being the preserve of the

Fig. 26 The Matthew Paris Shields, *c.* 1244 (London, British Library, Cotton MS Nero D.I, f. 171v.)

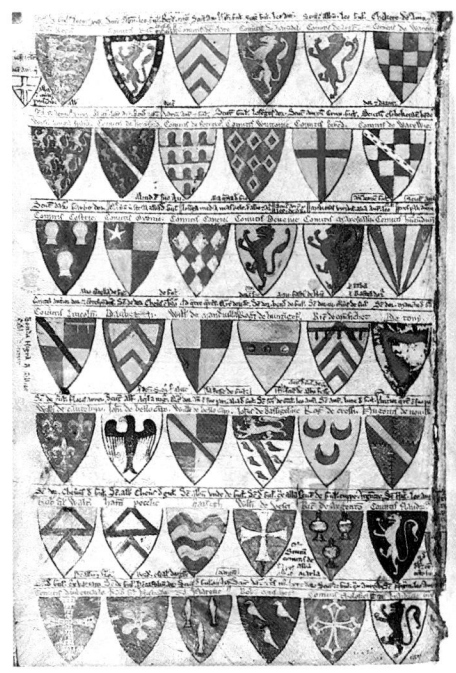

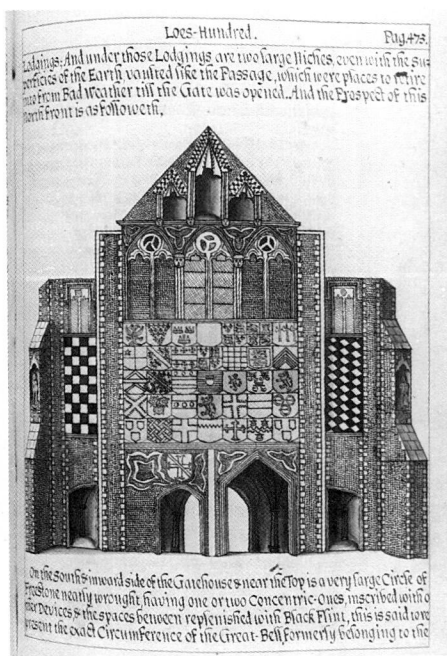

Fig. 27 Robert Hawes, drawing of the early fourteenth-century gatehouse of Butley Priory, 1712 (London, British Library, Add. MS 33247, f. 249)

sovereign and great seigneurial families, the use of seals extended to a much wider group; so too did the adoption of arms. Tenants or neighbours of a feudal lord took his arms with a difference in colouring or an adaptation of the charge. Arms appeared on the seals of simple knights, of esquires and of the more junior members of knightly families. Cities and boroughs began to place shields of arms on their official seals. At first these merely depicted the royal arms of the king as their overlord; but in the latter years of the thirteenth century they started to use their own distinctive devices. Even merchants, such as Henry le Callere (Cat. 200), gave a heraldic guise to their personal devices or merchants' marks by placing them upon shields. From the fourteenth century shields of arms were attributed to dioceses and to religious houses, hospitals and colleges.

Women too employed armorial bearings on seals. One of the earliest of all heraldic evidences is the seal of Rohese, Countess of Lincoln, who died in 1156, incorporating the famous chevrons of the house of Clare. A rare example of a woman's seal of equestrian type is included in the exhibition (Cat. 142); it shows Joanna de Stuteville, wife successively of Hugh Wake and Hugh Bigod, bearing a shield of the Stuteville arms. Not until the end of the thirteenth century was it common for women to bear the arms of both husband and father on the same shield.

Further evidence that heraldry had already established the foundations of a system is provided by the appearance around 1250 of various Rolls of Arms – rolls or books containing collections of coats of arms either painted or blazoned (described in heraldic language). The earliest of these occur not as separate collections, but as part of a group of 'illustrative' rolls, in which arms are used in chronicles, cartularies or liturgical books to illustrate or decorate the text. Best known are the shields used by the monastic historian Matthew Paris (Cat. 437) in several of his manuscripts: shields and other pictorial symbols (e.g. crosiers or mitres) are painted upside-down in the margin when the death of the owner is recorded. Matthew Paris also compiled about 1244 a sheet of painted and unpainted arms in his *Liber Additamentorum* (fig. 26), probably as a reference aid for writing his chronicles. These are the shields usually said to constitute the earliest English roll of arms. Another such series, the collection of twenty-one shields painted in the margins of a psalter illuminated in part by William de Brailes, has recently been assigned a date in the 1230s and may therefore pre-date Paris's groups of shields.[3]

Other classes of rolls were compiled as heraldic collections for their own sake: general rolls, which were random and varied collections (see Cat. 153); occasional rolls recording those present at a particular gathering – a tournament, siege or battle; local rolls, which in England are usually grouped by county; and ordinaries, where the arrangement is by subject. Unlike the illustrative collections, the content of these rolls and the developed heraldic language of blazon employed in them, suggest the work of those with specialist knowledge. Although they are for the most part anonymous, some at least seem certain to have been compiled by heralds, whether for a patron or for their own professional use.

In the thirteenth century heralds still occupied a humble position in society, virtually indistinguishable from that of wandering minstrels. Certainly they had not achieved the control over the granting and regulating of arms which they were later to attain. In a famous heraldic treatise, *De Insigniis et Armis* (*c.* 1350), the Italian lawyer Bartolus of Sassoferrato propounded the view that a man might assume arms at will as long as they had not been adopted by another; this bears out the evidence of seals. But growth in the popularity of the tournament, with which they were closely associated, brought the heralds to prominence; they became the acknowledged experts in the recognition and later the ordering of armorial bearings. When, in 1417, the Crown sought to control the use of arms, the heralds were the obvious authorities to undertake their regulation.

From the middle years of the thirteenth century heraldry played an increasingly important part in all branches of artistic activity. The attraction of a boldly-coloured shield of arms as a decorative motif is easily apparent. At the same time it was an effective way to proclaim ownership or pride in family and alliances. Domestic plate, furniture, and above all the prized illuminated books, which alone of such personal goods survive in any numbers, were adorned with the arms of their owners. Similarly,

Fig. 28 The Royal Arms embroidered on a seal bag of the City of London, 1319 (London, Corporation of London Records Office, charter 26; cf. Cat. 206)

the vestments and liturgical vessels used in churches, private chapels and monastic houses often bore the arms of lay benefactors or founders. From the late thirteenth century heraldic charges are common on tombs, and soon after the turn of the century they begin to appear in one of their most spectacular forms on monumental brasses (see Cat. 234–5). Heraldry may even have had an effect on technical developments in the arts: as has been pointed out in connection with the beautiful enamelled Valence casket (Cat. 362), it seems hardly to be chance that the increased use of enamelling to give colour to metal should coincide with the growth of interest in heraldic ornament.[4] It is worth noting that the French word for enamel, *émail*, from the fifteenth century means also heraldic tincture.

Architecture gave striking opportunities for heraldic display. Some of the more ambitious architectural schemes even provided equivalents to rolls of arms. The thirty-five stone shields arrayed on the early fourteenth-century gatehouse of Butley Priory in Suffolk (fig. 27) form a combined general and local roll; and the east window in Gloucester Cathedral can be seen as an occasional roll, since it portrays the arms of nobles associated with Edward III's French campaigns of 1346–7.

As might be expected, the royal arms have always been among the most widely displayed of all armorial bearings. In 1198 appeared the coat which still occupies the first place in the royal arms of the United Kingdom – the three leopards, known also in heraldry as three lions passant guardant. The earliest known representation of these arms is on the second Great Seal of King Richard I, cut in 1195 and brought into use in 1198. The tinctures of the shield are subsequently confirmed from the rolls of arms. Matthew Paris attributes the same coat to earlier kings, William the Conqueror and his successors. This is of course an anachronism, on a par with the fictitious arms invented for legendary figures, saints of the Church or renowned pre-Conquest kings such as Edward the Confessor (see Cat. 332).

The simple red shield with the three gold leopards remained the arms of all English kings down to 1340. During the reign of Henry III these arms were widely used in the decoration of the king's ambitious building projects, above all at Westminster. The series of shields carved in the stonework of the choir aisles in Westminster Abbey between 1245 and 1269 is the first known instance of heraldry used in an architectural context, and naturally included Henry's own arms. A splendid set of floor tiles in the chapter house laid between 1253 and 1258 provided a further opportunity to display the royal arms. Again, they are the earliest known heraldic examples in the medium. Although instances of heraldic glass rarely survive from before 1300, there are records to show that it was used in royal palaces and castles from the middle years of the thirteenth century. Entries on the Liberate Rolls indicate that Henry ordered armorial glass for Rochester Castle in 1247 and for Havering-atte-Bower in 1251 and 1268. Though early wall paintings are also rare, antiquarian evidence reveals that the now-lost cycle in the Painted Chamber at Westminster included at least one prominently displayed shield of England (Cat. 332), and that heraldry was an important element in the overall design. On a smaller scale, and among perhaps the most pleasing of all illustrations of the early arms of England, are examples of the beautiful *opus anglicanum*: a fragment of a horse trapping (Cat. 12) and an embroidered seal bag holding the seal attached to a City of London charter of 1319 (fig. 28; cf. Cat. 206). These chance survivors serve to remind us how much must have gone.

The first change in the royal arms came in 1340 when Edward III expressed his renewed claim to the French throne by quartering the arms of France, Azure semé with fleurs-de-lis or (later called France ancient) with those of England (Cat. 629). Richard II used the same arms, and so did Henry IV, until during the first decade of the fifteenth century the French quartering was changed to Azure three fleurs-de-lis or (France modern). Edward III's use of quartering was not unprecedented. Eleanor of Castile had introduced the idea into England with her father's quartered arms of Castile and Leon (Cat. 369). It was however the adoption of the quartered coat as the royal arms which gave direction to later heraldic practice. Quartering became the accepted method of representing lordships and alliances, and subsequently for showing all forms of descent.

The fourteenth century saw an increasing elaboration in armorial bearings and

more extravagant forms in their display. Much of the reason for this may be sought in the popularity of the tournament. The famous miniature of the Lincolnshire knight, Sir Geoffrey Luttrell (d. 1345), in the psalter which bears his name, shows just how lavish could be the heraldic display of a knight prepared for the tournament (Cat. 575; fig. 29). Sir Geoffrey bears the arms of Luttrell (Azure a bend between six martlets argent) on his surcoat, ailettes, and the fan crest, trapper and saddle of his horse; they appear on the lance pennon and the fan crest of the helmet handed to him by his wife Agnes Sutton, and on the shield held by his daughter-in-law, Beatrice Scrope. Both ladies are dressed in heraldic gowns displaying the arms of their husbands and fathers.

With the unique and marvellous exception of the funeral achievements of the Black Prince (Cat. 626–33), practically nothing remains of the more perishable items of armorial martial equipment. Our knowledge of their forms must be taken from other sources. Sir Geoffrey Luttrell's pennon illustrates well the type of flag displayed by the ordinary knight. Higher-ranking knights banneret and senior commanders bore their arms upon banners. Good examples of the proportions of these can be seen in miniatures such as that of St George and the Earl of Lancaster (Cat. 151). Documentary evidence of the early thirteenth century also records the use of such armorial banners for military purposes by the aldermen of London, but nothing is known of their design.[5]

The growing complexity of fourteenth-century heraldry provoked a need for a simpler form of recognition. This need provided, at least in part, the reason for the sudden increase in the popularity of the badge. Displayed alone and not associated with the shield, the badge was a distinct device adopted by a person or family and frequently used as a mark of allegiance. Much of its significance and the occasions for its use remain obscure. While earlier badges are known – the *planta genista* or broom badge of the Plantagenets is one famous example – they first became widely fashionable at the Court of Edward III. From the fourteenth to the sixteenth century royal badges are found more frequently than the royal arms in many forms of decoration (see Cat. 70, 725); they even make their appearance on the coinage. But the heyday of the badge was the age of livery and maintenance, and perhaps the best known of all such devices, along with the Prince of Wales's feathers, are those associated with the houses of York and Lancaster during the Wars of the Roses. Many of these derive from devices in use in the fourteenth century. Such is the Lancastrian Swan badge, represented here by the exquisite enamelled Dunstable Swan Jewel (Cat. 659). This badge was used in the fourteenth century by a number of English families – the Tonys, Bohuns, Beauchamps and Courtenays – who were proud of their descent from the Swan Knight of courtly romance. The marriage in 1380 of a Bohun heiress to Henry of Lancaster brought the use of the badge to the Lancastrian royal house (Cat. 697).

Figuring prominently among the badges, and also frequently used by the badge's owner for a crest or supporter, are many of the creatures that have come to be regarded as typical heraldic beasts: the lion, the griffin, the dragon and the antelope. The inspiration for some of the more fanciful of these creatures can be found in the bestiaries (Cat. 252–3). These reached the height of their popular appeal as picture-books in the late twelfth and early thirteenth centuries. Bestiary creatures and bestiary lore clearly exerted a powerful influence on the heraldic imagination. Beasts were especially popular as a crest, which in fourteenth-century heraldry became the most important adjunct to the shield. A two-dimensional form is still evident in the fan-shaped crest of Sir Geoffrey Luttrell's 'portrait'; but no doubt under the influence of the tournament many later crests were elaborately moulded confections of wood and leather (Cat. 627). It was this extravagant tournament crest which was introduced into heraldic art. Beasts were also commonly adopted as supporters to the shield. Such supporters, alone in the achievement of arms, have no martial origin. The most likely explanation for their appearance may be sought in the seal engravers' art; in the decorative devices, particularly dragons or wyvern-like creatures, introduced to fill the space between the shield and the circumference of the seal. By the end of the fourteenth century supporters were no longer purely ornamental but had gained a hereditary, and therefore heraldic, significance. The final culmination of this elaboration in armorial bearings was the full achievement of arms: the shield, crest, mantled helm and supporters.

Heraldic art reached its maturity in the fourteenth century. At the same time heraldry remained more than mere ornament. The celebrated contest of Scrope versus Grosvenor for the arms Azure a bend or gives a measure of how far this was so. Hearings in the Court of Chivalry continued for almost five years until in 1390 the king confirmed judgement to Sir Richard Scrope. Several hundred witnesses were heard, among them – testifying for Scrope – John of Gaunt, his son the future Henry IV, and the poet Geoffrey Chaucer. Evidence cited included arms displayed in glass and paintings, manuscripts, charters and seals, on walls, vestments, tombs (see also Cat. 678) – even on inn signs. But more important than any of these was the constant refrain that 'Scropes had always possessed arms in high knightly honour and bore them in royal wars and expeditions of the King'.[6] Not only pride in lineage, but the idea of doing 'honour to arms' in combat, represented a powerful ideal. It was this which imbued heraldic practice with vitality and vigour and made it in the thirteenth and fourteenth centuries a living art.

NOTES

1. British Library, Harley MS 5801, f. 6
2. Wagner 1956, p. 12.
3. Morgan 1982, no. 68.
4. Williamson 1986, p. 195.
5. Goodall 1959, pp. 1–5.
6. Nicolas 1832, p. 445.

Paul Crossley English Gothic Architecture

From the beginning, mankind has been divided into three parts, among men of prayer, men of toil, and men of war.

Gerard, Bishop of Cambrai (1012–51)

In this famous tripartite image of medieval political theory, 'the men of prayer' and 'the men of war', clerics and warriors, dominate our idea of the Middle Ages. They do so chiefly, and most immediately, through their architecture. At Norwich, Lincoln, and Rochester, castle confronts cathedral, and in hundreds of villages in England and Wales the twin accents of parish church and manor house still remind us of a world sharply divided between a secular and a spiritual power.

But the third of these estates, 'the men of toil', have left few visible remains before the year 1400. The growth of the rural population in the thirteenth and fourteenth centuries meant the expansion of settlements and the building of more houses, either mud-walled, timber-framed, or stone. The manor saw an increase in the scale and variety of its domestic and agricultural buildings, and their more orderly distribution, often around courtyards. But little of all this remains above ground. Today the agricultural wealth of the High Middle Ages is most easily measured, not by the dwellings of its peasants or yeomen, but by the barn and the manorial hall, both buildings reflecting the presence and authority of the lord.

Great stone or timber barns, the grandest of the agricultural buildings, often stood in the granges of wealthy abbeys, like the fourteenth-century barn of Beaulieu Abbey's grange at Great Coxwell in Berkshire, praised by William Morris as 'the greatest piece of architecture in England' (Cat. 218, fig. 30). The manorial hall doubled as the court and residence of the local lord; and as the nucleus of the estate and the heart of the manorial household it acquired a literary and symbolic significance. From the Venerable Bede onwards medieval commentators saw the warmth and radiance of the hall, sheltering the household against winter cold and darkness, as an image of life itself. The earliest and largest halls were aisled, like a church, the majority built of wood, but the grandest examples in stone, like Henry III's three-aisled hall at Winchester Castle (c. 1222–35, Cat. 261), with its tall transomed windows characteristic of large stone halls of the later Middle Ages (e.g. Cat. 189, 190). Throughout the thirteenth and fourteenth centuries manorial halls show a growing concern for domestic comfort and privacy. A wing of private rooms,

Fig. 30   Tithe barn at Great Coxwell, Berkshire

with the lord's solar or bed-chamber in the upper floor, was attached to it, usually at the high table end; while at the other end of the hall, separated by the 'screens passage', were placed the service rooms of buttery, pantry, and later, kitchen. Such additions created something resembling a standard medieval plan. Penshurst Place in Kent (Cat. 190), built after 1341 by Sir John de Pulteney, merchant, draper, and Lord Mayor of London, is one of the most complete fourteenth-century manor houses of this type in England.

Penshurst, however, represents only the highest class of manorial architecture. Most housing in town and country continued to be of wood, and even in stone buildings, particularly barns and halls, roofs provide ample evidence of the skill of the carpenter. The barn at Great Coxwell supports its vast timber roof on low stone walls and on two rows of slender timber posts dividing the interior into a sequence of separate bays reminiscent of the bay-dividing shafts of stone-built churches (Cat. 218). Up to the later thirteenth century, medieval halls solved the problem of covering their wide spans by supporting the roof on similar lines of timber posts (Hereford Bishop's Palace, Great Hall, c. 1160; Leicester Castle Hall, c. 1150), or stone pillars (Cat. 261). But as the technology of timber improved, new and more traditional roof types were used to cover the building without intermediate supports. One form was the cruck frame, where the roof was supported on pairs of large curved timbers extending from the ground or lower side walls to the ridge of the roof, creating a sequence of huge pointed arches (fig. 31). Other systems consisted of tie beams or hammer beams, often combined with a crown post at the roof top. The king's carpenters pioneered some of the most inventive and daring constructions of the later Middle Ages. In the octagon at Ely Cathedral (1322–42, Cat. 492) the royal carpenter William Hurley devised a unique solution to a unique problem: to throw a vault over an octagonal span of 70 ft (21 m) and to break it open at the centre with a polygonal lantern 152 ft (46 m) high. An ingenious system of interlocking timbers supports the lantern, but Hurley concealed it behind the wooden vaults of the octagon, so that the whole structure, painted to resemble stone, seems to float miraculously over the vast void of the crossing. Royal carpenters also invented new types of open timber roof for wide-span halls. For the great hall at Windsor (now destroyed) constructed c. 1362, the king's carpenter William Herland assembled a series of collar beams, supported by rows of large curved arches decorated with carved tracery. At Westminster Palace a colossal roof was erected between 1394 and c. 1400 over the old Norman hall (Cat. 692). The carpenter, William Herland's son and successor, Hugh Herland, combined the tracery and curved arches of Windsor with a system of braced hammer beams to create the largest medieval timber roof in Europe, and the acknowledged masterpiece of English carpentry.

All these royal halls, and many manorial houses, were given varying degrees of fortification. At the weakest end of the scale was that hybrid category known as the 'fortified manor' and referred to in Domesday Book as *domus defensabilis*. At Acton Burnell, Bishop Robert Burnell of Wells, Lord Chancellor of Edward I, built a comfortable manor house in the 1280s with no serious military pretensions apart from decorative battlements; while at Stokesay, also in Shropshire, the hall of c. 1270–80 was at first unfortified and a little later given its flanking tower (Cat. 189). But many great halls were protected by the full defences of a castle. As a stronghold, the great Norman stone tower – the keep or donjon – continued to enclose the residential apartments and to form the nucleus of the defence well into the thirteenth century. Whether in the traditional square or rectangular form (Dover, Newcastle upon Tyne, Richmond, – all built by Henry II), or cylindrical (as favoured in the Welsh Marches, e.g. Pembroke Castle), or polygonal (Orford Castle) or even quatrefoil (Clifford's Tower in York), the keep or *magna turris* played an essentially passive role of resistance: it remained the supreme expression of the idea that defence is a question of thick walls. Henry II's massive and dominating keep at Dover Castle (fig. 32), raised by the master mason Maurice 'the engineer' in the 1180s, marks the high point of a development which began with William the Conqueror's tower-keep in London. But the late twelfth and early thirteenth-century fortifications at Dover also looked forward to new techniques of fortification: in the Constable's Gate, with its drum-shaped towers flanking the entrance passage, in its curtain walls with their regularly-

Fig. 31 Cruck-framed barn at Cholstrey Court, Leominster

Fig. 32   Aerial view of Dover Castle, Kent

spaced mural towers, and in its use of an inner and outer circuit of such walls, anticipating the concentric castles of a century later.

The castle as a work of military engineering reached its apogee in the reign of Edward I, and particularly in the royal castles built or begun between 1274 and 1295 as an accompaniment to his conquest and settlement of Wales. Each major castle employed a workforce of between one and three thousand men, many of them impressed from all parts of England. The total cost, for the ten castles, including five with fortified towns, amounted to £80,000–£100,000, – a prodigious sum, even though spread over twenty-five years (Henry III's Westminster Abbey [1245–69] cost a little over £42,000). The overall master in charge of the work was James of St George, an engineer and mason from Savoy, where he had built similar castles for the counts of Savoy, vassals of Edward I. The six major royal Welsh castles (Flint, Rhuddlan, Conway, Caernarfon, Harlech and Beaumaris) all bear the imprint of Master James's ingenuity, and constitute, as a group, the high point of military architecture in Christendom. Conway and Caernarfon (fig. 33) enclose irregular spaces behind a single circuit of walls and towers; the rest are defended by a double concentric ring of walls, the inner taller than the outer so that both could be employed simultaneously against besiegers. All of them, apart from Flint, reject the old idea of the single defensive tower and rely on an integrated system of powerful mural towers. With no keep, the residential accomodation is often in the upper storeys of the gatehouse, but far from being the bastions of final resistance, the gatehouses of Edwardian castles, potentially the most vulnerable to attack as entrances, became the strongest and most aggressive points in the front line of the defence. Composed of an entrance passageway flanked by two mural towers and divided into deadly sequences of murder holes, portcullises and arrow loops, the gatehouse of Harlech (Cat. 323) and the King's Gate at Caernarfon concentrate a defensive power far in excess of any real threat brought against them.

Only the greatest magnates could afford to build castles to the sophisticated standards set by James of St George. Significantly, the two most impressive castles of the later thirteenth century which match the royal experiments in large gatehouses and concentric planning were both constructed in south Wales by great marcher lords: Kidwelly Castle by the Chaworth family and Henry of Lancaster, Caerphilly at the initiative of the powerful Gilbert de Clare, Earl of Gloucester (Cat. 133).

In the north of England, Edward's failure to conquer the Scots meant constant fortification throughout the fourteenth century. Most of the new castles were either small in scale, or took the form of a 'pele tower', a fortified residence shaped like a square or rectangular tower; the diminutive descendant of the old keep. But at Dunstanburgh Castle in Northumberland, John of Gaunt rebuilt the gatehouse in about 1380 as a great tower; and at Warkworth, at about the same time, the powerful Percy family constructed on the site of the old motte a colossal tower-keep on a Greek cross plan (Cat. 134), providing formidable defence, and ample well-lit accommodation.

The castle was always a residence, and the interiors of even the earliest castles never lacked comfort. Henry II spent heavily on residential amenities at Nottingham, Windsor and Winchester castles, but little survives. The Close and Liberate Rolls of Henry III's reign record lavish sums spent on decorating and rebuilding Windsor, Ludgershall, and especially Winchester, where now only the hall recalls the king's sumptuous standard of living (Cat. 261). But it was Edward III, more than any other English monarch, who elevated the residential aspect of the castle to a point of unprecedented splendour. In his new castle at Queenborough (see fig. 2) on the Isle of Sheppey in Kent he set up the earliest recorded mechanical clock in England, and between 1350 and 1377 he erected in his birthplace at Windsor what one authority has called 'the Versailles of its age'. But of Queenborough (figs 1, 2) not one stone remains, and little survives of the palatial extensions at Windsor. A seventeenth-century engraving shows the interior of its great hall (see above), but the scale of Windsor is best measured by its surviving imitations, in particular John of Gaunt's grandiose reconstruction of Kenilworth Castle in the late fourteenth century.

Fig. 33   Caernarfon Castle

From their earliest beginnings castles were built to express as much the pretensions as the substance of lordship. The keep was a symbol of status and nobility. At Caernarfon Castle (fig. 33) Edward I deliberately copied the banded coloured masonry and polygonal towers of the Theodosian walls in Constantinople, in order to stress the Welsh city's links with its Roman past, and to underline his own quasi-imperial status as lord of England and Wales. Edward I also projected himself as a new King Arthur, and throughout the latter Middle Ages English castles were designed to evoke images of chivalry and literary romance. Edward III instituted a Round Table at Windsor in 1344 in an effort to recreate Arthur's legendary Court; and in the wake of his triumphs at Crécy and Poitiers he rebuilt Windsor as a symbol of majesty, and a centre of his new order of chivalry, the Garter. As castle building declined in the fifteenth century through the relative poverty of the English kings, the increasing concentration of population and warfare on the towns, and the continuing emphasis on comfort rather than defence, so the military devices of castles were reduced to symbolic show.

The fortifications of castles were easily adapted into the walls and gates of towns. The steady growth of the English economy in the twelfth and thirteenth centuries brought agricultural surpluses disposed of, and also created by, a flourishing number of towns. Wool and cloth were the chief bases of large-scale commerce in medieval England; and it is, significantly, the individual wool merchants who have left us most of the few remaining traces of urban housing in the thirteenth and fourteenth centuries. Excavations have shown that the waterfronts and quays of Southampton were, from the late twelfth century, lined with fine stone merchants' houses; while at Chipping Campden in the Cotswolds, at the very centre of English sheep farming, in the late fourteenth century, William Grevel, the greatest wool merchant of his day, built a large town house of stone (Cat. 191), and described himself proudly on his brass in the church as *flos mercatorum tocius Anglie* ('the flower of merchants in all England'). The wool ports of East Anglia and the cloth-making cities of Norwich and York built some of the most extensive fortifications of the Middle Ages. Hull had brick walls with thirteen towers; York and Norwich were both ringed with over two miles of walls, and the latter, with its numerous gates or 'bars', is the longest and best-preserved circuit in England. Civic buildings of the later Middle Ages were modest compared to the great town and cloth halls of northern Germany and Flanders, and indeed most of the surviving guild halls in England belong to the fifteenth century. One notable exception is St Mary's Hall in Coventry (Cat. 192), which evokes, as eloquently as the slender steeple of its parish church (Cat. 695), the spectacular rise of this cloth town in the second half of the fourteenth century. But few of these wealthier towns convey such a vivid picture of medieval urban architecture as the small city of Chester. Apart from its cathedral and churches, Chester has preserved a good number of its secular and domestic buildings, including the Dee Bridge (Cat. 188), the whole circuit of its medieval walls and, not least, a series of late thirteenth-century vaulted cellars (Cat. 187), supporting not only houses, but also a unique set of covered walkways above the street at first floor level known as 'the Rows'.

The impressive unity of town fortifications may have influenced other institutions, such as monasteries and cathedrals, to encircle their precincts with walls and gates. Licences for enclosure were given to Norwich Cathedral Priory in 1276, to Lincoln, York and St Paul's in 1285, to Exeter in 1286, to Lichfield in 1299 and to Canterbury in 1309. These enclosures clearly marked out the areas of the institution's judicial immunity, and although not defensive in any serious military sense, gave protection from marauders, mobs, or a discontented peasantry. The idyllic peace of the English 'close', in contrast to the bustling streets that surround most Continental cathedrals, is to the modern tourist one of the most appealing aspects of English Gothic; but it was born out of the need of an increasingly unpopular English Church to protect itself from the social and economic unrest of the fourteenth century. As in the castle, the focal point of the defence was the gatehouse, and in the first half of the fourteenth century a number of monastries built grandiose entrances: the Cistercians at Whalley in Lancashire, and the Benedictines at Norwich, Chester, St Augustine's Canterbury (Cat. 327), and Bury St Edmunds in Suffolk, many displaying the same worldly heraldry which was by then invading the interiors of churches (Bristol Cathedral, Lady Chapel reredos, Cat. 487). The series culminated in the magnificent gatehouse of the Austin Canons at Thornton in Lincolnshire (fig. 34), begun in 1382, a year after the Peasants' Revolt.

Within this precinct the great church rose out of a complex of smaller buildings, most of them grouped, on the model of the standard monastic plan, around a cloister. To this traditional nucleus was attached a variety of buildings. Great churches in post-Conquest Britain belonged to three broad classes: secular cathedrals (composed of secular canons, and administered by a dean and chapter), monasteries (the majority Benedictine, Cluniac, Cistercian and Augustinian), and – a British peculiarity – cathedral priories (the seats of bishops, but staffed by a community of monks and ruled by priors). Thus the layout of a great cathedral priory – for example Durham – is distinguished by separate groups of buildings for the bishop and for the priory, the former lying to the north, the latter placed to the south of the church. Monasteries proliferated with residential, communal, and service buildings. The southern range of the cloister contained the refectory, among the grandest of the monastic buildings. For

Fig. 34   Gatehouse of Thornton Abbey, Lincolnshire

Fig. 35   Refectory pulpit at Chester Cathedral

the daily meal had a quasi-sacramental dignity, its silence broken only by readings from scripture and the Rule of St Benedict delivered from a stone pulpit. Two 'thirteenth-century pulpits are preserved from the Cistercian house at Beaulieu in Hampshire and the Benedictine monastery of St Werburgh (now the cathedral) at Chester (fig. 35). By contrast, the secular cathedrals, with their non-resident canons, needed few of these monastic amenities. Great churches like Wells, Salisbury, and Lincoln constructed cloisters more for show than necessity, the dormitory or refectory often giving way to a library. An aerial view of Wells exemplifies particularly clearly the functions of the secular cathedral (fig. 36): to the south, beyond a 'show' cloister with no attached buildings, lies the fortified palace of the bishops; to the north, a line of fourteenth-century terraced houses were built for the vicars choral (see pp. 83–4).

In all three types of institution only one building was consistently given a prominence second only to the church: the chapter house, so called because here a chapter of the rule of the order was read to the assembled community. This large room, usually opening off the east wing of the cloister, was set aside for the community to administer punishment and to discuss the practical administration of the institution. Many English chapter houses are distinguished from the standard rectangular plan of their Continental counterparts by their centralised shape and their prominent fan of ribs supported on a single central column. The centralised chapter house first entered the mainstream of English Gothic at Lincoln Cathedral (*c.* 1220–30; fig. 37), where the successful combination of polygonal planning and lavish rib vaults assured the popularity of the type in England and Scotland down to the end of the Middle Ages. At least twenty-five of these centralised chapter houses were built, many on a scale that dwarfs all the other conventual buildings, and with a richness of decoration that rivals the adjoining church (Wells, Cat. 328).

But no group of buildings, not even chapter houses, could surpass the church in scale and decoration. Churches were the most incomparably splendid buildings medieval people ever entered. Over nine thousand were built in England and Wales during the Middle Ages, each, as its dedication ritual clearly stated, a symbol of the whole church of Christendom and of the celestial church existing outside time (cf. Cat. 109). Two characteristics of the new Gothic style made this symbolism particularly vivid: the niche, and coloured light. Gothic sculptors often depicted the inhabitants of Heaven under tokens of the Heavenly City in the form of canopies. The space enclosed

Fig. 36   Aerial view of Wells Cathedral showing the bishop's palace and vicar's close

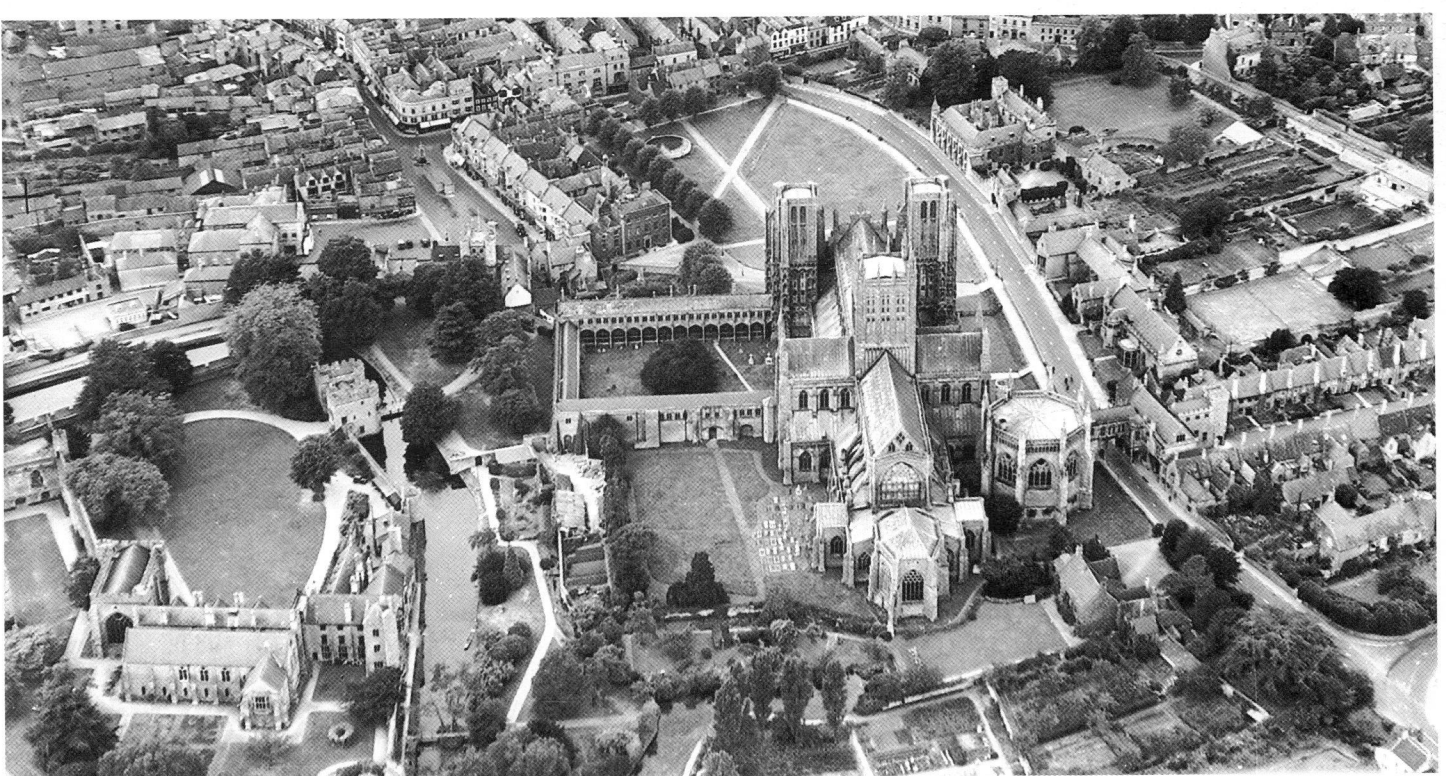

Fig. 37   Lincoln Cathedral chapter house

by these niches thus became special, separate, and holy; and the conclusion was soon drawn that the whole Church could be made a more comprehensive image of Heaven by multiplying these niches throughout the building. In a Gothic church elaborate architectural canopies crown fonts, tombs (Cat. 326), choir stalls (Cat. 524), Easter Sepulchres (Cat. 493), figures in stained glass (Cat. 741), buttresses, sculpture on façades (Cat. 239), and even the most precious liturgical objects like censers, aumbries, and reliquaries (Cat. 121–2, 25).

Moreover, the architectural forms of these niches were seen as microcosmic versions of full-scale architecture, so that large steeples could imitate reliquary canopies, and vaults resemble huge baldachins enclosing a sacred space. Indeed, Gervase, a monk of Canterbury writing in the late twelfth century, described the new rib vaults of Canterbury Cathedral as 'ciboria', a term usually referring to a canopy over an altar or shrine. By endowing vaults and towers with the sacred implications of the niche or baldachin the whole Gothic church was transformed into what Sir John Summerson called 'a multiple pile of heavenly mansions'.

Canopies and other structural forms were painted in bright primary colours, and walls whitewashed with false masonry joints painted in red. There was nothing new in polychrome church interiors, since Christian teaching had always identified light as the most potent symbol of divinity, and coloured churches as God's special habitation on earth. But the prominence given by the Gothic style to the stained-glass window added a new resonance to this symbolism of light. First in France at St-Denis near Paris, then in England at Canterbury (Cat. 17), churches were constructed specifically to display large windows, their images radiant with coloured light, their materials resembling precious stones. In the Book of Revelation St John described the Heavenly City as an actual building, with its walls '... of jasper ... of pure gold, like unto clear glass ... the foundations garnished with all manner of precious stones ...'. From the sombre glowing colours of twelfth-century Canterbury, to the light brilliance of fourteenth-century York or Gloucester, English Gothic churches must have seemed like miraculous recreations of the Heavenly Jerusalem on earth.

The church functioned at every level of medieval life. Its towers, besides housing bells and even sometimes lanterns to guide home ships, proclaimed the wealth of its builders and the identity of a community. (Cat. 489, 694). Façades of cathedrals served as backdrops for courts, judgements, and theatrical performances. And in particular, the religious and ceremonial life of local England was centred in hundreds of parish churches. Their porches often served, in their upper storeys, as school rooms, and in their lower as places for sealing business transactions or marriage contracts. The nave, whose upkeep was usually the responsibility of the laity, saw the beginning of Christian life at its font, and the end (if you were rich enough) in its tombs and chapels. Its walls were covered with paintings, depicting, especially over the choir arch, sensational representations of Doomsday, Heaven and Hell (Cat. 557). And as sermons grew longer, permanent seating was introduced, the bench ends often carved with their own sets of moralising images.

The choir was the province of the clergy. Separated from the nave by a large painted screen, above which rose an awesome sculpture of the Crucifixion, the choir was treated like a secret church within a church. In parish churches choirs remained relatively undeveloped, but in larger churches staffed by communities of canons or monks the choir and sanctuary became the theatre for the most advanced experiments in Early Gothic architecture. All secular cathedrals, and a number of prominent monastic churches, from the middle of the twelfth century onwards, followed the late Romanesque choir at Canterbury Cathedral in starting their choirs in line with the eastern piers of the crossing, so that the liturgical divisions coincided with the architectural ones, and an extensive eastern limb was created, consisting of a long choir and its sanctuary beyond. But in the late twelfth century even this expanded chancel came under pressure from the need to provide more altars, and from the growing popularity of relics. Altars were required partly because more and more monks were becoming priests and needed to say their daily masses, partly because the growing cult of the Virgin Mary resulted in new masses in her honour, and above all because of the proliferation of chantries – endowments for masses for the dead intended to redeem their souls from Purgatory. In the fourteenth and fifteenth centuries chantries had a profound influence on the shape of the church. At the wealthy end of the social scale men like Sir John de Cobham (Cat. 139) would found and endow whole colleges of priests to pray for their souls in perpetuity, providing them with their own domestic quarters and church, the choir of which was set aside as a large family mausoleum (Cat. 136). Other patrons – town guilds or great ecclesiastics – added chantry chapels to existing churches, either pushing them up against the sanctuary or tucking them between the pillars of choir or nave, as in William of Wykeham's chantry at Winchester Cathedral (Cat. 601).

But in the late twelfth century, when great churches were beginning to be transformed into what Coulton called 'Mass-machines'[1], a more systematic arrangement of altars was thought necessary. In addition, the growing cult of relics prompted radical changes in the design of choirs. Saints not only interceded for sinners in Heaven; their mortal remains could work miracles of healing on pilgrims who visited them. The choir of St-Denis, the first and most celebrated of Gothic churches, had continued a Romanesque practice for displaying relics which was already in use in England by 1100: the reliquary was removed from the crypt and set up on a high stone or marble base, standing in a special sacred area behind the high altar (cf. the shrine bases of St Albans and Chester, Cat. 19, 20). From now on, pilgrims in any great Gothic church had to be conveyed discreetly around a shrine that was visible, even accessible, and placed in a magnificent architectural setting. All these liturgical problems were solved in the new choir of Canterbury Cathedral, intended to house the popular relics of its martyred archbishop St Thomas Becket (Cat. 17).

Canterbury is important in the history of medieval architecture for a number of reasons. In the first place, we have an eye-witness account of the construction of the new choir from a monk and chronicler, Gervase of Canterbury: the fire of 1174 which destroyed the Romanesque choir, the appointment of the French architect William of Sens, the progress of the work season by season, William's fall from the scaffolding in 1178, the occupation of the choir by the monks in 1180, and the completion of the extension beyond the choir (the Trinity Chapel and Corona) under the architect William the Englishman in 1184. William of Sens emerges from Gervase's account as a professional master mason typical of his age: well travelled, something of a diplomat (he persuaded the more reluctant monks to demolish large parts of the old Romanesque choir), and with a mastery of carpentry as well as stone. Like all medieval architects, his training was not theoretical, but acquired by practical experience in the workshop. The building's general dimensions were determined by a few simple mathematical and geometrical rules of thumb handed down within a craft tradition, and the details of the building were worked out during construction. Although William drew details ('he handed templates for shaping the stones to carvers') no accurate scale drawings were made in advance, for after he fell from the scaffolding there were no plans to guide his warden on the site: 'he had to ordain what was to be done from his bed'.

Canterbury is not the first building in England to show the influence of the new Gothic style of northern France, and nor did it mark the end of Anglo-Norman Romanesque; but it brought English church architecture into line with the most progressive achievements of French Early Gothic. Its pointed arches, delicate rib vaults and detached shafts, its large aisle windows, rich capitals and use of marble have their nearest French counterparts in Notre-Dame in Paris, St-Remi at Rheims, and the cathedrals of Laon, Arras and Valenciennes. Canterbury's pressing liturgical needs may have also prompted this *rapprochement* with northern France. More altars were housed in the new choir by placing some of them in additional eastern transepts preserved from the old choir and aligned with the new sanctuary, an idea probably borrowed from the double-transept Romanesque church at Cluny. And the provisions for displaying the shrine seem to come straight from St-Denis: the sanctuary and Trinity Chapel raised above the crypt, the shrine (now lost) displayed behind the high altar, and the pilgrims circulating around it in a spacious ambulatory. No building in England had made a shrine so accessible and its setting so elaborate.

Canterbury's influence was widespread. For the next seventy years most of the greater churches of England had their east ends rebuilt in connection with a relic cult. In almost all, Canterbury's Purbeck marble and lavish decoration were eagerly adopted; its extended plan became a norm; and both at secular establishments – Lincoln, Salisbury, and Beverley – and Benedictine houses – Worcester and Durham – the grandiose double transept scheme reappeared. But Canterbury answered special needs, and as such it was never completely copied. The Trinity Chapel's French plan of apse and ambulatory was only adopted for shrine churches at Westminster and Hailes Abbey, both, significantly, under royal patronage. Otherwise the English reverted to their preference for rectangular east ends. In the West Country the favourite solution – first at Winchester and then most perfectly at Salisbury (Cat. 489, 18) – was to end the tall sanctuary wall just east of the high altar, and return the choir aisles behind it in the form of a low, crypt-like vaulted hall, containing the shrine, and opening directly eastwards into chapels, including the Lady Chapel. In the north of England and East Anglia – at Whitby, Beverley and Ely – the sanctuary ran its full height to the east end, sometimes projecting a little as a chapel, but usually ending flush with the aisle eastern walls to form a cliff-like termination (see Cat. 242, 399).

These deviations were part of a fundamental rejection of the principles of French Gothic which Canterbury embodied. The French had invented a new structural system by combining relatively thin walls with stone rib vaults, the thrusts of which were supported at the points of real stress by internal props and later by flying buttresses. This skeletal construction allowed walls to be replaced by windows, and interior spaces to expand to colossal heights. The English showed little interest in such structural innovations: they used flying buttresses reluctantly, hiding them beneath aisle roofs; they never built to great heights, preferring long horizontal vistas; and

Fig. 38 York Minster, north transept showing the 'five sisters' window and the elevation of the east wall

they remained faithful to the old Anglo-Norman practice of supporting vaults on very thick walls. When Gothic appeared at Canterbury only its decorative possibilities were really understood; and with a mixture of perversity and ignorance the English set about transforming an essentially structural style into a vehicle for linear ornament. Lincoln Cathedral (Cat. 240), begun in 1192, is the closest imitator of Canterbury, but the walls seem thicker, the ornament more congested, and the structural forms of shaft and arch reduced to linear accents. In particular, the simple French vaults of Canterbury, logically tied, like canopies, to the individual bays beneath them, become dense bunches of palm-like ribs, concealing the bay divisions, and echoing the rich wall surfaces below. Structural logic gives way to decorative unity.

Similar rejections of both Canterbury and French Gothic characterise regional versions of Early Gothic in the West Country and in the north of England. Paradoxically, the north had anticipated Canterbury by importing, in the 1150s and 1160s, the most advanced French Gothic forms into the choirs of York (now destroyed) and Ripon Minsters. But Continental contacts were quickly severed. By the time the choir of Whitby had been begun in around 1220 (Cat. 242), and the transepts of York Minster a decade later (fig. 38), the north had developed its own ponderous but monumental style, distinguished by massive walls and magnificent groups of lancet windows. The West Country and south Wales evolved an equally distinctive vocabulary, rejecting Purbeck marble and 'palm' vaults, encircling pillars with dense groups of triple shafts, omitting capitals between jambs and their arches, and placing exquisitely carved paterae against plain ashlar masonry. In its early stages the style also depended on French influences (both from Romanesque Burgundy and Gothic northern France), but it soon settled into an unmistakably English manner. At Wells Cathedral, begun around 1180, the walls have thickened, and verticality is replaced by unbroken horizontal storeys (Cat. 238).

Salisbury Cathedral is both a summation and a critique of these regional experiments. Begun on a virgin site in 1220, and completed without substantial alteration in 1268, Salisbury has a unity and perfection unique in English medieval architecture. The double transepts and Purbeck marble echo Canterbury and Lincoln (Cat. 489); the four-part vaults and insistent horizontality recall Wells (Cat. 238); the low retrochoir, perhaps designed to house the shrine of St Osmund, is borrowed from Winchester (Cat. 18). But a new regularity – sharp, austere, and elegant – grips the whole structure. Inside, the walls are clearly framed by marble shafts and string courses; outside (Cat. 489), they are linked by repetitive groups of lancet windows; and in the retrochoir the drainpipe-thin columns extend into the Lady Chapel to form a miniature hall church. Such clarity and delicacy may resemble French Gothic in a general sense, but as a whole Salisbury is as English as Lincoln or Wells. Its thick structure, its angular massing, and its constrictions of space in nave and choir, have nothing in common with the spatial magnitude and diaphanous splendour of the contemporary High Gothic cathedrals of Amiens or Rheims.

The insularity of English Early Gothic, what Thomas Rickman in 1817 called 'the Early English Style',[2] coincided with a growing sense of national identity in English political life. In particular, the gradual absorption of the Norman conquerors into Anglo-Saxon society found one expression in the renewed promotion of the cults of Anglo-Saxon saints: St Frideswide at Oxford, St Etheldreda at Ely, St Edmund at Bury. The 'Early English' showed similarly retrospective tendencies. At Wells Cathedral posthumous effigies of its Saxon bishops were laid round the new choir (Cat. 238). At the same time, and only a few miles away, the monks of Glastonbury Abbey defined their opposition to the episcopal claims of Wells, and stressed their ancient pre-eminence in the monastic life of the West Country by constructing a new Gothic church with a consciously old-fashioned elevation: the main arcade and the triforium were – as in the Romanesque churches of Oxford and Tewkesbury – contained within a colossal arch order. Similar considerations may have prompted, at Wells and Salisbury, the use of screen façades on the Anglo-Norman model of Malmesbury Abbey. Instead of the 'harmonic' façades of French cathedrals, with their clear indications of the nave behind them, and their concentration of sculpture in large portals, Salisbury and Wells (Cat. 239) dwarf their portals beneath tiers of statues, so that the whole façade, once brightly painted, would have resembled a huge altar reredos. And the bizarre reversal of this format in the west façade of Peterborough Cathedral (*c.* 1220; fig. 39), where the portals have been enlarged into gigantic porches, must also be a Gothic paraphrase of the great Romanesque 'arch-façades' of nearby Bury St Edmunds and Lincoln (Cat. 694).

These insular tendencies were dramatically interrupted in 1245 by Henry III's re-construction of the abbey church at Westminster (Cat. 262, 418, fig. 41). Henry's taste was as cosmopolitan as his dynastic relations, and he was particularly impressed by the new 'Rayonnant' French Gothic of his brother-in-law, King (later Saint) Louis IX of France. The new church, built entirely at his own expense, was designed as a mausoleum and coronation church for Henry and his heirs, and a shrine for the body of Henry's beloved St Edward the Confessor, last of the Anglo-Saxon kings. Accordingly, the architect, Henry of Reyns (from Rheims?) laid out a radiating system of chapels similar to the French kings' coronation cathedral in Rheims (fig. 44), he filled the transept ends with rose windows copied from the French royal burial church

Fig. 39   Peterborough Cathedral west front

at St-Denis, and he covered the interior surfaces with an unprecedented wealth of polychromatic ornament in imitation of the brilliant interior finish of King Louis' palace and shrine chapel of the Ste-Chapelle in Paris. All these buildings used bar tracery – thin bar-like lines of stone dividing windows into geometrical patterns, – and Westminster Abbey is the first great church in England to adopt bar tracery on a large and public scale. These French quotations, together with its soaring proportions and exposed flying buttresses, made Westminster Abbey the most French-looking building in England since Canterbury. Its influence on subsequent English architecture was considerable, probably because the impact of its French forms was mitigated by the use of traditionally English features, such as Purbeck marble and decorative vaults. The combination is particularly successful in the chapter house, completed *c.* 1253, where the English polygonal plan and the French bar tracery contrive to enclose the spectator in a ring of vast windows resembling a kind of centralised Ste-Chapelle. This Westminster solution set in motion the splendid series of English late thirteenth-century chapter houses, starting with its almost exact copy at Salisbury, and concluding with the upper chamber of the chapter house at Wells (*c.* 1285, Cat. 328) where bar tracery is combined with picturesque cones of ribs.

As if impelled by a logic of its own, tracery began in the second half of the thirteenth century to dominate almost every aspect of church building. Colossal tracery windows filled terminal walls in place of the old grouped lancets (as in the Angel Choir, Lincoln, Cat. 321), and the clerestorey was extended down into the elevation by dispensing with the traditional tall gallery openings and adopting the low French triforium passage (Exeter Cathedral, Cat. 589; York Minster, fig. 47). By 1300 new types of tracery – Y-shaped and intersecting – were filling windows with a complexity of pattern unparalleled on the Continent (see Wells chapter house, Cat. 328). And around 1320, in the dioceses of York and Lincoln, masons developed 'curvilinear' tracery by inserting the double-curved ogee arch into their windows, thereby softening hitherto regular and geometric patterns into sinuous lines resembling flames, raindrops, or the veins of gigantic leaves (York, west window, Cat. 495).

Masons saw nothing incompatible between these linear fantasies and their old traditions of thick walls and sculptural ornament. At Exeter, Bishop Grandisson's architect continued to build the nave into the mid-fourteenth century with the same thick walls and massive vaults as in the choir (Cat. 589). And in the north-east of England, around 1330, architectural furnishings – invariably topped by gables and bulbous ogee arches – become smothered in dense seaweed-like foliage. (Cat. 494, 493). In the Lady Chapel at Ely (Cat. 491) the whole architectural structure is disguised behind an accumulation of such niche-like motifs, once brightly painted. With the destroyed stained-glass windows (their scenes also enclosed in fictive niches) and the polychrome vaults, they would have created an overwhelmingly sumptuous décor.

Contemporary architecture in the west of England showed a similiar preference for exotic ornament, but combined it with devising new arrangements of interior space, and new types of decorative vault. No doubt inspired by centralised chapter houses, the octagonal Lady Chapel at Wells Cathedral or the hexagonal north porch of St Mary Redcliffe at Bristol (Cat. 490) break open the box-like masses of Early English planning with more expansive and fluent spaces, all crowned with vaults of almost Islamic elaboration. The polygonal choir at Tewkesbury, remodelled by the Despensers as their family mausoleum (Cat. 496), supports a lavish net vault, complicated even further at the crown by the addition of small matchstick-like ribs called 'liernes'.

Such excesses of two- and three-dimensional ornament no doubt justify Rickman's description of this early fourteenth-century style as 'Decorated', but they have their ultimate origins in a 'Court style' of architecture created by the masons of Edward I. Henry III's Westminster Abbey, by setting up a 'Royal Works' and a body of royal masons, had made the king the leading patron or architecture in England, a position which the monarchy was to hold, intermittently, to the end of the Middle Ages. Three of Edward's enterprises of the 1290s – the Eleanor crosses (Cat. 377) the tombs of Aveline and Edmund Crouchback in Westminster Abbey, (Cat. 326) and St Stephen's Chapel in Westminster Palace (Cat. 324–5) – were all inspired by French fashion: the first by the 'Montjoies' of St Louis, the second by the royal canopied tombs in St-Denis, and the third by the two-storeyed Ste-Chapelle of St Louis in Paris. But all three elaborated their French models with an unprecedented wealth of ornament, including the earliest known uses, in England, of the ogee arch, of tracery with curvilinear patterns, and of a prominent crenellated cornice motif that may owe something to wooden structures. These ornamental transformations of conventional French 'Rayonnant' inspired some of the most extravagant achievements of the Decorated style. St Stephen's Chapel in particular set the tone for the more ambitious projects of the early fourteenth century: the lierne vault in its lower storey anticipated those in the West Country, particularly in the Lady Chapel and choir of St Augustine's at Bristol (Cat. 487); the lavish finish of its upper storey found an immediate response in the Lady Chapel at Ely (Cat. 491); and its cornice motif became one of the main characteristics of English late medieval architecture.

Indeed, St Stephen's Chapel was not only a fountainhead for the Decorated, but also a prototype for the style which succeeded it, called – again by Thomas Rickman – 'Perpendicular'. Even before St Stephen's was complete the new style had made its début in the choir and south transept of Gloucester Cathedral (Cat. 498). In 1327 the body of the murdered Edward II was buried there. An unlikely cult grew up, and his son Edward III encouraged it by commissioning a splendid tomb for his father, the effigy in suave alabaster, the canopy as intricate as a shrine's (Cat. 497). Starting first in the south transept and then moving into the choir, the royal masons demolished the Norman clerestorey but retained the Romanesque walls below it, and extended over the old gallery openings and arcades screens of blind or open tracery, transforming the choir into an apparently aisleless, chapel-like space. The terminal walls were opened by colossal windows filled with similar grids of tracery, so that choir and transept, held in curtains of stone and glass, seem to stream vertically upwards in a series of delicate linear recessions and gradations (fig. 49). The lavish sculptural and sinuous vocabulary of the Decorated style has been hardened and flattened into a brittle cage of tracery, the simplicity of which suggests a source not in interior architecture at all, but in the exterior treatment of walls. Indeed, the earlier exterior of St Stephen's Chapel (Cat. 324), and the exactly contemporary exterior of the chapter house of Old St Paul's in London (Cat. 386) show similar curtains of tracery running down walls and openings. But Gloucester demonstrated that such veneers of mouldings and tracery could also transform the interior of a church, and at the same time disguise the masonry of older structures without the expense of demolishing them. Not suprisingly, Gloucester provoked immediate imitators, in the details of its south transept (Edward III's new Dean's Cloister at Windsor), and in the rectangular, chapel-like form of its choir (chancel of St Mary's Warwick, c. 1370). But its real merit was to show the adaptability of Perpendicular (a better term would be 'rectilinear') to all kinds of great church design. In the late fourteenth-century naves of Canterbury and Winchester cathedrals (Cat. 693, 601), the delicate surface effects of Gloucester were taken out of the specialised context of a royal chapel choir and applied to large basilican naves. Like Gloucester, Winchester is a 'face-lift' of the old Norman structure, much of which had to be preserved. Its upper parts were overlaid with grids of blind tracery, its thickness disguised by a horizontal balustrade and delicate gradations of mouldings, and its massive piers recut into slender shafts and profiles. At Canterbury the same subtle recessions of tracery and moulding articulate the tall, well-lit side aisles; and the vertical sweep of its majestic sequence of pillars is enhanced by extending their mouldings upwards, to frame both triforium and clerestorey.

Both Winchester and Canterbury have ordinary lierne vaults, but already in the choir at Tewkesbury in the 1330s attempts had been made to apply window tracery – in this case the rose pattern in its eastern window – to the vault's surface (Cat. 496). A more systematic solution to the problem of harmonising Perpendicular vaults with Perpendicular walls and windows was the fan vault. The visual unity achieved between these conoids of tracery and the adjacent surfaces is evident in the east walk of the cloister of Gloucester Cathedral (1351–77, Cat. 499), the first surviving examples of the type. Almost all the early fan vaults are on this small scale, usually placed over porches or tomb canopies. Only from the mid-fifteenth century did architects have the technical confidence to transfer this 'micro-architectural' form to the high stone vaults of a large church. Until then, fans over wider spaces had to be constructed in wood (as in Winchester College Chapel, Cat. 600).

The special emphasis on tracery in English late medieval architecture implies rigorous standards of craftsmanship in the masons' lodge. The creation of complicated windows demanded sophisticated draftsmanship, precision carving, and a knowledge of applied geometry. No architectural drawings survive in England of the kind preserved from German cathedral workshops of the fourteenth and fifteenth centuries; but above the north porch of Wells, and the chapter house vestibule of York, we can still see architects' tracing floors, with complicated details scratched out, full scale, on the plaster (Cat. 474–5). Master masons had no theoretical understanding of the science of geometry, using it simply as a practical tool for design; but their brilliant manipulation of tracery – which is, in effect, geometry made visible – gave them a new intellectual and social status. William Ramsey, the king's chief mason after 1336, had his own seal and coat of arms. William Wynford, architect of the Winchester nave, appeared with the royal carpenter Hugh Herland in the east window of Winchester College Chapel (Cat. 600, 612). And Wynford and Henry Yevele, the architect of Westminster Hall (Cat. 692), frequently dined at high table in New College, Oxford at the invitation of William of Wykeham, who had risen from 'chief keeper and surveyor' of Edward III's works at Windsor to Bishop of Winchester (in 1367) and Chancellor of England. Wynford as architect and Wykeham as patron formed one of the outstanding partnerships of English medieval architecture. Apart from their remodelling of the Winchester nave, they introduced the Perpendicular style to the universities in New College at Oxford, founded by Wykeham in 1379 on a scale unprecedented in university architecture. Working in a plain and monumental style, Wynford's integrated composition of buildings was to have a profound influence on subsequent collegiate architecture in Oxford: a quadrangular plan, with hall and T-shaped chapel aligned together on the north side, a cloister to the west (Cat. 599), and gatehouses worthy of a monastic or cathedral precinct. The scheme was successful enough to be copied by Wynford for Wykeham's foundation at Winchester College in 1382 (Cat. 600).

The pragmatic and adaptable vocabulary of Perpendicular is nowhere more evident than in the parish church. The Fourth Lateran Council of 1215 had instigated a reform of parish life in England which found one expression in a series of grandiose thirteenth-century parish churches (such as West Walton in Norfolk, c. 1240, Cat. 89). But in the early fourteenth century a revolutionary change took place in their scale and character, largely through the establishment and influence of the preaching friars. West Walton could be described, like most other large parish churches of its period, as a reduced version of cathedral architecture, in this case nearby Lincoln (Cat. 240). But in the now-destroyed Greyfriars church in London, founded in 1306 by Queen Margaret, second wife of Edward I, a type of open hall-like structure was created that bore no resemblance to a great church except in its scale. Suitable for preaching to large congregations, with its slender piers, wooden roofs, and simple rectangular plan, the London Greyfriars set the pattern for a series of friars' churches (now mostly destroyed) built in the prosperous towns of later medieval England. In turn, these became the model for the parish churches of East Anglia and the West Country (e.g. Yeovil, Cat. 91), and the great town churches of the fourteenth and fifteenth centuries (such as St Michael's in Coventry, Cat. 695, or Holy Trinity in Hull, Cat. 90). The choir of the latter, begun around 1320, is a close copy of the London Greyfriars.

Yeovil (Cat. 91), like many other larger parish churches of its period, is dominated by a western tower. The later Middle Ages was the age of great steeples. Usually the last addition to a building, steeples offered splendid opportunities for architectural virtuosity. They not only crowned churches, but signalled the wealth and pride of a community (see St Michael's, Coventry, Cat. 695). Most cathedrals and abbey churches were also completed with towers and spires in the fourteenth and fifteenth centuries. Some were built at the western end, and some over crossings never intended to receive them, necessitating, in Wells and Salisbury, the hasty erection of supporting 'strainer arches' (Cat. 238). All of them gave to the prevailing horizontality of the English church a contrasting vertical power. The fashion for crossing towers began with Lincoln and Hereford cathedrals in the early fourteenth century (Cat. 694), and continued with Worcester, York, Durham, Gloucester and Canterbury. But the most spectacular of the series, and perhaps the earliest, is the steeple at Salisbury (Cat. 489), an incomparable monument to architectural extravagance. Until the last years of the fourteenth century all towers were built to support spires, some of them wooden. Lincoln's central spire was destroyed by storm (1548), Old St Paul's colossal needle by lightning in 1561. Only Lichfield Cathedral retains its three stone steeples of the fourteenth century.

Whether spire or tower, steeples were the most public and prominent reminders of the presence of the Church in medieval life, of the Celestial City on earth. Rising above village, farmland and city, the steeples, churches, colleges and castles of the Middle Ages still dominate the landscape of modern England. In its beliefs and customs medieval society was very different from our own, and to understand it requires an effort of the imagination. But its material remains are perhaps its most eloquent legacy. To enter the grandest or humblest of Gothic buildings is to go back into the physical setting of medieval life; and in their craftsmanship of wood and stone, glass and paint, we can still recapture, at first hand, something of the tastes, ideals and attitudes of the people who lived and worshipped in them.

NOTES
1. G.G. Coulton, quoted by Cheney 1951–2.
2. Rickman 1817.

The English Response to French

Christopher Wilson

Gothic Architecture, c. 1200–1350

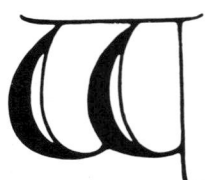

hen William the Englishman succeeded William of Sens as architect of the choir of Canterbury Cathedral in 1178, the change-over would have seemed at the time nothing more than an expedient necessitated by the Frenchman's crippling fall from the scaffolding. With the advantage of hindsight, however, the appointment of the Englishman seems prophetic of the situation during the rest of the Middle Ages in England, for throughout those three and a half centuries there was not a single occasion on which a foreign architect took charge of a major church building project.[1] Of course this was not the end of English interest in French Gothic architecture, but William of Sens' departure marks the close of a twenty-year period of French participation in the genesis of English Gothic, as well as the beginning of a much longer period, about sixty years, during which English architecture remained virtually impervious to outside influences.

Why then was England so unreceptive to the splendours of French Gothic during what is customarily regarded as its greatest period, a regard reflected in the stylistic label 'High Gothic'? Put this way, the English response sounds obtuse, wilful even; but was it really? Even in northern France the reception accorded to the three main High Gothic cathedrals of Chartres, Rheims and Amiens was in general a guarded one, and a complete contrast to the enthusiastic welcome extended both in France and beyond to the next phase of Gothic, the Rayonnant style pioneered at St-Denis from 1231. Yet it is still legitimate to ask why England produced no equivalents to Marburg and Trier, the only German churches which show perfect mastery of French High Gothic. One would have thought that the end of the Interdict in 1214 and the return of the English prelates from exile in France provided the ideal opportunity to introduce at least some elements of French cathedral architecture. That this did not happen on any significant scale must have been due at least partly to the existence in England of an architectural tradition which was something more than a provincial offshoot from its French parent. The major English churches of the early thirteenth century are obviously far lower than their French counterparts, but they are comparable in aesthetic sophistication and they must have been more than comparable in cost.

There can be no doubt that one bay of the nave of Lincoln Cathedral cost a great deal more to build than a bay of the nave of Chartres, for the extra height at Chartres is achieved with plain masonry such as occurs hardly anywhere at Lincoln (Cat. 240, fig. 40). It would be particularly interesting to know the respective costs of the simply profiled arches used at Chartres and almost all other thirteenth-century French churches and their infinitely more complicated English counterparts (fig. 42). Structurally considered, these rich arch mouldings are a by-product of the thick walls which English Gothic inherited from Anglo-Norman architecture, but it is clear that they were thought important in themselves, for they are present even in comparatively plainly detailed churches like Salisbury (Cat. 241) and Beverley. Since no thirteenth-century English architect imitated the thin, plate-like walls of the French Gothic churches, it seems safe to assume that this feature was disliked. The ability of so small a country as England to build large numbers of exceptionally elaborate and expensive churches is an under-researched question which cannot be explored here. However, an important part of the explanation must be the inordinate size and wealth of the English bishoprics, whose number had not increased since the early Middle Ages. In the thirteenth century no fewer than twelve of Europe's forty richest sees were in England; and in this situation even institutions which were not rich would become obliged to compete at the high level set by the cathedrals and major abbeys.

Fig. 40 Chartres Cathedral, north side of the nave seen from the south transept, after 1194

Fig. 41 Westminster Abbey, east wall of the south transept, southernmost bay

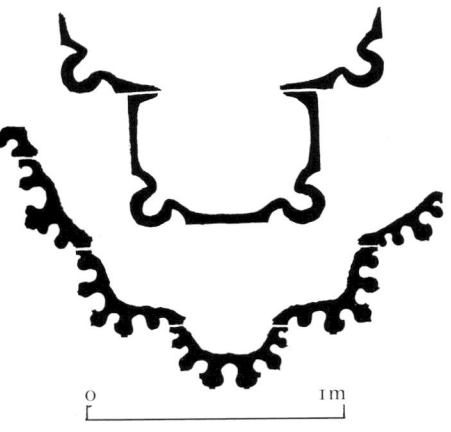

Fig. 42 Sections through the main arcade arches of Chartres Cathedral (*left*) and the presbytery of Ely Cathedral (drawing by C. Wilson)

Apart from clerical wealth and artistic tradition, there was another major factor working to sustain English insularity in architecture whose importance is very difficult to assess, namely the xenophobic and specifically anti-French feeling current during the reigns of John and Henry III. The loss of Normandy in 1204 and the French invasion of 1214 certainly promoted consciousness of a national, English identity among those of the aristocracy who chose to keep their English rather than their Norman lands. However, Henry III was the very last man in England to think of himself as an Englishman, and his Continental ambitions were one of the main causes of division between him and his English subjects. It therefore seems very apt that when the insularity of English Gothic was finally breached in the 1240s it was the Crown which led the way. Yet French influences would no doubt have prevailed sooner or later even without Henry III's patronage, for by comparison with the phenomenal momentum behind the formal development of early thirteenth-century French Gothic, English Gothic of the same period presents a static picture. It is hardly an exaggeration to say that by around 1215 all the main early thirteenth-century themes had been enunciated and that the next thirty years were spent in devising beautiful if none too surprising variations.

Henry III's reconstruction of Westminster Abbey (Cat. 262, fig. 41) was the building which drew the attention of England as a whole to many of the most spectacular aspects of the thirteenth-century French cathedrals, but this was not the first use of High Gothic ideas by its designer, Henry of Reyns. In 1240, five years before

Fig. 43 St Mary's Priory, Binham Norfolk, west front, before 1244

work on the Abbey began, he had received from his royal namesake the commission for a much less public building, a chapel of St Edward the Confessor in Windsor Castle. The small part of this building to have survived shows a knowledge of the detailing of Rheims Cathedral, so there is a strong chance that its long-destroyed windows incorporated the bar tracery invented at Rheims (fig. 44). Positive evidence that they did is the reference to circular cusped openings of different sizes in an account for glazing repairs in 1295. But if the windows of St Edward's Chapel were French, its basic structure could hardly have been more English, for in plan it was a simple rectangle, it had no figure sculpture on its west door and its vault was of timber imitating stone.

A similar combination is to be found on the contemporary west front of Binham Priory in Norfolk (fig. 43). The lighting of the central vessel by a single window of upright format rather than by a rose window can admittedly be paralleled at lesser French churches, yet it is clear that the Binham front does not owe this feature to a wish to imitate any French façade. The small portals and arcading-clad buttresses are an English framework into which are fitted tracery patterns that look like trophies from a tour of the most famous French High Gothic cathedrals. Thus the four-light, foliate-cusped tracery of the nave clearstorey at Amiens Cathedral (*c.* 1225) becomes the basis of the central window, and the linked clearstorey and triforium of the main apse at Rheims Cathedral (fig. 44) are turned into two-level windows which light the aisles and galleries of the Romanesque nave behind the façade while playing down the presence of the horizontal division between the two storeys. The ingenuity of this adaptation of the Rheims elevation illustrates a recurrent feature of the English response to French Gothic: the readiness to take account of French organisational principles if and when they could be made to serve as the basis for empirically conceived solutions to specific problems. French schemes were hardly ever to be adopted for their own sakes in thirteenth-century England.

Detailed knowledge of Rheims Cathedral is only one of several aspects common to Binham and Westminster Abbey which provide grounds for thinking that they were both designed by the same man. Most scholars concede that Henry of Reyns's surname is far more likely to denote Rheims than the only English alternative, the small Essex village of Rayne; and the debate about Henry's nationality and training seems to have subsided leaving a majority in favour of his being English. There appear to be no parallels for a medieval architect's taking the name of a foreign city but it can hardly be a coincidence that Rheims Cathedral was the most fundamental French influence on Henry of Reyns's design. Westminster is of course not a literal imitation of Rheims for, as at Binham, the English tradition is much in evidence and the French sources drawn on include more modern buildings than Rheims. Nevertheless, Westminster owes surprisingly much to what was in French terms an outdated design. To present this simply as a reflection of conservative taste would fail to acknowledge that there was a special factor in play here, namely that the normal concern to be up-to-date was given a lower priority than the need to assert parity with the coronation church of Henry III's greatest rivals, the Capetian kings of France. At Westminster ideology is of paramount importance, and indeed it could hardly be otherwise for this was the one and only occasion in the history of Gothic architecture when a head of state met the entire cost of a church of cathedral scale. The cost was in fact a staggering £42,000 plus, as compared to the equivalent of about £10,000 in English money spent by Louis IX on his most lavish architectural project, the Ste-Chapelle. Henry's average annual income during this period has been put at around £34,000. It follows that the motivation behind this uniquely ambitious act of patronage must have transcended mere enthusiasm for art, although this was a factor as Henry was the greatest Maecenas of his day. The contemporary historian Matthew Paris says simply that the rebuilding was undertaken out of devotion to St Edward the Confessor, whose relics stood in the place of honour behind the high altar.

But besides being a symptom of Henry's extreme piety, the cult of St Edward was a central element in his quasi-priestly conception of kingship, according to which he was God's vicar and lord of all men in his realm, clergy as well as laity. The ancient idea of the priest-like ruler had virtually fallen into abeyance in England during the twelfth century, and after Becket's martyrdom in the cause of defending the Church's rights against an oppressive king, its revival was hardly a practical proposition. Henry's determination to revive it had already aroused stiff opposition before 1245 and was to be one of the causes of the baronial revolt of 1258–65. Sacral kingship had survived in France partly because in the twelfth century the higher clergy and the kings had needed each others' help in order to overcome their common enemy, the lawless aristocracy of the region around Paris. Henry's rebuilding of the English coronation church on the model of its French equivalent was thus an integral part of his attempt to refashion the image of the English monarchy along French lines. The Abbey was to combine the functions and some of the architectural features of the two other churches beside Rheims which were most closely associated with the French crown, the abbey of St-Denis, royal burial place and repository of the coronation regalia, and the Ste-Chapelle, chief royal showpiece in the capital and the setting for the Crown of Thorns – a relic whose possession brought to the French Crown a prestige comparable to that which St Edward's relics gave to his successors on the English throne. In 1245 Henry III had still not seen any major French Gothic church, so he may not have realised how far the Abbey was from being a French design. If, however, he was aware that much of the structural and decorative detailing was English, the possibility arises that Westminster was consciously conceived as an amalgam of French and English traditions paralleling the carefully cultivated binational character of his Court and administrative machine. The hybrid character of Westminster contrasts strikingly with those exported French cathedrals, León, Cologne and Strasburg, none of which makes any concessions to the primitive versions of Gothic current in their respective regions.

Rheims Cathedral is successfully evoked at Westminster by the use throughout both upper and lower levels of windows with two lights under a cusped circle (figs 41, 44). If modernity had been the paramount consideration, the clearstorey would have had the four-light windows which became *de rigueur* after their invention at Amiens.

Fig. 44 Rheims Cathedral, upper storeys of the main apse, after 1211

For the paired two-light tracery units of the gallery, Robert Branner suggested as sources a number of minor Île-de-France churches such as Brie-Comte-Robert, and he compared the narrow clearstorey windows to those at Louis IX's Cistercian foundation at Royaumont.[2] Neither of these comparisons is really satisfactory, not because they are not sufficiently close – they are – but because they are with buildings unlikely to have attracted the attention of an architect commissioned to build the most sumptuous church in mid-thirteenth-century Europe. Brie-Comte-Robert is just too lowly a building to have been considered, and Royaumont's narrow windows were not so much the result of aesthetic choice as demonstrations of Cistercian simplicity and austerity, which made them irrelevant to Westminster. It may be proposed that the clearstorey at Westminster was influenced by the other great thirteenth-century church in Rheims, St-Nicaise, which, as a lavishly detailed Benedictine abbey church, was a far more appropriate model than Brie-Comte-Robert or Royaumont. St-Nicaise's clearstorey windows were not a source for Westminster in the sense of inspiring a copy or near-copy, but rather an authorisation to adhere to traditional English formulas, for whereas their narrowness was very unorthodox in north French Rayonnant architecture it was absolutely normal in English Gothic churches before Westminster.

This same process of selecting French precedents on the basis of their compatibility with English usage can be detected behind other components of the main elevations at Westminster. Virtually the only first-class French Gothic building of the early thirteenth century whose middle storey is fronted by a pair of large tracery designs is Amiens Cathedral, and to a designer determined not to jettison his English heritage the Amiens triforium could well have been seen as sanctioning the retention of a gallery of the kind which the influence of Canterbury had made the norm in early thirteenth-century England (Cat. 13, 240). The fact that the likeness is superficial is not an objection to the connection. This is true also of the pier design, a scheme modelled on the piers with four attached monolithic shafts at Salisbury (Cat. 241) but surely selected for its value as an approximation to the normal High Gothic pier-type introduced at Chartres, in which the four shafts are structurally integral with the cylindrical core (fig. 40).

It has very properly been emphasised by Jean Bony[3] that the main long-term effect of the building of Westminster Abbey was simply to introduce England as a whole to the tracery window. Rayonnant was not presented there as a coherent system of great church design, despite quite strong intimations in the chapter house, whose windows void the walls into screens of tracery and glass comparable to the clearstoreys of Amiens or St-Denis. But even if Westminster had been a purely French building like Cologne or Strasburg, it would probably not have resembled them in bringing about the almost instantaneous substitution of Rayonnant for the local style. That the French innovations of Westminster had become tainted through their association with a king unpopular on account of his French-inspired view of kingship cannot be formally proved, but a clear pointer in this direction is the fact that the plan of the east end was copied only at Battle and Hailes, two abbeys which were in different senses royal. Yet there was one important practical consideration which militated against acceptance of Westminster's innovatory French format, particularly its height. As in the period before 1245, most major church building projects were extensions to existing fabrics. The choir of Old St Paul's Cathedral in London and the Angel Choir at Lincoln (Cat. 321), both begun in the mid-1250s, are two such projects, typical in the concern they evince for the maintenance of the same internal and external levels as the older work to which they were joined. Of course it was possible successfully to add a high Rayonnant choir to a lower Romanesque body, as the case of Tournai Cathedral shows, although there was inevitably a greater loss of overall coherence. The tall format of Westminster was probably ruled out in such contexts as Lincoln not just on account of practicalities or unwelcome royal connotations, but because it would have violated an indigenous tradition of horizontal continuity which had been in existence since around 1100 when an extremely long and low choir was added to the post-Conquest cathedral at Canterbury.

The insistence that new extensions follow the broad proportions and thick-wall structure of older work obviously acted as a powerful brake on innovation in matters other than decoration. Thus most late thirteenth-century English buildings were essentially improvisations designed to contain as far as possible the disruptive consequences of introducing tracery into elevations which otherwise conformed very closely to early thirteenth-century ideas. The architect of the Angel Choir (Cat. 321) was typical of his generation in his refusal to think of tracery as anything more than a specialised form of the richly moulded arches discussed earlier in relation to the nave at Lincoln. In applying complex mouldings to tracery, he was only following Westminster's lead (fig. 41), but his use of amply moulded tracery as an equivalent for the inner layer of lancets in the clearstorey of the adjoining early thirteenth-century work makes it impossible to 'read' the outer, glazed tracery. The unfavourable verdict of contemporaries can be inferred from the lack of imitations elsewhere. The east wall illustrates in another way this architect's reluctance to face up to the full implications of using tracery. The disparity in curvature between the head of the east window and the high vault results in a residue of solid wall strangely at odds with the neat fit of the jambs against the side walls of the main vessel. Clearly the architect did not feel that a single large and complex opening required to be related to its surroundings more rigorously than the traditional grouped lancets. The basic French Gothic principle that tracery expands to fill the space available was completely foreign to him, although it was really no more than an extension of the logic of tracery itself, where there can be no left-over areas. Two mutually incompatible modes of architectural thought are operating here side by side. The actual window is one of the early triumphs of the great English tradition of very large-scale tracery compositions, a tradition which was enabled to flourish by the rejection of French apsidal east ends and of façades given over to large portals and rose windows.

Apart from the importation of some tracery designs and a few moulding profiles, there is no sign of further English interest in Rayonnant until the end of the thirteenth century, the very period when the growth of nationalism throughout Europe was beginning to undermine the political and artistic hegemony of France and to favour local versions of Gothic better adapted to local conditions. The completely unheralded appearance of ambitious Rayonnant architecture at York Minster in the late 1280s can hardly be explained except as a consequence of the appointment of John le Romeyn as archbishop in 1286. Le Romeyn was a theology professor in Paris during the 1270s and early 1280s and had presumably become enthused for French architecture then. The vestibule to the York chapter house has the earliest English elevations entirely given over to tracery (fig. 45). However, comparison with any similar Rayonnant interior reveals a curious anomaly: the verticals of the blind tracery on the dado are not linked up to the window mullions, which are set back a few centimetres. In the nave at York (fig. 47), designed around the same time as the vestibule, this motif of 'linkage' is correctly used in the upper storeys – the context where it originated (fig. 46) – so it is strange not to find it combined with the French principle successfully applied in the vestibule, namely the elimination of all solid wall around the windows. The designer of the vestibule and nave obviously felt no commitment to Rayonnant as an all-embracing system, for in the nave he retained several established English usages besides narrow clearstorey openings, notably the complex profiling of the main arcades and elaborate wall arcading in the aisles. His northern colleagues received with enthusiasm the elegant Parisian detailing of the wall arcade but they completely ignored the Rayonnant linkage of the upper storeys. There is nothing paradoxical about this response: the aisle wall decoration confirmed and renewed an established English taste for complex and varied ornamental effects, whereas linkage threatened this tradition because it limited the independence of each upper storey. The welcome accorded to the incidentals of French Gothic and the rejection of many of its fundamentals were an almost exact recurrence of the reception given to Westminster Abbey some fifty years before.

In Edward I's two major undertakings of the early 1290s the ornamental rather than the systematic aspects of Rayonnant are again to the fore. The decorative canopy work invented on mid-thirteenth-century French cathedral portals (fig. 48), and virtually unknown in England before its use on the Eleanor crosses (Cat. 369), was given pride of place in the main room of St Stephen's Chapel in Westminster Palace, begun in 1292 (Cat. 324–5). St Stephen's pioneered a new architecture of contrasted

Fig. 45 York Minster, vestibule to the chapter house, late 1280s (engraving from John Britton, *History and Antiquities of the Metropolitan Church of York*, 1819)

Fig. 47 York Minster, north side of the nave; designed in the late 1280s, construction begun in 1291

Fig. 46 Church of La Trinité, Vendôme, upper storeys of the choir, after 1271

modes, diametrically opposed in spirit to the integrated systems of thirteenth-century great church architecture. Thus the canopy-encrusted main chapel was totally different from the massive architecture of the lower chapel and both were unrelated to the lean, linear mode of the exterior which was based on the same kind of Rayonnant internal elevations as the upper storeys of the York nave (fig. 47). On the gatehouse of St Augustine's Abbey, Canterbury, the architect of St Stephen's, Michael of Canterbury, deploys all three modes on a single façade (Cat. 327). Arguably the most impressive use of this concept of multiple modes is the series of variously vaulted and planned spaces at the east end of Wells Cathedral (figs 60, 61)

In view of the general European move away from the certainties of Rayonnant by 1300, a movement in which St Stephen's occupies a prominent place, one might have

Fig. 48 Noyon Cathedral, west front, detail of the jamb of the south portal, mid-thirteenth century

Fig. 49 Gloucester Cathedral, south wall of the presbytery (*left*), Romanesque crossing pier (*centre*) and east wall of the south transept (*right*)

thought that the tracery-clad turrets at St Augustine's would be nothing more than a valedictory gesture to the linkage concept; and it is indeed the case that early fourteenth-century English architects forgot all about the French prototypes behind the detailing of the Canterbury gate in their enthusiasm for the picturesque eclecticism pioneered here. However, around 1330 the remodelling of the eastern parts of Gloucester Cathedral was begun in the south transept by an architect who was less interested in Michael of Canterbury's formal innovations than in the empirical approach which generated them. His solution to the extremely difficult problem he faced – how to modernise the interior elevations of the Romanesque church while retaining its antiquated galleries – was to adapt the exterior elevations of St Stephen's, in which the flat Rayonnant grid of tracery also serves partly to disguise necessary openings, in this case the windows of the lower chapel (fig. 49, Cat. 324). At Gloucester the tracery is more authentically Rayonnant in its organisation than at St Stephen's, but this was not necessarily the result of on-the-spot study of French architecture. If, as is virtually certain, the designer was the second architect of St Stephen's, Thomas of Canterbury, he would probably have been able to study the French sources of the chapel without leaving the Royal Works office at Westminster, for it is inherently likely that the archive of drawings recorded as being there in the fifteenth century reflected the continuity of major building works in the palace, starting with the foundation of St Stephen's in 1292. The architects of Strasburg Cathedral in the late thirteenth and fourteenth centuries certainly had access to accurate drawings of major French buildings. The design of the Gloucester south transept was revised in the slightly later presbytery so that the upright rectangular 'panels' derived from Rayonnant triforia (which give the Perpendicular style its name) become the leitmotiv of the entire design, window tracery included (fig. 49, Cat. 498). In the cloister, panelling based on French rose window tracery even spreads over the vault surfaces (Cat. 499). There is a very real sense in which Perpendicular is Rayonnant taken to its ultimate conclusion.

We can only guess what it was about the Perpendicular version of Rayonnant that gave it a success in England enjoyed by none of its predecessors. The aesthetic qualities of the work itself surely provide much of the answer, for the Gloucester presbytery is incomparably more powerful and impressive than any other English church building of the early fourteenth century. But we can be certain that other factors were involved. For one thing, Gloucester was the most radically new approach to great church design seen in England in over a century, so it had the advantage of novelty. Also it was uniquely flexible and adaptable for use in less ambitious buildings. But possibly the most important factor of all in Gloucester's success was non-architectural. Whereas royal associations had probably diminished the influence of Westminster Abbey, they were now working in favour of Perpendicular. The Gloucester east end was a royal building not only in style but in its function as a mausoleum for Edward II, whose canonisation was canvassed by his far more popular son. Moreover the earliest monuments of the other, London branch of Perpendicular were either royal buildings or buildings designed by the royal architect William Ramsey (Cat. 386). Edward III understood, as Henry III never did, what were the keys to the successful rule of England; and during the years when Perpendicular began to gain acceptance as the national style, Edward's success in the war against France brought him greater prestige than any other European ruler. The Rayonnant roots of Perpendicular probably went unrecognised except by its earliest exponents, yet it does seem highly ironic that the triumphant progress of this French-inspired style took place at a time of unprecedented bitterness in Anglo-French relations.

NOTES

1. A probable exception has been published since this essay was completed: the emphatically French-sounding Berengar, architect of the Westminster-style chevet added from 1271 to Hailes Abbey under the patronage of Henry III's brother, Edmund, Earl of Cornwall; Harvey 1987, p. 1 (and Cat. 443). Nevertheless, the extant details of the chevet are not specially French in style.

2. Branner 1964, pp. 8, 12–13.

3. Bony 1979, pp. 4–6.

Peter Draper Architecture and Liturgy

The continuity of worship in our medieval churches all too easily allows us to forget the profound changes that have taken place in these buildings since the Reformation. Even where the buildings have survived intact, altars, shrines, tombs, screens, stained glass, paintings and furnishings have been destroyed or moved from their original positions. These fundamental alterations to the liturgical arrangement of the church have changed more than the appearance of the architecture; they have changed its meaning and obscured much of the subtlety of the design. Significantly, the two most extensive medieval descriptions of churches – Gervase's account of Canterbury in the twelfth century and the Rites of Durham, written in 1593 but describing the church and its customs on the eve of the Reformation – concentrate as much, if not more, on the altars, shrines and furnishings as they do on the architecture. Medieval churches, from cathedrals to parish churches, were designed to accommodate the performance of a liturgy which differed considerably from that current today. Liturgy in this context may be taken to include not only the ritual of the regular services performed by the clergy, but other forms of public or corporate worship such as pilgrimage and the cult of relics. If we are to understand the architectural design of medieval churches, we must examine carefully the specific purposes for which they were built, and not be tempted to consider them purely as works of art.

This is not to suggest that all aspects of architecture can be explained in these terms, nor is it to deny that there are difficulties in establishing a direct correlation between architectural design and liturgical practice. Considerable variations in the liturgy can be accommodated within very similar buildings, and conversely, similarity of architecture does not necessarily indicate a comparable similarity of liturgical rites. It was possible, for example, for the Benedictines at Durham to copy quite closely the form of the Nine Altars of the Cistercians at Fountains even though in the eastern extension at Durham provision had to be made for a splendid shrine for St Cuthbert. It is also true that some major changes in architectural design, such as the abandoning of the apsidal plan of Anglo-Norman buildings in the twelfth century, cannot be related to any obvious change in the liturgy.

By the thirteenth century there was in fact considerable uniformity in liturgical practice, although this had never been imposed by papal authority. The broad structure of the liturgy had been largely established by the great reform movement of the tenth century, but local peculiarities were often tenaciously retained. In England the customs of the cathedral and diocese of Salisbury (known as the Use of Sarum) came to be the most influential. By the fifteenth century they had been adopted by most of the cathedral chapters, including those in Wales and Scotland. These customs, which codified existing practices in a very clear, orderly way, were almost certainly drawn up by Richard Poore when he was Dean of Salisbury between 1197 and 1215. Apart from their seminal importance, they are of particular interest because in 1220 the cathedral of Salisbury was moved from an inconvenient site at Old Sarum and re-established on a new site near the river Avon under the direction of Poore, who was now the Bishop. As the new design had to accommodate these newly-codified liturgical practices, an analysis of Salisbury (fig. 50) provides a particularly clear demonstration of the way in which the form of the liturgy could influence architectural design, although similar observations could be made about almost any other major building.

Salisbury, like York, Lincoln and Wells, was a secular cathedral served by a

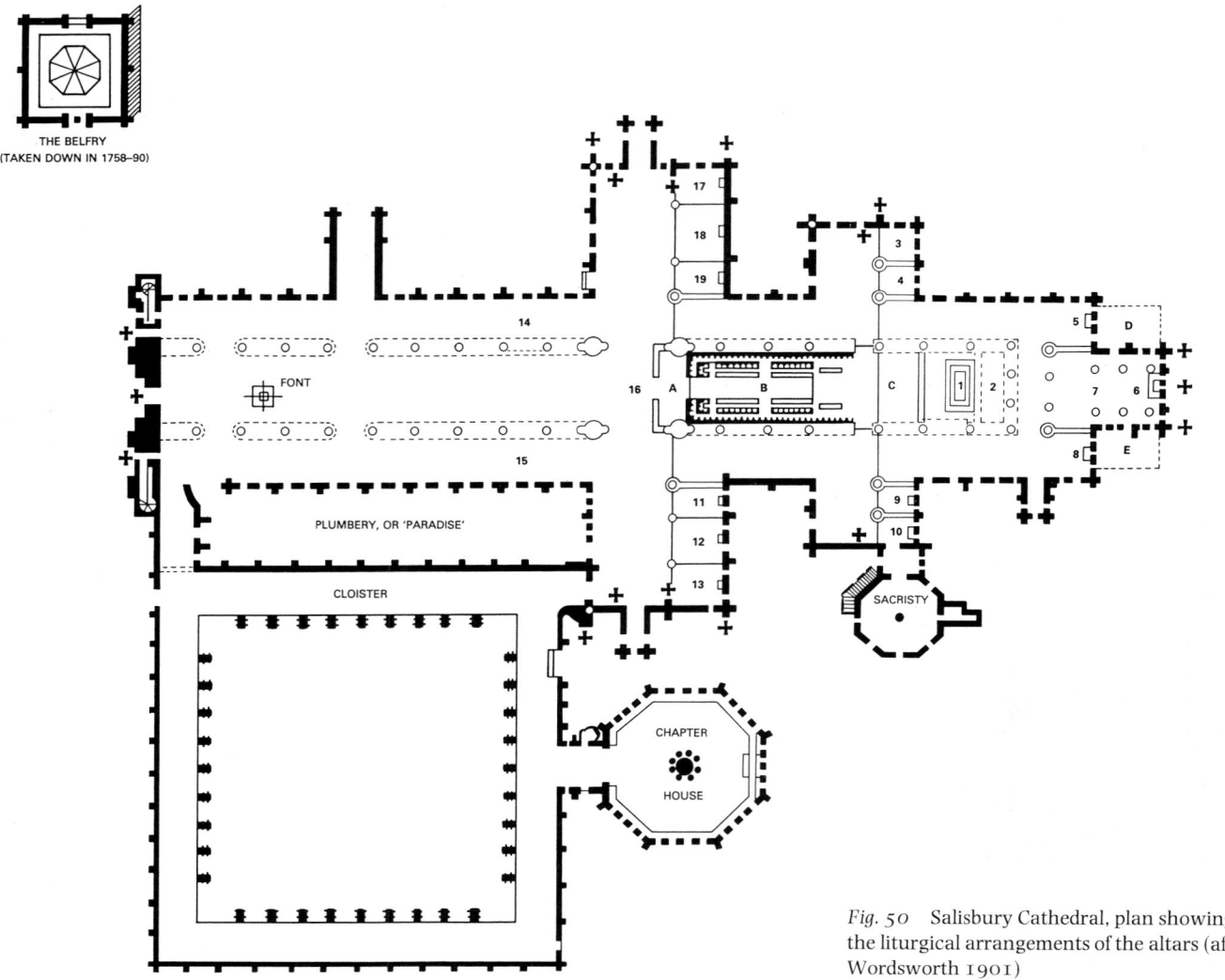

THE BELFRY
(TAKEN DOWN IN 1758–90)

FONT

PLUMBERY, OR 'PARADISE'

CLOISTER

CHAPTER HOUSE

SACRISTY

Fig. 50 Salisbury Cathedral, plan showing the liturgical arrangements of the altars (after Wordsworth 1901)

Key
1 High alter
2 Probable position of the shrine of St Osmund
3 Altar of St Martin
4 Altar of St Katherine
5 Altar of the Apostles
6 Trinity altar (All Saints)
7 Position of St Osmund's shrine from the fifteenth century
8 Altar of St Stephen
9 Altar of St Mary Magdalene
10 Altar of St Nicholas
11 Altar of St Margaret
12 Altar of St Lawrence
13 Altar of St Michael
14 Parochial altar of the Holy Cross (precise position unknown)
15 Altar of St Denis
16 Parochial altar of the Holy Cross (precise position unknown)
17 Altar of St Thomas of Canterbury
18 Altar of St Edmund the Confessor
19 Altar of St John the Baptist
A Pulpitum with Rood above
B Choir stalls
C Step marking entrance to the presbytery
D Site of Hungerford chantry chapel
E Site of Beauchamp chantry chapel
✛ Remains of consecration crosses on buttresses

community of priests, known as canons, whose daily life had much in common with that of the regular (monastic) clergy, although the seclusion of monastic life entailed some differences in the arrangements in monastic churches. For example, in monasteries the dormitory usually lay adjacent to the church, so a staircase was provided in the transept to give direct access for the night services. It was also common to find more altars and chapels in the naves of monastic churches, as they did not have to serve the needs of a lay congregation. On the other hand, the churches of the mendicant orders (the friars) were specifically designed to accommodate the large congregations that assembled to hear these popular preachers.

There were fifty canons at Salisbury, each of whom had to be provided with a stall in the choir and in the chapter house. In general, however, the scale of a church was more often determined by its status than directly related to the size of the community it served, which in secular cathedrals included the vicars choral who deputised for the canons for the many hours of services that had to be performed every day. On special feast days these services might take more than eight hours. To avoid distraction and disturbance during these services the religious community was separated from the laity by screens. The most substantial of these was the pulpitum, which divided the choir from the nave (fig. 51). The pulpitum was of solid construction, normally of stone, and upon it an altar (and sometimes an organ) might be placed, often surmounted by the Rood. The pulpitum had a central entrance and the choir stalls were returned against its east face. On the west side stood the nave altar of the Holy

Fig. 51 Exeter Cathedral, west face of the pulpitum, 1317–25. Altars would have been placed in the two side arches, which originally were not open to the choir

Fig. 52 Interior of Salisbury Cathedral in 1754 showing the thirteenth-century pulpitum with later balustrade and the Renatus Harris organ (engraving by Biddlescombe from B. Winkles, *Illustrations of the Cathedral Churches of England and Wales*, 1838)

Cross. In monastic churches the monks' choir was usually situated beneath the main crossing with the pulpitum in the eastern bays of the nave and a second (usually wooden) screen stood one bay further west, surmounted by the Rood. At Salisbury the pulpitum survives only in fragments, but originally it stood between the eastern piers of the crossing (fig. 52).

East of the pulpitum the canons were provided, in effect, with a complete cruciform church with its own transepts. At Salisbury, as at Canterbury (Cat. 17), these eastern transepts form a crossing which divided the choir from the presbytery, as they had at Cluny which was the probable source for this feature. At the cathedrals of York and Worcester the eastern transepts are set either side of the high altar, and a further variation is found at Fountains and Durham where they are at the extreme east end of the church and provide an impressive row of nine altars. These eastern transepts were undeniably a majestic feature which added greatly to the grandeur of the church, but the variations in their arrangement suggest that they did not have a consistent liturgical function other than to provide additional chapels.

The stalls of the canons' choir at Salisbury occupied three bays east of the pulpitum. A step on the east side of the eastern crossing marked the entrance to the presbytery, and another step led up to the high altar which was probably raised, as usual, on a further three steps although the original setting is not known. Up to the eleventh century altars were free-standing as the priest normally celebrated facing the congregation from the far side of the altar, so any decoration of the altar had to be confined to the frontal. By the twelfth century the priest had come to stand in front of the altar facing east, and it became possible to have an altarpiece or screen behind the altar with carved or painted images. The altar itself generally had no permanent furnishings on it: the pyx for the reservation of the Host was suspended above (Cat. 102), and candlesticks were usually placed around the altar. But increasingly the furniture in the presbytery, such as sedilia (Cat. 136) and even the Easter Sepulchre (Cat. 493), became permanent stone structures, like small-scale architecture. A comparable architectural quality is to be found in elaborate wooden choir stalls (figs 82–4), and, at its most grandiloquent, in the bishop's throne at Exeter (Cat. 488). The paschal candlestick at Durham is said to have reached within a few feet of the vault. Great expense was also lavished on the liturgical vessels, service books and vestments required for the Mass, many examples of which may be seen in the exhibition. During this period the prominence of altars was enhanced by the development of the retable (Cat. 329), a carved or painted altarpiece, into the much grander, usually sculptured, screen known as a reredos (fig. 53). When placed behind the high altar the reredos also served to further the process of enclosing the clergy within the choir and presbytery.

At Salisbury there were screens separating the choir and presbytery from the aisles, with access to the choir provided by doors at the crossing. Processions constituted an

Fig. 53 Durham Cathedral reredos, known as the Neville screen, 1376–9. The two entrances provide access to the shrine behind the altar

important part of the ritual; their protocol specifically related to the importance of the feast day in the calendar. On a normal Sunday, after the sprinkling of the high altar with holy water, the clergy processed through the north choir entrance to asperge each altar in turn, proceeding around the ambulatory and down the south aisle to the west end of the nave. On important feasts the procession went round the cloister and re-entered the church through the door at the south-west corner of the nave. A break in the continuous plinth between the piers of the nave (Cat. 241) allowed the clergy to pass from the aisle into the nave where they would reassemble to process up to a station in front of the pulpitum before returning to their stalls. (The position of stations was often marked by stones set in the floor.) On the grandest feasts, such as Palm Sunday, the procession included the precincts as well, pausing at set stations to sing psalms and hymns, ending up at the west front where anthems were sung with some of the choir concealed within the architecture of the façade. The procession would then pass beneath a reliquary held aloft, through the west door to proceed up the nave. The normal entrance for the laity was through the north door of the nave, which was provided with a splendid two-bay porch.

The elaboration of processions and the importance attached to them made it essential for all the altars to be easily accessible. This probably accounts for the demise of the Anglo-Norman gallery with its altars at an upper level to which the only access was by a narrow winding staircase. Seventeen altars are recorded at Salisbury in the thirteenth century, all of them conveniently placed on one level and all facing east. The correct orientation of altars seems to have been of particular importance in England, and is almost certainly the main reason for the adoption of the rectangular east end in place of the apsidal form with radiating chapels which remained the normal arrangement on the Continent.

The largest chapel outside the choir at Salisbury, large enough in fact to accommodate the whole community of vicars and canons, was like a hall church at the east end of the cathedral (Cat. 18). Although dedicated to the Trinity, this chapel was from the beginning used for the celebration of the important daily Mass to the Virgin. This was in addition to the daily Mass performed at the high altar, which at Salisbury (and commonly elsewhere) was dedicated to the Virgin, since by custom two masses could not be performed at the high altar in one day. In the early twelfth century the Lady Mass was celebrated only on Saturdays, but the marked increase in the importance accorded to the cult of the Virgin during that century, particularly in England, led to a parallel increase in the outward devotion paid to her in the form of special services. In the 1120s the Feast of the Conception of the Virgin was introduced, and by the end of the century the daily celebration of a full sung Mass of the Virgin had been widely accepted by monastic and secular communities. The practice is explicitly recognised in the annals of the monastery of St Albans, the *Gesta Abbatum*, where it is recorded that Abbot William of Trumpington (1214–35) ordained, with the consent of the convent, that a solemn Mass to the Virgin should be celebrated not only on Saturdays as hitherto but daily, 'seeing that this was done in all the noble churches in England'.

This evidence confirms what might have been surmised from the architectural evidence of the addition of Lady chapels to many large churches in the late twelfth and early thirteenth centuries. These chapels were often at the east end of the church, though they could be sited elsewhere. In a small but important group of foundations, mostly in the east of England, the Lady Chapel was built adjacent to the north transept. The best known of this group is the magnificent fourteenth-century chapel at Ely (Cat. 491). The need to add these Lady chapels to existing churches is the clearest instance of direct correlation between changes in liturgical practice and architectural design.

Another aspect of devotional practice which acquired greater importance in this period was seeking the intercession of saints through the cult of their relics. The increasing popularity of pilgrimage had important consequences for architecture. In the early Middle Ages sacred relics had usually been kept safely in crypts, but during the eleventh and twelfth centuries, particularly following the example of Abbot Suger's rebuilding at St-Denis, it became fashionable to set them in a conspicuous shrine behind the high altar. The relics of the major Anglo-Saxon saints had been honourably translated into the new Norman churches, but the setting of these shrines came to seem too modest and the provision for pilgrims inadequate. Through the thirteenth and fourteenth centuries the east ends of most of the major churches were extended or reconstructed to provide a more sumptuous setting for the relics of an important saint, largely inspired by the lavish provision made for the shrine of Thomas Becket at Canterbury (Cat. 17). Most of these refurbishments were of the shrines of Anglo-Saxon saints such as Sts Oswald and Wulfstan at Worcester (1224), St Chad at Lichfield (c. 1200), St Etheldreda at Ely (1234) and St Erkenwald at St Paul's (1256), but the thirteenth century also witnessed the significant growth of the cults of contemporary bishops, such as St Hugh of Lincoln (canonised 1220), St William of York (canonised 1226) and St Richard of Chichester (canonised 1262). It is probable that provision for a shrine was made in the new design at Salisbury, for in 1228 a petition was made to the Pope for the canonisation of Osmund, Bishop of Old Sarum from 1078 to 1099. Although this was not successful, Osmund continued to be venerated locally and he was finally canonised in 1453. In the later Middle Ages his shrine was in the centre of the Trinity Chapel. This may have been the original intention, but a site behind the high altar is more likely.

Aside from this uncertainty about the intended position of the shrine of St Osmund, it is evident that the overall layout of the new church at Salisbury, including the spacious cloister and the chapter house, was carefully designed to fulfil the major requirements of the liturgy. Reconsideration of the architectural details reveals that these too have been used to differentiate unobtrusively but unmistakably the various parts of the church which served different liturgical functions. The piers of the main arcade throughout the church are supported on a low plinth, which is continuous except in those bays kept clear to allow movement to and from the aisles. This plinth is higher in the choir than it is in the nave, and the level rises again for the presbytery. The identity of these liturgical divisions is reinforced by the use of different designs of arcade piers, whereas west of the crossing all the piers are identical to give coherence to the nave (Cat. 241). In the transepts the chapels are defined by being raised a step above the main floor level and by subtle additional ornament in the mouldings of the arcade arches. Originally all the chapels were enclosed by screens, as is shown on the plan made before James Wyatt's reorganisation in the late eighteenth century (fig. 54). Such parclose screens could be of stone, wood or metal.

The interrelationship between architecture and liturgy may go beyond this practical use of architectural features to define the liturgical arrangements: the character of the liturgy may be reflected in the style of the architecture. The best-known example of this is the early architecture of the Cistercians where, especially

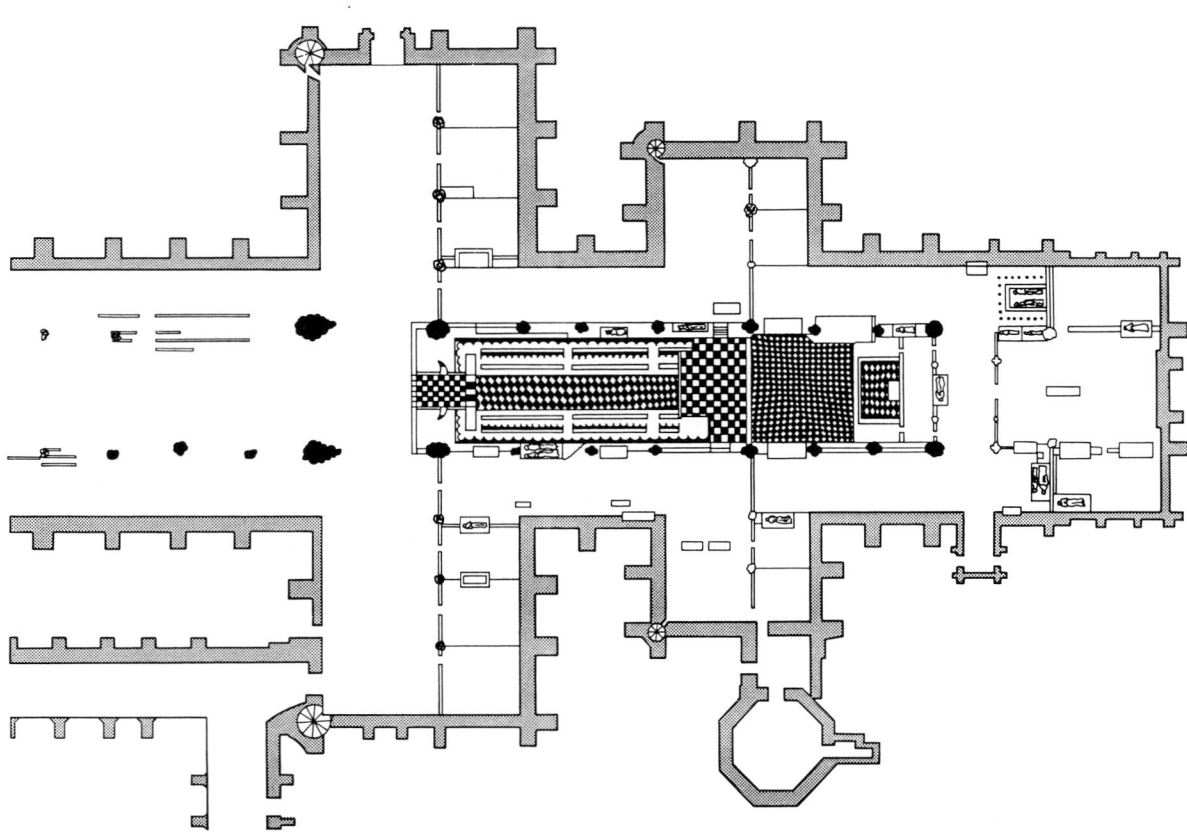

Fig. 54 Salisbury Cathedral, plan of the east end showing screens and furnishings before Wyatt's reordering of the liturgical arrangements and the demolition of the chantries flanking the Trinity chapel (from Gough 1786–96)

under the influence of St Bernard, unnecessary ornament was eschewed in favour of simplicity, to the point of austerity. At the other extreme was the richness of materials and lavish ornament displayed around shrines. Viewed in this light, the architecture of Salisbury (Cat. 18, 241), when compared with the extravagant richness of Lincoln (Cat. 240), acquires a significantly distinctive character. The extensive use of marble provides the sense of grandeur appropriate to a cathedral, yet the orderly way in which this is employed and the lack of sculptural detail give a restrained and chaste quality to the architecture. The Use of Sarum is an elaborate rite, yet it is organised down to the smallest detail with precision and clarity: the same qualities that characterise the architecture of Salisbury. This sense of decorum is an important element in architectural design, although it is often ignored in discussions of artistic style.

In parish churches the ritual was naturally much simpler, but the separation between the clergy and the laity could be as pronounced. In most churches there was a screen surmounted by a Rood at the entrance to the chancel, to which the laity was forbidden entry. The upkeep of the chancel was the responsibility of the rector, and the reconstruction and enlargement of many chancels during this period reflected the assertion of the institutional authority of the Church which, arguably, reached its high point in the thirteenth century. This makes an interesting comparison with the later Middle Ages, where it was more often the nave that was rebuilt and enlarged by the laity. In fact during the thirteenth and fourteenth centuries, in both cathedral and parish church, the laity played an almost incidental role in the liturgy. Though expected to attend services regularly, they did not take communion very often: a minimum of once per year was stipulated in the canons of the Fourth Lateran Council of 1215. At this same Council, Transubstantiation was defined as a matter of faith. With the greater solemnity being accorded to the Mass, it had become the practice to withhold the chalice from the laity. Increasingly, therefore, the clergy celebrated Mass on behalf of the laity, and the performance of the liturgy took on more of the quality of a theatrical spectacle. Significantly, this period witnessed the greatest elaboration of ecclesiastical vestments, particularly the embroidered copes which showed to full advantage when the priest with his back to the congregation raised his arms at the Elevation of the Host, a practice which only became widespread at this time. For many parishioners, however, the experience would have been very different, for the records of episcopal visitations reveal that many parishes lacked even the most basic liturgical vessels or books and had few if any vestments. As few could understand Latin, the Bidding Prayer in the Sarum Rite was said in the vernacular. The intervening chancel screen also meant that most of those present could see little of what went on at the altar, so it became customary to indicate the progress of the Mass by ringing bells at the Sanctus and the Elevation of the Host.

The most obvious example of masses being said on behalf of the laity without their participation is that of Chantry masses. These were masses of intercession for the dead said by a priest whose stipend was paid by an endowment, usually the income from a grant of land. The practice was established in the thirteenth century and became increasingly popular during the two subsequent centuries. Chantries could be endowed at existing altars, but new altars were founded and furnished for this purpose wherever space could be found in the church, even up against a pier. Only the grandest chantry altars were enclosed by elaborate screens like those of the Wykeham Chantry at Winchester (Cat. 601). Sometimes a special chapel was built on to the church. These chantry chapels came to constitute an important architectural feature in the later Middle Ages, but at the Reformation all chantries were suppressed, their assets sequestrated and, in many cases, the altars and chapels destroyed.

A considerable number of parish churches have retained some of their medieval furnishings, though these are not always found convenient for contemporary liturgical practice. It is, however, the larger churches that have suffered most by subsequent loss and rearrangement. A good illustration of this is the cathedral at Ely, where the choir has twice been moved. Originally the pulpitum stood at the eastern end of the nave with the choir stalls set beneath the crossing (fig. 55). There they remained even when the octagon was built in the early fourteenth century (fig. 56).

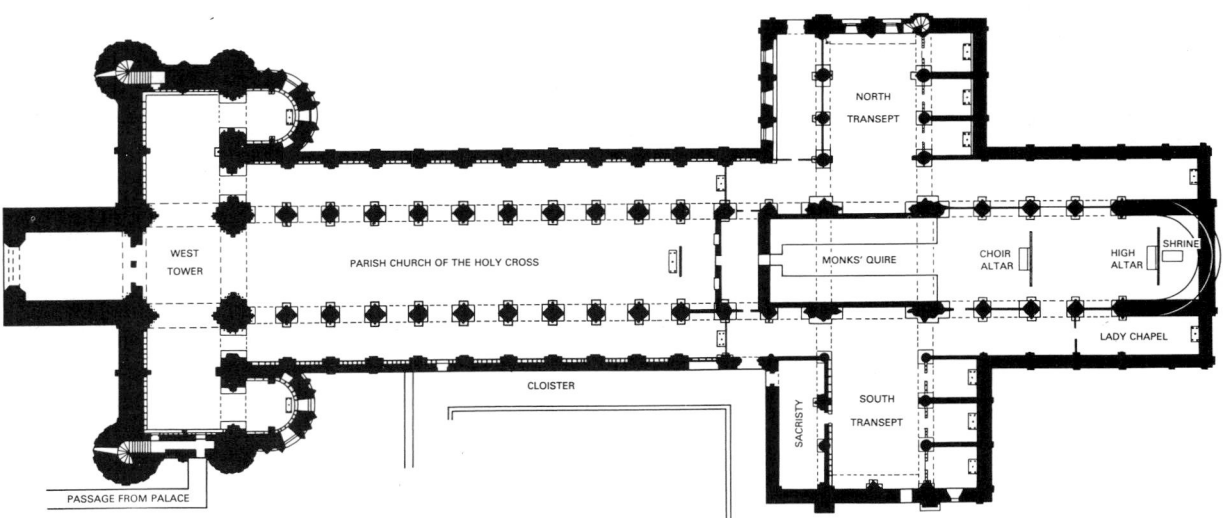

Fig. 55 Plan of Ely Cathedral *c.* 1225 (reconstruction after Atkinson 1953)

The high altar was in the fifth bay east of the crossing with the shrine of St Etheldreda behind it in the six-bay extension built for that purpose in the mid-thirteenth century. A row of chapels lined the east wall. Following the destruction of the shrine at the Reformation, the eastern bays were redundant, so the high altar was brought closer to the choir stalls. At the end of the eighteenth century the high altar was placed against the east wall and the choir stalls moved to where the shrine had been (fig. 57). This left the octagon space clear (Cat. 492), but in the process the splendid Romanesque pulpitum was destroyed. The arrangement was changed once again by Scott in the mid-nineteenth century. The choir stalls were moved westwards and set against a new screen placed at the east side of the octagon, and the high altar was brought into the third bay from the east, leaving space behind it for chapels and a procession path (fig. 58). At the time when it was built each part of the church had a precise liturgical function but this became obscured with each subsequent reorganisation, and in consequence the historical interpretation was distorted.

Fig. 56   Plan of Ely Cathedral *c.* 1530
(reconstruction after Atkinson 1953)

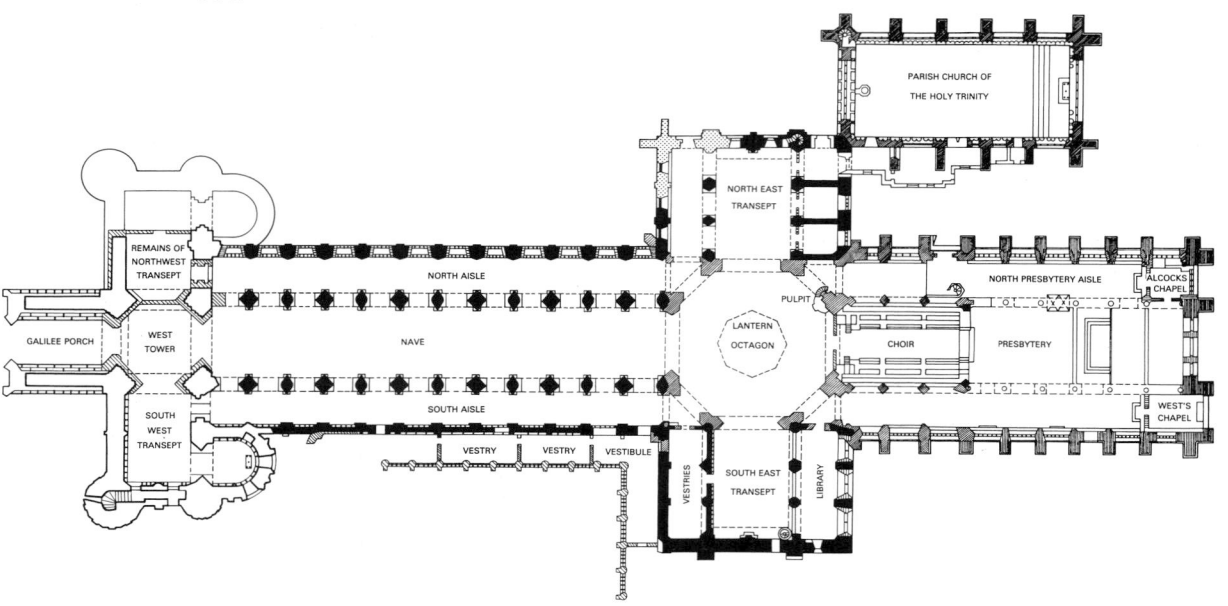

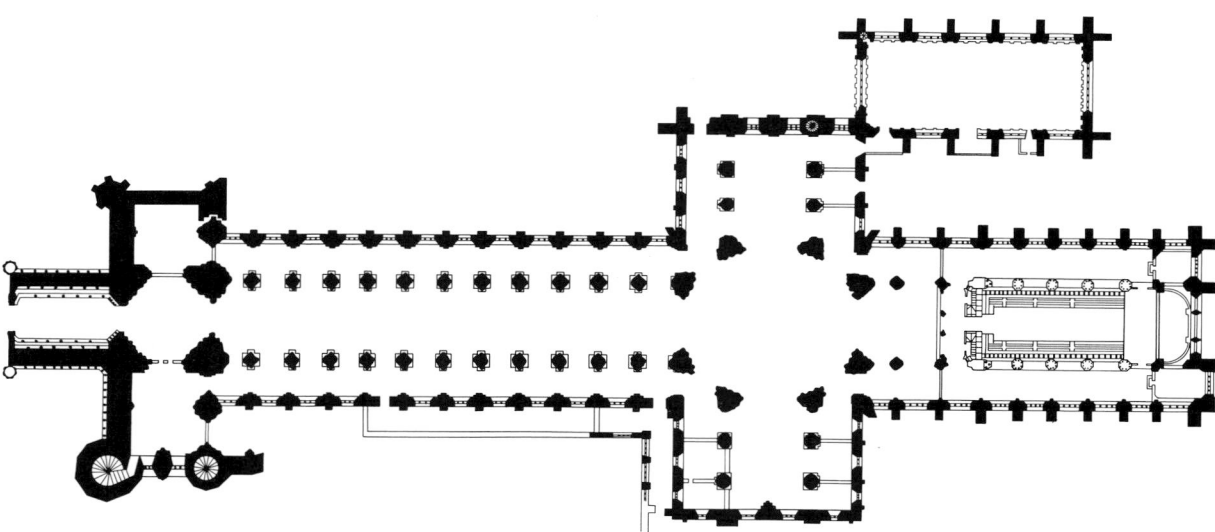

Fig. 57   James Wyatt's reorganisation of Ely
Cathedral, 1769–72 (after Bentham 1771)

Medieval churches were complex buildings, and our historical interpretation must take into account the many and varied factors that determined their design and decoration. Among these is the form and the character of the liturgy which was perfomed within the church. The adoption of a particular liturgy by a religious community, or the determined retention of a local variant, could have significant consequences for the architectural design of a church. It also is important to remember that there were changes in liturgical practices as in architectural style. The introduction of fashionable new elements in the liturgy might require substantial alterations to existing churches, such as the addition of a Lady Chapel or the refurbishment of a shrine. It is difficult for us to visualise the original appearance of the medieval churches, as we can see them only through the work of generations of restorers. So many of the liturgical furnishings have been lost or rearranged, and so much of the stained glass and painted decoration has been destroyed, starting with the drastic changes which occurred at the Reformation, and followed by the cumulative

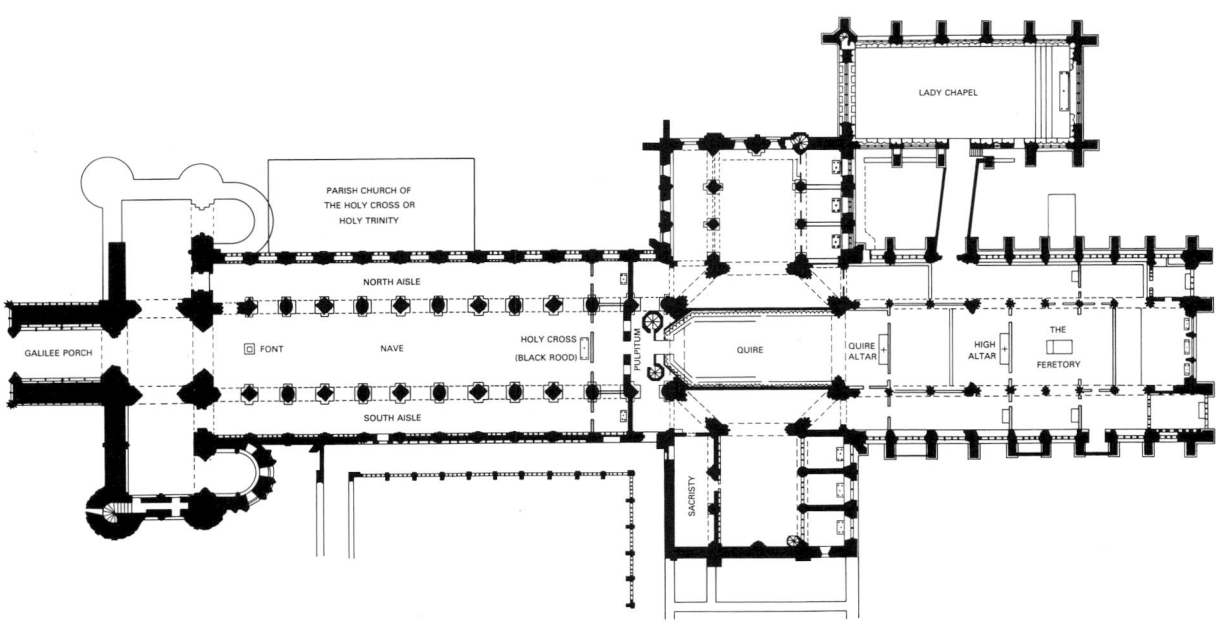

Fig. 58 G.G. Scott's reorganisation of Ely
Cathedral, 1844–68 (from Atkinson 1953)

efforts of Puritan iconoclasts, eighteenth-century restorers, and zealous ecclesiologists, up to the enthusiastic 'modernisers' of our own time. Yet the furnishings and the decoration were an integral part of a medieval church, and formed an essential element in that vital interrelationship between liturgy and architecture.

LIT.
Cobb 1980; Cook 1963; Frere 1898; Hamilton-
Thompson 1925; King 1955; Knowles 1963; Morris
1979, ch. 6; Vallance 1947; Wordsworth 1901.

The Kingdom of Heaven:

Nicola Coldstream ## Its Architectural Setting

n the long list of those who have destroyed things fair and lovely ... Henry VIII and Thomas Cromwell ... must find a place of note.' Thus the restrained eloquence of Dom David Knowles.[1] To these might be added the name of Oliver Cromwell, whose Puritan supporters finished what the Henrician reformers had begun. In the name of religion, successive outbursts of bigotry and hatred destroyed the medieval Church; but because many of the buildings themselves remain standing we can be deceived into thinking that at least the physical surroundings have survived.

The architecture, the bare bones of piers, arches, mouldings and vaults, has indeed survived remarkably well; but medieval churches were considerably more than architecture. The decoration, now almost wholly destroyed, would have been at least as important to contemporaries, having a meaning which emphasised to them the individual significance of a particular building, be it a private chapel or a more accessible church choir. The present atmosphere of an English Protestant church would have been wholly alien to medieval people; we ourselves are persuaded by the denuded aspect of our churches to concentrate too much on the architecture.

It is fully accepted by modern scholars that a seventeenth-century architect such as Bernini achieved the effects he wanted by combining architecture with ornament and sculpture, sculpture which included figures living, dead and imagined; to realise his idea, Bernini needed to use all these arts together. But his attitude of mind was not new in the seventeenth century: it already existed in the Middle Ages. In a building such as Chartres Cathedral, where the stained glass and sculpture survive, it is obvious that the architecture is the background to the figurative arts, that the architecture was designed to support and exhibit the vast *summa* of Christian history represented on the doorways and windows. In the damaged churches of Protestant England it is less obvious, not entirely because the figured work has been destroyed, but partly because, in the middle of our period at least, the architecture itself is so obtrusive. It is enormously tempting to study the swoops and curves of early fourteenth-century architecture for their own sake, and to forget that, like the undulating façades of seventeenth-century Rome, these architectural designs were never intended to be seen in isolation.[2]

Church art responds to religious ideas, and the reason for the change which came over church interiors in the course of the thirteenth century should be sought in changing religious attitudes. The figured art of the later Middle Ages is more approachable and naturalistic than the awe-inspiring, remote and minatory figures of the twelfth century; the inward concentration of later medieval decoration may reflect both religious thinking and the more personal, even mystical, relation of the individual to God which characterised those years. The church building, poised symbolically between everyday life and the life to come, was the place where earthbound sinners could glimpse the Heavenly Kingdom: every week the lay congregation entered the cloudy region between reality and symbolism when in the ceremony of the Eucharist the bread and wine became the body and blood of Christ. Much medieval literature explores the relation of inner states of being to the outer world, and it came naturally to medieval people to see individual objects in the world as symbols or representations.[3] The saints and prophets on the church walls were the Church Triumphant made actual; these divine beings were seen to be intercessors, offering a path to individual salvation amid the warnings of judgement, and they were an essential part of the experience of being in the church building.

An apparent need to make these figures into more than merely two-dimensional representations perhaps encouraged the use of large-scale sculptures inside the building as well as outside. It is with the appearance of these sculptures that the change can be said to begin. A heavily moulded, coloured interior was not new in itself, figured art being part of the church building from the earliest times; in the twelfth century we have William of Malmesbury's remarks about the richness and colour of the newly rebuilt choir of Canterbury Cathedral;[4] and the late twelfth-century Trinity Chapel of Canterbury glowed with coloured marble, stained glass and floor mosaics as the setting for the shrine of Thomas Becket (Cat. 17).

Nevertheless, the rebuilding of Westminster Abbey in the 1240s brought a new kind of interior, forerunner of what was aptly characterised by Geoffrey Webb as 'illuminated architecture'.[5] Its immediate inspiration was the Ste-Chapelle in Paris, with its great areas of stained glass, mural decoration and large-scale interior sculptures.[6] To its contemporaries the Ste-Chapelle, founded to house the relic of the Crown of Thorns, had strong connotations of a reliquary casket turned outside inwards: the miniaturistic, detailed ornament and the figures disposed one on each pier do recall a metal reliquary and the meaning was not lost on those who knew of it.[7] As a reliquary chapel it influenced the great shrine churches of Cologne and Westminster.[8] At Westminster (Cat. 262), the whole interior surface was painted with whitewash, colour or gilding, and it was also sculptured. The blind arcading on the lower walls followed established tradition, but the upper walls were tooled all over with rosette diaper, and with foliage ornament in the arches of the triforium. Apart from its association with the punched background decoration of reliquaries,[9] clearly here intended to emphasise the shrinelike qualities of the church, as decoration the diapered wall surface constantly caught and reflected light. The end walls of the transepts held sculptured figures of censing angels with Edward the Confessor and John the Evangelist representing Henry III's favourite story of the Ring and the Pilgrim. These figures, agile and full of movement, were carved almost in the round, and although the carved heads of angels had been used for interior sculpture, the large-scale figures were a new departure.[10]

The Westminster scheme was at once reflected in another great shrine church, the Angel Choir of Lincoln Cathedral (Cat. 321), begun 1256.[11] Although Lincoln was in many ways a building in an English tradition which owes nothing to Westminster, among those details which clearly do derive from Westminster is the large-scale figure sculpture inside the building, the angels in the triforium spandrels representing an angelic orchestra and symbolising judgement and salvation. Standing figures were placed in the triforium of the nave of York Minster a generation later, but the relation of Westminster to shrine chapels ensured that the future of illuminated architecture lay as much in chapels as in great churches.

The theme of building as reliquary was visually expressed in the use of ornament common to architecture and metalwork: buildings sprouted niches, gables, pinnacles, foliage cresting, openwork parapets and other devices which sat equally well in miniature on reliquary caskets; these were themselves garnished with tiny flying buttresses and tracery motifs. In England the introduction of micro-architectural ornament is mainly associated with the works of piety of Edward I, the Eleanor crosses (p. 361), the tombs (Cat. 326) and St Stephen's Chapel in the Palace of Westminster (Cat. 325).[12] The association with the Court at Westminster should not, however, obscure the equally important patronage of the greater magnates, the bishops and the monasteries. A society linked by interconnected households allowed artistic ideas to spread quickly,[13] and in the peculiar circumstances of the early fourteenth century the bankruptcy of Edward II compelled masons who might otherwise have worked for the king to go elsewhere, taking with them the designs and motifs of the Westminster workshops. It was not until the Despensers put Edward's financial affairs in order shortly before 1320 that he was able to pay for other than essential building work.[14]

Late thirteenth- and early fourteenth-century buildings can look very elaborate, the octagonal crossing at Ely (fig. 59) and the polygonal Lady Chapel at Wells (fig. 60) being notable essays in complicated planning; but many of them are architecturally very simple, deriving their lush visual effects from applied ornament. The Lady Chapel of Ely (Cat. 491) and the presbytery of Wells (fig. 61) are plain rectangular boxes covered in decoration. Nowadays they are plainer than they should be, for without the

Fig. 59 Ely Cathedral octagon (cf. frontispiece)

Fig. 61   Wells Cathedral presbytery

Fig. 60   Wells Cathedral retrochoir and Lady Chapel

figured work the surviving ornament presents a distorted picture. These buildings were alive not only with niches and foliage but with figures, three-dimensional, painted sculptures, for which the whole encrusted scaffolding of masonry was designed merely as a support.

The first surviving chapel to explore these possibilities is St Etheldreda's, Holborn (fig. 63), built in 1284 as part of the London residence of the bishops of Ely.[15] Rectangular, wooden-roofed and much restored, it exemplifies the English habit of adapting French ideas to suit local preferences, but its descent from the Ste-Chapelle is apparent at least in the fully decorated interior. The pedestals between the windows, surmounted by arch-and-gable in relief, held life-sized statues, and there would have been more figures in the stained glass. The mouldings and foliage were picked out in colour, but with the original figures in place the architectural ornament would have receded into the background.

The iconographic programme of St Etheldreda's is lost to us, but of the new Lady chapels built in these years the mutilated survivors at St Albans and Ely still give clues to their original appearance.[16] At St Albans (fig. 62), finished by 1315, the figured work was not completely destroyed. Sculptured decoration is concentrated mainly on the windows: in the jambs the small niches with nodding ogee heads contain figures, while more figures are carved on the window mullions. As at St Etheldreda's, the

Fig. 63 Church of St Etheldreda, Ely Place, London

Fig. 62 St Albans Cathedral Lady Chapel

iconographic programme is no longer clear, but as one figure represents John the Baptist a series of saints or prophets was evidently part of it.

The Lady Chapel at Ely, begun 1321 (Cat. 491), is much bigger than at St Albans and it had a much more ambitious programme. Like its predecessors it is rectangular, but it is literally enclosed with moulded decoration, on the walls and in the net pattern of the vault.[17] Masonry is cut to the minimum necessary to support windows and vault, and most of the interior stonework is carved and decorated. At dado level the stalls are framed in elaborate niches with arch-and-gable over them, nodding ogees rippling along the surface of the wall, the movement enhanced by the seaweed-like foliage carved as cresting on each one. The upper levels and the window jambs are all moulded into shallow suggestions of niches, as at St Etheldreda's, with flanking pinnacles and nodding ogee hoods. As the wall is thick, and the window glass is on the outer plane, the stalls and jambs are deep and the buttresses prominent; the whole wall seems to undulate. Enough traces of colour remain to show that the Lady Chapel was fully painted, and the surviving fragments of stained glass have architectural motifs, so that glass and masonry shared both designs and colour.

What we see now is only the background to the true decoration of the chapel, the huge crowd of carved figures for which it was designed. Small-scale figures survive at the lower level, but the life-sized figures on the upper walls are known to us from drawings, from paint marks on the wall surface (and one pair of carved feet high in the north-east bay), and from some recently identified fragments.[18] Ely was once alive with human figures, two-dimensional in the windows, three-dimensional on the walls. In the back of every stall a clerical figure stands on a fluted shaft, and others once stood on the apices of the nodding ogees; one miraculously survives on the west wall. All are headless, as are the other survivors, the scenes of the life and miracles of the Virgin, carved in relief on the spandrels of the dado. Interspersed with the ancestors of Christ seated in niches on the buttresses, is an exceptionally long series of over a hundred scenes telling the story of the Virgin;[19] as each coloured scene was set against a background of gilded diaper it must indeed have resembled an illustrated story book. On the niche marking the old entry to the Lady Chapel from the choir the nodding ogee is decorated with little figures bending out and forward as if in welcome. Almost every scene is attended by angels, and it is all but certain that saints and angels appeared in profusion on the upper walls.[20]

A recent study of Prior Crauden's Chapel (Cat. 393–8) at Ely, built in the 1320s when the Lady Chapel was in its early stages, reveals the same artistic attitude.[21] All that survived the chapel's reincarnation as a dwelling house in the seventeenth century was the architecture itself and some of the carved ornament; but Binski and Park have shown that Annunciation and Crucifixion scenes were painted on the

Fig. 64   Ely Cathedral Lady Chapel

western walls, sculpted and painted figures occupied the niches at the east, and extra architectural motifs were painted on to the stonework. This study demonstrates how the destruction of the painted work has distorted the way we have looked at this and other monuments, and has helped to destroy our understanding of their original meaning.[22]

The two chapels at Ely, the Lady Chapel and Prior Crauden's Chapel, give some idea of the difference between a private decorative scheme and a more public one. The cult of the Virgin was still at its height, and she was central to both programmes. In the larger chapel she was commemorated and represented on the walls as well as on the altar dedicated in her name (appropriately for a Benedictine house, several of the miracle stories show monks and nuns being rescued from the consequences of their own folly); in the prior's private chapel the theme was more personally redemptive, expressed in images which invited contemplation and prayer. But both chapels should also be understood as settings where the live congregation could experience the Mass in the presence of members of the Heavenly Kingdom surrounding them on the walls, and in the creation of this fusion of the actual and transcendental the essential ingredients were glass, paint and sculpture.

In Ely, as it happens, the patrons of the two chapels were drawn from the monastic community, and the iconography was concerned with universal as well as individual salvation. Lay or episcopal patrons might, in expressing faith through works, more overtly suggest their personal connections with the transcendental world. At Tewkesbury Abbey, which came by marriage into the Despenser family, the choir was transformed into a burial chapel designed to glorify the family name. Ending a sequence of the Life of Christ which begins in the nave, the roof bosses of the choir show Him after the Resurrection; it has been plausibly suggested that the flowery patterns in the vault (Cat. 496) are intended to symbolise Paradise, and the huge windows show the Lords of Tewkesbury, Hugh Despenser the Younger prominent among them, in the company of Old Testament prophets, patriarchs and kings (Cat. 742).[23] Here the Despensers associated themselves firmly with the Kingdom of Heaven and, as at Ely and elsewhere, this Paradise was created in paint, sculpture and ornament.

These traits were most richly manifested in the two buildings with strongest royal connections, St Stephen's Chapel, Westminster, and the choir of Gloucester Abbey (now Cathedral). St Stephen's (Cat. 325) was refounded in 1292, rather before most of the buildings previously discussed, but it was built and decorated according to the fortunes of Edward I, his son and grandson, and it was not finished until the 1360s.[24] The interior was drenched in colour from the windows, the walls were thickly moulded and decorated with paint and stamped gesso, gilded and diapered. No surface was left untouched. Narrative scenes here were painted (Cat. 678), and in both materials and subject-matter naturalism and fantasy were freely mingled. On the altar wall, in a picture with layers of symbolic meaning, Edward III, Queen Philippa and their children, accompanied by their patron saints, were shown in the presence of the Adoration of the Magi, living and dead, human and divine, portrayed in the same contrived space (Cat. 681).

At Gloucester (Cat. 498) the path to salvation was displayed in the east window, with the Coronation of the Virgin, attended by saints, angels, kings and founders of the abbey. Again, the iconography is modified to suit the circumstances: what at St Stephen's was a private royal chapel was at Gloucester the burial chapel and anticipated shrine of Edward II. The delicate tomb canopy with its superimposed pinnacles is among the most shrinelike of tomb canopies. The choir is a closed world, fenced in a very literal sense by the net of tracery which covers it in; an angelic orchestra plays in the roof bosses over the high altar, and the stage is set.

These set pieces, offering a glimpse into the life to come, were at once remote and inviting: remote in that the Kingdom of Heaven remained a vision to be contemplated; inviting in that the sculptured figures, increasingly shown in contemporary costume, made the vision both alive and real. Illusionism was essential to the effect: at St Stephen's stone figures in niches stood beside other figures, painted in grisaille to imitate stone, and there and at Ely real architectural mouldings were combined with painted ones.[25] Nothing was what it seemed to be, and the spectator was both within and outside the spectacle. Distinctions were blurred further: the great screens, the Eleanor crosses (Cat. 369, 373–4), the tomb canopies are carved on an architectural scale but they are decorated with micro-architectural motifs, and in their fake enamel and marble decorations these smaller pieces resemble larger buildings.[26]

For a brief period monumental architecture seems to have been designed deliberately to add to these illusionistic effects. The octagon at Ely and the Lady Chapel at Wells, which is attached to the choir by a low, deceptively rambling antechapel (figs 59, 60), suggest depths and spaces beyond the immediate limits of the building. The canopies rippling round the walls of the chapter house of York, in St Stephen's (Cat. 324) and at Ely (Cat. 491) similarly render indistinct the outer planes of the walls. At Ely mouldings seem to vanish only to reappear, at Bristol vault ribs are detached from the ceilings they theoretically support. That these designs were consciously stylish and sophisticated there can be no doubt, but they were not an end in themselves. The east end of Wells, for instance, which is much admired for the fusion of Lady Chapel and retrochoir in one continuous space, was designed to allow the easy passage of processions,[27] and although the change of style in the presbytery is ascribed to a change of architect,[28] the different function of the presbytery required different treatment.

The effects of these ideas, expressed for the most part in great churches or rich chapels, filtered quickly into the humbler domain of the parish church, no doubt because many of the grandest new chancels of the fourteenth century had patrons with royal connections.[29] The common aim was to give tangible form to symbols and representations of spiritual experiences or hopes. It is becoming clear that different buildings had specific individual meanings, illustrated in the way they were decorated. We may have lost all but the shadows of the faith, but recognition of its existence and its forms greatly enhances the study of a church building.

NOTES

1. Knowles 1976, p. 272.
2. Scholarship since the Second World War has not sufficiently taken this into account. For the effect on the study of later medieval English architecture, see Coldstream, *Bulletin Monumental* 1987. Happily, the balance is now being restored; see nn. 17, 22 and 28 below.
3. Lewis 1958; Medcalf 1981.
4. William of Malmesbury 1870 edn, p. 138.
5. Webb 1965, p. 135. For a bibliography of Westminster, see Wilson *et al.* 1986.
6. Branner 1965, pl. 63.
7. Branner 1965, p. 57.
8. Branner 1965, p. 123 ff.
9. Wilson *et al.* 1986, p. 55.
10. The figures were deployed in a very un-French way, but during the middle years of the thirteenth century large-scale figure sculpture was used elsewhere in France, e.g. the west wall of Rheims cathedral, and in Germany at e.g. Cologne, Naumburg and Bamberg.
11. Dean 1986.
12. Hastings 1955; Colvin 1963, pp. 479–86, 510–27; Wilson 1980a; Prestwich 1985.
13. Coldstream 1985, pp. 10–11.
14. Work was done on the castles, but not on, e.g., St Stephen's before 1320: see Colvin 1963, *passim*; Fryde 1979, p. 88.
15. Sleigh 1952, pp. 17–18.
16. VCH, *Hertfordshire*, II, 1908, p. 490; VCH, *Cambridgeshire*, 1970, pp. 359–61; Coldstream 1979, *passim*; Lindley 1986a, esp. pp. 126–7. For a highly decorated Lady Chapel which did not survive, see James 1895a, pp. 142–3.

17. Although Woodman 1984 dates the Lady Chapel vault to the fifteenth century, Binski & Park 1986, p. 33, produce convincing reasons why the traditional fourteenth-century date is acceptable.
18. The fragments were identified by Phillip Lindley. Drawings were made by Burges (London, Victoria and Albert Museum, Dept of Prints and Drawings, 93. E. 5).
19. James 1895b. This is the longest known cycle of Virgin scenes, either sculptured or painted on walls.
20. Burges (n. 18), 95. E. 5, pp. 23–4; Binski & Park 1986, p. 33.
21. Binski & Park 1986.
22. Lindley 1986b makes a similar point about the decoration of the octagon, but this essay was written while his article was still in the press. See, however, Lindley 1986a, p. 128.
23. Morris 1974, p. 143.
24. Hastings 1955; Colvin 1963, pp. 510–27; Bony 1979, *passim*; Wilson 1980; Coldstream 1985, pp. 7–8; Roberts 1986. The paintings are illustrated in Tristram 1955, pls 2–6.
25. Binski & Park 1986, p. 32, compare techniques at Ely and St Stephen's.
26. Binski & Park 1986, p. 32. The faking of precious materials may, of course, have been done for reasons of economy.
27. Klukas 1981.
28. Harvey 1982, p. 87. See Lindley 1986a, p. 128.
29. The most likely patron of the new chancel at Heckington, Lincolnshire, was Richard de Potesgrave, royal chaplain; see Sekules 1986, p. 123 and n. 46.

Sculpture

uring the abbacy of William of Trumpington at St Albans, between 1214 and 1235, much building work was done on the church. Fortunately there exists a wonderfully informative and almost contemporary account of the building programme by the famous chronicler and artist Matthew Paris. In this he marvels at the work being carried out inside the church:

> In his [William of Trumpington's] time also Master Walter of Colchester, then sacrist, who was an incomparable painter and sculptor, constructed the screen in the middle of the church with its great cross, also Mary and John and other sculptures and suitable stonework, at the expense of the sacristy, but by the diligence of his own labour.[1]

He goes on to describe another sculpture made by Walter of Colchester:

> In Abbot William's praise it should be added that he presented to our church a most elegant figure of Our Lady which the oft-mentioned Walter of Colchester had most carefully carved, and he had it consecrated by the Bishop John above mentioned. The figure of Mary which was formerly in the place where he installed the new one, he moved to the altar where the Mass of Our Lady was celebrated daily with music. He also installed a candle, which he used to decorate with flowers, to be burned day and night before this noble figure of Mary on principal feasts and during the procession which was made at her commemoration.[2]

In their different ways these two excerpts are extremely useful for the light they shed on working practices in the first half of the thirteenth century and because they refer to types of sculptures which, once common, have since virtually disappeared. The great rood screens which spanned the centre of major and minor churches alike were so comprehensively destroyed at the time of the Reformation and the Dissolution of the monasteries in the sixteenth century that nothing of this sort now exists in England; to represent large-scale English wood sculpture of the thirteenth century in the exhibition it was necessary to obtain loans from Scandinavia, where considerable amounts of this material had been exported at the time (Cat. 290).[3] There is also scant evidence of smaller altar figures, although fortuitously the rare oak Virgin and Child from Langham (Cat. 249) is of about the same date as the Virgin and Child referred to by Matthew Paris. These single figures were to be found on altars in every church and are sometimes seen in contemporary manuscript illuminations, such as the well-known Apocalypse manuscript of the late thirteenth century in Lambeth Palace Library, where the monk Theophilus prostrates himself before the altar (fig. 65; see Cat. 438). These figures were often considered to have miraculous properties, as in this illustration, and stories of statues coming to life were legion. It is also of interest to note the presence of the small altar cross in the same illustration, similar in type to a rare survival in gilt bronze in the exhibition (Cat. 125).

Master Walter of Colchester, as Matthew Paris describes him, was a craftsman of the first rank, equally expert in painting and sculpture (and probably metalworking); the chronicler tells us that Walter 'fortunately was attracted and persuaded by Brother Ralph Gubiun to take on the religious habit in our church'.[4] In his versatility Walter is the thirteenth-century counterpart of master Hugo of Bury St Edmunds, who, as the *Gesta Sacristarum Monasterii Sancti Edmundi* tells us, was responsible not only for the illumination of the Bury St Edmunds Bible of about 1135, but also for the double doors at the west end of the church at Bury, the casting of a bronze bell, and 'a cross in the choir with Mary and John incomparably carved'.[5] Both worked in the context of large monasteries, and Walter certainly devoted all his energies to embellishing the church to which he was attached; he therefore fits fairly and squarely into the tradition of the previous century. However, by the middle of the thirteenth century a new class of craftsman was already active: this was the lay sculptor who belonged to a workshop which would travel from one commission to the next. Because of the increase in contemporary documentation from this time onwards the names of many of these workmen are known, some of them appearing time and again in records of payment.[6] Not surprisingly, because the records connected with the Crown have survived better than others there is some imbalance in the coverage. From these documents it is not always clear whether the craftsman referred to is a 'sculptor' rather than a stonecutter or mason, and indeed in many cases such a distinction would have been irrelevant. So while Alexander of Abingdon, the sculptor of the statues on the Eleanor Cross at Waltham of 1291–4 (Cat. 374) is unequivocally described as *le ymagour* (the imager), another sculptor engaged on carving similar figures for the Hardingstone Eleanor Cross, William of Ireland, is called both *imaginator* and *cementarius* (mason).[7] At the same time William Torel, described as *aurifaber* (goldsmith), was commissioned to cast two life-sized effigies of Queen Eleanor, one for her tomb at Westminster Abbey (Cat. 377), the other for the tomb containing her entrails at Lincoln (Cat. 379).[8] Even at the end of the fourteenth century, among the men who designed and executed the lavish tomb of Richard II and his queen, Anne of Bohemia (Cat. 446), there is not one who would comfortably fit into the currently accepted definition of a sculptor: Henry Yevele and Stephen Lote, described as masons, designed the tomb chest and had it made, while the effigies were cast by the coppersmiths Nicholas Broker and Godfrey Prest.[9]

In any exhibition of Gothic sculpture, the major shortcoming must be that the largest pieces and those still attached to buildings cannot be included. In many cases the detachment of a figure from its architectural setting renders it less effective visually and often destroys its intended function, and the vast majority of the large-scale statuary of the thirteenth and fourteenth centuries should ideally be seen with the original setting in mind. In addition, it requires a certain amount of imagination to reconstruct the original appearance of much of the sculpture, as the vast majority of surviving pieces are now weathered and have lost their original polychromy (cf. Cat. 438–9). It cannot be over-emphasised how important this coloured decoration was to the medieval congregation: only rarely before 1400 were sculptures left unpainted, and even external figures were picked out with bright colours.[10]

Fig. 65 Page from the Lambeth Apocalypse showing the Legend of Theophilus, late thirteenth century (London, Lambeth Palace Library, MS 209 f. 46v.; Cat. 438)

No individual piece of sculpture, no particular ensemble can be singled out as the first example of Gothic sculpture in England. The transition from the Romanesque style – normally in England associated with the twelfth century – to a recognisably Gothic idiom was a gradual process over a long period. The move towards a greater naturalism, a gentler and less hieratic aspect (both marked features of the fully-developed Gothic style of the late thirteenth century) started in the late twelfth century; the decoration of the voussoirs around the outer south porch at Malmesbury Abbey, of around 1170, with small, twisting figures enveloped in swirling drapery which emphasises the contours of the bodies beneath, although belonging to the Romanesque world anticipates the precision and dramatic narrative of the early thirteenth century. This is borne out by comparison with the north door of the Lady Chapel at Glastonbury, of about 1220–30, where similar figures fill the voussoirs. But here, fifty years later, the draperies are not treated in the same way as at Malmesbury; whereas the latter were made up of fabulous configurations of cloth, almost abstract patterns which bore no relation to reality, the later figures are dressed in entirely believable garments, in elegant, less frenzied poses. The draperies are heavier, with thick, deep folds giving substance to the figures. In the half century between these two works the manner had changed more than the arrangement.[11]

Although this transitional phase can clearly be seen in other parts of the country as, for instance, in the life-sized standing figures from St Mary's Abbey, York, of about 1190 which reflect the influence of the Île-de-France, the West Country seems to be where the embryonic Gothic style developed and flourished at the beginning of the thirteenth century. At Worcester Cathedral the small figures in the historiated spandrels of the Lady Chapel and transepts (c. 1220–30 where they have not been restored in the nineteenth century), while following on in the tradition of Malmesbury and Glastonbury, clearly acted as prototypes for later, similar, schemes at Westminster and Salisbury. A now badly defaced but still very impressive figure of Christ in Majesty in a quatrefoil flanked by the four Evangelist symbols in the refectory at Worcester, of about the same date as the spandrel figures, also looks both backwards to the Romanesque and forwards to the major sculptural programme of the first half of the thirteenth century, the west front of Wells Cathedral (Cat. 239).[12]

Contemporary with the west front of Amiens Cathedral, the statues at Wells in their figure style certainly betray a knowledge of French sculpture, and in some cases the relationship of certain figures closely follows French models. Because of this strong French influence the sculptures of the west front make a clear break from the transitional sculptures of the preceding fifty years in England and usher in the new Gothic style. But the end result is distinctly un-French; the entire west façade acts as a screen on which to hang the sculpture, and the portals, so important in the great French cathedrals, are insignificant. The majority of the sculpture on the west front – originally consisting of 176 full-length statues (fig. 66), thirty half-length angels (e.g. Cat. 243) and 134 smaller reliefs of Old and New Testament scenes (e.g. Christ among the Doctors, Cat. 244) – should be dated c. 1230–50.[13] Unfortunately, owing to the destruction of much valuable evidence, it is not now possible to reconstruct the activities of the Wells workshop before, during and after the work on the west front. It is sensible to accept the suggestion that a French mason was employed in the early stages at least, and there are certainly variations in quality among the figure sculptures on the front, suggesting the participation of both experienced and apprentice workmen. A tantalising fragment here and there points to the input of the Wells workshop: a fragmentary life-sized Virgin and Child at St Bartholomew's Hospital, Bristol, is undoubtedly by a sculptor who had worked at Wells, and two seated knights from the town gate at Hereford, until recently on loan to the Victoria and Albert Museum, may also be connected with this 'school'.[14] Other significant sculptures of the second quarter of the century in the West Country, such as the effigy of William Longespée in Salisbury Cathedral, have long been associated with Wells.[15]

Most of this workshop's output is now lost, but as mentioned earlier there is valuable evidence outside England to show the creative wealth of its work and the considerable influence it exerted. Thanks to Aron Andersson's pioneering book[16] it is possible to see that the products of Wells-influenced workshops were exported to Scandinavia and have survived there in good numbers. Andersson convincingly demonstrated by stylistic means that many of these wood sculptures, often painted and in good condition but unknown to English scholars before 1949, are intimately connected with the figures on the west front at Wells. He identified a number of pieces as by English workshops, and went on to isolate other groups probably carved by Scandinavians under English training or influence. It is clear that this export of sculptures went on throughout the thirteenth century and that the products of other, slightly later, English workshops (such as London) are to be found in Scandinavia also.

Not surprisingly, sculpture of the type now found only in Scandinavia, the single figure in wood, was the most vulnerable at times of iconoclasm and a great deal of it was also probably destroyed in peaceful times as a result of accidental fires. Happily, architectural sculpture has fared comparatively better, often forming part of the structure of a building or positioned high up and out of reach of vandals. This is especially fortunate because it was in the decoration of capitals, corbels and bosses that the English thirteenth-century sculptor came into his own. Perhaps the major difference between Romanesque and Gothic sculpture may be seen in the decoration of capitals. The Gothic sculptor turned away from decorating capitals with narrative scenes, so omnipresent in the twelfth century, towards a simpler, less cluttered, formula usually incorporating foliage sprays. The most popular in the first half of the thirteenth century was the so-called 'stiff leaf', seen at an early stage in its development at the east end and in the transepts at Wells. Here, right at the beginning of the century, many of the capitals are still inhabited with figures engaged in various forms of activity, but the large leaf forms are starting to dominate the composition.

Fig. 66 Two deacons on the west front of Wells Cathedral, 1230–50

Fig. 67 Capital in the south transept of Wells Cathedral, *c.* 1210

Moreover, the little figures on these capitals are already far removed from their rather anonymous Romanesque predecessors; each one is distinct from the next in its face type and some are especially well observed, such as the justly celebrated bust of a man with toothache (fig. 67).[17] Leaf forms of various types continued to be popular decoration on capitals and bosses throughout the century, this kind of elaboration reaching its apogee in the 1280s and 1290s in the luxuriant and brilliantly successful foliate decoration in the chapter houses at York (Cat. 343) and Southwell minsters, where a dazzling variety of superbly executed leaf types sprout from the capitals and arches.

Likewise, the acute observation of heads, first seen in the Wells capitals, carried on and developed, especially on corbels: the extraordinarily naturalistic head from Clarendon Palace, of about 1240 (Cat. 295), is an example of the increased interest in 'portraiture'. Of course, this heightened naturalism must be viewed as a corollary of a study of classicism generally, an interest in the antique which had spread throughout Europe in the second quarter of the thirteenth century, producing the beautiful but enigmatic female figure from Winchester (Cat. 245), the clearly classically-inspired figures at Chartres and Rheims and their derivatives, such as the Visitation group at Bamberg, and the even purer classical figures produced for the Hohenstaufen Emperor Frederick II in south Italy, on his Porta Romana at Capua.

Before Henry III initiated his massively expensive rebuilding of Westminster Abbey from the 1240s onwards, the evidence for a 'London school' of sculptors is slight. Henry demanded the best workmen, presumably drawing them from over a wide area, and it is known that some of the sculptors at least emanated from the West Country. However, by 1250 it could fairly be said that a Court workshop existed and, not surprisingly, some of the best sculpture of the Gothic period in England, much of it fortunately still surviving, was created at Westminster. The heart of the Abbey was the Shrine of St Edward the Confessor, upon which Henry spent a colossal sum of between £4,000 and £5,000, adding jewels and other precious materials over the years. Although Roman craftsmen were employed on the shrine base and the pavement beneath, the other sculptural embellishments were executed by Englishmen, as is shown by records of payments made, for example, in 1257 to Simon of Wells and William of Gloucester, who were contracted to make a gilt-bronze figure for the tomb of the king's daughter Katherine: this has since disappeared.[18] The major surviving sculptures of the middle of the century at Westminster – the censing angels high up on the end walls of the north and south transepts (fig. 68), the bust-length angels in medallions on the soffits of the windows in the north transept, and the chapter house Annunciation group (Cat. 287–8) – have a majesty and a serenity which set them apart from the figures on the Wells west front, and which show clearly the contribution of master craftsmen influenced by French stylistic developments, at the centre of an élite workshop. However, it is especially to be regretted that the mid-thirteenth-century north portal at Westminster, the main ceremonial entrance, has perished, and that we have to rely on interior sculpture for an impression of the work of the Court workshop. With drawings and monumental derivatives from the north portal, such as those at Higham Ferrers in Northamptonshire and the Judgement Porch at Lincoln, it is possible to reconstruct its original form fairly accurately. It is clear that it departed from the north French practice of placing jamb figures to each side of the doors in rows, and that instead these figures were placed apart from each other on socles, as at Lincoln. The side portals had tympana which were not divided horizontally but had numerous small scenes contained in cinquefoils.[19] As might be expected, the stylistic and compositional formulas worked out at Westminster in the 1250s were taken up elsewhere, most notably at Lincoln in the twenty years following. The south portal of the Angel Choir (the so-called Judgement Porch), as already noted, has a number of features inspired by Westminster: the single standing figures at the sides of the door (fig. 69), the large figure of Christ (now much restored) in a quatrefoil, and the beautiful, gently-swaying, small figures enclosed in a cage of foliage in the voussoirs, which derive from the similar (although less graceful) figures around the doorway into the chapter house at Westminster. The masons responsible for the Judgement Porch moved on to Crowland Abbey, where they executed the west front sculptures, now badly mutilated and weathered – only the reliefs of the tympanum and a single figure representing Synagogue (once identical in style to that figure at Lincoln) of this period have survived.[20]

Returning to Lincoln, the magnificent Angel Choir itself was also much influenced by Westminster, the numerous angels filling the spandrels taking as their stylistic lead the censing angels in the transepts of around 1255. These sweetly smiling angels, with finely carved outstretched wings and soft, deeply creased draperies, were to remain popular until the beginning of the following century, and were often employed on tomb canopies and liturgical furnishings (e.g. the Sawley angels, Cat. 341–2).

Sepulchral effigies now constitute a large proportion of existing English Gothic figure sculpture. A great number of secular effigies survived the depredations of the iconoclasts, presumably because they represented personages worthy of note, rather than figures of religious superstition.[21] Considering the inherent limitations presented in the representation of a single recumbent figure, the thirteenth- and fourteenth-century English sculptor showed a quite outstanding originality. These effigies, especially the knights, are far from stiff, lifeless figures: during the course of the thirteenth century both the straight-legged, solemn type exemplified by the effigy of William Longespée, and the dynamic, twisting figures of the second half of the century – such as the magnificent freestone knight at Dorchester and the wooden effigy of Robert 'Curthose' at Gloucester (Cat. 2) – existed alongside one another. The latter type, with legs crossed and right hand poised ready to draw sword from scabbard, is an especially exciting composition and a brilliant solution to a potentially dull arrangement.[22] Throughout the fourteenth century experimentation continued, although the older types were still employed. Many different materials were used for the effigies: Purbeck 'marble', a limestone capable of taking a polish, quarried at Corfe in Dorset, was popular until about 1300, when the fashions for covering the effigies with stamped and moulded gesso and paint made it pointless to use such a relatively expensive material; freestone (loosely speaking, any good-quality building stone), which had been used throughout the thirteenth century, was cheaper and was thus preferred, and wood was an easily-carved and inexpensive alternative. By about 1340 alabaster, quarried at Chellaston, near Nottingham, started to be employed on effigies.

Of course, the wealthiest patrons of all were the royal family and those associated with them. It is therefore in Westminster Abbey, where Henry III and his son

Fig. 68   Censing angel in the south transept of Westminster Abbey, *c.* 1255

Fig. 69   Figure of Synagogue in the
Judgement porch of Lincoln Cathedral, *c.* 1265

Edward I had established the royal mausoleum and coronation church, that one must look for the masterpieces of English Gothic funerary sculpture. Around the tomb of St Edward, in the area known as the Confessor's Chapel, it became customary from the second half of the thirteenth century until the end of the fourteenth (when all the spaces had been filled) to place the tombs of the kings and (sometimes) queens of England. Thus in this small space there are the tombs of Henry III, Edward I and his queen, Eleanor of Castile, Edward III and Philippa of Hainault, and the double tomb of Richard II and Anne of Bohemia. This area therefore became a dynastic resting-place, a royal shrine where the monarchs were laid next to the great patron saint of the king's church. There can be no doubt that in setting up this great mausoleum, both Henry III and Edward I were responding to developments in Paris, where the Capetian Louis IX had created his royal shrine at St-Denis, making new tombs for the Carolingian and Capetian monarchs.[23]

The royal effigies are of the greatest importance not only because of their obvious historical significance but also because it is possible through them to chart stylistic changes over a period of a hundred years. The two earliest effigies at Westminster are those of Henry III and Eleanor of Castile. Although Henry had died in 1272, it was not until 1291–3 that the present gilt-bronze effigy surmounting the tomb was made. It was ordered by Edward I together with the tomb of Eleanor, and thanks to detailed accounts of payments left by the executors of Eleanor's estate a very full record of the circumstances surrounding the making of these tombs has come down to us.[24] William Torel, a goldsmith of London, cast both the life-sized gilt-bronze effigies for the tombs in Westminster and, as already mentioned, another for Eleanor's second tomb in Lincoln Cathedral: this was destroyed in 1641, but a drawing made before then shows that it was almost exactly the same as the effigy at Westminster.[25] The effigies of Henry and Eleanor are both extremely heavy castings and vary in thickness between 5 and 10 cm, leading some authorities to suggest that Torel, as a goldsmith, was unfamiliar with large-scale casting.[26] Certainly the effigy of the king, splendid as it is, is not a startlingly new work for the end of the thirteenth century; it belongs rather to the world of the sombre and simpler figures of the first half of the century, and in spirit is not very far from the Purbeck marble effigy of King John at Worcester, which was probably carved by a London workshop around 1232. Its refinement lies in the richness of the material, the surface chasing of the cushions and base beneath the figure, and the pious majesty of the pose.

Because of the extraordinarily full documentation surrounding Eleanor's death in November, 1290, and the funeral arrangements which followed, we know the names of all the craftsmen employed on her tomb (Cat. 377), how much they were paid and exactly what they all did. This information extends also to her other tomb at Lincoln, her heart memorial at the Dominican church of the Black Friars in London, and the twelve Eleanor crosses (Cat. 368–79). Although only three of the crosses survive, at Geddington, Northampton and Waltham, they show that despite all being commissioned from London they were entrusted to different workshops. Even without the documentary evidence, by comparing the figures of the Northampton (Hardingstone) and Waltham crosses the differences are clear; the former, with deep, abundant folds of drapery, are the work of William of Ireland and could not be more different from the restrained, elegant figures by Alexander of Abingdon on the Waltham Cross. Alexander was a central figure in the Court workshop (he made the base of Eleanor's tomb at Lincoln and also worked on the Eleanor Cross at Charing) and his statues of Eleanor come very close to the effigy on her tomb at Westminster. Both show her as an idealised, highly dignified figure with little movement and with straightforward, simply-conceived draperies: she is frozen and impassive, as if suspended between life and death.

It is ironic that Edward I, who commissioned both these magnificent tombs, does not himself have an effigy: a bare Purbeck marble tomb chest to the west of Henry's tomb suffices for his memorial. His son, Edward II, fared much better (after death at least) and his tomb at Gloucester, of the early 1330s, with its beautifully extravagant canopy, its Purbeck chest and sublime alabaster effigy, is one of the glories of the fourteenth century (Cat. 497). Returning to Westminster, on the south side of the Confessor's Chapel, next in date comes the tomb of Philippa of Hainault (d. 1369); her marble effigy was commissioned from the celebrated sculptor Jean de Liège in Philippa's lifetime, the large sum of £133.6s.8d being paid in 1367.[27] This tomb therefore stands outside the tradition of English sculpture and has more to do with the contemporary tombs Jean de Liège made for the French royal family, for Charles V, Margaret of Flanders, Blanche d'Évreux and others.[28] It must have presented a luxurious appearance, with thirty-two statuettes (weepers) in niches along the sides of the tomb chest (only one complete figure now survives) and with inlaid glass and imitation jewels on the canopy and elsewhere. Almost ten years later, in 1376, the tomb was further embellished when John Orchard the lattener added six copper-gilt angels, which are now also lost. Philippa's effigy is important in the context of English Gothic sculpture because it shows for the first time an attempt at true portraiture, in contrast to the idealised images of Henry III, Eleanor and Edward II. This is especially noticeable as the representation of Philippa is far from flattering: she is shown as a rather matronly, plump woman.

When Edward III died in 1377 his effigy was made in gilt bronze, returning to the material of the earlier royal tombs. Like Philippa's effigy it shows signs of real portraiture (fig. 70) and it seems likely that the features were based on the death mask and wooden effigy made for his funeral. This increasing realism is taken one step further in the last tomb to be installed in the Confessor's Chapel, that of Richard II and Anne of Bohemia. As would be expected, it is an expensive and elaborate monument, and the most highly esteemed craftsmen of the day were employed on it. Anne died in 1394 and by the following year Richard had commissioned his masons and coppersmiths (see above) to make a double tomb; the work appears to have been finished by 1396, although the effigies were only actually gilded in 1398–9.[29] Sadly, the effigies and the surrounding features on the tomb have been much mutilated, so that the tomb now presents a comparatively bare appearance. But enough remains to show how splendid it once was: the technical execution of the bronze casting is much more advanced than before, the figures being assembled from a number of separate pieces, but it is the surface decoration – the punching and chasing of exquisite designs on to the surfaces of the draperies – which sets the work apart. It is worth noting that in the contract for the tomb it was specifically ordered that the effigy of the king should 'counterfait' – exactly copy – his real appearance.

Outside the series of royal burials in the Confessor's Chapel, other important developments in the design of tomb monuments were taking place at Westminster. On the north side of the presbytery are three 'ciborium' tombs, of Aveline of Lancaster (d. 1273, but the tomb probably of c. 1295), Aymer de Valence (d. 1324) and Edmund Crouchback, Earl of Lancaster (d. 1296; see Cat. 326). With the tomb of Archbishop Pecham (d. 1292) at Canterbury Cathedral these show an effigy lying under a vaulted canopy, a central gable with a trefoil, and small weepers beneath an arcade running along the tomb chest.[30] It is mainly in the arrangement of the canopy, a miniature version of French architectural forms, and in the minute attention to detail that these tombs differ from their predecessors. However, precisely because they were so elaborate, they were not widely emulated: simpler wall tombs became common and the earlier type of canopy tomb, exemplified by those of Bishop Giles de Bridport (d. 1262) at Salisbury and Archbishop Walter de Gray (d. 1255) at York, continued to be popular into the fourteenth century. There is the occasional instance of a tomb of foreign workmanship: the sole surviving example is the effigy of William de Valence (d. 1296) in the Chapel of Sts Edmund and Thomas the Martyr at Westminster, made by craftsmen from Limoges. This was made up of plain and enamelled copper sheets applied to a wooden core, in the manner of the numerous caskets made by the same workshops and exported all over Europe. Because of the cost of such commissions, these Limoges effigies are hardly likely to have been produced in great numbers and do not appear to have been influential. Other materials, especially alabaster, were preferred in the fourteenth century.

Intimately connected with the canopy and ciborium tombs are the shrines which once provided the major focus for every important cathedral or church. Unfortunately they were the prime targets for vandalism, as they often housed precious reliquaries, and are now nearly all destroyed or in very fragmentary condition. The shrine of Edward the Confessor, of which only the base survives, has already been mentioned;

Fig. 70 Head of the effigy of Edward III in Westminster Abbey, 1377–80

other notable extant shrines (albeit reassembled in most cases) may be seen at Oxford (St Frideswide), Hereford (St Thomas Cantilupe, Cat. 86), St Albans (St Alban, Cat. 19), and Chester (St Werburgh, Cat. 20), to name only the four best preserved, and there are many fragments of the early fourteenth-century 'tomb' of St William at York (Cat. 513–16).[31] All date either from the end of the thirteenth or the first half of the fourteenth century and they of course closely resemble ordinary tombs, being the burial places of the saints. Hardly surprisingly they are usually more elaborate, often with numerous small figures and sometimes with sculpted scenes around the canopy.

Generally speaking it would be fair to say that in the thirteenth century sculptural styles were determined by the West Country and London schools. Although both continued to exert considerable influence nationwide in the fourteenth century (the latter especially in tomb sculpture), the major trend was towards diversification, with independent workshops operating in different parts of the country. In the first half of the fourteenth century these different centres were bound together with a common guiding aesthetic, now commonly known for convenience as the Decorated style. As the name suggests, in these years (c. 1290–1350) there was a love of decorative ornament and detailed figure work on buildings, tombs and church furnishings which in many cases separated the sculpture from its setting, lifting it apart from the architectural context it embellished. This is seen perfectly in the decoration of the Prior's Door in the cloister of Norwich Cathedral, of the first years of the fourteenth

Fig. 71 The Prior's Door in the cloister of Norwich Cathedral, *c.* 1310

century (fig. 71). Here the beautifully carved little statuettes seem to be stuck on to the arch which supports them; the traditional 'flat' space of the tympanum – the usual place for figured compositions up to this time – has disappeared altogether. This audacious use of applied ornament gives the door a lightness, and the figures a floating quality, not seen before. In the second quarter of the century at Ely, in the decoration of the Lady Chapel (Cat. 491), the Decorated style is taken to its logical conclusion (see p. 95).[32] In comparison with the historiated spandrels at Worcester, about a century earlier, the figure work dominates the architecture rather than filling the empty space provided by it.

The beginnings of this 'spreading' sculpture are seen in the application of luxuriant foliate decoration in the chapter houses at York and Southwell, at the end of the thirteenth century. By the first half of the fourteenth century, the Decorated style had firmly taken hold in the East Midlands and Yorkshire, and some of the finest existing sculpture of this kind is to be found in those regions. Especially noteworthy, and absolutely typical, are the Easter sepulchres and other liturgical furnishings in the chancels at Hawton (Cat. 493) and Heckington, where the extravagant foliate decoration and extremely fine figural work covers every available surface.[33] The most important surviving monument of the second quarter of the century in Yorkshire, the Percy tomb in Beverley Minster (Cat. 494), is the culmination of the style worked out in the Easter sepulchres of the East Midlands: the canopy seems to crawl with plants and small figures.

After the masterpieces of the Decorated style, the sculptures of the second half of the fourteenth century come as an anticlimax. Despite the progress of portraiture in the royal effigies at Westminster there is precious little else to compare in terms of quality with the products of 1200–1350. The decoration of the west front at Exeter with the seated figures of kings, of about 1350–65, and the Exeter workshop sculptures of the stone reredos at Christchurch (fig. 72), show a marked decline in the treatment of the human body; both ensembles make up for their deficiencies only by the sheer scale and grandeur of the compositions. However, it should not be forgotten that the now empty niches on the Christchurch reredos would have been filled with statues, probably of wood covered with silver plate, so that the overall impression would have been most striking. The vast majority of the rather dull alabaster tombs produced in this last fifty years largely followed stereotyped patterns, and the mass production of alabaster panels for retables began towards the end of the century. It can hardly be coincidence that this downturn in the quality of sculpture comes directly after the Black Death had devastated English society in 1348–9.[34] It is quite possible that many master masons succumbed to the plague, and that work outstanding at the time or commissioned in the years after had to be carried out by inexperienced sculptors.

Apart from the tomb he ordered for Anne of Bohemia and himself, the only sculptural commission securely associated with Richard II is the series of life-sized standing figures of kings, of which only six now remain, in Westminster Hall (Cat. 708–9). These statues, fifteen of which were made by Thomas Canon in 1385, anticipate the sculptural style of the fifteenth century, as seen in the first great work of the new century, the choir screen with six standing kings in Canterbury Cathedral (the figures probably 1411–30).[35] They are thus heralds of a new era, and although undeserving of the elevated status accorded the near-contemporary sculptures of Claus Sluter at Dijon, they belong to the same courtly, refined world. Richard II, regardless of his other limitations, may be seen to have promoted the arts with as much energy as his illustrious forefathers. His mixture of piety and self-aggrandisement was typical of his age, so that in the thirteenth and fourteenth centuries it was the Crown, not the monasteries (as before), which gave the greatest impetus to art. Sculptors were among the major beneficiaries of this patronage, and the best products of their workmanship bear witness to a creative talent and fertile imagination hardly surpassed elsewhere.

Fig. 72 The stone reredos in Christchurch Priory, Dorset, *c.* 1350–60

NOTES

1. Excerpted from Vaughan 1984, pp. 48–9.
2. Ibid., pp. 51–2.
3. Andersson 1949, *passim*.
4. Vaughan 1984, p. 24.
5. See Kauffmann 1975, no. 56.
6. Harvey 1984 includes a large number of 'sculptors'.
7. Ibid., pp. 1, 158.
8. Colvin 1963, pp. 479–82.
9. Ibid., pp. 487–8.
10. See Cat. 243–4; detailed analysis of English Gothic sculpture at the Victoria and Albert Museum and at Wells Cathedral has revealed considerable amounts of pigmentation on external sculptures. Cf. also Williamson 1987, pp. 20–4.
11. For Malmesbury see Saxl 1954, pls LXVII–LXXXIII; the portal at Glastonbury is now much decayed, but for an illustration see Stone 1972, pl. 77B.
12. Pevsner & Metcalf 1985b, fig. 183.
13. The most recent discussion of the Wells sculptures is Tudor-Craig 1982.
14. For the Bristol Virgin and Child see Andersson 1949, fig. 13. The Hereford Knights were sold at Christie's (London), 13 December 1985, lots 67 and 67A (illustrated in Sale Catalogue).
15. Tummers 1980, pp. 79–81.
16. Andersson 1949.
17. See Gardner 1956.
18. Colvin 1963, pp. 478–9.
19. For its form see Wilson *et al.* 1986, pp. 43–8; see also Roberts 1985.
20. Henderson 1985b.
21. See Prior & Gardner 1912, pp. 545–721; Tummers 1980, *passim*.
22. Tummers 1980, pls 96, 97.
23. Hallam 1982, pp. 371–5.
24. Colvin 1963, pp. 479–83.
25. Ibid., pl. 35B.
26. Plenderleith & Maryon 1959, pp. 87–8.
27. Colvin 1963, pp. 486–7.
28. For Jean de Liège see most recently Paris 1981–2, nos 65–7, 70, 78.
29. Colvin 1963, p. 488.
30. For a discussion of the group see Gee 1979 and Lindley 1984.
31. Coldstream 1976; for York (and shrines generally) see Wilson 1977.
32. Coldstream 1985 and Lindley 1985, pp. 189–225.
33. Sekules 1983.
34. Evans 1949, pp. 74–8.
35. Stone 1972, p. 204, pl. 153A; for an alternative date for these figures, of around the middle of the fourteenth century, see Woodman 1981, pp. 188–98.

Neil Stratford   Gothic Ivory Carving in England

ittle is known about the European trade in elephant ivory during the Middle Ages. Judging by survivals, it must have been, to say the least, spasmodic before *c.* 1270–80, brisk during the following century and a quarter, tailing off again during the fifteenth century. No direct political, economic or cultural causes herald its emergence in the thirteenth century, yet with hindsight it would be surprising if ivory had not begun to get through to the European markets during the century which saw a vast expansion of trade, both overland with the Orient (Marco Polo is the best-known witness to this) and, above all, through Mediterranean sea trade, with the Levant and North Africa. Throughout the Romanesque period, elephant ivory, whether Indian or African,[1] must have been extremely rare, if the very few survivals reflect the true state of things, and even some of these may have been older tusks or recarved from earlier, perhaps Roman or Late Antique ivories, as also happened in the ninth and tenth centuries.

In northern Europe, various other tusks and teeth were in demand as substitutes; the walrus tusk was the most prized, bone the humblest.[2] Scandinavia was the major source of walrus ivory. Although more restricted in size than the elephant tusk, when carved it takes on a lustrous sheen of its own, and it produced some of the great masterpieces of English Romanesque art. It continued to be highly prized throughout the Middle Ages. Four magnificent walrus-ivory chess pieces and three reliefs are exhibited here (Cat. 145–8, 307–9); they bear witness to its popularity with the best artists well into the thirteenth century. In 1327 walrus tusks from Greenland were used to pay tithe to the Archbishop of Trondheim, and were then sold in Bergen to a Flemish merchant from Bruges.[3] Gaming pieces, knife handles, writing tablets and other domestic artefacts of fourteenth- and fifteenth-century date are still sometimes of walrus ivory, though more commonly of bone (Cat. 428).[4] Yet by the second quarter of the thirteenth century it was beginning to be possible occasionally to buy the big elephant tusks, if you were rich enough, and this in spite of interdicts on trade with the 'sons of the Prophet'.[5] There are a few important Early Gothic elephant ivories, mainly French, others possibly English (Cat. 248), and we know that Queen Eleanor in London paid for $3\frac{1}{2}$lb of ivory in 1251–3 for the carving of images.[6] Ivory had inspired the description of King Solomon's throne (1 *Kings* x, 18–20), had been prized throughout the ancient world for its surface texture of translucent whiteness and its ability to take the finest of cutting with hard, minute chisels, and had continued to serve as a *topos* for all that was rich and rare with poets such as Chrétien de Troyes.[7] Finally, in the last quarter of the thirteenth century, it became more than just an exotic rarity, and by the 1320s and 1330s there was a relative abundance of elephant tusks in northern Europe. The Florentine merchant Francesco Balducci Pegolotti, a servant of the Bardi, writing *c.* 1310–40, listed *denti di liofante* among the many luxury goods, spices, exotic woods, pigments, silks, etc., which could be bought in Acre, Alexandria, Famagusta, Majorca and Venice.[8]

It was probably Italian merchants like Pegolotti who acted as direct agents in the provision of elephant tusks to Gothic Europe. For instance, in 1301, a Genoese vessel was freighted by the Piacenza merchant house of Scotti with a luxury cargo from Famagusta and Lajazzo, which included ivory for the ports of Marseilles or Aigues-Mortes.[9] Later fourteenth-century Genoa customs lists record Alexandrian cargoes with ivory (*dentes*); the destinations of two ivory cargoes are specified as Provence and Flanders. These are only two examples. An extensive inquiry into the shipment of ivory, particularly through Italian ports like Genoa and Venice, now needs to be made. As for England, so few Particular Customs accounts have survived from the fourteenth century that we will probably never be able to judge the quantity of ivory coming into England, or from which ports it had been shipped.[10]

But even if the Italian ports were the important route for the European ivory trade, whether with Aden via Cairo and Alexandria, or with Acre and Cyprus, curiously (and again on the strength purely of what has survived) Italy never seems to have been a centre of ivory carving during the great period *c.* 1270–1400. All the evidence points to Paris as the important centre. Of course there were minor workshops elsewhere (we know for instance of an ivory carver in Tournai in the late fourteenth century),[11] and a few Italian Gothic ivories have indeed survived (the most famous being the Giovanni Pisano Madonna in Pisa), but they are very few, and the same must be said for the German lands, the Low Countries, Spain, Scandinavia and England.

This claim for the dominance of Paris in the thirteenth and fourteenth centuries is controversial and has been much debated. For one thing, the ivory carvers did not sign or date their work, so that subjective criteria of stylistic attribution are left as the only means by which to localise it. Yet not only does the vast majority of the two or three thousand surviving Gothic ivories hang together as a coherent, serial production, with the stamp of one artistic tradition, even if of several distinct workshops, rather as do the *opus anglicanum* textiles (Cat. 576–9) and the 'Nottingham' alabasters (Cat. 699–707), but also documents reveal professional 'corporations' and a lively ivory-carving quarter in Paris.[12] Stylistic comparisons with documented Paris works of stone sculpture, metalwork and manuscript illumination further confirm the claim. Conversely, it is much harder to find ivories of the late thirteenth and fourteenth centuries which bear the stamp of other cultural traditions; they are often one-off pieces (such as a crucifix in Halberstadt and a Virgin in Hildesheim) and the various efforts which have been made in recent years to define a 'Cologne' production, or an 'Italian' production have not been convincing.

How and why the tusks should have been funnelled towards a Paris market is far from clear; perhaps it was simply a reflection of the fact that by the end of the reign of Louis IX (1226–70) Paris enjoyed a supreme reputation as the leading artistic centre in Europe, a reputation reflected not only in architecture (see pp. 75–7) but sculpture, painting and the 'minor arts'. That Paris was a true market for ivory is abundantly documented. Combs, boxes, knife handles, writing tablets, mirrors, crucifixes, tabernacles, all were carved and sold there, many undoubtedly exported. The quality of this production varied and was by no means always high; the artists themselves may not always have been French by birth or even training; but in the fourteenth century if you could afford it, it was fashionable to buy Parisian ivories, just as it was fashionable to 'build French'.

Why and when did the fashion pass? Probably by the early fifteenth century, again if survivals can be trusted. There are still certain groups of domestic artefacts, for instance ivory caskets and combs, which were apparently made in the Low Countries in the fifteenth century. There are also a few major fifteenth-century ivory statuettes, and the richest men of the time, for instance Henry V, owned ivories, just as their fathers and grandfathers had;[13] often, indeed, these ivories seem from surviving inventory descriptions to have been elaborate pieces, and some were no doubt commissioned, rather than inherited. However, the main Paris production of religious and secular ivories dates from the fourteenth century. Why so? Ivories are still included in luxury cargoes coming into the English ports in the fifteenth century. However, these are difficult to assess: first, the scarcity of surviving fourteenth-century Particular Customs accounts in England prevents comparison with these later lists; secondly, such references as there are in London, Southampton and Bristol lists are often to ivory combs, beads, handles and other mass-produced artefacts for everyday use, rather than to the raw material, or to fine ivory objects already carved.[14] We do not know whether the tusks themselves became scarcer, or whether other economic factors led to a falling-off in the production of Gothic ivories in the fifteenth century. Certainly as far as Paris is concerned, there are very good political reasons why ivory carving, based as it was on long-distance trade, might have declined drastically during the period of English occupation in the second quarter of the fifteenth century.[15] The best evidence for a halt in supply, rather than a shift in taste away from ivory, comes from the introduction of substitutes: towards the end of the fourteenth century new workshops associated with the name of the Genoese family of the Embriachi, whose dynasty subsequently appeared in Florence, then in Venice and northern Italy, started working in animal bone, treated and prepared to take on the superficial appearance of elephant ivory.[16] Men of the status of Giangaleazzo Visconti and Jean de Berry, bought the Embriachi 'ivories' as well as the elephant ivories, out of a shortage one presumes. Thereafter there seems to have been little major ivory carving in either northern Europe or Italy before the early seventeenth century. As Richard Randall has recently said, it is a striking fact that not a single major Renaissance artist has left behind an important work in ivory.[17]

It is against this rapid survey of the European ivory trade of the thirteenth and fourteenth centuries that the 'English' ivories must be judged. The sixteen ivories exhibited here form a small part of the total of sixty-one ivories catalogued by Porter (1974), in the most recent general survey of English Gothic ivory carving, which however includes a number of pieces whose only claim to being 'English' seems to be that they are 'provincial'. These figures should be set against the two to three thousand Gothic ivory carvings which survive in collections on both sides of the Atlantic. Some of these are fakes (though fewer than it is currently fashionable to dismiss);[18] others are single elements from larger medieval ensembles, broken up in the nineteenth century when dealers and collectors fostered a major trade in Gothic ivories, which were as popular in the Paris, Cologne and London salerooms as were the Limoges enamels. Hence two for the price of one was a law of the time, which led to the breaking-up of objects (cf. Cat. 307–9, 594–5), as well as the faking of fourteenth-century ivories in a world which enjoyed an abundance of elephant tusks – note the vast production of ivory billiard balls and piano keys at the same period.

Nevertheless, even if one were to accept Porter's entire corpus, England can claim only a tiny percentage of what survives. At first sight this seems most unlikely, for English medieval inventories and wills are liberally studded with references to ivories.[19] Church inventories, for instance, contain numerous references to ivory combs (no less than ten in a 1245 inventory of St Paul's);[20] pastoral and precentors' staffs, horns, and boxes for the Host or for relics (called *pyxis*, *scriniolum*, *coffrus*, etc.) are very common. On the other hand crucifixes, tabernacles, paxes (cf. Cat. 624), and images of the Virgin Mary are rarer, and ivory forms only a small element in these lists when put against the precious textiles and goldsmiths' work. Indeed it is often combined with other materials, precious metals or woods (such as cypress and ebony) or stones (such as jasper) or crystal or jet. In secular lists and wills boxes, combs, mirrors and cups appear, and we find chess and dice sets, sometimes of great splendour, boards and counters for games such as draughts and backgammon; but also devotional objects, including tabernacles (as in King Edward I's inventory of 1299–1300),[21] and horns. However, we do not know that these 'ivories' were made of elephant ivory (the combs and boxes could well be of bone or antler) and their place of origin is always unknown. Many were no doubt imports.[22] There is certainly no documentary evidence of an ivory production in London on the scale of that in Paris, and surely records would survive?[23] The iconoclasts of the sixteenth century destroyed images for their own sake (they could not even recycle ivory, as they could precious metal), and the nineteenth-century art market further obscured the early history of the few survivors, so that the art historian is left in a vacuum. Only one English Gothic ivory survives with a history that goes back as far as the late seventeenth century (Cat. 146); all the others first appear in the nineteenth century: total loss of history, loss of physical context, loss of relevant written sources. Even excavations have so far failed to produce more than a few minor pieces of evidence.[24]

By 'English' what is meant throughout this essay, and in the catalogue entries, is ivories whose style appears to establish them as related to English monuments, whether the buildings *in situ* and their decoration, or paintings of English origin. Medieval artists, English or not, were peripatetic, and so were ivories. No claim is made here that all the ivories exhibited were necessarily carved in England, any more than it is claimed that they were all carved by Englishmen; for instance, London had an international population, including Parisian merchants, painters and other artisans shuttling to and fro between London and Paris;[25] the English Court was

Fig. 73 Central plaque of an ivory triptych showing the Coronation of the Virgin and the Descent from the Cross, English(?), late thirteenth century (London, British Museum, MLA 88, 2–8, 2)

cosmopolitan and French-speaking. Yet whatever the nationality of the artists working in thirteenth- and fourteenth-century England, when an ivory can be attached to a group of known English monuments or paintings, it is labelled here as 'English': the surviving evidence of the great English Gothic buildings and their decoration, the stone and wood carvings, the glass and manuscript painting has been used as a touchstone of style for 'English' ivories. It is probable that many more surviving Gothic ivories were carved in England than we can now recognise. If so, this is because the artists who carved them did not noticeably adapt their stylistic language to local fashion. One further point: in selecting the ivories for the exhibition, there seemed no reason to assume that because a Gothic ivory was of inferior workmanship, or in some sense uncanonical by the standards of the French ivory carvings of the time, it must therefore be 'English'. For instance, the plaque in the British Museum (fig. 73)[26] which is universally accepted as English and of late thirteenth-century date may well be so, but it is not easy to secure close stylistic comparisons with it in English art; very little stone sculpture of the period descends to this level of mediocrity. The ivories which are known with certainty to be English, those made for Bishop John Grandisson of Exeter (Cat. 593–6), give the lie to the idea that the best English sculptors could not work ivory, even if there is no reason to suppose that they did so on a regular basis.

No surviving Gothic ivories anywhere in Europe are signed or dated, and they almost never bear inscriptions. The Grandisson ivories are unique in that they bear a shield of arms. A few surviving ivories can be identified in early inventories, but that does not tell us where, when or how they were made, and indeed none of these inventories is English. The absence of identity of the ivories points to two facts: first, their context is lost (e.g. if they were pinned to a shrine, or used on a chessboard) and we have also lost their frames (in metal, or painted or rare woods), which could well have been inscribed with the information we need; we can only speculate on the original appearance when mounted of such ivories as the Copenhagen reliefs (Cat. 307–9) or the Salting Diptych (Cat. 520). Secondly, many of them were mass-produced, and hence were never inscribed. Their appearance has been altered in a more fundamental way, for almost all were originally painted. Only the Salting Diptych with its nineteenth-century colouring gives any impression of how the medieval polychromy was distributed: borders of garments, flesh-tones perhaps, hair certainly were coloured or gilded, so that the whiteness and texture of the ivory was set off by a brilliant palette of gold, red, pink, blues and greens. We have occasional survivors, again none of them English, which show how Gothic ivories would originally have looked.[27]

By *c.* 1200 England could look back on over 200 years of ivory carving, almost always in walrus ivory; the recent Anglo-Saxon and English Romanesque exhibitions illustrated this insular tradition,[28] while chronicles and other sources indicate that English twelfth-century treasuries already boasted many ivories. From *c.* 1180 onwards an insular tradition is more difficult to isolate, because English artists were so closely in touch, and indeed in sympathy, with the latest fashions emanating from the Low Countries/Rhineland and northern France. The two walrus ivories in the English Romanesque exhibition, fragments of a Last Supper and a Deposition (both now in the Victoria and Albert Museum),[29] perhaps of *c.* 1200–10, may or may not be English, so intimately does their style relate to Early Gothic monuments on both sides of the Channel.[30]

As to the impact of the Early Gothic style of northern France in both England and Scandinavia, it creates peculiarly delicate problems of attribution: parallel interpretations of a common stylistic vocabulary, which lead to similar-looking results or, as is usually assumed, leading English artists exporting their interpretations in person to Scandinavia.[31] The Wells façade of *c.* 1220–42 (Cat. 239) represents an episode in the development of English Gothic sculpture which can be closely paralleled in wood and stone sculpture in Norway. For instance, it is remarkably difficult to decide whether wood sculptures like the Enebakk Madonna in Oslo (Cat. 250) are by a Wells sculptor. To this phase belong a mutilated group of the Adoration of the Magi in the British Museum[32] and four walrus-ivory chessmen: three knights (Cat. 146–8) can be dated

on the basis of their armour towards the middle of the thirteenth century. Most remarkable of all is a piece, perhaps a rook, in the form of a castle defended by a king and soldiers (Cat. 145), which even in its sadly battered condition still stands as a small masterpiece of English art of the Wells period, and in its exploitation of realistic detail and 'illusionism' (little figures look out of round windows, like portholes) comparable to sculpture of the Lincoln workshop at Trondheim in Norway (Cat. 299–306). Nothing is more evocative of the taste of the baronial class of Henry III's reign than these small images of knights, soldiers and castles; chess was a favourite pastime, and the thirteenth- and fourteenth-century English inventories contain many references to chess sets ('families'), often of ivory and occasionally magnificent.[33] As for the Hamburg Virgin and Child (Cat. 248), she may again belong to the 'Wells phase' of English art, if indeed she is not Norwegian. The problem is posed, not resolved, by showing her alongside her English and Norwegian contemporaries in wood, one of the rare early thirteenth-century ivory Madonna statuettes to have survived (most of the others are French). As cult images they were to become immensely popular, but nothing could be more remote in mood from this hieratic figure than the lyrical charm of the New York Madonna of *c.* 1300 (Cat. 518). There is documentary evidence to prove that such Virgin cult statuettes were relatively common in England by the end of the thirteenth century.[34]

The three openwork reliefs in Copenhagen (Cat. 307–9) can be assigned to the 1250s, their style and iconography closely related to the work of the Sarum Illuminator; compare particularly the Resurrection (Cat. 309) with the same scene in the Amesbury Psalter (fig. 74, Cat. 316) and in the Missal of Henry of Chichester (Cat. 108). Here English painting supplies the evidence for a firm English attribution of an ivory, even if it is perfectly possible that the shrine or altarpiece from which the reliefs come was made for, indeed in, Denmark. Similar large-scale commissions were executed later, most notably in the fourteenth-century Paris workshops[35] but also in England *c.* 1330, as is proved by the recent discovery in London of a remarkable applied figure of a sleeping soldier from a scene of the Resurrection (fig. 75 – cf. fig. 74 for the sleeping soldiers), which must have been on a scale to compete with the biggest

French reliefs;[36] and *c.* 1320–30, if Cat. 519 is indeed by an English artist. We also catch occasional glimpses in the inventories of big ivory ensembles: at Peterborough in the early fourteenth century Abbot Godfrey presented a towered shrine of ivory, its base decorated with three images showing the story of the Virgin Mary.[37] Ivory reliefs presumably also formed parts of altar antependia and retables; 'tabernacles' are referred to in the documents, and these were either like the small triptychs and polyptychs which have so often survived (Cat. 593, 596), or they could have been bigger altarpieces.

With the ivory Christ at Herlufsholm on Zealand (fig. 76), which is no less than 72 cm high, the Danish owners felt unable to risk its transport to London, and we are thus deprived for the best of reasons of a unique opportunity to test the claim that this, one of the great masterpieces of Early Gothic in Europe, is the work of an English sculptor.[38] The case is nicely balanced between an artistic origin *c.* 1250 in the milieu of Henry III's Court and Westminster, and a Danish sculptor who left his mark on other local but less remarkable ivories.[39] After all, stylistic evidence points strongly to

Fig. 76 Ivory crucifix figure, English(?), mid-thirteenth century, with detail of head (Herlufsholm, Denmark)

Fig. 77 Ivory Virgin and Child, *c.* 1260–80 (Oslo, Kunstindustrimuseet)

the fact that a major Westminster sculptor worked at Trondheim in Norway at this very time in the 1250s (cf. Cat. 290).

The second half of the thirteenth century and the years *c.* 1300 are peculiarly difficult to assess so far as English sculpture goes. Crucial monuments such as Vale Royal Abbey have been destroyed, and there seems to have been a certain conservatism, harking back to the sources of the High Gothic style, which emerges in Paris in the second quarter of the thirteenth century, in England somewhat later, probably in the 1250s. A mutilated ivory Virgin and Child in Oslo (fig. 77) may well be English and, if so, it must be about contemporary with the famous angels of the Lincoln Angel Choir.[40] The Christ in the Victoria and Albert Museum (Cat. 310) seems to belong to the late thirteenth century, as do the Lincoln cloister bosses, but its true place in the English art of the time, if indeed it is English, is enigmatic. Within the context of this exhibition, however, it stands for the Gothic ivory crucifix figure which so seldom avoided the hammers of the Puritans; but which occasionally speaks to us from the inventories,[41] and must have been fairly common. So too were the ivory Virgin statuettes, like Cat. 518. Here at least the attribution to England is less tenuous; together with a Virgin in Yale, which was too fragile to come to the exhibition, it shares a close relationship to some mutilated stone figures at Glastonbury, also of *c.* 1300 and perhaps from a screen or reredos.[42]

To compare the figure (Cat. 518) with Paris sculpture of the same period is to see how far it is still based firmly in the thirteenth century, and how directly this image speaks to us, with none of the svelte elegance of French contemporaries. The expressive Trinity relief (Cat. 519) is, on the contrary, deeply influenced by Parisian art of the succeeding generation, that associated particularly with the name of Jean Pucelle in the 1320s. But then so is a major group of English manuscripts, grouped around the Queen Mary Psalter (cf. Cat. 570), and it may well have been within this artistic milieu that the Trinity ivory was carved. As for the Salting Diptych (Cat. 520), always accepted as an English ivory, probably because its architectural elements are so obviously 'Decorated', it is here dated rather later than has been customary. Instead of a direct relationship with the Westminster Court school *c.* 1300 which is normally proposed, it seems more likely that we should look towards north-eastern England, in fact to sculpture in Yorkshire and particularly the Percy tomb at Beverley of *c.* 1340. This was not originally a diptych, so that the unusual, not to say uneasy relationship between the two leaves, with the blessing Christ a pendant to the Virgin and Child, needs no special explanation. Perhaps the two ivories were framed as front and back elements of a polyptych of wood or metal?

At the same time, in the 1330s but at Exeter, the three ivories with the arms of Bishop John Grandisson were being carved (Cat. 593–6). Their subject-matter reflects absolutely the preferred themes of Exeter and of Bishop John's own personal piety; the Italianism of certain scenes can only be explained in terms of contemporary Siennese panel paintings which John could have brought with him to Exeter from his years at the Papal Court at Avignon. Yet the hand of their sculptor is not easily recognised among the many hundreds of carvings at Exeter. Thus, even when we know where and when these English ivories were carved, we are faced with the anonymity of the artist and the special demands of ivory carving, so different in effect from wood or stone, closer to that of alabaster which was just becoming the medium of high fashion at the very moment when the Salting Diptych and the Grandisson ivories were carved. Finally, it is with the Midlands alabaster production that the pax of the Trinity (Cat. 624) can be most obviously compared. Unfortunately there is no ivory which can be placed confidently within the sphere of the International Gothic of Richard II's London at the end of the fourteenth century.

Few of those secular caskets, mirrors, knife handles, combs and writing implements which were so much a part of the life of the great household in fourteenth-century England can with any degree of probability be attributed to England (with the notable exception of Cat. 428). This may be because such artefacts were imports or carved by foreign artists in England. It could equally well be that these ivories were supposed to look 'French' to meet the demands of fashion, so that with our limited knowledge of who made which Gothic ivories where, we simply cannot recognise the English products.

NOTES

1. Under the microscope, closely similar: MacGregor 1985, pp. 17, 22 n. 9. See Heyd 1885–6, II, pp. 629–30, for the view that most European ivory was African; but this is still an open question.

2. MacGregor 1985, *passim*, for walrus and other ivories, as well as bone, antler and horn.

3. Munch 1864, p. 25.

4. For bone working in Winchester, see Keene 1985, I, p. 282. For bone knife handles, see Howe 1983.

5. Schaube 1906, p. 184. For the African trade, see Heyd 1885–6, I, pp. 9, 35, 379; II, pp. 443, 497, 629–30; Labib 1965, pp. 48, 98, 295, 312, 335, 374.

6. Public Record Office, E. 101/349/18 (Queen Eleanor's household account); [36–7 Henry III] payment '*pro tribus libris et dimidio eboris ad faciendos imagines ad opus regine per manus Ricardi Scriptoris*, xiiis.vd.' (personal communication, Elizabeth Gue).

7. E.g. a richly carved ivory saddle and ivory thrones in *Erec et Enide* (vv. 5335–53, 6713–809, ed. W. Foerster, 1890).

8. Pegolotti 1936, pp. 63, 69, 78, 123, 141.

9. See Heyd 1885–6, I, p. 8 n. 1; Day 1963, I, pp. 269, 487; II, p. 698 (Alexandrian cargoes); I, p. 531 (to Provence); II, p. 725 (to Flanders).

10. Gras 1918, *passim*.

11. For the Aubert family and its origins at Tournai, see Koechlin 1924, I, p. 13.

12. The corporations specialised in types of artefact, not in ivory as such, which was just one of the materials worked: *Paintres et Taillières Ymagiers, Ymagiers-Tailleurs et ceus qui taillent cruchefis, Pingniers et Lanterniers, Coutelliers feseeurs de manches, Ceus qui font Tables à escrire, Deiciers, Pat[r]enotriers*, i.e. painters and carvers of images (probably those who made reliefs, crosiers, tabernacles and statuettes), image carvers and those who carve crucifixes, makers of combs and lanterns, makers of knife handles, those who make writing tablets, dice makers and rosary makers. For the *Livre des Métiers* and other Paris documents, see Lespinasse & Bonnardot 1879, pp. 41, 81, 127, 138, 140, 149; Koechlin 1924, I, pp. 1–34, 531–40. See also Gaborit-Chopin 1978, pp. 16, 131; Randall 1985, pp. 178–88.

13. For references to ivories in the inventory of Henry V's goods (1423), see *Rot. Parl.*, IV; a box and two 'pyndes' (pint-pots?) (p. 221), a pair of flagons with silver-gilt mounts (p. 225), a 'tabulet' with images (p. 226), two pairs of knives with ivory handles (p. 238), a cypress-wood 'tabulet' with ivory images inside (p. 240).

14. For 15th-century cargoes, including ivory, see Gras 1918, pp. 514 (London, 1420/21 – combs), 569, 572, 574, 579 (London, 1509 – ivory, combs and beads), 688 (London, Venetian galley, 1409/12 – combs); Quinn & Ruddock 1937–8, I, pp. 47, 51 (Southampton, 1469–70 – combs); Carus-Wilson 1937 pp. 51 (Bristol, early 16th century, cargo from Flanders – combs), 110 (Bristol, 1456–62, vessel from Bordeaux – ivory). Helen Robinson refers me to several unpublished London ivory cargoes, between 1390 and the mid-15th century: these again confirm that the Italian galleys were mainly involved, that some tusks were still being shipped uncarved but combs were an almost invariable part of such cargoes, and that handles (for knives) and 'refutz' (reject tusks) are mentioned from time to time; there are also references to tables of ivory in 1392, a cross of ivory for a bishop in 1437–8, and an ivory lock in 1438 (Public Record Office, E. 122/71/17, f. 3; 77/3, f. 14; 73/10) (personal communication, Derek Keene, Helen Robinson).

15. Cf. Favier 1974, pp. 346–8.

16. Schlosser 1899.

17. Randall 1985, p. 242.

18. For an extreme view, see Leeuwenberg 1969.

19. For many of the English inventories and wills, see Lehmann-Brockhaus 1955–60, *passim* (index: *ebor, eburneus*, etc). Porter 1974, pp. 195–205, conveniently prints some of these texts, but out of context.

20. Lehmann-Brockhaus 1955–60, no. 2737.

21. Ibid., no. 6264.

22. For the import of combs and a few already carved items in the 15th century, see note 14, above.

23. Ivory carvers do not appear in the long London 14th-century list of crafts, for which see Unwin 1938, pp. 87–8. On the other hand, the cost of ivory is given in the 1507 book of rates; see Gras 1918, p. 699.

24. E.g. a 13th-century ivory-headed staff found in a coffin in St Mary's, Winchester.

25. Williams 1963, pp. 12, 106–7.

26. British Museum, MLA 88, 2–8, 2; cf. Dalton 1909, no. 243; Ottawa 1972, II, p. 153 (no. 70).

27. For recent remarks on polychromy, see Gaborit-Chopin 1978, pp. 15–16, 153 pl. 230, 208; Randall 1985, pp. 186–7.

28. London 1984a; London 1984b.

29. London 1984a, nos 220–21.

30. Sauerländer 1971, p. 512. Already in the 11th and 12th centuries, individual figures or groups are cut out in silhouette, to be glued against flat backgrounds, cf. London 1984b, no. 119; London 1984a, no. 210.

31. Andersson 1950, *passim*.

32. British Museum, MLA 56, 6–23, 145; cf. Dalton 1909, no. 248; New York 1970, I, no. 66; Sauerländer 1971, p. 511.

33. For ivory chess sets, see Lehmann-Brockhaus 1955–60, nos 2969, 6150; see also Murray 1913, pp. 449–50; Porter 1974, p. 200, 203. Three crystal sets, and an ivory board with a set in ivory and ebony, are included in a list of possessions of Hugh Despenser the elder, forfeited in 1321 (1397, the year of petition, is cited by Murray and by Porter); see *Rot. Parl.*, III, p. 363a; *GEC*, vol. IV, p. 264 (Despenser).

34. Lehmann-Brockhaus 1955–60, nos 1913 (Glastonbury, 1292), 1957 (Gloucester, 1284–1306), 6264 (Edward I, 1299–1300).

35. Paris 1981–2, nos 133–8.

36. British Museum, 1986, 6–4, 1; w. 10.2 cm. Perhaps of antler (personal communication, Richard Burleigh). Found on the Thames foreshore in the City of London (Customs House Quay) in 1985. Sold Sotheby's, 22 Apr. 1986, lot 183. The details of the armour (small heart-shaped shield, cut-back surcoat) suggest a date c. 1330 (personal communication, Claude Blair).

37. Lehmann-Brockhaus 1955–60, no. 3510.

38. Young 1977; Gaborit-Chopin 1978, pp. 134, 204; Liebgott 1985, pp. 33 ff.

39. E.g. the Horne book cover and the group of the Adoration of the Magi, both in Copenhagen; see Liebgott 1985, pp. 36–40.

40. Oslo, Kunstindustrimuseet, OK.10875 (unpublished).

41. Lehmann-Brockhaus 1955–60, no. 5885 (St Albans, gift of Richard of Wendover, a canon of St Paul's, London, but it had formerly belonged to Pope Gregory IX [1227–41], i.e. it was an import).

42. Stratford 1983. For an ivory Virgin given to Glastonbury in 1292, see Lehmann-Brockhaus 1955–60, no. 1913.

English Seals in the Thirteenth and Fourteenth Centuries

T. A. Heslop

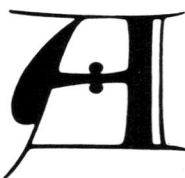lthough the wax impressions of seals in this exhibition are or were once attached to charters, that is to say legal documents, this is not the only way in which they were originally used. Things as varied as personal gifts, or correspondence, caskets of relics, or bundles of wool could be sealed. But no matter what it accompanied, the seal indicated three things; first, the source of the document or object to which it was attached (if it bore the seal of the archbishop, that is who sent it); second, if the seal was used to close something up, that the contents had not been tampered with or exposed since the sealing (if they had been the seal would be broken); and third and most important, it demonstrated authenticity. If the seal was genuine, in theory the thing to which it was attached could only have been issued by or with the consent of the seal's owner, or the person whose office entitled them to use it. From this, in England by the thirteenth century, there followed two legal consequences. On the one hand, if your genuine seal appeared on a document you were bound to honour the contents, but on the other, something without a seal could be regarded as void.

In the burlesque Latin doggerel the *Descriptio Norfolkensium*[1] a group of peasants who can no longer stand the oppression of their lord decide to buy their freedom. He issues them with a sealed charter, and they repair to the tavern to celebrate. Having need of a light as night falls they try to buy a candle, but none is to be had. One of their number, seeing the wax seal with the cord or strip of parchment passing through it, suggests that it would make an excellent substitute:

> *Pendet ad cartulam cera pulcherima*
> *Qua potest fieri candela nimia*[2]

and so, temporarily, they lighten their darkness. Their lord hears this with glee, knowing that he can reduce them to servitude once more. For the document has no legal validity without its authenticating seal. The point of this story, which is to ridicule rustics, would be lost if the world at large had not known that the seal was crucial as validation.

The seal's importance as an authenticating sign led to various felonies, such as forgery and misappropriation (forgery of royal seals was counted as high treason). These are commonly cited reasons for the making of a replacement die. At Salisbury Cathedral the disruption caused by the Interdict allowed repeated misuse (*multiplices excessus*) of the chapter's seal and so, in 1214, a new one was commissioned.[3] Other cathedral chapters and monastic convents may have felt the same need, since stylistic evidence suggests that there was an upsurge of seal-making activity shortly after the end of King John's quarrel with the papacy. But mismanagement and falsification are recorded less frequently than those other banes, simple theft and the sealing of blank charters. The danger of the latter was that any financial or contractual commitment could subsequently be written on the pristine parchment, and because it bore a genuine seal it would still be legally binding. Renegades were prone to taking blank charters with them, and such action usually resulted in a flurry of disclaimers which were the medieval equivalent of our reactions when a banker's card or credit card gets stolen.[4]

The importance of guarding the seal matrices of major institutions resulted in their providing small, iron-bound chests in which to put them. These had several locks (usually four), each with a different key kept under separate custody. It was only when all the keyholders were together and in accord that a matrix could be taken out and a document sealed. Careful storage of private matrices was also a matter of concern;

husbands were advised not to leave their seal where wife or servants might find it, since it might be used irresponsibly to run up debts or other obligations which they would then be bound to honour.

There were a number of choices which confronted someone wishing to have a seal made. To begin with an engraver had to be found, but such people were not concentrated within a single specialised craft. A matrix made of silver, or very rarely gold, would be produced by a goldsmith, whereas base-metal seals probably would not be. Nearly all the surviving documentation, whether general legislation or relating to individual commissions, concerns dies of precious metal. This is because of the larger quantities of money involved and because records are preserved only from the upper levels of society. From these we learn, for example, that the kings always approached either a goldsmith of London or a master of the mint, who would himself be a goldsmith. In the latter cases it is not always clear that it was the master who made the object. Instructions such as 'you should cause to have made' (cf. Cat. 276) might imply that the work was to be farmed out.

As well as royalty many of the wealthier institutions, both ecclesiastical and secular, and private individuals wanted matrices of precious metal (Cat. 454–5, 198). Making these might involve techniques of greater complexity than just engraving. For example when an engraved stone was set into a mount it had to be soldered at a relatively low temperature because of the danger of heat cracking the gem. In practice this meant that it had to be of gold or silver. One of the difficulties facing the purchaser of a gem matrix was knowing how much of the weight of the finished object was precious metal, and how much was stone or padding. Statutes, for example that of 1300, required goldsmiths to be honest when assessing the quantities so as not to overcharge customers for the raw materials.[5] Short of taking the object to pieces again there was not, and still is not, an easy way of achieving an accurate estimate. Apart from the setting of gems there were two other reasons for having a silver matrix. It was prestigious, and it was also easier to cut and hence achieve a fine finish. This helps to explain why the quality of the 'art' is usually high, but it is not the whole explanation. Skill in figure drawing and lettering were obviously essential for a medieval goldsmith. We are badly informed about the teaching methods of their apprenticeship systems, but it is clear from the records that someone who made seals of silver would also have made belt buckles and drinking cups and must have had a wide training.[6]

In the middle and at the lower end of the market matrices were usually of bronze, though in the early thirteenth century lead was quite widely used. Some of these seem to have been made by specialist seal makers called *sigillarius* or *factor sigillorum* in the records. But an instance was recently discovered of a 'latoner', that is someone who worked in high-grade copper alloy and produced such things as monumental brasses, making a seal for a royal official in Plymouth.[7]

It is natural for us to suppose that a craftsman had a workshop in one centre and that customers came to him to place a commission. All of the seals attributed to Walter de Ripa are likely to have been made in London. Geographically the most remote of his seals so far discovered was the result of a commission from no further afield than Colchester.[8] The works of other makers also show local concentration. Four early fourteenth-century seals of Norfolk religious houses by a single engraver suggest the existence of a workshop catering for the area between Lynn and Norwich.[9] Three of the four seals of Richard of Bury (e.g. Cat. 685, but not Cat. 686) are by the hand of an artist who worked for a contemporary bishop of Carlisle, which implies his residence at a centre in the north of England.[10] On the other hand some distribution patterns are more enigmatic. Oliver Sutton's counterseal as bishop of Lincoln is by the artist who made the beautiful seal of Oseney Abbey, just outside Oxford, c. 1290 (fig. 78).[11] One engraver working in the mid-1330s was employed by monasteries as distant as Quarr, Isle of Wight and Louth Park, Lincolnshire.[12] Another, who made the matrix for Southwick Priory, Hampshire (Cat. 462) seems also to have been employed by the city of Carlisle. One faces the temptation in these cases to suggest London as a place of origin simply because it must have been the most visited city in the kingdom, as well as having a thriving community of goldsmiths and other craftsmen. Against this easy assumption one may caution that some engravers clearly did travel. An item in the

Fig. 78 Seal from Oseney Abbey, c. 1290: photograph from a cast (Society of Antiquaries of London)

Canterbury Cathedral accounts for 1221 records 4s.1d spent on preparing the little house for Simon, the goldsmith, for making the new seal,[13] and this suggests that he had no established workplace near at hand. More study is needed before the implications of the various patterns of distribution can be fully worked out. At present the evidence is as contradictory as it is for other media, such as manuscript illumination. But because seals are so often made for known patrons they should eventually yield a clear picture of the relative instances of centralised as against local production on the one hand, and of itinerant craftsmen on the other.

The form a seal took was constrained by tradition in a number of ways. Size, for example, seems to have been indicative of status. If it was large, it belonged to an important person or institution (the reverse does not necessarily follow). There are instances where a seal matrix was renewed because the size of its predecessor was no longer considered appropriate (Cat. 195). Increase in size may be referred to in descriptions (Cat. 670), and the relative size of the seals used within an institution, for example a diocese, mirrors the overall hierarchy. There are some indications that attempts to produce a grandiose seal could result in censure. Early in 1283 the priory of Great Malvern, in Worcestershire, wrote to its parent house, Westminster Abbey, explaining that a new common seal had been adopted by the priory because the old one had been misappropriated. An impression of the new seal is attached; it measures 87×64 mm.[14] Within a very short time yet another seal appears, apparently by the same maker, which is significantly smaller (78×54 mm). It is tempting to suppose that this scaling down of their aspirations was as a result of criticism of their earlier hubris.

For the vast majority of seals it was not only size that was determined by convention, but subject-matter as well. Virtually all the seals of noble lords in the thirteenth century show them in armour, on horseback, with some heraldic indication of their descent. Similarly, nearly all thirteenth-century bishops are shown standing (but see Cat. 285-6), and without exception they wear episcopal garb, hold a crosier in the left hand and bless with the right (e.g. Cat. 281). Slightly different patterns were followed in various other parts of Europe, but the differences are not so great that they render the meaning of the image unintelligible. European seals among the international élite of institutions and lay and ecclesiastical magnates speak essentially the same language. Civic and royal seals as much as episcopal ones can have a strong family resemblance. Where seals differ most is at the lower end of the market. Here regional distinctions are stronger and the range of options wider, and perhaps this is because these cultures were more segregated by language and by lack of opportunity for travel than was the case in high society.

Looked at in a negative sense this essential uniformity, or at least the very slow rate of change, at the upper end of the market could be taken as evidence of a serious lack of artistic invention. If we adopt this attitude, however, we entirely mistake the intention of both artists and patrons, and the purpose of seals. Patrons wanted an image that was readily understandable in terms of a pre-existing vocabulary. Artists must frequently have been given a brief which specified that a basic model should be followed, with perhaps one or two variations (see Cat. 143, 278). What mattered most in the execution of the work must therefore have been performance rather than invention. Perhaps the common function of a seal, which was to 'stabilise' an agreement, also meant that anything innovatory in the design would be suspect.

For reasons that are not at all clear, the period from about 1280 saw far more experimentation than had been common earlier in the thirteenth century. Once again this is most noticeable at the lower end of the market. In particular the range of animal motifs was considerably extended, and combinations of animal, human and emblematic devices allowed for much greater invention and variety. This has its counterpart in legends, where the French and English vernaculars become far more common than hitherto, and the message is extended far beyond simple statements of the 'Seal of Jack Smith' type. A particularly playful and enigmatic example is the seal of Thomas Fishborne (fig. 79). The image shows a hare being borne by a fish! The legend HER IS N[O MOR]E BOT A FISCH AND HAR[15] encourages us in the idea that there is indeed more to the image than meets the eye; it is an excellent conceit. The

Fig. 79 Seal of Thomas Fishborne, *c.* 1300–15 (London, Public Record Office, E43/561)

Fig. 80 Seal of Walter de Grendon, *c.* 1320–35: photograph from a cast (Society of Antiquaries of London)

Fig. 81 Seal of John de Warenne, *c.* 1306(?): photograph from a cast (Oxford, Magdalen College)

wonderful seal of Walter de Grendon shows the Man in the Moon with his dog and his bundle of thorns (fig. 80). This is an earlier expression of the folk belief that re-emerges in Shakespeare's representation of Moonshine in *A Midsummer Night's Dream*.[16] The legend, in Latin, may be translated as 'Why do I carry thorns from the sun, I will teach you, Walter!' Nothing so inventive as these two seals had appeared in the first eighty or ninety years of the thirteenth century, but in the years around 1300 there is a steady trickle of them. In rare cases the effects of this experimentation and wit are found higher up the social scale. John de Warenne, Earl of Surrey, uses the conventional equestrian image on one side of his seal and shield of arms on the other. But the latter is seen against a woodland backdrop inhabited by stags, swans and other birds, a squirrel, a porcupine(?) and, crucially, rabbits (fig. 81). The rabbits matter because they indicate that this is a warren, and hence the scene is a canting reference to John's name.[17] These three examples should not be taken as representative, but they do serve to indicate that there was a new freedom of approach to the business of seal design. The motivation for this must have come from the patrons at least as much as from the artists, but there was certainly no shortage of talent among the engravers who were available to fulfil the commissions.

At a conservative estimate some 30,000 English seals survive from the period covered by this exhibition. Choosing fifty for display thus involves telling a very partial story, or rather sketching out only a few episodes in a complex saga. None the less, the principles which underly the commissioning and execution of these few may with reasonable safety be extended to apply to the vast majority of what must have been a huge total output.

NOTES

I should like to express my thanks to Elizabeth Wright for reading and commenting on this and my other typescript, and to J. A. Goodall for his enthusiastic help with the heraldry.

1. *Descriptio Norfolkensium* in Wright 1844, pp. 94–106, and better in Rigg 1965, pp. 146–56, and notes pp. 356–70. The version with the seal episode is found in Cambridge, Trinity College MS O.9.38.
2. 'There hangs on the charter some very fine wax/Which could serve as a great big candle . . .'
3. Wordsworth & Macleane 1915, pp. 40–1; and Lehmann-Brockhaus 1955–60, no. 6387.
4. For example the Oseney Chronicle, in Luard, 1869, pp. 109–10; and see Heslop 1986b, pp. 269–70.
5. Heslop 1986a, p. 52, for the techniques; Henig & Heslop 1986, p. 306, n. 9 for the legislation.
6. Henry Lyrpol was accused of making the harness for a girdle, cups and a seal of false silver; see Reddaway & Walker 1975, pp. 4–5.
7. Blair 1985, p. 129
8. Birch 1887, I, no. 2985.
9. Ibid., nos 3050 (Premonstratensians of Dereham), 3292 (Benedictine priory of Horsham

St Faith), 3585 (Carmelite Friars of King's Lynn), 4296 (Augustinian priory of Westacre).
10. Heslop 1980, *passim*.
11. Birch 1887, I, nos 1721 reverse (Oliver Sutton), 3801–4 (Oseney). The date of the latter is suggested in VCH, *Oxfordshire*, II, 1907, on the basis of Wood 1890, II, p. 214. This states that the Jews forged the old Oseney seal during Abbot Roger's time (1285–97) and this is likely to have been the cause of making a new one.
12. Heslop 1986b, p. 279.
13. Heslop 1982, pp. 94–5.
14. Westminster Abbey, Muniments 22944.
15. Ellis 1981, p. 1397, on a charter of 1316, and compare Greenwell & Blair 1911, VIII, DS. 1478, of 1292–5.
16. Ellis 1978, p. 348; for the Man in the Moon see Emerson 1906, pp. 840–5.
17. This is the first of John's seals as Earl of Surrey (1306?–47); for his second seal see Hope 1915, pp. 4–5. This photograph is from a cast at Magdalen College, Oxford and is reproduced with the kind permission of the President and Fellows. Sadly, the original impression is not now traceable.

Woodwork

ngland can boast the finest collection of thirteenth- and fourteenth-century ecclesiastical woodwork in Europe. The richness of our inheritance is such as to enable the art historian to reconstruct the medieval furnishing of, say, a great church, despite the subsequent alterations, destruction and decay of the last seven hundred years. On the other hand, our medieval domestic furniture has largely disappeared, as has most of that of Europe. Attempts to reconstruct the interior furnishing of palaces and castles must depend upon the written testimony of contemporary literature, wills, financial accounts and inventories, and the visual representations afforded us in illuminated manuscripts and panel paintings.

In the often frustrating but rewarding study of medieval art we are sometimes made privy to the most trivial details concerning an object whose fate has either gone quite unrecorded or is definitely known to have been an unhappy one. For instance, the Close Rolls for the 1240s provide the first record of an English state bed, in the medieval Palace of Westminster. It was presumably a four-poster with a wooden canopy.[1] It had green posts powdered with gold stars and was painted by Master William for twenty marks. A few years earlier we find the king personally specifying the details of the furnishings in the chapel of St Peter at the Tower of London. He stipulates: '... the stalls made for the king and queen, are to be well and suitably wainscotted ... painted and the small figure of St Mary with her tabernacle, the images of St Peter, St Nicholas, and St Katharine, the beam above the altar of St Peter, and the small cross with its images are to be repainted and refreshed with good colours.'

What remains to us of domestic furniture is a few chests – a tiny fraction of the original number – and a bench, a table, and perhaps a cupboard or two. The domestic equipment of our ancestors – beds, settles, forms, tables, 'copebordes' (buffets), cupboards ('armoires'), chairs, stools, and cradles have vanished. By comparison, surviving ecclesiastical furniture is strikingly plentiful and varied: choir stalls, parclose and rood screens, sedilia, Easter sepulchres, bishops' thrones, lecterns, pulpits, font covers, alms boxes, cope chests, and cupboards.[2] Much of it has been terribly neglected and misused, and has suffered misguided restoration. But it is, notwithstanding, a priceless legacy.

The chest was the commonest and most ubiquitous item of medieval furniture. At Château Cornillon, in Burgundy, which boasted forty-two chambers and offices, seventy-four chests were listed.[3] In the Middle Ages there were so many different kinds of chest that several words were used to describe them – *arche*, *bahut*, *cista*, *coffre*, *huche*, etc. Some chests were intended to stay put like the primitive 'dug-out' and iron-banded planked types still to be found in churches today. On the other hand there was a very large class of chest or 'trunk' designed for carriage. Either on account of the value of their contents – textiles and clothing, plate, jewellery – or, occasionally, the fine workmanship of the chest itself – an outer casing of hardened leather was provided for protection from the knocks and jolts of a medieval excursion. These trunks were loaded on to great horse-drawn covered wagons like the ones depicted in the pages of the mid-fourteenth-century Luttrell Psalter (Cat. 575), or carts. Much smaller 'sumpter' chests were designed to be carried on horseback.

Large decorated chests, like Cat. 103 remind us that coffers would have been nearly always adorned in some way, either carved, displaying decorative ironwork (fig. 121), or painted. The Richard of Bury chest (Cat. 523), made for the use of an important administrative establishment to store deeds and other legal documents, was painted inside the lid as well as, presumably, outside, as was the chest in Newport Church, Essex (Cat. 345).

Chests were commissioned by secular magnates such as Robert of Bethune, Count of Flanders, in whose inventory of 1322 we read: '*Item, une huge qui est en le tressorie del eglise de Courtray*'.[4] There may well have been occasions when a deposited chest was never reclaimed. Moreover, we know that inheritance coffers were often given to the warding institution at the coming-of-age as a thank offering. Chests had a bewilderingly large number of functions. At Oxford and Cambridge colleges, in the great religious houses, and in every parish church, they were used for storing books. Moreover, in a church they were essential for keeping vestments and plate. They also served as collecting boxes, being provided with a slot for money in the lid, and a till underneath, with a secret compartment below. In 1206 Pope Innocent II mandated on behalf of the Crusades that Christians should put their offerings in a hollow 'trunk'. To prevent the possibility of fraud, a system of three locks and key holders was introduced. The holders – the parish priest and, probably, two church wardens – had to be present together before the chest could be opened. In a secular context chests would be used as a tradesman's counter (cf. Cat. 204). They had many mundane functions also, for storing candles, corn, bread, spices, tools, salted meat, paints, saddles and harness, or medicines.

From the very considerable body of surviving English ecclesiastical furniture of the thirteenth and fourteenth centuries, most of it fitted and still *in situ*, it is the choir stalls which must bear the palm. The form started in England in the standard northern European mid-thirteenth-century type of either plain canopy-less seating, as at Salisbury Cathedral,[5] or the fully-canopied 'double-screen' design, as formerly at Westminster Abbey. The extraordinary early fourteenth-century double-screen choir stalls at Winchester Cathedral (Cat. 528; fig. 84), however, with their arrangement of two seats per bay surmounted by an elaborate and intricately carved superstructure, signalled a tendency in England to experiment. There is nothing in Europe at this time to compare with the Winchester stalls for size, ingenuity and architectural ambition.

As the century advanced they became progressively more daring – at Ely, Gloucester, Lincoln (fig. 82) and, finally, at Chester (fig. 83). Ely, like Winchester, was a brave attempt to amplify the French prototype. But it was the aesthetic of Perpendicular architecture which enabled the master carpenter eventually to discard the traditional conventions and create a style that best exploited the medium. The fibrous nature of wood offers the possibility, which English master carpenters grasped, of creating tall, insubstantial structures liberated from a mason's servitude to gravity. The Rayonnant aesthetic, which carried on into the fourteenth century, of the repetitive replication of standard units of design, inevitably imparted a static, earthbound character to the movement.

Fig. 82 Lincoln Cathedral choir stalls, *c.* 1370

Fig. 83 Chester Cathedral choir stalls, *c.* 1390

Fig. 84 Winchester Cathedral choir stalls, *c.* 1308–10

Another potential of wood is the ability to create forms by building up from a body of component parts. Joiners exploited this to produce highly-wrought complex canopies. These did not weigh very much because they were assembled from thin carved members glued and nailed together. The combination of tenuous verticality and intricate, almost metalwork-like detailing produced in buildings such as Lincoln, Chester and Nantwich a new impressionistic effect quite different in kind from Rayonnant, and distinct from, although not unrelated to, English Perpendicular. Without doubt the choir stalls at Lincoln, c. 1370, are an early manifestation of late Gothic. Yet the attention to detail ensures that on every arch each crocket is still individually treated, and a different species of foliage represented. At the same time, when seen from afar, the component motifs of the design start to merge one into another to produce an effect very considerably enhanced by the overall application of gaudy colour and gilding.

On a great set of choir stalls there would have been surprisingly few operatives. Even at Lincoln Cathedral, where there were 110 seats, probably only two carvers worked on the misericords (if a misericord took a month to carve, two men could have completed the job in about four years). It is occasionally possible to follow an artist from one monument to another. And hard evidence can be adduced on occasion that one designer copied the work of another. One of the important opportunities that English medieval woodwork offers the art historian is to monitor the development of architectural ornament. Misericords, in particular, offer a treasury of foliage specimens many of which, because they are attached to important monuments, are datable. Specimens of foliage in stone can be so weathered that they are of little use, whereas the examples in wood are often as good as new. The career of the voluted 'trefoil' leaf in the fourteenth century (Cat. 533), a motif which crops up in all media, can be plotted precisely in woodwork.

The extent to which the carpenter in the thirteenth and early fourteenth centuries was in the thrall of the mason has been the subject of much debate. However, we have only to recognise the social and economic importance of master carpenters such as William Hurley and Hugh Herland in the fourteenth century to realise that this is most unlikely to have been the case. The master mason was dependent upon the carpenter for the centerings of his arches and the provision of scaffolding. The absolute interdependence of the crafts is nowhere better exemplified than in the fabric accounts of Exeter Cathedral[6] where the coordination of specialist effort can be seen to represent the very bedrock of the building process. Whilst the mason needed the carpenter, by the same token, the carpenter looked to the mason for foundations; to the smith for nails, hinges and tools; to the painter for the all-important embellishment of his handiwork; and to others for glue, fish skin, and the other necessities of his craft. There is also much evidence that a good carver was equally confident with wood or stone.

To revert to the argument about inter-craft influence: if anything, the impulse may have been in the other direction, from carpenter to mason. Thirteenth-century oak screens, such as those at Rochester Cathedral, Stanton Harcourt, Oxfordshire, and St Mary's Hospital, Chichester are essentially unrelated in design to contemporary stone masonry. It has been suggested that such designs in wood may have developed from the form of temporary tribunes used by the king in tournaments.[7] The introduction of the three-tier cornice in early fourteenth-century architecture may be derived from wooden furniture. Moreover the introduction of the technique of panelled construction in furniture in the middle of the thirteenth century may, it has been adduced, have been the inspiration for the tracery panelling at St Stephen's Chapel, Westminster, and later the stiff rectangular window tracery of Perpendicular architecture. The Exeter Cathedral bishop's throne, with its audacious presentation of the cusped nodding ogee arch, the first such in England to be used on a large scale, could only have been the conception of a master carpenter (Cat. 488). The use of reticulated ornament was another innovation copied later by masons, as at Wells.

High-class woodcarving and joinery, as opposed to most structural woodwork, was still a peripatetic trade in this period. Master carpenters, like their mason colleagues, were of the gentry class. A master carver could also attain the same status in recognition of his genius as an artist. Such men travelled widely, associating closely with great prelates, magnates and officers of state. In the day of the packhorse as the

Fig. 85 Eagle lectern from Exeter Cathedral, *c.* 1320 (Exeter, Church of St Thomas)

NOTES

1. Eames 1977, p. 75.
2. Howard & Crossley 1917, 1927.
3. Eames 1977, p. 108 n. 280.
4. Eames 1977, p. 110 n. 281.
5. Tracy 1987a, pp. 5–7, pls I, 12–25.
6. Erskine 1981–3.
7. Bony 1979, p. 21.
8. Harvey 1984, p. 226. However, most of the fabric accounts of the greater churches have long since disappeared.
9. Erskine 1981–3, p. 71.

fastest means of passenger transport it is surprising how quickly and how far new fashions spread. At the same time we must expect to contend with a deep innate conservatism. Among the up-to-date diaper ornament of a mid-fourteenth-century lectern (Cat. 105) lurks an elephant typical of an early thirteenth-century bestiary!

The surviving accounts of the royal works confirm the importance of the few privileged craftsmen called upon to work for the Court. We know how much they were paid and the details of their considerable perquisites. In connection with ecclesiastical commissions, which in the fourteenth century overshadowed royal works in importance, we are less well informed. We do know that Master Page of Newport, Essex, who in 1317 had agreed to make new choir stalls for Hatfield Regis Priory, received thirty pounds and substantial allowances for the duration of his employment. He was entitled to two white loaves a day, a gallon of ale, and cold meat or fish from the kitchen or four herrings or six eggs.[8]

At Exeter Cathedral, however, the surviving records provide some compensation for this. The design and manufacture of the bishop's throne (Cat. 488), the only structure of its kind in Europe of that date, is recorded in minute detail. In the summer of 1313 the item 'Cost of timber for the bishop's throne'[9] appears in the fabric rolls. The material for its construction was obtained from the bishop's woods at Newton and Chudleigh at a cost of £6.12s.8½d. Master Thomas of Winton, the master mason resident at Winchester at that time, came to Exeter and selected the timber. In the summer of 1317 it is recorded that Robert of Galmeton and his associate William of Membiri, both evidently Devonians, made the throne at the contract price of four pounds. According to a recent analysis of the monument by the Exeter Archaeological Unit it seems that the final design represents an amendment to the original intention. We find that medieval craftsmen often resorted to making the design up as they went along. At least two other examples of this practice in woodwork could be cited: at Ely (Cat. 532) and at Gloucester. Such methods manifest a lack of day-to-day supervision by the designer, and the relative autonomy of the craftsmen on the spot.

Many of the most important examples of woodwork are part of the structure of the building for which they were made. For an appreciation of the glories of English structural carpentry such as the rib-vaulted ceiling of St Albans Abbey choir, or the open hammer-beam roof at Westminster Hall, London, it is necessary to seek the monuments out for oneself. There are, however, a few cases where fitted furniture or structural woodwork has become detached from its original situation because the building has been demolished or for other reasons. The roof bosses from Bishop Grandisson's extension to the bishop's palace at Exeter have been preserved since 1865 in the Victoria and Albert Museum (Cat. 590–2). A canopy from the choir stalls at St Katharine's-by-the-Tower (Cat. 533), a large royal charitable college demolished to make way for the new St Katharine's Dock in 1826, was preserved in the former Royal Architectural Museum, and bought by the V & A in 1921. Fragments of carving from the Winchester, Lincoln and Wells cathedral choir stalls have been accumulated by the same museum. A fragment of the early fourteenth-century choir stalls at Exeter Cathedral, given during the seventeenth century to a parish church in the city, has been built into a chantry door of the cathedral (Cat. 522). This chance survival is lucky since the ejected woodwork was destroyed by bombing in 1942. Another *disjectum membrum* from Exeter Cathedral is the remarkable early fourteenth-century lectern (fig. 85). This and the lecterns in the exhibition (Cat. 104–5) are the earliest English specimens to survive. Another very rare object is the putative pyx canopy from Wells Cathedral (Cat. 102), a valued refugee from institutionalised iconoclasm. But without doubt the most spectacular woodwork monument in the exhibition is the pair of choir stalls from Lancaster Parish Church (Cat. 524). Most choir furniture has been on the move for centuries, and has suffered grievously in consequence. At least in this instance, where a set of furniture has been arbitrarily and ruthlessly chopped up into different parts, we are afforded a segment which is eminently exhibitable! The Lancaster stalls are one of the most impressive sets of English medieval church furniture in England. They manifest in a brilliant way the flowering of the Decorated style in the north of England, itself a phenomenon of great importance. Their decoration might seem untypically exotic, yet they are as indigenous as *Quercus sessiflora*, the oak of northern England from which they were almost certainly made.

Christa Grössinger   Misericords

Day and night for a monk were divided into long periods of prayer and devotion in a standing position.[1] Misericords were invented to give support to old and sick monks, who could lean against the upturned seats, without actually sitting down.

The thirteenth-century misericords at Hemingborough, North Yorkshire, and Christchurch (Cat. 251) still give an impression of the block of wood underneath the ledge, which has been broken up into patterns of foliage or a combination of foliage and dragons. Trefoil or cinquefoil was the type of foliage used; this is also well represented by the Exeter Cathedral misericords which adorn the earliest remaining set of stalls in England (_c._ 1230–60). Over the long period of carving, the trefoil pattern there changes to a more naturalistic type of foliage. From the beginning, except at Gloucester Cathedral, supporters were added; a uniquely English feature. At Exeter interaction takes place between the central motif and the supporter, in the case of the centaur who shoots backwards at a dragon forming the supporter (fig. 86). There is also experimentation with a large variety of figural and animal motifs which have parallels in contemporary stone carvings and manuscript illuminations.

The animals and foliage in Winchester Cathedral (_c._ 1308–10) are naturalistic, although in a hard style comparable to that of a stonemason (Cat. 528). A development of these motifs can be found in the profusion of wildlife and domestic scenes in the misericords of Wells Cathedral (_c._ 1330–40) treated in a more delicate style.

The misericords of Winchester Cathedral are from a period when marginal subjects became a favourite device of manuscript illuminations, and a parallel development can be seen in the decoration of the misericords in Ely Cathedral (_c._ 1339–41) where the scenes in the supporters become more complex and are often related to the central scene, thus expanding the narrative. While earlier misericords rendered a single motif, the Ely misericords show complete scenes with a story to them, often placed in architectural settings (Cat. 106).

As the stories expanded, so the problem of fitting the desired figures into the given space increased. These difficulties are exemplified in Lincoln Minster, where complex agricultural scenes have been squeezed into the confines of the misericords; for example, two men ploughing a field with the help of two oxen and two horses are made to move around in a circle, with one of the horse's heads turned at a sharp angle. In a comparable marginal illumination (the Luttrell Psalter, Cat. 575, f. 170), men and beasts can move horizontally on even ground (figs 87, 88). The Gloucester misericords (_c._ 1350) have no supporters, enabling the figures to move in sweeping style across the whole width of the misericord (fig. 89). There are many examples of reclining figures, and in scenes like St Michael slaying the dragon, St Michael spears the dragon, not standing upright but from a horizontal position. Many of the scenes on the Worcester Cathedral misericords are placed on pedestals which create a stage for them and lift them off the background, giving them a more sculptural quality.

Dating misericords presents difficulties: the type of foliage, style of costumes and armour can give only an approximate date, as carvers often copied from earlier models. The shapes of the seat ledges, too, can give a very general indication of date as they change from a semi-oval curve in the thirteenth century to a concave front with central point in the late fourteenth century.[2]

The names of misericord carvers are unrecorded and more than one master would have worked on the larger sets. Some of the misericords in Exeter Cathedral have what seems to be a carver's mark of concentric circles, and the consistency of style and long

Fig. 86   Exeter Cathedral misericord showing a centaur shooting a dragon, _c._ 1230–60

period of carving suggest that a very small number of carvers was responsible for them. The larger centres influenced the surrounding parishes; for example the Worcester models were transmitted to Malvern, Worcestershire, and Astley, Warwickshire, and the style and iconography of the Wells Cathedral misericords were transmitted to Hereford Cathedral and then to All Saints, Hereford. Closest of all are the associations between the misericords of Lincoln and Chester cathedrals (*c.* 1370 and *c.* 1380–90) and then Nantwich Parish Church (*c.* 1400), where the style deteriorates, indicating the movement of carvers from one centre to another and the use of pattern books.[3] A scene which did have to be invented in Chester was that concerning St Werburgh, the saint to whom Chester Cathedral is dedicated.

Fig. 87 Lincoln Cathedral misericord depicting ploughing, *c.* 1370

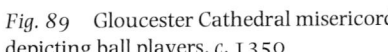

Fig. 88 (above right) Ploughing: marginal illustration from the Luttrell Psalter, *c.* 1325–35 (London, British Library, Add. MS 42130, f. 170; Cat. 575)

Fig. 89 Gloucester Cathedral misericord depicting ball players, *c.* 1350

The subject-matter of misericords is rarely religious, and only the Worcester Cathedral misericords have Old Testament scenes, probably because of a tradition of typological wall paintings of the twelfth century in the chapter house.[4] Generally, the carvers delighted in humorous depictions from everyday life, fables, proverbs and romances, and the large number of misericords required an imaginative repertory of monstrous beasts and foliage. There is rarely a consistent scheme of iconography, indicating that the carvers were free to choose their subject-matter, probably according to the availability of patterns. The monsters depicted are exactly those which St Bernard had already condemned in 1125, fearing their power of distraction from holy thoughts:[5] monkeys, lions, fighting knights, hunters, monstrous centaurs, half-human beings, many bodies with one head or many heads with one body. The animals carved on the misericords are generally of mythical and symbolic types, for example a lion fighting a dragon, symbolising Good fighting Evil: patterns for these could be copied from the bestiary. However, only a small selection of animals is repeated, probably those of which the carvers understood the symbolic meaning,[6] such as the pelican which feeds its young with its own blood, as Christ shed His blood on the Cross for the salvation of humanity; or the unicorn which could only be caught when it laid its head in the lap of a virgin, symbolic of Christ, born of a virgin and crucified. The elephant was usually depicted as a war machine with a tower on its back, but the example in Exeter Cathedral looks very natural, except for its hooves, and can be identified as an African elephant. In 1255 Louis IX of France presented an elephant to Henry III, of which Matthew Paris made a drawing from life (British Library MS Cotton Nero D. I f. 169v.), and the Exeter carver may have used a sketch similar to that of Matthew Paris.[7]

In order to hold the attention of their parishioners, preachers would often spice their sermons with anecdotal matter, everyday events and romances. The English Benedictine monk Odo of Cheriton (d. 1247) used animal fables for his parable-sermons. The fox as the cunning deceiver became very popular, and on a misericord in Chester Cathedral the fox, as described in the bestiary, lies on his back and feigns death; the birds come to peck at him and are unexpectely snatched by him. Generally, the story is taken from the Romance of Reynard the Fox, and the most common illustration is that of the fox making off with the goose. On a misericord at Ely Cathedral, a housewife is following the fox in hot pursuit with her distaff – a new addition. In the left supporter of the same misericord the fox stands preaching to a cock and two hens, disguised in a monk's cowl and holding a pastoral staff. In the supporter of the fox feigning death in Nantwich Parish Church, the foxes, dressed in friars' habits, are revealed as hunters; one is armed with bow and arrows, the other is carrying his loot of rabbit and goose. In this way wandering friars who travelled around the countryside preaching were satirised, because they had become notorious for their greed and for failing to adhere to their vow of poverty. The congregation would fall victim to the wiles of the friar as the geese would to the cunning of the fox. Also popular from medieval romances were the Flight of Alexander the Great (Cat. 530), Tristram and Isolde meeting under the tree (Cat. 535), the portcullis falling on Sir Ywain and his horse, and wodehouses or wild men (Cat. 537). The last three were first used by the Lincoln carvers and transmitted to Chester.

In scenes of everyday life women as viragos are most prevalent, possibly because of adverse preaching, women being castigated as temptresses, leading men to sin. They are usually seen victorious in the battle of the sexes, grabbing men by their hair or beards and belabouring them with washing beetles or distaffs (Cat. 538). Also, women were considered great gossips, worst of all in church. A misericord in Stepney, The Royal Foundation of St Katharine, Butcher Row, shows two women in the grasp of the Devil while a subordinate devil, Tutivillus, in the left supporter, takes down their chatter, to be reproduced on the Day of Judgement (see pp. 35, 41). The same happens to a couple at Ely Cathedral. Women's finery, and especially the horned headdress, was considered the snare of the Devil, who found a cosy abode between the horns.

The Christian was always reminded of the temptations of the Devil. Thus a mermaid is often seen with her comb and mirror, symbols of vanity, bent on seduction, or with a fish in her grasp, representing the successful catch of a Christian soul. The monkey, as the most nearly human of animals, is most suitable to mock human behaviour and is often shown examining a urine flask, in derision of the medical profession. Music-making was often associated with animals such as the pig, symbol of lust and lechery (fig. 90). Music, especially from the pipe and tabor or the bagpipes, would bring out man's animal instincts and lead to wild dancing and sinful abandonment (Cat. 531). Gambling and drinking, helped along by women, would eventually lead out into the jaws of Hell. Other diversions included wrestling, bear-baiting, ball games and hunting, and also more serious pursuits such as agriculture and the Labours of the Months (Cat. 219–20).

On the whole, therefore, misericords lack religious scenes, although some seemingly humorous depictions have moral implications. The playfulness of the subject-matter relates them to marginal drolleries, and in important cases sources of inspiration may have been illuminated manuscripts; but more often the craftsmen derived their ideas from pattern books or other misericords in neighbouring centres.

Fig. 90 Winchester Cathedral misericord depicting musical dogs and pigs, *c.* 1308–10

NOTES

1. The Offices to be said daily were Matins, soon after midnight, followed by Lauds, Prime, Terce, Sext, Nones, Vespers and Compline. There was also a High Mass every day, attended by the whole community.
2. Remnant 1969, p. xx.
3. Anderson 1967.
4. Cox (Anderson) 1959.
5. St Bernard's letter or *Apologia* to William, Abbot of St-Thierry, *c.* 1125.
6. Anderson in Remnant 1969, p. xxvi.
7. Ibid., p. xxix.

David Park Wall Painting

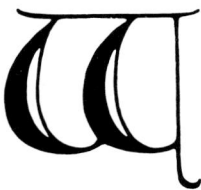

all paintings are integral to their support, and so are subject to the vicissitudes of the buildings they adorn – to alteration and to deterioration. They are superficial and easily eradicated. Particular susceptibility to these paired forces of destruction – to changing tastes and to decay – has meant that only a small proportion of wall paintings survive, often in exasperatingly fragmentary condition. Mural painting was the most usual form of interior ornament, frequently covering every available surface, so this loss seriously distorts its relative importance within the arts. None the less, hundreds of wall paintings survive from the period 1200 to 1400, since eradication may often mean no more than obliteration beneath a protective limewash.

In their style, Gothic wall paintings conform to the general trends of the period, especially in the assimilation by regional centres of successive waves of Continental influences. In subject-matter they respond to the requirements of patron and location, ranging from elaborate history cycles in royal contexts (Cat. 330–9) to unsubtle moral injunctions in rural parish churches (Cat. 557). Patrons are sometimes recorded in accounts, or may be inferred from heraldry or circumstantial evidence, but mostly remain anonymous. Similarly, there are instances of named painters, particularly in relation to royal schemes, but these are exceptional. The dependence of wall paintings on their architectural context is self-evident, and the progressive breaking up of wall surfaces during this period has implications not only for the role and format of wall paintings, but also for their relationship to other media within decorative programmes. Innovations in technique are also directly linked to developments in other media, with an increasing use of oil, glazes, stamped gesso, and metal or other attachments, all tending to greater sumptuousness as the period unfolds.

The transition from late Romanesque to Early Gothic which occurs in wall painting in the decades around 1200 can be most conveniently traced at Winchester Cathedral: in the Chapel of the Holy Sepulchre and the Chapel of the Guardian Angels. In the former, constructed in the twelfth century for liturgical ceremonies at Easter, a Passion and Resurrection cycle painted *c.* 1170–80 was damaged by subsequent

Fig. 91 Winchester Cathedral, Holy
Sepulchre Chapel, vault: Pantocrator, *c.* 1220

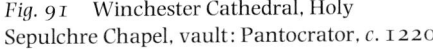

Fig. 92 Winchester Cathedral, Holy Sepulchre Chapel, painting from east wall: the Deposition (detail), *c.* 1220

architectural alterations and overpainted *c.* 1220 with a closely similar scheme, now the most important surviving Early Gothic wall paintings in England (figs 91, 92). The still complete vault decoration of the Guardian Angels Chapel (*c.* 1230), of angel busts in roundels (fig. 93), most likely belonged originally to an extensive depiction of Heaven over the entire vaulting of the east end of the cathedral, the likely model for the slightly later *Coelum* in a similar location at nearby Salisbury Cathedral (unfortunately whitewashed in the eighteenth century and later repainted).

The shift away from the Byzantine influences which dominated late Romanesque painting is clearly revealed by a comparison of the earlier and later schemes in the Holy Sepulchre Chapel. The Romanesque painting (partially uncovered in the 1960s when the painting of *c.* 1220 on the east wall was detached and replaced elsewhere) is as heavily Byzantinising as the contemporary illumination by the Morgan Master and others in the great Winchester Bible, anticipating the even more monumental, classicising style of *c.* 1200 seen at its apogee in the chapter house paintings of Sigena, Aragon, executed by travelling English artists, perhaps from Winchester. In the later scheme at Winchester this all-embracing Byzantinism is considerably diluted (figs 91, 92). Iconographical changes include the framing of the Pantocrator within a Gothic trefoil surrounded by Evangelist symbols (fig. 91) at the east end of the vault (probably derived from a similar figure in the twelfth-century paintings); a unique conflation of this Byzantine iconographical type with the Western Christ in Majesty. The heavy facial modelling survives (fig. 92), yet the exaggerated expressions, restless poses and emotional explicitness are new, with a special sweetness reserved for the face of the now benevolent Saviour. Draperies are arranged for decorative rather than naturalistic effect, concealing rather than revealing form. Such stylistic developments are closely paralleled in a group of manuscripts of *c.* 1220, probably illuminated at Peterborough, such as the Psalter of Robert de Lindesey (Cat. 254).

Reduced monumentality of form is accompanied by a lightening of palette and decreased density of images. The thirteenth-century vault decoration of the Holy Sepulchre Chapel, with roundels enclosing Infancy scenes and busts of prophets, is Romanesque in format but Gothic in its light, unsaturated ground. More divergent still from Romanesque models is the vault of the Guardian Angels Chapel (fig. 93), where angels, set within roundels, appear against a blue sky, while on the rest of the vault spindly foliage trails across the plain, light ground. The roundels are no longer compartments for narrative, but holes punched in the vault with figures looking through. Similarly, the gilded wooden stars and rosettes (mostly modern copies) are set against blue grounds. Lead stars and crescents from the period of Henry III have been excavated at Clarendon Palace; relief attachments become increasingly complex, leading eventually to such conceits as metallic mirrors set into vaults to reflect the light below.

Such exploration of levels of reality – the vault a real surface, yet shown as if pierced; the stars in relief, yet meant to appear as if behind the vault membrane – is characteristically Gothic. In the second quarter of the thirteenth century roundels move down to the wall plane: at Romsey Abbey, Hampshire, they are secured by a grid of symmetrical foliate sprays while the *dramatis personae* freely transgress their frames in enacting the narrative. In the surviving section (fig. 94) of a once extensive scheme of *c.* 1240–50, two scenes from the life of St Nicholas are distributed unequally between the upper roundels, the first scene occupying all but half of one roundel. In both format and disposition of scenes across roundels, close parallels are provided by contemporary manuscripts illuminated by William de Brailes (Cat. 436). Though similar roundel layouts occur elsewhere in wall painting – at Brook, Kent, and in paintings discovered in the 1960s in the royal apartments in the Lower Ward of Windsor Castle, renovated for Henry III in the 1220s and 1230s – narrative cycles at this date may alternatively be disposed as tiers of scenes under arcades, as at West Chiltington, West Sussex, where the arcading with angels in the spandrels clearly imitates contemporary sculptured examples.

It is, however, precisely at this period that the coherence of organisation and subject-matter of all but the most major schemes begins to break down. Even at Romsey and West Chiltington this tendency is already apparent: at the former, despite their orderly layout, the destroyed roundels contained an odd diversity of subjects. At

Fig. 93 Winchester Cathedral, Chapel of the Guardian Angels, vault, *c.* 1230

Fig. 94 Romsey Abbey, Hampshire, ambulatory: scenes from the life of St Nicholas, *c.* 1245–50

Fig. 95 Rochester Cathedral, north wall of the choir: the Wheel of Fortune, *c.* 1245–50

West Chiltington a huge St Christopher, rapidly becoming the most popular subject in Gothic wall painting, interrupts the scale and narrative of the arcade scheme. The expansion of the repertory to include new subjects, particularly moralities, and a much greater range of single images and scenes of saints, combined with the continued reduction in available wall space, were to result in the fourteenth century in such complex anthologies of *exempla* as Longthorpe Tower (Cat. 137). One of the earliest surviving examples of a morality subject, and also one of the finest is the Wheel of Fortune above the prior's stall in the choir of Rochester Cathedral (fig. 95). Doubtless very similar to those once painted for Henry III at Winchester Castle and Clarendon Palace, it is perhaps more subtle as a reminder of the fickleness of fortune than the mechanical wheel made for one French abbot in the previous century.

Location often functioned as a component of meaning, sometimes continuing earlier traditions (as in the positioning of the Last Judgement above the chancel arch), while in other cases responding to new subjects, for example in the painting of St Christopher by or opposite a doorway, visible to passers-by who believed themselves protected from evil by seeing his image. Similarly, certain types of buildings such as refectories had their own typical subject-matter, as did particular features such as tombs. The earliest surviving tomb paintings date from the mid-thirteenth century and thenceforward are consistent in their repertory of subjects: interecessory figures of the Virgin or the Trinity, the Crucifixion, obsequies, or angels bearing the soul of the deceased to Heaven.

The splendid mid-thirteenth-century scheme at Horsham St Faith (Cat. 263) is typical for refectories in its subject-matter, but is important chiefly as a paradigm of the style at this period, comparable yet superior to that of the illumination of Matthew Paris. St Faith herself is daunting in her uncompromising frontality, her broad face, staring eyes with solid black pupils, small pursed mouth and heavy chin, some of these features the last residues of earlier Byzantine influences. Compared with a celebrated sheet of drawings by Matthew Paris (Cambridge, Corpus Christi College, MS 26, f. vii), the similarities are obvious, yet the marked surety of the drawing of St Faith sets it off as even higher in quality. That relatively provincial wall paintings can surpass contemporary manuscripts produced at a leading English abbey with close Court connections, reminds us that the relative importance and innovation of wall paintings is consistently undervalued, particularly with respect to perfectly preserved manuscripts. The style of the Horsham paintings is matched in sophistication by their technique: to elaborate incised drawing and final gilding of details can be added unlooked-for complexities such as a lead white ground, and layers of glazes added to the secco painting. Similarly refined in technique is the slightly later roundel with Virgin and Child in the Bishop's Palace at Chichester (fig. 96). Here the exquisite pale palette, modified only by the expensive blue background (blue being the costliest of colours), the silver (now oxidised) and gilded ornament, matches the Gothic intimacy as Christ embraces the Virgin in a new emotional explicitness.

The richest materials were also used for the murals of the Painted Chamber, Westminster Palace, carried out in various campaigns for Henry III and Edward I in the second half of the thirteenth century. Totally destroyed by fire in 1834, they are known from antiquarian copies and descriptions (Cat. 330–9). Though virtually no secular wall painting survives from the thirteenth century, a great deal is known of royal schemes from royal account rolls. Of the fastidious and art-loving Henry III, we know, for example, that he had the legend of Dives and Lazarus painted in the hall of his castles at Guildford and Ludgershall, and a figure of Winter beside the fireplace of the queen's chamber at Westminster. At Clarendon Palace the crusader subjects in his 'Antioch Chamber' included the legendary duel between his uncle Richard I and Saladin (cf. Cat. 16), and at Geddington he ordered the paintings over his bed to be renewed in 1240 after they had been damaged by rainwater. Henry's choice of subjects thus shows a mixture of the religious and purely secular. The accounts also supply considerable detail about artists and materials: quantities of oil were purchased for the Painted Chamber, presumably for use as a binding medium; a manuscript of the 'Gests of Antioch' was borrowed from the Master of the Temple in 1250, which probably formed a model for another Antioch Chamber, at Westminster, painted shortly afterwards; and the king's painters included Peter of Spain, and his

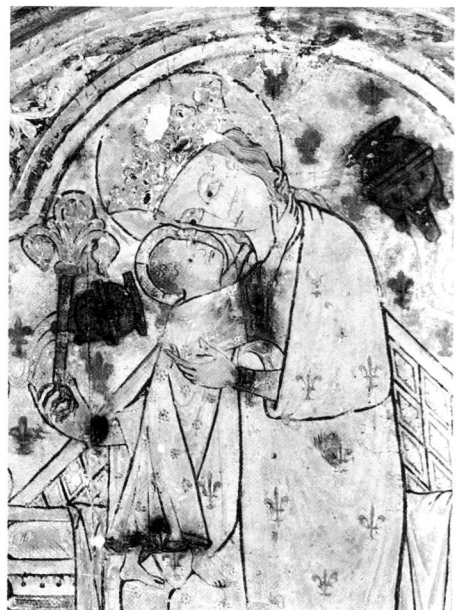

Fig. 96 Chichester Cathedral, chapel of the Bishop's Palace, south wall: the Virgin and Child (detail), *c.* 1260

chief painter from the 1260s on, Walter of Durham. It seems clear that virtually all Gothic wall painting was carried out by professional lay painters, often travelling from one centre to another, and although some of the king's painters are also recorded as having undertaken panel painting, there is no evidence that they also illuminated manuscripts.

The Painted Chamber decoration was in the self-consciously elegant 'broad-fold' style introduced from France into Court painting in the third quarter of the century. Seen at its finest in the superb painting of the Westminster Retable (Cat. 329), the new style is extraordinarily delicate and mannered, with its modelled rather than delineated forms, improbably attenuated figures with tiny, elegantly twisted hands, and angular draperies with self-generating, convoluted folds. Wall paintings in this style still survive in Westminster Abbey: the Doubting Thomas and St Christopher in the south transept, and the altar recess of St Faith's Chapel (Cat. 556), as well as the painted bases of the tombs of Edmund Crouchback and Queen Eleanor of Castile, the latter – sadly now almost invisible – probably painted by Walter of Durham. The identical subject of a standing St Faith in the Abbey and at Horsham St Faith offers a convenient point of comparison between the two styles. The robust St Faith of mid-century, with her heavy crown and summarily delineated, conventionalised features, gives way to the effete saint at Westminster, her unattractively long face fully modelled, and details such as the iris of the eye meticulously included. In this later painting a greater naturalism accompanies a pronounced mannerism.

The elegant style of the Westminster paintings spread rapidly to the provinces, especially to East Anglia, appearing in splendid manuscripts such as the Gorleston Psalter (Cat. 574), and in important wall paintings in the Ante-Reliquary Chapel of Norwich Cathedral and, less well-known, in the Suffolk churches of Brent Eleigh and Little Wenham. At Little Wenham (fig. 97), three female saints stand in exaggerated S-curves, their hands elegantly curled. Though intended to be read as fictive statues, continuing the conceit of the painting in St Faith's Chapel at Westminster (Cat. 556), they are, however, less convincing for being less obedient to the confines of their tabernacles. The exuberance of the style infects even the architectural setting, the tabernacles forming only an element of an entire building complete with central tower and spire. The delicate palette is as mannered as the figure style, with the dominant turquoise (verdigris) very characteristic of this phase of East Anglian painting. The equally typical black flesh areas, now lending the figures an even more exotic air, are merely the underpainting for flesh tones since fallen away.

To account for such splendid decoration in this remote, single-celled parish church, one probably need look no further than the equally fine contemporary manor house adjacent to it. Yet very little is known of the patronage of parish church wall paintings. Kneeling 'donor' figures are frequently represented but less often individualised, though at Brent Eleigh a tonsured figure labelled RICA[RDUS], accompanied by a beer barrel and jug, may be the sacristan of St Osyth's Priory, Essex, which owned the living of the church.[1] At South Newington, Oxfordshire, shields identify the donors as members of the Mortain and Giffard families, connected with the cause of Thomas of Lancaster, which doubtless accounts for the pairing of his execution (fig. 98) with the martyrdom of Becket in an implied canonisation by association.

Though the painted shields recently discovered in the lower hall range at Chepstow Castle, completed in 1285 before a visit by Edward I, are among the earliest to survive, Henry III ordered shields to be painted on the window shutters of a chamber in the Tower of London as early as 1240. Elaborate heraldic schemes reached the height of their popularity in the first half of the fourteenth century, with a spectacular instance provided by the chancel of Hailes, Gloucestershire, the chapel outside the gates of the Cistercian monastery founded by Henry III's brother, Richard, Earl of Cornwall. The heraldry, arranged variously in grids and a diaper, covers the lower two-thirds of the side walls, leaving only a narrow band above for the narrative (fig. 99). Among the arms depicted, which typically are not all correctly tinctured because of the painter's restricted palette, are the black spread eagle of Richard as king of the Romans, and those of his successive wives. The overall effect of repeated shields finds many contemporary parallels in other media, as in the carved stonework of the gatehouse façade of Butley Priory (fig. 27).

Fig. 97 Church of All Saints, Little Wenham, Suffolk, chancel east wall: St Margaret, St Catherine and St Mary Magdalene, *c.* 1310–20

Fig. 98 Church of St Peter ad Vincula, South Newington, Oxfordshire, north wall of north aisle: the execution of Thomas of Lancaster, c. 1340

Fig. 99 Hailes parish church, Gloucestershire: chancel north wall, c. 1320–30

Prominent grotesques, arranged in confronted pairs above the windows, are the other most striking feature of the Hailes programme, and ironic in this Cistercian context in view of the *Pictor in Carmine* text (c. 1200), attributed to an English abbot of the Order, which lists subjects appropriate to wall painting and specifically decries the grotesques introduced by the 'criminal presumption of the painters'.[2] The creatures at Hailes, and in other wall paintings of the period as at Bushmead Priory, Bedfordshire, closely resemble those in the margins of contemporary manuscripts such as the Ormesby Psalter (Cat. 573). Indeed, the popularity of such 'marginalia' in wall painting may have preceded that in manuscripts, occurring already in the Romanesque period at Winchester and elsewhere.

Heraldry and marginalia both feature prominently in the Great Chamber of Longthorpe Tower (Cat. 137), the major surviving monument of medieval secular wall painting in England, and one of the most impressive north of the Alps. This virtually intact scheme covers the vault as well as all the walls; the overall effect is quite overpowering. The deft disposition of subjects, as in the Ages of Man following the curve of the vault in its rise from infancy and descent towards decrepitude, camouflages to some extent the disparity of the subject-matter, which includes the purely religious and the purely secular as well as moralities. This tendency to assemblages of favoured themes is common also to many parish church schemes of the period, such as Barton, Cambridgeshire, and Belchamp Walter, Essex. At Longthorpe marginal subject-matter is again confined to the peripheries of wall surfaces: birds, depicted as naturalistically as in contemporary manuscripts, occupy the dado zone, while the mythical Bonnacon defecates at its pursuer above a doorway.

Amongst the subjects which show the greatest increase in popularity in the fourteenth century, and which contribute to a disruption in the coherency of programmes, are the apocryphal legends of the Virgin, and the moralities. Inclusion of Marian subjects reflects her increasing veneration, particularly in her intercessory role, as when she tips St Michael's scale with her rosary (e.g. Nassington, Northamptonshire, c. 1330). Depictions range from single images to extensive cycles based on the Apocrypha, such as the scenes of her death at Chalgrove (Cat. 93). Moralities include the Acts of Mercy and the Deadly Sins, the Warning against Idle Gossip (Cat. 557), and, most frequent of all, the Three Living and Three Dead, with some thirty examples known from the fourteenth century. The earliest representation of this subject in English illumination, in the De Lisle Psalter (Cat. 569), is closely paralleled by representations in wall painting. At Belchamp Walter the poses and costume are so close to those in the De Lisle Psalter that there must have been a common source. In general, however, moralities, with their emphatic message to the people, were more common in wall paintings than in manuscripts. One of the earliest Three Living, at Wensley, North Yorkshire, has, like the De Lisle Psalter, an inscription in English: [AS] WE A[RE] NOVE [THUS] SAL THE BE [B]EWAR WYT ME (see p. 39). It is in this period, in the early fourteenth century, that the vernacular makes its first appearance in wall painting, and the Wensley inscription is interesting in including an apparently otherwise unrecorded use of 'beware with', as well as for its northern dialect (personal communication, Prof. R.I. Page). Inscriptions tended, however, to remain in Latin, though French occurs as appropriate to the audience (e.g. Cat. 330–2, 137). Similarly, long texts or glosses on the subject-matter were generally eschewed except in the most major schemes (e.g. Cat. 680). In most contexts, these would have been inappropriate to the directness of the message aimed at the faithful, and inscriptions are commonly restricted to name labels or kept short, as at Melbourne (Cat. 557), where the reversed 'S' suggests the painter was working to the limit of his own literacy.

'One universal blaze of splendour and magnificence' was Topham's impression of the recently rediscovered mid-fourteenth-century painted decoration of St Stephen's Chapel, Westminster (Cat. 680), as 'the walls of which in the year 1800 ... were swept away with a haste so barbarous, as scarcely to allow a moment to artists to endeavour to preserve them by copies'.[3] The royal accounts for the scheme, as well as antiquarian descriptions and copies (Cat. 681), and a few original fragments of painting (Cat. 680) survive of the most ambitious decorative programme of the century. Painters were impressed into service under the direction of Hugh of St Albans from many different parts of the country. The paintings, over eighty scenes and many individual figures, filled the available surfaces, with the biblical narratives occupying the spaces below the windows of the lateral walls, and scenes of the Infancy of Christ and the patron, Edward III, and his family on the altar wall (Cat. 681). The 'blaze' was provided by the sumptuous materials and lavish technique – gilded relief gesso grounds and translucent oil glazes. Analysis of the technique was undertaken during conservation in the 1970s.[4] Although the complex technique of lead grounds, tempered colours, oil glazes, and stamped relief ornament relates closely to panel painting such as Cat. 564 and the Despenser Retable (Cat. 711), it is also consistent with other approximately contemporary mural painting techniques in England[5] and even in Italy. In Bologna, a painting of 1348 has recently been shown to have varnished metal foil, and a red built up of ochre in fresco, then vermilion in tempera, finished with red lake in oil.[6]

Yet a more obvious link between St Stephen's Chapel and Italy is in the introduction of Italianate modes of representing space through the use of perspectival architecture. The buildings which dominate the surviving scenes of Job and Tobit (Cat. 680) are decidedly Tuscan in their forms and colouring, and the empirical two-point perspective of obliquely placed structures is an Italian device. But the style of the St Stephen's Chapel paintings is hybrid. The Italian elements grafted on to the northern idiom lack fluency. The architecture is too small for its figures and its spatial function is diluted by anti-illusionistic raised grounds in a manner alien to monumental Italian painting. The undeniably Italian sources for some elements, including, for instance, the rocky landscapes, are likely to have been panel paintings, the 'tables of Lombardy' increasingly imported into England, and of which an example was owned by Hugh of St Albans.[7] Furthermore, there are several styles evident in the chapel; at least three hands were distinguished on the altar wall by the Georgian copyists, and the Job and Tobit scenes are by different hands again. The sources for these paintings need further study, but northern as well as Italian models undoubtedly lay behind the subjects of the Infancy of Christ and the royal patrons on the east wall.

From the end of the period covered by this exhibition, two major monuments of wall painting survive in the International style of around 1400, international in the exceptional similarity of works of art produced in centres as distant as London and Prague. The first is the great Last Judgement and Apocalyptic scheme in the chapter house of Westminster Abbey, paid for by John of Northampton, a monk of the Abbey from 1372 to 1404. The Judgement, with its central Christ flanked by cherubim, commands the eastern bays while the extensive scheme of Apocalypse scenes, originally numbering ninety-six, extends round the walls (fig. 100). The texts which accompany these scenes are even longer than those of St Stephen's Chapel, and are the work of a scribe, written on parchment and pasted to the wall. Although it has recently been argued that the Italianate style of the Judgement calls for a dating closer to that of St Stephen's Chapel and prior to John's arrival at the Abbey, this conflicts with the documentary evidence. The simultaneity of styles – that of the squat, bulbous-nosed Apocalypse figures which is close to contemporary Flemish and German painting, and that of the softly modelled cherubim with elegantly patterned haloes – is entirely appropriate to this most international of phases. We know, moreover, that German and other foreign artists were working in England at this time, and the price differential recorded in the accounts (the Judgement was costlier than the more extensive Apocalypse) seems entirely explicable by the respective quality of the paintings.

The second major scheme from this period, the painting of the Byward Tower (Cat. 696), apparently executed for Richard II in the 1390s, is of still higher quality. With its restrained elegance and melting colours, this is the International style at its most sophisticated. These wall paintings, the finest surviving of their date, and discovered only in the early 1950s, now require further conservation treatment, while the scheme in the chapter house at Westminster is only now being liberated of its discoloured 'preservative' coating, misguidedly applied in the past. These cases once again demonstrate the extreme fragility of the medium and again reveal why wall paintings have been so consistently undervalued.

Fig. 100 Westminster Abbey chapter house, north-western bay, second arch: angel musician and Apocalypse subjects above confronted beasts (Tudor), late fourteenth century

NOTES

I should particularly like to thank Sharon Cather for her help in the preparation of this essay.

1. Norton, Park & Binski 1987.
2. James 1951, p. 141.
3. Topham 1795–1813.
4. Van Geersdaele & Goldsworthy 1978.
5. Binski & Park 1986, pp. 30, 32.
6. Rossi Manaresi 1986, p. 70.
7. Binski & Park 1986, p. 40.

Pamela Tudor-Craig # Panel Painting

Introitumque chori maiestas aurea pingit
Et proprie propria crucifixus imagine Christus
Exprimitur, viteque sue progressus ad unguem
Insinuatur ibi. Nec solum Crux vel imago
Immo columnarum sex, lignorumque duorum
Ampla superficies, obrizo fulgurat auro[1]

Metrical Life of St Hugh of Lincoln [1220–35]

The gilt Majesty and crucifix were no doubt wooden sculptures, but the incidents of Christ's life would have been painted on the 'timbers', probably by the same man. The technique was the same, nor did it differ in essentials from that used on stone sculpture. A thin coat of gesso was applied to the wood, followed by the paint layer, sometimes in tempera, but frequently in Britain from the early thirteenth century, in oil.[2] Certainly from the time of the Westminster Retable (Cat. 329), and almost certainly before, glazes were applied,[3] as well as leaf gold, as in manuscripts.

The Gothic panel painter had many opportunities to practise his art. At the top of his profession he would be engaged on altarpieces, but Gilbert Prince, painter to Richard II, was also expected to paint the royal barge with a white hart, and to make banners and standards of the arms of the king and those that were ascribed to Edward the Confessor.[4]

The largest single area of panelling calling for a painted scheme was the semi flat ceiling of a Romanesque church. The earliest survivor is the vast nave ceiling (62.7 m by 10.7 m) of Peterborough Cathedral, usually dated to the thirteenth century.[5] But would not the painters have kept pace with the scaffolding as it went westward? Such a progression might explain why the iconography, rational at the east end, tails away into confusion and monsters towards the west. The decorative lozenges are still thoroughly Romanesque, and it is dangerous to date draperies that were repainted thoroughly in the 1740s and again in 1834. Essentially, the Peterborough ceiling belongs with the prodigious Romanesque painted ceilings at Zillis in Switzerland, at Hildersheim, and no doubt originally in Ely Cathedral.

Where later English ceilings were of wood simulating stone (Lichfield, York, Peterborough choir itself), the painter collaborated in the deception, which could involve painting wooden bosses and ribs, trails of foliage and figure subjects perhaps in roundels in the vault webs. Rarely did such a commission include anything as ambitious as the gigantic Synagogue occupying an entire vault web from the chapter house ceiling at York (Cat. 344).

Something of the range and excitement of it all is remembered in the 1593 Rites of Durham.[6] We admire the architecture of the Nine Altars today. What would we have made of it when 'All the fors'd nine altars had their severall shrines and covers of wainscote over head in very decent and comely forme, havinge likewise betwixt everye altar a very faire and large p[ar]tition of wainscott all varnished over, with fine branches & flowers and other imagerye worke most finely and artificially pictured and gilted . . .'?[7] The shrine of St Cuthbert was even richer, with a costly green marble base and a carved, painted and gilded cover, with four lively images either side, and on the ends Christ in Judgement upon the rainbow, and the Virgin and Child, the whole trimmed with a cresting of carved dragons and other beasts. That 'sounds' thirteenth century. The Durham artists embellished the doors of the relic cupboard with little images 'very seemly and beautiful to behold', and the inside of the opening statue of Our Lady of Boulton with green varnish strewn with gilt flowers. They painted the retable of the Jesus Altar in the nave, with the whole Passion of Christ 'most richly and curiously sett furth in most lyvely colours all lke y burni'ge gold, as he was tormented & as he honge on ye cross wch was a most lamentable sighte to beholde'. They adorned the Lady Altar in the Galilee with wainscot 'furnished wth most heavenly pictures so lyvely in cullers and gilting . . . .'[8] As the quotation placed on the feretory of the Venerable Bede in 1373 said: 'Christ to the maker sence did give/And to ye giver gold'.[9]

The Durham author's favourite adjective, 'lively', is the essence of English panel painting as it gathered pace in the 1230s under the most impatient and insatiable of great patrons, Henry III. His earlier commissions of paintings on panel have not come down to us, but we may make some deductions by combining the witness of illumination of the 1230s and 1240s with the group of Scandinavian panel paintings which speak the same visual language.

In 1248 the celebrated Matthew Paris went on a mission to King Haakon at Bergen, taking with him an invitation to join Louis IX on crusade. From Bergen Matthew Paris travelled to Trondheim, and thence returned the following year to England.[10] What could be more natural than to claim for his hand the great painting of St Peter from the wing of the Faaberg tabernacle (Cat. 311)? It bears the closest comparison with his drawings. It seems improbable, however, that the great man charged with royal and ecclesiastical embassage would have made time, during a few crowded months, to roll up his sleeves and paint an altarpiece. It is surely more likely that he distributed works of art on a smaller scale which were eagerly imitated by local artists. The notable similarities in economy and vitality between the Ulvik altar frontal, now in the Bergen Museum (fig. 101) and the illumination of William de Brailes (Cat. 314) goes further than a period resemblance. The flanking saints, striding across hummocks of their arcaded setting and the urgent, clean-cut knife pleats of Christ's drapery are akin to sculptural mannerisms of the late 1240s and early 1250s at Westminster Abbey itself (Cat. 287–8).

Fig. 101 Ulvik altar frontal, mid-thirteenth century (University of Bergen, Norway, The Historical Museum)

The Liberate Rolls[11] give detailed accounts of Henry III's expenditure. Mandates describe five pictures of the Majesty, the Blessed Virgin Mary, the Crucifixion with Mary and John, the Coronation of the Blessed Virgin and the Transfiguration, ordered in 1237 for the king's processions. Paintings on panel included histories of St Nicholas and St Catherine for the Church of St Peter within the Tower of London in 1240, a painting (no doubt of St Thomas) for his chapel in Winchester Palace in 1241; a complex of the Crucifix with the Virgin and St John in panel and wall painting for the Royal Palace at Woodstock in 1250, and two panel paintings of bishops for the king's Great Chapel there two years later. The account for 12 December 1251 makes it clear that altar frontals and altarpieces were often considered at the same time, and that both were frequently paintings. The king was never satisfied. At Clarendon Palace, on 12 July 1256, there was an order to paint the picture above the altar of the king's chapel. On 7 December of the same year and again in 1260, the painting of the panels of the same chapel was to be renewed.[12]

A motif of great importance in the artists' repertoire first appears in the Liberate Rolls for 29 June 1246. The lower parts of the walls of the king's lower and upper chambers at Clarendon Palace were to be wainscoted and the wainscot painted green. In the lower chamber that wainscot was to be treated with a border bearing the heads of kings and queens. In the more splendid upper chamber the green wainscoting was to be spotted with gold 'and heads of men and women thereon, all painting to be in good and exquisite colours'. A new range of head types and facial expressions was being explored at the same time in carving at Westminster Abbey, and there survives one sculpted head from the same Clarendon context (Cat. 295).[13] A later example of the same usage in the royal works is provided by the heads beneath the paterae from the wooden ceiling of the Painted Chamber at Westminster Palace.[14]

Henry III's artistic involvement went beyond his own projects. On 5 March 1256 he gave £20 (a prodigious sum) to the Abbot and Prior of Bury St Edmunds to finish the picture in front of their high altar. Such is the background that prepares us for the miraculous survival of the climax of Henry III's artistic endeavour: the retable for the high altar of Westminster Abbey which was, I believe, in place for the dedication of the sanctuary in 1269 (Cat. 329). The ten years running up to this occasion were darkened by rebellion, by lesser treachery among his artistic employees, and by depleted resources. Small wonder that some at least of the collection of antique cameos with which the border of the Westminster Retable was intended to be studded were mere paste. But the painting of the retable, where it survives, is of a quality unmatched by anything of its generation in western Europe. Only in contemporary English manuscripts, pre-eminently the Douce Apocalypse (Cat. 351), is there any comparison for the subtle draughtsmanship, the smoky colouring, the veiled sophistication of this work.[15] The central section was filled by a standing figure of the blessing Christ flanked by Our Lady and St John, bearing palms. Christ's orb is the actual globe, where birds and animals disport themselves in their natural elements, and men ride in a little boat. This comforting image of our world resting in the divine hand answers the cosmic pattern of the abbey's sanctuary floor, a cryptic microcosm of the Creation and its temporal limitations. Here, through Christ, His healing and His Sacraments, we are safe beyond the end of time.

There is no evidence of a late arrival among Henry III's artists. It was at Westminster that the feverish and cosmopolitan[16] artistic activity of Henry's Court had evolved this precious – in both senses – visual idiom.

As Paul Binski has shown,[17] Edward I's interest in Westminster Abbey and Palace quickened towards the end of his reign. In 1299–1300 Master Walter of Durham, the king's painter, was in charge of both the making and decoration of the Coronation Chair to enclose the Stone of Scone, captured by Edward I five years before.[18] The painting, which included a seated king, foliage, birds and inscriptions, was entirely in punched gilding. Walter of Durham had painted the base of Eleanor of Castile's tomb (a ghost remains) a decade before, and the Thomas of Westminster who painted the sedilia in 1307–8 was surely his son. Here two graceful kings 2.4 m high survive. They could be Sebert and Henry III as first and second 'founders' of the abbey. Between them an ecclesiastic, probably St Peter as legendary consecrator, has been savagely deleted. On the back were two pairs, of which only the lower parts remain: the Annunciation and St Edward with the Pilgrim. The style, for all its sprays of flowers and drooping gloved hands, is the art of the Westminster Retable inflated, but all its intensity has blown away.

Meanwhile, the later thirteenth-century had absorbed the Westminster conventions in the delightful assembly of the Newport Chest (Cat. 345). And now we realise that the Musée de Cluny panel is the frontal for a retable in Suffolk of c. 1335 (Cat. 564), we have a complete altar ensemble, as recorded in Henry III's earlier documents. Sts Dominic and Peter Martyr point to a Dominican preference, probably in East Anglia, though the descent of the Cluny panel through the Howard family could suggest one of their seats. This gives an idea of what an altarpiece of something more than parochial standing was like. The Dominicans, with their university connections and their popularity as confessors to the great, would have had choice liturgical furnishings.[19]

If the chapel of Forthampton Court, a grange of the abbots of Tewkesbury, was always the home of the panel of St Edward and the Pilgrim (Cat. 35), it is virtually alone among English Gothic panel paintings in having stayed quietly and unvan-

Fig. 102 Virgin with angel: panel from Park Farm, St Osyth's Priory, Essex, late fourteenth century (Colchester and Essex Museum)

Fig. 103 Canterbury Cathedral, head of St Matthew (detail) from the tester of the monument to the Black Prince (d. 1376)

dalised where it belonged. The Estouteville Triptych in the Courtauld Collection, with heraldic evidence suggesting Bruges, is similarly undesecrated, itself an argument against an English origin.[20]

It is the fashion to decry the adverse influence of the Black Death, but a certain slackening of the pulse in the generation after 1348–9 is surely evident in most fields. The puppet figures of the Norwich Retable (Cat. 711), cocooned in their wrap-around draperies, disarm us. For all his gold leaf and his exotic textiles, the artist of the Norwich Retable has a clear simplicity. Damage has shifted the emphasis from the original climax of the Crucifixion to the better-preserved Resurrection, which captures that wonderful surprise still conveyed in performance of the Mystery Plays.

The relatively fallow third quarter of the fourteenth century was followed by an artistic renaissance under Richard II. Modest panels were painted during his reign, such as the ceiling of St Helen's, Abingdon, proud achievement of the Guild of Our Lady, and the panel of the Entombment from Christchurch Mansions, Ipswich (Cat. 712), a parochial alternative to an alabaster altarpiece. But not all the best figurative art of the late fourteenth century was carried out for Richard II or William of Wykeham; lovely things can be overlooked in the humblest places. At Park Farm on the estate of St Osyth's Priory in Essex there survived a screen wall, partly of timber and partly of plaster, with a unified iconographic scheme of which two units, isolated from a much larger context, are now in the Colchester Museum (fig. 102). What survives is a panel painting, originally nearly life-sized, of the Virgin, freshly painted in brilliant pinks, blues and reds, with a small attendant angel with blond corkscrew curls, and a standing lady in green. A linking inscription in Gothic black letter ran over the timber arch between them.[21] Here we abandon any lingering conception of the panel painter as a specialist in one medium. Not far away at Great Wakering the splays of a late fourteenth-century window have a wall painting of Our Lady and Gabriel surely from the same hand.

By the reign of Richard II a new context for major panel paintings was well established: the tester. Surviving examples are all from monuments, but they had their secular counterparts. The earliest survivor is over the double tomb, once chantry chapel, of Sir John Harrington and his lady at Cartmel Priory, of the mid-fourteenth century. The effigies gaze in prayer at a fine life-sized painted Christ in Majesty, flanked by four Evangelist symbols. There followed two testers by painters, or a painter in royal employ: the first a Trinity over the tomb of the Black Prince (d. 1376) at Canterbury. It is desperately worn, but the face of St Matthew (fig. 103) shows a new mastery, not subservient to Cologne, Italy or even Paris. Little enough remains at Canterbury: less of the next great tester, that of Richard II and Anne of Bohemia at Westminster Abbey, part of the monument that Richard II put in hand upon Anne's death on 7 June 1394. The contract was drawn up in April 1395, and the work was finished, bar some of the gilding of the effigies, by 1397.[22] The painting of the tester is surely that described in the Sacrist's Roll of 14 December 1395.[23] The same account lists a picture in the likeness of a king made for the choir, surely the portrait of Richard II (Cat. 713).

A year before Anne's death Richard's authority was challenged in the Cheshire uprising of Sir Thomas Talbot.[24] His image in coronation robes refers to that challenge: 'The power of the king lay singly and wholly in the king'.[25] Richard's personal interest in what coronation had conferred, sacramentally, upon him is also expressed in the *Liber Regalis* at Westminster Abbey and in the third of the great works of art that he commissioned during the critical two years between Anne's death and his remarriage in October or November 1396. The Wilton Diptych (so called from the house where it was preserved) has been attributed to every possible nation, and to dates varying from Richard's accession, in 1377, to the reign of Henry V (fig. 104).[26] Richard's actual accession and crowning appear to be the moment commemorated, with the eleven angels referring to the eleven 'Angels' (coins) for his eleven years, which he then dedicated to Our Lady of the Pew in Westminster Abbey. At the other end of the time span, as Francis Wormald has demonstrated, the artistic affiliations of the celestial group are with illumination of 1413–15.[27] Wormald's comparisons are compelling, yet an artist illuminating for royal patrons in 1413–15 could have been working in the summer of 1394. The closest comparison is with the little Tondo of the Pietà in the Louvre. Links with the French Court had been close since at least 1392.

Fig. 104 The Wilton Diptych: Richard II presented by his patron saints to the Virgin and Child, here dated 1394 (London, National Gallery)

The single most obvious feature of the Wilton Diptych is that it was portable. It is not a small painting for a private chapel: that would more probably have been a triptych, with penitential subjects for meditation on the closed panels. Rather, it is a diptych for more secure closing, and on the outside it carries not food for meditation, but clear means of identifying royal ownership, with intention as explicit as a luggage label. It was designed for campaign, and the condition of the royal arms suggests that it has served the purpose for which it was made.

In the spring of 1394, before Anne died, Richard was already thinking of a personal visit to Ireland to establish his peace there. He set out in the autumn, and did not return until May 1395. Richard II was twenty-seven in the summer of 1394. The pudginess we detect in the full-length portrait of 1395 does not appear in the pre-restoration photograph of it. George Richmond, in restoring the face, may have been influenced by the bronze effigy, not completed until 1396–7.

The last document for Gilbert Prince is of Easter 1396, and the first for his successor, Thomas Litlyngton, painter of London, is of January 1397[28] for work of several months before. If Prince was fully engaged on the coronation portrait, the travelling altarpiece could have gone to the younger man soon to succeed him as King's Painter. The delicate profile of Richard II on the Wilton Diptych, extrapolating from his appearance at twenty-seven what it might have been fifteen years before, is just possible from a courtly artist of genius.

Richard would not have needed such a portable altar for ordinary journeys: his English chapels were all fully furnished with images. But in taking it to Ireland to quell violence, the Diptych assured him of the divine protection that guarded 'royal majesty, established at howsoever tender years ...'.[29] It also brought that most rare and piercing of consolations: extreme beauty.

On 6 January 1643 William Dowsing recorded in his diary that he and his mates destroyed one hundred 'superstitious images' in Haverhill Church, thirty at Hundon, one each at Wixoe and Withersfield, but one thousand at Clare.[30] Panel paintings made that most satisfactory of all iconoclastic gestures – the bonfire. Here we learn patience in deciphering the sad condition of what remains to us.

To have preserved the Wilton Diptych or the Forthampton St Edward and the Pilgrim could have been treasonable in the sixteenth and seventeenth centuries. Yet the spirit that commissioned masses for three or four voices to be sung in the woods from William Byrd in Elizabeth's reign did preserve a few paintings, and we honour those who saved them. The two great retables of Westminster Abbey and Norwich Cathedral survived as handy expanses of planking. The Norwich Retable was reused upside-down with corners hacked out of it to take legs and the upper part broken off, in a space for the workmen over one of the eastern chapels at Norwich. The Westminster Retable continued to linger in the upper part of Abbot Islip's Chapel for nearly a century after George Vertue had declared its importance. If not positively heretical, medieval paintings were regarded as worthless curiosities. Only in recent years have they acquired a new dimension which this exhibition will do nothing to reverse: they have become valuable. Bearing the scars of their near escape from destruction, they are part of our identity.

NOTES

1. He paints the entrance to the choir: a gold [Christ in] Majesty; and Christ crucified Himself is made manifest by His own image, and the progress of His life is included down to the last detail. Not only the Cross or the image, but the broad surface of six columns and two timbers shines with pure gold.

2. An oil medium has been traced in paint samples on the exterior sculpture of Wells Cathedral from the 1230s. There are frequent payments for oil in the accounts of paintings in the Liberate Rolls from the time of Henry III. References to the calendar of Liberate Rolls published by the Public Record Office, for the reign of Henry III, are too numerous to specify.

3. Mr Ushak Roy found glazes in the painting of the Coronation of the Virgin over the west door at Wells. They are unlikely to be later than the 1240s.

4. Harvey 1961a, p. 7. Observe that Gilbert Prince was expected to paint on cloth or panel.

5. For the Peterborough painted roof, see VCH, *Northamptonshire*, vol. II, 1906, p. 446; Cave & Borenius 1937, p. 297; Tristram 1944, pp. 141 ff.

6. *The Rites of Durham being a description or brief declaration of all the ancient Monuments, Rites and Customs belonging or being within the Monastical Church of Durham before the Suppression* 1593, published by The Surtees Society in 1844 and again, from the collated texts, in 1903.

7. *Rites of Durham* 1903, p. 2.

8. Ibid., p. 43.

9. Ibid., p. 45.

10. All writers on English medieval painting have made much of this expedition, for example Lindblom 1916, pp. 14–15.

11. Calendar of the Liberate Rolls (Public Record Office, Texts and Calendars), *passim*.

12. Borenius 1943, pp. 43–50.

13. For the Clarendon Palace Documents see Eames 1965, pp. 57–85.

14. For the paterae over heads ornamenting the flat ceiling of the Painted Chamber in Westminster Palace, Binski 1986, p. 15, pl. XXXIII; and Tudor-Craig 1957, p. 99, arguing a date of 1262–5 for the heads.

15. Binski 1986, pp. 56–63; Wilson, Tudor-Craig, Physick & Gem 1986, p. 102.

16. Artists included William of Florence, John of St-Omer and Peter de Hispania, with Master William, a Westminster monk, 'the King's beloved painter'. Members of the Roman Cosmati dynasty were also working at Westminster.

17. Binski 1986, pp. 96–112.

18. Ibid., pp. 61, 74, pl. LIII(b).

19. For these two panels see Norton, Park & Binski 1987.

20. We owe this suggested identification to Nicholas Rogers and Lynda Dennison.

21. Something of this framework appears in an old photograph of the interior of Park Farm in RCHM, *Essex*, vol. III, 1922, p. 206 & pl. opp. p. 101.

22. The documents are summarised by Harvey 1961a, p. 8, n. 6.

23. Ibid., p. 12, n. 2.

24. See, for instance, Tuck 1973, p. 165 ff.

25. Sermon preached at the opening of Parliament, 17 September 1397, by Edmund Stafford, Bishop of Exeter, on the text *Ezekiel* XXXVII, 22 (*Rot. Parl.* 1783, vol. III, p. 34).

26. The profuse bibliography of the Wilton Diptych is summarised in Harvey 1961a, pp. 1–18, the most illuminating study of this controversial work.

27. Wormald 1954, pp. 191–203.

28. Harvey 1961a, p. 7, nn. 2–3.

29. Richard II in a letter of 1397 to the Count of Hainault; quoted by Harvey 1961a, pp. 27–8.

30. Dowsing 1885 edn.

Stained Glass, *c.* 1200–1400

comparison of the figures of Hezekiah and the king (Cat. 3, 748) demonstrates the transformation in English stained glass during the two centuries covered by this exhibition. Both figures are from Canterbury Cathedral and belonged to high windows (Hezekiah from the choir clerestory and the king from the great west window of the nave); they were therefore designed to be 'read' from a distance. Provenance, location and medium are the only factors in common between the two panels. In respect of composition, colour-tone, figure style and even some technical features the two figures differ markedly. Hezekiah is sinuous and elegant with the draperies falling in regular and multiple folds; the king is solid and monumental with few and broad folds. The panels are equally distinct in composition and technique. Hezekiah is linear, with no attempt to give an impression of depth by modelling and is set against a ground enriched with foliage; the use of washes of paint on the drapery of the king imparts to it a three-dimensional sculptural effect and he is set on a formal latticework ground. Both panels are predominantly green and white, with considerable use of ruby and blue glass, but the tone of the panel with the king is much lighter and more translucent than the earlier one. Apart from the less intense colour, other reasons for this are that the glass used is much thinner and the individual pieces much larger. The processes by which the transformation outlined above took place were the result of a combination of changes in the architectural context and design of windows, developments and advances in the technique of glass-making and glass-painting, and of changes in figure style and colour.

The methods by which glass was made and painted did not differ fundamentally in the Gothic period from the processes used in the eleventh and twelfth centuries as described by Theophilus and other writers,[1] although several innovations occurred between 1200 and 1400. From the time of the earliest surviving treatises in the twelfth century down to the late fourteenth century, full-sized cartoons for glass windows were drawn on boards or trestle tables prepared with chalk or whitewash and sized with water or ale. None of these boards has yet been discovered in England, although recently a pair of whitewashed tables bearing designs for stained-glass panels and dating from the early fourteenth century appeared at Gerona in Spain.[2] Cartoons were still being prepared by this method in 1351–2 at St Stephen's Chapel, Westminster.[3] These tables were inconvenient and cumbersome: each time a new design was required the previous one had to be erased (there is evidence of this on the Gerona tables) and it must have been difficult to use the same design repeatedly, although the virtually identical panels depicting the Virgin and Child at Fladbury and Warndon demonstrate that this did happen (Cat. 472–3). The introduction of cartoons traced on parchment greatly facilitated the glazier's work, for they could be rolled up, stored and reused very easily. The earliest evidence for the replacement in England of glaziers' cartoons drawn on wooden tables by those on parchment is in connection with Robert Lyen's contract of 1391 for the reglazing of the great east window of Exeter Cathedral (Cat. 746).[4] The passing-down of such cartoons from one generation of glass-painters to the next is well documented in York in the fifteenth and early sixteenth centuries.[5]

The other main technical advance was the introduction of yellow stain. The painting of white glass with silver oxide which turned yellow when fired freed the glass-painter from the restrictions of leading and thus enhanced the translucency and liveliness of windows. For example, until the use of yellow stain, the hair of a figure had to be painted on a separate piece of glass from the face, if the former was to be of yellow and the latter of white glass; yellow stain enabled both to be achieved on the one piece of glass, as on the Virgin from Hadzor and the donor at Aldwincle (Cat. 740, 232). The recipe had been known in Egypt since the sixth century for the decoration of vases and reached western Europe at the end of the thirteenth century by means of a work written between 1276 and 1279 by King Alfonso of Castile.[6] The date and location of its first application to stained glass is still disputed: it is claimed that the technique had appeared in France in the last decade of the thirteenth century, although the first securely dated example of its use there is in a small church at Mesnil-Villeman (1313). Yellow stain is, however, present in the Heraldic Window in York Minster, which is datable to c. 1307–10 (Cat. 5). It seems likely that the technique was known in both England and France around the turn of the thirteenth century. At about the same time improvements in the manufacture of glass in France (from where came much of the coloured glass used in England in the fourteenth century) resulted in the production of larger and thinner sheets which further facilitated the transmission of light. The introduction of an improved range of brushes in the early fourteenth century permitted subtle modelling by stipple and various forms of shading; other means of decorating and ornamenting the glass involved the picking out of elaborate foliate designs on backgrounds by stickwork.

Already by the thirteenth century glass-painting in England seems to have been a highly organised craft. Individual glaziers are recorded from this time, with a large proportion coming from the major towns and cities such as Bath, Canterbury, Chester, Colchester, Lincoln, London, Norwich and Oxford.[7] No names of York glass-painters have been discovered for the thirteenth century, but the craft took swift root there in the following century: between 1313 and 1363 fourteen names are recorded, and twenty-one between 1363 and 1413; many others are recorded later.[8] By the late fourteenth century the York glaziers were sufficiently numerous to form their own craft guild. Rules for the London guild of glaziers were drawn up in 1364–5.[9] By the middle of the fourteenth century glaziers were very widely distributed: the writ for the collection of craftsmen for the glazing of St Stephen's Chapel, Westminster, covers twenty-seven counties.[10] It seems that during the late Middle Ages the average urban glazing firm consisted of no more than the master glass-painter, one or two servants and perhaps an apprentice. Robert Lyen employed one servant at Exeter towards the end of the fourteenth century (Cat. 746) and Thomas Glazier of Oxford also had one assistant (Cat. 612–13, 747)[11].

The earliest glass that can be attributed to an identified glazier are the panels executed in 1303–4 by Master Walter for the great east window of Exeter Cathedral (Cat. 739). The great west window of the nave of York Minster was glazed in 1339 by Master Robert (possibly Robert Ketelbarn; Cat. 741) and the two flanking windows by Master Thomas. In the 1390s Robert Lyen incorporated the earlier glass together with some of his own panels in the redesigned east window at Exeter (Cat. 746) and his contemporary, Thomas Glazier of Oxford, was employed by Bishop William of Wykeham to glaze the chapels of his foundations at New College, Oxford, and Winchester College (Cat. 612–13, 747).[12]

For new projects, as opposed to repair and maintenance, glaziers in the period 1200 to 1400 appear mainly to have been paid on the basis of an agreed sum per square foot. In 1253 the glaziers employed on the windows of Westminster Abbey received 8d per square foot for coloured glass and 4d for white (clear) glass.[13] The same applied in the contract drawn up in 1339 between the chapter of York Minster and Master Robert for the glazing of the great west window (Cat. 741). For this work Robert was to be paid 6d a foot for white and 12d per foot for coloured glass inclusive of the cost of the glass itself.[14] Robert Lyen's agreement of 1391 for the Exeter east window did not differentiate between white and coloured glass. He was paid 20d for each foot of new glass and 3s. 4d per week for setting the old glass (Cat. 739, 746).

The patrons who commissioned windows in this period were primarily the leading members of society and the great ecclesiastical corporations. There is little direct evidence of stained glass patronage in the thirteenth century, apart from the lavish expenditure of Henry III on his royal residences and Westminster Abbey (Cat. 735–6).[15] The ordering of stained-glass windows occurs quite frequently in the royal accounts of this reign. Later sovereigns also commissioned glazing as part of their building projects, notably Edward III at St Stephen's Chapel, Westminster, and Windsor.[16] Other members of the royal family are also associated with stained glass, for example Beatrix van Valkenburg, the wife of Richard Earl of Cornwall (Cat. 226) and John of Gaunt, Duke of Lancaster (Cat. 745).

The prelates and prince-bishops of the realm were active patrons of stained glass. The cost of glazing the great west window of York Minster was met by a gift of 100 marks from Archbishop Melton (Cat. 741). One of the most lavish patrons of the arts in these two centuries was William of Wykeham. The endowments of his foundations of New College, Oxford and Winchester College met the cost of their sumptuous glazing by Thomas Glazier of Oxford (fig. 110; Cat. 612–13, 747). Wykeham also left the sum of 500 marks in his will for the glazing of the Winchester Cathedral nave.[17] Important cathedral dignitaries also commissioned windows. At the end of the thirteenth century Henry de Mamesfeld met at least some of the cost of glazing Merton College Chapel, of which he was a Fellow (fig. 109; Cat. 738). Clerics attached to York Minster are associated with windows in the nave, notably Peter de Dene, a canon and vicar-general to Archbishop Greenfield (Cat. 5), the archbishop himself and Robert de Riplingham, chancellor of the diocese from 1297 to 1332. Elsewhere clerical participation took the form of a corporate rather than individual programme. The lack of evidence for individual gifts of windows at Canterbury, Lincoln and Salisbury perhaps indicates that their thirteenth-century glazing was paid for from a central fabric fund administered by the respective chapters. This certainly happened at Exeter in the late thirteenth and early fourteenth centuries (Cat. 746). Here the bishop, cathedral officials and the canons made large annual gifts to the fabric fund from their income according to an agreed formula.[18] It is likely that a similar arrangement was in operation at Wells in the same period, for the names of a number of canons and other officials occur in the Lady Chapel glazing.[19]

Fig. 105 Wine-sellers in an early fourteenth-century glass panel in York Minster

Parochial clergy (Cat. 232) and the laity, both nobles and commoners, were also major sources of patronage. Evidence for windows paid for by the laity is sparse before 1300, although two men named Philip and Solomon were depicted in a now destroyed thirteenth-century window at Upper Hardres in Kent.[20] Manorial lords were prominent donors of windows in their local parish churches. Two of them are shown in the exhibition, John de Newmarch at Carlton Scroop and Sir James Berners (who was beheaded in 1388) at West Horsley (Cat. 227, 744). Several of the early fourteenth-century nave windows at York Minster were the gift of members of the laity, who included a wealthy goldsmith and bell-founder, Richard Tunnoc, whose window has scenes of bell-casting. Two panels in the nave clerestory probably depict wine-selling and appear to have come from a window commissioned by tradesmen (fig. 105). Such trade and craft scenes are rare in English medieval glass, although they are quite common in France and Germany.[21] Windows could also be collective gifts from a guild or other group united by a common purpose, such as the penitentiaries who paid for a York nave window.[22]

Medieval donors or patrons normally expected their gifts to be suitably acknowledged. The position adopted by one John de Beverley was perhaps not untypical. In 1380 he bequeathed 40s for alterations to the windows in three churches on condition that a shield of his arms was placed in each one.[23] Commemoration of donors was almost invariably by inscription, shield of arms or by a representation of the patron(s) dressed according to their station in life; usually two, or even all three of these elements occur together. The donors themselves were depicted in much the same way in English as in Continental glass,[24] although unlike France and Germany, none survives in England before the second half of the thirteenth century. The earliest surviving donor figure in English glass is Beatrix van Valkenburg (died 1277; Cat. 226) and there are numerous examples dating from the fourteenth century. Patrons are most commonly shown kneeling in prayer, in either the main or the tracery lights (Cat. 226–7, 232, 612, 738, 744). Sometimes they hold the window they have presented (Cat. 231); at Lowick in Northamptonshire and Bere Ferrers in Devon, there are early fourteenth-century donors holding models of churches. Merchants and artisans are often represented plying their trades and crafts, as in the wine-selling and bell-founding windows in York Minster mentioned above, and in the stonemason panel at Helmdon (Cat. 477).

England is not rich in thirteenth-century glass. The principal monuments are the final phases of the Canterbury Cathedral glazing and fragments of the once very extensive schemes at Lincoln Cathedral, Salisbury Cathedral and Westminster Abbey. There is also some historiated glass of the period at Beverley Minster and fragments can be found in parish churches throughout England, with a concentration in Kent and Oxfordshire (Cat. 28, 737).[25] The material is far too scanty for any identifications of regional stylistic groupings to be valid, but it is possible to outline various developments between c. 1200 and 1300.

When the century opened the glazing of the eastern parts of Canterbury Cathedral had been in progress for approximately twenty-five years.[26] It is a fully historiated programme and the iconography had long been settled in broad outline. The clerestory contained a series of more than eighty large figures depicting the ancestors of Christ with the sequence broken by three narrative windows in the Trinity Chapel apse. In the choir aisles, eastern transepts and presbytery was a series of twelve typological windows. Above them in the trefoil 'triforium' openings and in the windows of the four eastern transept chapels were scenes from the lives of various saints. The major hagiographical cycle was in the twelve ambulatory windows of the Trinity Chapel, which were devoted to St Thomas Becket. The programme was completed by the lower windows of the Corona, one of which was typological, and the others probably included a Tree of Jesse and christological or narrative subjects. Much of this glass still survives, although some of it is heavily restored.

By 1200 the glazing appears to have been largely finished except for the Becket windows in the Trinity Chapel ambulatory and some of the ancestors of Christ which were destined for the clerestory of the Trinity Chapel. The completion of the scheme was evidently protracted, with delays caused by financial problems and political difficulties, including the exile in France of the archbishop and monks between 1207 and 1213. The work seems to have been ready in time for the translation of Becket's relics into the Trinity Chapel on 7 July 1220.[27] Although styles changed during the prolonged campaign, the repeated use of certain ornamental motifs and the recurrence of individual hands over the entire period have led Professor Caviness to the conclusion that the Canterbury glass was the product of a single workshop.[28] Compared with the earlier phases at Canterbury, the glass of the early thirteenth-century campaign is distinguished by elegance of pose and a balance of gesture (Cat. 3). In the narrative scenes (Cat. 27) the elements in the composition are reduced almost to shorthand compared with the minute attention to such details as landscape and foliage forms present in the pre-1200 glass. The loss of detail is more than counterbalanced by the dramatic silhouetting of the figures and their agile gestures against the plain blue grounds. Borders and ornamental motifs between the figural panels are reduced and simplified in the last, Gothic phase of the work. In these features, together with the intensity and combination of colours, the later Canterbury windows have many affinities with those of the contemporary French cathedrals at Chartres, Bourges and Sens. Indeed, a number of the glaziers working at Canterbury in this period appear to have been active in France during the years of exile before returning home.[29]

At Lincoln Cathedral the remains of a once extensive series of historiated and grisaille windows survive in the east windows of the choir aisles, and the north transept rose window and the lancets below this rose and that in the south transept.[30] They include a Last Judgement, Old Testament scenes, eight panels from the life and miracles of the Virgin and scenes from the lives of various saints as well as some single figures. Most of this glass dates from just before 1200 and c. 1220. In border designs, colour and general figure style the Lincoln glass is related to Canterbury and the contemporary northern French cathedrals, but the parallels are not sufficiently close to attribute any of the Lincoln glass to workshops active elsewhere. The hand responsible for the Virgin panels is distinct from the Canterbury glass. In his attenuated figures and treatment of facial features this artist is comparable with local miniature painting such as the Life of St Guthlac (Cat. 37).

In addition to the historiated panels there are remains of contemporary grisaille windows at Lincoln. These are best considered with the extensive collection at Salisbury Cathedral, glazed between 1220 and 1258.[31] Very little figural glass

Fig. 106 Grateley parish church, Hampshire: the martyrdom of St Stephen from Salisbury Cathedral, c. 1220–30

Fig. 107 Unpainted grisaille from Salisbury Cathedral, 1220–58: watercolour by Charles Winston (London, British Library, Add. MS 35211, part IV, f. 191)

survives at Salisbury apart from the fragments of a Jesse Tree, and medallions depicting the Angel appearing to Zacharias in the Temple and the Adoration of the Magi. At Grateley in Hampshire is a fine Martyrdom of St Stephen from Salisbury (fig. 106), which is unlikely to be much later than the Canterbury Becket windows. Grisaille played a major role in the Salisbury glazing. There are at least fifteen different designs amongst the surviving grisaille panels. Together with those at Lincoln and others in York Minster, Westminster Abbey and various parish churches the Salisbury panels are the principal evidence for a form of glazing that must have been very common in England during the first half of the thirteenth century.[32] The reasons for this were partly economic – grisaille was cheaper than coloured glass – but aesthetics may also have played their part. Coloured windows, as at Chartres, permit very little light to filter through and consequently the interior is difficult to discern and architectural details such as mouldings, profiles and carvings are obscured. Grisaille, by contrast, transmits more direct light and enhances architectural and sculptural details. Salisbury, Lincoln, York and Westminster all have a profusion of surface decoration, elaborate mouldings and rich marble columns.[33]

Grisaille windows can be classified under two main types: those of plain glass with vegetal and geometrical designs formed entirely by the leading and those decorated with painted designs of flowers and stems. Both varieties are also frequently embellished with bosses, borders and edgings in coloured glass. The first appears to be the more ancient of the two and examples can be found dating from before 1200 in a number of Cistercian abbeys on the Continent.[34] A late twelfth-century ornamental window at Brabourne in Kent shows that this type was also known in England. The largest quantity of grisaille designs formed by leading is at Salisbury (fig. 107); others are known from the former Cistercian church at Abbey Dore, Herefordshire, and Hastingleigh, Kent, as well as the lancet exhibited here (Cat. 734).[35] Grisaille windows with painted decoration survive in much larger numbers, notably at Salisbury and Lincoln and in a group of parish churches in Kent (fig. 108). Although the designs are much the same as those found in contemporary grisaille windows in France and Germany, the composition of English windows of the period differs from their Continental counterparts. The chief distinction lies in the predilection of English glaziers for designs founded on regular, rather than (as on the Continent) interlacing,

Fig. 108   Painted grisaille design from Salisbury Cathedral, 1220–58: watercolour by Charles Winston (London, British Library, Add. MS, 35211 part III, f. 177)

geometrical forms such as circles, lozenges, quatrefoils and diamonds. Grisaille windows made up of a latticework of diamond or square quarries bearing foliage on cross-hatched grounds also appear to be an indigenous type rarely found in France before the fourteenth century. A number of these quarry patterns are similar to those found on floor tiles and craftsmen working in both media must have used similar pattern books.[36] The glaziers were very imaginative in their designs; so much so that no two windows of this period from different buildings are exactly alike.

English glass of the second half of the thirteenth century is sparse and for the most part confined to comparatively modest buildings; for this reason it has largely escaped attention. Nevertheless, it is in this period that certain innovations took place which paved the way for the achievements of the first half of the fourteenth century. The principal monuments are the few remains of the Westminster Abbey glazing (Cat. 735–6), Stanton Harcourt, Oxfordshire, Chetwode (Cat. 737), Kempsey in Worcestershire, St Michael at the North Gate and Merton College Chapel (Cat. 738) in Oxford, and the chapter houses of Salisbury Cathedral and York Minster.[37] The Westminster glass dates from between c. 1246 and 1259. The grisaille windows here were similar to those at Lincoln and Salisbury and the surviving figural panels also conform to the same stylistic and compositional canons (Cat. 735–6). In one respect, however, Westminster marks an important innovation. The three shields of arms that are now set in St Edmund's Chapel formed part of Henry III's glazing and are among the first occurrences of English monumental heraldry, together with the armorial tiles in the abbey chapter house. From this time onwards heraldry became an important element in English window design (Cat. 7, 229, 745). An architectural development of fundamental importance for the glazier is also seen for the first time on a large scale in England at Westminster: the introduction of bar tracery windows made much larger spaces available for translucent decoration than hitherto.

Many of the changes which were to lead the way to the developments of around 1300 are present in the Chetwode glass of c. 1260–80 (Cat. 737). The grisaille still consists of stylised leaves and stems, but unlike the grisaille of the first half of the century they are not contained within the leading but form part of a coherent overall design passing over the lead-lines. The same phenomenon is present (rather tentatively) in the Five Sisters window in York Minster, in the Salisbury chapter house and at Stanton Harcourt.[38] Another change in the aesthetic of grisaille which is apparent at Chetwode is the abandonment of cross-hatching in favour of clear grounds, which greatly increased the translucency of the glass. The same trend is evident in French glass of the 1260s and 1270s, notably in the Château de Rouen and St-Urbain at Troyes.[39] This move toward more transmission of light was facilitated by other changes. The Chetwode window has vesica-shaped panels containing figures in coloured glass set in the grisaille. These figures are composed of larger pieces of glass than had been the norm in the first half of the century and the colours are also less dense and sombre. Moreover, the figure of St John the Baptist marks a great stylistic change: the calligraphic, multiple folds of the first half of the thirteenth century are here replaced by a few, sharply angular and broken draperies; the figure is also represented in an S-shaped stance. This new figure style was to endure for nearly a century. Although its origins lie in French early thirteenth-century sculpture, it probably only became widely known through painting associated with the French Court.[40] And what was fashionable in Court circles in France soon became *de rigueur* for patrons among royalty, higher nobility and prelates throughout northern Europe; their English counterparts proved to be no exception. The first signs of infiltration of the broken-fold High Gothic style into English art manifest themselves in the 1260s. The new mode of treating figures was adopted for Henry III's second Great Seal (c. 1259; Cat. 276) and appears in a number of manuscripts and monumental paintings associated with the royal Court at Westminster.[41] The new style was soon disseminated fairly widely, as is apparent from the Chetwode glass; early examples of it are also present in the glazing of Salisbury chapter house, Stanton Harcourt, Kempsey and St Michael's in Oxford. The versions in this medium are comparable with the figures in manuscripts such as the Cuerden Psalter (Cat. 355) and the Oscott Psalter (Cat. 352). There are also affinities between the architectural frameworks encompassing the figures in the above churches and the same manuscripts.

Chetwode does not exhibit all the changes that took place in English glass during the second half of the thirteenth century. One of the most far-reaching was the replacement of stylised by naturalistic foliage. This was not a development peculiar to English glaziers, but was part of a new interest in the depiction of the natural world found throughout Europe during the same period. The first major displays of naturalistic leaf forms occur in French architectural sculpture at Rheims and Notre-Dame in Paris; they had appeared in English sculpture at Windsor and Westminster by c. 1250 and the fashion soon spread into other media. Vine and oak leaves occur occasionally in La Estoire de Seint Aedward le Rei (Cat. 39), dating probably from c. 1255–60; by the time the Douce Apocalypse (Cat. 351) was painted in c. 1270 naturalistic foliage had become well-established in English manuscript illumination. The sparse evidence available suggests that both English and French glass-painters may have lagged a little in their adoption of the new forms. In France the first manifestations are at St-Pierre at Chartres, St-Urbain at Troyes and the chapel at St-Germer-de-Fly.[42] These all date from the 1260s and early 1270s and the presence of stylised trefoil-headed leaves side by side with naturalistic foliage suggests that the latter was only adopted hesitantly. It was not until the 1280s that naturalistic leaf forms appeared in English glass, in the vestibule to the chapter house of Wells Cathedral and in the chapter house proper of York Minster.[43] The speed of adoption of naturalistic foliage was not uniform throughout the country. The east window of Selling in Kent can be dated 1299–1307, yet there is still no trace of naturalistic leaf forms in the grisaille.[44] This is probably an exception and it seems that by the turn of the century naturalistic foliage had almost everywhere supplanted the older designs in grisaille and border decoration. It is also principally in borders that other components of the natural world begin to be represented during the late thirteenth century. A window of c. 1270 recently excavated at Bradwell Abbey in Buckingham-shire has borders composed of birds set among a climbing foliage trellis which are a far cry from the formal borders of Canterbury, Lincoln and Salisbury.[45] The birds at Bradwell are an early example of a taste for zoomorphic decoration which was to be a major element in English glass during the fourteenth century.

All the various developments described above were at the end of the thirteenth century fused into a new aesthetic which led to the creation of some of the greatest masterpieces of English medieval glass-painting. The late thirteenth and first half of the fourteenth centuries witnessed a series of outstanding works: the nave of York Minster (Cat. 5, 563), the choirs of Exeter (Cat. 739), Wells, Bristol (Cat. 558), Tewkesbury (Cat. 742) and Gloucester and the Lady Chapel of Ely (Cat. 230, 743). Morever, the glass from Merton College Chapel (Cat. 738), Credenhill (Cat. 29), Carlton Scroop (Cat. 227), Halvergate (Cat. 34), Beckley (Cat. 30–1), Helmdon (Cat. 477), Stanford on Avon (Cat. 560–1), Woodwalton (Cat. 559), Warndon (Cat. 473), Fladbury (Cat. 472), Brinsop (Cat. 33), Hadzor (Cat. 740), St Denys Walmgate (Cat. 231) and Mere (Cat. 32) demonstrates that glazing of high quality was not confined to the great cathedrals and monastic churches in this period.

Two more important innovations at the end of the thirteenth century which were absorbed together with the changes that have been traced above became standard features in English glass during the period c. 1300–50. Both are present in an important series of windows in the chapter house of York Minster (c. 1285) and in its vestibule (Cat. 4).[46] In the former are bands of historiated scenes in polylobed medallions set within borders containing a climbing trellis of naturalistic foliage and against a grisaille ground. The foliage in the very disturbed grisaille of each light springs from a central stem running vertically through the window from bottom to top. This arrangement became the norm for English grisaille until the middle of the fourteenth century; good examples can be seen at Merton College Chapel (Cat. 738), the nave of York Minster, Chartham in Kent and Stanford on Avon (Cat. 560–1). The overall arrangement of the York chapter house windows is also important as marking the first appearance of the band window in England. In essence the band window consists of one or two horizontal strips of coloured figural or historiated glass running across the window, the rest of which is filled with grisaille. The practice of placing coloured glass compositions in grisaille windows was known in the early thirteenth century, as at Petham in Kent and West Horsley, Surrey, and also occurred later in the

Fig. 109 Merton College chapel, Oxford: band window, *c.* 1294

century, notably at Stanton Harcourt and Chetwode (Cat. 737).[47] The band window proper, however, seems to have appeared in France during the 1260s and developed over the succeeding decades, notably at Tours Cathedral, St-Pierre at Chartres and St-Urbain at Troyes.[48] The glaziers of the York chapter house may have been aware of the Saint-Urbain windows: the use of polylobed medallions in bands is common to both. The fully evolved formula with figures in coloured glass panels entirely filling the width of each light is present in two works of the 1290s: the chapter house vestibule windows at York and the side windows of Merton College Chapel (Cat. 738; fig. 109) and there are numerous other examples of this kind of window dating from the first half of the century, including Selling and Stanford on Avon (Cat. 560–1).

At Selling, Merton College and Stanford on Avon the figures are each set under a cusped arch surmounted by a steep crocketed gable capped by a finial and flanked by pinnacled shafts. The source of this canopy design, which is found (with local variations) throughout northern Europe can be traced back to the crocketed gables over the windows of the Ste-Chapelle in Paris (1243–8). Professor Becksmann has shown that the glass-painters of the Rhineland borrowed the design from architectural drawings and it is highly probable that the same process occurred in England.[49] These canopies are found in almost all branches of artistic activity at the end of the thirteenth and first half of the fourteenth centuries; so much so that it seems as if master masons/architects were striving for a uniformity of design throughout churches which affected all their component parts. The windows of the York chapter house and vestibule (Cat. 4) mark some of the first appearances of this type of canopy in stained glass.

Present in the York nave glazing is another characteristic feature of English early fourteenth-century glass: the interest in the depiction of birds already evinced at Bradwell Abbey expanded in this period to include all manner of creatures, both real and fantastic, as well as drolleries. Birds occur in the borders of several windows in the south aisle of York Minster; the animal scenes in the borders of the Pilgrimage window in the north aisle are very similar to those found in *bas-de-page* illustrations in contemporary illuminated manuscripts (see p. 155) and demonstrate once again the common repertoire of designs used by Gothic craftsmen working in various media.[50] Zoomorphic representations, hybrid men and drolleries were not confined to borders. The Pilgrimage window has a series of monsters, griffins and centaurs in the small roundels which enliven the grisaille panels between the main historiated scenes. Elsewhere, heads of kings, of Christ and various saints were often used in these roundels (Cat. 6).

Decorated stained glass throughout England exhibits a high degree of uniformity: the glazing of Merton College Chapel (Cat. 738), the York chapter house vestibule (Cat. 4), Exeter east window (Cat. 739), the Bristol Cathedral angel (Cat. 558), and the glass at Beckley (Cat. 30–1), Credenhill (Cat. 29), Stanford on Avon (Cat. 560–1), Helmdon (Cat. 477) and Carlton Scroop (Cat. 227) all belong to the same 'family' in the range of colours used, design and figure style. Nevertheless the picture did not remain static and some important developments took place. One of these was the introduction of yellow stain. As was mentioned above, one of its first applications in England is in the York Heraldic window of *c.* 1307–10 (Cat. 5). The use of yellow stain spread very quickly and contributed to the trend towards greater translucency and lighter tone that characterises subsequent windows. It also led to a preponderance of white glass with yellow stain over coloured glass, which is very much a feature of the period 1350–1400. The impact made on the tonality of windows by the extensive use of yellow stain can be seen by comparing the figures of St Peter from Stanford on Avon and St Catherine from Wood Walton (Cat. 560, 559) with the Hadzor Virgin and the west window glazing of York Minster (Cat. 740–1). On the first two, which date from the first quarter of the century, yellow stain is employed very sparingly; on the Hadzor and York panels it is used extensively. Comparison of the two groups also emphasises other changes. Whereas in the earlier works canopies are represented parallel with the front plane of the picture, at Hadzor and York various devices are used to give an illusion of spatial depth. Part of the superstructure of the Hadzor canopy is tipped forward in 'bird's eye' perspective. In the York canopies a similar three-dimensional effect is created by the depiction of the vaulted interiors. This impression is heightened at Hadzor by the placing of the Virgin in front of the right side-shaft and slightly overlapping the border to the light, as if she is partly stepping out from the confines of the canopied niche. The folds of her drapery are all delicately modelled by washes of smear shading, sometimes on both sides of the glass.

This trend was not confined to the medium of stained glass and can be traced in English manuscript illumination of the 1320s and 1330s.[51] In the Crucifixion page in the Gorleston Psalter (Cat. 574), and in related manuscripts the interest in the rendering of space and modelling of figures is derived from Siennese painting. The same ultimate source lay behind an analogous development in French art, principally the manuscripts illuminated by Jean Pucelle and the closely related glass of the 1320s and 1330s at Évreux and Rouen.[52] The influence of this Pucellian art was felt in England, notably in the work of the Majesty Master in the De Lisle Psalter (Cat. 569) and in the glazing of the York nave west windows.[53] The workshop headed by Master Robert, the glazier responsible for the great west window (Cat. 741), exhibits the closest affinities with glass in Normandy in head-types, tightly curled foliate patterns on backgrounds and in the use of certain motifs, such as niched figures in canopy side shafts. The workshop of Master Robert was responsible for an important series of glazing schemes in the north, including windows in the Minster and parish churches of York and as far distant as Carlisle. Although this glass affords the nearest comparison with the French monuments, workshops active elsewhere in England were touched by the Pucellian taste. Notable examples are in East Anglia and the West Country. In the former the remains of the Ely Lady Chapel glazing (Cat. 230, 743) and the St Christopher from Halvergate (Cat. 34) were influenced by French glass. The Wells Cathedral atelier and the glaziers responsible for the important series of windows in the choirs of Bristol Cathedral, Tewkesbury Abbey (Cat. 742) and Gloucester Cathedral were also aware of developments on the other side of the Channel.[54] The east window of Gloucester seems to have been erected around 1350. It is designed to act as a gigantic triptych of tiers of canopied figures, with the central section rising higher than the wings. The style of figures and canopies is fully in the Decorated spirit, but in other respects the glass points the way to the achievements of the fifteenth century, in much the same way as the architectural framework with its reduction of wall to rectilinear, thin membranes of mullions and transoms signalled the introduction of the Perpendicular style. Indeed, the two go hand in hand. The creation of a new architectural aesthetic, with walls consisting merely of a translucent screen, demanded in its turn much less heavy colouring and a reduction of ornament, not just with white glass dominating, but also a lightening in tone of coloured glass. In this respect the Gloucester east window glazing points the way to the future; compared with the comparatively dark tones of Tewkesbury (Cat. 742), which creates an enclosure and a denial of external matter, the Gloucester glazing opens up and transmits the outside world to the interior through a transparent screen. Similarly in its tiers of figures, Gloucester anticipates the most common glazing scheme of the fifteenth and early sixteenth centuries.

The Gloucester glass was indeed anticipatory, for it was to be almost half a century before its aesthetic innovations took root in English glass-painting. If the first half of the fourteenth century ended on a high note with the series of outstanding works at York (Cat. 741), Wells, Tewkesbury (Cat. 742), Gloucester and Ely Lady Chapel (Cat. 230, 743), not to mention the lost schemes of St Stephen's Chapel, Westminster (c. 1349–52) and St George's, Windsor (1351–2),[55] the years between c. 1350 and 1380 come as an anticlimax. There are few surviving monuments of major importance from this period. With the exception of the remains of the glazing of Edington Priory in Wiltshire (c. 1358–61), the figures under canopies in the Latin Chapel of Christ Church Cathedral, Oxford and some panels in the choir of York Minster,[56] almost all of the surviving glass is to be found in parish churches, notably at Heydour in Lincolnshire (c. 1360 and 1382–3).[57] The trend towards increased use of white glass and yellow stain at the expense of coloured glass accelerated, while coloured glass was relegated to backgrounds behind figures. The band window fell out of favour and the overall trelliswork foliate pattern on grisaille was replaced by quarries bearing individual designs. In canopy design there is a continuation of the move which had already begun in the 1340s away from the very close affinities with

Fig. 110 New College chapel, Oxford: a royal female saint painted by Thomas Glazier, 1380–6

architectural and sculptural designs which was a feature of early fourteenth-century canopies; now they carry a stage further the illusion of spatial depth. Solid three-sided structures and multiple buildings grouped above the main arch occur separately and combined together: similar designs are also found in manuscripts like the Fitzwarin Psalter (Cat. 685). In figure style there is no marked change in the period *c*. 1350–70 from that of the 1340s. In this decade there was a predilection for very heavily modelled, rather unattractive facial features which show close affinities with the late East Anglian manuscripts, notably the Luttrell Psalter (Cat. 575). There was also a retreat from the mannered sinuous elegance of the early fourteenth century in favour of angular, twisted and exaggerated figural poses; an analogous development can be seen in contemporary manuscripts such as the Fitzwarin Psalter (Cat. 685).

In the 1370s and 1380s two new figure styles emerged, once again closely paralleling those found in manuscript painting. Bodies are no longer slender and elongated but tend to be squat. The first of the two styles to appear is closely associated with the Bohun group of manuscripts (Cat. 686–91).[58] Although this group is by no means uniform, the predominant style is characterised by heavily painted faces with beady eyes and thin, narrow mouths. The glazier's version lacks the heavy facial modelling of the Bohun manuscripts but in other respects the affinities between the two media are close. Examples of this style in glass can be seen at Bardwell in Suffolk, Wormshill in Kent, Aston Rowant, Oxfordshire, Raunds and Aldwincle (Cat. 232) in Northamptonshire, Maxey, Cambridgeshire, Weston Underwood in Buckinghamshire and Old Warden in Bedfordshire (this list is not exhaustive).[59]

During the 1380s the Bohun-related style was supplanted or joined by a figure-style related to that found in the group of manuscripts centring around the Lytlington Missal of 1383–4 (Cat. 714). The faces painted in this manner are distinguished by strongly emphasised eyes and arched brows, as in the figure of Sir James Berners at West Horsley (Cat. 744). Other examples can be seen at Birtsmorton in Worcestershire, Farleigh Hungerford in Somerset and the Bodleian Library, Oxford.[60] This style lasted into the first decades of the fifteenth century in more remote areas, as is demonstrated by the heads of Ralph Nevill, Earl of Westmorland, and his wife Joan at Penrith in Cumberland.[61]

By the time the Penrith glass was executed the Lytlington-related mode had been replaced in the principal centres of production by International Gothic. This style, which extended across Europe and embraced all branches of artistic activity, was established in England during the 1390s. In stained glass its early pioneers were Thomas Glazier of Oxford, Robert Lyen of Exeter and the anonymous glazier of the Canterbury west window. Thomas Glazier's work for William of Wykeham at New College, Oxford, and Winchester College (Cat. 612–13) is of particular significance in the development of the International Gothic style in this country. New College was built between 1380 and 1386 and most of the chapel glazing probably dates from this time (fig. 110).[62] The figures and canopies show that at this stage of his career Thomas still adhered to current glazing fashions: in facial features and figure style as a whole, the New College figures are related to those in the Lytlington Missal. The Jesse Tree executed for the chapel (now in York Minster) shows distinct differences from the rest of the New College glazing, as does the Winchester College glass (Cat. 612–13, 747). The Winchester College glazing was in progress in 1393 and so close is the New College Jesse to the Winchester glass that there are strong grounds for supposing that the Jesse also dates from the 1390s. The chief difference between Thomas Glazier's output of the 1380s and that of the 1390s lies in the modelling of his figures. In the New College Jesse and Winchester College they are sturdy and heavily swathed in drapery. The use of a soft and painterly treatment of draperies and features (especially by means of sensitive stipple-shading), created a three-dimensional, sculptural impression in conformity with the norms of the International Gothic style. At some time around 1390 Thomas must have come into contact with International Gothic. The resulting transformation parallels, albeit in less dramatic fashion, the change that took place between the Lytlington and the Lapworth Missals (Cat. 714, 717). In certain other aspects Thomas's work at Winchester College seems to have had a profound effect on subsequent English glazing. The multiple crocketed arches, shafts and pinnacles in the side windows and east window of the chapel (Cat. 612–13, 747) became the basic canopy design used by English glaziers throughout the fifteenth century. Similarly the 'seaweed' pattern used on the coloured backgrounds to the figures at Winchester was adopted as the standard method of embellishment for coloured grounds throughout most of the century.

The other early International Gothic monuments are Robert Lyen's four figures in the east window of Exeter (Cat. 746), executed in 1391, and the kings in the west window of Canterbury Cathedral (Cat. 748), which date from between 1396 and 1411. In both the Exeter and the Canterbury panels the general treatment of figures is similar to Thomas Glazier of Oxford's work, although each glazier has his own distinctive traits. No other glass by Lyen nor by the anonymous master responsible for the Canterbury west window has so far been identified. Thomas of Oxford, on the other hand, is known to have had a very long career and can be connected with important commissions. In addition to his work at New College and Winchester College he can be associated on stylistic grounds with glass in the east window of Merton College chapel and in the nave and choir clerestory at Winchester Cathedral.[63] He was still active in 1421–2 and thus overlapped with the second generation working in the International Gothic idiom.[64] The most important of these was John Thornton of Coventry, whose workshop was responsible for the great east window and other windows in York Minster, in addition to many other commissions in the north and the Midlands. His work, which exhibits many affinities with Thomas Glazier of Oxford, lies outside the scope of this exhibition.[65]

NOTES

1. Theophilus in Dodwell 1961; Heraclius in Merrifield 1849, I, pp. 166–257. The best modern account of the techniques used is Frodl-Kraft 1970; for English descriptions see Le Couteur 1926, pp. 1–21.
2. Vila Grau 1985.
3. Salzman 1926–7, p. 35.
4. Drake 1912, p. 238.
5. Knowles 1936, p. 38.
6. Grodecki & Brisac 1985, p. 176.
7. Woodforde 1954, p. 8.
8. Knowles 1936, pp. 11–12.
9. Ashdown 1948, p. 17
10. *Cal. Pat. Rolls* 1348–50, p. 481; *Cal. Pat. Rolls* 1350–4, p. 308.
11. Drake 1912, p. 8; Woodforde 1951, p. 4.
12. Woodforde 1951; Harvey & King 1971.
13. Colvin, 1971, p. 286.
14. French & O'Connor 1987, p. 85.
15. Borenius 1943; Colvin 1963; Colvin 1971.
16. Salzman 1926–7; Salzman 1927–8, pp. 188–9.
17. Woodforde 1951, pp. 6–7.
18. Erskine 1983, pp. ix–xii.
19. Marks 1982, pp. 139–40.
20. Toke 1935.
21. O'Connor & Haselock 1977, p. 345; Legge 1931–2.
22. O'Connor & Haselock 1977, pp. 353–4.
23. Gibbons 1888, p. 34.
24. Becksmann 1975.
25. For the Oxfordshire material see Newton 1979.
26. Caviness 1977; Caviness 1981.
27. Caviness 1977, pp. 100, 151, 154.
28. Ibid., p. 36.
29. For affinities between the Canterbury glazing and France see ibid., pp. 84–96 and Grodecki & Brisac 1985, p. 184.

30. Morgan 1983.
31. Winston 1865, pp. 106–29; Fletcher 1930–2.
32. Winston 1865, loc. cit.; Day 1909, pp. 136–48, 158–73; Morgan 1983, pp. 38–41.
33. Grodecki 1949.
34. Zakin 1979; Marks 1986, pp. 213–15.
35. For Abbey Dore see Marks 1986, p. 214, pl. 89.
36. Morgan 1983, pp. 40–1 n. 14.
37. For Stanton Harcourt see Newton 1979, pp. 182–8, pls 43, 44; Kempsey is published in Green 1942, pp. 42–4, and Salisbury chapter house in Blum 1978.
38. O'Connor & Haselock 1977, pp. 325–7, pl. 92; Winston 1865, pp. 116–18; Newton 1979, pp. 182–6, pl. 43 (f–i).
39. Lillich 1973; Grodecki & Brisac 1985, p. 154.
40. E.g. in the Ste-Chapelle glass and the Psalter of St Louis (Paris, Bibliothèque nationale, MS lat. 10525).
41. Binski 1986.
42. Lillich 1978, pp. 26–7; Grodecki & Brisac 1985, pp. 157, 172–5.
43. Marks 1982, p. 132; O'Connor & Haselock 1977, p. 108, pl. 98.
44. Winston 1847, II, pl. 8.
45. Croft, Mynard & Kerr 1986.
46. O'Connor & Haselock 1977, pp. 334–41, pls 98–100.
47. Councer 1952; Eeles & Peatling 1930, pp. 50–1; Newton 1979, pp. 182–6, pl. 43 (f).
48. Lillich 1970; Lillich 1978; Grodecki & Brisac 1985, pp. 137–9, 156–64.
49. Becksmann 1967.
50. O'Connor & Haselock 1977, pp. 357–8, pls 113, 114; Randall 1966a.
51. Pächt 1943. The best survey of the stained-glass material is in Newton 1961.

52. Morand 1962; Lafond 1954; Perrot 1972, pp. 18–20.
53. Sandler 1970; Sandler 1983; French & O'Connor 1987.
54. Marks 1982; Smith 1983; Winston 1865, pp. 285ff.; Kerr 1985.
55. Smith 1807; Salzman 1926–7; Salzman 1927–8, pp. 188–9.
56. Edington is unpublished. For York see O'Connor & Haselock 1977, pp. 370–2, pls 119, 120.
57. Woodforde 1933.
58. James & Millar 1936.
59. Several of these are unpublished. For Wormshill see Newman 1976, p. 499, pl. 59; Aston Rowant is published in Newton 1979, pp. 26–7, pl. 14 (f, g) and Old Warden in Marks 1986, pp. 225–7, pls 103, 104.
60. For Birtsmorton see Rushforth 1926; Farleigh Hungerford is published in Woodforde 1946, ill. on p. 17 and the Bodleian figure, which comes from Adderbury church, in Newton 1979, pp. 20–1, pl. 13.
61. Hudleston 1951.
62. Woodforde 1951.
63. Le Couteur 1920, pp. 25–6, 29–34.
64. For a full account of Thomas Glazier's documented career see Woodforde 1951, pp. 3–7.
65. For Thornton see esp. Newton 1961, pp. 98–124 and O'Connor & Haselock 1977, pp. 364–7, pls 117, 118; see also a forthcoming thesis by T. Owen.

Manuscript Illumination
of the Thirteenth
and Fourteenth Centuries

Nigel J. Morgan

& Lucy Freeman Sandler

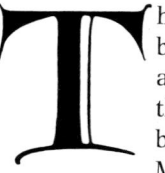

The years around 1200 heralded a period of change in the production of illuminated books. The types of books that were produced changed, as did the status of the patrons and the ways in which artists and scribes operated. New developments in society and the increasing importance of urban centres in part explain the differences between book production in the Gothic period and that of the Romanesque and the earlier Middle Ages.

In the twelfth century the main patrons were the monasteries, above all those of the Benedictines. Most of their books were large in format, with those for the library or use in the liturgy predominating almost exclusively over private, personal books. Texts of the commentaries of the Church Fathers and huge lectern bibles vastly outnumbered devotional books. Even these scholarly commentaries often received illumination of the highest quality. A personal devotional book which did begin to receive rich decoration, the psalter, gradually gained in popularity during the twelfth century, and by 1200 this book had become an important subject for illuminators. Throughout the thirteenth and fourteenth centuries and for the rest of the Middle Ages the psalter and Book of Hours, which served as prayer books for both lay people and religious, received the most elaborate decoration of all texts. These were books for individuals rather than institutions, and book production changed to cater for such a market.

Although the rise in popularity of the illuminated psalter and Book of Hours indicates a shift in taste, it is but one aspect of a shift towards a different form and organisation of book production. In the thirteenth century the market for scholarly books still existed, but in the universities rather than the monasteries. Oxford became established in the closing years of the twelfth century and Cambridge early in the thirteenth. These universities required texts of contemporary commentaries on the scriptures, the most accurate Paris texts of the Bible, the works of Aristotle and law books, above all those concerning canon law. Compilations of those works of Aristotle or of canon law which were studied for the course for the bachelor's and master's degrees were bound together as sets. Usually these received little or no illumination, but occasionally (e.g. Cat. 318) luxury copies were made. Bibles of small size (pocket bibles) were produced in large numbers for study; they contrast with the lavish lectern bibles of the twelfth century. Again, this production reflects a shift to personal book ownership.

The evidence so far gathered from archival sources which mention scribes and illuminators is insufficient to provide anything like a complete picture. An impressive documentation is available for Oxford from 1200 onwards. Only in the case of William de Brailes, recorded in Oxford *c.* 1230–50, are there extant signed works by a named artist (e.g. Cat. 314). For all other manuscripts attributions of date and location of place of production depend on a combination of evidence from liturgical texts, figure style, ornament, script and contemporary ownership. Manuscripts can be grouped on the basis of this evidence, and hypotheses of centres of artists' workshops have been put forward. As the material is subjected to closer analysis, and interrelationships of manuscripts more closely defined, some of these suggestions of places of production and chronological development will assuredly need revision. In the thirteenth century Oxford, London and Salisbury are considered to be the main centres of luxury book production. Only on a small scale was such work perhaps done at Canterbury, Worcester, York and in various places in East Anglia and the north Midlands. In the fourteenth century London, Oxford, Cambridge, Norwich and York may have been the leading centres but as yet firm evidence has to be found. It is still very much an open question whether illuminators and scribes were working in organised workshops in the large cities, or whether two or three collaborators moved from place to place wherever commissions could be found. So few records exist of contracts or payments for books in this period that only years of scholarly study to piece together such evidence as we do have may eventually refine our understanding of the situation.

An exception to the general trend towards illuminated book production by lay people (both men and women are recorded as illuminators) is the work of Matthew Paris, a Benedictine monk and the chronicler of the Abbey of St Albans. He illustrated his chronicles with marginal drawings (e.g. Cat. 437), and also made lives of the saints, most notably a Life of St Alban (Dublin, Trinity College, MS 177; fig. 111), the

Fig. 111 The martyrdom of St Alban, *c.* 1250 (Dublin, Trinity College Library. MS 177, f. 38)

saint whose relics rested at his abbey. Until recently it was considered that Matthew was the centre of a 'school' of artists based at St Albans, and that many of the great illuminated psalters and Apocalypses of the middle years of the thirteenth century were made there. It has now been argued persuasively that most of these books were produced in London, Oxford and Salisbury. Matthew Paris is best viewed as an exceptionally talented individual somewhat apart from the professional artists of his time. Although some books were made 'in house' in monasteries such as St Albans and elsewhere in the thirteenth century, it is only those decorated by Matthew which can hold their own among the great works of illumination of the period.

The style called Gothic is more easily definable in terms of architecture than for the figure arts of painting and sculpture, and the terminology of description of these arts is necessarily of quite a different order. The conventional division of English Gothic architecture into Early English (*c.* 1190–1250), Decorated (*c.* 1250–1360) and Perpendicular (*c.* 1330–1550) is only in a general sense appropriate for the history of painting, which has different phases of development. Perhaps only with the Decorated period is there a coincident phase. The beginning of Gothic painting in the years *c.* 1180–1220 has been termed the Transitional period. The mannered abstractions and distortions of Romanesque figure style became disciplined into a calm, dignified, sometimes even stolid, manner of composition. In many ways this is a counterpart to the clear-cut forms of the architectural style of those years, with the lines of the building still not masked by the decorative elements of elaborate mouldings and tracery which were introduced during the thirteenth century. A second phase of painting, *c.* 1220–60, can be termed Early Gothic as it was the period in which the essentials of the Gothic style were established in English painting. A small-scale fussiness of composition, combined with elegantly posed gesticulating figures and emphasis on linear elements, replaced the calm, solid figure forms of the Transitional period (e.g. Cat. 253–5). Decorative ornament gradually expands into a diverse repertoire of forms: line endings, border bars extending from the initials, pen flourishes, and, towards the end of the period, border decoration of birds, animals and fantasy hybrid forms (e.g. Cat. 315).

This second phase was comparatively little influenced by French art, but around 1260 in both painting and sculpture stylistic and decorative fashions penetrated from the other side of the Channel (e.g. Cat. 354–5). From that time until the early years of the fourteenth century the main trends in English painting paralleled developments in France, particularly those of Paris. Most English painters evolved an idiosyncratic variant of French styles which was distinctively different in appearance, and was a mature assimilation of the new forms into their own traditions. It is likely that in the last quarter of the thirteenth century such English work may have influenced some painters in France (see Cat. 356).

The French taste of this period is a reflection of the immense international prestige of Parisian Court culture, which had been a model for Western courtly society since the middle of the thirteenth century. Both Henry III in the latter part of his reign, and his son Edward I, in their patronage of art and architecture showed a preference for styles whose appearance, albeit in English guise, was French (e.g. Cat. 357–8). In the reigns of Edward II and III painting evolved without much influence from France; these specifically fourteenth-century developments will be considered further.

During the Gothic period, as a result of more diverse patronage of book illumination, the range of book types and subjects illustrated increased. Another factor which may explain this expansion is an artistic self-confidence in which invention of new images predominated over eclectic dependence on the past for models and traditions. It may be that Romanesque or Anglo-Saxon painting contrasted so much in appearance with the mature Gothic style that it could seldom provide inspiration. The tendency towards elaboration of small-scale figure decoration in initials, borders and *bas-de-page* ornaments led to the creation of programmes of overwhelming complexity. The manuscripts made for the Bohun family during the second half of the fourteenth century (Cat. 686–91) are prime examples of such a tendency. It sometimes seems that artists were given instructions to paint as many subjects as they could possibly fit into the initials and borders. Such proliferation of illuminated decoration is by no means only a characteristic of the fourteenth century, for the trend began as early as the middle of the thirteenth as in the Oscott and Cuerden Psalters (Cat. 352, 355). Personal patrons willing to pay the high price for such extensively decorated books must have stimulated artists to excesses of elaboration.

The combining of very different, even opposite, genres of subject within the same decorative scheme is a distinctive feature of Gothic manuscript illumination, particularly in the century between 1250 and 1350. Religious subjects from the Old and New Testaments, apocryphal legends and scenes from the lives of the saints compete for space in borders of the same page with secular imagery ranging from the humorous to the obscene. Such secular imagery had been important in Romanesque art in sculpture and the decorative initials of manuscripts. In the initials it had been enmeshed in the foliage coils, disguised by the intertwining stems and leaves. During the thirteenth century this fantastic menagerie escaped from its cage of the foliate initial and entered the borders. This troupe of monsters, animals, birds, humans and fantastic hybrids multiplied in the fourteenth century until in the second half of that century the fashion for this sort of imagery in book illumination waned.

There was an increase during the thirteenth century in books whose illustrations are so numerous in relation to the text that they can be termed picture books (e.g. Cat. 42, 348). The audience of lay people (or perhaps children in some cases) for which these were intended was able to read the story in the pictures, which often had only short titles or inscriptions to clarify their meaning. Bestiaries, Apocalypses, Lives of the Saints and the series of pictures included in psalters and Books of Hours are examples of this picture-book tendency. Pictures probably had an educative purpose, in some cases at an elementary level, and it cannot always be assumed that a higher meditative or intellectual contemplation of images was intended.

Certain types of book rose and fell in fashion. Psalters, and from *c.* 1250 also Books of Hours, were continuously popular. Illustrated bestiaries of great luxury (e.g. Cat. 252–3) were much in evidence in the first half of the thirteenth century but from then on their popularity declined. Bibles were produced in sufficiently large numbers in the thirteenth century to have provided for the subsequent century, in which very few were made. During the thirteenth century there were also numerous imports from France.

The fashion for illustrated Apocalypses is strongest in the periods 1250–80 (e.g. Cat. 347–51) and 1310–40 (e.g. Cat. 203). The reasons for the interest in this text are complex and still insufficiently defined. Certainly there was always a curiosity concerning predictions of the fearful events which would precede the end of the world, of which the visions of the Apocalypse were considered allegories. Dates for the coming end were always news, most notably that of 1260 favoured by the followers of Joachim of Fiore, a Calabrian monk writing in the last years of the twelfth century. The Franciscans in particular produced these Joachist prophetic writings. The memorable events of the Book of Revelation could be interpreted at different levels as allegories of past and present events, as predictions of future calamities, and in a personal sense as a description of the moral struggle of the Christian individual in the passage through life. The text ends with the triumph over evil, the mystical contemplation of the New Jerusalem with the river of the Water of Life, and the union of the righteous with Christ who appears to St John in the final vision. The illustrated copies must have had a multiplicity of interpretations from their owners, ranging from the courtly and romantic to the prophetic and the moral.

Devotional and moral treatises seldom received decoration (Cat. 42 is an exception) but their texts influenced the choice and type of illustration in psalters and Books of Hours. The programme of devotions described in the *Ancrene Riwle*, a manual of instructions in English for anchoresses written *c.* 1215–20, or the *c.* 1240 meditations on the life of Christ in the *Speculum Ecclesiae* of St Edmund of Abingdon (translated into Anglo-Norman as the *Mirour de Seinte Eglyse*) have direct reflections in the earliest Books of Hours such as the Egerton Hours (British Library, MS Egerton 1151, Cat. 41) and the Nuremberg Hours (Nuremberg, Stadtbibliothek, MS Solger 4.4°) made by the Parisian workshop of Maître Honoré for an English patron. Meditations on the Joys of the Virgin such as those of the Cistercian Stephen of Sawley (d. 1252) or of the poet Guillaume le Clerc (early thirteenth century) are also paralleled by pictorial equivalents. Pictures were used for meditations on the life of Christ or the Virgin before the various Hours or before recitation of the Psalms, and the choice of subject in Books of Hours and psalters may reflect literary sources. Such an interrelationship between texts and pictures was of particular importance in the development of the intensified imagery of the Passion in the late thirteenth and fourteenth centuries. Icon-like devotional images were created, such as those of the Veronica head of Christ and the Instruments of the Passion (*Arma Christi*) as aids to meditations on the Passion. Some of these images were attached to prayers granting indulgences, which enhanced their popularity.

Another important change was the increase of texts in the vernacular. For most of the period this vernacular was Anglo-Norman French rather than English, it being the languge spoken in aristocratic circles until supplanted by English during the fourteenth century. Apocalypses, bestiaries, Lives of the Saints, devotional and moral treatises, and even works on medicine (e.g. Cat. 312) occur in Anglo-Norman translation, or sometimes, as in the case of the romances, were originally composed in that language.

The workshops of thirteenth-century illuminators in some cases show continuity of ornamental and stylistic forms over a long period of time. This is most clearly seen in Oxford and London work. In the early years of the century there seems to be a continuity of production in those areas where there had been important monastic centres in the Romanesque period, such as Canterbury and Winchester. The early thirteenth-century group of bestiaries (Cat. 252–3) were probably made in the north Midlands or north of England, and Lincoln has been suggested as place of origin. From around 1200 there was continuous production in Oxford. The earliest group of manuscripts was around a lavishly illustrated psalter now in Munich (Stadtbibliothek, MS Clm. 835) and in *c.* 1210–20 was followed by a group of artists whose main work was the Huntingfield Psalter (New York, Pierpont Morgan Library, M.43). This second group laid the foundations for the workshop of William de Brailes(Cat. 314, 436) which operated in the period 1230–60. In ornamental forms and figure style a further continuation in workshops of the period 1250–80 produced psalters, bibles and copies of Aristotle (e.g. Cat. 354–5, 318). The important and long-lived workshop whose manuscripts (Cat. 354–5) are grouped around the Bible of William of Devon (London, British Library, MS Royal 1.D.1) may have been located in Oxford, but this is controversial.

The other thirteenth-century centre with a continuous tradition was London, where the earliest works were of c. 1230, such as the Glazier and Trinity Psalters (Cat. 8, 255). London production attained a peak of activity in the period 1250–75, in which years it is likely that many of the Apocalypses were made there. There has been much discussion as to the existence of a Court School associated with Westminster Abbey and Palace, but the extensive records of Henry III's art patronage offer no concrete evidence for such a group of illuminators. Some of the finest products of London artists are, however, associated with the patronage of the Abbey or the royal family (e.g. Cat. 9). These form a nucleus around which other manuscripts can be grouped. The evidence for the production of most of the Apocalypses in London is not strong, but it is the most satisfactory of the current hypotheses. Their close ties in style and iconography imply that their artists had close interrelationships, and these could best be explained by a single centre for their activities.

The Salisbury–Winchester region may also have played a role. The royal residences of Clarendon and Winchester and numerous rich monasteries and nunneries in the region resulted in a wide range of potential patrons. Almost certainly one of the greatest artists of the period, the Sarum Master (see Cat. 108, 316), was based in Salisbury. His work is quite distinct in style and ornament from that of London and Oxford, although some of his collaborators may also have worked in London.

At the end of Henry III's reign, in works such as the Douce Apocalypse (Cat. 351), English illumination had achieved a height of brilliance almost without rival in Europe. Even though that book owed much to French art it also relied much on English traditions, and the result unquestionably surpasses its Parisian models.

By the last decades of the thirteenth century the characteristics that gave rise to the term 'Decorated style' in English Gothic architecture had also appeared in manuscript painting. Graceful linearity, delicacy of scale and elaboration of ornamentation based on natural motifs were found not only in the treatment of walls, piers, shafts and arches, and in the echoes of architecture in borders and frames of miniatures and initials, but were fundamental to the refined figure style, the rich surface texture and pattern, and the elegantly tooled gold grounds of pictorial images.

In manuscript illumination these features are identified with the Court style, a term used in connection with a number of manuscripts produced between the time of the Alphonso Psalter of 1284 (Cat. 357) and the Tickhill Psalter of 1303–14 (Cat. 568). Some of these books were owned or commissioned by the royal family – the Alphonso Psalter, the Ashridge Petrus Comestor (London, British Library, MS Royal 3.D.VI), and the Isabella Psalter (Munich, Bayerische Nationalbibliothek, Cod. gall. 16). Others are connected with members of the Court, for example the Mazarine Bible (Cat. 360), or served as Court records, such as the Bodleian genealogical roll (Cat. 10). Some Court style books, however, are of uncertain provenance and destination, among them the Windmill Psalter (Cat. 358), the 'Peterborough Bestiary' (Cambridge, Corpus Christi College, MS 53), and the Jesus College Psalter (Oxford, Jesus College, MS D.40; fig. 19). And finally, the term, at least as far as its stylistic features are concerned, also applies perfectly to a few manuscripts whose owners or origins were monastic, not secular, above all to the first parts of the Peterborough Psalter in Brussels (Cat. 567) and the Tickhill Psalter (Cat. 568).

Where the Court style manuscripts were actually made can only be surmised. The style was not the product of a single group or a linear succession of artists. Since it appears in manuscripts made for royal use in various locales, including York, where the Court was lodged for much of the time between 1295 and 1305, it could be that miniaturists travelled around with the king, as members of the royal household, although documentary evidence for this practice is indirect at best. But since the main scene of Court life was the Palace of Westminster, which was the primary centre of government, it seems reasonable to conclude that the centre of the Court style was in London, the chief city of the realm, where patrons from outside Court circles could have had more ready access to Court style artists.

During the fourteenth century the illustration of a single luxury manuscript was often the work of several individuals. These artists might work in succession, perhaps over a long period, and occasionally with significant chronological gaps. They might work together on different portions of a volume, or they might work on different aspects of the decorative programme. Among the chief manuscripts identified with the Court style are some whose programmes of decoration were carried out in sharply divergent styles. The Alphonso Psalter (Cat. 357), for example, was only begun in an elegant and refined manner; most of the volume was decorated in the bold and exuberant style known as 'East Anglian'. A similar division marks the Brussels Peterborough Psalter, the Mazarine Bible, and to a degree the Tickhill Psalter (Cat. 567, 360, 568). Except for the Alphonso Psalter, where work by the original artist stopped abruptly with the death of its destined owner in 1284 and was taken up again only in the fourteenth century, the divergent styles in these manuscripts appear to be contemporary, or to follow immediately one upon the other.

The fundamental attributes of the East Anglian style – exuberant, fantastic and humorous pictorial imagery, accurate representation of details of nature in bold and arbitrarily varied scale – are characteristic of a considerable number of English manuscripts produced between 1300 and c. 1325. These books fall into several groups, some warranting the name 'East Anglian' by virtue of their geographical origins or destinations, and others not, but 'East Anglian' in style none the less.

The earliest East Anglian manuscripts are contemporary with those in the Court style, and belong to the first decade of the fourteenth century. One small group is centred around the second – and larger – portion of the Brussels Peterborough Psalter (Cat. 567), and includes the Ramsey Abbey Psalter (Cat. 565–6) as well as the inserted leaves in the Gough Psalter (Oxford, Bodleian Library, MS Gough liturg. 8). The destinations of these manuscripts were Benedictine abbeys in the Fenland, on the borders of East Anglia.

Another group of manuscripts of the first decade of the century, 'East Anglian' in style if not in known origin, includes the Grey-Fitzpayn Hours (Cambridge, Fitzwilliam Museum, MS 242), the Vaux Psalter (London, Lambeth Palace Library, MS 233), the McClean Bible (Cambridge, Fitzwilliam Museum, MS McClean 15), an Aristotle in Paris (Cat. 597), and the second part of the Tickhill Psalter (Cat. 568). Marked by the same bold scale and exuberant marginal décor as the Fenland group, these manuscripts are usually known collectively as the Tickhill group, although they resemble only the second part of that book, whose first portion was painted in the Court style. Although the Tickhill Psalter itself was written and decorated, at least in part, by John Tickhill, Augustinian prior of Worksop, Nottinghamshire, the circumstances of production of the rest of the group are difficult to ascertain in view of the diversity of owners and the indications of destination and provenance both in the northern and southern ecclesiastical provinces of England.

Between 1310 and 1325 English manuscript illumination developed in two broad artistic currents, the East Anglian and the Queen Mary, whose tributaries sometimes merged. To the first stream, the term 'East Anglian' applies accurately, since it identifies manuscripts connected by origin or destination with the counties of Norfolk and Suffolk and the dioceses of Norwich and Ely, and in style with the bold, exuberant manner already associated with the Fenland books of the first decade of the century. East Anglian manuscripts of this period fall into two groups, one centred around the Ormesby Psalter (Cat. 573) and its chief artist, and the other around the Gorleston Psalter (Cat. 574). The patronage of the Ormesby Psalter group seems to have been monastic; the earliest known owners of the books were Benedictine (as with the Ormesby Psalter and Gregory, *Moralia* [Cambridge, Emmanuel College, MS 112], and perhaps the Dublin Apocalypse [Dublin, Trinity College, MS 92]), or Cluniac (as with the Bromholm Psalter [Oxford, Bodleian Library, MS Ashmole 1523]). The owners of the Gorleston Psalter and the related Howard Psalter (London, British Library, MS

Fig. 112 God creating the birds and the beasts, from the Queen Mary Psalter, 1310–20 (London, British Library, MS 2 B. vii, f.2)

Arundel 83.1), and the Longleat Breviary (Longleat House, Marquess of Bath, MS 10) were secular clerics. These books seem to have been commissioned by lay patrons for priests in their service. They were meant to be used in parish churches and chapels in a variety of places in Suffolk, Norfolk and Huntingdonshire, again raising the question as to the actual place of origin or mode of production.

The second decade of the fourteenth century was also marked by the appearance on the scene of a profoundly influential artist known only as the Queen Mary Master, after his *chef d'œuvre*, the Queen Mary Psalter (London, British Library, MS Royal 2 B. vii; figs 6, 7, 112). The name 'Queen Mary style' is applied to a group of about twenty surviving books executed during the second, and into the third decade of the century. The term evokes a manner that is graceful and delicately linear, often more coloured drawing than full-bodied painting, and gentle and restrained in expression. In elegant refinement the Queen Mary style is the Court style in a new guise.

Several distinctive artists as well as a number of lesser figures worked in the Queen Mary style; their products exhibit a wide variety in provenance, patronage, and types of texts illustrated. But the uniformity of iconography, the adherence to a shared set of pictorial models, is striking. This balance of diversity and uniformity has suggested to most recent students that the Queen Mary manuscripts originated in a single place: an established workshop operating over a long period, perhaps organised along the lines apparently characteristic of Parisian manuscript production. The consensus is that this place of production was London; reasonable, as London is prominent among the known destinations of the Queen Mary books.

Artists working in the Queen Mary style remained active past the middle of the third decade of the fourteenth century, but around 1325 several new developments in manuscript illumination occurred. First, a wave of self-conscious Italianism swept over the East Anglian style – the St Omer Psalter (London, British Library, MS Yates Thompson 14) and the Gorleston Psalter Crucifixion (Cat. 574) are the chief examples – replacing bold scale, heavy outline and flat pattern with delicate scale, sculptural modelling and illusionistic textural effects, and even introducing three-dimensional spatial settings, all the time retaining the thematic absurdities and drolleries characteristic of indigenous English iconography. This variant of the East Anglian style persisted up to the middle of the fourteenth century, especially in a few books associated with the diocese of Ely, such as the Psalter of Simon of Montacute (Cat. 684). Other East Anglian manuscripts, however, continued the style of the Ormesby and Gorleston Psalters, although somewhat simplified and reduced in marginal richness (for example, the Stowe Breviary, London, British Library, MS Stowe 12).

In contrast to the continuity of the East Anglian style, the manuscripts produced in the orbit of the king, or in Court circles, during the 1320s and 1330s, were no longer distinctly courtly in style. In fact, to the extent that royal manuscripts survive from the second quarter of the fourteenth century, they no longer form a cohesive group. The Douce Psalter (Cat. 683), the Anglo-French Coronation Order (Cat. 11), the Psalters of Philippa of Hainault, the Brunetto Latini of Edward III and Philippa (Cat. 205) and the Treatise of Walter of Milemete (Cat. 682) exemplify this diversity, suggesting that the king and Court received or ordered manuscripts from a wide range of sources, and did not maintain miniaturists as personal *luminours*. Some of these books, above all the Milemete Treatise, were produced by the collaboration of unusually large numbers of artists (five contemporary hands in the Milemete volume, for example), whose hands recur widely in de-luxe exemplars of legal and scholarly texts that required only a few illustrations. These volumes could have been written in Oxford or Cambridge where there were many text models and potential owners, and could have been illustrated in these university centres – or elsewhere.

The Black Death devastated artists and patrons alike, but did not produce a distinctive 'post-Black Death' style in manuscript illumination. Heightened dramatic expression – achieved by devices such as exaggerated gestures, contorted poses and caricatured facial features – to create vivid and even terrifying pictorial images had always existed in English manuscript illumination, and had come to the fore in the 1320s in such picture books as the Holkham Bible (Cat. 22), perhaps in conjunction with the rise of vernacular literature and religious drama. This current was particularly strong around the time of the Black Death, affecting the illustration of service books, and giving new vitality and urgency to the illustration of standard themes of the Infancy and Passion of Christ (e.g. Walters Hours, Cat. 152). Not until the end of the century were texts written in English illustrated (Cat. 718).

The most important English illuminated manuscripts of the second half of the fourteenth century, the Bohun group, although Latin psalters and Books of Hours, introduced an incomparable wealth of pictorial imagery, most of it narrative, vividly evoking the actions and events of the Old and New Testaments, the Lives of the Virgin and the Saints in pictures – often historiated initials – that run into the hundreds in each manuscript (Cat. 686–91). In style the Bohun manuscripts echo such East Anglian books of 1325–50 as the St Omer Psalter, the Douce Psalter and the Montacute Psalter that are marked by Italianate techniques of shading and rendering of surface texture, and they also continue the East Anglian taste for marginal drolleries of fantastic and amusing hybrid construction. Details of figure proportions, facial types, clothing, and decorative motifs, however, are all changed. In these elements the Bohun style is comparable to contemporary manuscript illumination on the Continent, that of the Boqueteaux group in Paris and the artists of Count Louis de Male in Flanders.

Fig. 113 The coronation of the Queen from
the *Liber Regalis*, *c.* 1380–1400 (London,
Westminster Abbey, MS 38. f, 29)

The Bohun manuscripts were made between *c.* 1360 and *c.* 1380–90 for two successive Earls of Hereford, Essex and Northampton – Humphrey de Bohun, sixth earl and his nephew, Humphrey de Bohun, seventh earl – and their immediate descendants, by a cohesive group of artists who seem to have worked only for this family. The artists, two of whom were John de Teye and Henry Hood, both detached Augustinian friars, were treated as family retainers, and worked, so it seems, in the Bohun castle at Pleshey, Essex. The fortuitously preserved information about the production of the Bohun manuscripts suggests that the contemporary sovereigns of England might have maintained illuminators in a similar way, but the only tangible evidence of royal manuscript patronage during the later fourteenth century is associated with Richard II (1377–99) rather than Edward III. It would seem from such works as the *Liber Regalis* (London, Westminster Abbey, MS 38; fig. 113), the Historical Compilation in the British Library (Cotton Nero MS D.VI), and the Oxford Astrological Handbook (Bodleian Library, MS Bodley 581) – all linked with Richard II – that the king's patronage was shared with the monks of Westminster Abbey (Lytlington Missal, Cat. 714), the Carmelites at Whitefriars (Carmelite Missal, London, British Library, Add. MS 29704–5), and various individual owners of service books made, probably in London, during the last two decades of the century. Some of these manuscripts are conservative in style even though lavish in format, such as the Lytlington Missal with its numerous historiated initials filled with stock groupings of plump, stiff figures and its elaborate borders composed of repeated stylised foliate motifs, masks and heraldry. Other volumes, however, contain initials and miniatures in an English version of the International Style (*Liber Regalis*, and Cambridge University Proctor's Book), with large, softly-moulded figures swathed in graceful drapery, recalling contemporary painting in Bohemia, the Netherlands, Cologne and Paris.

The visual parallels between English Gothic illuminated books and works of art in other media are clear: figural style, iconographic motifs and decorative vocabulary are shared by wall painting, panel painting, stained glass and embroidery, and the decorative vocabulary recurs not only in two-dimensional form but in the carving of architectural mouldings, bosses and capitals, of tombs, and of ecclesiastical furniture from episcopal thrones to misericords. Among the striking instances of direct relationships across the media are the miniatures of the Douce Apocalypse (Cat. 351) and the Westminster Abbey Retable (Cat. 329), those of the De Lisle Psalter (Cat. 569) and the Westminster Abbey Sedilia, and those of the Hours of Alice de Reydon (Cat. 570) and the Swinburne Pyx (Cat. 571). What are not known, however, are the particulars of chronological relations between instances of close similarity, nor how frequently book illuminators crossed into the realms of painters of panels, walls and glass, or vice versa. It seems probable that for most of the thirteenth and fourteenth centuries professional illuminators of books were usually associated with practitioners of other aspects of the complex art of book production and rarely with artists identified as 'painters', who worked in a larger scale. But few paintings have survived, while manuscripts are abundant, and often preserved in a remarkably fresh state. Worthy of appreciation in themselves as characteristically medieval amalgams of image and text, illuminated manuscripts provide the only detailed and comprehensive view of pictorial art in England during the Gothic period.

Donald King Embroidery and Textiles

elatively few textile fabrics survive for six or seven centuries in a presentable condition. Hence the textile content of an exhibition of English Gothic art is comparatively small, consisting almost exclusively of religious embroideries which have outlasted the centuries in the protective environment of the church. Beautiful and fascinating though these embroideries are, it seems appropriate, before considering them, to take a slightly wider view of textiles in Gothic England.

In the present age of cheap mass-produced fabrics and artificial fibres, it is important to remember that in the Middle Ages textiles occupied a much larger place in a more limited stock of material possessions. They were relatively more costly, they absorbed a larger proportion of personal incomes, and they were more important as external signs of wealth, power and social status. Fine textiles were considered appropriate gifts for kings, popes and other great personages. The very wealthy spent fantastic sums on their dress and textile furnishings. Officials regularly received suits of clothes as part of their salaries. Everyone, however poor, needed clothing and bed coverings of some kind. This universal demand gave rise to the most complex of all medieval industries, engaged in many different countries in the cultivation and preparation of natural fibres and dyes, in the weaving, dyeing and finishing of cloth and in various ancillary activities. The industry employed vast numbers of workers and a great deal of sophisticated machinery, mostly hand- and foot-powered, but making use of water power where appropriate. It also employed large amounts of capital and played a crucial role in the development of the European capitalist system. Associated with the industry was a complex network of commercial activity, buying and selling the raw materials and the finished textiles, and transporting them by sea and land throughout Europe and beyond. Besides their economic importance, the industry and commerce of textiles were potent political forces, both nationally and internationally. In the case of England, for example, exports of wool and imports and exports of cloth were essential factors in political and economic decision-making, both for the country itself and for its relations with other European powers.

With regard to textiles used in England in the Middle Ages, one is struck by the great number and variety of types and qualities available. All available natural fibres were employed, the main ones being the vegetable fibres cotton, hemp and linen, and the animal fibres wool and silk.

Cotton, imported from Mediterranean and Asian sources, was much used in the raw state as padding for quilts and quilted garments. Fine cotton cloth known as bokeram (derived from Bokhara; the cloth was originally imported from Asia) was used for garments, linings and banners. A rather stouter fabric, used for garments and bedding, was fustian (originally derived from Fustat in Egypt, but it was also woven in Europe) which had a cotton weft and linen warp. Hemp served for cordage. Canvas was employed for tents, sails and beds. Linen was used for sewing thread. Linen cloth, in many different qualities, served for shirts and other garments, and for sheets, pillows, tablecloths, towels and much other household equipment. A good deal of linen cloth was produced in England, for instance at Aylsham and Wilton, but much of the finer cloth was imported from Continental centres such as Rheims and Paris. Though most of the foregoing were plain white cloths, they could also be dyed in various colours. For furnishing purposes they were sometimes woven with small-scale white-on-white lattice patterns, or with decorative bands at each end. For other uses the plain cloths might receive painted decoration in watercolour or body colour, or with gold leaf. Cloths with block-printed patterns were available in Europe, but there is no firm evidence of their use in England.

Exports of raw wool and woollen cloth were a principal source of national income and of the revenues of the English Crown. Fine English wool was an indispensable raw material for the weaving industries of the Netherlands and northern France and even, to some extent, that of Italy. Woollen cloths were employed for dress and furnishings in an enormous range of types and qualities. Near the bottom end of the scale came burel, woven in London, Winchester and other English towns, and used for the dress of servants and the poorer classes. Rather higher stood such varieties as camelin, kersey, say and worsted. At the top of the range and affordable only by the very rich was scarlet, finely woven from the best wool, beautifully finished, and dyed with the costly imported dyestuff called grain, made from dried insects.

Great importance was attached to fine dyes and colours. Besides scarlet, we find many references in England to blanchet (white), bluet (blue), burnet (brown) and a rainbow of other hues such as acole (columbine colour), applebloom, azure, green, murrey (mulberry colour), paonaz (peacock colour), russet, sanguine, tawny, violet and many more. Most of these cloths were in plain colours, but some were variegated, such as marbryn (marbled), medley, motley and ray (striped).

Although the great majority of woollen cloths used in England were woven in English centres, such as Beverley, Lincoln, Stamford, York and many others, a significant number of the finest cloths were imported from overseas, from towns such as Brussels, Ghent and Ypres. A few woollens came from much further afield, such as camlets, woven in the Near East and elsewhere from the hair of the angora goat. All the foregoing were normally unpatterned cloths, but there were some patterned woollen cloths, notably tapestries, which became increasingly important in the domestic arrangements of the wealthy during the fourteenth century. Many had heraldic designs, but the more elaborate examples, particularly those imported from Arras, had pictorial scenes, such as the stories of Charlemagne, Godfrey of Bouillon, Saladin, Guy of Warwick and many other subjects drawn from history, romance or scripture. Woollen carpets with geometrical and animal patterns were available, but it is not clear how far they were used in England at that period.

Silk, produced in Asia and in southern Europe, was imported in the form of thread and a very wide variety of woven fabrics. The commonest type, extensively used for garments, linings, furnishings and banners, was cendal, a light silk cloth in plain weave, available in many different colours. It was woven in all the silk-weaving areas of Asia and southern Europe; examples used in England were recorded as coming from Lucca and from Tripoli. Other silk cloths of related types were attabi, sarsenet, taffeta and tarteryn, all originally from the East, though subsequently woven in Europe also. A heavier, more lustrous type of plain silk cloth, widely used for dress and furnishing, was known as samite on account of its peculiar twill weave (*examitum*, six-thread). Still glossier was satin, originating from Zaitun in China, but also produced in all the silk-weaving areas. The heaviest and most luxurious of the silk cloths was velvet, woven mainly in Italy and increasingly used for dress and furnishing in the fourteenth century (Cat. 12, 577).

All the foregoing were chiefly produced as dyed but unpatterned fabrics, though they were sometimes provided with patterns, either during weaving or by painting or embroidering on the finished cloth. Many other types of silk textiles, however, were habitually woven with repeating patterns. For example, cloth of aresta (fishbone cloth) had small-scale patterns of birds and other motifs executed in a characteristic herringbone twill, which gave rise to the name. Diasper (double white), with patterns of animals and foliage woven generally in white on a white background, was a forerunner of later damask. Baudekin (the name derives from Baghdad) had patterns woven partly in gold thread. And there were many other varieties of gold-patterned silks, such as camaca, ciclaton, imperial, nak and racamas, most of which originated in the East and were later imitated by Western weavers.

The current of influence flowing from East to West affected not only the types and techniques, but also the designs of woven silk textiles. Many twelfth- and thirteenth-century examples were characterised by a certain stiffness in motifs and arrangement – heraldic insignia, rectilinear lattice patterns, ranks and files of circles containing symmetrically confronted animals or birds. The Mongol conquests, however, threw open the whole of Asia, and subsequently Europe, to liberating influences from the design traditions of China. Patterned Tartar cloths (*panni tartarici*) arrived in Europe in great numbers. From the late thirteenth century onwards Near Eastern and European silk designers generally abandoned their constricting rectilinear or circular frames and allowed their birds, beasts and, sometimes, human figures to twist and move asymmetrically among free-flowing compositions of foliage and flowers. An Italian textile, a chasuble in the Victoria and Albert Museum, is an example of a high-quality patterned silk cloth of the late Gothic period, woven in brilliantly dyed silk and silver-gilt thread with a typical asymmetrical design of birds and plants. Production of silk textiles with elaborate designs such as this depended on the complex technology of the pattern-weaving loom known as the drawloom, which was widespread in Asia and the Mediterranean lands, but almost unknown in northern Europe at this time. Silk pattern-weaving in England was generally limited to narrow bands or ribbons with small-scale geometrical or animal patterns produced by simpler techniques such as tablet weaving. Thus the English contribution to silk design was negligible; but on the other hand it is very possible that silk designs exercised some influence on English art. Certainly the constant influx of patterned silks from distant lands must have made artists familiar with at least some of the decorative idioms of China, Persia, the Near East, Italy and Spain.

The textile product which carried English art and design to every country in western Europe was embroidery in silk and gold thread. The Vatican inventory of 1295 includes well over a hundred embroideries designated as English work, *Opus anglicanum*, and innumerable examples are recorded in other Continental inventories of the Gothic period. A considerable number of such embroideries are still preserved, not only in England but also in Austria, Belgium, France, Germany, Italy, Sweden and Spain. Some arrived in these countries as diplomatic gifts from kings and other magnates; some were commissioned from English suppliers. In a ironical anecdote in his *Chronica Majora*, under the year 1246, Matthew Paris records that Pope Innocent IV,

> ... having noticed that the ecclesiastical ornaments of certain English priests, such as choral copes and mitres, were embroidered in gold thread after a most desirable fashion, asked whence came this work. From England, they told him. Then exclaimed the Pope, 'England is for us surely a garden of delights, truly an inexhaustible well; and from there where so many things abound, many may be extorted.' Thereupon the same Lord Pope, allured by the desire of the eye, sent letters, blessed and sealed, to wellnigh all the abbots of the Cistercian order established in England, desiring that they should send to him without delay, these embroideries of gold which he preferred above all others, and with which he wished to decorate his chasubles and choral copes, as if these acquisitions would cost him nothing. This command of my Lord Pope did not displease the London merchants who traded in these embroideries and sold them at their own price.

The names of some of these suppliers are known. We have, for instance, lists and prices of large numbers of silk cloths and embroideries supplied to King Henry III between 1238 and 1260 by the wealthy merchant Adam of Basing, who was Sheriff of London in 1243 and Mayor in 1251. Sometimes, however, the authorities dealt not with the merchants, but with the embroidery workshops themselves. Between 1239 and 1244 Henry III commissioned several embroideries from Mabel of Bury St Edmunds. Popes Alexander IV (reigned 1254–61) and Urban IV (1261–4) had a gold embroiderer, Gregory of London, attached to the papal household. From the 1330s onward King Edward III had an official embroidery workshop operating in the Tower of London under the direction of the Royal Armourer, John of Cologne.

Embroidery is a craft requiring very little apparatus and can be carried on almost anywhere. No doubt there were competent embroiderers in various parts of England, particularly in religious houses. The only signed English embroidery surviving from the Middle Ages (Cat. 442) was worked by a nun, Johanna Beverlai, which reminds one of an injunction addressed in 1314 to nuns in Yorkshire, forbidding them to absent themselves from divine service on account of their silk work. Without exception, however, the professional embroidery workshops that we know of – for instance those of Alexander Le Settere, William Courteray, Thomas Carleton, Stephen

Vyne and Robert Ashcombe, to name a few of the more prominent fourteenth-century embroiderers – were all situated in London. The reasons for this are fairly obvious. The materials used, fine cloth, silk thread, silver, gold, pearls, sometimes jewels, were costly. The production of the embroideries required the labour of teams of skilled operatives – designers (at about 12d per day in the royal accounts of the 1350s) and workers (at 3d to 9d per day) – sometimes over long periods of time; under Henry III, for example, four women worked for three and three-quarter years on an altar frontal for the high altar of Westminster Abbey. The embroideries therefore represented a considerable outlay of capital; at the beginning of the fourteenth century, for instance, an embroidered cloth was sold to the Earl of Lincoln for £200, equivalent to the lifetime wages of the lower-paid workers mentioned above. Clearly a craft as luxurious as this could hardly flourish except in the capital, in immediate proximity to the patronage of the Court.

Much of the embroidery was worked for secular dress and furnishings. Many elaborate beds are recorded, comprising coverlet, tester, celer (canopy), cushions and matching hangings, embroidered with heraldic and other devices. One example, belonging to the widow of the Black Prince, was of red velvet 'embroidered with ostrich feathers of silver and heads of leopards of gold, with boughs and leaves of silver issuing out of their mouths.' There are many records of embroidered dress, such as the robes made for Edward III and Queen Philippa in 1351, of red velvet 'embroidered with clouds of silver and eagles of pearl and gold, under each alternate cloud an eagle of pearl, and under each of the other clouds a golden eagle, every eagle having in his beak a Garter with the motto *hony soyt qui mal y pense* embroidered thereon.' Among the very few surviving examples of this secular embroidery are the Black Prince's heraldic surcoat at Canterbury Cathedral and the remarkable fragments, perhaps from a horse trapper, which Edward III may have left behind in Germany on the occasion of his state visit there in 1338 (Cat. 12). More modest examples of secular embroidery are the heraldic seal bags made for the City of London in 1319 and still preserved by the Corporation (Cat. 206).

Embroideries made for church use have survived in greater numbers. The most elaborate of them are the copes and chasubles embroidered throughout with religious subjects, which are often framed in rows of Gothic arches. The Bologna cope (Cat. 576), for example, which is thought to have belonged to Pope Benedict XI (reigned 1303–4), has two concentric rows of arches, the upper row framing scenes of the Passion and Resurrection (the Easter cycle) and the lower row with scenes of the Infancy of Christ (the Christmas cycle), terminating with an additional scene, the

Fig. 114 The Pienza cope, 1315–35 (Capitolo della Cattedrale di Pienza)

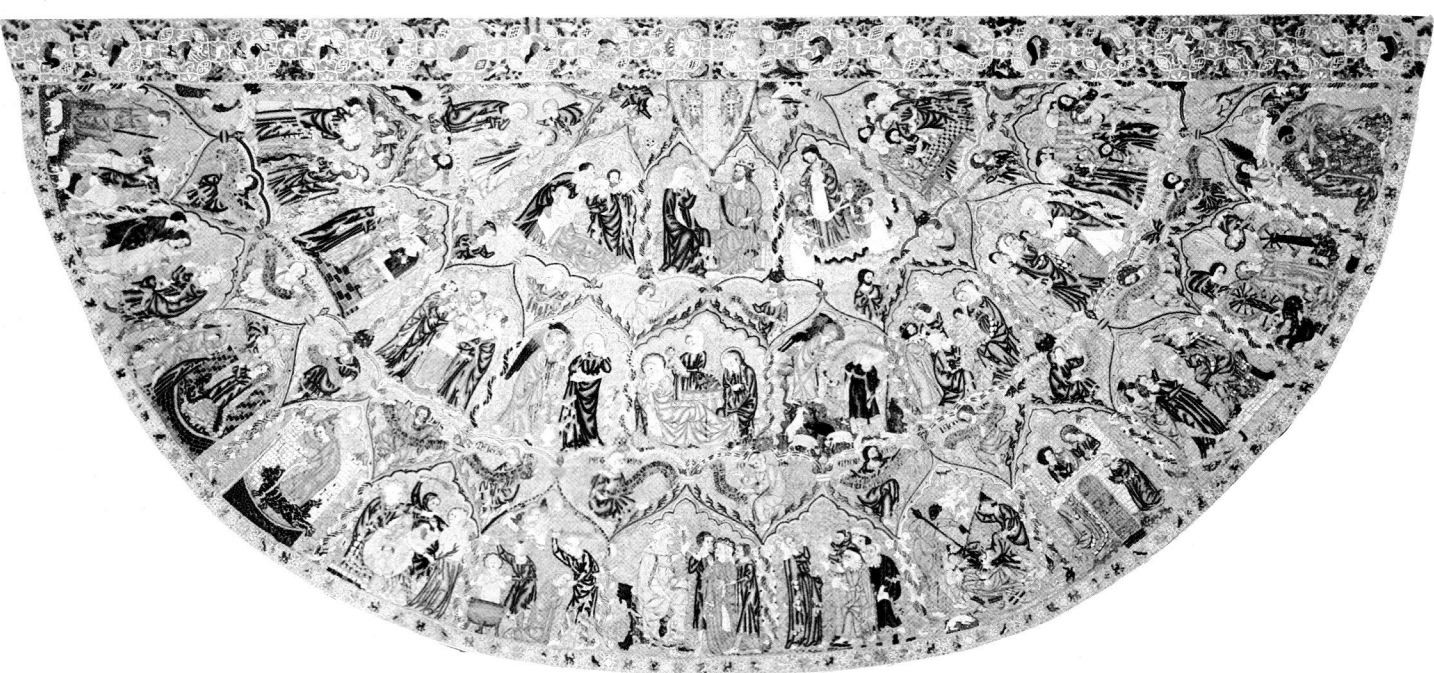

martyrdom of the most celebrated English saint, Thomas of Canterbury (on 29 December, and hence associated with the Christmas cycle). The slightly later Pienza cope (figs 21, 114), which belonged to the family of the Byzantine emperors, has three rows of arches, the two upper rows with the Life, Death and Assumption of the Virgin Mary and the lowest row with scenes from the lives of the virgin martyrs Margaret and Catherine. The New York chasuble (Cat. 577), likewise with three rows of arches, has an abridged version of the story of the Virgin, and figures of Apostles and saints. Altar frontals and orphreys depict similar scenes of the Passion (Cat. 578–9), the story of the Virgin, Apostles and saints (Cat. 598) and scenes of martyrdom.

The work is sometimes executed on backgrounds of dyed silk cloth or velvet (Cat. 577), but often on undyed linen cloth which is entirely concealed by the embroidery. The silk threads of the embroidery are mostly worked in split stitch, an exquisitely refined yet reasonably strong technique in which each stitch passes through the silk thread of its predecessor, producing the effect of a fine chain. The silver and gold threads (actually silver or silver-gilt strip wound spirally on a silk thread) are generally worked in underside couching, a laborious method which locks the metal threads very securely to the supporting material, while at the same time allowing them reasonable flexibility, so that the embroidered garments are not uncomfortably rigid. Often the entire background of the embroidery is worked in gold thread. Sometimes, particularly in early examples, these gold backgrounds are unpatterned. In the late thirteenth and early fourteenth centuries, however, they were frequently worked with gold-on-gold curvilinear patterns including animals and foliage (Cat. 578–9). Later, these were replaced by rectilinear lattice patterns (Cat. 598). Originally, many details of the richer embroideries were enhanced by the use of vast numbers of small pearls, but nearly all of these have now been lost. Some embroideries were also enriched with metal ornaments, enamels, gems and glass (Cat. 12, 606).

Occasionally, where the embroidery is worn away, it is possible to catch a glimpse of the underlying designs, which were drawn on the supporting material by a draughtsman for the guidance of the embroiderers. As these designs are generally outline drawings in ink, it seems that responsibility for the colours and shading may have been left to the embroiderers themselves. Sometimes the latter chose to ignore details of the designs provided for them; in the Bologna cope, for example, the designer supplied patterns for the gold backgrounds, but the embroiderers have worked plain gold backgrounds instead. Occasionally the designs included some colour; in the Pienza cope, the embroiderers have only partially worked many of the faces, leaving exposed the flesh tints in the underlying painting. It is also possible that, in addition to the designs drawn on the supporting material, the embroiderers could refer to fully coloured cartoons, perhaps something like the roll of Passion miniatures preserved at the cathedral of Velletri in Italy.

Designing for the embroidery workshops was presumably an occasional job undertaken by professional painters, and it is not surprising that the styles of the surviving embroideries are very close to those of surviving English paintings. Some embroideries, such as the Bologna cope, are related to paintings at Westminster Abbey, and some to East Anglian and other manuscripts of the fourteenth century. It is also interesting to find that embroideries may have exercised a certain influence on painting styles. That John Grandisson, Bishop of Exeter from 1327 to 1369, owned Italian embroideries has long been known from documentary evidence (see pp. 463–7); quite recently an actual example of Italian embroidery which belonged to him has been discovered and is now in Baltimore. In relation to this, it is noteworthy that the designs of embroideries and other works of art produced for Grandisson in England show apparent traces of Italian influence (Cat. 598). Evidently embroideries imported from overseas were one of the channels through which foreign influences could affect English painters. At the same time, the numerous embroideries which were exported from England may well have conveyed influences from English painting to many parts of Europe.

Metalwork in England,
Marian Campbell **c. 1200–1400**

The ultimate goal for Chaucer's pilgrims was Thomas Becket's shrine in Canterbury Cathedral. For many the wish to give thanks or do penance must have mingled with curiosity about the shrine itself, which impressed the sophisticated visitor as much as the naïve. A vivid description is that of an Italian, writing about a hundred years after Chaucer's death:

> But the magnificence of the tomb of St Thomas the Martyr . . . is that which surpasses all belief. Notwithstanding its great size, this is entirely covered with plates of pure gold; but the gold is scarcely visible from the variety of precious stones with which it is studded, such as sapphires, diamonds, rubies, balas-rubies, and emeralds; and on every side that the eye turns, something more beautiful than the other appears. And these beauties of nature are enhanced by human skill, for the gold is carved and engraved in beautiful design, both large and small, and agates, jaspers and cornelians set in relievo, some of the cameos being of such a size, that I do not dare to mention it: but everything is left far behind by a ruby, not larger than a man's thumbnail, which is set to the right of the altar. The church is rather dark, and particularly so where the shrine is placed, and when we went to see it the sun was nearly gone down, and the weather was cloudy; yet I saw that ruby as well as if I had it in my hand.[1]

A few years later the scholar Erasmus was impressed by the Cathedral treasury, 'before which Midas or Croesus would have seemed beggars', as by the shrine:

> A coffin of wood (covered) a coffin of gold which, being drawn up by ropes and pullies, an invaluable treasure was discovered. Gold was the meanest thing to be seen there. All shone and glittered with the rarest and most precious jewels of an extraordinary bigness; some were larger than the egg of a goose. When this sight was shown, the prior with a white wand touched every jewel one by one, telling the name, the value, and the donor of it.[2]

Only a few years later, in 1538, spoils from the shrine made up a good part of the twenty-six cartloads of gold and silver taken from Canterbury Cathedral by Henry VIII's commissioners.[3] His spoliation of the most spectacular prizes, the cathedrals and abbeys, was followed by his son Edward's more systematic attention to the minor churches, chapels and chantries.

The exhibition bears witness to the remorseless thoroughness of the royal commissioners: isolated fragments are all that remain of the magnificence of the medieval English metalworker's art. It has been calculated that the desecration of shrines and suppression of the monasteries yielded $289,768\frac{7}{8}$ oz of plate and jewels to the Crown;[4] in the summer of 1542 the French ambassador reported that men were employed at the Tower night and day to coin money from this silver.[5]

Of precious metal items intended for ecclesiastical use not a single cross, candlestick, shrine, reliquary, monstrance or jewelled mitre is left; in the base metals the story is little better. The earliest surviving pieces of English gold plate, Bishop Fox's gold chalice and paten of 1507,[6] are barely even medieval. Virtually every item of ecclesiastical use has survived either because deliberately hidden – as with the St Martin's chrismatory (Cat. 123) – or because buried as the trappings of office as was customary – as in the case of almost all chalices (Cat. 111), the Wells crosier (Cat. 257) and episcopal rings – or because they were lost (like the Ramsey Abbey censer and boat, Cat. 121–2), thrown away like the pewter cruets (Cat. 117) or preserved because institutional piety revered the memory of the donor (Wykeham's crosier, Cat. 608), where it no longer had regard for the object itself.

The fate of medieval domestic plate was far worse: until comparatively recently it was normal to have silver melted down and remodelled when it went out of fashion. And in an age without banks, plate and jewellery were seen as assets readily realisable, to be melted and sold. For different reasons base metal plate was equally expendable, cheap to produce, and to replace. As a result, medieval domestic plate is extraordinarily rare, preserved once more through institutional piety or conservatism in the ancient City Companies (Cat. 216), the ancient universities (Cat. 543, 545, 546, 722), and corporations (Cat. 207, 541). Two of the most beautiful fourteenth-century pieces, the Bermondsey dish (Cat. 156) and the Studley bowl (Cat. 728) were until comparatively recently in use as alms basins. Sometimes pieces found their way abroad, like the enamelled hart badge of Richard II (Cat. 725) or the immense and splendid girdle, covered in crystal and enamel, probably given to the Spanish Ferdinando de La Cerda (d. 1275), plausibly a gift by Henry III to Thibaut, Count of Champagne on the occasion of the coronation of Richard of Cornwall in 1257 (cf. Cat. 14, 275).[7] The crowns and sceptres of the King's Regalia fared scarcely better though unlike the shrines they survived until 1649[8] when they were melted down under the Protectorate. The only remaining medieval pieces – not in this exhibition – are the Coronation spoon of c. 1200[9] and the Black Prince's ruby (set into the State Crown) reputedly the gift in 1366–7 of King Peter the Cruel of Castile,[10] which is probably the same stupendous ruby of 181 carats, priced at £603.6s.8d, listed in an inventory of Richard II as part of the 'Crown of Spain'.[11]

'Vor Engelonde is vol ... of selver or and of gold, of tyn and ek of led' wrote the chronicler Robert of Gloucester in about 1325,[12] and with allowance for patriotic exaggeration he was right. Cornwall was Europe's chief tin producer at this date, averaging 700 tons a year by the mid-fourteenth century. An Italian work of c. 1332–42 describes Cornish tin as being exported in long square slabs to Venice, where it was smelted, divided into rods and stamped with the lion of St Mark before sale.[13] Lead was mined in Devon, Somerset, Durham, Cumberland, Shropshire and Derbyshire, and the total produced has been estimated as at least the equal of central Europe. The steadiest producer of lead was Derbyshire, and it was Derbyshire lead which was being exported from Boston in the twelfth and thirteenth centuries;[14] lead from Yorkshire was exported from Hull, reaching a total of fifty-two shiploads, worth £1,219.18s.4d, in 1305–6.[15] In England silver was obtained as a by-product of lead mining, since the galena (lead sulphide) contained small quantities of silver. The Devon mines had the richest ore, producing for example between 1292 and 1297 £4,046 worth of silver, and about £360 worth of lead.[16] Their productive period was short, however, from c. 1290 to 1340. Gold was principally imported, often in the convenient form of coins; although often prospected for in England, it was rarely found, and then in negligible quantities.[17]

Apart from iron, metalworkers used principally gold and silver, both alloyed with copper, and the white and yellow base metals: pewter, an alloy of tin with lead and copper, and a variety of copper alloys, indiscriminately called latten, maslin or brass. Copper was not apparently mined in quantity in medieval England, but recent work suggests that at least some copper alloys were being made in England in the fourteenth century, although much was imported both in sheet form or as made-up articles often listed simply as 'pots':[18] in 1310–11 seven shiploads worth £158.13s.4d were imported into Hull, one cargo alone containing 11,400 items.[19]

The tools used by all metalworkers throughout the period 1200 to 1400 were unchanged from those described in his treatise by Theophilus c. 1100. The two basic ways of working metal were by casting it and by forging it with the hammer. In all methods of casting, the metal was melted until liquid and poured into the mould, different types of mould being suited to different objects: simple open moulds for items like badges or jewellery, with the pattern on only one side, closed moulds (sometimes complex) for objects where shape and pattern were important (jugs or dishes). The *cire perdue* (lost wax) method of casting enabled the finest detail to be achieved; in this a wax model was made and covered with clay, leaving pour-holes and vents. When heated, the clay hardened, and the wax melted out, leaving the hollow mould empty to receive the molten metal. Although in theory a one-off method, duplicates could be made by casting a metal 'master' from which the waxes could be modelled,[20] or by using a carved wooden master.

Casting was the most efficient way of making large objects such as bells, or those needed in quantity of the same pattern, such as sets of dishes or jugs. But it was a method comparatively extravagant in its use of metal and so probably used more sparingly by goldsmiths than by other metalworkers, only for small details: figures (cf. Wykeham crosier, Cat. 608), finials, crestings (King John cup, Cat. 541), and architectural details (Wykeham crosier, Ramsey Abbey censer, Cat. 121). Since moulds were an expensive part of a metalworker's stock-in-trade, they were naturally passed down from him to his successors; the wills of pewterers, goldsmiths and braziers alike frequently mention this practice.[21] The use of the same moulds over several generations is sometimes demonstrable even from the comparatively few objects which survive, and there can be no doubt that this must have curbed innovation.[22] A type of mass production different from casting was die-stamping, possible in both precious and base metal – a method seen on the Guy of Warwick mazer (Cat. 155) and the spangle-mould (Cat. 450).

Metal was forged with the hammer, using sheets of an appropriate size cut into the basic pattern of the intended object, annealed (softened by heating and then allowed to cool) and shaped by being hammered over a series of different anvils. The surface might then be embellished in a number of ways: by embossing, engraving, enamelling, the use of niello, gilding and setting with gems. It should not be forgotten that the craft of the goldsmith encompassed that of the jeweller at this date. Very few gems were cut; they were simply polished, colour and 'virtue' being their chief attraction to medieval eyes.[23] They were used not merely on jewellery but on clothing and above all on ecclesiastical and secular plate of any distinction, quite apart from on shrines. Chalices and drinking cups, crosiers and salts might be studded with gems – only the All Souls mazer, with its jewelled knob, remains to us as a hint of this.

Engraving and enamelling are technically close, since one follows the other. Yet their popularity in England is difficult to chronicle; both could be carried out on precious or base metals. Some of the most splendid examples of engraving (aside from seals) in the exhibition are the thirteenth-century Dolgelly chalice and paten (Cat. 258), covered with elaborate foliage and figures, but they stand almost alone until the Studley bowl of c. 1400 (Cat. 728). The technique of enamelling was in essence to place glass powder on a metal surface, at this date usually engraved with a design, and to fire it, so fusing the two. The method had the distinction of allowing a metal surface to be permanently coloured, either with pure pattern as it might be with gems, or with heraldic badges, or figurative scenes from the Bible or romance, as though it were an illuminated manuscript page.[24] In England it seems likely that although a fitful tradition of enamelling survived from Roman and Anglo-Saxon times, it was not strong enough to have spawned, by the thirteenth century, an industry of the scale and prestige of Limoges. It must surely be significant that it was Limoges alone, from the late twelfth century and into the thirteenth, that produced and exported the enamelled reliquary caskets depicting St Thomas Becket, England's premier saint (Cat. 87). Further evidence of this early dominance of Limoges enamel in England is the commissioning by the executors of Walter de Merton, Bishop of Rochester (d. 1277) of an effigy from Master John of Limoges.[25] Well over £40 was spent in the construction of the effigy in Limoges and its carriage to Rochester and erection there. Though this was destroyed at the time of the Reformation, a contemporary, undocumented Limoges tomb survives in Westminster Abbey, that of William de Valence, whose son probably owned the Valence casket (Cat. 362).

But it seems likely that enamelling on a modest scale, perhaps principally heraldic, was being carried out in thirteenth-century England, and certainly continued into the fourteenth century, from when date so many of the heraldic badges or 'horse ornaments' (Cat. 157–64, 725) found in England. At least one English enameller is recorded working in Paris in 1292;[26] in London the first to be mentioned is a John 'the Enameller', goldsmith, in 1311.[27] At about this date, too, an English manuscript gives a recipe for the making of enamel.[28] Later in the century, however, comes evidence that some of the raw material for making enamel was being imported: in 1390 4 lb of 'amayl' were assessed at 6s.8d, on another occasion 1½ lb cost 8s.[29] The differences in cost must reflect different types or perhaps colours of enamel, the difficult *rouge cler*[30] presumably being one of the most expensive. Enamels specified as *clari*, what we call translucent, are mentioned as early as 1317 (10 Edward II), when the king gave the Pope a gold ewer and basin so enamelled, bought from the London goldsmith Roger Frowyck for £147.1s.8d.[31] An early English mention of *rouge cler* occurs in 1380, as colouring a wreath of roses enamelled on a gold cup belonging to Edmund, Earl of March.[32]

Niello – the goldsmith's equivalent of grisaille – was a sulphide of copper or silver usually inlaid into silver or gold, and a popular technique found in thirteenth-century Europe.[33] No English examples are known to survive, save on jewellery, but silver chalices, candlesticks and book-covers inlaid with niello appear, for example, in the 1245 and 1295 inventories of St Paul's Cathedral, though not necessarily native work.[34]

Although most of the metalworking trades did not form themselves into separate guilds until about the fourteenth century, some specialism must have occurred earlier, especially in London;[35] in the provinces the term smith or goldsmith must often have embraced a competence in all types of metalworking. The Englishman Alexander of Neckham in *c.* 1200 vividly portrayed a goldsmith of this sort of versatility:

> The goldsmith should have a furnace with a hole at the top so that the smoke can get out . . . Let there be an anvil of extreme hardness on which iron and gold may be softened and take the required form. They can be stretched and pulled with the tongs and the hammer. There should be a hammer also for making gold leaf, as well as sheets of silver, tin, brass [*oricalceas*], iron, or copper. The goldsmith must have a very sharp chisel by which he can engrave in amber, diamond, or *ophelta* [?], or marble, or *jacinth*, emerald, sapphire, or pearl, and form many figures. He should have a touchstone for testing metals, and one for distinguishing steel from iron. He must also have a rabbit's-foot for smoothing, polishing, and wiping the surface of gold and silver, and the small particles of metal should be collected in a leather apron. He must have . . . gold and silver wire, by which broken objects can be mended or properly constructed. The goldsmith should be skilled in engraving[?] [*in opere plumiali*] as well as in bas-relief, in casting as well as in hammering. His apprentice must have a waxed table, or one covered with clay, for portraying little flowers and drawing in various ways. He must know how to distinguish solid gold from brass and copper.[36]

The earliest ordinances concerning goldsmiths, of 1238, forbid them to plate base metal with gold or silver,[37] a regulation later relaxed into an embargo only on secular plate: it was permissible to make and gild church vessels in base metal, but forbidden to set them with real stones, as it was forbidden to set gold with false ones.[38] The constant fines listed in the early minute books of the Goldsmiths' Company illustrate how frequently these rules were breached.

The first royal charter of the London Goldsmiths' Company was granted in 1327, but the foundation of its authority was a statute of 1300.[39] The paramount intention was to protect the buying public from the use of inferior metals by dishonest goldsmiths. Gold and silver plate were to be of fixed alloys, gold of the standard of Paris, and silver (as in theory before) of the same standard as the coinage, that is, the 'sterling alloy' of 92.5% purity. Novelty lay in the introduction of a mark – *une teste de leopart* – to be punched on silver vessels before they left the possession of their makers by the wardens of the Company, as evidence that the metal had been assayed (tested) and found good. The leopard's-head mark thus began as a sterling mark, a proof of quality (fig. 116).

The London Goldsmiths' Company had jurisdiction over all workers of gold and silver in England, under the terms of its charter, which stated that provincial goldsmiths were to send representatives to London to have the 'sure touch' or leopard's-head mark verified by the Company. This authority, however, appears rarely to have been exercised, and goldsmiths' provincial centres in the fourteenth century, such as Chester, Exeter, Norwich and York, may have been fairly independent.[40] An ordinance of 1378–9 laid down that in towns with a mint, the

master of the mint was to mark plate with the mark of the city or borough where the assay was.[41] A further safeguard to standards was the ordinance of 1363 which ruled that each master goldsmith was to have his own mark, to be known to the supervisors or wardens of the Company. After an item of plate had been assayed it was to be marked twice – with the maker's mark, and with what is called 'the king's mark', that is, the leopard's head.[42]

The engraved leopard's head on the back of the Bermondsey dish (fig. 115) has been suggested as being an ownership mark – perhaps a royal one – using as a badge the leopard taken from the royal arms, and thus perhaps being the prototype 'king's mark'.[43] Despite the regulations, little medieval silver bears any mark at all – the only piece in the exhibition is the Manchester spoon (fig. 116) stamped with a form of leopard head of perhaps *c.* 1300–50. It is likely that pieces made to order, often from a customer's own old plate, escaped marking, while stock items intended for retail sale, like spoons, were easier to control.

A number of fourteenth-century inventories exist, showing the wide range of items a goldsmith had in his shop. One, that of the London goldsmith Walter Pynchon, 1398,[44] reveals a stock of loose gems (rubies, sapphires, pearls), jewellery (chaplets, a gold collar, rings, brooches), a mitre worth £20, a gold saddle (£10), three gold 'tabblettys' (cf. Cat. 582–4) (total £13), a silver pax (6 oz), three 'bikers' of silver gilt (total $45\frac{1}{2}$ oz) and twenty-four silver spoons (wt $23\frac{1}{2}$ oz). The silver was valued by weight here at 2s.4d per oz; gold would have been worth between ten and thirteen times more.[45] The weight (often a useful indicator of size) is almost invariably given in documents where other details are omitted, since value was directly related to it, and was usually placed at about a third more than the weight of the metal, to account for the workmanship.[46]

Contracts between goldsmiths and their customers have very rarely survived. One, dated 1292, illustrated the pull of London as a centre of excellence, as well as the relation of goldsmith with customer:

> Roger de 'Faringdon', goldsmith, servant of William de 'Farindon' [sic], goldsmith, covenants to make for the Chapter of St. John de Beverle[y] a shrine $5\frac{1}{2}$ feet in length and $1\frac{1}{2}$ feet in breadth, and of proportionate height, in honour of St. John the patron of the church of Beverle[y]; the shrine to be made of gold and silver provided by the Chapter and refined by the said Roger; to be adorned with columns and cunningly worked statues, in size and quantity as the Chapter may direct; and to have tabernacles and pinnacles and other ornaments of goldsmiths' work both behind and before.[47]

Craftsmen working in copper alloy were known by a number of names – potters, girdlers, brasiers, founders, belyeters (bell-founders), coppersmiths, and latteners – names which seem to reflect differences in technique (casting versus hammering) as well as in the products they produced, but the distinctions were often blurred.[48] Goldsmiths are also known to have worked in casting the metal; William Torel, for instance, who made the effigy of Eleanor of Castile (Cat. 377), and Edward FitzOtho, the king's goldsmith, who cast several bells.[49] By the early fourteenth century base-metal vessels for the table were mostly of pewter;[50] and the main use of copper-alloy products was for the kitchen (cauldrons, jugs), the church (bells, reliquaries, censers, etc., cf. Cat. 88), and everyday items (buckles, spurs, brooches).

The pewter industry, based principally in London and York, first became important in the fourteenth century, producing articles which competed with silver in appearance at a fractional cost: c. 2d per lb.[51] The 1348 ordinances of the London Pewterers specify two distinct types of pewter: fine, with a high tin content for flat dishes, square cruets and chrismatories; and an inferior alloy (equal parts of lead and tin) for round cruets, pots and candlesticks.[52] It is not known whether the punched marks occasionally found on medieval pewter signify standard of maker: different ones appear on the two saucers (Cat. 208, 215), one at least having a high tin content. It is interesting that the square Weoley cruet (Birmingham Museum and Art Gallery) has been found to be high in tin,[53] and the round Cardiff example (Cat. 116) high in lead, as specified in the ordinances. Other than the makers of pewter chalices – chalicers[54] – and those who produced pilgrim badges, pewterers do not appear to have subdivided themselves into specialisations.

England was no different from the rest of Europe in the shapes of the metal vessels it produced, many being based on prototypes in humble materials. The wide shallow drinking bowls, whether silver or silver-mounted mazer, clearly derive from turned wooden bowls; another form of drinking vessel, the beaker, is thought to be modelled on the shape of a segment of horn filled at one end;[55] and the word for spoon derives from the Anglo-Saxon for wood-chip. Conversely, the baser metal probably also aped the noble: acorn-tipped spoons are found in all metals (Cat. 209); pewter flagons and saucers can thus perhaps suggest what has been lost in silver. But these are the items for everyday use – our greatest losses have been the exotic: the gold peacocks set with gems, owned by Henry III in 1272,[56] or the gold peacock-shaped washing basin given to Henry by his sister-in-law, the French queen;[57] the ceremonial salts, such as the one shaped as an elephant and castle with flags, owned by Queen Philippa in c. 1369; an enamelled turtle owned by John of Gaunt, a silver-gilt lion and dog by Edmund, Earl of March, one enamelled with apes and little birds by Edward III.[58] Of all the cups enamelled with arms or jeux d'enfans or butterflies, just one is left: the marvellous 'King John' cup (Cat. 541).

It is not easy to imagine the scale of the losses, or to reconstruct, either from what remains or from the records, the changes in technique or in fashions of decoration:

Fig. 116   The Manchester spoon: detail of the hallmark, the 'Persian' leopard's-head standard mark, silver, c. 1350 (Manchester City Art Gallery; Cat. 212)

links between England and Scandinavian goldsmiths in the early thirteenth century had veered away by the late thirteenth century and throughout the fourteenth to a close relationship with France; then, by the early fifteenth century, a steady influx of 'Dutch' goldsmiths into England becomes apparent.[59] And all the while the greatest patrons, such as Queen Isabella, John of Gaunt, the Black Prince, Richard II, both owned foreign plate, most commonly 'of Paris', and also often employed alien goldsmiths. Herman van Cleve, the possible maker of Henry Bolingbroke's sword (Cat. 730) is not exceptional. Yet the internationalism of style particularly evident in goldsmiths' work is qualified by such dominant English motifs as leopards' heads, acorns and roses, and more rarely by the English language itself, as 'all is for the best', the Panglossian motto inscribed upon a salver of Richard II.[60]

NOTES

1. Sneyd 1847, pp. 83–4, n. 49.
2. Erasmus 1849 edn, pp. 49, 55–6.
3. White 1896, p. 13; Lewis 1877, p. 143.
4. Collins 1955, p. 85.
5. Ibid. p. 84, n. 4.
6. Jones 1907, introduction; Campbell 1981–2, pp. 20–44.
7. Fingerlin 1971, no. 61; Collin 1955.
8. Legg 1901, pp. 272–5.
9. How 1952–7, I, p. 24, pl. 1.
10. Collins 1955, p. 12, n. 3.
11. Palgrave 1836, III, p. 309.
12. Wright 1887, p. 2, ll. 11–15.
13. Singer et al. 1956, II, p. 67; Francisco Pegolotti 'La pratica della mercatura' quoted by Hunt 1884, p. 47.
14. Salzman 1923, pp. 42f.; Singer et al. 1956, p. 67; Uhler 1975, p. 61.
15. Uhler 1975, p. 114, table 26: PRO E 122/55/19.
16. Salzman 1923, pp. 63–4; Singer et al. 1956, pp. 43–4.
17. Salzman 1923, pp. 67–8.
18. Blair & Ramsey (forthcoming).
19. Uhler 1975, p. 134, table 35.
20. Theophilus trans. Hawthorne & Smith 1979. pp. 132, 163; Tylecote 1986.
21. Blair & Ramsey (forthcoming): articles by Blairs, Campbell, Homer. Specialist mould-makers appear in records from the 14th century, for example two in York, Gilbert and Richard, admitted as Freemen in 1337 and 1352 respectively (Collins 1896, pp. 30, 45).
22. Examples in English silver of the 15th and 16th centuries cited by Wilson 1980–1, pp. 13–14; Campbell 1983–4, p. 49.
23. The cutting of gems is discussed by Lightbown (forthcoming); for their magical and other powers, see Evans 1922.
24. Gauthier 1972, ch. 1; Untracht 1968.
25. Highfield 1964, p. 137 no. 111; William de Valence's tomb is illustrated in Gauthier, 1972, fig. 141, pp. 192–3.
26. Richardin de Londres assessed at 3 sous: Géraud 1837, p. 23.
27. Sharpe (ed.) 1900, Cal. Letter Book B, pp. 32, 39.
28. London, British Library, Sloane MS 1754, f. 231, printed in Way 1845a, p. 172.
29. PRO E 122/71/13 f. 5, 8.
30. See Paris 1981–2 (Gaborit-Chopin) p. 222; Campbell 1980, pp. 421–2, n. 30.
31. Stapleton 1836, p. 322.
32. Nichols 1780, p. 114.
33. Rosenberg 1924–5; Cologne 1972, nos M 3–7; Stratford 1986 discusses niello in 12th-century England.
34. Lehmann-Brockhaus 1956, nos 2735, 2901.
35. See p. 51.
36. De Nominibus Utensilium, printed in Scheler, 1867, pp. 114–16, trans. Holmes 1952. p. 142, and Lightbown 1978a, pp. 4–5. Neckham (d. 1217) taught for many years in Paris, and his description may be based on Parisian goldsmiths. Some of the terms are problematic.
37. Salzman 1923, p. 139.
38. 1370 ordinance: Salzman 1923, pp. 139–40; 1403–4 statute: Jackson 1921, pp. 9–10; Oman 1962b, p. 195.
39. 1327 charter: Reddaway & Walker 1975, pp. 222–4; 1300 statute: How 1952–7, III, p. 1, London 1978c, p. 14.
40. Ibid. pp. 24–32; How 1952–7, III, pp. 2–3, 86–7; for Chester see Ridgway 1968; for Norwich see Barrett 1981; for York see Swanson 1980–1, pp. 181f. It is not clear whether the leopard's head was used on provincial silver at this date; How (1952–7, III, p. 2) considers it a London mark.
41. Ibid; the ordinance was never enacted and may have had little effect.
42. London 1978c, p. 14.
43. Oman 1952, pp. 23–4; How (1952–7, III, pp. 11–12 n. 2) disagrees.
44. The total stock of the shop, in 'Cornhulle', was worth £600.3s.6d (Riley 1868, p. 550).
45. For units of weight and value see Zupko 1985; for the relative values of gold and silver in the 13th century see Carpenter 1986, in the 14th see Watson 1967.
46. Costs of workmanship and materials are detailed in some of John of Gaunt's commissions 1379–83 (Lodge & Somerville 1937, no. 556) and those of Queen Isabella 1357–8 in London, British Library Cotton MS Galba E XIV, f. 48.
47. Sharpe 1899, Cal. Letter Book, pp. 180–1.
48. Blair & Ramsay, op. cit.
49. Salzman 1923, p. 150; for both see Harvey 1984, sn., and for FitzOtho, Lancaster 1972, pp. 96f.; Stahlschmidt 1884, 1887, s.n.
50. Hatcher & Barker 1974, p. 59.
51. Ibid. p. 63.
52. Salzman 1923, p. 142.
53. Brownsword (forthcoming).
54. Oman 1957, p. 40, n. 1; Homer 1985, pp. 54–7; surviving pewter chalices are most usefully summarised in Tweddle 1986, pp. 207–9.
55. Oman 1959, p. 18; although no plain English beakers have survived, one, of 1352–5 commissioned by an Englishman, William Bateman, bears his enamelled arms inside, and an Avignon hallmark. It is preserved by the College he founded, Trinity Hall, Cambridge (Lightbown 1978a, p. 93). Beakers are discussed and illustrated by Fritz (1982, nos 372–6).
56. Lehmann-Brockhaus 1956, p. 289, no. 6223.
57. Described by Matthew Paris: ibid. p. 283, no. 6208.
58. Nicolas 1846b, pp. 353, 377; Lodge & Somerville 1937, no. 910, p. 287; Nichols 1780, pp. 112–13; Ord 1792, p. 247; Campbell 1983–4, p. 43 (which also discusses the ceremonial).
59. Reddaway & Walker 1975, pp. 120 ff.
60. In an inventory dated 1378: Oxford, Bodleian Library MS Bodley Eng. hist. c. 775, p.1.

Claude Blair Arms and Armour

ew examples of armour likely to have been used in England during the Middle Ages survive: most are helmets hung as part of funeral achievements in churches and only a handful fall within the period covered by the exhibition. None is provably of English origin, though the distinctive group of helms represented here by that of the Black Prince (Cat. 626–33) were probably made in London. Our knowledge of English medieval armour is therefore based almost exclusively on contemporary documents and illustrations, and contains many gaps, especially concerning undergarments and under-defences. The picture presented in the text-books has been slightly modified in recent years by the redating forward of the early military brasses (e.g. Cat. 234–5) – and in consequence also many comparable effigies in the round – all of which must now be ascribed to the period *c.* 1320–45, rather than *c.* 1277–1330. This has had the effect of bringing the armour styles depicted on English monuments into line with those found on the Continent.

For the first century or more of our period, the heavy cavalryman – the knight – wore mail armour that was still basically of a form that had remained in use since it had been adopted in the later Roman Empire. This was supplemented by a heater-shaped shield, which was suspended round the neck in the charge with the lance, or strapped to the left arm for close-quarter fighting. Minor developments that had taken place in the twelfth century had been the introduction of the textile gown (now usually called a surcoat), the closed great helm (see Cat. 626), and the extension of the sleeves of the mail hauberk to form mittens with leather palms, slit so that they could be thrown back when not in use (see Cat. 234). The introduction of the face-concealing helm probably gave an impetus to the development of heraldry, and from almost the beginning it was frequently surmounted by its owner's crest (see Cat. 627). Around 1250 illustrations start to appear of shaped reinforcing plates, either of metal or of hardened leather (cuir-bouilli) attached over the mail at the knees and elbows, those on the former being common from the end of the century onwards. For obvious reasons padded garments were worn under the armour, as at all periods.

English brasses and monumental effigies continue to depict armour that, externally at least, appears to consist entirely of mail, apart from plate knee reinforcements, until the 1330s (see Cat. 234–5). Literary evidence suggests, however, that from the beginning of the thirteenth century or before some kind of plate body defence was sometimes worn under the gown or the hauberk. Glimpses of defences of this kind, fastened by horizontal side straps, are visible through the armholes of the gowns of effigies of *c.* 1250 and *c.* 1270–80 respectively in the Temple Church, London and Pershore Abbey, Worcestershire. It is probable that these were originally painted to give the effect of being studded all over with rivets, and that they represent the defence known simply as the plates or pair of plates, which was constructed of a series of metal plates riveted to the inside of a textile or leather garment. The many examples found on the site on the Island of Gotland of the Battle of Wisby (1361) illustrate the form used all over Europe.

References both to the plates and also to knee and lower-leg defences of plate begin to occur regularly in documents from the 1290s onwards: the last named were presumably at first usually worn under the mail hosen since they are depicted only rarely in art before the late 1320s. Henceforth, however, they are increasingly common, together with comparable plate defences for the arms and feet, and also gauntlets constructed like the body plates. By the 1340s they become normal. At the same period the globular helmet (bacinet) formerly worn under the mail coif began to be worn over it, and eventually the coif lost its top and became an attachment to the helmet. Pivoted visors also came into use, usually made detachable so that the bacinet could be worn under the great helm (Cat. 678).

These constructions remained the normal ones for the rest of our period, and developments were concerned mainly with improving details, including the reduction in the amount of mail worn underneath, and with refining forms. Armour for the body continued normally to be covered and held together by textiles, but the main general tendency was for the plates in the pair of plates to become larger and fewer and to develop towards the full, polished steel cuirass of the fifteenth century and later. This trend must have been influenced also by the separate development of special armour for the tournament, something that had started as early as the thirteenth century, and which already by the 1330s involved the addition of reinforcing pieces, including breastplates, to the type of armour used for war.

No specifically English style of medieval armour has been identified. We know that much of that used here was imported from Italy, the Low Countries and Germany, and that by the fourteenth century at the latest foreign armourers were also working over here. There was, however, a well-established native craft, apparently centring mainly on London, but important enough in York for a separate guild of armourers to be established there in the second half of the fourteenth century. Regulations for the trade, involving makers of plate, mail and textile armour, were approved in London in 1322, and in 1347 the plate workers were recognised as a separate company under the name of Heaumers (makers of helmets), which they shortly afterwards changed to Armourers. Their regulations and the wills of many of the members show that they were actively engaged in making armour and not merely importing it.

The main knightly arms were the sword, the lance, and the dagger, of which the first and most important retained the same simple cruciform shape throughout our period (Cat. 170, 176–7), with a blade that was normally straight and double-edged (but cf. Cat. 165). These, and the various forms of axe, club and staff weapon, were both made in England – there was a long-established cutlery craft in London – and also imported. The longbow is regarded as the English medieval weapon *par excellence*, though the crossbow was also used and made over here. The longbow was not a new invention, and it was its tactical use by the English that gave it its national reputation.

England early adopted firearms and, despite Chinese claims, the earliest un-equivocal evidence for the existence anywhere of weapons projecting a missile by the force of exploding gunpowder are a Florentine ordinance of 1326 and the famous illustration of a vase-shaped, arrow-firing cannon in the treatise of Walter de Milemete of 1326–7 at Christ Church, Oxford (Cat. 682). The shape of the Milemete cannon is exactly that of a fourteenth-century pot (cf. Cat. 727), no doubt because it was the metal potters (eventually called brasiers) who were amongst the first gunmakers. The Royal Wardrobe Accounts show that from *c.* 1340 onwards cannon were increasingly used by the English forces, and that hand firearms had been introduced by the 1370s at the latest. The latter seem to have been of little tactical importance during our period.

NOTES

The main sources for this introduction are: Hewitt 1855–60, I, II; Riley 1868; Thordemann 1939; Hoffmeyer 1954; Blair 1958; Oakeshott 1964; Norman 1971; Norman 1976; Pollard 1983; Contamine 1984.

Paul Binski   Monumental Brasses

ngland preserves more medieval monumental brasses than any other European country. The origins of English brasses lay in the metalworking industries of Germany, north France and the region of the River Meuse, in the twelfth and thirteenth centuries.[1] A number of experiments in the use of metal for tombs, whether cast (Cat. 377) or enamelled, occurred in thirteenth-century Europe. The critical development in the emergence of the English monumental brass was the combination of separate metal inlays made of a medieval form of brass called latten – an alloy mostly of copper and tin largely made on the Continent in this period – and marble tomb-slabs. The English brass is thus a composite product. It is unlike the work of fourteenth-century Flemish brass manufacturers, huge and expensive-looking rectangular plates smothered in detailed ornament, and it was probably most closely allied to French inlaid memorials of the thirteenth and fourteenth centuries, of which only one, of c. 1320, remains in Noyon Cathedral. The drawing together of stone and metal occurred in England at some point in the second half of the thirteenth century. The first and most authoritative exponents of the art were London marblers, working with Purbeck marble, who from the late thirteenth century produced the type of brass familiar throughout the later Middle Ages, consisting of an effigy with a canopy and an inscription, and other, often coloured, adornments such as heraldic shields. As Purbeck marble was an innovative ingredient in English Gothic architecture, so was it also in English tomb manufacture.

The distinctive separate-inlay English brass began initially not with effigies, but with inscriptions consisting of large, individually-cast Lombardic letters set in stone; the first brasses were texts. The earliest important surviving example is on the presbytery floor of Westminster Abbey, a work consisting of a floor of ornamental mosaic of a Roman type produced by the Cosmati family, bearing the date 1268, and containing lengthy and abstruse texts concerning medieval cosmography, composed of metal letters. Although Cosmatesque works were associated with pompous inscriptions, none elsewhere had lettering in brass; this seems to be an English innovation. It was an important one, because it helped to establish a basic type of brass memorial which lasted throughout the next century: the simple inscription brass without an effigy, but sometimes adorned with a cross, an alternative to the brass with effigy, canopy and so on. Two examples of such brasses commemorating members of the Valence family and dating to the late 1270s remain at Westminster Abbey. Thus English brasses were from the start a flexible commodity, by the very fact of their consisting of separately-composed elements.

This effectively assured their commercial success. A large brass with full-length effigy, canopy and shields cost in the region of £15–£20, but a simple cross with inscription cost only about £6 and an inscription alone £3. In other words, brasses could be bought by a very wide section of the population, from bishops to fishmongers. In diversifying their production, London marblers quickly exploited this obvious asset; the larger workshops produced both ambitious and humble brasses. Although brasses have been associated with the decline of the Purbeck marblers' trade, it seems more likely that they were a sign of the healthy responsiveness of the marblers to new market conditions: a growing population; a developing concern for the well-being of souls in Purgatory; and the increasing preference for burial in church. Marblers were, if anything, attaining greater commercial and metropolitan prestige in the early fourteenth century, and continued to make brasses in the later Middle Ages.

By the late fourteenth and fifteenth centuries, the monumental brass was

Fig. 117 Brass to Sir Richard de Buslingthorpe, *c.* 1330 (Buslingthorpe parish church, Lincolnshire)

principally a memorial for the middle ranks of society. But figure brasses began, in the late thirteenth century, as a memorial for highly-placed ecclesiastical patrons. The figure brasses made before 1300 have almost entirely disappeared, leaving their traces in the form of indents where the metal was set in the stone. Examples of such indents remain on tombs such as that of Bishop William de Luda at Ely Cathedral (*c.* 1298), and St Thomas de Cantilupe at Hereford Cathedral, in place by 1287; a small subsidiary figure survives from the latter, and is the earliest surviving fragment of an English monumental brass (Cat. 86).

Around 1300 to 1310 a workshop was established in London, almost certainly under Adam of Corfe, the principal dealer in Purbeck marble in London and Westminster. This workshop was important in two respects: it manufactured brasses suited to a wide range of pockets, and it produced a standardised form of memorial. It carried on making figure brasses to standard designs into the 1330s, and made figure and cross brasses in the Camoys style, named after the earliest surviving product in the sequence, the brass of Margaret de Camoys (*c.* 1310) at Trotton in Sussex (Cat. 138). This workshop also made the most famous early brasses commemorating knights such as Sir Robert de Bures (d. 1331) at Acton in Suffolk (Cat. 235), and appears to have taken on an artist in the 1320s who designed such brasses as that of Sir William de Setvans (d. 1322) at Chartham in Kent (Cat. 234). The market for this workshop stretched throughout most of southern England and East Anglia, a sign of its commercial acumen. By the early fourteenth century brass workshops were established independently in other areas, notably in Lincolnshire, and their products, like the small brass to Sir Richard de Buslingthorpe (fig. 117), are distinct from but related to London work of the period.

In the period roughly from 1330 to 1360 English brass production underwent a crisis. Superb memorials were made in the period before the Black Death, and London producers still retained their commercial hegemony in southern England. A typical London product of the period would be the brass of Sir John d'Abernon (*c.* 1340; Cat. 236); slim, aloof and polished. But the character of brasses was changing. Having become widely established, brasses increasingly reflected the religious and social sentiments of the time. They became more picturesque, by incorporating represent-ations of favourite saints, especially the iconography of the Virgin Mary, or the Trinity (Cat. 625); the most pictorial of English brasses is that of Sir Hugh Hastings (d. 1347) at Elsing in Norfolk (Cat. 678), surrounded by a panoply of weepers (some of whom were founder members of the Order of the Garter) including Edward III, and surmounted by St George and the Coronation of the Virgin. They incorporated more texts; the early bold separate-letter inscriptions, sometimes granting days of pardon in Purgatory in return for prayers said for the deceased (Cat. 235), gave way to strips or plates of metal with small black-letter inscriptions holding more lettering, and so saying more about the patron and his spiritual concerns. The unusual appearance of Bishop Wyvil's brass at Salisbury (Cat. 98) can only be understood by reference to its lengthy text. Brasses also became more family-minded, by referring to the lineage of the deceased in an inscription, by showing married couples – for the first time at Westley Waterless, Cambridgeshire, in the 1340s – and eventually by showing children.

Brasses, having made an austere start, thus became a distinctive vehicle for the ordinary concerns of middle-ranking people, showing their personal piety, their growing sense of family intimacy and continuity, and their desire for social approbation through a conspicuous display of achievements biographical and heraldic. The English brass of the fifteenth century is a domesticated phenomenon; hence its revealing nature to the historian.

Most of the characteristics of brasses at the time of their greatest popularity – in the fifteenth century – had already emerged before the Black Death of 1348–9. The Black Death undoubtedly interrupted the sequence of English brass manufacturing, and although there are links between pre- and post-1350 brasses in design and content, those made in the period 1350 to 1400 tend to a greater degree of accomplished uniformity. Stylistically, brasses went through three phases in the course of the century. At first their design elements and engraving were bold and fluent. By the 1330s and 1340s the figures occasionally showed greater mobility and the engraving considerable finesse, as on Sir Hugh Hastings's brass. Elaborate canopy-work took on an increasingly important role in unifying the design of brasses, containing the effigy and subsidiary figures in an intricate pattern of enclosures; brasses conformed to the general taste of the century for architectural fantasy (Cat. 98). By the 1370s and 1380s London workshops were making highly standardised brasses to set patterns first identified by J.P.C. Kent; these were of splendid quality (Cat. 140), but they were marked by a symmetry and gauntness which contrasts with the lively experiment-ation of the 1330s and 1340s.[2] The growing use of repeat patterns for brass design is precisely matched by the methods of stained glass makers of the period (see p. 54 above). While the early brasses have rightly been described as 'children of the Decorated style', the later ones are emphatically a counterpart to the aesthetic frigidity of Perpendicular architecture. Thus, as the art form tended to cater more and more for the personal wishes of the client so, paradoxically, did greater stylistic uniformity come to prevail.

In the years immediately after the Black Death, possibly as a result of the annihilation of the producers themselves, English clients occasionally turned to Flemish workshops for their memorials. Sometimes these patrons had international tastes, like Abbot Thomas de la Mare at St Albans, who had a Flemish brass and bought an Italian panel painting for the high altar of his abbey. More often than not, however, they were associated with the trading communities on the North Sea coast. Impressive examples of Flemish engraving survive in eastern England at such places as King's Lynn and Newark. However, because English brasses, through their flexible separate-inlay designs, always manifested an independence of spirit, they seem never to have been influential on the Continent. Flemish brasses attained a much greater degree of commercial success throughout Europe, from the Iberian Peninsula to Poland and Scandinavia, demonstrating that it is often the most systematic-looking and even predictable of art forms – like French Rayonnant architecture in the thirteenth century – that gain the widest international acclaim. Their short-term success in England, however, indicates the underlying strength and popularity of the distinctively insular separate-inlay memorial in later medieval England.

NOTES

1. For the early history of brasses, see Binski 1987, Blair 1987 and Rogers 1987; in general, see Norris 1978 a and b.
2. Kent 1949. Kent defined categories of brasses according to characteristics of engraving and design, and designated the categories 'Series A', 'Series B' and so on (see Cat. 140, 237).

Jane Geddes Decorative Wrought Iron

he main survivals of medieval decorative ironwork are found on church furnishings, principally doors and chests (Gardner 1927; Geddes 1978; Geddes forthcoming). In the thirteenth century smiths reached a peak of technical accomplishment. This was achieved by the use of two types of specialist tool: moulded swages or dies, and curved punches individually shaped and resembling biscuit cutters. These enabled smiths to repeat small decorative motifs with great precision. By taking impressions of these stamped and cut-out designs it has been possible to identify works made by individual blacksmiths, or workshops using the same tools. The use of dies to produce stamped terminals on naturalistic scrollwork seems to have begun around Liège, possibly in the goldsmith's workshop of Hugo of Oignies (*fl. c.* 1230). His techniques were employed on a larger scale on the ironwork of the west doors of Notre-Dame, Paris (*c.* 1225–45), possibly made by a smith practised in working both gold and iron. The new French fashion first appeared in England at St George's Chapel, Windsor (1240–9), where the smith boldly stamped his name 'Gilebertus' on some of the terminals. From there the technique spread rapidly, extending roughly south of a line from York to Oxford (with an isolated exception at Chester, Cat. 365). The chapter house doors of York Minster (*c.* 1280–5) repeat the spiral 'Tree of Life' design used at Windsor but with much smaller, more delicate stamps (fig. 118).

Thomas of Leghtone, the only documented smith from this period whose works survive, made the grille over the tomb of Queen Eleanor at Westminster in 1293–4 for £12 (fig. 119). The king's master smith Henry of Lewes had just died in 1291, so Thomas was summoned from Leighton Buzzard in Bedfordshire to deliver the royal commission. He had already made the decorative ironwork on the doors of the churches at Turvey and at Leighton Buzzard (completed *c.* 1288), and he used many

Fig. 118   York Minster, doors to the chapter house vestibule, *c.* 1280–5

Fig. 119   Westminster Abbey, the Eleanor grille, 1293–4

Fig. 120   Lichfield Cathedral west door, 1290s

Fig. 121   Chest from the Church of All Saints, Icklingham, Suffolk, *c.* 1300

of the same stamp designs from his earlier works on the Eleanor grille. The grille was designed to project outwards from the top of the tomb, preventing access across Eleanor's effigy (Cat. 377) to the Confessor's shrine (Cat. 380). Details of its construction, such as the use of stamped scrolls riveted to iron bars, and rosettes along the lower edge of the frame, were also found on a very similar grille from St-Denis, Paris (now lost, Viollet-le-Duc 1866, VI, p. 61) suggesting that Thomas, in spite of his provincial smithy, was fully conversant with the latest French styles. A particularly fine group of stamped ironwork was produced by the smith who worked at Carnary College, Norwich (1316–37). The very distinctive, bold stamps he used on the door are also found on ornamental ring plates at the churches of Wickhampton, Filby and Stokesby, Norfolk.

Carving a die sufficiently strong to make an impression on wrought iron was a skilled task only attempted by accomplished smiths. An easier way to achieve the effect of identical terminals was to hammer the iron flat and simply punch an outline. This could be cut around a template or punched with an individually designed cutter. The earliest known use of this technique is at St Elizabeth's Church, Marburg (1270s), and it first appears in England at Lichfield Cathedral, on the west doors (1290s, fig. 120). The earliest cut-out work tended to follow the same designs as stamped work, using tight scrolls and delicately lobed terminals, as on the Icklingham chest (fig. 121; Geddes & Sherlock 1987). But by the mid-fourteenth century designs became generally cruder and simpler, as on the Richard of Bury chest (Cat. 523) although there were some magnificent exceptions such as the south doors of Worksop Priory, Nottinghamshire, and Eastwood Church, Essex.

Iron decoration on doors and chests reached its finest flowering just as fashions began to change in favour of geometric tracery designs. On doors, the tracery was applied with raised wooden ribs which eventually covered the whole surface of the door, leaving no room for iron decoration apart from discreet ring plates. The earliest example was found on the entrance gates of St Augustine's, Canterbury (1309). When smiths attempted to copy the accurate geometric designs, they had to treat their iron bars as if they were wood. The iron was worked cold, on a bench, using chisels and files instead of hammer and tongs, while joints were no longer forge-welded but were made with rebates and mortises as in carpentry, and riveted. Early examples of this technique can be seen on the screens put up by Prior Eastry at Canterbury Cathedral (1304–9) and over the tombs of Bishops Simon of Ghent (d. 1315) and Roger Mortival (d. 1330; fig. 122) at Salisbury Cathedral. Thereafter during the Middle Ages, decorative ironwork was increasingly confined to tomb railings and door rings, as the carpenters usurped the smiths' traditional areas of decoration on doors and chests.

Fig. 122   Salisbury Cathedral, tomb grille for Bishop Roger Mortival, 1330

John Cherry Jewellery

In 1774 the body of Edward I was examined in his tomb at Westminster Abbey; it was found to be 'richly habited, adorned with ensigns of royalty' (Cat. 382–3). The rich vestments included a tunic of red silk damask on which lay a stole decorated with gilt filigree quatrefoils adorned with transparent glass, between which an immense quantity of small white beads was powdered. Over this was worn the royal mantle of rich crimson satin fastened on the left shoulder with a gilt ring brooch ornamented with red and blue stones set in collets with twenty-two beads between them. The head of the pin of the brooch was formed by a long piece of uncut transparent blue paste, shaped like an acorn. Although the eighteenth-century description is not as precise as we should like today, and leaves many questions unanswered, it does provide a description of a surviving example of the richness of the jewellery that would have adorned the kings of England and their Court in the thirteenth century.[1]

One of the difficulties of defining the contribution of the kings of England to the development of jewellery in the thirteenth century is the lack of jewellery that can be clearly associated with them. This is in contrast to the evidence of the royal inventories, which clearly indicate the richness and quantity of jewels used at Court. King John's royal robe is described in an inventory of 1205 as a mantle of Eastern silk, studded with sapphires, cameos, and pearls, fastened with a clasp set with four emeralds, sapphires, and balas rubies and a turquoise. Henry III deposited with his sister in Paris four crowns, forty-five gold brooches, one hundred and ninety-three rings and seventy-six belts as well as other pieces. Edward I's *Liber Quotidianus* records many brooches, among which were a gold square with a sapphire in the middle surrounded by pearls and precious stones, and an eagle of gold set with rubies and emeralds. Clearly royal patronage must have played a great part in the development of the art of jewellery in England. Yet none survives.

The ring brooch that fastened the mantle of Edward I represented one of the most popular types of brooch in the thirteenth century. Often used for fastening a garment at the neck, as the inscription on the brooch from Writtle (Cat. 644) demonstrates, it was decorated with inscriptions, stones, or worked gold and silver. One of the gold brooches owned by Henry III in 1272 is described as being *cum duobus amantibus* (with two lovers). The decoration of the ring of the brooch in this sculptural manner as a pair of human figures may be reflected in the little silver brooches (Cat. 641). The exhibition offers an opportunity to compare a range of ring brooches from very small examples (Cat. 643, 650) to the fine example set alternately with rubies and sapphires that recall the red and blue stones of Edward I's mantle brooch. The French inscription on the back of this brooch, IO SUI ICI EN LIU [*sic*] DAMI: AMO (I am here in place of a friend: love), is not necessarily an indication of French origin, since French was the language of the Court. The use of the ring brooch can be seen on sculptured figures from both France and England in the thirteenth century. In England the best examples are to be seen on the west front of Wells Cathedral, though there are also such brooches on the statue of St Mary Magdalene at Lanercost Priory, *c.* 1250–75, and on the thirteenth-century effigy identified as Constantia de Frecheville at Scarcliffe in Derbyshire. The ring brooch began to be used in the twelfth century and continued to be popular until the end of the Middle Ages. The Oxwich brooch (Cat. 653), with earlier cameos set in beaded settings, indicates the greater emphasis on decoration in the fourteenth century.

Cameos such as those set in the Oxwich brooch were prized throughout the Middle Ages, as were all precious stones. There is very little evidence for the exact location of the cutting of cameos and intaglios, and the simple faceting of stones. Many stones were imported via Italy and France, after having been cut there, and then set in rings or brooches in England. There was also considerable reuse of stones that had already been set in crosses or earlier jewels. It is often difficult to be certain to which country in north-western Europe a particular brooch or ring should be assigned. Simply because a ring or a brooch has been found in England or belonged to an Englishman, it does not follow that it was necessarily made in England. English inscriptions do not occur on jewellery before the fifteenth century. It is therefore difficult to present a group of specifically English jewellery from the thirteenth and fourteenth centuries. The jewellery gathered for this exhibition has been found in either England or Wales, is associated with English people, or is of a type that may be assumed to have been in England in the period.

The series of bishops' rings found in their tombs provides one of the firmest groups of English origin. One can only regret that no ring was found in the tomb of Edward I. The series from bishops' tombs in this exhibition continues that from the 1984 exhibition of Romanesque art.[2] The fine early thirteenth-century ring from Wells (Cat. 634) may be compared with that from Durham.[3] It is not possible to draw a clear distinction between Romanesque and Gothic rings. The 'stirrup-shaped' ring, so called from the shape of the hoop, was known in the twelfth century and continued in the thirteenth century with the ring of Archbishop Ludham (Cat. 636). The use of the shape was not confined to episcopal rings, since it occurs on secular examples such as that from Hatfield Forest (Cat. 646). The pontifical ring of Archbishop de Gray (Cat. 635) provides an actual example of this type of ring, worn at principal festivals by the Archbishop. Matthew Paris in his drawings of the rings at St Albans illustrates two examples of pontifical rings[4] with the same characteristics of smaller stones set around a larger one. Woodlock's ring from Winchester (Cat. 637) is one of the most impressive bishop's rings but still in the tradition of a large sapphire held in a claw setting. The rings associated with Bishop Grandisson (d. 1369; Cat. 638) and Archbishop Wytlesey (d. 1374; Cat. 639) indicate the change in the fourteenth century. Grandisson's ring has an enamelled bezel and Wytlesey's ring, although set with a fine stone in the traditional manner, has enamelled shoulders. They both represent a new decorative attitude to rings, brought about by the introduction of enamel. Grandisson's ring may be French, and so also may be the Thame ring (Cat. 657) whose combination of amethysts, openwork gold with lettering, and enamelling make it one of the most sumptuous of medieval rings. The later fourteenth century is characterised by a greater variety of shapes of rings. In particular the Hornsey ring (Cat. 655) with its French proverbial inscription recalling that on the Ashanti ewer (Cat. 726), suggests a greater appreciation of literacy.

By the mid-fourteenth century the wearing of jewellery had become a matter of rank and was formally restricted by law. The sumptuary legislation of 1363 decreeed that handicraftsmen and yeomen were not to wear belts, brooches, garters, chains or seals of gold or silver: that knights were not to wear rings or brooches made of gold or set with precious stones, and that only esquires with land or rent of 200 marks a year or merchants and their families with good or chattels of £500 value were to be permitted to wear apparel reasonably garnished with silver, and their wives to have headdresses garnished with stones.[5] This attention to costume, even though it appears never to have been enforced, is a mark of the changes that were taking place in the middle of the fourteenth century. Fashion in clothes and jewellery was now much more important, bringing with it changes in jewellery. Brooches pinned to the outside of garments gained new popularity. This period was also characterised, particularly among Court circles, by an increasing decorativeness in jewellery well represented by the New College brooch (Cat. 640). This achieves its effect not only by the stones but also by its combination of sculptural figures of Gabriel and Mary and the use of enamel, particularly on the wings of the Archangel.

The close affinities of the brooch at New College with that formerly in the treasury at St-Denis suggests that both may have been made in France. Paris was certainly an important source for jewels in the thirteenth and fourteenth centuries. Eleanor of Castile ordered jewels from Paris in 1290[6] and Bishop Grandisson in his will refers to purchases made in Paris.[7] Yet of the purchases made by John of Gaunt recorded in his register (1379–83), none were purchased in Paris and all were bought from goldsmiths in London, some of whom, like Nicholas Twyford, were men of very considerable standing.[8] English goldsmiths prospered on the increasing taste for luxury in the second half of the fourteenth century.

Another influence that lay behind the popularity of gold jewellery was the increasing amount of gold available, as indicated by the successful introduction of a gold coinage from 1344. For almost every year after 1344 the value of gold minted exceeded that of silver, and for the period 1357 to 1438 the weight of gold struck and turned into coins often exceeded that of silver. Gold jewellery was often used as security for loans and was, as such, highly valued.

Towards the end of the fourteenth century the decoration of gold jewellery with white opaque enamel increased. From the 1370s animals, particularly swans and eagles, were being depicted on belts and dress ornaments in such a way that the use of white enamel was stressed in the inventories. In 1373 John of Gaunt gave as a gift an eagle of gold enamelled in white.[9] White swans were enamelled on the clasps of the psalter which Humphrey de Bohun (d. 1373) left to his daughter Eleanor. Both these early references, as well as the depiction of white enamelled harts on the Wilton Diptych, suggest an English origin for the Dunstable swan jewel (Cat. 659).

The Wilton Diptych gives an impression of the richness of the furs, clothes, and jewellery with which Richard II would have surrounded himself. The crowns of Richard, St Edmund, and St Edward the Confessor, the cloak clasp of St Edmund, the ring of St Edward, the collars of Richard and the angels, and the white harts attest a delight in the colour of precious stones and the use of white enamel on gold. It is not easy at this courtly level to define exactly what is meant by English Gothic jewellery. Many Courts had goldsmiths working at them drawn from different parts of Europe and there was a constant interchange of designs, decorative features and techniques. The crown of Blanche of Lancaster (Cat. 13) is an excellent example. The technique used might suggest a French origin, but French influence was strong in the Court of Charles IV at Prague from which Anne of Bohemia came to marry Richard II in 1382. The crown is likely to have belonged to a queen of England: it certainly belonged to a daughter of a king of England and was part of the English royal treasury. It conveys an excellent impression of the rich elegance of the Court of the last Plantagenet king.

NOTES

1. Ayloffe 1786, pp. 381–3.
2. London 1984a, pp. 290–1, 293.
3. London 1984a, no. 313.
4. Cherry 1982, nos 115, 128.
5. *Statutes* 1810.
6. Parsons 1977, p. 84.
7. Hingeston-Randolph 1894–9, nos 1511–23.
8. Lodge & Somerville 1937.
9. Ibid., p. 191 no. 132.

John Cherry Pottery

he contribution of medieval pottery to an exhibition of Gothic art is to illustrate an art form produced by the poorer parts of the population, who were unlikely to be able to read. Inscriptions on pots are rare, and where they do occur are often unintelligible. It therefore presents an art very different from the subtleties of illuminated manuscripts, ivories and enamels, or even the finer medieval tiles from Chertsey or Tring. It is vigorous, direct, and has a strong sense of volume and modelling.

Pottery making in the Middle Ages was never profitable. Mrs Jean le Patourel has shown that where potters can be identified in late fourteenth-century poll tax returns, they are assessed at 4d, the lowest rate paid by the mass of the peasantry, rather than the 6d paid by most small craftsmen.[1] In the thirteenth and fourteenth centuries pottery was often a part-time activity carried on together with farming. There were urban potteries, notably in Scarborough (Cat. 548) and Nottingham (Cat. 180, 555), but the general pattern is for potteries to be sited in the country, as at Laverstock (Cat. 181), Mill Green (Cat. 185) and Brill (Cat. 551).

Many of the pots here (Cat. 548, 550) were discovered in the 1840s or 1850s. In 1854 Charles Roach Smith commented that 'medieval pottery was completely void of beauty, taste, or sightliness'.[2] It is worth contrasting this attitude with the appreciation of the nobility and strength of form that a modern potter, such as Bernard Leach, found in medieval pottery. The type of pot that appealed to him was that of the Mill Green pitcher (Cat. 185), in which he perceived a severe dignity of form. It is true that many medieval pots attract us through their simple form, combined with an attractive speckled or rich dark-green glaze; but there is no evidence that any of these virtues had an appeal to medieval customers. They may have regarded the green-glazed pot simply as a cheaper version of the bronze jug. By the end of the thirteenth century they appear to have appreciated highly decorated pottery, since it became increasingly popular.

Decoration could be achieved by a number of techniques: incised lines (Cat. 550), combing (Cat. 185), applied slip (Cat. 184), applied scales (Cat. 551, 548), or modelling (Cat. 180). Sometimes the whole pot was conceived as a person or animal. The Scarborough aquamanile (Cat. 548), a vessel for holding water, is in the form of a ram, while the jugs from Worcester (Cat. 553) or London (Cat. 550) are in the form of people. The most common form of modelling was applied ornament. The use of clay to create animals and people provided an opportunity for the medieval potter to produce pottery whose decoration, while often adding little to the form of the pot, gives it a vitality and charm.

The selection for this exhibition has concentrated on the use of animals and the human face for the decoration of jugs. The face is one of the most common decorative features. We do not know whether it derived from the gargoyles or corbels on medieval churches, or whether it is simply part of the fascination with the human face in the Middle Ages. Sometimes the face is depicted alone, as in the roof finials (Cat. 554, 555), and sometimes the whole figure is represented, as in the matchstick-like figure of applied lines from Coventry (Cat. 549). There is no evidence for the use of names to describe pottery jugs, in the manner in which names were sometimes applied to metal jugs. Some figures on the jugs are identifiable as knights. The Moot Hall jug (Cat. 180) has an upper frieze of knights riding above, with hounds and stags below. We do not know who used these highly-decorated jugs, but it is unlikely that it was those who spent most of their time jousting or hunting. Animals were a common decorative theme: there are dragons on the jug from Cannon Street (Cat. 184) reminiscent of those found on tiles, stags on the Oxford puzzle jug (Cat. 551) and an 'elephant' on the Rye jug (Cat. 552), perhaps recalling the grander reproductions of the theme on misericords or in manuscripts.

It would be misleading to end with the impression that medieval pottery was a purely peasant art. The last twenty years of archaeological excavations have brought about great advances, not only in the dating of medieval pottery and the understanding of the sequence of development,[3] but also through the identification, study, and excavation of the manufacturing sites with their kilns such as Grimston (Cat. 182), Laverstock (Cat. 181) or Scarborough (Cat. 548). This in turn has led to a greater understanding of the distribution and trade in medieval pottery.[4] For instance, Scarborough ware was distributed not only in England (Cat. 548) but also across the North Sea in Scandinavia.

Conversely, English pottery was subject to the influence of styles of pottery from abroad, particularly France. There are slip-decorated jugs in London which are copies of Norman jugs,[5] and it is clear that the Cannon Street jug is a copy of a French jug. Likewise the puzzle jug from the Ashmolean has been seen as a copy of a south-west French polychrome jug found at Exeter. Although some foreign influence did exist, the fabric of the pottery indicates clearly that the jugs were made in England and not on the Continent. In that way medieval pottery is a more satisfactory subject for study than, say, goldsmith's work, since it is clear what is really English.

NOTES

1. Le Patourel 1968, 111.
2. Roach Smith 1854, p. 113.
3. Vince 1985, pp. 25–93.
4. Davey & Hodges 1983.
5. Vince 1985, p. 46.

John Cherry Tiles

In the south-eastern part of the floor of the chapter house of Westminster Abbey are the remains of an inscription describing the building as the work of King Henry III and praising its beauty.[1] This 'incomparable chapter house' according to Matthew Paris was completed by 1253 and the magnificent tile pavement was completed by 1258/9. The pavement still provides the visitor with a demonstration of the importance of royal patronage in the development of inlaid tiling in the thirteenth century.

In inlaid tiles a stamp is used to make a depressed pattern, which is then subsequently filled with clay of a contrasting colour. In the vast majority of thirteenth-century tiles the body colour of the tiles was red and the decoration inlaid in white clay. The technique may well have been brought to England from France in the second quarter of the thirteenth century. Both Anjou and Normandy have been suggested as sources, and although Normandy is perhaps more likely than Anjou, the origins are not yet certain.

It is clear, however, that tile production flourished in monasteries and palaces with which Henry III was directly concerned. The completion of his father's abbey at Beaulieu and the extensive remodelling and redecoration of the castle at Winchester may have played their part in this development. The Great Hall at Winchester (Cat. 261) had a tiled floor, but this does not survive. Tiling of the royal palaces can best be appreciated in the floors of the King's Chapel and the Queen's Chamber from Clarendon that are now on display in the British Museum (Medieval Tile and Pottery Gallery, nos 15 and 16).[2] The circular pavement from the first-floor chapel has alternating wide bands of inlaid tiles and narrower bands of green-glazed tiles. This pavement can be dated to the period 1240–4, and the kiln in which it was fired and later excavated is also now on display in the British Museum (Medieval Tile and Pottery Gallery, no. 14). The Queen's Chamber pavement of 1251–2 is laid as a series of rectangular panels including tiles of lions and griffins in circles facing each other.

The Westminster chapter house pavement was completed by 1258–9. One of the most outstanding designs used there is the four-tile design of the royal arms with figures of dragons and centaurs in the space left by the curve of the shield. The pavement is arranged by panels, but the southern part of this scheme is broken by the inclusion of designs including figures of a king, queen and abbot, two minstrels, St Edward giving his ring to a beggar and a hunting scene. The high quality of the depiction of the figures suggests that they may have been designed for a floor in a royal palace, perhaps Westminster Palace itself. The interest of the chapter house floor is that it is the first securely dated appearance of such fine representations of human figures.

The most famous series of historiated tiles is the series of roundels with scenes drawn from the Romance of Tristram found in the mid-nineteenth century at Chertsey Abbey (Cat. 320). We do not know who designed these tiles, but he was clearly an artist of high quality. The portrayal of Gormon hastening to view the body of Morhaut is full of anxiety. Although found at Chertsey, it is likely that they were first designed for a royal palace; this may have been Westminster itself, though none have been found there. Likewise the series of combats from Chertsey of which that of Richard and Saladin is displayed here (Cat. 16) would have been more suitable to a royal palace than a Benedictine abbey. Both the Tristram series and the combat series may be seen as part of Henry III's patronage, but the link between Westminster and Chertsey was clearly continued in the reign of Edward I. The three panels of the king, queen, and archbishop (Cat. 367) which occur at Chertsey may well have been designed for the paving around the tomb of Queen Eleanor at Westminster. Chertsey was always a rich monastery and was near Windsor, but the exact reasons for the Westminster–Chertsey connection have never been worked out.

It was not only the patronage of Henry III that inspired the development of the tile industry. At Hailes the patronage of his half-brother Richard of Cornwall encouraged the use of tile paving in his new Cistercian foundation. It is not yet clear which tiles, if any, were included in the new church consecrated in 1251. What is certain is that the new work connected with the extension of the east end to house the new relic of the Holy Blood was paved with tiles. Yet this part of the church was not paved with the historiated tiles used at Chertsey, but with a series of heraldic tiles commemorating the connections of Richard and Edmund of Cornwall (Cat. 131). It was this repetition of single motifs that was to provide the impetus for the development of the tile industry. The fashion for tiled floors in monasteries, castles and churches spread quickly, and craftsmen began to produce tiles on a wider scale to satisfy this demand. For instance, in Wessex in the late thirteenth and fourteenth centuries mass-produced tiles were made on kiln sites such as Nash Hill,[3] to designs similar to those used earlier at sites such as Clarendon. In a similar manner the use of tiles at Hailes and Halesowen led to a development of mass-produced tiles in the Midlands.

In the early fourteenth century another technique was being employed to produce tile designs. This is the use of tiles of different colours and shapes to make a picture, usually of light figures on a dark background. No example of this is shown in the exhibition, but the most notable example occurs in the floor at Ely in the chapel built by Prior Crauden, c. 1324. Here, before the altar, is a rectangular panel with Adam and Eve and the serpent in the tree. A similar effect of light figures on a darker ground is achieved by a quite different technique in the series of tiles from Tring, Hertfordshire (Cat. 217). Here the whole surface was coated with slip, the decoration was outlined with incised lines and the slip removed from the background. The details such as the hair, facial expressions and clothes were added by incised lines in a sgraffito technique, cutting through the white slip to produce a red line. This technique is used with great vigour and vivacity. The scenes illustrate the miracles of the Infancy of Christ recorded in the Apocryphal Gospels. The pictures are related to the Bodleian MS Selden Supra 38 (Cat. 203; figs 22–4), and the exhibition provides an opportunity to compare them. The tiles were probably meant to be set on a wall rather than a floor, and so represent a rare attempt to use tiles in a didactic way, rather like some wall paintings or stained glass.

In the fourteenth century the use of tiling became widespread, and there was a considerable number of local production centres turning out on the whole very repetitive tile designs. The two-colour tile from Wells (Cat. 260) is an example of a later Wessex design, and the panel of relief-decorated tiles from Bawsey (Cat. 132) illustrates the products of a kiln site from which they were widely distributed in the hinterland of the Wash. One of the designs includes an inscription asking for prayers for the soul of Nicholas de Stowe, Vicar of Snettisham. He died in 1376, and the stamp was probably cut in that year to cover his grave or surround his tomb. Tile-making in the Gothic period shows a descent from the royal patronage that gave it a new impetus in the thirteenth century to the production of repetitive designs for local patrons.

NOTES

1. Colvin 1963.
2. Eames 1980, pp. 134–8.
3. Eames 1974, pp. 131–5.

The Wheel of Fortune:

Thomas Cocke

The Appreciation of Gothic since the Middle Ages

The Gothic art of thirteenth- and fourteenth-century England, the age of the Plantagenets, forms one of the most enduring and influential contributions to the national culture of later centuries. In spite of losses much still surrounds us, not only in great monuments such as Salisbury Cathedral but in the humbler forms of inlaid tiles, corbel heads or cusped roof timbers. My purpose is to explain how the evidence survived and how its interpretation, as it varied over time, affected not just the treatment of the objects themselves but the course of later art.

To focus on England is not to deny the international nature of Gothic but simply a condition of making a coherent exhibition. The same constraint entails treating the Gothic Revival only as it affected the treatment of medieval buildings and works of art.[1] Inevitably architecture is discussed at a greater length than the other arts since it was here that Gothic was first perceived as a style and its nature debated and defined. In the exhibition this architectural emphasis will act as a complement to the other sections, where smaller objects predominate; some items, such as Hollar's view of the chapter house of Old St Paul's (Cat. 386), illustrate buildings that have vanished, others record stylistic features, as in Wilkins's studies of Prior Crauden's Chapel at Ely (Cat. 393–8). In others the vision of an artist such as Turner conveys an impression of the space and light in a building, which surpasses words or photographs in explaining that 'peculiar quality ... we may call emotional power, that separates Gothic ... and raises it to the supreme height'.[2]

Attitudes to Gothic are deep-seated and emotionally charged, even in late twentieth-century England. It is acknowledged as *the* medieval style of the country, whereas Romanesque, even in its English guise as 'Norman', remains appreciated only by a few. What has given Gothic such an identity and appeal?

First, the monuments remain prominent features of the landscape, not just as museum objects but, in the case of many cathedrals, churches and castles, still in use. Second, the institutions of the nation, the Crown, the Church, the Law, Parliament, preserve medieval concepts and ceremonies. Basic forms of Gothic architecture and ornament, the pointed arch, the traceried window, the quatrefoil, have become coded in people's memories as symbols to be perceived on many levels, from a key to a map to a more complex reference to traditional beliefs or learning.

Our image of the Middle Ages has not remained fixed. Each period has focused on the elements relevant to its own preoccupations. In the seventeenth century men delved into medieval law for precedents in their constitutional struggles, in the nineteenth century into medieval religious imagery and history for ecclesiological arguments. The same applies today. Interest in the late fourteenth-century female mystic Julian of Norwich has been stimulated by the growth of the women's movement.

The visitor to the exhibition cannot have a total, unprejudiced view of the objects. However, the need to read Gothic as a palimpsest of many layers, to see it in its own terms, in those of our own day and also cumulatively through the changing viewpoints of intervening centuries, is not a limitation but an enrichment of our understanding of art.

The use of the curious word 'Gothic' as a name for medieval art helps to explain how understanding of it developed. When Italian Renaissance writers, notably Vasari, attempted to distinguish their revived antique forms of art from those very different used before, they needed a name for the earlier style. Vasari chose *tedesco* (German) or *moderno* but, more importantly for the future, he blamed the destruction of classical art on the 'savage and barbarian invaders' who overran the Roman Empire of the West, the Vandals, Visigoths and Ostrogoths.[3] Although Vasari did not use the word *gotico* he occasionally used the phrase *la maniera de' Goti* as a neutral term for works of art of the twelfth or thirteenth century, long after the Goths had disappeared.[4] This dual meaning of Gothic persisted into the nineteenth century, the term sometimes retaining its barbarian associations, but more often signifying a chronological period.

'Gothic' as an adjective applied to a building first appeared in print in 1610 referring to the late medieval Bourse at Antwerp, but the introduction of the word to England was probably direct from Italy where it would have been known to the cosmopolitan patrons of Charles I's Court such as Lord Arundel.[5] In England the term retained its original ambiguity. John Evelyn described York Minster objectively in his diary for 1655 as 'a most intire, magnificent piece of Gotic [*sic*] Architecture',[6] but later used 'Gothic' as the climax to a bitter attack on the 'Fantastical and Licentious manner of Building, which we have since call'd Modern (or Gothic rather)'.[7]

Nevertheless, the term did not become universally accepted until the present century. This was chiefly because the name of the style was inextricably involved with debate about its origins. It was early recognised as absurd to attribute to the Goths, barbarians associated with the destruction of art, works created centuries after their time especially when, as early as the mid-seventeenth century, critics began to distinguish the first round-arched style of medieval architecture from its successor, the pointed.[8]

There were differences of approach even within Evelyn's generation, almost the first in England to be conscious of the historical succession of styles. John Aubrey in his pioneering chronology of English architecture prudently collected his examples by reign, with little stylistic commentary beyond marking the evolution from type to type, for example from lancet windows to traceried (Cat. 387). Christopher Wren, although he accepted that the Saxon and Norman round-arched style was 'not much altered from the Roman',[9] claimed that the pointed style was inspired by a more exotic source, the Saracens of the Levant; thus, 'what we now vulgarly call the Gothic, ought properly and truly to be named the Saracenic Architecture'.[10]

In the mid-eighteenth century William Warburton expounded a radical variant of the theory. He saw the Saracen influence as operating not in the Near East but in Spain on a style already introduced by the Goths and derived from the northern groves in which the Goths had worshipped 'during the gloom of Paganism'.[11] Warburton seems to have been the first English writer to give a wide currency to the analogy between the pointed arcades and vaults of a Gothic cathedral and an arching 'avenue of well-grown trees'.[12] The theory, scorned by scholars, has yet had lasting influence from the force of the visual image.[13] Even more significant was the way in which he reversed the charge against Gothic of a lack of classical order into praise of the Goths' 'new species of architecture, unknown to Greece and Rome; upon original principles and ideas much nobler than what had given birth even to classical magnificence'.[14]

This confidence in Gothic as a serious style of art led to further attempts to find a worthier name. Even the uncontroversial James Bentham, who used 'Gothic' for convenience, admitted 'the reason ... is not very apparent'.[15] The proliferation of alternative names went together with an increase in the number of books on the style. In 1835 John Britton could publish a list of sixty-six such books and articles, two-thirds of which had been written in the years 1800–35.[16] In them the origins and essential characteristics of Gothic were debated by antiquaries whose conclusions coloured their choice of name. The main contenders were 'Pointed', 'English' or 'Christian', though Mitford in 1809 put in a plea for 'Plantagenet'. John Milner combatively referred to 'that beautiful style of architecture properly called the pointed, and abusively the Gothic, order'.[17] Milner scorned the Saracen theory, preferring to see the pointed style evolving from the intersection of round-headed arcading as at the church of St Cross near Winchester.[18] 'Pointed' became the name favoured by the nineteenth-century enthusiasts of the Gothic Revival. Their historian Eastlake could claim around 1870 that Pointed 'has ... been universally accepted as a generic term for the Architecture of the Middle Ages'.[19]

This apparent success was despite the different choice by Thomas Rickman, in whose definitive book *An Attempt to Discriminate the Styles of Architecture in England*

(Cat. 400), first published in 1815 and often reprinted, each stage of medieval architecture was accurately described. He preferred 'English', partly because 'in many instances' the English were stylistically ahead of the Continent but more particularly because medieval architecture abroad lacked 'that pure simplicity and boldness of composition which marks [sic] the English buildings'.[20] Yet it is Rickman's subdivisions of the style, 'Early', 'Decorated' and 'Perpendicular English' which have endured (his 'English', except in the first case, abandoned). The association of Gothic with religion is so deeply rooted in English attitudes to the style that the proposal of 'Christian' as an alternative to 'Gothic' is not surprising. Both the Protestant Britton and the Catholic Pugin favoured the usage.[21]

In the twentieth century Gothic has become an objective term, free of controversy. W.R. Lethaby, surveyor of Westminster Abbey from 1902 to 1928, had a last attempt at substituting the term 'Romance' – as in language – but even he returned to Gothic.[22] Ruskin's use of 'Gothic' rather than 'Pointed' in his widely-read books must have been influential. He rejected any equation with 'Christian' and reversed the original opprobrious meaning of barbaric: 'It is true ... that the architecture of the North is rude and wild; but it is ... in this very character that it deserves our profoundest reverence.'[23] The wheel had come full circle.

An appreciation of Gothic buildings is found much earlier than the first use of the term. Already in 1562 a survey by officials of the Duchy of Lancaster discussed the ancient castles belonging to the Duchy in sympathetic terms and recommended their preservation, rather than their destruction as obsolete.[24] Pontefract was 'an honourable Castle to be ... kept for the goodlynes of the house' and nearly £2,000 was spent on it. Sixty years later James I was also determined to 'prevent the Ruynes of a Monument of such antiquity and goodly building'.[25] Such an attitude was encouraged by the contemporary passion for the medieval pursuits of heraldry, chivalry and even jousting which created a neo-feudal cult, the world of Spenser's Faerie Queen, with its apparatus of knights in armour and battlemented castles.

In the seventeenth century this harking back to secular Gothic was cast into insignificance by a renewed interest in the ecclesiastical. The combined impact of Reformation and Dissolution had halted the development of late medieval art in churches and destroyed the treasures of the religious houses. Of their metalwork and textiles hardly anything survives; of their libraries only a fraction. Although more survives of their buildings many, such as the great friaries of London, have vanished with scarcely a trace.

However, the institutional conservatism of the Elizabethan Settlement which preserved the traditional hierarchy and parochial structure of the Church did ensure the survival of cathedrals and parish churches as 'in times past'.[26] The features at risk were those which were superfluous or offensive to the reformed religion. Metalwork was destroyed not only for its intrinsic value but because the liturgy no longer required shrines and crucifixes. Sculpture was in danger if idolatrous but not, as with misericords or roof corbels, where it adorned a functional element and depicted moralising or secular subjects. Most stained glass was left intact, to be later whittled away by wear and tear, and a desire for more light, rather than iconoclasm. Economy joined with conservatism to limit destruction; it was cheaper to conceal obsolete or offending features with whitewash and plaster than to knock them out with a hammer.

Elizabethan church building was untraditional, but when ecclesiastical work revived under the Stuarts it was the thousands of medieval churches up and down the land which provided the model. Such a use of earlier forms was no blind following of late medieval models but a deliberate selection from the various periods of Gothic. The flowing tracery, elaborate vaulting and pinnacles of the fourteenth century were especially favoured sources. The chancel screen installed in 1618 at Geddington, Northamptonshire, had a pierced tracery head derived from the Decorated east window.[27] The east window installed in 1628–30 in the rebuilt church of St Katharine Cree, London, copied the late thirteenth-century east window of Old St Paul's Cathedral with lancets of equal height surmounted by a vast rose.[28]

The inspiration for this enthusiasm for Gothic was local pride and admiration of intricate medieval workmanship, untroubled by theories of taste, and not Catholic sympathies among high churchmen. Archbishop Laud and his adherents encouraged church maintenance and restoration but their artistic model, if any, was the Baroque of the Counter-Reformation.

Thomas Fuller defended native medieval art against the new foreign ideas in a panegyric of the chapter house at York Minster. 'Now as it follows not that the Usurping Tulip is better than the Rose, because preferred by some Foreign Fancies before it; so it is as inconsequent that Modish Italian Churches are better than this Reverend Magnificent Structure, because some humorous Travellers are so pleased to esteem them.'[29]

The important contribution of this period was the maintenance of so many medieval churches. Episcopal visitations, energetically pursued under James I and Charles I, revealed many buildings to be in a poor state and ill furnished. Their recommendations, though not always executed, encouraged repairs. A model restoration was that of John Cosin, later Bishop of Durham, at Brancepeth Church, County Durham, in the 1630s, where roof and masonry were repaired and the furnishings lavishly replaced, partly following Gothic forms. All over the country dates on a roof beam, battlement or pulpit, when not removed by disapproving Victorians, testify to the contribution of early Stuart England.

The Civil Wars had a catastrophic effect on major medieval monuments both secular and ecclesiastical. Castles were obvious military targets and suffered accordingly (fig. 123). Some cathedrals suffered similar fates, in particular Lichfield which was comprehensively wrecked by three successive sieges. Cathedrals were also targets for iconoclastic 'purifying'. Damage was concentrated on anything connected with the hated Laudian ritual – vestments, choir books, organs – and on tombs. Tombs were desecrated more in the hope of plunder than as an expression of religious or political radicalism. John Evelyn was told in 1654 of the 'hellish' greed of the soldiers who 'knocked off all or most of the Brasses' in Lincoln Cathedral, as well as presumably the bronze effigy of Queen Eleanor (Cat. 379).[30]

Parliamentarian iconoclasm, however, did less damage to the fabric of buildings than Royalist propaganda asserted. The serious damage was financial. With the abolition of the Church hierarchy and the confiscation of their lands there were neither corporate bodies nor funds to maintain the buildings. Yet this threatened ruin of the medieval heritage stimulated interest in it, especially in its recording by books or drawings. Even before the Civil War the *Antiquitas Rediviva*, a prescient group of antiquaries led by Sir Christopher (later Lord) Hatton, had foreseen 'the near-approaching storm' and William Dugdale with the heraldic draughtsman William Sedgwick had travelled in the Midlands and Yorkshire making 'exact draughts' of monuments and copying their epitaphs and any coats of arms, including those in stained glass.[31] Thus many tombs, such as that of Queen Eleanor at Lincoln or those of the medieval bishops at Lichfield, were recorded before destruction (Cat. 379). The Protectorate saw two important books on great medieval buildings, in 1655 the *Monasticon Anglicanum* prepared by Richard Dodsworth and William Dugdale and in 1658 the *History of St Paul's* by Dugdale alone. They were both documentary histories, the former of all the religious houses of the land; both were generously illustrated.

The period after the Civil War marked a watershed in attitudes to Gothic as well as to the physical fabric of its monuments. Refugees from the troubles such as John Evelyn or Roger Pratt, the 'Modish Travellers' complained of by Fuller, returned from their Continental travels not just with the word Gothic but with visions of a politer way of life and of classical rules of regular design which made medieval forms functionally as well as aesthetically redundant. Thus, although in the years after the king's return in 1660 the great medieval buildings damaged or neglected during the Interregnum underwent extensive repair, their rationale was no longer accepted.

The age of Wren would appear to have been peculiarly unfavourable to the understanding of medieval art. Old St Paul's was totally swept away after the Great Fire and the new cathedral gave authority to the classical style. In other cathedrals, though the medieval structure was repaired, the choir, still the home of the daily Offices and so the working heart of the building, was furnished with contemporary splendour and convenience. The canons of Canterbury gradually modernised their

Fig. 123 View of Pontefract Castle, Yorkshire, traditionally attributed to J. de Momper, *c.* 1625–30. The castle was virtually demolished *c.* 1649 (Collection of H.M. The Queen)

quarters (Cat. 404). In 1676 the parclose screens were panelled and in 1704–5 a Baroque archbishop's throne was installed and the late thirteenth-century stalls were replaced by a classical design on the model of those at the new St Paul's. The same held true for both secular and ecclesiastical medieval buildings which, however carefully repaired, were arranged and furnished in a contemporary style. The shell of the London Guildhall was retained in the post-Fire rebuilding but the new roof, windows and decoration made no concession to it. The Temple Church in London was restored by Wren in 1682–3 with no external alterations but internally it was panelled, pewed and given a Renaissance reredos and pulpit (Cat. 405).[32]

Perhaps this distancing from medieval ways, combined with an awareness of Gothic as a distinct if inferior style, helped to create a new attitude. Wren in the course of his long career was responsible for the maintenance of an assortment of official buildings such as the thirteenth-century chapter house of Westminster Abbey (then used as a Record Office) as well as the royal palaces, and was consulted on many others. Wren's report of 1669 on Salisbury Cathedral and the 'memorial' on Westminster Abbey that he prepared in 1713 became classic texts in any later discussion of Gothic. Wren regarded both Salisbury and Westminster with a critical, scientific eye, as examples of a particular structural system and not as absurdities.

The perception of Gothic buildings as monuments led to some precocious attempts at their preservation. There had been major programmes of repair at Westminster Abbey in the 1620s and 1660s, but in 1697 the Dean and Chapter successfully petitioned Parliament for 'State Aid', a proportion of the coal tax, to finance a comprehensive restoration which took fifty years to complete. The policy set out by Wren and continued by Dickinson and Hawksmoor was to retain (or on new features, such as the west towers, to create) authentic Gothic forms but to simplify decayed mouldings and sculpture. Dickinson's design of 1719 for the north transept, approved by Wren and his colleagues, exemplifies this confident and, for its time, purist approach (Cat. 418). Even bolder and more conservationist was the contemporary treatment of the outward-leaning north transept of Beverley Minster. Hawksmoor, together with the York joiner William Thornton, devised an immense apparatus of five trusses which cradled the north wall from ground to gable while it was screwed back to the vertical by jacks (Cat. 416–17). His colleague at the Works, John Vanbrugh, attempted to defend medieval Woodstock Palace from his patrons at Blenheim, the Duke and Duchess of Marlborough, urging the value of ancient buildings both for their 'Magnificence or Curious Workmanship' and for their associations.[33] He pointed out the values of such ruins to make an 'agreeable object' in the landscape, so anticipating the later treatment of sites such as Fountains Abbey integrated into the park of Studley Royal.[34]

Preservation was differently interpreted by the Society of Antiquaries of London, founded in 1717. Physical assistance was limited to paying for two oak posts to protect Waltham Cross (Cat. 373) from passing traffic but preservation on paper was enthusiastically pursued through the publication of meticulously prepared engravings (e.g. Cat. 380). These were collected and issued in volumes called *Vetusta Monumenta* which later included detailed drawings with explanatory text on particular themes, such as, in 1790, the Eleanor crosses (Cat. 370–1). In 1771 the Society organised the regular publication of the papers and exhibits presented to it in *Archaeologia*, a journal still current today. Here again medieval topics of all sorts featured prominently. Typical of the wide sympathies of the Society was its publication in *Archaeologia* of the careful description and reconstruction of Prior Crauden's Chapel, Ely, by the young William Wilkins, better known as a standard-bearer of the Greek Revival. In his illustrations Wilkins treated each Gothic detail with as much precision as the moulding of a Greek temple (Cat. 393–8).

The stress given by the Antiquaries to depiction and recording is clearly associated with the contemporary flowering of English topographical art. The quantity of drawings, engravings, watercolours and oils of medieval subjects, varying in quality from amateurs' scribbles to masterpieces by Turner, witnesses to the keen demand for them. The Buck brothers (see Cat. 389) produced and sold about 500 separate views of antiquities between 1723 and 1753. John Buckler (see Cat. 399) drew over 13,000 sketches, many worked up into watercolours, from whole cathedrals to details of doorways and fonts.[35] These pictures provide invaluable records of features since altered or destroyed and, when by artists of the calibre of Girtin or Turner, can convey the essential character of a building, the vast, complex shape of the Decorated octagon at Ely or the luminous balance of the Early English chapter house at Salisbury (Cat. 391–2).

The emotional power of Gothic appealed to the Romanticism of the early nineteenth century and helped to win appreciation of the style not as an apologetic second best to classical art but a proud alternative to it. Milner used the principles of the Sublime, its emphasis on height and length and an 'artificial infinity', to explain the qualities of a Gothic cathedral.[36] The associational power of Gothic was given much wider currency through literature and, in particular, the novels and poems of Walter Scott.[37] The Middle Ages became a living world which could be imitated. The same message was also found in *The Broad Stone of Honour* by Kenelm Digby, first published in 1822 and later expanded, which portrayed an idealised, chivalrous Middle Ages.[38]

Isolation during the Napoleonic Wars and national pride stimulated by their victorious conclusion encouraged Englishmen to study their own ancient monuments rather than the masterpieces of Graeco-Roman art. Even Sir William Chambers, the classical architect, urged dilettanti and antiquaries to abandon 'the gleanings of Greece' and publish to the world 'the riches of Britain, in the splendor [*sic*] of her ancient structures'.[39] In the first four decades of the nineteenth century the publisher and self-publicist John Britton produced literally scores of volumes illustrating medieval buildings and describing their history and architectural development.[40]

Parallel with this romantic enthusiasm for Gothic ran a serious interest in the technical aspects of the style, particularly in Cambridge. The architect and antiquary James Essex made a series of studies on the geometry of arches and windows and the structural problems of vaulting, partly as a result of his restorations of Ely and Lincoln cathedrals and partly as illustrations for his projected History of Gothic, of which several drafts survive (Cat. 408). The University Librarian, Thomas Kerrich, acquired Essex's papers and further developed this aspect of Gothic studies, introducing further examples particularly from Italy.[41] Yet another Cambridge Gothicist was William Whewell who eventually became the grand Victorian Master of Trinity but who had earlier travelled through Picardy, Normandy and Germany analysing medieval buildings and motifs. His younger contemporary and friend Robert Willis was the most gifted and influential of them all. He combined a profound knowledge of written sources with a keen archaeological eye and uncommon clarity of thought. His studies of the building histories of Canterbury and Winchester cathedrals have never been surpassed.

This analytical approach to Gothic was bound to conflict with the romantic vision of the style. And as the Victorian Gothic Revival advanced, it was the latter which dominated, however much supported by scholarship. Pevsner wrote of an antiquarian tour of Normandy made in 1823 by Kenelm Digby and Whewell, his incompatible tutor: 'Poor Kenelm Digby, exposed to the searching scholarship of Whewell, but poor Whewell and Willis also, who were soon to find their clear world of scholarship clouded by the passions of Catholics and Anglo-Catholics and Anti-Catholics and Ruskin.'[42]

The involvement of Gothic in passionate religious controversy was largely achieved by one man, A.W.N. Pugin, and two parties, the Tractarian Movement originating at Oxford and the Camden (later the Ecclesiological) Society at Cambridge.[43] Pugin followed eighteenth-century French critics in his appreciation of the rational structure of Gothic but for him Gothic was not just admirable, it was the only true style because it was Christian, by which Pugin meant Catholic. Pugin had embraced Rome in 1834 but just at that time there was a reawakening within the Church of England of Catholic thinking on the significance of tradition and liturgy, and on the role of church buildings and furnishings in bearing fit witness to the Faith. The idea that medieval forms were the prerequisite of acceptable worship transformed not just ecclesiological and architectural studies but the fortune of existing medieval monuments as well. It became the duty of right-thinking men to expunge all evidence of intervening centuries and to restore buildings to their hypothetical condition in the golden age of Gothic between rudeness and decadence, the thirteenth and fourteenth centuries.

John Ruskin shared some of these attitudes, although he attacked Pugin and was too Evangelical to succumb to the Tractarian 'beauty of holiness'. He too considered medieval art morally right, reflecting the wisdom of the Creator and the creative thinking of the workmen. However, he tended to deprecate northern and, in particular, English Gothic for 'its great mouldering wall of rugged sculpture and confused arcades', contrasting it unfavourably with the brilliant surfaces and decoration of Venetian art.[44] He was also appalled by the readiness of English Gothicists to indulge in the drastic restoration of buildings and sculpture. Through his immensely popular books and lectures, Ruskin propounded a vision of Gothic which transcended national and confessional boundaries and offered inspiring ideals of art and society for his own time.

William Morris, last of the nineteenth-century prophets of Gothic, was an avowed disciple of Ruskin in his conviction of the intrinsic virtues of the style and of the liberating effect it could have on contemporary life, precisely because it was based on such different principles. He regarded Ruskin's celebrated chapter on the nature of Gothic in *The Stones of Venice* as one of 'the very few necessary and inevitable utterances of the century'.[45] Morris understood that Gothic was the expression of a whole society and had not been confined to an esoteric, ecclesiastical élite. For him the thirteenth-century barn at Great Coxwell, Oxfordshire (Cat. 218) was as noble an expression of Gothic as a cathedral. He shared with the architect William Burges, who created the fabulous interiors of Cardiff Castle, a fascination with the diversity of Gothic art, the metalwork and textiles as well as the manuscripts, sculpture and carpentry.

To mention a handful of men, however great in themselves, is not to explain the

Victorian contribution to Gothic. Nineteenth-century England turned to the Middle Ages with a fervour that matched that of fifteenth-century Florence for classical antiquity. In 1855 G.G. Scott could speak of the Gothic Revival as 'a deep-seated, earnest and energetic revolution in the human mind'.[46] The enthusiasts of the previous century had maintained a rational distance. Even the serious-minded Thomas Gray considered it 'mere pedantry in Gothicism ... to sit upon nothing but Coronation chairs, nor drink out of nothing but chalices and flagons'.[47] Three generations later, such common sense demonstrated the superficiality of Gray's approach.

It was not caprice that sent the High Victorians reaching past the Perpendicular preferred in the early nineteenth century to the more perfect models of the thirteenth and fourteenth centuries, the periods of the First and Middle Pointed. As early as 1669 Wren had commended the 'stately and rich Plainness' of the Early English of Salisbury Cathedral,[48] and Essex a century later saw the period as the high-point of Gothic art; but these aesthetic judgements were mild compared to the nineteenth century's championship. Ruskin asserted that 'the art of the thirteenth century is the foundation of all art'[49] and for once he was in full agreement with G.G. Scott.

The paradox is that the Victorian passion for Gothic often destroyed the object of its devotion. Especially in the thirty-year heyday of ecclesiological restoration from 1840 to 1870 authentic medieval features were destroyed at a much faster rate than in the previous three hundred. William Butterfield in 1851–2 replaced the large Perpendicular east and west windows of Amesbury Church, Wiltshire, with Early English lancets to suit the style of the eastern parts of the building. The early medieval font was broken up and used as rubble under the chancel floor along with all the funerary monuments ancient and modern; two fifteenth-century wooden screens were discarded, one luckily into a stable whence it would be recovered fifty years later.[50] Restorers who could take such an attitude even to medieval features that were inconvenient or of the 'wrong' date were ruthless in their destruction of later elements. The Temple Church was restored in 1840–3 at great cost, all the columns of the Round being replaced and the interior completely stripped. Conservatives regarded the proceedings as 'an act of Vandalism' but the progressive rejoiced to see the 'plague-spot' of whitewash swept from the ceilings, the 'pew lumber' from the floors, the 'monstrous pagan altar screen' and 'glaring' monuments from the walls and pillars and the 'preposterous' organ screen from the arch to the Round.[51]

G.G. Scott was perhaps the archetypal Victorian restorer, prolific, scholarly and sure of the rightness of his conduct. For example, at Ely he was in charge of the cathedral's restoration from 1847 during which years he eradicated Essex's achievements of a century before.[52] His most conspicuous contribution internally was the moving and refurbishing of the choir. Externally it was the reconstruction in 1860 of the lantern over the central octagon, not because it was in poor condition but because its Georgian Gothic detailing was no longer considered acceptable. Scott's design was archaeologically researched but it has the robust profile of its period (Cat. 409).

These ideas of restoration penetrated to almost every church in the country. In Betjeman's succinct summary:

> The Church's Restoration
> In eighteen-eighty-three
> Has left for contemplation
> Not what there used to be.[53]

A typical example is the unexecuted scheme of 1875 by G.E. Street for All Saints, Great Driffield, North Humberside (Cat. 410–15). Street, one of the most devoted architects of the Gothic Revival, proposed few structural alterations beyond the standard raising of roof gables to a steep pitch and the additions of vestry with boiler room below, organ chamber and south porch. But the wholesale replacement of floors, roofs and furnishings would have given the church an appearance entirely of the 1870s.

It was this aspect of the nineteenth-century attitude to Gothic which so angered its prophets, John Ruskin and William Morris. Ruskin reiterated that it was impossible 'to restore anything that has ever been great or beautiful. . . . The life of the whole, that spirit which is given only by the hand and eye of the workman, can never be restored.'[54] Morris pursued this mission with vigour. On behalf of the Society for the Protection of Ancient Buildings, itself founded in 1877 on his initiative, he protested to the Dean and Chapter of Westminster about the restoration of the Abbey by Scott and Pearson. Scott had created on the exterior 'a modern building, imitating . . . work of the thirteenth century'.[55] It was no longer art but work of the architect's office. The eighteenth-century masons had at least 'put some of their own thought into it, poor as that was'.[56] The only aim of restoration should be to secure structural stability.

Morris's philosophy of restoration is now generally accepted, in theory if not in practice. Gothic is no longer a spiritual crusade but an art-historical period. Yet however remote or even absurd the debates of earlier centuries may now seem, they have shaped our vision and can still enrich our understanding. Their passion can recapture for us the excitement and splendour of Gothic, especially that of the age of the Plantagenets when, in William Morris's words, 'All over the intelligent world was spread this bright, glittering, joyous art, which had now reached its acme of elegance and beauty.'[57]

NOTES

1. There is no comprehensive modern account of the Gothic Revival. C.L. Eastlake's book of 1872 (reprinted in 1970 with a valuable introduction by J.M. Crook), remains the classic text. The brilliant essay by K. Clark of 1928 has become outdated even in the revised edition of 1962.
2. Kingsley Porter 1909, II, p. 253.
3. Vasari 1966 edn, *testo* vol. II, p. 18.
4. The origins of the term Gothic are discussed in de Beer 1948, *passim* and Frankl 1960, pp. 252–314.
5. De Beer 1948, p. 150.
6. Evelyn 1955 edn, III, p. 129. It is not certain how much Evelyn may have altered his original wording when later rewriting his diary entries.
7. Evelyn 1723, pp. 9–10. The quotation is from his 'Account of Architects and Architecture', written before 1697 but first published in 1707 as an appendix to the second edition of his translation of the *Parallele de l'architecture antique et de la moderne* by Roland de Fréart.
8. For a discussion of the development of the nomenclature of the Romanesque see London 1984a, p. 360.
9. Wren 1750, p. 296.
10. Ibid., p. 306.
11. Pope 1751, III, p. 267.
12. Ibid. Warburton's theory was shared by his contemporary Stukeley.
13. Sir James Hall at the end of the 18th century went further and claimed that Gothic derived from interwoven willow rods and had models made, or rather grown, to support his theory.
14. Pope 1751, III, p. 267.
15. Bentham 1771, p. 37.
16. Britton 1835, pp. xiii–xv.
17. Milner 1809, II, p. 161.
18. Op. cit., pp. 163–4.
19. Eastlake 1970 edn, p. 120.
20. Rickman 1817, p. 37.
21. Pugin published a book in 1841 with the title *The True Principles of Pointed or Christian Architecture*.
22. Lethaby 1949, p. 103.
23. Ruskin 1903–12, X, p. 185.
24. Colvin 1975, p. 288.
25. Ibid., p. 289.
26. The Book of Common Prayer; introductory

rubric to the Order for Morning and Evening Prayer.
27. The screen was moved in the 19th century to the south chapel.
28. The great east window of Old St Paul's was restored, together with the rest of the Gothic choir, as part of Inigo Jones's reconstruction of the cathedral in the 1630s.
29. Fuller 1662, III, p. 226.
30. Evelyn 1955 edn, III, p. 132.
31. Dugdale 1716, p. viii.
32. Details of the restoration were published in Wren Society, X, 1933, pp. 58–9.
33. Green 1951, pp. 303–4.
34. Ibid.
35. Colvin 1978, p. 155.
36. Taylor 1808, p. xvii.
37. There is an outline of the earlier literary influences on the Gothic Revival in Clark 1962, pp. 28–45. Clark questioned the importance of Scott (ibid., pp. 71–2) but it was stressed by Eastlake (1970 edn, pp. 112–15).
38. The subtitle of the first edition was 'Rules for the gentlemen of England', of the second, more ambitious version, published in 1827–9, 'The true sense and practice of chivalry'.
39. Chambers 1791, p. 24.
40. Britton's contribution to Gothic studies is described by Crook 1968, *passim*.
41. See Kerrich 1812, *passim*.
42. Pevsner 1972, p. 109.
43. For a summary of how these university movements came to dominate national attitudes to church buildings see Eastlake 1970, pp. 195–206.
44. Ruskin 1903–12, X, p. 78.
45. Ibid., p. 460.
46. Scott 1857, p. 11.
47. Gray 1937, II, p. 765.
48. Wren 1750, p. 304.
49. Ruskin 1903–12, XII, p. 100.
50. Cocke 1985, *passim*.
51. Burge 1843, pp. 16, 26.
52. Heseltine 1981, p. 30.
53. In his 'Hymn' first published in 1932; Betjeman 1970, p. 3.
54. Ruskin 1903–12, VIII, p. 242.
55. Morris 1910–15, XXII, p. 413.
56. Ibid., XXII, p. 414.
57. Morris 1936, I, p. 278.

The Catalogue

I Kingship

> This royal throne of kings, this sceptred isle,
> This earth of majesty, this seat of Mars,
> This other Eden, demi-paradise;
> This fortress built by nature for herself
> Against infection and the hand of war;
> This happy breed of men, this little world;
> This precious stone set in the silver sea.
> Which serves it in the office of a wall,
> Or as a moat defensive to a house,
> Against the envy of less happier lands;
> This blessed plot, this earth, this realm, this England,
> This nurse, this teeming womb of royal kings,
> Feared by their breed, and famous by their birth,
> Renowned for their deeds as far from home –
> For Christian service and true chivalry –
> As is the sepulchre in stubborn Jewry
> Of the world's ransom, blessed Mary's son;
>
> (WILLIAM SHAKESPEARE, *Richard II*, Act II, Scene I)

England in the thirteenth and fourteenth centuries was remarkable for the extent and uniformity of the king's authority throughout his realm. He controlled a government of increasing sophistication: in its executive and judicial functions and in its linking of the local government of the counties to the centre. There was a steady increase in national self-consciousness, stimulated especially by the hostility between the English and the French, and demonstrated by the emergence of English as a written language – witness notably Chaucer – after a long slumber following the Norman Conquest. However close their links with the Continent, underlined especially by their marriage ties, the Plantagenet kings were Englishmen.

The Plantagenet dynasty took its name from Geoffrey, Count of Anjou, father of Henry II of England, who used broom (Latin: *plantagenista*) as his emblem. The five Plantagenet kings of the thirteenth and fourteenth centuries had long reigns: Henry III reigned from 1216 to 1272, Edward I from 1272 to 1307, Edward II from 1307 to 1327, Edward III from 1327 to 1377, and Richard II from 1377 to 1399 (cf. fig. 124).

Prerogative power was certainly in the hands of the monarch, and the political stability of the nation was largely dependent upon the abilities and strength of purpose of the individual king, especially in controlling the magnates and in waging war. Yet royal authority could never be absolute, and only the unsuccessful kings overreached themselves and were deposed. Royal government was far stronger than personalities: it could survive minorities, as of Henry III between 1216 and 1227, and it could survive baronial revolts, whether led by Simon de Montfort between 1258 and 1265 or by Thomas of Lancaster in 1321–2; it crushed the Peasants' Revolt of 1381.

Royal government grew and developed. There was no conceivable alternative to it. The king's achievements were achievements for the nation: Edward I's conquest of Wales, and Edward III's military successes against the French in the Hundred Years War, at Crécy in 1346 and at Poitiers in 1356, and the gradual emergence in the middle of the thirteenth century, and rapid development thereafter, of the English Parliament.

However, we cannot understand English society just by studying the fortunes of kings. The universities – in England Oxford and Cambridge (cf. Cat. 318–19) – which emerged in the late twelfth and early thirteenth centuries became institutions of great importance in the thirteenth and fourteenth centuries. Learning, still a prerogative of

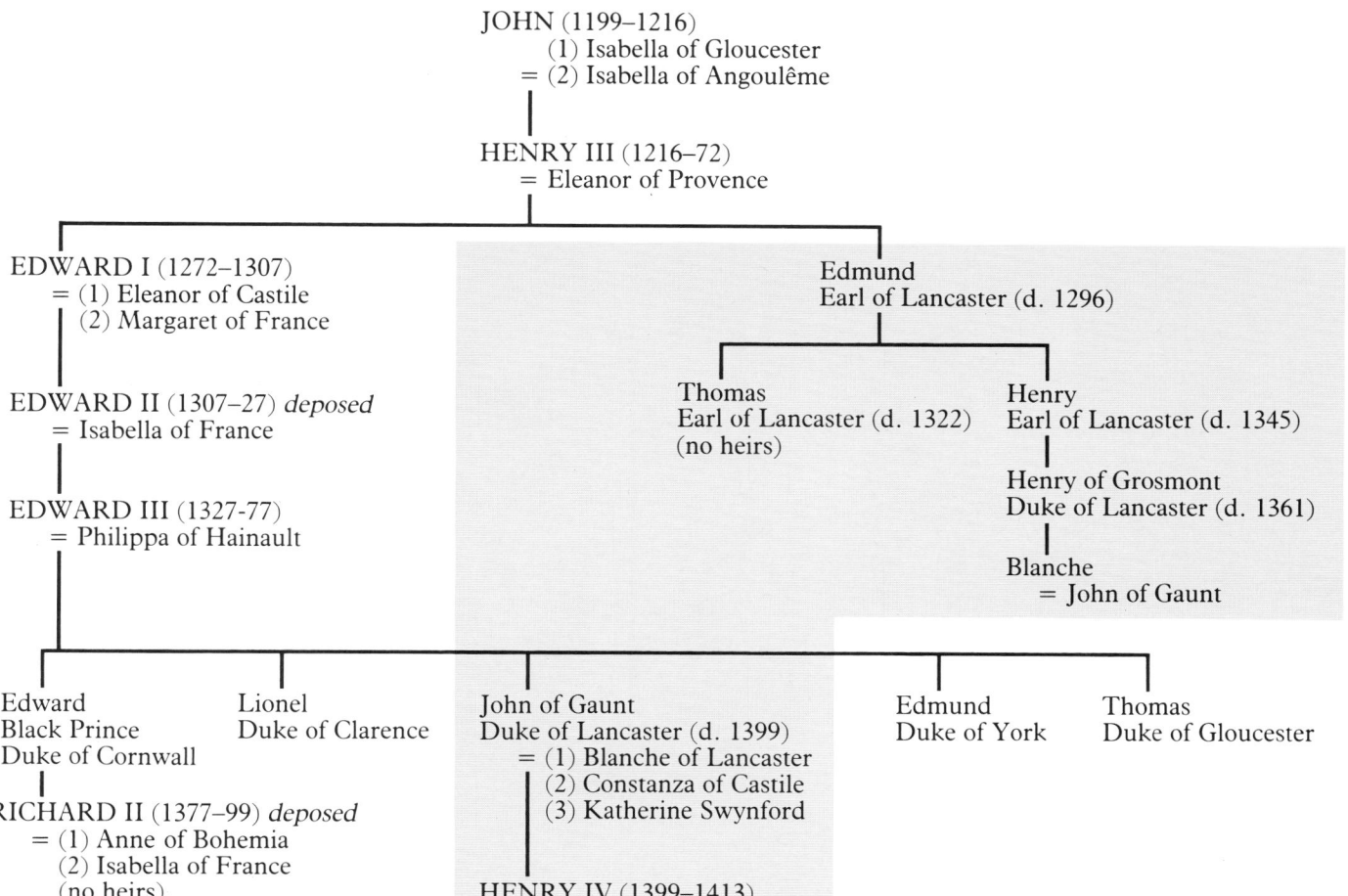

JOHN (1199–1216)
　　　(1) Isabella of Gloucester
　= (2) Isabella of Angoulême

HENRY III (1216–72)
　= Eleanor of Provence

EDWARD I (1272–1307)
　= (1) Eleanor of Castile
　　(2) Margaret of France

Edmund
Earl of Lancaster (d. 1296)

EDWARD II (1307–27) *deposed*
= Isabella of France

Thomas
Earl of Lancaster (d. 1322)
(no heirs)

Henry
Earl of Lancaster (d. 1345)

EDWARD III (1327-77)
= Philippa of Hainault

Henry of Grosmont
Duke of Lancaster (d. 1361)

Blanche
= John of Gaunt

Edward
Black Prince
Duke of Cornwall

Lionel
Duke of Clarence

John of Gaunt
Duke of Lancaster (d. 1399)
　= (1) Blanche of Lancaster
　　(2) Constanza of Castile
　　(3) Katherine Swynford

Edmund
Duke of York

Thomas
Duke of Gloucester

RICHARD II (1377–99) *deposed*
　= (1) Anne of Bohemia
　　(2) Isabella of France
　　(no heirs)

HENRY IV (1399–1413)

Fig. 124　Genealogical tree of the House of
Plantagenet and the Earls and Dukes of
Lancaster

the Church, spread into all branches of government and into most levels of society. The work of the Church was fostered by the new orders of Friars, the Franciscans and Dominicans. The thirteenth century was a period of economic stability, with the population rising to between four and five million. Instability came in the fourteenth century. The Black Death of 1348–9 killed about a quarter of the population, which continued to decline into the next century. But decline in numbers was a stimulus to change. With labour in demand, the bonds which tied peasants to landlords were weakened, and towns thrived. The fourteenth century saw a questioning of the old order, marked by the teaching of John Wyclif and the grievances of the peasants in 1381. But grievances and new visions could change only slowly the established social institutions, from the king downwards.

The king's great power and status were bolstered by ceremonies and symbols. Most important was the Coronation (Cat. 11) when he was invested by the Archbishop of Canterbury as head of the English Church with spiritual power as God's anointed like the Kings of Israel before him (David crowned by Samuel, Cat. 8). The crown (Cat. 13) and sceptre (Cat. 14) are constant symbols of kingship in medieval representations.

Though the king had to be accepted at the Coronation by the nobility doing homage for their lands in the feudal gesture of joined hands (Cat. 9), and had also to agree to uphold the customs and laws of the land (as described in Magna Carta, Cat. 1), he acquired his kingdom by inheritance. Edward I succeeded his father almost immediately in 1272, though he was absent on crusade at the time and was not crowned until his return to England in 1274. Edward II in turn was the first king to date his regnal years from the day after his father's death. In this way continuity was assured and a closer association was forged between the royal dynasty and the royal office. It is significant, therefore, that the arms of the Plantagenet dynasty, Gules three lions passant guardant or, became those of the kingdom of England (Cat. 7, 12). The same idea of family descent is symbolised in biblical terms by the Tree of Jesse showing the royal ancestors of Christ (Cat. 3).

The most potent symbol of feudal nobility and chivalry is the sword. The king is recorded on various occasions as giving the sword from his own side as a mark of special favour, and the Bristol sword (Cat. 15) may have been a royal gift in 1373. The image of the knight kneeling before the king in the Westminster Psalter (Cat. 9) is a crucial representation not only of the relationship of mutual responsibility imposed by the feudal system, but also of the chivalric code of which the Christian king, especially in the Crusades, was the supreme exponent. He it was who knighted his followers and upheld and rewarded the chivalric virtues of prowess and courtesy. The 'Matter of England', the tales of King Arthur and his Round Table, were perhaps the most popular of all the chivalric literature of the time throughout Europe. Edward I in his Welsh and Scottish wars consciously appealed to the Arthurian legends to legitimise his conquests (Cat. 10, 322).

The burial of the king was also an occasion for ceremonial. Since it has been impossible to contemplate moving any of the royal tombs for the exhibition, the commemorative effigy of Robert Curthose, eldest son of William the Conqueror, from Gloucester (Cat. 2) must serve to demonstrate how the Plantagenets linked together religious devotion and the continuity of their dynasty.

bearing the king's Great Seal, as once did this example). In addition to the confirmation of the charters, it was conceded that certain financial exactions would in future be taken only 'with the common assent of the whole kingdom and for the common benefit of the same kingdom'. The magnates then agreed to grant a tax of a ninth to support the war against the Scots. On 5 November King Edward, who was then at Ghent, confirmed the reissue of Magna Carta and the other concessions.

Edward resented being compelled to do this and in 1305 obtained from Pope Clement v a bull that released him from his obligation to observe the additions to the charters made in 1297 and in subsequent years, as being contrary to his coronation oath. However, the bull explicitly protected the rights of the

1 Magna Carta

12 Oct. 1297
Parchment: 60.5 × 45 cm
Public Record Office, London, DL 10/197

Magna Carta, the Great Charter of Liberties, was exacted from King John in 1215 by a group of the leading English magnates. It was made known throughout England by the despatch of sealed copies to a variety of people and places, and four of these original copies survive (at Lincoln and Salisbury cathedrals, and two in the British Library). It had been produced in haste in an attempt to settle grievances and it concerned the rights and privileges of the barons, the Church and the cities and towns. It was an attempt to curb the harsh policies of King John but was not in origin about any high-minded or theoretical notion of liberty.

Magna Carta was kept alive in the thirteenth century by being reissued, sometimes with changes, at various times from 1216 onwards. It soon gained a great degree of permanence because it rose beyond being an answer to particular baronial complaints: it gave protection to what were coming to be seen as the rights of all English freemen. Especially notable in this respect was the statement that no freeman shall be imprisoned except by the lawful judgement of his peers or by the law of the land. In the later Middle Ages the text of Magna Carta that was best known was the enrolled version which was confirmed in 1297, and of which this is an exemplification.

In the crisis of 1297, when Edward I was determined to go on a military expedition to Flanders and William Wallace was posing a major threat in Scotland, the magnates in Parliament insisted on Magna Carta and the Charter of the Forest being issued anew. These were accordingly confirmed in the king's absence by his son Edward, the future Edward II, in the form of letters patent of inspeximus dated 12 October (that is, as a document without any list of witnesses but

people existing before the concessions of 1297. The crisis of 1297 was the last occasion when Magna Carta was at the very centre of political controversy and most of its clauses were becoming more and more distant from the realities of the king's relations with his subjects. Even so, Magna Carta had come to be accepted as an unchangeable part of the laws and customs of the kingdom. NLR

PROV. Archives of the Duchy of Lancaster, incorporated in the Public Record Office, 1868.

LIT. *Statutes* 1810–28, I, pp. 114–22; Thompson 1925b; Edwards 1943; Thompson 1948, p. 5; Holt 1965.

2

2 Effigy of Robert Curthose, Duke of Normandy

c. 1250
Oak: h. 60.9 cm, l. 213.4 cm, d. 68.6 cm
The Dean and Chapter of Gloucester

Robert Curthose (*c.* 1053–1134), the first son of William the Conqueror, was not the favourite. William left him Normandy, but left England to his second surviving son, William Rufus. Squalid quarrels between the brothers led to Robert spending the last twenty-eight years of his life as a prisoner in Cardiff Castle. Gloucester, a cathedral from 1541, was then a Benedictine abbey in the diocese of Worcester. Curthose was buried here, perhaps first in the chapter house, where his father and the barons convened to organise the Domesday Book. His remains, however, were moved to the position of signal importance before the high altar where, having been shifted about in the meantime, they lie again today. This is the position reserved for founders and great benefactors, but Robert was only a disgraced duke. The puzzle is not elucidated by the fine tomb chest of *c.* 1500 on which he reposes. This is ornamented with the shields of the Nine Worthies. Curthose had two qualifications for special honour in the mid-thirteenth century: he was Duke of Normandy, and Henry III did not finally relinquish Normandy until 1259. He distinguished himself on the First Crusade, and Henry III pledged to go on crusade in 1250.

This effigy is the *locus classicus* for the legend that crossed-legged knights must be crusaders. John of Eltham (died 1337) has a cross-legged effigy in Westminster Abbey, but he was not a crusader. It is far more likely that the pose was intended to suggest the vigour of the Knight of Christ, ready to leap to his Lord's service at the last trump. Note that Curthose's hand reaches for his sword. The way in which the effigy-makers conveyed latent action in the knightly effigies of the century from 1250 is nascent here.

The longitudinal mail of the arms and mail over the chin can be found on the knightly figures on the west front of Wells, as can the hooked nose. His knees are not clad in poleyns: they are bare, explaining the nickname. The coronet is an anachronism of the restoration.

A drawing of the monument made in 1569 by Robert Cooke, Clarenceux King of Arms, in the College of Arms, shows all the main features as they are now, and records the painting of his surcoat with the leopards of England. The monument was broken up during the Civil War, but reassembled fairly speedily after that. Sandford's engraving of 1677 indicates a semé of roses upon the surcoat. A watercolour of 1786 (Cat. 390) still shows the gold leopards. However, the paint was renewed in 1791 (dated), and his surcoat has been unadorned since then. A photograph of the mid-nineteenth century and a print of 1856 show the Duke's left leg missing from the mid-calf. No reliance can be placed on his spurs. The most recent restoration was carried out *c.* 1980 under the aegis of Clive Rouse. The eighteenth-century paint was cleaned without stripping the varnish; new wood and damaged areas of pigment were touched in.   PT-C

LIT. Prior & Gardner 1912, pp. 665, 666, fig. 745; Crossley 1921, pp. 181, 209, repr.

3 King Hezekiah

After 1213, probably *c.* 1220
Stained glass: h. 157.5 cm, w. 68.5 cm
Inscr. in Lombardic letters EZECHIAS
Dean and Chapter of Canterbury, window S.XXVIII

The seated figure of Hezekiah within a quatrefoil is part of the great series representing the genealogy of Christ which originally filled the clerestory windows throughout the eastern part of the cathedral. This particular panel and its companion Josiah were originally in a north clerestory window (N.V) in the Trinity Chapel. Most of the figures are from the genealogy recorded in *Luke* III, 23–38, and Hezekiah and Josiah with several others are from *Matthew* I, 1–16. Hezekiah holds the attribute of a sundial which according to *Isaiah* XXXVIII, 8 turned ten degrees backwards as an indication that the king would be cured of his illness; Hezekiah and this

3

sundial occur as an Old Testament type of the Ascension in the east window of the Corona in Canterbury Cathedral. The panel is very well preserved, the only significant restorations being the border to the quatrefoil and the lower ornamental lobe. The colours conform to the general green, white and purple formula found throughout the clerestory figures. In addition there is considerable use of ruby and pot-metal yellow, and the ground on which the figure is placed is blue.

The figure style and the *rinceaux* indicate that the panel dates from the last phase of the Canterbury glazing, which was undertaken after the return of the monks from exile in 1213. The glass of this period is distinctly Gothic in feeling, with an emphasis on soft, ornamental and elegant draperies, compared with the late Romanesque and classicising earlier phases of the glazing. The figure of Hezekiah is remarkable for the gracefulness of its pose and the rhythmic fall of the drapery concealing the bodily forms beneath. It has been compared with English early thirteenth-century manuscript illumination, and has also been related in style to the clerestory figures of David and Ezekiel in the clerestory of the chevet at Chartres Cathedral (1220–25?). RM

LIT. Caviness 1977, *passim*; Harrison 1978, no. 2, colour pl.; Caviness 1981, pp. 7–16, 44–6, fig. 74; Grodecki & Brisac 1985, pp. 183–4.

4 King of England

c. 1290–5

Stained glass: h. 158 cm, w. 45 cm

The Dean and Chapter of York, chapter house vestibule, window c/H.NVIII.2b–3b

There are eight figures of kings and queens in the Royal Window in the vestibule. A bearded king in pot-metal yellow robe and

4

5

crown, and blue mantle and shoes, holds a spray of white lilies and points upwards. He stands against a ruby ground within a mainly white canopy with pinnacled masonry side shafts, crocketed arch and gable, and crenellated arcading topped by a sloping blue roof. The finial extends into a trellis design of oak and acorn grisaille with balanced trails of foliage springing from a central stem. There are borders of white maple leaves on ruby grounds. Some plain modern glass was inserted in 1959, and some paint has been lost through corrosion.

The glazing of the vestibule followed closely on that of the chapter house (*c.* 1285) and on heraldic evidence was probably completed before 1300. Without inscriptions firm identifications are impossible but they probably represent Edward I, Queen Eleanor and their immediate predecessors. Edward was closely associated with York, especially after 1296 when the city became an administrative centre during the Scottish wars. The figures in the window find very close parallels in the royal figures on Chertsey tiles (Cat. 367), possibly connected with the tomb of Queen Eleanor, suggesting that Edward may even have commissioned the window himself, either as another memorial to his queen, or simply as another piece of royal propaganda like the genealogical rolls from St

Mary's Abbey, York (Cat. 10). This cult of kingship is reinforced by the adjacent window (c/H NIX) with its figures of saintly kings of England.

The solution to the multiplicity of architectural forms in the vestibule was a band scheme with single figures under canopies, an effect not unlike the Eleanor crosses. The architectural forms are simpler than those at Merton College (Cat. 738), or in the Heraldic Window at York (Cat. 5) which continues the royal theme. DO'C

LIT. Harrison 1927, pp. 56–7; O'Connor & Haselock 1977, p. 341, repr. pl. 102.

5 Canopy with kings of France and England

c. 1307–10

Stained glass: h. 91 cm, w. 91 cm

The Dean and Chapter of York, nave window NXXIII.6b

This canopy from the Heraldic Window consists of a central structure with cusped arch, crocketed gable and two-light niche, joined by flying buttresses to side niches containing kings. Architecture and grounds are in a variety of pot-metal and ruby colours, and the kings wear pot-metal yellow crowns and white mail with rowel spurs and sword fittings in yellow stain. The left knight's surcoat bears the arms of France ancient, and his companion's those of England. A high percentage of original glass survives but most of the blue surcoat is modern.

The donor, Canon Peter de Dene, was a king's clerk who travelled widely in royal service. A quarrel with Archbishop Winchelsea deprived him of numerous benefices in the Canterbury province but he found a supporter at York in Archbishop Greenfield, the donor of the window opposite. The choice of subject, St Catherine, was appropriate given his legal and academic background. The elegant figures, sumptuous ornament, display of heraldry and precocious technique also proclaim his Court connections. The window develops many of the ideological concerns already present in the chapter house vestibule (Cat. 4).

Besides armorials with the arms of England and other royal houses, in the borders of the central light are figures of magnates, queens, kings and members of military orders identified by heraldic surcoats and gowns. On the basis of the heraldry Winston and Walford dated the window to c. 1306-7 and identified the kings shown here as Philip IV and Edward I. But the heraldry may be less specific in intention and reads more like a general roll of arms, partly determined by aesthetic considerations. Dene is recorded in York by 1307, and with the fall of Thomas of Lancaster in 1322 he retired to St Augustine's, Canterbury. On various grounds an earlier rather than a later date within this period is to be preferred, not least because the inclusion of a Templar in the central border would be most unlikely after the dissolution of the Order in 1312. The proposed dating produces one of the earliest examples of yellow stain in English glass.

DO'C

LIT. Winston & Walford 1860; Harrison n.d., repr. colour pl. V; O'Connor & Haselock 1977, pp. 349-50, repr. colour frontispiece.

6 Head of a king

c. 1335-50
Stained glass: diam. 31.5 cm
The Yorkshire Museum, York

This is a medallion consisting of the head and shoulders of a king placed frontally on a plain ruby ground within a green border. He has a white face, yellow-stained hair and beard, pot-metal yellow crown and robe, and blue brooch. The left piece of crown is nineteenth-century.

In the late thirteenth century busts of kings were used to decorate panels of grisaille, an example of the widespread interest in royal imagery in the art of this period. This combination of medallion heads and foliage became increasingly common in the second quarter of the fourteenth century as a

means of glazing the complicated shapes inherent in flowing tracery designs.

This finely-balanced decorative panel combines a precise, linear drawing technique with transparent modelling washes carefully applied to both surfaces of the glass. There are marked stylistic similarities to the French-inspired glazing of the Master Robert workshop in York (Cat. 562-3, 741). DO'C

PROV. James Fowler Coll.; acq. by Yorkshire Museum, 1887.

LIT. Yorks. Phil. Soc. 1891, p. 176, no. 11g.

7 Royal arms of England

Early 14th century
Stained glass: diam. 27.7 cm
The Burrell Collection, Glasgow Museums and Art Galleries, 45/129

Placed within a roundel with a beaded border is a shield bearing the royal arms, differenced by a label of three points azure. The label, indicating an eldest son, was borne successively by Edward I, Edward II and Edward III prior to their accessions. The style and design of the roundel suggest that the shield either represented the arms of Edward of Caernarfon, Prince of Wales and Earl of Chester in 1300/1, king as Edward II in 1307; or his son Edward, created Earl of Chester, Duke of Aquitaine and Count of Ponthieu in 1325 and crowned King Edward III in 1327 (Humphery-Smith & Heenan 1962-3, pp. 21, 82). RM

PROV. Dr Philip Nelson; bt by Sir William Burrell, 1946, donated to Glasgow as part of Burrell Collection, 1948.

LIT. Glasgow Art Gallery 1962, no. 17.

8 The Glazier Psalter

London (?), *c.* 1230
Vellum, ff. 182: 33 × 22 cm
Pierpont Morgan Library, New York, MS Glazier 25

Six full-page miniatures precede the psalter text, a full-page B introduces Psalm 1, and ornamental and historiated initials mark the nine liturgical divisions of the psalter. The full-page pictures are arranged as diptychs of facing scenes of the Virgin Mary, Christ and David. Each figure is on one side in a scene of humility (the Annunciation, the Crucifixion, David threatened by Saul) and on the opposite page in glory (the Virgin enthroned with the Child, Christ in Majesty, the coronation of David). The figure style is a key example of the developed Early Gothic in England. Forms tend to be somewhat attenuated and angular with elaborate troughed drapery folds

7

6

8

important for an understanding of manuscript illustration of the period. The City seems to have been an important centre of manuscript production from the second quarter of the century onwards. The style of these Westminster Psalter drawings provides a contrast to that of Matthew Paris, to whom they have sometimes been attributed. The Westminster work has more detailed, refined faces, and contours and internal folds show more jagged effects of line. There is a sophisticated professionalism about the drawing which contrasts with Matthew's accomplished but somewhat naïve style.

A number of English manuscripts of the mid-thirteenth century (e.g. the Evesham Psalter [London, British Library, MS Add. 44874] and the Lambeth Apocalypse [Cat. 438]) contain the picture of the Veronica head of Christ, attesting the image's popularity at this time. A prayer is attached.　NJM

PROV. Benedictine Abbey of Westminster; John Theyer (1597–1673); bt for the Royal Coll., *c.* 1678; passed to British Museum, 1757.

LIT. Wormald 1949, pp. 163–4; Lewis 1985, p. 102; Morgan 1987, no. 95, repr.

10　Genealogical roll of kings of Britain

End of 13th century
Parchment, 6 membranes: 416 × 52.3 cm
Oxford, Bodleian Library, MS. Bodl. Rolls 3

Not all of the original roll is preserved in the Bodleian Library; the last two membranes are in the British Library (Cotton, Galba Charter XIV.4). The main part traces the ancestry of the rulers of Britain from ancient Greece down to Edward I, and the second displays the pedigree of the kings of England and Scotland. At the top of the roll is an ex-libris, *c.* 1300, of St Mary's Abbey, York, which was the repository of government records between 1298 and 1305 during the campaign against the Scots, when York was the centre of royal administration.

The purpose of the roll was undoubtedly to substantiate Edward's claim to overlordship in Scotland. Twenty large roundels at the top constitute a pictorial narrative – accompanied by written text – of the founding of Britain, based on the *Historia Regum Britanniae* of Geoffrey of Monmouth. These medallions are followed by 220 smaller ones that show early British, Anglo-Saxon, Anglo-Norman and Plantagenet rulers from Brutus to Edward I. Then there are seventy-two further roundels (the part now in the British Library) showing sovereigns of England and Scotland, their collateral relations and their intermarriages, down to the time of Edward I.

The masterful wash drawings of the Bodleian roll are by a superb pictorial story-teller who may also have done the large coloured drawings of religious subjects in a picture book in Cambridge (Fitzwilliam Museum, MS 370). His drawing style is generally re-

strongly delineated in black lines. Related manuscripts (e.g. Cat. 255) suggest the possibility that the artists working in this manner were based in London.

The litany may give a clue to the owner of this richly-decorated psalter, for it has an exceptional emphasis on St Silvester, which may be the name of the patron. Possibly it might have been made for Silvester of Everdon, who became keeper of the Great Seal in 1244 and Bishop of Carlisle in 1246. Another Silvester, Bishop of Worcester (1216–18) is probably too early to have owned the book.　NJM

PROV. André Hachette, 20th century; bt by William Glazier, 1953; Pierpont Morgan Library, New York, 1962.

LIT. Schapiro 1960, pp. 179 ff.; Wormald 1960, pp. 307–8; New York 1970, no. 258; Morgan 1982, no. 50, figs 160–2, frontispiece.

9　The Westminster Psalter (added drawings)

Westminster, *c.* 1250
Vellum, ff. 3: 22.8 × 15.6 cm
British Library, Royal MS 2 A.xxii

This psalter was made for Westminster Abbey *c.* 1200. In the middle years of the century five high-quality tinted drawings were added at the end of the manuscript. Two, of St Christopher and the Veronica head of Christ, fulfil a devotional function. It is uncertain for what reason the other three, a king, a knight and his squire, and an archbishop, are included.

As it is certain that the psalter was at Westminster Abbey in the middle years of the thirteenth century, these drawings (ff. 219v.–221v.) are clear evidence for an artist working in London for Westminster. The definition of London styles of drawing is

9

9

lated to that of the well-known Ashridge Petrus Comestor (London, British Library, Royal MS 3 D. VI), a Court style work of 1283–1300, and also to a pair of leaves showing the Three Living and the Three Dead now inserted in an unrelated Bible in Baltimore (Walters Art Gallery, MS W. 51), images framed with heraldic motifs of Edward I and his uncle, Richard, King of the Romans. Apparently the artistic ambiance of the Bodleian roll was the Court, whether at Westminster or in the north.   LFS

PROV. Henry Savile of Banke, beq. to Bodleian Library, 1617; part in British Library detached, and acq. in an unknown manner by Robert Cotton, 1571–1631.

LIT. Brussels 1973, no. 60; Sandler 1986, no. 16, II, pp. 26–7, repr. I, figs 35–6.

11   Apocalypse and Coronation Order

c. 1330–9(?)
Parchment, ff. 72: 37 × 24.8 cm
The Master and Fellows of Corpus Christi College, Cambridge, MS 20

The heterogeneous contents of this manuscript include the Apocalypse, the Apocryphal Visions of St Paul and a Coronation Order of the kings of England, all written as a unit by a single scribe, and illustrated by a single artist. The Latin text of the Apocalypse is accompanied, paragraph by paragraph, by a metrical version and a prose commentary, both in Anglo-French; the Visions of St Paul, in Anglo-French verse, are followed by a Latin prose version; and the text of the Coronation Order, which refers to a Prince

Edward, is also in Anglo-French, with only a few Latin cues to the beginning of the Coronation Mass. The combination of the Apocalypse with the Visions of St Paul, itself apocalyptic in character as the visions are of Hell, is found in at least one other manuscript (Toulouse, Bibliothèque municipale, MS 815), but the addition of the Coronation Order to these texts is unique. The original owner can be identified tentatively as Baron Henry de Cobham from the heraldic surcoat of the knight in the historiated initial at the beginning of the Apocalypse text (f. 1). Lord Cobham may have participated in the coronation of Edward II or Edward III by virtue of his office as a warden of the Cinque Ports. A

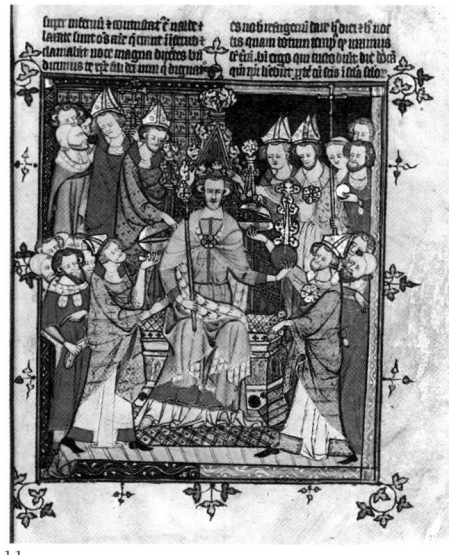

11

layman might have appreciated the vernacular versions, not only of the Coronation Order, but also of the apocalyptic texts.

One hundred and six illustrations accompany the Apocalypse (a pictorial cycle duplicated iconographically in Toulouse, MS 815, and London, British Library, Add. MS 18633), and fourteen more text miniatures are found in the Visions of St Paul, but the volume is best known for its Coronation miniature (f. 68), which has been called a 'Glory of Regality'. In general, the miniature style of the Corpus Christi manuscript is reminiscent of that of the Taymouth Hours (London, British Library, Yates Thompson MS 13; fig. 18) of *c.*1325–35 and the Smithfield Decretals (fig. 130) of *c.*1330–40. All share not only the same general features but also the same peculiar decorative motif of background grids filled with rows of smiling outlined faces, as in the Coronation miniature of the Corpus Christi volume.   LFS

PROV. Henry de Cobham, d. 1339(?); Juliana de Leybourn, Countess of Huntingdon, d. 1367; given to St Augustine's, Canterbury; Matthew Parker, Archbishop of Canterbury, d. 1575; beq. to Corpus Christi College.

LIT. Legg 1900, pp. xxxi–xxxvii; Sandler 1986, no. 103, II, pp. 113, repr. I, figs 262–3.

10

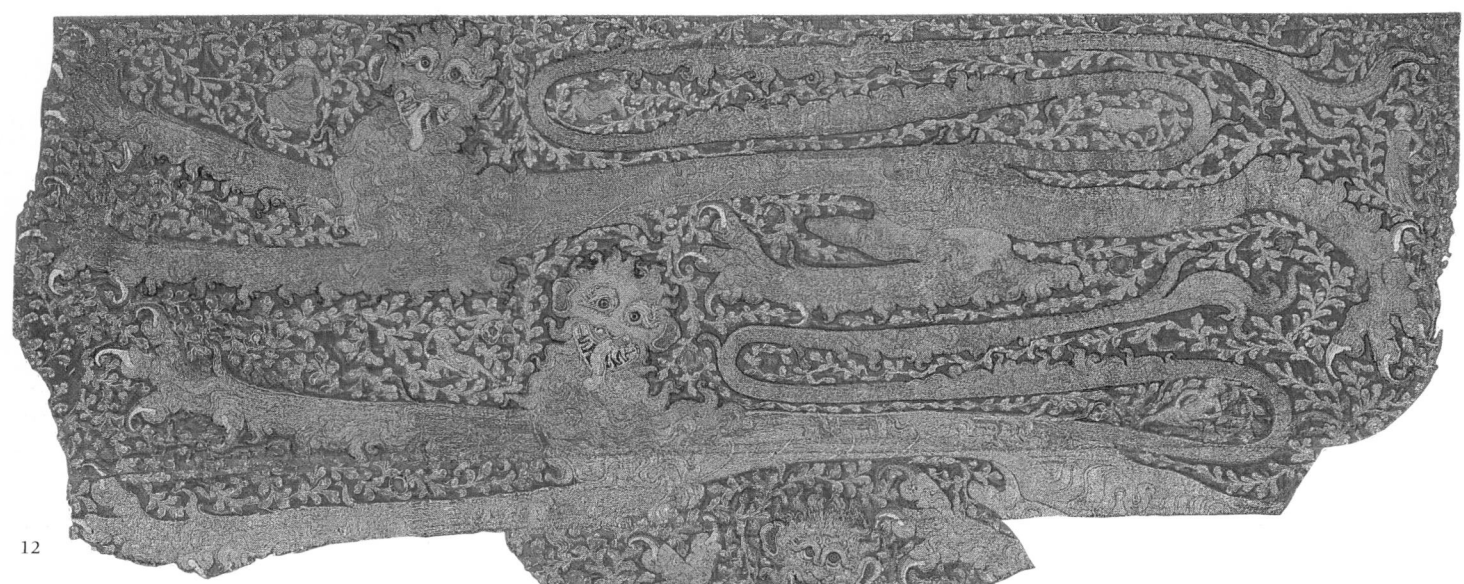

12

12 Heraldic embroidery, possibly from a horse trapper

Second quarter 14th century
Silver and silver-gilt thread and coloured silks in couched work and split, stem and satin stitches, with raised work, pearls and cabochon crystals, on velvet; two pieces, each, h. 59.5 cm, l. 130 cm
Paris, Musée National des Thermes et de l'Hôtel de Cluny, Cl. 20367

The embroidery shows the leopards of England, with foliage trails and small figures of men and women. Though later converted into a chasuble, this must originally have been a secular object, possibly a horse trapper. Probably made for royal use, it provides an admirable illustration of the extravagant secular embroideries recorded in the royal wardrobe accounts. It is likely to date from before 1340, since it shows only the leopards, not the new arms, quarterly France and England, which were adopted that year. The provenance of such an English royal object from Altenberg on the Lahn suggests that it may have been used by Edward III on his state visit to his brother-in-law, the Emperor Ludwig, at Coblenz in September 1338.

The style of the small figures is reminiscent of the Luttrell Psalter (Cat. 575) and other East Anglian manuscripts.   DK

PROV. Convent of Altenberg on the Lahn; Prince Solms-Braunfels; Paris, Heilbronner Coll.

LIT. London 1963, no. 76.

13 Crown

French (?), c. 1370–80
Gold set with sapphires, rubies, diamonds, pearls, and decorated with enamelling: h. 18 cm, diam. 18 cm
Bayerische Verwaltung der Staatlichen Schlösser, Gärten und Seen, Munich

This crown is one of the finest achievements of the Gothic goldsmith. It consists of an elaborate twelve-part circlet from which rise twelve golden lilies, large and small alternating and with beaded edges. Each element of the circlet consists of a circular gold ring on which is mounted an hexagonal enamelled band filled with openwork gold tracery. At the centre of each hexagon is a sapphire. The hexagons are enamelled alternately blue and red with white enamel applied in spots to form a pattern of five-petalled flowers over the enamel. Each point of the hexagon is set alternately with a ruby or with a diamond surrounded by pearls. On red-enamelled hexagons the ruby is at the top, and on blue hexagons the diamond and four pearls are at the top. The six tall lilies have trefoil leaves at the top and sides. In the centre is set a ruby with four sapphires around it, and on the stem is a diamond with four pearls and a sapphire. The six smaller lilies have a sapphire in the centre of four rubies, and alternately an emerald or a ruby on the stem.

13

Each part of the circlet is numbered I to XII so that each lily stem can be fitted into the correct place.

The crown was clearly made for a princess. It came to Bavaria as part of the marriage dowry of Blanche, daughter of Henry IV, who married Ludwig III in 1401. Where did Henry IV obtain it? It is first recorded in England in 1399 in a list of jewels and gold and silver plate delivered from the Treasury to the King's Chamber and which formerly belonged to Edward III, Richard II, his queen Anne, the Duchess of York, the Duke of Gloucester and Sir John Golafre. It is described as follows (no. 175): *Item I corone de XI overages garnis de XI saphirs XXXIII baleys et CXXXII perles XXXIII dyamants dont VIII contrefaitz. Item VI florons chescun de un baleys V saphirs chescun de IX perles dont defaut en tout VII perles. Item VI menners florons chescun d'un saphir III petitz baleys I esmauraude dont defaut un esmaraud et II petitz perles en chescun. Pois – V marcez VII unc.*

It is most likely, though not certain, that the crown belonged to Anne, wife of Richard II. If so it could have been brought by her from Bohemia when she married Richard II in 1382. The beaded edges to the lilies and the enamelling certainly suggest a Parisian origin. If it was produced in Bohemia, it is likely that it was made by a French or French-trained goldsmith in Prague, but alternatively it could have been produced in Paris for Anne. This crown illustrates the difficulty of assigning an exact origin to a major piece of goldsmith's work. Richard II's personal taste for jewels set a fashion at his Court, and this crown illustrates the value and richness of the jewellery in the possession of the English royal family. The crown may be compared with that of Joan of Navarre, queen of Henry IV, on her effigy at Canterbury Cathedral, where there is the same alternation of tall and short lilies. JC

PROV. Part of dowry of Blanche, daughter of Henry IV, when she married the Wittelsbach Prince Louis III, 1401.

LIT. Palgrave 1836, no. 175 p. 339; Biehn 1957, pp. 139–40; Twining 1960, p. 67; Brunner 1971, pp. 23–6.

14 Sceptre of Richard of Cornwall

c. 1260
Silver-gilt: h. 86 cm
Aachen, Domschatzkammer, G51

The stem consists of two hollow rods, held together with modern screws, with plain knops in the middle and at either end. Soldered to the topmost knop is a dove, cast and chased. The sceptre has been restored since 1865, when it measured only 55.4 cm (Bock 1865, p. 9). Judging by Bock's engraving, where the lower part of the stem is much the shorter, the present lower section must be a replacement. The gilding is probably all renewed.

The sceptre was first identified by Bock as that of Richard of Cornwall (1209–72), who in 1262 is recorded as having given Aachen Cathedral insignia to be used at all future coronations of the kings of the Romans. These gifts consisted of a gem-set gold crown,

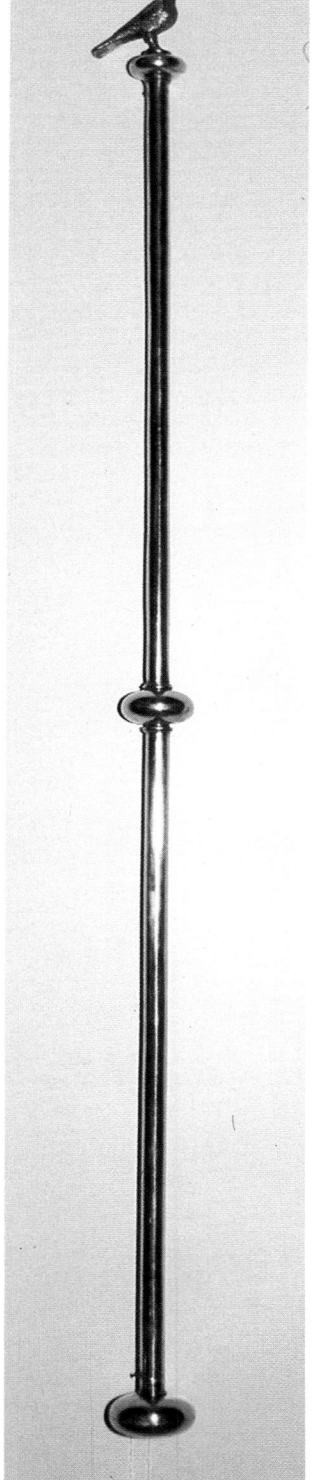

vestments, a sceptre and a gilt apple. There is no description of the sceptre, making certain identification impossible, but the association seems plausible. Richard was crowned King of the Romans (in effect, ruler of part of Germany) in Aachen Cathedral on 17 May 1257 (Denholm-Young 1947, pp. 90–2). Richard, brother of Henry III, was the only Englishman ever to be King of the Romans (cf. Cat. 275). Believed to be the richest man in England, a lover of pomp and magnificence, he had been present as a child at the coronation of his older brother. It seems highly likely that he should choose the distinctively English form of royal sceptre, topped by a dove, to give to Aachen. This type is known first from the Great Seal of Edward the Confessor (1043–66) (Wyon 1887, p. 3, pl. I). Its design may have been inspired by the eleventh-century German imperial eagle-headed sceptre (Dolley 1970, pp. 220–1). The use of the dove-headed sceptre had probably become standard in England by the time of Richard I (Legg 1901, p. liii; Alexander 1983, p. 142 n. 5); it appears on Great Seals of Henry III (Wyon 1887, nos 43, 45, pl. vii), continuing in use into the fifteenth century. Edward I is known to have been buried with an enamelled dove-topped sceptre of *c.* 1.8 m (6 ft), drawn when his coffin was opened in 1774 (Cat. 382–3). MLC

PROV. Richard of Cornwall; probably given to Aachen Cathedral, 1262.

LIT. Bock 1865, pp. 9–11; Grimme 1972, no. 51.

14   14 (detail)

15 The mourning sword of the City of Bristol

1373(?), grip and scabbard later but the latter with some original mounts

Blade steel, hilt iron covered with silver-gilt, grip wood bound with silver wire, scabbard mounts silver-gilt: l. 120 cm, w. 36 cm

City of Bristol

This is a hand-and-a-half sword. The straight, tapering double-edged blade has a maker's mark, a tripod cross, stamped on each face. The cruciform hilt has an oval wheel pommel, bordered by a hollow chamfer and with the centre of each face set with

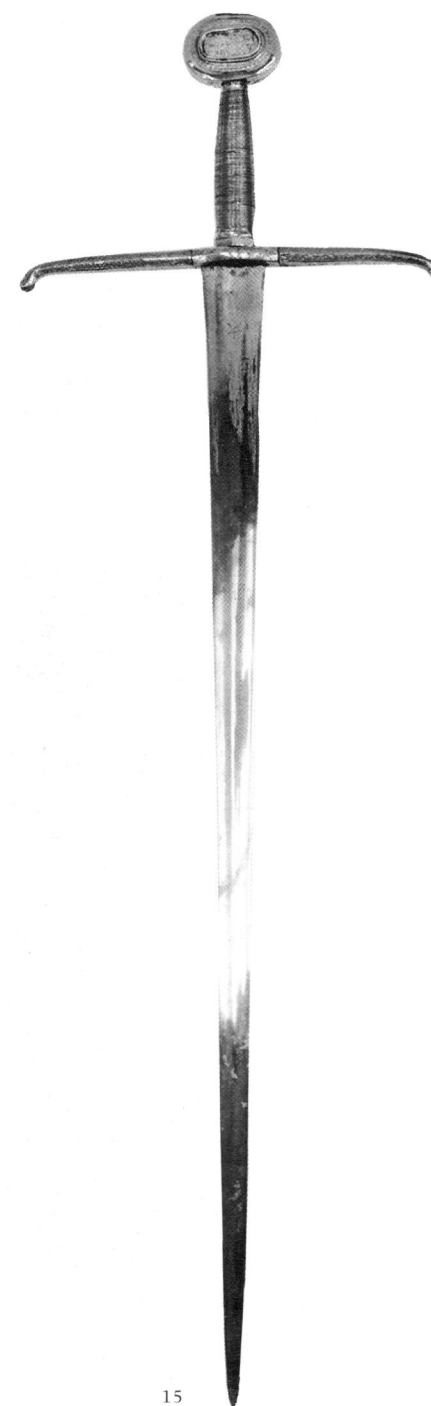

15

an oval recessed silver cartouche; the straight, slender cross tapers to downturned tips. The main surfaces are engraved with a design of running foliage, and the cartouches, which contain traces of translucent enamel, with respectively the arms of Bristol and two shields, one with the cross of St George and the other with the royal arms as borne 1340–1405. The later scabbard is of wood covered with velvet and the mounts comprise a mouth locket, a chape and two central lockets, of which the upper one carries belt mounts; a star is set in each of the spaces between. The chape and adjacent locket are embossed with scrolling foliage and, perhaps with some of the stars, are original to the sword; the other mounts have been replaced or redecorated.

It is not known when the Mayor of Bristol was given the right to have a sword borne before him, but it was probably in 1373 when the city was granted a major royal charter. The style of this sword is consistent with such a date, and it is therefore probably the earliest surviving English civic sword. CB

LIT. Jewitt & Hope 1895, I, pp. 235–7; Laking 1920–2, II, pp. 313–16, fig. 692; London 1952, no. 192, pl. XLV; Hoffmeyer 1954, II, p. 25, no. 11; Williams 1984, no. 32.

16

chard, identified by the three leopards of England on his shield and the crown on his helmet, rests his lance between his horse's ears and charges at a gallop. Saladin, a turban on his head, drops his curved sword as his horse collapses. The subject of Richard's victory over Saladin was a favourite theme of Henry III. It was painted on the walls of the Antioch Chamber at Clarendon Palace.

There are a number of other portrayals of combats in the Chertsey tiles. They are all made of four quarter tiles rather than one roundel, and all have a band around the edge which distinguishes them from the Tristram series (Cat. 320). Richard and Saladin is the only example in the combat series where the scene is spread over two roundels. The mosaic arrangement framing the roundels in this modern reassembly is authentic, but the choice of these particular tiles is purely arbitrary. It is unlikely that the crown (design 648) was originally used to frame the roundels since there exist segmental tiles with letters making words such as RICARDUS, and these probably surrounded the tiles. Two contrasts may be drawn between the Richard and Saladin and the Tristram series. The first is that the use of quarter tiles and the elaborate mosaic sur-

16 Chertsey tiles: Richard I and Saladin

1250–60

Earthenware, each roundel composed of four quarter tiles in mosaic setting of crowns and foliage: l. of whole setting 171.4 cm, w. 104.2 cm, diam. of roundels 15.5 cm

The Trustees of the British Museum, London, tile design nos Richard 468 and Saladin 467 in mosaic framework composed of designs 602, 611, 614, 616–18, 648

These two tiles show in highly dramatic form the victory of Richard I over Saladin. Ri-

round represent an earlier phase than the Tristram series, where each scene is on a single roundel and the surrounding tilework is reduced to one design. The other is the higher quality of the drawing on the combat roundels than in the Tristram series. Although the tiles were found at Chertsey it is more likely that they were designed for a royal palace, perhaps Westminster. JC

PROV. Found on site of Chertsey Abbey, Surrey, probably in 1852–3.

LIT. Loomis 1916, pp. 82–6; Ottawa 1972, no. 97; Eames 1980, p. 145.

11 Pilgrimage:
The Devotion to the Saints

Pilgrimage has been a vital part of Christianity from the earliest times, and in the Middle Ages the cult of most saints was focused geographically on the particular place where they were buried or their venerated relics were preserved. Healing and other miracles took place at their shrines, and pilgrims visited them to make their offerings, especially on the saints' appointed feast days. Pilgrimage as a physical journey was a metaphor for spiritual growth. Of the international pilgrimages Jerusalem and the Holy Places of Jesus's life took first place, succeeded by Rome, and Santiago de Compostela in north Spain. Jerusalem is shown at the centre of the world in the Hereford Map (Cat. 36). In England the shrine of St Thomas Becket at Canterbury (Cat. 17) was pre-eminent, but every great cathedral and abbey had its own venerated saints (St Edward the Confessor at Westminster, Cat. 380; St William of York, Cat. 513–16; St Alban, Cat. 19; St Swithun at Winchester, Cat. 23–4; cf. fig. 126). Particularly popular places of pilgrimage included Bromholm for the Holy Rood and the shrine of Our Lady of Walsingham (Cat. 71–4).

All the saints' tomb shrines were damaged or destroyed at the Reformation or by the Puritans, so that only fragments survive (Cat. 23–4). The precious-metal shrines and reliquaries were also all melted down, so we only have contemporary representations (fig. 125), or accounts of them. The lead pilgrim souvenirs alone survive in quantity to witness to popular devotion to the different cults.

Representations of the saints in art included both narrative pictures of their lives, especially their miracles and their sufferings (Cat. 27), and cult statues or paintings of them with identifying attributes (Cat. 34). Images also fostered public and private devotion to the Virgin Mary or to Christ's Passion (Cat. 30–1, 41–2).

Fig. 125 Pilgrims at the thirteenth-century shrine of St Edward from The Life of St Edward the Confessor (Cambridge University Library, EE. 3.59, f. 30; Cat. 39)

Fig. 126 Pilgrimage sites in later medieval England

17

17 Christ Church, Canterbury, choir and presbytery looking east to the Trinity Chapel

1175–86
Photograph

The architecture of the east end of Canterbury as rebuilt after a fire in 1174 had a decisive influence on the development of the Gothic style in England. The artistic vocabulary was closely related to contemporary practice in north-east France because the reconstruction was entrusted to a French master mason, William of Sens, who brought with him sculptors and glaziers from that region. Following William's enforced retirement after a fall in 1178, he was succeeded by William the Englishman, who despite his name was also conversant with current French practice. He enlarged the Trinity Chapel (the area behind the high altar) and raised the level of the pavement in order to display more effectively the relics of the martyred archbishop Thomas Becket, who had been canonised in 1173. The spectacular shrine, erected in 1220, was destroyed at the Reformation but once formed the visual and liturgical focus of the church.

An appropriately sumptuous setting for the shrine was provided by using various kinds of marble (mostly from the Isle of Purbeck) for the shrine base, the piers, and the pavement in the Trinity Chapel and for the shafts throughout the elevation. This use of marble, which added both colour and richness to the interior and served to accentuate the linear qualities of the design, was to prove the most influential aspect of Canterbury. The fashion for marble decoration, which began in the mid-twelfth century, was undoubtedly associated with the extensive use of marble in Roman and early Christian buildings. Some of the French features at Canterbury, such as the foliage carving and the sexpartite vault, found little favour in

England, but the varied ways in which this architectural idiom could be interpreted in the thirteenth century can be seen at Lincoln (Cat. 240) and Salisbury (Cat. 18, 241).

The ascending liturgical importance of the choir, presbytery and shrine area is indicated by the rising levels and by the increasing elaboration of the architecture. The high altar was originally set lower, flanked by the shrines of St Dunstan and St Alphege. The choir stalls are largely nineteenth century but the arcaded stone screens were erected by Prior Eastry in 1304–5. In the presbytery and the crossing these screens have been partially replaced by the tombs of pre-Reformation archbishops. PD

LIT. Woodman 1981; Pevsner & Metcalf 1985a.

18 Salisbury Cathedral, Trinity Chapel looking north-east from the south choir aisle

1220–5
Photograph

Although dedicated to the Trinity, the spacious eastern chapel at Salisbury always served as the Lady Chapel, being the only chapel outside the choir which could accommodate the whole community for the customary daily masses to the Virgin (see p. 86). In the fifteenth century the shrine of St Osmund was in the centre of the chapel, and the unusual aisled arrangement of this eastern chapel, which derives from the retrochoir of Winchester Cathedral, may indicate that it was always intended as the setting for this shrine.

The sparing use of sculptural ornament, the simple lancet windows and the plain quadripartite vaults supported on slender,

18

polished marble shafts impart an elegant clarity to the design, which complements perfectly the orderly liturgical customs at Salisbury. The use of marble shafts *en délit* for structural supports, and not just for decorative features as at Canterbury (Cat. 17) or Lincoln (Cat. 240), was technically daring as the shafts were made up of separate lengths of marble joined end to end by unobtrusive brass rings. To indicate the entrance to the chapel from the ambulatory the single shafts are replaced by five thinner marble shafts grouped beneath a circular abacus. The plinth beneath the pier in the foreground defines the chapel at the east end of the presbytery aisle.

The north and south walls were extensively restored following the demolition in the eighteenth century of two late medieval chantry chapels which formerly opened out on either side of the Trinity Chapel. PD

LIT. Pevsner & Metcalf 1985a; RCHM, *Salisbury* (forthcoming).

19 Base of the shrine of St Alban, St Albans Cathedral

c. 1302–8
Photograph

This shrine base typifies the arrangement of a major shrine in post-Conquest England, where the reliquary containing the holy bones was placed behind the high altar on a base tall enough to be visible above the altar.

At St Albans the shrine base is in its original place in the shrine chapel, but it is now separated from the high altar by a fifteenth-century screen. Literary evidence suggests that the grave of St Alban was believed to be close by. This base, probably datable to 1302–8 when Abbot John de Maryns is recorded as having 'moved and adorned' the shrine, is possibly the third on the site: the foliage cresting, the lowest step and the trefoil bases for candlesticks beside the shrine are part of an earlier structure, intermediate between this and the shrine to which the saint was translated in 1129.

The base was reconstructed from pieces discovered in 1872, and although the ends and south side are reasonably complete, the north side is fragmentary. It is made of Purbeck stone, except for the niche vaults which are of clunch. Brick, oak and iron clamps were used in the restoration. There are traces of polychromy inside the niches.

The base has a box-like lower section, with rhomboid openings of uncertain purpose. The ten vaulted niches above were for pilgrims to benefit from the saint's healing powers by praying close to his bones, and for votive offerings. The base is a variant of a type which became popular in the later Middle Ages, initiated at Westminster *c.* 1269 and continuing into the fifteenth century.

The ecclesiastical figures along the sides

19

possibly represent abbots and abbey patrons, while the scenes at the ends illustrate the martyrdom of St Alban. The polychromy and the main decorative motifs of arch-and-gable, varieties of foliage, cusped arches, decorative vaults and a very early example of reticulated flowing tracery, are related to the late thirteenth-century works of Edward I at Westminster and elsewhere. NC

LIT. *Gest. Abb.*, ii, p. 107; Micklethwaite 1872; VCH, *Hertfordshire*, II, p. 493, repr. opp. p. 494; Coldstream 1976, p. 20, repr. pl. VIIIB.

20 Base of the shrine of St Werburgh, Chester Cathedral

c. 1340
Photograph

Like the shrine of St Alban (Cat. 19), this shrine base is in two parts, here a solid lower section with six niches for praying pilgrims, and an upper level with traceried windows, gables and a parapet, which represents a miniature chapel. But this base is nearly twice the normal height, and it is likely that the reliquary was placed inside the 'chapel' rather than on top. St Werburgh's royal and Mercian connections are emphasised in the sculptured figures on the panelled buttresses, originally numbering forty, identifiable by inscriptions still visible in the eighteenth century as kings and saints of Mercia.

The shrine probably stood behind the high altar, but after the Dissolution the base was dismantled and incorporated in the bishop's throne. It was correctly reconstructed by Blomfield when several missing pieces were discovered in 1873.

The shrine base has been compared to the chapel-like thirteenth-century tombs of bishops, e.g. Giles de Bridport of Salisbury; in style, however, the mouldings and flowing

tracery are related to work dated to the 1340s in the south transept of Chester Cathedral, and comparable to slightly earlier work in Yorkshire, notably at Selby and Beverley. Unfinished detailing in the mouldings indicates that to avoid damage some of the decorative work was not executed until the shrine base had been set in position. NC

LIT. Scott 1863–5; Barber 1904; Maddison 1984.

20

21 The 'Slipper Chapel', Houghton St Giles, Norfolk

c. 1340
Photograph

Penitence was a significant part of pilgrimage for all ranks of society, and although the 'Slipper Chapel' is undocumented in medieval times, the tradition has been accepted that here pilgrims to the shrine of Our Lady at Walsingham discarded their shoes to walk the last one-and-a-half miles of their journey barefoot.

The great shrines were supported on the strength of popular religion, and the decoration of this luxurious little building, suggesting a date towards the middle of the fourteenth century, is evidence that the pilgrimage to Walsingham was already flourishing at that time, part of the circuit of East Anglian shrines which also included St Edmund at Bury and the Rood of Bromholm. The decorative quatrefoils, miniature battlements, seaweed-like foliage and flowing tracery are standard details of the period, but the tracery in particular has local connections, being related to designs at Great Walsingham and Norwich.

After the Reformation the chapel was converted to cottages, but it was bought in 1894 and restored, opening for Roman Catholic worship in 1934. Drawings made in 1828 by A. C. Pugin show that the ornamental details have been accurately restored. NC

LIT. Bolingbroke 1914; Dickinson 1956, pp. 26, 141–2; Pevsner 1962, p. 174; Etherton 1965, p. 177, Cat. CI, 34b; Wedgwood 1977, [11].6, [12].13.

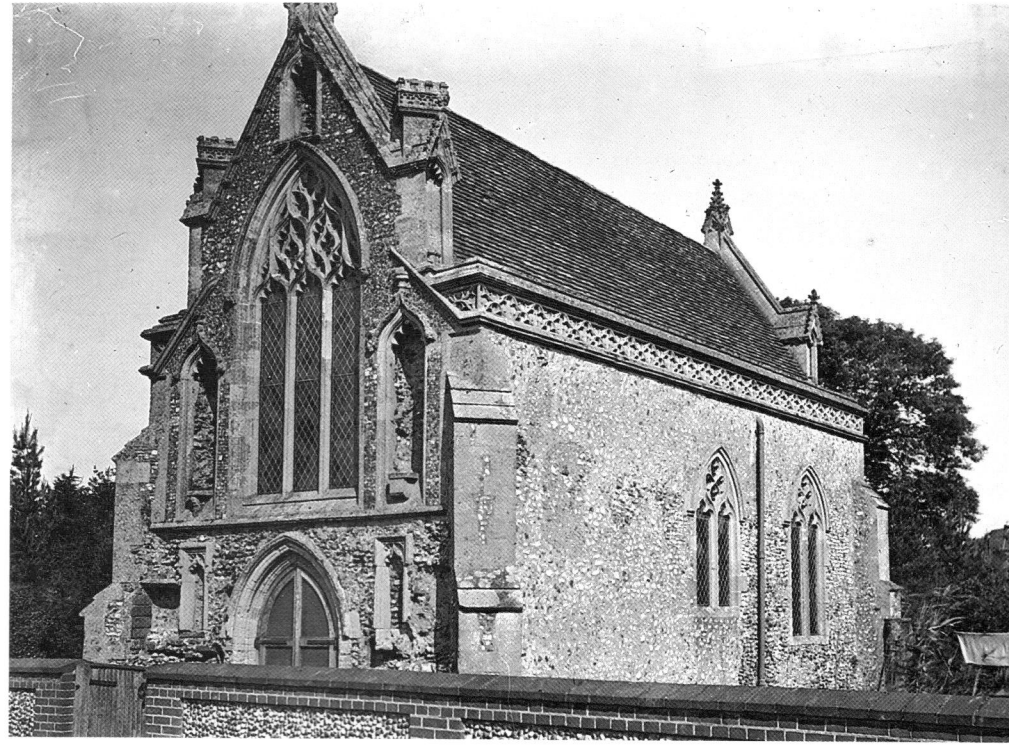

21

22

22 Effigy of a layman

c. 1250

Purbeck marble: l. 213.4 cm, h. 30.5 cm,
  d. 71.1 cm

The National Trust, Ramsey Abbey

According to monastic tradition, Ramsey Abbey was founded about AD 969 by Ailwyn, Ealdorman of East Anglia and fosterbrother of King Edgar, with the help of St Oswald. William Stukeley knew and engraved this effigy, which he called Ailwin (see Cat. 388). Thus it would seem to be a case of a thirteenth-century founder effigy of unusual splendour. The fashion for retrospective effigies was at its height in the early to mid-thirteenth century – compare the series of Anglo-Saxon bishops at Wells, and of bishops at Peterborough. But according to the thirteenth-century chronicler William de Godmanchester the founder's effigy was of metal, 'of subtle and sumptuous artifice, and splendidly gilt'.

So who is represented in this splendid Purbeck effigy? Clearly it is a layman, and not a king. At the Dissolution Ramsey had the shrines of St Felix, first Bishop of East Anglia, and Ethelred and Ethelbreth, two Saxon princes. Could this effigy be a retro-

spective image of a Saxon prince? Its individual iconography, with the soul of the deceased being carried to heaven in a napkin over the gable, recalls the equally striking iconography of the contemporary Purbeck effigy of Bishop Hugh de Northwold at Ely Cathedral. Nor was this the only distinctive mid-thirteenth-century Purbeck effigy at Ramsey Abbey. In 1914 the lower half of a magnificent figure of an Abbot of Ramsey flanked by attendant monks was found in the yard of an inn at Alconbury. The exhibited effigy shows the subject bearing a ragged staff, and with his feet resting against two beasts which are half-buried in the lead which fell from the roof at the demolition of the abbey.   PT-C

PROV. Known to Stukeley by 1719, and reputed to have been dug up 'many years ago' near abbey buildings; old photograph published by RCHM shows it in the house, but now kept in gatehouse, owned by National Trust.

LIT. RCHM, *Huntingdon*, 1926, pp. 207–9, pl. 115 opp. p. 212.

23

23 Spandrel carrying relief with figure of bishop

c. 1260

Purbeck marble carved on both sides: h. 73 cm,
  w. 62.5 cm, d. *c.* 20 cm

The Dean and Chapter of Winchester

24 Spandrel carrying figure of monk

c. 1260

Purbeck marble carved on both sides: figure h.
  57.5 cm, w. 31.5 cm, d. *c.* 20 cm; head h.
  22.4 cm, w. 21.5 cm, d. *c.* 14.4 cm

The Dean and Chapter of Winchester

A study of these pieces and a number of related fragments (Tudor-Craig & Keen 1980) concludes that they formed part of a screen which probably enclosed the shrine of St Swithun. Comparison with the arcaded fragments which had already been identified as forming part of the actual shrine base

indicated that all formed part of a rich Purbeck marble complex created during the episcopate of Aymer de Valence, 1250–60, and rather towards the end of that decade. There are strong similarities between this work and his Purbeck marble heart effigy in the cathedral. The 'rubber' fingers and smiles indicate a knowledge of the latest Westminster sculpture. The drapery bears comparison with that of the Sawley angels (Cat. 341–2). Some of the tracery that belongs to the same complex is grooved for glass, or for inner cusps in a thinner material.   PT-C

PROV. Found under 'Bishop's stairs' leading from south retrochoir aisle, 1907; most pieces deposited in crypt, but head of monk taken to tribune gallery thus deceiving Le Couteur and Carter (1921) into thinking this was part of shrine base proper.

LIT. *Hampshire Chronicle*, 31 Aug. 1907; *Hampshire Independent*, same date; Le Couteur & Carter 1924, pp. 25–70; Atkinson 1936, pp. 159–67; Tudor-Craig & Keen (1980) 1983, pp. 63–72; Crook 1985, pp. 125–31.

24

25 Reliquary

c. 1330

Red sandstone: h. 39.4 cm, w. 20.8 cm,
  d. 20.8 cm

Church of All Saints, Brixworth,
  Northamptonshire

The reliquary is in the form of a small casket carved on three sides with blind pointed cusped arches on cylindrical pilasters, beneath gables ornamented with crockets. The top of the lid is much damaged, and dowel holes there indicate that the gables and summit were probably originally crowned with decorative finials. In 1809 it was cleaned and opened, and in a cylindrical cavity in the base a wooden box was found containing a sliver of human throat bone, and a strip of paper which disintegrated before its inscription could be read. It has been suggested that the bone may have been a relic of St Boniface. Brixworth, Northamptonshire, had a guild uniquely dedicated

25

approximate dating for the carving. The arms are, left to right: Ireland (Gules six fleurs-de-lis argent), Foljambe (Sable a bend between six escallops or) impaling Ireland, and Foljambe alone; they must commemorate the marriage of Sir Godfrey Foljambe (d. 1376) and his second wife, Avena (d. 1382), daughter and heiress of Sir Thomas Ireland. That it was carved for Sir Godfrey, despite the prominence given to his wife's arms, is clear from the presence of his family's crest of a leg (*folle jambe*) on the helm on the right.

The two left-hand shields are shown as hanging from hooks, that on the right from a tree which also supports the helm. Above, the four armed knights, with leg-harness and wearing bascinets, advance upon Becket, who kneels at the altar; above him stands the priest Grim, receiving a sword-thrust from the second knight.

There are considerable remains of paint, of which some is probably original (e.g. the white lacing down the sides of the knights' jerkins [?] and leg-harness), but the blue-green background paint, which also covers a break (top left corner), is post-medieval. The cornice at top continues round the left side; the lower portion has been cut away smoothly at the left, possibly at a medieval date, while the shelved edge at the bottom continues round the right side. This could reflect the exigencies of the panel's original location.

The alabaster of which this is carved was no doubt quarried in Derbyshire or Nottinghamshire, and it is probable that the panel was carved locally; it has a certain stiffness which, together with its wealth of careful detail, sets it apart from other alabaster panels of this date (e.g. Cat. 703–5, 706). Prior and Gardner compared its cornice's combination of battlementing and frilled tracery with the cornice of the Southwell choir screen, adding strength to the suggestion that the panel was carved locally. NLR

PROV. Supposedly from Beauchief Abbey, near Sheffield; Aldwark, Ecclesfield (Yorks.), by 1801; by descent to the present owner.

to the saint, and his feast was celebrated annually with a vigil and three-day fair. Although the reliquary closely resembles the kind of miniature Gothic gabled pinnacle that one might find as architectural decoration, its form is of some antiquity and is ultimately derived from a type of Roman sarcophagus. Numerous stone reliquaries of this type have been found, dating at least from the sixth century, in Asia Minor and in Italy. However, this seems to be an unusual survival in England. English stone reliquaries tended to be undecorated and made for insertion within or near an altar where they remained concealed, probably having been placed there during the altar consecration ceremony. The nearest relative to this Brixworth example was discovered in 1849 in the north nave wall of the parish church at Kew Stoke, Somerset. It consisted of a thirteenth-century image niche behind which was an arched chamber containing an oak vessel for a relic. Presumably it was for reasons of security that these tiny shrines were built into the fabric. VS

LIT. Dryden 1893, pp. 79–82; Conway 1918–19, pp. 218–41; Parsons 1980–1, pp. 179–83; Parsons 1983; Bickerton-Hudson 1905; Cabrol & Leclercq 1907, vol. 1, col. 1774, vol. 2, cols 2345–7.

26   Murder of Thomas Becket

1370s
Alabaster: h. 59.5 cm, w. 53 cm, d. 10 cm
Private Collection

Unlike every other surviving devotional panel of alabaster, this large representation of the murder of Thomas Becket by four knights at Henry II's behest (1170) is adorned with heraldry that enables the presumed donor to be identified, and thus gives an

26

LIT. Pegge 1801, pp. 246–7, pl. ix; Cox 1875–7, i, p. 79; ii, pp. 10–17; London 1910, pp. 76–7, pl. xxviii; Prior & Gardner 1912, pp. 460–1, fig. 534; Borenius 1932a, pp. 81–2; London 1972, no. 264.

27 Miracles of St Thomas Becket

1213–20

Stained glass: h. 6.70 m, w. 1.57 m

Dean and Chapter of Canterbury, window S.VII

This is one of the seven surviving windows in the Trinity Chapel ambulatory depicting the life and posthumous miracles of St Thomas Becket. The series originally consisted of twelve windows and commenced with scenes from the saint's life in the two westernmost windows on the north side of the ambulatory: one of these scenes survives in the Fogg Art Museum, Cambridge, Massachusetts. The miracle windows are unique to Canterbury and include miracles which occurred at Becket's tomb in the crypt or cures for which an offering was made at this tomb. All of these took place between 1171 and 1173 and were recorded in two prose accounts, one by a monk named William who held an office at the tomb, and the other by Benedict, Prior of the Cathedral Priory until 1177 and subsequently Abbot of Peterborough. These accounts were used by the glaziers, although the wording of the verse inscriptions in the windows is not close to either of them. The relics of Becket were translated from the crypt tomb to a magnificent new shrine in the Trinity Chapel on 7 July 1220. The windows of this part of the church, with their brilliantly coloured glass, were a major feature of the architectural framework which in itself acted as a monumental reliquary for the shrine. The window exhibited here is the last in the miracle series and contains six episodes expounded in twenty-two figural panels. The scenes are the Cures of Geoffrey of Winchester, of James son of the Earl of Clare, of Eilwin and Walter of Berkhamsted(?), of Brother Elias and the Miraculous Rescue of William of Gloucester; the sixth episode, at the base of the window, depicts a woman praying at the altar in front of Becket's shrine, one of only two surviving representations of the shrine in the Trinity Chapel glass.

The window has been attributed to a glazier identified as the Fitz-Eisulf Master and appears to date from after the return of the monks from exile in 1213 and before the translation of the relics in 1220. The glass was very heavily restored by Samuel Caldwell and his son in 1897 and subsequently. Six of the figural panels are entirely their work and only a few fragments of ancient glass remain in a seventh. Only two of the border panels are largely original, and much of the ornamental ground is also by the Caldwells. RM

LIT. Caviness 1977, *passim*; Caviness 1981, pp. 157–64, 208–14, figs 349–66.

27

27 (detail)

28 Archbishop Asterius commissions St Birinus

c. 1225

Stained glass: medallion excluding modern border
diam. 41 cm

Inscr. BER/NIVS

Dorchester Abbey, Oxford, window n III.2b

The medieval glass at Dorchester dates mainly from the late thirteenth and early fourteenth centuries, a period of great rebuilding there. This panel, the earliest in the church, is the sole survivor of a window depicting the life of the local saint, Birinus. Consecrated bishop by Asterius, Archbishop of Milan, he was sent by Pope Honorius I to evangelise Wessex. In 634 he baptised King Cynegils at Dorchester, where he established his see. His relics were moved to Winchester in the seventh century, but the Austin canons, established at Dorchester around 1142, also claimed his body, and these relics were translated into a more prominent place in the church in 1225. Birinus holds his bishop's crosier and takes hold of Asterius' cross-staff while he is blessed. A bearded layman on the right witnesses the scene.

The figures and throne are executed in a combination of bright green, pink, purple, ruby, yellow and white glass, against a blue background. Heads, drapery and ornament are exquisitely drawn in a dry manner, with a minimum of shading on both surfaces. Although the outside is corroded, the inner surface and the paint are well preserved. The original shape of the panel has been disturbed and there are a few insertions. The glass was conserved by King & Sons in 1969.

The problems of dating this isolated medallion are discussed by Newton who, while noting archaic elements, tentatively proposes a mid-thirteenth-century date. On stylistic grounds an earlier date is equally plausible, suggesting that the glass might be associated with the translation of the relics in 1225. DO'C

LIT. Newton 1979, pp. 12, 84–5, repr. pls 31a, b; Grodecki & Brisac 1985, p. 264, repr. pl. 172.

29 St Thomas of Canterbury and St Thomas of Hereford

c. 1300

Stained glass: h. 61 cm, w. 35 cm

Inscr. CATVAR : THOMAS : DECATVLVPO

St Mary's Church, Credenhill, Hereford, window s IV.2a

Apart from a few fragments in the nave, this panel, probably still in its original position in the chancel, is all that remains of the medieval glazing. The two blessing saints stand against a background of white foliage quarries, Becket on the left with pall and cross-staff, Cantilupe holding a crosier. The vestments are in blue, green, ruby, white and pot-metal yellow with Becket's head and hands in white glass and Cantilupe's in pink. The borders consist of golden castles and fleurs-de-lis on blue and ruby grounds. It is a remarkably well-preserved panel, although a few pieces are heavily corroded, and there is a little patching and disordering.

Represented beside the martyr saint of England is his namesake, Thomas Cantilupe (1218–82), Bishop of Hereford from 1272. His vigorous defence of the see brought him into conflict with Archbishop Pecham, and he died on his way to Rome to seek the Pope's support. His bones were returned to Hereford by his successor, Richard Swinfield, who keenly promoted the cult. The new tomb erected in Hereford in 1287 (Cat. 86) led to an outbreak of miracles and an upsurge of popular devotion in the neighbourhood (Finucane 1977 ch. 10). The inscription is arranged to stress the parallels which bi-

29

ographers have noted between the men. The shared Christian name is in the centre, flanked by Cantuar and the family name of Cantulupo, no doubt chosen to heighten the play on words.

Havergal and subsequent writers have dated the panel to after the official canonisation process of 1320. However this would make it an exceptionally conservative piece on grounds of style and technique. Representations of 'unofficial' saints are not that rare, and the ambivalence suggested by the absence of haloes and *sanctus* inscriptions presupposes an image designed to stimulate a cult, rather than the celebration of a successful canonisation process. DO'C

LIT. Havergal 1884, pp. 4–6, repr. p. 3; Baker 1960, p. 110, repr. pl. 22.

30 The Assumption of the Virgin

c. 1300–10

Stained glass: h. 56 cm, w. 46 cm

The Revd Anthony de Vere and Churchwardens of the Church of the Assumption of the Blessed Virgin Mary, Beckley Oxford, chancel window s IV.A1

The strong Marian element in what survives of the glazing and the presence of a second Assumption panel (Cat. 31) are explained by the dedication of the church.

This tracery light, the earlier of the panels, presents a very static, balanced image in which Mary, dressed in white, is placed centrally on a ruby ground within a pot-metal yellow mandorla. She is accompanied by six angels, executed in a variety of pot-metal and ruby colours, on a white oak-leaf ground; four carry the mandorla upwards and two are censing. A linear painting technique is used with a small amount of smear shading, some of it on the outside. Despite exterior corrosion most of the glass is

28

30

31

being the best preserved.

In a quatrefoil opening is an equestrian figure of Martin turning in his saddle and cutting his cloak for a semi-naked and bearded beggar who stands on the right. White with a little yellow stain is used for the saint and horse; the cloak is purple and the scabbard and saddle pot-metal yellow. The beggar is in darkened brownish-pink and wears a white loincloth. The foils are filled with a bold design of white oak leaves and acorns; the ground is plain ruby. The saint's head, some foliage, and some smaller pieces are restorations probably executed in 1852 when main light glazing by Ward & Hughes was inserted. Minor repairs were carried out by the Salisbury Cathedral glaziers in 1982.

As one of the most prodigious miracle workers in the West, St Martin of Tours (d. 397) became the focus of a widespread cult which the life of Sulpicius Severus and the extensive account of his miracles by St

32

original, although the heads of the bottom and centre right angels, and a few other pieces were restored, probably c. 1895 when Hardman & Co. inserted the main light glazing. Recently conservation has been carried out by Chapel Studios.

Dating the panel is problematic. It seems to be in situ but appears to be earlier than the rest of the chancel glazing of c. 1325–50. Newton, who points to general parallels with late thirteenth-century glass at Merton College, Oxford (Cat. 738), proposes a date after 1310, claiming that yellow stain is used. However, the colour looks to be pot-metal yellow, allowing for a dating nearer to 1300. Perhaps the panel was very skilfully reused in its present setting, or the chancel glazing was produced by glaziers working in very different techniques and styles.   DO'C

LIT. Newton 1979, p. 31, repr. pls 1d, 16c, d.

31   The Assumption of the Virgin

c. 1325–50
Stained glass: h. 70 cm, w. 55 cm
The Revd Anthony de Vere and Churchwardens
    of the Church of the Assumption of the Blessed
    Virgin Mary, Beckley, Oxford, east window
    (I.A2)

This panel, like the other Assumption from Beckley (Cat. 30), comes from a quatrefoil tracery opening where it is flanked by a Coronation of the Virgin; a third missing panel probably represented her Dormition or Burial. It is much less iconic than the earlier version. Mary, with yellow-stained hair, purple robe and pot-metal yellow mantle, is placed horizontally and carried upwards in a winding sheet by four angels with white albs and yellow-stained wings. At the top is the blessing hand of God, and below, by the empty tomb, kneels St Thomas in green robe, about to receive the Virgin's girdle. Although

in better physical condition than the earlier panel, less original glass survives. Most of the angel on the left and some of the ground was restored in the nineteenth century, probably by Hardman. Recent conservation was carried out by Chapel Studios.

In colour and technique the panel is different from its predecessor. Yellow stain is used here and more modelling and depth are created by greater use of smear shading and backpainting. The somewhat awkward adaptation of the design to the shape of the opening contrasts sharply with the poise of the earlier panel.

The episode of St Thomas and the girdle is a late addition to the legend, stressing yet further the parallels between Christ and His mother, who leaves her girdle behind on earth to convince the doubting Thomas of her bodily resurrection. Newton discusses the iconography in detail and stresses the popularity of the theme in English art c. 1290–1340, which might be connected with the acquisition of a relic of the girdle by Westminster Abbey.   DO'C

LIT. Newton 1979, p. 30, repr. pls 1b, 16a, b.

32   St Martin and the beggar

c. 1325–30
Stained glass: h. 60 cm, w. 50 cm
Vicar and Churchwardens of the Parish Church of
    St Michael the Archangel, Mere, Wiltshire,
    window sv.A2

Since John Aubrey visited Mere in the seventeenth century virtually all the heraldic glass he recorded has disappeared. Fortunately the figures of 'St. Nicholas and some other Saints' which he saw in the Bettesthorne Chapel have survived. Four tracery lights in a south window contain St Nicholas raising the three boys, St Martin, St Christopher and a papal saint, the panel exhibited

Gregory both helped to spread. The scene most commonly represented by artists is that shown here, the famous incident at Amiens, when the soldier saint, prior to becoming a monk, shared his cloak with a beggar. Martin is here presented as an image of the perfect Christian knight with the sign of the Cross displayed on the trappings of his horse.

The panel forms part of the glazing of a chantry chapel founded in 1325, a date consistent with the style of the glass which, as Woodforde suggested, shows marked similarities with contemporary glass at Wells (Robinson 1931; Marks 1982).   DO'C

LIT. Jackson 1862, p. 387; Woodforde 1946, pp. 20–1.

33   St George

c. 1330–40
Stained glass: h. 94 cm, w. 70 cm
St George's Church, Brinsop, Hereford, east
    window I.2b

The figure exhibited forms part of the original glazing of the east window, rearranged and

33

extended by Ninian Comper in 1923. All the medieval glass in the church dates from the second quarter of the fourteenth century and is contemporary with the building.

The patron saint of the church is shown without a halo and wearing mail armour, poleyns and white surcoat with red cross; his arms are repeated on his shield and the pennon attached to his lance. His swordbelt is pot-metal yellow and the scabbard and pommel white. There is a ruby fretwork background of blue quarries containing lions rampant and eagles displayed. The canopy consists of a crocketed ogee arch with ball-flower ornament, and side shafts of traceried windows with crocketed pinnacles, all in pot-metal yellow, white and yellow stain. There are heraldic borders of France on the left and England on the right. Apart from a few modern insertions and severe corrosion of the face, plinth and some pieces of canopy, the condition is good. Prior to the exhibition Barley Studios carried out some cleaning.

This is a powerful secular image of the soldier saint who enjoyed a widespread cult in the later Middle Ages, especially in Court circles (Newton 1961, 1, pp. 254–5). Edward III showed particular devotion to the saint, who became one of the patrons of the Order of the Garter in 1347. The image at Brinsop does not include a dragon and is perhaps designed to stress the saint's role as patron and protector of England. There are close parallels at Gloucester (Kerr 1985, pl. XXXVIB) and Wells (Marks 1982, pl. 69). The borders may well be an allusion to Edward's claims to the French throne. A date of c. 1330–40 is proposed here on stylistic grounds. Many of the architectural details anticipate the canopy work at Tewkesbury (Cat. 742) in the 1340s, though it is only the plinth which is shown in perspective. The mail worn by the saint is clearly earlier in

type than the Transitional armour worn by the Tewkesbury knights but the panel comes from a window which has strong proto-Perpendicular elements.   DO'C

LIT. Nelson 1913 p. 98; Woodforde 1954, p. 12.

34   St Christopher

c. 1340–50
Stained glass: h. 37 cm, w. 38 cm
Vicar, Churchwardens and Parochial Church Council of Halvergate Church, Norfolk, nIV.AI

Apart from some fragments from the rectory, this panel in a Y-traceried window is all that remains of the medieval glass. Its position on the north of the nave is traditional for representations of the saint, who is shown here in gown, mantle and cap, wading across a river containing a crab, an eel and another fish. Christopher holds a staff and carries on his shoulder the Christ Child who holds an orb and blesses him. The figures are painted

34

on white glass decorated with yellow stain. The background is ruby and there is a border of green *rinceau* ornament with decorative designs in yellow stain. Delicate washes of smear shading give depth to the drapery; backpainting is used to create the illusion of water. Prior to restoration in 1983 by King & Sons the panel was inside out.

As patron saint of travellers Christopher was one of the most popular saints of the Middle Ages. A devotional image of the kind seen here was thought to be particularly effective against sudden death and plague, and it was popular in such public art forms as stained glass and wall paintings (Rushforth 1936, pp. 222–4). The story of the giant, converted by a hermit and enjoined to serve Christ by carrying travellers across a dangerous river, was made popular by the Golden Legend (Ellis 1900, pp. 111–19). The child he carries over and who grows heavier and heavier is revealed as Christ: 'Christopher, marvel thee nothing, for thou hast not only borne all the world upon thee, but thou hast

borne him that created and made all the world, upon thy shoulders.'

The elegantly modelled style of the figures suggests comparisons with French-inspired glazing of the mid-fourteenth century.   DO'C

LIT. Norwich 1983, no. 82.

35   Panel painting of St Edward and the Pilgrim

c. 1370
Tempera on wooden panel: h. 77.5 cm, w. 73.5 cm
Private Collection

These simple figures recall the silver figures of the king and St John the Pilgrim which stood on either side of the shrine of St Edward in Westminster Abbey (fig. 125). The Confessor was not widely portrayed outside royal circles. Forthampton Court, however, was a residence of the Abbot of Tewkesbury, and the abbots of Tewkesbury were immersed in royal affairs. Edward le Despenser, Lord of the

35

Manor of Tewkesbury and Knight of the Garter from 1358 until his death in 1375, is commemorated in Tewkesbury Abbey: the Confessor was his titular saint.

The hairstyles, the fitted waist, and the long sleeve of the king's undergarment partly covering his wrist recall the effigy and weepers of Edward III in Westminster Abbey, made between 1377 and 1380, and Bohun-style manuscripts of the 1370s (Cat. 686–91). This painting was carried out on two boards, held together by a frame. The condition of the paint layer, where it has not been seriously abraded, is remarkably fresh. There is no evidence of deliberate defacing by scratching or gouging out eyes, which suggests that the panel was concealed where it has since remained, at Forthampton Court.

The last Abbot of Tewkesbury, John Wakeman, embellished Forthampton with carved bosses, a gargoyle and probably ashlar from the destroyed Lady Chapel. He brought here from the Abbey the effigy of William de la Zouche (d. 1335). This panel could have been among the pieces he rescued. Alternatively, it might have always belonged to the chapel in the house. At the bottom of the back an upright rectangle, approximately 49.5 cm × 30.5 cm, is bare but the rest, a narrow border for the original frame, is painted scarlet.   PT-C

PROV. Forthampton Court.

LIT. Tristram 1943, pp. 160–5; Spencer 1972, no. 32, illus.

36   The Hereford World Map

Lincoln and Hereford(?), c. 1277–89
Vellum: 162.6 × 134.6 cm (without frame)
The Dean and Chapter of Hereford

The Hereford World Map is the finest and grandest surviving map of the thirteenth century. A closely related, slightly earlier German example, probably devised by the Englishman Gervase of Tilbury, the Ebstorf Map (formerly Hanover, Bibliothek des his-

torischen Vereins für Niedersachsen) was destroyed by bombing in the last war. A fragment of the bottom right-hand corner of an English world map similar to the Hereford one has recently been discovered in the archives of the Duchy of Cornwall. Other English thirteenth-century world maps, now lost, are recorded as wall paintings or wall hangings of vellum, tapestry or embroidery. Examples were in the Great Hall of Winchester Castle, painted by Master Nigel in 1239, and at Waltham Abbey and Westminster Palace. On a small scale they are found in manuscripts, such as a psalter (London, British Library, Add. MS 28681).

The structure of the map is based on a division of the globe into three parts with an east-west orientation and surrounded by the winds. The whole of the upper semicircle contains Asia, and Europe and Africa (their names are reversed owing to an error of the scribe) each occupying half of the lower semicircle. Jerusalem is in the centre, at the top in the extreme east is Paradise, and at the

bottom in the extreme west is the ocean beyond the Straits of Gibraltar. The continents have small drawings of figures, animals and buildings representing cities. The peoples of the world and historical events from the Bible or classical antiquity are indicated by single figures or symbols of the events. In the right-hand bottom perimeter on the coast of Africa, for example, are the fantastic monstrous races said to inhabit this region.

The world map was not only a topographic representation but presented the story of the world in its historical development and as an image of man's destiny. The world has at the four diagonal points of the perimeter extensions containing the letters MORS – Death. At the bottom on the left the Emperor Augustus sends out surveyors. On the right a horseman and his squire may represent man's journey through the world, the horseman gesturing to it as he rides on. The life of man is but a short span, and the map has at the top a reminder of the eventual judgement which will come to all at the Second Coming of Christ. The map of the world is viewed both in the sense of a chronicle of past events and as a presentation of the Christian belief in God's total plan of Creation, man's fall, his redemption and eventual salvation.

The name of the author of the map is given in the bottom left-hand corner as Richard of Haldingham and Lafford (Sleaford). There is considerable controversy concerning the identification of this man. He was probably Richard de Bello, Canon of Lincoln 1264–83, prebendary of Lafford by 1277, and he may have come to or resided at Hereford in the period 1283–9. A man of this name is recorded in the company of Richard Swinfield, Bishop of Hereford, in 1289. The map may have been some time in the making, begun at Lincoln in the 1270s and completed at Hereford in the 1280s.   NJM

PROV. First recorded in Hereford Cathedral 1682, but probably there since time of its completion in late 13th century.

LIT. Crone 1954; Emden 1957, p. 556; Destombes 1964, pp. 197–202, no. 52.3; Crone 1965, pp. 447–62; Yates 1974, pp. 165–72; Arentzen 1984, passim; Morgan 1987, no. 188, repr.

37   The Guthlac Roll

Crowland(?), c. 1210
Vellum roll: 16 × 285 cm
British Library, Harley Roll Y.6

Rolls were used throughout the Middle Ages for certain texts and forms of illustration such as genealogies, obituaries, and occasionally Lives of Saints. This roll has seventeen scenes of the Life of St Guthlac in roundels in penwork tinted with light washes. The only text is as inscriptions within the illustrations. It has been suggested that the roll form may

36

37

indicate a use as a source of designs for stained-glass windows, but no surviving roll has any evidence of being designed for such a function. The relics of St Guthlac were at the Benedictine abbey of Crowland, Lincolnshire, which, in addition to the physical remains of the saint, possessed the scourge given to Guthlac by St Bartholomew to defend himself against devils. The story of the scourge is illustrated on the roll. Scenes of miracles at Guthlac's tomb, and of the benefactors of Crowland, are at the end.

The technique of penwork drawing tinted in colour has a continuous tradition in England from the tenth century onward. The drawing style is an early thirteenth-century form of that used by Matthew Paris and the artists of the Apocalypses (Cat. 437, 348) in the middle years of the century.

The production of the Guthlac Roll has been associated with a translation of the relics of the saint in 1196, but there is no reason to connect it with this event. The figure style suggests a date well into the first quarter of the thirteenth century, as evidenced by comparisons with stained glass and manuscript painting.   NJM

PROV. Crowland Abbey; Robert Harley (1661–1724) or Edward Harley (1689–1741); bt by British Museum with Harley manuscripts, 1753.

LIT. Warner 1928; London 1980, no. 35; Morgan 1982, no. 22, figs 72–5; Henderson 1985b, pp. 84ff.

38   Life of St Thomas of Canterbury (fragment)

London(?), c. 1230–40
Vellum, ff. 4: 30.3 × 22.3 cm
J. Paul Getty, KBE

These four leaves are a fragment of a fully-illustrated life of St Thomas of Canterbury, the only example of such an illustrated life with accompanying text in any English manuscript. Rectangular pictures as tinted drawings are set above a text in Anglo-Norman French verse.

Such illustrated Lives of the Saints are

particularly associated with the St Albans monk, Matthew Paris (see Cat. 39, 315, 437), and the text of this has been controversially attributed to his authorship. The illustrations are definitely not by his hand although they might derive from models devised by him if he was, in fact, the author of the text. This Life of St Thomas seems earlier in date than Matthew Paris's Life of St Alban of c. 1250 (fig. 111). The drawings in the Thomas are closer to London work than to the style of Matthew Paris. A good parallel is a set of tinted drawings of the Life of Christ in a psalter (now fragmentary) made for the Benedictine Abbey of Chertsey (Cambridge, Emmanuel College, MS 252). The Thomas

38

fragment is central to the whole issue of the relationship of the work of the monk Matthew Paris to that of lay artists in London. The problems of its dating and the authorship of its text need further careful investigation.

NJM

PROV. Jacques Goethals-Vercruysse (d. 1838): Goethals family; Sotheby's, 24 June 1986, lot 40.

LIT. Meyer 1885; Morgan 1982, no. 61, figs 206–8.

39   Life of St Edward the Confessor

Westminster, c. 1255–60
Vellum, ff. 37: 28 × 19.2 cm
Syndics of Cambridge University Library, MS Ee.3.59

Henry III had a particular devotion to his royal predecessor St Edward the Confessor, best evident in his patronage of the building and decoration of Westminster Abbey. In 1252 the king ordered paintings of the Life of St Edward for his chapel in the Abbey. This illustrated copy of the Life has a text in Anglo-Norman French and is dedicated to his queen, Eleanor of Provence, and may have been a presentation copy for her.

Sixty-four tinted drawings are set at the head of a two- or three-column text, a format commonly used for illustrated Lives of the Saints at this time (see Cat. 38; fig. 111). The authorship of the text has controversially been attributed to Matthew Paris, and the original set of illustrations of which these could be copies have been considered also to have been by him. There is general agreement that the Cambridge Life of Edward is by

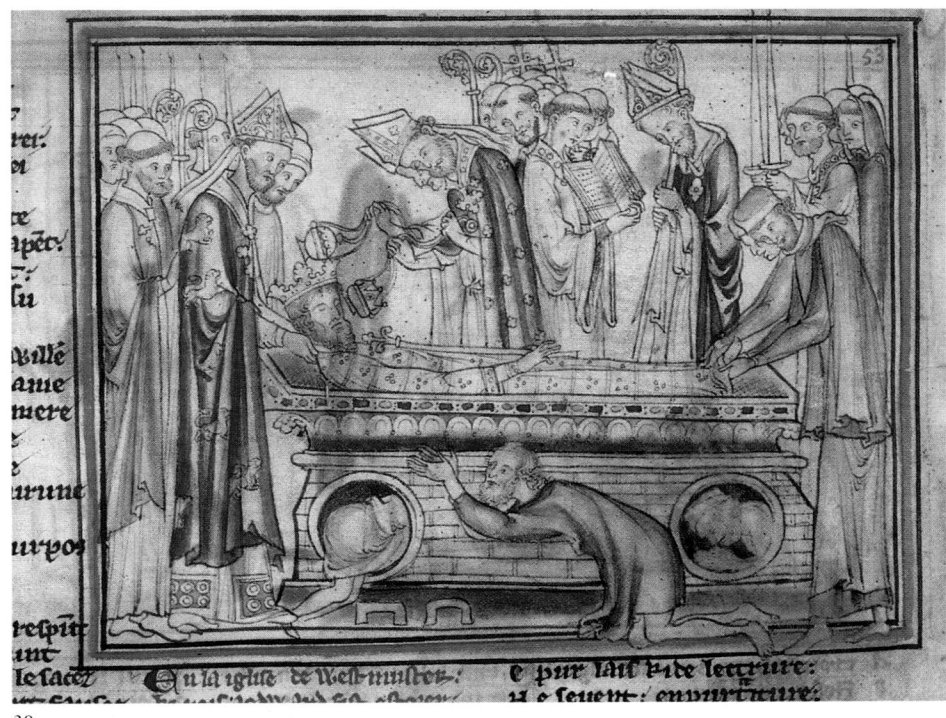

39

paralleled in the thirteenth-century Matthew
Paris Life from Cambridge (Cat. 39) and in a
series of fifteenth-century reliefs carved on
the presbytery screen in Westminster Abbey.
The exhibited pages (ff. 42v.–43) show two
miraculous events from Edward's life, his
death, and the veneration of his shrine at
Westminster. The style of the drawings,
which are by more than one hand, is not a
distinctly English one. It can more readily be
related to Dutch or Flemish work of the late
fourteenth century.   JB

PROV. John Whitgift (d. 1604); given to Trinity
College, of which he was Master 1567–77.

LIT. Simpson 1978, pp. 153–4, repr. pls 295–7;
Sandler 1986, no. 153.

41   Book of Hours

Oxford(?), c. 1260–70
Vellum, ff. 159: 16.2 × 10.7 cm
British Library, Egerton MS 1151

The Book of Hours as a devotional text
independent from that of the psalter first
appeared in England around the middle of

artists working in Westminster in a quite
different manner from that of Matthew Paris,
but they could be copying a series of pictures
devised by him. There are two artists, and the
second, who does the work from f. 5v.
onwards, shows a gradual assimilation of
French influence. His figures are smaller in
scale than those of the first artist, with
emphasis on refined facial features and head
types of pear shape with neatly curled hair
and beards (fig. 125). The drapery folds have
broad angular shapes rather than a system of
multiple troughed folds. This tendency in
English painting culminates in work such as
the Douce Apocalypse (Cat. 351).   NJM

PROV. Queen Eleanor (?) (d. 1291); Laurence
Nowell (d. 1576); William Lambard (d. 1601); Sir
Anthony Cope (d. 1614); John Moore, Bishop of
Ely 1707–14; Bishop Moore's library bt by George
I, 1715, and presented to Cambridge University.

LIT. James 1920; Henderson 1967, pp. 8off.;
Ottawa 1972, no. 19; Brussels 1973, no. 48;
Binski 1986, pp. 39, 40, 42–3, 52, 53, 54, 108,
pls XXXVIIb, XXXVIIIa; Morgan 1987, no. 123,
repr.

40   Apocalypse and scenes from the Life of Edward the Confessor

c. 1380–c. 1400
Vellum, ff. 44: 36.5 × 25 cm
The Master and Fellows, Trinity College,
    Cambridge, MS B. 10. 2

The manuscript contains two distinct items,
an Apocalypse richly illuminated in gold and
colours and a series of tinted line drawings
illustrating the Life of St Edward the Confessor. Although they are so very different in

40

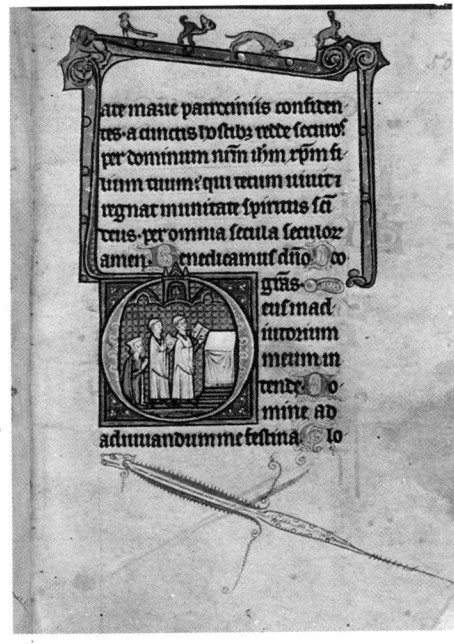

41

appearance, the two may not be far removed
from each other in date. The fashionable
costumes depicted in the drawings suggest a
date in the last decade of the fourteenth
century. The Apocalypse is close in style to
work in the Litlyngton Missal (Cat. 714),
which was made at Westminster in 1383–4.
The connection with Westminster is underlined by the close relationship between the
Apocalypse cycle and the late fourteenth-
century paintings of the same subject in the
Abbey chapter house.

Twenty-four scenes from the Life of the
Confessor are illustrated. Episodes can be

the thirteenth century, and rapidly increased
in popularity during the later thirteenth and
fourteenth centuries. This is probably due to
the text providing short devotions in a struc-
tured form, usually combined with illustration, which well suited the piety of the
laity. This example contains the Hours of the
Virgin Mary and of the Holy Spirit, and the
Offices of the Passion and of the Dead. Its
intended owner seems to be the woman
shown kneeling on ff. 7 and 50. The initials
for the hours of the day over which the
devotions are spread show activities at various times. Compline, for example, is illus-

trated by two figures preparing beds for the night.

The work is by the William of Devon workshop, named after the scribe of the Bible in the British Library (MS Royal I.D.I; Cat. 354–5), which uses a characteristic ornament of grotesque figures, birds and hybrid creatures on the decorative border bars which extend from the initials. These features are well shown in this small Book of Hours whose figure style, like that of other manuscripts of the workshop, derives directly from that of a Parisian workshop. Where the workshop was based is a controversial topic. Several of its products have liturgical evidence connecting them with the dioceses of Lincoln or Worcester. It is possible that Oxford was the centre of its operation. This Book of Hours has a calendar connecting it with the diocese of Worcester. The text contents reflect the sort of devotions prescribed in the early thirteenth-century *Ancrene Riwle* which also may have contacts with the Worcester region.   NJM

PROV. Thomas Mazya, 15th century; Mistress Felys, 16th century; Robert Colston, 17th century; bt for British Museum from Thomas Rodd, 1848.

LIT. Ottawa 1972, no. 25; Morgan 1987, no. 161, repr.

42   Canticles, hymns and Passion of Christ

c. 1280–90
Parchment, ff. 96: 31.5 × 21.6 cm
The Master and Fellows of St John's College,
   Cambridge, MS 262 (K.21)

Pictorial narratives accompanied by vernacular 'captions', in which the ordinary relation between text and illustration is inverted, constitute a distinct category of manuscript illumination – the picture book. The long Passion cycle of the St John's volume is an example, along with the Old Testament cycle of the Queen Mary Psalter (London, British Library, Royal MS 2 B VII), the Holkham Bible (Cat. 221), and the Egerton Genesis (London, British Library, Eger. MS 1894); in all these, each miniature is accompanied by a short explanatory text beginning '*Comment* [How] . . .'. What distinguishes the St John's manuscript is the integration of the pictorial cycle and its Anglo-French captions into an imposing liturgical book, intended to be used in services at the Benedictine Abbey of St Augustine's, Canterbury.

Probably the main textual contents were originally a psalter (now entirely lost); what survives is a calendar of St Augustine's, the monastic canticles and a hymnal for use at the same abbey. The Passion miniatures are placed between the hymn for the Last Supper and the hymn for Easter. We can imagine that the words of the Psalms, hymns and canticles were chanted by rote; the role of the pictures and their vernacular explanation

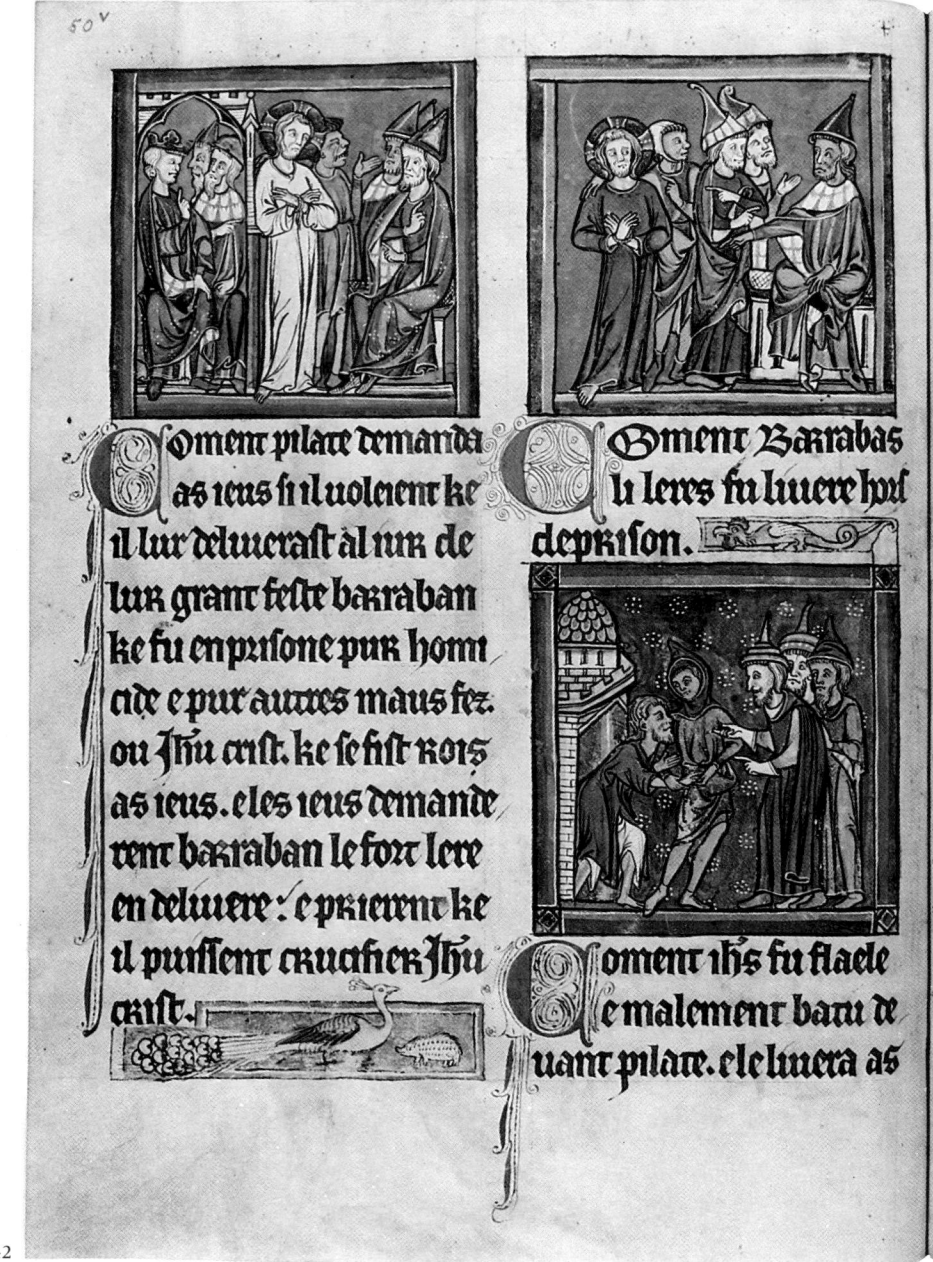

42

was perhaps to rekindle the sense of emotional participation in the events of the Passion.

The text of the manuscript gives no indications of its date. The work of the three artists, however, suggests the 1280s; it is reminiscent of the series of images of English kings painted during the reign of Edward I (London, British Library, MS Cotton Vitell A. XIII) or the New College Apocalypse (Oxford, New College, MS 65), whose original owner was probably Lady Johanna de Bohun, d. 1283.   LFS

PROV. St Augustine's, Canterbury; Edward Benlowes, beq. to St John's College, 1631.

LIT. Camille 1985c, pp. 140–1, repr. fig. 8; Sandler 1986, no. 8, II, pp. 18–9, repr. I, figs 18–20.

Pilgrim souvenirs

By 1200 the word 'ampuller' had come into use to describe a new craft, the purpose of which was to produce cheap souvenirs for Canterbury's pilgrims. It so happened that then and for another hundred years Canterbury water proved to be the means by which devotees of St Thomas Becket most frequently secured miraculous cures. The water's thaumaturgic property was based on the belief that it was tinged with the martyr's blood, collected from his mortal wounds in 1170 and continuously diluted to ensure its conservation for later generations. Even before the end of 1171, pewter ampullae had been devised to meet the huge demand for souvenirs of England's new saint and as containers for his miraculous medicine. These ampullae were worn suspended round the owners' necks as talismans as well as proof of pilgrimage and were soon hung up by returning pilgrims, for the benefit of neighbours, in churches throughout the land.

Archaeological evidence suggests that at first they were rectangular and scallop-shaped, and that by 1200 another form had begun to predominate: a pouch-like, flat-sided vessel, large enough to contain scenes commemorating St Thomas's posthumous miracles (Cat. 43) or episodes from his life, or his martyrdom, burial and reception into Heaven. Exalted figures of Becket the arch-bishop in the act of intercession, depicted initially in semi-relief, also featured regularly on these ampullae (Cat. 47). In scenes of the martyrdom, the number of knights depicted was soon reduced from four to one or two and Becket shown (in spite of evidence to the contrary) as praying at an altar at the time of the assault (Cat. 46).

Other forms of ampulla were introduced, among them a boat in which Becket, en-throned and accompanied by a steersman and a kneeling devotee, is shown returning from exile in France (Cat. 50). Further sorts appear to have been added for the centenary of Becket's martyrdom in 1270 and con-tinued to be made into the early years of the fourteenth century, some based on contem-porary pottery costrels (Cat. 53), others on the gabled reliquaries that were still being made by Limoges craftsmen as receptacles for relics of St Thomas. As with the reliquaries themselves, the rectangular sides of these ampullae invited a frieze-like treatment of the martyrdom and burial (Cat. 51–2). Many ampullae also included allusions to the cath-edral itself (Christ Church) and its famous Rood, which in the thirteenth century had still not been overshadowed by the Becket cult.

Though Canterbury had English rivals (Cat. 71, 77) and plagiarists producing com-parable ampullae, no Continental sanctuary of the thirteenth century sent away its pilgrims with such eye-catching propaganda for its saint. Many ampullae bore inscrip-tions, mostly claiming that 'Thomas is the best doctor of the worthy sick'. This was also the message of Canterbury's miracle books. Ordinary doctors are shown up as expensive failures. But Thomas's success depended on expectant faith. Those who failed to benefit from a pilgrimage or a dose of Canterbury water or from the possession of a pilgrim sign were deemed unworthy, lacking sufficient belief and piety.

Although they had been in use at a few of the major Continental shrines from the sec-ond half of the twelfth century, pilgrim badges appear not to have been introduced at Canterbury (or anywhere else in England) until the early fourteenth century, when several sorts were devised to commemorate the principal holy places in the pilgrim's tour of Canterbury Cathedral. One important station was a reliquary that took the form of a life-sized bust and contained the portion of Becket's skull that had been hacked off at his martyrdom. This reliquary was refashioned and gorgeously enriched for the third jubilee of Becket's martyrdom in 1320. Subsequent popular interest in this object is borne out by the evidence of pilgrim signs. Badges depict-ing the reliquary occur in a variety of sizes and settings (Cat. 54–8) and, on their own, far exceed the number of surviving souvenirs from any other shrine in medieval Christendom.

Pilgrim souvenirs also provide us with an important, if schematic, record of the shrine of St Thomas in the fourteenth century. They show the gabled chest containing Becket's bones, raised high on pillars, encrusted with jewels and topped with larger votive offer-ings, and they provide the earliest evidence of the existence of a little statue which pointed to the shrine's chief glory, the jewel given in 1179 by the King of France and claimed as the largest in existence (Cat. 63).

Other badges that were widely popular in Chaucer's time commemorated Becket's last days, his return from France (Cat. 59), his triumphal ride into Canterbury (Cat. 60, 451) and his murder, with the full comple-ment of four knights, wearing bascinets, body armour and low-slung belts (Cat. 61). Here are to be found all the elements of the martyrdom as they had come, with growing realism, to be depicted by the middle of the fourteenth century. Becket kneels before an altar on which stand a chalice and crucifix (and, on other versions, a retable and a missal). Reinforcing the sense of sacrilege, his vestments are trampled on as his assailants strike from behind, while the clerk, Edward Grim, looks on, aghast but as yet unharmed.

It was at an altar set up on the spot, variously known as the Martyrdom, the Sword or the Sword-Point, where Becket had been slain, that the actual murder weapon was exhibited to pilgrims. This sword, and in particular its point, was a relic of consider-able importance in the thirteenth century and may have accounted for the pointed configuration of many ampullae (Cat. 47–9). In the fourteenth century, however, miniature replicas of the sword were sold as pilgrim signs, some of them designed to slot into matching scabbards (Cat. 62).

The year 1376 was one of the peaks of the Canterbury pilgrimage. Offerings then ex-ceeded those even of the jubilee years 1320 and 1370, when special indulgences and the sense of occasion had boosted the throng of pilgrims. In 1376 the Black Prince's funeral took place at Canterbury in an atmosphere of unprecedented national grief (Cat. 626–33). Four months were required for the prepar-ations, and these are likely to have included such details as the making of funerary badges (Cat. 68–70) and of stylish pilgrim souvenirs (Cat. 65–7). The interest of a courtly clientele in Canterbury at this period doubtless helped to ensure that the artistry of this minor mould-cutting craft transcended both the materials and the methods of multiple pro-duction on which it was based.

The opposing tendency towards naïvety and even banality in this field of popular art is also represented here (Cat. 75), as are the souvenirs of a few of Canterbury's competi-tors, such as Bromholm, St Albans, Bury St Edmunds, Pontefract, Westminster (Cat. 76–81) and, in particular, Walsingham, where the chief attractions were a miracle-working image of the Virgin (Cat. 72) and the Holy House, a replica of the house in Nazar-eth where the Virgin was greeted by Gabriel (Cat. 73–5). Finally, pilgrim signs are set in a wider context by reference to the multitude of devotional (Cat. 82–3) and purely secular (Cat. 84) ornaments that were also products of the English mould-maker's craft in the thirteenth and fourteenth centuries.   BS

43 Ampulla: Pilgrims arriving at Canterbury and miracles at St Thomas's tomb (for reverse, Cat. 44)

43

Early 13th century, before 1220
Tin or tin-lead alloy: h. 9.7 cm, w. 8 cm
Inscr. + EXILITAS OMNIS : OFFERT DOLOR
  EXCIDIT OMNIS : SANA[TVS] BIBIT · COMEDIT ·
  M(?ALVM) CV[M] MORTE RECEDIT (All
  weakness and pain is removed, the healed man
  eats and drinks, and evil and death pass away)
Paris, Musée National des Thermes et de l'Hôtel de
  Cluny, 18063

PROV. Victor Gay Coll.; Musée de Cluny, 1909.

LIT. Gay 1883, pp. 30–1; Spencer 1975, pp. 245–6.

44 Ampulla (very similar to Cat. 43): St Thomas preaching, his murder and burial

Early 13th century, before 1220
Tin or tin-lead: h. 9.5 cm, w. 6.7 cm
The Medieval Collection. Historical Museum,
University of Bergen, Norway

PROV. Excavated at Bryggen, site of the medieval
Hanseatic wharf at Bergen.

LIT. Herteig 1969, pp. 208–9; Bergen 1978, fig.
27 (extreme right).

45 Ampulla: Demi-figure of St Thomas and (on reverse) his murder and burial

Second quarter 13th century
Tin: h. 8.2 cm, w. 7.5 cm
Inscr. OPTIM[V]S EGRORVM : MEDICVS FIT TOMA
BONORVM (Thomas is the best doctor of the
worthy sick)
Museum of London, 8778

PROV. Found in London.

LIT. Guildhall Museum 1908, p. 332, no. 123;
Rydbeck 1964, fig. 3; Spencer 1975, p. 246, fig.
237, no. 3. For virtually identical ampullae found
at York and Lödöse, Sweden (1961), see Smith
1852, pl. XVIII and Rydbeck 1964, fig. 1; for a
closely-related stone mould from the site of 16
Watling Street, Canterbury, see Spencer
(forthcoming).

46 Ampulla: St Thomas giving his blessing and (on reverse) his martyrdom

Mid-13th century
Tin: h. 9.7 cm, w. 8.6 cm
Inscr. +O[P]TIMVS EGRORVM MEDICVS FIT
THOMA BONOR[VM]
Museum of London, TL74 1671

PROV. Found in association with a mid- to late
13th-century waterfront structure excavated at
Trig Lane, Upper Thames Street, London.

LIT. Spencer 1982, pp. 306–7, p. 305 pls 1, 2.

47 Ampulla: St Thomas and his martyrdom

c. 1270
Tin: h. 8.3 cm, w. 8.1 cm
Inscr. OPTIMVS EGRORV[M] + MEDICVS FIT
T[HOMA]+
Southampton City Museums, SOU 163 267

PROV. Found during excavation of cesspit
belonging to 13th-century house in Cuckoo Lane,
Southampton, 1966; among a rich assemblage of
associated finds was the seal of Richard of
Southwick (d. c. 1290). Identical ampullae were
found at Bull Wharf, London, 1980 (private coll.)
and Billingsgate, London, 1984 (Oxford,
Ashmolean Museum, 1986. 1).

LIT. Spencer 1975, fig. 236, no. 2.

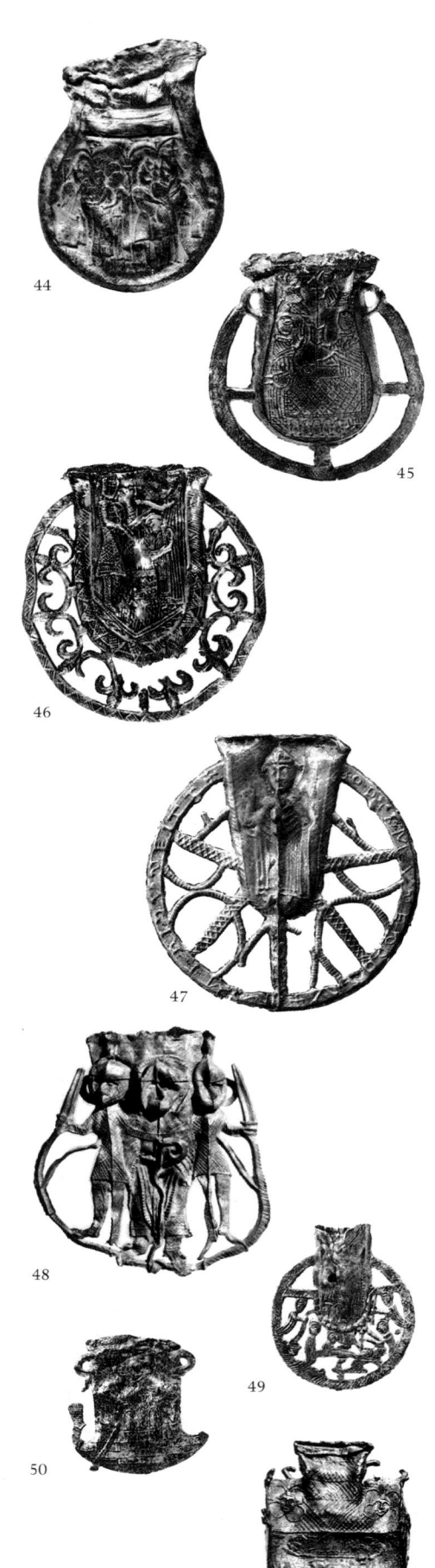

44

45

46

47

48

49

50

51

48 Ampulla: St Thomas between two knights and (on reverse) his martyrdom

First half 13th century
Tin: h. 9.5 cm, w. 8.7 cm
Inscr. + OPTIM[VS] EGROR[VM] MEDIC[VS] FIT
TOMA BONOR[VM]
The Trustees of the British Museum, London,
MLA 1921, 2–16, 62

PROV. Coll. of Thomas Greg; given to British
Museum, 1921. Closely-related ampullae, in
which two angels bearing up Becket's soul take
the place of the knights, have been found at
London (British Museum and private coll.) and in
a mid-13th-century context in High Street, Perth
(Perth, Museum & Art Gallery PHS75,
A04–0682).

LIT. Borenius 1929, p. 33; Borenius 1932a, p. 77,
fig. D.

49 Ampulla: St Thomas, his murder and his burial

Last quarter 13th century
Tin: h. 6.3 cm, w. 5.3 cm
Museum of London, 82.8/1

PROV. Found during redevelopment of Thames
waterfront site of the Newfoundland Company,
Bull Wharf, Upper Thames Street, London, winter
1979–80.

50 Ampulla: St Thomas in a boat, returning from exile, and (on reverse) the Crucifixion with Longinus and Stephaton

First half 13th century
Tin: h. 5.3 cm, w. 5.2 cm
Museum of London, 84.407 (see also Cat. 59)

PROV. Found during archaeological watching-
brief on redevelopment of former market lorry
park, immediately to west of Billingsgate Market,
Lower Thames Street, London, 1984.

51 Ampulla: St Thomas's burial, (on reverse) penance of Henry II and (ends) St Thomas's martyrdom and the Crucifixion

Last quarter 13th century
Tin: h. 4.9 cm, w. 4.5 cm, d. 2 cm
Peter J. Shaffery Collection

PROV. Found at Billingsgate, London, 1984 (see
Cat. 50).

52 Ampulla: St Thomas's martyrdom, (on reverse) penance of Henry II and (ends) St Thomas enthroned and the Crucifixion

Last quarter 13th century
Tin: h. 5.5 cm, w. 4.5 cm, d. 2 cm
Museum of London, 8779

PROV. Found on site of the Steelyard, headquarters of the Hanseatic merchants, Upper Thames Street, London, 1864.

LIT. Cuming 1865, pl. 9, figs 1, 2; Guildhall Museum 1908, pl. LXXIX, 5; Borenius 1929, p. 33, fig. 1.

53 Ampulla: (on one end) St Thomas enthroned and (on other) his martyrdom

Third quarter 13th century
Tin: h. 5.6 cm, w 5.5 cm, d. 3 cm
The Trustees of the British Museum, London, MLA 1985, 10–9, 1

PROV. Found at Billingsgate, London, 1984 (see Cat. 50); identical ampulla recovered from Thames at Billingsgate, 1984 (Cardiff, National Museum of Wales, 1985. 634); similar ampulla recovered (1981) from deposit at Swan Lane, London, datable to 1250–79 (Egan 1986b).

LIT. Cf. Egan 1986b, fig. 11.

54 Pilgrim badge: Head of St Thomas reliquary

c. 1320
Tin-lead: diam. 38 mm; this badge, and all the others listed below, provided with a pin and clasp at the back
The Trustees of the British Museum, London, MLA 1955, 10–1, 1

PROV. Found in River Dove at Tutbury, Derbyshire, 1831, with a hoard of silver pennies; hoard has been linked with the flight of Thomas of Lancaster (cf. Cat. 80) from Tutbury Castle in 1322.

LIT. Tait 1955, p. 39, pl. xvd; Spencer 1968, fig. 1d, p. 138.

55 Pilgrim badge: Head of St Thomas

First quarter 14th century
Tin-lead: h. 8 cm, w. 8 cm
Inscr. + CAPVT SANCTI THOME
Private Collection

PROV. Found at Billingsgate, London, 1984 (see Cat. 50).

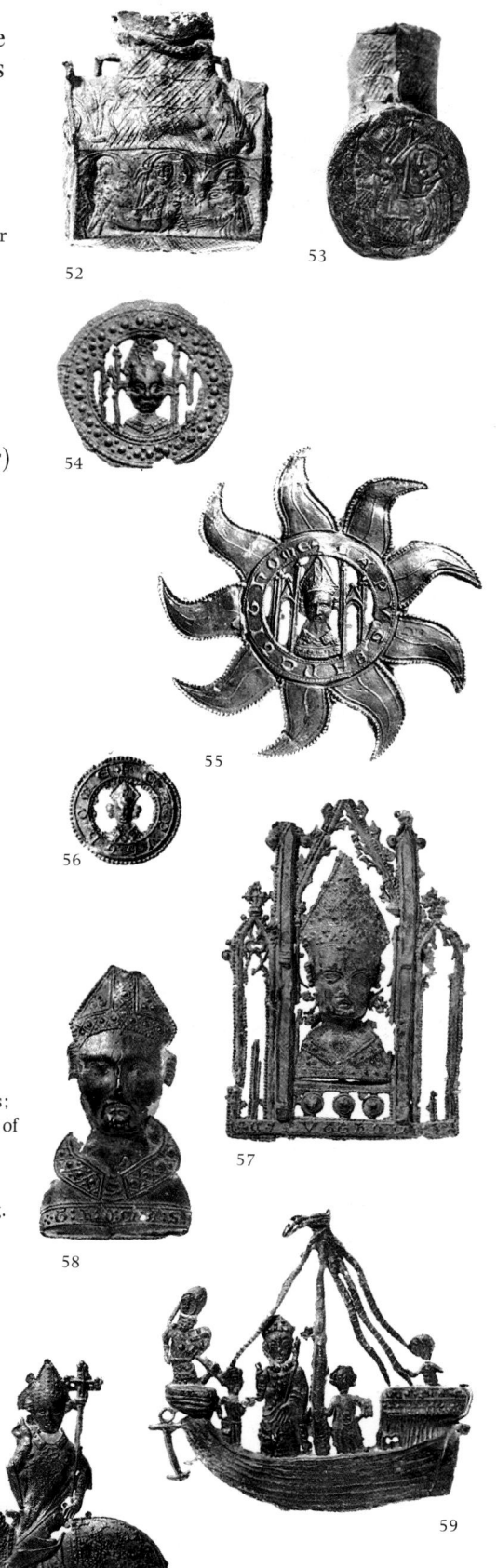

52

53

54

55

56

57

58

59

60

56 Pilgrim badge: Head of St Thomas

Second half 14th century
Tin-lead: diam. 2.4 cm
Inscr. + CAPVT THOME
Museum of London, BC72 2241

PROV. Found during the excavation of 'Baynard's Castle' dock, 1972, in back-fill dated to last quarter of 14th century.

57 Pilgrim badge: Head of St Thomas

Mid-14th century
Tin-lead: h. 9 cm, w. 5.8 cm
Inscr. + CAPVT THOME
Museum of London, 8788

PROV. Found at Dowgate, Upper Thames Street, London.

LIT. Guildhall Museum 1908, pl. LXXVIII, 8.

58 Pilgrim badge: Head of St Thomas

Second half 14th century
Tin-lead: h. 7.8 cm, w. 4.2 cm
Inscr. T : H : O : M : A : S
Museum of London, 80.65/9

PROV. Found at Bull Wharf, London, 1979 (see Cat. 49).

59 Pilgrim badge: St Thomas returning from exile

Late 14th century
Tin-lead: h. 7.5 cm, w. 7.9 cm (see also Cat. 50)
Museum of London, 82.8/3

PROV. Found at Bull Wharf, London, 1980 (see Cat. 49).

LIT. Museum of London 1983, fig. 12; Museum of London 1985, p. 27.

60 Pilgrim badge: St Thomas riding to Canterbury

Second half 14th century
Tin-lead: h. 8.4 cm, w. 8.2 cm (see also Cat. 451)
D. Morgan, Esq.

PROV. Found at Billingsgate, London, 1984 (see Cat. 50).

LIT. Cf. Spencer 1968, pl. VI, 1 & 9; Spencer 1982, pp. 309–11.

61 Pilgrim badge: St Thomas's martyrdom

Mid-14th century
Tin-lead: h. 6.6 cm, w. 6.6 cm
Messrs R. and I. Smith

PROV. Found in Thames at Brooks Wharf, London, 1983.

62 Pilgrim badges: Souvenirs of the sword that killed Becket

Late 14th century
Tin-lead (59.6% : 40.4%): overall h. 14.5 cm, w. 3.6 cm
Museum of London, TL74 602; SWA81, 915; and 79.135/4

PROV. Found respectively at Trig Lane, London, 1974, on a patch of foreshore datable to before *c.* 1440; in a context datable to *c.* 1390–1400 at Swan Lane, Upper Thames Street, London, in the course of watching brief during redevelopment of car park site, 1981; and on Thames foreshore at Queenhithe, 1977.

LIT. Spencer 1982, pp. 313–14; Museum of London 1985, p. 27.

63 Pilgrim badge: Shrine of St Thomas of Canterbury

Second half 14th century
Tin-lead: h. 7.5 cm, w. 5.7 cm
Museum of London, BC72.1555

PROV. Found at 'Baynard's Castle' dock, London, 1972 (see Cat. 56).

LIT. Spencer 1982, pp. 311–12.

64 Pilgrim sign: Canterbury bell

Late 14th century
Bell tin with bismuth (99% : 1%), clapper and split pin tin-lead (65% : 35%): h. 6.5 cm, diam. 6 cm
Museum of London, 80.65/10

PROV. Found at Bull Wharf, London, 1979 (see Cat. 49).

65 Pilgrim badges: Virgin and Child (?Our Lady Undercroft, Canterbury) flanked by St Edward the Confessor and St Thomas of Canterbury

Second half 14th century
Tin-lead: h. 13.5 cm, w. 8.7 cm; fitted with two pins at the back
Museum of London, 84.394 and BWB83.201

PROV. Found at Billingsgate, London, 1984 (see Cat. 50); the smaller fragment (the supporting angel) found separately, probably from a different badge cast from the same mould; part of a variant from same site has St Thomas as the large central figure.

LIT. Egan 1986b, fig. 10.

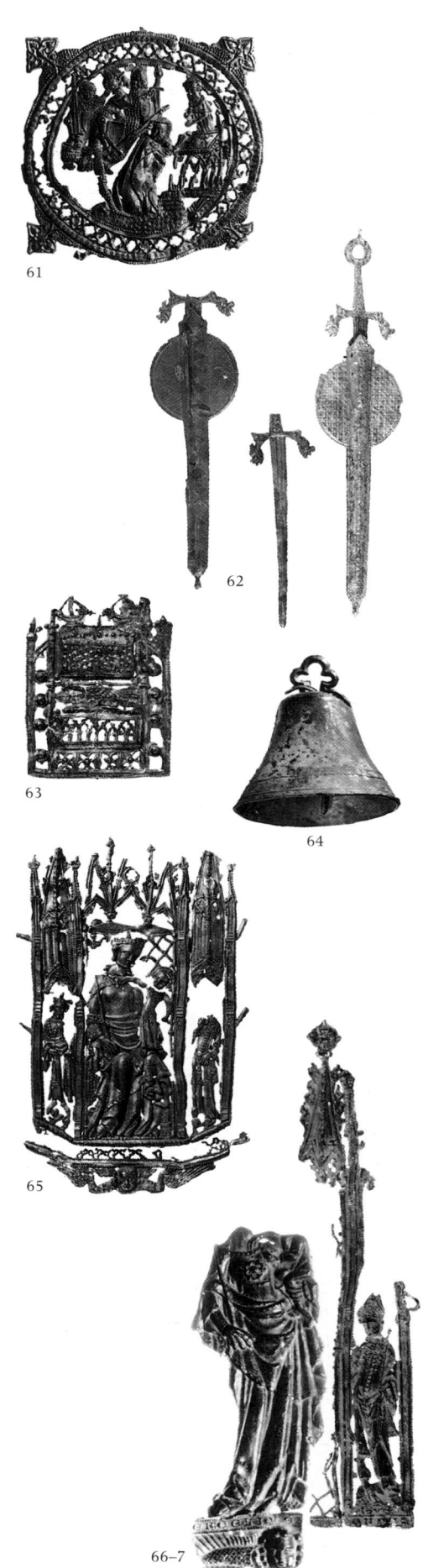

61

62

63

64

65

66–7

66–7 Pilgrim badges (variants of Cat. 65)

Second half 14th century
Tin-lead, with vermilion in the folds of the Virgin's garment: figure h. 9 cm, w. 3.5 cm; side panel h. 12.2 cm, w. 2.5 cm
Inscr. (DEI MA)TER : CELI·REG(I)NA MONDI: beneath the figure of St Thomas, SA[NC]TVS T[HOMA]S
Norfolk Museums Service (King's Lynn Museums), PB 28 (Virgin); Museum of London, A14581/1 (side panel)

PROV. Figure of the Virgin found in River Purfleet, King's Lynn; collection of Thomas Pung; Greenland Fishery Museum, Lynn; King's Lynn Museum, 1946. Side panel found in Thames at London Bridge.

LIT. London, London Museum 1940, pl. LXXII, 52; Spencer 1980, p. 28.

68 Funerary badge: The Black Prince worshipping the Trinity, within the Garter

c. 1376
Tin-lead: h. 10.2 cm, w. 7.9 cm
Inscr. in black letter *honi soyt ke mal y pense*
The Trustees of the British Museum, London, MLA OA 100

PROV. Not recorded.

LIT. Nicolas 1846a, pp. 140–1; Hume 1863, pp. 120, 142; Hope 1913b, pp. 260–3, fig. 153; Spencer 1972, cover; Marks & Payne 1978, p. 129, no. 255; Spencer 1982, pp. 318–20, fig 2b p. 317.

68

69

69 Funerary badge (variant of Cat. 68)

c. 1376
Tin-lead: h. 8.6 cm, w. 6.6 cm
Inscr. in black letter *the : trynyty (& seynt geor)g : be at : oure : endyng :*
Museum of London, TL74 1428

PROV. Found during excavation of a late 14th–early 15th-century deposit at Trig Lane, Upper Thames Street, London, 1974.

LIT. Spencer 1982, pp. 316–20, fig. 2a.

70   Funerary badge: The Black Prince's ostrich feather

c. 1376
Tin-lead: h. 11.1 cm, w. 5.2 cm
Inscr. in black letter *ich dene*
Museum of London, BC72 1821

PROV. Found at 'Baynard's Castle' dock, London, 1972 (see Cat. 56).

71   Ampulla: Church with an image of the Virgin (?Our Lady of Walsingham) and the Coronation of the Virgin

Mid-13th century
Tin: h. 5.5 cm, w. 4.5 cm, d. 1 cm
Inscr. flanking Coronation ECCE/SVA D/EXT/RA MA/TRE/M DE/VS I/PSE C/ORO/NAT flanking image ECCE/ CORO/MATE/[*sic*] GLO/RIA/ NA/TVS/ HO/MO
Private Collection

PROV. Found at Bull Wharf, London, 1980 (see Cat. 49); identical examples excavated from an early 14th-century context at High Street, Perth, 1979 (Perth, Museum and Art Gallery, PHS 77, A04–0214) and from a deposit datable to *c.* 1270 at Swan Lane, London, 1981 (Museum of London, SWA 81 2097).

72   Pilgrim badge: Our Lady of Walsingham

End 14th century
Tin-lead (62.7% : 37.3%): h. 5.2 cm, w. 4 cm
Museum of London, 82.8/4

PROV. Found on Thames foreshore at Brooks Wharf, Upper Thames Street, London, 1979.

LIT. Cf. Spencer 1980, p. 10.

73   Pilgrim badge: The Holy House of Walsingham with the Annunciation

Late 14th century
Tin-lead: h. 3.8 cm, w. 3.3 cm
Collection of Mr E. G. Lake

PROV. Found on Thames foreshore at Swan Wharf, London Bridge, 1976.

LIT. Cf. Spencer 1980, pp. 11–12.

74   Pilgrim badge: The cult of the Annunciation at Walsingham

First half 14th century
Tin-lead: h. 8.6 cm, w. 5.9 cm
Inscr. ECCE ANC[I]L[A]DOMIN[I]/ AVE: MARIA
Museum of London, A17216

PROV. Found in Thames at Tower Bridge, London, 1891.

LIT. London, London Museum 1937, pl. XXV, 2; London, London Museum 1940, p. 257, pl. LXIX, 14; Spencer 1968, pl. II, no. 1.

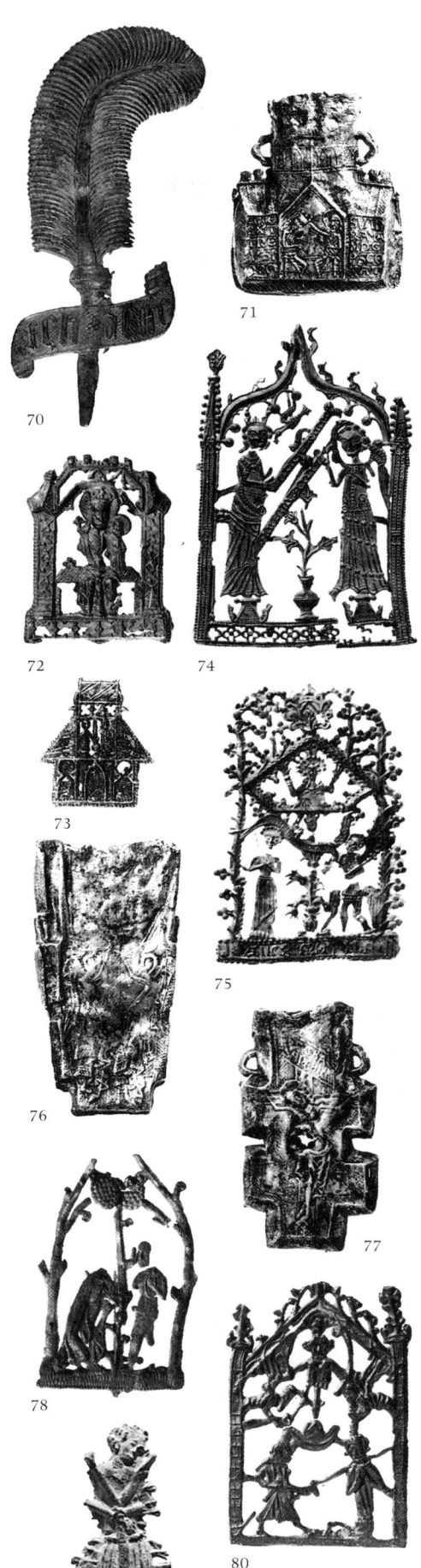

75   Pilgrim badge: The Annunciation with God the Father

Early 15th century
Tin-lead: h. 7.6 cm, w. 4.8 cm
Inscr. in black letter *Aue gras[i]a plena*
Messrs R. and I. Smith

PROV. Found at Bull Wharf, London, 1979 (see Cat. 49).

76   Ampulla: The Holy Cross of Bromholm, Norfolk, and the Feast of the Exaltation

Mid-13th century
Tin: h. 7.5 cm, w. 4 cm
Museum of London, TL74 1672

PROV. Found at Trig Lane, London (see Cat. 46).

LIT. Spencer 1982, pp. 307–9, pls 3, 4.

77   Ampulla: Bromholm Holy Cross

Second quarter 13th century
Tin: h. 6.9 cm, w. 3.6 cm
Inscr. (front) IESVS NA/SARENVS
        (back) RA/DI/X
Museum of London, 83.367

PROV. Found at Billingsgate, London, 1983 (see Cat. 50), fixed by a nail to a piece of wood (not conserved).

78   Pilgrim badge: The martyrdom of St Alban

Second half 14th century
Tin-lead: h. 7 cm, w. 4.3 cm
The Trustees of the British Museum, London, MLA 56, 7–1, 2095

PROV. Found in London; C. Roach Smith Coll.

LIT. Spencer 1969, pp. 34–5, fig. 7.

79   Pilgrim sign: The martyrdom of St Edmund

Late 13th/early 14th century
Tin, hollow-cast: h. 6.6 cm, w. 2.7 cm
John Auld, Esq.

PROV. Found at Bull Wharf, London, 1979 (see Cat. 49).

80   Pilgrim badge: The execution of Thomas of Lancaster and the ascent of his soul

Second quarter 14th century
Tin-lead: h. 9.1 cm, w. 6 cm
The Trustees of the British Museum, London, MLA 1984, 5–5, 2

PROV. Found at Billingsgate, London, 1984 (Cat. 50).

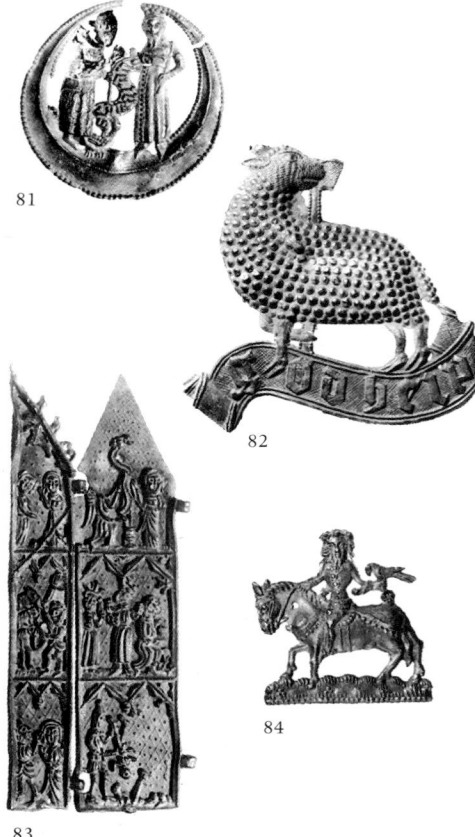

81

82

83

84

85

224

81 Pilgrim badge: St Edward the Confessor and the Pilgrim

Last quarter 14th century
Tin-lead: h. 5.3 cm, w. 5.2 cm
Inscr. in black letter *s edwardus*
Norfolk Museums Service (King's Lynn Museums), PB 67

PROV. From the Mill Fleet, King's Lynn (cf. Cat. 67); upper half of the Pilgrim lost during World War II.

LIT. Spencer 1968, fig. 3a; London 1972, no. 207, xxiii; Spencer 1980, p. 21.

82 Devotional badge: The Paschal Lamb

Last quarter 14th century
Tin-lead: h. 7.6 cm, w. 7.7 cm
Inscr. in black letter *god help* (cf. epigraphy of Cat. 68–70)
J. T. Dartnall, Esq.

PROV. Found on Thames foreshore at Queenhithe, 1979.

83 Leaves from triptych

First half 14th century
Tin-lead: h. 11.5 cm, w. 6.7 cm
Norfolk Museums Service (King's Lynn Museums), PB89

PROV. From River Purfleet, King's Lynn (see Cat. 66–7).

LIT. Tait 1955, pl. XIVc; London 1972, no. 207, xl; Spencer 1982, pp. 26–8.

84 Decorative badge: Man hawking

Late 14th century
Tin-lead: h. 4.4 cm, w. 4.1 cm
Museum of London, 82.8/15

PROV. Found at Bull Wharf, London, 1979 (see Cat. 49).

85 Statuette of a queen enthroned, probably the Virgin

First half 14th century
Tin or tin-lead: h. 8.6 cm, w. 2.8 cm, d. 2.6 cm
Private Collection

PROV. Found in River Avon, Salisbury, 1986.

86 Part of the brass of St Thomas Cantilupe

1282–7
Latten: h. 10.1 cm
The Dean and Chapter of Hereford

The figure of St Ethelbert, King and Martyr, is seated on a chest-like throne with his feet on a footstool, dressed in flowing robes, and holding his crowned head against his chest.

The brass comes from the tomb of St Thomas Cantilupe, Bishop of Hereford, who died at Montefiascone, Italy in 1282. The tomb still retains a coffin-shaped Purbeck

86

slab with indents for the full-length figure of a bishop under a canopy, two small figures (including the present exhibit), detached fleurs-de-lis, and a marginal inscription on a fillet. In the accounts of miracles at his tomb collected by the Papal Commissioners for his canonisation (in 1320) is one relating to the cure of John Tregoz who in November, 1287, kept vigil at the tomb and had a vision of a bishop in white vestments who 'came out from under the image of brass which is fixed upon the sarcophagus of the man of God'. This must have been the one to which the present figure belongs, so establishing its date and making it the earliest identifiable portion of a figure brass in the country. It cannot be related closely in style to the next earliest group (see Cat. 138), but there is no reason to doubt that it was made in England, though probably under French influence.   CB

PROV. Hereford Cathedral.

LIT. Emmerson 1980; Binski 1987, pp. 70–3, figs 17, 50.

87

87 Becket reliquary châsse

Limoges, c. 1200–10
Copper alloy, with champlevé enamels, and oak:
  h. 17.2 cm, w. 12.1 cm
The Burrell Collection, Glasgow Museums and Art
  Galleries, 26/6

The enamel plaques are mounted on a solid wooden core (not original); a side and centre back panel are missing, also part of the roof cresting (now in two pieces) and an assassin's head. The front is enamelled with the martyrdom of Thomas Becket, with the apotheosis of the saint above.

Becket is mitred, before an altar on which stand a chalice and paten, book and pyx (indicated by h̄: host): two knights attack him, while a *Manus Dei* (Hand of God) emerges from a cloud above. The personified soul of Thomas rises to Heaven supported by two angels.

The side panel shows an unidentified saint standing under an arch. The heads of all figures save this and that of Thomas are cast separately and pinned on. The back (roof) is enamelled with a double row of five four-petalled flowers, bordered by a row of crosses. The colours used are opaque blues – light, mid and dark – red, green, yellow and white.

Base-metal pilgrim souvenirs for Becket's cult were made in Canterbury, but the enamel reliquary châsses, of which over forty-five still survive, were produced in Limoges, mainly c. 1200–50. Thomas is invariably shown at Mass, attacked by between one and three murderers, although it is a historical fact that there were four (Rupin 1890, pp. 396–9; Barlow 1986). These caskets were merely a version of the basic design of Limoges reliquary, themselves a variation upon a common type of relic container produced throughout Europe (Braun 1940, pp. 163–85). The (missing) centre back panel here would have covered a lid, hinged to allow access to the relics, the original casket being hollow.

Limoges was in the Middle Ages a large-scale manufacturer of champlevé enamelled objects; more of its products have survived than from anywhere else. Characterised by vivid blues and stylised rosettes, the enamels were widely exported; many have been found in England. Limoges basins are known to have been given to Rochester Cathedral by the Prior Elias (*fl.* 1214–15), and in 1240 Henry III bought two pairs of Limoges basins for St Stephen's Chapel, Westminster (Lehmann-Brockhaus 1955–60, no. 3752).

This is one of the few Becket reliquaries with an English provenance of antiquity. Its association with Becket's own county by adoption is unique; it may originally have belonged to a Kentish church (Borenius 1933, pp. 177–8).　　　　MLC

PROV. John Batteley (1647–1708), Archdeacon of Canterbury; Thomas Barrett (d. 1758), of Lee Priory, near Canterbury; sold London, 21 Feb. 1758 (Barrett sale, no. 80) to Horace Walpole of Strawberry Hill; beq. to Mrs Damer; given to Dowager Countess of Waldegrave; sold by her to Walter Sneyd, 1842; possibly disposed of before 1862 (Caudron 1975, pp. 37–8); in Leopold Hirsch Coll., by 1933; bt by John Hunt; bt by Sir William Burrell, 1934; given by him to Glasgow City Art Gallery, 1958.

LIT. Cole MS 1762, ff. 151–2; Borenius 1933, p. 177, repr.; Caudron 1975, no. 3, pp. 34–8, 65–8, 102–3, 121–2; London 1975, no. 372.

88 Reliquary casket

c. 1400
Copper alloy, engraved, enamelled and gilt:
  h. 15 cm, l. 11.5 cm, w. 6.6 cm
The Board of Trustees of the Victoria and Albert
  Museum, London, 634–1870

The sheet-metal box is riveted and soldered together; the feet and figures are cast. On the front of the lid a plaque enamelled (in opaque red and black) shows St George on horseback lancing the dragon, the rescued princess kneeling on the right. Holes and patches bare of gilding on the casket indicate the position of the figures on the sides and a roundel on the back. On the body of the box are engraved: (front) a tonsured priest with dragon, beside the Virgin and Child; (left side) a female saint with sceptre, holding a church, perhaps St Etheldreda; (right side) a female saint, perhaps St Hilda, holding a bird.

On the back is a ring handle, riveted on, and engraved acanthus scrollwork springing from a devil's head. Similar acanthus is engraved beneath the St George plaque. The six small cast and chased figures are of differing sizes, and stylistically of two different dates: the Virgin, St Lawrence with gridiron, and boy in tunic, c. 1400; bishop with crosier, St Etheldreda (?) with church, and a male saint with a corn sheaf, of the later fifteenth century. All may then have been added, with the enamel plaque and gilding.

This form of reliquary casket is found throughout Europe in the Middle Ages (Braun 1940, pp. 121–30), and might have contained relics of one or more saints depicted on it. The style of the acanthus compares with that on the Godsfield pyx (Cat. 119); St George wears armour current c. 1400. If St Etheldreda, patron of Ely Cathedral, is correctly identified this may point to an East Anglian origin for the casket. The awkward combination of enamel, engraving and relief figures is a clumsy imitation of goldsmiths' work (cf. Cat. 582).　　　　MLC

PROV. G. Phillips; bt by V&A, 1870.

LIT. Wall 1905, pl. 6; Oman 1962b, pp. 203–4; Norwich 1973, no. 83.

88

III The English Church

Medieval society below the king was divided by contemporaries into men of prayer (*oratores*), that is the members of the Church who had taken religious vows, men of war (*bellatores*), that is the feudal nobility and knights, and men of toil (*laboratores*), that is the peasantry.

By the thirteenth century the English Church was highly organised: a hierarchy of ecclesiastical courts and ordained clergy descended from the Archbishops of Canterbury and York to the large numbers of minor clerks giving assistance to the beneficed clergy in the parishes. England comprised a large number of parishes (in the region of 9,500) but, compared with other European countries, a small number of dioceses: three in the province of York and a total of eighteen in the province of Canterbury (fig. 127). Even so, there was a great variety of bishoprics, from the extremely wealthy like Winchester, to the extremely poor, like St Asaph. A few dioceses were very large: Lincoln (with eight archdeaconries), Coventry and Lichfield, and York (each with five archdeaconries). The superiority of Canterbury to York was no longer in any kind of doubt. Indeed, Pope Nicholas III is reported to have said in 1278 that the Church of Canterbury was second only in importance to the Church of Rome. The English Church with its spiritual and ever-developing administrative and legal powers, had at its head the pope, and its law was Roman canon law.

The parish clergy were controlled more and more by their bishops, especially as a result of the bishops' newly acquired right to institute to benefices, that is to take the final step in the process of appointment. Efforts were being made by many bishops to ensure that the men in charge of the cure of souls had at least a basic level of learning. Each rector of a church enjoyed its income, derived mainly from a tenth of the produce of the land of the parishioners – the tithes. But the rector, often in fact not an individual but a monastery, could put a vicar in charge of the church and the vicar was paid a stipend. The incomes of churches varied very greatly, and it is clear that many of the clergy, including the chaplains who assisted in the church, were among the poor of the parish. But there was certainly scope for the able and well-placed to gain advancement and wealth within the Church. It remained possible for clerics, despite legislation to the contrary, to accumulate benefices, especially the prebends of collegiate churches, the most important of which were cathedral churches.

Ecclesiastical advancement was secured largely through the influence of patrons: monasteries, bishops, nobles and, of course, the king. Patronage rights in churches and in monasteries, although often in dispute, were long-established rights stretching back to the early twelfth century and beyond. It was the twelfth century which had seen the rapid expansion in monastic orders, notable among them the Augustinian canons with about two hundred and fifty houses, and the much wealthier Cistercians with over one hundred houses, the most important being Fountains and Rievaulx (Yorkshire), Furness (Lancashire) and Waverley (Surrey). Despite these developments the large Benedictine houses, many of which were of much more ancient foundation, remained the most influential of all the monasteries. Some of these had become cathedral churches: Christ Church Canterbury, Rochester, Ely, Norwich, Winchester, Worcester, Bath, Coventry and Durham. Among the rest there were many that were large and wealthy: the great abbeys of Abingdon, Bury St Edmunds, St Augustine's Canterbury, Chester, Crowland, Evesham, Glastonbury, Gloucester, Malmesbury, Peterborough, Ramsey, Reading, St Albans, Tewkesbury, St Mary's York, and, of course, Westminster.

The new spiritual drive of the thirteenth century was away from these land-owning and church-owning corporations. Houses of mendicant friars, mostly Franciscans (Grey Friars; see Cat. 107) and Dominicans (Black Friars), spread into the towns from the early years of the thirteenth century (see fig. 128). Soon they influenced most

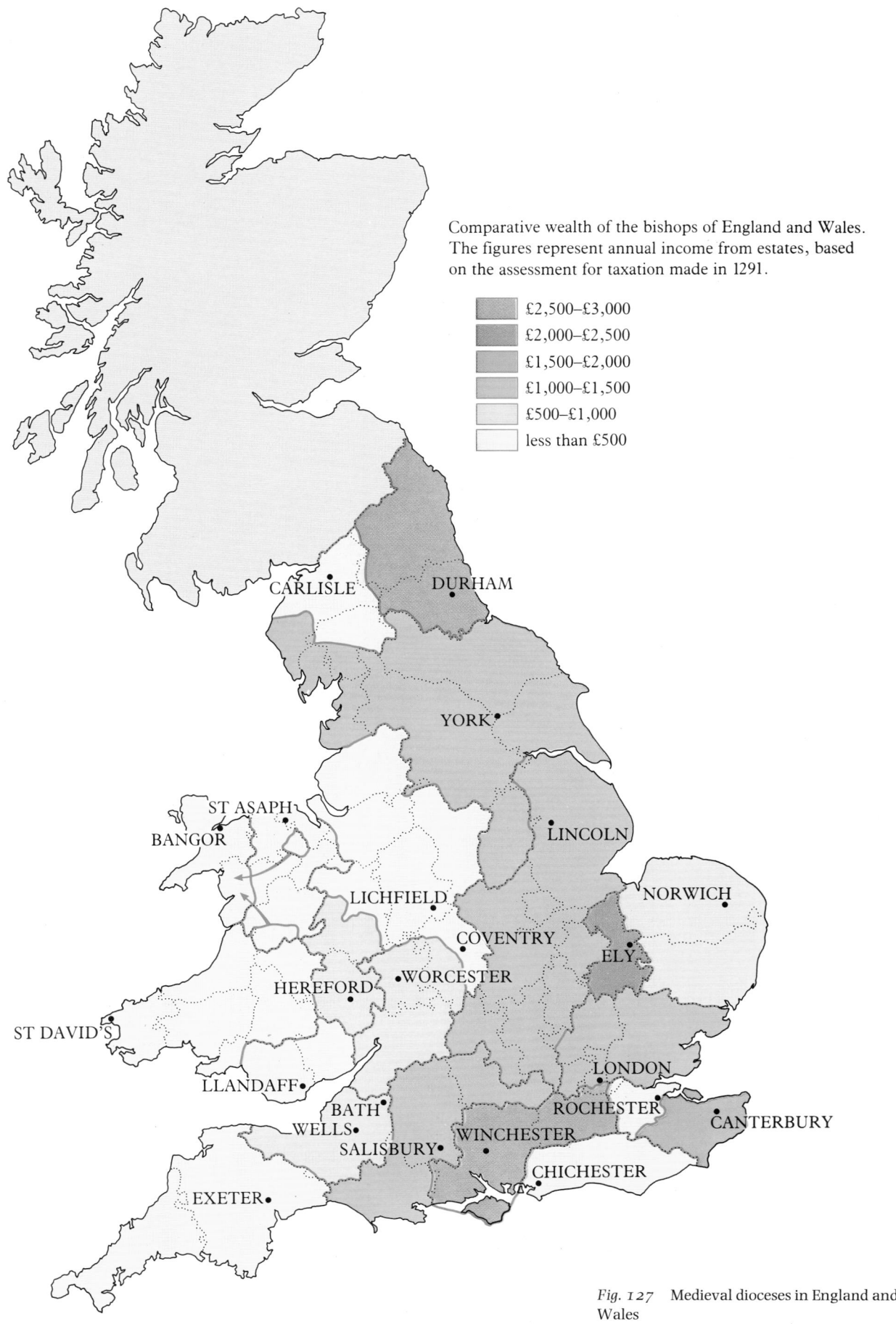

Comparative wealth of the bishops of England and Wales.
The figures represent annual income from estates, based
on the assessment for taxation made in 1291.

- £2,500–£3,000
- £2,000–£2,500
- £1,500–£2,000
- £1,000–£1,500
- £500–£1,000
- less than £500

CARLISLE
DURHAM
YORK
ST ASAPH
BANGOR
LINCOLN
NORWICH
LICHFIELD
COVENTRY
ELY
HEREFORD
WORCESTER
ST DAVID'S
LONDON
LLANDAFF
BATH
ROCHESTER
WELLS
CANTERBURY
SALISBURY
WINCHESTER
CHICHESTER
EXETER

Fig. 127 Medieval dioceses in England and
Wales

aspects of the Church's work, from the universities and the royal Court down to the parishes. As preachers, teachers and confessors, the mendicants called for relatively little by way of grants and endowments. The magnate class, however, continued to be active ecclesiastical patrons. The foundation of monasteries was superseded by the foundation of chantries, that is the establishment of chaplains, with endowments to support them, in colleges (see Cat. 136) or parish churches. These provided special masses on which the ultimate salvation of the founder depended and often, though incidentally, to provide works of charity, as for the support of a school or an almshouse. While the popularity of chantries in the later Middle Ages is partly explained by the comparatively small endowments needed, even so the rich provided extremely elaborate chantry chapels and costly tombs. The work of the Church and local family interests were still closely linked.

89

90

89 West Walton Church, Norfolk, nave from north aisle looking south-east

c. 1240
Photograph

West Walton is one of the most elaborate parish churches of the mid-thirteenth century, demonstrating the prosperity of the towns and villages around the Wash. It displays characteristics of the Early English style clearly derived from Lincoln (Cat. 240) and rarely found outside the great churches. The nave arcade has cylindrical piers with circular bases and abaci, surrounded by four, occasionally eight, detached shafts of Purbeck marble, some now modestly replaced in wood. The prominent shaft rings were needed because the marble was despatched from the quarries in short lengths to reduce the risk of breakage in transit. The capitals have luxuriant, fully-developed stiff-leaf foliage, and the wide arcade arches have complex mouldings, including hood moulds on both sides. The deep-splayed clerestory windows are contained within a continuous row of arches which, curiously, do not coincide exactly with the main arcade. The aisles were greatly enlarged in the late Middle Ages, and the shields in the spandrels are also a later addition.   PD

LIT. Pevsner 1973a.

90 Holy Trinity Church, Hull, choir looking east

c. 1320s and later
Photograph

Holy Trinity was built after Edward I refounded Kingston-upon-Hull as a new town and royal borough in 1299. Although not of full parochial status, it was for parochial use, and it is one of the earliest churches to reflect the influence of the great new preaching churches of the friars, both in the ground plan, a rectangle with barely projecting transepts, and the details of the elevation.

Built externally of brick with stone dressings and internally of stone, Holy Trinity is a thin, light, wooden-roofed structure with wide interior spaces, slender supports and large windows. The main elevation has two storeys, with two clerestory windows to each bay. The pier form, a quatrefoil shape of four shafts separated by sunk chamfers, later to become a standard pier design for parish churches, seems to be derived from a mendicant context: although the Hull piers are among the earliest to survive, similar piers existed in the choir of the Franciscan church in Newgate, London, built from *c.* 1306, probably by the royal mason Walter of Hereford.

The Hull choir probably dates from *c.* 1320s, but the flowing tracery of the windows is almost certainly later. Its near parallels are with buildings of the 1340s, a date also indicated by the more rectilinear appearance of the main east window.   NC

LIT. Clapham & Godfrey 1913, p. 253; VCH, *Yorkshire, East Riding*, I, pp. 18, 20; Morris 1978, p. 31; Wilson 1980a, p. 370, n. 64; Harvey 1984, p. 137.

91 St John's Church, Yeovil, exterior from south-west

Begun before 1382
Photograph

St John's, Yeovil, Somerset, is an outstanding example of a Perpendicular parish church built to a unified design in one continuous campaign. The will of Robert de Sambourne, rector from 1362 to his death in 1382, left money 'to the works of Yeovil Church begun by me'. Presumably building had started with the chancel, the part for which rectors were legally responsible. Yeovil Church was begun just as Somerset's late medieval church building boom was getting under way, and many features of its design were to be influential, notably the hall church format and the simple 'honeycomb' tracery. The east window and the end windows of the transeptal chapels have slightly richer tracery than the rest. By fifteenth-century Somerset standards the west tower is both modest and

91

creating the arches across the central aisle. The latter arches support cambered collar beams. connected to the ridge by king posts. The side aisles repeat this construction in miniature: braced tie beams support vertical struts which, in turn, support the principal rafters which butt into the continued uprights of the pillars below the main collars.

PC

LIT. Crossley 1937. p. 134; Crossley 1940; Horn 1958, pp. 2–23; Alexander & Crossley 1976, p. 120.

92 Church of St James and St Paul, Marton, Cheshire, interior of nave

14th century and later
Photograph

With the Church of St Oswald in Lower Peover, Marton is possibly the earliest surviving example of a longitudinal half-timbered church in Europe. It was founded by Sir John Davenport at some time in the reign of Edward III (about 1350?). A deed of 1390 by

another, later, Sir John Davenport, gives four messuages and sixty acres of land to maintain a priest for the chapel of Marton, by which date the present building may have been substantially complete. In the eighteenth century the chancel and side chapels were rebuilt in brick, and restorations of 1850 and 1871 removed the north door, refaced the brick exterior with half-timbering, and gave the belfry its present shape. Originally the western porch was wider, so that the aisles of the church may have run back to include the porch and its tower. This, together with the type of belfry construction (with large scissor braces across the central space) is reminiscent of the medieval wooden belfries of Essex (e.g. Blackmore).

The roof runs in a single span over main and side aisles. The nave is divided into three bays by four octagonal wooden pillars. Arch braces spring from their capitals on three sides, the eastern and western forming the arcade arches, the northern and southern

in proportion to the body of the church. Bequests to the fabric were still being made in 1400, so the tower was probably not complete before then. Along with the bell tower at New College (Cat. 599), the Yeovil tower is among the earliest of innumerable late medieval flat-topped church towers, a characteristically English type very consonant with the general rectilinearity of Perpendicular architecture.

CW

93 Chancel scheme: scenes from the Life of Christ and the Death of the Virgin; Tree of Jesse; Last Judgement

c. 1325–30
Wall painting in Church of St Mary, Chalgrove, Oxfordshire
Photograph

This virtually complete scheme provides one of the best impressions of a fully painted parish church interior of the period. On the north side, following a Tree of Jesse at the west end, a christological cycle of the Infancy and Passion culminates on the east wall in the Resurrection and Ascension. Similarly, on the south side a cycle of the Death of the Virgin ends on the east wall in her Assumption and Coronation, paralleling the scenes on the other side of the east window. The Virgin, interceding with bared breast, also features prominently in the Judgement at the west end of the south wall, with its two tiers of resurrecting souls still draped in their grave shrouds.

With its three-tiered division of scenes and the consistency of its subject-matter, the

92

93

scheme is unusually coherent for the period (cf. Cat. 136). Yet the apparent order is belied by the eccentric narrative sequence, which proceeds in a zigzag fashion up the centre of the side walls. The exceptionally long cycle of eleven scenes from the Death of the Virgin, including the Gathering of the Apostles and the Attack on the Bier by the Jewish 'prince of priests', conforms closely to the account in the *Golden Legend*. The concentration on the Virgin is obviously appropriate to the dedication, but such subject-matter is particularly popular in wall painting and other media at this date: see e.g. the early fourteenth-century wall paintings at Croughton, Northamptonshire (Tristram & James 1927) and the Taymouth Hours.

The recent cleaning of the paintings (completed 1986) reveals them as competent though unexceptional provincial work. They are clearly coeval with the chancel, rebuilt *c.* 1325–30 (Maynard 1986). DP

LIT. Tristram 1955, pp. 84–6, 153–5, pls. 30–40; Ashby 1980, pp. 122–4; Maynard 1986.

Seals and ecclesiastical hierarchy

The seals in use at Exeter Cathedral from *c.* 1280 to 1340 demonstrate clearly the ways in which relative importance was indicated by size. Not surprisingly, the cathedral itself had the largest seal (85 mm high), and the bishops' came next. The archdeacon merited something less pretentious (58 mm) but still grander than those at the lowliest level, the canons. Even those canons with titles, such as the precentor, had seals only about 40–45 mm in height. The archdeacon's official ranked at this level. TAH

94 Second seal of Exeter Cathedral

c. 1280
Wax: h. 8.5 cm, w. 5 cm
Inscr. SIGILLUM ECCLESIE BEATI PETRI EXONIE
British Library, Add. Charter 15453

The mid-eleventh-century seal of Exeter Cathedral was still in use in 1279 (London, Public Record Office, E329/213). The elegant pose of St Peter on the new seal and the style of his vestments suggest a date of origin very soon after this. The only anomaly is the canopy, which may perhaps be an updated version of a design common in the second quarter of the century (Cat. 283). Peter Quivel was consecrated Bishop of Exeter in 1280. At some point during his eleven-year episcopate he used a seal which showed him enthroned (cf. Cat. 285–6) and with a canopy over his head (Birch 1887, I, no. 1550) very much in the manner of the cathedral seal's image of St Peter. The two

94

seals in use together must have been intended to indicate the equation between St Peter as Christ's vicar on earth and the bishop as St Peter's vicar at Exeter. Peter is indeed shown with the two symbols of his Christ-given authority; a church ('... thou art Peter, and upon this rock I will build my church') and the keys ('... I will give unto thee the keys of the kingdom of heaven' – *Matthew* XVI, 18–19). He is vested as pope, wearing the papal tiara with a single crown.

This seal is remarkably modest for a cathedral. Both before and after *c.* 1280 it was common for cathedrals having a new seal made to commission a large, round, two-piece matrix. Exeter was content with a single-sided oval, albeit a rather large one. TAH

LIT. Birch 1887, I, no. 1579.

95 Seal of John Grandisson, Bishop of Exeter 1327–69

Before April 1328
Wax: h. 7 cm, w. 4.1 cm
Inscr. S' IOHIS DEI GRA EPI EXONIENSIS above shield of arms in base DE GRANDISONO
British Library, Add. charter 15453

Grandisson was consecrated bishop in Avignon and did not arrive in England until 3 February 1328. There is an impression of this seal on a charter of 7 April 1328 (Hereford Cathedral Library A 1433), so Grandisson either had the matrix made immediately after his return, or quite possibly it is of foreign manufacture. Like so much of Grandisson's artistic patronage (pp. 463–7) this seal is eccentric. It is rather small, and the attenuated form of his body is hard to parallel in England at this period. The source for the understated ogee arch above his head is the second seal of Louis X of France. Not only the form of the arch, but the small pinnacles which frame it and the central trefoil with two crockets to either side, are direct borrowings (cf. Cat. 670). Also from Louis' seal is the

95

lion-headed throne draped in an identical manner with a heavy cloth. Grandisson was probably unique among bishops in using a royal seal as a partial model for his own.

The appearance of an enthroned figure on the seal of an earlier bishop of Exeter has been noted above (Cat. 94). Among Grandisson's contemporaries, Adam of Orleton as Bishop of Hereford had used the form (Birch 1887, I, no. 1607).

Birch neglects to mention the tiny counterseal showing a half-length image of the Virgin and Child with the legend EGO SUM MATER MISERICORDIE. TAH

LIT. Birch 1887, I, no. 1557; Morgan & Morgan 1966.

96 Seal of Thomas de Massington, Archdeacon of Exeter 1331–45

1331–7
Wax: h. 5.8 cm, w. 3.6 cm
Inscr. S' THOME DE MASSINGTONE ARCHIDIACONI EXONIE P T M P
British Library, Add. Charter 15453

The P T M P between the pinnacles at the top of the legend rim identifies the four saints represented; from left to right they are Peter, Thomas Becket and Paul, with Mary above. Becket's presence is probably to be explained by the archdeacon's own Christian name.

96

Seals showing a small figure kneeling in prayer beneath an arch at the base had been common since soon after 1200 (Cat. 282, counterseal), but it was unusual to include more than two saints before the mid-fourteenth century. Both in that sense and by virtue of its elaborate architectural surround, Massington's seal is precocious. It shows that innovation is not the prerogative of the wealthy and powerful. Indeed they were often more reluctant to break with established traditions. TAH

LIT. 1887, I, no. 1586.

97 Seal of the Official of the Archdeacon of Exeter

c. 1330
Wax: h. 4.5 cm, w. 2.5 cm
Inscr. s' OFFICIAL ARCHIDIACONI EXONIE
British Library, Add. Charter 15453

As the legend does not mention the name of any individual, it is clear that this seal was intended for use by whoever held the post of archdeacon's official. It is one of at least three seals used by successive officials over the period 1267–1367. The three are very similar in size, legend and motif. Presumably it was loss, damage or forgery that caused each in its turn to be replaced.

All three show the head of a cleric in a trefoil surmounting a forward-facing figure.

97

Presumably this is an image of the archdeacon presiding above the head of his official. In other words it shows both the source of the official's authority and his subservience. TAH

LIT. Birch 1887, I, no. 1589.

98 Brass of Robert Wyvil, Bishop of Salisbury

c. 1375
Rubbing: l. of castle design 228 cm
Inscr. in Gothic letters on marginal fillet, now
  incomplete, but recorded: (*Hic iacet bone
  memorie Robt̄us Wyvell huius ecclīe Salisburie
  Epūs qui ecclīam istam quatraginta quinque annos
  & amplius pacifice & laudabilit' rexit, dispsa*

98

*eiusdm̄ ecclīe prudenter) congregauit & congregata
vt pastor vigilans conseruauit Int[er] enim alia
beficia sua minima·Castrum dc̄e ecclīe de Schirebon̄
p[er] ducentos annos et amplius manu militari
violent (occupatum eidem ecclīe ut pugil) intrepidus
recup[er]auit ac ip̄i ecclīe chaceam suam de la Bere
restitui p[ro]curauit qui quarto die Septemb̄ʒ anno
dn̄i millio CCC^{mo·} lxxv^{to} et anno consecr sue xlvj^{to}
sicut altissimo placuit in dc̄o castro debitum
reddidit (humane natur' Cujus aie ppiciet' ille in
quo sp'avit & credidit cuncta potens)*
Rubbing by Derrick A. Chivers (original in
  Salisbury Cathedral)

The inscription can be translated as follows: 'Here lyeth Robert Wyvell, of happy memory, Bishop of the Church of Salisbury, who ruled that Church peaceably and laudably for more than forty-five years; he prudently gathered

together the dispersed possessions of the Church, and they having been collected, as a vigilant pastor he prudently maintained the same, for, among the least of his other benefits, he recovered, like an intrepid champion, the Castle of Sherborne to the said Church, which for two hundred years and more had been withheld therefrom by military violence, and he also procured the restoration to the same Church of its Chace of Bere; who on the fourth day of September, AD 1375, and in the 46th year of his consecration, according to the will of the Most High, paid the debt of human nature in the said Castle; On whose soul may He have mercy in whom he so devoutly trusted and believed.'

The slab was originally set with four quatrefoils bearing the symbols of the Evangelists, of which only St Luke survives, in the British Museum, and four shields, of which two remain bearing the Bishop's arms. (The lost shields and St Luke symbol have been restored on the rubbing.) This unique brass is a product of the London 'Series A' workshop. The castle enclosing the Bishop must represent Sherborne, and the land in the foreground with rabbits Bere Chace, both of which, as the inscription indicates, were regained for the see of Salisbury by Wyvil. The process instituted by him for the recovery of the Castle in 1337 involved trial by combat: the champions appointed by the two sides met, but did not fight, because it was discovered that the Bishop's, Robert (or Richard) Shawell, was wearing charms under his clothing, and a cash settlement eventually ensued. Shawell is depicted in the gateway, with the equipment laid down for such contests, that is without metal armour, carrying a shield and a cowhorn-headed double pick. CB

LIT. Hewitt 1855–60, I, pp. 375–7; Kite 1860, pp. 14–19; Benson 1943–51; Waller 1975, p. xiv, no. 21; Clanchy 1978; Norris 1978a, p. 78, fig. 62, 1978b, pp. 57, 61.

99 Crucifix figure

Anglo-Norwegian, *c.* 1230–45
Oak: h. 77 cm, w. 70 cm
The Historical Museum, University of Bergen,
  Norway, M.A 244

The figure of Christ is crowned; there are three nails. The polychromy is original, remarkably complete and beautiful: the hair, beard and crown are gold glazed over silver, the crown with black, white, red and green geometric and foliage designs; the flesh tones are pink with the ribs, nipples, lips and wound in the right side picked out in a darker shade; the eyebrows and lashes are brown; and the double loincloth is gold with red inside, and white with blue-green inside. This figure comes from a small rood or altar cross, such as was standard in most English churches before the Reformation. Andersson

99

100

revenues were assigned by Dean Oliver Sutton to the support of the Vicars Choral of the Cathedral.

The statue probably dates from a little later than this and is likely to have been described as Germanic because of the sturdy proportions and powerfully modelled face. Similar expressiveness is characteristic of other local work, especially among the angels carved in the clerestory of the Lincoln Cathedral retro-choir, c. 1280. However, the drapery of St Giles is less bulky and angular and approximates to the more delicate carving of the seated Virgin at Anwick, Lincolnshire, which is likely to be nearer c. 1320 in date.

I am grateful to David Stocker for supplying me with information about the provenance of this figure. VS

LIT. Prior & Gardner 1912, p. 326, repr. fig. 364; Clay 1966, p. 163; VCH, *Lincoln*, vol. 2, 1906, p. 233; Stone 1972, p. 152, repr. pl. 114; Ryan & Ripperger 1969, pp. 516–19.

attributed it to the Master of the Hove Madonna (Andersson 1950, fig. 49), whom he believed to be English, the leading figure of a workshop which was active in west Norway, probably at Bergen. Since no thirteenth-century wood crucifix figures survive in England, direct comparisons are impossible, but in style the Christ would seem to be of the 1230s or 1240s – cf. King John's effigy at Worcester, which is precisely dated to 1232 (Colvin 1963, I, p. 478). NS

PROV. From the church of Fresvik-Leikanger, Sogn, Norway.

LIT. Lindblom 1916, p. 127; Andersson 1950, pp. 130–4, fig. 51; Blindheim 1986, pp. 141 (repr.), 148.

100   Figure of St Giles

c. 1300
Limestone: h. 157 cm, w. 50 cm, d. 20 cm
Dean and Chapter, Lincoln Cathedral

This figure was found near the old Hospital of St Giles, Lincoln, and is probably a rare representation of St Giles tonsured and vested as a priest. He is wearing an alb and amice, crossed stole, and a maniple over his left arm. The outer garment is a cope, here shown unusually joined across the front. It is fastened with a morse decorated with diaperwork. His right hand was probably originally raised in blessing and his left holding a pastoral staff. Under his feet is a quadruped, probably a hind, referring to the episode in the legend of St Giles when he was a hermit near Arles and protected a hind which was being chased by Charlemagne's hunters. Subsequently, while celebrating Mass, the saint obtained miraculous forgiveness on Charlemagne's behalf for a terrible sin which the king had committed. Thereafter it became known that any sinner could invoke his saintly powers to obtain forgiveness, provided that the sin was never repeated. St Giles was also a healer and became the patron saint of cripples. Some twenty-five hospitals were dedicated to him in England. The Lincoln hospital was founded in the thirteenth century and, around 1280, its

101

101 Boss with an abbot kneeling before the Virgin and Child

Early 14th century
Stone: h. 62.6 cm, w. 84.2 cm, diam. 54.7 cm
The Rector and Churchwardens, Abbeydore,
  Hereford and Worcs.

This is one of a group of early fourteenth-century bosses to survive from Dore Abbey, a house of Cistercian monks founded in 1147. An abbot, almost certainly the benefactor responsible for the vaulting, is shown kneeling in prayer before the Virgin, for whom the Cistercians had a special reverence and to whom all churches of the Order were dedicated. The profile of the ribs which the boss was designed to receive, consisting of a double roll and fillet flanked by detached fillets, corresponds to that of a springer at the south-east corner of the nave, suggesting that the bosses originally formed part of the vault erected over the central vessel of the earlier and now largely destroyed nave. ND

PROV. Dore Abbey, Hereford and Worcs.; built into face of a tomb, probably in 17th century when choir and transepts were restored for use as parish church; removed during repairs carried out 1901–3 by Roland W. Paul, FSA, and deposited at east end of church.

LIT. Paul 1904, pp. 123–4; Sledmere 1914, pp. 55–6, repr. opp. p. 55; Paul 1927, p. 271; RCHM, *Herefordshire*, 1931, p. 9, repr. pl. 78; Gardner 1951, pp. 117, 196, repr. fig. 389; Pevsner 1963, pp. 61–2; Morgan 1984, p. 6.

102 Pyx cover

Late 13th century
Oak: h. 1.26 m, diam. 35.8 cm
The Dean and Chapter of Wells

Cylindrical in form, the top and the base consist of a moulded wooden ring. From inside the upper ring two pairs of iron rods emerge which originally joined at the top to form a double loop. Between the loops is a wrought-iron ring in which works a swivel

102

hook. One of the rods has at some time been broken and has been replaced by a thicker one which was incorrectly fixed to the ring from the swivel (Hope 1897). Much of the original wood has been replaced in deal. Considerable areas of the original polychromy remain.

This is the only surviving example from this period in England of a cover, or baldachin, used to protect the pyx – that is, the container suspended above the altar in which was stored the consecrated Host. The double loop arrangement for suspension of the Wells cover conforms closely with the account in the Rites of Durham of the pyx canopy at Durham Cathedral. The established practice of the reservation of the sacrament became, after the fourth Lateran Council of 1215, a matter of priority. Injunctions on the subject abounded, including one from the Constitutions of Archbishop Pecham of Canterbury in 1281. CT

PROV. Wells Cathedral.

LIT. Hope 1897a.

103 Chest

Late 13th century
Oak: h. 46 cm, w. 49 cm, l. 197 cm
A West Sussex church

The construction (Eames 1977, hutch type 1) is the one used in the well-documented group of late twelfth- and thirteenth-century English chests (Johnston 1907b) displaying chip-carved ornament. The front and back consist of a single panel flanked by stiles. These vertical members are higher than the main body of the chest and raise it clear of the ground. This chest has lost the lower section of its uprights. From a nineteenth-century engraving (Shaw 1836) we know that these were decorated with panels of honeycomb ornament surrounded by a row of nail heads. The end panels are reinforced by framed rails. The lid is pivot-hinged, the pivot protected on the outer surface by an iron plate, and equipped with an apron at the sides. There are three metal straps on the main plank at the back which formerly continued across the lid to link up with three locking devices, now missing, at the front. The straps are fitted with a fixed staple from which chains are attached for securing to the wall.

This chest stands out from others in its class (e.g. Chichester Cathedral, Midhurst and Stoke D'Abernon) on account of the quality and ambition of its decoration, and its comparatively late date. The design of the roundels at either end is jewel-like in its delicacy and complexity. The arcade of trefoils with thin columns and stepped bases provides a satisfying link between one end and the other. Most of the comparable hutch chests are of the early thirteenth century whereas this example cannot be earlier than *c*. 1280. Eames adduced the blank arcading

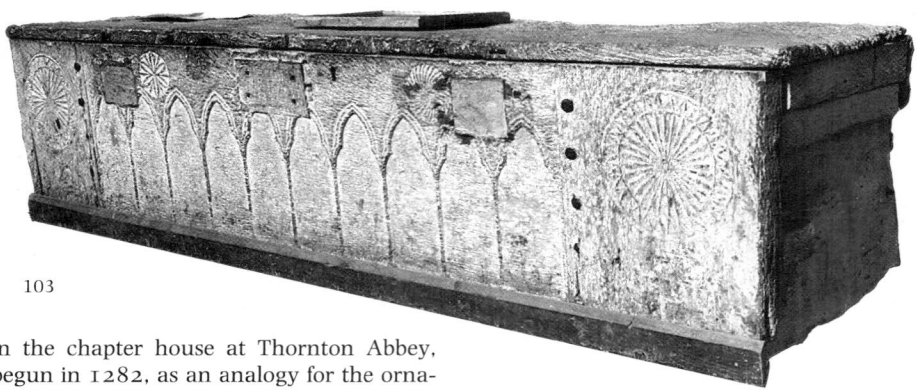

103

in the chapter house at Thornton Abbey, begun in 1282, as an analogy for the ornament. The treatment of the underside of the lid of the Newport Chest (Cat. 345) provides a relevant stylistic comparison in the same medium. CT

LIT. Shaw 1836, pl. XXIX; Johnston 1907, pp. 286–9, repr. fig. 17 p. 286, fig. 18 p. 287, fig. 19 p. 288, pls XIII, XIV; Eames 1977, pp. 108, 143–5, repr. fig. 17 p. 109, pl. 35B.

104

104 Lectern

Early 14th century
Oak: h. 119 cm, w. (of desk) 51.5 cm, d. 25 cm
The Church of the Holy Cross, Bury,
    Cambridgeshire

This is the simplest kind of lectern with only one book rest. It is supported on a thin shaft. There is no evidence for the form of the original, presumably wooden, base. The desk is a triangular box accommodating one book only. The unpretentiousness of the structure is echoed in the rather eccentric design and provincial quality of the carving. The lectern is considerably knocked about. But, the modern book rest and frieze underneath apart, it survives in an authentic state. CT

PROV. Holy Cross Church, Bury, Cambs.

LIT. Twopeny 1859, pls I, II.

105 Lectern

c. 1330–40
Oak: h. 150 cm, w. (of desk) 73 cm, d. 56 cm
A Kent church

This is a fine specimen in design, decoration and workmanship. Each of the book rests displays a different configuration of 'window tracery' – spherical triangles, mouchettes, oculi and half circles. The lectern appears to

have been left outside for some time. The carving of the ornament has lost its former sharpness. The ledge extension is missing on two sides of the desk. The supporting column and base are carved out of one piece of wood. The tenon at the top of the central column probably supported candlestick arms.

In the greater churches in the Middle Ages there were at least two lecterns, one at the high altar, the other in the choir. In addition a lectern would have been needed to read the Gospel on the greater feast days from the pulpitum. This lectern is traditionally said to have come from either Boxley or Leeds Abbey. Its high artistic quality makes the provenance from a great church a certainty.

The use of diaper-type patterning evokes

105

the decorative treatment of the wall surfaces at St Stephen's Chapel. However, the absence of the ogee arch in the 'window tracery' evinces a somewhat conservative approach. The choir stalls at Ely Cathedral (c. 1342), themselves the work of metropolitan craftsmen, provide the closest analogy in wood (Cat. 532). There is a kinship in the handling of ornament and the use of certain motifs. A feature is the use of the voluted 'trefoil' leaf characteristic of Ely. CT

LIT. Cox 1915, pp. 187–8, repr. pp. 186, 187; Howard & Crossley 1917, pp. 197–206, repr. pp. 207, 209.

106 Misericord: Men dicing

1339–41
Oak: h. 30.7 cm, w. 64.5 cm, d. 20 cm
Dean and Chapter, Ely Cathedral, north side stalls
    from west, upper row, no. 23 (of 65)

Two bearded men dressed in hoods and tunics sit by a table and look intently at the dice just thrown by one of them. Game pieces lie on the corner of the table, and the degenerate scene of gambling is completed by the figures in the supporters: a woman holding a sprig of flowers and sitting by a large barrel, and a man approaching with a tankard of ale. Gambling is therefore associated with drunkenness, and the woman is the temptress who, by the flowers, may be a personification of May, the month of love. Often, too, gambling would lead to violent brawls; it was strongly condemned by the Church as leading into the jaws of Hell.

A misericord in Gloucester Cathedral also depicts two men sitting by a table, playing with five game pieces.

The supporters of the Ely misericords do not only contain decorative motifs; they often have elaborate compositions which add to the narrative in the central part, enlarging on the story in the same way as marginal illuminations, where scenes of gambling are also very popular.

Some of the carvings of the Ely misericords can be compared with specific marginal illuminations, pointing to contacts with centres such as London. They were carved between 1339 and 1341, after the choir bays, ruined by the fall of the tower, were reconstructed. William Hurley, master carver to Edward III, is mentioned at Ely (1334–5, 1336–7, 1339–40, 1345–6 and 1349–50). He was therefore in a position to transmit new ideas to the carvers from the capital (cf. Cat. 492, 532). CG

PROV. Ely Cathedral.

LIT. Pevsner 1970, pp. 358, 359.

106

107

108

107 Alexander Neckham, miscellany

c. 1240–50
Vellum, single sheet: 18.2 × 14 cm
Syndics of Cambridge University Library, MS
   Gg.6.42

A single leaf inserted into a collection of texts of the Augustinian canon, Alexander Neckham (1157–1217) has two illustrations of friars, the first of St Francis and a Franciscan, and on the reverse two friars of another Order, possibly Dominicans, although their habits are unspecific. The date of these tinted drawings is only some twenty years after these new Orders had first come to England in 1221 and 1224, and provides one of the earliest depictions of them in English art.

The style of the drawings has some affinity with that of Matthew Paris but is not close enough to suggest production at St Albans. It may be an early version of that found in a tinted drawing Apocalypse in the Bodleian Library (MS Auct. D.4.17).   NJM

PROV. Maurice Gyffard, 17th century; John Moore, Bishop of Ely 1707–14; Moore's library bt by George I, 1715, and presented to Cambridge University.

LIT. Little 1937, pp. 41, 64, pl. 7; Morgan 1982, no. 84, figs 280–1; Hunt 1984, *passim*, pl. 11.

108 Missal of Henry of Chichester

Salisbury, *c.* 1250
Vellum, ff. 256: 30.5 × 20 cm
John Rylands University Library of Manchester,
   MS lat. 24

The owner of this richly decorated missal, Henry of Chichester, was precentor of the collegiate church of Crediton, Devon, until 1264. In 1277 the missal was given to Exeter

Cathedral, of which Henry was a canon. He must have acquired it earlier in his career, perhaps in the vicinity of Salisbury, for which area other books by the same artist were made. This artist, one of the leading figures of the time, has been named the Sarum Master in view of his Salisbury associations. English illuminated missals of this period are rare, and it is exceptional at any time for this text to contain a series of full-page miniatures as does this example. In addition the masses for major feast days and the Canon prayer have historiated initials.

The Sarum Master and his collaborators decorated a Bible (London, British Library, Royal MS I.B.XII) by the scribe William of Hales and dated 1254, for Thomas de la Wyle, Master of the Schools at Salisbury. Psalters by the workshop were made for the nearby nunneries of Amesbury (Cat. 316) and Wilton (London, Royal College of Physicians, MS 409). The large-scale miniatures in the missal and the Amesbury Psalter show the monumental aspect of the style of the Sarum Master himself, which may reflect contemporary wall painting. The elongated figures with elaborate systems of strongly delineated troughed folds represent the mature English Early Gothic style whose early phase is evident in works such as the Glazier Psalter (Cat. 8).

This manuscript is one of the earliest examples of the Sarum Missal, and was used for Wickham Legg's edition of the text (1916).   NJM

PROV. Henry of Chichester; Exeter Cathedral, 1277; 26th Earl of Crawford (1847–1913); Crawford Coll. bt by Mrs Enriqueta Augustina Rylands for library founded in memory of her husband, John Rylands, 1901.

LIT. Legg 1916; Hollaender 1943, pp. 232–8, pls I–IV; Paris 1968, no. 237; Marks & Morgan 1981, pp. 54–7, pls 8–9; Morgan 1987, no. 100, repr.

109   The Anian (Bangor) Pontifical

c. 1320–8
Parchment, ff. 169: 25.8 × 17.5 cm
Dean and Chapter, Bangor Cathedral

An inscription in the hand of the main scribe (f. 164v.) identifies the book as the Pontifical of Bishop Anianus of Bangor, probably Anianus II, who held the office from 1309 to 1328. A pontifical contains the text of liturgical ceremonies performed by bishops, such as consecrations, ordinations and benedictions. The only miniature in the manuscript, showing the dedication of a church, (f. 8v.), is painted in the distinctive style of the Queen Mary Psalter (London, British Library, Royal MS 2 B VII), not by the artist known as the Queen Mary Master but by another hand, perhaps that of the miniaturist of the Hours of Alice de Reydon of 1320–4 (Cat. 570). In

109

general, the Queen Mary style is marked by a balance of pale, transparent washes of colour articulated by black linear patterns and strong opaque hues, both set out against tooled gold grounds. Figures are tall, slender, and swaying, and are clothed in simple drapery, only slightly shaded; their faces have high, sloping brows and deep-set eyes; their hair is delicately textured in finely outlined waves. This refined style characterises more than twenty surviving manuscripts of the years between 1310 and 1330 (e.g. Cat. 110, 570, 572) – the largest cohesive group of English illuminated manuscripts of the fourteenth century from the point of view of style. Yet the books were apparently made for a wide range of owners, clerical and secular, bourgeois, noble and royal. It is widely agreed that this group of artists was centred in London.   LFS

PROV. Anianus II, Bishop of Bangor, before 1328; Ednam, Bishop of Bangor 1465–94; returned to cathedral by Humphrey Humphrey, Bishop of Bangor, 1701.

LIT. Sandler 1986, no. 69, II, pp. 77–8, repr. I, figs 177, 178, 181; Dennison 1984.

110   Theological miscellany

c. 1310–25
Parchment, ff. 53: 20.5 × 13 cm
Paris, Bibliothèque nationale, MS fr. 13342

The chief text in this volume is an illustrated manual in Anglo-French, with the introductory rubric, Ceo qe vous devez fere & penser a chascon point de la messe [What you should do and think at each stage of the Mass]. The thirteen text miniatures show priest, server and congregation at various points in the celebration of the Mass. Like the instructions for the Mass, the other components of the manuscript – a catechism on Baptism and the Speculum Ecclesie of Edmund Rich, both in Anglo-French, and the Latin Psalter of St Jerome – are also directed toward the pious layperson. Originally the miscellany included additional devotional texts, of which a few fragments are now preserved in Oxford, Bodleian Library MS Douce 79 (Cat. 572).

110

As in Douce 79, the illustrations of the Paris manuscript, the historiated initials and borders, the unframed *bas-de-page* compositions and the smaller decorative initials are all the work of the artist of the Queen Mary Psalter (London, British Library Royal MS 2 B VII). Characteristic of his style is the sensitive, delicate drawing using broken outline, the colour applied either in transparent near-grisaille washes (as in the *Speculum Ecclesie*) or in a full range of hues, and the decorative motifs – graceful dragons, curving fronds of foliage, and above all deeply-fringed profile leaves, doubled over lengthwise.

Like most manuscripts of the Queen Mary group, the Paris miscellany has no indications of date and, in this case, no indications of its original destination either. Those manuscripts that do offer some internal evidence for dating, none by the Queen Mary Master himself – for example, the Bangor Pontifical of *c*. 1320–8 (Cat. 109) and the Hours of Alice de Reydon of 1320–4 (Cat. 570) – suggest that the artists were active during the 1320s and perhaps during the previous decade. LFS

PROV. In France by 1740.

LIT. Wormald 1968, pp. 39–45, repr. pls 37–42; Sandler 1986, no. 58, II, pp. 67–8, repr. figs 144–5; Avril & Stirnemann 1987, no. 179, repr. pls L, lxxii–iii.

111 Chalice and paten of Bishop Gravesend

c. 1200–70

Silver, parcel-gilt; inside of chalice split at junction with stem, knot cracked, foot holed, cracked and pitted: h. of chalice 12.4 cm, diam. of paten 11.4 cm

Dean and Chapter, Lincoln Cathedral

The bowl of the chalice is shallow with a pronounced lip; the upper and lower stem are engraved with a simple zigzag pattern, the fields left alternately plain or wheel-engraved; the knot consists of eight tripartite lobes separated by bands of cross-hatching; the foot is round and plain. There is gilding inside the bowl, around the outside lip and on the stem. The paten has a single depression, a cusped quatrefoil, with a central *Manus Dei* engraved within a circle.

Although found in the grave of Richard de Gravesend, Bishop of Lincoln 1258–79, the chalice and paten cannot be very precisely dated. The lobed knot is a simpler version of the Dolgelly chalice of *c*. 1230–50 (Cat. 258). These comparatively humble pieces contrast with the 'precious gold chalice', image of the Virgin Mary and other silver-gilt images, copes and silver given by Gravesend to the cathedral (Poole 1857, p. 41).

The chalice and paten may have been old when buried; they reflect the practice, common until the end of the Middle Ages, of burying a priest with his emblems of office, a chalice and paten, and in the case of an abbot

111

or bishop also his crosier and ring (cf. Cat. 256–7, 634–9). If not silver, these burial chalices were often pewter, some made expressly for the purpose; numbers have been found including eight in Lincoln of thirteenth-century date (Bruce-Mitford 1976), one with a knot close to the Gravesend example. MLC

PROV. Lincoln Cathedral; found in grave of Bishop Gravesend, 1791.

LIT. Hope & Fallow 1886, pp. 143, 154, 365, 376; London 1930, nos 173–4; London 1939, no. 38; Oman 1957, pp. 41, 304–5; Ottawa 1972, no. 49a; London 1978c, no. 2.

112 Chalice and paten of Archbishop de Melton

c. 1320–40

Silver, parcel-gilt; h. 14 cm, diam. of paten 13.5 cm

The Dean and Chapter of York

The bowl of the chalice is conical, the stem round with an eight-lobed knot, the foot round and plain, except for an engraved Crucifixion. A similar chalice from a church in western Sweden differs only in having a

112

foot decorated with a cast and applied crucifix (Oman 1957, p. 42, pl. 8b). The paten, repaired under Dean Duncombe (Hope & Fallow 1886) is engraved with the *Manus Dei* within a sexfoil depression.

The chalice is characterised by a new form of bowl which superseded the earlier hemispherical type. Only one other English fourteenth-century chalice with a foot engraved with the Crucifixion is known, that at Aston-by-Sutton (Oman 1957, p. 43, pl. 10) with a coat of arms in addition. It is rather later, and the engraving cruder than Melton's chalice, which was perhaps commissioned by him from his kinsman, Henry Melton, a York goldsmith known to have made silver vessels for him (Butler 1951, p. 66). If so, the chalice and paten would be the earliest known pieces of York silver, York being the city second only to London in the number of its medieval goldsmiths (Swanson 1980, pp. 181f). MLC

PROV. William de Melton; found in his grave in the Minster, 29 May 1732.

LIT. Gent 1733, pp. 108–9; Poole & Hugall 1850, pl. XXV; Hope & Fallow 1886, p. 208, repr.; London 1930, nos 178–9; London 1939, no. 39; Oman 1957, pp. 43, 304–5.

113 The Hamstall Ridware chalice and paten

c. 1350

Silver, parcel-gilt, unmarked; scratched and pitted, chalice patched on point of foot, stem repaired: h. of chalice 11.9 cm; diam. of paten 12 cm

Parochial Church Council, St Michael and All Angels, Hamstall Ridware, Staffordshire

The chalice has a wide, shallow bowl, short stem and prominent knot, with a broad, incurving hexagonal foot. A gilt band runs around the rim of the bowl, which is gilt inside, the gilding covering deep scratches and probably therefore new, as is a butterfly nut holding together stem and bowl. The paten with gilt rim is embossed with a sexfoil depression within which is engraved a circle framing a *Manus Dei*.

The chalice is the earliest surviving English example with this form of foot, which succeeded the circular shape. The will of Sir John Foxley (1378) mentions a chalice *cum pede de forma molette sex punctorum* (with a mullet [star]-shaped foot of six points; Oman 1957, p. 43 n. 2). However, variations upon this shape are found earlier on French silver such as the Copenhagen ewer (Lightbown 1978, pl. 31) and the Avignon cup (ibid., pl. 69), both of *c*. 1330. It seems likely that chalice makers took up this particular shape for practical reasons: a new liturgical custom was to lay the chalice on its side to drain after the Mass, the bowl resting on the paten (Wickham Legg 1916, p. 228 no. 55); the angular foot would prevent rolling, the shal-

113

114

115

low bowl facilitate draining. The prominent 'writhen' knot was by then old-fashioned, its style comparable to that of the Børsa chalice of *c.* 1250 (Oman 1957, pl. 7).　　MLC

PROV. Found at Hamstall Hall Farm by W. Jaggard, tenant farmer, while digging drain in meadow formerly called the Sheepwash, opposite the Rectory meadow, *c.* 1817 (notes of Revd John Coussmaker [d. 1921]); given to Hon. Mary Leigh, of Stoneleigh Abbey; given by William, Lord Leigh, to parish of Hamstall Ridware, 7 May 1874, after repairs by Cobbett of Coventry (Vestry minutes, 18 June 1874); on loan to V&A 1930–83; on loan to Lichfield Heritage Centre, 1983.

LIT. Hope & Fallow 1886, pp. 145–6, 156, 366; London 1930, nos 392–3; Birmingham 1948 no. 7; Oman 1957, pp. 43, 484.

114　Paten

c. 1250
Silver, parcel-gilt; splits along edge repaired at
　back with silver patches: diam. 14.2 cm
Inscr. around rim CVNTA CREO VVIRTUTE ŘEGO
　PIETATE REFORMO
Rector and Churchwardens of St Matthew,
　Weeke, Winchester

In a central depression is engraved a Lamb of God holding the standard of the Resurrection. This is framed within an octofoil depression, in whose spandrels are engraved fleshy palmettes against a matted ground. (The inscription engraved around the rim means: I am the Creator of the Universe. My power guides all things. My mercy restores them.) Only the inscription and engraving are gilt.

The *Agnus Dei* and the *Manus Dei* were the commonest subjects for English medieval patens. The perkily-rendered Weeke Lamb is in the same stylistic tradition as that on the Chichester paten of the late twelfth century (London 1984a, no. 322c), though finer. Unlike many inscriptions found on patens,

which derived from the psalter and were probably routinely used by goldsmiths, the Weeke inscription may have been especially composed.　　MLC

PROV. Parish Church of St Matthew, Weeke, Hants., at least since 1845.

LIT. Winchester Archaeological Institute 1845, p. xliii; Hope & Fallow 1886, pp. 138, 154, 375; Oman 1957, pp. 51, 56–7; Ottawa 1972, no. 49d.

115　Chalice case

c. 1373–82
Leather (cuir-bouilli): h. 21.5 cm, diam. 22 cm
Inscr. on lid + IHESUS NAZARENUS REX
　IUDEORUM +
Rector, Churchwardens and Parochial Church
　Council of St Agnes, Cawston, Norfolk

The lid is decorated with a griffin on a background of punched quatrefoils, surrounded by a lobed circle and a cut inscription. Two holes punched in the lid originally held a thong handle. The sides display seven heraldic shields, the spandrels between them

being filled with stylised foliage. Only one coat of arms, that of de Ufford (Sable, a cross engrailed), can be closely connected with Cawston. The de Ufford family held the principal manor of Cawston from 1330 until 1382, and the other shields may represent personal friends at arms of the de Uffords. No chalice with case appears in the church inventory of 1373, suggesting a later date of manufacture. Cawston passed in 1382 to the de la Poles. It seems unlikely that they would

have commissioned a case on which the coat of arms of their predecessors appeared.

Hardened leather (cuir-bouilli) was particularly useful as a protective covering for precious portable objects such as church plate. The main advantage of the material was its malleability before treatment and its durability and rigidity after. Franks suggests that the case might have contained a crown commissioned by guilds to be placed on the head of a statue of St Agnes on her feast day. However, no such crown appears in the church inventories of 1552 or 1613. There seems no reason to doubt that the case originally contained a chalice and paten. MA

PROV. Church of St Agnes, Cawston, Norfolk.

LIT. Micklethwaite 1883, p. 328; Franks 1892, pp. 246–50; London 1930, no. 310 p. 58.

116　The White Castle cruet

English(?), 14th century
Pewter: h. 12.1 cm, w. 5.4 cm
The National Museum of Wales, Cardiff, 27.92/1

A splayed hollow foot supports a pear-shaped body with slender neck and hinged lid, on which is engraved a Lombardic A. The lid now fits badly; signs of repairs to the edge of the neck suggest that this, like most known examples, originally had a spout. It is made

116

in four parts: neck, body and base are soldered together and lathe-turned. Differences in metal colour and thickness between the lid and the vessel suggest the use of different alloys. A sample from underneath the base was analysed by spectrography as 61.2 per cent tin, 36.9 per cent lead, 1 per cent copper, 0.2 per cent iron.

The purpose of this piece is indicated by the A on the lid, for *aqua*. Altar cruets were used in pairs, sometimes marked A and V (*vinum*); one held the water, the other the wine, used for the Mass, which were mixed together in the chalice by the priest. Cruets were small because only small quantities were needed, since the laity did not partake of the wine at this date (Rock 1905, I, pp. 125–7).

Close parallels to the shape and size of the White Castle cruet exist in thirteenth- and fourteenth-century pottery cruets excavated in England (Lewis 1968, pp. 147–9) and an unmarked pewter cruet found in Bergenhus, Norway with coins dated to between 1215 and 1471 (Grieg 1933, pp. 127–8). Other similar cruets in silver are a fourteenth-century pair (South German?) from the Bastle Treasure (Fritz 1982, pl. 615), a fifteenth-century silver-mounted amber pair (Flemish?; Trusted 1982, no. 1), and a silver pair of *c.* 1500 made in Lübeck (Fritz 1982, pl. 616). All are marked A and V; most lack handles, but have spouts.

The vessel form clearly did not change over a considerable period, and probably evolved from a domestic jug (cf. Paris 1981–2, no. 180). The date of this cruet may be deduced from the architectural history of White Castle, where the chapel was in a tower rebuilt in *c.* 1267, derelict by 1437 (Lewis 1965–9); no greater precision is possible.

Other forms of pewter cruet have been found in England (Cat. 117); two more, nearly identical, are of hexagonal vase shape from Weoley and Ludlow Castles (Hatcher 1974, p. 28, pl. 6). The Weoley cruet is made of a high tin pewter thought characteristically English, very different from the White Castle cruet; although the results of analysis of the latter may be misleading, a German source for it, as suggested for the Bergenhus piece, cannot be discounted. MLC

PROV. White Castle (Llantilio Cressenny), Gwent; found in well, *c.* 1927; given to Museum by Sir Henry Matheson Jackson of St Mary Hill, Abergavenny.

LIT. Lewis 1965–9, pp. 127–39.

117   Cruet

c. 1400
Pewter: h. 11.8 cm, w. of base 5.3 cm, w. of rim 2.6 cm
Inscr. on two panels on body THOMAS HUNTE HONORIFICABILIUT
The Board of Trustees of the Victoria and Albert Museum, London, M. 26–1939

The body, of hexagonal section, has stepped mouldings at base and rim; a recurving spout of polygonal section is soldered to the body, the mouth formed as a dragon's head; the plain handle has a loop at the top and two flanges with the fragment of a hinged lid; a broken section of a pierced circular plate linking the spout to the body is still attached to the body.

This is one of three similar cruets, two of which have an English provenance. Another, formerly in the Figdor Collection, Vienna, may have been acquired in France. The best preserved of the group was discovered in 1977 at Tong Castle, Shropshire, and is at present on loan to Rowley's House Museum, Shropshire. It was found in a well within the building of the keep. It bears a maker's mark, has an early hammer-head thumbpiece and was found with fourteenth-century material. The exhibited cruet and a bronze ewer were found in a well at Ashby de la Zouche Castle during conservation work on the building. It is of special interest as it bears contemporary inscriptions: the name of the owner, and an abbreviation of the medieval tongue twister HONORIFICABILI-TUDINITATIBUS. The Zouche family are known to have lived in Ashby and Tong in medieval times. This cruet differs slightly

117

from the other recorded examples in the form of the spout and handle. AN

PROV. From Ashby de la Zouche Castle; found 1937 in well-filling associated with construction of Great Tower for Lord Hastings in 1476; given by the Countess of Loudon, 1939.

LIT. Berling 1920, p. 38; Boucaud & Fregnac 1978, pl. 35; *J. Pewter Soc.* vol. 1 no. 3, 1978; Simms 1983, p. 178; *Brit. Pewter* 1960, p. 2.

118   Pyx

c. 1300
Pewter: h. 6.4 cm, w. 7.9 cm
Inscr. within border on upper section of body AVE MAIIA GRACIA PLENA DOMINUS TECUM BENEDIT
    on label on top surface AVE
The Board of Trustees of the Victoria and Albert Museum, London, 4474–1858

118

The body, of hexagonal form, is supported by three cast feet and fitted with a hinged lid; the lid is cast in relief with the scene of the Annunciation and with the arms of France and England, as used before 1340; on the other side of the hinge is a dragon courant also cast in relief. The knop is formed as a seated hound. The panels forming the sides are decorated with scrolling foliage and a frieze; in the centre of four panels and on the top is a device roughly engraved in 'wriggle work', probably representing a candlestick – an owner's mark.

This is one of a number of hexagonal pyxes decorated with cast work. A close parallel both in form and decoration is to be found in the Cluny Museum, Paris; like this example it has a flat lid decorated in relief with the Annunciation. In the London Museum is the lid from a similar pyx found at Bankside. This is cast with the scene of the Annunciation, the arms of England and France and the Coronation of the Virgin. On most surviving pyxes of this form, the knop is formed as a seated hound, a feature found on several contemporary flagons. Cf. Cat. 102, 571. AN

PROV. Acq. by the V&A, 1858, for £2.4s.

LIT. Massé 1910, p. 161; Berling 1920, pl. 31; Boucaud & Fregnac 1978, pl. 34; *Brit. Pewter* 1960, pl. 1.

119

119   The Godsfield pyx

c. 1350–1400
Copper alloy, engraved and gilt: h. 9 cm
The Board of Trustees of the Victoria and Albert
  Museum, London, M.360–1921

Both box and cover are heavy castings,
turned on the lathe (the cross-finial and
hinge are modern restorations), and elaborately engraved with acanthus-like foliage.
The style of this is close to that on the St
George casket (Cat. 88), and the English
Reliquaire du Saint-Esprit of *c.* 1410 in the
Louvre (Paris 1981–2, no. 221), which in
turn resembles foliage drawn in contemporary manuscripts.

The pyx is the only known English
example of this form, one found throughout
northern Europe, and produced most prolifi-
cally by Limoges enamellers (cf. Cambridge,
Mass., 1975, nos 9–12). The pyx was found
near the chapel of an ancient Commandery
of the Knights Hospitallers at Godsfield, near
Alresford, Hampshire, and was probably part
of the chapel's furnishings.   MLC

PROV. Found while grubbing up a hedge called
Wield Row, Godsfield, Hants., 1870; Mr A.
Houghton (owner of Wield Row); Mrs Buck (niece
of Mr Houghton); bt by V&A, 1920.

LIT. *Proc. Soc. Ants.*, 2nd ser., 31, 1918, p. 63;
London 1930, no. 180; Oman 1962b, p. 203.

120   Pax

c. 1400
Copper alloy: l. 13.8 cm, w. 9.1 cm
St Edmundsbury Museum Service, 1976–501

Cast in one piece, the plaque is engraved with
the Crucifixion, the Virgin Mary and St John
the Evangelist against a lightly cross-hatched
ground, framed by a rope-moulding border.
A cresting of trefoils is pinned on, and bears
traces of gilding. A hinged handle fixed

longitudinally to the back of the pax consists
of a milled strip.

Paxes originated in the Early Christian
custom in which members of the congregation gave each other a kiss of peace at Mass
(Way 1845b, p. 145). At an uncertain date,
but certainly not later than 1250 (ibid., pp.
146–7; Oman 1962b, p. 201) the custom
was modified in England, and the pax became
an object which was passed around the
congregation to be kissed, known variously
as an *osculatorium* and *tabula pacis* (tablet of
peace). Paxes formed part of the furnishings
of all churches (Oman 1962b, p. 201) and
might be made of precious or base metal,
enamel or even wood (Way 1845b, p. 8), and
often depicted the Crucifixion. Few English
examples have survived, the Bury pax being
among the earliest.

Base-metal paxes were produced *en masse.*
They are of two types, as above, with its

120

design engraved, or with the design cast, as
on copper-alloy and pewter examples (Oman
1962b, pl. XIXA, B, p. 201). While the
techniques and metals used vary, their basic
designs are close, suggestive of widely-
diffused pattern books.

There are numerous medieval literary allusions to quarrels over the order of pre-
cedence for kissing the pax; attacked by
English Protestants, the ceremony was abol-
ished at the time of the Reformation (Bossy
1973, pp. 141–3).   MLC

PROV. Revd C. H. Bennet; given by him to
Museum, 1853.

LIT. *Proc. Bury W. Suff. Arch. Inst.*, 1, 1853, p.
218; St Albans 1905, no. 105; London 1930, no.
466; Oman 1962b, p. 201, repr.; Norwich 1973,
no. 60.

121   The Ramsey Abbey censer

c. 1325
Silver-gilt: h. 10.8 cm; diam. 5.3 cm,
  wt *c.* 47 troy oz
The Board of Trustees of the Victoria and Albert
  Museum, London, M.268–1923

The censer appears to be modelled on the
design for a chapter house. The top half takes
the form of a six-sided tower, in which gabled
windows of decorated tracery alternate with
groups of lancets surmounted by window
heads set back behind battlemented parapets.
The steep pyramidal roof, engraved with
chevrons, rises to a cluster of trefoil leaves
which hold the chain for raising the cover.

This is the finest surviving piece of English
Gothic ecclesiastical metalwork; workmanship and design combine in harmonious
dignity. Until the discovery of the Cambridge
example (London, Victoria and Albert
Museum) it was the only known English
Gothic censer. The architectural motifs can
be paralleled in English architecture of the
early fourteenth century, the most notable
features being the hexagonal plan, found on
Eleanor crosses of 1291, the abundance of
miniature crenellations, as in Ely Cathedral
octagon and choir (Bony 1979, pls 246–8),
especially the way in which crenellations
define the horizontal cornice from behind
which rises a gablet (ibid., pp. 21–2, pls 120,
123), as on the canopy over the prior's seat in
Canterbury Cathedral chapter house (personal communication, Christopher Wilson).

The 'cinquefoil' heads to the lights are an
English feature rather than French, the 'voluted trefoil' leaves on the finial resemble
those on the Swan mazer (Cat. 543) and King
John cup (Cat. 541). If goldsmiths' patterns
lagged a little behind those of the architect,
the censer may date from *c.* 1325. Its metal
content, like the technique in which its
crenellations are made, is significantly different from that of the incense boat – they are
unlikely to have been made as a pair.   MLC

PROV. Whittlesey Mere, Cambs.; found *c.* 1850 by
James & Frank Coles while fishing for eels; acq.
William Wells, Lord of the Manor; on his death
sold with Cat. 122, Christie's, 3 June 1890, lots
95–6; bt by C. Davis on behalf of William, 5th Earl
of Carysfort of Elton; inherited by Col. D.J. Proby,
1909; on loan to V&A, 1914–19; sold by him to
V&A, 1923.

LIT. Hawkins 1851, pp. 195–6; Cambridge 1895,
nos 192–3; London 1901, pp. 133–4, pl. XXIV,
fig. 2; London 1930, nos 362–3; Braun 1932,
nos 526, 549, pp. 606, 620, 639–40; Oman
1957, pp. 89–91; Paris 1968, nos 467, 478.

122   The Ramsey Abbey incense boat

c. 1350
Silver, parcel-gilt: h. 12 cm, l. 9.5 cm, wt 17.25
  troy oz
The Board of Trustees of the Victoria and Albert
  Museum, London, M.269–1923

121–2

The boat has a narrow, battlemented edge and a finial at each end in the form of a ram's head (one with horn missing) rising from the sea, set on a mullet-shaped foot. The body is decorated with punched gilt strapwork; the top is engraved with two stylised double roses and one half is hinged to act as a lid, having a pointed diamond-knop (cf. the spoon finial, Cat. 213).

The boat held incense for the censer; the shape is found in all metals, Limoges enamel examples often having finials with dragons' heads (Braun 1932, no. 526). The rams are undoubtedly placed in punning allusion to the name Ramsey, probably referring to Ramsey Abbey, whose arms included a ram (Dugdale 1846, II, p. 554) and which was geographically close to Whittlesey Mere. A punched ram's head appears on two sixteenth-century pewter plates found at the same time (Brownsword *et al.*, 1984, p. 241).

The style of foot is characteristically fourteenth-century, similar to that of the Hamstall Ridware chalice (Cat. 113). The double rose is not a Tudor device as has been suggested (Cambridge 1895, no. 192) but a motif (perhaps a badge) found long before, as on the Grandisson diptych (Cat. 594–5) of *c.* 1340, on Wykeham's crosier (Cat. 608) and on the cover of the wardrobe book of Henry of Bolingbroke, of 1391–2 (Blair & Delamer [forthcoming]).

Although censer and incense boat are probably fairly close in date, they seem to have been made by different goldsmiths: the style of their battlementing is discernibly different, as is their metal content.   MLC

PROV. As Cat. 121.

LIT. As Cat. 121.

123 Chrismatory

c. 1350
Copper alloy: l. 15 cm, h. 10.8 cm
The Rector and Churchwardens of St Martin and St Paul, Canterbury

The casket is made of sheet metal; it has a hipped roof, decorated by a cresting (damaged) pierced with quatrefoils. Inside, a plate holds in place three phials (lead or pewter?).

A chrismatory was the receptacle used in ritual for the holy oils: *oleum infirmorum*, used for the sick; *oleum catechumenorum*, used at baptism; and *chrisma*, or balm, used for confirmation, ordination and certain consecrations. Such containers took various forms; English examples of this type are extremely rare. A comparable chrismatory in pewter, of *c.* 1400, found at Granborough, Buckinghamshire, now on loan to Christ Church Cathedral, Oxford (Watson 1880), retains its containers, each with a lid attached to a hooked metal prong, with which

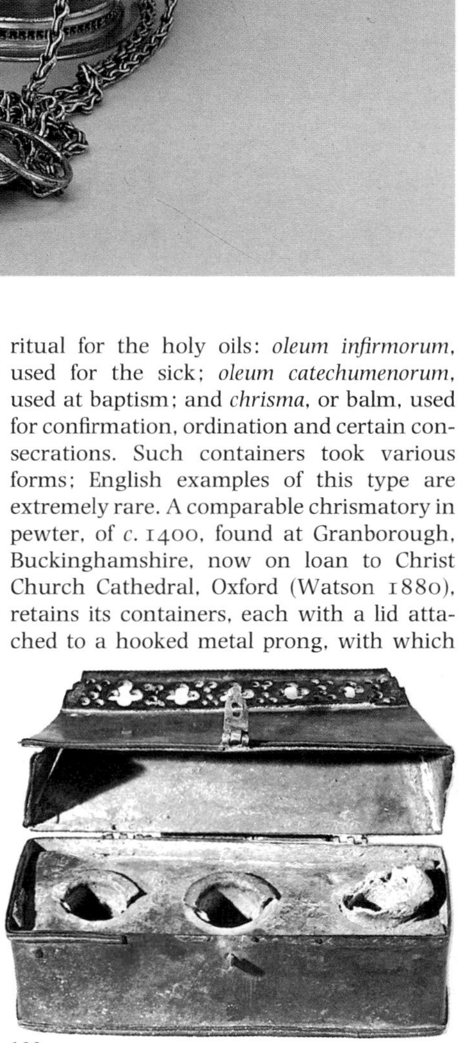

123

the tow (for anointing) might be lifted from the oil pot. The Canterbury chrismatory, lacking these, was at first thought to be an inkstand (Canterbury 1844). The style of its roof cresting suggests a date of c. 1350–1400.   MLC

PROV. Canterbury, St Martin's; found on wall plate of nave when roof was removed, c. 1844.

LIT. British Archaeological Association 1844, pp. 141–2; British Archaeological Association 1845, p. xliii; Watson 1879–81, pp. 429–31, repr.; St Albans 1905, no. 99; Cox & Harvey 1907, pp. 52–3; Oman 1962b, p. 264.

124   Holy-water stoup

Third quarter(?) 14th century
Copper alloy: h. 20.1 cm, diam. 21.1 cm
Inscr. round lip in relief Lombardic capitals
   + PRIES . PUR . LALME . G . GLAUILLE [sic]
The Parochial Church Council of St Mary's, Wreay, Cumbria, on loan to Carlisle Cathedral Museum

The stoup is cast, of inverted bell shape, on three straight ribbed legs ending in stylised paws; on the lip are a pair of pierced lugs holding an iron swing handle. Round the middle are three rectangular relief panels, of which two, each framed in an arch, together form an Annunciation scene. The third shows an enthroned man with a hunting horn held to his lips with his right hand, a small bell raised aloft in the other, and a lion or hound sejant at his feet. The style of the scenes indicates a date of c. 1200, so the dies used to reproduce them were already old when the stoup was made, and they have been truncated at top and bottom to make them fit. They are unlikely to have been designed as dies and probably came originally from a casket or small house altar, and the third panel may not even have belonged to the others. The figure on it has not been identified, but he may represent one of the tones of music: comparable figures are shown, for example, in an eleventh-century Cluniac troper from St-Martial de Limoges in the Bibliothèque nationale, Paris (MS lat. 1118). Other suggestions are that he repres-

124

ents one of the winds or the month of March, or, perhaps, St Oswald, who was depicted blowing a horn in a window formerly in Durham Cathedral. The style of lettering in the inscription (Pray for the soul of G. Glanville) suggests a mid-fourteenth-century date for the stoup, but, since old dies may have been used for this also, it could be somewhat later.

The Glanvilles were prominent in East Anglia and, when the stoup was exhibited to the Society of Antiquaries on 17 June 1790, it was in private possession in Suffolk. Possible candidates for the member of the family commemorated are Geoffrey de Glanville who succeeded to the manor of Felsted, Essex, in 1329 and was dead by 1365, or William [Guillaume] de Glanville who was presented to the Rectory of Chevington, Suffolk on 9 July 1367.   CB

PROV. Mrs Motte of Suffolk, 1790; presented to Wreay church (consecrated 1842) by its founder, Sara Losh.

LIT. Smith 1792; Longstaffe 1876, p. 129; Allen 1896, p. 106; Cal. Inq. P.M., VII, p. 150; Cal.Pat.R.1340–3, p. 392; Webster 1938; Evans 1950, fig. 208b; Instrumenta Ecclesiastica, f. 15; Scott n.d., pl. XIV, fig. 3.

125   Altar or processional cross

1220–50
Gilt bronze: h. 28.8 cm (including tang), h. figure 11.8 cm, w. 19.9 cm
The Board of Trustees of the Victoria and Albert Museum, London, M.13–1952

The cross and figure (cast hollow) retain traces of heavy gilding. The cross has been broken near its foot and repaired. There are four holes (presumably not original) drilled through the bottom of the cross and its tang to take pins or rivets, and two holes through the cross behind the figure of Christ. The back is plain. The piece is badly rubbed front and back.

W.L. Hildburgh, assigned the cross to England and the first third of the thirteenth century, comparing manuscript illuminations such as the Crucifixion miniature in the psalter of Robert de Lindesey, c. 1220–2 (Cat. 254). While that has stiff-leaf foliage running the length of the cross, the present cross is decorated only at its ends, with foliate decoration represented as flattened capitals. Closer still are two Norwegian wood crucifixes (Universitetets Oldsaksamling, Oslo), from Faaberg and Tretten (Andersson 1949, figs. 90, 91), with less flamboyant stiff-leaf than that in the Lindesey Psalter; the figure of Christ on the Tretten cross is the closest in type to the present figure. Andersson recognised the debt such Norwegian sculptures owed to English prototypes, but he was unaware of any three-dimensional examples of the latter. Two slightly later, gilt copper crucifixes provide additional evidence for an English provenance for the present cross: the

125

first, from Bellinge (Nationalmuseet, Copenhagen), was attributed by Andersson to an English workshop of the third quarter of the thirteenth century. The second, in Hölandet Church, slightly rougher stylistically, he considered to be a Norwegian copy of an English work (ibid., pp. 243–6, figs 131, 134). Perhaps the most convincing evidence for an English provenance and for the cross's original function is the pen-drawing of an archbishop, of around 1250, in the Westminster Psalter (Cat. 9), f. 221: he holds a cross of remarkably similar type (James 1925–6, no. 129, p. 25, pl. XXVIII).   PW

PROV. Bt by Dr W. L. Hildburgh in Paris, 1927 (said to have come from the Auvergne); on loan to the V&A, 1927–52; given to the V&A by Dr Hildburgh, 1952.

LIT. Hildburgh 1942; Oman 1962b, p. 199, pl. XVa.

126   Pair of Limoges candlesticks

c. 1230
Copper, champlevé enamel and gilt: h. 31.2 cm
Diocese of Bristol: from St Thomas the Martyr, on loan to St Nicholas Church Museum, Bristol

These candlesticks are decorated in the Limoges tradition with geometrical patterns picked out in bright enamels and gold. The only figurative work on the candlesticks is to be found on the bases. A mythical figure of a dragon with a human torso is holding a shield and fighting a lion. One of the applied human heads remains in situ. Relief work on such small objects was relatively unusual; however, a head in relief can be seen on a similar sized candlestick in the Victoria and Albert Museum.

It is probable that such objects would have been produced on a large scale in the Limoges workshops in France. It is thought that these particular candlesticks were brought from Limoges to Bristol as early as 1232, the date of the consecration of the church of St

126

the purchase of 10 lb of verdigris at 7d per lb which was passed to Alexander the chandler.

JC

PROV. Given to Jesus College, Cambridge by Sir Ninian Comper, 1945; according to him, found in a recess in the chapel during restoration by A. W. Pugin, 1846–9; design on candlestock was certainly used by Pugin on brass tops to the candlestocks on the lectern he provided for the chapel.

LIT. RCHM, *Cambridge* 1959, pp. 90–1, pl. 68.

128   Candlestock

14th century
Wax, painted and gilded: h. 55 cm
The Trustees of the British Museum, London,
  MLA 1965, 4–3, 1

The decoration and measurements of this candlestock are so close to those of Cat. 127 that it is impossible to escape the conclusion

127   128

Thomas the Martyr; possibly they were presented to the church on this occasion. This would make them the earliest pair of Limoges candlesticks in England. Their low material value would have spared them during the Reformation.

Each candlestick is made up of ten pieces: a pyramidal base with feet on to which was bolted a shaft terminating in a conical spike or pricket. On to this shaft were slotted four decorated cylinders, three spherical nodes and finally a drip pan. The sections, all made of beaten copper, would have been enamelled and gilded before being assembled. The pricket has now been replaced by a nozzle and the height of the candlesticks reduced from *c.* 35 cm to 31.2 cm. On one candlestick the nodes seem to have been wrongly reassembled.   JS

PROV. Church of St Thomas the Martyr, Bristol; acq. by St Nicholas Church Museum.

LIT. *Trans. Brit. Gloucs. Arch. Soc.*, vol. XXVII, pp. 340–351; vol. XXX, pp. 174–5.

127   Candlestock

14th century
Wax, painted and gilded: h. 54.5 cm, diam. 6.5 cm
The Master and Fellows of Jesus College,
  Cambridge, on loan to the Fitzwilliam Museum,
  E 63

A candlestock stood on a pricket candlestick and supported, with the aid of a metal fitting on the top, a smaller wax candle which could be replaced when necessary. The intention, since the candlestock was tapered, was to give the impression that very large candles were being burnt. The candlestock is decorated with a pattern of six and a half spirals. This consists, first, of a green line with gilding on both sides. On each side of this there are red four-petalled flowers and in the centre a white naturalistic vine scroll, each tendril of which terminates in three leaves. On the top of this spiral decoration is a gilded horizontal band, with white painted spots, from which rise six fleurons alternating with six red trefoils. The order of painting appears to have been first the green, then the gold, and finally the red and white paint. The white may have been painted through a stencil.

This candlestock and its fellow (Cat. 128) are without parallel and present a remarkable survival of a decorative altar fitting in wax. The naturalistic vine scroll suggests a date at the very end of the thirteenth century or the beginning of the fourteenth century. A representation of a similar candlestock appears in an early fourteenth-century manuscript (Cat. 110). The candles used by Queen Eleanor of Castile were coloured with various substances including vermilion and green. In her wardrobe account for December 1289 (Parsons 1977, p. 80) there is a reference to

that they were made as a pair whatever their subsequent history. This candlestock has been repaired in the middle. JC

PROV. Bt from Captain George Kett, MC, in 1965; according to him found by his great-grandfather George Kett, of Wymondham and Norwich, somewhere in Norfolk where, prior to 1846, he had carried out much restoration work (James Rattee was apprenticed to George Kett, and in 1843 came to Cambridge where he worked for Pugin).

129 Church bell

c. 1320
Bronze: diam. of mouth 73.5 cm
Inscr. + IHC: NAZARENUS: REX: IUDEORUM
Norfolk Museums Service (King's Lynn
   Museums), KL 47.974

The bell is from Lynn foundry, Norfolk. The fine inscription is in Lombardic capitals, with the letters almost equally spaced round the bell. The insides of the letters are decorated and the Z is on its side; the initial cross is ornamented and the two-dot stops between the words plain. The six canons, or loops on the crown, have cable moulded faces.

A bell formerly at Woodrising, Norfolk,

130

bore the same initial cross, stop, lettering and the same inscription with the addition of the name of the founder, Thomas de Lenne. He is thought to have been Thomas Belleyetere of Lynn, whose name appears in the Subsidy Roll of 6 Edward III (1333). RC

PROV. Hales Church, Norfolk, now redundant; to King's Lynn Museum, 1974.

LIT. L'Estrange 1874, pp. 22, 139, 201.

130 Mortar

Dated 1308
Copper alloy: h. 23.5 cm, diam. 30 cm
Inscr. in Lombardic capitals round lip MORTARĪV
· S̄C̄ I · JOH̄IS · EWANḠEL · DE · INFIRMARIA
BE · MARIE EBOR
above base FR · WILLS · DE · TOVTHORP · ME ·
FECIT · Å · D̊ · M̊ · CCC · VIII
The Yorkshire Museum, York

The cast mortar is bucket-shaped with everted lip and base, respectively above and below raised mouldings, and a pair of roped handles. The body is encircled by a wide band, set between raised, roped mouldings and decorated in bas-relief with an overall design of quatrefoils framing figures of animals and birds, some grotesque.

One inscription (Mortar of St John the Evangelist of the Infirmary of the Blessed Mary of York) indicates that this is a pharmacy mortar from the Infirmary of St Mary's Abbey, York. The other is the maker's signature (Brother William of Towthorpe made me 1308). The quality of the mortar suggests that he was a professional founder, but nothing is known about him. He would have changed his name on entering the abbey, of which Towthorpe was a prebend. CB

PROV. Fairfax family, 1714; given to the Yorkshire Philosophical Society Museum, St Mary's Abbey, by S. Kenrick, 1835.

LIT. Yorks. Phil. Soc. 1858, pp. 106–8, no. VI; Benson 1898, pp. 19–20; Hemming 1929, pp. 1–3, fig. 1.

129

131 Eight heraldic tiles

1270–7

Earthenware, inlaid: h. (min.) 12.5 cm
  (max.) 14 cm, w. (min.) 13.2 cm, (max.)
  14.2 cm, th. (min.) 2.5 cm, (max.) 3 cm
Cheltenham Art Gallery and Museums 1926.30,
  nos 11, 40, 60, 37, 42, 24, 9, 43

The Cistercian abbey of Hailes, Gloucestershire, was founded by Richard, Earl of Cornwall, brother of Henry III, in 1246. In 1270

131

Edmund, second son of Richard, presented a
phial of the Holy Blood to the community.
This important relic needed a worthy setting,
so the east end of the church was rebuilt and
extended in the form of a chevet of chapels
radiating around the apse. This was completed in 1277. Excavation in the chevet and
north presbytery aisle have revealed large
areas of paving *in situ*. This was arranged in
panels in a chequered appearance of oxidised
(red) and reduced (dark blue) tiles. These
eight tiles illustrate some of the heraldic tiles
with which the eastern arm of the abbey
church was decorated. All the heraldry on
the tiles is connected with Richard, Earl of
Cornwall or his second son Edmund. They
are (11) England; (40) Richard, Earl of
Cornwall; (60) Provence for Sanchia of Provence, Richard's second wife; (37) von Valkenburg for Beatrix von Valkenburg,
Richard's third wife (cf. Cat. 226); and four

baronial families, (42) Warenne, (24) Ferrers, (9) Stafford, and (43) Peveril. The tiles,
now rather worn, would originally have
provided a bright and colourful heraldic floor
demonstrating not only the royal descent
and marriages of Richard and Edmund, but
also their connections with many of the
principal baronial families of the time. JC

PROV. From Hailes Abbey; W. St Clair Baddeley
Coll.

LIT. Baddeley 1908; Eames 1980, pp. 202–3.

132 Bawsey tiles

c. 1376

Earthenware, twelve tiles with relief decorated
  designs: average size l. 10.1 cm, w. 9.7 cm,
  th. 1.9 cm
The Trustees of the British Museum, London, nos
  7546, 7415, 7449, 7093, 7057, 7321, 6820,
  11,131, 11,132, 7301, 11,119, 6843

All these tiles were produced at the kiln site at
Bawsey near King's Lynn, Norfolk. Ten of
these were found on the actual kiln site while
the other two were found at Beachemwell

Church and Castle Acre Church. They were
produced in the second half of the fourteenth
century; the kiln mainly supplied churches
and manor or town houses in East Anglia.
The twelve tiles are arranged so that light
and dark glazed tiles alternate. The designs
include dragons, stars, stamps, and a number
of heraldic shields. One (6843) shows the
arms of the Beauchamp family who inherited
West Acre in 1310. One closely datable tile is
represented by three examples (6820,
11,131, 11,132). This bears the inscription
*Orate pro anima d[omi]ni Nich[oli]; de Stowe
Vicari.* Nicholas of Stowe was vicar of Snettisham, Norfolk and died in 1376. The tile
bearing his name was originally designed
either to surround his tomb or to mark the
place of his burial. The Bawsey tiles are
therefore good examples of the type of mass-
produced tiles that a priest might order in the
reign of Richard II. JC

PROV. From Bawsey kiln, Norfolk, except no.
11,132, Beachemwell Church, Norfolk, and no.
11,119, Castle Acre Church, Norfolk.

LIT. Eames 1955, pp. 162–81; Eames 1980, pp.
109–15.

132

IV Nobility and Knights

Along with the bishops, the great lay magnates – the tenants-in-chief who held their lands directly from the Crown – occupied a central position in English politics and society. Their relations with the king were governed by mutual responsibilities and were particularly successful during the first part of Edward I's reign, that is from 1272 to 1294, and, despite inauspicious beginnings, during the long reign of Edward III (1327–77). When royal policies faltered (weakness was chiefly measured by reliance on favourites at Court, military failures and high taxation) strong opposition came from the nobility: Simon de Montfort, Earl of Leicester, led the rebellion against Henry III; Thomas, Earl of Lancaster, led the first rebellion against Edward II; Henry Bolingbroke, Duke of Lancaster, toppled Richard II.

The nature of the aristocratic hierarchy was ever changing, as the fortunes of noble families waxed and waned. By long tradition the earls occupied the top rung of the social ladder, but they declined in numbers and in political importance during the thirteenth century. Edward III's reign saw a revival, as new earldoms were created. Also a new stratification of the aristocracy was taking place: the first duke was created in 1337 when the king's six-year-old son and heir, Edward of Woodstock – the Black Prince (pp. 476–81) – was made Duke of Cornwall; and a hereditary peerage tied to the House of Lords emerged. The fourteenth century was a golden age for the nobility.

Knights were usually below the highest ranks of the nobility. They were traditionally able to equip themselves with a horse and all the necessary arms of a cavalryman. Great occasions, such as a feast day or a battle, were sometimes chosen for mass knightings. By far the biggest was held in Westminster Abbey in 1306, when a further campaign in Scotland was needed after the success of Robert Bruce. Nearly three hundred young men were knighted along with the king's eldest son, the future Edward II. The feast after the ceremony was called the Feast of Swans: two swans richly adorned with gold were brought in and the king swore 'before God and the swans' to reconquer Scotland. The knights pledged themselves to fulfil the royal vow.

Knights were also closely involved in local government: they were the leaders of county society. By the fourteenth century representatives from the towns and two knights sent from each shire formed the House of Commons.

Nobility of birth was itself a virtue; so was success in arms. Both were linked in the cult of chivalry. Tournaments were spectacular social occasions, and they were also the training grounds for knights. The code of chivalry, idealised in romance literature, was institutionalised in England in the Order of the Garter (see p. 490). It was closely associated with beliefs in Christian endeavour, and fighting on crusade continued to represent the pinnacle of knightly courage and endurance.

The endemic nature of warfare had a profound influence on many social developments, and some of its most tangible manifestations were the castles which the nobility built both for defence and for display (Cat. 133–4). The self-image which the nobility left on their tombs after their death was of the man-at-arms (Cat. 135, 224), and the constantly repeated representations of them on horseback in the objects they used during their lives, for example on their seals (Cat. 143) and on their plate (Cat. 154–6), reiterated their distinguishing status as mounted cavalry. The ever increasing use of heraldry served to reinforce the concept of noble birth (Cat. 153).

Any assessment of medieval nobility must stress that women were clearly subordinate. Even so, their importance in relation to the specific problems of landholding, quite apart from any other considerations, must not be overlooked. In the first place, there had been, from the twelfth century, a new emphasis on legitimacy for succession, and the lawfully wedded wife thus became the sole source of legitimate heirs. Also, a woman could succeed to her father in the absence of male heirs and could pass on her lands to her husband and to her sons (Cat. 141–2). Sole control over inherited lands, however, was usually acquired only if a woman was widowed. A third share of lands, the dower share, went to a widow for life. Dowager peeresses could, therefore, hold a large part of an inheritance for many years. No doubt wives, daughters, heiresses and dowager countesses played a vital part in many aspects of the cultural and religious life of the realm and were on occasion important patrons (see p. 44). But in these centuries there are few examples of women who had in their hands direct political power: Queen Isabella, who plotted successfully against her husband, Edward II, was for a short time rather an exception.

133

133 Caerphilly Castle, Gwent, from the air

1268–1326
Photograph

Gilbert de Clare, Earl of Gloucester (1243–95) began the castle in 1268 with the intention of securing Glamorgan from the incursions of the Welsh prince Llywelyn ap Gruffydd. Building was interrupted in 1270–1, when it was besieged and burnt by the prince. But Earl Gilbert repossessed it in 1272 and by c. 1280 it was largely complete, according to the latest chronology (Johns 1978), though additions were made by the Despensers in 1326 (Taylor 1952). Caerphilly was the first new English castle to be built on the principle of concentric defence, and it anticipates many of the technical achievements of Edward I's Welsh castles. The rectangular inner ward with its corner towers and twin gatehouses is very similar to those of Harlech (begun 1283; Cat. 323) and Beaumaris (begun 1295), and displays knowledge of earlier French plans (e.g. Dourdan, begun c. 1220). The two great fortified

dams which hold back Caerphilly's impressive water defences may in part be influenced by Byzantine architecture. The south dam (1268–71) in particular invites comparison with the fifth-century Fildami cistern at Bakirkoy near Constantinople whose retaining walls have the same rhythm of stout buttresses and concave interstices. The castle was heavily restored by the Marquesses of Bute in 1868, 1900 and 1928–39, but the work was in all instances based on clear archaeological evidence.   JMM

LIT. Taylor 1952; Rees 1974; Johns 1978.

134 Warkworth Castle, Northumberland, donjon from the south

c. 1380–90
Photograph

The tower house or donjon was built by Henry Percy, first Earl of Northumberland, and is the most distinctive of his additions to the great castle that was granted to his family by Edward III in 1332. Its exact date is uncertain, but the lion rampant of the Percys which decorates its northern salient would, after 1390, have been quartered with the arms of the Lucys; this and the style of its architectural details argue for its construction during the previous decade. In its formality and purposeful symmetry Warkworth is the most striking representative of an increasingly architectural approach in the fortifications of the late fourteenth century. The designs of Queenborough (1361–77; fig. 2), Bolton (c. 1378) and Bodiam (1386) all suggest a powerful initial architectural concept to which the interior planning has been made to conform, and at Warkworth more than twenty rooms of different volumes and relationships have been ingeniously interlocked to fit into the compass of a square with semi-polygonal projecting towers on each face. Some of the keeps of the early twelfth century show a similar preoccupation with external symmetry but are far less ambitious in their internal arrangements.

The donjon stands on the site of a Norman predecessor, and the notion that it is a conscious revival of the Anglo-Norman keep remains an open question. The idea was refuted by Simpson (1938), who preferred to characterise it as a purely architectural expression of the needs of late fourteenth-century feudalism when families like the Percys, who relied on armies of mercenaries rather than on loyal feudal levies, required a powerfully fortified and well-appointed inner fortress within the walls of their own castle. It has been suggested (Simpson 1941) that its architect may have been John Lewyn (*fl.* 1364–1398), Bishop Hatfield's master mason at Durham and the designer of Lord Scrope's castle at Bolton. JMM

LIT. Simpson 1938; Simpson 1941; Harvey 1984, pp. 181–4.

135 Reepham Church, tomb of Sir William de Kerdiston

c. 1361
Photograph

The architecture of this tomb, like that of another in Norfolk, the similar but grander and earlier monument to Sir Oliver de Ingham (d. 1344) at Ingham, is in the style of the royal master mason William Ramsey, who ran an important tomb workshop in London as a sideline. Ramsey died in the Black Death in 1349 but his style of tomb architecture survived him, no doubt because, as has emerged recently, his shop was carried on by his daughter Agnes. In 1358–9 she supplied the tomb of Queen Isabella in the London Greyfriars (destroyed).

The gablets and upright cusped panels of the canopy derive ultimately from mid-thirteenth-century French Rayonnant portal architecture (see fig. 48). Like the similar features on William Ramsey's main work, the chapter house of St Paul's Cathedral (Cat. 386), they are closer to their ultimate source than to more recent English interpretations (e.g. Cat. 325). The relationship exemplifies the kind of links between the Rayonnant and Perpendicular styles which are hardly explicable unless one posits the existence of drawings of thirteenth-century French buildings preserved by the Royal Works organisation. Although extremely accomplished, the architecture of the Kerdiston tomb is essentially a framework for the fashionably clad weepers

134

135

here for five priests, and in 1370 licence was granted for the construction of their domestic quarters, which still exist. Besides the splendid series of brasses (just visible beyond the communion rail; see Cat. 139), the spacious thirteenth-century chancel retains some of the fittings which in 1362 Lord Cobham agreed to provide. In their crisp detailing the piscina and sedilia typify the London version of Perpendicular established by William Ramsey in the 1330s and 1340s and practised by other designers after Ramsey's death in 1349 (see Cat. 135). For statuary possibly from the destroyed reredos at Cobham see Cat. 508.   CW

LIT. Hussey 1944.

137   Great Chamber murals

c. 1330
Wall painting in Longthorpe Tower,
   Cambridgeshire
Inscr. in Latin and French
Photograph

The tower, with the Great Chamber on the first floor, was added *c.* 1300–10 to an earlier manor house, and was probably built by Robert de Thorpe, steward of nearby Peterborough Abbey until 1329, with the paintings executed either for him or his son Robert. They were uncovered and waxed in 1946, and are currently being cleaned. The programme includes, on the north wall, the Ages of Man, Nativity and Apostles' Creed;

on the tomb chest and for the superbly carved and highly detailed effigy. The strange twisting pose and the even odder motif of a 'bed' of cobbles recur at Ingham.   CW

LIT. Sayer 1972, pp. 18–19; Wilson 1980a, pp. 45–54; Blackley 1983.

136   Cobham Church, piscina and sedilia looking south-west

c. 1370
Photograph

Cobham Church, Kent, is a good example of a parish church made into a mausoleum and showplace by an important local family. In 1362 John, Lord Cobham founded a college

137

over the doorway, Three Living and Three Dead; on the east wall, the Wheel of Five Senses; on the south wall, enthroned kings, heraldry, Bonnacon; on the west wall, the angel appearing to St Anthony, prophets; and on the vault, Evangelist symbols, King David and other musicians.

This almost complete survival of a medieval secular scheme is unique in England, where otherwise only fragments of secular wall painting remain (Cat. 696). Although a few reasonably complete schemes survive in France – e.g. one of *c.* 1300 at Pernes (Vaucluse), showing battle and other subjects (Deschamps and Thibout 1963, pp. 229–34, pls CXL–CXLI) – they are less varied in subject-matter than Longthorpe which has been justly described as a 'spiritual encyclopedia'. The unexceptional context of these paintings suggests that such

136

pictorial schemes were once not uncommon. Several extremely rare subjects are included, e.g. the Wheel of Senses, appropriately located above the fireplace, with the senses represented symbolically – Taste as a monkey eating, Touch as a spider's web – around the rim. In wall painting, the only other surviving example of this subject in wheel format dates from the thirteenth century, in the Cistercian Abbey of Tre Fontane near Rome (Nordenfalk 1976, p. 24, fig. 13).

Contrasting with the sophisticated iconography, the technique of the paintings is markedly ordinary. Although they have been compared to Peterborough manuscripts such as the Psalter of Hugh of Stukeley (Cambridge, Corpus Christi College, MS 53) of between 1304–21, they seem slightly later in style. DP

LIT. Rouse & Baker 1955; Tristram 1955, pp. 92–4, 107–8, 219–21, pls 41, 64b; Rouse 1964; Nordenfalk 1976, pp. 24–5, fig. 14; Yapp 1978; Nordenfalk 1985, p. 2; Sears 1986, pp. 137–8, fig. 78.

138 Brass of Lady Margaret de Camoys

c. 1310
Rubbing: l. of figure 160 cm
Inscr. in separate Lombardic letters around slab
  (indents only) MARGARETE : DE : CAMOYS :
  GIST : ICI : DEVS : DE : SA : ALME : EIT :
  MERCI : AMEN
Rubbing by Derrick A. Chivers (original in
  Church of St George, Trotton, Sussex)

The figure is full-length with hands in prayer. She wears a veil, a wimple that covers both chest and throat, and a gown with loose, three-quarter-length sleeves and a scooped neckline marked by a plain border below a low standing collar round the sides and back. The close-fitting buttoned sleeves of an undertunic are visible on the forearms and the tips of the pointed shoes below the hem, where a small dog crouches. On her robe are the indents of nine small shields which were presumably originally set with enamelled copper arms. The slab, which is of Purbeck marble, bears the indents of the inscription ('Margaret of Camoys lies here. God have mercy on her soul. Amen'), and indents of border fillets, a cusped and crocketed canopy, eight shields, and numerous background stars and other unidentified devices.

This magnificent figure and the contemporary one of Joan de Cobham at Cobham, Kent, have considerable claim to being the finest female brasses in existence. Margaret de Camoys (née de Braose), wife of Ralph de Camoys, was dead by 1311–12, so her monument can be ascribed with reasonable confidence to *c.* 1310. This makes it the earliest full figure brass known to survive in Britain. Stylistic analysis shows that the workshop that produced it was also responsible for most of the major figure brasses of

138

the first four decades of the fourteenth century (cf. Cat. 139, 234–5), so 'Camoys' has been adopted as an eponym for it. CB

PROV. Church of St George, Trotton, Sussex.
LIT. Norris 1978a, fig. 124 1978b, pp.13–15, Binski 1987, pp. 78–82.

139 Brass of Sir John de Cobham

c. 1360 (1362?)
Rubbing: l. of figure 152.4 cm
Inscr. in Gothic letters on marginal fillet,
  incomplete, but partly recorded (*De terre fust
  fait) Et en terre a terre suis (retourne Johan de
  Cobham founder de ceste place qui fut nomme)
  mercy de malme eit la seinte Trinite*
Rubbing by Derrick A. Chivers (original in Parish
  Church of St Mary Magdalene, Cobham, Kent)

The full-length knight is under a single canopy; shafts, pinnacles and a figure of the Virgin above are modern replacements, as are his feet and the lion on which they rest. He holds a miniature church with a central spire. He wears a bacinet with a short medial ridge at the apex and a narrow mail aventail laced under it; a sleeveless, close-fitting, waisted coat armour with an invected hem;

from below this project the invected hem, set with rosette-shaped rivet heads, of the coat-of-plates, and, below that, the straight hem of the mail habergeon, both worn beneath; complete closed plate vambraces, opening on hinges, with laminated spaudlers on the points of the shoulders, and cowters with very small circular side wings with central rosettes; fingered gauntlets with short cuffs, and two laminations across the back of each hand, studded with rivets which indicate that they were textile-covered; cuisses studded with rivets, indicating that they were of textile lined with small plates, and carrying rounded poleyns, each with a central vertical reinforcing strip; closed, hinged, plate greaves; and laminated, pointed sabatons with rowel spurs (all replacements). Round his hips is a broad belt composed of

139

rectangular ornamental plaques and with a larger central clasp; on the right and left respectively are a cruciform dagger and sword (the external quillon of the latter replaced).

This is a London 'Series A' brass. Sir John de Cobham, 3rd Baron Cobham, died in 1408, but the brass is clearly much earlier. The armour on the brasses of Sir Hugh de Hastings (Cat. 678) and Sir John de Wautone at Wimbish, Essex, both of whom died in 1347, is only a little less developed, and that on the effigy of Hugh, Lord Despenser (d. 1349), at Tewkesbury, is markedly similar. The brass itself, apart from the miniature church, closely resembles one to the 2nd Baron (d. 1354) also at Cobham. On the other hand, it also closely resembles the figure of Thomas Cheyne (d. 1368) at Drayton Beauchamp, Buckinghamshire, suggesting a common date for the Cheyne and Cobham brasses of *c.* 1360. In 1362 Sir John refounded Cobham church as a collegiate one, an action that is both mentioned in the inscription and represented by the church he holds (see Cat. 136).   CB

PROV. Parish Church of St Mary Magdalene, Cobham, Kent.

LIT. Gough 1786, II (ii), p. 22, pl. VI; Norris 1978a, p. 65, fig. 38.

140   Brass of Sir John and Lady Harsick

c. 1384
Rubbing: l. of male figure 155 cm
Inscr. in Gothic letters on marginal fillet, incomplete and apparently not all in its original position, but partly recorded + *Hic iacet dns Joh̄es H (arsick miles ejusdem nominis) tercius qui obiit sc̄d̄o die sept̄ebr Anno dn̄i mill̄o CCC lxxxiiii cuius aīe p[ro]piciet[ur] d̄s arn̄e et dn̄a katerina Vx(or)[…]*
Rubbing by Derrick A. Chivers (original in Parish Church of St George, Southacre, Norfolk)

Sir John and his wife hold hands, he with his left hand on his sheathed sword. Sir John wears a more developed version of the armour depicted on the John de Cobham brass (Cat. 139), differing in the following details: the aventail is fuller and laced over the edge of the bacinet; the cowters are laminated above and below, and have fully-developed oval side wings; the mail habergeon is visible at the armpits, the inside of one elbow, and below the coat armour; the left gauntlet, the only one worn, is of hour-glass form; the cuisses are of plate with articulated poleyns and strong medial ridges extending down the greaves. It has laminated pointed sabatons with spurs with large many-pointed rowels, and the coat armour bears the arms of Harsick. The hip belt is decorated with quatrefoils within circles, and the large circular front clasp bears a cinquefoil flower. The cruciform sword attached on the left has an oval wheel pommel with a button, wire-

140

bound grip and trumpet-shaped quillons. The armour is of the same type as the Black Prince's achievements (Cat. 626–33).

She wears a gown under an open mantle – fastened by a cord which she hold with one hand – both reaching to the ground. The gown is close fitting with full skirt, square neck-opening, and tight buttoned trumpet sleeves (perhaps actually on an undergarment), and bears her own arms, Calthorp, impaling Harsick. Her head is bare, and her hair dressed in two stiff plaits on either side of her face, linked by a decorated band across the top of the forehead. Between their heads is an indent for a shield, and above, set at right angles, is a canted shield bearing the Harsick arms, under a mantled helm crested with a bush of feathers encircled by a wreath; the fringed lower edge of the lining is represented. The Calthorp arms and the upper parts of the Harsick ones are recessed and hatched and would originally have been filled with lead or perhaps pewter (to represent the silver of ermine) and coloured composition. This is a London 'Series B' brass.   CB

PROV. Parish Church of St George, Southacre, Norfolk.

LIT. Gough 1786, I (ii), p. 146, pl. LVIII; Norris 1978a, p. 70, fig. 161; 1978b, pp. 54, 70.

Seals of lords and ladies

Beginning in the twelfth century, the usual image on a knight's seal showed a mounted warrior, and on a lady's a standing woman. During the early thirteenth century heraldry began to play an increasingly important role in the designation of aristocracy, and it is thus no surprise to find shields of arms being added to the established formats. Normally a single shield is chosen to show the lineage of a man, whereas on a woman's seal there may well be two: her father's arms would normally be to her left (sinister) while her husband's would be on the more important dexter side. At this early period it is very difficult to establish hard-and-fast rules, and the two ladies' seals chosen in this section indicate independent behaviour.   TAH

141   Seal of Margaret de Quincy, Countess of Winchester 1207–35

c. 1207–18
Wax: h. 8 cm, w. 5 cm
Inscr. SIGILL : MARGARETE : DE : QUINCI : COMITISSE : WINTONIE
President and Fellows, Magdalen College, Oxford, Brackley Charter B.180

Margaret is standing under a rounded archway which supports crenellated parapets, presumably indicating the entrance to a castle or city. To her right (dexter) hang two shields of arms, de Quincy at the top and FitzWalter below. A pairing of the same two shields occurs on an early seal of her husband, Saher, as Earl of Winchester (a title which he had been granted by early 1207) and on the matrix of Robert FitzWalter (Cat. 454). The choice of a tree to support the shields on Margaret's seal cannot connote family descent, since the relationship between FitzWalter and the de Quincys was military and political rather than genealog-

141

ical. The cinquefoil on the gateway may be a family emblem since her son, Robert, used it on his shield.

The flower which Margaret holds in her right hand commonly appeared as an attribute on ladies' seals (cf. London 1984a, no. 337). T A H

LIT. Birch 1892, II, nos. 6700–1; GEC 1910–59, vol. 12, pt 2d, 750–1, n. j, app. 1; Blair 1943, p. 20; Henderson 1978, pp. 33–4.

142 Seal of Joanna de Stuteville

1266(?)
Wax: diam. 6 cm
Inscr. . . . . EVIL . . (for Stuteville)
British Library, Cotton Charter XXIX.63

Joanna adopts an unusual format, riding sidesaddle (a rarity in itself) and carrying the shield of Stuteville, from her father Nicholas whose sole heir she was, rather than of her first husband (Hugh Wake, d. 1241) or her second (Hugh Bigod, m. 1244, d. 1266). Both of these men came from aristocratic families; the latter was Justiciar and brother of the Earl of Norfolk.

The image of Joanna on horseback derives from the seal of Alice, widow of Henry III, Duke of Brabant and Lotharingia (Demay 1873, I, no. 238, pl. opp. p. 37, on a charter of 1260) or something extremely like it. But rather than carrying a hawk as Alice does, Joanna chooses to display her inheritance by holding a shield of arms. Other 'Netherlandish' seals of this equestrian or hawking type showing a lady riding sidesaddle are known (e.g. Demay, op. cit. no. 145, pl. opp. p. 29) and seem also to have belonged to female aristocrats who held estates in their own right, perhaps indicating an association between equestrian imagery and 'lordship'.

T A H

LIT. Birch 1892, II, no. 6719; Tremlett & London 1967, p. 148; Clay 1952, IX, pp. 21–3, 130.

142

143 Seal of Roger de Quincy, Earl of Winchester and Constable of Scotland 1235–64

Probably 1235
Wax: diam. 7.8 cm
Inscr. obv. SIGILL : ROGERI : DE : QUINCI :
  COMITIS : WINCESTRIE
  rev. SIGILL : ROGERI : DE : QUINCI :
  CONSTABLLARII : SCOCIE
Public Record Office, London, DL27/203

Roger was not granted the title Earl of Winchester until after his mother, Margaret (Cat. 141), had died early in 1235. In the previous year he had become Constable of Scotland in right of his wife whose father, the previous Constable, had died without direct male heir. Thus Roger's seal, which carries these two titles, probably dates from the mid-1230s. The designs of obverse and reverse substantially follow those of a seal made for his father, Saher, probably c. 1218 (Henderson 1978, pls 19, 20). The only differences are the dragon, added on Roger's seal beneath the horse on the equestrian side, and the six-petalled rose on the side where he is shown on foot fighting a rampant lion. Despite at least fifteen years' difference in date, the two seals are virtually identical in style. The engraver must have been told to copy Saher's, but to add dragon and flower to make a distinction between them. This was thought necesary because legends, in a vulnerable position round the edges of seals, were easily broken away, and as a result motifs which would facilitate differentiation were often employed on similar seals. T A H

LIT. Birch, 1892, II, nos 6346–52; Stevenson & Wood 1940, III, p. 55; Henderson 1978; Ellis 1981, II, no. P 1916.

143

144

144 Seal of Richard of Cornwall as Count of Poitou and Earl of Cornwall 1227–72

1227(?)
Wax: diam. 8 cm
Inscr. obv. SIGILLUM RICARDI COMITIS
  PICTAVIS
  rev. SIGILLUM RICARDI COMITIS
  CORNUBIE
British Library, Loose seal XXXVI, 215

Richard, younger brother of King Henry III, was knighted early in 1225 and was styled Count of Poitou by August that year and Earl of Cornwall by mid-1227. The equestrian side of his seal is a more energetic version of the king's seal of November 1218 (Cat. 453). Despite this difference of mood, the details of lettering, arms and armour, are very similar on these two seals and it is likely that Richard's is also the work of Master Walter de Ripa. The reverse shows a shield of arms surrounded by scrolls of foliage which not

only help to integrate the shield into an overall design but have the connotations of flourishing success.

Although the identification of an individual by means of heraldry had been an option from the later years of the twelfth century, the greater nobility had continued to employ the equestrian image as the main indicator of their status. The use of the shield on its own was, at first, usually confined to small seals. Gradually, though, the scale increased until, as here, it attained an importance comparable with the representation of the knight on horseback. This signals the coming of age of heraldry as a means of stressing lineage and legitimate title. T A H

LIT. Birch 1892, II, nos 6328–9; Blair 1943; Posse 1909, I, pls 36 no. 3, 37 no. 2.

145 Chessman, probably a rook

c. 1220–40
Walrus ivory; extensive damage to top, many heads and weapons; traces of blackened paint in deeply-cut sections and foliage: h. 10.1 cm, w. 6.5 cm
The Board of Trustees of the Victoria and Albert Museum, London, A.8987–1863

The piece is carved in the round from an exceptionally large walrus tusk. A castle

145

with two tiers of battlements is defended by seven soldiers and a king. The upper tier, crowned by a central dome (with a modern hole pierced through it) is almost completely destroyed. Of the soldiers in the lower tier, two wear kettle-hats, one a helm(?), and all have mail shirts with hoods. Three have long triangular shields decorated with simple patterns, including one with a rampant lion. Beneath the lower crenellated parapet of the castle, the wall is pierced by round windows, out of which figures (one with a sword) are looking. Tendrils of exquisitely engraved stiff-leaf foliage further embellish these lower walls.

Murray believed that this was not a chessman, since the castle form of the rook does not appear in chess until the sixteenth century; Longhurst claimed it as a king. However, it could well have originally had crowning side turrets (now broken off); early rooks traditionally had a two-headed shape (cf. a German Romanesque rook in Berlin, Wichmann 1960, p. 287, pl. 22). Although the castle structure can be paralleled in mid-thirteenth-century manuscripts (Vaughan 1958, pl. vi), the device of creating an illusion of reality with small figures leaning out of 'windows' is something that would not normally be expected before the second quarter of the fourteenth century, as with the figures looking down at the spectator from

the triforium gallery of Selby or the west porch of Exeter Cathedral. It is remarkable in the preceding century, but compare the Lincoln Cathedral west gable (Courtauld Lincoln 1/5/45-7) and the roundels on the octagon at Trondheim (Fett 1908, fig. 29 p. 22). The stiff-leaf foliage, the armour and the drapery style can all be paralleled on the Wells Cathedral west front, probably largely finished in 1242. Even in its sadly mutilated condition, this small masterpiece can claim to be one of the finest of early thirteenth-century ivories.   NS

PROV. Bt in Paris, 1863.

LIT. Maskell 1872, pp. 38–9; Murray 1913, p. 762 n. 9; Koechlin 1924, I, p. 470 n. 1; Longhurst 1926, pp. 38, 99, no. XLVI, pl. 42; Longhurst 1929, p. 8, pl. II; Porter 1974, pp. 73–5, no. 20.

146–8   Three chessmen

c. 1240–50

In spite of doubts expressed by Murray, there seems no reason to question the traditional view that these are knights for chess. In scale, technique of cutting, approach to subject-matter, details of armour and style they share enough common features to suggest a single walrus-ivory workshop. A fourth chesspiece with a knight on horseback (ex Figdor Collec-

tion, now Berlin; see Wichmann 1960, pp. 292–3, pl. 54) does not seem to belong to the same group. Porter compared the group to English seals and manuscripts, dating it to the third quarter of the thirteenth century. However, details of the armour, the type of helm and triangular shield and the flying fold of the surcoat suggest a somewhat earlier date (cf. Morgan 1982, fig. 271; Hunter Blair 1943, pls IIIf–g, VIIa). Indeed, the armour and drapery would not seem out of place on the west front of Wells Cathedral, largely complete in 1242. The elegant but still stylised plant-forms, although not typical stiff leaf, also have close English parallels (e.g. Morgan 1982, fig. 293), as do the remarkably characterised horses and dragons (Morgan 1982, figs 206, 209, 271). These small-scale sculptures are among the most vivid surviving expressions of the taste of the feudal aristocracy of Henry III's reign. Chessmen were made in the image of the contemporary knight, who himself played chess, just as that same knight often commissioned a rider image for his seal (Cat. 144) or bought similar rider figures for his table (Cat. 154, 183).   NS

LIT. Oxford 1656, p. 38; Oxford 1685, no. 587; Way 1846, pp. 242–3; Leeds 1868, p. 209 (Gallery J, no. 721); Maskell 1875, p. 165, no. 14; Westwood 1876, p. 292; Koechlin 1911, p. 11, pl. 10; Pératé 1911, no. 18, pl. XV; Murray 1913, p. 762 n. 9; Koechlin 1924, I, pp. 469–70; II, no. 1256–57–58, pl. CCXII; London 1923, no. 88, pl. XXVIII; Goldschmidt 1926, p. 54, nos 261, 266, 267, pl. LXXII; Longhurst 1926, pp. 39, 99–100, nos XLVII–XLIX, pl. 41; Wichmann 1960, pp. 292–3, pls 52, 55; Paris 1970–1, no. 177; Ottawa 1972, I, pp. 151–2; II, nos 68A–c, pls 91–3; Porter 1974, pp. 64–73, nos 16–19; Greygoose 1979, pls 16–17, 39; Oxford 1983, pp. 284–5, no. 236, fig. 73.

146   Chessman

Walrus ivory with traces of green paint and gilding: h. 7.5 cm, w. 5.8 cm, d. 3.6 cm
The Visitors of the Ashmolean Museum, Oxford, 1685, A 587

This is the masterpiece of the group, exceptional in that the composition of the two sides

146

differs: each shows a knight on horseback in great helm with mail shirt under a surcoat, mail hose and carrying a shield; one knight has a raised sword, the other looks back at his right hand which holds the butt of a lance as if to throw it. Plants with long delicate leaf tips bend around the sides of the ivory and complete the ends.   NS

PROV. Coll. John Tradescant, by 1685; given to University of Oxford by Elias Ashmole, 1683.

147

147   Chessman

Walrus ivory; right arm and weapon broken off: h. 7.9 cm, w. 6.6 cm
New York, The Metropolitan Museum of Art, gift of J. Pierpont Morgan, 1917.190.231

This is cut through as a single figure in the round, with the foliage on only one end: a similarly accoutred knight attacks a winged dragon.   NS

PROV. Paris, Hoentschel Collection, 1911; given to Metropolitan Museum by J. P. Morgan, 1917.

148   Chessman

Walrus ivory: h. 6.5 cm, w. 6.5 cm
Musée Vivenel, Compiègne, France, V 347

Double-sided, like Cat. 146, this repeats its composition on each face: a knight attacks a dragon, but here the knight is on foot.   NS

PROV. Given to town of Compiègne by Antoine Vivenel, 1843.

148

149

149   Misericord: A joust

c. 1379
Oak: h. 30 cm, w. 63 cm, d. 15 cm
The Dean and Chapter of Worcester, south side stalls from east, no.9 (of 42)

The joust takes place on a piece of undulating ground; the horses and knights are well modelled. One knight charges against his opponent with his lance and throws him off his rearing horse, while a drummer and bugler add to the excitement with their din. The knights sport drooping moustaches, and their armour is of the type found on the effigy of the Black Prince in Canterbury Cathedral. The shield of the winning knight is embossed with a floral pattern. As the helmets are without visors, the full horror on the face of the tumbling knight is revealed. A comparable scene is found in the margin of the Luttrell Psalter (Cat. 575, f.82), showing a knight charging and unseating a Saracen.

Jousts involved single combat between two knights and are to be distinguished from tournaments, which were chaotic mêlées and more like real battles. Both, however, were extremely expensive pursuits owing to the cost of armour and horses, and were restricted to the nobility. Many a knight would travel from place to place challenging his opponents in honour of his lady. Chivalry was supported by the royal Courts, and associated with courtly love and the literary romance.   CG

PROV. Worcester Cathedral.

LIT. Keen 1984.

150   Peraldus, *Summa de Vitiis*, bestiary and miscellaneous texts

c. 1240–55
Vellum, ff. 192: 27.8 × 17.2 cm
British Library, Harley MS 3244

The Dominican friar kneeling before Christ on f. 27 seems to have been the owner of this compilation of texts as aids to preaching. These include a moral treatise of Alain of Lille, the *Ars Predicandi* of Richard of Thetford, the *Templum Domini* of Robert Grosseteste, Bishop of Lincoln, a bestiary and a work on the vices by Gulielmus Peraldus written c. 1236.

The treatise of Peraldus is preceded by a symbolic diagram showing a knight on horseback armed with the shield of faith, accompanied by doves representing the seven gifts of the Holy Spirit, confronting an army of devils and dragons representing the vices. The armour of the knight and the trappings of his horse are labelled with names of virtues. Chivalric allegory is used to present the moral struggles of the Christian life (cf. Cat. 438). The other text illustrated is the bestiary, whose anecdotal moralising tales of the various creatures could provide examples for sermons. *Exempla* (moral tales) are found in the other text sections of the manuscript, and the compilation served as a preaching manual. It is very rare to find a book of this type with illustrations. These pictures are in tinted drawing in a style difficult to parallel.   NJM

PROV. Richard Edwards, 17th century; Robert Harley (1661–1724) or Edward Harley (1689–1741); bt by British Museum, 1753.

LIT. Evans 1982, pp. 14–46; Morgan 1982, no. 80, figs 267–70.

151   Book of Hours

c. 1325–30
Parchment, ff. 113: 15.6 × 10.8 cm
Oxford, Bodleian Library, MS Douce 231

A calendar including both the Deposition and Translation of St Hugh of Lincoln (ff. 7–18v.) precedes the text of the Hours of the Virgin (ff. 19–72v.), the Penitential Psalms (ff. 73–87v.) and Gradual Psalms (ff. 88–100v.), and a Litany invoking Bishop Robert Grosseteste (never officially

148

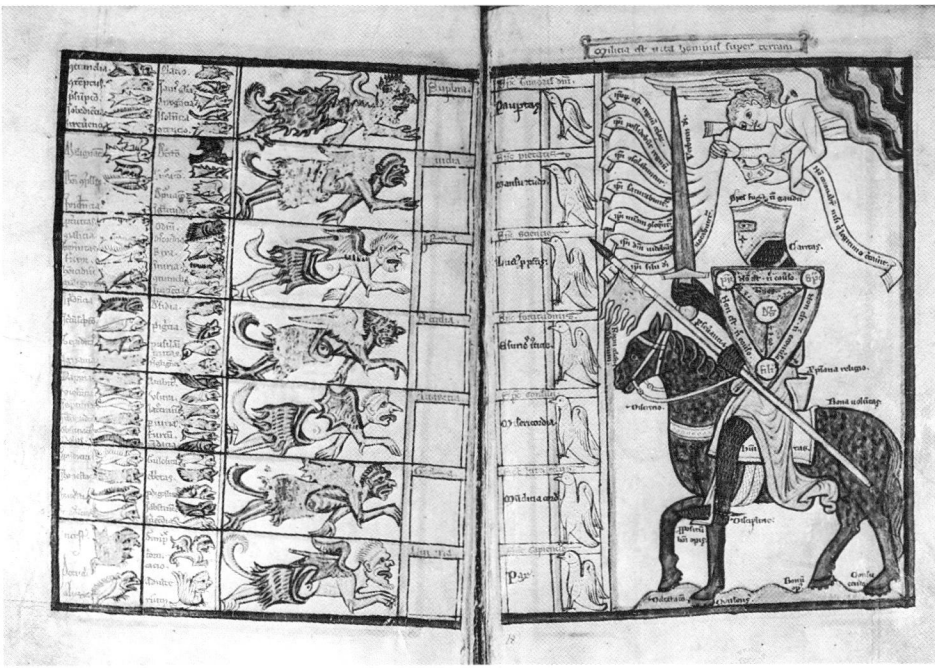

150

151

canonised) as well as Sts Hugh and Hilda follows (ff. 109–13v.) – all suggesting intended use in the diocese of Lincoln. The unidentified owner may have been a partisan of Thomas, Earl of Lancaster (d. 1322), who is represented alongside St George in the first miniature (f. 1) of a series at the beginning of the book that shows pairs of popular saints. Indeed, the position of Thomas in the Douce Hours suggests that he is being put forward as a saint, reflecting a widespread belief, supported by Edward III himself, that Thomas had been a patriotic martyr deserving of canonisation. A similar composition, but with the royal figure identified by his surcoat and shield as the King of England rather than the Earl of Lancaster, is in the Milemete Treatise (Cat. 682), which contains a number of illustrations directly related in style to those of the Douce Hours.

Aside from the full-page miniatures of saints, the Douce volume has a series of historiated initials with full foliated borders and *bas-de-page* animals at the subdivisions of the Hours, and the other text divisions.

The artist of the Douce Hours worked in an unpretentious, even inelegant manner, characterised by awkward, flat, outlined figures whose nearly chinless faces have elongated eyes. His idiosyncratic style recurs in the DuBois Hours (New York, Pierpont Morgan Library, M.700), whose compositions of the Annunciation, Visitation, Adoration of the Magi and Resurrection are identical, as well as elsewhere among the manuscripts of the Milemete group.   LFS

PROV. R. G. [Richard Graves?], 18th century; London, Count Justin MacCarthy-Reagh Sale, May 1789, bt by Francis Douce; beq. to Bodleian Library, 1834.

LIT. Dennison 1986, p. 62; Sandler 1986, no. 87, II, pp. 95–6. repr. I, figs 218, 226; Michael 1987.

152   Book of Hours

c. 1340–50
Parchment, ff. 56: 21 × 14 cm
The Walters Art Gallery, Baltimore, MS W. 105

Like many Books of Hours, the Walters manuscript was made for lay use; its original owners are shown at Mass in a full-page miniature (f. 15) and can be identified by the coat of arms at the beginning of Matins as the Butler family, Lords of Wem, Shropshire, in the diocese of Lichfield. The liturgical calendar, however, seems to have been based on a stock Sarum model of an outdated type.

In addition to the Hours of the Virgin (including illustrated memoriae at Lauds), the Walters volume contains the Short Office of the Cross (with historiated initials) and Suffrages for St Thomas of Canterbury and 'St' Thomas of Lancaster, both originally facing full-page miniatures (f. 14, that of Thomas of Lancaster is lost, cf. Cat. 151), as well as an indulgence of Pope Innocent facing the miniature of the Butlers at Mass. The text illustrations are historiated initials with full or partial borders. Two illustrated pages missing from the manuscript are in the Nationalmuseum, Stockholm (MSS B.1726–7), and at least one other is in private hands.

Not all the work is by the same artist and some is in poor condition, but one of the hands – the painter of the Butler family and the text illustrations – recurs in a Book of Hours now in Dublin (Trinity College, MS 94). This artist painted in the typical large-scale, awkward yet expressive style of the mid-fourteenth century, as exemplified by the Fitzwarin Psalter (Cat. 685).   LFS

PROV. Butler family, 14th century; T. Taylor, Wakefield, 1879; L. Gruel, Paris, bt by Henry Walters; Stockholm leaves bt from Georges Ryaux, Paris, 1955.

LIT. Sandler 1986, no. 117, II, pp. 130–1, repr. I, figs 305–6.

152

153   The Camden Roll

c. 1280
Vellum roll, 3 membranes: l. 1.59 m, w. 15.7 cm
British Library, Cotton Roll XV.8

The Camden Roll is important as one of the few surviving original painted rolls of arms of the thirteenth century. On the face of the roll are 270 shields of arms, and on the dorse 185 corresponding blazons, in French, written in

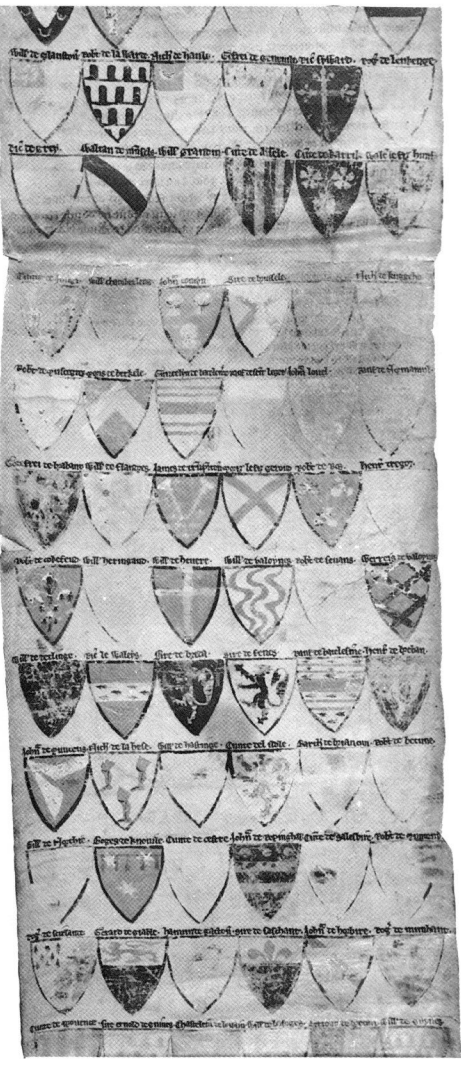

153

154 Aquamanile

Late 13th century
Copper alloy; lance, shield, lid of helmet, both feet
of knight and horse's tail missing: h. 33.7 cm
The Trustees of the British Museum, London,
MLA 53, 3–15, I

This aquamanile was filled through the top of
the helmet and emptied through the spout on
the forehead of the horse. The knight is firmly
seated in the saddle and turns to his lance
side. He has a flat-topped helmet with a thin
slit for the eyes ending in a relief trefoil. There
is another trefoil at the front of the helmet. He
wears mail over which is a surcoat engraved
with alternating fleurs-de-lis and stars in a
diamond pattern with cross-hatched lines.
The bridle and breastband (peytrel) are in
relief, and are both decorated with rosettes.

A number of aquamaniles with knights on
horseback have survived, but this example is
not particularly close to any of them. The
modelling of the horse and knight is of
particularly high quality. The find place has
been taken to mean that this aquamanile
was produced in England, and there is
nothing in the armour or decoration to
contradict this.   JC

PROV. Found in River Tyne near Hexham, before
1853.

LIT. Laking 1920, fig. 314; Falke & Meyer 1935,
no. 290, fig. 257; Paris 1968, no. 503.

155 The Guy of Warwick mazer

c. 1300–50
Maplewood, mounted in silver-gilt: h. 13.2 cm,
diam. 22.7 cm
Inscr. in Lombardic letters + GY DE WARWYC AD
A NOWN KECI OCCIS LE DRAGOVN
The Prior, Brothers and Sisters of St Nicholas's
Hospital, Harbledown, Canterbury, on loan to
the Poor Priests' Hospital

The bowl is lathe-turned, mounted with wide
silver-gilt bands and a flaring foot (perhaps

a contemporary or near contemporary hand.
Following the pattern of a general roll, it
begins with the King of Jerusalem and other
sovereigns and continues with English and
foreign nobles in no readily discernible order.
Among the English arms (many unfortunately grievously rubbed and faded) are
those of Lovel, Valence, de Quincy, Tiptoft
and Bardolph. This is also the only roll to
include the arms of the young Prince Alphonso ('Sire Aunfour'), the eldest son of
Edward I, who died in 1284 in his eleventh
year.

Authorship of individual rolls of arms is
not known before the fifteenth century; the
roll's title derives from its later ownership
about 1605 by the antiquary William Camden, Clarenceux King of Arms.   AP

PROV. William Camden, Clarenceux, d. 1623; Sir
Robert Bruce Cotton, d. 1631; acquired by the
nation with the Cotton collection in 1702.

LIT. Wagner 1950, pp. 16–18; Denholm-Young
1965, pp. 46, 62–3, 78; Brault 1972, p. xx, pl. 3;
Brault 1973, pp. 8–9, 68–76; Wright 1973, pp.
8–9, 12; London 1978, no. 12.

154

155

PROV. St Nicholas Hospital, Harbledown, since at least 1784; lent to V&A, 1968–86; lent to Poor Priests' Museum, Canterbury, 1986.

LIT. *Gent. Mag.* 1784, pp. 257, 349–50; Duncombe 1785, p. 18, repr.; Summerly 1843, p. 77; Hope 1887, no. 2; Ottawa 1972, no. 50.

156   The Bermondsey dish

c. 1335–45
Silver, parcel-gilt, with traces of enamel: diam. 26.4 cm
The Rector and Churchwardens of St Mary Magdalen, Bermondsey

The dish is set with a shallowly engraved central medallion, showing a lady in a low-cut dress, her hair in *cornettes*, placing a helm upon the head of a kneeling knight in armour with mail coif and sabatons. The medallion is wreathed by a gilt embossed vine-stem, encircled by sixteen radiating spiral tear-shaped lobes, alternately raised and depressed; in the spandrels are engraved triple-pointed leaves, on the back an uncrowned leopard's head. This highly decorative dish was probably made as a piece of display plate, intended to adorn a sideboard. Although too fragile to stand much use, it may be a spice plate, used to serve the 'spices' which were taken with sweet wine after a meal. No medieval spice plates are known to survive, although they are much mentioned in documents.

The leopard's head is probably an owner's mark, conceivably that of Bermondsey Ab-

fifteenth-century) with openwork quatrefoils around the edge; in the centre of the bowl is a medallion of silver-gilt: cracks and holes in the maplewood have been mended in antiquity with silver patches and staples.

The inscription on the medallion ('Guy of Warwick is his name; here he kills the dragon') describes the scene: the legendary Guy, Earl of Warwick, carries a shield with the arms of Beauchamp, the family name of the earls: Gules a fess between six crosses trefly. Mounted on a horse, he is lancing the dragon, thereby, according to legend, saving the lion it had been attacking (Loomis 1924, pp. 125–7). He wears coat armour and a bacinet with camail, of a sort comparable to that on the effigy of John of Eltham (*c.* 1340) in Westminster Abbey. Guy, one of the most popular heroes of English romance, had strong patriotic appeal, because he was thought to have saved the country from the Danes. His cult, fostered by his alleged descendants, the Earls of Warwick – centred upon Guy's Cliffe near Warwick Castle, where he is ultimately supposed to have retreated and become a hermit. Illustrations in English fourteenth-century art include the Taymouth Hours, ff. 12–14 (London, British Library, Yates Thompson MS 13) of *c.* 1330 and a tapestry showing the story hung in Warwick Castle in 1400 (Loomis 1924, pp. 127–31) where Guy's Tower had just been completed in 1394 (Pevsner 1966b, pp. 452–4).

The mazer's medallion or 'print' (Hope 1887, p. 131) has been stamped outwards, probably using a die, which would allow some degree of mass production. The language of the inscription is Anglo-Norman shown by the use of OV for the nasalised O, and K for QV (personal communication, B. Cottle). Prints for mazers were otherwise often enamelled, with arms of with saints dear to their owners.

Despite the apparent inconvenience, it is clear that mazers were used as drinking

vessels (Hope 1887, pp. 133–4). Large ones like this were perhaps used communally as a grace cup, as at Durham where the monks drank from a 'great mazer' after grace (ibid., p. 134). The word 'mazer' is derived from the Old High German *masa*, spot, from the spotted maplewood burrs of which they were often, but not invariably, made. The broad and shallow burrs dictated their form; greater depth was given by metal mounts (Pinto 1969, pp. 43–7). This shape probably served as a model for the bowls made by goldsmiths (Andersson 1983; Fritz 1982, figs. 377–82).   MLC

156

bey whose arms included a lion (or leopard) passant guardant or. Equally various families included the leopard in their arms, most conspicuously that of the king. Royal inventories frequently mention plate *signo cum leopardo* (marked with a leopard) which may signify an ownership mark rather than a hallmark. If so, the dish would be the earliest surviving piece of royal plate after the Coronation spoon (How 1952–7, I, pp. 24–5); a date in Edward III's reign is likely, judging by the lady's appearance, and the knight's armour, comparable with that on the 1347 Wautone brass (Norris 1978, II, fig. 20).

MLC

PROV. Church of St Mary Magdalene, Bermondsey; in use as an alms dish from pre-1880 to c. 1951; on loan to V&A, 1951 to present.

LIT. Victoria and Albert 1883, p. 54 (no. 1880–45); Cooper 1900, p. 152; London 1936, no. 58; Oman 1952, pp. 23–4, repr.; London 1978c, no. 6.

Pendants

Horses were often elaborately decorated and caparisoned in the Gothic period. All the elaborate horse trappings have now vanished but for the fragments of heraldic embroidery from the Cluny Museum (Cat. 12) which may indicate their quality. What have survived in much greater numbers are the cast copper alloy pendants, often enamelled, that were used either for the breast strap (peytrel) or on the head harness. They were popular in the late thirteenth and fourteenth centuries, and the military campaigns of Edward I may have provided a stimulus for the production of these pendants (Griffiths 1986a, I). No pendants are known in gold or silver, and it may be that most copper alloy pendants were used for the decoration of the horses of servants or retainers. The selection made for this exhibition concentrates on the heraldic pendants, though many pendants are known without heraldry. It includes the royal arms and the arms of Richard of Cornwall, Court officials, and gentlemen. JC

157 Pendant

Late 13th century
Copper alloy with traces of enamel, h. 4.4 cm, w. 5.3 cm
The Trustees of the British Museum, London, MLA OA 2132

This pendant combined two shields on the rectangular pendant. They are of England and of the earldom of Cornwall, Gules a lion rampant or within a bordure bezanté. JC

PROV. Not known.

158 Pendant

Early 14th century
Copper alloy, gilded and enamelled: h. 4.5 cm
The Trustees of the British Museum, London, MLA 88, 6–8, 8

This pendant bears the royal arms of England before they were quartered with those of France in 1340, Gules three lions passant guardant. The red enamel is well preserved and the lines retain traces of gilding. The presence of the royal arms suggests that it might have decorated the horse of a royal official. JC

PROV. A. W. Franks Coll.

LIT. London 1978a, no. 172 p. 106.

159 Pendant

Late 13th/early 14th century
Copper alloy with traces of red enamel. l. 4.1 cm, w. 2.4 cm
The Trustees of the British Museum, London, MLA 82, 10–11, 7

This shield-shaped pendant bears the arms of Cornwall, Argent a lion rampant gules within a bordure sable bezanté. JC

PROV. A. W. Franks Coll.

160 Pendant

Early 14th century
Copper alloy with enamel: h. 4.5 cm, w. 2.5 cm
Salisbury and South Wiltshire Museum, 85/1956

The arms on the pendant (Gules three lions passant, a bendlet azure) are those of the Fitzpayn family. At least two members of the family could have borne these arms, Sir Robert Fitzpayn (d. 1315), his son Robert Fitpayn (d. 1354). Of the two the first Sir Robert Fitzpayn is most likely. A soldier and a courtier, he was Constable of Corfe Castle, Constable of Winchester Castle, Steward of the King's Household and Keeper of the Forests south of Trent. Such a person would no doubt have many occasions to visit Clarendon Palace where the pendant was found.

JC

PROV. Found just beyond the north-east end of Clarendon Palace, 1939; Borenius Coll.

161 Pendant

Early 14th century
Copper alloy: h. 4.6 cm, w. 2.9 cm
London Borough of Greenwich Museum Service, 1981.154

The Hausted family emerged from almost total obscurity, and, as a result of their royal service, attained baronial rank in the mid-fourteenth century. Sir Robert de Hausted was a knight in the household of Eleanor of Castile, and Marjorie his wife was a lady of the chamber and Keeper of the Queen's Jewels (Parsons 1977, 29–37). A pendant with the arms of Hausted, Gules a chief

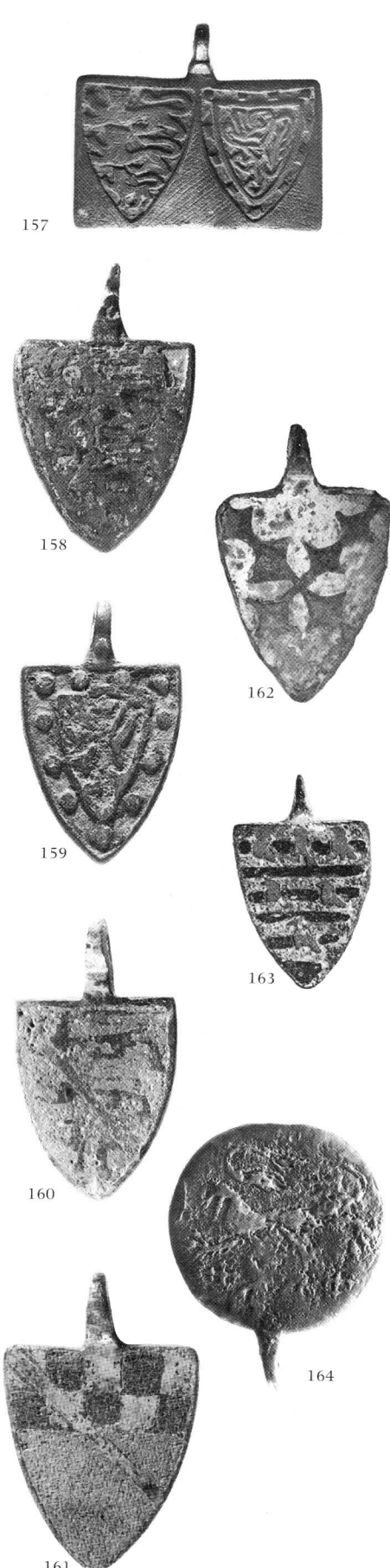

157

158

162

159

163

160

164

161

checky or and azure, was found in 1959 in Teffont, Wiltshire (Salisbury Museum, 11.G.24, 52/62). This pendant bears the arms of Hausted differenced with a band. This indicates that it is likely that it belonged to a servant of Sir John de Hausted who fought for Edward II at Boroughbridge in 1322 and was acting marshal of the royal household in that year. He died before 1336. A seal on a charter dated 1332 (Birch 1894, no. 10,570) shows that he was using these arms.   JC

PROV. Not known.

162   Pendant

Early 14th century
Copper alloy with enamel: h. 4.3 cm, w. 2.7 cm
Devizes Museum, 1984.94

The arms (Argent a saltire engrailed gules) are very well preserved on this pendant. The silvered ground is slightly tarnished and the red enamel inlay is complete. The arms are those of the family of Tiptoft, who owned both Castle Combe and Bathampton Manor in Wiltshire in the fourteenth century.   JC

PROV. Found at Edington, Wiltshire, 1983.

LIT. Griffiths 1986b, pp. 221–3.

163   Pendant

Before 1324
Copper alloy with enamel: h. 4 cm
The Trustees of the British Museum, London, MLA
    1947, 10–7,1

This shield-shaped pendant bears the enamelled arms of the Valence family, Earls of Pembroke (Barry of twelve argent and azure an orle of six martlets gules). The last Valence Earl of Pembroke was Aymer, who died in 1324. The enamelled arms may be compared with that on the Valence casket (Cat. 362) and on the tomb of William de Valence (died 1296), half brother of Henry III, in the Chapel of St Edmund in Westminster Abbey.   JC

PROV. Found near Mitcham Green, Surrey, 1909.

LIT. Clinch 1910, p. 212; London 1978a, no. 16.

164   Pendant

1351–61
Copper alloy with enamel: h. 3.9 cm, w. 5 cm
Salisbury and South Wiltshire Museum, 123/1948

This pendant was fixed at the side and is decorated with arms on both sides. These arms (Or powdered with crosses crosslet azure, a lion azure and argent, two chevrons gules and on a sinister quarter a molet of six points) have been identified as those of the Lovells of Castle Carey (Somerset) and St Maur differenced with the sinister quarter. Muriel Lovell married Nicholas St Maur in 1351; he died in 1361.   JC

PROV. Found on Mere Down, Wiltshire, c. 1900.

LIT. Shortt 1951, pp. 72–4.

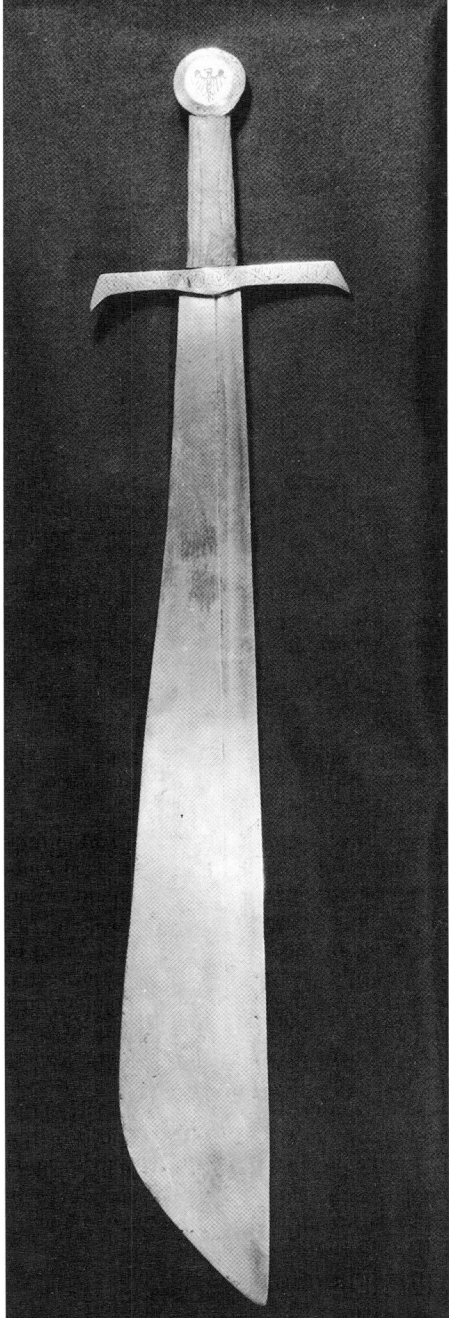

165

165   The Conyers falchion

English(?), 1257–72 (grip later)
Blade steel, hilt of enamelled copper-gilt, grip
    wood: l. 89 cm
The Dean and Chapter of Durham

The spatulate cleaver-shaped blade has a straight back bordered by fullers. The hilt is cruciform with a short, straight cross with beaked ends, chamfered disc pommel and plain grip. The chamfer of the pommel and the cross are engraved with a design of running foliage, on the latter forming a prolongation of dragon-like monsters; in the centre of each face of the pommel is a shield enamelled respectively with the arms of England and of the Holy Roman Empire.

This is a unique survival in unexcavated condition of a once common type of medieval sword depicted, for instance, in the scenes once in the Painted Chamber at Westminster, and also a very rare example of a thirteenth-century enamel that may have been produced in England. It was used until 1860 by the Conyers family as a sword of tenure of their lands at Sockburn from the Bishop of Durham: it was presented to each new Bishop on his first entry into the diocese, and then returned. The heraldry, however, suggests that it may have belonged originally to Richard, Earl of Cornwall, King of the Romans from 1257 until his death in 1272 (see Cat. 131, 144).   CB

PROV. Conyers family of Sockburn; Durham Cathedral.

LIT. Hodges 1892; Blackett & de Cosson 1893; Laking 1920–2, I, pp. 128–9; Oakeshott 1964, p. 124, figs 94, 103; Paris 1968, no. 512.

166   Rowel spur

c. 1240–c. 1300
Copper alloy, gilt: l. spur body (without moving
    parts) 9.5 cm, span 6.4 cm, rowel diam. 2.2 cm
Claude Blair

The introduction of the rowel spur was an important development. An early example is depicted on the heel of a mounted pilgrim on one of the Miracle windows in Trinity Chapel, Canterbury Cathedral, 1220–30. By the mid-fourteenth century most spurs had

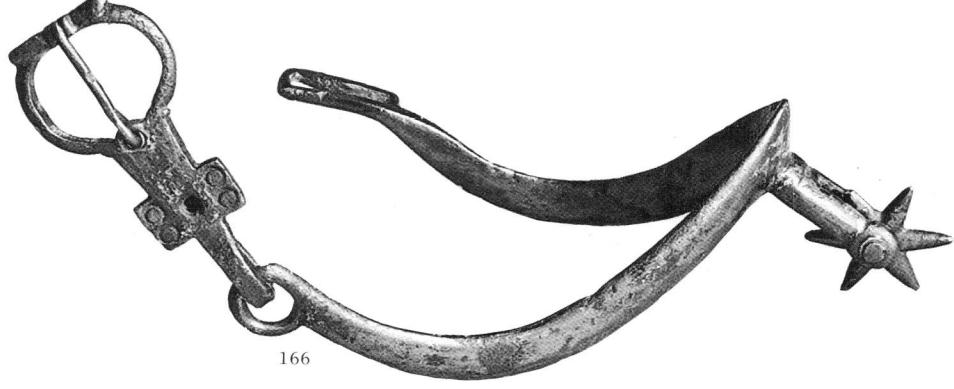

166

rowels, although on the Hastings brass when complete (Cat. 678) Sir Hugh wore rowel spurs while the royal and noble figures in the canopy still use the old prick form.

This spur has deeply curved D-section sides, one with a single ring terminal supporting the buckle. Buckles were worn on the outside of the foot, in this case the left. The inner terminal is vertically pierced with an hour-glass-shaped slot. The sides join in a pointed crest behind the wearer's heel; this point and the neck below it are defined by simple mouldings. The spur has an extremely short, straight neck of oval section with a six-point rowel. The slender buckle body, below the decoratively moulded frame, broadens into a rectangular area with an impressed circle at each corner; in the centre a rivet (of which only a fragment remains) secured the extremity of the loop attaching the buckle to the spur terminal. Late prick spurs, and contemporary early rowel spurs which gradually replaced them, were of similar form with curved sides; the combination of one ring and one slot terminal often featured on both types, e.g. those excavated at Ragnildsholmen, Sweden, before 1320, including a similar iron spur, but with a curled crest (Statens Historiska Museum, Stockholm, 7040; Ward Perkins 1940 fig. 30, 2 & 4).

The equestrian statue of the Emperor Otto the Great, c. 1250 (Reitzenstein 1972), at Magdeburg, now in the Museum, has a very similar spur but without the pointed crest. From the outer ring terminal its single leather runs beneath the foot, passing up through the inner slot terminal and over the foot to the buckle. Small curved-side rowel spurs with minimal necks and inner slot terminals appear on the incised monumental slab of Sir Johan le Botiler, c. 1285, in St Bride's Major Church, Glamorgan (Greenhill 1976, II, pl 46b.) Gilded spurs were symbolic of knighthood. BE

PROV. Walbrook, London; colls C.R. Beard, R.E. Oakeshott.

LIT. Oakeshott 1960, p. 278, repr. fig. 136.

167   Rowel spur

c. 1300–c. 1340
Copper alloy, gilt and enamelled: l. 12 cm, span (outer terminal distorted) 7.6 cm, l. of rowel box 3 cm
Norfolk Museums Service (King's Lynn Museums), KL 100.970 (A928)

This spur is for the left foot, and is decorated with eleven shields of arms (Vert a cross engrailed or) inlaid with green enamel. The triangular section curved sides, each bearing three shields, have terminals as Cat. 166 with another shield decorating the slot terminal. A round stem projects forward from the ring terminal, curling to display the shield it supports. A similar stem with shield forms a crest above the junction of sides and neck. The rowel box divides most of the

167

plunging S-shaped neck; the rowel is missing. Rust indicates that the missing rowel pin and buckle pin were iron. The buckle, of similar form to Cat. 166, and the hook attachment for the leather, each join the ring terminal by a round loop with zoomorphic head finial. Both bear triangular shields.

This spur was found on the traditional site of the lost village of Leziate (Allison 1955–7) now within Ashwicken, a medieval manor of the Noon (Nugon or Noion) family, so that it may be the Noon arms, Or a cross engrailed vert, which appear on this spur with the tinctures reversed, perhaps differenced to denote a younger son or cousin.

The heraldic prick spurs of King Sancho IV of Castile and Leon, 1284–95 (in the Tesoro Mayor, Toledo Cathedral, Spain) are similar except for their necks. They retain their leather-lined woven galoon leathers with monsters' heads on their end mounts (Blair 1959). Most spur necks are straight. The very unusual form of neck of this spur also occurs on a plain copper-alloy rowel spur from Litcham, Norfolk, (Norwich Castle Museum, 136.29) and a large plain iron one, probably from London (Museum of London, 86.426/1), both of which are mid-fourteenth-century.

I am indebted to Miss A.S. Mottram for details of the find site, and to Mr John Chaplin for his help with the Noon genealogy. BE

PROV. Dug up at East Farm, Ashwicken, Norfolk, 1970, and given to King's Lynn Museum by Mr A. Brand.

LIT. Allison 1955–7; Blair 1959.

168   Rowel spur

c. 1400
Copper alloy, gilt: l. 1.3 cm, span approx. 7.5 cm, rowel diam 6.5 cm
D.S. Neal, on loan to St Albans District Council, Verulamium Museum, AM 722751

The gently-curved D-section sides have single ring terminals. A raised flange behind the heel, with an ogee piercing at each side, rises into a curling crest with ball finial. The slightly distorted neck now curves upwards along its length. The large rowel has six lozenge points. The sides and neck are decorated with scrolling foliage in relief against a cross-hatched ground, the crest with two Ss entwined along a horizontal bar. One hook attachment remains. Two more and the buckle are lost, as are the two spur leathers, of leather or fabric; the upper one was probably strengthened with small studs across the foot as on the Kerdiston effigy (Cat. 135; Stothard 1817).

Spurs of this basic form were common in England. They are worn by Sir Nicholas Dagworth on his monumental brass, 1401, at Blickling, Norfolk (Beresford 1975). Several excavations including Goltho, Lincolnshire, and Pleshey Castle, Essex, revealed undecorated iron ones (Beresford 1975; Williams 1977). The Royal Armouries have a gilded rowel identical to that of Cat. 168, within a fragment of neck decorated with

168

stylised feathers; it was probably found in London (AL.116/455). The length of the neck of the present exhibit illustrates the transition to the fashionable long spurs of the fifteenth century.   BE

PROV. Found 1970 against outside wall of inner gatehouse of King's Langley Palace, 1970; deposited by site owner in Verulamium Museum, St Albans.

LIT. Stothard 1817, pl. 63; Beresford 1975, p. 90, fig. 42, nos 131–2; Neal 1977, pp. 143–4, repr. fig. 53; Williams 1977, p. 181, fig. 40, no. 46.

169   Dagger

English(?), 14th century, probably second half
Blade steel, hilt iron with cuir-bouilli grip
  mounted in copper alloy (latten): l. 38.8 cm
Norfolk Museums Service (King's Lynn
  Museums), KL37.960 (A905)

The tapering, single-edged blade is of flat triangular section, with a maker's mark – an oval with a projection at one end – inlaid in copper in one face. The flat, hollow, disc pommel has a narrow chamfer round each face, and is made in two halves. The arched cross has a triangular projection over the centre of each face of the blade, and is of flat rectangular section, with the broader faces, which widen towards rounded tips, in the same plane as the blade, and the taper in the other plane. The grip is of oval section, swelling in the centre and inlaid with four narrow longitudinal strips of latten(?) incorporating what appear to be collets for pastes or stones (missing), with pairs of diagonal engraved lines between.

This is unique among later medieval daggers in having been set with stones, but otherwise represents a form – with simple cross-guard and circular pommel – that was used widely from the thirteenth to the fifteenth centuries. At least one somewhat similar dagger is illustrated in the well-known mid-thirteenth-century French Maciejowski Bible in the Pierpont Morgan Library, but it is particularly close to daggers depicted on the brasses of Sir Miles de Stapleton (d. 1364), formerly at Ingham, Norfolk, and John Cray (d. 1392), at Chinnor, Oxfordshire.   CB

PROV. Found on site of ford on Ten Mile River (Ouse), Southery, Norfolk, 1940; given to Lynn Museums by Great Ouse River Board, 1960.

LIT. Laking 1920–2, III, pp. 3–4, figs 726–30; London 1940, pl. VI (2), fig. 8 (1).

170   Sword

English(?), the blade probably German,
  c. 1250–1330
Blade steel, hilt iron: l. 95.5 cm
Inscr. on fullers of the blade, inlaid in latten on
  one face, a series of letters of unknown
  meaning in a mixture of Roman and Lombardic
  characters
The Trustees of the British Museum, London,
  MLA 58, 11–16, 5

The broad, straight double-edged blade has a wide double fuller on each face; there is a thick wheel pommel and slender, straight cross of polygonal section swelling towards the tips which are cut off straight. The end of the blade has been broken off and rejoined with a modern weld.

This is a very fine example of the classic

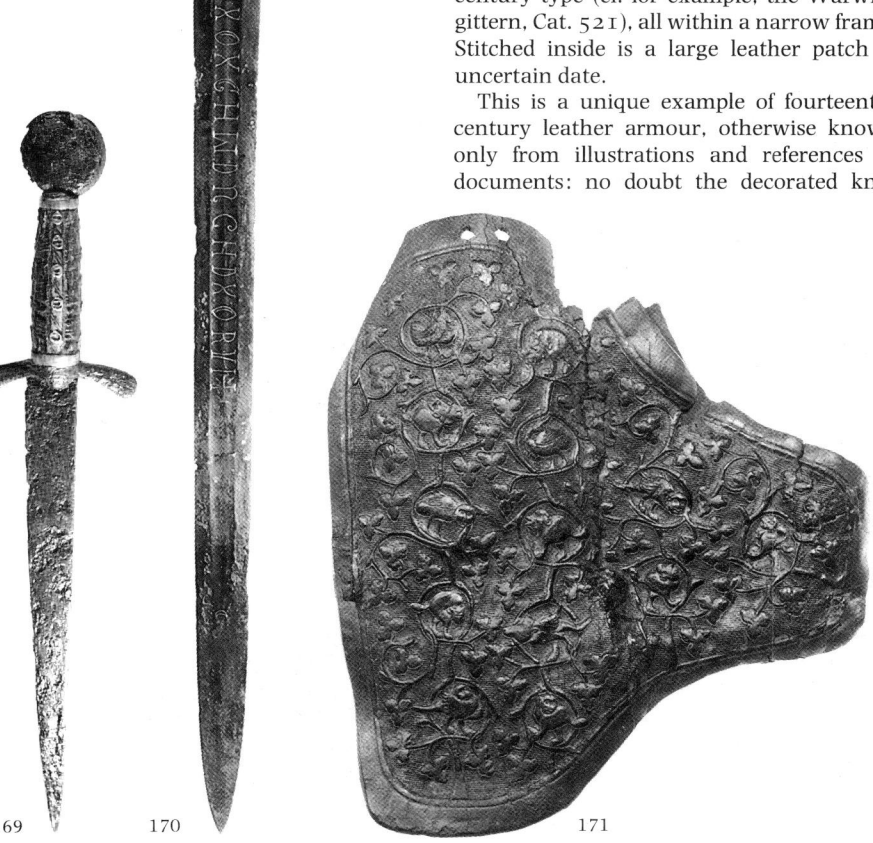

169   170   171

'knightly' sword of its period, as depicted on many effigies and brasses (cf. Cat. 234–5). The letters inlaid in latten on the blade are perhaps the initials of the words of a religious invocation (cf. Cat. 172). The other side is inlaid in a similar technique with crosses, crescents and quatrefoils containing saltires.
                                                    CB

PROV. Found in River Witham, Lincs., July 1825; presented to Royal Archaeological Institute by Robert Swann, Registrar to Bishop of Lincoln; British Museum, 1858.

LIT. Gent. Mag. XCVI (2), 1826, p. 300; Lincoln 1850, p. xxxiv (repr.); Way 1850, p. 290 (repr.) see also p. 373; Hoffmeyer 1954, II, pp. 17–18, no. 34, pl. XIIId; Oakeshott 1964, pl. 6c.

171   Arm defence

English(?), first half 14th century
Leather (cuir-bouilli): h. 28.5 cm, w. 24.2 cm
The Trustees of the British Museum, London,
  MLA 56, 7–1, 1665

This is for the right upper arm, to the form of which it would have been curved, though it is now flat. Shaped approximately like a letter T on its side, with the stem pointing inwards, it is pierced at the top with a pair of lace-holes for attaching it to the sleeve of a mail shirt, and has traces of straps which would have buckled round the arm. The surface is tooled in low relief with an overall design of scrolling tendrils carrying trefoil leaves and involving grotesque birds and animals of a common late thirteenth and early fourteenth-century type (cf. for example, the Warwick gittern, Cat. 521), all within a narrow frame. Stitched inside is a large leather patch of uncertain date.

This is a unique example of fourteenth-century leather armour, otherwise known only from illustrations and references in documents: no doubt the decorated knee defences depicted on contemporary effigies and brasses (for example, Cat. 235), were of similar design. Its form, but not its decoration, is paralleled closely by arm defences on a group of Neapolitan effigies of the period *c.* 1330–60.   CB

PROV. Charles Roach Smith Collection (and therefore certainly a London find), 1854; British Museum, 1856.

LIT. London 1940, pl. XLVII; Norman 1974–6.

172   Sword

Scandinavian(?), blade probably German, 13th century
Blade steel, hilt iron with traces of tinning(?): l. 95.2 cm
Inscr. on fullers of blade, inlaid in tin or pewter, a series of letters of unknown meaning in a mixture of Roman and Lombardic characters
Private Collection

The broad, straight, double-edged blade has a wide central fuller on each face. The pommel is multi-lobed, almost fishtail-shaped, the cross slender, strongly arched, swelling slightly towards the tips and with a small triangular central projection over each face of the blade.

This sword provides an interesting actual example of the very late survival of a Viking lobed type of pommel in England, otherwise known mainly from representations on twelfth- and thirteenth-century monuments, most of which are in the north of England (but see also the Robert of Gloucester effigy, Cat. 2). For the inscription, cf. Cat. 170. A

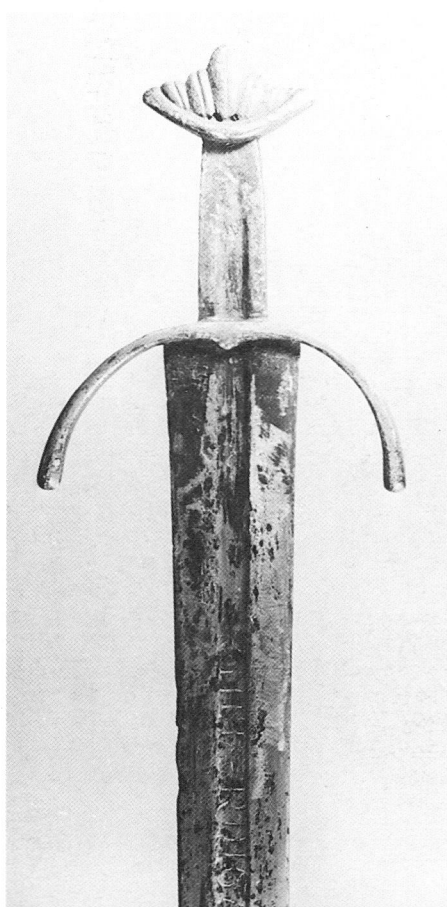

173

closely similar sword in the Oldsaksamling, Oslo, bears a runic inscription datable to the period *c.* 1100–1300.   CB

PROV. From River Ouse, opposite Cawood Castle, Yorks.; Abraham Kirkman, 1861; Thomas Lister Parker of Browsholme Hall, Lancs.; Sotheby's, 21 Dec. 1956, lot 36.

LIT. London 1861, I, p. 151; Read 1915; Ward Perkins 1941b; Hoffmeyer, 1954, I, p. 35; II, p. 7, no. 8, pl. III; Oakeshott 1964, fig. 3, C, D; Ryder 1985, p. 18.

173   Mail shirt (habergeon)

Probably 14th century
Iron or steel: h. from shoulder to hem 90 cm, w. 60 cm, external diam. of rings approx. 1.3 cm
Museum of London, 35.52

Made of alternate rows of riveted and one-piece rings, it is shaped slightly to the waist, with a straight lower edge at mid-thigh level, three-quarter length sleeves, and rather wide neck opening, shaped square at the front and rounded at the back. It opens up the full

length of the back, and has a short vertical slit in the front of the lower edge.

This is the only recorded complete mail shirt with English associations. Like all mail, it is difficult to date, but the combination of riveted and one-piece rings is in favour of a period before the fifteenth century.   CB

PROV. Said to have been found 'on the site of an old house in the Whitechapel Road', London; Sir Guy Laking, who gave it to the London Museum.

LIT. Laking 1920–2, II, p. 179, fig. 520.

174   Knife-dagger

Mid-14th century
Steel blade, copper alloy (latten?) hilt mounted in silver and copper-gilt: l. 41 cm, w. 4.5 cm
Inscr. on silver strips on grip and pommel, repeated, in Lombardic capitals AVE MARIA GRATIA PLENA
Museum of London, 7681

The blade is slightly recurved, stiff and single-edged, the back flat except for a short gable-shaped section towards the centre. The square-section grip and globular pommel are cast as a single unit. Each face of the grip is recessed, the recesses in line with the edge and back of the blade continuing right round the pommel, which also has a saltire-shaped recess on each side and a transverse central hole containing a copper(?) sleeve. This last served to secure a rosette on each side, of which one survivor, now missing, is visible on old photographs of the dagger. The bottom of the grip is shaped to fit inside the missing guard, which was further secured by a tubular double-ended rivet now loose in a

174

hole in the base of the blade. The recesses in the grip and pommel are filled with copper-gilt and silver strips, of which the former are confined to those in line with the edge and back of the blade. The silver strips are stamped with the repeated inscription in low relief, cut haphazardly from what was obviously a long prefabricated strip, and overstamped at regular intervals with a sexfoil framing the figure of a heron(?) with its head raised and bill open. The copper-gilt strips on the sides are each engraved twice with a female figure holding a dragon's head (St Margaret?) standing under a canopy, and once, at the top, with a crowned female head, all reserved against a ground recessed for enamel. At the top of the pommel is a small ring.

This belongs to a small group of closely-similar engraved daggers found in England. Another example, from Billingsgate and bearing unidentified coats of arms, is in the Museum of London (86.100), a third, and fragments of a fourth, from the same source are respectively in the Royal Armouries (x.799) and in private possession. A fifth,

found at Duston, near Northampton, and now in the Metropolitan Museum of Art, New York, retains much of its enamel. Comparable figures under gable canopies occur in other English enamels of the period (Cat. 585) and in the margins of the Hastings brass of 1347 (Cat. 678).   CB

PROV. Guildhall Museum (M.XVII.129), and therefore certainly a London find.

LIT. Guildhall Museum 1903, p. 273, no. 128; Laking 1920–2, III, pp. 13–16, figs 758 a, b; Dean 1929, no. 61; London 1930, no. 315.

175 Short sword (baselard)

Late 14th century
Steel blade, wooden hilt mounted with iron
      plates: l. 78 cm, w. 11.5 cm
Museum of London, 80.34

The broad, tapering, single-edged blade is inlaid in copper alloy (latten?) on one face with a maker's mark, a Y on its side and a saltire. The one-piece hilt is of characteristic I shape, the grip of flattened octagonal section, and the top of the pommel and the underside of the guard each reinforced with an iron plate. The pommel, instead of being symmetrical as on the normal double-edged baselard, has been slightly curtailed on the side in line with the back of the blade.

This is a typical example of a civilian weapon very widely used in the second half of the fourteenth and first half of the fifteenth centuries, and depicted on many effigies and brasses (e.g. Cat. 237). The name is derived from the city of Basle where it apparently originated.   CB

PROV. Excavated at Bull Wharf, London, 1979.

EXH. Shown in the Museum of London 'Capital Gains' exhibition, 1986–7.

LIT. Blair 1984; London 1940, pp. 48–50.

176 Westminster Bridge Sword

English(?), second quarter 14th century
Blade steel, hilt iron, scabbard mounts silver:
      l. 108.5 cm, w. 21 cm
Inscr. on scabbard mounts several times in Gothic
      minuscules wiste . i
Museum of London, 52.12

The sharply-tapering, straight, double-edged blade is of flat, hollow-diamond section. Each face of the thick wheel pommel is bordered by a hollow chamfer; the slightly arched cross is of chamfered oblong section, tapering towards the tips which terminate in small rounded knobs, turned up slightly towards the pommel. Stamped on each face of both the blade and the pommel is a maker's mark resembling a stylised standing quadruped, formed of two lines, under a circle. The scabbard mounts comprise a mouth- and central-locket – of which the former carries a fixed suspension ring on both sides and the

latter one on one side – and a chape. The top and bottom edges of the lockets and the upper edge of the chape are each bordered by a row of small punched quatrefoil flowers within a pair of applied roped mouldings; the lower edges of the locket below the mouldings are also cut and engraved as a row of conventional leaves. The outer face of each of the lockets is engraved on one face with a rectangular, cross-hatched panel containing a stag's head caboched over a horizontal scroll bearing the inscription twice in succession; the corresponding face of the chape is

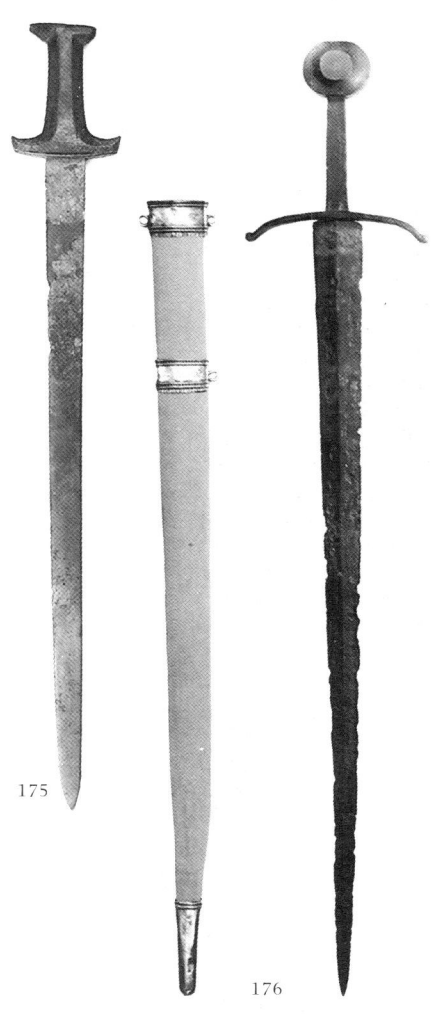

175

176

similarly engraved but with a vertical scroll inscribed only once. The inscription may be Middle English, meaning 'knew I'.

It is unusual to find a sword with the same maker's mark on both the hilt and the blade. The form of cross appears to represent a typological development immediately before that found on the Bristol sword (Cat. 15). A similar form of three-ring scabbard attachment occurs on a sword from the tomb of Can Grande della Scala (d. 1329), in the Verona Museum, and is also represented on an effigy of c. 1330–5 of Maurice, seventh Lord Berkeley, in Bristol Cathedral. This is the finest of all surviving fourteenth-century one-hand swords with English associations, and clearly belonged to someone of importance. Unfortunately, neither the stag's head badge nor the motto have been identified.　　　　CB

PROV. Found in River Thames, either 'in 1739, when excavating for Westminster Bridge' (Hawkins) or in 1745 'about eight feet below the bed of the river, by Mr Smith, who contracted for drawing ballast out of the river for the roads' (Gough); given to Royal United Services Institute Museum, Whitehall, by Walter Hawkins, mid-19th century; London Museum, 1963.

LIT. Hawkins 1846; Gough 1786–96, I (i), p.cxlvii, pl. opp. p. cxlvii, II; Laking 1920–2, I, pp. 132–3, fig. 161; Crossley 1921, p. 211; Beard 1933; London 1940, pp. 37–8, pl. v; Oakeshott 1960, pp. 307–8, 326, fig. 149; Paris 1968; London 1972; RUSI, no. 2210.

177　Sword for a child

English(?), first half 14th century
Blade steel, hilt iron: l. 78.5 cm
Society of Antiquaries of London, Mus. Cat. 625

The straight, tapering, two-edged blade is of flattened hexagonal section for half its length changing to flattened diamond section to-wards the point. The wheel pommel has a chamfered rim and low pyramidal button, and the slightly arched cross of rectangular section tapers to the tips in the plane at right angles to that of the blade.

The fact that the proportions are those of a full-size sword leaves little doubt that it was designed for a child, rather than as a short sword for an adult. The hilt form is one that is found on nearly all the earliest English military brasses (see Cat. 235).　　　　CB

PROV. From River Thames, Westminster.

LIT. London 1940, p. 38, fig. 7; Hoffmeyer 1952–4, pp. 31, 38; Hoffmeyer 1954, II, p. 26, no. 23.

178　Thigh defence (cuisse)

Italian or possibly English, late 14th century
Polished steel: l. 45 cm
James Pickthorn Esq., on loan to the Royal
　　Armouries, AL.23/224

This is for the left leg. It has a low medial ridge running its entire length, and consists of a main plate, its upper edge shaped to the groin and slightly thickened, and with a stop rib riveted just below it on the left, and its lower edge shaped to a double cusp meeting in a central point; a knee piece (poleyn) boldly embossed over the kneecap and with a heart-shaped side wing, and a narrow and a deep articulating lame above and below respectively, the top lame overlapped by the main plate, and the bottom one with a double cusp and central point at the bottom. The side wing has been broken off and riveted back in place. Various rivet holes indicate where the straps and buckles for securing it to the leg were formerly attached.

Although this piece is of Italian form, that does not necessarily mean that it was made in Italy. The author of this entry was informed by the late Sir James Mann that its first recorded owner, the Baron de Cosson, told him that he had acquired it 'from an old English family': it is possible, if not probable, therefore, that it is a unique example, apart from a few gauntlets and headpieces, of a piece of fourteenth-century armour with English associations that has survived above ground from the time when it was in use. The general type is one that is depicted on most English military effigies and brasses of the late fourteenth and early fifteenth centuries (see Cat. 140).　　　　CB

PROV. 'An old English family'; Baron C. A. de Cosson, before 1883; de Cosson sale, Christie's, 2–3 May 1893, lot 101; Sir Edward Barry, Ockwells Manor, Berks.; Sir James Mann, 1948.

LIT. Costume Society 1883, pl. v; Boccia 1980, figs 34–5; Boccia & Coelho 1967, nos 34–5; Gwynn 1977, p. 4, no. 13.

179　Horse's head defence (shaffron)

Probably English, second half 14th century
Iron or steel: h. 91.4 cm
The Board of Trustees of the Royal Armouries

Of large size, this is designed to enclose all but the underside of the horse's head completely. It has a prominent medial ridge extending from top to bottom and is made of two sheets of metal: a large main plate shaped to the front of the head and extending on either side to behind the line of the ears, where it overlaps and is riveted to a plate which forms an arch over the top of the head and extends down either side to the level of the mouth. The main plate is embossed out over both the eyes and muzzle, where it is also pierced with numerous small holes, and its edges are scalloped where it overlaps the other plate: two large circular holes at the top, encircled by rivets, indicate where tubular ear protectors were once attached (a fragment of the flanged edge of one remains on the right). The other plate extends back at the top to protect the rear of the pate and top of the neck, and is pierced here with three pairs of holes for attachment-laces. Numerous internal rivets and a series of small holes along the edges served to secure a lining.

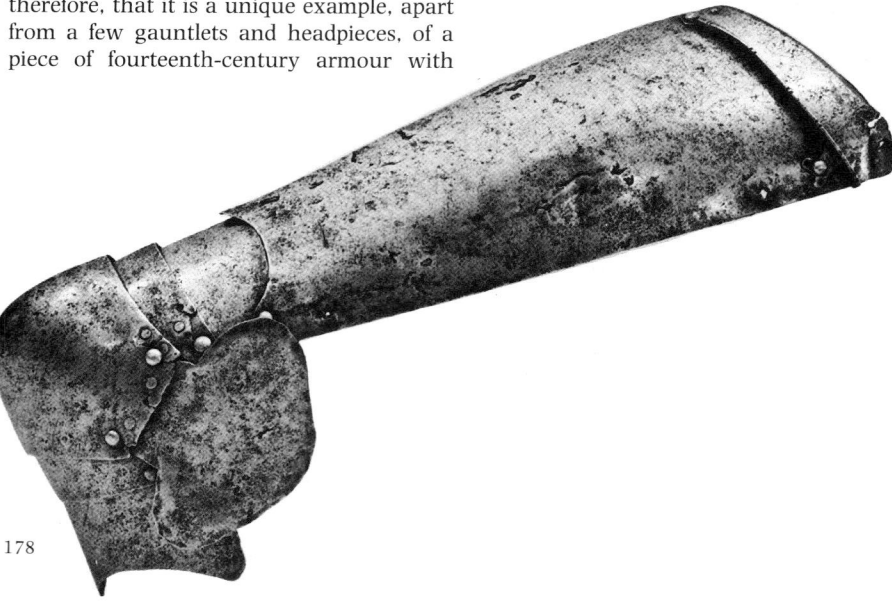

177　　178

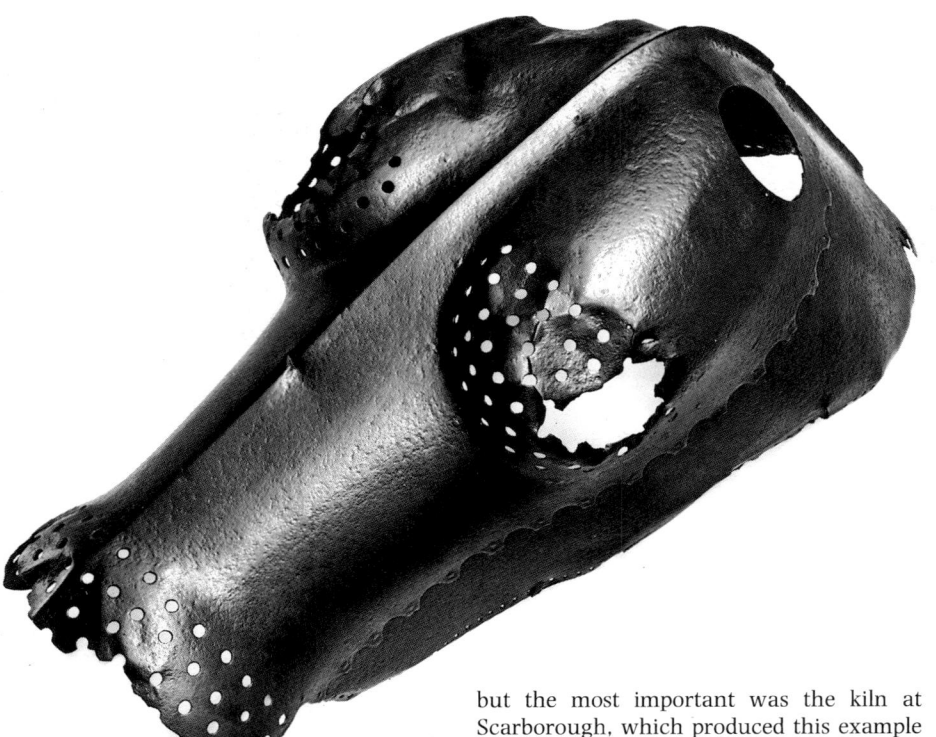

179

Various parts have suffered from rust damage, especially the eye and muzzle defences.

According to a tradition, recorded as early as 1656 by Dugdale, this piece belonged to the legendary Guy of Warwick, which no doubt accounts for its survival. Shaffrons of similar type are represented in English and French art from c.1350 until the second quarter of the fifteenth century, but no other example appears to have survived.   CB

PROV. Warwick Castle, before 1656.

LIT. Dugdale 1656, p. 343; Grose 1786, pl. 42; Laking 1920–2, III, pp. 151–2, fig. 957; Mann 1935–6, pp. 153–9, pl. XI, 2; Nickel 1969, p. 180, fig. 18; London 1972.

180   Knight jug

Late 13th century, possibly c.1250–70
Earthenware, with figures, green glaze, restored: h. 35.6 cm, diam. 21 cm
Nottingham Castle Museum, 56.11 NCM

This is the finest example of the group of highly-decorated jugs known as 'knight jugs' from the figures of knights on them. This jug has two knights on horseback on each side of the rim riding towards the tubular spout, which is in the form of a man. Beneath there is a stag hunt with three stags being attacked by four hounds. Although the restoration of the three heads of the knights and in other places may be recognised by the matt surface, enough remains of the original modelling, covered by a glossy dark green glaze, to appreciate the fineness of the quality. Knight jugs were produced at a number of kiln sites

but the most important was the kiln at Scarborough, which produced this example as well as the ram aquamanile (Cat. 548). The products of the kiln were exported over the North Sea, and this knight jug appears to have inspired copies in Nottingham. The decoration of this example combines the pursuits of warfare and the chase.   JC

PROV. Found on site of Moot Hall, Nottingham, at corner of Friar Lane and Wheeler Gate; Sir Cecil Armitage Coll.

LIT. Dunning 1955, pp. 18–23; Dunning 1968, p. 41; Rackham 1972, p. 10, pl. D; Farmer 1979, p. 56.

180

181   Jug

Probably 1250–75
Earthenware, bridge spout, rod handle, yellow-green and brown glaze: h. 38.8 cm
Salisbury and South Wiltshire Museum, 10/1960

This jug was found among the last load of pots to be fired at the kiln no. 6 at Laverstock. This kiln site lay in the royal forest of Clarendon and may have owed its origin to the needs of the royal palace, which it supplied with pottery. The jug has a well-balanced shape and is decorated with strips and applied stamps in a dark brown glaze, but yellow-green when superimposed on the brown. Strips and stamps are marshalled in order to give a quasi-heraldic impression to

181

the decoration, though no identifiable heraldry is indicated. Palaeomagnetic dating suggests a date range of 1230 to 1275 for the kilns; kiln no. 6 is placed at the end of the sequence of kilns.   JC

PROV. Found in the excavation of kiln no. 6, Laverstock, Wilts., 1958.

LIT. Musty et al. 1969, p. 123, no. 130.

182   Jug

Late 13th century
Earthenware, green and brown glaze: h. 42 cm
The Trustees of the British Museum, London, MLA 68, 3–18, 10

This is decorated with overlapping leaves in the form of scales (cf. Cat. 551, 548) which are coloured alternately green and brown. The fabric and decoration are characteristic of the medieval pottery produced at the kiln site at Grimston, Norfolk. Jugs from this site were exported widely across the North Sea to

182

183

Bergen from King's Lynn. The use of the face mask on the side of the jug provides a contrast with the jugs from Worcester (Cat. 553), Coventry (Cat. 549), and London (Cat. 550), where the mask is on the front.   JC

PROV. Found in Cambridge; A.W. Franks Coll.

LIT. Hobson 1903, p. 61 no. B.30.

183   Rider aquamanile

Late 13th century
Earthenware, in form of rider on horseback; face of horse and arms of rider missing, right front leg of horse restored with plaster: h. 26.5 cm, l. 25 cm, d. 13 cm.
Sussex Archaeological Society, A 010.17

Rider aquamaniles in pottery were no doubt inspired by metal examples such as the Hexham acquamanile (Cat. 154). While that clearly showed a knight, the figure here is a male in civilian clothes with hat, boots, and prick spurs, and so is more likely to represent a huntsman than a knight. The arches of the saddle are represented as being of extraordinary height. The acquamanile would have been filled by the hole at the end of the handle, and emptied through the mouth of the horse. If the figure is a huntsman, this acquamanile, like the jug from Nottingham (Cat. 180), demonstrates the popularity of hunting as a subject in medieval pottery.   JC

PROV. Found at southern end of tunnel on Keymer branch of London, Brighton and South Coast railway at Lewes, 1846; Mr W. Figg's Coll.

LIT. *J. Brit. Archaeol. Assoc.* II, 1847, 1846, p. 343; *Archaeol. J.*, IV, 1847, p. 79; Rackham 1972, p. 20 pl. 13.

184   Jug

Late 13th century
Earthenware, decorated with three diamond-shaped panels with four-legged animals, rod handle: h. 17.5 cm
The Trustees of the British Museum, London, MLA 56, 7–1, 566

The different-coloured glazes are produced by the addition of iron for the brown and copper for the dark green. Against an overall plain lead glaze the diamond-shaped panels contain a rampant lion or dragon standing out from a brown glaze. This effect is not dissimilar to that produced on the Tring tiles (Cat. 217). The diamond-shaped panels alternate with dark-green inverted chevrons. The rim of the jug is decorated with a dark-green glaze over a pattern of lozenges created by applied lines. Although the jug was probably made in Surrey, the polychrome effect is probably copied from a French jug, since a similar jug with yellow animal decoration in brown roundels was found in mid-thirteenth-century levels at the West Hall site in Southampton in 1970 (R. Thompson,

184

186

185

personal communication). It therefore shows a French influence on the decoration of English pottery in the second half of the thirteenth century. JC

PROV. Found in Cannon St near London Bridge; Roach Smith Coll.

LIT. Roach Smith 1854, p. 115 no. 593; Hobson 1903, p. 63 no. B 40; Rackham 1948, pl. B.

185 Jug

Late 13th/early 14th century
Earthenware, green glaze over white slip:
    h. 38 cm
Museum of London, 5630

This type of tall, elegant green-glazed jug was much admired by art potters such as Bernard Leach. It was probably produced at the kiln site of Mill Green in Essex, which provided London with a considerable amount of pottery around 1300. It is covered with a white slip, then the green glaze, and finally decorated with combing. The vigorous treatment of the thumb-pressed base contrasts with the simpler treatment of the baluster jugs. JC

PROV. Found on the site of the Royal Exchange, London, before 1848.

LIT. Guildhall Mus. Cat., 1908, p. 181, no. 63, pl. LXVI; Pearce, Vince & White 1982, p. 271, fig. 3, no. 3.

186 Jug

Mid-14th century
Earthenware, of baluster form with turned base, rod handle, applied white slip and glaze:
    h. 40.8 cm
The Trustees of the British Museum, London, MLA 54, 12–27, 102

The tall baluster jug has often been admired for its majestic proportions. The bulbous body of the jug is echoed by the shape of the neck, of a form sometimes termed 'tulip-necked'. These jugs are invariably undecorated with only a slight cordon to divide body and neck. The average capacity of this type of jug may well correspond with Henry III's 1260 nine-gallon measure. JC

PROV. Found in Cannon St, London, Crofton Croker Coll.

LIT. Hobson 1903, p. 58, no. B9; Pearce, Vince & Jenner 1985, p. 24.

V Towns and Merchants

Urban life was flourishing in England. London was a major commercial and industrial centre; the ports on the east coast – King's Lynn (Cat. 541), Boston, Hull (Cat. 90) and Newcastle – prospered. A few important new towns were established, sometimes because of the shifting coastline as at New Winchelsea and New Romney. Towns had developed a measure of self-government, with mayors in a number of them from the early thirteenth century. Corporate life was marked by the setting up of Guildhalls (Cat. 192) and the use of common seals (Cat. 197).

By modern standards towns were small: few probably exceeded a population of 10,000 and even London may only have reached about 40,000 by about 1300. But their importance to the surrounding areas was far greater than these figures suggest, and small market towns were spread over the whole country. Some towns obtained royal charters stating their rights. A charter did not mark the beginning of a town's corporate existence; it confirmed – and in some cases may even have restricted – a town's liberties.

Guilds and fraternities in towns, and also in rural society, had been of a varied kind. It was in the fourteenth century that the formal organisation into guilds of separate trades in English towns emerged for the first time. This development gave a new and special sense to the term 'guild'.

Important towns developed by both local and international trading, which was various and widespread. Trade was affected in the fourteenth century by warfare and by the government's financial needs. For example, the large imports of wine from the Bordeaux region and the large exports of wool for the Flemish cloth industry (Cat. 237) steadily declined. The fluctuating fortunes of trade stimulated industries at home: notably, the English cloth industry expanded. A professional class of English merchants emerged, some of whom became very rich. One such was Lawrence de Ludlow, who rebuilt Stokesay Castle (Cat. 189). He negotiated a massive wool tax for the king in 1294 (40s for each sack), but was drowned in a ship laden with wool later in the year: this, some thought, was retribution for his sins against the wool producers.

187 Cellar at no. 11 Watergate Street, Chester

c. 1270
Photograph

Measuring 13.4 m long, 6.7 m wide and 3 m high, the cellar is divided into two aisles of four bays. Eight four-part vaults, with chamfered ribs, are supported on octagonal columns with moulded capitals. Chester has preserved twenty-five of its medieval cellars, grouped along the main streets of the old Roman town: Bridge Street, Eastgate Street, Northgate Street, and – most densely – Watergate Street. Although some have tunnel vaults, some are single- and some double-aisled, they seem to form a homogeneous group in date and building technique. Lawson dates them to 'not later than 1270', J. T. Smith to '1270–80'. The cellars run back at right angles to the street, and are half below and half above street level. At its street end each cellar supports part of a continuous walkway at first-floor level, known as 'the Rows'.

The Chester Rows are raised footwalks running continuously above the street at first-floor level, covered by the upper floors of houses which project over them to form pedestrian galleries. The origin and purpose of these walkways is still controversial. Lawson argued that the idea evolved gradually through the twelfth and thirteenth centuries; Smith considered all the Rows to have been built in a short period, soon after the city fire of 1278 – an opinion given some weight by the presence of Edward I in Chester after 1278 (the city was his operational base for the Welsh wars). The king's new town in Winchelsea, founded in 1287, has similar cellars, while his *bastide* town at Monpazier (founded 1284) in southern France has footwalks running below the projecting upper storeys of houses. The Chester Rows are, however, unique in medieval town planning in combining the footwalk with the raised vaulted cellar, thus creating pedestrian walkways above the street level.   PC

LIT. Lawson & Smith 1958; Wood 1965, pp. 87–9; Alexander & Crossley 1976, p. 110.

187

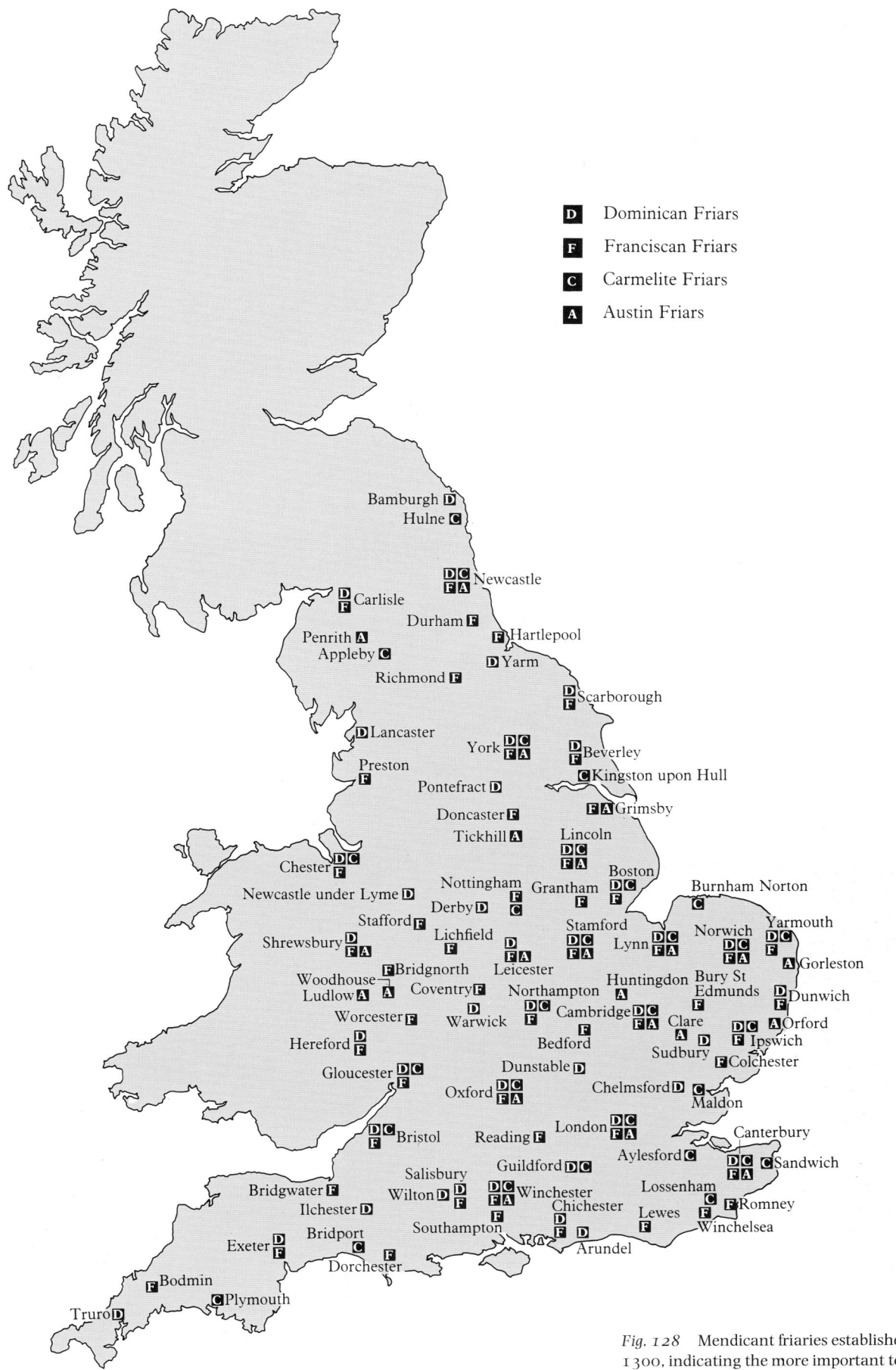

Fig. 128 Mendicant friaries established by 1300, indicating the more important towns

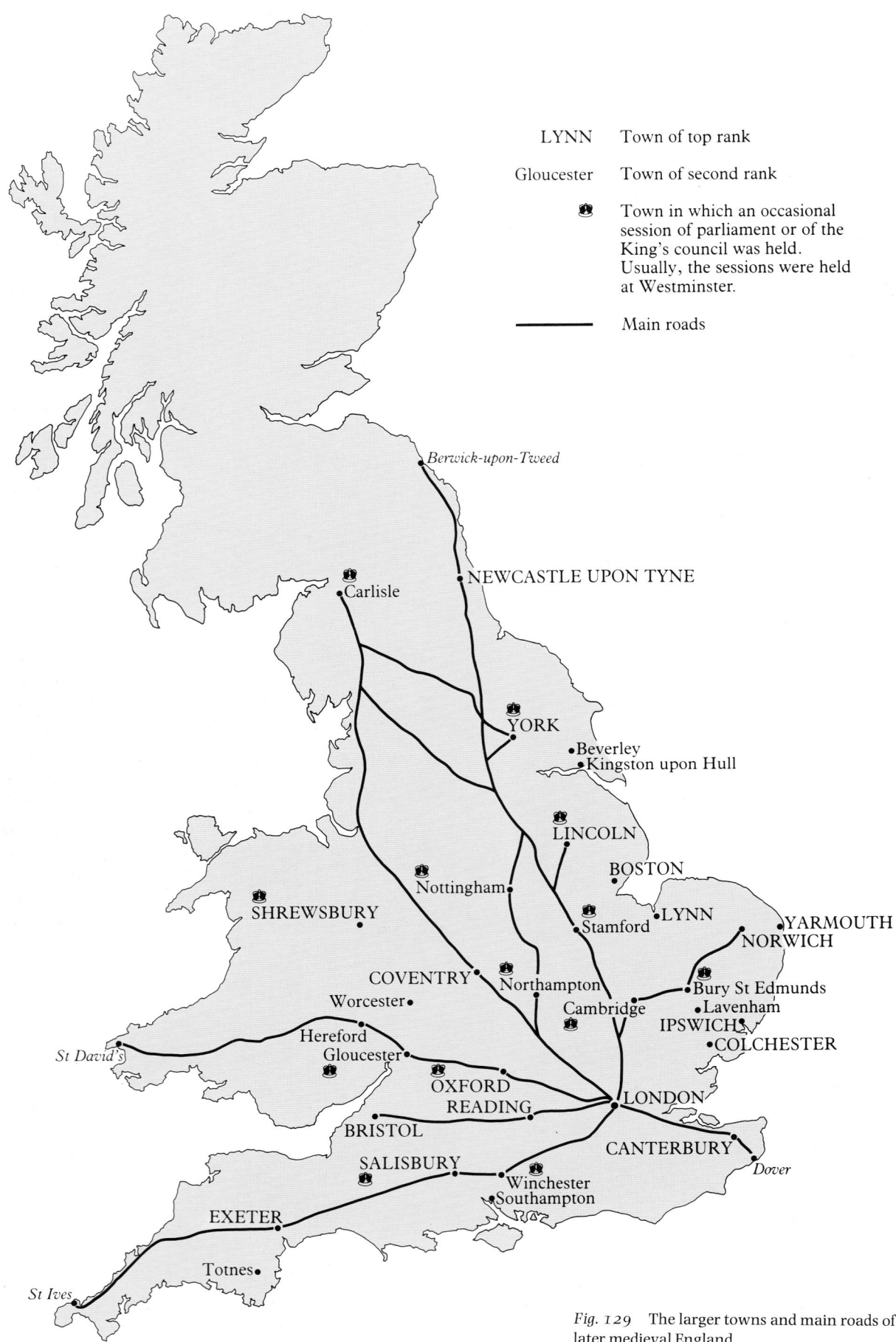

LYNN   Town of top rank

Gloucester   Town of second rank

      Town in which an occasional session of parliament or of the King's council was held. Usually, the sessions were held at Westminster.

      Main roads

Fig. 129   The larger towns and main roads of later medieval England

188 The Dee Bridge, Chester

Late 14th–15th century
Photograph

A wooden bridge over the Dee is mentioned in Domesday, but it could hardly have been reliable, for there are repeated records of the wooden structure being damaged or destroyed by flood in 1277, 1280 and 1297. In 1346 the bridge was evidently in bad repair, and Sir Thomas de Ferrers, the Justiciar of the County, took in hand the repair of the arches. These repairs were in stone, but much of the bridge was probably still wooden, for another flood, of 1353, seriously damaged it. The disaster may finally have prompted the erection of the present stone structure, for in 1387 Richard II allowed the citizens to use the murage, normally assigned to the repair of the walls, for the rebuilding of the bridge. A tower standing between the last two arches at the city end was also begun in Richard's reign, but it was still unfinished by 1407, when the Prince of Wales (later Henry V) granted murage for its completion. In 1499–1500 the 'further end' (perhaps the wider, penultimate arch at the south end) was 'buylded', but timber continued to be used for either a drawbridge or a carriageway to the south end well into the reign of Elizabeth. The bridge tower was demolished in 1593 and replaced by a stone gatehouse, which in turn was destroyed at the end of the eighteenth century. The bridge was widened in 1820 but its medieval appearance, especially from the west, has altered little. It is 115 m long and has seven arches, each with two orders of double-chamfered mouldings.

PC

LIT. Harrison 1896, p. 67; Stewart Brown, 1933, p. 63; Alexander & Crossley 1976, p. 111.

188

189 Stokesay Castle, Shropshire, from the south-west

12th–14th century
Photograph

Stokesay belonged to the de Saye family for much of the twelfth and thirteenth centuries. Of their castle only the twelfth-century north tower remains. The great hall of c. 1270–80 is the only example to preserve unaltered the window gables that are known to have been a feature of so many thirteenth-century secular halls. That such large windows could be risked in a defensive building at this date is of considerable interest, but Acton Burnell Castle nearby (licensed in 1285) is equally bold in its display of vulnerable glazing. These buildings were residences rather than castles in the true sense, and since they could not perform a useful military role were unlikely targets for attack. It is significant therefore that Lawrence de Ludlow, who acquired Stokesay in 1281, was not a soldier but a wool merchant. The great south tower for which he obtained licence to crenellate in

189

1291, although it provided a useful place of ultimate retreat in troubled times, is more a gesture of the new owner's social pretensions than a military necessity. Its ambitious compound polygonal plan, tall crenellations and careful use of contrasting local sandstones all suggest an attempt to emulate Caernarfon Castle, begun by Edward I in 1283 (fig. 33).

Stokesay has an important place in the development of English carpentry. The timber-framed upper storey of the north tower embodies the remains of a thirteenth-century tower-hoard, a great rarity. Opinion is divided on the original form of the hall roof. It has been argued (Smith 1956) that it was originally an aisled structure, but its significance is enhanced if it can be accepted that the huge crucks which, unsupported, span the full width were actually the original arrangement of c. 1280 (Cordingley 1963). JMM

LIT. Smith 1956; Cordingley 1963.

190 Penshurst Place, Great Hall

Licence to crenellate 1341
Photograph

Penshurst Place, Kent, was the main country seat of Sir John de Pulteney, an epitome of the successful late medieval London merchant. Its crenellations, like the paintings of men-at-arms between the wall windows, are just so

190

much fashionably martial swank, for Penshurst was not defensible and its owner never took part in battle.

This is the best preserved great hall of its date. Only the louvre which let out the smoke has gone, although the central hearth survives. The mid-sixteenth-century screen in front of the usual three doors to the services may replace an original screen. The roof incorporates crown posts and collar beams carried on purlins and is unusually highly finished, with masonry-derived mouldings and caryatids under the arch braces. The stonework was probably designed by some leading London mason, for the tracery pattern is exactly the same as that of the slightly earlier choir enclosure of Old St Paul's Cathedral.

Soon after the completion of the hall it became fashionable for the head of the household to eat not in the hall but in his first-floor great chamber; and Penshurst accordingly acquired a spacious staircase connecting this room to the hall. CW

LIT. Binney 1972.

191   William Grevel's House, Chipping Campden, exterior

Late 14th century (before 1401)
Photograph

Built some time before William Grevel's death in 1401, this is a rare survival of 'middle-class' stone domestic architecture of the fourteenth century. The majority of merchants' houses in town and country were wooden, but the prosperity of the Cotswolds and its good local stone meant the construction of stone houses in this area from a relatively early period. But Grevel's house was still exceptional for its day in its size and decoration. Its most distinguished feature is its bay window, decorated with Perpendicular tracery, its central stone panels marking an original floor division. According to Margaret Wood it is one of the earliest stone houses in Britain still to possess its oriel window at the dais end of the hall. Oriels, in the sense of projecting window embrasures at ground level, had been used (in incipient form) at Nassington Prebendal house, Northamptonshire, in the first half of the fourteenth century, and perhaps at Stanton's Farm, Black Notley in Essex, dated *c.* 1340; but they only became frequent in the fifteenth century.

William Grevel made his fortune in wool. By the end of the fourteenth century the Cotswolds had become the chief centre of the wool trade in England, and Chipping Campden was its emporium. Woolmen like Grevel or John Thame of Fairford profited from sales to the local cloth-making towns of the Stroud valley, and from exports abroad, the bulk of which had been under the control of English wool merchants since the early fourteenth century.   PC

LIT. Wood 1965, pp. 99ff.; Bridbury 1962.

192   St Mary's Hall, Coventry, looking south-east

Begun in 1394, structurally complete by 1399
Photograph

In 1340 Coventry's merchants formed a guild in order to enforce their privileges, and by 1342 they had built 'la sale nostre dame'. The replacement of this first hall by the present building was done for the Trinity Guild, which during the late fourteenth century absorbed the merchant guild. Coventry was at this period the main Midlands centre for cloth manufacture and ranked as fourth richest English town after London, York and Bristol.

The low end of the hall features the usual three doors to the buttery, kitchen and pantry. Typologically, the side elevations are interesting as they combine traditional transomed windows (cf. Cat. 261, 190, 189) with the tall dado made fashionable by Westminster Hall, also begun in 1394 (Cat. 692). Influence from John of Gaunt's hall at nearby

191

192

wording of the legend. Although there was a mayor and commune in London in the 1190s, the earliest reference we have to a seal comes in 1219 (Tait 1936, pp. 236, 266, 303, 314; but cf. Stow 1908, II, p. 153). This date fits well with the style of the seal exhibited here in general terms; compare the figure of St Paul on the counterseal of Eustace de Fauconberg, Bishop of London 1221–8 (Birch 1887, I, no. 1907). More specifically, the similarity between various details and features of Henry III's first Great Seal (Cat. 453) suggests that the London seal, too, is the work of Master Walter de Ripa, active in the late teens and twenties of the century.

Like York (Birch 1892, II, no. 5542, pl. I), London adopted the expensive double-sided matrix type (see p. 462), which allowed quite complex imagery. On the obverse St Paul, holding a standard with the leopards of England, looms up from his cathedral as protector of the City. The reverse shows citizens kneeling in prayer before St Thomas Becket, himself a Londoner and adopted as a secondary patron. The legend reads 'Thomas do not cease protecting me who gave thee birth'. Below this scene is a 'view' of the City, but it is the larger panorama on St Paul's side which merits most attention. It seems to have a general topographical accuracy, with the Tower of London and Baynard's Castle to either side and the cathedral in the middle. The large number of spires indicates both how fashionable they were at the time and the density of the City's churches. The subtle gradations of relief and the diagonally set buildings lend a plausible perspective to the view which, enhanced by the minuteness and elegance of the engraving, makes this one of the outstanding civic seals of medieval Europe.   TAH

LIT. Birch 1892, II, no. 5068; Jewitt & Hope 1895, II, pp. 118–21; Tait 1936, pp. 236, 257–8; Pedrick 1904, pp. 84–5, pl. XI.

Kenilworth (completed by 1391) is evident in the bay windows at the high end (not visible in the photograph) and probably also in the low-pitched tie-beam roof. Indebtedness to the two most splendid great halls of the day speaks eloquently of the high ambitions of Coventry's ruling élite. A carving of Richard II's white hart badge on the roof is the evidence for completion by 1399.   CW

LIT. Lancaster 1948; VCH, *Coventry*, 1969, pp. 141–3.

Seals of the City of London

The earliest English city or borough seals do not appear until the 1190s but thereafter are remarkably consistent in form. They are invariably round with a representation of a crenellated and turreted wall, often with flags and watchmen surmounting it. If the town is a port, water will be shown, and perhaps boats. To identify the place more specifically the patron saint of its major church or some canting symbol (such as an ox on the Oxford seal) can be included. Most of these features occurred first on the Conti-

nent where some of the major communes had employed seals from before the mid-twelfth century.

In some of the more important cities (e.g. Cologne) a smaller, supplementary seal was made during the thirteenth century. London followed suit acquiring, in the 1270s, a seal for the mayoral office. Presumably it had a different function from the common seal, but precise details are hard to come by in this early period. Because it was smaller than the main borough seal, and single-sided, it was easier and cheaper to use: it did not require a seal press and needed less wax.   TAH

193   Seal of the barons of London

1219(?)
Wax: diam. 7.2 cm
Inscr. obv. + SIGILLUM BARONUM
            LONDONIARUM
       rev. + ME QUE TE PEPERI NE CESSES
            THOMA TUERI
       background of rev. SCS THOM AP
Public Record Office, London, E 329/428

As early as the 1140s it was noted that the citizens (aldermen?) of London were entitled to be called barons, which explains the

193

194

194 First seal of the mayors of London

Before 1278
Wax: diam. 4.6 cm
Inscr. SIGILLUM MAIORATUS LONDON
background SS Th SS P
Dean and Chapter of Westminster, W.A.M. 41

St Thomas Becket and St Paul are shown seated beneath elaborate gabled arches; the leopards of England are strewn below and on either side. This seal has stylistic features in common with the second seal of St Paul's Cathedral (Birch 1887, I, nos 1966–7), and may well be by the same maker. The latter seal is from before 1276 (St Paul's charter A26–40.973). The mayoral seal itself appears on a Durham charter of 1277–8 (Durham Cathedral Library, Misc. 5574), where it is used to give 'greater surety and testimony' to a document issued by William FitzLuke of Durham, Citizen of London. In the charter exhibited here, we are told 'because the said Roger's seal [Cat. 197] is not generally known, John Lovekin, Mayor of London, has appended the seal of the city [sic]'. The mayoral seal was often used to give greater authority to a private grant.

The architectural surround to the figures, with its crocketed gables and tower pinnacles, is reminiscent of the Westminster Retable (Cat. 329). TAH

LIT. Greenwell & Blair 1919, XVI, no. 3737; Jewitt & Hope 1895, II, 121.

195 Second seal of the mayors of London

1381
Wax: diam. 6 cm
Inscr. *sigill' maioratus civitatis london*
British Library, Loose seal XXXVI, 41

A document of 17 April 1381 (Sharpe 1907, pp. 164–5) records that the old seal of the

mayoral office should be destroyed because it was 'small, crude and ancient, ugly and unworthy of the honour of the said city' (*parvum, rude et antiquum erat, ineptum et indecens*), and another new one, 'commendable and skilful [*honorificum et artificiosum*], which the mayor [William Walworth] has had made for the said office, should take its place . . . in which seal, as well as the images of Peter [*sic*; cf. Cat. 194] and Paul, which were crudely rendered on the old one [*que in antiquo ruditer fiebant*], has been carved in the base the arms of the city . . . and above are two serjeants at arms, and two tabernacles on which stand two angels, between which, and above . . . Peter [*sic*] and Paul, sits the image of the Glorious Virgin'. Some of the implications of this record are discussed on p. 32.

195

The design, with its projecting canopies and auxiliary figures, is based on Edward III's 'Brétigny' seal (Cat. 672). TAH

LIT. Birch 1892, II, no. 5074; Pedrick 1904, p. 86, pl. XXXIV; Sharpe 1907, pp. 164–5; Jewitt & Hope, 1895, II, pp. 121–2; Stow 1908, I, pp. 220–1.

Seals of merchants, citizens and freemen

It was the right of all those who were 'free' to own and use a seal. Despite the wide range of motifs available in the early thirteenth century the vast majority of commoners employed devices based on a fleur-de-lis, a star, a bird or a lion. The matrix was usually a lead disc or pointed oval of small size. By the end of the century considerable changes had come about. Circular matrices of bronze with faceted, bell-shaped handles were normal (see p. 115), and a greater variety of imagery was in vogue including religious subjects, a wider range of animals, quasi-heraldic devices and merchants' marks. The repertoire of messages contained in the legend, which might be written in French or English, as opposed to Latin, also expanded considerably. So many of these seals survive, either as matrices or in wax impressions from them, that it is possible

to produce statistics charting the relative popularity of these variables between regions, sexes, trades and social groups.

A small selection of such seals, as exhibited here, cannot be regarded as representative, but it nevertheless gives an indication of the richness and variety of this neglected area of English medieval production. It also gives us some access to the taste of people whose material possessions have otherwise hardly come down to us. TAH

LIT. Greenwell & Blair 1910, 1911, 1912, 1913, 1914; Rigold 1977; Ellis 1978; Ellis 1981; Spencer 1984; Margeson 1985; Henig & Heslop 1986.

196 Quitclaim to William de Walworth and William de Halden, by the nine men whose seals are attached, of tenements and land in London and its environs, including the manor of Westfield and the advowson of the church there

1377
28 × 34 cm, with seals hanging an additional 15 cm below
Public Record Office, London, E. 329/434

The following descriptions follow the order of the seals from left tag to right, the upper seal on each tag being described first. This order is the same used for the names of the grantors listed at the beginning of the charter. The seals are catalogued in Ellis 1978, vol. I. In one or two cases alternative readings are proposed for legend or subject-matter.

(i) Seal of John Middleton

Wax: diam. 2 cm
Inscr. S' *Iohannis de Midelton*

A lion curled up beneath a tree. This very popular subject was often accompanied by the English legend WAKE ME NO MAN or something in that vein. In one instance a bold squirrel up the tree is pelting the lion with nuts; legend I NOTIS CRAK ON LION BAK. TAH

(ii) Seal of Alexander de Whitby

Wax: diam. 1.8 cm
Inscr.(?) HEYL OWL

A monkey scratches its bottom and gazes at an owl perched on his hand. This is an abbreviated form of the burlesque hunting scene where a monkey or hare rides on a dog or a donkey and holds an owl in his hand. Such satire was occasionally used as a comment on the degenerate modern world, for example in Richard of Bury's *Philobiblon* (1344): 'now slothful Thersites handles the arms of Achilles and the choice trappings of

196

warhorses are spready upon lazy asses, winking owls lord it in the eagle's nest.' Joke legends such as MOR NO LESSE BOT APE OULE ASSE are discussed above (p. 117). TAH

(iii) Seal of Nicholas Heryng

Wax: 2.5 × 1.7 cm
Inscr.(?) SIGILLUM ... HERENGNE

A man, the owner of the seal, kneels before St John the Baptist, who holds a disc with the Lamb of God upon it. He is frequently chosen to appear on personal seals. Surprisingly few people used their own Christian name as a basis for their choice of saint.   TAH

(iv) Seal of John Bays

Wax: diam. 1.4 cm
No inscr.

This has a letter form like a Lombardic T.

(v) Seal of Martin Ellis

Wax: diam. 1.7 cm
Inscr. *PRIVE (?) PRIVE

The legend and the motif, which is a quatrefoil leaf, are about as anonymous as it is possible for a seal to be at this period. The leaf was sometimes used on its own like this, or combined with other forms (Cat. 199).   TAH

(vi) Seal of Roger de Farringdon, clerk

Wax: diam. 2.5 cm
Inscr. SIGILL ROGI DE FAREDON

The owner kneels in prayer, on the right, before the enthroned Virgin and Child. The whole group is enclosed in a double-arched frame. Seals of this type, with patron saints and suppliant, were used by men and women, by merchants as well as religious. Not surprisingly, though, they are found most commonly belonging to ecclesiastics and to clerks, as here. The Virgin Mary was the most popular of female subjects on such seals; St Catherine was next.   TAH

(vii) Seal of Richard de Warmington

Wax: diam. 1.9 cm
Inscr. PRDIVE < S'I

The seal shows the Lamb and Flag. A considerable proportion (perhaps one in ten) of seals from the cheaper end of the market have garbled legends or ones which are partly illegible or unintelligible, even on a matrix which survives in good condition (v, above and Cat. 458 are other examples). The first part is presumably intended for PRIVE.   TAH

(viii) Thomas Broundich alias Thomas de Santon

Wax: diam. 2 cm
Inscr. SIGILL . THOME . BROUNDICH

This bears a tall-stemmed covered cup between two brooches. The motif, later adopted

275

as part of the shield of arms of the Goldsmiths' Company, is explicable as an indication of its owner's trade; as a gold- and silversmith whose output largely consisted of jewellery and tableware. Such men frequently made seals as well (see the note on Henry Lyrpol in the introductory essay) and Thomas may well have made this well-cut and well-inscribed matrix for his own use.   TAH

(ix) Seal of William Stowe

Wax: diam. 2 cm
Inscr. VEI[...]TE BATAILE

The seal shows a lion attacking a dragon. Scenes of combat, so common in medieval art generally, are quite rare on seals. It may be that they were felt too disruptive on an object the purpose of which was to confer stability. Dragons, too, were eschewed. Their evil connotations made them as unpopular on seals as they were in heraldry.   TAH

LIT. Ellis 1978, (i) P. 537, (ii) P. 867, (iii) P. 389, (iv) P. 50, (v) P. 269, (vi) P. 280, (vii) P. 847, (viii) P. 132, (ix) P. 758.

197   Seal of Roger De Depham

c. 1340
Wax: diam. 1.9 cm
Inscr. NUNCIUS EST VERUS LE[...]MITTO ROG[.]
Dean and Chapter of Westminster, W.A.M. 41

This is another interpretation of the sleeping lion theme (cf. Cat. 196i). In the bestiary it was noted that the lion slept with its eyes open. This no doubt rendered the beast a vigilant guardian of any document to which such a seal was attached. Disregarding this entirely, the legend claims that 'the lion is a true messenger'!

Although Roger was an alderman, the charter states that his seal was not generally known, so the mayoralty seal of London (Cat. 194) was also affixed for greater surety. TAH

197

198   Intaglio gem set in a gold handle

c. 1300
Gold and jasper: h. of handle 2 cm;
   die 2.5 × 2.1 cm
Inscr. CLAUSA SECRETA TEGO
The Trustees of the British Museum, London,
   MLA 81, 3–12, 1

The beautifully engraved jasper shows a woman's face in profile. Her headgear is typical of the thirteenth century and shows how high the quality of the best medieval

198

intaglios could be. The gold handle has the faceted bell shape which did not appear until the end of the century, and the lettering too suggests a date around 1300.

The legend may be rendered as 'I conceal the enclosed secrets', and must mean that the seal was most often used for private correspondence of a confidential nature, rather than for legal documents. On gem seals in general, see Cat. 456.   TAH

PROV. Not known.

LIT. King 1864; Tonnochy 1952, no. 705; Dalton 1915, no. 1,119.

199   Copper-alloy 'love and loyalty' matrix

c. 1320
Copper alloy: h. of handle 2 cm, diam. of die 1.9 cm
Inscr. * LOVE ME AND I THE
The Trustees of the British Museum, London,
   MLA 65, 3–24, 18

'Love and loyalty' seals employ a number of devices, either singly or in combination, of which the most common are a male and a female figure or their facing profiles, a heart, flowers, and clasped hands. The legends are

199

usually in the vernacular, most commonly French but occasionally, as here, in English. The engraving is very similar to the seal of Christian Sprotforth (Cat. 459) and may well be by the same maker.   TAH

PROV. H. Godfrey Fausset, 1786; British Museum, 1865.

LIT. *Gent. Mag.*, lvi, 1786, p. 570; Tonnochy 1952, no. 739.

200   Silver seal matrix/signet of Henry le Callere

c. 1330
Silver: h. of handle 2.7 cm; diam. of die 1.9 cm, centre 1.4 cm
Inscr. * SIGILLUM HENRICI LE CALLERE
The Trustees of the British Museum, London,
   MLA 75, 6–24, 1

Merchant's marks first begin to appear on English seals around 1300, and are distin-

200

guished by the flag and cross which surmount them. In many cases they are used on seals in a quasi-heraldic fashion, within a shield shape. Like Cat. 459, this matrix has a screw-out centre so that it can be used without its legend. Here, however, the central motif is specific enough to make it recognisably the mark of its owner. The matrix is a fragment, having lost its outer, bell-shaped casing.   TAH

PROV. found at Chard, Som., before 1849.

LIT. Kingsford 1924, p. 254; Tonnochy 1952, no. 341; *Archaeol. J.* (1849), vi, p. 77.

201 Copper-alloy matrix with squirrel

c. 1300
Copper alloy: h. of handle 2.5 cm; diam. of die 2.4 cm
Inscr. I CRAKE NUTIS SWETE
Society of Antiquaries of London

Squirrels are normally seen in English art of this period as womens' pets (see also Cat. 367) and it has been suggested that there may occasionally be a bawdy meaning intended (Sandler 1985a, p. 159). However, ownership of squirrel seals is not exclusively female (e.g. Ellis 1981, P. 1322, P. 1925) and it is possible that the analogy here is between the cracking of a nutshell to obtain the sweet kernel and breaking the seal to reach a sweet message inside a letter. Often the squirrel will

201

be joined by other creatures, particularly the lion and sometimes stags and rabbits, in a 'woodland' scene. For the inscription, cf. Tonnochy 1952, no. 754; Greenwell & Blair 1910, vii, no. DS. 203 etc.   TAH

PROV. Not known.

202 Charter of Edward III to the City of Bristol

1347
Vellum: 18.5 × 36 cm with pendent seal
City of Bristol Record Office, no. 01250 (1)

The charter grants to the mayor, bailiffs and citizens of Bristol the right to construct a cage for prisoners and to incarcerate in it all

evildoers and disturbers of the peace found wandering in the City by night. They are also empowered to punish bakers found guilty of selling short-weight bread by drawing them through the public streets on a hurdle. The charter is dated 24 April 1347. Similar powers had been granted to the civic authorities of London in 1281.

The document is remarkable for the large decorative initial which, although crudely executed, provides lively illustrations of both forms of punishment. Although illuminated manuscript volumes of collected legal material are quite common in the early fourteenth century, individual decorated charters are comparatively rare. The painted initial would have been ordered and paid for by the recipients of the grant, in this case the mayor and citizens of Bristol, and not by the royal chancery.   JB

PROV. Bristol, from 1347 to the present.

LIT. Harding 1930, pp. 108–9; Bristol 1984, no. 9, repr. p. 19.

203 *Gesta Infantiae Salvatoris* and Apocalypse

c. 1315–25
Parchment, ff. 129: 20.4 × 15 cm
Oxford, Bodleian Library, MS Selden Supra 38

Gesta Infantiae Salvatoris and *Liber de Infantia* are Latin titles for an Anglo-French text that recounts the story of the childhood of Christ from the Annunciation to the Wedding at Cana, including numerous apocryphal episodes. The Bodleian copy is profusely illustrated with sixty text miniatures, often several to an episode of the narrative. One series shows Jesus riding on sunbeams while another child falls off, the dead child's parents complaining to Joseph, and Jesus reviving the child (ff. 24–24v.). In another, Jesus is apprenticed to a dyer of cloth (f. 25); ignoring orders, He puts all the cloth in one dye-vat (f. 26v.), but He then removes the cloth, dyed in the proper colours (f. 27).

The Bodleian manuscript is the only work in which pictures and this text occur together, but an incomplete series of contemporary incised wall tiles from Tring in Hertfordshire (Cat. 217) once constituted a closely related pictorial cycle, and such manuscripts as the Taymouth Hours (London, British Library, Yates Thompson MS 13) and the Holkham Bible (Cat. 221) also contain extensive cycles of Infancy miracle illustrations, testifying to their popularity in the fourteenth century.

The Bodleian Infancy miniatures are appealing, energetic tinted drawings with bright blue and red backgrounds. The illustrations of the Anglo-French Apocalypse that follows (ff. 37–129), probably by the same artist, are fully painted. They are identical in style to those of an Apocalypse in Brussels (Bibliothèque royale, MS 11.282), as

202

203

well as to the prefatory miniatures of the Vernon Psalter (San Marino, California, Huntington Library, MS EL.9.H.17), which can be dated after 1316. The places of origin and destination of the Bodleian and Brussels books are unknown; the Vernon Psalter was probably made for use in the diocese of Lichfield (see also figs 23–4). LFS

PROV. Jehan Reynzford, 15th century; John Selden, beq. to Bodleian.

LIT. Eames 1980, pp. 39–40, 56–61; Sandler 1986, no. 54, II, pp. 62–3, repr. I, figs 131–3.

204 Guillaume le Clerc, bestiary

c. 1265–70

Vellum, ff. 85: 21.5 × 14.3 cm

Paris, Bibliothèque nationale, MS fr. 14969

Guillaume le Clerc's Anglo-Norman French bestiary was written c. 1210 and survives in several illustrated versions made in thirteenth-century England. This copy is unique in having pictures of both the creatures and the moralisations about them. These illustrate virtues and vices by means of contemporary situations in which friars and other preachers are involved. The pictures

are a record of the contents of moralising sermons in which preachers used examples from the bestiary to make their points, for example on the evils of avarice. The preaching compilation made for a Dominican (Cat. 150) included a bestiary.

The artist is very close to the second artist of the Lambeth Apocalypse (Cat. 438), and if not the same hand must have been a close collaborator. The technique is tinted drawing set against coloured grounds. It has been suggested that, in view of the frequent inclusion of Franciscans in its illustrations, this manuscript was produced in the circle of the Franciscan Archbishop of Canterbury, John Pecham (1279–92). This theory is on the basis of an attribution of the related Lambeth Apocalypse to Canterbury. Both on the grounds of date, and the weak evidence for Canterbury for the Apocalypse, this attribution is unlikely. NJM

PROV. Margaret of Flanders, wife of Philippe le Hardi, Duke of Burgundy (1364–1404); Burgundian ducal library until 1748; transferred to French royal library; Bibliothèque nationale.

LIT. Muratova 1978, pp. 142–8; Avril & Stirnemann 1987, no. 144, pls H, LI, LII, LIII; Lewis 1986, pp. 549, 552, 554, 560, figs 6, 11, 14, 23; Morgan 1987, no. 129, repr.

205 Miscellany

c. 1320–30

Parchment, ff. 150: 33.1 × 23.2 cm

Paris, Bibliothèque nationale, MS fr. 571

Although two scribes were employed, a single artist illustrated all the surviving components of this volume, which has a

204

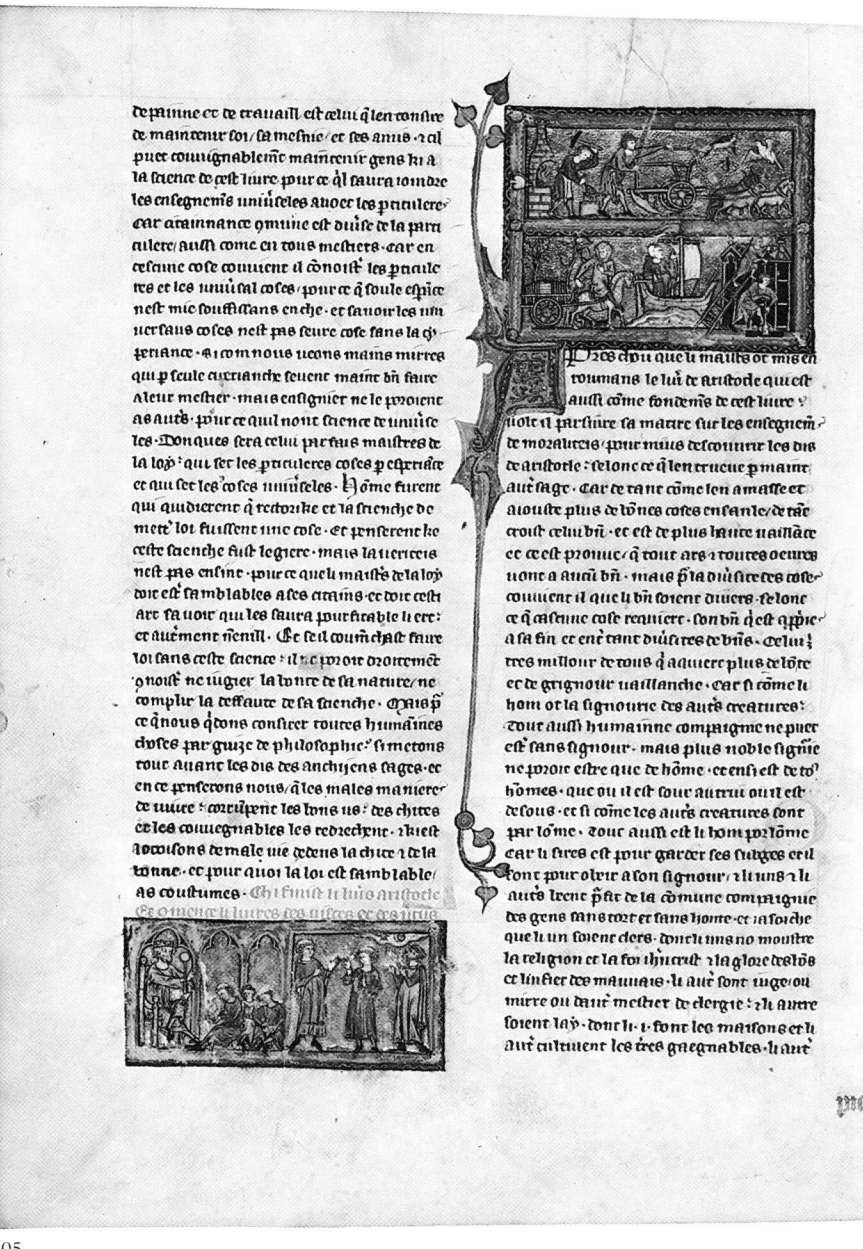

205

206

206 Charter and seal bag

1319

Seal bag embroidered with silver-gilt thread and
coloured silks, in underside couching, split
stitch, eyelet holes and two forms of cross-
stitch: each h. 13 cm, w. 13 cm

Charter, parchment: h. 53 cm, w. 57 cm

Corporation of London Records Office, Charter 25

A charter, granted by Edward II at York on 8
June 1319, confirming and extending the
privileges of the City of London and regulating matters of dispute in the administration
of the City. The City paid 1,000 marks into
the king's wardrobe in respect of these
documents.

The heraldic seal bag protecting the wax
seal was no doubt specially commissioned
from one of the London embroidery workshops. The bag has on one side the arms of
the City of London: a shield Gules, with a
figure of St Paul robed or, holding a sword
argent in the dexter hand and a book sable in
the sinister hand. On the reverse of the bag is
a shield Gules, three lions passant guardant
or, the royal arms of England. In style and
colouring the bag is reminiscent of the Syon
cope in the Victoria and Albert Museum,
providing a valuable pointer to its probable
date (cf. also fig. 28). DK

LIT. London 1963, no. 44.

207 Moot horn

c. 1252

Copper alloy, leather covered; two repair patches,
mouthpiece possibly 16th century: l. 67 cm,
diam. of mouth 15.1 cm

Inscr. around mouth in Lombardic capitals

+ RICARDVS : IVVENVS : ME : FECIT

Faversham Town Council

It is made of beaten sheet metal with two cast
suspension lugs and a mouthpiece soldered
on. Stitched leather covers everything except
the mouthpiece and a band at the other end,
around which the inscription (Richard
Young [?] made me) is roughly engraved in
uneven letters. The unknown Richard may

fourteenth-century table of contents listing
several now lost texts and in addition others
whose titles have been erased. One of the
erased titles may have referred to a *Statuta
Anglie* now at Harvard (Harvard Law School
Library, MS 12), which has the same format
as the Paris volume, and was illuminated by
the same artist and written by one of the two
scribes. The texts, all in French, include
Brunetto Latini's popular encyclopaedia of
history, nature and morals, *Le livre du trésor*,
illustrated with scenes of labour and commerce, the *Secreta Secretorum* of the pseudo-
Aristotle, a manual of instruction for a ruler;
and the *Dit de Fauveyn*, an allegory of the
triumph and defeat of Deceit, by the Picard
poet, Raoul le Petit. Among the lost texts
were the *Gouvernement des princes* of Giles de
Rome and a *Livre de Julius Cesar*, possibly a
Roman history or a romance.

This richly illustrated collection may well
have been put together as a gift of Philippa of
Hainault to Edward, the heir apparent of
England, on the occasion of their betrothal in
Hainault in 1326, a gift recorded pictorially
at the beginning of the *Trésor* (f. 6).

Although the manuscript was probably
written and illustrated in the province of
Hainault, one of the scribes has been identified as English and the artist was certainly of
English origin as well; many aspects of his
work, especially as found in the drawings of
the *Fauveyn*, resemble the miniatures of the
Barlow Psalter of 1321–38 (Oxford, Bodleian
Library, MS Barlow 22) and the contemporary Canonici Apocalypse (Oxford, Bodleian
Library, MS Canon. Bibl. 62). LFS

PROV. Edward III(?); Henry de Grosmont, Duke of
Lancaster, d. 1361; Louis, Duke of Orleans, 1396.

LIT. Långfors 1914; Michael 1985, pp. 582–98;
Sandler 1986, no. 96, II, pp. 103–5, I, fig. 246.

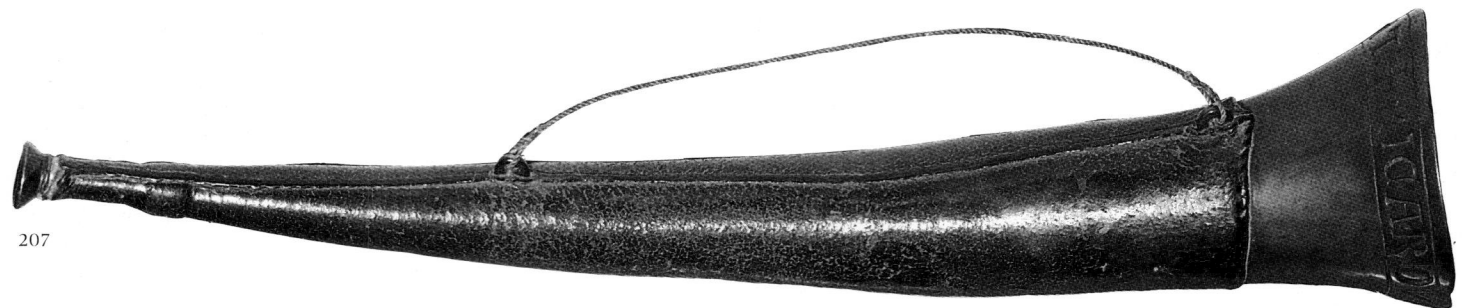

207

have been the man who commissioned the horn, rather than its maker. The horn was repaired in 1540–1 for 16d (Giraud 1897), and also in 1566 and 1567.

This moot horn is one of the earliest to survive, although its appearance does not facilitate precise dating; the lettering is of a style used until at least *c.* 1350. It seems likely that the horn was made in *c.* 1252, when Faversham was granted its first charter (Murray 1935, p. 61); mention of 'the common horn' occurs in 1257 when Faversham Abbey attempted to limit the blowing of the horn to occasions such as calling a burghmoot (common assembly), or signalling a fire or someone's death (ibid., pp. 65, 96). That such horns were a focus of civic identity is shown by an instance in 1257, when the Canterbury citizens were led in riot to attack the abbot of St Augustine's mill, to the sound of their burghmoot horn (Urry 1967, p. 168). This incident was paralleled in Faversham in 1301, when the Chronicle of St Augustine's Abbey describes a violent dispute between the abbot and monks of Faversham and the townspeople in which the mayor summoned his fellows with the common horn (Davis 1934, pp. 349–50) presumably this one. The Customs of the Cinque Ports, as recited at a court of brotherhood at New Romney in 1503–4, required the Faversham horn to be blown to summon those concerned in the election of Mayors, Bailiffs and Jurats (Giraud 1879, p. 8); it is now blown only by newly-elected Councillors.

PROV. Faversham. MLC

LIT. Jewitt & Hope 1895, I, p. 332, repr.; Bridge 1905, pp. 138–9; London 1930, no. 323; Davis 1934, pp. 349–50.

208 Saucer

c. 1290
Pewter, cast and hammered: diam. 12.7 cm
Southampton City Museums, SOU 163.206

The saucer is deeply dished. A capital P has been applied with a punch or die to the rim; this mark may be that of either owner or maker. There is an old repair at the side of the bowl; slight splitting at the junction of rim and bowl, and on the edge; hammer marks are visible on the rim, and numerous knife marks in the bowl.

The saucer was found with material of the late thirteenth century. Although pewter

208

saucers abound in contemporary inventories (Hatcher & Barker 1974, pp. 39, 75) few examples survive, least of all with marks, a rare one being the Tong Castle saucer (cf. Cat. 117, 215). The knife marks suggest that this saucer was used for cutting bread or meat. Silver saucers also frequently occur in inventories, but their appearance was unknown until one was excavated in October 1986 in a pre-1350 context at Shrewsbury, bearing the earliest-known English mark and of very similar appearance to the pewter examples. Pewter vessels of this form in various sizes continued to be made until at least *c.* 1700.

MLC

PROV. Southampton, excavated in Cuckoo Lane (A site, house 1, pit 14), 1968.

LIT. Michaelis, in Platt & Coleman-Smith 1975, pp. 250–1.

209 Spoon

c. 1300
Silver, unmarked: l. 14.9 cm
The Board of Trustees of the Victoria and Albert Museum, London, 699–1902

The finial is shaped as an acorn, the bowl figshaped; on the back of the bowl is engraved a Gothic capital S, probably an owner's initial. The surface is slightly pitted.

Spoons were made of wood or horn for general use, with metals confined to the comparatively wealthy; acorn-shaped finials were popular for fourteenth-century spoons. The earliest English hallmark, the 'Grecian' leopard's head, thought to be datable to

209

c. 1300–50, appears on an acorn-knopped spoon (How 1952, I, pl. 15, p. 64; III, p. 55) very like this, the bowl and stem of which are considered typically English in form, of perhaps just pre-1300 (ibid., I, pl. 14, p. 62). Acorn knops were made elsewhere, as evidenced by the Rouen-marked silver spoons in the Victoria and Albert Museum (Lightbown 1978c, nos 10, 11); English base-metal examples survive too, for instance in pewter (Cat. 210) and copper alloy, excavated in Coventry in the 1930s (Chatwin 1934, pp. 56–8, pl. XIII). The engraved S compares with inventory references to initials marked on plate, undoubtedly to denote ownership: such as spoons marked P for Queen Philippa in a 1369(?) document (Nicolas 1846b, p. 337).   MLC

PROV. Found in Coventry during building, late 19th century; acq. by Mrs M. Haywood, Coventry; bt from her by V & A, 1902.

LIT. Jackson 1911, p. 486; London 1930, no. 782; How 1952, I, pl. 14, p. 62

210 Spoon

c. 1300
Pewter: l. 18.1 cm, w. 4 cm
Dr Ronald F. Homer

The bowl is of leaf shape, the junction with the stem formed as a grotesque animal's head; the long, tapering stem of diamond section terminates in an acorn knop.

Certain features of this spoon such as the shape of the bowl, the animal's head motif and the acorn knop are found on a number of spoons which have been dated to the thirteenth and early fourteenth centuries. The most significant parallels include a silver spoon dated to about 1190 found in Iona, a silver spoon from the Rouen Treasure dated to about 1330 and a pewter spoon in the collection of the Worshipful Company of Pewterers. This is the earliest medieval English spoon at present recorded, and is preserved in fine condition. It has been suggested that it was made for ecclesiastical use in association with an incense boat.   AN

PROV. Not known.

LIT. Worshipful Company of Pewterers 1968, p. 46 no. 451; Homer 1973, pp. 263–4; Homer 1975, p. 16.

211 Flagon

English or Flemish, first half 14th century
Pewter: h. to lip 19 cm, h. overall 24 cm
Dr A. S. Law

The body is of baluster shape and octagonal section, set on an octagonal foot with a flat base; there are plain mouldings at the edge of the base and rim, a solid handle with attention terminal, a domed lid of octagonal section with octagonal knop and twin-acorn thumbpiece; it is stamped under the lid with a maker's touch-mark.

This flagon is related in form to a number of other flagons of presumed fourteenth-century date preserved in European collections, including examples in the Landesmuseum, Zurich: the Rijksmuseum, Amsterdam; and the Victoria and Albert Museum. Evidence for the date of these is suggested by a comparison with two flagons which formed part of a hoard excavated from the ruins of Homberg Castle, Aargau, destroyed by an earthquake in 1356. The hoard is now preserved in Schloss Lenzburg Museum, Switzerland. As surviving examples have been found from a range of provenances, it is not possible at present to establish definitely where these vessels were produced. It is, however, likely that they were made in either the Low Countries or England. The Tonbridge flagon is perhaps the best preserved of this group, and it has been pointed out that the hard oxide covering the surface indicates that a good alloy was used in its manufacture. The owner has established its capacity as 1.1 l. (42 fl. oz.).   AN

PROV. Found in Medway basin near Tonbridge Castle; Sotheby's, 31 October 1985, lot 33; A.S. Law Coll.

LIT. Bossard 1934, p. 33 pl. I nos 1,2; Verster 1957, pl.9; Brett 1981, p. 17; Law 1986.

210

211

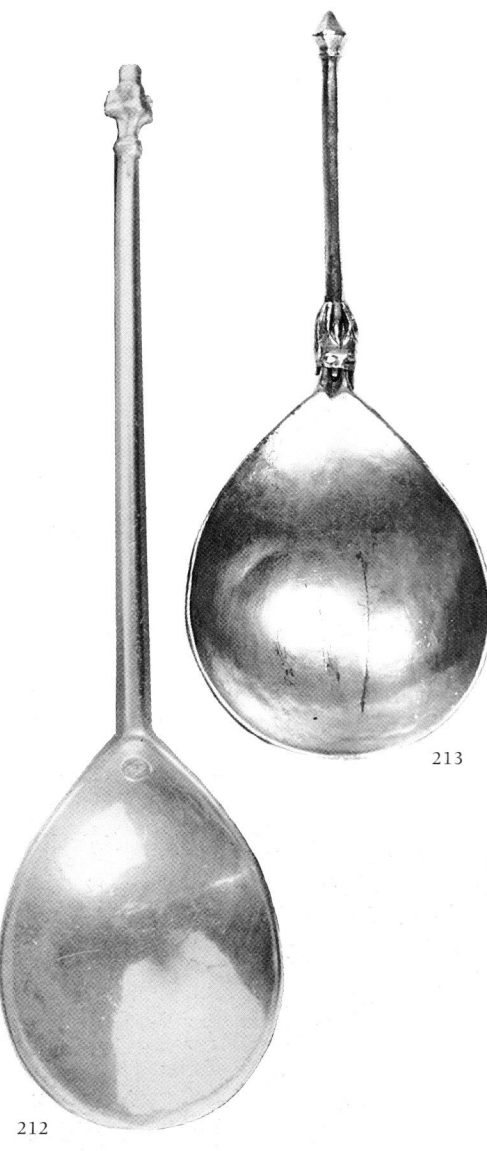

213

212

(Chatwin 1934–5, pp. 57–8, pl. XIII, fig. 2), all perhaps of the sort known in documents as 'fruitlet' (*Test. Ebor.* II, 74).   MLC

PROV. Coll. Mr & Mrs E. Assheton Bennett; given to Manchester Museum, 1957.

LIT. How 1952, I, pl. 16 p. 6; III, p. 13; Manchester 1965, no. 28; London 1965, no. 96.

213   Folding spoon

c. 1350–1400
Silver: l. 12.8 cm
Rotunda Museum, Scarborough Borough
    Council, 47.39

The bowl of the spoon is fig-shaped, the stem hexagonal with a pointed, faceted finial (a 'diamond' point); the junction of bowl and stem is hinged to allow the spoon to fold. A decorative sliding piece cast in the form of a dragon's head with long ears (cf. the Queen's College horn, Cat. 546) can be moved to enable the spoon to fold, or to cover the junction, holding the stem firm for use.

This is the only surviving English medieval example of a spoon type known otherwise from documents (Hope 1889). Animal heads are commonly found at the junction of bowl and stem of horn spoons, as from Chichester (Waterman 1959, pp. 85–6, fig. 15, no. 3), and in silver, most notably on the twelfth-century Coronation spoon.

Dating is difficult: the style of bowl has been interpreted as a forerunner of the English fig-bowl of the fourteenth and fifteenth centuries (How 1952, I, p. 58). The diamond-knop form was undoubtedly inspired by the 'point cut' used for actual diamonds, based on the natural octahedral shape of a diamond crystal, as seen on Blanche's crown (Cat. 13). This cut is unlikely to have been well enough established in England to be mimicked by goldsmiths until the fourteenth century.   MLC

PROV. Scarborough, St Mary's Parish Church; found while digging a grave, 1836.

LIT. Hope 1889, pp. 308–10; How 1952, I, pp. 58–60.

214   Dish

c. 1400
Pewter: diam. 28.9 cm, d. 3.2 cm
Stanley Shemmel

Circular, with a plain rim, this dish has a central panel of domed section. On the rim is stamped a maker's mark: a pewterer's hammer.

This is one of the earliest English dishes so far recorded. The plain rim and raised centre are features found on a number of early

212   Spoon

c. 1350
Silver, marked on bowl with leopard's head
    within dotted circle:
l. 18.1 cm, w. 4.9 cm
Manchester City Art Galleries, Assheton Bennett
    Bequest 1979. 288

The bowl of the spoon is fig-shaped, the stem hexagonal with a crocketed bud as finial, cast separately and soldered on with a V-joint. The mark of the uncrowned leopard's head, 'the Persian's head', has been interpreted as the second oldest London mark (How 1952, I, p. 66) in use before 1478. It has equal claims to be the silver standard mark used in the provinces as well as in London, following Edward I's statute of 1300 requiring silver to be marked with the leopard's head (London 1978, nos 14–15). The spoon's proportions are considered by How (op. cit., pp. 33–5, 66) as 'the English national form', standardised by *c.* 1350, found also in the Whittington spoons (Cat. 216). The finial is of a rare type, with related versions found on a fifteenth-century silver spoon (How 1952 I, p. 356, repr.) and one of base metal from Coventry

214

dishes, including the spice plate found in the well at Tong Castle (Cat. 215) which can be dated on archaeological grounds to the fifteenth century. The proportions of this dish are much larger, and, like other pewter dishes dating from before 1500, it is of substantial thickness and weight. The Tong spice plate also bears a pewterer's hammer mark. AN

PROV. Not known

LIT. Shemmel 1978, p. 2; Amsterdam 1979, nos 53, 267; King 1980, p. 28.

215 Spice plate

c. 1400
Pewter: diam. 13.7 cm, d. 1.6 cm, w. of rim 1.6 cm
The Worshipful Company of Pewterers, INV 516

This is circular with a plain edge, flat base and moulding under the rim. The plate is stamped with two marks on the rim: a pewterer's hammer within a circle and the letter E in Lombardic lettering. This spice plate and a pewter cruet were excavated from a well in the keep of Tong Castle, Shropshire. It was found associated with fifteenth-century material. This plate may be compared in style with the larger dish from a private collection, also struck with a mark of a pewterer's hammer (Cat. 214). AN

PROV. Excavated from well at Tong Castle, 1978.

LIT. Shemmell 1978, p. 2; Worshipful Company of Pewterers 1979, p. 16.

215

216 Richard Whittington's spoons

c. 1410
Silver, unmarked, knops gilt: l. 18.4 cm
The Mercer's Company

The two spoons form part of a set of four, each with hexagonal knops, faceted stems and fig-shaped bowls; on the back of each bowl is engraved a shield with Whittington's arms: Argent, a fesse checky, or and azure, in

dexter chief an annulet for difference. The legendary Dick Whittington (d. 1423), thrice Mayor of London, was a rich and powerful merchant who frequently lent large sums to the Crown (Richard II, Henry IV and Henry V). He was a great benefactor of the Mercers' Company and founded Whittington College. His spoons are all that remain of his plate and jewellery, which included a gold rosary, with beads enamelled in white and *rouge cler*, a collar of Ss, quantities of cups, bowls and at least three different seals. One of these shows a classical bust, a design more typical of Italian Renaissance than of medieval English taste, and quite exceptional among merchants' seals of this date; another includes a variation of Whittington's arms as on the spoons (Barron 1969). Both have the Whittington arms, not impaling those of his wife

216

Alice Fitzwaryn (d. before 1414), which suggests she may have been dead by the time they were made. The shape on the spoons of the armorial shields indicates a date of *c.* 1410 (How 1952). MLC

PROV. Whittington College (?), mention in MS inventories, 1511, 1582; Mercers' Company 1756 or earlier; Acts of the Court, July 8, 1756 (see MS notes at Mercers' Hall).

LIT. London 1951, no. 1; How 1952, I, pp. 78–80; Barron 1969, pp. 230–1; Lane 1985, pp. 34–5.

217 The Tring tiles

1320–30
Earthenware, eight tiles of red fabric with sgraffito decoration showing scenes from the Infancy miracles of Christ: l. 32.5 cm, w. 16.2 cm, th. 3.5 cm
The Trustees of the British Museum, London, MLA 1922, 4–12, 1–8

It is most remarkable among medieval tiles to have a series of historiated scenes so vividly depicted. The tiles are not worn and it is suggested they may have been made for a series on a wall. Ten complete tiles are known, of which two are in the Victoria and Albert Museum, and there are also three fragments of the same series of tiles. The subjects were identified by M.R. James as the Infancy miracles of Christ. They are:

1. A man dies because he spoilt a pool that Jesus made.
2. He is brought to life and walks away.
3. A boy dies because he jumped on Jesus's back while they stood before the schoolmaster.
4. He is brought to life and walks away.
5. A man locks his son in a tower.
6. Jesus frees the boy by pulling him out through a hole in the wall.
7. The schoolmaster slaps Jesus on the face.
8. Jesus and two cripples are with the schoolmasters.
9. A boy pitchforks a sheaf of miraculously-grown corn into a horse-drawn cart (see fig. 22).
10. Jesus and three men stand in front of the door of an oven in which the men have imprisoned their sons.
11. Jesus, the Virgin, St Joseph, and two other men look at three lion cubs.
12. Jesus straightens the beam of a plough.
13. Jesus turns the water into wine at the wedding at Cana in Galilee.

It is clear that there is a close relationship between these scenes on the tiles and Bodleian MS Selden Supra 38 (Cat. 203, figs 23–4). The similarities are considerable, but neither is a slavish copy of the other and there are considerable differences in scale. It is possible that both the cartoons for the tiles and the manuscript were based on a common source.

The technique is unusual. The surface of the tiles was covered with white slip and the outline of the design cut through this. Internal details on the faces and clothing were indicated with lines incised through the slip, and finally the white slip was scraped away from the whole background.

The scenes are depicted with great humour, and the economy of line produces a vividness of expression that borders on caricature. There is no external evidence for dating and it is likely that the tiles were produced at the same time as Selden Supra 38, i.e. *c.* 1315–25. They were probably made in the east of England, where sgraffito was used on pottery and occasionally on tiles such as the pavement of Prior Crauden's Chapel at Ely, dated 1324–5. JC

PROV. Bt at a 'curiosity shop' in Tring between 1843 and 1857 by Revd E. Owen; Coll. of his son Revd J.R.B. Owen; sold at Sotheby's 3 March 1922.

LIT. James 1923b, pp. 32–7 and pl. f p. 34; Eames 1980. pp. 56–61.

217

VI Peasants

Between the late twelfth century and around 1300 the population of England probably doubled to between four and five millions. Then the reverse happened. Between 1300 and the early fifteenth century the population was halved, largely because of famine and plague: especially the famine of 1315–17, the Black Death of 1348–9 and the successive returns of the plague in 1360–1, 1369 and 1375.

The agricultural economy failed to keep pace in the thirteenth century with the increase of population. It seems likely that by the early fourteenth century most of the peasants had scarcely sufficient in arable holdings or in livestock to maintain a family. Naturally it was the poorest sections of the peasantry that suffered most in the fourteenth century from bad harvests and from disease. Even the houses of richer peasants were rarely substantial. Most peasant houses were built of wood, mud and thatch, were frequently being rebuilt and comprised only one small room, open to the roof with a central hearth. The cost of building cottages in Northamptonshire around 1300 was in the region of 10 to 30s.

Among the peasants there were many different degrees of freedom and servility. But a large proportion were villeins: they were unfree by birth and were tied through the land that they held to a particular lord. The most important aspect of this servility was the owing of labour services. But these bonds were weakening; labour services were being changed to money rents. In the period after the Black Death the movement away from labour services was decisive. In the Bible the curse of labour came with the Fall of Adam and Eve and their expulsion from Paradise (Cat. 219, 221). Other common scenes representing peasants at work were the Labours of the Months (Cat. 220, 222) and the Annunciation to the Shepherds (Cat. 228).

218 Great Coxwell barn, interior looking south

First decade 14th century
Photograph

This barn is 46 m long, 13.4 m wide (an external measurement not counting buttresses), and 14.6 m high at the ridge. Horn and Born consider this and the barn of Parcay-Meslay, near Tours, to be the earliest surviving vernacular examples of a medieval 'purlin roof', (*Pfettendach*), in which the major weight of the roof is transmitted by purlins to principal trusses. The vast roof rests on purlins held in place by six intermediate trusses of cruck construction rising directly from the aisle walls, and seven principal trusses supported on two rows of slender timber posts set on high stone bases. Three-way double braces rise from these posts to their connecting longitudinal and cross beams, locking the frame together and reinforcing the beams which support the rafters. The total effect is of a powerfully vertical space, divided into sequences of bays by braces and posts reminiscent of the shafts and arches of masonry churches. In the Middle Ages the barn was entered only from the side, through two transeptal porches, one of which housed, in its upper storey, the office of the monastic granger. The barn belonged to the grange of Great Coxwell, a dependency of the Cistercian abbey of Beaulieu in Hampshire. PC

LIT. Horn & Born 1965; Horn & Born 1979, II, pp. 102–14.

219 Misericord: Woman spinning, man digging

c. 1379
Oak: h. 30 cm, w. 63 cm, d. 15 cm
The Dean and Chapter of Worcester, north side stalls from east, no. 16 (of 42)

The Worcester misericords are exceptional in that they include Old Testament scenes which look back to the lost twelfth-century wall paintings of the chapter house. They show close similarities to the Old Testament scenes in the thirteenth-century Eton College Manuscript (MS 177), and the Peterborough Psalter (Cat, 567) dated *c.* 1300.

The exhibited misericord could portray one of the Labours of the Months (digging in March replaced pruning of trees in England; see Webster 1938, p.89). However, the comparison with the same arrangement of the figures in the Huth Psalter (London, British Library, Add. MS 38116, f. 9) makes it probable that the figures represent Adam and Eve. Adam places his foot on the same type of

218

spade, and Eve holds her implements in like manner. The Temptation and Expulsion illustrated on the same page of the psalter are also found among the Worcester misericords, and here, too, the quite unusual portrayal of the Temptation is identical: the serpent's body coils around the tree; it has wings and a monster's head with large ears; and Eve takes the apple from the serpent's mouth, hands it to Adam, and he puts it into his mouth. This iconography goes back to the English Romanesque St Albans Psalter (Hildesheim, Basilika St Godehard; f. 17). CG

PROV. Worcester Cathedral.

LIT. Willis 1863, p. 120; James 1901, pp. 99–117; Webster 1938, p. 89; Cox 1959, pp. 165–78.

220 Misericord: Three men mowing

c. 1379
Oak: h.. 30 cm, w. 63 cm, d. 15 cm
The Dean and Chapter of Worcester, south side stalls from east, no. 3 (of 42)

The three men with scythes, dressed in the fashion of the last quarter of the fourteenth century, stand on pedestals. They represent the Labour of the Month for July.

The Labours of the Months in Worcester are the first almost complete cycle on misericords. The figures sit or stand in stiff frontal poses and, in their motionless activities, can be compared with those in twelfth-century psalters, e.g. the York Psalter (Glasgow, University Library, MS Hunter U 3.2). The Worcester misericord for June shows three men weeding, the tools for this having first been depicted in the twelfth century.

The Worcester Labours were used as models by the carver of the Malvern misericords. This enables us to reconstruct the missing Worcester months, January and September. The suggested list of occupations for Worcester is: January, feasting; February, warming by the fire; March, sowing; April, riding out; May, picking flowers; June, weeding; July, mowing; August, reaping; September, harvesting grapes; October, horn-blowing; November, feeding pigs; December, slaughtering the ox.

The supporters represent the topsy-turvy world: the wolf in clerical robes places its paws on a sheep's head on an altar, mimicking the priest blessing the host at Mass. In the margin of a fourteenth-century manuscript (Cambridge, Trinity College, MS B. 11.22, f.4), an ape in bishop's cloak and mitre lifts the skull of a sheep as at the Elevation of the Host, assisted by a cat. CG

PROV. Worcester Cathedral.

LIT. Webster 1938.

221 The Holkham Bible

c. 1320–30
Parchment, ff. 42: 28.6 × 21.2 cm
British Library, Add. MS 47682

The Holkham Bible recounts the story of man from Creation to the Last Judgement in 231 miniatures accompanied by short explanatory passages in Anglo-French.

The pictorial narratives of the Holkham Bible, mostly arranged in two unframed compositions per page, are fast-paced, but no detail of a vivid or dramatic kind is glossed over. Numerous apocryphal Infancy subjects are included (cf. Cat. 203) and many narrative sequences are expanded: for instance, the usual number of incidents between Christ's Entry into Jerusalem and the Flagellation are multiplied from six to thirty-six episodes. Individual miniatures are enriched with details derived from or paralleled by a wide range of literary sources, probably including contemporary religious drama, as well as observation of daily life (cf. fig. 11).

The Holkham Bible shares a tendency towards the pictorial vernacular general in English illumination of the second quarter of the fourteenth century, also to be found, for example, in the Taymouth Hours (London, British Library, Yates Thompson MS 13) and the Smithfield Decretals (fig. 130). In the Bible, this vernacular style is expressed in large-scale figures, crowded compositions and harsh colours, the streaky shading recalling *opus anglicanum* (Cat. 576–9). LFS

PROV. Thomas William Coke (Coke of Norfolk), 1816; acq. by British Museum, 1952.

LIT. James 1923a, pp. 1–27, repr. pls 1–19; Hassall 1954; Pickering 1971; Sandler 1986, no. 97, II, pp. 105–7, repr. I, fig. 247.

219

220

Oment vn auugel de vn espese. Gardoit la porte tla vese. Re adam
ne enceist. Por la defens deu q̇ fl valest. E dit adam va fuer tere.
Car ich ne arez iames a fere. Adam vne beche prist. Sicu le auugel ls̃ a
noist dist. E semost ble ↄ fruit tere. E eue filoist por vesture fere. Adam
uuoist a sees desauuz. E engendrat deus enfauuz. Carin le esne ↄ li
autre Abel. Li premier taus ↄ le dreyner tel.

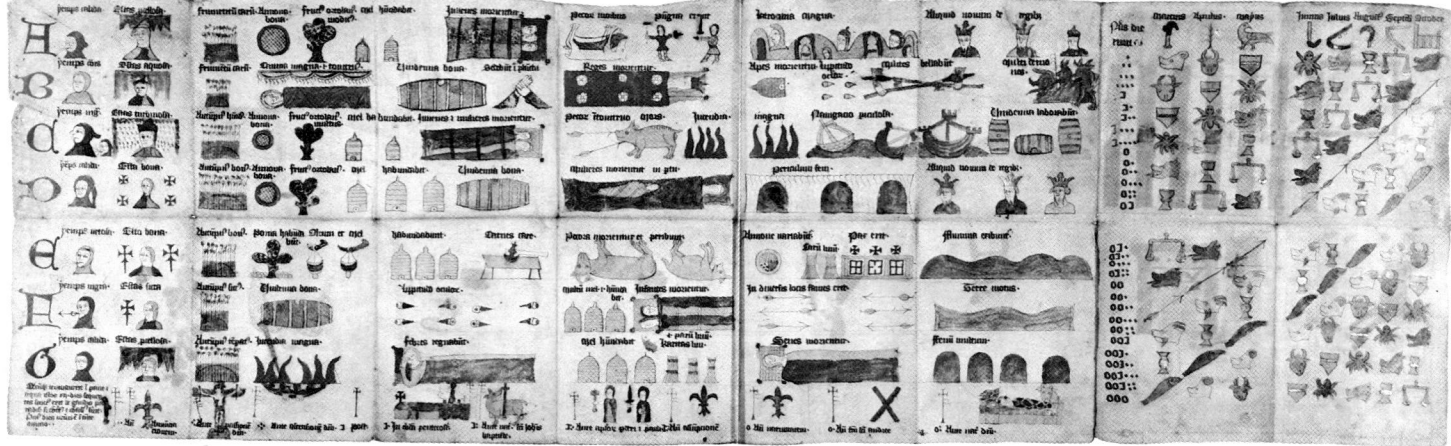

222

222 Astrological and ecclesiastical calendar (almanac)

Late 14th century
Parchment, 6 sheets folded individually to pocket
size: approx. 14 × 11 cm
Oxford, Bodleian Library, MS Rawl. D. 939

Each sheet is ingeniously cut and folded so as to organise a large quantity of useful information, historical, current and prognostic, in an easily accessible pocket format. The texts, diagrammatic or tabular in form, include a Sarum calendar, an Easter table for 1235–1677, planetary and zodiacal spheres, and calendrical prognostications regarding harvests, weather, war, pestilence, birth and death. Most of these are embellished by illustrations, either pictograms, such as a barrel for the grape harvest and a hive for the honey crop (sheet 4), or images of the major saints of the church year (sheet 2), the occupations of the months (sheet 2), Harry the Haywarde (manorial official in charge of fences and enclosures, sheet 1) and Perys the Pyndare (manorial official responsible for impounding stray animals, sheet 3), and the story of Adam and Eve (sheet 4).

The coloured drawings are rudimentary, but full of engaging descriptive detail that provides considerable information about medieval agricultural technology, one sheet alone (3) showing at least nine different kinds of hand tools. These almanacs must have once been common; those that survive (such as London, British Library, Eger. MS 2734, close to the present example but fifteenth-century in date) are well thumbed.   LFS

PROV. William Fleetwood, Bishop of Ely, given to Thomas Hearne, 1719; Richard Rawlinson, beq. to Bodleian Library, 1756.

LIT. Macray 1898, IV, cols 209–11; Oxford 1952, no. 98, repr. pls XVIII–XIX; Pächt & Alexander 1973, no. 749.

223 William Langland, The Vision of Piers Plowman

1427
Vellum, ff. 112: 22 × 15 cm
Oxford, Bodleian Library, MS Douce 104

The Middle English alliterative poem commonly entitled Piers Plowman provides a view of the contemporary life of the lower classes of society in late fourteenth-century England. More than sixty manuscripts of the poem have come down to us. What little is known of the author, who was inspired by a vision while walking in the Malvern Hills, has been gleaned solely from the occasional personal references included in the text. Three successive versions of the work were made and their composition seems to have occupied a period of at least twenty years, beginning about the middle of the 1360s.

The exhibited manuscript, which is a fairly late copy of the 'C' text and has recently been associated on linguistic grounds with Ireland, is unusual because it includes a series of marginal illustrations. These apparently represent various figures mentioned in accompanying passages of the poem. Illustrations are very rare in English literary manuscripts but when they do occur it is not uncommon for them to be placed in lateral margins, where earlier and more elaborate illuminated books such as the Luttrell Psalter (Cat. 575) would have had grotesques or decorative figures. Formal miniatures such as those seen in Sir Gawain and the Green Knight (Cat. 718) are very rare indeed.   JB

PROV. Sir James Ley (d. 1628); Francis Douce (d. 1834); beq. to Bodleian Library.

LIT. Skeat 1873, no. xxxviii; Pächt & Alexander 1973, no. 886; Watson 1984, no. 455.

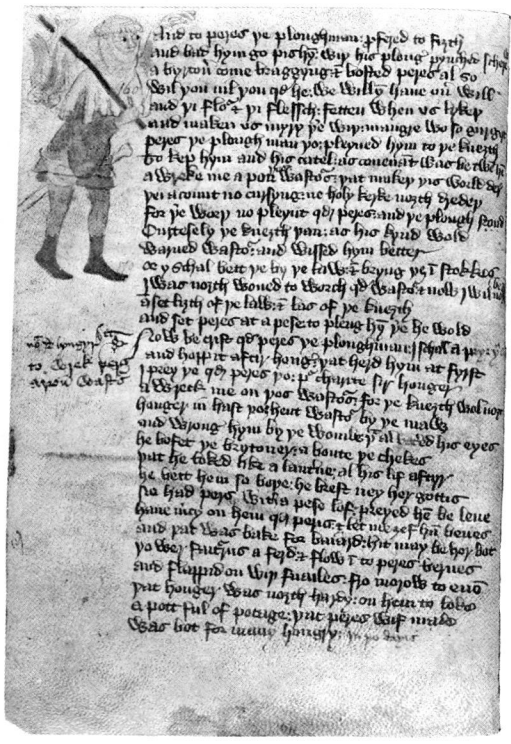

223

VII Lords Lying on High on their Graves

This section illustrates the way that the great and the wealthy had themselves commemorated in funeral effigies on their tombs and in donor portraits recording their gifts of stained glass to churches. The portrait of Beatrix van Valkenburg is the earliest such donor portrait surviving in English stained glass. In Piers Plowman reference is made to such portraits as signs of pride and worldly glory and the author of Handlyng Synne speaks of the lords 'busy about acquiring proud stones, lying on high on their graves' (cf. p. 30 above). In spite of such criticisms, parish churches throughout England still retain numerous monumental tombs and brasses, even if the majority of the stained-glass windows which once existed have been destroyed. The peasants, if represented at all, are shown as a class, not as individuals (Cat. 228, 230).

224   Effigy of a Knight and a Lady

Knight *c.* 1346–9; Lady *c.* 1340
Oak: knight l. 206 cm, lady l. 204.5 cm
The Rector and Parochial Church Council of
   Paulerspury, Northamptonshire

The two effigies were made by different carvers and do not seem to be of the same date. The lady is an accomplished figure made by a carver familiar with courtly work of the second quarter of the fourteenth century. Her sleeveless open-sided tunic falling in multiple folds over her feet, her long cloak caught up under her arms and the quantity of hair revealed on either side of her face over the wimple, indicate a date around 1340. The male effigy is by comparison rather stiff and provincial. Certain distinctive details of his armour, such as the close-fitting surcoat extending below the knees at the back, the ribbed poleyns and the bacinet laced to an aventail covering his shoulders, can be found *c.* 1345–50, for example, carved with much better detail on the effigy of Peter, Lord Grandisson at Hereford Cathedral (repr. Crossley 1921, p. 9). It is likely that the male effigy represents Sir Robert de Pavely, Lord of the Manor of Paulerspury, Northamptonshire, and former Sheriff of Northampton, who died in 1346, or his son Laurence, who died aged twenty-two in 1349. The female effigy may represent Robert's wife, who certainly predeceased him, but whose identity and precise date of death are unknown.   VS

PROV. Church of St James the Great, Paulerspury, Northamptonshire.

LIT. Whalley 1791, pp. 311–3; Baker 1836–41, pp. 200–1; Hartshorne 1876, p. 66; Prior & Gardner 1912, p. 669; Fryer 1924, pp. 20–1; Cal. Inq. 20 E III, no. 666; 22 E III, no. 124; 23 E III, no. 215.

224

225   Incised slab

London, second quarter 14th century
Purbeck marble: l. 114.5 cm, w. 46 cm
   Inscr. in Lombardic capitals . . . AM
The Board of Trustees of the Victoria and Albert
   Museum, London, A. 53-1935

The slab has been cut down at top and bottom and much of the right-hand side has been broken away. It has been suggested that

225

the inscription at the top right-hand corner may be the end of a surname (*Ant. J.* 1934).

The figure is clearly a civilian; by comparison with brasses, the dress may be dated to the second quarter of the fourteenth century. This particular type of tunic with hood may be seen on the brass of Nicholas de Aumberdene at Taplow, Buckinghamshire, *c.* 1350 (Haines 1861, repr. pl. clxii); this figure also holds his hands together in prayer and has a similar hairstyle.   PW

PROV. Discovered during reconstruction of the Bank of England, 1934, coming probably from Church of St Christopher-le-Stocks (destroyed 1780); given to the V & A by the Governors of the Bank of England, 1934.

LIT. *Ant. J.* 1934, p. 279; *Review* 1935, p. 2; Greenhill 1958, p. 220; Greenhill 1976, I, pp. 66, 204; II, p. 13; Williamson (forthcoming), no. 19.

226   Beatrix van Valkenburg

c. 1270–80
Stained glass: h. 60 cm, w. 26.5 cm
Inscr. in Lombardic letters BEATRIX DE
   VALKENBURGH REGINA ALLEMANNIE
The Burrell Collection, Glasgow Museums and Art
   Galleries, 45/2

Beatrix van Valkenburg was the daughter of Dirk II, Lord of Valkenburg (Limburg), and third wife of Richard, Earl of Cornwall and King of the Romans (Cat. 275). She died in 1277 and was buried in the Church of the Minorite Friars in Oxford, from where this panel may have come. The figure of Beatrix is depicted in conventional donor pose, kneeling in prayer. She is crowned and wears a mantle decorated with alternate ruby and black bands. On the blue ground are a series of roundels charged with the imperial eagle.

Since the destruction by fire several years ago of the figures at Upper Hardres in Kent, the panel depicting Beatrix van Valkenburg has become the earliest known surviving representation of a donor in English glass.
   RM

PROV. Church of Minorite Friars, Oxford (?); George William Jerningham, 8th Baron Stafford of Costessey, Norfolk; Sir William Burrell; donated to Glasgow as part of Burrell Coll., 1944.

LIT. Steinberg 1938; Glasgow 1962, no. 1.

227   John de Newmarch

c. 1307
Stained glass: h. 93 cm, w. 49 cm
The Parish of St Nicholas, Carlton Scroop,
   Lincolnshire, east window, I.B.3

The surviving medieval glass is *in situ* in the east window; there is grisaille in the heads of two main lights and, in the tracery, foliage designs, an armorial of St Edmund, and two donors beneath a modern Christ in Majesty. The panel exhibited depicts a knight kneeling on a pot-metal yellow plinth, and holding a Newmarch shield, Gules five fusils conjoined in fess or. His face is pink, and he wears white

226

mail, poleyns, prick spurs and sword belt, with surcoat and aillettes again displaying his arms. White foliage fills the top and right foils; the ground is blue. A few pieces of foliage and ground were restored in the nineteenth century, and in 1975–6 the York Glaziers Trust cleaned the heavily corroded glass.

A shield identifies the other donor as a member of the Briddeshall family. Described as a woman by the antiquary Holles, this figure has the restored head of a priest, an identification which is plausible, given the blue fur-lined gown the figure wears. Fortu-

227

nately an entry in Bishop Dalderby's Register (Lincoln Archives Office, Bishop's Register no. 2 [Dalderby], f. 20) clarifies the situation as it records that John de Newmarch, lord of the manor of Carlton Newmarch, as the village was then known, presented William de Briddeshall, chaplain, to the vacant living of the parish in 1307. The tracery of the east window was a record of this event, with priest and patron kneeling before a lost figure of a saint.

John de Newmarch was dead by 1310 when his brother, Roger, had inherited. This suggests a narrow bracket of 1307–10 for the dating. The style, the type of armour, and the absence of yellow stain confirm a date early in the fourteenth century, and suggest that Woodforde's attempt to link the Carlton Scroop glazing with later fourteenth-century work at Barton on Humber, Heydour and Long Sutton, must be abandoned. DO'C

LIT. Holles 1911, p. 230; Nelson 1913, pp. 136–7; Woodforde 1954 pp. 13–14.

228

228 Annunciation to the shepherds

c. 1325–50
Stained glass: diam. 29.2 cm
The Board of Trustees of the Victoria and Albert
Museum, London, 2270–1900

In this small roundel the archangel appears from a cloud before two shepherds with their dog tending horned sheep. The standing figure, who is clad in a cowled cloak over a short tunic, hose and boots, leans on a club-shaped staff; at his waist is a woven openwork pouch. His companion, wearing a long cowled robe, hose and shoes, is sitting on a bank playing the bagpipes. The figures and beasts are all in white and yellow stain, and the foliate diapered background is on blue glass. The ground at the top and bottom as well as the sun and stars are not original. Although this roundel was included in the Vienna exhibition of art around 1400, the figure style and painting indicate a date of at least fifty years earlier. The motif of the shepherds playing music occurs in representations of the same scene in illuminated manuscripts, e.g. the De Lisle Psalter (Cat. 569) and Queen Mary Psalter and in the lost wall paintings in St Stephen's Chapel, Westminster (Cat. 680). RM

PROV. Henry Vaughan; beq. to V & A, 1900.

LIT. Rackham 1936, p. 46, pl. 14B; Baker 1960; Vienna 1962, no. 221.

229 Arms of Somery

c. 1330–50
Stained glass: h. 52.6 cm, w. 44.5 cm
The Burrell Collection, Glasgow Museums and Art
Galleries, 45/109

Set within a pointed ruby quatrefoil on a green ground is the shield of arms, Or two lions passant azure, of the Somery family of Dudley Castle, Worcestershire. This family

229

held the barony of Dudley from 1194 until the death in 1322 of the last male heir, Sir John de Somery. The foliate diapering on the shield and the green ground is delicately picked out on a matt wash. The shield and its enframing, together with two others in the Burrell Collection, are outstanding examples of English medieval heraldic art and may be compared with the heraldic glass of *c.* 1344 in the choir clerestory windows of Tewkesbury Abbey (Rushforth 1924).   RM

PROV. Bruce Coll.; Christie's, 28 June 1935, bt by Sir William Burrell; donated to Glasgow as part of Burrell Coll., 1944.

LIT. Newton 1962, pp. 13–16; Glasgow 1962, no. 14, colour pl. p. 5.

230   Peasants

c. 1340–49
Stained glass: h. 77 cm, w. 20 cm
Dean and Chapter, Ely Cathedral, on loan to the
 Stained Glass Museum, Ely, 78/10/2

These four men in peasant costume are companions to the soldiers in Cat. 743 and belong to a similar canopy from the first window from the east on the south side of the Lady Chapel. They are executed in white and yellow stain and are set in niches on a matt ground and under steep crocketed gables. Modern stippled glass has been inserted between two pairs of figures and in the lower left panel.   RM

231   Robert Skelton

c. 1350
Stained glass: h. 75 cm, w. 57 cm
  Inscr. + ORATE P̄ ANIMABZ ROḂT
The Rector and Churchwardens of St Denys
 Church, Walmgate, York, window nIV.2a

This panel from a window in the north choir aisle was given by a donor called Robert, his wife Johanna and son John, who kneel below St Margaret, the Virgin and Child, and a lost St Catherine. The inscription is damaged but Henry Johnston recorded the end of the surname as LTVN in 1669. The mercer Robert de Skelton, Chamberlain of York in 1353 and Bailiff in 1355/6, is a possible donor and a member of a class which directed large sums of money into the parish churches. He is shown presenting the window, and has a white head, yellow-stained hair and beard, parti-coloured blue and ruby gown with pendent sleeves, and pot-metal yellow shoes. The butterfly quarry background is in white and yellow stain, and there are borders of gold lions on ruby grounds. The inscription, which continues across the other two lights, requests prayers for the souls of the donors. The panel was restored in 1896 by J.W. Knowles, who replaced half of the quarries and ten lions. The blue glass is heavily corroded.

Much of the glazing of the north aisle survives, including another window (nIII) by the same designer and with a donor based

230

231

on the Robert Skelton cartoon. J. A. Knowles suggested that this glass showed the influence of Wells (Knowles 1936, pp. 112–14), but his Richard de Welles, freeman of York in 1359, was an ironworker not a glazier. The style, technique, and even the iconography of the St Denys glass owes much more to the York workshop of Master Robert (Cat. 6, 562–3, 741). The costume and the developed perspective of the canopies in the window suggest a mid-century date.   DO'C

LIT. Henry Johnston, Church Notes and Drawings 1669–70, Oxford, Bodleian Library, MS Top. Yorks c. 14, f. 107; RCHM, *York*, 1981, p. 18.

232 Rector William de Luffwyk

1335–80

Stained glass: h. 65 cm, w. 41 cm

Inscr. in Lombardic letters ORATE PRO VITA WIL (LUFFWYK R)ECTORIS ISTIUS ECCL(ES)IE

The Rector and Parochial Church Council of Aldwincle, Northamptonshire, window 1

This panel is from the tracery (light A2) of the chancel east window. William de Luffwyk is shown kneeling in prayer. He is tonsured, with yellow-stain wavy hair and wears a rust-red cassock and shoes in dark brown edged in white. The figure is set on a blue ground with a foliate diaper pattern of heart-shaped leaves and stems picked out on a matt wash, and overlaps the border with its in-

232

scription. The lower lobe in the border has a flower and bosses in yellow stain. The panel is complete except for part of the inscription and the ground in the right lobe, which are modern. William de Luffwyk was rector of Aldwincle St Peter's between 1335 and 1380, and the inscription shows that the glazing was carried out during his lifetime. In the use of heavy modelling and the delineation of facial features this panel is comparable with glass of the 1340s, but the Perpen-

dicular tracery of the window precludes such an early date. Possibly the construction of the window was connected with the endowment in 1372 of a priest to celebrate at the high altar. The other medieval glass in the tracery of this window (not exhibited) comprises an inscription for Luffwyk's predecessor Roger Travers (rector 1321–35) and parts of three angels.   RM

LIT. Newton 1961, I, pp. 11–12, 89–92, II. pp. 312–23.

233 Brass of Laurence de St Maur (Seymour)

c. 1337

Replica: l. of figure 160 cm

Inscr. in Gothic letters across base *Hic iacet laurēci [us] de s͞c͞o Mauro q° ndā rector ist [ius] ecc͞e cui[ius] āie p[ro]piciēt[ur] deus*
across chest *Fili dei miserere mei;*
along lower canopy *Suscipiat me xpistus qui uocauit me & in sinu abrahe angeli deducant me*

Bryan Egan Esq. (original in Parish Church of St Mary the Virgin, Higham Ferrers, Northamptonshire)

The figure is of a full-length priest, his hands in prayer, bareheaded, with a tonsure and bushy sidelocks, standing on a pair of dogs fighting over a bone. He wears Mass vestments, with decorated apparels. There is a slender cusped and crocketed ogee canopy, and a rectangular super-canopy supported on tower-like side shafts, the top crenellated. The super-canopy and shafts are formed of rectangular panels (three and most of a fourth missing from the right-hand side), each containing a sacred personage under a gable canopy: in the super-canopy, Christ (God the Father?) is enthroned with the deceased's soul held before him in a napkin by two angels, and flanked by Sts Andrew, Peter, Paul and Thomas; at the top and bottom of each side shaft is an Evangelist with his symbol below; in the right-hand shaft there are remains of St Christopher at the bottom; in the left-hand shaft, an angel, St John the Baptist, St Stephen and an abbot (?). Struck on the super-canopy is a mark – a plater's hammer(?) over a reversed N between a fleur-de-lis(?) and a star – almost certainly that of the maker of the latten plate.

St Maur died in 1337, and the brass certainly dates from this period. It represents a departure from the Camoys/Setvans style (Cat. 138, 234–5), though possibly from the same London workshop. This workshop also produced, *inter alia*, the De Creke brass of *c.* 1340–5 at Westley Waterless, Cambridgeshire, which bears the same mark, and that of Sir John D'Abernon III, *c.* 1340–5, at Stoke D'Abernon, Surrey, which bears a defaced mark which may originally have been the same one or a version of it. The Hastings brass of *c.* 1347 (Cat. 690) has a comparable arrangement of inhabited side

233

shafts, and may be a later product of the same workshop. The present brass is the earliest of its style to survive, and 'Seymour' has therefore been chosen as the eponym for the whole group.   CB

PROV. Parish Church of St Mary the Virgin, Higham Ferrers, Northants.

LIT. Gough 1786, II (III), p. 332, pl. 118; Hudson 1853, (p. 294); Norris 1978a p. 72, figs 70, 132; 1978b, pp. 21–2, 52; Binski 1987, pp. 106–16.

234 Brass of Sir William de Setvans

c. 1322

Replica: l. of figure 188 cm

Inscr. in separate Lombardic letters round slab, now illegible, recorded as including the words LE FILS SIRE ROBERT DE SETVANS

Studio 69 Monumental Brass Facsimiles (original at St Mary's, Chartham, Kent)

The figure is full-length, with crossed legs, the feet resting on a lion (now incomplete), the bare head unsupported and the hands in prayer. He wears a mid-thigh length mail shirt with close-fitting sleeves, and coif and mittens attached, the former thrown back over the shoulders, and the latter from the

234

235

sword belt with a cusped inner border, except where it passes through the buckle, and a central row of rosettes, of which some form eyelets for the tongue. The buckle is attached directly to the top of the scabbard: immediately below is a locket carrying a ring on the other side, through which is passed another ring on the end of the belt proper. The straight, double-edged sword is cruciform, with slightly arched cross and disc pommel, the latter decorated with a quatrefoil and a pyramidal button. The grip and scabbard are decorated with a trellis and quatrefoil pattern, on the latter between a series of plain lockets. The somewhat unusual (for a brass) bare head shows the hair framing the face in a bouffant style with the ends curled inwards. The lines of engraving where the two plates forming the brass meet, just below the hands, are slightly offset, indicating that they must have been engraved separately. Also, in addition to the main convention for representing mail, two others are used, respectively inside the mittens and on the left foot. The Purbeck slab contains indents for two corner shields in addition to those for the letters of the inscription identifying the tomb as that of the son of Sir Robert de Setvans.

Only two sons are possible candidates, of whom one, also called Robert, died in 1304, and the second, William, Sheriff of Kent, in 1322. Evidence is strongly in favour of the latter. The brass now gives its name to a small group of London products, contemporary with and related to the Camoys group (see Cat. 138), but not apparently by the same hand, though perhaps by another designer or engraver in the same workshop. The style shows certain affinities with drawings in the early fourteenth-century De Lisle Psalter in the British Library (Cat. 569). The hairstyle gives it a superficial similarity to some Continental and Yorkshire effigies, but is merely the characteristic masculine one of the period.   CB

PROV. Parish Church of St Mary, Chartham, Kent.

LIT. Waller 1975, no. 4; Norris 1978a, pp. 71,85; figs 120–1; 1978b, pp. 9, 13, 84–5, 168, 191; Binski 1980; Binski 1987, pp. 83–90, figs 74–6.

235   Brass of Sir Robert de Bures

c. 1331
Replica: l. of figure 201.9 cm
Inscr. in separate Lombardic letters around slab (recorded, but now completely illegible) +
ROBERT : DE : BURES : GYST : YCI : DEVX : DE : SALME : EIT : MERCI : XPI [error for KI ?] : PVR : SA : ALME : PRYERA : QVARANTE : IOVRS : DE : PARDON : AVERA
Studio 69 Monumental Brass Facsimiles (original at All Saints, Acton, Suffolk)

The figure is full length, with crossed legs, the feet resting on a lion, the head unsupported and the hands in prayer. The armour, sword,

hands. Underneath is a vertically-quilted hacketon, visible just above the knees and at the wrists, with close-fitting buttoned sleeves. On the legs are mail hosen over which are strapped vertically-quilted thigh defences (cuisses), perhaps lined with riveted plates, carrying small cusped plate (or cuir-bouilli?) knee defences (poleyns). Over all is a sleeveless gown, girded at the waist and with a rather full, mid-calf length skirt, split up the front: it is charged with winnowing fans from the canting Setvans coat of arms. On the heels are prick spurs, a pair of rectangular fringed ailettes charged with winnowing fans is shown behind the shoulders, and covering the upper left side is a strongly concave, heater-shaped shield, similarly charged. Buckled diagonally round the hips is a broad

and type and position of the shield are basically the same as on the Setvans brass of *c.* 1322 (Cat. 234), but without ailettes and with a few other differences. The head is covered by a separate mail coif, extending over the shoulders and covering a rounded skullcap, arched slightly over the brow and secured by an encircling strap round its lower edge. The hands are covered by mail mittens with supporting thongs round the wrists. The hacketon is not visible. The plain gown has a fringed lower edge with a border of repeated trefoils, and is held at the waist by a plaited cord with a plaited button at the front. The thighs are covered by cuisses which are presumably of padded (gamboised) textile since they appear to be embroidered with a trellis pattern of thread framing fleurs-de-lis and lyre-like motifs, and with a rosette set at each intersection: they extend to just below the knees, which are additionally protected at the front by ornamental poleyns, strapped over the cuisses, and apparently made of cuir-bouilli, each decorated with two panels of foliage framed in riveted reinforcing strips. The sword belt is of the type with the section bearing the buckle forked and with the upper part laced round the scabbard just below its mouth, and the lower part linked diagonally to the end of the main belt where it passes round the scabbard lower down. It has narrow plain borders and is set at intervals with transverse bars with circular central eyelets alternating with simple stitched(?) eyelets, for the tongue of the buckle. The sword pommel is decorated with a cross within a circle within a rosette, and the grip with trelliswork as on the cuisses, but framing stars and rosettes. The spurs are set with similar rosettes, and the buckled guige of the shield, decorated with a lozenge and fylfot pattern, is visible by the left shoulder. The shield bears the arms of Bures: Ermine, on a chief indented sable, two lioncels or. The slab bearing the inscription (Robert de Bures lies here. God have mercy on his soul. Whoever will pray for his soul shall have forty days of pardon) is of Purbeck marble

This is from the London Camoys workshop (cf. Cat. 138). Jennifer Ward's article establishing that, despite a 'traditional' date of 1302, the only possible candidate for ownership was the Robert de Bures who died in 1331, was the prime mover in the process of redating all the early military brasses, of which it is perhaps the finest example. It demonstrates very clearly that armour made almost entirely of mail survived well into the fourteenth century.　　　CB

PROV. Parish Church of All Saints, Acton, Suffolk.

LIT. Ward 1963–8; Blatchly 1975, p. 39; Waller 1975, no. 3; Norris 1978a, p. 34; 1978b, pp. 9, 83, 190; Binski 1987, pp. 94–7, fig. 88.

236　Brass of Sir John D'Abernon III

c. 1340–5
Replica: l. of figure 165.1 cm
Inscr. in French in Lombardic letters on marginal fillet, fragmentary, no longer in original position
The Board of Trustees of the Royal Armouries (original in Parish Church of St Mary, Stoke D'Abernon, Surrey)

The figure is a full-length knight, under an ogee canopy (now incomplete but reconstructed in the Catalogue illustration) with side pinnacles, his bare hands in prayer, his feet supported on a lion. He wears full armour, comprising a fluted ogee-shaped bacinet with its lower edge bordered by lining rivets, and an applied finial shaped as a cross

with heart-shaped terminals; close-fitting aventail (?separate mail hood) fitting under the bacinet; close-fitting coat armour laced up the sides, sleeveless, but extending over the points of the shoulders, and with a full, knee-length skirt, cut short at the front; visible below this last are successively the lower edges of the coat-of-plates, habergeon and hacketon; also visible is one of the three-quarter-length sleeves of the habergeon, with a closed, hinged, plate vambrace beneath; strapped over the upper arms are gutter-shaped rerebraces with small pointed cowters; circular besagews, with engrailed inner borders, over the fronts of the shoulders and elbows, held respectively by a rosette-headed rivet and a knotted lace; mail hosen covered by globular poleyns with applied, engrailed medial ribs, plate schynbalds secured by straps, laminated sabatons over the tops of the feet and prick spurs; round the hips is a broad sword-belt linked to the locket of the scabbard by side rings; cruciform sword with slightly arched quillons, ovoidal,

236

faceted pommel and bound grip; on the left arm is a small, heater-shaped shield bearing the D'Abernon arms – Azure, a chevron or – with the field cut away and hatched for a coloured filling (missing). Two subsidiary shields were originally attached to the Purbeck slab, one on each side of the canopy. Struck near one edge of the main figure is a defaced mark, possibly the remains, or a version, of the one discussed under Cat. 233.

This is a Seymour style brass (see Cat. 233), closely similar to that of Sir John de Creke at Westley Waterless, Cambridgeshire. It was once attributed to the Sir John D'Abernon who died in 1327, but this attribution and date cannot now be sustained: a date of 1327 would not only put the monument of a comparatively minor Surrey knight in advance of the effigy of John of Eltham, Earl of Cornwall, in Westminster Abbey, but also, even more improbably, suggest that English armour styles were in advance of Continental ones. Of the three recorded John D'Abernons – father, son and grandson – who died respectively in 1277, 1327, and between 1335 and 1350, it is clear from the style of the armour depicted on the brass that it commemorates the last of these.　　　CB

PROV. Parish Church of St Mary, Stoke D'Abernon, Surrey.

LIT. Stothard 1817, pl. 60; Percival 1871, p. 65; Johnston 1907a, pp. 36–43, 61–4; Clift 1909, pp. 77–101; Stephenson 1921, pp. 482–3; Gawthorp 1934–42; Norris 1978a, fig. 128; 1978b, pp. 11, 17, 21; Binski 1987, pp. 108–14.

237　Brass of an unknown wool merchant and his wife

Late 14th century
Replica: l. of man 142 cm
Studio 69 Monumental Brass Facsimiles (original at Parish Church of St Peter and Paul, Northleach, Gloucestershire)

The figures are full length, in separate slabs, both with hands in prayer, he with his feet on a rectangular woolsack tied at four corners, she with a small dog with belled collar at her feet. He is shown as middle-aged, bareheaded, bald and with a small forked beard. He wears a gown with an ankle-length buttoned skirt and loose, wrist-length sleeves, covering an undergarment, of which all that is visible are the cuffs of the close-fitting, buttoned sleeves with mitten-like extensions half-way up the hands: over all is a long ankle-length cloak with large buttons at the top, and, round his shoulders, a hood with buttons up the front, partly undone. On his feet are pointed shoes with ankle straps, while his waist is girded with a broad belt, set at intervals with discs bearing rosettes alternating with pairs of pellets, and with an ornamental buckle and chape which bears a Lombardic letter T, presumably the owner's initial. Suspended from it on a cord on the left

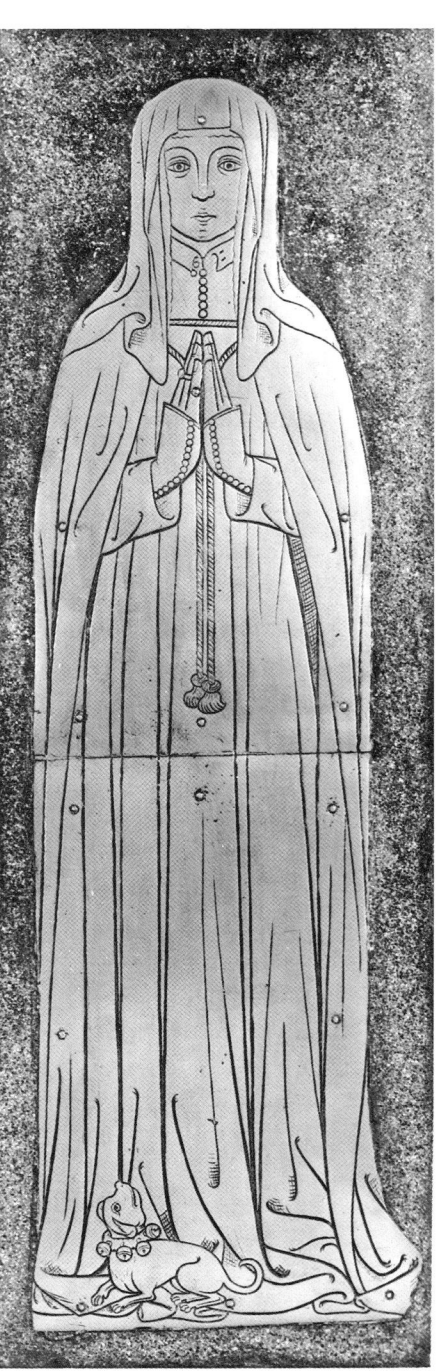

237

is a baselard (cf. Cat. 175) with scalloped mounts at the top and bottom of the hilt, and the locket and chape of the scabbard decorated with Gothic arcading. She wears a similar undergarment, robe and cloak, but the last two reach to the ground, while the robe has a high, buttoned neck, unfastened at the top so that the upper part falls over, and the cloak is secured by a cord with pendent tasselled ends. She wears a veil over her head, which may indicate that she was a widow when the brass was laid down.

This is a London 'Series A' brass of a kind widely found commemorating the professional and merchant classes from the middle of the fourteenth century onwards. The woolsack refers to England's chief late medieval industry, like the modern one upon which the Lord Chancellor sits in the House of Lords.   CB

PROV. Parish Church of St Peter and Paul, Northleach, Gloucestershire.

LIT. Norris 1978b, pp. 58, 60, 66, fig. 80.

VIII The Cathedrals and the Beginnings of Gothic Style

The English episcopate was unusual in two important respects. A large number of the cathedral churches were monasteries, rather than secular colleges with a dean and canons: seven were Benedictine monasteries and Carlisle was an Augustinian priory. Monk-bishops were, however, very much the exception by the end of the thirteenth century; more and more bishops were university-trained, especially at Paris and Oxford. Second, the bishops held their estates 'in barony', that is directly from the Crown. They were thus, as a whole group, regarded as 'barons' on a par with those magnates who were tenants-in-chief; and so the bishops were summoned by the king, along with a number of the abbots, to the highest court of the realm, developing under the name of 'parliament' during the second half of the thirteenth century, and in the fourteenth century they sat in the House of Lords, already distinguished from the House of Commons. The very close relationship of bishops and their bishoprics to the Crown is indicated by the fact that diocesan boundaries and boundaries of archdeaconries often corresponded to county boundaries (fig. 127).

Though the Normans had by 1200 rebuilt the majority of the English cathedrals, the thirteenth century saw further additions and modifications which in many cases, for example Canterbury, Wells, Salisbury, and Lincoln, were to result in totally new structures. A poem on the building of the new cathedral at Salisbury, moved from Old Sarum, referred to the king's virtue, the bishop's devotion and the workmen's faith as responsible for its completion.

The Gothic style of architecture, with its rib vaults, pointed arches and large stained-glass windows (Cat. 27–34, 732–48), was brought from England to France in the 1160s and 1170s. The new choir of Canterbury Cathedral, begun in 1174 by a French architect, William of Sens, made the style obligatory for large churches; but the English quickly developed distinctive regional forms of Gothic (e.g. Whitby Abbey, Wells Cathedral, Cat. 239, 242), and their preference for horizontal vistas, linear surface patterns and thick walls (e.g. Lincoln, Salisbury, Cat. 240–1), produced a highly original English version of the style, at odds with the verticality and lightness of the French cathedrals. In sculpture and painting it is not until the second decade of the thirteenth century that we begin to find the first signs of elegant elongation, swaying poses and layered overlapping spatial constructions which are characteristic of the fully developed Gothic style of the thirteenth century (Cat. 254). The political and religious prestige of Louis IX of France (canonised in 1297) is paralleled by the hegemony of French architecture and art centred on Paris and the Île-de-France. Architecturally, Henry III's rebuilding of Westminster Abbey marked the emergence of the king as the most important patron in England, and it reflected a new interest in the latest architectural fashions in France (see pp. 74–82)

238 Wells Cathedral, nave looking east

1190s–c.1220
Photograph

Begun shortly before 1180, the building of the cathedral at Wells was contemporary with the reconstruction of the east end of Canterbury (Cat. 17) and yet it represents a very different and a highly original approach to the emerging Gothic style. The Gothic quality here resides not in the vertical articulation of the elevation into bay units nor in any sense of skeletal structure of the wall (cf. the west front [Cat. 239]) but in the pronounced linearity of the design and in the consistent use of pointed arches throughout, including the quadripartite rib vault. The structure remains fundamentally Anglo-Norman with a clerestory passage, but the sculptural possibilities of the massively thick wall have been fully exploited in the elaborate mouldings of the arches of the main arcade and of the insistently horizontal triforium where the arches have continuous mouldings. The piers are made to seem equally complex by having eight groups of three shafts clustered symmetrically around a simple cruciform core; but a sharpness and clarity is preserved by the polygonal abaci and bases and by the subtle keeling on the diagonal shafts. The sculptural richness is

238

239

further enhanced by the flowing rhythms of the stiff-leaf foliage of the capitals, and additional decoration is provided by the extensive use of head stops and of paterae in the spandrels of the triforium.

The nave is dominated by the massive strainer arches inserted in the mid-fourteenth century to strengthen the crossing following the heightening of the central crossing tower between 1315 and 1322. Although out of scale with the existing building, the bold design of the intersecting ogee arches successfully captures an essential quality of the twelfth-century design. PD

LIT. Colchester 1982; Pevsner & Metcalf 1985a.

239 Wells Cathedral, west front

c. 1230–1250
Photograph

The west front of Wells has the most extensive display of sculpture of any English cathedral. The plan of this exceptionally wide west front, with the towers projecting beyond the nave aisles, was laid out with the nave, but the architectural vocabulary employed for the screen-like façade, particularly the extensive use of marble shafts (originally of local blue lias to simulate Purbeck marble but later restored with Kilkenny marble), indicates a decisive change of style in the building of Wells. This new idiom was almost certainly introduced by Thomas Norreys, who succeeded Adam Lock as master mason

in 1229. The prominent buttresses indicate that the thirteenth-century design included towers, which would have been surmounted by spires. The tall lancets that form the lower stages of the towers were originally open, which would have given the façade a much lighter and more skeletal appearance. The infilling dates from the late fourteenth century when the present towers were built in the then fashionable Perpendicular style. Behind the lowest row of quatrefoils are hidden openings through which, it has been suggested, voices or instruments could have been heard responding to the chants of the Sunday procession stationed outside the west door.

Despite deterioration and loss, recent restoration has revealed the high quality of much of this sculpture, which shows stylistic affinities with contemporary developments in French sculpture. In contrast to French practice, however, the portals at Wells are insignificant and the programme of the sculpture less obviously coherent. Over the central door is a Virgin and Child, with the Coronation of the Virgin above. Surmounting the central lancets, in ascending order, are the Resurrected, the Orders of Angels and the Twelve Apostles, culminating in Christ in Majesty. In the lowest tier the quatrefoils contain angels and, to south and north respectively, scenes from the Old and New Testaments. The middle tiers, with statues of prophets, patriarchs, martyrs and confessors,

including many local saints, constitute a vision of the Heavenly Jerusalem. Surviving traces of pigment, and further evidence recorded in the nineteenth century, show that the sculpture was originally coloured. PD

LIT. Colchester 1982; Pevsner & Metcalf 1985a.

240 Lincoln Cathedral, nave looking east

c. 1220–30
Photograph

Notable for its exceptionally spacious proportions, the nave of Lincoln epitomises the most elaborate phase of the Early English style. The main arcade occupies half the height of the elevation and, as the arches are unusually wide, the aisles are fully integrated into the spatial effect of the nave. The variety and the complexity of the architectural features employed throughout, together with the lavish use of Purbeck marble, make this a conspicuously extravagant building, in marked contrast to the chaste clarity of the contemporary work at Salisbury (Cat. 241). The consistently linear quality in the design is evident in the varied forms of the complex piers, in the elaborate mouldings of all the arches, and it even extends to the tierceron vault. With seven ribs rising from each springer to a ridge rib and with all the intersections emphasised by sculptured bosses, the same richness of decoration was being applied to the vault as to the wall surfaces and arches. All the capitals have deeply carved stiff-leaf foliage, as have the corbels from which the slender vaulting shafts rise. The delicacy of these shafts seems to deny the structural weight of the vault, and a similar impression of lightness is achieved in the aisles by setting the vault responds free-standing in front of the continuous wall arcading. The thickness of the wall construction in the main elevation is shown by the use of a clerestory passage in the tradition of Anglo-Norman buildings, but the solidity is lightened by the use of pierced trefoils and quatrefoils in the middle storey, which also serve to enhance the overall decorative effect.   PD

LIT. Pevsner & Metcalf 1985b.

240

241

241   Salisbury Cathedral, nave looking north-east from south aisle

c. 1230–40
Photograph

Too often taken as a paradigm of the Early English style, the consistent and orderly design of Salisbury should rather be seen as a deliberate reaction to the mannered complexity of the recent and contemporary work at Lincoln (Cat. 240). Certainly the rich effect of coloured marble is exploited at Salisbury and the mouldings of the arches could hardly be more elaborate, yet the architecture exhibits a clarity and restraint wholly in keeping with the qualities of the liturgical customs for which it was designed (see pp. 83–91). The coherence of the nave, as the part of the building reserved for the laity, is established by the unbroken continuity of the main arcade of uniform piers of coursed marble with four detached marble shafts on the main axes, and by the sharply defined horizontal string courses. The piers rest on a continuous plinth which is interrupted only to provide access between nave and aisles (see p. 86). The simple quadripartite vaults spring from the clerestory sill, allowing the abaci of the short vaulting shafts to be integrated with the upper string course. The most awkward feature of the design is the depressed relieving arch in the middle storey, which serves to define the bay unit in the absence of strong vertical elements in the elevation. The clerestory passage shows the continuing use of the Anglo-Norman thick wall construction and the seeming determination of English masons to take no account of contemporary developments in constructional techniques in France. The present tidied appearance is due to a late eighteenth-century rearrangement by Wyatt.   PD

LIT. Pevsner & Metcalf 1985a; RCHM, *Salisbury* (forthcoming).

242   Whitby Abbey, east façade looking north-west

c. 1220
Photograph

No documentary evidence exists concerning the rebuilding of the Benedictine Abbey of Whitby, Yorkshire, in the thirteenth century, so the present remains are datable only on stylistic grounds and may be somewhat earlier than the widely accepted date of *c.* 1220. The reconstruction was probably connected with the fashionable refurbishing of the shrine of St Hilda. The form of this imposing extension, with the aisles extending eastwards as far as the high gable of the presbytery, is closely related to other east ends in the north, including St Andrews Cathedral, the Augustinian Hexham Priory and the Cistercian Rievaulx Abbey. This type of east end, characteristic of the north and east of England, may derive from the (destroyed) choir of York Minster of the 1160s.

The interior is appropriately ornamented but on the exterior architectural detail is kept to a minimum; a 'stylistic' feature determined by the weathering quality of the stone in this exposed coastal site. The majestic lancet windows, which fill the entire wall, have simple chamfered mouldings, only the upper tier being enriched with dogtooth ornament. The continuous shafts linking the two lower tiers of windows stress the verticality of the design, which is scarcely interrupted by the lightly-drawn horizontal mouldings beneath the windows. The three openings in the gable served only to illuminate the roof space.

The three-storey elevation of the ruined choir can be seen to have had a large gallery, an old-fashioned feature by this date but characteristic of the region. Only the small clerestory would originally have been exposed on the exterior.   PD

LIT. Pevsner 1966a.

242

243

243 Quatrefoil angel

c. 1230

White lias: h. 76.2 cm, w. 73.6 cm, d. 19 cm
The Dean and Chapter of Wells

It would appear that only nine out of a series of thirty angels in quatrefoils above the lowest pairs of life-sized standing figures on the west front of Wells Cathedral have been lost. They carry as emblems mitres, crowns, scrolls, books or palms. This angel carries two crowns upon a cloth which passes behind his back. The emblems ought to help identify the pairs of figures beneath them, but where the group is complete the emblems seem inappropriate. One carries a mitre over a pair of deacons, another a mitre over a pair of Evangelists and a third a mitre over a prophet or patriarch. If there was any clear intention in the distribution of emblems, it seems to have been lost in the assembling, as happened in the sequence of the Resurrected on the north side. Our angel presides over a pair of niches now empty, but which should have contained figures of Old Testament patriarchs.

The motif of half-length angels emerging from clouds was extremely popular both sides of the Channel. It was chosen for the spandrels of the arcading around St Hugh's Choir at Lincoln a generation earlier. The source, as with so much of the decorative

articulation of Early Gothic stone sculpture, was metalwork. Compare the deployment of half-length angels in, for example, the Mosan shrine of the Virgin of 1205 in Tournai Cathedral. The resemblance would have been the more striking if the Wells angels were originally gilt. Evidence has been found that they once bore a coat of red or yellow paint, surely as a base for gold.   PT-C

LIT. Hope & Lethaby 1905, pp. 186–8, pl. XXIVa; Stone 1972, p. 111, pl. 81a; Colchester 1982, pp.116, 130 n. 3.

244 Quatrefoil of Christ among the Doctors

c. 1230

White lias; (i) Holy Family h. 109.4 cm, w. 60 cm, d. 16.5 cm; (ii) Doctors h. 126.3 cm, w. 60 cm, d. 17.4 cm
The Dean and Chapter of Wells

Nearly all the narrative scenes from the Old and New Testaments on the west front of Wells were designed to be placed in quatrefoils that were bent either backwards or forwards at an angle of 45 degrees. The complex shape, of which the only imitation appears to have been in the Prior's Lodging at Glastonbury, made peculiarly awkward demands upon the sculptor, which were met

with great agility. Where, as in this case, the quatrefoil turns inwards, he composed his figures on two separate blocks of stone in such a way as to take full advantage of the re-entrant angle. Originally the ninth of a run of thirty quatrefoils devoted to the New Testament, this subject closed the cycle of nine Infancy scenes. This extensive sequence has allowed for some iconographic innovation. Here Mary and Joseph, having returned to Jerusalem in search for the missing Christ Child, find Him in the Temple (*Luke* II, 46). The involvement of the Doctors is expressed through their poses of concentrated attention. The exaggeratedly crossed leg of one of

244

244   (detail, after cleaning)

them was not a gesture of relaxation but of command in thirteenth-century body language. The charming conceit of the Christ Child using the lectern as a chair involves making Him unwarrantably small for twelve years. The composition of this subject is reflected in the ghost of a relief of the same subject in St David's Cathedral, and in the Queen Mary Psalter, both nearly a century later.

The coving of the balcony, treated with a foliage arabesque, has preserved more of the original paint surface than any other part of the Wells façade. Much of the west front sculpture was fully painted in oil-based colours. PT-C

LIT. Prior & Gardner 1912, fig. 305 p. 209.

245 Female figure

1230-5
Limestone: h. 128 cm, w. 48 cm
The Dean and Chapter of Winchester

Now headless, weathered and with its lower arms missing, this figure is nevertheless one of the finest surviving examples of English thirteenth-century sculpture. Originally the carved surface would have been enlivened with metal fittings, the positions of which are indicated by pinholes: a belt at the waist, the end of which hung down at the front to the ground, jewellery at the neck and possibly a metal object held in the left hand. At the base are the weathered remains of stiff-leaf decoration. The back has been hollowed out.

The identity of this figure is unfortunately not clear; various suggestions have been made, such as Ecclesia, Synagogue and Fortitude, but the lack of any attributes or a particularly distinctive pose militates against convincing attribution. Atkinson (1936) proposed that the figure came from a niche (one of four) above the porch of the Deanery – formerly the Prior's House – at Winchester, but even if this were its original position (and that is far from certain) it would not help to identify it. The overtly classicising nature of

245

the figure has led to some speculation that the sculptor responsible for the work had seen and copied classical sculptures (Roosen-Runge 1961), but it is more likely that the style was derived from French sculpture of the 1220s and 1230s, itself heavily indebted to classical prototypes. Especially close in this respect and clear evidence of an interest in the antique at this time are the life-sized figures of St Modesta on the north porch at Chartres (1220-30) and the Queen of Sheba on the west portal at Rheims c. 1230-3 (cf. Sauerländer 1972, pls 98 and 204). PW

PROV. Dug up in the Dean's Garden, Winchester, before 1912; currently displayed in the south retrochoir aisle.

LIT. Prior & Gardner 1912, pp. 317-18, fig. 355; London 1930, no. 113; Atkinson 1935, pp. 161-2, pl. XLVII, fig. 1; Andersson 1949, pp. 41-3, fig. 10; Gardner 1951, p. 140, fig. 266; Stone 1972, pp. 112-13, pl. 86; Brieger 1957, p. 126, pl. 41a; Roosen-Runge 1961; Paris 1968, no. 50, pl. 9.

246 Foliage boss

After 1233
Local 'Selborne rock' from quarry opened 1222 to supply stone for works at Winchester Castle: l. 70 cm, w. 47 cm, d. 26 cm
Mark Beach, Priory Farm, Selborne, on loan to the Gilbert White Museum, Selborne, Hampshire

The Selborne boss, like the thirteenth-century bosses of Durham Cathedral, is of the flat 'dish' variety common in France but foreign to English practice, which favoured a convex form. The effect at Selborne is of a cruciform foliate design applied to a concave dish, of which the chamfered rim is decorated with a row of punched holes. Even more unusual is the treatment of the two main sides. The space between the ribs to north and south of a rectangular bay was too narrow, but the wider spaces to east and west have been carved. The normal English bulbous boss carried the carving back to the vault web where that could be appreciated from below. Here the dished top is combined with the full treatment of the flanks which from the floor would be visible only from an oblique angle. One flank carries typically English stiff leaf and part of a dragon. The other, however, is ornamented with two sprays of foliage of varieties not found in English work between 1200 and 1244. Leaf forms somewhat resembling the frilly leaf can be identified forming parts of larger designs on the capitals of the Canterbury choir apse. The Canterbury bosses illustrate the gradual rejection of these French-derived shapes for the stiff-leaf convention which was broken only in works associated with Henry of Reyns, first at Windsor and then from 1245 at Westminster Abbey. He introduced the full naturalistic leaf forms from Rheims.

246

It would be against the evidence to suggest that the vault of Selborne Priory choir was completed much later than the foundation of the house by Bishop Peter de Roches of Winchester in 1233. There is every indication that works proceeded swiftly. The remarkable character of this boss, therefore, must have sprung from the background of those involved in the establishment of Selborne Priory. They included the omnipresent Elias de Dereham, who witnessed Selborne Charters when he was at Winchester between 1233 and 1245. Peter Kidson has cited in correspondence a boss from the ambulatory of Chartres Cathedral as the nearest parallel for the Selborne example.

The hole through the boss suggests that it was used for suspension, either of a corona or a pyx, in the centre of Selborne choir. PT-C

PROV. Found in centre of choir, face downwards, where it had fallen from vault on to original floor level, August 1966.

247 Boss with dragons

c. 1240
Limestone: l. 40 cm, w. 40 cm, d. 28 cm
The Dean and Chapter of Winchester

The brilliantly executed boss of two biting dragons is of the same family as other Winchester work such as the deeply undercut, crisp boss in the centre of the Guardian Angels Chapel, or the foliate carving of the thirteenth-century alterations to the Chapel of the Holy Sepulchre. It could have been displaced from either the earlier Lady Chapel vault or that of the adjacent

247

south-east chapel, both of which received new vaults as part of their later medieval development. The weathered condition of this boss, and the traces of limewash upon it, suggest that it may have spent some of its subsequent history out of doors. Maybe, like the sculptures from high altar screen and chantry chapels, it was reused in the Close partition walls. Bearing no offensive religious significance, it could have been reset with the carving visible, and the limewash might represent an attempt to arrest its resultant decay.

These dragons are first cousins to the dragon eating a grape in the 'lizard alerted' position which forms a corbel in the eastern aisle of the north transept at Wells. That corbel, associated with leaves that relate it to the chapter house undercroft at Wells, belongs to the last years of Bishop Jocelyn (d. 1242). Nothing about the Winchester dragon boss suggests the suavity of the carvings carried out in the Aymer de Valence episcopate, which began in 1250 (see Cat. 23–4). These beasts could have been modelled on the Limoges enamel ones which feature so largely upon crosiers of the very early thirteenth century. Fifty-eight of these survive, one of the best preserved being the St Michael and the Dragon crosier at Wells (Cat. 257). PT-C

PROV. Presumably from party-wall in Winchester Cathedral Close, and ultimately from the cathedral.

248 Virgin and Child

English(?), c. 1220–40
Elephant ivory: h. 11.8 cm, w. 8.4 cm
Museum für Kunst und Gewerbe, Hamburg, 1893.199

The back is not elaborately finished, and the back of the throne is flat and hollowed out, so that the group must have been conceived for a niche, probably as the centrepiece of a tabernacle. The Virgin is crowned and seated on a throne decorated with round-headed trilobe arcading (with vestiges of painted roundels in the spandrels); the base of the throne is embellished with a foliate motif, the flat cushion with a pearled lozenge diaper filled with four-petalled flowers; rich stalks of stiff-leaf foliage sprout up around the cushion. The Virgin's pose is strictly frontal. Beneath her feet are the lion and asp of Psalm XC (XCI in A.V.), 13: 'Thou shalt walk upon the asp and the basilisk; and thou shalt trample under foot the lion and the dragon'. Acting as the Virgin's footstool, the beasts are borrowed from representations of Christ triumphant. Her left foot and knee are raised, so that the elaborate folds of the mantle fall asymmetrically around her legs. A large foliate brooch decorates her breast. On her left knee is the uncrowned Christ Child with a small bunch of stiff-leaf foliage in His left hand, blessing frontally although His legs are turned to the right. The Virgin's right hand is a replacement, so that the brownish patina, also found on the flesh areas and hair, may not be original, even if such an ivory would certainly have been conceived to be painted. The new right hand has introduced an air of false balance, as if the two blessing gestures were intended to echo each other; originally the Virgin probably held an attribute.

This magnificent group is a key document in the dissemination of the Early Gothic style, one of the rare early thirteenth-century ivory Virgins which were to become so fashionable by the fourteenth century; other related, though inferior, statuettes are in Berlin and Copenhagen (Goldschmidt 1923, nos 135–6, pl. XLVII). Northern Germany, northern France and the Mosan region have all been suggested for the Hamburg Virgin, but none of these attributions has proved entirely convincing. On the other hand, compare the first seal of Henry III of 1218 (Cat. 453) and the sculpture on the west front of Wells Cathedral, from the early Virgin and Child over the main door (Courtauld, Wells 1/4/170), to some of the later angels (1/2/152) and standing figures (1/2/52–3, 1/4/124, 126); the iconography of the lion and asp is standard in thirteenth-century England (cf. not only the Wells Virgin and Child but also the Amesbury Psalter (Hollaender 1943, pl. VII); so is the exceptionally broad throne with foliate ends (cf. Morgan 1982, figs 267, 277, 291, 303; Hollaender 1943, pls III, VII, IX). Above all, the stiff-leaf foliage, with trefoil heads on long stalks, is a typically English and early form of Gothic foliage, found already in the late twelfth century at Wells. However, the possibility that the sculptor of the Hamburg Virgin was Norwegian cannot be excluded, since many of the elements cited here as 'English' are just as much at home in Norway – see Cat. 250. NS

PROV. Coll. Frédéric Spitzer, by 1890; Spitzer sale, 1893; given by Frau M. Gaiser, 1893.

LIT. Spitzer 1890, no. 37, pl. IX; Spitzer 1893, no. 72; Goldschmidt 1902; Goldschmidt 1923, no. 133, pl. XLVII; Hamann 1927, p. 87; New York 1970, I, p. 48, no. 55; Sauerländer 1971, p. 511; Gaborit-Chopin 1978, pp. 132, 204, no. 193; Hamburg Museum 1980, p. 58, no. 106; Liebgott 1985, p. 48, pl. 33.

248

249

(ibid., pp. 127–33). In this connection there can be little doubt that a sculpture very like the Langham Virgin and Child provided the model for a number of Madonna and Child groups now preserved in Sweden: the eccentric, exaggerated U-shaped curving loops of drapery just above the Virgin's belt are repeated on Madonnas at Over-Järna and Rimbo, of the middle of the thirteenth century (Andersson 1964–6, vol. II, fig. 50, v, pl. 64).   PW

PROV. Langham Church, Essex; Langham Hall; Willis's Rooms, London, 23 December 1925; bt and donated to the V & A by E.R.D. Maclagan, through the National Art-Collections Fund, 1925.

LIT. *Review* 1935, pp. 2–3, pl. 1; London 1930, no. 20; Andersson 1949, pp. 31–2, Stone 1972, pp. 104, 107, 249 (n. 32), repr. pl. 78; New York 1970, no. 33; Williamson (forthcoming), no. 1.

250   Virgin and Child

Anglo-Norwegian, *c.* 1220–40

Oak; the back deeply hollowed out, one hole drilled on top of the head and three under the socle, perhaps for pinning while the oak trunk was carved (Blindheim 1952, pp. 8–10, 87–111); Virgin's right arm and three fingers of Christ's right hand broken off, wood broken through between the Virgin's legs, edges of mantle chipped, flowers of both crowns and bottom right corner of plinth restored in birch wood; traces of red paint on skirt: h. 98 cm, w. 32.5 cm, d. 24.5 cm

Oslo, Universitetets Oldsaksamlingen, c. 7490

This is among the most imposing of the many wooden Virgin and Child groups which have survived in Norway with close stylistic connections with English stone sculpture, for

250

249   Virgin and Child

1200–20

Polychromed oak: h. 47.5 cm, w. 24.1 cm
The Board of Trustees of the Victoria and Albert Museum, London, A. 79–1925

A considerable amount of paint in several layers remains on the surface of the sculpture; the present colour scheme is approximately that of the earliest layer (see Williamson [forthcoming]).

This Virgin and Child group represents the transitional phase between Romanesque and Gothic, retaining recognisable twelfth-century features while looking forward to the stylistic advances of the thirteenth century. It was probably originally an altar figure.

English medieval figure sculpture in wood, excluding effigies, is of the utmost rarity.

Although there can be no doubt that such figures were made in large numbers, they suffered more than stone carvings at the Dissolution of the Monasteries as they rarely formed part of the fabric of a building and were thus easily carried off and burned. There are very few medieval wood sculptures remaining in England which can be assigned with certainty to English workshops, however Aron Andersson has demonstrated that large numbers of English wood sculptures were exported to Scandinavia in the late Romanesque and Gothic periods: a good number still survive such as the St Michael from Mosvik (Cat. 290) and the Madonna from Austrät (Andersson, 1949 pp. 108–18). Andersson also postulated that there were workshops of English sculptors working in Norway in the thirteenth century

instance with figures on the Wells Cathedral façade of *c.* 1220–42 (Courtauld, Wells 1/4/170, 1/2/108, 1/2/112, etc.). See also Cat. 249 for a wooden Virgin, which is a unique survival in England. The Enebakk Madonna is exhibited here because '... quantitatively the most important type of English thirteenth-century sculpture was the cult image ... Norway maintained the closest economic, political, and cultural relations with England during the twelfth and thirteenth centuries, and did not experience the iconoclastic zeal of early Protestantism in quite so ruthless and methodical a form' (Stone 1955, p. 127). For other sculptures from Norway which may stand for this lost English wood-carving tradition of cult images, whether or not they were actually carved by English sculptors, see Cat. 99, 290.

NS

PROV. From Enebakk Church, Akershus, near Oslo, Norway.

LIT. Fett 1908, fig. 62 p. 42; Andersson 1950, pp. 138–45, fig. 56.

251 Misericord: Entwined, foliated dragons

c. 1200–20
Oak: h. 30 cm, w. 65 cm, d. 20 cm
The Churchwardens, Christchurch Priory
    Church, Dorset, north side stalls from east,
    lower row, no. 8 (of 39)

The dragons, their necks entwined, bite each others' wings; their tails sprout foliage and two heads appear from under two leaves.

The trefoiled foliage is of the type found in the first quarter of the thirteenth century, for example on the capitals of Ivinghoe Church or Salisbury Cathedral, and the style of the heads can be compared to sculpture of the beginning of the thirteenth century in the Wells Cathedral transepts. The Christchurch misericord, therefore, is one of the earliest remaining, together with the one in the Church of the Blessed Virgin Mary in

Hemingborough, North Yorkshire, which has foliage only. The dragons added in Christchurch, in their writhing and biting, are reminiscent of Romanesque manuscript illuminations and sculptures. Another new element is the two heads emerging from between the two leaves below either end of the ledge. Heads emerging from foliage are already known from the Bury Bible of *c.* 1135 (Cambridge, Corpus Christi College, MS 2) and f. 201v. combines all the elements inherent in the Christchurch misericord: two winged animals (griffins), spiralling foliage and heads clasped by leaves.

Thus the Christchurch misericord goes back to an older tradition for its inspiration, and translates this into the style of the beginning of the thirteenth century. There is only one other misericord of this date in Christchurch Priory; the rest belong to the fourteenth and sixteenth centuries.

CG

PROV. Christchurch Priory, Dorset.

LIT. Bond 1910, p. 202.

252 The Cambridge Bestiary

North Midlands/Lincolnshire (?), *c.* 1200–10
Vellum, ff. 74: 28.2 × 19.2 cm
Syndics of Cambridge University Library,
    MS Ii.4.26

Illustrated bestiaries seem to have been particularly fashionable during the first half of the thirteenth century, and as yet there is no satisfactory explanation of their popularity at that time. The text is concerned with accounts of various creatures accompanied by a moralisation of their habits. Twelfth-century examples have smaller and simpler illustrations, but around 1200 luxury bestiaries were produced with large pictures, both painted and drawn. The Cambridge Bestiary uses both techniques for its illustrations, ninety-nine in all, and it is uncertain whether it was intended that all the drawings should be painted. Fortunately, in view of the great refinement of the drawings, few were

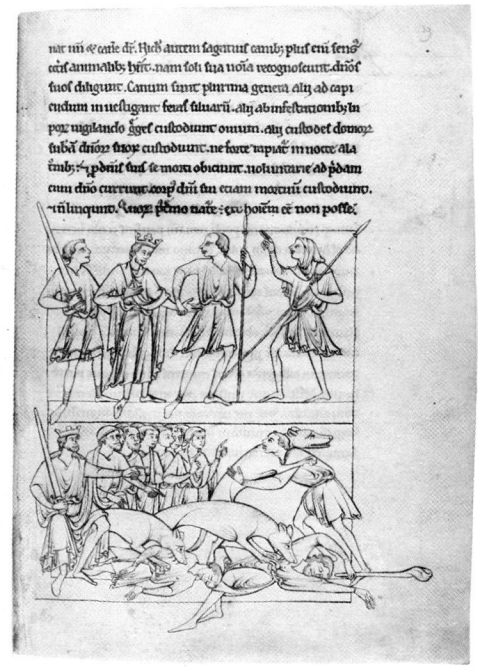

252

overpainted by the less able artist who was the painter.

The style of the figures is very close to that of the Guthlac Roll (Cat. 37), and many of the illustrations have similarities of composition to those of the Ashmole Bestiary (Cat. 253). The place of production of this and the related Leningrad, Aberdeen and Ashmole bestiaries is controversial. The Cambridge Bestiary has a very damaged ownership inscription of an abbey whose name can perhaps be read as Revesby (Lincolnshire). The close stylistic connection with the Guthlac Roll also suggests that the artists worked in the Lincolnshire region.

NJM

PROV. Cistercian Abbey of Revesby (?); James Thomas Herison, 16th century; Osbert Fowler, 17th century; Cambridge University Library, 1655.

LIT. James 1928; London 1939, no. 26; Manchester 1959, no. 40; Brussels 1973, no. 39; Morgan 1982, no. 21, figs 66–70.

253 The Ashmole Bestiary

North Midlands/Lincolnshire (?), *c.* 1210
Vellum, ff. 105: 27.6 × 18.3 cm
Oxford, Bodleian Library, MS Ashm. 1511

The Ashmole Bestiary, with 121 bestiary scenes and 8 miniatures of Creation scenes, all on burnished gold grounds, is the most luxurious of the bestiaries of the early thirteenth century. It is closely related both in style and iconography to a copy almost as fine in Aberdeen (University Library, MS 24), but it has been argued that they must be the work of two different artists. The group of bestiaries to which this exhibit belongs originates in two late twelfth-century examples in New York (Pierpont Morgan Library, M. 81) and Leningrad (State Public Library, Salty-

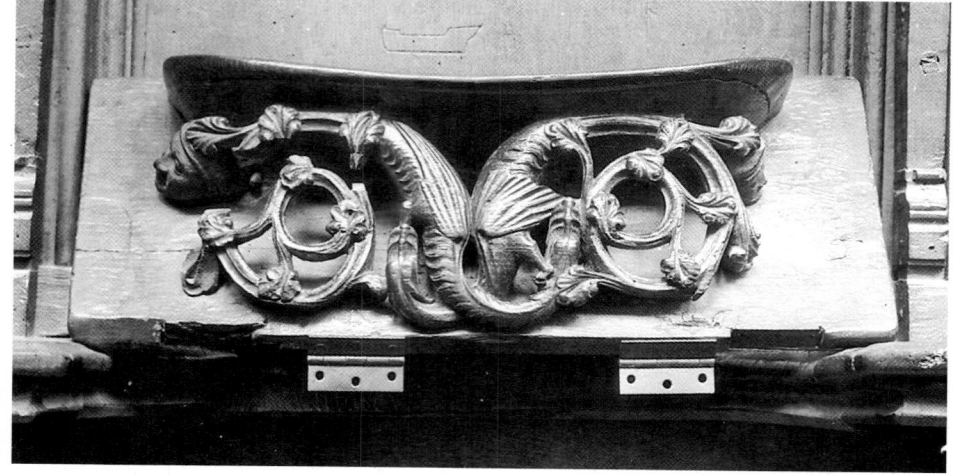

251

253

254

painted and gilded full-page miniatures of the Crucifixion and Christ in Majesty, three pages of tinted drawings of scenes of the Life of Christ, and eight historiated and ornamental initials at the liturgical divisions of the psalter text. The two miniatures and the initials are by an artist whose elegant, delicately-posed figures are prime examples of the Early Gothic style in English painting. The artist of the tinted drawings uses figures which still show traces of rigid ornamental fold patterns of earlier Romanesque drawing. Tinted drawings, although popular for Apocalypses and Lives of the Saints (e.g. Cat. 38–9, 347–8) are rarely found in prefatory pictures for psalters.

Although in its set of full-page illustrations and illuminated initials this Benedictine psalter resembles contemporary luxury psalters (e.g. Cat. 255), the very simple decoration of the text pages sets it apart. Neither line endings nor initials containing grotesques are found, and this austerity of the page may be a reflection of the taste of the monastic patron.   NJM

PROV. Robert de Lindesey, Abbot of Peterborough 1214–22; Smart Lethieuiller (d. 1760); Charles Lyttleton, Bishop of Carlisle 1762–8; beq. to Society of Antiquaries, 1768.

LIT. London 1908, no. 37; London 1930, no. 124; London 1939, no. 28; Brussels 1973, no. 44; Marks & Morgan 1981, pp. 44–7, pls 3, 4; Morgan 1982, no. 47, figs 151, 156–9.

255 Psalter

London, c. 1230
Vellum, ff. 181: 28.5 × 20 cm
The Master and Fellows, Trinity College,
   Cambridge, MS B.11.4

A series of forty-eight pictures of the Old and New Testaments ending with the Last Judge-

---

kov-Shchedrin, MS Lat. Q.V.V.1) which are the earliest fully-illuminated English bestiaries. The Morgan Bestiary belonged to the Augustinian Priory of Worksop in Nottinghamshire, and this has led to a suggestion that these manuscripts were produced in the North Midlands or Lincolnshire (cf. Cat. 252).   NJM

PROV. William Wryght, vicar of High Wycombe, 16th century; William Mann, 17th century; Sir Peter Mancroft, 17th century; John Tradescant (d. 1637); Elias Ashmole (1617–92) who gave his manuscripts to Oxford University, 1677; transferred from Ashmolean to Bodleian Library, 1860.

LIT. Manchester 1959, no. 41; Morgan 1982, no. 19, figs 62–5; *Faksmile Ausgabe* 1982; Yapp 1983, pp. 134–9; Muratova 1986, pp. 118–44.

254 Psalter of Robert de Lindesey

Peterborough Abbey (?), before 1222
   Vellum, ff. 167: 24 × 15.5 cm
Society of Antiquaries of London, MS 59

This is one of the few thirteenth-century devotional books which can be connected by strong evidence to a named individual, Robert de Lindesey, Abbot of Peterborough 1214–22. The abbot is recorded as the owner in a fourteenth-century inscription on f. iii, and the provenance seems assured by the evidence of the Peterborough texts of the calendar and Litany.

The illumination consists of two fully-

255

very elongated and in mannered poses with lively facial expressions and gesticulating hands dramatically conveying the sense of the narrative. The general appearance is similar to contemporary stained glass in the Trinity Chapel of Canterbury Cathedral and at Lincoln Cathedral. The historiated initials in fully-painted work are in a different style, close to that of the Glazier Psalter (Cat. 8).

The calendar is of the London diocese, and has a connection with the Augustinian canons, but also includes some saints of the Winchester region. In the historiated initials to Psalms CI and CIX an abbess and nun are represented, which suggests that the book may have belonged to the abbess. Some of the habits worn are of Augustinian canonesses, but in Psalm CIX the abbess is in Benedictine habit. Possibly these are women of the same family but in different religious orders. Some psalters show various members of a family in the initials.   NJM

PROV. Dame Ida de Ralegh, 14th century; Walter Hone, Abbot of Cistercian house of Newnham, Devon, 14th century; Dame Johane de Roches (?), Benedictine nun of St Mary's, Winchester; library of Trinity College, by early 17th century.

LIT. London 1908, no. 38; London 1930, no. 120; Brussels 1973, no. 45; Morgan 1982, no. 51, figs, 167–74.

256   The Hyde Abbey crosier head

c. 1200–50
Copper alloy, gilt; pitted, knop partly restored:
   h. 32 cm, w. of crook 9.2 cm
The Board of Trustees of the Victoria and Albert
   Museum, London, M. 88–1920

A crosier was the staff of office of a bishop or abbot, representing his authority over, and responsibility for, his flock.

The crook is hammered, not cast, formed as an eight-sided stem from which spring finely-chased leaves and grapes (?). The lower part of the stem, the knop and the staff below it are of round section, unadorned.

Several English Romanesque crosiers are decorated with florid leafwork (London 1984a, nos 268–70), but none of this delicacy. Leaves and fruit in a similar style are found in English manuscripts of *c.* 1200–50, such as Cambridge University Library, MS ii.4.26, f. 37v. (Cat. 252; Morgan 1982, fig. 7). The abbot for whom it was made is unknown, but its date would fit the abbacy of either Walter de Aston, 1222–47, or Roger de St Walery, 1247–63 (Dugdale 1819, II, p. 431).   MLC

PROV. Hyde Abbey, Winchester; found while digging foundations of new gaol (Milner), *c.* 1788; bt by G. Percy Elliott of Winchester, before 1851; inherited by granddaughter Mrs E.S.M. Bowker; bt from her by V & A, 1920.

LIT. Milner 1809, II, pp. 237–8; Elliott 1851, pp. 319–20; Watts 1924, no. 1; London 1930, no.169.

ment and the Torments of Hell precedes the psalter text. There must have been a larger series extending to now-lost pages. This sort of picture-book preface to the psalter had become popular in the late twelfth century. The narrative sequences relating to Old Testament figures may have been intended to present them as exemplars of virtuous conduct or as warnings of evil ways. In addition Labours of the Months and signs of the zodiac decorate the calendar, and nine historiated

initials are placed at the liturgical divisions of the Psalms. The text pages have decorative initials and elaborate ornamental line endings which give additional richness. As Gothic illumination develops there is an increasing interest in integrating illumination with the text page as an overall decorative system.

The Old and New Testament scenes are drawings painted with overall washes of colour rather than tinted. The figures are

256

257

257 Crosier head

French (Limoges) *c.* 1205–15
Copper alloy, gilt, enamelled in champlevé, set
  with stones, mounted on a (modern) wooden
  staff: h. 31.5 cm, w. of crook 13.2 cm
The Dean and Chapter of Wells

The crook encloses the winged figure of St
Michael fighting the Dragon, its back studded
with turquoises. The upper part of the crook
takes the form of a blue and gold scaly
serpent with serrated crest, its head nudging
the wing of the saint. The hollow metal knop
is encased by openwork hemispheres, embossed with dragons. The lower part of the
crosier is engraved with three spiralling
bands of scrolling foliage, against a blue
enamel ground, separated by diagonally-
placed bejewelled dragons, head downwards.
The crosier was given a new rod and ferrule
in 1834 (Robinson 1916–17, p. 155).

The theme of St Michael and the Dragon –
the victorious struggle of good against evil –
was an apt form of decoration for a crosier,
and one much favoured by Limoges enamellers; it is third commonest among surviving
examples (Vasselot 1941, pp. 85 ff.). Of about
fifty known St Michael crosiers, only four are
closely comparable with this, respectively at
St-Amant-de-Boixe (formerly) and Tarbes
(op. cit., pp. 281–2), and at Amiens and
Gloucester City Museum (Colchester 1984,
p. 21). Since it is not known exactly where
the crosier was found, certainty about its
original owner is impossible. Presumably it
was one of the many Bishops of Bath and
Wells buried in the Cathedral. A likely con-
tender on grounds of date is Jocelyn, Bishop
1206–42, who was buried in the choir
(Colchester 1984, pp. 21–2).   MLC

PROV. Wells Cathedral; found in the precincts in
time of Dean Lukin (1799–1812).

LIT. London 1862, no. 1097; London 1874,
no. 872; London 1897, no. 54; Bristol 1938,
no. 14; Vasselot 1941, no. 145; Colchester 1984,
pp. 18–23.

258 Dolgelly chalice and paten

c. 1230–50
Silver-gilt: h. of chalice 18.3 cm, diam. of paten
  18.6 cm, wt 46 troy oz
Inscr. in Lombardic letters on chalice, under foot
      NICOL'VS . ME . FECIT. DE HERFORDIE
      on paten INNOMINIE [*sic*]. PATRIS . ET
      FILII : ET SPIRITUS SANCTIAM [*sic*]
      MATEVS IOHNES MARCVS LVCAS
Her Majesty The Queen, on loan to the National
  Museum of Wales, Cardiff

The chalice is made in three parts. The stem is
engraved above and below the knot with
stiff-stalked trefoil leaves; the knot is divided
into twelve complex lobes. The circular foot is
embossed with two rows of twelve
downward-radiating trefoil-shaped lobes,
the upper row plain, the lower engraved with
trefoil stiff-leafwork against a hatched

258

ground, as are the spandrels between the lobes. The chalice is entirely gilt, including under the foot (renewed?).

The paten, gilt on both sides, and spotted with metallic (?) accretions, is embossed with concentric depressions, a circular one enclosing a sexfoil, in the centre of which is engraved a Majesty encircled by the inscription. The spandrels of the sexfoil are engraved with the symbols of the Evangelists and scrolling trefoils.

The chalice and paten are among the largest and finest surviving English medieval chalices. Their size must indicate that they were made for a monastic foundation, perhaps Cymer Abbey nearby (Owen 1953–6, p. 184), where Communion would be taken in both kinds by the congregation. The chalice is most closely paralleled by chalices from Børsa and Dragsmark in Sweden (Oman 1957, p. 41, pls 5, 7), but part of Norway in the Middle Ages, and Iceland (Oslo 1972, nos 27–30). The engraving style and trefoil motifs are particularly close. The Dolgelly chalice-knot is clearly an elaborate version of that on the Gravesend chalice (Cat. 111).

The Majesty on the paten is the only surviving English example of a fairly commonplace subject, but also one of the most elaborate surviving pieces of thirteenth-century engraving. The rounded solidity of Christ's figure compares with the drawing

style practised in England c. 1200–50, latterly by Matthew Paris (d. 1259). Paris, a versatile artist and accomplished goldsmith, is known to have visited Norway in 1248 (Cat. 437); other English goldsmiths, including Walter of Croxton and Edward FitzOtho, worked there c. 1225–50 (Kielland 1926, pp. 130–6, 502–3). While there is no evidence to link them with these chalices, nor firm grounds for dating the group, their stylistic similarities and the survival of several in Scandinavia is suggestive. It has been suggested that Nicholas de Hereford, the presumed maker, came from Erfurt in Germany – unlikely in view of the Englishness of his work (Owen 1953–6, p. 184). Chester has also been proposed (Ridgway 1968, p. 7), but there is no evidence for this.   MLC

PROV. Cwn Mynach, near Dolgelly; found amid boulders on mountainside, 1890; acq. by Thomas Roberts, Dolgelly; acq. by Mrs Owen, Dolgelly, 1891; sold by Robert Griffith, Christie's, 4 March 1892, bt by W. Bloore; bt by Baron Schroeder, 1892; beq. on his death (1910) to Crown, by arrangement with Treasury after belated treasure trove inquest.

LIT. Hope 1893, pp. 575–6, London 1930, no. 175; Braun 1932, nos 45, 155, pp. 92, 94; London 1934, no. 1384; Birmingham 1948, no. 1; Owen 1953–6, pp. 180–90; Oman 1957, pp. 41, 47–8, 53; Paris 1968, no. 402; Taylor 1977, pp. 252–62.

259   The Book of Llandaf Christ in Majesty

c. 1250–65

Copper alloy, hollow-cast, engraved and gilded; middle finger of right hand broken off:
   h. 17.1 cm, w. 11.4 cm, d. 3 cm
Aberystwyth, National Library of Wales, NLW MS 17110 E

The alloy is 93.1 per cent copper, 1.4 per cent zinc, 1.3 per cent lead and 3.8 per cent tin, similar to other mercury-gilded twelfth- to thirteenth-century 'bronzes' (XRF analysis, British Museum Laboratory; cf. Oddy 1986). The mercury-gilding cannot be original, as it occurs in scratches, but the figure was probably gilded from the start. The complicated history of the Book of Llandaf (*Liber Landavensis*) and its binding cannot be used to elucidate the origins of the Christ: until recently it decorated the twelfth-century lower board but earlier pinholes prove that it was not part of the original decoration of this binding, although probably added in the fifteenth century. Christ is seated on a rainbow, blessing, a book on His left knee. His feet rested on a rounded shape, probably a smaller rainbow. The form of the ends of the longer rainbow suggests that there was a framing mandorla, cf. the Majesty image in the Westminster Psalter (Cat. 9 – see Morgan 1982, fig. 9). Such a large-scale 'bronze' Majesty would be appropriate to the gable end of a house shrine or the centre of an altar antependium or retable.

The youthful head of Christ, so delicately chiselled with minutely rendered features, would not be out of place in manuscripts associated with the Sarum Illuminator (Cat. 108, 316; Hollaender 1943), but the broadly-treated surfaces of the drapery, with softly moulded channels, are now broken up by hard edges and V-folds, which presuppose a knowledge of the new Paris style of the second quarter of the thirteenth century. In so far as the reception of this new style in England can be dated with any certainty, it seems first to appear in the 1250s with the Westminster transept sculptures and the 1259 Great Seal of Henry III (Cat. 276). But there are no really close parallels to the style of the magnificent Llandaf figure, so different from its French contemporaries such as the Évreux shrine (Paris 1970–1, no. 86); it is a unique survival of major English bronze casting of the third quarter of the thirteenth century. NS

PROV. On the lower board of *Liber Landavensis*, by 1659.

LIT. Rees 1840, p. XXVII, repr. frontispiece; Evans & Rhys 1893, p. XVIII n. 32, repr. frontispiece; Jones 1945–6, pp. 125–7, pls 16–17; Huws 1987.

260   Nash Hill tile

Late 13th century
Earthenware, inlaid two-colour tile: l. 12.7 cm,
    w. 12.7 cm, th. 2.5 cm
The Dean and Chapter of Wells

This tile shows a stylised west front of a great church inlaid in white clay against a green-glazed background. On each of the outer towers stands a bird. The same design is

260

known from St Nicholas's Church, Stoke-under-Ham, Somerset, and Muchelney Abbey, Somerset. It also occurs rather oddly at the church of Barton, near Cambridge (*Arch. Journ.*, VI, 1849, pp. 81–2). A similar design was produced at the late thirteenth-century tile kiln excavated at Nash Hill, Wiltshire, and examples have also been found at Glastonbury Abbey, Somerset. The depiction of buildings on tiles is unusual, although castles do occur on tiles from Chertsey and Hailes. Birds in pairs with heads either turned towards each other or away are common in the Wessex school of tile-making. This tile illustrates the type of tile design used in Wessex in the late thirteenth century when the tile industry developed from the initial royal patronage at Winchester, Clarendon and Hailes. JC

PROV. Found in excavations of Lady Chapel by cloister, Wells Cathedral, 1978.

LIT. Ward Perkins 1941a, p. 54 pl. IX no. 6; McCarthy 1974, p. 138, fig. 26, no. 14; Rodwell 1979, cover illus.

259

IX Henry III (1216–72)

When King John died at Newark on 18 October 1216 the country was in the throes of civil war caused by his repudiation of Magna Carta. The claim of Louis of France, son of Philip Augustus, to the English throne, had won baronial support, and Prince Louis had captured London. John's nine-year old son was hastily crowned as Henry III at Gloucester on 28 October in a ceremony which was hardly regular, for there was no Archbishop of Canterbury and no royal regalia. The Archbishop, Stephen Langton, was in Rome, and the coronation regalia along with the rest of the king's treasure had been lost in the Wash on 12 October. Henry's supporters with the aid of the papacy won over the rebels by reissuing Magna Carta in 1216, 1217 and again in 1225. The 1225 reissue became the law of the land and by the end of the century appeared first among the Statutes of the Realm. It derived its authority both from the force of the baronial checks upon arbitrary royal control and also from the reinstatement in 1216 of the Plantagenet dynasty.

King John's biggest political disaster had been the loss of control to the King of France of his Continental territories north of the Loire. Above all, Normandy had been lost in 1204. But to re-establish the influence of the English king on the Continent was a central aim of Henry III, and Normandy, Maine, Anjou and Poitou were not irrevocably conceded to France until the Treaty of Paris of 1259. Even then the King of England remained Duke of Aquitaine. And Henry III, until the baronial rebellion of 1258, worked to widen his contacts in Europe. He shared a sense of common problems with rulers of the West and was closely related to the most important of them by marriage: Louis IX of France and the Emperor Frederick II, as well as Alexander II of Scotland and Charles of Anjou, King of Sicily. He had extravagant plans for increasing his prestige in Europe, building upon the fact that the English kings were renowned for their outstanding wealth. It was wealth based upon the extent of their administrative and financial control of the English kingdom. The English Exchequer flourished.

Following his minority which ended in 1227, there began a thirty-year period of emphasis upon monarchical rule. Henry sought to reassert his own family connection with Poitou. He was intent upon choosing his own ministers, and they were very often foreigners. In a notable *coup d'état* in 1232 Poitevins were brought into the centre of English government: Peter des Roches, who had experience in war and in financial administration, returned to the bishopric of Winchester, the richest of the English sees, and Peter des Rivaux was brought in to manage the king's finances. After Henry married Eleanor of Provence in 1236, his political interests turned to Provence and Savoy, areas of strategic importance in central Europe. The Provençal and Savoyard kinsmen of his wife became increasingly influential in furthering Henry's diplomatic causes in Europe and worked with him and for him in England. His wife's uncle, Boniface of Savoy, became Archbishop of Canterbury in 1245.

Henry's Continental schemes became more and more ambitious. In 1255 he agreed with the Pope to send troops and money to Italy in exchange for recognition of his younger son, Edmund, as King of Sicily. This was an attempt to prevent both the French and the Aragonese from gaining authority there. The sum that Henry agreed to pay the Pope, over £90,000, was huge by any standards and could only have been met by consent to taxation at home. At first Henry appeared to be achieving his aims. At Aachen his brother, Richard of Cornwall, was crowned King of the Romans, that is emperor designate (Cat. 14, 275). But Richard failed to get recognition throughout Germany, and Henry's Sicilian plans were crumbling. The king's policies were seen as reckless in England, and they caused a rebellion even more serious in its constitutional implications than the rebellion which King John had faced.

In 1258 Henry was compelled to submit to his baronial opponents, led by Simon de Montfort, Earl of Leicester, the king's brother-in-law. He agreed to expel his Poitevin favourites from the country, and his authority was put under strict control by the setting up of a baronial council. The central offices of state, the Chancellor and the Treasurer, were to be made independent of the royal household. Magna Carta was reissued. The magnates, with some support from the prelates, were attempting a revolution in government, with the king to be made a figurehead. But like Henry's schemes in Sicily, the baronial plan was over-ambitious. One highly significant development led to a revival of Henry's cause. He gained the support of Louis IX of France, but only at the heavy price of surrendering his claims to territory in France north of the Loire and also to Poitou. Only Gascony in the south-west corner of France remained in the hands of the King of England. The Pope also supported Henry, and the barons could not make good their claim to legitimate authority. In the civil war of 1264-5 they were victorious at the Battle of Lewes and the king became the prisoner of Simon de Montfort; but with his son Edward fighting for him, Henry's troops defeated and killed Simon de Montfort at Evesham in 1265.

The cause of monarchy triumphed and had been only temporarily shaken. Yet the concerns of the kings of England would now always be more firmly centred upon England itself. Henry's personal rule had resulted in no glittering political successes, but he had brought a new theatricality to the English monarchy. He ruled as God's vicar and emphasised the sacredness of royal authority. Huge sums of money were spent on works of art which demonstrated his conception of monarchy: for example, his palace chambers with their paintings of Alexander the Great and of the combat of Richard and Saladin (Cat. 16). He saw the newly built Ste-Chapelle in Paris on his visit to Louis IX in 1254, and a French song related that he coveted it so much that he wanted to carry it off in a cart to London. His disastrous Continental scheming had been intended to bolster the prestige of his English hereditary title. He gave his sons English names – Edward and Edmund – and venerated Edward the Confessor (Cat. 380-1), though he was not directly descended from him. He had his own tomb in Westminster Abbey placed within the aura of sanctity of the tomb of Edward the Confessor, and it was constructed of identical mosaic materials. The administration of royal justice was enhanced and extended during his reign, which saw the birth of the English Parliament, and justice was seen to stretch back to the Anglo-Saxons.

There are important indications during this period of a growing sense of English identity and especially of a sharpening distinction between the English and the French. The English language was very slow to regain its status in competition with French, and with Latin, and Henry did not extend his patronage to native writers; but he did extend it to native artists and craftsmen. The focusing of political interests upon the realm of England meant, as the next reign demonstrated, the increasing importance of the English claims to overlordship in Wales and Scotland. Henry's last years were marked by policies of settlement and conciliation, and Magna Carta was yet again affirmed. The king fell seriously ill in 1272 and died in his great palace at Westminster on the evening of 16 November; he was buried in the Abbey four days later.

261 Winchester Castle, Great Hall interior looking west

1222-35
Photograph

Built by Henry III as part of a well-documented reconstruction of Winchester Castle, the Great Hall is the finest surviving aisled hall of the thirteenth century. Divided into five bays, the overall dimensions of the plan are 34 × 17 m. The hall has architectural features comparable to those in the contemporary work on the retrochoir of the cathedral. The spacious arcades are supported on slender Purbeck marble piers composed of four shafts *en délit* (the two lengths of marble joined unobtrusively with brass rings) set into a coursed marble core of quatrefoil shape, giving the impression of a cluster of eight shafts, all with plain moulded capitals bound together beneath a circular abacus. The mouldings of the arches are comparatively simple, being dominated by plain chamfers. The heavily restored windows consist of two trefoil-headed lights divided by a transom and surmounted by a quatrefoil. Although still plate tracery, this arrangement comes close to the delicacy of bar tracery, which had recently appeared at the cathedral of Rheims. The door was placed in its present central position only in 1789.

The form of the wooden roof was altered substantially in the mid-fourteenth century (the delicately-panelled braces corbelled from the spandrels of the arcade may be of this date), but the entire roof was extensively restored in 1875. The present paving replaces the original tiled floor, and there was

261

windows of normal upright format became the favoured centrepiece for façades (fig. 43; Cat. 321). The original tracery of the Westminster rose was very advanced, being closest to that of the north transept rose at Notre-Dame in Paris (*c.* 1245). Apparently only its detailing was altered when it was replaced after 1451, and subsequent renewals have not entailed further departures.

The main change suffered by the interior is the loss of the brilliantly coloured stained glass (Cat. 735–6) and the equally brilliant painting of surfaces, particularly the diaper ornament on the spandrels. The diaper must in fact have been an afterthought as it is absent from the earliest part of the main arcades to be built, the southernmost springer of the east arcade in the south transept (fig. 41). The plain masonry interrupting the lowest arcading on the south wall indicates the position of the destroyed night stair, and the flight of steps immediately above is part of the route by which Henry III could come privately from Westminster Palace to the 'king's seat', a kind of royal box on the west side of the transept.   CW

LIT. Branner 1964; Bony 1979, pp. 2–5; Wilson *et al.* 1986, pp. 22–31, 37–67.

once a daïs at one end of the hall. The circular table hanging on the wall dates from the late thirteenth century, and is probably connected with the interest of Edward I in the chivalric legends of King Arthur.   PD

LIT. Colvin 1963; Biddle & Clayre 1983.

262   Westminster Abbey, south transept looking south-east

Begun 1246, completed by 1259
Photograph

Westminster Abbey is unique among English medieval churches in the extent to which it reproduces the tall proportions and architectural detailing of the French High Gothic cathedrals. The reasons for the imitation, its superficiality and the sources of the lateral elevations are discussed on pp. 75–8. The end wall of the south transept is among the most impressive and original parts of the church, incorporating a beautifully organised transition from the solidity and darkness of the lowest arcading to the delicacy and brilliance of the rose window. This is separated from the high vault by a shallow void (fig. 41) which allows the spandrels above the rose to be glazed, an arrangement probably derived from the chapel of the royal castle of St-Germain-en-Laye, west of Paris (late 1230s). At Westminster the aim seems to have been to subordinate the rose to the pointed profile of the vault. In England, as in Germany, the impossibility of reconciling the self-contained character of circular windows to the Gothic ideal of integrated elevations was soon acknowledged, and tracery

262

263

263 Refectory murals

c. 1250
Wall painting in Horsham St Faith Priory, Norfolk
Photograph

The painting covering the refectory east wall of this Benedictine priory comprises three distinct elements. The upper area is occupied by a Crucifixion, over twice life-size (Christ, unfortunately, destroyed from the waist up), flanked by a male and a female saint. Below, a series of small scenes illustrating the foundation legend of the priory runs the entire width of the wall in a single register, while blank arcading is painted at dado level. Although partially retouched *c.* 1440, and

also damaged by post-Reformation architectural alterations (when the refectory was converted into a house), the paintings survive in places in excellent condition, and form the most impressive surviving scheme of mid-thirteenth-century wall painting in England. The Crucifixion was discovered in the 1920s, but the foundation scenes and the splendid female saint to the left of the Crucifixion were revealed only in 1969.

The priory was founded *c.* 1105 by Robert and Sybil Fitzwalter, and it is the story of their pilgrimage, capture by brigands in the south of France, their miraculous rescue by St Faith, and the building of the priory as an *ex-voto* which is recorded in the narrative scenes. These diverge slightly from the only literary account, a seventeenth-century transcription of an earlier text, now lost. The scenes include many fascinating details; e.g. representations of a golden image of St Faith, one in a depiction of the Fitzwalters in the abbey church of Conques, which seems to be based ultimately on the famous reliquary of the saint still surviving there. In the fifteenth-century retouching no essential alterations were made, though details of armour, architecture, etc., were updated.

In its emphasis on the Crucifixion, with its obvious eucharistic significance, and representations of the founders and patron saint, the scheme conforms to the medieval tradition of refectory iconography which was developed in the Renaissance. For example, founders and benefactors were represented in paintings in the refectory at Cluny; while, in the hall of Eastbridge Hospital, Canterbury, scenes of Becket, the dedicatee, were shown in the thirteenth-century paintings on the east wall (Tristram 1950, pp. 520–1, suppl. pl. 49). In this context the female saint beside the Crucifixion at Horsham is almost certainly identifiable as St Faith herself. A similar representation of the saint on the priory's seal shows the founders kneeling on either side, Robert with his shackles cast off before him (Pedrick 1902, p. 90, pl. XVIII).

For the style and technique of the paintings, see p. 127   DP

LIT. Tristram 1926, repr.; Tristram 1950, pp. 360–1, 554, repr. pls 205–7, suppl. pls 56 f.; Purcell 1974, repr.; Sherlock 1976, pp. 207, 222; Whittingham, Rouse & Baker 1980; Binski 1986, p. 75, repr. pl. LV; Park & Cather (forthcoming).

English coinage in the thirteenth century

From about 1180 the English currency experienced a vast expansion in quantity. There may have been a twentyfold increase in the amount of coinage leaving the mints between 1180 and 1280, a factor of major influence on price levels. The bullion which fuelled this came from the newly-discovered silver deposits of central Europe, which sent immense quantities of the metal flowing through the Continent. England was well placed to attract the silver because of a consistently favourable balance of trade arising from her wool exports.

For most of the thirteenth century the silver penny remained the only coin minted in England. Smaller denominations were provided by cutting the coin into fractions. The fineness of the penny remained constant at 92.5 per cent silver, the sterling standard, while until 1279 its weight was set at $22\frac{1}{2}$

grains. The design of the penny was not so stable. It was sometimes revised as part of a general recoinage, when all the currency of the land was recalled and reminted. Such a recoinage was brought on not by a change in ruler but by the condition of the currency. After a recoinage its quality gradually declined through natural wear and tear, forgery, clipping and incursions of foreign coin. Furthermore, after a general recoinage the mints continued converting fresh supplies of silver into English legal tender, during which time the style of the coins tended to deteriorate, eventually to the point when a revival in standards was desirable.

A change in design was not a necessary consequence of a general recoinage. Until 1247 the pennies issued were all of the Short Cross type introduced by Henry II in 1180. The simple design of this coin featured a stylised royal bust with the legend HENRICUS REX on the front and on the back a short double cross with the names of moneyer and mint. This was to ensure that if coins were issued which deviated from the official standards, the responsible moneyer could be identified. The Short Cross type survived a general recoinage in 1205 which saw the improvement of the design, not its replacement. When Henry III succeeded the current Short Cross issue, class VI, was showing the signs of a renewed degeneration in style while retaining the characteristic features established in 1205.

By 1247 the state of the currency again made a general recoinage desirable and this time a new design was introduced, the Long Cross type. The cross on the back of the penny was extended to the edges of the coin to inhibit clipping: all four ends of the cross had to be visible for a coin to be legal tender. On the front a new, though still extremely stylised, royal head appeared. For the first time the ordinal was used in the legend to indicate the ruling king HENRICUS REX III, an innovation not repeated until the reign of Henry VII. The Long Cross coinage also featured a distinctive style of lettering, involving the ligation or conjoining of pairs of letters. The same design was used on Henry III's Irish coinage, though differentiated by the use of a triangle instead of a circle surrounding the royal head.

The great monetary experiment of Henry III's reign was the king's attempt to launch a gold coinage. After centuries of silver monometallism in its currency, western Europe experienced the revival of gold coinages in the mid-thirteenth century, the most important being the florin of Florence, launched in 1252–3. There was thus a precedent for Henry when in 1257 he ordered the striking of a penny in pure gold to be current at a value of twenty silver pennies. The king's

goldsmith William of Gloucester was responsible for the issue. The design on the front of the coin, the image of the king enthroned, had not appeared on English coins since Anglo-Saxon times. Henry's gold coinage failed to become established for reasons still the subject of debate. The traditional view is that the gold penny was undervalued against silver, though an alternative argument stresses the lack of a role for gold coins in the English economy at that time.

The issue of Long Cross pennies in Henry III's name continued after the king's death until 1279, though the output under Edward I was not large. As it was over thirty years since the last recoinage, the currency had again deteriorated. The new coinage ordered in August 1279 featured a variety of major innovations. For the first time in the century the weight of the penny was reduced, from $22\frac{1}{2}$ to $22\frac{1}{4}$ grains, to prevent the government from making a loss by exchanging full-weight new coins for old worn or clipped ones. Large quantities of round halfpennies and farthings were issued to eliminate the practice of shaving silver off the straight edges of the cut coins used previously.

A new denomination was also introduced under Edward I: the silver groat, worth fourpence. The appearance of multiples of the traditional penny or denier was a feature of European coinages in the thirteenth century most clearly represented by the *gros tournois*, worth 12 deniers, of Louis IX of France. Edward's groat was not issued in large numbers and made little impact on the currency. Many examples now surviving show evidence of gilding and mounting, indicating that they had been worn as decorations.

All Edward I's new coinage was of one basic design: on the front was the bust of a crowned king, and on the back a cross with three pellets in each angle. A new mint organisation made one individual officer responsible for the whole coinage, and so the moneyer's name was removed from the coin. This design was to remain in use on English silver coins for the next two centuries, and its influence extended far beyond England. The fineness of English silver made it popular on the Continent, where it was much imitated. The importation into England of such imitations of uncertain standards resulted in a major recoinage in 1300 to remove this incursive element. The classification of the series of Edwardian sterling pennies is done on the basis of small alterations in the lettering and the royal bust. There was no clear break in the series at any time during the reigns of Edward I and Edward II. Of great importance in establishing the chronology of the identified classes are the issues of the privileged ecclesiastical mint at Durham

where the bishops, from Anthony Bek onwards, took to placing personal marks on their pennies. Bek's own coins bear a cross moline at the start of the legends in place of the usual plain cross. BC

264 Penny of Short Cross type, class VI

264

Struck at London by the moneyer Abel, 1210–17
Silver, obv. crowned facing bust with sceptre in right hand, rev. short double cross with cross pommée in each quarter: wt 1.46 g (22.6 gr)
Inscr. obv. + HENRICVS REX
rev. + ABEL . ON . LVND
The Trustees of the British Museum, London, CM 1915, 5–7, 1527

PROV. From Eccles, Lancs., hoard deposited c. 1240–1, found 1864; bt by Sir John Evans; bt by J. P. Morgan, 1908; bt by British Museum, 1915.

LIT. Lawrence 1914a, p. 65; Brand 1964, pp. 65–6; North 1980, p. 179 no. 97.

265 Penny of Long Cross type, class VC

265

Struck at London by the moneyer David of Enfield, 1251–72
Silver, obv. crowned facing head with sceptre in right hand, rev. long double cross with three pellets in each quarter: wt 1.39 g (21.5 gr)
Inscr. obv. + HENRICVS REX III
rev. + DAVI ON LVNDEN
The Trustees of the British Museum, London, CM 1911, 9–3, 59

PROV. From Palmer's Green, London, hoard, deposited c. 1258–65, found 1911.

LIT. Lawrence 1912, p. 153; North 1980, p. 182 no. 993.

266 Groat of Edward I, class III

266

Struck at London, 1280–1

Silver, obv. crowned facing bust with flower at each side all within quatrefoil with flower in each spandrel, rev. long cross with three pellets in each quarter: wt 5.81 g (89.6 gr)

Inscr. obv. EDWARDVS DI GRA REX ANGL
rev. DNS HIBNE DVX AQVT LONDONIA CIVI

The Trustees of the British Museum, London, CM 1956, 4–12, 1

PROV. From Dover, Kent, hoard deposited c. 1295, found June 1955.

LIT. Fox & Fox 1910, pp. 125–7; North 1980, p. 19.

267 Penny of Long Cross type

267

Struck at Dublin by the moneyer Richard Olof, 1216–72

Silver, obv. crowned facing head with sceptre in right hand and pierced cinquefoil at left all within triangle, rev. long double cross with three pellets in each quarter: wt 1.34 g (20.7 gr)

Inscr. obv. + HENRICVS REX III
rev. + RICARD . ON . DIVE

The Trustees of the British Museum, London, CM E2901

PROV. Not known.

LIT. Dykes 1963, pp. 98–116; Dolley 1972, pp. 8–10.

268 Penny of Edward I, class IC

268

Struck at London, May–Dec. 1279

Silver, obv. crowned facing bust, rev. long single cross with three pellets in each quarter: wt 1.43 g (22.1 gr)

Inscr. obv. EDW REX ANGL DNS HYB
rev. CIVITAS LONDON

The Trustees of the British Museum, London, CM 1950, 10–1, 93

PROV. Coll. L. A. Lawrence; bt by British Museum, 1950.

LIT. Fox & Fox 1910, pp. 105–8; North 1968, p. 16; North 1980, p. 22, no. 1021.

269 Penny of Edward I, class IIIC

269

Struck at Bristol, 1280–1

Silver, obv. crowned facing bust. rev. long cross with three pellets in each quarter: wt 1.33 g (20.5 gr)

Inscr. obv. EDW R ANGL DNS HYB
rev. VILLA BRISTOLLIE

The Trustees of the British Museum, London CM 1915, 5–7, 1833

PROV. Coll. Sir John Evans; bt by J. P. Morgan, 1908; bt by British Museum, 1915.

LIT. Fox & Fox 1910, pp. 114–18; North 1968, p. 18; North 1980, p. 22 no. 1018.

270 Halfpenny of Edward I, class IV

270

Struck at London, 1282–9

Silver, obv. crowned facing bust, rev. long cross with three pellets in each quarter: wt 0.64 g (9.8 gr)

Inscr. obv. + EDW R ANGL DNS HYB
rev. + CIVITAS LONDON

The Trustees of the British Museum, London, CM 1950, 10–1, 94

PROV. Coll. L. A. Lawrence; bt by British Museum, 1950.

LIT. Fox & Fox 1911, pp. 139–41; North 1968, p. 20; North 1980, p. 25 no. 1046.

271 Farthing of Edward I, class IIIg

271

Struck at London, 1280–1

Silver, obv. crowned facing bust without surrounding inner circle, rev. long cross with three pellets in each quarter: wt 0.36 g (5.5 gr)

Inscr. obv. + E R ANGLIE
rev. + LONDONIENSIS

The Trustees of the British Museum, London, CM 1935, 4–9, 41

PROV. Coll. C. Roach Smith; bt by British Museum, 1856; transferred to Dept of Coins & Medals, 1935.

LIT. Fox & Fox 1910, pp. 122–4; North 1968, p. 18; North 1980, p. 25 no. 1053/2.

272 Penny of Edward I, class IVb

272

Struck at Durham under Bishop Anthony Bek, 1284–9

Silver, obv. crowned facing bust, rev. long cross with three pellets in each quarter: wt 1.40 g (21.6 gr)

Inscr. obv. EDW R ANGL DNS HYB
rev. CIVITAS DVREME

The Trustees of the British Museum, London, CM Grueber 243

PROV. Not known.

LIT. Fox & Fox 1912, pp. 189–96; North 1968, p. 19; North 1980, p. 23 no.1024.

273 Penny of Edward II, class XIb

273

Struck at Canterbury, 1310–14

Silver, obv. crowned facing bust, rev. long cross with three pellets in each quarter: wt 1.39 g (21.5 gr)

Inscr. obv. EDWA R ANGL DNS HYB
rev. CIVITAS CANTOR

The Trustees of the British Museum, London, CM 1915, 5–7, 2051

PROV. From Tutbury, Staffs., hoard deposited c. 1321–9, found June 1831; bt by Sir John Evans; bt by J.P. Morgan, 1908; bt by British Museum, 1915.

LIT. Fox & Fox 1913, p. 98; North 1968, p. 25; North 1980, p. 28 no. 1061.

274 Imitation sterling of Gui de Dampierre, Count of Flanders and Marquis of Namur

274

Struck at Namur, 1279–1305

Silver, obv. uncrowned facing bust, rev. long cross with three pellets in each quarter: wt 1.28 g (19.7 gr)

Inscr. obv. MARCHIO NAMVRC
rev. G COMES FLADRE

The Trustees of the British Museum, London, CM 1911, 2–1, 25

PROV. From Mallenden, Roxburgh, hoard deposited c. 1298, found 1911.

LIT. Chautard 1871, p. 26; Mayhew 1983, p.32.

315

English seals of the mid-thirteenth century

The second half of Henry III's reign saw a major reorientation in the styles of English art and architecture. But whereas the changes that took place in the design of buildings were under way by the mid-1240s, it was not until the later 1250s that a comparable shift occurred in the figurative arts. This hiatus of a dozen or so years makes it hard to believe that there was a single political, economic or social trigger activating the two transformations. None the less, these two separate developments have factors in common: both are to a large extent superficial, affecting the surface clothing of forms rather than their underlying structures, and both use as their starting-points ideas that had developed in northern France over the preceding three decades. The medium of seals demonstrates very clearly the pace and the direction of the metamorphosis that took place in the representation of the drapery of figures.

Bishops' seals, throughout the period, show a full-length standing figure vested for Mass. His weight is evenly distributed on either foot; only his forearms, the right raised in blessing and the other holding a pastoral staff, slightly disturb the basic symmetry. For four decades, from the late teens to the late fifties of the thirteenth century, the formula for the fold pattern of his outer garment (the chasuble) hardly varies. A series of pleats falls from the shoulders and then veers to one side. Below the stomach a new sequence of roughly symmetrical catenary curves hang as if suspended from the crooks of his elbows. In cross-section the folds form a series of relatively even corrugations, not unlike the profiles of contemporary architectural mouldings, for example on the nave arcades of Lincoln Cathedral or the presbytery of Westminster Abbey. The only noticeable developments are firstly the increasing density and fineness of the folds, and later, from the 1240s, a tendency to reduce this complexity, to create wider troughs and ridges, and to use a round-ended, tear-drop terminal on some of the depressions (Cat. 278).

Deviation from this 'trough-fold' style begins with the seal of Hugh Balsham, Bishop of Ely from 1257 (Cat. 279). Here, what had been looping folds, branching into the centre from either side of the chasuble, are straightened out, and the result is a series of small, incipiently triangular plateaux down the middle of the lower part. Once promulgated, this design was quite rapidly adopted, and developed within a decade into the 'broad-fold' style with larger, flatter areas of cloth separated by sharper fold lines.

It is possible that this shift resulted from a real change in the appearance of the garment, perhaps occasioned by a fashion for using a heavier weight of cloth or a development in tailoring. On the other hand, it did not affect just ecclesiastical vestments (the same tendency is seen on royal seals, Cat. 275–6), nor was it solely an English phenomenon. Indeed, the English were rather late in accepting a style that was already on the verge of becoming ubiquitous in Europe north of the Alps. The fact that these seals show a gradual adjustment in the direction of Continental forms rather than a wholehearted and immediate acceptance of them suggests that either the patrons or the group of goldsmiths who made seals were conservative in their tastes and practices. TAH

275 Seal of Richard of Cornwall, King of the Romans

Feb.–June 1257
Wax: diam. 9.5 cm
Inscr. + RICARDUS DEI GRACIA ROMANORUM REX SEMPER AUGUSTUS
Landeshauptarchiv Koblenz, Bestand 133 Nr. 18

On 31 January 1257 the news reached Richard that he had the necessary support to secure his election as King of the Romans (i.e. Germany). He left England on 29 April and was crowned at Aachen on 17 May (cf. Cat. 14). The seal appears on a charter of 16 June, issued in Cologne (British Library, Add. Charter 1051). Although it shows awareness in

275

its legend, regalia and throne type, of William of Holland's seal as King of the Romans (1248–56; Stuttgart 1977–9, I, no. 57), which must have been made in the Low Countries, Richard's is clearly by an English craftsman. There are other instances of English seal engravers borrowing selectively from the seals of Continental European rulers (e.g. Cat. 670), so these designs must have been quite well known.

The drapery style demonstrates a stage of

development before angularity has set in, but when the looping, tear-drop fold terminals are well developed. TAH

LIT. Birch 1900, VI, nos 21158–9; Posse 1909, I, p. 37 no. 3; Stuttgart 1977–9, I no. 59.

276

276 Second Great Seal of King Henry III

Probably Aug., but certainly before 9 Sept. 1259
Wax: diam. 10 cm
Inscr. obv. HENRICUS DEI GRACIA REX ANGLIE DOMINUS HYBERNIE DUX AQUITANNIE
rev. same as obv.
The Dean and Chapter of Durham, 1.2 Reg. 6a

The need for a new Great Seal came about as a result of the Treaty of Paris by which Henry III lost his right to the titles Duke of Normandy and Count of Anjou (cf. inscr. on Cat. 453 rev.). Contemporaries noted with shame that Henry also dispensed with the sword which earlier kings had carried on the majesty side of their seals, but the change of attributes had already occurred on the coinage (Cat. 266) and so cannot be a direct result of the treaty.

Henry was apparently personally responsible for the alterations. A record survives (among material dating from early August 1259) of a note to Master William of Gloucester, goldsmith and keeper of the mints of London and Canterbury, reminding him to have the two dies for the seal made in the form enjoined upon him and Edward of Westminster, the king's artistic adviser, by the king himself. This doubtless included instructions to show a leopard to either side of the throne to represent those bronze ones which Henry, on Edward's advice, had had made for his new throne in 1245: presumably a reference to those which flanked the throne of Solomon (I *Kings* X, 19 and II *Chronicles* IX, 18). The accounts returned by William specify the sum of £9.2s.3d 'for making anew the king's seal' (Public Record Office, Pipe Roll 104 [44 Hen III], m, 2d).

The influence of the seal of Henry's brother, Richard, as King of the Romans (Cat. 275) is readily apparent in the throne, pose and regalia (cf. Cat. 453), but, as well as being more elaborate, Henry's shows a greater angularity in the drapery folds. TAH

LIT. Wyon 1887, nos 43–4, pp. 22–3, 150; Birch 1887, I, nos 119–30; Greenwell & Blair 1915, XIII, no. DS 3026; Chaplais 1952, pp. 235–53; Wormald 1961, pp. 532–9; Lancaster 1972, p. 95.

277 Seal of John Climping, Bishop of Chichester 1254–62

Feb./Mar. 1254
Wax: h. 6.3 cm, w. 4 cm
Inscr. IOHANNES : DEI : GRACIA CICESTRENSIS : EPISCOP
President and Fellows, Magdalen College, Oxford, Sele Charter 29

The period c. 1240 to 1255 witnessed the coexistence of two rather different styles superimposed upon the basic format for bishops' seals. One, exemplified by this exhibit, shows the chasuble covered with

277

myriad fine folds with acute terminals. It came into vogue before the trough fold with looped ends and went out of fashion earlier. Climping's seal is one of the last to employ it; by this stage the undulations of the drapery had reached their maximum density.

The orphrey of the amice stands upright around the neck. Immediately below it is the 'rationale', a trilobed ornament often regarded as a Christian modernisation of the ephod, or breastplate of the high priests of the Old Testament. The inscription IOH II on the background indicates that John is the second bishop of Chichester with that name. TAH

LIT. Birch, 1887, I, no. 1460.

278

278 Seal of Robert Stichill, Bishop of Durham 1261–74

1261
Wax: h. 8 cm, w. 4.3 cm
Inscr. + ROBERTUS : DEI GRA DUNELMENSIS EPISCOPUS
The Dean and Chapter of Durham, 4.2 Pont. 2

The earliest surviving impression of this seal is on a document of December 1261, the first year of the bishop's rule (Durham, 4.6. Pont. 7). However, the design and style (with its trough folds with looped ends) follow very closely indeed those of the seals of his two predecessors, Nicholas Farnham (1241–9) and Walter Kirkham (1249–60). The fact that almost indistinguishable seals could be made as much as twenty years apart in date should caution us against using style as a criterion for dating purposes in a period such as this when there was little stylistic innovation (and cf. Cat. 143).

The placing of a head in a foiled recess to either side of the bishop echoes on the one hand complex three-part matrices such as that of Southwick Priory (Cat. 462) and on the other the use of classical gems set within the matrix (cf. Birch 1887, I, no. 1205). The first English prelate to use such heads seems to have been Archbishop Richard of Canterbury, 1229–31 (Birch 1887, I, no. 1201).
TAH

PROV. Durham Cathedral.

LIT. Birch 1887, I, nos 2449–50; Greenwell & Blair 1916, XIV, no. DS 3123, Blair 1922, pp. 5, 11.

279

279 Seal of Hugh Balsham, Bishop of Ely 1257–86

1257
Wax: h. 7.2 cm, w. 4.8 cm
Inscr. + SIGILLUM : HUGONIS : DEI : GRA : EPI : ELIENSIS
The Dean and Chapter of Durham, 2.1. Archiep. 12

With this seal begins the transformation from curving trough fold to triangular broad fold. Reminiscent of one version of the older format is the use of rounded or tear-drop ends to the channels of drapery (cf. Cat. 278). Symptomatic of what is to come are the flat area of drapery between the bishop's shoulders and the relative straightness of the lines of folds lower down the chasuble. Several details of costume are novel; the orphrey of the amice descends to form a sharp angle below the throat rather than encircling the neck (cf. Cat. 277), and the strongly-patterned orphrey and cuffs to the dalmatic help to distinguish that garment.

A legend beginning with SIGILLUM, and the bishop's name in the genitive, is far less usual than simply the name in the nominative at this period, and the curious use of two lines of beading between legend and effigy is also a rarity. All in all there are sufficient oddities here to suggest either that the artist was a stranger to English bishops' seals, or that self-conscious innovation was deliberately being sought. TAH

LIT. Birch 1887, I, nos 1498–9; Greenwell & Blair 1916, XIV, no. DS 3189.

280

281

282

280　Seal of Walter Giffard, Archbishop of York 1266–1302

Sept. 1266–Feb. 1268
Wax: h. 8.2 cm, w. 5.2 cm.
Inscr. WALTERUS DEI GRA ARCHIEPS EBORAC
ANGLIE PRIMAS
The Dean and Chapter of Durham, 3.1. Archiep.
10a

Giffard is the first archbishop of York to adopt the title Primate of England on his seal. It coincides with Canterbury's adoption of the term Primate of All England. This seal is the largest on display in this group, reflecting its owner's status as an archbishop rather than just a bishop. It is distinguished in other ways too. particularly by the inclusion of full-length figures of saints (Peter, dedicatory saint of York Minster, and Paul) in niches to either side of the prelate.

The folds of the chasuble are shown here as angled loops. There may well be a Continental prototype for this style, which was a popular alternative to the flat triangles seen on Walter de Merton's seal (Cat. 281).　TAH

LIT. Birch 1887, I, no. 2308; Hope 1887, pp. 267, 288–9; Porter 1891, pp. 51–2; Greenwell & Blair 1916, XIV, no. DS 3224; Rowe 1880, pp. 216–19.

281　Seal of Walter of Merton, Bishop of Rochester 1274–7

1274–7
Wax: h. 6.7 cm, w. 4.2 cm
Inscr. WALTERUS DEI GRACIA ROFFENSIS
EPISCOPUS
The Dean and Chapter of Durham, Misc. Ch. 816

Walter of Merton, founder of Merton College, Oxford, was twice Royal Chancellor (which meant among other things that he had custody of the Great Seal, Cat. 276) before becoming Bishop of Rochester in 1274. His

own episcopal seal shows that as late as the mid-1270s there was still a tendency to combine folds with distinctly looped terminals with flat triangles of drapery (cf. Cat. 279).

The size of this seal, only very slightly bigger than John Climping's but considerably smaller than those of the bishops of Ely and Durham, shows that in the mid-thirteenth century the relative wealth and importance of a diocese was indicated, albeit approximately, by the dimensions of the bishops' seals. Since there are no known written regulations on this subject, the hierarchy must have been established by common, perhaps even tacit consent.　TAH

LIT. Birch 1887, I, no. 2154; Greenwell & Blair 1916, XIV, no. DS 3207.

282　Seal of Richard Ware, Abbot of Westminster 1259–83

1259
Wax. h. 7 cm, w. 4.5 cm, counterseal h. 5.2 cm, w. 3.1 cm
Inscr. +:s' : RICARDI : DEI GRACIA ABBATIS
WESTMONASTERII
counterseal + VIR [....] DWARDU . XPO
CONIUNGE RICARDUM
President and Fellows, Magdalen College, Oxford, Oddington Charter 21A

Richard Ware was elected Abbot of Westminster in December 1258 and consecrated in the following year; by the autumn he was using this seal (e.g. Westminster Abbey Muniment 12802). Unlike other English abbots and bishops (e.g. Cat. 280, 284), he is not shown with his weight evenly distributed and facing forward but with a slight sway at the hips and looking a little to his right. This is the design which, beginning in the 1220s, had spread from the southern Low Countries

into northern France to become the most common formula for French episcopal and abbatial seals. The free-falling folds of the chasuble seen on Richard's seal were also current in French examples from about 1250. The counterseal, with the abbot kneeling in prayer below an image of St Edward and the Pilgrim, shows an even greater naturalism and breadth of handling. The prospect of a French or French-influenced goldsmith of this quality working at Westminster in the late 1250s is a tantalising one.

The seal attributed by Birch 1887, I, no. 4306 to Abbot Ware is really that of his predecessor, Richard Crokesley.　TAH

LIT. Ellis 1986, no. M917.

283　Seal of Merton Priory

Nov. 1241
Wax: h. 9 cm, w. 5.5 cm
Inscr. obv. SIGILL' ECCLESIE SANCTE MARIE DE
MERITONA
rev. MUNDI LUCERNA NOS AUGUSTINE
GUBERNA
edge AUGUSTINE PATER QUOS INSTRUIS
IN MERITONA
HIC CHRISTI MATER TUTRIX
ESTATQUE PATRONA
British Library, Cotton Charter XXI 25

The Annals of Waverley record that the Augustinian Priory of Merton (dedicated to the Virgin Mary) had a new seal brought into use on 12 December 1241. An early impression survives (Westminster Abbey Muniment 1915, before 1249).

The figure of Saint Augustine on the reverse is comparable with contemporary episcopal seals in the style of its drapery (cf. Cat. 278), but his extra importance is indicated by the elaborate canopy on columns – a feature which was not to be appropriated by

283

285

mere mortals for several decades! The obverse shows the Virgin and Child on a throne of English type, with a foliate frieze immediately below the seat (cf. Cat. 248, 453). In the background to either side is the bust of a member of the community, the one on the left apparently reflected in a mirror which Mary holds in her hand.   TAH

LIT. Birch 1887, I, no. 3637; Pedrick 1902, pp. 104–6; Luard 1865, II, 329; Lehmann-Brockhaus 1955–60, III, no. 6394.

284   Seal of Kirkstead Abbey

Shortly before 1278
Wax: h. 5.6 cm, w. 3.5 cm
Inscr. SIGILLUM ABBATIS DE KIRKESTEDE
British Library, Harley Charter 44. F. 3

By comparison with sealing practice in other monasteries that in Cistercian houses, such

as Kirkstead, was very simple. The convents possessed no matrices of their own; instead all important writings were sealed with the abbots' seals. As these did not have personal names on them they could be used by successive prelates, thus avoiding the unnecessary expense of replacement. They were also modest in size (well under half the surface area of that of Merton Priory, Cat. 283), and uniform in imagery; those made between about 1200 and the early fourteenth century showed the abbot standing holding crosier and book.

Notwithstanding their avoidance of pretension, the quality of the engraving of the matrices is of a high order, as we see here. Stylistically the seal of Kirkstead can bear comparison with the best work of the mid-1270s, showing fully-developed and graceful broad-fold drapery.   TAH

LIT. Birch 1887, I, nos 3371–5; Heslop 1986b, p. 271.

285–6   Seal of Anthony Bek, Bishop of Durham 1284–1311

1284
Wax: h. 8.5 cm, w. 5.7 cm
Inscr. obv. S' ANTHONII DEI GRA DUNOLM' EPI
     rev. ECCE EXALTATA ES SR CHORUS
     ANG'LOR'
The Dean and Chapter of Durham, Misc. Ch.
     1245 (obv.), 3. 2. Pont. 15a (rev.)

Bek's magnificence as a prelate was remarked upon by contemporaries and is entirely borne out by this seal. It is the only English bishop's seal to have two equal and large sides, and it is the first to show the chasuble embroidered with personal heraldry. Bek's is perhaps the first English bishop's seal for nearly a century and a half to show its owner seated (but see reference in Cat. 94). This not only has the connotations of royal majesty (cf. Cat. 275–6) but also, as is made clear on the reverse which shows the Coronation of the Virgin, of enthronement in Heaven. The images of Sts Oswald and Cuthbert, standing in niches on the cushion beside him, hardly contradict this message.

The style shows that Bek employed one of the best seal makers of the period. The work is almost comparable with Oseney Priory's seal of soon after 1285 (fig. 78). When, twenty years later, Bek was appointed Patriarch of Jerusalem and needed to have another seal made, he seems to have turned again to the same craftsman. This is a tribute both to the Bishop's enduring admiration for his episcopal seal and to the longevity of its engraver.   TAH

LIT. Birch 1887, I, nos 2452–4; Hope 1887b, pp. 278–9; Greenwell & Blair 1916, XIV, no. DS 3125; Blair 1922, pp. 5–6, 12–13.

286

287–8   Figures of the Virgin Mary and the Archangel Gabriel

c.1250
Virgin (287) Reigate stone: h. approx. 150 cm
Archangel (288) Tottenhoe chalk: h. approx.
     150 cm
English Heritage, Westminster Abbey Chapter
     House

This remarkable group comes from the niches flanking the inner portal of the chapter house, a building which Matthew Paris described as 'incomparable' in 1250. The figures have been associated with a payment of 53s.4d to William Ixeworth in 1253, but are unlikely to have been carved by the same hand. Are they a pair at all? They are not carved from the same stone. The Virgin is drawn out on a more modest scale. The Archangel is scarcely contained within the

284

287

288

289

niche, and if the single wing for which the slot survives were completed, it would have exceeded the bounds of the space. No doubt the wing was made of wood or light metal, gilded, and was large enough to hide the lack of a second, for which there is no slot and there was no room. Gabriel's wide foot and exaggerated pose already suggest the ambiance of the Westminster Retable (Cat. 329) and the Douce Apocalypse (Cat. 351), while the Virgin looks back to the queens of the west front of Wells Cathedral. The Gabriel Master could well have executed the corbel heads in St Faith's Chapel at the Abbey.

Annunciations, epitomising the narrow way whereby the Incarnation entered the world, are usually associated with doorways or windows, and in the chapter house here reference to the Virgin is underlined by all the iconography, from the floor tiles to the outer doorway. The trefoils over the once open-traceried entrance are peopled with angelic acolytes. A similar disparity between artists is also found in the transept bosses. As in the transept bosses, the more advanced sculptor chose the better stone.

This group has been divested of the darkened shellac with which Sir George Gilbert Scott had coated it, along with the rest of the Abbey sculpture. It may be possible to observe the original colour.   PT-C

PROV. Gilbert Scott found Virgin *in situ* behind panelling, presumably during restoration, 1866. Archangel recorded in vestibule, 1842.

LIT. Prior & Gardner 1912, p. 320, figs 356–7; Lethaby 1925, pp. 116–20; Stone 1972, esp. pp. 120–1.

289   Boss with Samson and the lion

Probably 1246–51
Cotswold stone: h. 70 cm, w. 90 cm, d. 49 cm
English Heritage, Hailes Abbey, 78207139

The Old Testament scene of Samson breaking the jaws of the lion was seen as a type for Christ breaking the jaws of death. The two scenes are found in juxtaposition in the Romanesque Winchester Bible (Winchester Cathedral Library). Samson is also found in the wall arcading in the passage approaching the chapter house of Southwell Minster of *c.* 1290.

The companions of the Samson boss are two stiff-leaf bosses which are so similar to stiff-leaf bosses found by Gilbert Scott and reused in his reconstructed vault of the chapter house at Westminster Abbey that they could have been carved by the same hand. The Samson boss is not of the same pre-eminence as the muniment room bosses of Westminster Abbey, but the lion recalls the lion in the capital foliage of the inner entrance to the Westminster chapter house. It would not be out of the way to suggest that Hailes chapter house was ornamented by members of the Westminster Abbey chapter house team. Hailes Abbey was begun in

1246, and dedicated on 5 November 1251 in the presence of Henry III, his wife and his brother Richard, Earl of Cornwall, King of the Romans, who had founded this, one of the last and most lavish Cistercian houses. After the first impetus, which had realised cloister, dorter and frater as well, funds at Hailes languished until in 1270 Edmund, second son of Richard, gave to the Abbey the relic of the Holy Blood which was to be the focus of notoriety at the Dissolution. The repute of this relic – again mirroring the relic of the Holy Blood given to Westminster Abbey by Henry III in 1247 – replenished the coffers of the fabric fund. The entrance to the chapter house was modified as part of this second building campaign. The Hailes bosses still bear traces of red paint, and gold was found on them when they were first excavated.

PT-C

PROV. Found on site of chapter house in excavations begun 1948.

LIT. Coad 1969, pp. 17, 23.

290   St Michael spearing the dragon

c. 1250–60
Oak, painted; St Michael's right hand and spear broken off, wings missing: h. 165 cm
UNIT-Vitenskapsmuseet Archaeological dep. Trondheim, Norway, T 2451

On the back of the shoulders are slots and pegs for the wings, which were separately carved. The back is hollowed out. Holes on top of the head and beneath the socle were for pegging during the carving process (Blindheim 1952). The original polychromy is in an exceptional state of preservation, with a palette of gold, silver, red, pink (for flesh tones), orange, brown-red, black, azure blue and green; the mantle is green and red scattered with gold fleurs-de-lis; the tunic is gold, silver, black and orange, the shield gold, silver and black; the two-headed dragon has vividly coloured jaws, wings, scales and feathers. The archangel, a narrow, attenuated figure with long, pointed shield, stands on tiptoe, legs crossed on the dragon's back, above a small rounded socle; the loss of the big wings and the diagonal spear has seriously modified the group's appearance. Nevertheless, the Mosvik St Michael remains one of the great masterpieces of early English Gothic sculpture; Fett's and Andersson's claims that this is the work of a sculptor closely associated with the Westminster chapter house Annunciation group (Cat. 287–8) are clearly correct. The chapter house Annunciation can probably be associated with payments to a William Yxewerth in 1253 (Colvin 1971, pp. 226, 230, cf. p. 236). Some of the voussoir figures of the Lincoln Judgement portal, begun after 1256, share the same dislocation of pose and gesture, with the same extreme elongation of the neck and the same head type (Courtauld, Lincoln 1/7/36, 42, 51, 53), but Lincoln seems to represent a further stage, beyond that of the Westminster and Mosvik groups.

That is not to say that the sculptor did not work in Norway, and other English or English-influenced oak sculptures survive near Trondheim: at Austråt, Horg and, again, at Mosvik (a crucifix). The cult of the archangel was exceptionally popular in Scandinavia from an early period, in Denmark (Nyborg 1977) as well as in Norway (Gjerlöw 1971), and several other wood St Michael groups have survived (e.g. Andersson 1950, fig. 34). Like their surviving German counterparts, these big St Michael groups suggest from their scale that they were placed free standing against a wall or pier, often near a doorway, rather than being parts of altar retables (Stuttgart 1977, I, nos 459, 463). Unfortunately nothing is known of the old stave church at Mosvik (first recorded 1589, partly rebuilt 1652, last mentioned 1664, present church built 1884 – information Kalle Sognnes). How did the St Michael find its way to this apparently obscure parish? Mosvik faces Trondheim in the inner fertile part of the fjord and the presence of Westminster sculptors during the period of the construction of the great nave and the earliest work on the west front of Trondheim Cathedral must remain a distinct possibility. For Trondheim, see Cat. 299–306, and compare the spandrel sculptures of the Trondheim nave, one of which shows St Michael spearing the dragon (Fischer 1965, I, pp. 338–40, 347). NS

PROV. From Mosvik old church (Nord-Trøndelag); passed to Trondheim Univ. Mus. from former Coll. of Royal Norwegian Soc. of Sciences and Letters.

LIT. Fett 1908, pp. 53–9 (fig. 92); Andersson 1950, pp. 108–13, figs 30–1; Gjerlöw 1971, p. 493, pl. XLVI (fig. 1).

290

291

291 Gloucester Cathedral head

c. 1242
Stone: h. 35.6 cm, w. 16.5 cm
The Dean and Chapter of Gloucester

In 1242 the nave of Gloucester Cathedral was vaulted. This vault rests on a series of corbels terminating in striking carved heads.

This head probably belonged to that sequence and may be assumed to have been replaced in the Victorian restoration. It is, therefore, an early example of the facial characterisation greatly favoured in Henry III's building works. The reliquary in the north transept of Gloucester Cathedral manifests a range of these character heads, probably of the following decade.   PT-C

292–4 Fragments from wall arcading of St John the Baptist's Chapel, Westminster Abbey

1245–50
Dean and Chapter of Westminster

The northern radiating chapels were part of the first building campaign of Henry III's Westminster Abbey, begun in 1245. From the incomplete survival of wall arcading round the radiating chapels, it would seem that the elaborate scheme of figure sculpture, carried round the north side and continued round that transept, was substituted on the south by spandrels filled with wall diapering like that on the main wall surfaces of the arcades.

The wall arcading of the northerly radiating chapels appears to have carried an iconographic theme: histories of divine intervention. It is possible that the motif of

292–3

historiated arcade spandrels was carried on from the Westminster Lady Chapel (begun 1220), then at the east end. The use of such a space for ambitious subject-matter, as opposed to the usual demi-angels in clouds, was native and established.   PT-C

PROV. Probably displaced by one of the Elizabethan monuments which have invaded wall arcade of Chapel of St John the Baptist; two fragments of 13th-century stiff leaf from same wall arcading found in tomb of Humphrey and Mary de Bohun in same chapel, 1949.

LIT. Peers & Tanner 1949, p. 134.

292 Standing headless figure of a deacon

Limestone, painted: h. 24.1 cm, w. 10.2 cm

293 Two parts of a figure

Limestone, painted: upper fragment
h. 11.4 cm, w. 12.7 cm, d. 6.3 cm; lower fragment h. 17.8 cm, w. 12.7 cm, d. 6.3 cm

This figure was designed to fit the lower point of a half-spandrel. Its angular pose and ribbon-like drapery are typical of the best Westminster sculpture of the first generation.   PT-C

294 Smiling head

Limestone, painted: h. 17.4 cm, w. 11.4 cm

This fragment comes from a hood-mould of the wall arcade. Henry III's fascination for the new capacity, developed in the Île de France, to express the nuances of facial expression, and above all the smile, is documented from 1241, when he ordered smiling

294

angels to go on either side of a rood for the Church of St Martin le Grand. This face might be a trial run for the head of the great censing angel high in the east spandrel of the south transept. PT-C

295

295 The Clarendon Palace head

Probably 1246–56

Limestone, painted: h. 22 cm, w. 14 cm, d. 25 cm

Salisbury and South Wiltshire Museum, 80/1956

The Liberate Rolls for Henry III's reign fully document his building activities at Clarendon Palace. Work on the king's private apartments, where this head was found, was unremitting during the decade from 1246. The documents describe two features for which this label stop might have been made. In 1249 the fireplace of the king's wardrobe was repaired and improved. In 1252–3 a window was provided for the king's wardrobe, with a pillar, a seat and a bench for his clothes. This record suggests a two-light window with a traceried head, no doubt with an internal hood-mould finishing in a pair of

heads. This head implies a pair, and as this one so clearly represents anguish we may argue that its pendant was of joy. The same device of showing the teeth, the same hair ending in a row of curls and the same long chin appear in the corbel heads of St Faith's Chapel at Westminster Abbey. The wrinkled brow appears in a corbel in St Benedict's Chapel at Westminster Abbey and in the combat bosses in the Muniment Room there. The furrowed brow appears in a mutilated corbel head of the same decade in Winchester Cathedral. PT-C

PROV. Found in excavation of a room (unspecified) of king's apartments at Clarendon Palace, summer 1935.

LIT. Paris 1968, no. 51, pl. 20, with bibliography.

296 Four heads and one torso from a reredos

c. 1250–70

White lias or Bath stone: A.191 h. 12.8 cm, w. 10.3 cm, d. 6.8 cm; A.192 (torso) h. 11.2 cm, w. 7.6 cm, d. 6.4 cm; A.193 h. 10 cm, w. 7.6 cm, d. 9 cm; A.194 h. 9 cm, w. 10 cm, d. 8.4 cm; unnumbered h. 12.8 cm, w. 19.2 cm, d. 12.8 cm

Glastonbury Abbey Trustees, A.191–4 and unnumbered

These fragments probably represent all that remains of a major stone altarpiece of Glastonbury Abbey. The scale is smaller than that of comparable reliefs, for example on the former *jubé* at Chartres Cathedral, or the relief of the stoning of St Stephen in the Dommuseum in Mainz, which probably came from a choir screen. It is comparable with the quatrefoil reliefs at Wells, but the Glastonbury figures were in exceedingly high relief, their heads carved fully in the round, and not part of blocks inserted into niches, as

at Wells. The profile head (A.193) is still attached to the beard of another figure. The idealised facial type and flowing hair of A.193 and A.194 correspond with the type of the *Beau Dieu* of Amiens Cathedral, as found at Wells in the biblical quatrefoils, and the large standing Evangelists on the lowest tier of figures on the north side of the north buttress. These heads, therefore, could have been of c. 1230–40. The character and condition of the unnumbered head, with its slightly dished face, more elaborately curled hair, and different relationship with the block, suggest a slightly different context and a slightly later date. Perhaps this was one of a series of heads punctuating a moulding around the framework. Compare the heads around the base of the tomb of William de Marchia (d. 1302) at Wells or, more nearly, the heads flanking the effigy of Peter de Acquablanca (d. 1268) at Hereford.

The comparable scale, material, damage and context of the head of an ecclesiastic (A.191) must imply that it comes from the same context as the others, though the strong individuality of this head has suggested a much later date. Observe the detail of a mole on his cheek, the crowsfeet and the double chin. Among the finest carvings at Westminster Abbey in the late 1240s there are a number of individual heads. The idea did not reach Wells until immediately after the west front had been completed, but appeared in the head corbels from the east walk of the Wells cloister, of c. 1255–60, reused in the library. This head, however, is specific, and must have been taken from the life. In any case these fragments represent the finest English sculpture of the third quarter of the thirteenth century. PT-C

PROV. Found on south side of the Galilee, with lesser drapery fragments, 1929; another draped shoulder (A.197) found in tomb in nave.

LIT. Tudor-Craig 1973, pp. 9–10, no. 2.

296

297

297 Head

Second half 13th century
Purbeck marble(?): h. 26 cm, w. 22.5 cm,
d. 17 cm
Dean and Chapter, Ely Cathedral

This head declares an influence from the Court school that was not apparent in the Purbeck marble monuments to Bishops Hugh de Northwold (d. 1254) or Kilkenny (d. 1256) at Ely Cathedral. It could have belonged to a screen completing the display of

the shrine of St Etheldreda. It compares in date with the figures from the Winchester shrine screen (Cat. 23–4). PT-C

PROV. Until recently mortared to back of one of walls between bays in south nave triforium; mortar perhaps of nineteenth-century date.

298 Head

Late 13th century
Stone: h. 24 cm
The Trustees of the British Museum, London,
MLA 1978, 12–1, 1

This fine head is among the many remarkable studies of facial variety that fall into the seventy years after 1250. The exploration of facial types, introduced at Westminster from Rheims, spread across the country within the decade, inspiring series of head corbels and head stops as the major decorative feature of cathedral and palace works, monuments and furnishings. The fashion never waned but, like the parallel interest in specific foliate forms, it settled down into a new range of conventional types in the early fourteenth century. The temptation is to think of portraiture. Such a head as this is undoubtedly taken from the life, but it would seem that the aim was to achieve individuality rather than to commemorate an individual.

Presumably this sculpture, of which the semi-octagonal abacus suggests the end of the thirteenth century, comes from the orbit

of Michael of Canterbury, the most famous architect of his time, and of Henry of Eastry, Prior of Canterbury from 1281 to 1331. The most ambitious architectural endeavour going on in Canterbury itself was the construction of the chapter house, for which Prior Eastry built two new gable walls. His upper part of the chapter house was replaced again in the late fourteenth century by the present wagon roof. A head like this could have carried ribs for Eastry's vault. The closest comparisons that can be made with Canterbury work still *in situ* are with the two heads of *c.* 1300 supporting the arch now in Prior Chillenden's garden. PT-C

PROV. Bt for British Museum; reputed Canterbury provenance, 1978.

299–306 Eight carved heads

Nidaros Domkirkes Restaureringsarbeider,
Trondheim, Norway, nos 3593, =233, =19,
3557, 3594, =236–7, =239

Nidaros (modern Trondheim) on the coast of Norway, some 270 miles north of Bergen, has been since 1153 the seat of the Archbishopric of Norway (from 1104 within the province of Lund). Nearby Stiklestad was the site of the battle in which King Olav died in 1030 and Norway's martyr-king soon became the focus of a major local and international pilgrimage; St Olav's holy well is built into the southern wall of the eastern octagon of the present cathedral.

Of the Romanesque buildings on the site, there survive major parts of the north and south transepts, and a chapel north of the choir. Archbishop Eystein (d. 1188) is normally credited with the decision to rebuild the Romanesque church, following a three-year exile in England (1180–3; Fischer 1965). Work began with the laying out of a remarkable eastern octagon and continued with the 'long choir' of six bays to the east of the Romanesque crossing. The chronology of this period of building is far from clear, but the major campaign on this east end seems to belong to the years *c.* 1200–35. The works of *c.* 1183–1235 have not survived intact, the 'long choir' in particular (except its outer walls) being a nineteenth-century reconstruction based on fragmentary surviving evidence found in its east and west bays, but enough has been preserved or can be deduced to show that throughout this period the building was in the hands of one or more English masons: there are particularly close links with the lodge at Lincoln, where St Hugh's Choir was begun in 1192, i.e. a few years after the opening of work on the Trondheim octagon, which is however clearly related in ground plan, elevation and decorative detailing to the late twelfth- and early thirteenth-century work at Lincoln. Cat. 299, 300 and 301 are fragments which probably belong to this early 'Lincoln phase' at Trondheim and may indeed have been

298

carved by English sculptors; another fragment (Cat. 302) seems to be related to the succeeding stage of work, when the crossing tower was given a Lincoln-style star vault, *c*. 1235–48. The 1230s and 1240s must also have seen the beginning of the building of a new nave, which continued well into the third quarter of the thirteenth century. Once again, what has come down to us is largely (except the outer walls) a nineteenth-century building; the evidence of the surviving fragments of this nave suggests the influence of Westminster as much as of Lincoln (Cat. 303; cf. Cat. 290). The foundation stone of a west screen façade, very much on an English model, was laid in 1248 and, although it was never completed, parts of five major statues and many other fragments survive from this vast and ambitious project, which was largely supplanted by a neo-Gothic façade in the present century.

Trondheim has suffered many fires, one of the worst of which in 1328 led to the renewal of the chancel screen wall between the octagon and the long choir in an English Decorated style, and a substantial rebuilding of the interior of the octagon. It may be to this campaign that the very realistic heads (Cat. 304–6) belong. From 1869 onwards a continuous masons' tradition has developed within the lodge at Trondheim, and there has been a systematic policy of replacing many of the exterior sculptures with modern copies. However, the originals have always been scrupulously preserved. In 1983 a fire destroyed the main stone depot where the vast majority of the replaced sculptures and mouldings had been stored. Fortunately many of the finest fragments had been removed for exhibition and these were saved.

The eight heads exhibited here may or may not be the work of English sculptors, but they are fully representative of the kind of minor decorative and grotesque sculpture which was such a special feature of English buildings of the thirteenth and fourteenth centuries – although already found in profusion in the last years of the twelfth century at Wells and Lincoln. The Trondheim heads are detached from their setting and therefore exhibitable, and they are joined here by heads from certain English buildings (Clarendon, Cat. 295; Glastonbury, Cat. 296; Westminster, Cat. 294, etc.).

It has often and rightly been said that this is not 'portraiture' in the modern sense, and indeed certain head types seem to migrate from one building to another, even from one country to another (i.e. between Rheims and Salisbury – see Sauerländer 1965 and 1972, pl. 257; Whittingham 1970), as if there was a stock repertory common to certain masons, perhaps transmitted by model books. It would however be foolish to deny the direct response to nature that is so clearly evident with many of these heads. Some were undoubtedly meant to be funny or to shock,

others to mirror a particular trait of character or health (such as the celebrated man with toothache at Wells), others may even represent persons living or dead, particularly kings (Cat. 299), bishops, masons, pilgrims (Cat. 306), and so on. Above all, they helped to add to the intricate and exotic richness of these buildings, often placed where they were virtually invisible from the floor of the church, simply there for their own sake, not because they contributed to some neo-Platonic 'ideal' of the Gothic cathedral. No exhibition of Gothic art would be complete without such heads, which can only be paralleled by the small *drôleries* in the margins of contemporary manuscripts (cf. Cat. 575) or the scenes hidden beneath choir seats (Cat. 531, 536). Such 'minor' sculptures are notoriously difficult to date; these heads enjoyed such prolonged popularity. Thus the dates offered here are provisional, based wherever possible on what is known of the original positions of the heads on the building. NS

299

299 Crowned head of a young man

c. 1210–35(?)
Soapstone: h. 21.1 cm, w. 19.5 cm, d. 23.5 cm
No. 3593

The leaves of the crown, much damaged, have the typical trefoil form of Lincoln 'stiff-leaf' foliage. If the provenance of this head is correctly recorded, then it is not strictly comparable to other heads from the octagon (Fett 1908, fig. 29 p. 22), but must be somewhat earlier than the first work (*c*. 1220) on the Lincoln nave (cf. Courtauld, Lincoln 1/3/88). NS

PROV. Said to be from the exterior cornice of the east chapel of the octagon.

300

300 Head of a young man

c. 1210–35(?)
Soapstone: h. 10.9 cm, w. 19.2 cm, d. 22.5 cm
No. = 233

Compare a drawing of a Trondheim corbel from the 'Lincoln phase', when altars were refurbished in the transept (Fischer 1965, I, p. 254; II, p. 648 n. 15 [repr.]). The head has much in common with the octagon heads (Fett 1908, fig. 29 p. 22). NS

PROV. Not known.

301

301 Man's head

c. 1220–35(?)
Soapstone: h. 23.5 cm, w. 23.2 cm, d. 40.7 cm
No. = 19

This is broadly carved and in places unfinished, extensively weathered and damaged. It is an extraordinarily bold, grimacing head of a man, with mouth agape and deeply-carved, apparently sightless eyes. Similar heads already occur at Lincoln on the choir buttresses and in the nave (of *c.* 1220–40: Courtauld, Lincoln 1/3/25–26, 1/5/101, 106).   NS

PROV. Found reused in the later walls of the 'long choir'; probably a corbel from its exterior cornice.

LIT. Fett 1908, fig. 69 p. 46; Fischer 1965, I, p. 225 (repr.), 226; II, p. 639 n. 149.

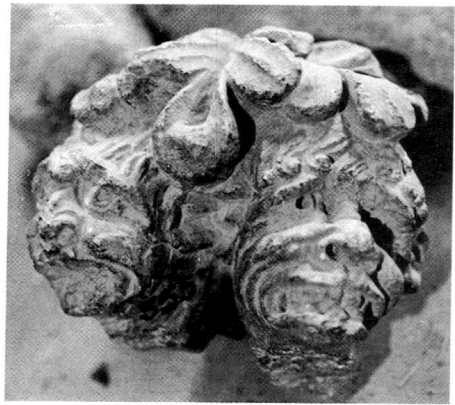

302

302   Two grotesque heads amid foliage

c. 1235–48(?)
Soapstone: h. 10.5 cm, w. 11.7 cm, d. 10.3 cm
No. 3557

This tiny fragment, of indeterminate origin (from a vaulting-shaft corbel, label stop or boss?), is similar to corbels probably made for a star vault in the lantern of the crossing

tower late in the second quarter of the thirteenth century (Fischer 1965, I, pp. 268–9; II, p. 652 n. 55). Grotesque masks with stiff-leaf foliage also decorated the somewhat earlier choir piers at Trondheim and are a typical feature at Lincoln, e.g. in the nave (Courtauld, Lincoln 1/5/96).   NS

PROV. Not known.

LIT. Fett 1908, fig. 156 p. 102.

303   Grinning head of a young man

Third quarter 13th century(?)
Soapstone: h. 21.9 cm, w. 25 cm, d. 28.4 cm
No. 3594

A similar but more fragmentary head is said to come from the nave (unnumbered). Fett dated this head *c.* 1300 but this seems too late; cf. the Westminster hemicycle triforium corbels (Carpenter 1972, pls IV–V).   NS

PROV. Not known.

LIT. Fett 1908, fig. 147 p. 97.

304   Head of a man

c. 1330–50(?)
Soapstone: h. 12.3 cm, w. 14.2 cm, d. 12 cm
No. =236

Like Cat. 305 and 306, this is probably a head stop. All three heads are closely related

304

in style and may belong to the period after the fire of 1328, when the screen wall between the octagon and the 'long choir', and the inner area of the octagon were rebuilt by English Decorated masons, employing a rich repertory of curvilinear tracery and ballflower ornament (see Fischer 1965, I, pp. 379, 381–3, for illustrations of similar corbels). 'Character' is achieved by a few chiselled lines, with deeply-drilled pockets accenting the eyes, ears, mouth and nostrils.   NS

PROV. Not known.

LIT. Fett 1908, fig. 151b p. 101.

305   Head of a man

c. 1330–50(?)
Soapstone: h. 11.1 cm, w. 13.6 cm, d. 13 cm
No. =237

Compare Cat. 304 and 306.

PROV. Said to come from the octagon.

305

303

306

306 Head of an old man wearing a hat

c. 1330–50(?)

Red sandstone: h. 14.8 cm, w. 8.7 cm, d. 12.2 cm

No. = 239

Compare Cat. 304 and 305. The right side of the hat is broken off; it had a tall crown and turned-back brim, perhaps a pilgrim's hat.

NS

PROV. Not known.

LIT. Fett 1908, fig. 151a p. 101.

307–9 Three reliefs

c. 1250–60

The Danish National Museum, Second
  Department, 5075, 5076, 5077

These three openwork reliefs, perhaps cut from the same tusk, show no traces of paint and have been scored on the backs with vertical and horizontal strokes. There are several pinholes for large ivory plugs, probably contemporary with the mends, which are numerous (Cat. 307: head of woman, top right; top of angel's wing, top left; top of spice pot, below right. Cat. 308: Christ's left leg and bottom of His drapery; top of cross; Adam's arm).

The three must come from the same ensemble (a shrine, antependium or retable?). They were applied against flat backgrounds, perhaps of painted ivory, wood or black marble, as part of a Passion series; presumably the framing would have been in a contemporary Rayonnant style with tracery, buttresses and finials, and brightly coloured. Fourteenth-century fragments survive to prove the existence of such ivory ensembles, both in France (Paris 1981–2,

nos 133–8) and in England (fig. 75), but none is intact or in its frame. Similar applied ivory reliefs were already being carved in the eleventh and twelfth centuries (London 1984a, nos 210, 220–1; London 1984b, no. 119). Liebgott (1985, pl. 40) compared Cat. 304 with a mid-thirteenth-century wood group, perhaps from the rood of Roskilde (see also Andersson 1970; Nyborg 1981). There are also close iconographic connections between Cat. 309 and the Resurrection scenes in two English manuscripts, the Amesbury Psalter (Cat. 316; fig. 74) and the Missal of Henry of Chichester (Cat. 108). The style of these two books, dating from *c.* 1250–60, is intimately related to the Copenhagen ivories. Similar heads and the same soft, 'moulded' folds of the draperies can again be found in the 1250s in the St Albans copy of the Lives of the Offas (Morgan 1982, figs 292–4). Andersson dismissed these reliefs as 'of inferior quality', whereas the English parallels argue strongly for a mid-century date and an English-trained artist of the highest order: his ivories are characterised by a minute attention to surface finish and to the rendering of the physical details of a scene, absolute mastery in the layout of his densely-packed compositions, above all an ability to imbue each episode with its own mood, from the introspective calm of the Women at the Tomb to the high drama of the wind-blown Resurrection. The possibility that this remarkable ensemble was made in or for Denmark cannot of course be excluded. NS

307 The Holy Women at the Tomb

Walrus ivory: h. 8.8 cm, w. 5.9 cm

Seated on the tomb chest, which is decorated with blank arcading, quatrefoils and a band of reversed trilobed leaves, an angel holding a long palm branch gestures towards the open tomb. The three women carry spice pots and one of them grasps the abandoned shroud which falls over the front edge of the tomb.

NS

307

308

308   The Harrowing of Hell

Walrus ivory: h. 9.2 cm, w. 6 cm

Christ on the left dominates the crowd of small naked figures emerging from the crenellated gate of Hell; Adam in the lead is grasped by Christ's hand. The shaft of Christ's long cross impales a horned devil beneath Adam's feet; on the right, two other devils torment three naked souls (one mitred, one with crown [?], one a woman) behind another set of battlements; one of the devils pours boiling liquid from a pot; below, a horned devil with wings, his arms bound and caught in the flames of Hell, is emerging from a big Hell-mouth, with teeth and fangs.   NS

309   The Resurrection

Walrus ivory: h. 9.2 cm, w. 6.4 cm

Christ steps from the tomb, His drapery blown up behind Him and the pennant of His cross cascading downwards on the right (His cruciform halo is broken off on the left); the wound in His side is visible, the lid of the tomb set diagonally behind Him; in front of the

tomb, three sleeping soldiers with drawn swords, wearing mail with hoods, are shown in various attitudes of sleep, unaffected by Christ's physical Resurrection.   NS

PROV. Bt from a farmer by Sheriff of Nykøbing Sjaelland (Northwest Zealand); given to Danish National Collection by 1839.

LIT. Andersson 1970, p. 135 n. 5; Liebgott 1985, pp. 42–5, pls 36–8.

310   Crucifix figure

English(?), late 13th century
Elephant ivory: trimmed at shoulders and shins to take new arms and feet; central looping fold of loincloth damaged and recarved; extensive traces of discoloured pigments on hair and loincloth: h. 24.3 cm
The Board of Trustees of the Victoria and Albert Museum, London, A2-1921

The original arms must have been carved separately. The back of the head and loincloth are completely finished, suggesting that they were meant to be visible; if so, the

309

310

vertical bar of the cross was narrow. The figure was pinned to the cross by three nails and there is a large dowel for attachment at the waist. In spite of surface cracks, the refined modelling of the face, torso, ribcage and belly is still intact, as is the spear-wound in the right side. The figure is from a large altar cross or retable, like the other rare surviving Gothic ivory crucifix figures, but none is comparable. However, the Christ of a Deposition relief in Oslo (Paris 1981–2, no. 136) has many features in common, although clearly of somewhat later date. The Oslo ivory has always been considered French, and this one English. The problem posed by this magnificent fragment can only be expressed in stylistic terms, and these are inconclusive. The drapery of the loincloth, even in its recut state, finds close English parallels, e.g. on some of the wooden cloister bosses at Lincoln of c. 1296–9 (Brighton 1985, fig. 92). On the other hand, nothing in English art remotely resembles this noble head, so deeply touched with suffering, even in death. Is this Christ, more linear and flattened than its Parisian contemporaries, an insular response to ivories like the Bargello Christ (Gaborit-Chopin 1978, figs 208 –9)? Or is it the work of a Frenchman, somewhat unusual in terms of late thirteenth-century Paris sculpture as we know it?   NS

PROV. Coll. Thomas Gambier-Parry (d. 1888), Highnam Court, Glos.; bt by V&A, 1921.

LIT. Koechlin 1924, I, p. 263; II, no. 738 bis; III, pl. CXXI bis; Longhurst 1926, pp. 43, 103, no. LVI, pls 8, 44; Longhurst 1929, pp. 6–7, pl. III (with modern arms and feet); London 1963, no. 169; Blunt 1967, p. 116, fig. 45; Porter 1974, pp. 102–5, no. 35; Gaborit-Chopin 1978, pp. 159, 210, no. 244.

311 St Peter from a tabernacle

c. 1250
Oak covered with gesso and paint: h. 185 cm,
    w. 75 cm
Oslo, Universitetets Oldsaksamlingen, C 3006

This panel is the sole surviving piece from a tabernacle shrine which probably held a sculpted wooden figure of the Virgin and Child. The panel is part of a system of shutters which closed around the tabernacle, and on their inner sides had attached wooden reliefs of scenes of the Life of Christ or of the Saints. Several examples survive in Norway and Sweden, mostly only in part. A good example of a complete system is the one from Fröskog (Stockholm, Statens Historiska Museum). On the reverse of the St Peter panel silhouettes can be seen where the wood sculptures were once attached.

The painting is on oak, whereas almost all works of Norwegian panel painting are on pine. There is a very thin application of a gesso ground. The figure, set against a red ground, has lightly coloured garments flatly painted but with pale green tinting in the

311

folds. Black lines are extensively used almost as if it were a coloured drawing.

The affinities with English tinted drawing and manuscript painting have long been recognised. Above all comparison has been made with the work of Matthew Paris (e.g. Cat. 315, 437). The drawing style of the St Peter is slightly more fussy in use of line than that of Matthew. It is perhaps rather closer to the drawings in the Westminster Psalter (Cat. 9). If the work can be associated directly with Matthew Paris, it could possibly have been brought with him when he visited Norway in 1248–9. Norwegian painting and sculpture in this period is strongly influenced by English art (Cat. 290, 299–306). It may be that English artists worked in Norway and trained Norwegian artists in English styles. Whatever the origins of its artist, this panel gives an idea of a form of art totally lost from England itself. NJM

PROV. Faaberg Church (Oppland).

LIT. Lindblom 1916, pp. 24, 40–1, 128–31, pl. 7; Fett 1917, pp. 72–3; Lethaby 1917, p. 51, pl. A; Andersson 1950, pp. 154, 160; Lange 1953–6, pp. 189–96; Vaughan 1958, pp. 205–7; Wichstrom 1981, pp. 268, col. fig. 3.10.

312   Roger of Salerno, *Chirurgia*

c. 1230–50
Vellum, ff. 50: 19.7 × 15.2 cm
The Master and Fellows, Trinity College,
   Cambridge, MS 0.1.20

Roger of Salerno's treatise on surgery was written in the third quarter of the twelfth century. This copy is a translation in Anglo-Norman French accompanied by fifty marginal tinted drawings of medical examinations, operations and the preparation of medicines. The lively drawings are full of expressive action. The instruments used for surgery, the stages in preparation of the potions and ointments, and the depiction of the various complaints of the sick persons are full of carefully-observed details. The pain of the patient and sympathy of the doctor are sometimes conveyed by the expressions of the faces.

There is some affinity in style with London work of the mid-century (e.g. Cat. 313), but it is not close enough to suggest that the artist was working there. This manner of drawing can be seen as a continuation of earlier styles such as that of the Cambridge Bestiary (Cat. 252). NJM

PROV. Thomas Gale (d. 1702); given to Trinity College by his son, Roger Gale, 1738.

LIT. London 1908, no. 78; Sudhoff 1914, pp. 33–42, pls v–vii; Morgan 1982, no. 78, figs 256–61.

313   Thomas of Kent, *Roman de toute chevalerie*

c. 1240–50
Vellum, ff. 46: 28 × 19.5 cm
The Master and Fellows, Trinity College,
   Cambridge, MS 0.9.34

Illustrated romances by English artists are rare in the thirteenth and fourteenth centuries. Perhaps such works, which were certainly widely read, were imported from France, from which country many more examples survive. The poem of Thomas of Kent is concerned with the life of Alexander the Great, and was written in the second half of the twelfth century. This illustrated copy is a fragment comprising less than half the full text. The illustration is very full with 152 framed tinted drawings. An early fourteenth-century copy (Cat. 361) has almost the complete text with over 300 pictures. The battle scenes and diverse narrative situations provide opportunities for a great range of anecdotal detail.

These drawings may be London work, having similarities with the style of the fragmentary Life of St Thomas of Canterbury (Cat. 38). These works have been attributed to a 'School of St Albans' supposedly under the direction of the Benedictine monk, Matthew Paris. Although the work of Matthew himself clearly shows that tinted drawing was done at the Abbey of St Albans, it is unlikely that he had a 'school' that produced illustrated copies of secular romances. NJM

PROV. Thomas Gale (d. 1702); given to Trinity College by his son Roger Gale, 1738.

LIT. London 1908, no. 79; London 1930, no. 127; Ross 1969, pp. 690–4; Brussels 1973, no. 50; Secomska 1975, pp. 60, 66, pls 8h, 8i; Morgan 1982, no. 81, figs 271–4.

314   Psalter

Oxford, *c.* 1240–50
Vellum, ff. 162: 35 × 25 cm
The Warden and Fellows of New College, Oxford,
   MS 322

The unusually large size of this psalter enabled the illuminators of the de Brailes workshop in Oxford to elaborate the decoration of the text pages and initials (cf. Cat. 436). In addition to historiated initials for the psalms of the liturgical divisions there are small figures in almost every psalm initial. Border bars formed of dragons, foliage or

313

314

312

penwork sprays extend from the initials into the margin, unifying the decoration of the page. The ornamental line endings complete this integration of decoration with text. This early use of border bars is a precursor of a form of decoration which becomes common in the later thirteenth and fourteenth centuries. The figure decoration is of the scenes of the Labours of the Months in the calendar, a full-page initial to Psalm 1 containing the Tree of Jesse, and scenes from the lives of Saul, David, Solomon and Christ for the nine initials of the liturgical divisions.

The patron of this psalter probably lived in the Winchester diocese, as evidenced by several Winchester saints in the calendar.

NJM

PROV. 14th century, a person associated with the Brewese, Le Marny and Wokingdon families whose obits are entered in the calendar; given by Henry Howell to New College, 1693.

LIT. London 1908, no. 59; Cockerell 1930, pp. 2, 7–11, pls II–XIII; London 1930, no. 152; London 1939, no. 31; Morgan 1982, no. 74, figs 239–40.

315

315 Fortune-telling tracts

St Albans, c. 1250–5
Vellum, ff. 72: 17.6 × 12.8 cm
Oxford, Bodleian Library, MS. Ashm. 304

Fortune-telling books, or Books of Fate as they are sometimes called, contain compilations of various systems of divination. Much of this text is concerned with geomancy, in which a number obtained by chance is applied to a series of questions and answers in diagrams which lead to a prediction. Matthew Paris (cf. Cat. 437) wrote the whole manuscript in his own hand save for two folios, and must have had a particular interest in fortune-telling in spite of the opposition of the Church to such superstitious practices. The tracts are associated with various pagan

philosophers and mathematicians, who were viewed as if they were astrologers. Pythagoras and Euclid are represented, and Plato stands at the shoulder of the writing Socrates. On the facing page to the latter is one of the tables of questions and answers which will lead on to other diagrams to obtain a final prediction. Later copies of the same text and illustrations are Cambridge, Magdalene College, MS Pepys 911 and Oxford, Bodleian Library, MS Digby 46.

The assured style of the drawings suggests a date during the last decade of Matthew Paris's activity before his death in 1259.

NJM

PROV. Thomas West, 1602; Mr Vaughan, 17th century; Edward Lluyd (1660–1709), from whom it passed to Ashmolean Library, which became part of Bodleian Library, 1860.

LIT. Wormald 1946, pp. 109ff.; Brussels 1973, no. 47; Oxford 1980, no. 53; Morgan 1982, no. 89, figs 299–300.

316 The Amesbury Psalter

Salisbury, c. 1250–5
Vellum, ff. 189: 30.5 × 21 cm
Warden and Fellows of All Souls College, Oxford, MS 6

The nunnery of Amesbury was a dependency of the French abbey of Fontevrault, the burial place of the Plantagenet kings: the tombs of Henry II and Richard I are there. This psalter was made for a nun of Amesbury, who in two miniatures is shown kneeling before the Virgin and Child and Christ in Majesty. As in the Missal of Henry of Chichester (Cat. 108)

316

by the same artist, the donor picture has an intimacy in the relationship between the kneeling figure and the Virgin and Child. The Virgin is shown suckling the Child, which is a favourite type in thirteenth-century England. It is debatable whether the psalter precedes or follows the missal in the development of the artist's work.

There are four miniatures preceding the psalter, ten initials to the liturgical divisions of the Psalms (fig. 74), and a scene of confession for the initial to the first of the canticles.　NJM

PROV. Benedictine Nunnery of Amesbury; John Grandisson, Bishop of Exeter (1327–69); Robert Manday, 16th century; Dr Daniel Lysons of Bath; beq. to All Souls, 1772.

LIT. London 1908, no. 41; London 1930, no. 157; London 1939, no. 29; Hollaender 1943, pp. 239–48, pls v–x, xii, xiii; Brussels 1973, no. 51; Morgan 1987, no. 101, repr.

317

317　Medical illustrations

c. 1260
Vellum, bifolium: 27 × 18.6 cm
Oxford, Bodleian Library, MS. Ashm. 399, ff. 33v–34r

This book is a compilation of medical texts of various dates from the mid-thirteenth to the early fourteenth centuries. A bifolium of *c.* 1260 has eight illustrations of the sickness, death and autopsy of a woman. The pictures lack inscriptions or accompanying text, and the interpretation of the story is uncertain. The most likely version is that it is a moral story about a woman who does not take the doctor's advice, resorts to unwise superstitious remedies and dies. The last picture in the series shows the doctor pointing out the moral to a group of women.

The drawings are not of the sophistication of contemporary London work, neither do they have the narrative vigour of Matthew Paris. None the less they provide an interest-

ing illustration of medical practices, above all in the gruesome scene of the autopsy.　NJM

PROV. John Gibbon of Trinity College, Oxford, 1628; Elias Ashmole (1617–92), who gave his manuscripts to Oxford University, 1677; transferred from Ashmolean to Bodleian Library, 1860.

LIT. McKinney & Bober 1960, pp. 251–9; Morgan 1987, no. 117, repr.

318

318　Averroes, *Commentary on the Metaphysics of Aristotle*

Oxford, *c.* 1260
Vellum, ff. 290: 29.8 × 21.4 cm
The Warden and Fellows of Merton College, Oxford, MS. 269(F.I.4)

In thirteenth-century universities the texts of Aristotle and their commentaries were an essential part of the curriculum for the bachelor's degree in the faculty of arts. Particularly at Oxford and Paris, scholars actively worked on commentaries on these texts.

Most copies of Aristotle are without decoration, except possibly in penwork initials. These were essentially scholar's books, and their use is frequently testified by copious annotations in the margins. A group of illuminated copies was made in the third quarter of the thirteenth century by a workshop probably based on Oxford. The Merton Averroes must once have had a complete set of figure initials to the various chapters, but some sadly have been cut out. The illustration of these philosophical texts must have produced problems for artists, as there was no tradition of decoration for the abstruse concepts of such books. The trial drawings for the historiated initials in the margins may suggest instruction by a master who had worked out some pictorial form suited to the text. Such marginal sketches may often have been used by artists, but were

probably usually erased later. Sketches do survive, mainly in manuscripts for which there had previously been little or no illustrative tradition. The conclusion might be made that for familiar subjects sketches were seldom necessary.　NJM

PROV. Library of Merton College, since late fourteenth century.

LIT. Camille 1985b, pp. 32, 36 n. 27, 41, fig. 16; Morgan 1987, no. 146(b), repr.

319　Charter of the University of Cambridge

London and Cambridge, 1291–2
Vellum: 40.5 × 47.5 cm; seal l. 15.8 cm
Deposited by the Keeper of the Cambridge University Archives, UA. Luard 7*

This charter of Edward I with the royal seal confirms the privileges of the University of Cambridge granted by Henry III in 1270. The historiated initial shows the king presenting the charter to Doctors of Canon Law, Civil Law and Theology.

Although the charter was probably written out in London there is some evidence that the illuminated initial was painted in the Cambridge region. A breviary-missal of the Benedictines of the nearby Cathedral Priory of Ely (Cambridge, University Library, MS ii.4.20) has a few small historiated initials close in style and ornament to the initial of the charter. It seems likely that the Ely manuscript was decorated at Cambridge, or by artists from Cambridge who also added a decorative initial to an unilluminated charter. If this hypothesis is accepted, these works are the earliest extant evidence for illumination in Cambridge.　NJM

PROV. Cambridge, University Archives.

LIT. *Docs Univ. Camb.* 1852, p. 3; Luard 1876, p. 387; Peek & Hall 1962, p. 54, pl. 12.

319

320 Chertsey tiles

1250–70

Earthenware, four roundels each showing a scene from the Romance of Tristram, set within four surrounding tiles decorated with human-headed serpents and foliage: frames l. 31.5 cm, w. 31.5 cm, roundels diam. 25.2 cm

The Trustees of the British Museum, London, design nos 478, 487, 492, 502, set within surrounding design nos 863, 864 repeated

The identification of these scenes as illustrating the Romance of Tristram was first made by Dr M. Shurlock (1885) and the scenes defined more precisely by Loomis (1916), who identified the version of the story used for the illustrations as the Anglo-Norman poem by Thomas of Erceldount. No illuminated manuscript is known with these particular scenes. The four scenes shown here are Tristram harping before King Mark (design 478), Mark kissing Tristram (design 487), King Gormon hastening to view the body of Morhaut (design 492) and Isolde (with broad hat seated before the oarsman) voyaging to see the dying Tristram (design 502). The emphasis on the choice of subjects from the Tristram Romance is on the heroic acts of Tristram rather than his love for Isolde. The Tristram scenes are skilfully drawn and full of expression, but do not have the vitality of the combat scenes (Cat. 16). Gormon's anxious expression and the fold of his cloak are good examples of the detail that may have been achieved not by hammering the stamp into fairly dry clay tiles but by placing the stamps in the bottom of a mould where moist clay was pressed down upon them. This enabled the fine red lines of the design to appear through the white inlay. Nothing is known of the actual craftsman involved. Like the combat series, it was probably originally designed for one of Henry III's principal residences and only afterwards used at Chertsey Abbey.

JC

PROV. Found on site of Chertsey Abbey, Surrey, probably in 1852–3; Shurlock Coll.

LIT. Shurlock 1885; Loomis 1916, designs 4, 13, 18, 29; Loomis 1938, pp. 44–8, figs 30, 41, 46, 58; Eames 1980, pp. 141–71.

320

X Edward I (1272–1307)

The choice of Edward as a name, unfashionable among the French-speaking aristocracy, reflected a new emphasis on English traditions and a veneration for Edward the Confessor. Edward, the eldest son of Henry III, played an active part in the royalist opposition to Simon de Montfort and also in Simon's defeat and death at the Battle of Evesham in 1265. When he became king in 1272 he was returning from a crusade to Acre, where he narrowly escaped assassination. In August 1274, at the age of thirty-five, he was crowned at Westminster with his queen, Eleanor of Castile.

The first twenty years of his reign, up to the early 1290s, were oustandingly successful, in two ways especially. In the first place, it was a time of legislation. A series of statutes gave definition particularly to the rights of the Crown and of the nobility. The legislation, which owed much to the king's Chancellor, Robert Burnell, Bishop of Bath and Wells, had an enduring importance in consolidating the king's control of his kingdom. The Statute of Mortmain, for example, sought to forbid, at any rate without royal licence, the granting of further lands to the Church.

His second major achievement in these years was in Wales. The position of the prince of Wales, Llywelyn ap Gruffydd, had been recognised, though only through his feudal allegiance to the King of England; when Edward became king, Llywelyn refused to do homage to him and in 1276 the king decided on military action, aiming to conquer the strongholds of Llywelyn in north Wales. Until 1284 Edward was mainly preoccupied with Wales, fighting two major campaigns in 1277 and 1282–3, the latter being by far the more expensive. His conquest of north Wales was consolidated by the building of castles (see Cat. 322) and the creation of the new counties of Flint, Anglesey, Merioneth and Caernarfon. After a further serious rising and campaign in 1294–5 the king's policies of enforcing English rule came to a successful end, the last chapter in a long story of English penetration in Wales which had begun at the time of William the Conqueror.

The early 1290s proved to be a major turning-point in the reign, with the deaths of his beloved queen, Eleanor (see Cat. 368–79), and of his Chancellor, Robert Burnell, and also of the Archbishop of Canterbury, John Pecham. There followed a period of political dissension and increasing financial problems, associated closely with wars and plans for wars against the Scots and the French. In none of these spheres, internal or external, were Edward's policies fully effective.

Difficult relations with France came to a head in 1293–4, when his brother, Edmund Crouchback, Earl of Lancaster (Cat. 326), had charge of negotiations in Paris. The king was tricked into accepting the supposedly temporary holding of the Duchy of Gascony by Philip IV of France. Since Philip refused to restore the Duchy, war was declared, but effective military action against the French was not possible, as the campaign in Flanders in 1297–8 demonstrated. Negotiation and Edward's marriage to Philip's sister, Margaret, in 1299 brought about a temporary settlement. Edward's extreme financial demands between 1294 and 1297 had caused an internal crisis which weakened his political position for the rest of the reign.

In Scotland Edward had acted as arbitrator between the claimants to the throne (the Great Cause of 1291–2) on the understanding that he be accepted as feudal overlord of the King of Scots. Edward's demand brought in its tow bitter dissension between the English and the Scots: the Scottish Wars of Independence. The throne of Scotland was adjudged to John Balliol, rather than his chief rival, Robert Bruce. But Edward's attempts to exercise his overlordship soon caused rebellion and, even more significantly for the future, a Franco-Scottish treaty.

The campaign of 1296 against the rebellious in Scotland was intended to be as decisive as the subjugation of Wales: Berwick was sacked, the defeated were compelled to do homage, the Stone of Destiny was removed from Scone to Westminster Abbey, and the government of Scotland was entrusted to Englishmen. But, in fact, this was the beginning, not the end, of the struggle. A popular rising in 1297 was led by William Wallace who defeated the English at Stirling Bridge; but an English triumph followed at Falkirk in 1298. A period of successful English pressure then culminated in a political settlement and the brutal execution of Wallace in London in 1305. Once again, however, a revolt was the result, this time led by Robert Bruce, who was crowned King of Scots in 1306. Edward resolved to fight again but died in the effort, at Burgh-on-Sands near Carlisle in July 1307. On his plain tomb in Westminster Abbey he was later described as the 'hammer of the Scots'. In truth, the Scottish wars had robbed him of political success during his last years. Even so, there is no doubting the prestige which he brought to the English monarchy, a prestige which in some ways at least reflected his physical prowess: when his tomb was opened in 1774 (Cat. 382–3), the body measured 6 ft 2 in.

Edward's reign saw the extension of Court patronage associated with his father's works at Westminster in the abbey and the palace, so that we can speak of a Court style as exemplified in wall paintings (e.g. Cat. 330–9) and manuscripts (e.g. Cat. 351, 357–8). As with his father, his patronage reflected his idea of the role and status of the monarchy. His presence both in Wales and in the north of England affected local architecture and art as he brought architects and craftsmen with him. This can be clearly seen in stained glass and manuscripts at York (Cat. 4–5, 10). In Wales his castles are unrivalled in Latin Christendom as works of military engineering. His other building projects such as the Eleanor crosses (Cat. 368–79), the tombs in Westminster Abbey (Cat. 326) and his chapel of St Stephen in the palace at Westminster (Cat. 324–5) display a new kind of ornamental Gothic, more exotic and inventive than its equivalents on the Continent.

321 Lincoln Cathedral, Angel Choir, looking north-east

Begun 1256, consecrated 1280
Photograph

The Angel Choir at Lincoln, named after the carved angels in the spandrels of the gallery, was founded in 1256 to provide a large space for the expanded liturgy of the thirteenth century and for the shrine of St Hugh of Avalon (bishop 1186–1200), which was moved from the north-east transept to an elevated position behind the high altar.

Although the Angel Choir shows the general influence of English thirteenth-century architecture and the more specific influence of Westminster, it is also rooted in the tradition of Lincoln itself. The tierceron vault, with five ribs at each springer, confirms the idea of the vault as a surface pattern rather than a structural member, which was adumbrated in St Hugh's Choir (1190s) and developed in the nave (c. 1200–40). The widely spaced main arcade is equally characteristic of Lincoln.

Typically English are the rectangular plan with flat east wall, the three-storey elevation with clerestory passage, and the vault corbelled in at arcade level. The highly decorated and coloured interior, using Purbeck marble, clustered piers with fillets, keels and shaft rings, and abundant foliage sculpture on capitals, corbels and window jambs, is an English tradition. Westminster Abbey inspired the window tracery (a double layer in the clerestory), the iconography of the south entrance door, and the idea of large-scale

321

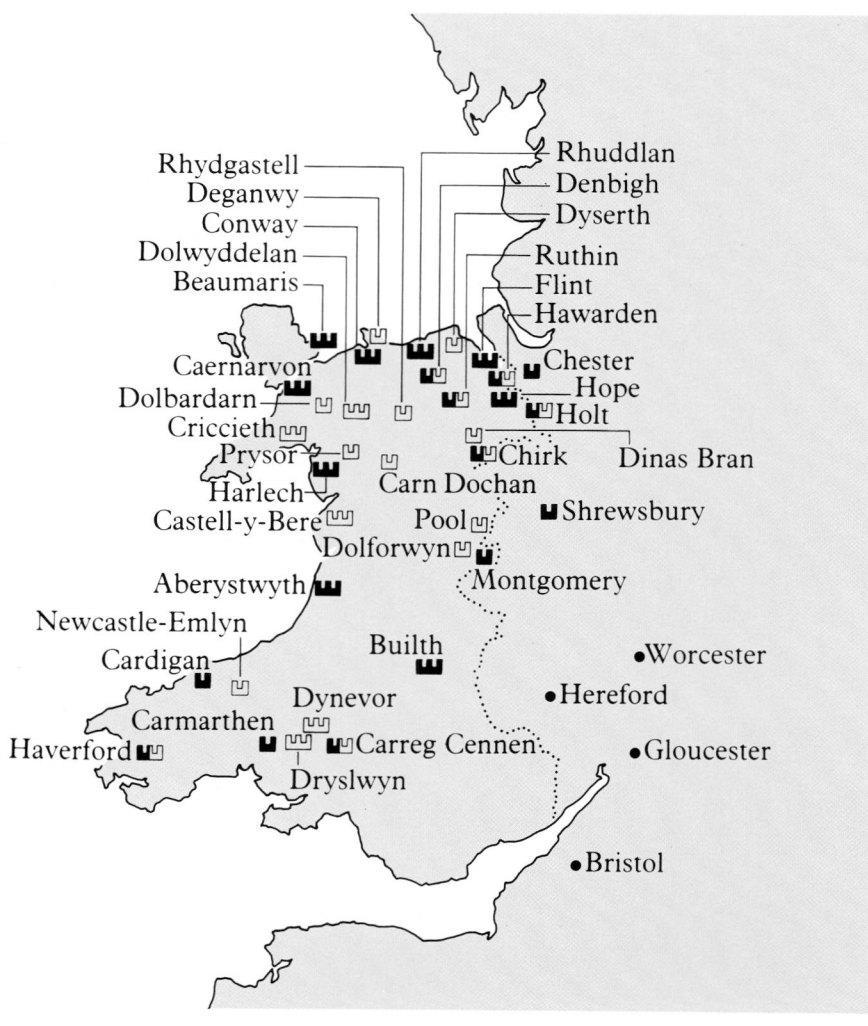

Rhydgastell
Deganwy
Conway
Dolwyddelan
Beaumaris
Caernarvon
Dolbardarn
Criccieth
Prysor
Harlech
Castell-y-Bere
Aberystwyth
Newcastle-Emlyn
Cardigan
Carmarthen
Haverford
Dryslwyn
Dynevor
Carreg Cennen
Builth
Dolforwyn
Pool
Carn Dochan
Chirk
Dinas Bran
Holt
Hope
Chester
Hawarden
Flint
Ruthin
Dyserth
Denbigh
Rhuddlan
Montgomery
Shrewsbury
Worcester
Hereford
Gloucester
Bristol

322

Castles built or wholly rebuilt by Edward I	Other Welsh Castles
Other Royal Castles	'Lordship' Castles built or rebuilt in the time of Edward I
Welsh Castles repaired by Edward I	

figure sculpture on interior surfaces. In the two eastern bays the spandrel angels, each with a musical instrument, represent a heavenly orchestra, while angels further west hold scrolls whose inscriptions are now indecipherable. Others form part of carved scenes symbolising judgement and salvation, the theme of the great south door.   NC

LIT. CPR Henry III, 1247–58, p. 506; Gardner 1952; Pevsner & Harris 1964, pp. 85–111; Brieger 1968, pp. 189–93; Stone 1972, pp. 130–3; Glenn 1986.

322   The castles of Edward I in North Wales

Edward I accomplished his conquest of Wales in three campaigns of 1277, 1282–3 and 1294. The Welsh territory was secured by ten new royal castles, several of which were built in conjunction with walled towns of English settlers. The castles are for the most part unusually well preserved and afford an unparalleled opportunity to study the design approach of a single medieval architect, the King's Master of Works James of St George, when confronted with a succession of widely different sites and defensive problems. Whereas the planning requirements of Gothic churches were circumscribed by a relatively stable liturgy and a series of powerful but gradually evolving conventions, military architecture was of necessity dynamic and idiosyncratic.

The two most impressive castles of the 1277 war, Flint and Rhuddlan, were strikingly contrasted essays in defensive planning; one a square with a massive cylindrical donjon at one corner, the other a rhombus with twin-towered gatehouse on the oblique

angles. The 1282–3 war instigated three of Europe's greatest castles; Harlech (Cat. 323), Conway and Caernarfon (fig. 33), each of which ingeniously exploited a well-chosen site. The building of Conway necessitated the displacement of a Cistercian monastery from its defensible rocky peninsula on the Conway estuary. Beaumaris, built on an unencumbered coastal plain after Madoc's revolt of 1294, perfected the now well-established principle of concentric defence but shows special cunning in the disposition of its various gates and passages and a new sequence of construction (the completion of the curtain wall before the raising of the towers) specially adapted to the defensive needs of a rising castle. Caernarfon, whose uncompleted northern curtain had been overrun by the Welsh in 1294, was Edward's seat of government (fig. 33). Its planning and decoration imitate the land walls of Constantinople (Caernarfon was once occupied by the legions of Constantine's father Magnus Maximus), endowing Edward's conquest with Roman imperial authority. Although Caernarfon's symbolism is particularly overt it must be recognised that all these castles were the signs as well as the means of political change, a consideration which must have contributed to their design.

Caernarfon and Beaumaris were still being completed in the early fourteenth century, but on other castles construction was remarkably swift: Rhuddlan for example took no more than five building seasons. The impressment of workmen from all over England was central to this kind of achievement, and is characteristic of the ruthlessly efficient conduct of the King's Works under Edward I.

JMM

LIT. Colvin 1963, I.

323   Harlech Castle, Gwynedd, from the south

1283–90
Photograph

Harlech is the most perfect of the castles built by Edward I to secure his conquest of Wales in the last quarter of the thirteenth century. Its architect was the King's Master of Works in Wales, James of St George, a Savoyard military engineer who at Harlech was granted the special honour of the constableship on the completion of the castle in July 1290. His design represents the high-water mark of thirteenth-century military architecture and possesses a clarity of plan, economy of means and an integration of functions which find analogies in the design of the French High Gothic cathedral. The site chosen was a rocky outcrop perched above the sea which provided a natural defence to the west and a ready source of supply by ship. There being no natural obstacle to the south and east, a great ditch similar to that at Beeston, Cheshire was hewn into the solid rock; one of several outstanding engineering achievements associated with Edward's Welsh wars. The castle is built on a classic concentric quadrangular plan with cylindrical corner towers, a strong, twin-towered gatehouse and a low outer curtain, in which respects it closely resembles the inner ward at Caerphilly Castle (Cat. 133), built in the previous decade. But the symmetry and precision of the plan at Harlech are more impressive. Most of the domestic offices, including the hall and chapel, were built around the wall of the inner courtyard but, as in most of the Edwardian castles, the great gatehouse accommodated its own set of apartments which provided safety and comfort when the castle was under attack. The whole layout was sufficiently compact to be held by a small garrison, a characteristic embodied in the design of James of St George's other castles at Flint (1277–86), Rhuddlan (1277–80) and Conway (1283–92). Since the Normans built the first castles in Britain late in the eleventh century there had been no more efficient instrument of conquest. JMM

LIT. Hughes 1913; Peers 1922; Colvin 1963, I, pp. 357–65.

323

324

324   St Stephen's Chapel, Westminster Palace, exterior elevation of part of south side by Frederick Mackenzie (1844)

1292–1348
Photograph

Edward I's rebuilding of St Stephen's was part of a general refurbishing of his principal palace which may have been undertaken in anticipation of his remarriage after Queen Eleanor's death. Its position, its two-storey format, its dimensions and its extreme richness all make clear that the aim was to rival the fifty-year-old Ste-Chapelle in the main royal palace in Paris. When construction was halted by financial crisis in 1297, the lower storey was finished and the upper completed to window sill level. The chequered fortunes of the first three Edwards are reflected clearly in the building history of St Stephen's, for the work was to be interrupted a further four times before the structure was completed in 1348. In the early 1320s it was decided to add a clearstorey and a wooden vault, features which must have made nonsense of elevations obviously intended to end with the emphatic horizontals immediately above the main windows. The vault and clearstorey were destroyed in 1692. There is substantial evidence to show that virtually everything of the upper chapel which survived until its demolition in the 1830s had been built in conformity to the original designs of 1292. As in most palace chapels, the upper storey was intended to be reserved for the royal family and their immediate

337

entourage, while the lower storey was open to the Court at large. Atrociously restored, the lower storey survives as the chapel of the House of Commons.

The windows and wall surfaces between the deeply projecting buttresses are treated virtually as if they were the internal elevations of the clearstorey and triforium of a French Rayonnant cathedral. But the exterior of St Stephen's was conceived in a very different spirit from any Rayonnant building. Far from being part of a lucid and perfectly integrated system, the tracery grid has become a means of concealing or at least playing down structural realities: there is no horizontal element marking the internal floor level and the mullions of the 'triforium' are continued down across the deeply-recessed lower chapel windows. At the same time the existence of these windows is stressed by the moulding framing each opening. It is a very sophisticated, not to say perverse cast of the mind which could relish this conflict between illusionism and structural honesty. Apart from the blind tracery on the Eleanor crosses (Cat.369), the lower windows are the first in England to incorporate ogees. Mackenzie's engraving shows the upper windows with conjecturally restored tracery and lights partly blocked by paintings on stone inserted c. 1351 (Cat. 680). CW

LIT. Mackenzie 1844, pp. 9–17, pl. 4; Harvey 1961 b, pp. 141–9; Colvin 1963, pp. 510–17, 523–5; Colvin 1966, pp. 42–3, 137–45; Wilson 1980 a, pp. 34–80.

325 St Stephen's Chapel, Westminster Palace, interior elevation of easternmost bay of north wall of upper chapel by Richard Dixon (c. 1800)

1292–1348
Pen and ink drawing: 94.5 × 60.3 cm
Society of Antiquaries of London

St Stephen's was designed by Michael of Canterbury, whose only previous royal commission was the Eleanor Cross in Cheapside, London (Cat. 375–6), so it can be no coincidence that the chapel incorporates the miniaturised architecture which the Eleanor crosses had been instrumental in transmitting to England from its original home on the portals of mid-thirteenth-century French Rayonnant cathedrals. The element of this so-called 'micro-architecture' which most clearly reveals its ancestry is the series of narrow upright panels of tracery on the canopies of the wall arcading under the windows, for these had appeared, combined with crocketed gablets, on the jambs of a considerable number of French portals and on the shaft of the Eleanor Cross at Hardingstone (fig. 48; Cat. 369). What was quite new about the main interior at St Stephen's was the extent to which micro-architecture

325

and its constituent elements were allowed to take over the elevations. The canopies of the wall arcading, the most complex and delicate arcading yet seen in Gothic architecture, were answered on the upper walls by enlargements of their panels and pierced tracery cresting (Cat. 680) and by tall, statue-sheltering canopies, the latter destroyed before any visual record was made. The essential prerequisite of this novel approach was the freeing of wall surfaces by the omission of vaulting, an omission unthinkable in thirteenth-century France. In fact the

only borrowing from full-scale Rayonnant architecture is the continuation of the shafts of the window mullions on to the wall behind the arcading.

The tracery grid on the outside of St Stephen's became the basis for Perpendicular architecture some forty years after 1292 (Cat. 386, 498), but the influence of the canopy-encrusted interior of the upper chapel was felt much sooner, notably the Lady chapels at St Albans (begun before 1308) and Ely (Cat. 491). In fact there is remarkably little in early fourteenth-century

English architecture that did not stem directly or indirectly from St Stephen's or from Michael of Canterbury's other works (Cat. 326, 327). CW

LIT. Topham 1795–1813.

326 Westminster Abbey, tomb of Edmund Crouchback, Earl of Lancaster

c. 1297
Photograph

This is the most ambitious canopy tomb of its date in Europe, made almost certainly on the orders of the earl's elder brother, Edward I, who is known to have paid for the funeral. The design has long been attributed to Michael of Canterbury, architect of Edward's important church building project, St Stephen's Chapel in Westminster Palace. During the century following the making of Queen Eleanor's tomb in 1293 by Richard Crundale, the royal tombs at Westminster seem to have been automatically commissioned from the leading royal architect of the day, the only exception being Queen

326

Philippa's tomb by Jean de Liège. The tripartite canopy, possibly derived from late thirteenth-century English prototypes, carries a prodigious array of forms drawn from very varied sources: Michael's earlier works, including Archbishop Pecham's tomb at Canterbury (the foliage bosses on the side gables); the architecture of the abbey itself (polychrome figures against diapered backgrounds); the retable of the adjacent high altar (the doubling of the side gables). Like many of the most important early fourteenth-century English tombs, this is an

innovatory and influential piece of architecture in its own right and not merely a decorative application of ideas borrowed from full-scale architecture. Enough of the original polychromy has survived to show that the original brilliance of the tomb must have rivalled the pages of the De Lisle Psalter (Cat. 569). CW

LIT. Wilson 1980a, pp. 83–4.

327 St Augustine's Abbey, Canterbury, gatehouse looking north-east

Completed c. 1308
Photograph

A royal licence to crenellate granted in 1308 is the only firm dating evidence for this most richly treated gatehouse of its date in Europe and prototype of a kind of late-medieval gate familiar from Cambridge colleges and Tudor palaces. Ambitious thirteenth-century English gateways generally had a gabled upper storey but no turrets.

The attribution of the St Augustine's gate to Michael of Canterbury, the most import-

327

ant and influential English architect of his day, rests on many detailed correspondences with his main documented work, St Stephen's Chapel in Westminster Palace (Cat. 324–5), and also on the fact that the gate is the earliest application on a single façade of the distinctive principle of design invented by Michael at St Stephen's, namely the use of highly contrasted modes. Thus the entrance has sturdy arches profiled like the ribs in the lower chapel at St Stephen's and similarly expressive of their supporting role; the upper storey has statue niches with

overhanging canopies comparable to those of the wall arcade at Westminster; and the free-standing parts of the turrets are covered by elongated tracery panels derived from those on the exterior of St Stephen's. The angle turrets themselves, which were no doubt meant to impart a military air, were based on the turrets at all four corners of St Stephen's. The doors decorated with tracery patterns in Michael of Canterbury's style (renewed to the original pattern) are an extreme instance of the architectural treatment of ancillary features whose design would normally have been left to the specialist craftsmen involved.

The first mention of Michael of Canterbury dates from 1275, when he was master mason to Canterbury Cathedral Priory, the great rival of St Augustine's. The building period of the chapter house and choir enclosure there must have overlapped with that of the gatehouse. CW

LIT. Wilson 1980a, pp. 97–100; Harvey 1984, pp. 45–6.

328 Wells Cathedral, chapter house looking north-east from entrance

c. 1293–1302
Photograph

The centrally-planned chapter house is one of the distinctive glories of English medieval architecture, although there are some fourteenth-century German and Spanish examples which look like adaptations of English designs to square and rectangular plans. Following the earlier octagonal chapter houses at Beverley and Westminster, Wells incorporates an undercroft serving as a treasury. The emphasis on vaulting rather than windows marks a reversion to the early thirteenth-century Margam–Lincoln type and a rejection of the tall, window-dominated scheme of Westminster and Salis-

328

bury. The profusion of tierceron ribs and the wonderful palm-branch effect which they create are clearly modelled on the presbytery of Exeter Cathedral (begun 1288), whereas the discreet use of ogees in the tracery betrays the designer's awareness of St Stephen's Chapel, Westminster (Cat. 324). The ball-flower decoration encrusting the window embrasures anticipates the over-use of this motif in the early fourteenth-century parts of Gloucester and Hereford cathedrals.   CW

LIT. Morris 1972, pp. 114–16; Draper 1981, pp. 18–20; Harvey 1982b, pp. 66–73.

329   The Westminster Retable

c. 1270–80
Oil and tempera over gesso, on oak; frame inlaid
   with numerous imitation enamel plaques,
   a cameo and gemstones, and decorative glass;
   thirteen compartments for figurative paintings,
   eight of which wholly, and one mostly, erased:
   h. 95.8 cm, w. 333.5 cm
Photograph

The outstanding Westminster Retable is the sole example of panel painting from the thirteenth-century Anglo-French Court milieu. It survived the seventeenth and eighteenth centuries as part of the container for Westminster Abbey's royal funeral effigies, although its right-hand paintings were destroyed *c.* 1780. The construction and appearance indicate that it was an altarpiece; its comparatively large size implies a location on the abbey's high altar. The St Faith mural in the abbey (Cat. 556) depicts a retable with similar eight-pointed medallions.

The iconography is curious. St Peter, the patron saint of Westminster Abbey, adorns the left-hand tabernacle and points across to four medallions enclosing scenes from the Ministry of Christ: the Raising of Jairus's Daughter, the Healing of the Blind Man and the Feeding of the Five Thousand are all that remain. At the centre stands Christ, blessing and holding a small globe filled with life, accompanied by the Virgin Mary and St John holding palms. The other paintings have perished, but probably comprised further Gospel scenes, and St Paul.

The Retable's date remains an open question. Its superb and affected paintings are essentially similar to Westminster products such as the Douce Apocalypse (Cat. 351) of *c.* 1270, and some murals once in the Painted Chamber (see Cat. 330–9) probably of the 1260s. The soft lustre of the paintwork and the convoluted hairstyles are also related to the courtly Alphonso Psalter (Cat. 357) of *c.* 1284. The Retable marks a major development in styles which culminated in the 1290s with the French *style Honoré* (Cat. 356) and in England with some work in the Bible of Bishop Bek (Cat. 360). Although the Retable is indubitably English, its exquisite micro-architectural enclosures and applied decorations are in a mid-thirteenth-century

329 (detail)

329 (detail)

French idiom consonant with the interior adornments of the Paris Ste-Chapelle of the 1240s.

The panel is in an extremely fragile state and accordingly has not been removed to the Royal Academy for exhibition. PB

PROV. First recorded in Islip's Chapel, Westminster Abbey c. 1725; framed by Edward Blore, 1827.

LIT. Wormald 1949, pp. 166–74; Tristram 1950, pp. 127–48; Binski 1986, pp. 49–69; Macek 1986; Binski 1987.

330–9   Copies of murals formerly in the Painted Chamber in the medieval Palace of Westminster

The Painted Chamber was one of the principal apartments of the Palace of Westminster. It stood near the River Thames close to St Stephen's Chapel, which was also decorated with important fourteenth-century murals (Cat. 680–1). In 1819 the great series of wall paintings that gave the room its name was uncovered, and copied by Charles Stothard and Edward Crocker. This was fortunate because although much of the scheme had already perished (only twenty-four items were copied), what remained provided the most important evidence for the decoration of a king's chamber in the thirteenth century. The murals were destroyed in the fire which consumed most of the palace in 1834, and no fragments survived. Stothard and Crocker worked independently of one another, but their copies are mostly in agreement. Crocker's palette is richer than

Stothard's more insipid colouration, but Stothard was the superior draughtsman.

The fabric of the Painted Chamber was mostly twelfth-century in date, with alterations by Henry III. Under Henry the room was used as a bedroom and audience chamber, but in the fourteenth century it was used as one of the first meeting-places of Parliament. The copied murals fell into two groups. The first, consisting of a large representation (1.73 m high by 3.23 m wide) of the coronation of Edward the Confessor together with paintings of St Edward giving a ring to St John and a series of Virtues and Vices on the window splays of the room (Cat. 330–2), was in all probability executed in the last years of the reign of Henry III, after a fire in the room in 1263. The paintings were orientated around the king's state bed in the chamber, and attest to Henry III's love of Edward the Confessor's virtuous kingship. The copies indicate a close resemblance between this group and the illustrations in the Douce Apocalypse (Cat. 351) made for Edward I or Eleanor of Castile before 1272. The figures, colouration, decorative motifs and architectural details of the coronation mural especially seem also to have corresponded to those on the Westminster Retable (Cat. 329). This suggests that elements in the style of this important but undated panel painting had already appeared before c. 1270, even if the Retable may itself be slightly later in date.

The second group (Cat. 333–7) comprised an extensive series of Old Testament stories arranged around the room in registers, with bands of French inscription between. Although traditionally assigned to the time

of Henry III, these were almost certainly executed for Edward I between 1292 and 1297 at the same time as the first campaign on the new St Stephen's Chapel. The architectural details in the paintings correspond to works of the years towards 1300, such as the Crouchback tomb in Westminster Abbey (Cat. 326), and the compositional formats already indicate the taste for architectural fantasy typical of the fourteenth century. The surviving imagery was unusual: a large cycle of paintings about Judas Maccabeus, doubtless chosen because of his association with heroic Arthurian exploits much favoured at Edward's Court, was set above paintings concerning good and bad kings, and prophets, illustrating passages from II *Kings*, *Judges* and II *Maccabees*. This combination of military events and moralising stories is unparalleled in contemporary secular decoration and was, so far as we know, without precedent in England. However, its emphasis on Judas Maccabeus anticipated later themes of interior decoration such as the Nine Worthies (who included Judas Maccabeus and King Arthur).

The comparatively plentiful documents for the execution and repair of the murals show that the master painter in charge of both groups of murals was Walter of Durham, whose activity can be traced from c. 1265 to 1300. Walter also worked in Westminster Abbey, and this connection should explain the general similarity in character between the palace murals and those of c. 1300 in the abbey church (Cat. 556). A document mentioning the repair of the Painted Chamber murals for the coronation of Edward II in 1308 is included in the exhibition (Cat. 444).
PB

330   The coronation of St Edward

C. A. Stothard, 1819
Watercolour with raised gilt detail: h. 18.3 cm,
w. 33 cm
Society of Antiquaries of London

This mural was originally at the head of Henry III's bed, and is probably to be identified with the paintings around the bed that were paid for in 1267. Stothard's copy should be compared with that by Crocker (Cat. 338). The iconography, with St Edward at the centre being crowned, and two archbishops and other ecclesiastics to either side, is similar to that of coronation scenes in the *Flores Historiarum* manuscripts such as that in Manchester (Cat. 346), which was associated with the abbeys of St Albans and Westminster. The main example of St Edward iconography under Henry III is the illustrated Life of the Saint dedicated to Eleanor of Provence (Cat. 39); this and the Douce Apocalypse (Cat. 351) closely resemble the style of the mural as copied. The bird-headed sceptre in Edward's hand is of the same type as that found in the tomb of Edward I (Cat. 382–3). PB

T. A. Stothard del.

The Coronation of Edward the Confessor.

Vetusta Mon. Vol. VI. pl. xxxvii.

330

C. A. Stothard del.

The Triumph of Debonerete or Meekness over Anger.

Vetusta Mon. Vol. VI. pl. xxxix.

331   332

331–2   The Virtues *Largesce* and *Debonereté*

C. A. Stothard, 1819
Watercolour with raised gilt detail: 331 h. 37 cm, w. 12.8 cm; 332 h. 37 cm, w. 12.6 cm
Society of Antiquaries of London

These faced each other on the splays of a window opposite the royal bed, and were probably contemporary with the coronation mural. The Virtues were shown being crowned from on high by angels, a motif resembling an illustration in Peraldus's *Summa* of Vice (Cat. 150). *Largesce* (Generosity) tramples on *Covoitise* (Covetousness); she is armed, and sticks a spear into the Vice, while also emptying coins into its mouth from a long purse. The block border contains the arms of England and the Empire (or of Richard, Earl of Cornwall [d. 1272], Henry's brother and King of the Romans). *Debonereté* (Tranquillity) stands on *Ira* (Anger) and holds a switch over the Vice. She wears a swan badge signifying patience, and holds a shield with the arms of England differenced by two bars; in the border are the arms of England and the royal saints Edward and Edmund (also the names of Henry's two elder sons).

PB

333   The warfare of Judas Maccabeus

C. A. Stothard, 1819
Watercolour with raised gilt detail: h. 14.8 cm, w. 42.1 cm
Society of Antiquaries of London

This illustration formed part of the extensive selection of scenes from 1 *Maccabees* added to the Painted Chamber by Edward I in the 1290s. Judas is seen in conflict with Nicanor (1 *Maccabees*, VII). The narrative is punctuated by small buildings, and the brilliant display of arms and heraldry may be compared with courtly illustrations of warfare such as those in the Cambridge Life of St Edward (Cat. 39), the contemporary Bodleian Roll (Cat. 10), and the *Roman de toute chevalerie* (Cat. 361). Edward I was compared to Judas Maccabeus, and the Maccabean Wars are invoked in the epitaph of the Westminster tomb of another warlike king, Edward III. Compare Crocker's version (Cat. 339).

PB

334   The miracles of Elisha

C. A. Stothard, 1819
Watercolour with raised gilt detail: h. 15 cm, w. 32 cm
Society of Antiquaries of London

Typical of the Westminster milieu is the use of stage sets, compared by Bony (1979, p. 22) to the temporary tribunes set up for the Court for tournaments or other ceremonies. The endless variation of architectural compositions is an English interpretation of somewhat less inventive French Rayonnant

333

334

micro-architectural forms. The iconography is based on II *Kings*, V, and tells how Elisha fed the hungry and cured Namaan (shown naked and crowned in the River Jordan) of his leprosy.   PB

335 The story of Abimelech

C. A. Stothard, 1819
Watercolour with raised gilt detail: h. 14.7 cm,
   w. 35.5 cm
Society of Antiquaries of London

Abimelech was one of the more unpleasant kings in the Book of Judges, and is shown here slaughtering his brothers and later receiving his just deserts when a woman dropped a millstone on his head, fatally wounding him. The *coup de grâce* is administered by his squire (*Judges*, IX). Abimelech was a type for Antichrist, and is shown with a surcoat semé with goat's heads, an emblem of immorality. According to the *Flores Historiarum*, Edward I was reminded of this story when he went unarmed too near the walls of Stirling during a siege in 1304. The iconography occurs in the earlier Parisian Maciejowski Bible, which also concentrates on military events in the Old Testament; it reappears in the Queen Mary Psalter.   PB

336 Antiochus and the Maccabean martyrs

C. A. Stothard, 1819
Watercolour with raised gilt detail: h. 14.7 cm,
   w. 38.2 cm
Society of Antiquaries of London

Drawn from II *Maccabees*, VII, this picture relates how the haughty tyrant King Antiochus disposed of the Maccabean brethren by torture. Placed near the bottom of the south wall of the Painted Chamber, this mural depicts one of Judas Maccabeus's chief antagonists.   PB

335

336

337 The story of Joab and Abner

C. A. Stothard, 1819

Watercolour with raised gilt detail: h. 14.7 cm,
w. 17.4 cm

Society of Antiquaries of London

The illustration is based on II *Samuel*, III. Joab is seen in conference with King David; the next incident, to judge from its outline, depicted Joab murdering Abner. This rare scene is matched in the episodes about King David in the Parisian Maciejowski Bible and in the Queen Mary Psalter. Its presence in the cycle implies the original inclusion of events about King Saul, another bad king, although no such illustrations remained in 1819.   PB

PROV. (330–7) Executed for the Society of Antiquaries by C. A. Stothard, 1819; thereafter in the Society's possession.

LIT. (330–7) Rokewode 1885; Wormald 1949; Tudor-Craig 1957; Binski 1986.

338 The coronation of St Edward

Edward Crocker, 1819

Watercolour with raised gilt detail: h. 22 cm,
w. 41.1 cm

The Visitors of the Ashmolean Museum, Oxford

Compare with Cat. 330.   PB

339 The warfare of Judas Maccabeus

Watercolour with raised gilt detail: h. 19.7 cm,
w. 64.2 cm

The Visitors of the Ashmolean Museum, Oxford

Compare with Cat. 333.   PB

PROV. (338–9) Executed 1819 by Edward Crocker II (c. 1757–1836), Clerk of the Works at Westminster 1818–29, with encouragement of Sir Gregory Osborne Page Turner (1785–1843); Douce bequest, 1834; formerly in the Bodleian Library.

LIT. (338–9) Wormald 1949; Tudor-Craig 1957; Binski 1986.

340 Seated Christ

c. 1260–90

Stone: h. 69.6 cm, w. 43.3 cm, d. 29.2 cm

English Heritage, Rievaulx Abbey, 81065601

This figure, found on the site of the abbot's house of Rievaulx Abbey, shows little sign of surface decay from weathering, suggesting that it occupied an interior or otherwise sheltered setting. The crisply-cut drapery, hanging vertically or falling in repeated V-folds, is in the tradition of the sculpture of the Judgement Porch at Lincoln (Stone 1955, pl. 98) but represents a more advanced stage in

340

337

338

339

the evolution of the style, anticipating in some respects the style of the Madonna and Child at the entrance to the chapter house of York Minster (Stone 1955, pl. 116[A]).

An inventory compiled for the Earl of Rutland, who acquired the site at the Dissolution, shows that a portion of the abbot's house had been set aside as a storage area for images removed from the church (Coppack 1986). Among the items listed in connection with this part of the building was a carved portal which could not have been the existing doorway to the abbot's house as the latter was mentioned separately. The size, subject and format of the Rievaulx Christ would suit a tympanum above a doorway and, in view of its place of discovery, the figure may well have come from the portal mentioned in the inventory. It is unlikely that a portal of this type and date would have formed part of the structure of the abbot's house, which was an early sixteenth-century remodelling of the twelfth-century infirmary hall, and it is more probable that the doorway had been removed from another part of the abbey and left in the abbot's house for storage.   ND

PROV. Rievaulx Abbey, North Yorks.; discovered Jan. 1931 on site of infirmary/abbot's house; no. 380 in list of finds compiled during clearance carried out by HM Office of Works.

LIT. Gardner 1951, p. 174, repr. fig. 332; Coppack 1986, pp. 109, 123.

341–2   Two censing angels

1270–80

Limestone: 341 h. 50 cm, max. w. 55 cm;
    342 h. 56 cm, max. w. 48 cm

Rector, Churchwardens and Parochial Church Council, All Saints, Sawley, Derbyshire, on loan to the Victoria and Albert Museum

These two angels originally formed part of a canopied tomb (dismantled in 1838) in the parish church of All Saints, Sawley. Seven other fragments also survived from the canopy: four portions of mouldings, the bottom half of a third censing angel and a

341

fourth complete angel, now restored from two large pieces (only the top half had been discovered when the fragments were first published by Sekules in 1981). It is of interest to note that while the angels are carved from limestone, the mouldings are sandstone (both from local outcrops; analysis by R. W. Sanderson, Institute of Geological Science). There are considerable remains of paint. A fine effigy of a priest still remaining in the north aisle of the church is in all probability from this tomb also, and has tentatively been identified as Ralph de Chaddesdon, Treasurer of Lichfield, Archdeacon of Coventry and Chancellor of the diocese; he probably died c.1275–6. Although this identification cannot be established with certainty the style of the sculptures tallies with a date in the 1270s.

These exquisitely carved angels must be contemporary with the spandrel figures of angels in the Angel Choir, Lincoln Cathedral (Gardner 1952; see also Cat. 321), and there is indeed the likelihood that they were executed by carvers associated with work there: the soft fall of the draperies and the beautifully studied faces are common features of both. Ultimately derived from the French-inspired censing angels in the transepts of Westminster Abbey of the early 1250s, they are works of the highest standard. To gauge their quality they may be compared with the censing angels from the spandrels of a canopy tomb at Gosberton

342

(Lincs), about twenty years later (Gardner 1951, fig. 344): the latter are rather lifeless and have none of the refinement of the Sawley angels. PW

PROV. Parish church of All Saints, Sawley, Derbyshire; on loan to the V&A, from 1980.

LIT. Sekules 1981; Williamson (forthcoming). nos 5–6.

343 Pendant

1280–95
York stone, painted and gilded: h. 14.8 cm, diam. of top 15 cm
The Board of Trustees of the Victoria and Albert Museum, London, A. 102–1916

The pendant has been broken into three pieces and repaired, but still retains its original polychromy, as evidenced by comparison with the unrestored capitals of the chapter house vestibule at York Minster. It would have been completed with a small decorated boss on its underside, which has been broken off.

This pendant once formed part of the decoration of one of the canopies above the stalls running around the walls of the chapter house at York Minster. These were heavily restored in 1845, and the present pendant had passed to the collections of the Royal Architectural Museum by 1877. As most of the remaining pendants and small capitals of the canopies were stripped or re-carved in 1845, this pendant is valuable evidence for the original colour scheme of the sculptures within the chapter house. The decoration of the chapter house at York cannot be securely dated (see also Cat. 344), although it was certainly finished by c. 1295 (see Coldstream 1972; Bassham & Gee 1974; Gee in Aylmer & Cant 1977, pp. 136–41; Pevsner & Metcalf 1985 b, p. 341). Its undoubted relationship with the decoration of the smaller chapter house at Southwell, of around 1290–1300 (Pevsner 1945), gives a probable date bracket of 1280–95.

With the sculptural decoration at Southwell, the capitals and pendants of the York chapter house represent the best examples of naturalistic carving of the Gothic period in England. This pendant is carved with precisely-studied maple leaves, but in the chapter house itself there are numerous other types of leaf carving, all identifiable in nature; the same variety is found at Southwell. PW

PROV. Chapter house, York Minster, until 1845; Royal Architectural Museum, Westminster; transferred to the V&A, 1916.

LIT. *Review* 1916, p. 5, fig. 3; Stone 1972, p. 256, n. 77; Williamson (forthcoming), no. 12.

344 Synagogue

c. 1290
Oil or tempera on 17 oak planks; prominent medieval nail heads show position of wooden vault rib behind: h. 283 cm, w. at top 130 cm, w. at bottom 75 cm
The Dean and Chapter of York.

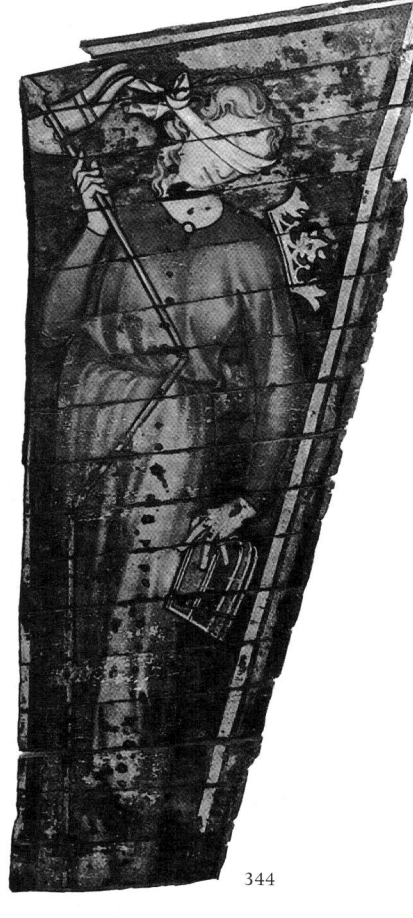

344

343

Synagogue is one of three surviving paintings from the medieval wooden vault of the chapter house of York Minster (the others being St Edmund and an archbishop, probably St William of York). The panels were taken down in 1798. Around 1690 James Torre identified the contents of forty of the forty-eight painted webs, some figural, some

345

345   The Newport chest

Late thirteenth century
Oak: h. 81.8 cm, w. 166 cm, d. 69 cm
The Vicar and Churchwardens of St Mary's,
Newport, Essex

The Newport chest with its painted lid is an intricate example of Victorian craftsmanship in the service of a frail medieval object. In the nineteenth century it was fitted with a lining of greater substance than the original timbers, and the single great plank which formed the lid was undergirded by an inner framework with four partitions between the paintings. This nineteenth-century frame for the lid presumably replaces something similar, if perhaps slighter. Indeed, the hinged member could be original. The locks were probably altered in the fifteenth century and the internal partitions at the same time, but the drop handles, of which there is another in the middle of the back, and the horizontal iron straps, are of the first construction. The decorative friezes across the front, including the lead lozenges, are reproduced from an original motif, now in the Victoria and Albert Museum (Department of Metalwork, 74737. 1860). The lead-pierced frieze incorporates a naturalistic leaf, and naturalistic leaves are painted on the mounds beneath the figures. A frieze of shields and recessed geometric shapes appears on the chest at St John's, Glastonbury, and also on the Lillebon panel, dated to c.1310–20, at Winchester Cathedral (the most comparable surviving painted lid of a chest). The chest formerly in the Chancery Court at Durham and possibly associated with Richard de Bury, Bishop of Durham 1336–45, also has a painted lid, though in that case the paintings are heraldic with grotesques. Penelope Eames considers the Newport chest to be an altar chest, and gives Burgundian and French parallels of 1388 and 1426.

The iconography – a crucifix flanked by Mary and John with Peter bearing his keys and Paul with his sword – is unexceptional. The quality both of woodwork and painting is high, so there is no reason to advance the date much beyond that of works like the Westminster Retable. Another parallel is the Oscott Psalter (Cat. 352), circumstantially dated to 1265–8. Compare also the Ulvik frontal in Bergen (fig. 101), or the Clare Chasuble of before 1284 in the Victoria and Albert Museum.   PT-C & JG

PROV. Presumably always at Newport, where there are other striking pieces of medieval woodwork: stalls, lectern (restored in 1837) and font cover.

LIT. (chest) Rose 1929, pp. 58, 65; Johnson 1907 b, p. 254; RCHM, Esesex, I, 1916, p. 200, repr.; Eames 1977, p. 134, pls 64b, 65; (lid) London 1923, no. 10, pl. VI; Borenius & Tristram 1927, p. 12, pl. 25; Rickert 1954, p. 163 no. 78.

---

decorative. Synagogue was paired with Ecclesia; other images included St Peter and St Paul, John the Baptist and Moses, saints, angels and mermen. Synagogue is blindfolded, and holds a broken flagstaff and the Tablets of the Law. She lacks the knotted waistband of the sculpted Synagogue figures on portals at Lincoln Cathedral and Crowland Abbey, but unusually, as at Lincoln and Crowland, she stood to Ecclesia's right. The medieval central boss of the vault comprises an *Agnus Dei*, complementing Ecclesia's covered chalice described by Torre. Ecclesia and Synagogue also figure in the glass of the chapter house vestibule, c. 1285–95.

The paintings were probably executed at the same time as the vault itself. The exact date of the completion of the fabric of the chapter house is not known; but as it was evidently in use by 1295–6, a date for the vault in the 1280s or c. 1290 is probable. The style of the paintings cannot be matched closely in monumental English work of the period, appearing to be rather closer to north French painting of the 1280s. This would be in keeping with the increasingly French orientation of the building works at York in the late 1280s and 1290s.   PB

PROV. York Minster, former chapter house vault.

LIT. Drake 1736, pp. 476–7; Browne 1847, p. 102; Aylmer & Cant 1977; Binski 1986, p. 81, pl. lxv.

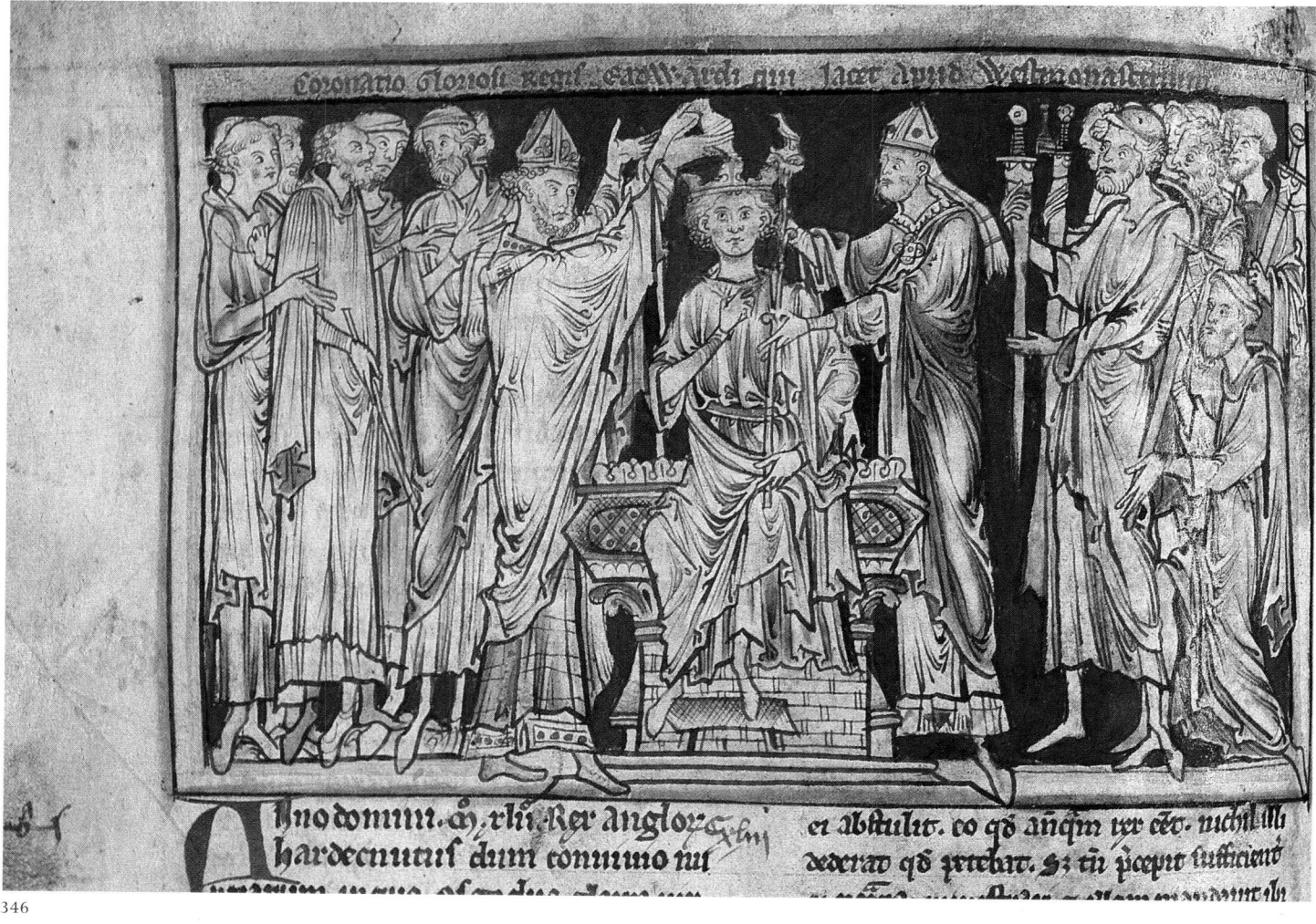

346

346 Matthew Paris, *Flores Historiarum*

Westminster and St Albans, *c*.1250–2 and later
Vellum, ff. 298: 24.8 × 19 cm
Feoffees of Chetham's Hospital and Library,
 Manchester, MS 6712

The *Flores Historiarum* is an abbreviated chronicle from the Creation to 1249 with continuations up to 1327. The part of the text from 1241 to 1249 is written by the hand of Matthew Paris (Cat. 315, 437), but the earlier part of the book, with illustrations of the coronations of the English kings from Arthur to John, is neither written nor illustrated by him. The text has interpolations referring to Westminster Abbey, and there is no doubt that the copy was specifically designed for that place, in whose ownership it definitely was from *c*.1265. The tinted drawings by various hands have parallels with the Westminster Psalter drawings (Cat. 9), and two other London works, the Life of St Edward (Cat. 39) and an Apocalypse (London, British Library, Add. MS 35166). The miniature of the coronation of St Edward resembles that formerly in the Painted Chamber (Cat. 330). It seems likely that the manuscript was begun at Westminster,

using a version of Matthew Paris's text which went up to 1240. It was then transferred to St Albans for the author to update the text with the section containing recent events 1241–9. Whatever the circumstances of its production were, the manuscript is if central to a consideration of artistic interrelationships between London and St Albans around 1250. A precise date of *c*.1251–2 has been argued (Vaughan 1958) for the completion of Matthew Paris's section of the text.   NJM

PROV. Benedictine Abbey of Westminster;
T. Gardener, 1503; given by Nicholas
Higginbottome, steward of manor of Stockport, to
Chetham's College in 1657.

LIT. Hollaender 1944, pp. 361–81; Vaughan
1958, pp. 92–103, 114–15, 152, 224–5;
Morgan 1987, no. 96. repr.

347 The Paris Apocalypse

Salisbury (?), *c*.1250–5
Vellum, ff. 50: 32 × 22.5 cm
Paris, Bibliothèque nationale, MS fr. 403

The format of illustration of many of the English Apocalypses is a rectangular framed illustration at the head of a two-column text. The abbreviated text of the Book of Revelation is either in Latin or, as in this example,

in Anglo-Norman French, and is usually accompanied by a commentary. This presents an interpretation of the visions of the Apocalypse as allegories of the struggles between good and evil, the presence of Antichrist in the world and the final triumph of Christ.

The Paris Apocalypse, like the Trinity Apocalypse (Cat. 349) is unusually large in size. Its ninety tinted drawings of the Life of St John and of the Apocalypse are related to those of two picture-book Apocalypses in the Bodleian Library (MS Auct. D.4.17) and the Pierpont Morgan Library (Cat. 348). All three derive from a common prototype which was probably in tinted drawing and made shortly before 1250, the earliest of the English illustrated Apocalypses. The Paris example may be the earliest to survive.

The use of Anglo-Norman French for the text, and the luxurious size and quality of this manuscript, suggests a rich lay patron, but there is no indication of the thirteenth-century ownership before its distinguished series of owners in the fourteenth and fifteenth centuries. Although in a different technique than their normal use of full illumination, the Apocalypse was probably produced by the Sarum Master's workshop.

347

A fully-painted initial at the beginning of the text is particularly close to the Sarum Master's style. (Cat. 108, 316). NJM

PROV. Charles V of France (1338–80); Charles VI of France (1368–1422); John, Duke of Bedford (1389–1435); Louise de Gruthuyse of Bruges (1422–92); Louis XII of France (1498–1515); French royal library; Bibliothèque nationale.

LIT. Delisle & Meyer 1900–1; Henderson 1967, pp. 104–14, Henderson 1968, pp. 110–13; Paris 1968, no. 123; Marks & Morgan 1981, pp. 58–61, pls 10–11; Otaka & Fukui 1981; Avril & Stirnemann 1987, no. 123, pls F, XLII; Morgan 1987, no. 103, repr.

348 The Morgan Apocalypse

London (?), c. 1255–60
Vellum, ff. 21: 27.2 × 19.5 cm
Pierpont Morgan Library, New York, M. 524

Some Apocalypses, like this example, are in the form of picture books with inscriptions and texts on scrolls held by the figures. Eighty-three illustrations in tinted drawing are set two to a page. At the end are two scenes of the Life of St John, which seem to be a fragment of a longer sequence now lost. The interpolated scenes of the life and miracles of Antichrist are not in the text of the Apocalypse. Antichrist is shown as a human figure, not as a beast as in some Apocalypses. The Witnesses come before him and are killed, and then he persecutes the people and performs miracles which are parodies of those of Christ, but is finally destroyed. For a contemporary reader he would be a type of the evil ruler.

The style of the artist is close to that of the first artist of the Life of St Edward the Confessor (Cat. 39). The iconographically related Apocalypses (Cat. 347 and Oxford, Bodleian MS Auct. D.4.17) are in the same tinted-drawing technique, but are by distinctly different artists probably working in different centres but having access to the same pictorial model. NJM

PROV. Vicomte Blin de Bourdon, 19th century; John Pierpont Morgan, whose coll. became nucleus of Pierpont Morgan Library, New York.

LIT. London 1930, no. 126; Baltimore 1949, no. 62; Freyhan 1955, pp. 218, 235–6, 241–2; Henderson 1967, pp. 105 ff., 131–7; Henderson 1968, pp. 109–13; Emmerson 1981, passim; Morgan 1987, no. 122, repr.

349 The Trinity Apocalypse

c. 1255–60
Vellum, ff. 32: 43 × 30.4 cm
The Master and Fellows, Trinity College, Cambridge, MS R.16.2

This fully-painted Apocalypse, by virtue of its size and rich colouring and gilding, is the most splendid example of the period. Eleven pages with scenes of the Life of St John are set

348

349

before and after the Apocalypse, which itself is illustrated with seventy-one framed pictures. These Apocalypse scenes are of varying size and set at various positions on the text page, an unusual alternative to the normal arrangement of placing the miniature at the head of a two-column text. The figures are set against rectangular panels alternately of red and blue. The painting is by four artists, two in a completely English tradition, and two showing influence from the new French style which made an impact on England from *c.* 1255 onward. The colouring shows an interest in modelling

drapery in light and shadow, even though linear elements persist in some of the work. The transition from the predominant linearism of the English Early Gothic to a more sculptural, painterly approach characterises the development of several artists in the third quarter of the thirteenth century. The artists of the Trinity Apocalypse are rather isolated, and it is uncertain where they were working. Two have some affinity with the Sarum Master's workshop but are not part of it.

In some of the miniatures such as the fight with the seven-headed beast, an aristocratic lady is given prominence. It has been sugges-

ted that in the Tree of Life the branches form an E, and that the lady may be Henry III's queen, Eleanor of Provence. Although it is plausible that such a sumptuous book would be appropriate for the queen, these arguments for her ownership are not strong. Several miniatures include figures of Franciscans, which suggest that the patron favoured that order. NJM

PROV. Anne Sadleir in note of 1649 commits book to Ralph Brownrigg, Bishop of Exeter (1592–1649) and instructs him to give it to Trinity College, Cambridge, where it arrived in 1660.

LIT. James 1909; London, 1930, no. 125; Henderson 1967, p. 117 ff.; Brieger 1967; Otaka & Fukui 1977; Marks & Morgan 1981, pp. 62–5, pls 12–13; Morgan 1987, no. 110, repr.

350 Apocalypse

London, c. 1270

Vellum, ff. 48: 26.5 × 18.2 cm

Paris, Bibliothèque nationale, MS lat. 10474

This is a companion book to the Douce Apocalypse (Cat. 351). Although smaller in format, it is undoubtedly by the same workshop, but very probably by a different artist as suggested by significant differences in the drawing of facial features. As in the Douce Apocalypse, its painting is unfinished with only the first few leaves being completed and the remaining illustrations left as drawings.

There is much controversy concerning the chronological relationship of the two Apocalypses. Unusual features in iconography or in

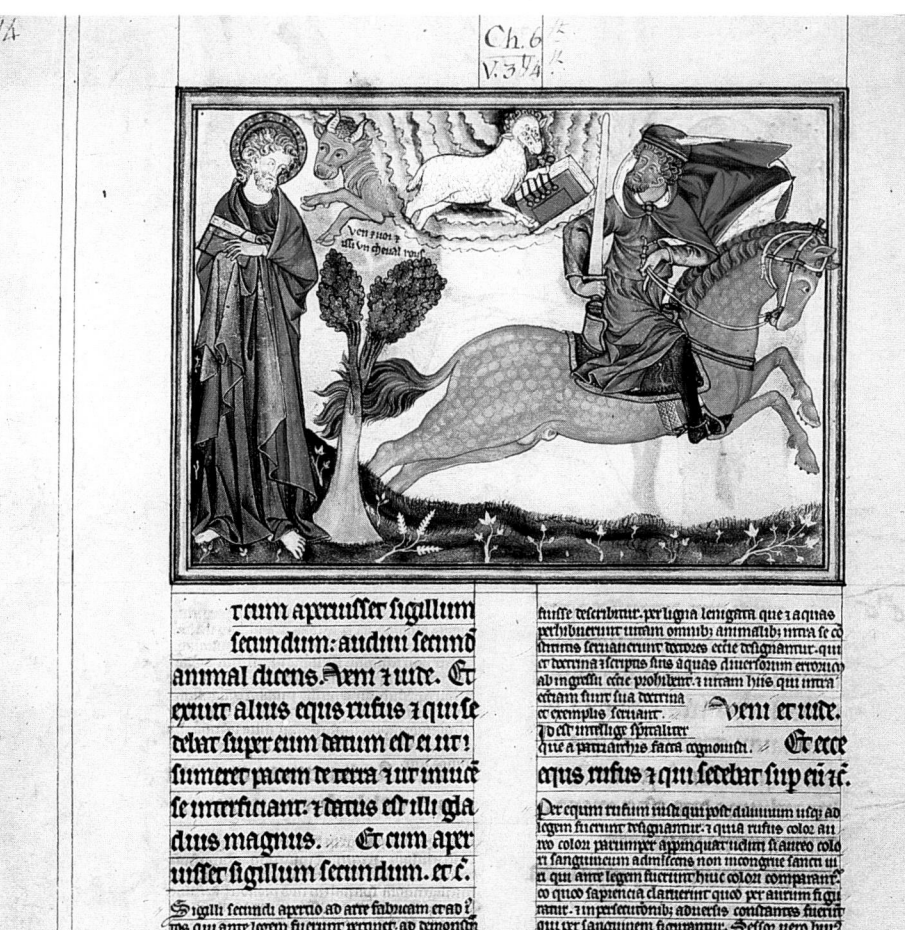

350

choice of scene can be paralleled in both, and it is possible that they derive from a common model now lost. The Paris Apocalypse has simpler compositions than Douce and it is extremely unlikely that these are derived from the more complex Douce versions. The use of colour in the two books is very different. The Paris manuscript has a less vivid palette and in some figures more developed painterly modelling. It is possible that the colouring was done at a later date than the drawings. This painting shows the softer, fluid modelled forms of painting of the 1270s and 1280s whose prime example, but in a different medium, is the Westminster Retable (Cat. 329). The ornamental decorative bands on the drapery have a remarkable resemblance to those on the borders of the garments of the figures on the Retable.   NJM

PROV. The Noalhes family, 17th century; Jesuit College of Lyon whose manuscripts passed to the Bibliothèque nationale, 1794.

LIT. Henderson 1970, *passim*; Klein 1983, *passim*; Binski 1986, pp. 50, 56–7; Avril & Stirnemann 1987, no. 146, pls F, LV, LVI; Morgan 1987, no. 154, repr.

351   The Douce Apocalypse

London, c. 1270

Vellum, ff. 63: 31.2 × 21.5 cm

Oxford, Bodleian Library, MS Douce 180

A French translation precedes an Apocalypse in Latin decorated with ninety-seven miniatures. The French section begins with a historiated initial containing kneeling figures of Prince Edward (later Edward I) and his wife Eleanor of Castile kneeling before the Trinity. This must give a date for the painting before 1272, when Edward became king. The book was probably begun shortly before

1270 when the prince and his wife went to the Holy Land, from which they did not return until 1274. The painting of the Apocalypse pictures was never completed, and several miniatures show illumination at various stages of completion.

The Apocalypse scenes are represented in an elegant courtly manner almost like a chivalric romance. The refined poses of the figures and delicate facial types are the English version of the French Court style of the closing years of the reign of St Louis (Louis IX). The early tendency towards this style is evident in the Life of St Edward the Confessor (Cat. 39). An interesting feature is the frequent inclusion of landscape settings with naturalistic foliage. A slightly later reflection of this style is in the English panel painting, the Westminster Retable (Cat. 329), and a precedent for the Douce Apocalypse style may be in the lost paintings of the Painted Chamber in the Palace of Westminster (Cat. 330–9). Like these works, the

351

Douce Apocalypse was produced by artists associated with the Palace and Abbey of Westminster.   NJM

PROV. Prince Edward (Edward I. 1272–1307) and his wife Eleanor of Castile (d. 1290); William Wilson, early 19th century; Francis Douce (1756–1834); passed to Bodleian Library at his death.

LIT. James 1922; Wormald 1949, pp. 170–3; Hassall & Hassall 1961; Henderson 1970, *passim*; *Apokalypse* 1982; Klein 1983; Binski 1986, *passim*, Morgan 1987, no. 153, repr.

352   The Oscott Psalter

c. 1265–70
Vellum, ff. 257: 30.2 × 19.6 cm
British Library, Add. MS 50000

The quantity of decoration in illuminated psalters varies considerably according to the commission. The Oscott Psalter is one of the most elaborately decorated. The calendar has the usual signs of the zodiac and Labours of the Months. Then follow twenty-two full-page miniatures of scenes of the Life of Christ, the Apostles, a Last Judgement, and King David harping. The complete text of the psalter, canticles, Litany, Psalter of the Virgin and Office of the Dead is elaborately decorated with historiated and ornamental initials, grotesques, border bars, line endings and penwork sprays in red and blue ink. Almost every element of illuminated decoration is present (see also fig. 8).

Some of the full-page miniatures have been lost, and in recent years one (now in the British Library, Add. MS 54215) was discovered at Ampleforth Abbey. It has a Tree of Jesse on one side and a seated mitred figure wearing a cope on the other. The mitred figure might be the portrait of the intended owner of the psalter. On the basis of some rare entries of south Italian saints in the calendar, and that the figure is not wearing normal episcopal insignia, it has been suggested that this person may be the papal legate Cardinal Ottobuono Fieschi, who at this time had only attained the order of deacon.

Several artists worked on the psalter, and some of them seem to originate in Oxford workshops. The work has been considered as of London, associated with the 'Court school', but these artists do not have any obvious contacts with that centre. It would be a better hypothesis to suggest it was made in Oxford.   NJM

PROV. Mary Airck, 17th century; Charles Blundell (?), 19th century; St Mary's College, Oscott; bt by C. W. Dyson Perrins, 1908; acq. by British Library after his death, 1958.

LIT. London 1908, no. 39; London 1930, no. 184; Turner 1969, pp. 10–19; Ottawa 1972, no. 22; Brussels 1973, no. 55; Marks & Morgan 1981, pp. 66–9, pls 14–15; Morgan 1987, no. 151, repr.

352

Two artists have worked on the miniatures, and as yet no other manuscripts have been attributed to their hands. The place of origin of the manuscript is problematic and no convincing attribution has been made. The date of production is equally controversial, and an early dating of *c.* 1260 has been suggested by some. The large figures suggest links with monumental painting in panels or on walls. There may be a third artist who has coloured part of the work, applying the paint thickly with a developed understanding of painterly modelling.   NJM

PROV. Holland family, late 14th century; Sir Thomas Holland, Duke of Surrey and 3rd Earl of Kent (?) (1374–1400); William Leeke, 16th century; Charles Baker, who gave it to St John's College, 1672, in memory of Francis Leeke, canon of Southwark.

LIT. London 1908, no. 48; London 1930, no. 183; Henderson 1968, pp. 145–7; Brussels 1973, no. 56; Morgan 1987, no. 179, repr.

354

354   Bible

Oxford (?), *c.* 1260–70

Vellum, ff. 349: 41.2 × 26.4 cm

The Master and fellows of Emmanuel College, Cambridge, MS 116(2.1.6)

Bibles in the thirteenth century are usually much smaller than twelfth-century examples, except in cases such as this were a lectern bible was required. The small copies, pocket bibles as they are called, were mainly for scholarly use, and their production is associated with university centres such as Oxford and Paris. Certain workshops of artists seem to have specialised in the decoration of this type of university book. This example is by the workshop of the Bible

353

De serpente decipiente adam et euam. Genij.

353   Prefatory miniatures to a psalter

c. 1270–80

Vellum, ff. 23: 27.8 × 17.5 cm

The Master and Fellows of St John's College Cambridge, MS K.26(231)

This series of miniatures of the Old and New Testaments ends with the figure of King David harping. Although they are now attached to a psalter of over a century later, the David picture is proof that they must originally have been designed for a psalter.

The forty full-sized pictures contain seventeen of Old Testament figures, and twenty-nine of the New Testament which include apocryphal scenes of the Life of the Virgin. These form a sort of collection of Bible stories; such cycles of pictures had been placed as a preface to the psalter since the twelfth century. They probably in many cases served an educational function. The psalter was used to teach children Latin by learning and construing passages from the Psalms. In a different way these narrative pictures could be used for didactic purposes.

of William of Devon (see Cat. 41, 355). The artists' origins are in French illumination, and some must have received their training in a workshop in Paris. Their work in England is partly by French and partly by English artists. As the psalters they produced have texts and other evidence associating them with the Midland region, and some of the bibles are linked with bibles produced in Oxford, it is possible that the workshop was centred on Oxford.

Almost every book of the Bible is given an historiated initial, and from some extend border bars with occasional grotesques. Parrots and figures with long-pointed caps are characteristic of the border decoration of this workshop. The figures are somewhat flatly painted with rather bland and unvaried facial types.   NJM

PROV. First listed in 1697 catalogue of manuscripts of Emmanuel College.

LIT. Bennett 1972, pp. 31ff., figs 5, 7, 10; Morgan 1987, no. 163, repr.

355   The Cuerden Psalter

Oxford (?), c. 1270
Vellum, ff. 241: 29.5 × 19.6 cm
Pierpont Morgan Library, New York, M.756

The patronage of illuminated devotional books was more extensive than that of any other type of book in the thirteenth and fourteenth centuries. In relatively few cases can the name or even social position of the patron be determined, particularly in the thirteenth century when the use of heraldry as a means of identification is still relatively rare. The Cuerden Psalter is an excellent example of the patronage of lay people, a husband and wife who kneel before the figure of the Virgin suckling the Child. Unfortunately there is no evidence, heraldic or otherwise, which identifies the two figures. The small historiated initials to the Psalms have further portraits of them (fig. 9). These initials also contain Dominicans, probably because this was the religious order favoured by the patrons.

There are eight full-page miniatures, seven being divided into six compartments, with scenes of the Life of Christ and a series of figures of saints. The saints include the rare St Fremund and possibly St Rumwald. Their relics were at Dunstable and Buckingham, and their cults were particularly centred on the Midland region. In addition to these miniatures the text pages of the psalter are elaborately decorated with figure initials for every Psalm, some illustrating the text, as well as the large initials for those of the liturgical divisions.

The artists are of the Bible of William of Devon workshop (see Cat. 41, 354). The Midlands associations of this psalter help in the evidence for possible location of the workshop in Oxford.   NJM

355

PROV. Peter Brooke of Astley, Lancs, 18th century; Towneley Parker family, 19th century; Reginald Arthur Tatton of Cuerden Hall; bt for Pierpont Morgan Library, 1929.

LIT. London 1930, no. 155; Watson 1970, pp. 34ff.; Ottawa 1972, no. 24; Morgan 1987, no. 162, repr.

356   Single leaf from Frère Laurent, *Somme le Roi*

Paris, c. 1300
Vellum: 17 × 12. cm
The Syndics of the Fitzwilliam Museum
   Cambridge, MS 368

The Parisian artist Maître Honoré and his workshop illuminated a Book of Hours for an English patron (Nuremberg, Stadtbibliothek, MS Solger 4.4°). The leaf exhibited is from another work by this artist, a moral treatise on the Commandments, the Creed and the virtues and vices by Frère Laurent, the confessor of Philip III of France. The complete manuscript is in London (British Library, Add. MS 54180), from which at some time in the past the two leaves now in the Fitzwilliam Museum (MSS 192, 368) were excised.

It has been suggested that Honoré's early style in the Nuremberg Hours may have had links with England. Works such as the Alfonso Psalter (Cat. 357) antedate the earliest work of Honoré and could have been influential in his development. Conversely, the art of Honoré could have been an ingre-

chaste. luxure.

Oloferne. Judith. Joseph q̃ fuit la fole dame.

356

dient in English (particularly London) style in the last fifteen years of the thirteenth century. The relaxed, swaying figures with cascading folds modelled in light and shade are features of Parisian and north French painting which are taken up by English artists in the closing years of the century. NJM

PROV. Given by Friends of the Fitzwilliam Museum, 1934.

LIT. Millar 1953, pp. 16, 40–1, pl. XII; Millar 1959, pp. 12–13; Cambridge 1966, no. 46; Turner 1968, pp. 53–65; Wormald & Giles 1982, pp. 369–70.

357 The Alphonso Psalter

c. 1284 and before 1316
Parchment, ff. 136: 24 × 14 cm
British Library, Add. MS 24686

Named after a son of Edward I, the Alphonso Psalter was most probably begun in 1284 in anticipation of the marriage of the eleven-year-old to Margaret, daughter of the Count of Holland, as we know from the juxtaposition of the arms of the heir apparant of England with those of Holland on the Beatus page (f. 11) of the manuscript. By the time of Alphonso's death, which occurred in the same year, before the marriage could take place, the text had been written and an elaborate programme of illustrations begun.

Only the first two gatherings (ff. 11–26v.) were executed according to the original plan. The first of these contains some of the most refined painting of the time of Edward I, subminiature in scale, subtle and nuanced in treatment of the surface, and convincing in representation of real or imaginary creatures.

The Beatus page with its appealing picture of the graceful young David is a superlative

example of the Court style, a term used for a group of manuscripts executed at or around the English Court at the end of the thirteenth century and in the first decade of the fourteenth. These include the Alphonso Psalter, the Ashridge Petrus Comestor (London, British Library, Royal MS 3 D VI), and the Mazarine Bible (Cat. 360). The style also characterises some important manuscripts not known to be connected with the royal family, in particular the Windmill Psalter (Cat. 358), the Mostyn Psalter (London, private collection), the opening pages of the Peterborough Psalter in Brussels (Cat. 567), and a psalter in Jesus College, Oxford (MS D. 40). LFS

PROV. Elizabeth de Bohun, daughter of Edward I, before 1316; Bohun family, 14th century;—Mannynge, d. 1584; Edward Graveley, 16th century; Archbishop Tenison; Sotheby's, 1 July 1861; Sotheby's, 27 May 1862, bt by British Museum.

LIT. Sandler 1986, no. I, II, pp. 13–14, repr. I, figs 1, 2, 4.

358 The Windmill Psalter

c. 1290
Parchment, ff. 167: 32 × 21.5 cm
Pierpont Morgan Library, New York, M. 102

The facing pages that open the text of the Windmill Psalter represent the height of the Court style at the close of the thirteenth century. The illustration of the Beatus initial (f. IV.) incorporates a Tree of Jesse, the Six Days of Creation, four animal-headed

357

style it is closest to the Mostyn Psalter (London, private collection); in fact, the compositions of the historiated initials for Psalms XXVI, LII and LXXX are nearly identical in both books. The calendar of the Mostyn Psalter points to London. LFS

PROV. H.H. Gibbs, 1st Baron Aldenham, *c.* 1860; William Morris, 1896; Richard Bennett; J.P. Morgan, 1902.

LIT. Bennett 1980, pp. 52–67; Calkins 1983, pp. 214–25, repr. colour pls 16–19, pls 118–24; Bennett 1985, pp. 15–30; Sandler 1986, no. 4, II, pp. 15–16, repr. I, figs 9–10, 12.

359 Book of Hours

c. 1290–1300
Parchment, ff. 105: 26.2 × 18.5 cm
The Walters Art Gallery, Baltimore, MS W.102

Although many folios are lost, the Walters manuscript once contained an unusually large range of devotional texts, including not only the Hours of the Virgin, but those of the Holy Spirit and of Jesus Crucified, as well as an Office of St Catherine, the Penitential and

359

Evangelists, and a host of supporting prophets, all woven into a wiry letter frame entwined with luxuriant foliage and clambering leaf-men. This full-page B is paired with a unique enlargement of the E of *Beatus* in which a windmill (the source of the name of the manuscript) and a vignette of the Judgement of Solomon are joined by a flying angel with a scroll bearing the phrase *(Be)atus vir qui non abiit* – all silhouetted against a gossamer mesh of red, green and blue penwork vine leaves and tendrils.

By contrast to the extravagant decoration

of the opening pages, the pictorial programme of the rest of the psalter is relatively austere, consisting of large, simply-framed historiated initials, without elaborate marginal extensions, at the text divisions. Throughout the manuscript, however, the short lines of the Psalms are filled with a remarkable assortment of fanciful creatures, both painted and penwork.

Since the Windmill Psalter no longer has a calendar or Litany, there is no way to date or localise the book by interpretation of internal evidence. Among manuscripts of the Court

Gradual Psalms, the Litany of the Saints, and the Office of the Dead, all with numerous historiated initials (of which thirty-three survive), painted line fillers and marginal illustrations. It seems possible that in addition a psalter once preceded the Hours.

The chief artist was an accomplished practitioner of the most elegant Court style of the end of the thirteenth century, as exemplified, above all, in the Windmill Psalter (Cat. 358). His hand can be recognised in other books, a Bible in Oxford (Bodleian Library, MS Auct. D.3.2) and a pair of leaves inserted in an

358

unrelated psalter in Cambridge (Trinity College, MS O.4.16), and he used identical compositions for several subjects that occur both in the psalter leaves and the Hours. In addition to standard themes, the Walters manuscript contains a considerable amount of inventive iconography, including a long marginal cycle of Reynard the Fox (by a second artist), many fantastic marginal pen-work drolleries, and a number of enlarged line fillers in the Litany.

Among the components missing from the Walters Hours is the calendar, which might have contained some clue as to the original destination of the manuscript. As it is, the remaining indications of provenance or destination are ambiguous, since the Litany is Franciscan and the rubrics of the Office of the Dead mention *freres*, while a laywoman is depicted frequently in the Hours of the Virgin and the Holy Spirit. LFS

PROV. Henry Walters, bt in Paris, c. 1930.

LIT. Sandler 1986, no. 15, II, pp. 24–6, repr. I, figs 26–8, 31.

360

360 Bible

c. 1300–10 and 1320s
Parchment, ff. 441: 38.1 × 24.1 cm
Paris, Bibliothèque mazarine, MS 34

According to a fifteenth-century inscription, in 1419 the Mazarine Bible was given to the Carthusian priory at Sheen, Surrey by its royal founder, Henry V. Indeed, the manuscript might have been in royal possession from the outset, since the arms of England, together with those of Bek (Anthony Bek, Bishop of Durham and adviser to Edward I), are painted on the first page. Perhaps Bishop

Bek (d. 1310) intended the Bible as a gift to Edward I (d. 1307), or Edward II (d. 1327).

The Bible has seventy-five historiated initials with partial or full borders, one at the beginning of each Book or main subdivision of the text. The illustrations at the beginning of the volume are typical of the Court style in their elegance, finesse, and choice of motifs and patterns.

The first illuminator executed only the Genesis initial (f. 5) and one other; starting with Exodus (f. 24) he was replaced by a second master of the Court style, an artist who also illustrated a psalter in Jesus College, Oxford (MS D. 40), and a bestiary now attached to a psalter in Corpus Christi College, Cambridge (MS 53). From Ruth (f. 97v.) to the Apocalypse (f. 432v.), the historiation of the Mazarine Bible was continued by two later artists, apparently in the 1320s, to judge by the resemblance of their work to that in the Stowe Breviary of 1322–5 (London, British Library, Stowe MS 12), the Barlow Psalter of 1321–38 (Oxford, Bodleian Library, MS Barlow 22), and, above all, the Milemete Treatise of 1326–7 (Cat. 682). This work is distinctly large in scale, comparatively awkward in drawing, and includes bold and humourous marginal hybrids. LFS

PROV. Henry V (?), given to Priory of Jesus of Bethlehem, Sheen, Surrey, 1419; James II (?), given to a Parisian religous house after 1688 (?).

LIT. Alexander 1983, p. 149; Bennett 1986a, p. 13, nn. 38, 40, 41; Sandler 1986, p. 25, II, pp. 31–2, repr. I, figs 52–5.

361 Thomas of Kent, *Roman de toute chevalerie*

c. 1300–10
Vellum, ff. 87: 32.2 × 22 cm
Paris, Bibliothèque nationale, MS fr. 24364

This is a later version of Cat. 313 with an almost complete series of illustrations to the romance. The series would be complete had the scribe not omitted certain sections of the text. The 311 pictures are inserted in various positions on the page within the two-column text. Only some of these have been coloured, others having been left as pen drawings. The pictures follow closely the mid-thirteenth-century version which may have been available as a model. A detailed comparison of the two sets of illustrations has not yet been carried out. The difference is that in this manuscript full colouring seems to have been intended rather than tinted drawing. It is a splendid example of the type of chivalric romance which was popular in aristocratic circles of the period.

The romance was illustrated shortly after the wall paintings of Old Testament scenes in the Painted Chamber in the Palace of Westminster (Cat. 333–9). On a small scale the battle scenes and architectural forms with canted-out battlements parallel those in the

361

wall paintings. On f. 1 are several heraldic shields including those of the families of Huntingfield, Zouche, Latimer, Basset and D'Engaine. That of D'Engaine occurs elsewhere in the book, suggesting ownership by that family. NJM

PROV. D'Engaine family (?); Montigny family; Jean-François-Paul Le Febvre de Caumartin, Bishop of Blois (1668–1733); Duc de la Vallière, 18th century; Bibliothèque nationale, 19th century.

LIT. Ross 1963, pp. 25–7; Secomska 1975, pp. 60–1, 66, 67, 69, 70–1, pls 4f, 5g, 6e, 6h–k, 7d–e; Foster 1977, pp. 6–10; Avril & Stirnemann 1987, no. 171, pls K L, LXVII–LXIX.

362 The Valence casket

French (Limoges) or English, c. 1290–1324
Copper alloy, enamelled in champlevé and gilt; parts restored: h. 9.5 cm, w. 17.5 cm
The Board of Trustees of the Victoria and Albert Museum, London, 4–1865

This is made of sheet metal riveted together, supported on paw-shaped feet (two restored). The lid is attached by two hinges (partly restored) made up of dragon-like creatures. The similar front hasp now backs on to a lock fitting (original?). The gilded handle terminates at each end in a snake's head: four holes in the lid might originally have held decorative rosettes. The enamel is opaque, in black, white, blue and red.

The armorial decoration covering the casket links it with the Valence family, Earls of Pembroke, who were fond of placing their own arms with those of their royal and noble relations. The arms are as follows: England (before 1340), Valence, Brittany (Dreux), Angoulème, Brabant, Lacy. Margaret, daughter of Edward I, married John, Duke of

357

362

Brabant, in 1290, which accounts for the presence of his arms. The casket was probably intended to hold valuables and would have been lined with wood and fabric. It perhaps belonged either to Aymer de Valence (d. 1324) or to his father, William (d. 1296), whose Limoges enamel effigy is in Westminster Abbey (see p. 164). The casket, which is unique, may have been made either in Limoges or England. A contemporary cup lid at All Souls College, Oxford, also enamelled with arms, is associated with Aymer de Valence's wife, Beatrice de Nesle (Ottawa 1972, no. 56). The increasing use of enamel on metalwork from the late thirteenth century coincided with a growth of interest in, and the use of, heraldic ornament; enamel was the only means of permanently colouring metal, and colour was a crucial element in heraldic language. MLC

PROV. Revd George Pocock; bt by the V&A, 1865.

LIT. Shaw 1836, pp. 50–2, pl. LXII; London 1862, no. 1122; Gauthier 1972, no. 143; Ottawa 1972, no. 51; London 1978c, no. 15.

363 Casket

1303–8
Silver-gilt, the present gilding early 19th century:
   h. 6.2 cm, l. 8.1 cm, w. 3.7 cm
The Trustees of the British Museum, London,
   MLA 72, 12–16, 1

This casket has its sides ornamented with

seven twin lancets and the ends with three twin lancets, above which is a trilobe with three leaves within it. On each side of the lid there are three quatrefoils containing on one side the arms of England dimidiate and of France semé entire, and on the other the same arms but with a three-point label over all. The dimidiate arms with a common label must be those of Isabella, daughter of Philip IV of France, who was betrothed to Prince Edward son of Edward I in 1303. The marriage was celebrated in 1308. The arms on the other side are those of Margaret, half-

sister of Philip IV, who married Edward I in 1299. The casket was therefore probably a gift from Margaret to Isabella before or upon her marriage. There are traces of a three-part division on the inside of the box and it may therefore have been a small chrismatory (cf. Cat. 123) or, less likely, a jewel case. JC

PROV. Coll. Dr Ducarel, 1779; Astle, Douce; Sir Samuel Meyrick; bt by Museum from Mr Thomas Whitehead, 1872.

LIT. Walford 1856, pp. 134–8; Ottawa 1972, p. 134 no. 48.

363

364 Grille

*c.*1250–75, with later frame
Wrought iron: max. h. 245 cm; w. 298 cm
The Board of Trustees of the Victoria and Albert
Museum, London, M. 591–1896

The grille is composed of eight different-sized panels attached to a framework of plain iron bars with a spiked cresting on top. The elements grouped in the panels are Y scrolls curled like rams' horns with a central stem which is either looped, lobed or circular; two sizes of spiral S scrolls; and back-to-back C scrolls ending in circular terminals stamped with a crude fleur-de-lis and rosette, one on each side. The scrolled elements are collared to each other and to slender vertical bars which end in an open circlet. The collars used within each panel are small and neat with a circular cross-section, while those attaching the panels to the main frame are crude and roughly clasped, indicating that the panels have been reassembled in their present frame. Traces of gilding and red paint were visible in 1896.

Similar elements of spiral S and Y scrolls are found on many French grilles of the late twelfth and early thirteenth centuries, at St-Aventin, Artonne, Billom, Conques, Le Mans and elsewhere (Delaine 1972; Delaine 1973), but the use of stamped terminals on the C scrolls suggests that the panels were made after *c.*1250. Another panel from Chichester (Victoria and Albert Museum, 592a–1896), constructed in the same way, has S scrolls with stamped terminals. The same S and Y elements were also recorded on a grille at Boxgrove Priory, Sussex, in 1825 (J. Buckler, British Library. Add. MS 36433, ff. 629,641).

The grille may have been part of the 'costly clausures' made for the relics of Bishop Richard in 1276 (Vallance 1947, pp. 57–61). When the shrine was demolished in 1538 the 'clausures' were removed and could have been reassembled in their present frame at that date. The grille was removed from the choir during a nineteenth-century restoration.   JG

PROV. Chichester Cathedral choir; sold to a marine store dealer during 19th-century restorations; bt by Duke de Moro; bt by Victoria and Albert Museum 1896.

LIT. Museum records; J.S. Gardner 1927, pp. 74–5; Vallance 1947, pp. 57–61; Delaine 1972. pp. 153–5; Delaine 1973, pp. 101–49.

365 Door from armoire

*c.*1260–90
Wrought iron on wood: h. 146 cm, w. 55 cm
The Dean and Canons of Chester Cathedral

The armoire is a composite piece with four doors coming from an earlier construction, a modern base and a late medieval body specially designed for the old doors. Inside it has wooden pegs designed for hanging vestments. The armoire has a frame and panel

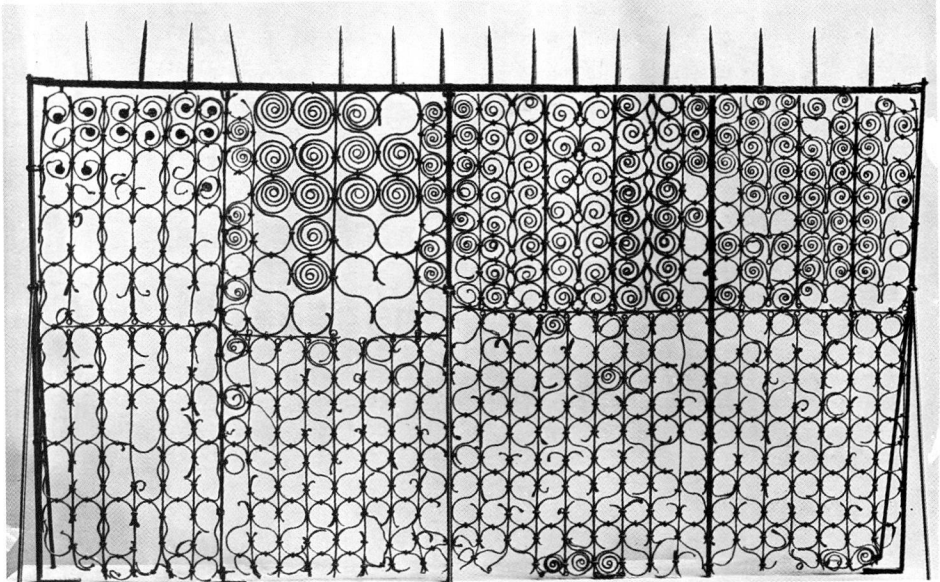

364

construction with a billet edging on top, and side panels made with overlapping boards covered by a lattice of rough iron straps. The crude iron hinges interfere with the scroll-work and are clearly a later insertion, although there are no traces of earlier hinges on the panels. The boards may have been trimmed to fit their present location. The armoire was until recently kept in a closely-fitting recess in the vaulted chamber to the north-west of the nave. It is possible that the door panels were designed to fit directly into such a recess, and would not originally have needed a wooden body.

The panel in the exhibition (the left door) is covered by three spirals arranged vertically.

Below the top spiral on the left, a long tendril fits awkwardly into the available space and immediately beside it a tendril from the edging bar has broken off, suggesting that the iron has been slightly rearranged. On this panel all the welds are bare but on the other panels they are frequently covered by folded, stamped leaves. Most of the scrolls have a roughly triangular section and all end in delicate stamped terminals. Nineteen stamp designs are used, including trefoils, rosettes and asymmetrical leaves. They are very closely related in style and scale to the stamps used on the York Minster chapter house doors, *c.*1280–5 (fig. 118), and one of the York cope chests. The door on exhibition is

365

also similar to the chest panel illustrated in the Life of St Edward (Cambridge, University Library MS Ee 3.59, f. 133v.; Cat. 39), produced at Westminster c. 1255–60. The general use of tight spiral scrolls and a central 'Tree of Life', together with the detailed parallels in stamp design, suggests that at least similar pattern books were used for the Chester and York ironwork, and they could even have been made in the same Yorkshire workshop.   JG

PROV. Chester Cathedral, chapter house.

LIT. Brandon 1847, section II, pl. 1; Gardner 1927, p. 82; Crossley 1939, pp. 172–3; Macquoid & Edwards 1954, I, p. 23; Manchester 1976, p. 107, no. 82; Eames 1977, pp. 44–6.

366   Doors with iron decoration

c. 1272–85

Wrought iron on wood: double doors, each leaf
  h. 244 cm, w. 76 cm

St Peter Hungate Museum, Norwich (Norfolk
  Museums Service), 102.940(1)

366

The doors are completely covered by five horizontal rows of scrolls with thin, straight dividing bars between them. Some iron has been lost, particularly at the bottom, but traces of it can be seen in the wood. The top semicircular area of the doors is filled with two affronted dragons whose tails turn into scrolls. All terminals are stamped with a pointed trefoil, asymmetrical leaf, stippled lobe, disc or rosette with linear petals. Many welds were originally concealed beneath folded leaves. The main straps originally had a raised rib profile, now considerably worn. The delicate stamps and the dragons at the

367

top of the doors are related in design to the ironwork on the doors of York Minster chapter house, c. 1280–5 (fig. 118). The boards of the doors are original but a new frame has been fitted to the back.

The doors came from Norwich Cathedral infirmary, c. 1180, where they probably replaced the originals after the fire of 1272. The building was demolished in 1804 and re-erected in part in Bracondale Woods, Norwich in 1813 by Philip Martineau.   JG

PROV. Bracondale Woods; bt by Messrs J. and J. Colman, 1877; presented by them to Norwich Museums, 1940.

LIT. Catalogue papers (where accounts contemporary with its demolition mistake the dormitory for the infirmary), Norfolk Museums Service; Whittingham 1949, pp. 86–7.

367   Chertsey tiles

1293–8

Earthenware; three groups of four tiles showing
  standing figures of an archbishop, a queen, and
  a king under elaborate canopies: upper three
  tiles l. 22.5 cm, w. 22.5 cm; bottom tile
  l. 22.5 cm, w. 13.5 cm

The Trustees of the British Museum, London,
  design nos Archbishop 1306–9, Queen
  1310–13, King 1306, 1314–16

All three figures stand under elaborate architectural canopies with tracery windows, pinnacles, and elaborate crocketed gables with ogee arches. Such elaborate decoration is paralleled on the Eleanor crosses erected by Edward I in the 1290s. A kiln excavated in

1922 at Chertsey was used to fire these designs and John Gardner and Elizabeth Eames, in publishing that kiln (1954), suggested that the designs were made between 1290 and 1298 in connection with works undertaken by Edward I to commemorate Eleanor of Castile (d. 1290). Norton (1981) has subsequently drawn attention to the payment of £7, a high price, to William the Paviour for making a pavement at Westminster for the executors of the queen. This pavement may have been on the ambulatory side of Eleanor's tomb (Cat. 377), and these designs may have been used for it. The blessing archbishop is probably St Thomas of Canterbury; the king with a martyr's palm may represent St Edmund for whom Edward I had a particular veneration, and the queen, holding a sceptre and a squirrel, towards whom they both look may be Eleanor herself. The designs were therefore first made for Westminster and subsequently manufactured at Chertsey for use there. They were also used at Winchester Cathedral in the medieval period. The terminal date of 1298 for their production is given because by that date the tilers at Chertsey had already moved on to Halesowen, where they made tiles for Abbot Nicholas (d. 1298). The style of the figures is solemn and severe, and the detail of the draperies provides an interesting contrast with the liveliness of the draperies of the combat or Tristram series (Cat. 16, 320).   JC

PROV. Found on the site of Chertsey Abbey, Surrey, probably 1852–3.

LIT. Shurlock 1885; Gardner & Eames 1954, pp. 33–42, pl. XII; Eames 1980, pp. 150–2; Norton 1981, p. iii.

The Eleanor crosses

The centrepiece of this section is the figure of Queen Eleanor from the Waltham Cross, one of twelve crosses erected by Edward I at the resting places along the route taken by his wife's funeral cortège in 1290 (Cat. 374). Only this and the crosses at Hardingstone and Geddington, Northamptonshire, and the queen's tomb in Westminster Abbey still survive largely intact (Cat. 369–70, 377). We therefore depend for our knowledge of the king's other commemorative works both on contemporary documentation (Cat. 372) and on such representations as were made of particular monuments, such as that in Lincoln Cathedral (Cat. 379), before their destruction.

368 Map of the funeral procession of the body of Queen Eleanor of Castile from Harby to London

Eleanor, born c. 1240, daughter of Ferdinand III of Castile and León, and Jeanne de Dammartin his second wife, married Edward, son of Henry III of England, in late October 1254 at the Cistercian house of La Huelgas near Burgos, and first arrived in England in the autumn of 1255. She was only rarely away from the side of Edward and between 1255 and 1284 she bore him at least fifteen children, many of whom died young. During this period the English royal family was more united than at any time between the Norman Conquest and the accession of the Stuarts. Eleanor went on crusade with Edward in 1270–2, and about fifty years later Ptolemy of Lucca in his chronicle told the significant, but probably spurious, story of her sucking the poison from Edward's wound after an attempted assassination. She was crowned with Edward in Westminster Abbey on Sunday 19 August 1274, and a feast was held in great splendour in Westminster Hall.

The only major sources of evidence for her position as Queen of England are household accounts. She was certainly personally involved in running her own estates and in keeping control over her own household, which was about 150 strong. Despite obvious reverence for her in England it is clear that both she and her ministers had a reputation as grasping estate managers. She died of fever on 28 November 1290 at Harby, Nottinghamshire, not far from Lincoln. Edward was with her and was deeply affected by her death, which came at a political turning-point in his reign. His deep devotion to her was marked by the erection of the famous Eleanor crosses, twelve in all, at the resting-places of her funeral procession from Lincoln to Westminster. Only those at Waltham (Essex), Geddington and Hardingstone (both Northamptonshire) survive (Cat.

369–70, 373). The queen's viscera were buried at Lincoln (Cat. 379), her heart at the London Blackfriars, and her bones in Westminster Abbey (Cat. 377).   JD

LIT. Colvin 1963, I, pp. 482–5; Parsons, 1977.

369 Eleanor Cross, Hardingstone, Northampton

1291–3
Photograph

Five of the twelve Eleanor crosses were made by John of Battle, previously undermaster at Edward I's foundation of Vale Royal Abbey. This is the only one of his to survive, and it has been modified and restored several times. The octagonal base is in three tiers: the solid lowest tier is decorated with arch-and-gable motifs separated by pinnacles, the arches enclosing shields of arms of Ponthieu (in virtue of Eleanor's mother, cf. Cat. 378), Castile, León and England, and open books (presumably once inscribed). The arches have continuous mouldings, and blind tracery and seaweed foliage complete the decoration. The open middle tier rises from an elaborate projecting foliate cornice. The four tabernacles housing statues of the queen are separated by pinnacles and defined by an arch-and-gable overlapping the solid gable roofs. The main decorative motifs are cusping, blind tracery and foliage, here more naturalistic. Similar motifs adorn the smaller top storey, from which rose the cross shaft, also with blind panelling behind the gable.

All the ornamental motifs of the cross base were to characterise the Decorated style in the following years. The ogee arch makes its first surviving appearance in England on a

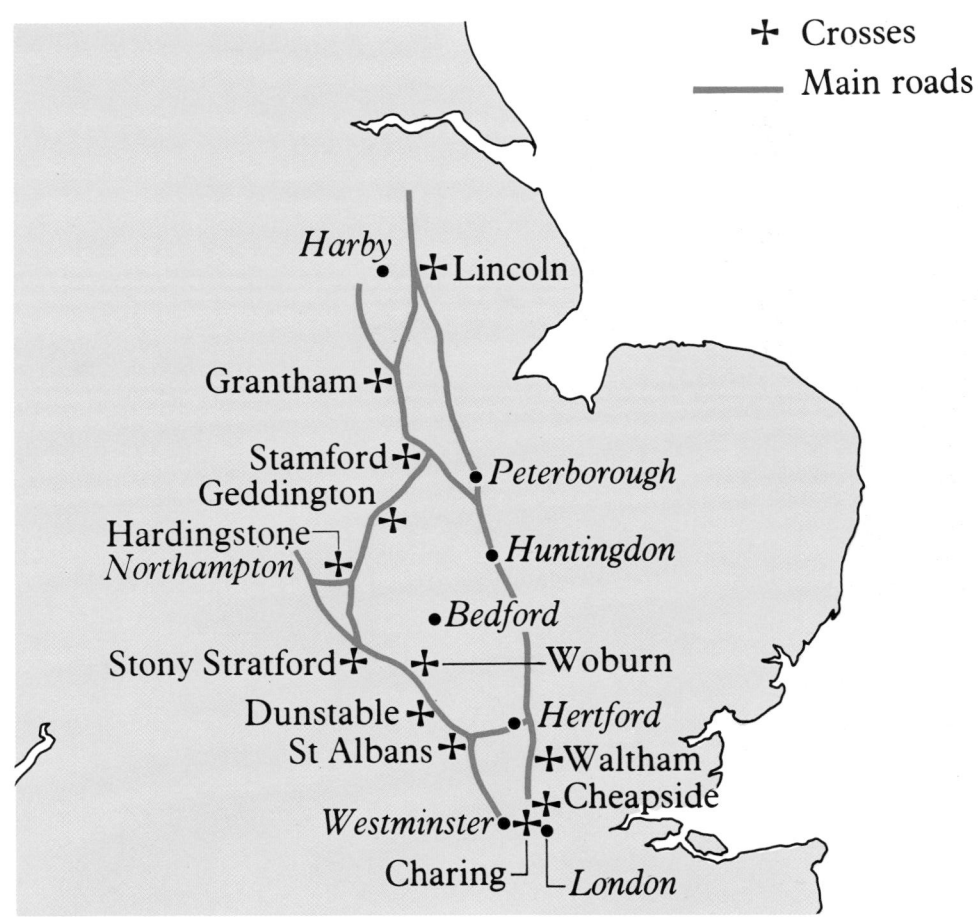

368

369

370

371

monumental scale, flattened in the blind tracery of the lowest tier, more overt in the arches over the statues. Equally characteristic are the polygonal ground-plan, the overlapping forms and illusionism, and the miniature architectural detailing which blurs the distinction between architecture and sculpture.

These ideas and designs were developed from the 1280s by masons working for the king and other leading patrons on both buildings and smaller pieces such as tombs and shrine bases (cf. the shrine of St Alban, Cat. 19), which began to share stylistic characteristics. The ornament is derived from French architecture, particularly the decoration of façades, e.g. the transepts of Notre-Dame, Paris, after 1250. The ogee appeared randomly in the last quarter of the thirteenth century in architecture, manuscripts and metalwork, but in architectural ornament it was the English who systematically developed its use from *c.* 1300.   NC

LIT. Vallance 1920, p. 95; Hastings 1955, pp. 24–5, repr. pl. 10; Colvin 1963, pp. 479–85; Stone 1972, pp. 143–4; Pevsner, rev. Cherry 1973, pp. 353–4, repr. pl. 68; Bony 1979, p. 20ff., repr. pls 126–8; Wilson 1980a, pp. 31–3.

370   The Geddington Eleanor Cross

J. C. Schnebbelie (1760–92)
1789
Watercolour: 49 × 33 cm
Society of Antiquaries of London

371   The Hardingstone Eleanor Cross

J. C. Schnebbelie (1760–92)
1789
Watercolour: 49 × 33 cm
Society of Antiquaries of London

These accurate but sensitive representations, together with details of the sculpture (not shown), were drawn by Schnebbelie, a topographical artist born in England of a Swiss father, and engraved for the third volume of *Vetusta Monumenta*, published in 1791 (XII–XVII). The accompanying notes by Englefield noted the stylistic connections with paintings and tombs of the same period at Westminster. The cross and sundials around the top of the Hardingstone monument were added, as well as an inscription, when the cross was restored by order of the Bench of Justices in 1713, a precocious example of preservation by a public body.   TC

PROV. Drawn for the Society of Antiquaries, 1789.

372   Payments for Eleanor crosses

1293
Parchment: approx. 62.5 × 22.5 cm
Inscr. *Liber[ationes] p[ro] A[lianora] quondam Regina Angl[ie], cons[orte] d[omi]ni Regis fact[e] p[er] manus. J. Bacon [et] R. de Kancia, post festum S[an]c[t]i Mich[ael]is, Anno Regni Regis E[dwardi] vicesimo finiente.*
Public Record Office, London, E 101/353/1

The crosses and tombs with which Edward I commemorated Eleanor of Castile were paid for by her executors – the Bishop of Bath and Wells, the Earl of Lincoln and a clerk called John of Berwick. Their duties were carried out by the two clerks named at the top of this roll, John Bacon and Richard of Kent, four of whose accounts (of which this is one) survive, providing extremely full details of the payments; nothing was sub-contracted.

The accounts form part of a chronological sequence, this one covering the terms from Michaelmas 1292 to the summer of 1293.

372

The document is a fair copy, but appears to follow the order in which the executors paid the various sums (although these are undated); the subject of each entry is indicated in the left margin, although only very approximately and inconsistently (*crux* [cross], Charringe, *expense* [expenses], *opus* [work], etc.).

A few of the payments are doubtless in

discharge of provisions in the queen's will (now lost), but most are concerned with her commemoration: for instance, 100 marks (£66.13s.4d) as a deposit for the setting up of a chantry for her soul at Herdeby (Harby, Nottinghamshire, where she died), or 8s.6d to Juliana la Potere for 300 pitchers on the anniversary of her death (presumably to be given away), quite apart from the many payments in connection with her tombs and memorial crosses; the payments were spread out over a long period of time (their average of over £300 per term perhaps corresponding to the income available to the queen's estate, although this had to be supplemented by grants from the Treasury). For instance, master William Torel who made and gilded the bronze effigies on her tombs at Lincoln and Westminster Abbey (Cat. 377–9) received many part payments of £2 or £4.

Only the craftsmen who made the costliest crosses are referred to as master (*magister*): master Richard of Crundale made the cross at Charing and master Michael of Canterbury that in the Cheap (see Cat. 375–6 for a fragment of this), for a total of over £900. Each of these men had other court connections (at least by 1292); on the other hand, Richard of Stow, who carved the cross at Lincoln, is otherwise known only to have worked for Lincoln. Edward evidently attached most importance to the crosses in London. NLR

PROV. Exchequer records, incorporated into the Public Record Office.

LIT. Turner 1841, pp. 116–30; Colvin 1963, I, pp. 479–85; Harvey 1984, pp. 45, 77, 286; Ekwall 1960, p. 95.

373   The Waltham Eleanor Cross

After William Stukeley (1687–1765)
1721
Engraving: 54 × 37 cm
Society of Antiquaries of London

After the destruction in the 1640s of the Charing and Cheapside crosses the Waltham Cross was the most prominent of those surviving, and early excited the interest of the Society of Antiquaries. In 1721, in an untypical conservationist gesture, they paid for two oak bollards to prevent the cross from being damaged by carts on the high road (Evans 1956, 72). They also commissioned this engraving, only the seventh in *Vetusta Monumenta* (the collection of prints commissioned by the Antiquaries and first published in one volume in 1747). The isolation in which Stukeley placed the cross was imaginary. Over thirty years later he himself complained that the bollards had been removed by the turnpike commissioners and had a protective brick plinth erected instead, but he could not prevent the affixing of road signs and the intrusion of the inn. TC

PROV. Engraved for Society of Antiquaries, 1721.

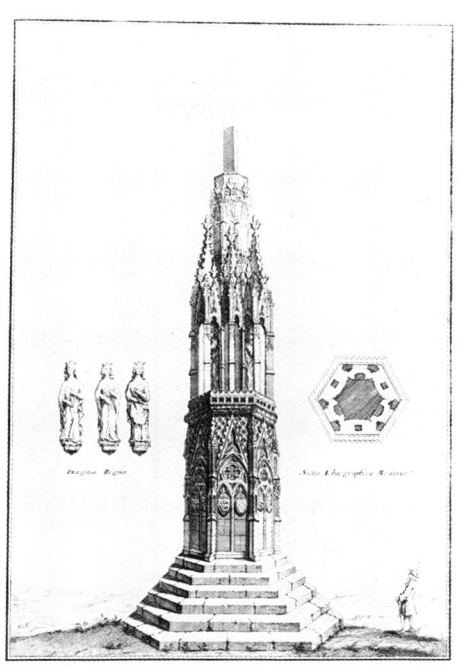

373

374   The Waltham Cross Queen Eleanor statue

Alexander of Abingdon, 1291–2
Caen stone, considerably weathered: h. 183 cm
Hertfordshire County Council, on loan to the
   Victoria and Albert Museum, London

Alexander of Abingdon is also documented as having carved the (lost) images of the Charing Cross, designed by Michael of Canterbury. With William Torel and William of Ireland, Alexander appears to have dominated English sculpture at the end of the thirteenth and beginning of the fourteenth centuries. Of this trio, Alexander seems to have been the most important *imaginator* in freestone. His earliest documented works – parts of the tomb for Queen Eleanor's viscera in the Lady Chapel of Lincoln Cathedral and the heart tomb in the Dominican church in London, and the Waltham and Charing Cross figures – are connected with monuments of such prestige and importance that he must already have been a sculptor of considerable repute. Alexander's style is intimately linked with that of Torel's effigy of Queen Eleanor at Westminster Abbey (Cat. 377), and is a parallel to that of the 'Madonna Master's' work in the De Lisle Psalter (Cat. 569). That Alexander's style is linked to Torel's is hardly surprising when it is recalled that he supplied wax models for the three metal images cast by William of Suffolk for the tomb of Queen Eleanor's heart in the London Blackfriars; it is possible that a model by Alexander also lies behind Torel's Westminster and Lincoln effigies.

The Waltham Queens reveal, in their elegantly swaying poses, their subtle draperies and their calm and aristocratic heads (one is a nineteenth-century replacement),

an idealised and restrained style which is in marked contrast to the fluttering draperies and taller proportions of William of Ireland's surviving Hardingstone Cross (Cat. 369) figures. Alexander's style is also seen in two undocumented works at Westminster, the tombs of Aveline of Lancaster (d. 1273) and Edmund Crouchback (d. 1296; Cat. 326). He was probably responsible for both effigies and for the weepers on the latter monument. The same characteristics of pose and garments are also found on female effigies at Aldworth and Chichester Cathedral and in the much damaged imagery of the tomb of Bishop de Luda (d. 1298) at Ely cathedral, and his participation in these works seems certain. PL

PROV. Waltham; on loan to V&A since 1985.

LIT. Prior & Gardner 1912, pp. 98, 100, 348–9, 645, repr. fig. 395; Gardner 1951, p. 167, repr. fig. 318; Stone 1972, pp. 143, 143–7, 155, 164, 167; Lindley 1984, p. 77.

374

375

376

375–6 Fragments of Eleanor Cross from Cheapside

c. 1291–5
Purbeck marble: 375 h. 96 cm, w. 101 cm,
 d. 19 cm; 376 h. 54 cm, w. 101 cm, c. 10 cm
Museum of London, 7240–1

The Cheapside Eleanor Cross was built by contract, like all the others except Richard of Crundale's Charing Cross. At a contract price of £300, the Cheapside Cross was second only in cost to that at Charing, on which over £700 had already been disbursed by March 1294. As these two fragments reveal, the lavish use of expensive Purbeck marble goes some way to explain the high cost of the two London monuments, which were doubtless intended to surpass all the others in quality of

materials, as well as size and workmanship. Michael of Canterbury, perhaps the most influential master mason of his generation, and the designer of St Stephen's Chapel, Westminster (Cat. 324–5), was responsible for the Cheapside Cross. In 1441, long before any accurate visual record of its appearance had been made, it was extensively rebuilt, and its original appearance is therefore lost. The Museum of London fragments were discovered in 1838 during reconstruction of the sewer in Cheapside; they show that Michael adhered to the formula of a plinth decorated with two-light tracery framing shields suspended from foliage, which can be seen on the surviving Waltham (Cat. 373) and Hardingstone (Cat. 369) crosses.

The identity of the sculptor to whom the imagery of this cross and the carving of the Purbeck marble plinth should be attributed is unknown. But it is possible that Alexander of Abingdon, whose Waltham images survive (Cat. 374), was also responsible for some of this work; at Lincoln he and Nicholas Dymenge carved the Purbeck marble tomb chest on which William Torel's gilt-bronze effigy of Queen Eleanor lay (Cat. 379), proving that he was an expert in the carving of marble as well as freestone. The designs for the latter work will probably have been furnished by Richard of Crundale, the designer of Eleanor's Westminster tomb chest, just as Michael of Canterbury presumably supplied the moulding patterns employed for the Cheapside Cross. PL

PROV. Cheapside Eleanor Cross; Museum of London (formerly Guildhall Museum Collection).

LIT. Botfield 1841, *passim*; Hunter 1842, *passim*; Lovell 1892. pp. 34–5; Vallance 1920, p. 102, repr. figs. 130–1; Colvin 1963, I, pp. 483–4; Wilson 1980a, p. 33.

377 Effigy of Queen Eleanor of Castile, Westminster Abbey

1291–3
Photograph

The effigy of the queen has long hair and is crowned. She wears a gown, kirtle and mantle; her left hand holds the cord of the gown, and her right hand probably once carried a sceptre. Her head rests on two superposed cushions, which are diapered with the arms of Castile, and there are two lions at her feet. The crown and the edges of the garments have holes for added jewellery.

The effigy, which was made by William Torel, goldsmith, is one of the earliest surviving large-scale bronzes in England. At the same time Torel made the effigy of Henry III and a second figure of Eleanor, for the lost tomb at Lincoln (Cat. 379). The figures, slightly over life-size, were each cast in one piece, except for the right hands which were cast separately. The thickness of the metal (4.5–10 cm) and the technique of casting, a lost-wax method normally used for making large bells, shows that the casting of large-scale figures was still an unrefined technique. Three hundred and fifty gold florins were bought from merchants of Lucca for the gilding.

The cord-holding gesture, similar to that on Eleanor's seal, is also found on the series of French royal effigies at St-Denis (commissioned 1263–4) on which the Westminster tombs were evidently based, but it was already commonplace in stone sculpture, appearing on the north transept of Chartres, *c.* 1205–10, and at Wells, *c.* 1230s. The linear drapery style, with straight folds softly overlapping at the feet, may be compared to that of contemporary works in the abbey, such as the weepers on the Crouch-

377

back tomb and the painting of St Faith (Cat. 556). However, the calm elegance and refinement produced by the original modelling have no exact parallels in other art forms. NC

LIT. Botfield 1841; RCHM, *London: Westminster Abbey*, 1924, pp. 29–30; Plendeleith & Maryon 1959; Colvin 1963, I, pp. 479f.; Stone 1972, pp. 142–3, repr. pls 108–9; Tummers 1980, *passim*, cat. 164, repr. pl. 160.

378 Westminster Abbey, shield on tomb of Eleanor of Castile

John Ruskin (1819–1900)
c. 1871
Wash over pencil: 40.5 × 33 cm
The Visitors of the Ashmolean Museum, Oxford, Ruskin Drawing School Collection, Rudimentary 11

In the winter of 1871–2 Ruskin gathered a collection of drawings and casts of details in Westminster Abbey. They were prepared not as works of art but as technical illustrations to aid students at the School of Drawing which Ruskin established at Oxford. This drawing of the arms of the County of Ponthieu on Eleanor's tomb demonstrates particular aspects of Ruskin's attitude to Gothic:

378

first, his conviction of its contemporary educational value, second, his hatred of restoration – the timeworn aspect of the stone, especially on the bottom right-hand corner, is exactly rendered – third, his ability to invest the smallest detail with significance. The faithful depiction of a simple shield of arms becomes a moving image of Gothic nobility. TC

PROV. Presented to Museum by the artist.

LIT. Ruskin 1903–12, p. 174.

379 Lincoln Cathedral, monument to Queen Eleanor

From Sir William Dugdale's *Book of Monuments*
William Sedgwick (b. *c.* 1617)
c. 1641
Pen and colour washes: h. 56 cm, w. 66 cm
The Rt Hon. Earl of Winchilsea and Nottingham, on loan to the British Library, Loan MS 38, ff. 98v–9, Winchilsea Settled Estates

The Lincoln monument to Queen Eleanor, defaced and now heavily restored and lacking the original effigy, was similar in design to the surviving tomb in the Abbey (Cat. 377). On the facing page are drawn shields of arms formerly in the stained glass of the great east window of the cathedral. These drawings were made as part of a far-sighted programme of recording monuments, in-

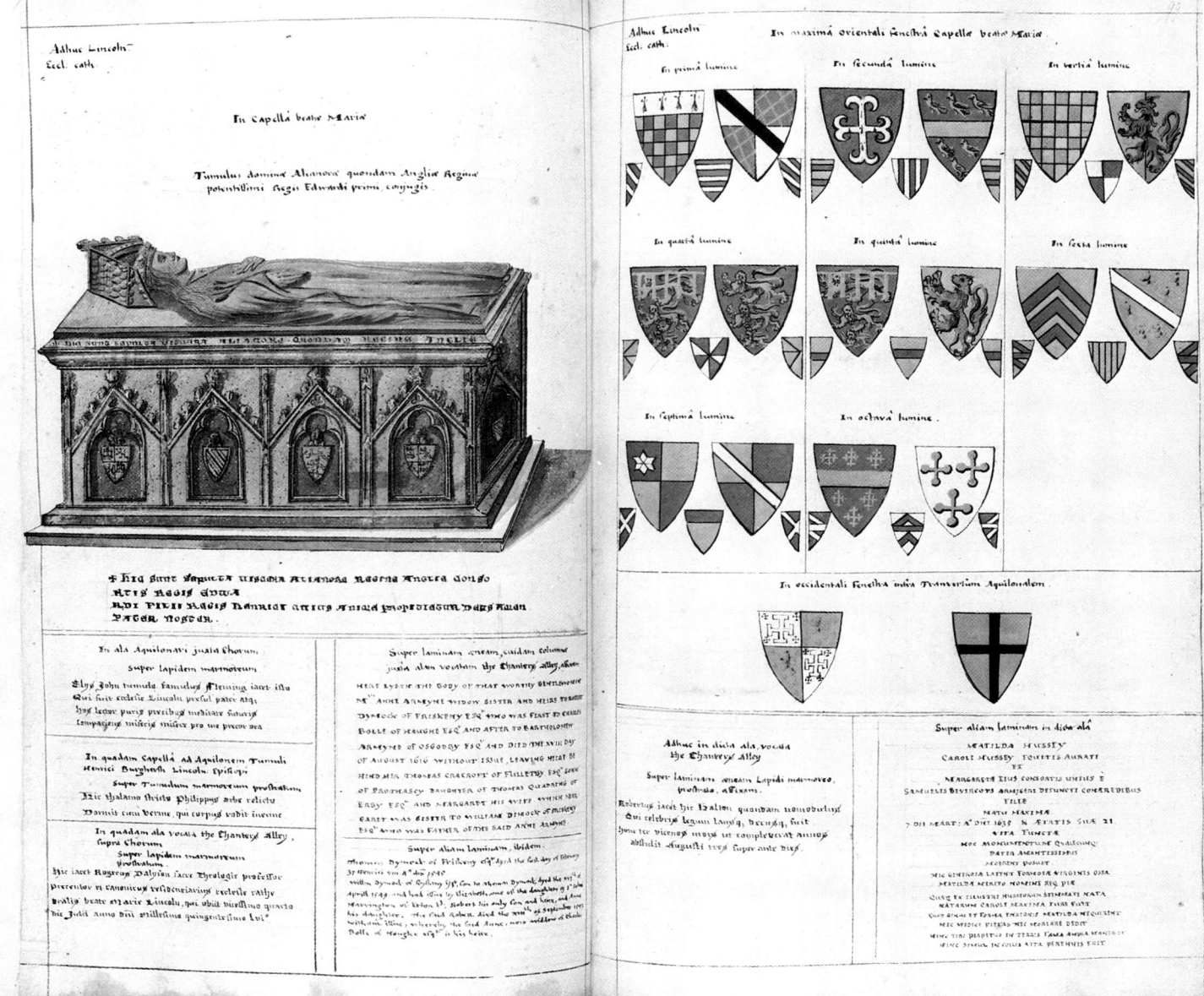

379

scriptions and stained glass at risk from war and Puritan iconoclasm, instigated just before the Civil War by Sir Christopher (later Lord) Hatton and carried out by William Dugdale and the heraldic draughtsman William Sedgwick. TC

PROV. By descent to present owner.

LIT. Colvin 1963, I, pp. 481–2; London 1978a; London 1984a, pp. 361, 367.

XI The Appreciation of Gothic Art and Architecture

The representations of Court works like the Eleanor crosses (Cat. 373, 379) or the Painted Chamber (Cat. 330–9) are vital evidence for the former appearance of damaged or lost masterpieces. Such visual records are linked to shifts in taste and the appreciation of Gothic art in later centuries. They also demonstrate how the appearance of buildings in particular, such as the Temple Church in London, could alter radically according to changing use (Cat. 405–6). The necessity of restoring and conserving Gothic buildings and works of art has continued to be a pressing concern, as it still is today (Cat. 407–19).

380 Westminster Abbey, shrine of St Edward the Confessor

After John Talman (1677–1726), engraved by
G. Vertue (1684–1756)
1724
Engraving with contemporary colouring:
62 × 39 cm
Society of Antiquaries of London

Henry III commissioned a magnificent new shrine for his royal predecessor and patron saint Edward the Confessor as part of his rebuilding of Westminster Abbey. It was erected in 1269 by 'Petrus Romanus', who gave it a Cosmatesque form with mosaic inlay and twisted colonettes to the base. He was perhaps the son of the Roman Odericus who signed the presbytery pavement in 1268. Although the gilded and bejewelled 'châsse' was despoiled at the Reformation the masonry base remained, the only major saint's shrine still *in situ* in England. The tiered wooden cover in a Renaissance style was added during the brief revival of the monastery under Mary I (Perkins 1938–52, ii, 82–5). John Talman, who made the original drawing for the engraving, was chosen as director of the Society of Antiquaries of London at its foundation in 1717 and helped to instigate its programme of illustrating the major monuments of the country in large-scale prints (later bound up as *Vetusta Monumenta*). Talman, son of the architect William Talman, had spent years travelling and collecting in Italy and included among his many interests a study of Italian medieval art which surely aided him in this meticulous rendering of the shrine, now seen as a major historical rather than religious treasure. Vertue also lectured on the shrine to the Antiquaries in 1741. TC

PROV. Engraved for the Society of Antiquaries, 1724.

LIT. Vertue 1770, pp. 32–9; Colvin 1963, p. 149.

MAUSOLEUM sive FERETRUM Sti. EDVARDI CONFESSORIS REGIS ANGLIÆ.
ex marmor. Porphyretico & Serpentino, Operoque insuper musivo elegantissimè ornatum uti hodie in Ecclesia Westmonasteriensi conspicitur
sumptibus Societatis Antiquariæ Londinensis MDCCXXIV.

380

382–3 Westminster Abbey, two sheets of drawings of the opened coffin of Edward I

(382) Attrib. William Blake (1757–1827)
1774
Pencil with ink outlines: 20 × 15 cm (trimmed)
Society of Antiquaries of London

(383) Attrib. James Basire (1730–1802)
1774
Pen and ink with wash: 23.5 × 45.4 cm
Society of Antiquaries of London

At the instigation of Daines Barrington, vice-president of the Society of Antiquaries, the tomb of Edward I in Westminster Abbey was opened in the presence of the Dean, John Thomas, and a selected group of observers including Richard Gough, on 2 May 1774. Contrary to expectation not only was the king's body almost intact, but so were his vestments, including a form of dalmatic decorated with imitation jewels, and two sceptres. The tomb was open only for about

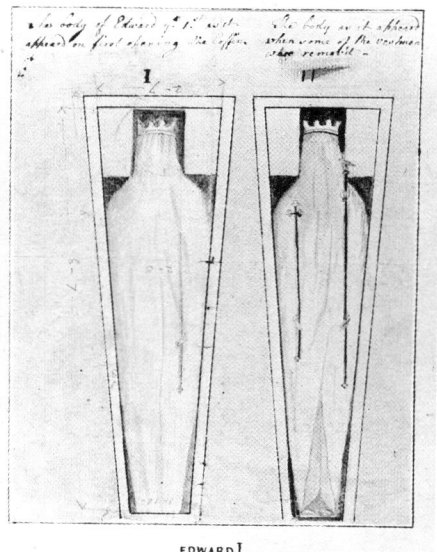

EDWARD I.

381

an hour, after which the Dean insisted that it be re-sealed without disturbing the remains or removing any of the contents. A detailed description was read to the Antiquaries by Sir Joseph Ayloffe. Barrington had considered it unnecessary to bring Basire (the Antiquaries' draughtsman), so the only known visual records made on the spot were 'rude sketches' by Gough (Nichols 1812–15, VIII, p. 612). Basire presumably worked up the larger drawing from Gough's description and drawings, with the idea of publication. Basire's brilliant but idiosyncratic apprentice William Blake is credited with the smaller drawing, but the style of the larger can hardly be his. TC

PROV. Presumably executed for Soc. of Antiqs.
LIT. Ayloffe 1786, *passim*; London 1978b, nos 6, 7.

382

381 Westminster Abbey, reconstruction of the medieval appearance and setting of the Confessor's shrine

William Burges (1827–81)
1852
Watercolour: 67 × 47.5 cm
British Architectural Library–RIBA, London, Arc. IV/2

Although the masonry shrine of the Confessor survived the Dissolution, by the nineteenth century the Abbey had become something of a museum, guarded by vergers and accessible only for a fee. Burges in this dramatic reconstruction tried to recapture the medieval shrine as an object of devotion, with Mass being celebrated at the altar at its

foot. Burges was, of all the architects of the Gothic Revival, the most committed to reviving medieval forms in all media for every department of contemporary life, although apparently he had no strong religious convictions. His collection of medieval objects, and the many drawings and photographs of them that he assembled on his travels in Britain and Europe, gave him the knowledge necessary for his elaborate drawing. As to restoration in general, Burges followed Scott rather than Ruskin in his confidence that he could reconstruct medieval detail: indeed Burges contributed sections on the tombs and metalwork to the second edition of Scott's *Gleanings from Westminster Abbey* (1863). TC

LIT. London 1852, no. 1220; Cardiff 1981, no. D.10.

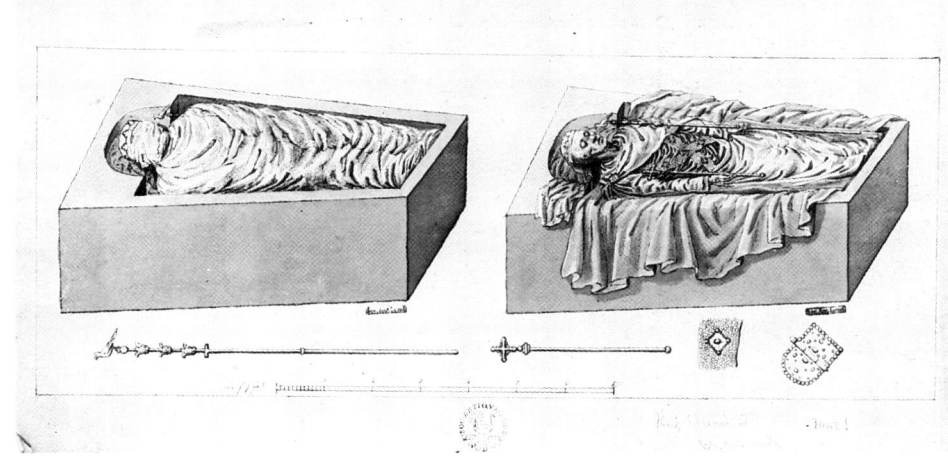

383

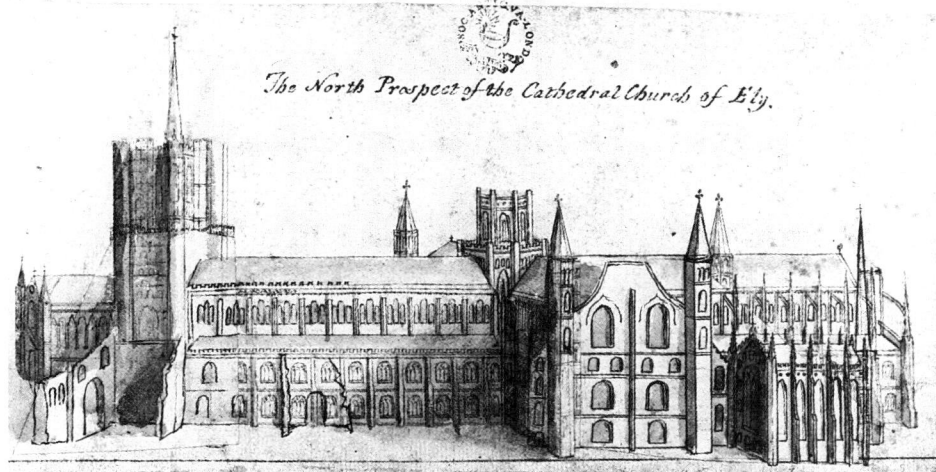

384

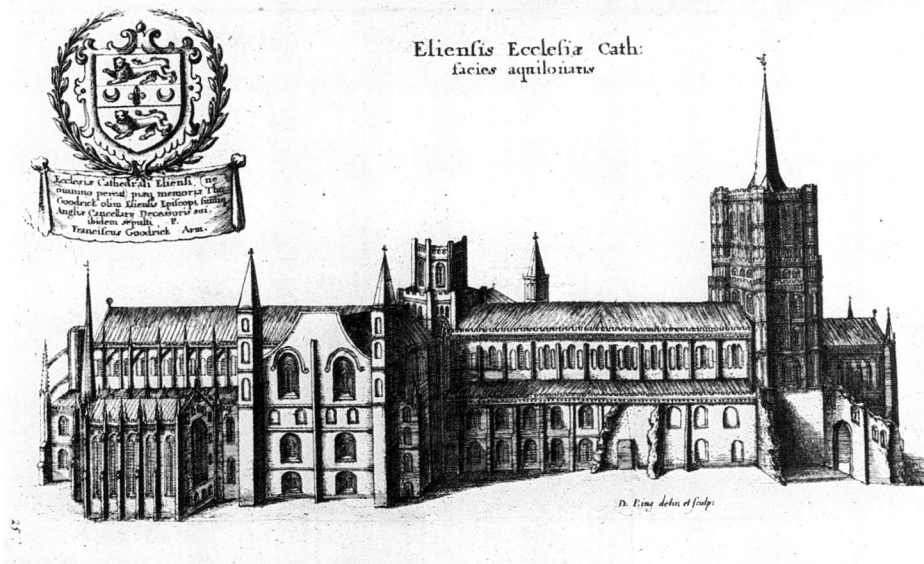

385

384 Ely Cathedral, view from the north

Daniel King (d. c. 1664)
c. 1650
Pen and ink with contemporary corrections and 2
  inserts in ink: 16 × 29.5 cm
Society of Antiquaries of London

This drawing was engraved as an illustration to the *Monasticon Anglicanum*, the history of the religious houses of England compiled by Roger Dodsworth and William Dugdale and published in 1655 (Cat. 385). Paradoxically the overthrow of Church and king by Parliament had stimulated antiquaries to preserve their monuments, on paper at least. This is the first representation of Ely Cathedral and, though small and crude, shows features such as the fourteenth-century octagon and lantern before post-medieval restorations (Cat. 399, 409). It also records the remains of the former parochial church of Holy Cross, cleared away in 1662, and more of the north-west transept than survives today. TC

PROV. Acq. Society of Antiquaries before c. 1850.

385 Ely Cathedral, view from the north

Daniel King (d. c. 1664), engraved after his own
  drawing
1655
Engraving: 21 × 34 cm
Society of Antiquaries of London

This engraving by King after his own drawing (Cat. 384) illustrates the history of the monastery, and from 1109 also the cathedral, of Ely in *Monasticon Anglicanum* (this engraving was opposite p. 88). Although the accounts were entirely documentary, there was an attempt to provide at least one elevation and sometimes a plan for each major building. King's plate lacks the scale and artistry of Hollar's similar views (Cat. 386) but does not try to classicise the medieval fabric. The dedicatory cartouche to the patron who paid for the engraving (son of a bishop of Ely) reveals the preservationist purpose of the *Monasticon*, to record the building *ne omnino pereat* (lest it perish utterly). The engraving was included in King's compilation, *Cathedrall and Conventuall Churches of England and Wales*. TC

PROV. Engraved for *Monasticon Anglicanum* (opp. p. 88).

386 Old St Paul's Cathedral, chapter house from the south

Wenceslaus Hollar (1607–77)
1658
Engraving: 19.5 × 28.5 cm
Guildhall Library, City of London, 460. PAU(1)Int.

By 1332, when the canons of St Paul's decided to follow most other secular cathedral chapters in building a chapter house and cloister, the only space available was their

DOMVS CAPITVLARIS S. PAVLI,
Meridie Profpectus.

386

former garden in the angle of the nave and south transept. Its smallness explains the placing of the chapter house inside the cloister, and its lowness relative to the floor level within the cathedral accounts for the very unusual two-storey design of the cloister. Despite being small this complex was highly important for, together with the south transept of Gloucester Cathedral (fig. 49), it ranks as the earliest example of Perpendicular architecture. The cloister was copied on an enlarged scale at Westminster Abbey from 1345, and its internal treatment inspired the piers in the nave of Canterbury Cathedral (Cat. 693). The tracery, destroyed by Hollar's day, had three lights under two hexagons like those shown in the chapter house windows. The designer was William Ramsey, chief royal architect from 1336.

The chapter house was retained in its Gothic form when the body of the cathedral was recased by Inigo Jones in the 1630s in the classical Tuscan style, visible in the background of the engraving. It survived the degradation of the cathedral in the Civil War, only to be destroyed in the Great Fire of 1666. The *History of St Paul's* by Dugdale, for which this was an illustration, was the first monograph on an English medieval building. Although the architecture was little discussed in the text, it was well illustrated by Hollar, the Bohemian-born artist whom Dugdale valued for his skilful recording. Hollar did not attempt to modernise the fourteenth-century detailing. The Great Fire fulfilled the gloomy prophecy of the dedicatory cartouche, leaving this as the only detailed record of the chapter house.   CW & TC

PROV. Engraved for Dugdale, 1658.

LIT. Wilson 1980a, pp. 197–226; London 1984a, pp. 361, 369.

387 *Chronologia Architectonica*

John Aubrey (1626–97)
c. 1670–90
Pen and wash: h. 31.5 cm, w. 39 cm
Oxford, Bodleian Library MS. top.gen. c. 25, ff. 155–156

John Aubrey included in his *Monumenta Britannica*, a vast manuscript account of native antiquities, the first chronology of English architecture ever attempted. Using as evidence his own observations, especially in his native Wiltshire, with other examples and dates provided by fellow antiquaries

such as John Evelyn and Anthony à Wood, Aubrey evolved a coherent account of the development of the successive styles. In the pages exhibited Aubrey successfully groups types of Early English windows under the reign of Henry III, citing as examples details from the Temple Church (Cat. 405–6), Westminster Abbey, Salisbury Cathedral, Dore Abbey and, particularly interesting because it was destroyed when Blenheim was built, the twelfth- and thirteenth-century palace at Woodstock. In 1672 Aubrey noted that the hall still retained its painted decoration.   TC

PROV. Acq. Bodleian Library, 1836.

LIT. Colvin 1968 passim.; London 1984a, p. 361, no. 505.

388 Ramsey Abbey, effigy of the founder Ailwyn (?)

After William Stukeley (1687–1765), engraved by E. Kirkall
1719
Engraving: 28 × 17.5
Society of Antiquaries of London

This mid-thirteenth-century effigy now preserved in the gatehouse to the mansion occupying the site of the Benedictine Abbey of Ramsey, Cambridgeshire, was identified by Stukeley as that of Ailwyn, the Saxon alderman who founded the house in 969 (see also Cat. 22). The attribution, though perhaps made earlier, when the effigy was recovered from a pond in the reign of Charles II, is probably not authentic. The effigy cannot be identified with the monument recorded as having been erected to Ailwyn in the thir-

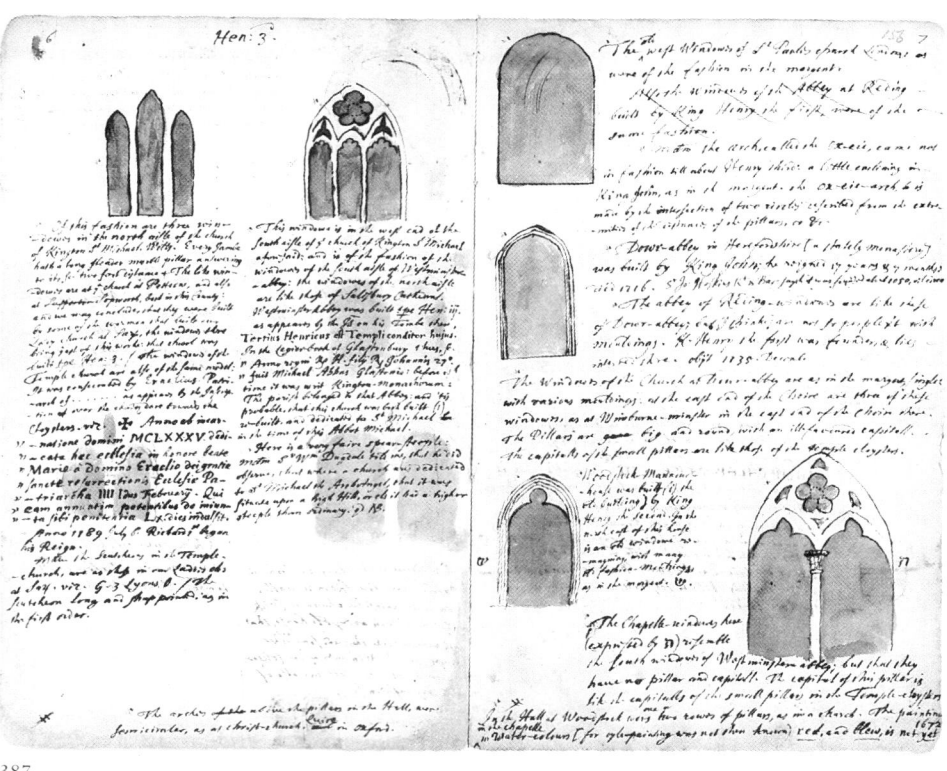

387

388

389

teenth century, which was of bronze. Stukeley, first a doctor and then a priest, was one of the most indefatigable and universal of eighteenth-century archaeologists. He recorded the effigy during a 'field trip' in 1719 studying all the antiquities along Ermine Street. Stukeley's depiction, in spite of its stylistic anachronisms, is faithful over details such as the keys and knotted staff and has added importance since it was made before the head was damaged by frost in 1745. The print, which illustrated his book, the *Itinerarium Curiosum*, is dedicated to Samuel Gale, fellow member of the Society of Antiquaries, whose father had edited the late twelfth-century chronicle of Ramsey Abbey.

TC

LIT. Stukeley, 1776, p. 81; Gough 1786, I, p. xcii.

389   Netley Abbey, view from the north

After Samuel Buck (1696–1779) and Nathaniel Buck (*fl.* 1727–53/9), engraved after their own drawing

1733
Engraving: 19 × 37 cm
Society of Antiquaries of London

The Cistercian abbey at Netley (Hampshire) on the Solent, was founded and for the most part built in the mid-thirteenth century. Its history after the Dissolution, first converted into a house and then partly demolished by a treasure-seeking owner, himself crushed in the ruins, left the shell of the church relatively intact, though overgrown with trees and ivy. The site, 'a most beautiful Ruin in as beautiful a situation' (Gray, 1937, I 428),

became much admired by tourists such as Thomas Gray in search of picturesque antiquity. The popularity of the views published by the Buck brothers – about 500, nearly all of medieval buildings – testifies to the interest taken in the architecture of the past by a wide section of the educated public in the mid-eighteenth century.   TC

LIT. Gray 1937 edn, II, p. 843.

390   Gloucester Cathedral, effigy of Robert Curthose, Duke of Normandy

John Saunders (*c.* 1750–1825)
1786
Watercolour, signed and dated 27.5 × 35 cm
Society of Antiquaries of London

The wooden effigy (Cat. 2) in the choir of

Gloucester Cathedral, though now considered thirteenth-century in date, is traditionally identified as representing Robert Curthose (d. 1134), Duke of Normandy and eldest son of the Conqueror. It was perhaps this royal connection that led to the effigy being removed and broken up during the Civil War. The pieces were bought by a Royalist squire in the county, Sir Humphrey Tracy, and were returned to the cathedral at the Restoration, when they were reassembled, perhaps with some alterations in the detailing of the armour and coronet. This episode shows a piety in preserving medieval monuments that is more historical than religious.   TC

PROV. Acq. by the Society of Antiquaries before *c.* 1850.

LIT. Sandford & Stebbing 1707, p. 15; Roper 1931, pp. 231–6.

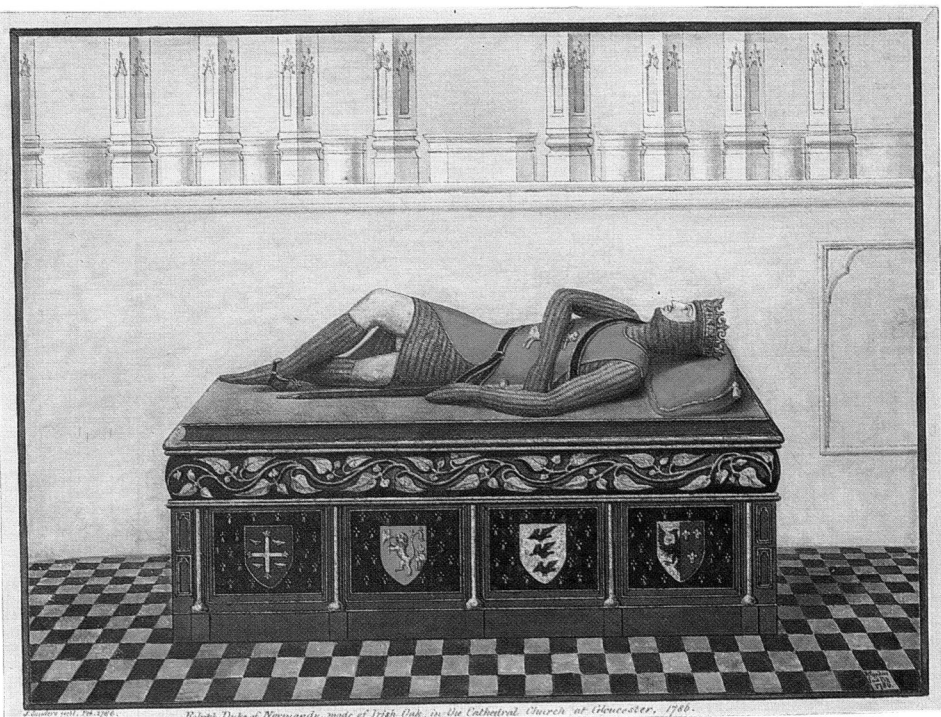

390

391

391 Ely Cathedral, octagon looking north-east

J.M.W. Turner (1775–1851)
c. 1796
Watercolour: 62.7 × 49.1 cm
Aberdeen Art Gallery and Museums, ABD AG
3016

The Romanesque crossing of Ely Cathedral was destroyed by the fall of the central tower in 1322 and replaced by a daring octagonal design, traditionally attributed to the sacrist Alan of Walsingham. The lantern above, used as a belfry, was threatening collapse by the mid-eighteenth century but was restored by James Essex in 1757 (see Cat. 408), who altered some of the roof carpentry and the detailing of windows and pinnacles. The great space under the octagon was until 1770 occupied by the choir which had remained in the original Romanesque position but which was then moved to the far east end. The new choir screen, designed by Essex, can be seen to the right of the picture. Turner's watercolour, which belongs to his early series of topographical views, conveys better than any photograph the complex scale and lighting of the octagon and how its eighteenth-century restoration exploited its sublime qualities. The picture was commissioned by the then Bishop Yorke, who promoted further refurbishings and restoration, especially of the west tower. TC

PROV. James Yorke, Bishop of Ely and his heirs; bt by Aberdeen Art Gallery, 1953.

LIT. London 1974, no. 13.

392 Salisbury Cathedral, interior of the chapter house

J.M.W. Turner (1775–1851)
c. 1799
Watercolour and pen and ink over pencil:
64.5 × 51.2 cm
Whitworth Art Gallery, University of Manchester

The polygonal chapter house of Salisbury Cathedral was built *c.* 1280. It remains one of the most perfect examples of its type, much

392

better preserved than the similar but earlier Westminster chapter house, restored in the nineteenth century with Salisbury as model. In this watercolour painted for the great patron of Wiltshire antiquities, Sir Richard Colt Hoare of Stourhead, Turner conveys the balanced proportions and luminosity of the structure. In the eighteenth century it escaped the sweeping restoration of the cathedral by Bishop Barrington and James Wyatt which, though execrated by later generations, established Salisbury with its regular architecture, uncluttered interior and landscape setting as the 'beau ideal' of the English cathedral. TC

PROV. Sir Richard Colt Hoare and his heirs; presented to Whitworth Art Gallery, 1891.

LIT. London 1974, no. 327; Paris 1979, no. 20.

393–8 Prior Crauden's Chapel, Ely, six drawings showing elevations, sections and details

William Wilkins Jnr (1778–1839)
1801
Pen and ink with grey wash: (i), (ii), (iii), (v)
42 × 25 cm; (iv) (vi) 44 × 30 cm
Society of Antiquaries of London

About 1325 Prior Crauden of Ely added to his lodgings a chapel which, though small, is one of the finest examples of English Decorated. At the Dissolution it became the dean's chapel, but after the Civil War confiscation of chapter property it was desecrated and the lead stripped from the roof. After the Restoration it was reroofed with tiles and adapted as a house. A floor was inserted approximately at the springing level of the former vault and a chimney stack against the north side, but much of the elaborate sculpted decoration and the rich tiled floor remained intact. Wilkins was able to make these detailed studies of the building for a paper he delivered to the Antiquaries in 1801, deleting the domestic intrusions, although they were not removed for another fifty years, and the steep-pitched roof which still survives. Wilkins is better known as the neo-classical architect of Downing College, Cambridge, and much later of the National Gallery, London; but for his generation enthusiasm for the antique was by no means incompatible with an equal knowledge of medieval art   TC

PROV. Drawn for the Society of Antiquaries, 1801.

LIT. Wilkins 1808, *passim.*

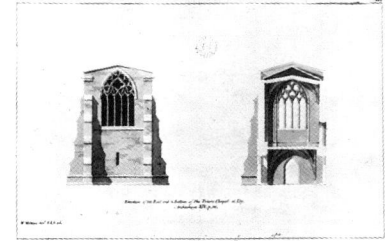

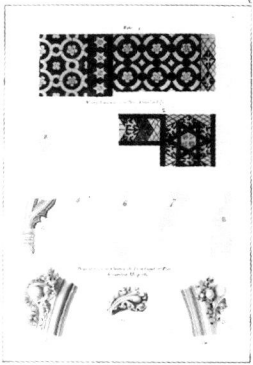

393–8

399 Ely Cathedral, view from the north-east

John Buckler (1770–1851)
1807
Watercolour: 45 × 66 cm
Dean and Chapter, Ely Cathedral

This view of Ely, one of a series by Buckler, shows the major thirteenth- and fourteenth-century additions to the Romanesque cathedral: the presbytery, the lantern and the Lady Chapel, then used as a separate parish church. Essex had restored the lantern in 1757 and, in an attempt to lighten it, had removed the upper flying buttresses and crowned it with a simple pinnacled parapet; he had also simplified the tracery in the windows. At the same time he had renewed the presbytery roof which was pushing out the east front and returned the wall to the vertical. Buckler was a prolific draughtsman of medieval buildings, combining accuracy of detail with a Romantic appreciation of their massing.   TC

LIT. Cambridge 1984, pp. 14, 32–3.

399

400

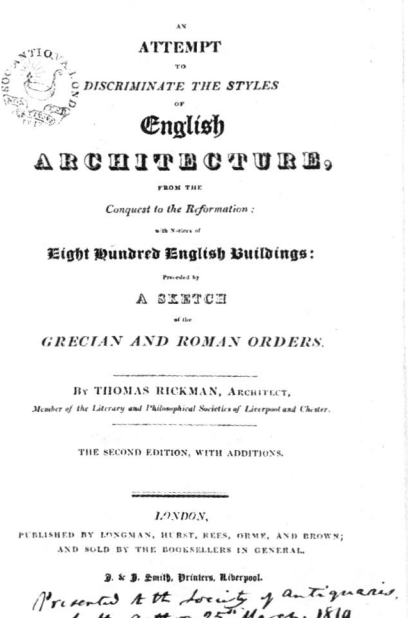

401

400   T. Rickman, *An Attempt to Discriminate the Styles of Architecture*: frontispiece and title page

After Thomas Rickman (1776–1841), engraved
   by W. Radclyffe
1817, this edn (2nd) 1819
Engraving, inscr. by the author: 21.7 × 12.3 cm;
   page 22 cm × 28 cm
Society of Antiquaries of London

In the eighteenth century no comprehensive account of Gothic was published in spite of attempts by, among others, James Essex (Cat. 408). Demand became such that a compilation first printed in 1800 of the essays on the subject by Wren, Warburton, Warton, Bentham and Milner went into three editions: a series of general histories followed. Rickman, a Quaker from Liverpool yet an architect devoted to medieval art, attempted something different, a manual which named, analysed and illustrated each successive style. First printed in 1815 in a Liverpool journal, it was then published in book form in 1817 and had six editions in the author's lifetime. The copy (of the second edition) exhibited is that presented by Rickman to the Society of Antiquaries, to which he was to be elected in 1829. The frontispiece, 'A Decorated interior', showing a hall church with groined vaults and ornamental niches has, like Rickman's own buildings, a thin, wiry quality which belies the accuracy of his archaeology. His terms 'Early English', 'Decorated' and 'Perpendicular' have stood the test of time as style names, but the general use of 'English' instead of 'Gothic' never succeeded.   TC

PROV. Presented by Rickman to the Society of Antiquaries, 1819.

LIT. Aldrich 1985, *passim.*

401   Prior Crauden's Chapel, Ely, south front

A.W.N. Pugin (1812–52)
c. 1848
Pen and ink on paper: 22 × 15.8 cm
The Board of Trustees of the Victoria and Albert
   Museum, London, E.77 (17)–1970

Pugin, an architect of precocious genius and fertile decorative imagination, had a profound influence not only on Gothic Revival architecture but also on the treatment of Gothic buildings by insisting that Pointed (his preferred term for Gothic) was both the only true Christian style and the only rational style, in which no feature or ornament was superfluous to the structure. Pugin almost certainly drew the chapel during his honeymoon tour of great medieval buildings

after his marriage to his third wife on 10 August 1848. He had previously visited Ely in 1842 with the medievalising young enthusiasts of the Cambridge Camden Society (see p. 189 above). His attention would have been drawn to the building by its recent repair (Cat. 402). In contrast with the cool precision of the neo-classical Wilkins (Cat. 393–8), Pugin stressed the verticality of the chapel and, in the details at the foot of the page, the intricacy of the tracery of the west and south windows.   TC

PROV. By descent; acquired by V&A, 1970.

LIT. Wedgwood 1985, pp. 52, 288.

402   Prior Crauden's Chapel, Ely, view showing windows and niche in south-east corner

William Burges (1827–81)
c. 1852
Pencil with coloured washes: 35.5 × 22 cm
British Architectural Library – RIBA, London,
   z.4/6

In 1846 the chapel was cleared of its domestic elements and thoroughly repaired, and eventually it was restored to worship. The great Cambridge Gothic scholar, Robert Willis, was intimately involved with the project and suggested the timber reconstruction of the vault based on evidence he had found in the surviving springing blocks. The chimney stacks, flues and brick cladding were re-

402

moved from the north wall and destroyed features replaced to match those opposite on the south side. Burges made a series of drawings of the chapel and other buildings at Ely, showing surviving polychromy, a subject in which he was much interested. The

restoration of the interior in 1986 has again revealed many traces of paint on architectural features. TC

LIT. Stewart 1868, pp. 244–8; Cardiff 1981, no. D. 1; Binski & Park 1986, pp. 32–4.

403 Rochester Cathedral, four drawings of the tomb of Bishop John de Sheppey

Edwin J. Lambert (exh. 1881–1928)
1894
Pen and ink and watercolour: whole card
48 × 74 cm
The Board of Trustees of the Victoria and Albert
Museum, London, 348–1894

The tomb of John de Sheppey, Bishop of Rochester from 1352 to his death in 1360, lies under an arch between the south transept aisle and the choir of the cathedral. Its high standard of preservation is due to its having been carefully walled up, either against iconoclasm or because of the threatened collapse of the crossing; it was revealed only in 1825 during repairs by Cottingham. The tomb was restored in 1840, the effigy and the polychromy being in part renewed, and at the same time the contemporary railing which bears the bishop's initials was placed by the tomb. The watercolours reveal the wealth of detail in the tomb preserved by its exceptional history. That they were ac-

quired for the South Kensington Museum, presumably for artists and designers to copy, shows the educational value still placed on Gothic in the 1890s. TC

PROV. Acq. from the artist by V&A Museum, 1894.

LIT. Kempe 1834, *passim*; Palmer 1897, pp. 99–103.

404 Canterbury Cathedral, choir viewed from the west

Artist anonymous
c. 1680
Oil on canvas: 122 × 99 cm
Dean and Chapter of Canterbury

The view, looking east from the pulpitum, shows the choir, sanctuary and the Corona chapel, built in 1175–84 and usually regarded as the first masterpiece of Gothic in an English cathedral. Canterbury survived the upheavals of both Reformation and Civil War relatively intact, except for the destruction of Becket's shrine in the former and of 'superstitious' stained glass, sculpture and liturgical objects in the latter. At the Restoration the choir regained its traditional liturgical functions but was gradually modernised by new furnishings in a classical style. The painting depicts the panelling along the parclose screens installed in 1676 and the organ of 1663 still coexisting with the late thirteenth-century stalls (replaced in 1705).

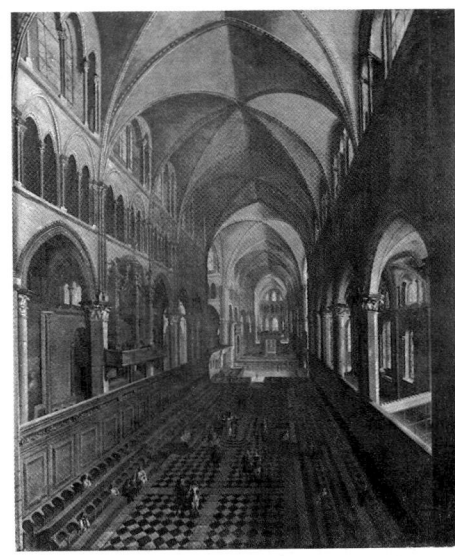

404

Though it lacks the astonishing accuracy of the similar view painted by T. Johnson in 1657 (London 1984a, no. 502), its very commissioning shows the respect the cathedral commanded even under Charles II. It also demonstrates how contemporary furnishings were introduced not to cloak but to complement the splendours of the medieval building. TC

PROV. Not recorded before late 19th century.

LIT. Caröe 1911, *passim*.

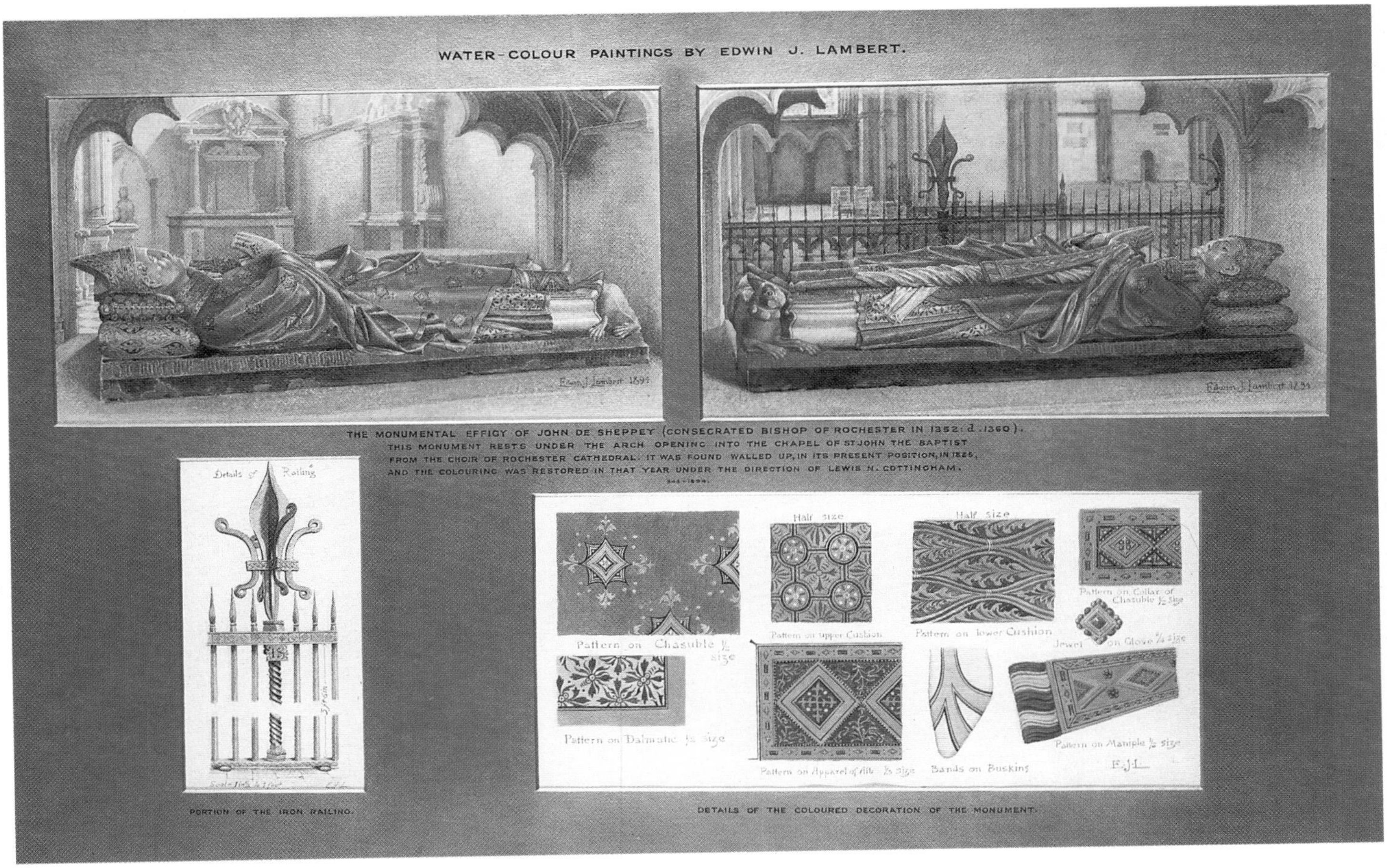

405

405 The Temple Church, London, interior of chancel looking east

After George Shepherd (c. 1765–1831), etched by
J. Skelton
1812
Etching: 17.3 × 23.6 cm
Guildhall Library, City of London, 570/TEM.CHU,
no. 62830

The east part or chancel of the Temple
Church in London was added to the twelfth-
century rotunda between 1220 and 1240. It
is 'one of the most perfectly and classically
proportioned buildings of the thirteenth century in England' (Pevsner 1973 b, p. 315).
After the dissolution of the Knights Templar
in 1308–12 the Temple eventually passed to
the Inns of Court, the Inner and Middle
Temple, which still possess it. The church,
thus having wealthy patrons and an influential congregation, was regularly altered to
suit contemporary modes of worship. The
engraving shows the building with classical
reredos, installed by Wren in 1682 as part of
his restoration of the building, central pulpit
with a rich sounding-board above, banked
panelled pews, and monuments attached to
walls and pillars. These were all swept away
in the restoration of 1840–3 (though the
reredos was returned in 1954).   TC

PROV. Engraved for publication in *Architectura
Ecclesiastica Londini*, 1819 (Adams 1983, pp.
298–305).

LIT. Esdaile 1933, pp. 2–9.

406 The Temple Church, London, interior of chancel looking west after restoration

After (W.) R.H. Essex (1802–55)
1843
Chromolithograph: 45.3 × 34.1 cm
Guildhall Library, City of London, 570/TEM.CHU

From 1840 to 1843 the east part or chancel
of the Temple Church was the subject of a
radical restoration under the direction of
James Savage and then, after a dispute, of
Sidney Smirke and Decimus Burton. Every
furnishing, including the Wren reredos and
all the post-medieval monuments, was removed in a determined effort to return the

building to its original Gothic state. Essex was
allowed to record the restoration as it pro-
gressed, from the scaffolding. Comparison
between Shepherd's picture of 1812 (Cat.
405) and this startling view of only thirty
years later, the subject almost unrecognis-
able as the same building, shows how fast
attitudes to Gothic were changing even in a
conservative institution like the Temple. The
church was now adorned with stained glass
and vivid medievalising paintings on the
walls and vaults of sacred and, on the west
wall, historical subjects by William Wille-
ment. Evidence of medieval painting on the
vaults was revealed but ignored. Savage
designed the Minton tiles after those in the
Westminster chapter house and installed
elaborate pews, also using medieval models
(the latter omitted here as they spoiled the
ecclesiological purity). Small wonder the
restoration cost at least five times the estimate! After damage during the Second
World War almost nothing remains today of
the nineteenth-century decoration and furnishing except for a little stained glass.   TC

LIT. Burge 1843, *passim*; Essex & Smirke 1845,
passim; Crook 1965, *passim*.

407 York Minster, choir, looking west

J. Harwood
1827
Oil on panel, dated on back: 95.5 × 79 cm
Michael Gillingham Esq.

The eastern part of York Minster dates from
the second half of the fourteenth century but
it was seriously damaged by arson in 1829.
A further fire in 1840 destroyed the interior
of the south-west tower and the nave roof.
This painting provides rare evidence of the
east end before the 1829 fire, with the

406

407

medieval vault intact, and the choir furnished with the Gothic throne, pews and pulpit designed by William Kent. Kent and his patron Lord Burlington were also responsible for the prominent geometric paving laid in 1731–8. The light and brilliant colour of the painting give a more authentic picture than monochrome prints or Puginian lampoons of the rich dignity of a Georgian cathedral choir. The painting was engraved with minor differences in staffage in 1829. The choral service in the Minster at this period was recalled even in 1866 as 'like the opening of a new world' and 'mingled with the most inspiring thoughts of the public worship of God' (Aylmer & Cant 1979, p. 293). TC

PROV. Not recorded before acquisition in York by present owner.

LIT. Wylson 1845, *passim*.

408

408 Ely Cathedral, section through presbytery

James Essex (1722–84)
c. 1768
Pen and wash: 39 × 25 cm
British Library, Add. MS 6772, ff. 220–1

The presbytery (or retrochoir) of Ely Cathedral was built in the mid-thirteenth century. James Essex, the Cambridge architect and antiquary who was surveyor for an extensive restoration of Ely from 1757 to 1771, prepared this section – no easy task with contemporary techniques – either in connection with his renewal of the roof in 1768, or as a study for his projected *History of Gothic*. He appears to show the fourteenth-century roof, similar to that of the nave. Essex, unusually for his period, was concerned with the structure of Gothic rather than its ornament. TC

PROV. Beq. to British Museum by Essex's nephew by marriage, Thomas Kerrich, 1828.

LIT. Cambridge 1984, p. 14 & no. 53.

409 Ely Cathedral, proposed restoration of octagon and lantern

G.G. Scott (1811–78)
1859
Pen and ink with sepia wash: 64 × 49.5 cm
British Architectural Library–RIBA, London, Arc I/30 SCGGS(40)3

The restoration of the Ely octagon and lantern was proposed as a memorial to Dean Pocock (d. 1858) who had instigated an extensive programme of repair and reconstruction starting in 1843. The project was motivated not by structural needs – Essex's fabric of eighty years earlier was still in good condition – but from a dissatisfaction with all the eighteenth-century contributions to the cathedral. Scott's chief alterations were in the treatment of the openings, the pinnacles, buttresses and the parapet which were restored with reference to early prints, particularly the *Monasticon* (Cat. 385) but which nevertheless now give a vigorous High Victorian profile to the lantern. The drawing was engraved and published in the *Ecclesiologist*, XX, 1859, opposite p. 328. TC

PROV. By descent; presented to RIBA, 1953.

LIT. Heseltine 1981, p. 30; Lindley 1987, *passim*.

410–15 Church of All Saints, Great Driffield, plan and five elevations for proposed restoration

G.E. Street (1824–81)
1875
Pen and coloured inks, each 37.5 × w. 55 cm
British Architectural Library–RIBA, London, RAN 2/K/4(1–6)

The church of Great Driffield, North Humberside, is a building largely of the twelfth and

409

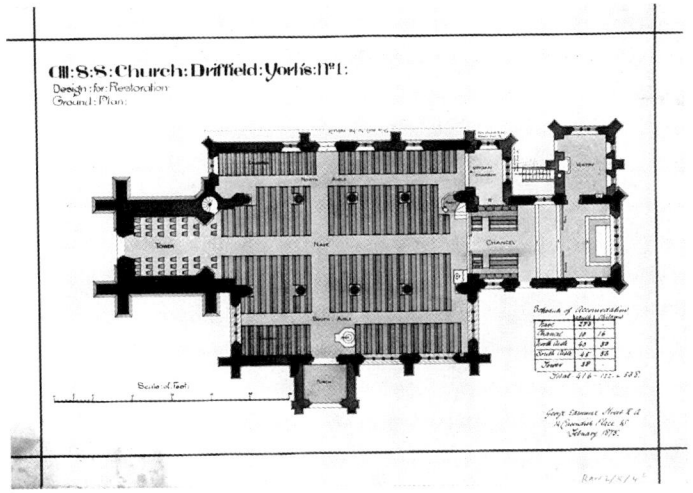

410

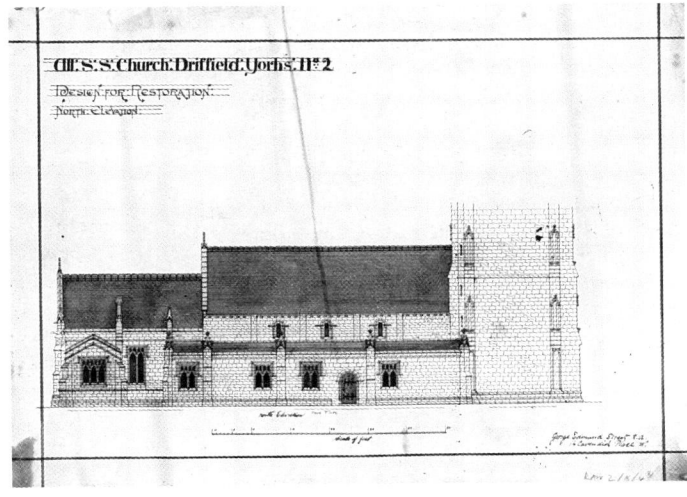

411

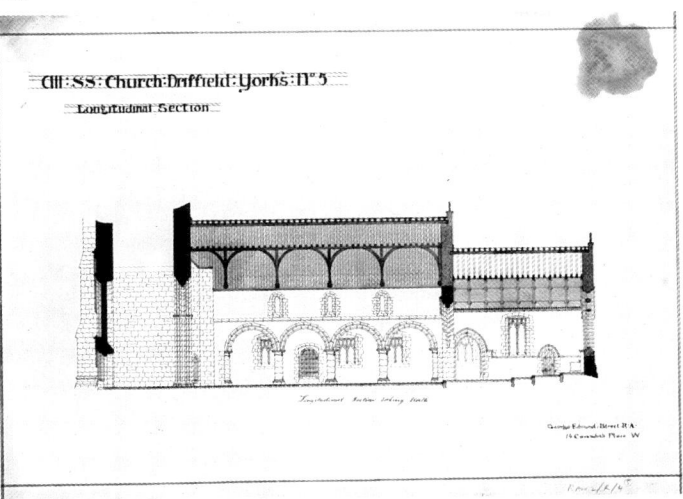

412

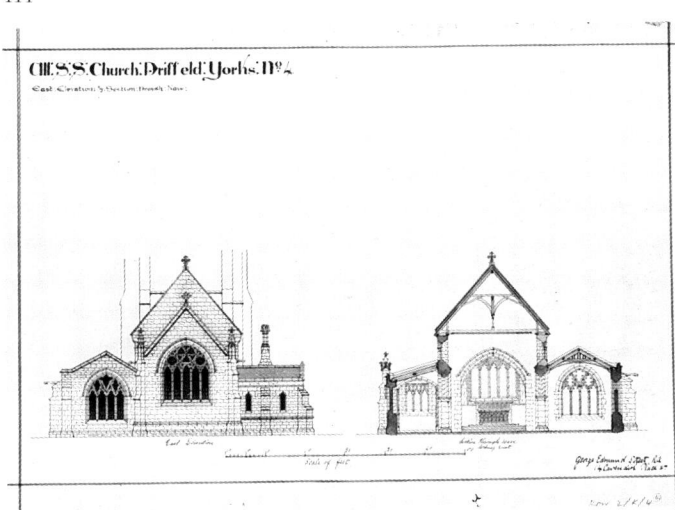

413

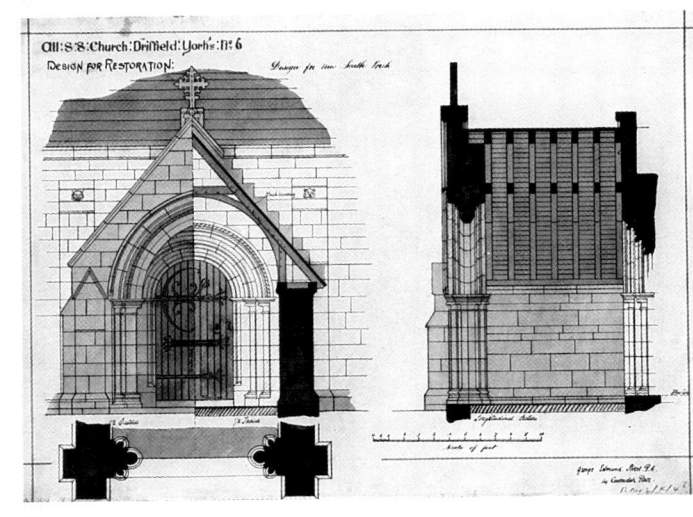

414

415

thirteen centuries. These proposals by Street for its restoration were rejected in favour of a scheme by G.G. Scott the Younger, executed three years later. The Street designs are a good example of an unremarkable, thorough High Victorian restoration in which the total impression is indelibly nineteenth-century although relatively little of the fabric was replaced, only those sections marked in red being new building. This was largely due to the complete renewal of all roofs, floors and furnishings. The annotations on the plan show the importance attached to squeezing the maximum amount of seating into the interior. Ironically the successful Scott designs, though more sympathetic in texture, were more radical in their additions and alterations to the structure. TC

PROV. By descent; presented on permanent loan to RIBA, 1967.

LIT. Richardson 1976, p. 120; Heseltine 1981, p. 131.

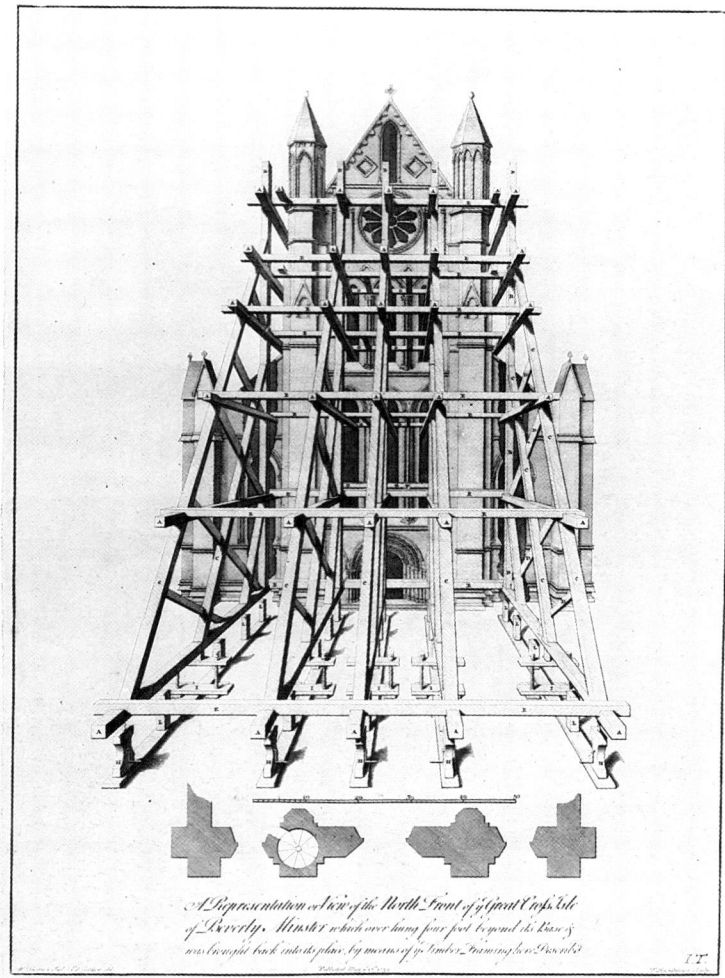

416

417

416–17 Beverley Minster, mechanism for the restoration of the north transept

(i) elevation; (ii) section
After Edward Geldorf, engraved by P. Fourdrinier
(fl. 1720–50)
1739
Engravings: (i) 45 × 32 cm; (ii) 33 × 30 cm
Society of Antiquaries of London

By the early eighteenth century Beverley Minster was in serious need of repair, especially the thirteenth-century north transept, the north front of which overhung 1.2 m beyond its base. A major restoration was launched in 1716 under the direction of Nicholas Hawksmoor which successfully repaired and refurnished the church. The most striking part was the straightening of the north front in 1717–19. Hawksmoor and William Thornton, the York joiner who supervised the restoration on the spot, devised a giant cradle of five trusses to hold the front which was then cut near the base, wedged and gradually screwed back to the vertical. The scale and ingenuity of the scheme, executed without the benefit of later technology, disprove the conventional idea of Georgian church work as inadequate and superficial.   TC

LIT. Hall 1973, pp. 20–6.

418 Westminster Abbey, design accepted for the restoration of the north front of the north transept

W. Dickinson (c. 1671–1725)
1719
Pen and wash: 53.6 × 38.7 cm
Dean and Chapter of Westminster, W.A.M.(P)
900,900A

The thirteenth-century north front of Westminster Abbey had fallen into serious decay by the end of the seventeenth century, despite repairs in the 1620s and again in the 1660s. Its ragged state, 'rather the skeleton of a church than any great comeliness' (Keepe 1683, pp. 23–4) was the more conspicuous as it housed the principal entrance. This drawing for the restoration of the transept was prepared in 1719 for the approval of the sub-committee in charge of the works begun in 1697 by parliamentary grant under the direction of Christopher Wren; by this stage everyday responsibility had been assumed by the under-surveyor to the fabric, Wren's pupil William Dickinson. The flap shows the contrast between the consistent Gothic proposed by Dickinson and approved by Wren 'to make the Whole of a Piece' and the existing mongrel, with the rose window stopped up with plaster, 'a little Dorick Passage' inserted below and the flanking pinnacles cropped (Wren 1750, p. 302). That the flap does not extend to the lowest stage may indicate that the portals had already been completed although the blind tracery in the tympana over the doorways as executed was more ambitiously Gothic than the simplified mouldings shown here. The result was one of the most assured and prominent restorations of the eighteenth century. Though the decayed medieval sculpture round the porch was cut away as an unsightly detraction from the beauty of the architecture, the detailing of the elevation as a whole and of the rose window tracery in particular was authentically conceived. The eighteenth-century work was swept away by G.G. Scott and J.L. Pearson in their radical restoration of 1875–92, to the dismay of William Morris and the Society for the Protection of Ancient Buildings.   TC

PROV. Acq. by the Dean & Chapter of Westminster, 1927.

418

419   York Minster, carpenters at work in the nave vault

Joseph Halfpenny (1748–1811)
1796
Watercolour, dated on mount: 47.2 × 61.5 cm
York City Art Gallery, R1784

The timber vault of York Minster was complete by 1354. Although disastrous fires have destroyed most of the medieval high roofs, including in 1840 that of the nave, the Minster is among the best-maintained medieval buildings in England, retaining a separate fabric fund and cared for even during the Interregnum. In 1770 John Carr of York had surveyed the structure and repaired the roofs. In 1796 further repairs of the nave roof proved necessary, which included the stripping away of the cells of the vault from the ribs. Joseph Halfpenny, a York artist interested in local antiquities, took advantage of the scaffolding to add drawings of the vault bosses to his great collection of architectural and scuptural details of the Minster, many of which he published in his book *Gothic ornaments in the cathedral church of York* in 1795. He also drew this picture, a rare illustration of the unsensational regular maintenance which is the chief cause of the survival of the great churches of England. TC

PROV. Bt in London, 1864; acq. by York City Art Gallery as part of the Evelyn Coll., 1931.

LIT. Halfpenny 1795; Ingamells 1972, pp. 285–6; York, 1972, no. 24.

419

XII Medieval Artists and their Techniques

Medieval artists' tools do not survive in any number and they are difficult to date in the absence of archaeological evidence. One group of tools gathered here is connected with the making of medieval manuscripts, the other with work in wood and stone.

It is well known that medieval artists relatively seldom signed their works and there are very few representations of them at work (Cat. 441). However, since by this period the majority were paid professionals, there is a considerable amount of archival evidence as to the names of artists, the work they were employed to do and the payments they received (see Cat. 443–6). From these it is clear that though the majority were men there were also some women, for example working as embroideresses (see Cat. 442).

An interesting aspect of their work is their dependence on earlier works of art as models. The use of pattern books to record and transmit imagery must have been widespread, though very few survive now. Some of the pattern books include drawings of mouldings for stonemasons, as does the famous Pepysian pattern book which could not be lent to the exhibition (Cat. 466), and the way these patterns transferred to the stone is seen on surviving stonework (e.g. Cat. 476). There is also a rare surviving example of a mason's sketch on a stone, a reduced version of a tracing floor (see Cat. 474–5). The materials used and the technical skill of the artist were valued above all in the Middle Ages. Works of art were also, however, produced serially by tracing and casting from moulds (see Cat. 447–63).

Fig. 130 The artist painting a statue of the Virgin and Child argues with the Devil, from the Smithfield Decretals (London, British Library, Royal MS 10 E.iv, f. 209v.)

420–1 Styli(?)

Excavations of sites ranging from before the Conquest to the fifteenth or sixteenth century have turned up bone implements that, when complete, are set with a short narrow tip, of iron or (less frequently) bronze or (occasionally) silver (MacGregor 1985, p. 124).

At one time these were readily identified as styli, for writing on a waxed writing table (cf. Cat. 428; e.g. Guildhall Museum 1908, pp. 42–3), but against this it has been pointed out that they lack any spatulate eraser at the head (the heads being commonly ovoid or spherical), while the implements are rather short to be held in the hand comfortably for long periods. The implements have been found (among other places) on school sites, suggesting some connection with academic activities (Woodfield 1981, pp. 103, 154).

Instead it has recently been suggested (MacGregor 1985, p. 125) that the implements are *punctoria*, prickers for making the holes in folded parchment sheets that would enable ruling by dry point or plummet (Cat. 427) to take place. The 'shoulder' formed by the bottom of the bone shank would have prevented the metal top from penetrating too deeply and making too large a hole, while the rounded head could have served as a burnisher to treat small blemishes in the parchment (and many of the heads do show signs of wear or polishing).

Against this, however, is the abundance of the implements; no systematic investigation of the pricking of later medieval manuscripts has taken place, but it is certainly very common to find that the pricking consists of longitudinal slits, such as would be made by the tip of a knife, rather than round holes. Furthermore, Horman's *Vulgaria* of 1519 refers to *poyntyllis* of bone (or silver, brass or stone) 'hauynge a pynne at the ende' (James 1926, p. 124; personal communication, A. MacGregor); 'poyntell' was translated by Horman as *stylus* or *graphium*, meaning a writing implement. It is also significant that a stylus which is still preserved as part of a set of waxed tables and their leather cover, at Namur, is short and thin and has a rounded top (Paris 1981–2, pp. 194–5; repr. Viollet-le-Duc 1871, II, p. 157). A stylus for writing on a waxed table is therefore the likeliest identification of these objects. NLR

420 Stylus

English(?), medieval
Bone and metal: l. of bone 88 mm; l. of metal tip 4 mm; max. w. of broad end 1 cm
Museum of London, 1328

This has a turned, tapering peg, with ovoid head and moulding below; a metal tip is inserted into the other end. NLR

PROV. Found in Backchurch Lane, Spitalfields; Guildhall Museum, by 1903.

LIT. London, Guildhall Museum 1908, p. 43, no. 293; MacGregor 1985, pp. 124–5.

421 Stylus

English(?), medieval
Bone and metal: l. of bone 71 mm; l. of metal tip 3 mm; max. w. of tip 1 mm; max w. of broad end 9.5 mm
Museum of London, 10964

The turned, tapering peg has a moulding at the broad end; a metal tip is inserted into the other end. The broad end has a flat surface on which has been cut what might be a merchant's mark; it is possible that this end of the implement served as the matrix for a merchant's mark stamp. NLR

PROV. Found at 34–40 Finsbury Pavement (i.e. Moorgate); bt from a workman (by permission of Sir Howell J. Williams, and the Anglo-Persian Oil Co.) by Guildhall Museum, 1921.

422 Metal pen

13th century(?)
Copper alloy: l. 105 mm, w. at knop 7 mm
Museum of London, 1574

The quill pen was the commonest writing instrument in medieval England, although none has survived. But metal pens cannot have been such a rarity, for several of this design have been found: each has a flattened knop at one end, and at the other end widens into four flanged grooves which taper to a point. When one such pen was found in the last century it was thought to be for use as a stylus on a waxed surface (Hussey 1848, pp. 161–2), but the grooves in the end are best explained as for ink: experiments have shown that with ink 'it is quite possible to make letters, and certainly to draw lines, although there is no way of achieving variation in the thickness of stroke' (Cook 1958, p. 178). Furthermore, another such pen was found with charters and other documents, under flooring at Canterbury Cathedral (Faussett 1868, p. 241).

Like certain of the other similar pens, this one has a round knop but a square stem out of which scoops have been cut: such patterning would make it easier to rotate between one's fingers. NLR

PROV. Guildhall Museum, London, by 1903.

LIT. Hussey 1848, pp. 161–2; London, Guildhall Museum 1908, p. 53, no. 71, repr. pl. xx fig. 11; Cook 1958, pp. 177–8, repr. pl. xx.

423 Penner

14th century?
Leather: lower part 109 × 23 mm; top 36 × 32 mm
Museum of London, 4670

As frequently referred to in contemporary sources as the inkhorn or inkwell (Cat. 425), the penner served to keep safe the quills used by medieval writers; as in this example, its top as well as bottom might have holes to enable it to be hung from the waist by a cord (up and down which the top might slide). Its top is made of a single, folded and stitched piece of leather; its lower part is similarly made, but contains two more folded and stitched pieces of leather that form tubes enabling the pens to be stored separately.

Both parts retain faint signs of the designs that were stamped or pressed on to them; these comprise shields of arms, and include three leopards (as on the English royal arms) on the lower part: the latter is closely paralleled on a knife sheath in the British Museum (repr. Russell 1939, pl. IV, opp. p. 135).

That pen cases might be elaborately decorated is perhaps implied by the bequest in 1436 by Thomas Damett, Canon of St Paul's Cathedral, London, of 'one penner with its appurtenances, of Paris work' (Harvey 1948, p. 183). NLR

PROV. Guildhall Museum, London, by 1903.

LIT. London, Guildhall Museum 1908, p. 147, no. 105.

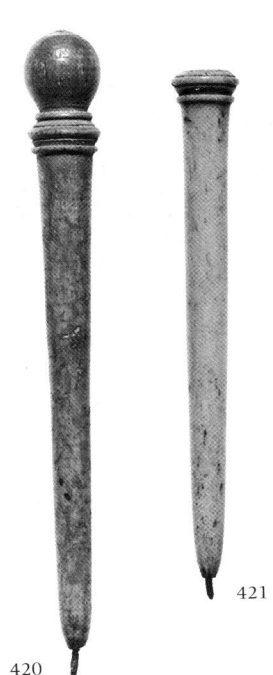

420   421

422   423

426

425

424

427

424 Metal pen

English(?), 15th century(?)
Copper alloy: l. 105 mm, max. w. 6 mm
Museum of London, 82.145/2

The cut (6 mm long) in its nib shows that this implement must have been made for use as an ink pen; it is puzzling, therefore, that its other end is scoop-shaped.

Numbers of such pens have been assumed in the past to be of Roman origin (see e.g. British Museum 1958, p. 48, no. 2; personal communication, John Clark); when lacking the split nib, they were thought to be styli for use on waxed tablets (cf. Cat. 428), or even ear-picks. This example was found with fifteenth-century material and is presumably of that date. It is made of a single piece of metal, folded over to form a tight tube (save at its nib and scooped ends). NLR

PROV. Found on River Thames foreshore, at north end of Southwark Bridge, 1982; bt by Museum of London, 1982.

LIT. Schuermans 1866; British Museum 1958, p. 48.

425 Inkwell

Late medieval
Horn and bone(?): h. 45 mm, max. diam. at top
56 mm, max. diam. at bottom 59 mm, max.
diam. of hole in top 26 mm, th. of horn c. 3 mm
Museum of London, A 292

With the penner (as in Cat. 423), the inkhorn was long an indispensable part of any writer's equipment; penner and inkhorn

were translated as *scriptorium* in the *Promptorium Parvulorum*, a lexicon of c. 1440. But later fifteenth-century memorial brasses show inkwells that are of this shape or have an even narrower top, which was far more convenient to use than a horn with its pointed end (see Cat. 440).

Horn was, however, cheap and light, and this inkwell, of horn with a bone(?) top (the base is missing), represents the transitional stage of using just a section of horn, before the displacement of horn by such materials as glass in the sixteenth century. The well's outside has been decorated with a compass-drawn pattern of incised overlapping double rings (with dots from the compass point). At the top are one hole and the remains of a second, for a cord by which it could be suspended from, say, a waist-belt. NLR

PROV. Found in Finsbury, London; bt by the London Museum, 1911.

LIT. Ward Perkins 1940, p. 292, repr. pl. xc.

426 Parchment clip(?)

1270–90
Copper alloy: l. 58 mm, w. 18 mm
Museum of London, SWA 81 (2232)

Several similar bows or tweezers have been found, with a movable collar and large heads decorated with patterns of punched dots; it has been suggested that they were to hold sheets of parchment, perhaps in a scriptorium (personal communication, John Clark). Their large, flat heads certainly indicate that

they were for holding in place one or more relatively light, flat-surfaced objects. NLR

PROV. Swan Lane, City of London, excavated by Dept. of Urban Archaeology, 1981.

LIT. Williams 1977, p. 184, repr.; Williams 1979, no. Cu. 73, repr. pl. 48.

427 Plummet

13th/first half 14th century
Lead: l. 70 mm
Inscr. ROGERVS
Private Collection

Modern pencils are of graphite, which was not used for writing instruments in England before the sixteenth century (Boon 1976, p. 115). But from the very late eleventh century, metallic lead was used to rule the parchment page: it superseded blind ruling (with a hard point) by the third quarter of the twelfth century (Ker 1957, pp. xxiv–xxv), and remained the commonest means of ruling until its gradual replacement by ink, including coloured inks for ornamental ruling, from the fifteenth century onwards.

Lead was expensive – which is why it was so little used for roofs – and so it was worth casting this plummet with a hole at one end, for securing it, and with the name Roger, presumably its owner. A very fine late thirteenth-century plummet or lead stylus found in the Seine was lettered KAROLI SCRIPTORIS, 'of Charles the Writer' (Vallet de Viriville 1866, pp. 75–6). Roger's plummet, unlike this and other plummets thought to have been used for writing (Henig 1976, p. 216), is not pointed at one end, but it is worn and perhaps once had a sharper point; and other uses (such as for a plumb-line's weight) seem unlikely. NLR

PROV. Found at Abbots Bromley, Staffs., deserted medieval village.

LIT. Vallet de Viriville 1866, pp. 72–7; Ker 1957, pp. xxiv–xxv; Ker 1960, pp. 41–2; Gilissen 1969, pp. 150–62; Henig 1976; Boon 1976, p. 115.

428 Writing tablet

English(?): second half 14th century
Bone: h. 7.8 cm, w. 3.5 cm, th. 0.35 cm
Southampton City Museums, SOU 122.179

Abbot Guibert de Nogent (d. 1124) in his autobiography said that 'I made no notes in my tablets for the composition of my works, but committed them to the written page without alteration, as I thought them out' (Bland 1926, p. 72). For most medieval writers, however, whether boys at school or Archbishop Anselm composing a philosophical treatise (Eadmer 1962 edn, p. 30), the possession of a writing medium that was readily alterable (unlike parchment) was a necessity of life. Writing tablets, usually in a pair but sometimes forming a booklet of several leaves, and usually of ivory but occasionally of bone (as here), silver or even

428

gold, were coated with a mixture of wax and pitch or some resin (so they were usually black): they were written on with a stylus (cf. Cat. 420–1), and by smoothing the wax the writer could then correct his mistakes or express a fresh thought. The tablets might be kept in a leather case and be as portable as a penner and inkhorn (cf. Serbat 1913, p. 311), and they could be used in the open air. In the *Canterbury Tales* (Chaucer 1966 edn, p. 94, ll. 1740 ff.), Chaucer says of the Summoner that

> His felawe hadde a staf tipped with horn,
> A peyre of tables al of yvory,
> And a poyntel polysshed fetisly,
> And wroot the names alwey, as he stood,
> Of alle folk that yaf hym any good.

(*poyntel*: see Cat. 420–1; *fetisly*: finely)

The Summoner's fellow lost no time in smoothing away his benefactors' names as soon as he could.

Like mirror cases and other ivory or bone objects, writing tablets were commonly decorated with romantic scenes. This tablet shows the encounter of two lovers in a garden (indicated by a tree in the background): the man offers his heart, which he holds in his hands, to his lady. The man wears a tunic belted below the waist and a hood with a long liripipe, and he and the lady each have long tippets to their sleeves; the carver was evidently intending to represent the couple as fashionably dressed, but the crudeness of the carving virtually masks the nature of the scene. None the less it is clear that the carver was seeking to emulate a finer ivory tablet, such as were being made in Paris at this date: his model must have been something like a pair now in the Namur Museum (Koechlin 1924, II, nos 1161–2; Paris 1981–2, pp. 194–5).

This tablet is one of a pair or 'booklet' of

several leaves: all save a narrow strip round the edge of its reverse is slightly recessed, and the recessed area has been scored slightly, the better to hold the wax in place. Inner leaves would have been covered with wax on both sides, and then the bottom leaf would have mirrored this one with wax on one side and a carved scene on the other. Slightly inconveniently, the leaves would have been held together by a pair of cords that passed through the holes cut at the left side of each leaf.   NLR

PROV. Excavated St Michael's House, Southampton, 1972.

LIT. Hughes 1897; de Beaurepaire 1897–9; Serbat 1913; Forsyth 1938.

429   Writing master's poster

Early 14th century
Parchment, ff. 2: 11.7 × 17.8/18 cm
Oxford, Bodleian Library, MS.e Mus. 198*, ff. 5, 8

Van Dijk discovered the four fragments of which two are shown here, used as pastedowns in the binding of a fourteenth-century manuscript connected by its contents with Oxford University. Since they contain discontinuous texts and musical notation written in different sizes and types of script on one side of the parchment only, he argued that they formed part of an advertisement in the form of a poster of an Oxford writing master of the fourteenth century. Customers would have been able to order different types of service books from the samples given. For example, on f. 5 there is specimen script for a large choir psalter and a large gradual. On f. 8 are smaller specimen scripts for portable liturgical books, and a larger script for a ritual with the collect for the dead, *Fidelium omnium conditor*.

It is interesting that the scribe is neither accurate nor, in Van Dijk's opinion, particularly skilful. Other such specimen sheets survive, though none from England. They give, therefore, an indication of how a book trade was beginning to develop, most manuscripts still being written to order at this date.   JA

PROV. Given by Sir Thomas Herbert, 1666.

LIT. Van Dijk 1956.

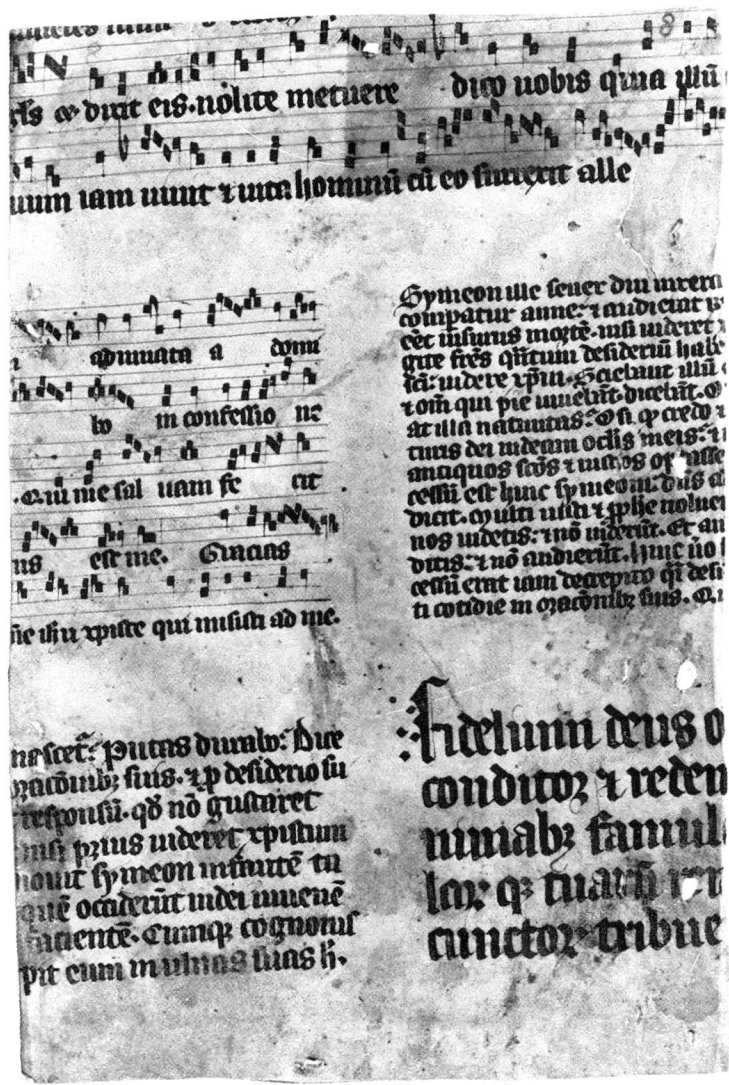

429

430–3 Bookbinder's stamps

The practice of decorating leather bookbindings with impressed designs seems to have waned as the Gothic style became fashionable in England. There are no Gothic bindings with architectural designs of a sort to parallel the Winchester Domesday's Romanesque arrangement of stamps; two tools that may be as late as the early thirteenth century are exhibited (Cat. 430–1), as well as one of the late thirteenth century (Cat. 432) and one of the fourteenth (Cat. 433), but the last may not have been made for use on book covers, nor was the third necessarily. Only a very few of the bookbindings that survive from the thirteenth and fourteenth centuries have had any decoration stamped upon them (see Cat. 435) and none of these is a de luxe manuscript. The most valuable books of the nobility were covered with whitened or red-coloured leather, or with velvet or some other fabric, and were undecorated apart from their clasps (which might be finely enamelled: see, for example, an inventory of the books of Thomas of Woodstock, Duke of Gloucester, in 1397; Dillond Hope 1897, pp. 298–9); a very few books were entirely bejewelled.

Bookbinders doubled as stationers and even illuminators (see p. 50), and not as workers in leather for other objects. Very little research has so far been carried out on the relationship of the decoration of leather bookbindings with that of other leather objects, such as knife or dagger sheaths or penners (Cat. 423) that had designs stamped on them (for which see Ward Perkins 1940, pp. 185–99); it appears, however, that the bookbinders and the other leatherworkers generally used different repertoires of designs. If Cat. 433 was not made as a book stamp it is hard to suggest an alternative function other than as a strap end.   NLR

430 Stamp

English(?) 12th/early 13th century
Copper alloy: working surface h. 28 mm,
   w. 17 mm, th. 3.5 mm; l. of shank 31 mm
The Trustees of the British Museum, London,
   MLA 65, 3–24, 24

Bookbinding stamps with representations of David playing the harp were popular in the twelfth and early thirteenth centuries, and G.D. Hobson noted at least ten variants from different workshops (Hobson 1938–9, p. 244); this pointed oval stamp closely resembles one that was used on the binding of Évreux, Bibliothèque municipale, MS 59, a glossed Gospel of St John written in the twelfth century (repr. Hobson 1929, pl. 21a), although that is less boldly cut. In each, David is shown crowned, seated, and playing the harp which is before him.   NLR

430

PROV. Rev. Henry Wellesley, Principal of New Inn Hall, Oxford; bt by British Museum, 1865.

LIT. Hobson 1929; Hobson 1934–5, pp. 164, 204, p. 164 fig. 3; Hobson 1938–9, p. 244, pl. vii, fig. 1.

431

431 Stamp

English(?), 12th/early 13th century
Copper alloy: working surface h. 28 mm;
   th. c. 10 mm; l. of shank 44 mm
The Trustees of the British Museum, London.
   MLA 72, 5–20, 28

This pointed oval stamp has been both deeply and elegantly engraved with a vigorous representation of a griffin passant. The griffin or gryphon was a feathered, four-legged creature with the head and wings of an eagle and the body of a lion, and sometimes with a pair of small horns or (as here) ears; Hobson noted two variants of this design as occurring on English twelfth-century bindings.   NLR

PROV. Purnell B. Purnell, of Stancombe Park, Glos.; Sotheby's, 8 May 1872, lot 569 or 570, bt by P. Albert, 39 Great Russell St, London, for British Museum.

LIT. Brown 1885; Hobson 1938–9. p. 244, pl. vii, fig. 2.

432 Stamp

English(?), c. 1275–1325
Copper alloy: working surface h. 24 mm,
   w. 20 mm, th. 14 mm; l. of shank 40 mm
The Trustees of the British Museum, London,
   MLA OA 7414

This rectangular stamp has been deeply cut with the representation of a fully armed man wearing a long hauberk (with an aketon below this) and a helmet with a domed top; with one hand he plunges a sword into the

432

belly of a lion rampant while with the other hand he holds up one of the lion's legs.

Men fighting monstrous beasts abound in Romanesque art, but in the thirteenth century the theme became more specific as certain legendary or literary exploits lent themselves to representation. Richard I's nickname of Lionheart was subsequently explained as referring to his tearing the heart out of a lion, but Richard is customarily shown unarmed (Loomis 1915); if then this stamp is not of Richard, its scene may be derived from some other lion fight, such as one presumably supposed to have been waged by Saher de Quincy, 1st Earl of Winchester (d. 1219), and shown on his seal of c. 1210 (Henderson 1978, pp. 31–2). The absence of a shield on the stamp may reflect a wish to avoid portraying any particular lion fight, for a shield would be likely to show a knight's arms.

Hobson thought that this stamp could not have been a binder's, since its square-sectioned shank has a blunt end (making it very difficult to insert into a wooden handle) and shows hammer marks. He assumed that binders in this period always limited themselves to hand pressure when tooling, but for a deeply-cut stamp such as this, where mechanical force might have been needed, the use of, say, a press has been suggested on at least one surviving binding (Paris, Bibliothèque nationale, MS lat. 6637 A; Vézin 1982, p. 248).   NLR

PROV. British Museum, MLA, Old Acquisition, accessioned 1981, but in British Museum before 1934.

LIT. 1915; Hobson 1938–9, pp. 243–4, pl. vii, fig. 5; Henderson 1978, esp. pp. 27–32.

433 Stamp

English(?), 14th century(?)
Copper alloy: working surface h. 42 mm,
   w. 24 mm, d. 21 mm; l. of handle 14 mm
The Trustees of the British Museum, London.
   MLA WT 853

433

The rectangular area of the stamp is engraved with a foliate scroll inhabited in its central roundel by a man-headed bird; the skimpy leaves are similar to those found in the marginal decoration of some manuscripts of c. 1300–50.

The stamp is large for a bookbinder's tool, but would seem likeliest to have been made for use on bookbindings; the short handle on its reverse is of a type found on binders' tools, and the relative shallowness of the cutting means that it would not have needed much force to make a clear impression.   NLR

PROV. Sir William Temple, Minister at the Court of Naples; beq. to British Museum, 1856.

434   Stamp or mould

English(?), late 12th/early 13th century
Copper alloy: l. 52 mm, w. 38 mm, th. 5 mm
The Trustees of the British Museum, London,

MLA 1927, 3–12, 1

434

The working surface of this implement is somewhat crudely cut in intaglio with a lion set on a hatched ground within an oval; at each of the four corners of the oval's irregular oblong setting is a fleur-de-lis. The semi-heraldic lion may be compared stylistically with seal impressions of the late twelfth and early thirteenth centuries, but the stamp's shape and design preclude its having been made as a seal. Although it is deeply cut, it could have been used as a bookbinder's tool; it is however, very large for a hand tool, deeply cut, and its reverse shows no sign of a handle or other attachment. It might therefore be thought to have been intended as a mould, but its bevelled edge that slopes away from the working surface suggests that it was a stamp of some kind.   NLR

PROV. Horndon-on-the-Hill Church, Essex, discovered below belfry (in a position stated to have been inaccessible since the 13th century), 1926; presented to British Museum, 1927.

LIT. Anon. 1926, pp. 447–8.

435   Bookbinding

14th century(?)
Leather: 33.5 × 25 cm
The Dean and Chapter of Durham, MS. A.iii.28

The survival of what appear to be Gothic bookbinding stamps (cf. Cat. 430–3,) is not matched by the clear-cut survival of any English Gothic binding. The Museum of London has what may be a *chemise* (or loose-fitting) binding of the thirteenth or four-teenth century, but this may have been to wrap around something other than a book

435

(no. A 27347; repr. Ward Perkins 1940, p. 198, fig. 64). Cosin MS V.II.8 in Durham University Library has been stamped with tools of late twelfth- or thirteenth-century design, but this was perhaps done in the fifteenth century. And there is no certainty that MS lat. 6637 A in the Bibliothèque nationale, Paris, was bound in England, although it belonged to an Englishman (who had studied in Paris) and two of its stamps have been suggested as being English (Vézin 1982, pp. 248–9).

That little binding with decorated stamps was carried out in the thirteenth and four-teenth centuries is also suggested by the fifteenth century's return to the favourite motifs of the twelfth century – leading to the suggestion that some of the fifteenth-century bindings were actually executed with twelfth-century stamps (Goldschmidt 1928,

I, p. 5; Hobson 1929, p. 5), although this supposition has been disproved. Graham Pollard argued that the surviving stamped bindings made before *c.* 1225 were the pro-duct of monastic binderies, and that an abandonment of bookbinding at most religi-ous houses (though not, for example, at St Albans or Bury St Edmunds) reflected a transfer of activity to lay, urban workshops, mostly situated in London, Oxford and Cam-bridge (Pollard 1962, pp. 18–19).

Durham Cathedral MS A.III.28 has been decorated with large tools of Romanesque or at least archaic design, while the text they enclose, a commentary on *Ecclesiasticus* by Stephen Langton (d. 1228), was copied *c.* 1200–50. The binder was using elderly or old-fashioned tools.

The book was rebound in the nineteenth century, the leather covers being laid down on new boards and new end leaves being added. NLR

PROV. Brother Godfrey of Kepier; his gift to Durham Cathedral Priory; Dean and Chapter of Durham.

LIT. Hobson, 1929, pp. 34–5, pl. 31; Doyle 1984.

436 Single leaf from a psalter, showing the artist W. de Brailes

Oxford, c. 1230–40
Vellum: 25.5 × 17.5 cm
The Syndics of the Fitzwilliam Museum
Cambridge, MS 330 iii

This is one of seven full-page miniatures surviving from a psalter whose text is lost. Six are in the Fitzwilliam Museum, and one is in the Pierpont Morgan Library, New York, (M. 913). They include Old and New Testament scenes, a Wheel of Fortune, David harping and a Tree of Jesse. The leaf of the Last Judgment is one of the two instances of the signature of the illuminator W. de Brailes, who is shown as a suppliant figure beside the angel with the sword in the lower right-hand corner. His arm is grasped by the angel who is rescuing him from being cast into Hell. A William de Brailes is mentioned as an illuminator in Catte Street, Oxford, in records dating from 1238 to 1252. Although tonsured in the miniature he must only have been in minor orders, as his wife Celena is mentioned in the documents.

The group of artists working with de Brailes seem to have specialised in bibles and psalters (e.g. Cat. 314), and several of their books have come down to us. Their stocky figures with alert faces show a liveliness of narrative composition conveyed by nervous gestures and expressive poses. The sources of the style earlier in the century, and its later followers in the period c. 1250–70, are in manuscripts associated with Oxford, which was perhaps the most important centre of book production in thirteenth-century England. NJM

PROV. Jean-Baptiste-Joseph Barrois of Lille (1784–1855); acq. by Bertram, 4th Earl of Ashburnham, 1849; sold to George C. Thomas of Philadelphia, 1901; A.S.W. Rosenbach; Sir Alfred Chester Beatty; bt for Fitzwilliam Museum, 1932.

LIT. Cockerell 1930, pp. 3, 15–28, pls XV–XVII; London 1930, nos 145–50; London 1939, no. 135; Pollard 1956, p. 204; Cambridge 1966, no. 29; Morgan 1982, no. 72(a), fig. 238; Wormald & Giles 1982, pp. 319–20.

437 Matthew Paris, *Historia Anglorum* and *Chronica Maiora*, pt III, showing the author's self-portrait

St Albans, 1250–9
Vellum, ff. 232: 35.8 × 25 cm
British Library, MS Royal 14 c. vii

436

Matthew Paris was the official chronicler of the Abbey of St Albans. His greatest work was a chronicle from pre-Christian times up to the middle of the thirteenth century, the *Chronica Maiora*, which has come down to us in three parts. An abbreviated version of it, concentrating mostly on English history, is the *Historia Anglorum*. These chronicles are illustrated by small marginal tinted drawings by the hand of the author. The choice of subjects for illustration emphasises the anecdotal, and is an interesting comment on

which events and incidents the author considered of particular importance. Illustrated maps and itineraries are also included in the volumes, as in this manuscript, which contains an itinerary to the Holy Land and a map of the British Isles.

The *Historia Anglorum* has an additional two pages of portraits of the kings of England from William I to Henry III, and a large picture of Matthew Paris kneeling before the seated Virgin and Child. The latter is the most monumental work of Matthew Paris's art. It

Osculta oscula Lactenus labus impressa. cu
inter crebra iudicia repramuf inf. ca ncie
utpote ver' er te fili' iuri alludvet cu
uctuus er patre & di genir' imparer

437

shows well the rounded contours of his drawing lines, which give a softness of form to the figures. This contrasts with the more jagged, intricate systems of lines found in the work of most of his contemporaries. The Virgin and Child has been compared with the panel painting of St Peter in Oslo (Cat. 311), possibly taken by Matthew on his visit to Norway (cf. also Cat. 315).   NJM

PROV. Benedictine Abbey of St Albans; Humphrey, Duke of Gloucester (1391–1447); John Russell, Bishop of Lincoln 1480–94; Henry Fitzalan, Earl of Arundel (1511–80); John, Lord Lumley (1534–1609) whose manuscripts were purchased by James I; Royal Library became part of British Museum, 1757.

LIT. James 1925–6, pp. 18–21, pls XIX–XXI; London 1980, no. 88; Morgan 1982, no. 92, figs 304–5, col. pl. p. 29; Lewis 1987b.

438 The Lambeth Apocalypse, showing a monk painting a statue

London(?), c. 1260–7
Vellum, ff. 54: 27.2 × 20 cm
The Archbishop of Canterbury and the Trustees of
     Lambeth Palace Library, MS. 209

This is the only one of the Apocalypses for which contemporary ownership and patronage are fairly certain. On f. 48 Lady Eleanor de Quincy, wife of the Earl of Winchester, is shown kneeling before the Virgin and Child. Her bearing of the de Quincy arms implies that the book was made before her second marriage to Roger de Leybourne in 1267.

It is unusual in having miniatures of a devotional nature in addition to the normal scenes of the Life of St John and the Apocalypse. These are of saints, miracles of the Virgin Mary (fig. 65), the Veronica head of Christ, the Crucifixion, and an allegorical picture of a woman armed with the shield of faith attacked by the Devil (cf. Cat. 150). In addition, at the beginning there is a Benedictine monk-artist painting a sculpted image of the Virgin and Child. It is likely that during the production of the Apocalypse illustrations it was decided to expand the pictorial decoration of the book. At the same time scenes of the Life of Antichrist were painted in the bottom margins on some pages of the Apocalypse. That this work may be an afterthought is suggested by it being in the most advanced style in the book. As in the Life of Edward the Confessor (Cat. 39) the new French style influences the artists during the course of the decoration of the book. The work is in full painting, although on some pages the figures are painted in the manner of tinted drawings set against coloured grounds.

The place of origin of this Apocalypse is controversial. It has been attributed on very weak evidence to Canterbury. The close interrelationships in style and pictorial cycles of English Apocalypses in the period c. 1250–75 suggest that their artists may

438

have been working in different workshops in one centre. This centre may have been London. The portrait of the Benedictine monk-artist may suggest his involvement in the illumination.   NJM

PROV. Lady Eleanor de Quincy (d. 1274); William de Barton(?), 14th century; John, Lord Lumley (1534–1609); Archbishop of Canterbury's library, probably 17th century.

LIT. London 1908, no. 87; London 1930, no. 161; Henderson 1967, pp. 88ff., 102ff.; Henderson 1968, p. 129ff.; Paris 1968, no. 239; Morgan 1987, no. 126, repr.

439 Unknown female figure

c. 1330–60
Limestone, traces of polychromy and gilding;
     h. 90 cm, w. 30 cm, d. 21 cm
Museum of London, 21216

This statue, recovered from the site of the house of Minoresses founded at London by Blanche of Artois in 1293, retains extensive traces of its original polychromy and gilding, indicating that it comes from an interior location. The back is unfinished, suggesting that the figure occupied a niche. Stylistically the statue is related to a group of sculpture of

439

c. 1330–60, including the statues of Ecclesia and Synagogue on the doorway to the chapter room of Rochester Cathedral and the weepers on the tomb of John of Eltham in Westminster Abbey (Hirschhorn 1977, Gardner 1951, RCHM, *London*, 1924). The elegant drapery treatment and lively, hip-shot stance reflect the influence of the French style associated with Jean Pucelle and his followers and are closely paralleled in other media, notably the mid-fourteenth-century stained glass at York (Cat. 563) and the work of the Majesty Master in the De Lisle Psalter (Cat. 569). ND

PROV. London, Nunnery of the Minoresses of St Clare; three stones composing the statue discovered among rubble used to block doorway in north wall of former conventual church, 1956.

LIT. RCHM, *London*, 1924, pl. 75; Gardner 1951, fig. 350 p. 184; Evans & Cook 1956, repr. opp. p. 104; Hirschhorn 1977, pp. 70–2.

440 Artist's palette

Before 1338(?)
Oyster shell: h. 2.5 cm, w. 7.6 cm, d. 7.6 cm
The Church of the Blessed Mary of Boyton,
  Wiltshire

Restoration work at Boyton parish church, Wiltshire, in 1956–62, revealed this painter's palette, a rare survivor of its kind in England. It was found at floor level, loosely covered by a slight scrabbling of stone, at the south-west corner of the tomb chest in the centre of the Giffard chantry chapel (personal communication, Canon R.D. Richardson); the tomb was of Lady Margaret Nevill, widow of John Giffard, who died in 1338, so the palette is presumably of c. 1330 or earlier. (Another suggestion is that the tomb was of Lady Sybil Giffard: Richardson 1980, p. 29.)

The shell has been painted on both sides, and retains considerable amounts of gold, as well as red and blue. It is said that the red and blue are the same shades as the paint formerly on the tomb chest.

An oyster shell would have made a cheap receptacle for a painter's pigments; horns are

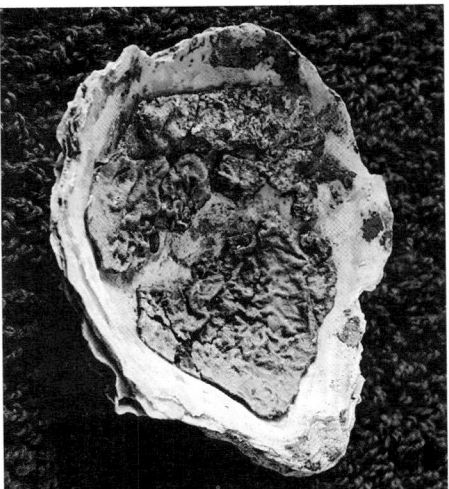

440

most commonly illustrated in representations of medieval artists, who had holes in their paint board so that their horns would stay upright (see e.g. Alexander 1978, pp. 110–11). NLR

PROV. Boyton Parish Church, discovered in the Giffard chapel, c. 1956–62.

LIT. Richardson 1980.

441 Misericord: Carver

1383–92
Oak: h. 26 cm, w. 61 cm, d. 16 cm
All Hallows, Wellingborough Parochial Church
  Council, Northamptonshire

The carving depicts a master carver at his bench carving a rosette. He wears a tippet secured with a brooch, hose and pointed boots, and a cap. His tools – mallet, chisels and gouges – can be distinguished. Behind him on either side are affronted birds. The supporters are of foliage type.

Six seats remain from the medieval choir stalls of unknown size. A shield bearing the arms of John White, rector of the church from 1361 to 1392, provides a broad dating bracket. The settlement of a dispute between the church and the monks of Crowland Abbey, to whom the living belonged, in 1383 provides a more specific *terminus post quem* for the making of the furniture. One of the conditions was that the members should repair the chancel at their own expense.

There is another version of this subject at the nearby church of Great Doddington, dated by Remnant to the late fifteenth century. It seems more likely, however, from the geographical proximity, coincidence of subject-matter, seat shape and handling of the supporters that the Great Doddington furniture was made by the same artist. CT

PROV. All Hallows, Wellingborough.

LIT. Martin 1896; Remnant 1969, pp. 120–1, repr. pl. 13d.

441

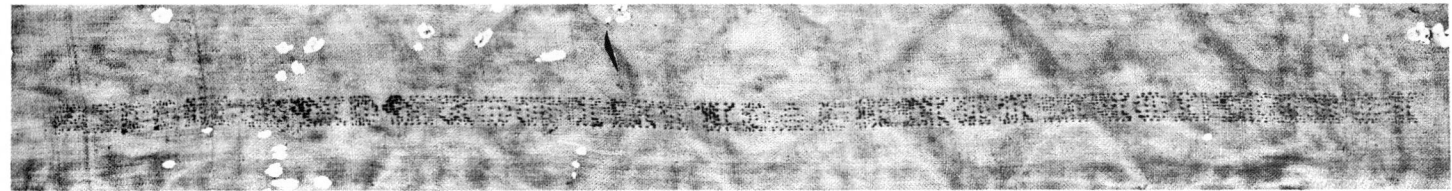

442

442 Frontlet for an altar

Late 13th/early 14th century
Silver-gilt thread and coloured silks in tent, satin,
stem and long-and-short stitches with couched
work on linen: h. 9 cm, l. 264 cm
Inscr. front IN HORA MORTIS SVCCVRRE NOBIS
DOMINE
back IOHANNA BEVERLAI MONACA ME
FECIT
The Board of Trustees of the Victoria and Albert
Museum, London, T. 70–1923

This embroidery by Johanna Beverlai, a nun,
is the only signed English embroidery surviving from the Middle Ages. It is also of a
unique type. The two facts are probably
connected, for it is natural that the work of
non-professional embroiderers should differ
from that of professional workshops, which
constitutes the overwhelming majority of
surviving embroideries. In the absence of
comparative material the date of the piece is
uncertain, but the green silk edging is very
similar to that of seal bags of 1319 (Cat. 206)
and may well be of roughly the same period.
In the centre is a shield of arms, Or a lion
rampant purpure (Lacy), and at either end
further shields, Or a cross sable (Vescy).
Henry de Lacy, last Earl of Lincoln of that
name, died in 1311. William de Vescy, last
Baron of that name, died in 1314.   DK

PROV. Lord Willoughby de Broke; Monsieur G.
Saville Seligman, who gave it to the Victoria and
Albert Museum, 1923.

LIT. London 1963, no. 43.

443 Account referring to Hailes Abbey

1272–3(?)
Parchment: 59.5 × 28 cm
Public Record Office, London, SC 6/961/6

Edmund of Almaine, Earl of Cornwall (d.
1300) followed his father, Richard of Cornwall, King of the Romans (see Cat. 14), in
supporting the Cistercian abbey of Hailes in
Gloucestershire. Several of the accounts for

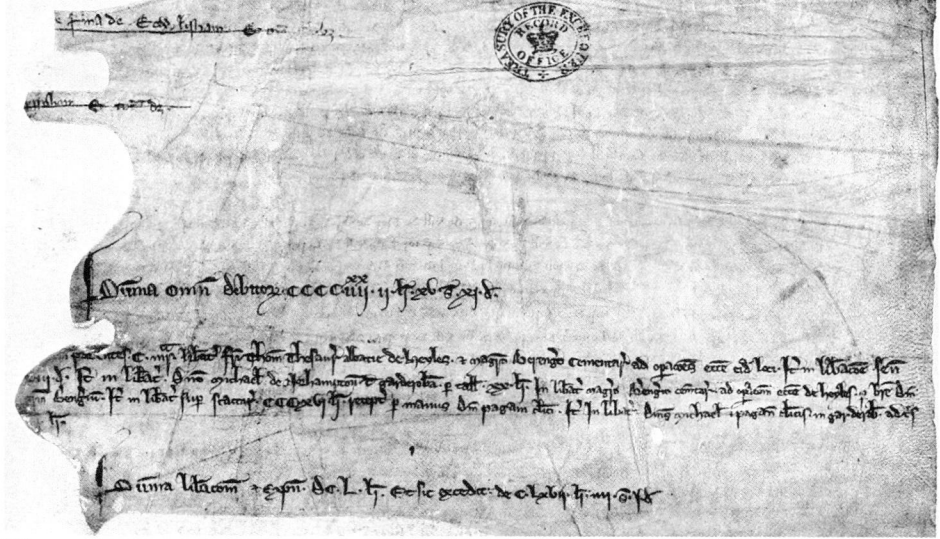

443

Edmund's estates survive; this document is
only a fragment from the middle of a roll, and
lacks a main heading, but from its reference
to a subsidiary account for two manors as
being of the first year of King Edward (i.e.,
Edmund's uncle, Edward I), it is probably of
1272–3.

Under the heading 'Total of all debts,
£482.15s. 11d' (Summa omnium debitorum;
these being sums due to the earl), follow
entries of expenditure. The manorial accounts record small sums, such as 6s. 8d in
alms to the prioress of Studley, Oxfordshire,
and 18d to the smith for repairing a cart, but
these notes of further expenditure are tan-
talisingly summary, although they come to a
total of £650. Some of these outgoings were
sums handed over to the Earl's wardrobe
clerks (one of whom, Michael of Northampton, was closely involved in Edmund's
affairs and a man of considerable authority;
in 1280 he was sheriff of Middlesex: Emden
1957–9, II, p. 1368), but 100 marks
(£66.13s. 4d) are recorded as handed over to
Thomas, treasurer of Hailes Abbey, and
Master Berengar, mason, for the works
(operaciones) of that church, and a further

sum (now illegible) is stated to have been
handed over to Master Berengar, mason, for
the works of the church of Hailes.

Major building works were in progress at
Hailes Abbey in the 1270s, both to provide a
suitable setting for the Relic of the Holy Blood
given by Edmund in 1270 and to make good
the damage caused by a fire in 1271; these
works, which must have been largely completed by 1277 (when the new work was
dedicated), included the Continental feature
of a chevet (set of chapels radiating out from
the apse). The name Berengar is rarely found
in thirteenth-century England but was common on the Continent (Edmund's maternal
grandfather was Raymond Berengar, Count
of Provence), while no trace of Master
Berengar the mason has been found in other
English documents. It is therefore very
tempting to see Master Berengar as a Continental mason, perhaps brought over by
Edmund or his father, and perhaps responsible for the design of the chevet.   NLR

PROV. Archives of Edmund, Earl of Cornwall,
incorporated in Public Record Office.

LIT. Baddeley 1908; Midgley 1942–5; Coad 1972.

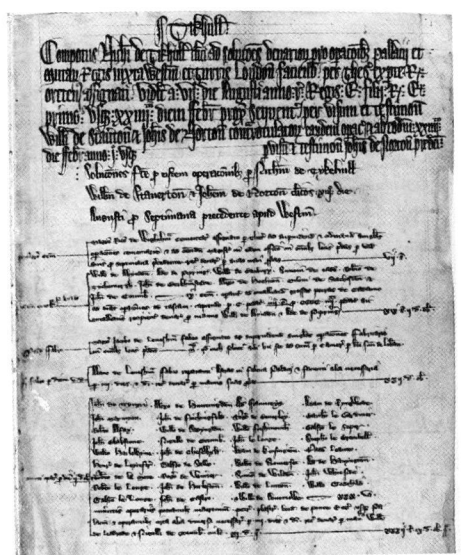

444

444 Building work at Westminster Palace, 1307–11

c. 1311
Parchment: h. 32.8 cm, w. 54 cm, d. 5 cm
Inscr. *Compotus Nicholai de Tikhull clerici ad soluciones denariorum pro operacionibus Pallacii et Mutarum Regis*[. . .]
Public Record Office, London, E101/468/21

When Edward II came to the throne in 1307 he decided to make good the damage that had been caused by fire at his palace of Westminster and to prepare the palace for his coronation. This was a major undertaking, whose costs in his first four regnal years were £3,091, £508, £80 and £98, and instead of just being recorded on rolls of 'works' expenditure, the costs were neatly copied into this book. Unusually, too, sets of memoranda were added to the book, summarising the achievements of these years.

As in almost all medieval accounts, the costs of materials (£1,038.14s. 6d in the first year) and wages (£1,966.7s. 11½d in the first year) were kept distinct; fortnight by fortnight in the first year, and then over longer periods of time, the expenditure is set out in minute detail: packthread, white lead, ver-

milion and other colours for the painters; white and coloured glass; timber from Master Robert Osekyn and Richer de Refham; and so forth, as well as all the daily payments to the craftsmen.

It seems clear that Nicholas of Tickhill, joint Clerk of the King's Works at Westminster and the Tower, and the man in whose name this account book was written, took a particular interest and even pride in the achievement. At the end of the book he also recorded the names of the principal craftsmen: the masters of the masons, carpenters, smiths, painters and glaziers, who were *ad hoc* appointees and were each paid according to his expertise (*scientia*).

The book has been rebound, preserving the original quiring but mounting each quire separately.   NLR

PROV. Alienated from Exchequer records; Craven Ord (d. 1832), who perhaps pasted in the signature of Thomas Martin of Palgrave (d. 1771); Ord's sale, Evans, 25 Jan. 1830, lot 1008, to Sir Thomas Phillipps; Phillipps MS 4099; bt by Public Record Office, 1956.

LIT. Colvin 1963, I, pp. 504–8; II, pp. 1041–4 (printing a set of the Memoranda).

445 Contract for the cornice of Westminster Hall

1395
Parchment: 15.9 × 39 cm
Public Record Office, London, E101/473/21

By this contract, dated 18 March 1395, Richard Washbourne and John Swalwe, masons, undertook to make the *table* or cornice of the walls of Westminster Palace hall, with 26 *souses* or corbels, for the new hammerbeam roof. Richard II must have decided to remodel the hall just over two years previously; the mason to whose oversight he entrusted the stonework was Henry Yevele, and the contract specifies that Washbourne and Swalwe are to execute the work according to his designs (*forme et molde*). The stonework was to be completed by February 1396; the roof timbers were prepared at Farnham at the same time, and were in place by 1397.

The immense roof remains intact (Cat. 692), but neither visual examination nor the contract makes clear whether the corbels are load-bearing and actually help support it. The contract's aim was simply to bind the masons, in considerable detail, to carry out what Yevele wanted.   NLR

PROV. Exchequer records, incorporated in Public Record Office.

LIT. Harvey 1961b, p. 5; Colvin 1963, I, pp. 528–9; Salzman 1967, pp. 472–3; Courtenay 1984, pp. 295–309.

446 Contracts for the tomb of Richard II and Anne of Bohemia

(i) 14 Apr.; (ii) 1 Apr. 1395
Parchment: (i) 19 × 35.3 cm; (ii) 21 × 33 cm
Public Record Office, London, E101/473/7

Griefstricken after the death in 1394 of his wife Anne of Bohemia, Richard II decided to have a monument made for both his queen and himself in Westminster Abbey. Contracts were entered into with leading craftsmen for a marble tomb with gilt copper images of Richard and Anne; the tomb was to be of the same height as that of King Edward III, completed only a few years previously, and it is very likely that Richard was seeking to enhance his own regal dignity by the way in which he and his predecessors were publicly commemorated.

As one contract records, the marble base of the tomb was to be made by Henry Yevele and Stephen Lote, for £250; the work was to be completed by Michaelmas 1397, and they were to have £20 extra if the work pleased Richard. Yevele had probably designed the tombs of Edward III and the Black Prince, and, among a string of other royal commissions, had just produced a design for the new cornice and corbels of Westminster Hall (Cat. 445). By then aged about seventy or more, he was no doubt glad to share this commission with his friend Stephen Lote; they were already collaborating on the tomb of Cardinal Langham in Westminster Abbey. The contract provides that the tomb shall be made according to a *patron* (pattern or design) that had already been made, presumably by the masons, and had been sealed by the Treasurer of England.

The other contract was made three weeks later with two London coppersmiths, Nicholas Broker and Godfrey Prest: it is stated that they are to make *ymages*, or effigies, of the king and queen of copper and latten, gilt, holding sceptres in their left hands and with their right hands joined, and with an orb between them. They are to work according to a *patron* shown to them; it is apparent that they were merely executing someone else's design (perhaps one by Yevele and Lote; Stone 1972, p. 193, has misunderstood the text here). The contract specifies payment of £400, but in the event they were ultimately

445

paid a further £300 for gilding the effigies; Yevele and Lote, by contrast, were underpaid by £16.13s.4d.

Richard's head has been described as 'a fine and unflattering piece of portraiture' (Evans 1949, p. 156), and Anne's is perhaps also a portrait, while their robes flow far more easily than those on the effigies of Edward III or the Black Prince; but technically the work is of mixed quality. Richard's effigy was skilfully cast in bronze about 1 cm thick, the head being made separately from the body, but Anne's, made in bronze about 2.5 cm thick, had to be recast in part, with fresh metal being poured into the mould for the front of the body, where it fused on to the portion already cast.

The effigies have lost their arms, cushions (replaced at the direction of Queen Victoria), orb, beasts at their feet, and other work, but retain their delicately executed pointillé surface decoration. The coppersmiths' contract only calls for the tomb's metal top to be made with a *frette* of fleurs-de-lis, lions, eagles and leopards, but the clothes are powdered with the letters A and R and the badges or devices of king and queen – the tree stock, sunburst, Plantagenet broom pod, and chained and couchant hart, for Richard, and knots and chained, collared ostriches for Anne.   NLR

PROV. Exchequer records, incorporated into Public Record Office.

LIT. Rymer 1739–45, III, pt iv, pp. 106, 105–6); Gough 1786–96, I, pt i, pp. 163–5; Nichols 1842, pp. 32–9; London 1945, pp. 6–7; Evans 1949, p. 156; Plenderleith & Maryon 1959, pp. 89–90, pl. XXII; Colvin 1963, I, pp. 487–8; Whittingham 1971, p. 12; Stone 1972, pp. 193–4.

447   Mould of Massacre of the Innocents

Probably 1245–57
Stone: h. 15.3 cm, w. 14 cm, d. 4 cm
St Peter Hungate Museum, Norwich (Norfolk Museums Service), 76.94(429)

This portion of a mould suffices to identify the subject as the Massacre of the Innocents. The bucket helm could scarcely be later than the mid-thirteenth century; the pose, drapery and head of Herod could hardly be earlier. The quality is high and the relief delicate, suggesting that the mould was used to cast in precious metal; compare St Edward before the King in the Cambridge Life of St Edward (Cat. 39), f. 5v. No other mould for the casting of repoussé work of this kind and date has yet been found. But such moulds must have been employed to cast book covers, small altarpieces, and above all plaques to adorn shrines. English examples of this technique would have been peculiarly vulnerable to melting down at the Reformation. They may have adorned any of the remarkable group of shrines to English saints erected or refurbished in cathedrals in the middle of the

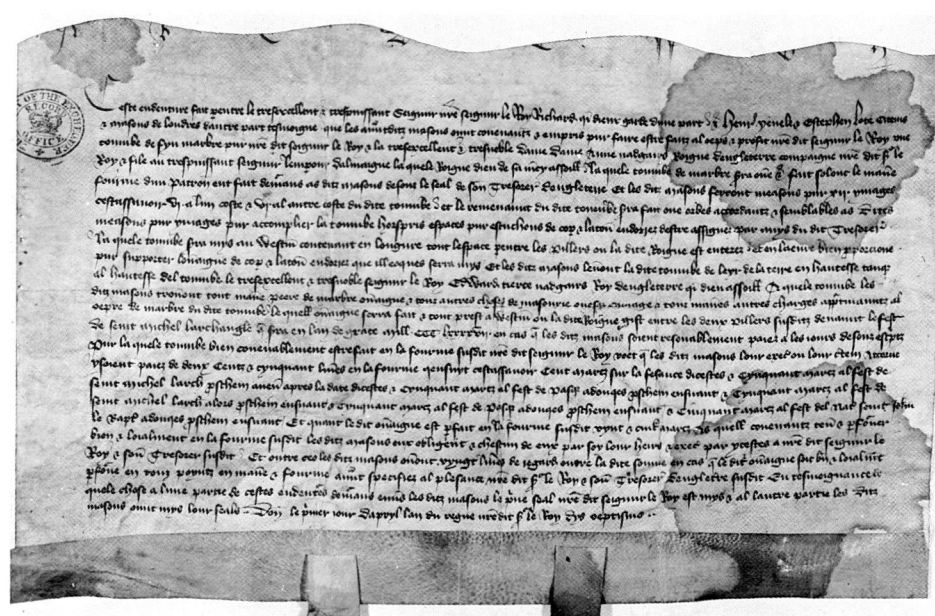

446

447

thirteenth century. Norwich treasured the relics of the child martyr St William. Francis Wormald suggested that a scene of the Massacre of the Innocents would have been especially appropriate for the casket of a child martyr (personal communication).   PT-C

PROV. Found in an archaeological context in Norwich.

LIT. *J. Brit. Archaeol. Assoc.* 1858, p. 170, pl. 15.

448   Mould for making hart badges

c. 1390–1400
Fine limestone, perhaps from Solnhofen, Bavaria: l. at front 4.6 cm, w. at front 6.6 cm, d. 2.2 cm
College of Guardians of the Anglican Shrine, Walsingham, on loan to St Peter Hungate Museum, Norwich (Norfolk Museums Service), L 1976. 27

Deepening of a well at the Anglican Shrine at Little Walsingham in 1971 revealed this half-mould for making badges of a hart. Walsingham was one of the leading pil-

grimage centres in medieval England, because of the fame of its miracle-working statue of the Virgin and Child (cf. Cat. 71–4); various forms of badges were made and sold there to pilgrims. Although this mould's subject cannot be connected with a shrine, it is likely that a mould carver at Walsingham should also have produced moulds for making badges, spangles and other secular objects.

Richard II is stated in the *Historia Vitae et Regni Ricardi Secundi* to have adopted the device of a white hart with a crown and gold chain at the Smithfield tournament in October 1390, and over the next decade he is known to have distributed to his followers badges with this device. In 1404 the Countess of Oxford, who was seeking to overthrow Henry IV, had many such badges made, of silver and gilt (Riley 1863–4, ii, p. 262). But Richard's device was of a white hart couchant (lying down) with a crown collar with a chain attached (see Cat. 725–6 and the Wilton Diptych, fig. 104) – perhaps echoing

448

449

his mother Joan's device of a white hind wearing such a collar – and the harts in this mould lack collar and chain (although the central hart has a loop by its neck which could conceivably be intended for a chain). The tree shown behind the hart is uncalled for if Richard's hart is intended (although a jewelled hart beneath a tree may have belonged to Richard II: Palgrave 1836, III, p. 356; see also Hope 1929, pp. 213–14, pl. XVIIIb for contemporary instances of a tree or tree stock as a device), whereas the crown's presence would doubtless have been seen as important because in the late 1380s Richard had distributed livery badges consisting simply of silver and gilt crowns (Given-Wilson 1986, p. 239 n. 160).

Although the mould must probably be excluded as for Richard's device, it was almost certainly for making badges for the retainers or followers of some magnate. The fashion for giving livery in the form of metal badges was at its height in Richard's reign, to the dislike of the Commons; many lords gave pewter or lead badges to their followers and numerous examples survive. They lack hooks and eyelets, but were sewn on to the shoulders or sleeves of men's clothes, or over their breast.

This mould was presumably for pewter or lead badges, as these were the commonest sort; the stone is broken, but clearly was once large enough for at least three badges to be made simultaneously. Imported stones like this were valuable; this one shows signs of having been repaired, with possible dowel holes at one end (personal communication, T.A. Heslop).   NLR

PROV. Little Walsingham, Norfolk, found in well at Anglican Shrine, 1971; loan to St Peter Hungate Church Museum, Norwich.

LIT. Nichols 1842, pp. 37–41; Harvey 1961a, pp. 6–8, 16; Stow 1977, pp. 131–2; Spencer 1980, pp. 28–9; Given-Wilson 1986, pp. 234–43.

449   Mould for belt or strap ends

Late 14th or early 15th century
Fine-grained limestone: l. 8.4 cm, w. 4.5 cm,
    d. 1.8 cm
Museum of London, 84.462

The importance of the belt in medieval dress made it well worth producing buckles in bulk, and the buckle's flatness made it easy to cast in a mould; one surviving mould was designed for six to be cast simultaneously (Edinburgh 1856, p. 64). This mould, which has the sockets for the counter-mould, was for an elaborate belt or strap end, with trefoil ornament. The stone's reverse forms part of a mould for a hinged circular object. A late medieval clay mould for making buckles was recently found in London (Armitage, Pearce & Vince 1981).   NLR

PROV. Found in River Thames at Billingsgate; bt by Museum of London, 1984.

LIT. Hume 1863, pp. 116–28.

450   Multiple die-piece

c. 1330s–1340s and later
Copper alloy: l. 11 cm, w. 4.5 cm, d. 0.9 cm
The Trustees of the British Museum, London,
    MLA 56, 7–1, 2242

This surviving portion of a die-piece has been cut on each face with a variety of designs: the exhibited side includes human faces (one within a quatrefoil), a bird with wings outstretched, a Wheel of Fortune (partly broken away), a crowned falcon with a scroll issuing from its mouth, a cock, a squirrel holding a nut to its mouth, what looks like a brooch with an immovable pin, and a bird with wings outstretched and with a human face. These have been relatively shallowly cut, and it is clear that the block served as a die on to which thin pieces of metal could be hammered so as to take the designs.

The human heads are all of comparable execution and likely to be the same engraver's work, whilst it is quite possible that he or a contemporary cut the other designs. But the Wheel of Fortune (with a human head comparable to the other heads) has been superimposed over the crowned falcon's tail feathers, so one must presume that the designs are not of quite the same date.

The other side of the die-piece has further designs, more miscellaneous in nature, including an acorn, an *Agnus Dei*, and part of a large (diam. c. 4.5 cm) circular piece enclosing a four-footed animal, possibly a lion. This last, perhaps together with the other designs on this side, appears to be of fifteenth-century date – suggesting that the die-piece remained in use for at least three or four generations.

It was a fourteenth-century European fashion to wear spangles of gold, silver, or silver-gilt, sewn on to garments, either loosely, so as to catch the light when the wearer moved, or in a careful arrangement that punctuated patterned embroidery (Newton 1980, p. 25, referring to them as *gaufres* or *bezants*). For instance, in the 1330s or 1340s Queen Philippa of Hainault's wardrobe purchases included 2,000 *despengles* (London, British Library, Add. Ch. 75855).

Sheets or small pieces of metal might have religious or secular designs imprinted upon them by stamping them, as with this die-piece, or by embossing them, as on a mid-fourteenth-century Norwegian piece (Brunswick 1985, vol. 2, no. 657; both sides are reproduced by F.A. Dreier, *Zeitschrift für Kunstwissenschaft*, XIII, 1959, pp. 32–3, and see pp. 30–6 for a discussion of these and of *Glocken* and other *Medaillons* generally) and a

450

Hungarian embossing block (Newton 1980, repr. p. 43). As the early twelfth-century writer Theophilus makes clear, die-stamping from a metal block such as this is not true repoussé work, as the metal sheet is much thinner than for repoussé work and the design is transferred by covering the sheet with a piece of lead and hitting this smartly with the hammer, just once (Dodwell 1961, pp. 135–6). NLR

PROV. Charles Roach Smith (d. 1890); bt by British Museum, 1856.

LIT. Newton 1980, esp. p. 25.

451 Mould for casting pilgrim signs

Late 14th century
Stone: h. 9.6 cm, w. 8.4 cm, th. 2.4 cm
The Trustees of the British Museum, London.
MLA 90, 10–2, 1

451

The face of the mould is carved with a figure of St Thomas of Canterbury mounted on a dappled stallion, led by a groom. Wearing mitre, gloves and ring and holding a crosier and cross-staff, the archbishop turns and gives his blessing. A dog and twisting shrubs help to fill in the openwork and to link the main figures to a base plate. This type of badge commemorated Becket's momentous return from exile and triumphal ride from Sandwich into Canterbury at the beginning of December 1170, only a month before his martyrdom. This moment in Becket's passion was celebrated liturgically by an annual festival, the *Regressio Sancti Thomae*.

The mould, which has been mutilated here and there by later scratchings, would have slotted against a two-piece counter-mould, carved with an ingate for the molten metal and with a matrix for the badge's pin and clasp. Numerous late fourteenth-century badges from similar moulds have been found (Cat. 57; Spencer 1982), occasionally with traces of their original paint. No badge from

this mould has yet been found, however, though a version very close to it has turned up at Salisbury (Spencer 1987).

Moulds for the production, sometimes mass production, of pilgrim souvenirs have been found at Canterbury, Walsingham and other major pilgrim centres. In a few instances discarded moulds have, like this one, migrated from the shrine concerned. BS

PROV. Found in digging foundations of Bonny Boat Tavern, Trinity House Lane, Kingston-on-Hull, Humberside; given to British Museum by John Symons, Esq., 1890.

LIT. Hull 1902, pp. 5–6; Spencer 1968, pl. VI, 1; Spencer 1982, pp. 309–11; Spencer 1987, no. 9.

452 Die

1225–50
Copper alloy: diam. 5.7 cm
Gray Art Gallery and Museum, Borough of Hartlepool HAPMG.124'86

The die was used in the production of fine metalwork, probably for stamping a pattern into silver sheet. It is engraved with a winged griffin with one front claw raised. From an inverted lion's head under the griffin's belly emerge strands of stiff-leaf foliage from which spring fruit and flowers forming a decorative background for the griffin. The griffin was a common subject in the thirteenth century and stiff-leaf foliage emerging from a lion's head occurs in the first half of the thirteenth century. The die may have been used for the production of silver mounts for caskets, but no examples of English metalwork decorated with griffins against stiff-leaf foliage appear to have survived. The fact that the die was lost in Hartlepool may have been mere chance, or it may be a rather surprising indication of high-class metalworking there in the thirteenth century. JC

PROV. Found in excavations in Church Walk, Hartlepool, in rubbish deposited after a 14th- or 15th-century building had gone out of use, 1972.

LIT. Cherry (forthcoming).

452

Techniques for making seal matrices and impression

In the Romanesque period seal matrices were made predominantly of ivory and bone and, in lesser numbers, of various types of stone and metal. By the late twelfth century this had changed and lead, copper alloy and silver and, very occasionally, gold were used to the exclusion of almost all other materials. So it remained for the rest of the Middle Ages except that during the thirteenth century lead became less and less popular. Apart from relative expense there was another consequence which followed from the material: the category of craftsman that the potential patron would approach to do the work. Precious metal matrices were made by goldsmiths, whereas the copper-alloy dies were worked either by specialist seal makers or else by latteners who might also produce other objects in base metal.

Early in the period all dies were engraved on flat discs or ovals ranging in thickness from about 3 mm to about 7 mm. Towards the end of the thirteenth century many smaller seals in particular were cut into the circular end of a faceted trumpet or bell shape (Cat. 201). These bell-bottomed seals were cast in two-part moulds (Cat. 457) before being filed and engraved to a finish. The trilobed apertures at the apex, and the survival of one or two with fragments of chain still attached (Cat. 458), indicate that these objects were to be fastened either to the person, perhaps from the belt, or to the container in which they were kept.

As well as casting and engraving, various other techniques were regularly employed. Several of the flat disc matrices of silver have elaborate handles soldered on to the reverse (Cat. 455). Precious metals were worked with punches, and from quite early in the period dies show signs of their use; in one case (Cat. 454) at least three are in evidence. However, such stamps seem to have been made only for small repeated patterns, not for figures or for letter forms. A final necessary skill, in demand particularly around 1300, was the setting of engraved gemstones. Again this technique only pertains to the goldsmiths (Cat. 198, 456).

In most cases the taking of a wax impression from a matrix was a simple process. Beeswax, usually with an admixture of resin and a colouring agent, was softened and kneaded in the hand. The matrix would be placed face upwards and a quantity of wax pressed into it with the thumb. The parchment strip or silk cords hanging from the charter were then laid across the back of this wax and attached to it by means of more wax being pressed on top. If it was desired, a small counterseal could be pressed into the back of the wax before the whole impression was removed from the larger matrix.

Some matrices, however, were in two parts of equal size, one for each face of the impression. In such cases it was necessary to employ a seal press (Cat. 460) to force the two dies together simultaneously, but first the wax had to be formed into two thin 'cakes' of the required diameter. Each was fitted loosely into its half of the matrix. Then the two dies were lined up and fitted together, one on top of the other, and kept in register by the rings and pins on their peripheries. The cords or tags were placed between the two parts and the whole inserted into the press which was then screwed down, forcing the wax into the dies and uniting the two cakes.   TAH

453   The first Great Seal of Henry III

October 1218
Wax: diam. 10 cm
Inscr. obv. + HENRICUS DEI GRACIA REX
    ANGLIE DOMINUS HYBERNIE
    rev. + HENRICUS DUX NORMANNIE ET
    AQUITANIE COMS ANDEGAVIE
British Library, Cotton Charter XI. 53

Henry's first Great Seal was made by Master Walter de Ripa, a goldsmith of London. Early in November 1218 he was reimbursed five marks of silver, which was the weight of metal that had been used to make the pair of

matrices, and was asked how much money he wanted for his labour. A month later he was paid 40s for the work. This was a considerable sum, the equivalent of several months' wages, for what was no more than a few weeks' work, and it may be that it was a token of the king's pleasure rather than the amount Walter asked for. In 1195, Master William had received only two marks (£1.6s.8d) for making a Great Seal for Richard I.

Master Walter was clearly a supreme technician and a very fine artist versed in the classicism of the later Transitional style. The image of Henry enthroned is characterised by an unusual depth and subtlety in the handling of relief. The design of the equestrian side set a pattern for barons' seals (Cat. 144) for decades to come. The balance and uniformity of the lettering, among other features, are distinctive and allow a corpus of other, distinguished seals to be attributed to this maker (Cat. 144, 193).

This seal had many imitators, ranging from Haakon Haakonson, King of Norway, to James, King of Aragon. The lion and the dragon beneath the king's feet are probably a reference to Psalm XCI, 13 and thus to divine support for Christian sovereignty (cf. Cat. 143).   TAH

LIT. Birch 1887, I, nos 100–17; Wyon 1887, nos 41–2, pp. 21–2, 149–50, 189; Powicke 1908, esp. pp. 222–3; Norgate 1912, pp. 73, 102, 113–14; Kingsford 1940, pp. 158–9.

454   Seal matrix of Robert FitzWalter

c. 1207–15
Silver: diam. 7.2 cm
Inscr. + SIGILLUM ROBERTI FILII WALTERI
The Trustees of the British Museum, London,
    MLA 1841, 6–24, I

The heraldry on this matrix indicates that its origins are inextricably bound up with seals belonging to the de Quincy family (e.g. Cat. 141). A date in the teens of the thirteenth century is likely. The short surcoat with very agitated hem is found on seals of this date (Ellis 1981, II, no. P. 1009), so too are the shield with rounded corners and the helmet with a flanged top and a visor that curves in under the chin (Ellis 1981, II, no. P. 2213; Blair 1943, pl. III d). A similar FitzWalter seal, but without the de Quincy shield, is on British Library, Add. Charter 21, 698.

The basic forms of the figure, lettering, etc. were engraved into the silver matrix, but certain details such as the quatrefoil dots seen both on the caparison round the horse's head and in the legend, were done with small punches. The silver handle, soldered onto the reverse, is in the form of a brooch pin, perhaps indicating that such seals were regarded as items of adornment even if they were not actually worn.   TAH

PROV. Found in Lincolnshire temp. Charles II; Robert Sanderson, Bishop of Lincoln; by descent to John King; Rev. Richard Neate, 1777; British Museum, 1841.

LIT. Tonnochy 1952, no. 332, p. lvii no. 4; New York 1970, no. 333; London 1978a, no. 8; Henderson 1978; Heslop 1986a, p. 52.

453

454

455

455 Seal matrix of Chichester Cathedral

c. 1220
Silver: h. 8.4 cm, w. 6.3 cm
Inscr. + SIGILLUM: SANCTE: CICESTRENSIS:
    ECCLESIE
    on background TEPLU JUSTCIE
The Trustees of the British Museum, London,
    MLA 1923, 10-15, 1

This matrix has principally been famous for its representation of a church with an elaborate tower in receding stages. Clapham argued that it showed with some accuracy an Anglo-Saxon wooden building type. But, as he recognised, the lettering of the legend indicates an early thirteenth-century date for the engraving. It remains a mystery why such an archaic structure should have been chosen as the motif for the Cathedral's seal.

Close examination of the surfaces of the silver reveals a number of interesting technical features. The front of the die was filed before being engraved: some of the marks of the file have been interrupted by the subsequent cutting (e.g. around the star to the right of the tower). After the basic form of the building had been cut, a series of fine guidelines (still visible to the naked eye) was scratched on it to aid the artist in positioning the lines of masonry. He did not adhere at all closely to these lines indicating a degree of freedom in taking decisions at a very late stage of production. As on FitzWalter's matrix (Cat. 454), there are indications that small punches were used.

The beautiful and elaborate foliate handle on the reverse was made separately and then soldered on. The style of its leafwork, with scalloped and fluted edges, is reminiscent of Mosan and Cologne work of the late twelfth century (e.g. The Anno Shrine, Cologne 1972, no. K.3, repr. p. 322).   TAH

PROV. Grimston family, Yorkshire; Lady Waechter, 1922; British Museum, 1923.

LIT. Birch 1887, 1, no. 1469; Clapham 1930, pp. 83, 96; Tonnochy 1952, no. 794; Moor 1923. p. 267; Heslop 1986a, pp. 51-2.

456 Antique intaglio in a thirteenth-century matrix

Early 13th century
Engraved sard set in silver; h. 2.9 cm, w. 2.2 cm
Inscr. + QUI ME PORTE SIEST LE MUS
The Trustees of the British Museum, London,
    MLA 96, 3-26, 1

456

Precious and semi-precious stones were often regarded in the Middle Ages as having magical properties; a category of book, the Lapidary, was devoted to describing their qualities. An engraved gem might be endowed with even greater powers: for example, a mid-thirteenth-century tract tells us that an image of Mercury on a stone grants to its owner irresistible wisdom and grace. The profile on this sard seems to be that of Hercules, and the legend claims that 'who carries me fares the best'. Because of their antiquity, relative rarity and potency such stones were prestigious and expensive. They could not be set in bronze since the heat necessary to accomplish this would crack them, so only silver or gold could be used (Cat. 198).

When the gem is antique, the only means of dating a matrix is by the style of the lettering. In this case the curvaceous, but thin forms suggest the period soon after 1200.   TAH

PROV. Said to have been found in Ireland; Mr J. Hill of Clifton; British Museum, 1896.

LIT. Tonnochy 1952, no. 760, Smith 1857, p. 75, pl. xviii, no. 10.

457 Blank seal matrix of bell-shaped form

c. 1300-50
Copper alloy: h. 3 cm, w. 2.1 cm
John Auld Esq.

457

Two uncut blank dies of this kind have been discovered in London in recent years (for the other see Spencer 1984, p. 382, no. 32). The casting flange up the handle and across the face on which the matrix would have been engraved indicates that such blanks were made in reusable two-part moulds. To produce a saleable finished product the engraver would have had to file off the rough excrescences before cutting the rim, central design and legend. Since the motifs used on these seals were relatively limited, much of this work could be done without a particular customer in mind. The legend, if it specified the owner's name, can have been cut only after a purchaser had appeared.   TAH

PROV. London, north Thames foreshore by Southwark Bridge.

458 Bell-shaped seal matrix with chain

c. 1325-50
Copper alloy; h. 2.5 cm, w. 2 cm, chain with
    hook and swivel l. 11.5 cm
Inscr. PREVE*SURE**CONU
Museum of London, 84.266/2

The contemporary swivel and chain indicate the way in which the matrix was secured,

458

either to a belt, a burse or some other container. Even though moderately well preserved, the central device is illegible and some letters of the legend are open to alternative readings, but the first word is probably PREVE. Similar legends continue in the vein *privé suis et peu/puis connu* (I am secret and little then known; cf. Spencer 1984, p. 380, no. 19). It suggests that such seals were often used for private correspondence. On late seals of this class legends are sometimes garbled, which casts doubt on the literacy of both engraver and owner.   TAH

PROV. London, Billingsgate lorry park, Lower Thames Street.

459   Seal matrix of Christian Sprotforth

c. 1330
Copper alloy: h. 3.5 cm, w. 2.6 cm
Inscr. * S'CRISIANI SPROTFOR'
The Trustees of the British Museum, London,
MLA 1929, 4–12, 1

459

At least eight examples of these small dies with screw-out centres are known. They are normally made of silver. The purpose of the screw thread is to allow the central motif to be advanced until it is 3–4 mm proud of the legend on the rim. With the owner's name thus effectively removed from the die, the seal could be used as a secret signet.

The device of the heart sprouting a flower (cf. Cat. 199), in this case with facing male and female profiles either side, was presumably felt to be appropriate to the owner, if indeed his name was Sprotforth!   TAH

PROV. Found in Suffolk; S. G. Fenton; F. H. Harman Oates Coll.; British Museum, 1929.

LIT. Tonnochy 1952, no. 624; Kingsford 1924, p. 255.

460   Thirteenth-century seal press from Canterbury Cathedral

1232(?)
Copper alloy with iron handle and oak base:
  h. 39 cm, w. 67 cm, d. 27 cm
Dean and Chapter of Canterbury

Seal presses of this type must have been made to accompany all large two-sided seals (e.g. Cat. 143, 193, 453, 456). Only by means of such machinery could the necessary pressure be applied simultaneously to both faces of the softened wax which was to constitute the

460

impression. As far as it is known, this press has always been at Canterbury Cathedral and there is thus a prima facie case that it was made for use with the 1232 seal (Cat. 461). The style of the capitals and bases on the columns of the press indicates an early to mid-thirteenth-century date, and the diameter of the matrix which the press was designed to contain was about 94 mm.

The press is as attractive for its accuracy as for its design. The screw thread, in particular, must have been complicated to cast and finish so that it worked smoothly. The unit of measurement employed was probably the same as the modern English inch: the central base-plate is a 5-in square, with a $2\frac{1}{2}$-in projection at either end, and the column height is $7\frac{1}{2}$-in.   TAH

PROV. Canterbury Cathedral.

LIT. Heslop 1982, p. 96.

461–2   Multiple die matrices

461   The third seal of Canterbury Cathedral Priory

1232
Wax: diam. 9.4 cm
Inscr. obv. SIGILLUM ECCLESIE XPISTI
     CANTUARIE PRIME SEDIS BRITANNIE
  rev. EST HUIC VITA MORI/PRO QUA DUM
    VIXIT AMORI, MORS ERAT ET
    MEMORI/PER MORTEM VIVIT HONORI
  edge SIT MICHI CAUSA MERA/STILUS
    APTUS LITERA VERA/CIRCUMSPECTA
    SERA/TENOR UTILIS INTEGRA CERA
British Library, Cotton Charter XXI.11

The abbey of St Augustine at Canterbury had a new seal made in 1198–9 which began a tradition for matrices with more than two dies. In the most complex examples, such as this exhibit, up to five separate engravings might be used. Most of the image was impressed by just two of these – each initially on a separate cake of wax. Small figures were pressed on the reverses of these cakes using two other dies (engraved on the front and back of a single metal plate, e.g. Cat. 462). Apertures were then cut through the fronts of the principal faces of the two wax discs so that, when they were placed back to back, the little images on the reverse of one half were visible through the holes in the front of the other. After the two wax laminae had been stuck together, the fifth die, a separate legend, was used round the edge of the completed seal to mask the joining of the two halves.

461

A surviving annual account rendered by the treasurers of Canterbury Cathedral Priory on 29 October 1233 records £7.6s.8d spent 'on the work of the new seal'. This large sum must refer to the complex seal before us (cf. costs in Cat. 453). The matrices and the press (Cat. 460) were actually finished in 1232, the date of a document in the Archives nationales, Paris, bearing this seal. The account probably represents the final reckoning. A later Canterbury charter is witnessed by 'Nigel, who made the seal'. This designation suggests that a degree of fame attached to this goldsmith for his work on the project.

The subject of the main face of this seal is an image of the cathedral itself with censing angels overhead and heads, including those of Sts Dunstan and Alphege, peering through openings in the towers. On the reverse is the scene of St Thomas Becket's martyrdom set, as it were, within the church. In the centre his soul is seen ascending to Christ who appears in the trefoiled gable. TAH

LIT. Birch 1887, I. nos 1373–8, Borenius 1932a, p. 75; Kingsford 1940, pp. 159–60; Heslop 1982, *passim*.

462

462 Three-part seal matrix of Southwick Priory

Soon after 1258(?)
Copper alloy: diam. 7 cm
Inscr. obv. SIGILLUM : ECCLESIE : SANCTE :
MARIE : DE : SUWIKA
rev. SIT : PRO : SUWIKA :/MEDIATRIX :
VIRGO : PUDICA/ET : PAX : ANGELICA :
/SIT : NOBIS : SEMPER : AMICA
Lady Lubbock

This is the most complex surviving matrix of its kind and shows how such seals as Canterbury Cathedral's (Cat. 461) were impressed. It must always have been time-consuming taking impressions in this way. At Canterbury Cathedral there was doubtless a secretariat that could cope; the small priory of Southwick was not remotely in the same league. No medieval impression from this matrix has yet come to light, so we have no idea how long it remained in use. We do know, however, that it had been replaced by *c.* 1380, the date of the matrix still in use at the Dissolution (Ellis 1986, no. M 791). Despite its being superseded, the three-part matrix was not destroyed and was probably kept at the priory. Originally there may have been an additional engraved plate with a long, narrow legend for use round the edge of an impression (cf. Cat. 283).

The overall design, as well as the idea of the many small apertures, derives from Canterbury Cathedral's third seal but, as Kingsford pointed out, the style and layout seem to derive more directly from the Norwich Cathedral seal of 1258. An earlier Southwick seal of *c.* 1200 was certainly still in use in 1242 (Oxford, Magdalen College, Selbourne Charter 337) and so this exhibit must anyway be later than that. The lettering and certain details of the image of the Virgin suggest that the matrix is a later work by the craftsman responsible for the seal of the city of Carlisle (Birch, 1892, II, no. 4792). TAH

PROV. Mr Smith, Attorney of Southwick; John Bonham of Petersfield; John Bonham Carter, 1831; Lady Lubbock.

LIT. Madden 1831, pp. 374–9; Birch 1887, I, nos 4061–3; Dale *et al.* 1917, pp. 101–7; Kingsford 1940, p. 161.

463 Canopy of memorial brass

c. 1375
Copper-alloy fragment: l. 34 cm, w. 27.5 cm
The Trustees of the British Museum, London, MLA, 1922, 12–5, I

This fragment of a canopy, crocketed and with cusped openings, from the brass of Peter de Lacy (d. 1375) at Northfleet, Kent, is of a commonly found type, and it is very likely that other brasses may survive with identical canopy work intact; at least for the early

463

fourteenth century, it has been shown that templates were used for such canopy work, for rubbings of parts of them can be superimposed exactly (Badham 1985, p. 141).

The technique of engraving a brass was to sketch out the design on the metal and then, for the broader lines or recessed areas, to cut the outlines on either side with a sharp tracer; the brass between these lines could then be chiselled out (Gawthorp 1926, p. 19). A burin, with triangular or rectangular section, was used where narrower lines were to be cut.

The black filling of the ground in this fragment may be original; recessed areas on many brasses certainly were originally filled with black inlay of bitumen or pitch or, occasionally, coloured enamel or even glass, although it is rare for any of this to survive; the roughly worked recessed areas were not intended to be seen.   NLR

PROV. Messrs Fenton Ltd, 33 Cranbourn St, London; bt by British Museum, 1922.

LIT. Gawthorp 1926, pp. 19–20; Norris 1978a, pp. 39–42; Badham 1985.

464   Resurrection

1370s
Alabaster: h. 38 cm, w. 26.9 cm
The Board of Trustees of the Victoria and Albert
    Museum, London, A 61–1926

Although severely weathered, with loss of surface smoothness and detail, this representation of Christ's Resurrection successfully conveys a sense of movement and drama – more so than the slightly later, more crowded carving (Cat. 465).

The panel's simplicity of design and chamfered edging are indicative of an early date, in the context of English alabaster sculpture's development; a date of around 1370–80 is indicated by the three soldiers' comparatively low bacinets, with central points and short aventails, as well as by their rather short gauntlets (personal communication, Claude Blair). W.L. Hildburgh suggested that the peculiarly English convention of showing Christ as stepping on to a sleeping soldier (cf. Cat. 465) reflected the representation of the Resurrection in contemporary Mystery Plays (Hildburgh 1949, pp. 91–2).

There are several other alabaster panels that may be related sculpturally to this (e.g. London, Victoria and Albert Museum, A 106–1946; see Hildburgh 1950, p. 13), doubtless reflecting the fact that alabaster panels were already being produced in substantial quantities, even if by a small number of sculptors, at this date.   NLR

PROV. Lt-Col. G.B. Croft-Lyons, by 1910; beq. by him to V&A, 1926.

LIT. London 1910, p. 51, no. 2, pl. IX; London 1930, no. 344; Hildburgh 1937, pp. 97–8; Hildburgh 1950, p. 13, fig. 21; Cheetham 1984, p. 272, no. 199, repr.

465   Resurrection

End 14th century
Alabaster: h. 43.3 cm, w. 28.1 cm
The Board of Trustees of the Victoria and Albert
    Museum, London, A 110–1946

Perhaps carved less than twenty-five years after Cat. 464, this panel of the same subject shows a far greater depth and detail of carving (partly reflecting the fact that this

464

465

panel is of a finer-grained stone), but it has lost some of the other's dramatic effect. Attention is focused on Christ by means of the garment (probably His shroud-cloth) flung over His shoulder and by the device of making the soldier below His feet lie at a diagonal that brings the spectator's eyes upwards – a schematisation that does not entirely avoid a sense of clutter.

The panel combines chamfered sides and top with battlementing, indicative of its being in the transitional state in the development of alabaster panels, between either having chamfered sides (as in Cat. 464) or having a battlemented top. The soldiers' bacinets are more sharply pointed than in Cat. 464, and their gauntlets and aventails are longer; they wear long-sleeved jupons. The soldier at the bottom has a rondel dagger, of a sort not common until after 1400 (personal communication, Claude Blair).   NLR

PROV. Count Paul Biver; Philip Nelson, by 1918; W.L. Hildburgh, by 1926; given by Hildburgh to V&A, 1946.

LIT. Nelson 1918, p. 320, pl. v, fig. 2; London 1930, no. 342; London 1939, no. 130; Hildburgh 1950, p. 19, fig. 30; Brussels 1967, no. E/15, fig. 8; Hodgkinson 1976, colour pl. 1; Cheetham 1984, p. 273, no. 200, repr.

466   The Pepysian model book

c. 1370–90 with later additions
Vellum, ff. 24: 240 × 205 cm
Magdalene College, Cambridge, Pepys MS 1916
Photograph

The manuscript contains painted, shaded and outline drawings mainly of single figures and of animals and birds. There are also two textile patterns, and three architectural drawings, two for moulding profiles and one for window tracery (fig. 20). The drawings are of different dates, the latest being of the fifteenth or even the early sixteenth century. M.R. James isolated two main groups, of which the first includes the figures on folios 2v.–9, 14–15v. These are the earliest drawings of probably *c.* 1370–90. The seated figures of Prophets or Apostles might have served for a Jesse Tree or a Creed cycle. The second main group includes the painted bird studies, folios 10–13v., 19, and the outline drawings of animals and birds. The birds have been compared to those painted by John Siferwas in the Sherborne Missal of *c.* 1396–1407. Scheller has also convincingly compared some of the animal drawings with the Holkham Bible Picture Book (Cat. 221), which suggests that earlier models are incorporated, as is often the case in such model books.

Whilst many of the drawings seem to be models for use in a workshop, others, especially the birds, have the appearance of nature studies. The book is thus transitional in terms of medieval artistic practice. Its varied contents make its purpose uncertain, though it

466

has been suggested that it belonged either to a glass painter's or to an embroiderer's workshop. There are stylistic links with Bohemian art, and Pächt and Wormald have stressed the similarities with Lombard nature studies, especially those of the Milanese artist Giovanni de' Grassi (d. 1399). A number of the animals and birds have English names written beside them, however, and an English origin is not in doubt. As such it is a unique survival among model books.   JA

PROV. Bequeathed by Samuel Pepys (1653–1703).

LIT. James 1924–5; Pächt 1950, pp. 18ff.; Wormald 1954, pp. 191, 194–5, pl. 29a; Scheller 1963, pp. 112–19; Jenni 1976, pp. 31, 33, 61ff., 80, 83, 85, Abb. 111, 117; Yapp 1981, *passim*, pl. 2, figs 10, 16.

467   Peter Lombard, Sentences

Early 14th century
Parchment, ff. 197: 42.4 × 27.4 cm
The Master and Fellows, Christ's College, Cambridge, MS 1

The manuscript is important for two leaves of an artist's working drawings (ff. 196v., 197v.). They fill blanks left at the end of an early fourteenth-century copy of the Sentences, which has an erased colophon, possibly once giving the name of the scribe or original owner. The sketches, some of which are very faint, have been described and interpreted by Michael A. Michael. Each page has a diagonal grid of stylus-ruled lines set in a broad rectangular framing band. Within the lozenge-shaped compartments are figure sketches, more or less finished, and similar

467

468

469

trials, though not calibrated with the grid structure, occur elsewhere on the two pages. In the framing band are some lightly-sketched ornamental motifs: stylised foliage and architectural tracery.

The chief subjects visible may be identified as an angel of the Annunciation (f. 196v.) and a standing Virgin and Child (f. 197v.). The Virgin and Child particularly engaged the attention of the artist, who made several separate studies of her head and of the drapery of the lower half of her body, as well as quick sketches of the entire image. The more detailed studies are shaded with consummate skill in monochromatic gradations equivalent to the modelled surfaces of the most refined Court style manuscripts and panel paintings of the early fourteenth century. As Michael concluded, the artist was clearly related to the chief master of the Robert de Lisle Psalter (Cat. 569), a manuscript discussed by Lucy F. Sandler in connection with the sedilia of Westminster Abbey of c. 1308. Indeed, the kind of finished study of drapery in these drawings suggests not what we know of the process of manuscript illumination but what we know of the stages of preparation for large-scale works from the practices of later artists. In these drawings we may have 'cartoons' for lost panels designed by the painter of the Westminster sedilia.

In the late fourteenth century the volume came into the possession of St Augustine's, Canterbury, where a verse summary of the Sentences was written on blanks between the end of the original text and the two pages of drawings. LFS

PROV. Canterbury, St Augustine's, late 14th century.

LIT. Michael 1982, pp. 230–2, repr. figs 39–41, 44–5; Sandler 1983, pp. 15–16.

468 Misericord: Crowned mask

c. 1370
Oak: h. 33 cm, w. 64 cm, d. 18 cm
Dean and Chapter, Lincoln Cathedral, north back
stalls from east, no. 18 (cf. Cat. 534–5)

The sets of choir stalls at St Katharine's Hospital, Lincoln and Chester cathedrals, manufactured over a period of some twenty-five years, appear to have been the responsibility of the same workshop. The gables at Chester with voluted 'trefoil' leaf crocket decoration are treated in exactly the same way, with the same plated stems and cusped termination, as the gable from St Katharine's, Stepney (Cat. 533). Plated stems occur at Lincoln Cathedral, and we must allow the probability that one artist, at least, worked in all three buildings.

The misericords at Lincoln and Chester of a king's head flanked by male profiles as supporters are strikingly similar in conception and execution. The head on the right at Chester must be by the same artist, with the characteristic Lincoln band over the hair. The quatrefoil rosette on this band is similar to that on the brooch on the profile head on the misericord at St Katharine's and along the sunk mouldings around the front of the projecting ledges on the seats at Lincoln. CT

PROV. Lincoln Cathedral.

LIT. Anderson 1967; Tracy 1987a, pp. 49–55, repr. pls 181, 183, 184.

469 Misericord: Profile head

c. 1365
Oak: h. 28 cm, w. 60 cm, d. 17 cm
The Royal Foundation of St Katharine, London,
by kind permission of Her Majesty Queen
Elizabeth The Queen Mother, Patron

The central carving shows the bearded head of a man in profile. He is possibly wearing a striped cloak clasped at the chest, and has knotted and trailing drapery at the back of his head. The supporters are winged beasts with human heads. There were originally twenty-four choir stalls at St Katharine's. The hospital was moved to Regent's Park in 1826 and, again, to Stepney after the Second World War. Thirteen misericords with their seating have survived.

As already mentioned in connection with the canopy arch from the St Katharine's choir stalls (Cat. 533) and the misericords from Lincoln Cathedral (Cat. 534–5), the vocabulary of architectural and sculptural motifs on both sets of furniture betrays their near contemporaneity. The tracery of the gables on the upper tabernacles at Lincoln is very similar to that on the gables at St Katharine's. Some of the foliage on the gable crockets at Lincoln is also very close, as well as the way that the leaf sprays emerge from grooved 'plates' of wood.

The clasp on the bust of the profile head on this misericord is precisely the device used throughout the Lincoln misericords on the

470

front mouldings of the seats. A profile head on a misericord from the Carmelite friary at Coventry is also closely comparable, and may well have been carved by a member of the same workshop.   CT

PROV. St Katharine's-by-the-Tower.

LIT. Druce 1917, repr. pls I–II; Majendie 1924, pl. p. 20; Tracy 1987a, pp. 49–55, repr. pls 165–75.

470   Misericord: Man slaying dragon

1335–40
Oak: h. 30.5 cm, w. 76.2 cm, d. 16.5 cm
The Dean and Chapter of Wells (cf. Cat. 530)

The Wells Cathedral choir furniture, with fifty back stalls originally, is the earliest of the three surviving West Country monuments (Tewkesbury Abbey, 1340–4; Hereford Cathedral, 1340–55, Cat. 531) designed during the second quarter of the fourteenth century. All three conformed to the canonical single-tiered double-screen format, almost certainly initiated at Westminster Abbey in the 1250s. In 1848 the super-structure of the Wells stalls was removed as part of a radical refurbishment by Salvin. The original appearance of the choir stalls is preserved in contemporary drawings by Dollman.

There were two master carvers working on the choir stalls: the master of the 'Flight of Alexander' (Cat. 530), clearly the younger of the two men working in an up-to-date style; and the master of the 'Animals', who quite possibly worked as a young man on the choir stalls at Winchester Cathedral. Important characteristics of the Alexander master's style – the use of the raised line, the swathed human figure and contorted pose, the handling of the dragon's ears and claws, and the stylised treatment of animal ribs – are clearly recognisable on this misericord, showing a

left-handed man slaying a dragon. The subject presumably depicts the power of good over evil.   CT

PROV. Wells Cathedral.

LIT. Church 1897, repr. fig. 2, p. 339; Tracy 1987a, pp. 25–9, repr. pls 78–90.

471   Misericord: Centaur stabbing monster

Mid-1340s
Oak: h. 26 cm, w. 61 cm, d. 14 cm
The Dean and Chapter of Hereford, south side upper stalls from east, no. 5 (cf. Cat. 531)

A centaur with flowing hair plunges its lance into the chest of a dragon. The supporters on either side are of foliage type.

This carving is one of the earlier type of misericords in the cathedral choir stalls. There were, originally, fifty back stalls the manufacture of which seems to have been extended over an unusually long period (c. 1340–55), probably owing to the visitation of the Black Death.

Although the making of the stalls is not

recorded, some assistance is provided by the close similarity in many cases of the carving style to that at Wells Cathedral. For example, a number of near comparisons can be made with the foliage on the misericord supporters. Interestingly, the subject of a man (at Hereford a centaur) slaying a dragon, left-handed, occurs in both places (see Cat. 470). Other examples in stone of dragon slayers at Wells and many in Somerset are also left-handed (the other dragon-slayer misericord at Wells is right-handed). Failing a survey of dragon slayers in Herefordshire, we cannot say whether the Hereford Cathedral treatment is typical of the locality or not. Some of the sculpture at Hereford is so close to Wells in subject-matter and general appearance that is is certain that the Hereford master carver must have visited the cathedral.   CT

PROV. Hereford Cathedral.

LIT. Tracy 1987a, pp. 30–3, repr. pls 93, 95, 96–100, 102–7.

472   Virgin and Child

c. 1330–40
Stained glass: h. 56 cm, w. 34 cm
Rector and Parochial Church Council of the Parish Church of St John the Baptist, Fladbury, Hereford and Worcester

The original location of this panel within the church is unknown, but it is contemporary with the present structure which was rebuilt in the second quarter of the fourteenth century. From about 1935 it was in a vestry window but more recently it has been set in a light box on a wooden cross erected in the south aisle of the nave as a memorial to a former rector, an extraordinary method of displaying medieval glass. Along with some fourteenth-century armorials in a north chancel window, this is all that survives of the medieval glazing.

The Virgin, who is crowned but not nimbed, is seated on a throne; she offers her breast to the Christ Child who is shown blessing her and holding a fruit, an image stressing Mary's roles as queen and mother. Apart from Mary's green robe and pot-metal

471

472

yellow mantle the figures are in white, the hair, crown, cross-nimbus and fruit stained yellow. The ground is green and the canopy, which consists of a cusped arch and crocketed gable, is in white, green and pot-metal yellow glass. A linear drawing technique is used with distinctive conventionalised drapery folds and little shading to create a direct and very expressive image. The artist has tried to suggest the texture of the linen veil by scratching out the diaper pattern from a backpainted wash. The lower section of the Virgin's mantle has been patched and various medieval fragments, many of them in the style of the original, have been used to extend the panel.

A companion piece from Warndon (Cat. 473), some ten miles from Fladbury, is based on the same design and is the work of the same local atelier. It gives a clearer idea of the original appearance of the Fladbury panel. Such reuse of designs and cartoons was a common practice with medieval glaziers. It was particularly useful for large commissions where full-scale outlines for figures, canopies and decorative elements in windows were painted on to wooden tables so that repeated copies could be cut to save time. DO'C

LIT. Green 1937, p. 2; Baker 1960, p. 100, pls xv, 52; Paris 1968, no. 216.

473 Virgin and Child

c. 1330–40
Stained glass: h. 71 cm, w. 54 cm, original glass
 h. 61 cm, w. 42 cm
St Nicholas, Warndon, Hereford and Worcester
 east window 1 2b

This panel is a second, much better preserved version of the Virgin and Child from Fladbury (Cat. 472). In most details the panels are virtually identical but at Warndon the Virgin has been given a blue nimbus, and there are some differences in colour with her robe in pot-metal yellow, her mantle blue and the crockets in yellow stain. The canopy design is similar to Fladbury but is complete with pinnacled side shafts and, behind the gable, a band of blue quatrefoil ornament beneath crenellation. The borders consists of rosettes in white and yellow stain on green grounds. In 1984 the panel, which was in poor condition, was restored by Barley Studios. A few replacement pieces were painted for the canopy and borders, and Christ was given a new right hand based upon the Fladbury design.

The glass is too narrow for its present setting but would fit in one of the lateral windows. Apart from a few fragments in some tracery lights, what survives of the medieval glazing has been gathered together in the centre light of the east window. Beneath the Virgin and Child is a panel in the same style depicting St Peter and St Paul, above is a slightly earlier Annunciation, and a fifteenth-century figure of St Andrew. Thomas Habington, the seventeenth-century antiquary, recorded lost armorials of Bracy in the east window and other windows. As lords of the manor and patrons of the church, they may well have commissioned the glass. DO'C

LIT. Green 1947, pp. 20–2; Woodforde 1954, p. 12, pl. 17.

474 Architectural sketch: Design for a window

13th century
Clunch: h. 20 cm, w. 21 cm, d. 75 cm
Cambridge University Museum of Archaeology
 and Anthropology, z.15088

Medieval architectural designs were usually carried around in the form of sketches on parchment or paper for elevations, or as wooden or metal templates for the cross-sections of mouldings. On site, designs could be transferred on to wood in a tracing house

473

474

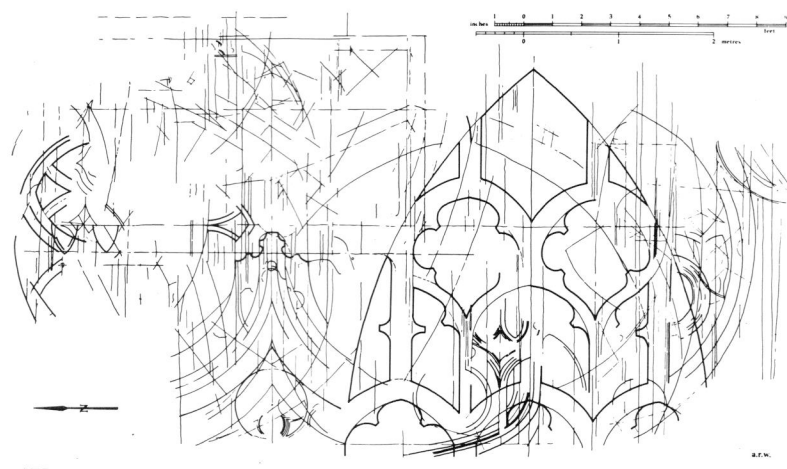

475

where a specially-made plaster tracing floor could have a large area of actual-size design marked out on it (Cat. 475). The working drawings made in the tracing house have very rarely survived, but this particular sketch has been preserved as a result of being made on clunch – soft enough to be easy to draw on, but hard enough to be used as building material.

The stone contains part of the design for a window; although much of the stone has been broken away, the design of the whole window can be reconstructed, for it appears to have been the window of the very east wall of St John's College Chapel in which the stone was discovered during demolition work in 1869. The chapel was very possibly built for St John's Hospital c. 1280, when scholars first came to live there. The stone was presumably discarded from the workshop of the mason in charge of the chapel's construction once he had had its design drawn out actual size.

The sketch has been incised using a pair of mason's compasses; the variation of the arcs results from his compass point having slipped. NLR

PROV. St John's College, Cambridge; discovered 1869.

LIT. Biddle 1961, pp. 99–108, repr. pl. XVI.

475 Masons' tracing floor, York Minster chapter house vestibule

c. 1360–*c.* 1520
Photograph

In medieval times full-size geometry was used for setting out the exact curves of vaulting ribs and tracery. This was often done in special tracing houses, which are well-known from documentary sources; in England there are three known survivors, at Ely Cathedral, Wells Cathedral (above the north porch) and this one, above the chapter house vestibule at York Minster.

The room is L-shaped, with a fireplace, and a garderobe built into one of the buttresses. The plaster floor on which the designs were drawn out occupies the north–south wing,

and about two-thirds of the original remains. The surface of the plaster is covered in scratches, some of which make up clear designs for tracery or mouldings, drawn out with compasses.

The largest and most complete design is for the presbytery aisle windows, built in the early 1360s. The design shows the outline of the window arch, the tops of the window lights, and details of the modified reticulations which make up the tracery pattern. The profiles of the mouldings are not given. The design on the floor is exactly the same size as the window itself, and measurement confirms that the radius of the window arch was derived from the width of the window in a proportional relation of $\sqrt{2}:1$. This proportion, easily obtained from the diagonal of a square, was one of the most commonly used systems of proportion in medieval architecture.

Other designs on the floor can be related to windows in or near the Minster, and it seems to have been in use until after 1500. NC

LIT. Harvey 1969a.

476 Double capital with stiff-leaf decoration

Late 13th century
Limestone: h. 23.5 cm, w. 45.5 cm, d. 28 cm
The Yorkshire Museum, York, 1986. 136

This capital, possibly from the clerestory of the church of St Mary's Abbey, York, was found during the excavation carried out between 1827 and 1829 under the auspices of the Yorkshire Philosophical Society. Scratched on its upper bed are setting-out lines which, showing the relative positions of the moulding under the uppermost unit and of the profile of the capital immediately above the necking, are evidence of the method by which the design for the block was transferred to the stone by means of a series of templates. ND

PROV. York; excavated at St Mary's Abbey, 1827–9.

LIT. Wellbeloved 1829, p. 15, pl. LVIIIG; Brook n.d., inv. 537, bk 2, p. 32.

476

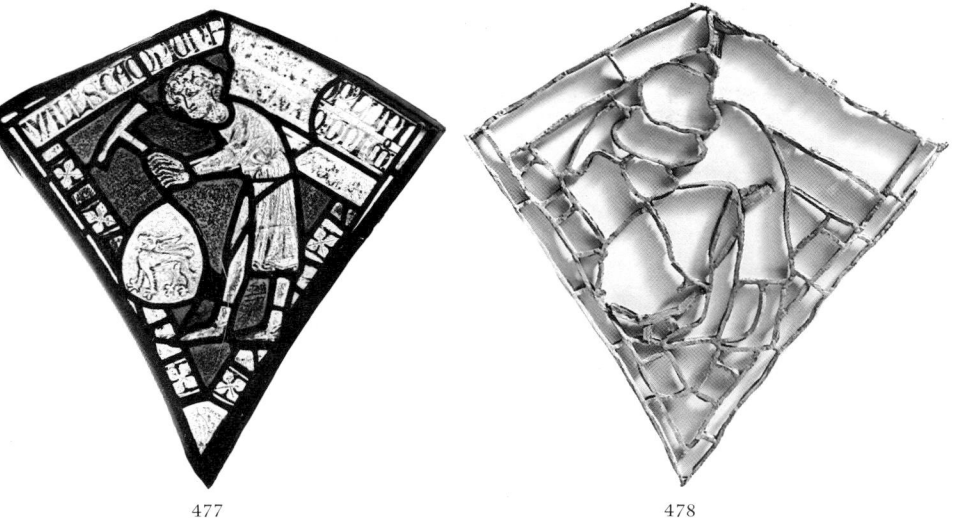

477   478

477   William Campiun

c. 1313
Stained glass: h. 42 cm, w. 39 cm
Inscr. in Lombardic letters: WILL'S ⁚ CAMPIUN ⁚ F
  [modern insertion replacing missing section]
OP' ⁚ LAP ⁚ O ⁚ DNI ⁚ Ṁ ⁚ C [modern insertion]
The Parochial Church Council of St Mary
  Magdalene, Helmdon, Northamptonshire,
  window n.v

This panel comes from its original location in
the apex of the easternmost window in the
nave north aisle at Helmdon. It depicts a
stonemason named William Campiun, who
is clad in a pot-metal yellow knee-length
tunic over blue hose and pointed shoes and
wields a pick. The ground is plain ruby and
the border consists of yellow quatrefoil
flowers separated by plain blue glass and the
inscription quoted above. The piece of white
glass with a lion statant guardant outlined
upon it is an alien insertion of contemporary
glass; the missing sections of the inscription
were replaced by pieces of white 'antique'
glass toned down by stippling during the
conservation of the panel by the York
Glaziers' Trust in 1976 and 1977. At the
same time the original sections of the inscription were strengthened by external plating
painted with copies of the original lettering.

The Helmdon panel is of exceptional interest as it is one of the very few in English
medieval stained glass to depict an artisan
with the tools of his trade. In France a
number of such windows survive, including
several with stonemasons plying their craft,
but apart from Helmdon the only known
examples of artisans in English glass are in
the Bell-founders' window and the masons
and carpenters in the borders of the Penan-
cers' window, both in York Minster; also the
west window of St George's Chapel, Windsor.
The last includes the figure of a mason who is
generally considered to represent William
Vertue (d. 1527). One further depiction of an
English mason is known from a copy made in
1822 of the original glass of *c.* 1393 in

Winchester College Chapel: this represents
the master mason William Wynford (see also
Cat. 612).

The incomplete inscription on the Helmdon panel can be reconstructed to be read as
follows: WILL'S ⁚ CAMPIUN ⁚ F[ECIT ⁚ HOC ⁚]
OP' ⁚ LAPI[DIS ⁚ ANN]O ⁚ DNI ⁚ ṀC[CCXIII].
The evidence for the date of 1313 comes from
notes made by an antiquary in 1873 and is
consistent with the style and design of the
panel. The inscription shows that William
Campiun worked on the fabric of Helmdon
Church; although this is the only reference to
him that has been traced, it is reasonable to
assume that he was associated with the oolite
limestone quarries at Helmdon which have
been in existence since the Middle Ages
(Parry 1986–7).   RM

LIT. Marks 1981, pp. 105–7.

478   Medieval window leading

c. 1313
Lead: h. 42 cm, w. 39 cm
The Parochial Church Council of St Mary
  Magdalene, Helmdon, Northamptonshire

The medieval leading of the stained-glass
panel depicting the stonemason William
Campiun (Cat. 477) was found to be almost
intact when it was conserved in 1976–7. It
was too weak to be reused when the panel
was replaced. Although the lead does not
differ very much from that used in contemporary stained glass, the rounded profile
indicates its medieval date. In this period it
was cast and not milled as today (Dodwell
1961, pp. 54–6).   RM

LIT. Marks 1981, pp. 105–7.

479   Crucifixion

c. 1400 or later
Alabaster, unfinished: 31.3 × 28.8 cm
  & 16 × 13 cm
Society of Antiquaries of London, Mus. Cat. 592

These fragments of alabaster show quite
clearly how the stone was prepared: the
design was incised on the flat surface of the
stone (as with the figure of Mary on one of the
left-hand fragments) and the figures were
then given their relief by the cutting away of
surrounding parts (as partly effected on the
central figure of Christ). Chisel marks are
clearly visible.

Puzzlingly, these fragments appear to be
from two different alabaster panels: the left-
hand pieces are from a Crucifixion scene that
would probably have comprised a simple
grouping of Mary, Christ and John the
Evangelist, whereas the right-hand fragment

479

is of some more crowded scene; the left-hand fragments also have an edging carved differently from that on the right. All the fragments are likely to be of the same date, however, partly because only the earliest type of alabaster panels (carved until about the end of the first quarter of the fifteenth century) have finished edges. Like some other panels of this type, these fragments lack any sockets on their reverse to fix them to, say, a wooden frame: at this period, it was presumably left to the patron to display them as he wished. NLR

PROV. St Peter's Church, Isle of Thanet, believed to have been found under floor during repairs; Joseph Carke, FSA, FRIBA, 1886; given to Society of Antiquaries, 1888.

LIT. *Proc. Soc. Ants.*, 2nd ser., XI, 1885–7, p. 175; London 1910, no. 1, repr. pl. IX; Nelson 1919, p. 93, repr. pl. VIII, fig. 1; Hildburgh 1950, pp. 2–3; York 1954, no. 65.

480 Triple auger

Probably 15th century
Iron: greatest w. 30 cm, l. of arms 16.5 cm, 16.9 cm, 17.5 cm
Museum of London, 77.176

This multiple tool consists of three conjoined augers of different sizes, producing holes of respectively 1 cm, 1.4 cm and 2.1 cm maximum diameter; two would serve as handles when the third was in use. Each arm carries a tapering bit, having a spiral channel with a cutting edge; each has a toothed stop at its upper end, similar to that on the small gimlet/auger from Brooks Wharf (Cat. 483), which would clear any burrs from the edge of the hole and perhaps countersink it slightly.

Bits of this form probably could not be used to drill holes in solid timber, but perhaps served to ream existing pilot holes to specified diameters and tapers. The closest parallels in more recent use would seem to be found among cooper's tap-hole boring and bushing tools (Salaman 1975, pp. 34–5, fig. 35c), and it may well belong with the equipment of that very specialised craft. JAC

PROV. From Thames foreshore at Queenhithe, Upper Thames Street, London, 1976.

481 Hammer head

15th century
Iron: h. 11 cm, w. over claws 3.4 cm, wt 160 g
Museum of London, 81.543/1

The face is octagonal, and shows signs of wear; the claws are slightly curved. The shaft hole is rectangular, 1.6 cm by 1.2 cm; it would take only a lightweight handle. The cheeks bear punched ornament.

Claw hammers, used to draw as well as drive nails, have been found in medieval contexts on a number of sites (Goodall 1981, p. 53, fig. 51 no. 9); examples include one of thirteenth- to fourteenth-century date from Alsted, Surrey (Ketteringham 1976, pp. 56–7, fig. 34 no. 11), and there are others from London Thames-side sites of late medieval date. Although as early as the thirteenth century a hammer of this type is shown in the hands of a farrier (Higgs 1964, fig. 48, from Oxford, Bodleian Library MS Douce 88), a craft with which it has remained associated up to the present day, it was also a carpenter's tool (Harvey 1975, fig. 1; Salzman 1952, p. 344 – though Salzman's assertion that the claw hammer was known to the Romans is ill-founded). Half the weight of a modern farrier's hammer, and about that of the lightest joiner's hammer, this tool with its slender handle was intended for relatively light use, presumably in small-scale woodworking. JAC

PROV. From Thames foreshore at Bankside, London, 1981.

482 Pointing tool

14th century
Iron: l. 18 cm, w. of blade 1.6 cm
Museum of London, 84.207

The blade is parallel-sided, but tapering slightly at the end to a squared tip. The offset handle is twisted and ends in a loop, a form found on other simple medieval tools, such as a cleaver dating from before 1250 from King's Lynn (Clarke & Carter 1977, p. 294, fig. 52 no. 4). Medieval mason's trowels were very similar in form to those of today (Goodall 1981, p. 53. fig. 52, no. 4; Harvey 1975, fig. 19; Treue *et al.* 1965, pl. 46), and this tool would seem to have been designed for finer work, such as pointing. JAC

PROV. From Billingsgate, London, 1984.

483 Twist auger or gimlet

15th century
Iron, with wooden handle: l. 13.2 cm, handle w. 8.2 cm, d. 3.3 cm
Museum of London, 85.494/2

The handle is turned to a barrel shape, with groups of three turned grooves at each end and in the middle; a slot houses the tang of the bit. The tang is lanceolate and projects through the handle, originally being capped with a square washer. The upper part of the shaft is octagonal in section, decorated with chiselled lines and with a punched maker's mark, and bears a faceted square collar. Below, a round collar carries four teeth on its

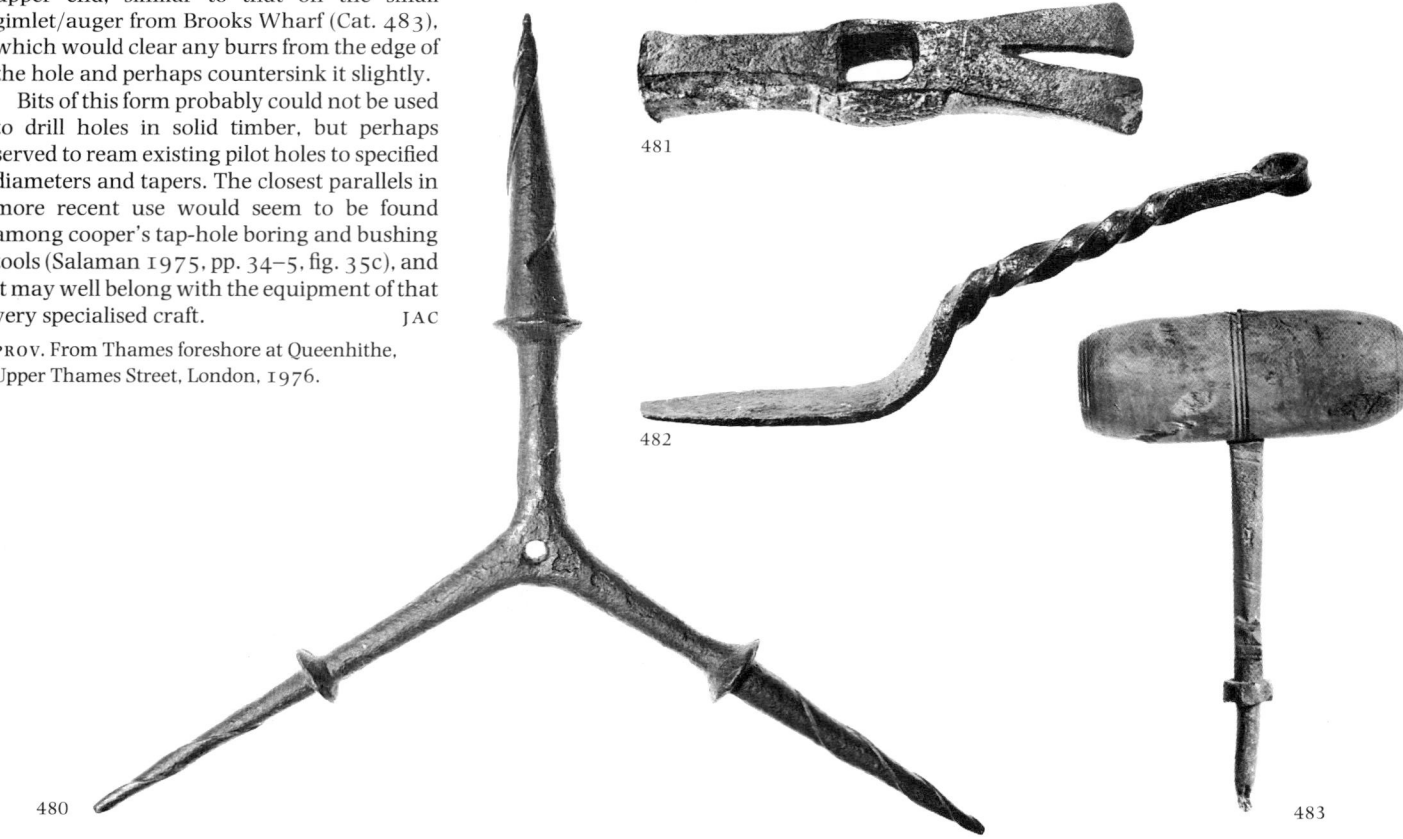

481

482

480

483

underside. The lower end of the shaft is circular in section, and is broken at the tip, though sufficient remains to show that the point was spirally grooved as on a modern gimlet. Little of the tip would appear to be lost, since in other surviving examples such grooving extends only a short way up the shaft.

The majority of medieval auger and drill bits known are of spoon or gouge form, similar to those of Roman and Anglo-Saxon date (Goodall 1981, p. 53, fig. 51 nos 10, 11). However, twist bits such as this are recorded from a number of medieval sites, as in late thirteenth- and fourteenth-century contexts at Custom House, London (Tatton-Brown 1974, p. 191, fig. 38 no. 57) and in Oxford (Durham 1977, p. 142, fig. 26 no. 21). A thirteenth-century example from Dublin retains its turned wooden handle, similar to that of the example exhibited here (Ó Ríordáin 1971, pp. 76–7, pl. X, B); another similar handle, separated from its tool, comes from a late thirteenth-century context at Southampton (Platt & Coleman-Smith 1975, II p. 231, fig. 229 no. 1635). The toothed collar or stop has been noticed on a number of late medieval augers from London and elsewhere; it would serve to countersink the hole slightly, presumably to take a nail head. JAC

PROV. From Thames at Brooks Wharf, Upper Thames Street, London, 1985.

484 Leatherworker's awl

English(?), 15th century(?)
Iron and wood, with copper-alloy capping; l. 10 cm, max. w. 1 cm
Museum of London, 86.108/6

This is probably a stabbing awl, the sharp-pointed implement that a leatherworker would hold in his hand to pierce leather so that he could stitch it. The craftsman's techniques in leatherworking can hardly have changed since the medieval period, given the unchanging nature of some of his tools, and what J.W. Waterer wrote of the technique of hand stitching in the twentieth century is doubtless true of the later Middle Ages: 'Most flat stitching ... is done "double-handed", the work being held down in a "clam" or "clamp" ... The made-up thread, with a needle at each end (or in olden times and still for fine work, a hog's bristle worked in wax) is pulled through to half its length. An awl held in one hand makes a hole, the needle held in the other hand follows the awl as it is withdrawn and the other needle, held in the awl hand, then enters from the opposite side. The stitches are drawn tight and the operation repeated' (Waterer 1968, p. 50).

Of iron, with wooden scales held to its tang by two copper alloy rivets and with a copper-alloy capping, this awl is a survivor from a very large range of such implements (see

484

485

486

Salaman 1986, e.g. pp. 84–7). It probably dates from the fifteenth century, having been found with material of that date; other awls in a less good state of preservation have been found in Essex and Scotland (Williams 1977, p. 176, repr. fig. 38, p. 175 no. 14; Good & Tabraham 1981, p. 112 no.11), repr. fig. 12, p. 114. I owe these references to John Clark. NLR

PROV. Found on River Thames foreshore, near the Anchor Tavern, Bankside, 1986; bt by Museum of London, 1986.

LIT. Waterer 1968; Salaman 1986.

485 Chisel

15th century
Iron: l. 18.2 cm, w. of blade 3.2 cm
Museum of London, 86.108/7

The shaft is octagonal, burred at the top by heavy use. The shouldered form of the blade is similar to that found on modern mason's chisels and pitching tools, and it is probably to that craft that this tool belongs. JAC

PROV. From Thames at Bankside, London, 1986.

486 Timber scribe

15th century
Iron, with wooden handle: l. 17.5 cm, w. 4.8 cm
Museum of London, 86.165/3

This tool carries a spike and an adjacent gouge-like cutter which could be used for marking timber with circles. An arm with a similar hooked cutting end folds into a recess in the handle; it is decorated with an incised lattice pattern. The wooden handle is oval in cross-section and ends in an iron cap.

Scribes or race knives of this type were used for marking the timbers of a framed building or similar structure before erection. Very similar tools have been in use into modern times, but the closest in form to this example, with its drag knife folding into the handle, is one illustrated by Salaman (1975, pp. 404–5, fig. 708c) which carries the prominent date 1774. JAC

PROV. From Thames foreshore at north end of Southwark Bridge, London, 1986.

XIII Edward II (1307–27)

Edward II was born at Caernarfon on 25 April 1284 and was made Prince of Wales in 1301 by his father who was eager to give him both military and political experience. On his accession in 1307 he inherited a difficult legacy: not only financial debts and a war in Scotland, but also continuing baronial distrust. A significant new clause was added to his coronation oath: he agreed to observe 'the just laws and customs which the community of the realm shall have chosen'. The clear intention was that the new king should not revoke agreements with the magnates, especially concerning taxation, as his father had done. One of Edward's first acts, however, was to recall from banishment his favourite, the foreign knight from Gascony, Piers Gavaston. In January 1308 when Edward went to Boulogne to marry the twelve-year-old Isabella of France, Gavaston, now made Earl of Cornwall, was left behind as Regent and at the coronation a month later he carried the crown and sword of St Edward before the king, parading himself in finer robes than was conventional. The queen's relations returned to France believing that the king was more devoted to Gavaston than to her.

Gavaston's position and influence aroused baronial indignation. He was banished once again but the king quickly recalled him. This led to the establishment by the opposition to the king of a group of twenty-one 'Ordainers', magnates and bishops. Their ordinances of 1311 aimed to control the king and included a detailed attack on Gavaston. When the king refused to accept his renewed banishment, there was a rebellion led by the king's cousin, Thomas, Earl of Lancaster. In 1312 Gavaston was murdered in Thomas's presence, an act the king was too weak to avenge.

Meanwhile, Robert Bruce in Scotland took advantage of the internal discord to rally his forces. The king, enjoying a brief period of accord with the magnates, led a great army to relieve the besieged Sterling. Military success might well have changed the king's fortunes, but his badly organised troops suffered a humiliating defeat at Bannockburn in June 1314.

There followed a disturbed period during which England was on the brink of civil war. Fortunately for the king his leading opponent, the wealthy Thomas of Lancaster, was not an astute political leader. Even so, regardless of the influence of some moderate men, including the Earl of Pembroke, dissension increased. Additional factors weakened the position of the king: harvests were ruined by heavy rain in 1314 and severe famine followed in 1315 and 1316, with high food prices and increased local disorder; and in the north it proved impossible to organise effective defence against Scottish raids. Once again the king built up a court circle of favourites, especially Hugh Despenser, the father, and Hugh Despenser, the son. Open conflict with the Earl of Lancaster came in 1321, and with it Edward's chance of vengeance for the murder of Gavaston. Lancaster was executed at Pontefract in March 1322, six days after his defeat in battle at Boroughbridge. It is an indication of Edward's weak hold upon power that the political advantages of this success were very short-lived.

In the last years of his reign the greed and monopoly of political influence of the Despensers increased the unpopularity of the king. External relations also deteriorated. A truce with the Scots in 1323 brought some respite, but Robert Bruce's achievements remained unchecked, leading to the affirmation of the Franco-Scottish alliance and to the renunciation, in 1328, of the king of England's claim to feudal overlordship. By way of contrast, the king of France was making good his claim to overlordship in Gascony, where England's control was challenged again in 1324. Despite negotiations and threats of war, Edward was unable to oppose the increased display of French authority. By 1325 opposition to the king was taking clearer shape. Queen Isabella had crossed to France with Edward of Windsor, her eldest son, and she refused to return until the king's favourites were removed. She became the mistress of Roger Mortimer, who, having escaped from imprisonment in the Tower of London, had fled to France. Isabella, Mortimer and the young Edward landed in Suffolk in

September 1326 with troops from Hainhault. They marched westwards in pursuit of the king and allies; as a result, both Despensers were seized and executed and the king was held captive at Kenilworth. Since there were no precedents to follow, attempts were then made to ensure that at least there was some demonstration of general assent to the deposition of the king. A parliament in London provided the occasion for the political manoeuvrings. Walter Reynolds, Archbishop of Canterbury, announced the deposition in a sermon in Westminster Hall, and then a deputation was sent to Edward which secured his abdication on 20 January 1327. Conditions, however, remained unstable, and Edward was cruelly murdered at Mortimer's command in September. In death he achieved veneration, for his magnificent tomb in the abbey at Gloucester, erected by his son, became a place of pilgrimage (Cat. 497). The feuding of the nobility did not end until Edward III assumed personal rule in 1330.

Edward II's incompetence as king had brought humiliation to the English monarchy, though not, it must be stressed, to the concept of kingship itself. Executions had followed executions. But Queen Isabella, the 'she-wolf' of France, had survived. In retirement from public life she became fond of hearing or reading romances and of collecting relics; having taken the habit of the Franciscan nuns, the Poor Clares, she died in 1358 and was buried in the Franciscan Church at Newgate, London.

Whatever the political upheavals, the years between 1300 and 1350 witnessed the most brilliantly inventive period in the history of English medieval architecture. Inspired by the ornamental richness of Edward I's enterprises, especially his chapel of St Stephen in the Palace of Westminster (Cat. 324–5), masons and carpenters felt free to experiment with polygonal arrangements of interior space, and to devise an exotic repertory of ornamental effects. Distinct art forms were fused by colour, decoration and the repetition of the same motifs in varying scales and media. The spectacular octagon at Ely (Cat. 492) and the picturesque polygonal planning of the chapter house at Wells (Cat. 328) are accompanied by seaweed-like foliage (Cat. 513–16), curvilinear tracery (Cat. 495), bulbous ogee arches (Cat. 491) and vaults of almost Islamic elaboration (Cat. 496). The same richness of decoration with many of the same forms, for instance the seaweed foliage, is seen in carvings in wood, such as the Lancaster Stalls (Cat. 524) or the Warwick Gittern (Cat. 521), and in stone, such as the tomb of St William of York (Cat. 513–16). The niches of the Ely Lady Chapel (Cat. 491), now all empty but once filled with polychrome figures, indicate the sheer volume of figure sculpture which must once have existed in the churches. The small number of stone statues which are gathered in this section give an indication of the skill of the carvers. But they also, in their sadly mutilated state and mostly lacking their original polychromy, indicate how thorough was the work of the Puritan iconoclasts.

The reaction against the excesses of the Decorated style began in the 1330s, with Edward III's remodelling of the Romanesque abbey church at Gloucester as a shrine for his father's tomb (Cat. 497–8). Its old walls were disguised behind flat upright panels of tracery, reminiscent of the tracery grids on the exterior of St Stephen's Chapel, and also resembling the cages of tracery that characterise French 'Rayonnant' architecture. In the cloister of Gloucester similar tracery panels were spread over the vault surfaces to create the first surviving example of a fan vault (Cat. 499). Associated from its beginnings Edward III, with the most successful English king of the later Middle Ages, Gloucester's austere and rigid style, the Perpendicular style, was to dominate English architecture right up to the Reformation.

487 Bristol Cathedral, Lady Chapel, looking north-east

Begun 1298
Photograph

The choir of St Augustine's Abbey, Bristol (a cathedral from 1542) is the most important English example of a hall church, a type not otherwise used at major churches except for subordinate chapels such as the axial chapel at Salisbury (Cat. 18). The Lady Chapel occupies the normal position, at the extreme east end, and matches in height and width the central vessel of the aisled part of the choir. The tall, transomed form of the side windows is only one among several features designed to emphasise the kinship between the choir and the traditional type of aisled great hall (Cat. 261). Such indebtedness to secular architecture is exceptional in a major church, and was only possible in late thirteenth- and early fourteenth-century England, when imaginative freedom in architecture was greater than in any other medieval milieu.

The hall church scheme provides a self-effacing backdrop for a series of ornamental set pieces which are spectacular even by the standards of Decorated architecture. Their originality stems partly from the extremely advanced character of their detail – the lierne ribs in the vault and the ogee-reticulated tracery in the east window are among the earliest examples anywhere – but also partly from the extraordinarily wide repertory of forms which major practitioners of Dec-

487

on each side and a wooden vault, above which are canopied and finialled tripods on the east, west and north sides. Set into the cluster of tripods is the second two-part stage, an open tower carried on four massive buttresses between which are panels of reticulated tracery enclosing the space between the tripods. From the level of the crown of the tripod vaults, smaller buttresses project to form a canopied statue housing. The third stage springs from the top of the upper tower gable and consists of a four-sided crocketed and finialled spire held together by cusped intersected tracery.

In 1982 a detailed investigation of the monument was made by the Exeter Archaeological Unit. Samples were taken for tree-ring dating from which the recorded date of manufacture was confirmed. The most interesting discovery is that the present tower section represents a 'second thought' on the part of the designer. The presence of carving

on the back of the inside tripod legs, rendered invisible from the ground by the crenellated panelling behind the main gables, indicates that the tripods were intended to be fully visible. Moreover, the rails which run from corner to corner within the central tower cut through the back legs of the tripods. Redundant mortises on these crosspieces, outside the existing tower, show that a larger second tier, possibly consisting of two massive intersecting gables, must have been intended in the first place.   CT

LIT. Tracy 1984, pp. 124–9.

489   Salisbury Cathedral, view from north-east

1220–c. 1260; tower and spire 1330s(?)
Photograph

The exterior of Salisbury has a consistency of design seldom found among English cathedrals. The clarity of the plan (fig. 50) is reflected in the clear articulation of each part of the building, from the low projecting eastern chapel (Cat. 18) to the high gable over the presbytery and the two sets of transepts. The uniformity of appearance is reinforced by the orderly fenestration with simple lancets grouped in pairs of triplets. The magnificent tower and spire rise to a height of 123 m to form one of the most familiar landmarks in England, and although brilliantly designed to appear a natural extension to the building, they were a later addition and such a grand feature was almost certainly not part of the original design. Despite the construction of extra internal buttressing, the enormous additional weight has caused the great crossing piers to bend alarmingly. The present tower is usually dated in the 1330s on the basis of the presumed association of the work with the appointment of Richard of Farleigh as master mason in 1334 and the stylistic comparison with other buildings in the west of England, particularly the towers of Hereford Cathedral and Pershore Abbey. The architectural details, however, could be taken to indicate a date nearer to 1300: most notably, the absence of the fashionable ogee arches would be surprising after about 1320. Contrasting with the elaborate decoration of the tower, the spire is plain but for the three bands of quatrefoils and the pinnacles around its base which effectively mask the transition from the square tower to the octagonal spire. The main bells were hung in a substantial, detached bell tower, constructed at the same time as the cathedral just north of the nave, but demolished in 1790.
                      PD

LIT. RCHM, *Salisbury* (forthcoming); Pevsner & Metcalf 1985a.

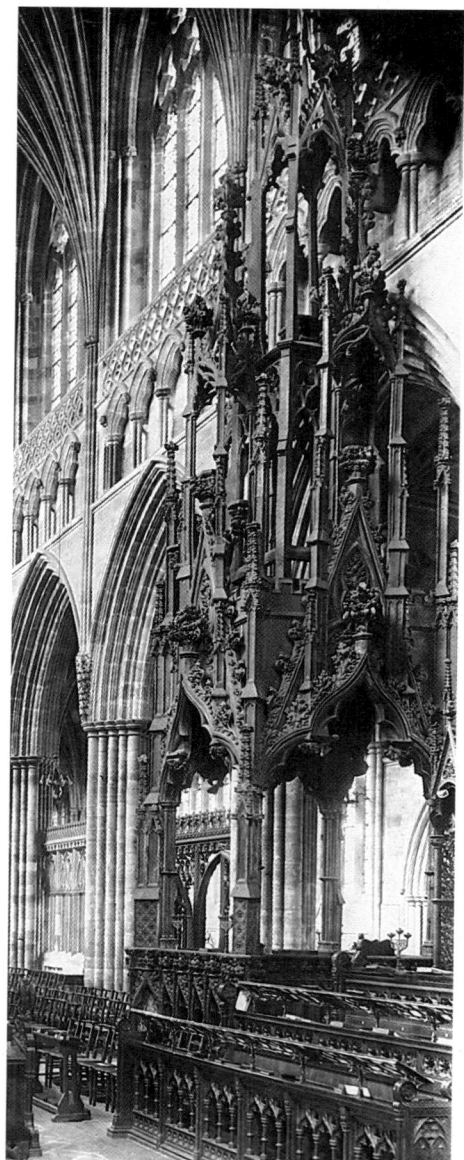

488

orated had at their disposal. This abundance can be illustrated by the forms of arch used: ogee in the recesses on the east wall, four-centred in the middle part of the east window, inverted on the sedilia (on the right), concave over the openings of the wall passage in the window jambs, half-octagonal in the tomb recesses. The inclusion of a series of recesses along the sides of the choir to house pre-existing effigies and provide for future needs is an extreme instance of an architect's exerting control over the use of 'his' building, but it is characteristic of the Decorated emphasis on architecturally sophisticated fittings (cf. Cat. 493). The comparatively unsophisticated treatment of the east wall below the window is due to the insertion in 1840 of the three central recesses in place of the defaced remains of a reredos incorporating image niches. The original recesses at each end include sculptural elements typical of c. 1300: diaper, ballflower and heraldic shields (the arms of England and of the abbey's patrons, Fitzhardinge and Berkeley). The polychromy dates from the 1930s and is by E. W. Tristram.   CW

LIT. Pevsner 1958, pp. 371–9; Cobb 1980, pp. 40, 42.

488   Exeter Bishop's throne

1313–17
Photograph

The structure is made up of three tiers. The base section is an arcaded plinth, originally probably resting on a stone base, with large buttresses at each corner supporting a gable

489

490

490 St Mary Redcliffe, Bristol, outer north porch, north side

c. 1320
Photograph

Redcliffe's mercantile wealth and its pride in having once been a separate entity from Bristol are the main reasons for the uniquely cathedral-like architecture of its parish church. The anomaly of the double north porch is attributable to the fact that at an unknown date before *c.* 1200 the inner porch of *c.* 1200 became the receptacle for a popular cult image of the Virgin. The outer porch was needed as a vestibule both to the cult area and to the church as a whole.

There appear to be no earlier examples of hexagonally planned porches, so it is probably reasonable to explain the choice in terms of the Decorated emphasis on the curious and the unexpected. The inspiration was presumably some earlier Gothic hexagonal structure such as the canopy over the shrine of St-Sernin at Toulouse (1258, destroyed) or the Eleanor Cross at Waltham (Cat. 373). No doubt the simple hexagonal porches at Chipping Norton, Oxfordshire, and Ludlow, Shropshire, derive from the Redcliffe porch. The only other work of full-scale architecture of the period which is to the same extent a support for image niches is the interior of the Lady Chapel at Ely (Cat. 491), where the canopies are also three-dimensional ogees backed by gablets. The arrangement of the niches as a band which spreads on to the buttresses is very reminiscent of the gatehouse of St Augustine's, Canterbury (Cat. 327), as is the studied contrast between the encrusted, crystalline aspect of the portal and the sinuous curves of the niche canopies. Despite its exotic appearance, the sources of the portal are strictly local. The reversed curves come from the tomb recesses in the choir of Bristol Cathedral (Cat. 487), probably an earlier work of the same designer, and the motif of undercut foliage running continuously from arch to jambs seems to be a clear debt to the 150-year-old portals of the Lady Chapel at Glastonbury Abbey. The exterior was completely but very accurately renewed from 1848. For sculpture removed from the porch see Cat. 502–5. CW

LIT. Dallaway 1834, pp. 105, 158–9. Pevsner 1958, pp. 397–8.

491 Ely Cathedral, Lady Chapel looking south-east

1321–49
Photograph

The Lady Chapel of Ely Cathedral exemplifies many of the characteristics of the Decorated style. Most noticeable, perhaps, is the structural ambiguity of a design which masks all the wall surfaces and even the window splays under an incrustation of statue niches. The

491

sculptural embellishment of the architecture was devastated at the Reformation. Only fragments of the one hundred and fifty large-scale figures survive, and the huge relief cycle showing the Life of the Virgin Mary is severely mutilated. Originally, they helped to disrupt the planar frontality of the architecture. The recessing of the windows, the employment of the nodding ogee arch, the texturing of the masonry, and the use of Purbeck marble for the shafts between the rhythmically-varied stall designs also have this effect. The huge windows (the west and east ones are sometimes wrongly thought to be later additions), relate the Lady Chapel to a number of other key buildings of the Decorated style, such as Bristol Cathedral (Cat. 487) and St Stephen's Chapel, Westminster (Cat. 324–5).

The lierne vault of the Lady Chapel is not a fifteenth-century addition as has been recently claimed, and is preceded at Ely by that of the choir, completed by 1337. It appears to have been painted in imitation of the latest net vaults. The simple rectangular ground plan of the Lady Chapel relates it to buildings such as the Wykeham Chapel at Spalding, complete by 1311. However, its shape, as well as its location and the absence of a crypt, should also be related to earlier East Anglian models. The Lady chapels of Peterborough Cathedral, Bury St Edmunds Abbey and Thetford Priory, for instance, were all aisle-less and cryptless rectangular buildings on the north side of the church's presbytery. Ely's Lady Chapel is exceptional, though, in its size and magnificence. It was entered by a vaulted, tiled passage from the choir and not through the present entrance, crudely cut

through the stalls in the late seventeenth century, an enduring legacy of its function as a parish church from 1566 to 1939. The chapel seems to have been intended from the outset to accommodate lay and particularly female worshippers, whose crowding round the old Lady altar in the early fourteenth century may have precipitated the decision to build a new chapel. So its post-Reformation function was peculiarly appropriate.   PL

LIT. Wharton 1691, pp. 651–2; Bentham 1771, pp. 159–60, 286; Stevenson 1817, pp. 61–7; Millers 1807, pp. 95–100; Stewart 1868, pp. 136–45; Atkinson 1953, pp. 60–2; Coldstream 1979, pp. 28–46; Bony 1979, *passim*; Woodman 1984, pp. 137–44; Coldstream 1985, pp. 1–16; Lindley 1985, pp. 100–28; Lindley 1986a, pp. 126–8.

492   Ely Cathedral, octagon interior

1322–53
Photograph

The octagon is one of the most spectacular buildings of the Decorated style. However, the open space in the heart of the building, permitting an uninterrupted vista across the cathedral, is a product not of the Middle Ages, but of the eighteenth and nineteenth centuries. Originally, the liturgical choir and stalls were placed under the octagon, which functioned as the bell tower over the crossing. These arrangements were swept away in the late eighteenth century, when the stalls were removed to the eastern part of the cathedral; the major casualties of the move, apart from the stalls and monuments, were

the pulpitum and the lateral screen walls. The loss of the latter was particularly unfortunate because the northern wall displayed a series of paintings of Anglo-Saxon benefactors to the convent, painted by an artist responsible for some of the paintings in St Stephen's Chapel, Westminster. When the eighteenth-century arrangements were destroyed in their turn, the choir stalls were not reinstated under the octagon, but were placed in their present location (cf. p. 89, figs 57–8, Cat. 391, 409).

Technically, the octagon is extraordinary. The search for precedents in kitchen, tower or chapter house design emphasises the unique and surprising nature of the building. The masonry work was begun in 1322, immediately after the collapse of the Anglo-Norman crossing tower, and was completed by 1328. Work on the timber lantern started immediately, and the building was structurally complete by 1339–40, when John of Burwell was paid 2s for carving the lantern's central boss. The lantern was given a lead covering in 1352–3. The carpenter responsible for the lantern was William Hurley, the king's master carpenter. His work consists of a regular timber octagon framed into the angles of the irregular octagonal masonry base, which absorbed a bay each of the nave, choir and transepts. The timber vaulting was originally painted to imitate stone vaults. It does not have an important structural function but serves to hide the massive timbers which actually bear the load. The extremely complicated design of the building indicates that it was carefully laid out before work began, in consultation with the patron, the monastic sacrist, Alan of Walsingham. The decision to build an octagonal crossing tower,

492

493

like the devising of the original iconographic programme, which was articulated in a variety of different media, may ultimately be attributable to Alan, who was a trained goldsmith.   PL

LIT. Wharton 1691, I, pp. 643–6; Bentham 1771, pp. 221–2, 283; Millers 1807, pp. 62–8; Stevenson 1817, pp. 61–8; Stewart 1868, pp. 82–128; Rowe 1876, pp. 70–83; Atkinson 1953, pp. 62–4; Coldstream 1979, pp. 28–46; Bony 1979, pp. 40–2, 55–6; Heyman & Wade 1985, pp. 1421–36; Lindley 1986a, pp. 120–3; Lindley 1986b, pp. 75–99.

493   Church of All Saints, Hawton, chancel interior, north side

c. 1335–40
Photograph

The chancel of All Saints, Hawton, Nottinghamshire, is the best preserved example of a small group in the East Midlands with exceptionally elaborate liturgical arrangements. The most distinctive and important of its furnishings is the Easter Sepulchre, or, more probably, sacrament shrine (shown on the right in the photograph). To the left of it there is also a founder's tomb and the entrance to a sacristy. Normally the Easter Sepulchre was a temporary wood or cloth furnishing set up to the north of the high altar, and used in the Easter services to represent Christ's tomb. On Good Friday a Host or cross was buried inside

it, and this was symbolically resurrected on Easter Sunday during a specially embellished ceremony. These sepulchres were removed at the end of Easter week. The Hawton monument rather follows the Continental tradition of permanent tombs of Christ as reliquaries and places of pilgrimage, providing symbolic solace for the tombs of mortals in proximity to them. With the establishment between 1264 and 1317 of Corpus Christi as a principal festival of the Church year, a new type of fully-fledged sacrament shrine was evolved in the Low Countries and Germany, in which the Host was permanently reserved in order that Christ's Body should be ever present. It is likely that the monument at Hawton is of this type and was inspired by the growing popularity of Corpus Christi in eastern England in the early fourteenth century. The sacrament shrine at Hawton is a variation of the design of that at Heckington, Lincolnshire. Other examples are at Arnold Nottinghamshire; Patrington, Humberside; and in Lincolnshire: Navenby, and Sibthorpe.   VS

LIT. Heales 1869; Mansell-Sympson 1895–6; Woolley 1924; Stone 1972, pp. 168–9; Sekules 1983, pp. 163–4; Sekules 1986.

494   The Percy tomb, viewed from the north

c. 1340
Photograph

The Percy tomb, situated on the north side of

the presbytery of Beverley Minster and abutting the screen staircase to the east, is the most lavishly decorated of a group of monuments whose basic design was derived from the tomb of Edmund Crouchback, Earl of Lancaster (d. 1296), in Westminster Abbey (Cat. 326). The canopy, a vaulted structure incorporating cusped nodding ogee arches surmounted by steeply pitched gables, is enriched with a wide variety of architectural ornament and an extensive programme of figure sculpture, creating a synthesis of decorative and figurative elements which may be seen as a development of the style seen at Ely (Cat. 491), Hawton (Cat. 493) and York (Cat. 513–16). Among the atelier responsible for the carving was a sculptor who may be accredited with an important series of statues at York and who may also have been responsible for carving the tomb of Aymer de Valence in Westminster Abbey (Dawton [forthcoming]). The existence of parallel traditions in other media is attested by the Salting Diptych (Cat. 520), which represents a slightly earlier stage in the development of the style, and a group of manuscripts, notably a set of illustrations to the Book of Genesis (London, British Museum, Egerton MS 1894), executed by an artist whose style reflects the influence of Italian Trecento painting (Pächt 1943).   ND

LIT. Pächt 1943, pp. 57–70, pl. 16a; Stone 1955, pp. 171–2, repr. pls 132(A), 133; Goldberg 1984, repr. pl. 1 p. 66; Dawton (forthcoming) (with bibliog.).

494

495 York Minster, west window of nave

*c.*1335
Photograph

The so-called 'heart of Yorkshire', named after the central motif of the tracery pattern, is one of the great designs of flowing tracery. It was used in English church windows in the first half of the fourteenth century, especially in East Anglia and Yorkshire.

Flowing tracery is based on the ogee or reversed curve, which was introduced on the Eleanor crosses and the tomb of Edmund Crouchback in Westminster Abbey in the 1290s (Cat. 326, 369). It allows the shapes to lead sinuously from one to the other, squeezing circles into ovals and dagger shapes. The York window has eight lights, the central mullion leading up through the tracery head, with the heart shape formed round it. The details of the pattern are based on the leaf-stem design also found at Lincoln Cathedral, Beverley Minster and Patrington.

The York window was glazed in 1338/9, at the expense of Archbishop Melton, and it is assumed that he also paid for the tracery. The design has been attributed to Ivo de Raghton, who may have been responsible for the typologically earlier east window of Carlisle Cathedral. Patrington and Beverley followed York, but the fully developed leaf-stem may have appeared first in the south transept of Lincoln, *c.*1330.   NC

LIT. Etherton 1965, p. 180, repr. pl. 8; French 1975; Aylmer & Cant 1977, p. 157; Coldstream 1980, pp. 94–6, repr. pl. III; Harvey 1984, pp. 238–9.

495

496

496 Tewkesbury Abbey, choir looking east

Remodelled *c.*1331–40
Photograph

The Tewkesbury choir embodies a frontal approach to the problem of modernising Romanesque fabrics, and in this respect makes an interesting foil to the choir of its neighbour, Gloucester Cathedral (Cat. 498). The drum piers of the eleventh-century choir were cut down and worked into a two-storey elevation whose plainness is offset by the high vault, an ambitious yet naïve design. There is no acknowledgment of the fact that a rib pattern which is pleasing when drawn out in plan, as this is, does not necessarily look well when stretched and bent round the curving webs of a vault. For instance, the diagonal ribs that extend across two bays instead of one stand out immediately in plan, whereas in most views they appear not as entities but as parts of a dense and almost chaotic mesh of lines. At Gloucester a similarly complex mesh is made 'readable' by its application to a vault of simpler three-dimensional shape. The inclusion of tracery elements follows recent south-western precedent, as does the use of similar patterns at the vault crowns and in the tracery of the east window. The tracery on the springings is one of comparatively many early fourteenth-century anticipations of fan vaulting (Cat. 499, 600).   CW

LIT. Bock 1962, pp. 61–4; Morris 1974.

497 Gloucester Cathedral, tomb of King Edward II, north side

1327–31
Photograph

Edward II was murdered on 21 September 1327 at Berkeley Castle and buried at Gloucester three months later. St Peter's Abbey (whose church is now the cathedral)

was selected because it was the most important monastic house near Berkeley and because the hostility of the Londoners to the régime of Mortimer and Isabella made a Westminster funeral too dangerous. There is no truth in the story fabricated by the Gloucester monks that the king's body was refused burial by several neighbouring abbeys fearful of reprisals from Mortimer's faction.

Edward II's monument belongs to a genre more highly developed in England than elsewhere in the late Middle Ages, the architecturally ambitious tomb. However, compared to tomb canopies of the previous generation, for example that of Crouchback at Westminster (Cat. 326), it is singleminded in its emphasis on tabernacles of complex plan. This eschewal of Decorated luxuriance foreshadows the remodelling of the south transept at Gloucester, begun *c.*1331 (fig. 49), and there can be little doubt that both are the work of one architect. As in the transept, the detailing indicates a close knowledge of London and Canterbury work consonant with an attribution to Thomas of Canterbury, architect of St Stephen's Chapel from 1320 to 1336 (Cat. 324–5). Evidence for the international reputation which south-eastern English designers enjoyed for tomb architecture is the still larger monument of Pope John XXII (d. 1334) in Avignon Cathedral, whose every detail can be paralleled at Canterbury or in St Stephen's.

The niches in the tomb chest are decorative versions of the prayer niches of shrines such as St Werburgh's (Cat. 20). The only traces of the short-lived cult of Edward II are crosses cut by 'pilgrims' into the surrounding stonework and the bracket inserted into the side of the tomb chest to carry a golden ship which Edward III presented after his deliverance from a dangerous sea crossing. The tomb must have been made at Gloucester, for the main material is local Cotswold oolite. The effigy, the earliest important English

497

example made from alabaster, was doubtless intended to emulate the late thirteenth- and early fourteenth-century French royal effigies in white marble. CW

LIT. Richardson 1951; Stone, 1955, pp. 158, 160–2, 172, 181, pl. 119; Wilson 1980a, pp. 113–21.

498 Gloucester Cathedral, choir looking east

Begun c. 1351, completed by 1367
Photograph

The remodelling of the eastern parts of the Romanesque church of St Peter's Abbey, Gloucester (made a cathedral in 1541) was partly financed by the offerings of 'pilgrims' visiting the tomb of the murdered Edward II (Cat. 497). The work was done in three distinct phases: the south transept (c. 1331–6), the choir, begun with the liturgical choir in the crossing under Abbot Staunton (1337–51) and continued into the presbytery under Abbot Horton (1351–77); the north transept (1368–73). The remodelling was essentially a refacing of the interior surfaces of the Romanesque main vessels which left the aisles, galleries and crypt virtually untouched. The main vessel of the presbytery was lengthened by demolishing the Romanesque apse and the central section of the ambulatory. The exigencies of building on top of the outer wall of the crypt-level ambulatory explain the main peculiarity of the easternmost bay: the way that its side walls swing outwards before joining the east wall. The consequences of this improvisation are breathtaking: an immense window-wall, the largest in medieval Europe, which appears from most viewpoints as if floating unattached to the side walls.

The elevations of the choir are a development from those of the south transept (fig. 49), where tiers of upright arch-enclosing rectangles have not yet become the leitmotiv of the design. It is much clearer there than in

498

the choir that this 'panel' motif develops from the version of the French Rayonnant triforium used to mask the remodelled openings of the gallery (see p. 82). The moulding which frames these openings is only the most important of several correspondences which prove that the immediate source of the idea of the masking was the exterior of St Stephen's Chapel in Westminster Palace. The screening of the south choir aisle from the transept has already taken on the panelled aspect adumbrated in the framework of the timber screens traditionally used in such a position, but only in the choir are its closely spaced horizontals extended to the whole height of the elevation. The result of this change is to give the choir much greater rhythmic and textural consistency. But the increase in the number of horizontals is offset by making them slighter in gauge than the mullions. Verticality is further stressed by eliminating all horizontals from the immediate vicinity of the vault responds and by extending the clearstorey far above the level of the Romanesque wall head still adhered to in the south transept.

The choir was influenced to a limited extent by local Decorated architecture. The basic form of its vault – a tunnel with penetrations – appears earlier in the choir aisles of Bristol Cathedral and the main vessels of the choirs of Wells Cathedral and Ottery St Mary; and the dense mesh of surface ribs includes elements found at Exeter and Tewkesbury (Cat. 496). Although the Gloucester choir vault could hardly be less like the fan vaults under construction in the nearby cloister during the same years (Cat. 499), both designs reject many of the basic premises of thirteenth-century vault design, in particular the use of prominent and steeply-curved diagonal ribs which reduce the general visibility of windows (Cat. 241). The other important feature drawn from local Decorated architecture is the tripartite arrangement of the east window (cf. Cat. 487, fig. 61). CW

LIT. Wilson 1980a, pp. 113–17, 127–39, 164–70.

499 Gloucester Cathedral, east walk of cloister looking north-east

c. 1351–64
Photograph

It can hardly be an accident that the Gloucester cloister contains the earliest known fan vaulting, a type of vaulting which is essentially a development of the concept of repetitive and infinitely extensible 'panels' invented in the slightly earlier elevations of the south transept and choir at Gloucester (Cat. 498). The walls and windows of the cloister are as consistently panelled as in the choir. The actual tracery pattern applied to the vaults appears to derive from the self-generating 'petals' of mid-thirteenth-century French rose windows like those imitated at

499

Westminster Abbey (Cat. 262). The three-dimensional shapes behind the tracery, like halved trumpet bells, grow out of a long and specifically English Gothic tradition of co-noidal rib clusters of which the most spectacular examples are those over the central columns of polygonal chapter houses (e.g. Cat. 328).

Designing and building fan vaults over square bays, as at Gloucester, was comparatively straightforward, but it was far more difficult to adapt them to the rectangular bays normally used in churches. The earliest surviving fan vault over rectangular bays is the timber example at Winchester College Chapel (Cat. 600). The Gloucester vaults are constructed entirely of jointed ashlar blocks each of which includes part of the tracery and part of the plain surfaces between. Many later vaults which are visually similar to Gloucester revert to traditional rib and infill construction. CW

LIT. Leedy 1980, pp. 7–9, 166–8; Wilson 1980a, pp. 260–77; Wilson 1981, pp. 138–9.

500 Water basin

c. 1280
Doulting stone: h. 58.5 cm, w. 88 cm, d. 53 cm
The Dean and Chapter of Wells

This stone basin was originally set into the south wall of the undercroft of the chapter house at Wells Cathedral, behind the entrance door. It has been suggested that because the undercroft formerly served as the treasury, this basin was used for rinsing ceremonial vessels before they were used

500

during Mass. The entrance to the drain shaft of the half-octagonal bowl is guarded by a carved figure of a dog chewing a bone. Similar amusing decorative devices are often found in semi-hidden places in churches. At Christchurch, Hampshire is another dog gnawing a bone, carved on a misericord. Animal figures are found inside the bowls of drinking vessels from the eleventh century onwards (e.g. London 1984a, nos 304, 306), but this seems to be a unique example of such a device in a stone basin in an ecclesiastical context.   VS

PROV. Wells Cathedral.

LIT. Colchester & Harvey 1974; Draper 1981, pp. 18–19; Clark 1956–7, pp. 114–15; Anderson 1938, pp. 34, 81.

501   Statue of an Apostle

Attrib. Guillaume de Nourriche, 1319–24
Limestone, both hands lost: h. 171 cm, w. 51 cm
Paris, Musée National des Thermes et de l'Hôtel de
    Cluny, Cl. 18759

This image comes from the chapel of the Confrérie de St-Jacques-l'Hôpital in Paris, where it was probably arranged in a modernised version of the layout in the Ste-Chapelle. It differs sharply from the other surviving statues (also in the Cluny Museum), for which there is good documentary evidence that they were carved by Robert Lannoy between 1319 and 1327, and it has been convincingly argued that this statue is one of the two executed by Guillaume de Nourriche between 1319 and 1324.

Dr Françoise Baron has suggested that Guillaume was of English origin, and has pointed to the variety of different spellings of his name as evidence that the scribes had difficulty with the pronunciation of the name of the English town of Norwich; it is difficult to provide any convincing etymological alternative to 'Norwich' for 'Nourriche'. William is also often found working in the company of men who are indisputably of English origin. He had been living and working in Paris from at least 1297, and was still alive in 1330.

By the date when he carved this figure William had already been working in Paris for two decades, and traces of his English training seem to have been all but obliterated. Certainly his statue has little in common with the surviving small-scale figure sculpture from Norwich. This is not solely because all the life-sized imagery from Norwich has disappeared for, fundamentally, William's work belongs not in an English milieu, but should be seen in the context of contemporary Parisian sculpture. The style of his Apostle has some affinities, despite the disparities of scale and technique, with the Virgin reliefs from the exterior of Notre-Dame de Paris's northern apsidal chapels, and it can also be partially paralleled in contemporary metalwork. What is interesting, though, is the evidence that English sculptors, as well as scribes and masons, were working in France. By the later 1330s there would appear to have been quite a number of English artists not only in Paris but also in such major centres as the Papal Palace of Avignon, and the international importance of English art is shown by such examples as the tomb of Pope John XXII (d. 1334), which was clearly designed by an English master mason (cf. Cat. 497).   PL

PROV. St-Jacques-l'Hôpital, Paris; Coll. M. Pommateau; Musée de Cluny, 1852.

LIT. Lavillegille et al., 1840, pp. 370–3; Bordier 1865, pp. 111–32; Bordier & Brièle, 1877, pp. 49–79; Baron 1968, pp. 37–121; Paris 1968, no. 137(B); Baron 1970, pp. 77–115; Baron 1975, pp. 29–72, repr. figs 5, 16; Gnudi 1975, pp. 41–6; Paris 1981–2, no. 10(A).

502–5   Four corbel figures

c. 1320
Doulting stone: h. (i), (ii), (iii) 51 cm, (iv) 76 cm
The Vicar and Churchwardens, St Mary Redcliffe,
    Bristol

The dual function of the north porch of St Mary Redcliffe (see also Cat. 490), as an antechamber to a chapel of the Virgin Mary as well as a principal entrance perhaps accounted for its profusion of carved ornament. Originally the exterior was decorated with two tiers of niches for statues, identified by William Worcestre as kings, and possibly therefore representing the ancestry of the Virgin. Beneath each figure was a corbel carved with a crouching caryatid figure.

Decorative corbel figures are a relatively common feature of the 1320s, though West

501

502

503

504

505

506   Standing female figure

c. 1320–30
Limestone, slight damage to nose and surface
  abrasions, right hand replaced: h. 170 cm
Rector and Churchwardens of St Mary's,
  Stamford, Lincolnshire

This large statue, almost certainly of the Virgin Annunciate, is an unusual survivor of a class of imagery which is generally known to us only in a fragmentary state (see Cat. 507, 508). Standing life-sized statues of saints were one of the primary targets of sixteenth- and seventeenth-century iconoclasts, but this figure seems to have escaped fairly lightly, with damage to the nose, the loss of the right hand (replaced in the restoration of 1890) and the breaking of the book she held in her left hand. She was hidden behind panelling until her discovery in 1853.

The date of the sculpture is intimately linked to that of a group of works of architectural furniture in Lincolnshire and Nottinghamshire. It can be seen as a reversed and gigantic enlargement of the figure of one of the Marys on the Navenby Easter Sepulchre; the shawl-like draperies and marked dehanchement of pose are particularly similar.

506

Country examples do not survive elsewhere in such great numbers. They are equivalent to the comic grotesques in the borders of manuscripts, providing a burlesque commentary or irreverent substructure to the serious purpose of the monument. Here, their ugliness and contortion is exaggerated in deliberate contrast with the composure of the statues that they supported. This is particularly striking in the case of the upside-down tumblers, the joke being that they are forever stuck in the same position. Much play is made for comic effect on the function of the corbels as illusionistic weight-bearers and several, like the female figure here, are supposedly holding back the wall. Other figures clutch parts of their anatomy in pain, some are straining to escape. The indignity of the position was also exploited and alongside the monsters, cripples and peasants, are well-dressed bourgeois gentlemen and clerks, leaning on their elbows and looking exceptionally bored by the tedium of their task. The homilist John Bromyard made reference to corbels like these in his sermons, likening their distressed countenances (which declared that their work was too heavy) to the characters of hypocrites, or of slothful clergy who complained of the smallest task.   VS

PROV. Church of St Mary Redcliffe, Bristol.

LIT. Dallaway 1834, p. 159; Brakspear 1922; Evans 1949, pp. 38–44; Owst 1961, pp. 238–9; Randall 1966a: Harvey 1969, p. 401; Bony 1979, p. 83, repr. pls 230, 232, 233.

The long face, wave-like hair and restless mobility of the hemline are characteristic of work in Lincolnshire during the third and fourth decades of the fourteenth century, and correspond to the luxuriant surface articulation of contemporary architecture. PL

PROV. St Mary's Church, Stamford, Lincs.

LIT. Pevsner & Harris 1964, pp. 662–3; RCHM, *Stamford*, 1977, p. 27, repr. pl. 33; Lindley 1985, p. 221, repr. figs 259–60.

507 Figure of female saint

c. 1320
Limestone, pigment: h. 91.5 cm
St Andrew's Church, Pickworth, Lincolnshire

507

This figure, with its head and left hand broken away, was revealed when a window in the north aisle was unblocked during restoration of the church in the 1940s. It represents a female saint supporting an attribute with her right hand, and is likely to have been situated originally on an image bracket or in a niche near an altar in the church. The attribute has suffered damage at the top, which makes its interpretation difficult. It has been identified in the past as the ointment pot of St Mary Magdalene. However, because of its wide base and the manner in which it is being held, it does not resemble

those carried by the saint in comparable images on sacrament shrines at nearby Heckington or Navenby. It may possibly have represented the tower of St Barbara. The figure was certainly made by a Lincolnshire carver. It is very similar stylistically to the Virgin and Child at Anwick and to figures on the west front of Sleaford church. It retains much of its medieval colouring. VS

PROV. Church of St Andrew, Pickworth, Lincs.

LIT. Rouse 1951.

508 Head of a queen

c. 1325
Limestone, with extensive traces of polychromy: h. 31 cm, w. 20 cm
The Vicar and Churchwardens of St Mary Magdalene, Cobham, Kent

This is the finest of a group of three large heads and eight small fragmentary figures, all with considerable remains of their medieval polychromy, which were discovered at the south-east corner of the chancel in 1860, during Sir George Gilbert Scott's restoration. All these fragments are extremely valuable as providing a good idea of the original appearance of medieval sculpture when it was brightly painted and gilt. Some of these sculptures, which must have been smashed and built into the wall at the Reformation, should be associated with John, Lord Cobham's 1362 transformation of the parochial church into a collegiate one, when he undertook to repair and decorate the church at his own expense (Cat. 136). The smaller images may come from the pre-1381

508

reredos, but the heads of the queens have generally been dated to *c.* 1325, on the basis of stylistic analogies with works such as the corbel heads of this date in the nave at St Albans Abbey. In this case they could be connected with the meeting held at Cobham in March 1327, when the Prior of Levesham was ordered by the Bishop of Rochester to put the chancel into a fit state of repair. But the

dating of both groups urgently needs to be re-examined. PL

PROV. St Mary Magdalene's Church, Cobham, Kent.

LIT. *Ecclesiologist*, 1861, pp. 110–11; Waller 1877, pp. 50–1; Prior & Gardner 1912, p. 360, repr. fig. 410; Vallance 1931, pp. 134–43; Gardner 1951, p. 185, repr. fig. 354.

509 Relief of St Helena from a screen or retable

c. 1325
Limestone, breakages and surface damage: h. 99.7 cm, w. 64 cm, d. 15.2 cm
The Vicar and Churchwardens of All Saints, Mattersey, Nottinghamshire

Both this and the St Martin relief (Cat. 510) were discovered under the chancel pavement in All Saints Church, Mattersey, when the floor was relaid in the eighteenth century. However, it is possible that they were originally part of a reredos or some object of architectural furniture in the nearby Gilbertine priory, which was dedicated to St Helen. They were clearly carved by the same hand, the pose of St Martin's torso echoing that of St Helena, and other features of style are also consistent. This style is related to that of a group of works in Lincolnshire and Nottinghamshire, including the Easter Sepulchres at Hawton and Heckington. A date of *c.* 1325 can be argued on the basis of comparisons with the eight reliefs of the Legend of St Etheldreda at Ely Cathedral, certainly executed between 1322 and 1328. The architectural setting of the Mattersey reliefs, under cusped ogee arches with foliate crocketing, reinforces this dating.

The first half of the fourteenth century saw a great expansion in the quantity of narrative sculpture, and small-scale figure work was widely used both to ornament and to focus the meaning of architecture.

Iconographically, the choice of the Invention of the True Cross is a somewhat unusual choice. It shows the point in the legend where, after St Helena, mother of Constantine, had the True Cross excavated from where it had been buried by Solomon, its identity as the cross of the Crucifixion was proved by a miracle: it raised a young boy from the dead after it was passed over his corpse. It seems likely that other, more familiar scenes from the Legend of the True Cross were also featured among the sculptures at Mattersey. St Helena's story was especially popular in Britain because she was believed to be British. PL

PROV. Mattersey Priory(?); All Saints Church, Mattersey, Notts.

LIT. Thoroton 1797, p. 442, engr. opp. p. 443; Scott-Moncrieff 1909, pp. 2–5, repr. opp. p. 3; Prior & Gardner 1912, pp. 70, 370–1, 462; Gardner 1951, p. 183; Lindley 1985, pp. 157–9 repr. pl. 167; Lindley 1986b, p. 79, repr. pl. XXVIII B.

509

510

510 Relief of St Martin from a screen or retable

c. 1325
Limestone, breakages and surface damage:
  h. 99 cm, w. 79 cm, d. 15.2 cm
The Vicar and Churchwardens of All Saints,
  Mattersey, Nottinghamshire

This relief shows an episode of St Martin's legend which was especially popular in the early fourteenth century: his sharing of his cloak with a beggar. The prancing horse and figure of St Martin may be compared with those of the king and his attendants in the Ely octagon relief of the Miracle of St Abb's Head.

The St Martin relief is wider than that of St Helena (Cat. 509), but very probably came from the same object, perhaps a reredos to the high altar; there may also, of course, have been an altar in the priory church dedicated to St Martin.   PL

PROV. Mattersey Priory(?); All Saints Church, Mattersey, Notts.

LIT. Thoroton 1797, p. 442, engr. opp. p. 443; Scott-Moncrieff 1909, pp. 2–5, repr. opp. p. 1; Prior & Gardner 1912, pp. 70, 370–1, 462, repr. fig. 422; Gardner 1951, p. 183, repr. fig. 345; Lindley 1985, pp. 157–9, repr. pl. 166; Lindley 1986b, p. 79, pl. XXVIII A.

511 Statue of standing figure

c. 1330–50
Limestone, head and upper shoulders broken off, sawn in half by iconoclasts, re-joined in 19th century: h. 70.2 cm, w. 28 cm, d. 18 cm
The Dean and Chapter of Winchester

Unique among the sculpture fragments at Winchester, which form an extremely im-

511

portant collection of Gothic imagery, this figure is carved in the round. This argues for its original placing in an open screen or on an altar where it could be viewed from the back. While it does not seem possible to associate the figure with any particular object of architectural furniture, an approximate date can be assigned to it on the basis of stylistic comparisons with work of the second quarter of the fourteenth century. The draperies fall in sinuous curves, suspended from the arms and pulled across the chest, but without the restless mobility and flicked hemline exhibited by the garments of images of the second half of the century such as the Flawford Madonna (Cat. 699).   PL

PROV. Winchester Cathedral.

LIT. Atkinson 1936, p. 162, repr. pl. L, fig. 4.

512 Boss with musician

First third 14th century
Stone: h. 61 cm, w. 51 cm, d. 34 cm
The Yorkshire Museum, York, 1986.135

This boss, carved with a fiddler skilfully composed to fit its circular format, is one of a group of keystones from a vault with ridge-ribs, most of which were found on the site of the warming room of St Mary's Abbey, York. Its rib mouldings match those of the wall-shafts of the warming room and chapter house vestibule, suggesting that it comes from the ceiling of one of these two buildings.

The sculptor of the warming-room bosses was also responsible for carving a monumental Coronation of the Virgin for St Mary's Abbey, fragments of which are now in the Yorkshire Museum (RCHM, York, 1975, pl.

512

40). To the same atelier may be attributed the statues from the east front of Howden Minster (Prior & Gardner 1912). The angular drapery treatment of the unpublished figure of St Cuthbert corresponds closely to that of the St Mary's Abbey Christ. This group of sculpture at York and Howden testifies to the existence of a flourishing early fourteenth-century workshop in Yorkshire, distinct both from the so-called 'Cheyne' atelier and from the sculptors whose arrival in the county is associated with the appearance of the richly decorated style seen in the tomb of St William of York (Cat. 513–16).   ND

PROV. York, St Mary's Abbey; found on site of warming room during excavation 1827–9.

LIT. Wellbeloved 1829, p. 14, repr. pl. LVIIH; Prior & Gardner 1912, figs 372–3 p. 334; Brook n.d., inv. 598, bk 2, p. 50; RCHM, *York*, 1975, 22, repr. pl. 12.

513–16   Fragments of the tomb of St William of York

c. 1330–40

The Yorkshire Museum, York, 1980.51. 1, 2, 3, 4, 5.

These fragments formed part of a magnificent cenotaph which stood in the easternmost bay of the nave of York Minster, marking the site of the tomb of St William, the twelfth-century Archbishop of York canonised in 1227. The two-tier monument consisted of a stone slab elevated on a series of nodding ogee arches and surmounted by a canopy incorporating openwork arches. The elaborately moulded members of this framework were encrusted with figure sculpture and architectural ornament, the spandrels of the lower stage being filled with a medley of grotesque creatures and subjects taken from daily life which strongly recall the marginalia of East Anglian manuscripts (Cat. 573, 575). The pillars supporting the upper stage of the tomb were adorned with images of the saints, each set beneath a canopy decked with an intricate arrangement of crocketed pinnacles.

Dated to the period of office of Archbishop Melton (1317–40), who donated £20 towards its construction, the tomb of St William signals the arrival in Yorkshire of the highly ornate style seen in the Lady Chapel of Ely Cathedral (Cat. 491) and the Easter sepulchres of Lincolnshire and Nottinghamshire (Cat. 493). The soft drapery treatment, seen to particular advantage in the image of St Margaret, may be compared to that of the figures carved on the parapet inside the choir of Selby Abbey (Pevsner 1967) – a capricious feature very much in the spirit of the St William tomb. Sculpture close in character to that at York and Selby is found on the sedilia at Heckington, Lincolnshire, and it would appear that one is dealing with the work of a single master engaged on a number of related commissions. The same sculptor later worked at Beverley, forming one of the ateliers responsible for carving the Percy tomb (Cat. 494; Stone 1955; Dawton [forthcoming]).

The figure style of the St William tomb is paralleled in a boxwood triptych with the Crucifixion exhibited at the South Kensington Museum in 1862 (London 1863). The triptych, which epitomises the taste for lavish decoration seen in the shrine, also provides convincing stylistic comparisons for the statue of St Mary Magdalen from Pickworth (Cat. 507), underlining the close connections existing between Yorkshire and the Midlands at this period.   ND

513   Block from the lower stage

Magnesian limestone: h. 54 cm, w. 36 cm, d. 32 cm

A gloved stonemason working with mallet and chisel is carved on the interior spandrel. The exterior face is enriched with rosette decoration and covered with cusped panelling in the manner of the spandrels of the great west window of York Minster.   ND

514   Corner of the lower stage

Magnesian limestone: h. 58 cm, w. 64 cm, d. 69 cm

A grimacing Atlas figure, his mouth twisted to the side and his eyes distorted with rage, crouches beneath the angle of the upper moulding; in the spandrels on either side are a hybrid hawker and the eagle of St John the Evangelist.   ND

515   Block from the lower stage

Magnesian limestone: h. 43 cm, w. 37 cm, d. 31 cm

A grotesque creature with the head and arms of a man and the hindquarters of an animal fills the outer spandrel; a pilgrim, barefooted and holding a pointed staff, is represented on the inner face.   ND

516   Fragment of one of the pillars supporting the upper stage

Magnesian limestone: h. 100 cm, w. 18 cm, d. 38 cm

This is adorned on the outside with images of St Margaret and an unidentified figure and, on the inside, with St Edmund and St Cuthbert holding the head of King Oswald.   ND

PROV. York Minster; fragments of the tomb, broken up and ejected from the cathedral by 1553, found in Precentor's Court, buried or reused as building material, on several occasions; two larger stones of 1980.51.3 (support with saints) and 1980.51.4 (corner with Atlas figure) excavated by F. Swineard, 1835, and presented to the Yorkshire Museum; 1980.51.5 (block with pilgrim) and, apparently, 1980.51.1 (block with stonemason, larger stone) discovered during alterations to No. 10 Precentor's Court, 1883; former presented to Yorkshire Museum by Rev. E.S. Carter, 1883; 1980.51.1 bt for Museum by W. Harvey Brook.

LIT. London 1863, no. 1037*; Prior & Gardner 1912, p. 373, repr. fig. 428 p. 373; London 1930, no. 249, repr. pl. 50; Stone 1955, pl. 133 A; Pevsner 1967, pl. 28b; Wilson 1977; Brook n.d., bk 2, pp. 198–207, 215, 226–9, 231–6, 238–41, 243–9, 255, 258–61; bk 3, p. 229; Dawton (forthcoming).

513

514

515

516

517

517 Boss with Christ showing His wounds

Second quarter 14th century
Dundry limestone: l. 68 cm, w. 54 cm, d. 27 cm
Diocese of Bristol

This boss, one of several salvaged from the Church of St Thomas the Martyr, Bristol, comes from the lierne vault erected over the north aisle of the church in the early fourteenth century. Christ, bare-chested and showing His wounds, stands surrounded by large, bulbous leaves, their engrailed edges emphasised by the depth of the carving. The thin, clinging drapery, falling in sharply-pointed folds, may be compared to that of the figures on the nave bosses at Tewkesbury (Cave 1929). This style flourished in the west and south-west of England during the second quarter of the fourteenth century, culminating in the dramatic poses and tightly stretched draperies of the seated kings on the west front of Exeter Cathedral (Gardner 1951). ND

PROV. Bristol, Church of St Thomas the Martyr; boss apparently procured by A. Edgar, Mayor of Bristol, when old church was demolished, 1789; T. Garrard, Chamberlain of Bristol, by 1821; sale of Garrard's effects, 1856, bt by Revd G. W. Braikenridge; given to Church of St Thomas the Martyr, 1883 (information Miss J. Stewart, citing Braikenridge n.d. and Stoddard 1983).

LIT. Taylor 1904, pp. 345, 350–1; Cave 1929, pl. XXIX fig. 4; Gardner 1951, pl. 434 p. 221; Stoddard 1983; Braikenridge n.d.

518 Virgin and Child

c. 1300
Elephant ivory; only part of one leg and foot of Child remaining; Virgin's left hand and right arm from above elbow missing, cavity in her breast for artificial or precious stone, or relic beneath crystal; throne carved separately and missing; dark brown patina, not original: h. 27.3 cm, w. 13.5 cm
New York, The Metropolitan Museum of Art, The Cloisters Collection, 1979.402

The claim (Detroit 1928) that the ivory was 'offered to Jean de Dormans at the time he was made Bishop of Lisieux in 1359' remains undocumented. The Virgin turns her regard tenderly towards her Child, who was clambering on her knee, but it is now impossible to tell how the figures related to each other. The group was either the centrepiece from a large altar tabernacle or a devotional image on its own. The deeply-cut draperies, still reminiscent of thirteenth-century conventions in their combination of channels and broad V-folds, relate this ivory closely to another in Yale (see p. 112); for further ivories of this English group and a close stylistic relationship to two stone sculptures at Glastonbury, see Stratford 1983. NS

PROV. G. J. Demotte, New York, by 1928; Coll. John and Gertrude Hunt, London and Dublin, from 1931; bt by Metropolitan Museum, 1979.

LIT. Detroit 1928, no. 69; London 1936, no. 24, pl. XXVII; Porter 1974, pp. 96–8, no. 33; Wixom 1980, pp. 22–3; Stratford 1983, pp. 208, 213, 215 nn. 9–10, pl. LXXXVIb.

519 The Trinity

English(?), *c.* 1330
Elephant ivory; extensive breakages, particularly arms of God the Father and Christ; fire damage: h. 16.1 cm, w. 8 cm
The Board of Trustees of the Victoria and Albert Museum, London, A49–1937

Carved from the outside of the tusk, the group has a concave back, except that God the Father's head is flat. Porter called this a pax (see Cat. 624), whereas the group was in fact a relief applied against a flat background, perhaps of ivory or painted wood. The technique of applied reliefs enabled ivory carvers to work with small quantities of the precious tusks and to supplement the ivory with other materials. Occasionally series of reliefs went to make up shrines or altarpieces (cf. Cat. 307–9). The Trinity is shown in traditional fashion with God the Father enthroned, holding His Son on the Cross, while the dove

518

519

of the Holy Spirit emerges from His mouth and touches Christ's head with its beak (cf. Cat. 623). Such images of the Trinity were extremely popular in fourteenth-century England. The iconography goes back at least to the early twelfth century and presents the three persons of the Trinity seated on the Throne of Mercy (Braunfels 1954, pp. XXXV ff.). The attribution to an English artist is not certain. Stylistic comparison with the Queen Mary Psalter group and later books (Cat. 109, 110, 570; Sandler 1986, figs 138, 147, 161, 166, 169, 194) must be judged against the undoubtedly French elements in these same books, elements normally associated with Paris illumination *c.* 1315–35. What marks this group as different from contemporary Paris ivories (e.g. Paris 1981–2, no. 135) is the elongation of the figures, the flattening-out of the draperies, and purposeful asymmetries such as the diagonal of the dove.   NS

PROV. Coll. H. Oppenheimer, by 1923; given to V&A by G. Durlacher, 1937.

LIT. London 1923, no. 101, pl. XXIX; Koechlin 1924, I, p. 142 n. 3; *V&A Review* 1937, pp. 3–4, pl. 3b; Porter 1974, pp. 105–7, no. 39.

520 Diptych

c. 1330–40

Elephant ivory: h. 21.6 cm, w. (each leaf) 7.9 cm, d. (each leaf) 2.6 cm

Inscr. on open book, probably 19th century *Ego su[m] d[omi]n[u]s tuus I[esu]s Chr[istu]s q[ui] creavi redemi et salvabo te*

The Board of Trustees of the Victoria and Albert Museum, London, A545–1910

Each leaf is exceptionally thick. The diptych is now hinged to shut like a box, although the present hinges were added when the inner borders were cut back. Originally the two leaves do not seem to have been hinged together, but pinned into a frame. Thus the original disposition of the leaves has been lost, but it is unlikely that they were carved as a pair. Perhaps they were set into a frame of wood or metal, with other architectural elements embellishing the spandrels. They could have been the two central plaques of a double-sided altar tabernacle. Left is the Virgin Mary with the Christ Child on her left arm, who holds an apple and touches the flowers in the Virgin's right hand. Right is Christ blessing, holding an open book. The figures stand within deep ogee-headed niches, with trefoil sub-arches, their hollow chamfered borders studded with rosettes, the main arches decorated with stylised crockets which spring from the base of the gables and terminate in a crowning foliate element. The sides end at the top in small half-buttress finials (on the inner sides these were destroyed when the hinges were added). The gold paint on the rosettes, the hair and the borders of draperies is modern, over traces of an original three-dot pattern on the garment borders, so that the general disposition of the colouring is probably medieval.

The style of the diptych has usually been compared with that of the Eleanor crosses (Cat. 374) and the Westminster Sedilia, but these figures inhabit a world of ultimate refinement alien to that of the best London sculpture and painting of *c.* 1300, where the silhouettes of figures are elongated, the poses angular. The architecture of the diptych, with simply cusped ogees decorated with rosette studs and stylised 'seaweed' foliage, can be paralleled on the Percy tomb at Beverley of *c.* 1330–40 (Cat. 494). Several of the figures on the tomb have similar delicately carved heads and dignified poses, with the draperies treated as flat surfaces from which small cascades fall away at the sides. It is within the general sphere of activity of the Yorkshire sculptors that the ivory was probably created (personal communication, Nicholas Dawton). Yet the precision of the cutting of the ivory and its surface polish remove it from direct comparisons with monumental limestone sculpture. Here everything is exquisitely finished, as with the early alabaster effigies in England, e.g. the head of Edward II at Gloucester, after 1327.

NS

520

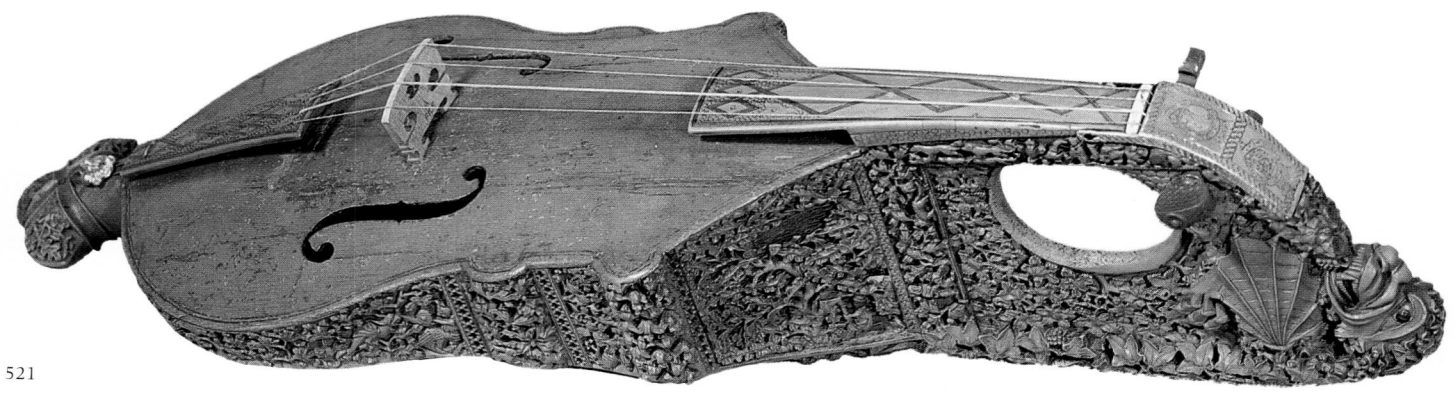

521

PROV. Coll. Francis Douce (d. 1834); Doucean Museum at Goodrich Court, Hereford and Worcs. (Coll. Sir Samuel Meyrick), by 1836; Coll. Frédéric Spitzer, by 1890; Spitzer sale, 1893; Salting beq. to V&A, 1910 (no. 1158).

LIT. Meyrick 1836, v, p. 586, no. 28; Maskell 1872, pp. xc, 179; Westwood 1876, p. 258; Spitzer 1890, no. 110; Spitzer 1893, no. 145; Molinier 1896, p. 255; Prior & Gardner 1912, pp. 363–4; Koechlin 1924, I, pp. 110, 149, 169; II, no. 113B; III, pl. XXXIII; Longhurst 1926, pp. 44, 103–4, no. LVII, pl. 9; Longhurst 1929, p. 6, pl. I; Evans 1949, p. 8, pl. 4; Natanson 1951, pp. 28, 38, no. 57; Stone 1955, pp. 148–9, pl. 104; Philippowich 1961, pp. 90, 92, pl. 71; London 1963, no. 168; Paris 1968, no. 357; Porter 1974, pp. 98–102, no. 34; Gaborit-Chopin 1978, pp. 159, 210, no. 246; Bony 1979, p. 22, pl. 125; Williamson 1982, p. 42, pl. 25; Victoria and Albert Museum 1986b, pp. 200–1.

521   Gittern

Probably English, early 14th century
Wood: l. 61 cm, w. (max.) 18.6 cm,
    d. (max.) 14.7 cm
The Trustees of the British Museum, London
    MLA 1963, 10–2, 1

The original parts are the back, sides and neck, which are carved from a single piece of wood. The form of the instrument, with rounded lower end and trefoil extension, is similar to the guitar illustrated in the Psalter of Robert de Lisle, c. 1300–20 (f.134v.; Cat. 569). A similar looking instrument is being played with a bow on a misericord at Chichester Cathedral (Cat. 529). A 'new' sound-board with vaulted profile has been inserted, as well as finger-board, tailpiece and bridge, to effect the post-medieval conversion to a bowed instrument. A silver plate engraved with the arms of Queen Elizabeth I and Robert Dudley, Earl of Leicester, has been placed above the pegbox. The centre part of the trefoil is a replacement.

The use of foliate borders, the oak leaf panel showing a typical Labours of the Month scene infested with hunters and animals, can be paralleled in the pages of early fourteenth-century English manuscripts such as the early part of the Ormesby Psalter (Cat. 573), of c. 1310. Analogues in wood are much harder to find. The best

comparison, particularly with its very naturalistic early Decorated foliage and figure carving in the spandrels, is the choir stalls at Winchester Cathedral, 1308–10 seqq. The lions on the back of the instrument resemble the one on a misericord from John of Glaston's choirstalls, 1309–10 (Cat. 522) at Exeter Cathedral, and also examples in stone of the same date at Exeter in the north transept and eastern bay of the nave. The hawthorn sprays are identical to those on the capitals in the crypt of St Stephen's Chapel, Westminster. The sharply-cut skeletal handling of the quatrefoil friezes is close to that on the trefoil friezes of Prior Eastry's choir screen at Canterbury Cathedral.   CT

PROV. Owned by Duke of Dorset, 18th century; bt by R. Bremner, 1769; Warwick Castle; bt by British Museum, 1963.

LIT. Remnant & Marks 1980, repr. pls 75–80, 83, 86, 87, 90, 92, 94, 96, 97.

522   Choir stall backing

1309–10
Oak: h. (original screen) 61 cm, w. 65 cm,
    d. 12.5 cm
Dean and Chapter of Exeter

The open-traceried stall backing of typically early fourteenth-century type has been reused as the top part of the door to the fifteenth-century Sylke Chantry in the north transept. The lower part of the door consists of a panel with applied tracery of mid-fourteenth-century date not dissimilar in style to the wooden parclose screens still in situ in the choir.

In the mid-seventeenth century it is recorded in the Act Book of the cathedral that a rector of St Lawrence's Church, Exeter, asked 'permission of the Dean and Chapter to have some of the woodwork lying in the south choir aisle . . .'. In the Devon County Library, Exeter, are two photographs of the interior of St Lawrence's showing the choir stalls. Behind the seating is open tracery of identical type to that of the fragment in the chantry door. These stalls must have been made by the Somerset joiner John of Glaston. A reference in the cathedral fabric rolls for Christmas term 1309–10 states: 'In wages of Master John de Glaston' removing the stalls

522

for fourteen weeks 52s.6d., 3s.9d. a week' (Erskine 1981). This entry has always been interpreted as meaning that Bishop Brewer's thirteenth-century choir stalls, the misericords from which are preserved to this day, were reused when the liturgical choir was transferred to the new eastern arm of the church under Bishop Stapledon. However, the photographs (St Lawrence's was completely destroyed in May 1942) and the fragment demonstrate that Stapledon retained only the misericords and commissioned completely new choir stalls.   CT

PROV. Exeter Cathedral.

LIT. Glasscoe & Swanton 1978, pp. 8–10, repr. p. 9; Erskine 1981, p. 49; Tracy 1986a, repr. figs 19–20 p. 92, figs 21–3 p. 101.

523   Richard of Bury chest

c. 1340
Oak: h. 63.5 cm, l. 230.2 cm, w. 66 cm
The Burrell Collection, Glasgow Museums and Art
    Galleries, 14/352

The planked construction is secured with wooden pegs, iron bracing and nails. Hinged carrying handles are at each end. There is a

523

locking mechanism at both ends for pad-locks. The space for a central lock is now filled in. Inside the lid, in red, yellow, white and blue tempera on a green field, and flanked by heraldic supporters, are four shields of arms as follows: (1) D'Aungervile of Co. Leicester; (2) unidentified but also probably D'Aungervile; (3) England and France quartered; (4) Nevill of Raby, created Earl of Westmorland in 1397. Richard of Bury, Bishop of Durham, 1334–45, was a member of the D'Aungervile family and Chancellor of England and High Treasurer under Edward III. The quartering of his emblem against a plain cross is probably an augment-tation of the bishop's arms. The royal arms of England on the sinister side are in the form used before 1340. It has been suggested that the arrangement of the shields repres-ents a deliberate juxtaposition of the Bishop of Durham on one side, and the soldier, Ralph, second Lord Nevill on the other. Nevill was the major magnate of the Palatinate and was a 'very dear friend' of de Bury.

Although many medieval chests were painted, only the smallest scraps of poly-chromy have survived to our day. It is perhaps the heraldic and iconographical importance

of the painting on the inside of this and the Newport chest (Cat. 345) lids which has ensured their survival.

The ironwork consists of six vertical split-curl straps on the front. Two horizontal brackets on each corner also end in split-curl terminals. The six hinge straps on the lid end in cut-out unlobed leaves with sharply bent stems. The datable heraldry on this chest provides an important fixed point for related but otherwise undated ironwork. Traces of very similar straps with cut-out foliage ter-minals can be seen on the lid of a chest from Mattishall, Norfolk (now in St Peter Hungate Museum, Norwich). On the chest at Bitterly, Shropshire, paired cut-out leaves spring from the base of each strap rather than from its terminal. The cut-out asymmetrical leaf is used most effectively on the south door of St Mary at Elm, Ipswich, and a simpler form is found on the church door at Clothall, Essex. A more developed version of the terminals may be seen in wood on the choir stalls at Ely Cathedral (c. 1342) and elsewhere.   CT & JG

PROV. Until c. 1855 in office of Chancery Court, Durham; bt by Revd W. Greenwell; bt by Captain N. R. Colville; bt by Sir William Burrell, 1941.

LIT. Cescinsky & Gribble 1922, pp. 8–9; Edwards & Macquoid 1924–7, II, p. 7; London 1930, no. 46; London 1934, no. 1261; Wells 1966, repr. pp. 14, 16, 17, 18, 31.

524   Pair of choir stalls

c. 1345
Oak: h. 433 cm, w. 143 cm
By Faculty and Permission of the Vicar of Lancaster

This pair of seats from the south return stalls includes that for the head of the college, with the carved head of a king underneath the seat capping, and the prior's on the elbow. The panelling behind the superstructure is miss-ing. The choir furniture is no longer *in situ* but chopped up and rearranged according to no particular logic. Moreover, it is uncertain that the stalls were even made originally for the priory. There is a tradition that they were removed from Cockersand Abbey. The chan-cel at Lancaster must have been rebuilt in the late fourteenth century. The stalls are not therefore coeval with the building.

Of all the major fourteenth-century Eng-lish choir stalls those at Lancaster are the least influenced stylistically by London. In-

525 Christ and the Virgin with Sts Peter, Paul, Matthew and John the Evangelist

c. 1350

Oak: Christ h. 31.8 cm; Virgin h. 33 cm;
St Peter h. 33 cm; St Paul h. 32.4 cm;
St Matthew h. 31.8 cm; St John h. 32.4 cm

The Board of Trustees of the Victoria and Albert Museum, London, 411 to 416–1889

524

525

deed, there is nothing directly comparable in England in wood or any other medium. The handling of the tracery is closer to the goldsmith's than the mason's craft. Such complexity of patterning was not realised in stone until the fifteenth century, on the Continent.

The impressionistic aesthetic of this furniture can be shown to stem from the North Country. It is most likely that the designer would have learnt about flowing tracery from across the Pennines. Monuments such as the Beverley reredos of the 1330s, and the Wakefield Bridge Chapel, of the middle 1340s, could have supplied most of the ideas incorporated here. If there is any doubt about the date of the choir stalls, close study of architectural and sculptural details can help us to fix their broad chronological and stylistic context. Some of the figures on the misericords are comparable with those in the Luttrell Psalter (Cat. 575), for instance. Moreover, the mouldings, especially those on the capitals, neckings and bases, are typical of those in English architecture of *c.* 1340. CT

PROV. St Mary's, Lancaster.

LIT. Bond 1910, pp. 40–4, repr. pp. 39, 41, 42; Crossley 1918, repr. opp. pp. 1, 6, 20, 32, 33, & app.; Tracy 1987a, pp. 40–3, repr. pls 129–44.

Together with the early thirteenth-century Langham Virgin (Cat. 249) these figures are examples of a now mostly lost genre of English medieval sculpture: the wooden altar image. They would presumably have been framed in an altarpiece and were in all probability painted, although none of this remains.

Stylistically, with their deep folds of drapery, these figures may be related to such mid-fourteenth-century sculptures as the voussoir statuettes of the Rochester chapter house doorway (Prior & Gardner 1912, fig. 414) and with ivory figures of the seated Virgin and Child of the third quarter of the century

428

(for an example in the Victoria and Albert Museum see Stratford 1983, pl. LXXXVIIa). Figures of this type must have been relatively inexpensive and would have been found in even the most humble parish churches. PW

PROV. Early history unknown; given to the V&A by Mr W. Maskell, 1889.

LIT. Prior & Gardner 1912, p. 524, fig. 613 (only three figures); London 1930, no. 340; Williamson (forthcoming), nos 28–33.

526–7 Annunciation group

c. 1363
Oak: Virgin h. 118 cm, base 68 cm;
   archangel h. 119 cm, base 68 cm
The Dean and Chapter of Wells

It is believed that this Annunciation group, which is now placed high up against the east wall of the Vicars' Choral at Wells, was made

for that position and is likely to be contemporary with the building, which was completed in 1363. No extant records indicate otherwise, yet the original setting of the group may well have been more elaborate. It is very unlikely that relief figures of this kind would be independent of niches, or at least canopies, and it is conceivable that originally they were set within wooden arcading similar to the stone canopy work in the Wells retrochoir. On the evidence of their style and dimensions, the two figures and their half-columnar corbels were clearly made for one another, although their subjects are not closely related. The Three Magi carved beneath the angel are looking up and outward, as if in the direction of a Nativity which may formerly have appeared nearby on a roof boss, though there is no record of this. Most unusually, the angel has no trace of wings, but its barefooted dancing stance is

characteristic of English Annunciations. Although the pose of Mary is also distinctively English, there are hints of French influence in her gracefully draped figure, which is similar, for example, to the Virgin Annunciate from La Gleize (repr. Cologne 1980, vol. 4, p. 86). The sinuous pose and the costume of both figures would be consistent with a date in the early 1360s. The loose hair and the flaring ankle-length buttoned robes worn by the angel and the Three Magi resemble those on the brass of the merchant Robert Braunche of King's Lynn (*c.* 1364), though examples from the 1370s and 1380s (e.g. in the Bohun manuscripts [Cat. 686–91] and the Litlyngton Missal [Cat. 714]) are more common. VS

PROV. Wells Cathedral.
LIT. Stone 1972, p. 187, repr. pl. 140; Scott 1986, pp. 17, 35.

528

528 Misericord: Cat and mouse

c. 1308–10
Oak: h. 24 cm, w. 69 cm, d. 10 cm
The Dean and Chapter of Winchester, north side
   stalls from west, upper row, no.28 (of 68)

The central scene is very naturalistically portrayed and shows the cat with its teeth sunk in the neck of the mouse and shaking it. The supporters of the Winchester misericords are unusually large in relation to the central carvings, and in the exhibited misericord the outlines of the supporters form the curving branches of a beech tree within which squirrels sit.

The depiction of natural animals and foliage, as opposed to creatures derived from the bestiary, is a characteristic of the Winchester misericords and must have been transmitted to the Wells carvers, where equally natural animals and foliage are found, translated into a later style. The Winchester carvings are knobbly and hard, with deeply drilled eyes and mouths, giving the impression of stone carvings, whereas in Wells they are smoother, not as tightly knit. A cat in Wells Cathedral (unfinished) has just pounced on the mouse and planted a massive claw on its back, illustrating the fleeting moment of the mouse's attempt to escape. A squirrel is also found at Wells, on a lead held by a monkey.

526

527

In a letter of 1308 Bishop Woodlock of Winchester asked John Salmon, Bishop of Norwich, for permission to keep on the carver William Lyngwode (perhaps a native of Lingwood near Norwich) to enable him to finish his work in Winchester. The request was renewed in 1309. Although the letter does not mention the misericords specifically, they may well have been among the work yet to be finished, especially as they fit into this period stylistically. CG

PROV. Winchester Cathedral.

LIT. Goodman 1927, pp. 125–6.

529 Misericord: Dancing

c. 1320
Oak: h. 63.5 cm, w. 25.5 cm, d. 14 cm
The Dean and Chapter of Chichester Cathedral, north side stalls from east, no. 7 (of 38)

The man and woman bend backwards towards each other, their faces touching, and the woman is about to turn cartwheels, as was done in some medieval dances.

Music-making and dancing was a popular theme in carvings and marginal illuminations at the beginning of the fourteenth century, and there are other misericords in Chichester Cathedral where humans and half-humans delight in musical performances. Especially close in style and iconography is a manuscript from Battle Abbey (London, British Library, MS Cotton Domitian A. II), which has a centaur beating the tambour – as on another misericord in Chichester Cathedral – and on f.7 is a depiction of a woman who bends double to dance to the strains of a fiddle played by a centaur.

Two main masters were responsible for the Chichester Cathedral misericords. One, as in the exhibited misericord, created rounded, lively forms, while another worked in a harsher, flatter style, with large faces and limbs. These two styles are also represented by two bosses in the Cathedral sacristy, which must therefore belong to the same

530

period. The misericords are related to those at St Mary's Hospital, Chichester, *c.* 1295, from which they take their inspiration; but they accord in style with the manuscripts and sculptures of the period *c.* 1320. CG

PROV. Chichester Cathedral.

LIT. Steer 1961.

530 Misericord: The Flight of Alexander

c. 1330–40
Oak: h. 29.2 cm, w. 63.5 cm, d. 15.2 cm
The Dean and Chapter of Wells, south choir aisle stalls (displaced when stalls were rearranged, 1848; total stalls 64, plus one in Victoria and Albert Museum)

Alexander the Great sits in regal pose, cross-legged with one hand on his knee, flanked by two griffins. This is a scene from the medieval Romance of Alexander. It portrays Alexander's journey to the end of the world. curious to discover what was beyond, where the sky sloped down. He therefore had a basket and wooden frame constructed, in order to be lifted up into the air by griffins. These he attracted by holding up two spears with pieces of meat on the points. He was

thus able to view the earth, encircled by a great serpentine ocean. He then turned the spears downwards in order to descend. In a moral interpretation of the scene, Alexander represents pride.

The story was also very popular with misericord carvers and, near Wells alone, there are two versions in Gloucester Cathedral and one in Tewkesbury Abbey.

The carving in Wells is most delicately done, with great feeling for the flow of the drapery and the movement of the beasts. The griffins do not face the king symmetrically as is usual: the one on the left has turned its back to him and twists its head right round towards the spear. Alexander's tongue is showing. The carving is by the same hand as the Dragonslayer (Cat. 470). It can be compared stylistically with the ruined Douai Psalter, dated after 1322 (Douai, Bibliothèque municipale, MS 171), where on f.1 a king sits cross-legged with his sword uplifted, comparable with Alexander in pose and arrangement of drapery.

New stalls were ordered for Wells Cathedral in 1325 as part of the eastward extension of the choir, but some of the misericords were still unfinished when the choir was completed in *c.* 1340. The style of the figures and the foliage, much of it naturalistic, fits into the period 1330–40. The master carpenter may have been John Strode (although he is not mentioned until 1341; his assistant was Bartholomew Quarter, first mentioned in 1343). CG

PROV. Wells Cathedral.

LIT. Loomis 1918, pp. 117–85; Friends of Wells 1981.

531 Misericord: Animal musicians

1340s
Oak: h. 27 cm, w. 66 cm, d. 15 cm
The Dean and Chapter of Hereford, south end stalls from east, lower row, no. 7 (of 39) (cf. Cat. 471)

A study of the costumes worn by the figures of the Hereford Cathedral misericords indi-

529

cates a date of *c.* 1340, and stylistic and iconographic comparisons with the Wells Cathedral misericords, dated to *c.* 1330–40, confirm this.

Many of the same types of animals are portrayed, often almost identically. The supporters of the Wells Cathedral misericords and all but two at Hereford display foliage. At Wells it is the cat alone that plays the fiddle, without lifting its body into an upright position.

The idea of animals mimicking human beings and making music was popular in medieval drolleries of the fourteenth century. The goat was seen as a lecherous animal and in the misericord its genitals are in prominent frontal view. To the Christians the goat represented the Devil and sinners were likened to the goat; Antichrist was sometimes shown in the shape of a satyr.

The cat was considered lazy and lustful. The scraping of the fiddle suggests the cat's own mewing, which is complemented by the bleating of the goat. Thus, disharmony and a world upside-down are created when the fiddle and lute, often played by angel musicians, fall into the hands of brutes.   CG

PROV. Hereford Cathedral.

LIT. Morgan 1966.

531

532   Choir stall canopy fragment

c. 1342
Oak: h. 1.48 m, w. 61 cm, d. 31 cm
Dean and Chapter, Ely Cathedral

Below is one of the projecting three-sided canopies which crown the choir-stall superstructure. Rising above is a hexagonal crocketed spire. To complete the design, to each side and slightly further back, are tall gabled and crocketed finials. Both components are mutilated, with ornamental details missing. The furniture itself has been moved twice from its original position under the octagon. These are two of the various *disjecta membra* now stored in the choir gallery.

The choir stalls were intended to be of the conventional double-screen type. However, it is clear that the design of the superstructure was changed at an early stage of its manufacture. The upper canopies, of which this fragment forms a part, seem to have been an afterthought. The 'double-decker' effect of the resulting composition is not an entirely happy one. We can only guess at the motivation for the change of plan, but the desire to use the fashionable French semi-hexagonal canopy form, instanced for the first time in England on the west front of St Stephen's Chapel, Westminster, is probable.

Fourteenth-century English choir stalls are notable for the development and perfection of tall and intricately detailed superstructures. The tendency to greater height and the piling up of design elements was facilitated by the increasingly sophisticated methods of jointing, which were paralleled in

532

the field of roof construction. The complicated detailing, typical of tabernacles like these, sometimes known as 'ciborium' canopies, was achieved by the building-up of forms from small components. A single canopy is assembled from dozens of separate parts, joined together by wooden pegs and iron nails. See also Cat. 106.   CT

PROV. Ely Cathedral.

LIT. Tracy 1987a, pp. 34–9, pls 114–28, fig. 4.

533   Canopy arch from choir stall

c. 1365
Oak: h. 108 cm, w. 66 cm
The Board of Trustees of the Victoria and Albert
    Museum, London, W.21–1921

This is probably from the destroyed church of the royal hospital of St Katharine's-by-the-Tower, London. The institution, founded in the twelfth century, received a new charter in 1351 from Queen Philippa. Rebuilding was slow, and it was not finished when the queen died in 1369. Druce (1917) maintained that it was probably not until about the time of King Edward's death in 1377 that the new choir stalls were eventually finished. The carving style of such of the furniture as still survives, however, suggests a date in the mid-1360s. Although only the seating remains, antiquarian records made before demolition in the early nineteenth century provide us with a reliable idea of the form of

533

this furniture. It is the only surviving witness of mid-fourteenth-century choir stalls made under direct royal patronage. The two other fourteenth-century sets of metropolitan choir stalls, at St Stephen's Chapel, Westminster and St George's Chapel, Windsor, are no longer extant.

The choir stalls were of the conventional double-screen 'London' type, as exemplified in the lower portion of the work at Ely Cathedral, or the furniture at Wells Cathedral of the late 1330s, except that the gables were allowed to break free of the crowning cornice. Our knowledge of the superstructure is limited to various drawings, the earliest, of 1780, by John Carter. See also Cat. 469. CT

PROV. Royal Architectural Museum; bt by Victoria and Albert Museum, 1921.

LIT. Druce 1917, repr. pls I–II; Majendie 1924, pl. p. 20; Tracy 1987a, pp. 165–75, repr. pls 49–55; Tracy 1987b, cat. 88.

534 Misericord: Falling knight

c. 1370
Oak: h. 33 cm, w. 64 cm, d. 15 cm
Dean and Chapter, Lincoln Cathedral, south side
  stalls from east, upper row, no. 30 (of 92)

The horse's forelegs have folded under it, the neck and head are twisted into a V-shape and the knight, who has just pierced the neck of the wyvern on the supporter with his lance, has been thrown forward and is about to slide off the horse's back, wounded by an arrow. He may be an unidentified hero from a romance but, in the splendour of his armour, he could also represent the Fall of Pride.

Many of the Chester misericords take their inspiration from the Lincoln set (see Cat. 537–8), and there too can be found a knight on horseback and wyverns in the supporters. There, however, the knight rides triumphantly on a proud horse, his coat armour incised with fleurs-de-lis, and he looks out confidently, his tasselled lance resting on his shoulder.

The great skill of the Lincoln carver is seen in the detail of the knight's armour and the horse's trappings and the total harmony in the movement of horse and rider. Even the

535

fastening of the armour at the back is shown precisely, a view rarely depicted. The style of the armour points to the 1370s. The combination of mail and plate armour, the fashioning of the joints, the shape of the basinet, the low belt and the stirrups can be compared to the effigy of the Black Prince in Canterbury Cathedral, dated *c.* 1377–80.

The canopied stalls at Lincoln show the influence of the king's master carpenters William and Hugh Herland, and the quality of the misericords indicates an association with a major artistic centre, more so as many of the patterns were transmitted to Chester Cathedral where another of the king's chief carpenters, William Newhall, was active from 1377 to 1411. Cf. Cat. 468, 535. CG

PROV. Lincoln Cathedral.

LIT. Anderson 1967.

535 Misericord: Tristram and Isolde

c. 1370
Oak: h. 33 cm, w. 64 cm, d. 15 cm
Dean and Chapter, Lincoln Cathedral, south side
  stalls from east, upper row, no. 26 (of 92)

The carving depicts the meeting of Tristram and Isolde underneath a tree which harbours King Mark, Isolde's husband, who is trying to spy on the young lovers. His presence, however, is discovered when they notice his reflection in the pool at their feet, and they accordingly adopt innocent behaviour. The supporters depict a squire (head missing) on the left, and on the right, a waiting-woman with a pet dog.

Although the Arthurian romance is well represented in English literature, Loomis says that England's contribution to the iconography is very limited, though found on thirteenth-century Chertsey tiles (Cat. 320). The Tryst beneath the Tree in Lincoln Cathedral is the first occurrence of such a scene on a misericord: it can be compared to ivory caskets and embroideries from the Continent, such as a German embroidery in the Victoria and Albert Museum (No. 1370–1864) and a tablecloth in Erfurt Cathedral of *c.* 1370.

Usually either Tristram or Isolde points at the reflection of Mark's face in the water and Isolde holds the dog on her arm. In the Lincoln misericord, however, the dog is by the edge of the pool and Tristram and Isolde lift their hands up to touch the face of King Mark. The misunderstanding of the story here demonstrated is further aggravated at Chester Cathedral where the same scene is based on the Lincoln model; the dog now laps up the water, thus ruining the reflection of King Mark, and Tristram presents Isolde with a ring.

The style of the costumes points to *c.* 1370: Tristram is dressed in a tightly-fitting cote-

534

hardie with closely-set buttons, a girdle round his hips, and pointed shoes; Isolde wears a low-cut, tight-fitting dress and a rectangular headdress. The rosettes that decorate Tristram's girdle and the top edge of Isolde's dress are also found around the ledge of the misericord itself. The woman-in-waiting is wrapped up for out of doors in a short cape and a hat. See also Cat. 464, 534.

CG

PROV. Lincoln Cathedral.

LIT. Loomis 1938, p. 138; Anderson 1967.

536 Misericord: The riddle

c. 1379
Oak: h. 30 cm, w. 63 cm, d. 15 cm
The Dean and Chapter of Worcester, north side
    stalls from east, no. 15 (of 42)

The carving illustrates a riddle concerning the posing of impossible demands and the resulting battle of wits. This kind of riddling combat was well known in the Middle Ages, according to MacColl, who quotes an example from a Transylvanian tale, *Der Burghueter und seine kluge Tochter*. The demand is made by a king, usually to a young woman, to come 'neither driving, nor walking, nor riding, neither dressed, nor naked; neither out of the road, nor in the road; and bringing something that is a gift and no gift'. The carving therefore shows a woman half-riding on a goat, with one foot on the ground, her nakedness covered only by a net and with a hare under her arm which will jump away when presented.

Another example of this riddle on a misericord is in St Mary's Church, Beverley, dated *c.* 1445. There, the king with sceptre is included, gesturing towards a man on the goat. The story is also illustrated in the margins of fourteenth-century manuscripts, e.g. the Ormesby Psalter (Cat. 573, f. 72).

The goat is also associated with lechery, and a nude woman riding on a beast is a symbol of lust and sensuality.   CG

PROV. Worcester Cathedral.

LIT. MacColl 1905–6, pp. 80–6.

537 Misericord: Wodehouse on a lion

1380s
Oak: h. 33 cm, w. 60.9 cm, d. 15.2 cm
The Dean and Canons of Chester Cathedral, south
    side stalls from east no. 12 (of 48, of which 5
    are Victorian)

The wodehouse gained great popularity in the second half of the fourteenth century. His name derived from the Anglo-Saxon *wude-wasa*, wild man. He lived in the forest, had a shaggy beard and was dressed in a hairy skin, covering all but his hands and feet. He got his furry garment by killing a lion and, in order to illustrate his great strength and power over animals, he was often shown in combat

536

537

with wild, mythical beasts such as dragons and wyverns. In his inability to control his sexual passions he was compared with the mythological satyr; he fought knights over ladies and assailed Castles of Love. Most frequently, as on the Chester misericord, he was shown in company with or riding on a ferocious animal, thus demonstrating his control over its wildness and his kinship with it. The lion symbolises loyalty and strength, which the wodehouse has made his own by taming it, and loyalty in connection with the wodehouse is also associated with his amorous intentions, so that the knot around the neck of the right supporter may be a love-knot.

There is another wodehouse misericord in Chester Cathedral, slightly different in style. A wodehouse riding cross-legged on a chained lion is also found on a misericord in Lincoln Cathedral, and this is one of the many examples of Chester misericords modelled on those in Lincoln Cathedral.

Although the wodehouse may often be seen on a lion, guiding it by means of a chain is rare, and M. D. Anderson has demonstrated that both the iconography and style are so closely related that the Lincoln models must have been transmitted through a sketchbook, and possibly travelling carvers. Some of these, such as the wodehouse on a chained lion, are also found on the misericords of Holy Trinity Church, Coventry.

The Lincoln misericords were carved *c.* 1370, and J. H. Harvey thinks that William Newhall (the king's chief carpenter at Chester from 1377–1411) probably collaborated at Lincoln with William and Hugh Herland, thus accounting for the close association between Lincoln and Chester.   CG

PROV. Chester Cathedral.

LIT. Harvey 1947, p. 56; Bernheimer 1952; Anderson 1967.

538

538 Misericord: Fighting couple

1380s

Oak: h. 33 cm, w. 60.9 cm, d. 15.2 cm

The Dean and Canons of Chester Cathedral, north side stalls from east, no. 12 (of 48)

The scene illustrates the battle of the sexes which is found in almost every set of stalls from the fourteenth to the sixteenth centuries and in which the woman, seen as the virago, is usually victorious. The model for this scene is found on a misericord in Lincoln Cathedral. In both cases the woman swings round with one foot forward, the other thrown back, and she picks up the man by the top of his head, belabouring him with a washing beetle. The Lincoln carving is more sculptural, revealing the energetic body movement underneath the drapery, while the figures on the Chester misericord are more delicate and the woman's dress spreads out like a fan. So, while many of the Chester misericords used the Lincoln misericords as models, their style may vary according to the hand of the carver. The man is dressed in the fashion of the end of the century, with wide, fan-shaped sleeves and pointed shoes.

A last, rather crude reflection of the Lincoln model is found in the misericords of the Parish Church in Nantwich, Cheshire, including the scene of the henpecked husband, here being beaten with a ladle and made to hold the distaff, the characteristic implement of the woman.   CG

PROV. Chester Cathedral.

LIT. Cann Hughes 1895; Wolfgang 1911, pp. 79–87; Bennett 1968.

539 Misericord: Acrobats

1386

Oak: h. 32 cm, w. 66 cm, d. 17.5 cm

The Warden and Fellows of New College, Oxford, chapel, south side stalls from east, no. 22 (of 62)

The two acrobats have two heads but four bodies, two of which hover horizontally one above the other and are joined by the vertically-positioned parts of the bodies, merging into each other. Feet and heads are at diagonally opposite ends and this, combined with the merging shapes, gives the impression of cartwheeling.

The figures wear tight-fitting garments of quilted material with closely-set buttons down the front and the lower part of the sleeves; the belts are tied low and the shoes are very pointed: a late fourteenth-century fashion. The face beneath the tumblers is smiling, an expression found on some of the other misericords.

Both New College, Oxford, and Winchester College were founded by William of Wykeham. At New College the first building phase lasted from 1379 to 1386, while Winchester College was founded in 1387 and the chapel consecrated in 1395. The close relationship between the colleges is also demonstrated by the misericords in both chapels, in the stylistic similarities of the foliage, the compositions, the figures and the facial characteristics. Particularly comparable with the Oxford acrobats is the contorted figure of a man holding up the seat in Winchester College Chapel. He is dressed in the same type of quilted garment, only here the quilting is raised and not incised, and he, too, wears pointed shoes and has curly hair. With his left hand he hides a dagger behind his back, a weapon also held in the extended arm of the bottom acrobat in Oxford. In his right hand he seems to hold a bauble and this, with the quilted pattern of his garment, may indicate the jester in his multicoloured dress, for the role of the jester included all manner of entertaining, including tumbling.

The style of the Oxford misericord is slightly harder than that in Winchester, but so close that carvers from the Oxford workshop must have moved to Winchester.   CG

PROV. New College Chapel, Oxford.

LIT. Wood 1786; Steer 1973.

540 Closing ring from a door

Late 13th–early 14th century

Copper alloy: w. 23.5 cm, diam. of ring 37.1 cm

Gloucester City Museums, Art 1174

This is cast as a flat, hexagonal back plate with, in its centre in high relief, the head and forequarters of a demon with ass's ears, long,

540

539

swept-back hair, bat-like wings, hairy front legs with claws, and slender neck round which the ring itself (a late replacement?) is passed; on his back is a second head with protruding tongue, while above and below on the plate are sprays of naturalistic foliage.

This is a unique, and splendid, representation in base metal of the kind of Decorated grotesque – often, as here, accompanied by naturalistic foliage – better known from carvings, for example at Exeter Cathedral, Heckington (Lincolnshire), the Percy Tomb at Beverley Minster and on the Warwick gittern (Cat. 494, 521). It is likely to have been produced in Gloucester, where there was an important and long-established bell-founding industry. Similar winged demons, perhaps copied from the closing ring, are carved on the base of the fifteenth-century spire of St Nicholas Church, Gloucester. CB

PROV. From south door of St Nicholas Church, Gloucester; purchased by Gloucester City Museum and Art Gallery, 1971.

LIT. Carter 1780–7, I, p. 53, unnumbered plate; Bagnall-Oakeley 1889, p. 131; Keyser 1912; NACF 1971, p. 29, pl. VIA; London 1972, no. 228; Mende 1981, pp. 283–4, figs 275–6.

541   The King John cup

c. 1340
Silver-gilt and enamel; h. 39.5 cm, diam. of foot
  c. 18.5 cm, wt. *c.* 69½ troy oz
Inscr. under foot
  New Enamled in 1692
  New Enameld & gilded in 1750. John Goodwyn, Mayor
  New Enameld gilded & repaired 1770. Sam Brown, Mayor
  Re-enameled gilt & repaired 1782. Edw Everard, Mayor
  John Bagge, Mayor 1711
Borough Council of King's Lynn and West Norfolk

The bell-shaped cup, on a five-sided enamelled stem, has a prominent knop, embossed with acorns and oak-leaves. The flat, round foot is edged with five projecting cusps. The flat cover has a cast gilt cresting of trefoil leaves, and a leafy finial surmounted by a ball and spike, the latter probably early sixteenth century (How 1946, p. 120). The foot, cup and cover are decorated with twenty-one panels of enamel, in translucent mid-blue, green, purple and opaque dark blue divided by decorative ribs consisting of stems sprouting fleshy trefoil leaves, apparently not embossed but solid castings (Maryon 1953).

The enamels depict elegantly dressed figures, some engaged in hawking and hunting, and animals (hares, hounds and a fox) in flight, many against a background of star-shaped flowers, often elaborately framed. There are twelve women (one holding a longbow, two with a hawk and nine men (one about to blow a horn, another with a sword).

Inside the base of the cup in a medallion is enamelled a woman holding a hawk in one

541

541 (detail of lid)

541 (detail of bowl)

541 (detail of base)

hand, a branch in the other; a medallion, now gilt, under the lid is engraved (worn) with a rose(?). The stem of the cup is embellished with architectural motifs: engraved pointed arches surmounted by projecting fleurons, and panels of dagger tracery. A bayonet joint between bowl and stem allows the cup to be used as a beaker.

This magnificent cup is an astonishing survival – it is the earliest secular medieval example in England, and one of the finest of its kind. Its closest parallel is the Avignon-made cup of c.1330 now in Milan (Lightbown 1978a, pp. 91–2, pls LXIX–LXXI), also with a foot and lid enamelled with secular subjects, but the cup itself of crystal.

The date of the King John cup can be established by the style and costume of the enamelled figures. The women with hair in cornettes, the long tippets, hoods with liri-pipes, generally close-fitting garments with numerous buttons point to a date c.1340 (Newton 1980, ch. 1) when these features became fashionable. The fleshy trefoiled-leaf ribs are less easy to parallel, but are found for example on misericords in Ely Cathedral of the 1330s. There is nothing comparable in surviving metalwork, except for the cresting on the lid, very close to that on the Lacock cup of c.1450 (exh. London [Christie's] 1955 no. 2) or earlier.

Its origin is uncertain; opinion has been divided between Flanders (Fox 1984, pp. 76–7) and England (Lasko in Norwich 1973), but the balance of probability seems to lie with England. The Flemish brass to Robert Braunche (d. 1364), Mayor of King's Lynn, is engraved with a feast whose participants bear only the most general resemblance to the figures on the cup (Cameron 1979, pl. XLIX). These, though not unlike figures in a Flemish manuscript (Oxford, Bodleian Library, MS 264), are closer still, in pose and angularity, to those in the Luttrell (Cat. 575), Gorleston (Cat. 574), Ormesby (Cat. 573) or Douce (Cat. 683) Psalters.

The technique of preparing the metal for enamelling is odd and without parallel; although the figures are finely chased, their backgrounds are crudely engraved with deep lateral grooves entirely dissimilar to the delicate patterns of the Victoria and Albert Museum triptych (Cat. 583) or the Swin-burne pyx (Cat. 571). It is not clear if any enamel is original after the repairs mentioned in the inscriptions; it seems possible that only the dark blue on the lid is old. The brilliant acid tones of the purple and green are not paralleled by other contemporary enamels; the purple now colouring the engraved leaves around the figures is eccentric.

The first known reference to the cup is in 1548, when it is called the King John cup in the town's Hall Book (ff. 92v.–93). The name may be due to mistaken association: the town was given its first charter by King John in 1204. It has been suggested that the cup was the gift either of the French King John (d. 1364) who spent some time in England (Trollope 1857, pp. 55, 58–9) or, more plausibly, of John IV, Duke of Brittany (d. 1399), son-in-law of Edward III. The latter owned and lived at Castle Rising near King's Lynn from c.1378, and may have recipro-cated the lavish gifts which he received from the townspeople (Bradfer-Lawrence 1922).

Of the guilds in King's Lynn, the largest was the Trinity guild which commemorated King John as one of its founders (Harrod 1874, p. 25). No trace of the cup appears among its extant records, but it is equally possible that the cup may owe its name and its survival to this guild. On the dissolution of the guild, the cup would have passed naturally into the possession of the town.   MLC

PROV. King's Lynn, in the possession of the Corporation by 1548 (Hall Book, ff. 92v.–93).

LIT. Mackerell 1738, p. 184, repr.; Carter 1785, II, pp. 1–3, repr.; Shaw 1836, pl. 67, p. 55; London 1850, no. 345; Manchester 1857, p. 14; London 1862, no. 8101; Harrod 1874, pp. 25–7; Jewitt & Hope 1895, II, p. 202; Bradfer-Lawrence 1922; Chamot 1930, no. 24; How 1946, p. 120; Penzer 1946, pp. 12–16, 64, 79–84, 120; Maryon 1953, p. 88; Norwich 1973, no. 35; Fox 1984.

542 Mazer lid

c.1350

Wood, turned and painted: diam. 24.2 cm. max h. 5 cm

The Prior, Brothers and Sisters of St Nicholas' Hospital, Harbledown, Canterbury, on loan to the Poor Priests' Hospital

The turned conical cover is painted on the outside with two lions combatant, separated by flowering plants (one oak) all on a dark-green ground dappled with groups of three white dots. Other colours used are yellow, black and red. Inside, the lid is painted a pale geranium red. The plain wooden stud at the apex of the cover no longer functions as a knob, and has either been broken and planed down, or is a replacement.

Although inventories mention painted wooden mazer lids, this is a unique survival. Its history is unknown; it was considered by Hope (1887) as belonging with the Smythe mazer (also at Harbledown), but the fit is poor, and the mazer rather earlier in date. The dishevelled manes of the lions and the lively drawing style have some resemblance to marginalia in the Queen Mary Psalter (Warner 1912, repr. pp. 206, 220).   MLC

PROV. Canterbury, St Nicholas's Hospital, Harbledown; on loan to Poor Priests' Museum, Canterbury, 1986.

LIT. Hope 1887a, p. 129.

543 Swan mazer

c.1350–90

Maplewood, mounted with silver-gilt: h. 7 cm, diam. 13 cm.

The Master and Fellows of Corpus Christi College, Cambridge

The turned bowl is mounted with a silver-gilt rim, decorated with three stylised 'strawberry' leaves, cast and soldered on, intended to hold steady the cover (missing). A crack

542

popular from *c.* 1300 onwards (Cat. 551). Its design is very close to the cup sketched by the French thirteenth-century architect Villard de Honnecourt, except that the French piece had a differently constructed foot (Cambridge 1895, pp. 7–9). The earliest college inventory, *c.* 1384, records the mazer as having a silver-gilt foot, and a cover so mounted. The voluted trefoil 'strawberry' leaves resemble those on the top of the Ramsey Abbey censer (Cat. 121) and on the King John cup (Cat. 541). MLC

PROV. John Northwode, admitted Fellow by 1388, d. by 1398 (Emden 1963, p. 427) given by him to college; listed in earliest inventory, post-1384 (James 1911–12, p. 114).

LIT. Hope 1887a, p. 145; Cambridge 1896, no. 11; James 1911–12, p. 144; Norwich 1973, no. 59; Cambridge 1975, no. MTD.2.

544　The Savernake horn

Horn 12th century; two silver and enamelled bands at bell of horn 1325–50; two silver fittings nearer mouthpiece early 18th century
Elephant ivory horn, silver bands with translucent enamelling: l. 63.5 cm
The Trustees of the British Museum, London, MLA 1975, 4–1, 1

The importance of the horn lies in the two silver bands, divided into sixteen compart-

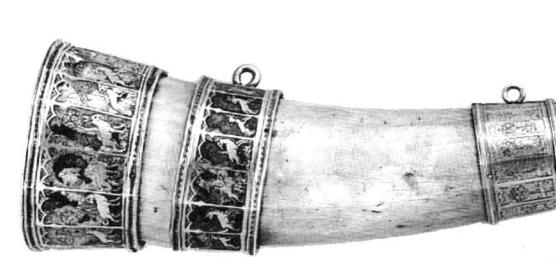

544

has been repaired anciently with rivets. A hollow six-sided column rises from the middle of the base, topped by battlements within which perches a swan. A hole in its beak connects with a tube which leads into the column. When the bowl is filled above the level of the battlements, the liquid is siphoned, via beak and column, into the lap of the unwary. The foot of the bowl is a sixteenth-century replacement; the original foot may have allowed the liquid to be channelled back into the bowl.

　This is a unique survival of a type of joke vessel analogous to pottery 'puzzle jugs'

544 (detail)

ments, at the bell of the horn. The top band is turned inwards to form a narrow flange decorated with sixteen birds, each beneath a canopy. On the sides of this band two adjacent figures frame the engraved figures of a bearded king and bishop. They face one another, each with a hand raised. Next to the

543

king stands a forester blowing a horn. Twelve of the remaining compartments show alternating figures of hunting dogs and forest animals. The thirteenth, diametrically opposite the king, has a seated lion. The second band has sixteen compartments all with hunting dogs and animals of the chase. The backgrounds of both bands have translucent enamel, while the figures of the people and animals are reserved and gilded. These two bands are among the few enamels of the period that are certainly of English origin. They may be compared with the central medallion in the base of the Bermondsey dish (Cat. 156), dated to *c.* 1335–45. Comparisons with the Smithfield Decretals (fig. 130) decorated in the second quarter of the fourteenth century, suggest a source in London. The king and bishop have not been identified.

JC

PROV. Hereditary horn of the Wardens of Savernake Forest; Marquess of Ailesbury.

LIT. Paris 1968, no. 433; Camber & Cherry 1977, pp. 201–11.

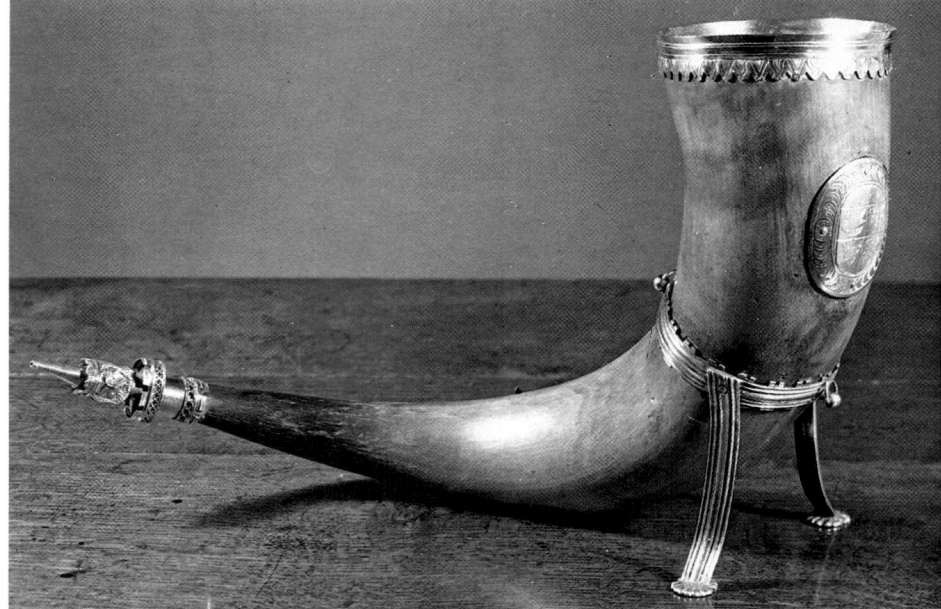

545

545 Drinking horn

Before 1347, with 17th-century additions
Horn mounted in silver-gilt: l. 62.2 cm
The Master and Fellows of Corpus Christi College, Cambridge

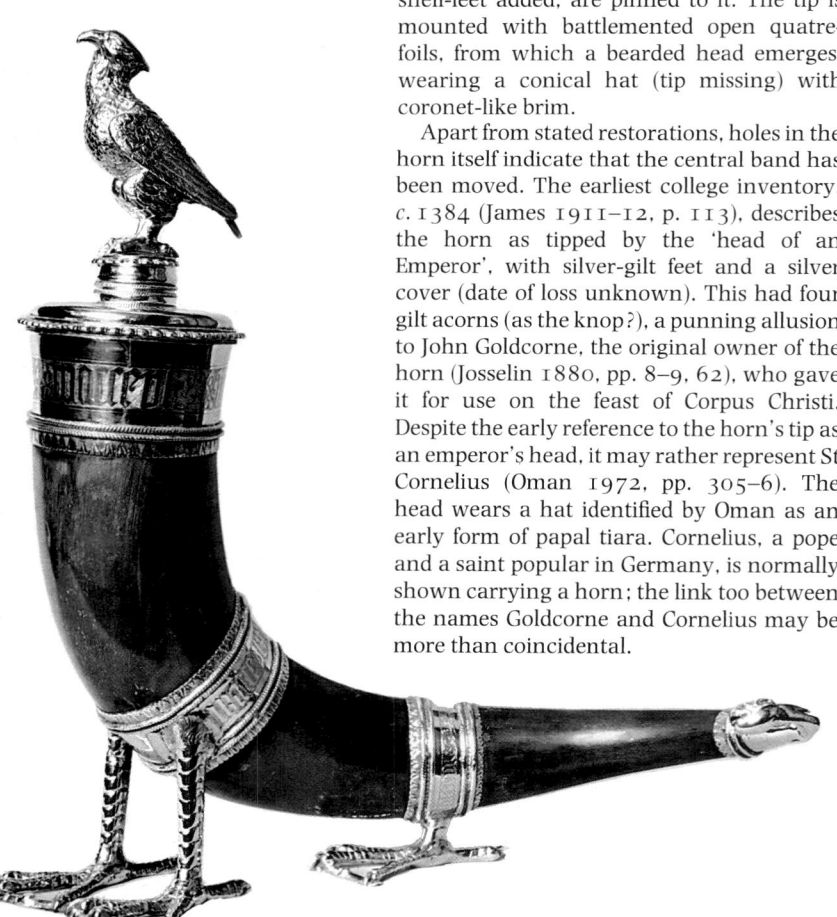

546

The horn (ox or aurochs) is mounted at the lip with a band and on the front with an oval shield with the college arms (probably seventeenth-century). A milled band encircles the middle; two strap-like legs, with shell-feet added, are pinned to it. The tip is mounted with battlemented open quatrefoils, from which a bearded head emerges, wearing a conical hat (tip missing) with coronet-like brim.

Apart from stated restorations, holes in the horn itself indicate that the central band has been moved. The earliest college inventory, *c.* 1384 (James 1911–12, p. 113), describes the horn as tipped by the 'head of an Emperor', with silver-gilt feet and a silver cover (date of loss unknown). This had four gilt acorns (as the knop?), a punning allusion to John Goldcorne, the original owner of the horn (Josselin 1880, pp. 8–9, 62), who gave it for use on the feast of Corpus Christi. Despite the early reference to the horn's tip as an emperor's head, it may rather represent St Cornelius (Oman 1972, pp. 305–6). The head wears a hat identified by Oman as an early form of papal tiara. Cornelius, a pope and a saint popular in Germany, is normally shown carrying a horn; the link too between the names Goldcorne and Cornelius may be more than coincidental.

But the hat may simply be a piece of exotica: such hats worn by Tartars are illustrated at this date (Newton 1980, pp. 92–3, fig. 31).

The horn is today used at High Table for feasts, and at the degree-day lunch, when each undergraduate drinks from it before taking his degree.

MLC

PROV. John Goldcorne, alderman of Guild of Corpus Christi (d. 1347); given by him to Guild, which in 1352 united with that of Blessed Virgin to found college.

LIT. Tyson 1786, p. 19, repr.; Manchester 1857, p. 15; London 1862, no. 3238; Gosselin 1880 edn, pp. 8–9, 61; Cambridge 1896, no. 1; Bridge 1905, p. 133; Oman 1972, pp. 305–6, Cambridge 1975, no. MD.1.

546 Wassail horn

Before 1349, with 17th-century additions
Horn mounted in silver-gilt: h. 48.3 cm
Inscr. in black letter *wacceyl*
on lid HP
The Provost and Fellows of the Queen's College, Oxford

The horn (ox or aurochs) is mounted with three broad bands; the inscription is engraved on each three times, divided by floral sprays, against a hatched ground. The tip-mount consists of a grinning lion's head (one ear missing) also engraved twice with the inscription and foliage (much rubbed). The horn has been cut in three and lined in silver-gilt. Two claw feet are soldered to one band, a third to another. The lid is mounted with an eagle knop and probably *c.* 1700, like the lip band and lining.

The horn is, with that of Corpus Christi College, Cambridge (Cat. 545), one of the earliest English survivals. Its convivial inscription 'wacceyl' is a Middle East variant of the Anglo-Saxon *wes hael* (may you be healthy, or fortunate) – an early instance of the use of English, and of black letter on plate, by contrast with the inscription on the Guy of Warwick mazer (Cat. 155). The Earl of March owned a silver cup called 'wassaill' in 1380 (Nicholas 1780, p. 115); it was probably a common tag for drinking vessels.

The replacement lid probably resembles the original: college accounts from 1416–17 onwards (Magrath 1921, pp. 22, 213, 226, 242) list repairs to the horn. The eagle is a punning reference to Robert de Eglesfield, the founder in 1341 of the college whose arms included eagles (ibid., pl. VI). Moffatt (1906) was the first to recognise that the horn must have been Robert's gift rather than that of Queen Philippa, after whom the college is named.   MLC

PROV. Queen's College; given by Robert de Eglesfield (d. 1349).

LIT. Storer 1822, p. 91, repr.; *Gent. Mag.* 1850, p. 171; Shaw 1836, pp. 52–3, pl. 63; Manchester 1857, p. 15; London 1862, no. 3220; Bridge 1905, pp. 134–5; Moffatt 1906, p. 46; Jones 1938, p. 17; Oman 1944, p. 22; Emden 1957, p. 632.

547 Straight trumpet

Late 14th century
Latten and brass: l. (assembled) approx. 154 cm
Museum of London, BWB83 (225)

The instrument is in four detachable sections, made from more than twenty pieces of sheet metal. The latten composition and soft-soldered overlapping seams of the mouth pipe and adjacent section contrast with the brass tubing and silver solder of the other two: these have elegant butt seams, developed in the flaring bell section into a fine coppersmith's joint. This points to as many as three phases of manufacture and redesign in which the two proximal sections, including the mouthpiece, are clearly later replacements. Additional soldered repairs elsewhere support the impression that it could have had a long working life (Lawson 1987).

The mouthpiece is, unusually, of an integral form, and lacks the internal refinements familiar from most later and many

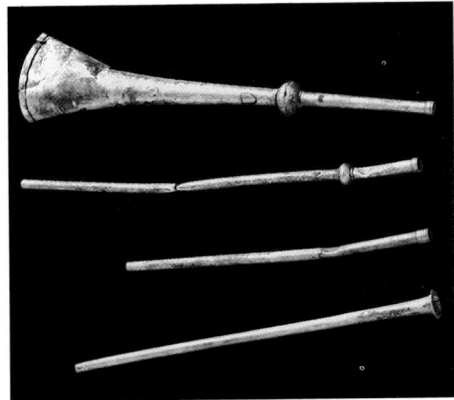

547

earlier excavated trumpet mouthpieces: namely, a hemispherical cup, narrow throat and gradually tapering back-bore. This open internal shape is crucial in determining the musical character of the instrument. However, the original mouthpiece may have been differently shaped. Finds of medieval trumpet components of any sort are extremely rare, though contemporary illustrations occasionally show external details suggestive of both types.

The broad throat and relative unsophistication of the surviving mouthpiece may argue for the trumpet's use, at least in later years, as a signal instrument, possibly as a ship's trumpet of the kind recorded in contemporary historical sources and illustrations such as the surviving fourteenth-century seals of Faversham and Dover (Remnant 1978, 151; Pedrick 1904, pls VIII, XXIII). Its detachable joints would have suited it to a military role. This need not preclude a more musical, ceremonial function as well, particularly in its earlier phases (Byrne 1971).

There is a single small perforation in the rim, perhaps for the attachment of a banner.
                                                    GL

PROV. Found Thames foreshore deposits on site of Billingsgate Lorry Park, Lower Thames Street, London, during post-excavation watching-brief examination of deposits adhering to landward face of modern river wall. Context probably late 14th century (Egan 1986a).

LIT. Museum of London 1985, pp. 28–9; Egan 1986a; Lawson 1987.

548 Ram aquamanile

Late 13th century
Earthenware, in form of ram, dark green glaze: h. 23.9 cm, l. 37 cm
Rotunda Museum, Scarborough Borough Council, 3.39.1

The ram is one of the most common animals chosen for the form of medieval pottery aquamaniles. Curiously enough, it is not

548

known in metal versions. This example has a twisted handle and horns, and is decorated with applied scales covered by a dark green glaze. It was certainly produced in Scarborough, since it was found in the kilns at Castle Road. These kilns were an important source for highly decorated pottery which was widely distributed both in England and over the North Sea. The Scarborough aquamanile is a most successful combination of the curved wheel-thrown cylinder to form the body of the animal, which is balanced by the wheel-thrown neck and moulded head.
                                                    JC

PROV. Found in kiln at Castle Rd., Scarborough, 1854.

LIT. London 1930, pl. 49 no. 232; Rutter 1961, p. 26 pl. I; London 1964, no. 63; Rackham 1972, p. 20 pl. F.

549 Jug

Late 13th century
Earthenware, with three handles, applied decoration, the base, upper part of handles, eyes of face and rim restored: h. 44.5 cm
Herbert Art Gallery and Museum, Coventry, 49/220/2

This tall jug of a white fabric covered with green glaze has three handles and on the front a figure indicated by applied strips of clay. The beard suggests that a man is represented. His body is hour-glass shaped with a belt at the waist. Details of dress are indicated by incised lines below the waist, by the belt, and by a circular brooch ornamented with seven circular impressions intended to represent stones on the chest between the raised hands. Below the left elbow is an incised cross whose meaning is obscure. The fabric suggests that the jug was produced at the Chilvers Coton kilns near Nuneaton. The jug has a strap handle opposite the figure and on either side are lateral handles, all elaborately grooved and incised. The handles are separated by an applied strip of clay with incised lines, and under each of the side handles is a pattern of incised lines representing a tree. The jug is a fine example of applied figural decoration.   JC

PROV. Found on site of Benedictine Priory, Coventry; Shelton Coll.

LIT. Webster & Dunning 1960, pp. 120–1 fig. 45.

550 Jug

Late 13th century
Earthenware, in the form of man pulling his
    beard, green glaze: h. 11 cm
The Trustees of the British Museum, London.
    MLA 55, 10–29, 11

This small jug provides an amusing contrast to the more stately jug from Worcester (Cat. 553). Like that jug, the features of the face and the arms are indicated by applied pieces of clay but the mouth, beard and hands are indicated by incised lines. There are a considerable number of small jugs in human form from London, some with brooches,

550

some in the form of a king. The quality of the copper-green glaze on this jug is particularly fine, and indicates the brightness and colour that such jugs would have given to the medieval table.   JC

PROV. Found in City of London, before 1855.

LIT. Hobson 1903, p. 72 no. B.119.

551 Puzzle jug

c. 1300
Pottery, formed of two chambers decorated with
    panels of leaf scales and human and animal
    decoration: h. 33 cm, w. 21 cm
The Visitors of the Ashmolean Museum, Oxford.
    1921.212

This elaborate puzzle jug was made in two separate sections which form two separate chambers. The lower chamber is filled through the hollow handle at the side and the liquid flows out through the stag's-head spout. If the drinker attempted to drink from the other side the liquid in the upper chamber ran out from the spout on that side. The puzzle was to find out how to drink without being soaked from one or other spout.

The jug is notable for the elaboration of its decoration. The spout in the form of a stag is strongly modelled, and around the outside of the rim of the jug are eight irregularly spaced human masks. The spout (now broken) on the upper chamber may well have represented a human figure, since there appear to be two arms curving down and holding on to a ridge around the pot.

From its fabric, the jug was certainly produced in the Oxford area and elements of the decoration such as the panels of leaf scales or the series of hands around the rim are typical of the region. The heads may be compared with those on another jug (Oxford, Ashmolean Museum, 1888.106). The manufacture is certainly local but it was found together with another similar puzzle jug (London, British Museum, B.6). It was suggested by Dr G. C. Dunning that both were copied from a more elaborate puzzle jug produced in the Saintonge in south-west France in the second half of the thirteenth century and found in Exeter (Exeter Museum and Art Gallery), to which town it had been exported in the Middle Ages. The principal difference is that the centre of the French jug forms an openwork structure in which figures stand and from which they lean out. The English potter was not able to reproduce the complexity of form of the French original but instead, by covering the surface with modelled decoration, produced one of the finest existing pieces of highly decorated pottery. JC

PROV. Found in digging foundations of new Town Hall, Oxford, 1895; P. Manning Coll. 1911; bt by Ashmolean Museum, 1921.

LIT. Dunning 19233, pp. 130–1; Hinton 1973, no. 12.

552 Jug

14th century
Earthenware, incised decoration, neck and rim
   missing: h. 27.5 cm
The Rye Museum Association

552

The kilns at Rye in Sussex produced jugs with a remarkably wide variety of incised decoration. It includes knights in combat, a figure of Christ blessing, a scene possibly of the Adoration of the Magi and subjects such as ships, fish, letters and animals. This jug is decorated with an incised pattern under the glaze, with a fish and what was probably intended to be an elephant and howdah. The animal actually shown is more like a pig, since it has cloven hooves and a ridge of hair along its back. The Rye pottery shows how finer designs were reproduced on a more popular level.   JC

PROV. Found in excavations of Rye kilns at St Bartholomew's hospital, Spital Field, Rye, 1933.

LIT. Vidler 1933, p. 53 pl. 1.

553 Jug

Early 14th century
Earthenware, in the form of a woman, strap
   handle, green glaze: h. 40 cm
The Trustees of the British Museum, London,
   MLA 1974, 10–1,1

The shoulder and neck of the jug represent the shoulder and neck of a woman. The face looks to the front. The arms are formed of applied strips and are bent at the elbow so that the gloved hands are pressed against the body at shoulder level. The hair is represented by a strip of clay above the top of the handle. This is decorated with pierced holes and short incised lines, probably representing braiding.

   Jugs decorated with faces on the front occur mainly in the south-east of England. The closest parallel to this example is a jug found in the well at Bristol Castle (Barton

551

553

554

555

1959, fig. 2 no. 7). In the Midlands, jugs with faces on the front occur as far north as Nottingham (Cherry 1976, p. 237). Possibly of local manufacture, this jug is the most westerly of the Midlands examples. As an interpretation of the simple elements of the human figures it may be compared with the examples from London and Coventry (Cat. 549–50). JC

PROV. Found near Worcester Cathedral, c. 1954.

LIT. Cherry 1976, pp. 236–8.

554 Roof finial

Late 13th/early 14th century
Earthenware: h. 17 cm
The Trustees of the British Museum, London,
  MLA 1966, 4–1, 1

This is half of a roof finial moulded in the form of a human face on each side with a hole at the top. Such finials were used to crown the ends of ridges. The strongly-modelled forms are built up by hand. The sharply-curved nose contrasts with the holes punched from the outside to form the eyes and mouth to provide a caricature of a face that may be compared with the expressions on the Tring tiles (Cat. 217). JC

PROV. Found in Reading; A. Derrett Coll.

555 Roof finial

Late 13th/early 14th century
Earthenware, with faces: h. 32.5 cm, w. 24 cm
Nottingham Castle Museum, 78.314 T.NCM

This roof finial, produced at the Nottingham kilns, may be compared with the example from Reading (Cat. 554). It has the shape of an inverted wheel-thrown flask with thumbed strips at shoulder and base. On each side there is an applied circle forming a face. The top is indented to represent hair and the bottom is pulled down to represent the chin. There are vestigial ears, the eyes stand out, and the mouth is a knife-cut slit. Intended to be seen from the ground, the features are emphasised to give a firm, almost crude profile. JC

PROV. From Parliament St, Nottingham, 1874; W.G. Ward Coll.

LIT. Parker 1932; Rackham 1972, pp. 4, 11, 31, pl. 14.

XIV The Decorated Style and the Figurative Arts

In the *House of Fame* Chaucer speaks of 'subtil compassinges ... babewinnes and pinacles, imageries and tabernacles'. The mention of 'pinacles' and 'tabernacles' serves to emphasise that in the early fourteenth century all the other arts make use of the complex forms of Decorated architecture for settings and frames. The many overlaps and reciprocal interconnections between architecture and the other arts are seen in the vocabulary of their ornamental forms, for example the architectural canopies in stained glass, the complex framing patterns of the *opus anglicanum* textiles, and the border ornament of illuminated manuscripts. The textiles of this period are particularly notable, since this was an English art form admired and exported all over Europe (Cat. 12, 576–9). They are also typical in the richness of their materials and textures, a richness of materials and colour also found in the enamels. Interconnections between the different media are shown by such well-known comparisons as that of the Swinburne pyx (Cat. 571) with the Reydon Hours (Cat. 570).

The range of pictorial narrative, both religious and secular, is also greatly extended in this period. English art of the fourteenth century is famous for its genre scenes, particularly on the misericords (Cat. 528–39) and in the margins of illuminated manuscripts. These are the 'babewinnes' referred to by Chaucer, meaning literally 'baboon scenes'. The term comes from the many parodies of human behaviour by animals including very often, but by no means exclusively, apes and monkeys. Also referred to as 'drolleries' this subject-matter, though marginalised (literally, for it occurs in the margins of manuscripts and beneath the seats of the choir stalls, the misericords), must have acted in some sense as a way of expressing and thereby defusing social tensions. The images have also been linked to the stories (*exempla*) used by the friar preachers in their sermons to hold their congregations' attention, and certainly there are parallels. Sometimes gently humorous, sometimes bitingly satirical, sometimes grotesque, sometimes even lewd or indecent, these representations draw even in the same manuscripts both on everyday life and on the weirdest of imaginary fantasies. The Luttrell Psalter (Cat. 575) is perhaps the most famous example of this. In addition to fantastic hybrid forms worthy of Hieronymus Bosch or Ken Russell, it contains a sequence of observed representations of the various social divisions from Sir Geoffrey Luttrell, the patron, to the peasants working in the fields (figs 15, 29, 88).

556 Altar recess in east wall: St Faith, Crucifixion and praying Benedictine

Early 14th century
Wall painting in chapel of St Faith, Westminster Abbey, London
Inscr. ME : QVEM : CVLPA : GRAVIS : PREMIT : ERIGE : VIRGO : SVAVIS : FAC : MIHI : PLACATVM : CHRISTVM : DELEASQVE : REATVM
Photograph

The painting is complex in its illusionism, imitating the combined media which would have comprised a contemporary altar. A fictive statue of St Faith, holding the brazen bed of her martyrdom, stands within a tabernacle above an imitation of a wooden retable. The depth of the altar recess is accentuated by a bold chevron pattern, interrupted by a quatrefoil enclosing a kneeling Benedictine monk, whose prayer ascends on the back wall towards the saint.

The arrangement resembles that of the altar recorded in a 1304 inventory of the Lady Chapel in the Abbey, where an image of the Virgin was placed above the retable. The conceit of imitating a painted wooden retable complete with frame occurs elsewhere in wall painting, e.g. Brent Eleigh, Suffolk (*c.* 1330–40). In the St Faith's example the central Crucifixion is typical of surviving retables (Cat. 345, 564, 711), while the flanking star shapes are identical to those of the Westminster Retable (Cat. 329), though here they evidently never contained subjects. The praying monk is more likely to be a generic representative of his Order than a specific donor.

The painting is one of a group of late thirteenth-/early fourteenth-century paintings in the Abbey in the Westminster Court style. It is closest in execution and conception, as well as in style, to the wall paintings of Doubting Thomas and St Christopher in the south transept. The drapery style is more

556

557

complex and mannered than in the Westminster Retable, and closer to that of the Sedilia paintings in the Abbey and to the work of the Madonna Master in the De Lisle Psalter (Cat. 569), suggesting a dating for the wall paintings after the turn of the century (Binski 1986, p. 80). New floor tiles were laid in St Faith's chapel in the early fourteenth century, and the painting may belong to the same phase of renovation. DP

LIT. Tristram 1950, pp. 121–6, 561–2, repr. pls 7–10, suppl. pl. 12; Wilson 1980b, pp. 93, 102, repr. fig. 2; Binski 1983, pp. 109–12, 117, 120, repr. pl. 79; Binski 1986, pp. 32, 56, 61, 78, 80, repr. pl. LXII.

557 Warning against idle gossip

Second quarter 14th century
Wall painting in Church of St Michael and St Mary, Melbourne, Derbyshire
Inscr. IC EST C[?]ELIA DEABOL
Photograph

This is one of the moralising subjects which became popular in Gothic wall painting.

Priests ran a high risk of losing their congregations who tended to fall asleep, to chatter, or simply to leave during the service. Idle gossip, encouraged by the Devil, was considered a compound sin for it also prevented others from hearing the word of God. According to contemporary preachers, it was chiefly women who chattered during sermons, while 'the fende sate on hor schuldyrs, wrytyng on a long roll als fast as he myght' (see Owst 1933, p. 387, and also pp. 35, 41 above).

In the Melbourne scene a large winged devil, holding an inscribed scroll, sits above two kneeling women with their heads close together, while two smaller devils (one blowing a horn) push the women from behind, and a fourth, impish devil appears between the women. The subject appears in various media (cf. Cat. 561), and there are at least nine examples known in wall painting: Brook (Kent) and Wiston (Suffolk) from the second half of the thirteenth century; from the fourteenth, Peakirk (Cambridgeshire), Colton and Little Melton (Norfolk), Grundisburgh (Suffolk), Lower Halstow (Kent), and Slapton (Northamptonshire), the last three

recently identified. All but Grundisburgh and Melbourne are, most appropriately, located towards the back of the church. Discovered in 1842, the Melbourne painting is on the west face of the north-west crossing pier, highly conspicuous to the congregation. The most elaborate of all the wall painting examples, it may also contain a witchcraft element, with the object the women are exchanging possibly to be identified as the Host. DP

LIT. Deans 1860–1, pp. 31–3, repr. p. 32; Tristram 1955, pp. 110–12, 222.

558 Angel

c. 1300
Stained glass: h. 46 cm, w. 23 cm
Craggaunowen Project, Co. Clare, Ireland

The angel wears a white full-length robe and is blowing a trumpet. Its hands and feet are flesh-coloured.

In 1848 this figure and parts of four companion music-making angels were in the choir east window of the former Augustinian abbey of Bristol (now Bristol Cathedral), where they were copied by Charles Winston, the pioneer of English medieval stained glass studies (British Library, Add. MS 33847, f.10v., Add. MS 35211, vol. 1, no. 69). Winston noted that none of the angels was *in situ* and that they had been collected from other windows in the church. The east end of Bristol Cathedral, including the Lady Chapel and choir, was begun by Abbot Knowle on 21 August 1298 and completed in about 1330 (Cat. 487). The figure style of the angel, and the lack of modelling in the facial features and drapery, suggest that it dates from the first phase of the building work. RM

PROV. Bristol Cathedral until at least 1848; present owner.

LIT. Westlake 1882, p. 3; Paris 1968, no. 203.

558

559

560

559   St Catherine

c. 1310–30

Stained glass: h. 76 cm, w. 30 cm

The Friends of the Friendless Churches, on temporary exhibition at the Stained Glass Museum, Ely, 80/2/1

One of a pair of panels (the companion, not exhibited here, depicts St Lawrence) from the north-west chancel window at Wood Walton in Cambridgeshire. St Catherine holds the wheel and sword (emblems of her martyr-dom) and wears a blue mantle over a pot-metal yellow robe and has a white veil and crown. The saint is set on a plain ruby ground below a trefoil cusped yellow stain arch with a steep gable and green crockets. The side shafts are white with yellow stain bands and are capped by steep yellow stain crocketed pinnacles. The ground flanking the gable is in white glass diapered with a foliate pattern picked out on a matt wash. The border to the panel, which has a trefoil head

to match the window tracery, is plain ruby, some of which is post-medieval. The flat canopy, absence of modelling from the figure and the sparing use of yellow stain suggest that the panel is of the same period as the Stanford on Avon chancel glass (Cat. 560).

RM

PROV. Parish church of St Andrew at Wood Walton, near Huntingdon, Cambridgeshire; on loan to Stained Glass Museum, Ely, from Friends of the Friendless Churches, since 1980.

LIT. RCHM, *Hunts.*, 1936, p. 298, pl. 157.

560   St Peter

c. 1315–26

Stained glass: h. 76 cm, w. 40.5 cm

Inscr. in Lombardic letters S : PETRUS

The Vicar and Parochial Church Council, Stanford, Northamptonshire, window n.11

Stanford contains one of the most extensive parish church glazing schemes of the first half of the fourteenth century. In the chancel side windows are an almost complete set of the twelve Apostles and associated grisaille. The heraldic glass in the east window suggests a date of *c*.1315–26 for the chancel glazing. Most of the surviving fourteenth-century glass in the nave is concentrated in the east windows of the north and south aisles and consists of several saints, a set of eight canopies and, in the tracery, two Crucifixion scenes, angels and other motifs. The nave glass is by a different workshop from the chancel windows and probably dates from *c*.1325–40.

The chancel side windows, in common with the Merton College glazing (Cat. 738), are good examples of the 'band' composition, with the Apostles arranged in a horizontal row across each window and set between grisaille ornamented with naturalistic foliage. The figure of St Peter comes from the first light of the north-east window. Face, hands and feet are a very light flesh colour and the figure wears a pot-metal yellow mantle over a blue robe and has a pot-metal yellow nimbus. The pair of keys in his left hand are in white and yellow stain. The figure is set on a ruby background with a trail of naturalistic foliage picked out on a heavy matt wash and below a canopy with white cusps and a pot-metal yellow crocketed gable. The canopy rests on pot-metal yellow capitals and blue columns; the side shafts are white with traces of painted patterns and embellished with pot-metal yellow and green quatrefoils, green bases and pot-metal yellow pinnacles. The background above the arch is

ruby and the borders consist of a climbing trellis of vine leaves and stems alternately in yellow stain and pot-metal yellow and on a plain blue ground. The letters of the label are in white and yellow stain on a matt wash. The panel still retains most of its original leading and is intact apart from minor insertions of medieval glass, principally in the lower right part of the figure.

St Peter's lugubrious expression and the multiple drapery folds are features of the workshop responsible for the chancel glazing. The absence of any perspectival devices in the canopy and in the placing of the figure is characteristic of English glass of the early fourteenth century.   RM

LIT. Winston 1849; Eden 1929–30; Newton 1961, I, pp. 2–3, 29–35, II, pp. 358–91.

561   Warning against idle gossip

c.1325–40
Stained glass: h. 29 cm, w. 33 cm
The Vicar and Parochial Church Council,
   Stanford, Northamptonshire, window n.II

Chattering or gossiping by the laity during church services was a common vice in the late Middle Ages. The clergy saw it as the work of the Devil and inveighed against it in sermons:

> … synners herithe no worde of God, but turnithe hem to dilectacion of synne, to which the devil temptithe hem. For the devil hissithe be mony diverse weyes in the sermon; and how? For he makith some to slepe that they her not the wordes of God; and some he makithe to chatir faste. (Owst 1926, p. 175)

Several occurrences of this subject have been noted in English medieval art, including wall paintings at Little Melton in Norfolk and Peakirk in Cambridgeshire. Another, dating from *c*.1500, is in a window at Old in Northamptonshire. The Stanford on Avon version, like those at Little Melton and Peakirk, has women as the protagonists. In the Stanford panel three ladies wearing various attire on their heads are beset on both sides by denizens of Hell. On the right is the upper part of a fierce monster in pale blue glass and on the left are the upper half of a green devil and the lower section of a ruby monster. There are several insertions and repairs, but the panel is still in its original medieval leading; however, its place in the apex of the north-east window in the chancel is not its original position. It is by the workshop responsible for the nave glazing at Stanford on Avon (see Cat. 562).   RM

562   Angel with gittern

c.1335–50
Stained glass: diam. 13.2 cm
The Yorkshire Museum, York

The roundel depicts a seated angel in robe and mantle, facing right and playing a gittern with a quill. The figure is reserved on white glass profusely decorated with yellow stain.

562

561

Such roundels became an increasingly common feature of English and French window design after the invention of yellow stain in the early years of the fourteenth century. They were often used with grisaille in both main and tracery light glazing, and occasionally decorated the gables of canopies. Grotesques and musicians were popular subjects, and stringed instruments such as the gittern (Cat. 521) were deemed appropriate for heavenly music. The artist

563

seems to have misunderstood the mechanics of the instrument, which has six pegs but only five strings. Although the drawing lacks control, the figure style and perspective design of the throne suggest an association with the workshop of Master Robert at York (Cat. 6, 563, 741). This and related workshops of the second quarter of the fourteenth century were responsible for a number of similar roundels in the north of England (French and O'Connor 1987, pp. 73–4).

DO'C

PROV. Not recorded.

563 The Annunciation

c. 1335–50
Stained glass: h. 101 cm, w. 93 cm
Inscr. *A(ve M)ar/ia [gracia]/ plena ⫶ domin(u)/s ⫶
tecum ⫶* (paint has been lost at the beginning and the third word is inserted)
The Dean and Chapter of York, nave window sxxxv.lb

This is one of a series of scattered panels depicting the Life of the Virgin, and the Infancy and Passion of Christ. They may have originated in the demolished Chapel of St Mary and the Holy Angels (St Sepulchre's) off the north-west end of the nave and under reconstruction from 1333. The Annunciation now forms part of a window created out of miscellaneous mid-fourteenth-century panels in 1951. The lower quarter of the panel is reconstructed, and alien inscriptions have been added at the top. All the coloured glass is inserted and the borders are modern.

Within an elaborate architectural setting with windows, corbels and crenellation in perspective, Gabriel holds a scroll and goes down on one knee before the Virgin. She stands against a diapered background, one hand raised, the other supported by a lectern and an open book with a text beginning *Domine veni*. At her ear is the dove, and at her feet a reconstructed lily pot. A ray of light descends towards her from God the Father who looks out of a window above.

White glass and yellow stain are exploited to the full, creating a grisaille effect similar to the east end of Gloucester or the Lady Chapel at Ely (Cat. 743). The delicate smear shading and tiny scratched-out ornament show great technical proficiency, and the style is typical of the French-inspired glazing produced by the Master Robert workshop (Cat. 6, 562, 741). Certain elements in the design and iconography derive from Ducciesque Trecento painting, probably transmitted to York by the intermediary of French manuscript illumination. There are close parallels with the Annunciation miniatures in the Hours of Jeanne d'Évreux and the Belleville Breviary, attributed to the Parisian illuminator Jean Pucelle and dated to the 1320s (cf. Cat. 569).

DO'C

LIT. Milner-White 1952; O'Connor & Haselock 1977, pp. 378–9, repr. pl. 128.

564 Retable with Crucifixion and (from left) Sts Dominic, Catherine, John the Baptist, Peter, Paul, Edmund, Margaret and Peter Martyr

c. 1335
Oil and stamped *pastiglia* decoration on oak:
h. 94 cm, w. 3.81 m
A Suffolk church

In this very high-quality painting – one of only a few English panel paintings surviving from the fourteenth century – the figures are disposed beneath a projecting arcade with carved foliage in the spandrels, and set against grounds lavishly decorated with repeated stamped *pastiglia* motifs, or with these motifs alternating with stencilled fleurs-de-lis. Although previously recognised as being closely related in style and technique (e.g. in employing identical background motifs) to a frontal in the Musée de Cluny (figs 131–2), Paris, it has recently been shown on the basis of construction, iconography and style that, in fact, the two panels originally belonged to the same altar (Norton, Park & Binski 1987). The left part of the frontal has been cut off, and on thematic and compositional grounds it has been demonstrated that the sequence of surviving subjects (Nativity, Death of the Virgin, Adoration of the Magi and St Anne Teaching the Virgin) would have begun with an Annunciation, balancing the Teaching scene at the opposite end. Thus reconstructed, the panels correspond not only in overall dimensions but also in vertical alignment, each frontal scene matching a pair of facing saints above and the central Death scene relating iconographically and in its shared gold ground (unique among the frontal scenes) to the Crucifixion above.

The inclusion of Sts Dominic and Peter Martyr indicates a Dominican provenance, most probably the priory at Thetford (Norfolk). This is not far from Stradbroke (Suffolk) where in 1778 the retable was in the possession of a family connected to the Howards, who had received part of the Thetford Priory

564

site after the Dissolution. The retable is similar both in format and in the positioning of the Dominican saints at the end to the only other two surviving Dominican retables from northern Europe: a thirteenth-century German example (Stuttgart 1977, no. 435), and a panel at Leeds (Kent), of *c.* 1400. The emphasis on the Virgin in the frontal iconography reflects the Dominicans' particular devotion to her.

Thetford Priory was founded in 1335, and such a dating is entirely consistent with the style and iconography of the panels. Although close stylistically to other work in East Anglia, such as the wall paintings at Brent Eleigh (Suffolk), of *c.* 1330–40, significant parallels are also provided by paintings elsewhere, e.g. wall paintings at South Newington (see fig. 98), and in a Book of Hours apparently illuminated for a Shropshire family (Cat. 152). The iconography is also typical of the period, when, for example, the subject of St Anne Teaching the Virgin was at the height of its popularity (Cat. 685). DP

PROV. Fox family, Rookery Farm Stradbroke (Suffolk); bt 1778 at sale of contents of farm (lot 171) by Sir John Major; discovered by Sir John's descendant, 1927.

LIT. Lillie 1933a, repr.; Lillie 1933b, repr.; Tristram 1955, pp. 41–2, 224–5, 257–9; Rickert 1965, p. 139, repr. pl. 144; Paris 1968, p. 184; Norwich 1973, p. 26, repr. ill. 32; Norton, Park & Binski 1987.

Fig. 131 Panel painting with scenes from the Life of the Virgin, *c.* 1335 (Paris, Musée National des Thermes et de l'Hotel de Cluny)

Fig. 132 The Adoration of the Magi and St Anne teaching the Virgin to read (detail of fig. 131) (Paris, Musée National des Thermes et de l'Hotel de Cluny)

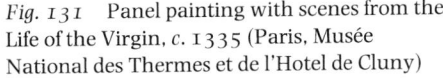

564 (detail)

449

565–6 The Ramsey Psalter

c. 1300–10

Parchment, ff. 173: approx. 26.8 × 19.5 cm

Benediktinerstift St Paul, St Paul im Lavanttal,
Austria, Cod. 58/1 (xxv/2, 19) and The
Pierpont Morgan Library, New York, M.302

The five folios of the Ramsey Psalter now in
New York were once ff. 6–10v. of the manuscript. The psalter bears abundant textual
and pictorial evidence of its Ramsey provenance: although the original Litany is lost, the
calendar has the dedication of the abbey
church and an obit of Abbot William of
Godmanchester (d. 1288). The manuscript
was apparently given to Abbot John of
Sawtry (1288–1316) by his cellarer William
of Grafham (appointed 1303), a gift recorded

pictorially in a medallion portrait of a
Benedictine inscribed 'May Grafham be
honoured' (St Paul, f. 16v.).

In addition to the miniatures relating
specifically to the history of Ramsey, the
manuscript also has a cycle of full-page
prefatory miniatures of Old and New Testament subjects (New York, ff. 1–4) and a
number of historiated initials of unusual
iconographic interest, such as Habakkuk
taken by an angel to feed the imprisoned
Daniel, for Psalm XCVII (St Paul, f. 105v.).

The artist of the Ramsey Psalter was one of
the masters of the East Anglian style who
also worked on the Peterborough Psalter,
another Benedictine book from the Fenlands.

LFS

566

PROV. John of Sawtry, Abbot of Ramsey, d. 1316;
Abbey of St Blasien, 15th century; removed to St
Paul im Lavanttal, 19th century; T. O. Weigelt,
19th century (New York leaves only); bt by
J.P. Morgan, 1907.

LIT. Sandler 1974, Bennett 1982, pp. 2–5;
Sinclair 1984, pp. 305–9, Sandler 1986, no. 41,
II, pp. 47–8, repr. I, figs 91–4.

567 The Peterborough Psalter

c. 1300–before 1318

Parchment, ff. 141: 30 × 19.5 cm

Bibliothèque Royale, Albert 1er, Brussels, MS
9961–62

In 1318 Geoffrey of Crowland, Benedictine
Abbot of Peterborough from 1299 to 1321,
gave, according to the chronicle of the abbey,
'a certain psalter written in gold and blue and

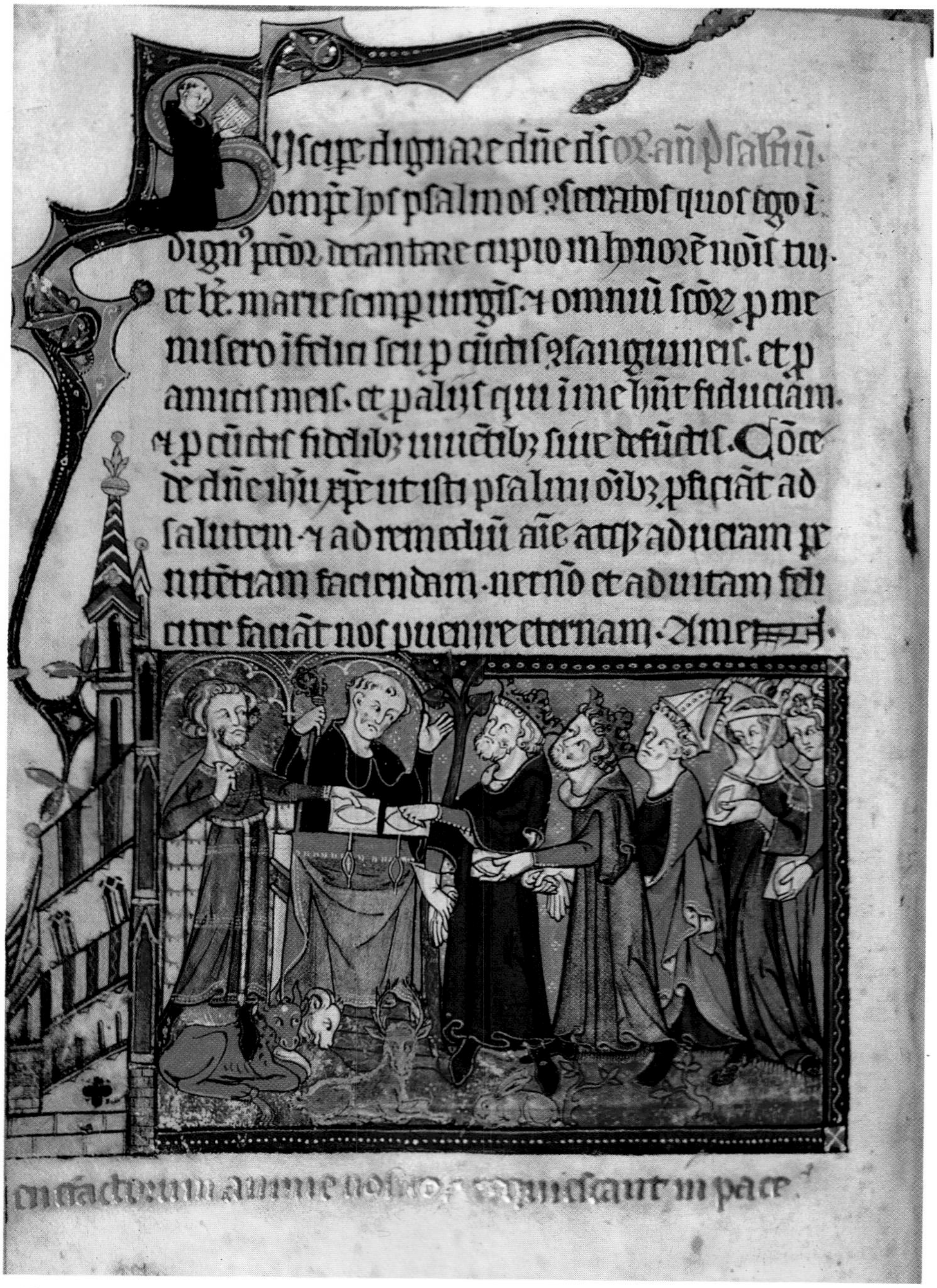

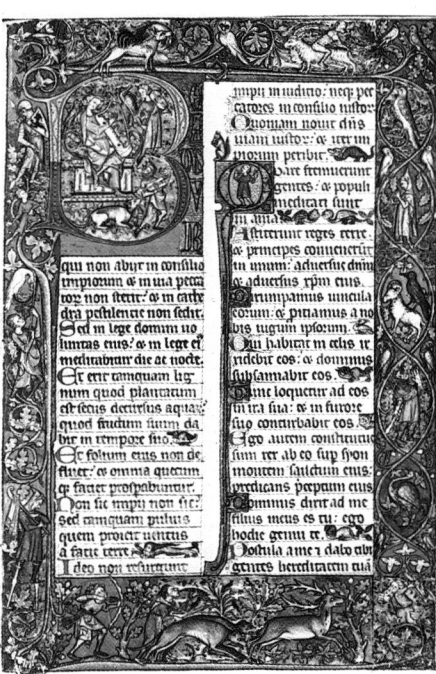

565

567

admirably illuminated' to Gaucelin d'Euse, papal nuncio and nephew of Pope John XXII. We know that this was the manuscript now in Brussels. Made expressly for Geoffrey, the psalter is one of the most lavishly illuminated books of the fourteenth century.

Not only is the text sumptuously written in alternating columns or pages of gold and blue, but the decorative programme is incomparably rich and varied. Distributed at each of the psalter text divisions is a series of 109 typological miniatures of Old and New Testament subjects, reflecting a now lost cycle painted in the thirteenth century on the backs of the choir stalls at Peterborough; in addition, historiated initials and full foliated borders complete with numerous marginal animals, human and hybrid figures and coats of arms (all altered) occur at each of the psalter divisions (fig. 14). The marginal scenes as well as additional framed vignettes often show chivalric subjects akin to those found in romances but representations of Benedictines are also frequent.

The decoration of the Peterborough Psalter was initiated by an artist who worked in the Court style of the end of the thirteenth century, as it is found in the Alphonso Psalter (Cat. 357) and the Mazarine Bible (Cat. 360), miniature in scale, accomplished in handling of shading, colour and gold, and rich in surface texture and detail, some of it remarkably true to life. The associates of this master completed most of the work in the style known as East Anglian, larger in scale and bolder in drawing. One of these artists illuminated a psalter of neighbouring Ramsey Abbey (Cat. 565–6), but where these Fenland masters worked is not certain.   LFS

PROV. Geoffrey of Crowland, 1299–1321: given to Gaucelin d'Euse, 1318; Pope John XXII. 1316–34; bt by Philip VI of France, c. 1328; Charles V of France, 1364–80; Philip the Good of Burgundy, 1419–67; Paris, Bibliothèque nationale, c. 1789; returned to Brussels after fall of Napoleon.

LIT. Brussels 1973, no. 61; Sandler 1974; Sandler 1986, no. 40, II, pp. 45–7, repr. I, figs 88–90.

568   The Tickhill Psalter

1303–14(?)
Parchment, ff. 154; 32.6 × 22.2 cm
The Spencer Collection, The New York Public
  Library, Astor, Lenox and Tilden Foundations,
  MS Spencer 26

According to a fifteenth-century inscription John Tickhill, Augustinian Prior of Worksop, Nottinghamshire, (appointed 1303), wrote and gilded this manuscript, but the gilding (probably referring to the *tituli* and first lines of the Psalms) and the programme of illustration were left unfinished, perhaps on account of Tickhill's removal from office in 1314. The projected decorative programme was extraordinary in design and thematic range, encompassing not only a full-page Tree of Jesse before the first Psalm (f. 5v.) but

568

nearly full-page historiated initials at each of the text divisions and *bas-de-page* illustrations on every page, all forming a continuous Old Testament cycle of 482 subjects from the lives of David and Solomon (progressively less finished and breaking off at f. 112). The lesser text decoration, although also unfinished, is composed of elaborate borders incorporating meticulously naturalistic as well as stylised foliage, hybrid and heraldic motifs.

The work of the chief artist of the Tickhill Psalter is most comparable to that of the chief artist of the Peterborough Psalter (Cat. 567). Although the Tickhill Psalter was written for monastic use in the Midlands (York Diocese),

the illumination is typical of the Court style. Indeed, the chief artist painted the psalter made for the wedding of Isabella and Edward II in 1308 (Munich, Bayerische Staatsbibliothek, MS Gall. 16), a manuscript that has York diocese liturgical features. He could have worked in the ambiance of the Court while it was in York in 1298–1305.   LFS

PROV. Worksop Priory, Notts., 14th–15th century; William, 3rd Marquess of Lothian, 1722–67; New York, Anderson Galleries (lot 7), bt by New York Public Library, 1932.

LIT. Egbert 1940; Sandler 1986, no. 26, II, pp. 32–3, repr. I, figs 56–8.

569   The De Lisle Psalter

c. 1310 and before 1339
Parchment, ff. 19: 33.8 × 22.5 cm
British Library, Arundel MS 83/II (ff. 117–35)

Traditionally and no doubt correctly called a psalter, the manuscript today consists only of a Sarum calendar and a series of twenty-three large miniatures comprising a narrative cycle of the Life of Christ and a group of theological diagrams and pictorial 'moralities'. The psalter text is lost and the surviving leaves are bound at the end of an unrelated contemporary book, the Howard Psalter (Arundel MS 83 pt I). An autograph calendar inscription of 1339 records the gift of the volume by Baron Robert de Lisle (d. 1344) to two daughters who were Gilbertine nuns at Chicksands Priory, adjacent to his manor at Campton, Bedfordshire.

More than any other manuscript of the first half of the fourteenth century, the De Lisle Psalter suggests the world of panel painting. The pictures are monumental in character and enclosed in architectural frames like those of altarpieces or like contemporary Decorated style church furniture. At the same time, the work of the chief artist is graceful, exquisitely nuanced and detailed with consummate skill in a manner representing the height of the Court style. This style is so close to that of the painter of the sedilia of *c.* 1308 in Westminster Abbey that it would be reasonable to suppose that the 2.4 m (8 ft) tall sedilia panels and the 30 cm (12 in) high miniatures were the work of the same individual – perhaps Master Thomas, the king's painter.

In the 1330s a second artist painted five miniatures on pages left blank by the first master of the De Lisle Psalter. He was an English follower of the Parisian illuminator, Jean Pucelle, who transformed Pucellian models by giving them a forceful monumentality.   LFS

PROV. Robert de Lisle, beq. to daughters Audere and Alborou, 1339; William Howard of Naworth, 1590; descended in the Howard family; given to the British Museum, 1831.
LIT. Sandler 1983; Sandler 1986, no. 38, II, pp. 43–5, repr. I, figs 84–5.

570   Book of Hours

1320(?)–4(?)
Parchment, ff. 135: 21 × 15.3 cm
Syndics of Cambridge University Library, MS Dd. 4.17

Although not by the hand of the master, the prefatory miniatures of this manuscript were certainly executed by an artist in the orbit of the painter of the Queen Mary Psalter (British Library, Royal MS 2 B VII; figs 6, 7, 112). The relatively precise dating of the Cambridge volume provides a valuable signpost in the morass of chronological problems in the Queen Mary group. The date can be determined by the inclusion of Thomas de Cantilupe (canonised 1320) among the Confessors in the Litany and the presence of the arms of Aymer de Valence, Earl of Pembroke (d. without heirs, 1324) on the opening page of the Hours of the Virgin (f. 19). Apparently the book belonged to Alice de Reymes, wife of Robert de Reydon of Wherstead, Suffolk. Her obit, with incomplete date MCCCX_, was added to the calendar and she was certainly dead by 1323. Reymes arms occur twice in the manuscript, once added to the garment of a woman praying before an archbishop-saint (f. 1v) and once original (f. 19).

The liturgical features are not very useful guides to the destination of the book. The Litany is long and eclectic and the calendar points toward Lincoln diocese in spite of the East Anglian origins of the owners. Perhaps to those who ordered devotional books these textual components – which would play little part in the private prayer of pious laypersons – were of slight concern. But the decoration is also heterogeneous, since the graceful miniatures in the Queen Mary style (cf. Cat. 109–10) precede the Hours text decorated in

569

570

571

(Cat. 570; fig. 25) even more closely. The goldsmith must have had access to patterns also available to the illuminators of these two early fourteenth-century manuscripts, produced either in the Peterborough region or in London. The pyx is the only surviving example of its kind in silver, and a unique demonstration of the close links between goldsmiths and painters at this date.

The Swinburne family are related to the same Alice de Reydon (d. after 1310) who appears as donor in the De Reydon Hours.

Gilbert de Reymes of Wherstead in Suffolk had two sons, the elder, Robert (d. 1295), whose son married Alice, and the younger, Hugh, who migrated to Northumberland in the 1280s and whose descendant Joan married William de Swinburne c. 1348. Although it is uncertain how the Swinburnes obtained the pyx, it may have come as an heirloom from the Suffolk branch of the family after Alice de Reydon's death (Oman 1950), and perhaps remained in use after the Reformation, since at least one of the Swinburnes was a recusant (Camm 1910, p. 116).

MLC

PROV. Mrs L. G. Swinburne, widow of the last of the Swinburnes of Capheaton, Northumberland; bt by V&A, 1950.

LIT. Oman 1950, pp. 337–41; Norwich 1973, no. 9.

572 Theological miscellany

c. 1310–25
Parchment, ff. 14; 21 × 13.3 cm
Oxford, Bodleian Library, MS Douce 79

The Douce fragment was once part of the Paris devotional miscellany (Cat. 110) illustrated by the artist of the Queen Mary Psalter. The incomplete Anglo-French text, resembling the *Golden Legend*, recounts the lives of Adam and Eve, King Solomon, the Passion of Christ, and the history of the Cross. It has numerous decorated initials whose graceful marginal extensions are tipped with foliage identical to that in the Paris fragment and other manuscripts painted by the Queen Mary Master. Preceding the text is a series of four full-page miniatures: Annunciation, Nativity, Assumption and Coronation of the Virgin (ff. 2–3v). While in the recognisable individual style of the Queen Mary Master, these miniatures differ in technique and

an East Anglian manner reminiscent of the Gorleston Psalter (Cat. 574).

LFS

PROV. Alice de Reydon, d. after 1310; Matilda or John Stranle, 14th century.

LIT. Oman 1950, pp. 337–41; Sandler 1986, no. 67, II, pp. 75–6, repr. I, figs 168–9, 171–2.

571 The Swinburne pyx

c. 1310–25
Silver, engraved, formerly enamelled, parcel-gilt: diam. 5.7 cm, d. 2.9 cm
The Board of Trustees of the Victoria and Albert Museum, London, M. 15–1950

A pyx (from Latin *pyxis*, box) was made to contain the consecrated Host; this one takes the form of a cylindrical box with a flat lid, fastened with a bayonet joint. All its engraved surfaces, inside and out, were originally covered in translucent enamel; only

minute fragments remain (black, blue, green, brown). Around the sides runs an arcade of six triple-cusped ogee arches, the area within each roughly scored, obliterating either simple drapery or more elaborate scenes. A gilt band of punched pellets decorates the base and the rim of the lid. Inside the box the sides are gilt (worn).

The lid (top) is engraved with a ground of stylised fur, as often shown lining the mantles of the nobility. Against this stand the Virgin and Child, the Virgin crowned, with flowers in her right hand; inside the lid is the Nativity. The base is engraved inside with the head of Christ with crossed halo within a sexfoil border; outside a similar frame encloses an *Agnus Dei*.

The depiction of the Virgin is very like one in the Peterborough Psalter (Cambridge, Corpus Christi College, MS 53); the Nativity resembles the related Cambridge University Library Book of Hours of Alice de Reydon

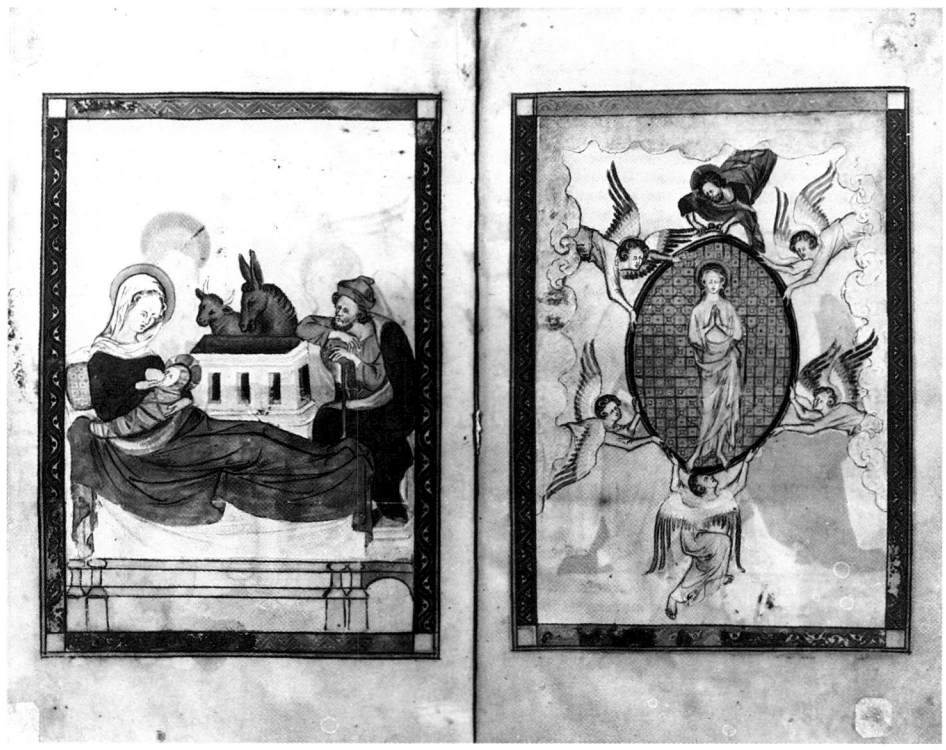

572

composition from his other representations of the same subjects: figures are placed at an angle to the picture plane, increasing the implication of pictorial depth; and some details are handled illusionistically, shaded without separate outlines. These features suggest a late stage in the career of the Queen Mary Master, perhaps around 1325 when similar 'Italianisms' occur sporadically elsewhere in English illumination (cf. the Gorleston Psalter Crucifixion, Cat. 574). LFS

PROV. Bound in Paris, 18th–19th century; Francis Douce, 1818; beq. to Bodleian Library, 1834.

LIT. Oxford 1984, no. 224, p. 157; Sandler 1986, no. 59, II, p.68, repr. I figs 146–7.

573 The Ormesby Psalter

c. 1250–60, *c.* 1310 & *c.* 1325
Parchment, ff. 213: 39.4 × 27.9 cm
Oxford, Bodleian Library, MS Douce 366

When the psalter was given to Norwich Cathedral Priory around 1325 by Robert of Ormesby, a Benedictine monk, it already had a long history. The text had been written and some of the decoration completed (ff. 10–21v. and parts of ff. 22–45v.) as early as the middle of the previous century; work was taken up again *c.* 1280 (text decoration of ff. 58–67v. and parts of ff. 70–81v.); the main historiated initial pages were done only between 1310–20, perhaps during a campaign in which patronage of the Foliot and Bardolf families played a part (especially f. 9v.); and finally, all the remaining decoration was completed at the time of the donation to Norwich. At this time also a Norwich

573

calendar and Litany were inserted in the book, some alterations in the latest Ducciesque style were made to the Beatus page, and the present binding was sewn round the volume.

The Ormesby Psalter provides a panorama of the stylistic development of East Anglian illumination, but nevertheless it is stamped with the strong personality of one master, who executed almost all the fully bordered pages at the text divisions. He was a brilliant inventor in the sphere of marginal illustration, mingling a wealth of interlace, foliate,

floral, human, animal, hybrid and fantastic motifs with figure compositions drawn from literary genres of the fabliau, the riddle, and the romance. The Ormesby Master was the painter of a number of surviving manuscripts that have Norwich diocese or Cathedral Priory connetions, including the Bromholm Psalter (Oxford, Bodleian Library, MS Ashmole 1523) and a *Moralia in Job* (Cambridge, Emmanuel College, MS 112), as well as the Dublin Apocalypse (Dublin, Trinity College, MS 64) of unknown Benedictine provenance.

LFS

PROV. Norwich Cathedral Priory, *c.* 1325; A. Gray, 1654; Francis Douce; beq. to Bodleian Library, 1834.

LIT. Cockerell & James 1926; Sandler 1985; Sandler 1986, no. 43, II, pp. 49–51, repr. frontispiece and figs 96–8.

574 The Gorleston Psalter

c. 1310–20 & *c.* 1325
Parchment, ff. 228: 37.4 × 23.5 cm
British Library, Add. MS 49622

The calendar of the psalter contains the feast of dedication of the parish church of St Andrew, Gorleston, Suffolk; hence the name of this, one of the most famous East Anglian manuscripts. The profuse illustrations include calendar roundels of signs of the zodiac, occupations of the months and busts of saints, a full-page Crucifixion patterned on a contemporary Siennese panel painting (f. 7, inserted *c.*1325), a Tree of Jesse Beatus initial within a broad frame incorporating heraldry of England and France and vignettes of the Infancy of Christ (f. 8), twelve great historiated initials with full foliated borders and marginal drolleries at the main divisions of the text, and innumerable smaller figured initials attached to vertical bars with foliated extensions and marginal drolleries. The marginal motifs represent every category of human activity, sometimes parodied by animals and hybrid creatures (figs 12, 16). Among the non-figural motifs are variegated foliage, flowers, berries, birds, and an extensive armorial, including royal, noble and county families as well as ecclesiastical foundations, in particular Westminster Abbey and Ely Cathedral Priory (Benedictine), Thetford Priory (Cluniac) and probably Gorleston itself. The inclusion of the arms of Gilbert Peche, the last of his line, suggests a date before his death in 1322. Expressing considerable reservation, Cockerell dated the Gorleston Psalter before 1306 on the basis of the occurrence of the arms of Roger Bigod, Earl of Norfolk, who died without heirs in that year. But since Bigod arms were adopted for use by the Bigod family foundation at Thetford, the date of the Psalter is not limited absolutely by the death of Roger.

The book was the product of a complex collaboration of five artists, one of whom was the painter of the Beatus page and almost all

574

ties, and of Christian, chivalric and folkloric narratives (figs 15, 88). But still more striking are the endlessly varied monstrous beings, humorous or nightmarish creatures all the more 'real' by being rendered with the same sophisticated techniques used for the representation of nature.

Although the Luttrell Psalter was made for use in the diocese of Lincoln (cf. figs 87–8), it is related in style to a number of manuscripts of East Anglian (Norwich diocese) destination, among them the Cluniac Psalter at Yale (Beinecke Rare Book and Manuscript Library, MS 417) and the Douai Psalter of 1322–5 (Douai, Bibliothèque municipale,

MS 171). Some work in the Luttrell Psalter (five artists participated in the project) resembles that in the Stowe Breviary (London, British Library, MS Stowe 12), another East Anglian manuscript of 1322–5. In addition, the leading artist of the Luttrell Psalter shared with the chief master of Douce 131, a psalter in the Bodleian (Cat. 683), possibly made for Edward III, the same Italianate technique of modelling forms with neither exterior nor interior outlines.

The Luttrell Psalter must have been executed before the death of Agnes Sutton in 1340, and Millar thought it had been made between 1335 and 1340, but the relation-

the figural components of the manuscript, and the others designers of the decorative ensembles in successive sections of the text. The figure painter is closely related to the artist of the Howard Psalter (London, British Library, MS Arundel 83, I) and the Longleat Breviary (Longleat House, Marquess of Bath, MS 10) of 1316–22.   LFS

PROV. Church of St Andrew, Gorleston, Suffolk ; Norwich Cathedral Priory, 14th century; Thomas Cornwallis, 1519–1604; Jane Neville and the Misses Cornwallis; descended in the Neville family; C.W. Dyson Perrins, 1904; beq. to British Museum, 1958.

LIT. Cockerell 1907; Sandler 1986, no. 50, II, pp. 56–8, repr. I, figs 115–22.

575 The Luttrell Psalter

c. 1325–35
Parchment, ff. 309: 35.4 × 24.4 cm
British Library, Add. MS 42130

The Luttrell Psalter takes its name from its original owner, Geoffrey Luttrell (1276–1345), Lord of Irnham, Lincolnshire, who is depicted in a miniature preceding Psalm CIX, together with his wife Agnes Sutton and daughter-in-law Beatrice Scrope, all clothed in heraldic garments (fig. 29).

Of all East Anglian Psalters, the Luttrell volume makes the boldest impression: the script is large, black and formal; line initials and line fillers are elaborately patterned; the margins of every page are filled with a profusion of figural and foliate motifs of iconographic range unusual even in this period of thematic inventiveness; the handling of colour is startling and the technique, especially of shading and rendering textures, reaches heights of virtuosity. There are hundreds of marginal images of daily activi-

575

ships to East Anglian works of the 1320s suggest a somewhat earlier date. LFS

PROV. Geoffrey Luttrell; Fitzalan family, Earls of Arundel, late 14th century; William Howard of Naworth, 1563–1640; Thomas Weld, Lulworth Castle, Dorset, late 18th century; Weld family until 1929; bt by British Museum with the assistance of J.P. Morgan, 1929.

LIT. Millar 1932; Grössinger 1975; Sandler 1986, no. 107, II, pp. 118–21, repr. I, figs 274–8, 280, 282.

576 Cope

Late 13th/early 14th century
Silver and silver-gilt thread and coloured silks in underside couching, split stitch and laid-and-couched work on linen: l. of front edge 323 cm. d. neck to hem 147 cm
Museo Civico Medievale, Bologna, Italy

The scenes in the lower row of arches, reading left to right, are: (1) the Annunciation (2) the Visitation, (3) the Nativity, (4) the Annunciation to the Shepherds, (5) the Flight into Egypt, (6) the Massacre of the Innocents, (7) the Presentation in the Temple, (8) the three Kings consulting Herod, (9) the Journey of the Kings, (10) the Adoration of the Kings, (11) the Dream of the Kings, (12) the Martyrdom of St Thomas of Canterbury. In the upper row of arches, from left to right, they are (13) the Entry into Jerusalem, (14) the Betrayal, (15) the Flagellation, (16) the Crucifixion, with the Virgin and St John, (17) the Resurrection, (18) the Harrowing of Hell, (19) Christ appearing to St Mary Magdalene.

This vestment may well be identical with a gold cope with figures, recorded at S. Domenico, Bologna, in 1390, as having belonged to Pope Benedict, i.e. Benedict XI, who was Pope from 1303 until his death in 1304. The figure style, with crisply-drawn heads and well-modelled draperies, is unusual in English embroidery, but is related to contemporary paintings at Westminster Abbey. Where the embroidery is worn, the underlying drawing is visible. The draughtsman designed various patterns to be worked in the gold background, but the embroiderers ignored this and made a plain background. DK

PROV. Church of S. Domenico, Bologna.

LIT. Christie 1938, no. 86, repr. pl. CXII, CXIII; King 1963, no. 53; Montefusco 1970.

576

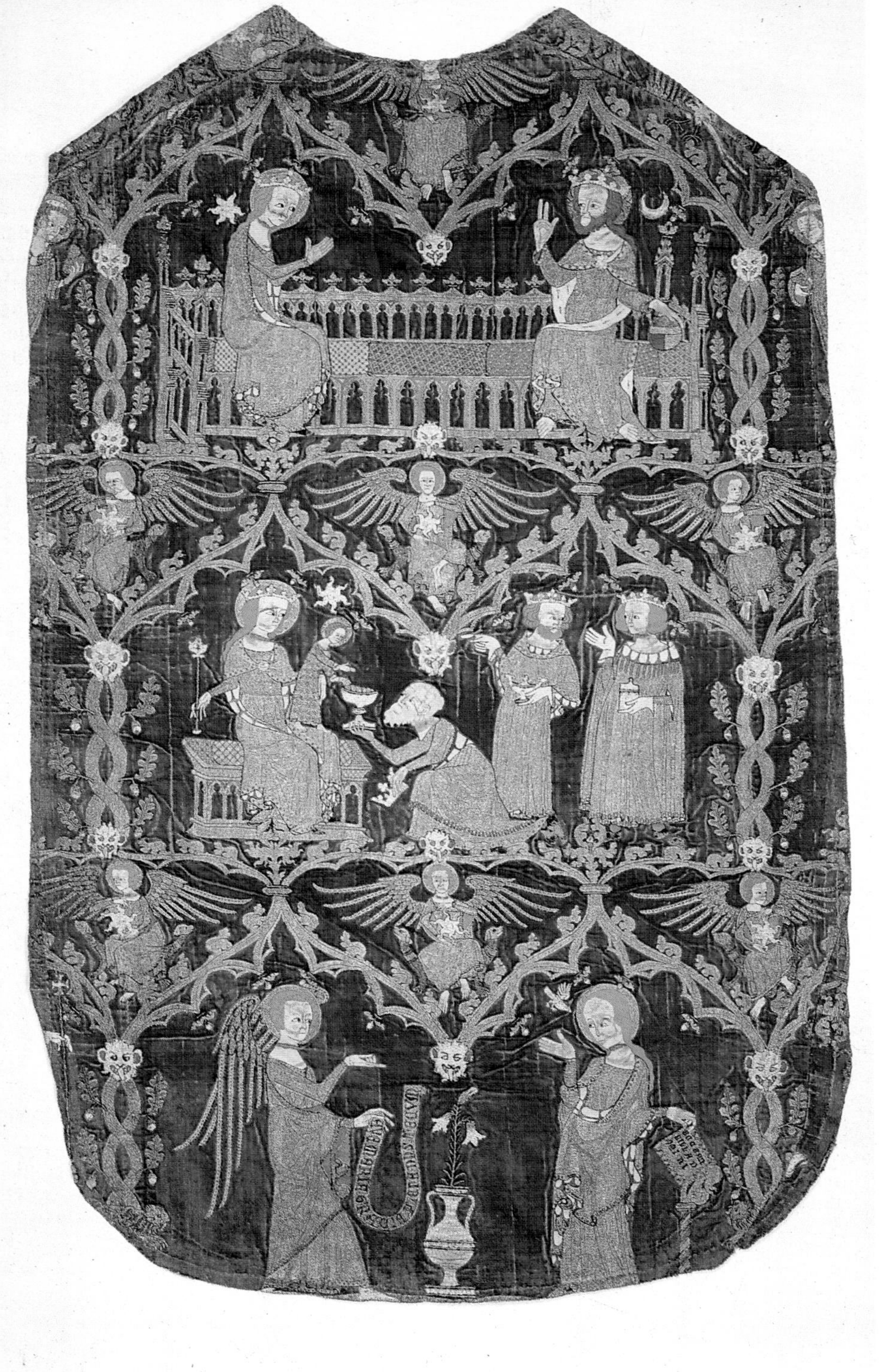

577

578 Cross-orphrey for a chasuble

First half 14th century
Silver and silver-gilt thread and coloured silks in
   underside couching, split stitch and couched
   work on linen: l. 109 cm., w. 44 cm
The Board of Trustees of the Victoria and Albert
   Museum, London, T. 31–1936

Reading upwards, the subjects are: the Flagellation; Christ carrying the Cross; Christ
crucified, with the Virgin and St John; Christ
in Judgement, with angels holding the instruments of the Passion; in the cross-arms,
St Peter and St Paul. In the spandrels of the
arches are shields of arms, Gules a lion
rampant argent crowned or, for Wokyndon.
Joan, widow of Sir Nicholas de Wokyndon,
founded a chantry at St Paul's Cathedral; her
will, dated 1322, is in the cathedral archives.
   DK

PROV. The Presbytery, Marnhull, Dorset; given to
the Victoria and Albert Museum by the National
Art-Collections Fund, 1936.

LIT. Christie 1938, no. 72, repr. pls XCI, XCII;
London 1963, no. 58.

578

577 Chasuble

Second quarter 14th century
Silver and silver-gilt thread and coloured silks in
   underside couching, split stitch, laid-and-
   couched work and raised work, with pearls, on
   velvet: h. 129.5 cm, w. 76.2 cm
New York, The Metropolitan Museum of Art,
   Fletcher Fund, 1927. 162.1

On the back, reading upwards, are: the
Annunciation (the archangel's scroll is in-
scribed AVE MARIA GRACIA PLENA DŇS
TECUM, the Virgin's book ECCE ANCILLA
DOMINI), the Adoration of the Kings, the
Virgin enthroned with Christ. On the front,
reading upwards, are: St Andrew with a
cross, St James with pilgrim's hat, staff and

wallet, St Peter with keys, St Paul with a
sword, and parts of St John the Evangelist
and St John the Baptist. Further figures of
saints were mutilated when the vestment
was reduced in size and the cuttings used to
make a stole and maniple.

   In iconography, composition and style, the
chasuble is very closely related to the Butler-
Bowden cope in the Victoria and Albert
Museum.   DK

PROV. Lieutenant-Colonel Raleigh Chichester-
Constable and his ancestors; possibly the 'antient
vestment' bequeathed in the will of Lady Margaret
Constable, 1599.

LIT. Christie 1938, no. 92, repr. pls CXXXI–
CXXXIV; London 1963, no. 78.

579

580

579 Part of an altar frontal

First half 14th century
Silver-gilt thread and coloured silks in underside
  couching split stitch and laid-and-couched
  work on linen: h. 51 cm, w. 60 cm
The Trustees of the British Museum, London,
  MLA 84, 6–6, 6

The surviving scenes are Christ's Charge to
Peter and the Betrayal. The presence of a
scourge at the right edge indicates that the
third scene was the Flagellation, which was
presumably followed by further Passion
subjects.

On the foliate capital between the two
extant scenes is an embroidered inscription,
MCCCXC ROMA. It is perfectly credible that
the embroidery was in Rome in 1390. The
scene of Christ's Charge to Peter, unique in
English medieval embroidery, suggests that
the work may have been commissioned for
papal use. A papal inventory taken at
Avignon in 1369 records 'a great altar
frontal of English work with scenes of the
Passion of Christ'. In 1403 the collection of
Jean, Duc de Berry, included 'a frontal of

English embroidery with a number of scenes
of the Passion of Christ within tabernacles
made like masonry'; this frontal had a border
of cloth of gold with applied coats of arms and
the restricted height of English altar frontals
like the present example is no doubt to be
explained by the use of such borders.   DK

PROV. Sir A. Wollaston Franks, who gave it to the
British Museum, 1884.

LIT. Christie 1938, no. 69, repr. pl. LXXXV;
London 1963, no. 56.

580 Pendant

Early 14th century
Gold, formerly enamelled: h. 2.2 cm
The Trustees of the British Museum, London,
  MLA 1959, 7–6, 1

This lozenge-shaped pendant is engraved for
translucent enamelling, but every trace of
enamel has been lost. On one side are the
Virgin and Child, and on the other the
Crucifixion with figures holding the sponge
and lance. On both sides the background is

scattered with six-petalled flowers. The engraving of the figures is of high quality and
the Crucifixion in particular has a strong
sense of movement. The figure of Christ is
similar to that in the Crucifixion in the centre
of the Beatus page from the Gorleston Psalter
(Cat. 574).   JC

PROV. Coll. R. & M. Norton.

LIT. Connoisseur, vol. 147, no. 591, Feb. 1961, p.
41; London 1976, p. 225 no. 372.

581 Pendant-case

English (?), c. 1325–40
Silver-gilt with translucent enamel: h. 5.1 cm,
  w. 5.3 cm
Inscr. in Lombardic letters AVE MARIA GRACIA
  PL[ENA]
The Board of Trustees of the Victoria and Albert
  Museum, London, 218–1874

The rectangular book-shaped case is topped
by a balustrade of openwork quatrefoils; the
vertical edges consist of miniature pinnacled
buttresses. Each side is inset with an enamelled plaque, surrounded by a border of
punched pellets. A lug is soldered to each side
and a loop attached to the top panel, which
slides to open. This panel is engraved with
trelliswork, formerly enamelled. The inscription fills both the narrow sides and is covered
with blue and yellow enamel. On the bottom
panel is engraved a reclining wodewose
enamelled in blue and green (damaged). On
one side a mounted knight, wearing a helm,
coat armour and riveted plate gauntlets,
gives his lance to a lady. Except for the heads
and hands, it is entirely enamelled in green,
blue, purple, yellow, dark and pale grey. On
the reverse a mounted knight in a similar
pose, differently coloured and wearing a
broad-brimmed hat, rides out of a twin-
turreted castle. He lances a wodewose, who
carries a club and heart-shaped shield.

The rarity of medieval secular enamels
makes the comparative neglect of this piece
all the stranger. The story seems to show, in
part, a scene from Sir Enyas and the Wodewose, a lost romance. The story was one

exemplifying ingratitude rewarded: a maiden, rescued from the embraces of a wild man by the elderly knight Enyas, spurns him for a younger one, and is ultimately eaten by lion. Two English manuscripts, the Taymouth Hours and the Smithfield Decretals (London, British Library), of c. 1325–40, show a number of episodes; French fourteenth-century ivory caskets depict only one, close in iconography but not style to this enamel (Husband 1980, no. 11). The only other piece probably depicting the romance is a fourteenth-century silver-mounted ivory horn in Maastricht (St-Servais Treasury). Louis, Duke of Anjou in 1364-5 owned cups and a basin depicting Enyas and the wodewose (ibid., no. 69). The other large plaque

581

may be unconnected with the Enyas story – perhaps from a legend attached to Gawain or Lancelot – but is associated with it as on the ivory caskets.

The case, now empty, possibly originally held an amulet; the lugs would allow it to be worn, perhaps suspended from the girdle. In style it does not resemble French enamels, but its English attribution, suggested first by Evans (1921), can only be tentative. The simple coiffure and dress of the woman, the style of armour and lettering, suggest a date no later than c. 1340.   MLC

PROV. John Webb, London; bt by V&A, 1874

LIT. Evans 1921, p. 35, pl. XI, no. 7; Chamot 1930, no. 28; London 1930, no. 820.

582 Diptych

English (?), c. 1325–50
Silver-gilt: h. 6 cm, w. 4.6 cm
The National Trust, Anglesey Abbey

Two frames linked vertically by loops and a pin hinge enclose two scenes: on the left is the Annunciation, on the right the Nativity, each in bas-relief under cusped trilobed arches against a ground hatched with a diagonal trellis pattern. The openwork relief components were probably cast separately

582

and soldered to the background panels, which slide into grooves in the backs of the frames. The backs of the panels are plain. The inner edges of the front of the frame are decorated with punched pellets; four rough holes, now functionless, pierce the inner frames.

Similar in purpose to its enamel and ivory counterparts (Cat. 583–4) the diptych is difficult to date or localise with certainty. It bears little stylistic resemblance to the other goldsmiths' work exhibited, and rather more to pieces thought Parisian, such as the Salzburg miniature altarpiece (Paris 1981, no. 199), or German, such as the Blumka diptych (Cleveland 1967, no. V–12). Both of these combine silver-gilt relief scenes with enamelled ones; enamels may likewise have decorated the back of the Anglesey diptych.
      MLC

PROV. Lord Fairhaven; beq. to National Trust, 1966.

583 Triptych

c. 1325–50
Silver-gilt with enamel: w. 11.2 cm, h. 6.5 cm
The Board of Trustees of the Victoria and Albert Museum, London, M. 545–1910

The triptych consists of three panels, enamelled on both sides in opaque red, black and turquoise, and translucent blue, green, yellow, and light grey, dark and speckled

brown. The panels slide into a frame, open at the bottom; heads and hands are reserved in the metal and gilt. The front shows (centre) the Resurrection; (left) the Mocking and Scourging of Christ; (right) the Descent from the Cross and Christ carrying the Cross. The back shows (centre) the Crucifixion: (left) the Holy Women at the Sepulchre, with the Harrowing of Hell below; (right) Christ appearing to Mary Magdalene and St Thomas.

The triptych has been wrongly reassembled: if the centre panel were reversed, the scenes would be chronologically coherent, reading anticlockwise, as often found on ivories. The range of colours and the detail of the scenes are exceptionally fine, the iconography of outstanding interest.

The crowded Crucifixion scene is unique among northern Gothic enamels in showing the more dramatic and realistic rendering favoured by artists from the thirteenth century onwards (Schiller 1972, II, pp. 151–4). To the left of the Cross the fainting Virgin is supported by the Holy Women, to the right the centurion stands amid soldiers. Although the Italians, notably Pisano (1286: ibid., fig. 507) and Duccio (1308–11: ibid., fig. 511) also explored this theme, it was known earlier in England (Cat. 108, f. 152). It is seen in the Queen Mary Psalter (ibid., fig. 514) as well as in the Jeanne d'Evreux Hours, Paris, 1326–7, by Jean Pucelle (Avril 1978, p. 16). A further iconographic rarity is the depiction of the Mocking of Christ, where Christ's head is shown shrouded as according to Luke XXII, 64, a rendering found, for example, by Jean le Noir 1372–5 in the Petites heures (Meiss 1967, I, fig. 108).

However, the figure style and subtle colours of the triptych are quite unlike anything found on enamels known to be French (cf. Paris 1982, nos 183–91, 199), or in French painting. The tree in the Noli me tangere scene and the fleshy acanthus spandrel-infills are again reminiscent of Italian art; such acanthus occurs also on a

583

459

fourteenth-century retable (Cat. 564). A more obviously English feature is the Resurrection scene, strongly reminiscent of Easter sepulchres (e.g. Cat. 493). The poses of the sleeping soldiers, are closely paralleled by those at Patrington (Sekules 1986, pl. xxvi d) of c. 1356. The scale armour worn by the soldiers is of a type found on the Stoke D'Abernon II brass (Cat. 236). Some of the cusped frames surrounding the scenes are paralleled in enamel by those on the King John cup (Cat. 541) and in illumination (less closely) by the St Omer Psalter of c. 1330–40 (Rickert 1965, pl. 133).

Hitherto randomly called French or English for no cogent reason, the triptych awaits a detailed study. Although so different from the Grandisson ivories (Cat. 593–6), the triptych, like them, bears rare witness to the influence of Italian art in England in the mid-fourteenth century.   MLC

PROV. George Salting: beq. to V&A, 1910.

LIT. London 1901, pl. v, fig. 2, pp. 135–6; Chamot 1930, no. 29; London 1930, no. 950; Gauthier 1972, no. 211, pp. 262–3; Campbell (forthcoming).

584 Diptych

c. 1335–45

Silver, enamelled, parcel-gilt: h. 4.1 cm, w. 6.3 cm; wt 1.85 troy oz
The Board of Trustees of the Victoria and Albert Museum, London, M.544–1910

The diptych consists of two panels, enamelled on both sides, set into a silver-gilt frame. The plaques are enamelled in translucent blue, green, yellow, lime green, grey, purple, brown and opaque red, some features (heads, hands) reserved in the metal. On the inside are (left) the Annunciation above the Adoration of the Magi; (right) the Crucifixion. Outside are (left) the Ascension above the Resurrection; (right) the Coronation of the Virgin above Sts Christopher and George. All scenes are framed by architectural canopies, two with prominent leopard's-head cusps. The diptych is notable for the range and brilliance of its colours.

The original function of such miniature enamels was devotional, like their ivory counterparts; their scenes were intended to inspire private meditation. A will of 1359 describes just such a piece as a *tabula*, 'accustomed to stand in my chapel on the altar' (Campbell 1980, p. 423 n. 16).

Since these pieces were often made to order, the iconography probably reflects individual choice. The presence of St George here may suggest an original male owner. His swaggering pose and armour are closely paralleled by that of his counterpart in stained glass in Wells Cathedral, c. 1330, and the figure of Sir Hugh Hastings, d. 1347 (Cat. 678) in brass.

St George is associated with St Christopher elsewhere in English art: in enamel (Cat. 587), glass in York (Rushforth 1936, pp. 216–17), and in a manuscript of c. 1380 (Oxford, Keble College, MS 47; Sandler 1986, no. 146, fig. 388). The depiction of the Crucifixion is very close to that on the Melton chalice (Cat. 112) of before 1340.   MLC

PROV. Spitzer Coll.; sold Paris 1893, lot 1786: bt by George Salting; beq. to V&A, 1910.

LIT. London 1897, no. 219; Chamot 1930, no. 31; London 1930, no. 826; Victoria and Albert Museum 1986a, p. 207.

585 Triptych

c. 1350–70

Gold and enamel: h. 7.1 cm, w. 8.1 cm; wt 2.8 troy oz
Inscr. *Eliabetha Vaux DD Rmo Claudio Aquavivae Societ Jesu Gener praep^to*
Campion Hall Oxford

A gold frame, open at the bottom, holds the four plaques enamelled on both sides in opaque red and black, and translucent blue, green, grey, brown, yellow and purple. The inside shows: (top) the Coronation of the Virgin; (centre) St Anne and the Virgin, the Visitation, John the Baptist; (lower row) St James of Compostella, St Edmund, St Giles; (left wing) St Christopher; (right wing) All Saints (?). The outside shows: (top) the Holy Trinity; (centre) the Circumcision, the Agony in the Garden, the Flagellation; (lower row) the Crowning with Thorns, the Crucifixion, the Resurrection; (left) the Annunciation; (right) the Adoration of the Magi. Heads and hands are reserved in the metal; a pink rose decorates each wing of the triptych.

This beautiful piece demonstrates the richness imparted to enamel colours by the use of gold. The particular choice of saints and scenes from the Life of Christ were probably selected by the person who commissioned it, perhaps someone named Edmund, as the most prominent figure is St Edmund, East Anglian king and martyr, dear to the English.

The cult of St Anne is found in England from the early fourteenth century, where she is depicted in most media before 1350, as well as on another enamel which may be English (Campbell 1980, p. 420, n. 19; Chamot 1930, no. 30). St James, patron of pilgrims, and in particular St Giles, patron of cripples and lepers, are less commonly found. There were hospitals dedicated to both in or near London, and to St Giles in Norwich (Campbell 1980, p. 420). It may be significant that an English thirteenth-century manuscript, perhaps from Oxford, the Cuerden Psalter (Cat. 355), includes on f. 9 the same selection of saints as the triptych. Scenes from the Life of Christ were an obvious choice for an altarpiece but the inclusion of the Circumcision is unique on an enamel, and rare in English art until the late fourteenth century (Campbell 1980, p. 420 n. 21). The closest iconographic parallel is in an English breviary of c. 1350 (Bodl. Laud Misc. 3 a, f. 49: Pächt & Alexander 1973, no. 642, pl. LXIV).

The figure style, with large feet and stiff beards, cannot be closely paralleled in any manuscript, although there are affinities with the Cambridge, Fitzwilliam Museum MS 48 (Sandler 1986, no. 130, figs 344–5) of 1350–60. It is a unique record for an English medieval goldsmith that four examples of his work should survive (Cat. 586, 587). Yet their style is unlike other English enamels, probably because they represent the work of a different generation. A curious technical feature is the use of opaque rather than translucent red enamel. Translucent red alone could be used to dramatic advantage on gold (but not on silver), as on the royal gold cup, c. 1380 (Paris 1981–2, no. 213, colour pl. 31). The technique of producing this sought-after colour was probably perfec-

584

585

586

fixion plaque alone measures about 3.75 cm high by 3 cm wide, which makes it, perhaps coincidentally, of precisely the right dimensions to have formed the missing centrepiece for the Cologne plaques. Unlike them, or the Campion Hall triptych, it is enamelled on one side only; if it was originally part of a triptych the reverse might have consisted of a relic.

MLC

PROV. J.P. Morgan; given to Metropolitan Museum of Art, 1917.

LIT. Campbell 1980, pp. 418–23.

587 Pair of plaques from a triptych

c. 1350–70
Gold and enamel: (i) h. 3.7 cm, w. 1.5 cm;
(ii) h. 3.7 cm, w. 1.4 cm
Cologne, Kunstgewerbe Museum der Stadt Köln, nos G. 998, 998 Cl.

On one plaque is the crowned figure of St Catherine, looking right, holding her emblems, the wheel and sword. On the reverse, also looking right, is the figure of St George, wearing a mixture of mail and plate armour with a pointed helm. The second plaque depicts St Catherine with dragon, looking left, and on the reverse St Christopher also facing left, bearing the Christ Child, his staff formed as a tree. Each figure stands under a

587

cusped ogee arch; heads, hands and feet are reserved in the metal, the enamel fields are surrounded by a broad gold border. The colours are translucent green, blue, yellow, grey, purple and opaque red.

All figures bear a striking similarity to those on the Campion Hall triptych (Cat. 585): that of St Christopher is almost a mirror image of his figure on the triptych, while the heads of Sts Margaret and Catherine resemble that of the Virgin, and that of St George the soldier's head visible in the Resurrection scene. The pairing of Sts George and Christopher parallels that on another diptych (Cat. 584), where it is discussed further; that of Sts Margaret and Catherine seems more

---

ted in Paris before *c.* 1330 (Campbell 1980, pp. 421–2); its absence on the triptych may suggest a provincial or technically unsophisticated goldsmith.

MLC

PROV. Elizabeth Vaux, acc. to tradition given to her by Mary Queen of Scots; given to Claudio Aquaviva by her acc. to inscription; listed as possession of Wittelsbachs, the Bavarian ruling house, 1617 (Geheimes Hausarchiv München 6/3 nr. 1588); there noted as gift of Aquaviva and former possession of Mary Queen of Scots; sold by Wittelsbachs to Paul Drey, Munich, *c.* 1933–9; Fritz Mannheimer, *c.* 1939; owned by Mr & Mrs J. Hunt after 1945; given by Mrs Engelhardt (formerly Mrs Mannheimer) to Father D'Arcy, SJ for Campion Hall, Oxford, 1952.

LIT. Enzler *et al.* 1876, 17, pls 19–20; London 1953, no. 234; Chicago 1970, no. 15; Gauthier 1972, no. 214; Campbell 1980, pp. 418–23; Munich 1980, vol. II/2, no. 335.

586 Pendant

c. 1350–70
Gold, silver-gilt and enamel: h. 4.2 cm, w. 3.5 cm
New York, The Metropolitan Museum of Art, Gift of J. Pierpont Morgan, 1917.190.916

On a gold plaque is engraved the Crucifixion, with the Virgin Mary and St John; faces and hands are reserved in the metal, otherwise the enamel colours used are translucent (green, blue, purple, brown, grey) and opaque (red, black). The plaque is held in a frame of silver-gilt on a chain.

The similarity in composition and palette between this and the same scene on the

Campion Hall triptych (Cat. 585) is striking, no less so than the similarity of the style and technique of the two pieces when compared with the Cologne plaques (Cat. 587). All are clearly products of the same goldsmith. It is likely that the frame of the Crucifixion pendant is not original; it lacks wear and is of silver-gilt rather than gold, by contrast with that of the Campion Hall triptych. The Cruci-

commonly found in England than elsewhere. In the fourteenth century it occurs, for example, in the Queen Mary Psalter (London, British Library; Warner 1912, p. 163), on a retable (Cat. 564) and on another enamel, a triptych of Anglo-Flemish origin (Chamot 1930, no. 30).

Each plaque is stamped on the border with two hallmarks: one now obliterated, and the eagle's-head (Chadour & Joppien 1985, I, repr. p. 588), the standard mark as used in Paris on gold from 1847 to the present (Carré 1971, p. 208). Ancient objects, like the Rouen treasure (Lightbown 1978c, nos 6, 7, 9), were frequently marked in the nineteenth century. Here the position of the marks may indicate that the plaques then already lacked their frame. MLC

PROV. Wilhem Clemens, 1910 or earlier; his gift to the Kunstgewerbemuseum, 1919–20.

LIT. Chadour & Joppien 1985, nos 416–17.

588 Figure of a Virtue (?)

c. 1350
Copper alloy, chased and gilt; h. 12 cm
The Board of Trustees of the Victoria and Albert
    Museum, London, M. 179–1926

The figure, partly hollow-cast, is that of a fashionably-dressed woman, in the act of plunging a sword into an unseen opponent. The end of the sword blade is smoothly broken off. The woman wears a cote-hardie with close-cut bodice and full skirts, the sleeves attenuating at the elbows into tippets; the long close-buttoned sleeves of an undergarment are visible.

The figure clearly formed part of a group (three attachment holes pierce it), perhaps a series of Virtues overcoming Vices. This was a popular theme in the Middle Ages, depictions being derived from the *Psychomachia* by the fifth-century writer Prudentius. Virtues and Vices are found in English twelfth- and thirteenth-century sculpture and metalwork (e.g. London 1984a, nos 282, 283) and wall painting, notably in the Painted Chamber at

588

Westminster (Cat. 331–2; Binski 1986, pp. 41–2), while a book of Virtues and Vices was bequeathed in 1399 by Eleanor, Duchess of Gloucester, to her son Humphrey (Nichols 1780, p. 181). It is not clear which of the Virtues the figure may be, though she stands in a posture often adopted by Humility overcoming Pride (Green 1968, p. 154). MLC

PROV. Dr W. L. Hildburgh; given by him to V&A, 1926.

LIT. Stone 1972, pp. 187–8.

XV Three Fourteenth-Century Patrons

John de Grandisson, Bishop of Exeter (1327–69)

The English Grandissons were a cadet branch of an important family in Savoy, whose principal residence was at Grandson on Lake Neuchâtel; Otto, the bishop's uncle, was a leading figure under Edward I and thereafter members of the family remained extremely influential, particularly in the west of England in the fourteenth century. Born in 1292, John de Grandisson devoted himself to learning early in his life: by 1306 he was already studying civil law, perhaps at Oxford, and within a few years theology at Paris. Success in the universities brought ecclesiastical preferment: the archdeaconry of Nottingham, and canonries of York, Wells and Lincoln.

He was consecrated Bishop of Exeter in 1327 at Avignon, where he had become a close friend and chaplain of Pope John XXII and an international diplomat. He returned to England to take up his bishopric in 1328. He was a firm and diligent bishop, devoting himself almost exclusively to his large diocese and rarely travelling outside it, except to attend Parliament or the Convocation of the Canterbury province. He wrote a Life of St Thomas Becket, a copy of which he presented to his cathedral library where it still survives; and he also compiled an *Ordinale* for the regulation of services within his diocese.

Grandisson must be credited substantially with the building of the nave and the west image screen of Exeter from the evidence of the surviving account rolls, though those for the years 1335–40 and 1354–69 are lost. He also refounded and built the great collegiate church at Ottery St Mary, Devon, in the years following 1337. His taste was cosmopolitan. This is clear both from descriptions in his will, for example of objects as bought in Paris or 'in the Roman manner', and from the surviving works of art which owe much to Italian sources. His ownership is established for these works by the presence of his coat of arms (Paly of six argent and azure on a bend gules a mitre between two eagles displayed). His will also contains an impressive list of precious textiles, goldsmiths' works, jewellery and manuscripts. Among the textiles were bequests to the king and Westminster Abbey: the Walters Art Gallery altar frontal (which could not be lent to the exhibition for conservation reasons) may be identifiable with that bequeathed to the Black Prince who in turn bequeathed it to Canterbury Cathedral (Randall 1974). Grandisson's ring (Cat. 638) is exhibited with a selection of ecclesiastical and secular jewellery. Grandisson was buried at Exeter in a chapel beside the west door within the screen façade.

589 Exeter Cathedral: nave looking east

c. 1318–*c.* 1350
Photograph

With its richly decorated stonework and its sumptuous fourteenth-century furnishings, Exeter Cathedral is the epitome of the Decorated style. Thanks to its surviving building accounts it is one of the best documented of English Gothic churches.

Construction of the new Gothic church began at the east end some time before 1279, and the choir was finished by 1310. The first bay of the nave was up by 1318–19, but work on the nave began in earnest only under Bishop Grandisson who saw its structural completion probably by 1350. The nave was designed by the long-serving master mason Thomas of Witney (active at Exeter *c.* 1313–*c.* 1342), who also designed the pulpitum (1317–25; fig. 51) and probably the wooden bishop's throne (Cat. 488) – another indication of the medieval mason's familiarity with carpentry. Thomas and his patrons obviously valued uniformity, for the nave closely follows the design of the choir; the main differences are confined to moulding profiles, roof bosses, and window tracery.

Exeter's interior takes to an extreme point the English Gothic preference for thick walls and lavish surface ornament: it has pillars of clustered Purbeck marble shafts, intricate arch mouldings, and tierceron vaults, copied from those in the nave at Lincoln (Cat. 240) or the choir of Old St Paul's, but increasing each bunch of ribs from seven to eleven. The windows, many of intersecting tracery inspired initially by London fashions, are also exceptionally elaborate. To give them greater prominence the clerestory is extended down into the elevation by replacing the traditional tall gallery openings (see Lincoln Cathedral nave and Angel Choir, Cat. 240, 321) with a low triforium passage, a format first used in French High Gothic cathedrals and a few years before Exeter in the choirs of St Albans Abbey and Chester Cathedral. Even so, the windows remain lost in the general effect of thick masonry, and it may be significant that Exeter's design was never copied in a great church, though its vault cones reappear in the chapter house at Wells (Cat. 328). PC

LIT. Bishop & Prideaux 1922; Jansen 1979; Erskine 1981; Erskine 1983.

590–2 Three rib-vault bosses

1335–40
Oak: diam. 49.5 cm
The Board of Trustees of the Victoria and Albert
Museum, London, 119, 123, 124–1865

These come from one of the first-floor chambers of the extension to the Bishop of Exeter's palace erected by Bishop Grandisson. The new apartments were added to the extreme west end of the existing complex of buildings, substantially the work of Bishop Brewer (1224–44). The conjectural plan is reproduced in Chanter 1932. The extension was demolished in the mid-nineteenth century.

It was recorded that one of the rooms was furnished with a floor of decorative tiles and an oak roof of 'ornamental cross beams'

590

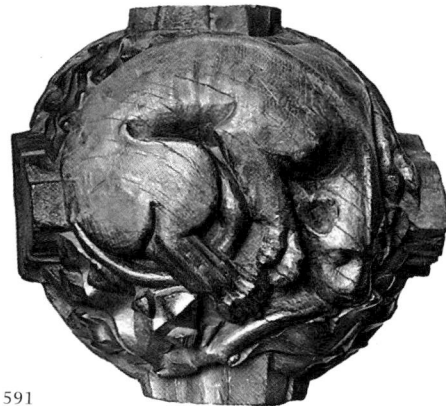

591

592

(Tucker 1846). In particular, the bosses of this roof were mentioned, one of which displayed the carving of a mitred bishop, wearing amice and chasuble. Another showed a female in a hood, and both were surrounded by foliage. Two adjoining cross beams carried the arms of Grandisson and Montacute on separate shields. It was suggested that the bosses were portraits of Bishop Grandisson and his mother, who was of the Montacute family. A third boss was mentioned in the form of a crouching hound (this is presumably the museum's lioness), and three other bosses of foliage only.

There is no documented date for the extension to the bishop's palace but, given the pattern of lacunae in the records (Erskine 1983), it seems likely that the building work was undertaken between 1335 and 1340. If so, the wooden roof would have been designed by the master mason, Thomas of Witney, in collaboration with the master carpenter. Although of considerably later date, the style of the bosses can be compared to the bishop's

589

throne in the cathedral (Cat. 488) and the stone roof bosses in the eastern bay of the nave.   CT

PROV. Bishop's Palace, Exeter; HM Office of Works; given to South Kensington Museum, 1865.

LIT. Tucker 1846; Chanter 1932, repr. facing p. 27; Erskine 1983, p. viii; Tracy 1987b, cat. 5–9.

593–6   The John de Grandisson ivories

c. 1330–40

Even if the heraldry did not guarantee that these ivories were made for Grandisson, their subject-matter would suggest Exeter: the cathedral high altar was dedicated to the Virgin Mary, with Sts Peter and Paul, and other altars to Sts Stephen, John the Evangelist, John the Baptist, Thomas Becket, and the Archangel Gabriel. Grandisson himself was instrumental in updating the Exeter calendar of saints (Orme 1986, pp. 22–3, 82–6), he wrote a life of Becket, and during his episcopacy the Coronation of the Virgin, the Crucifixion, the Annunciation, St Paul, St John the Baptist and St Thomas Becket were all carved on roof bosses at Exeter and Ottery St Mary. Stylistic comparison with the Exeter sculpture is more difficult: traditionally the ivories have been compared with the earliest figures of the west front's image screen, begun *c.* 1340, but they have none of the new dynamic intensity of the façade sculptures, belonging rather to a phase at Exeter when the nave was being constructed in the 1330s and similar corbels and bosses were carved (Prideaux & Holt Shafto 1910, repr. pp. 166, 197, 205). It is also to this decade that the foliage of Cat. 596 most obviously belongs, and the ogee-arches of Cat. 593–5 are most closely similar to the upper storey of the Exeter pulpitum and the arch into Bishop John's burial chapel of *c.* 1329. In spite of the much lower relief of Cat. 596, a single sculptor was probably responsible for all three works. He shows an intimate knowledge of near-contemporary Italian painting: the Virgin's resigned acceptance of her divine role at the Annunciation, the Crucifixion with the swooning Virgin and onlookers, and the axe at the root of the tree are all iconographic motifs found in Siennese art of the 1320s and 1330s; the Virgin *Eleousa* (of tenderness), Cat. 596, must be based on a group by Ambrogio Lorenzetti (Saxl & Wittkower 1969). Even the format, with a double register of standing figures in the wings, is more reminiscent of panel painting than of contemporary French ivories. But these Italianisms, absorbed perhaps from works of art in Bishop John's own possession, made no impact on this sculptor's style, which is wholly English. Above all, Grandisson's taste is reflected in his coat of arms: these beautiful ivories are unique within the whole corpus of European Gothic ivory carving in being decorated with a patron's coat of arms.   NS

LIT. Debruge-Duménil 1847, no. 164; Fould 1861, p. 96 no. 1689, pl. XXVI; Franks 1861; Musée Sauvageot 1861, p. 57 no. 226; Soltykoff 1861, no. 238; Molinier 1896, pp. 252–5 no. 122; Dalton 1909, pp. 88–91 nos 245–6, pls LIV–LV; Prior & Gardner 1912, pp. 357, 374–5; Koechlin 1924, I, pp. 118, 161–2; II, nos 209, 272A; III, pls L, LXXI; Dalton 1926; Longhurst 1926, pp. 44–7, nos LX–LXII, suppl. p. 47, repr. p. 171; Rose-Troup 1928; Evans 1949, pp. 49–51, pl. 31; Stone 1955, pp. 173–4, pl. 135; Paris 1968, no. 363; Saxl & Wittkower 1969, no. 33, pl. 11; Porter 1974, pp. 123–52, nos 49–51; Randall 1974; Gaborit-Chopin 1978, pp. 159, 210, no. 247; London 1978a, p. 23, no. 18.

593   Triptych

Elephant ivory: h. 23.8 cm, w. (overall) 20.2 cm; (central leaf) 10.2 cm, (each wing) 5 cm
The Trustees of the British Museum, London.
   MLA 61, 4–16, 1

This is in two registers, with figures and scenes framed by depressed ogee-headed ar-

ches with crockets and finials: on the central leaf are the Coronation of the Virgin and the Crucifixion; on the left wing St Peter and St Stephen; on the right wing St Paul and St Thomas Becket. The spandrels are studded with large rosettes and Grandisson's arms at bottom left and right.   NS

PROV. Coll. Debruge-Duménil, Paris, by 1847; Coll. Juste; Coll. Prince Soltykoff, by 1861; bt by British Museum from J. Webb, 1861.

594–5   Two leaves of a polyptych(?)

Elephant ivory: 594 h. 24 cm, w. 11.3 cm; 595 h. 24 cm, w. 11.5 cm
594 The Trustees of the British Museum, London, MLA 61, 4–16, 2; 595 Musée du Louvre, Paris, OA 105

Although of almost identical dimensions and therefore always considered a diptych, the two leaves can never have been hinged together, since the hinge holes on their inner edges do not correspond. They must, however, come from the same object. The framing elements are as on Cat. 593, with minor

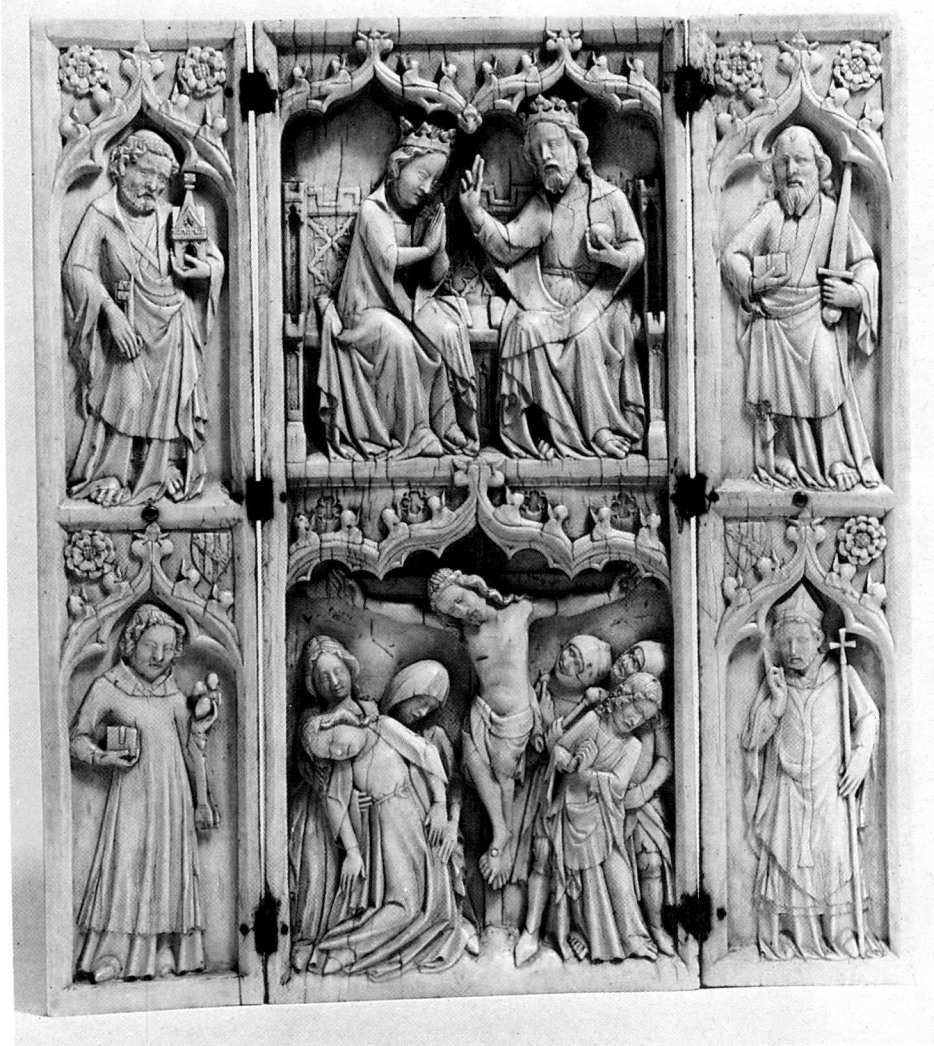

593

595

variants. The Grandisson arms, almost erased, are on Cat. 594 at bottom left; a shield with crudely carved cross, apparently a later addition, on Cat. 594. Cat. 595 shows the Annunciation, and St John the Baptist seated in a rocky landscape with two trees, one of which has an axe in its roots, echoing his saying: 'And now also the axe is laid unto the root of the trees' (*Matthew* III, 10; *Luke* III, 9). Cat. 595 depicts the Coronation of the Virgin, and St John the Evangelist accompanied by his eagle, writing his Gospel. NS

PROV. 594 Coll. Louis Fould, Paris, sold 1860; bt by British Museum from J. Webb, 1861. 595 Coll. Charles Sauvageot, Paris: given to Louvre by Sauvageot, 1856.

596 Triptych

Elephant ivory; central leaf broken on left; patina not original: h. 21 cm, w. (overall) 16.9 cm, (central leaf) 8.5 cm, (each wing) 4.2 cm
The Trustees of the British Museum, London.
  MLA 1926, 7–12, 1

This is cut in lower relief than Cat. 593–5 and with less elaborate ogee arches. The spandrels are decorated with tracery or stylised 'seaweed' foliage, the arms of John Grandisson on the central leaf at bottom right. On the central leaf are the Crucifixion (the mourning Virgin lost) and the Virgin and Child embracing, cheek to cheek; on the left wing are St Peter and St John the Baptist; on the right are St Paul and St Thomas Becket. NS

PROV. Bt by British Museum from Miss Seaborne of Southampton, 1926.

594

596

598 Orphreys for a chasuble

Mid- 14th century
Silver-gilt thread and coloured silks in underside
  couching and split stitch on linen: l. 109 cm,
  w. 23 cm; l. 91 cm, w. 23 cm
Private Collection

The orphreys depict half-length figures, On
the back orphrey, reading upwards, are: an

598

597 Aristotle, *Metaphysica* and *Metheora*

c. 1310
Parchment, ff. 168: 37.2 × 24.5 cm
Paris, Bibliothèque nationale, MS lat. 6299

Once in the Visconti Library in Pavia, at the
end of the fifteenth century the manuscript
was brought to France, but it was originally
intended for an English owner, since it
contains the arms of England and Grandisson (possibly John Grandisson, b. 1292,
Bishop of Exeter 1327–69), and its decoration was painted by an English artist.

The Paris Aristotle is a luxury copy of a
university text (Grandisson had studied theology in Paris), with historiated initials showing Aristotle lecturing on his work and
elaborate full or partial borders incorporating flowers, foliage, heraldic motifs, birds,
animals and hybrids. The precision of observation of natural details, and the humour,
are characteristically 'East Anglian', but
more specifically the manuscript belongs to a
group centred around the Vaux Psalter (London, Lambeth Palace Library, MS 233), including the work of one of the artists of the
Tickhill Psalter of 1303–14 (Cat. 568) as
well as the Grey-Fitzpayn Hours of *c.* 1300–8
(Cambridge, Fitzwilliam Museum, MS 242)
and the McClean Bible (Fitzwilliam Museum,
MS McClean 15).   LFS

PROV. Galeazzo II Visconti, d. 1378 (?); Visconti
Library, Pavia; Louis XII, King of France, 1499.

LIT. Sandler 1986, no. 33, II, pp. 38–9, repr. I,
figs 69–72; Avril & Stirnemann 1987, no. 176,
repr. pls LXIX–LXX.

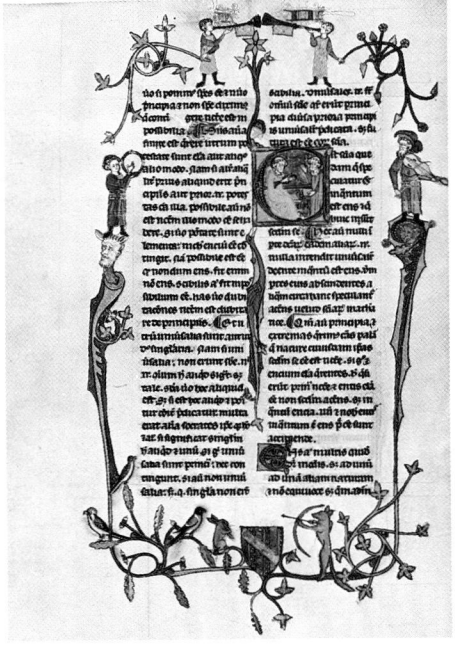

597

inverted fragment of St Mary Magdalene
with a jar of ointment, St Mary of Egypt with
three loaves, St Margaret with a cross, St
Catherine with a wheel and sword, the
Virgin and Child (originally with angels in
the cross-arms, now lost), Christ blessing. On
the front orphrey are: the shield of arms of
John Grandisson, Bishop of Exeter 1327–69,
St Andrew with a cross, St John the Baptist
with a lamb, St John the Evangelist writing,
St Paul with a sword.

The type of the Virgin and Child is markedly Italianate, as in the ivory triptych in the
British Museum (Cat. 596). Grandisson is
known to have owned Roman embroideries,
namely an altar cloth with the Crucifixion,
which he bequeathed to King Edward III,
and a frontlet with figures, which he
bequeathed to Westminster Abbey.   DK

LIT. London 1963, no. 89.

William of Wykeham, Bishop of Winchester (1367–1404)

William of Wykeham (1324–1404) inherited his name from his Hampshire birthplace (Wickham) and his great height from his father, John Long, a man of not impoverished free peasant status but a shade inferior to his wife, Sybil. As an able and pious schoolboy William was taken up by the local bishop, William Edington of Winchester. He took holy orders, but it was his obvious administrative talents which were increasingly borrowed by Edward III. He achieved fame through his work as overseer of the king's buildings, especially of the new constructions at Windsor Castle, 1356–61. His formal offices are only the outline of his standing: consecutively King's Secretary from 1361, Keeper of the Privy Seal from June 1363, Chancellor of the Realm from 1367. For all this he was amply rewarded, holding at least twenty-six Church preferments, many concurrently and all *in absentia*, between 1357 and 1366.

His succession in 1367 to his old patron Edington at Winchester (a see rivalled in wealth only by Milan in all Christendom) was resisted for a while by Pope Urban v for diplomatic reasons. Forced out of office on 24 March 1371 by parliamentary criticism of the failing war effort, his own integrity was not in question, and he in turn was willing to make sharp criticisms of the Court of the senile king in 1376. John of Gaunt, his erstwhile friend, recriminated bitterly and, for supposed misconduct in office, the bishop suffered internal exile and impoverishment from 17 November 1376 until 31 July 1377 when a clerical tax-strike and the accession of a new boy-king obliged the government to relent. Thereafter Wykeham played the respected elder statesman, close to the royal family (including Gaunt) but still on occasion a respectful but candid critic of Richard II's financial administration. On 4 May 1389, after the brutal political crisis of 1386–8, he was recalled as Chancellor to demonstrate to a suspicious country Richard II's good faith and intent on sound government. He was not really averse to his final dismissal as Chancellor on 27 September 1391 and remained in contact with councils and parliaments until his last two years. He could now give nearly all his time to his diocese and foundations.

Wykeham himself had had scant academic education – unusually little for a bishop by 1400 – but he had always provided for many young scholars in his household and at Oxford. His integrated foundations of New College, Oxford (26 November 1379), and Winchester College (20 October 1382) were of a scale hitherto undreamed of in English education, a model for Henry VI's Eton and King's College, Cambridge, as well as a deliberate monument to the bishop's wealth and influence. His close personal interest and supervision of his building projects is documented in the frequent meetings recorded with his architects, William Wynford and Henry Yevele, and the carpenter Hugh Herland, builder of Richard II's great hall at Westminster (Cat. 692).

By enjoining theology, not law, as the Fellows' principle study he resisted the fourteenth-century trend and pioneered that of the fifteenth: he championed the career he would have liked rather than the (vastly more lucrative) one he had followed, and by his provisions offered his protégés a vocation rather than wealth. They were to 'cure the general disease of the clerical army which we have observed to be grievously wounded owing to the fewness of the clergy, arising from pestilences, wars and other miseries of the world', and·be 'fruitful to the Church of God and to the king and to the realm'.

There was no self-effacement: the colleges must reflect his achievement to posterity and pray for the soul of himself, his patrons, family and friends. He himself was prominently represented in prayer to the Virgin on the college gateways (Cat. 602) and in stained glass (Cat. 612). Meanwhile, on 29 September 1394 he inaugurated the rebuilding of his cathedral's nave, largely at his own expense. It proved too great a task even for him to complete, though he was buried there in his chantry tomb after his death on 28 September 1404 (Cat. 601). Just one month before, with characteristic efficiency, he had sealed the contract with the cathedral convent for perpetual masses to be said there. To the end a superb administrator, but one with a sense of purpose and imagination, he had served God and his king with equal fidelity, the model of a medieval churchman that all men could (and nearly all did) admire.

599

599 New College, Oxford, chapel, cloister and bell tower, looking east

Chapel 1380–6, cloister and bell tower
  c. 1396–1400
Photograph

William of Wykeham, Bishop of Winchester, founded New College in 1379 and its 'feeder' school, Winchester College (Cat. 600), in 1382. Wykeham occupied the richest see in England, and so was well able to make handsome architectural provision for his foundations. No doubt the knowledge of building he gained in 1356–61 while clerk of works for Edward III's reconstruction of Windsor Castle proved invaluable when he became a patron himself; indeed the influence of the upper courtyard at Windsor can be traced in the planning of the main quadrangle of New College. Until comparatively recently Wykeham was thought to have been his own architect; hence his statue among those of great English artists on the front of the Royal Academy. Although the name of the architect of New College is not recorded, it is likely to have been William Wynford, the designer of Winchester College.

The inverted T-plan of the chapel was derived from Merton College where the nave had remained unbuilt, leaving the transepts to function as a vestibule to the liturgical choir in the eastern arm. The west front of New College chapel is much obscured by the cloister, an anomaly due to the fact that Wykeham had to acquire the land piecemeal; that for the cloister and bell tower was bought only in 1388–9. Perhaps the aim was to give parity with Winchester College, where a cloister was consecrated in 1395.

Both cloisters were primarily cemeteries. The bell tower doubles as an interval tower in the city wall. CW

LIT. Jackson-Stops 1979.

600 Winchester College, vault of chapel

Early 1390s
Photograph

At the time of its foundation by William of Wykeham in 1382, Winchester College was

600

probably the largest and best-endowed school in western Europe. The statutes in their final form of 1400 provided for seventy 'poor and needy scholars', sixteen choristers and no more than ten 'commoners', i.e. paying scholars from rich families. The first stone was laid in 1387, and the chapel was dedicated in 1395.

Timber imitations of Gothic stone vaulting had become an English speciality since the early thirteenth century. Responsibility for the design probably lay entirely with the master carpenter Hugh Herland, since its detailing is strongly reminiscent of the canopy of Edward III's tomb at Westminster (after 1386), which Herland would have designed in his capacity as chief carpenter of the royal works. The Winchester vault is a very effective solution to the problem of fitting fan vaults into rectangular bays. The horizontal ribs defining the upper limits of the conoids cannot be semicircular as at Gloucester (Cat. 499), and are therefore given an elongated, pointed form. The scarlet and white colour scheme was recreated in 1952 from original traces. Wykeham clearly had a high estimation of the men whose expertise he needed to realise his great project, for the glass of the east window contains figures of Herland, William Wynford the master mason, and Simon of Membury the clerk of works. CW

LIT. Harvey 1965, pp. 118–19; Harvey 1984, p. 138.

601 Winchester Cathedral, Chantry Chapel of Bishop William of Wykeham

1394–1403
Photograph

The reconstruction of the Romanesque nave of Winchester Cathedral was begun at the west end by Bishop William Edington, but was apparently abandoned at his death in 1366. William of Wykeham, bishop from 1367 to 1404, continued the work (to revised designs) from 1394, when the buildings of his foundations of New College, Oxford (Cat. 599) and Winchester College (Cat. 600) were virtually complete. The unusual site for his chantry, about half way along the south side of the nave, was chosen by Wykeham ostensibly because it was where he had been accustomed to pray as a boy, but it was also a very effective means of indicating that the nave was his personal achievement. Three times every day three monks recited Mass here. In the 1390s it was still a fairly recent innovation to make a stone enclosure surrounding both the tomb and an altar reserved exclusively for the founder's soul masses. The earliest extant example, Bishop Edington's chapel at the east end of the nave, was the model for the screenwork of Wykeham's chantry, but the tall triple arches above this are adapted from

601

well-established types of tomb canopy (Cat. 135, 326). The designer of both chantry and nave was William Wynford, whom Wykeham also employed at Winchester College. Wykeham's chantry set standards of display not surpassed until well into the fifteenth century. The genre of chantry chapel is an extreme and specifically English manifestation of late medieval spiritual privatisation achieved at the expense of the church interior as a communal space.   CW

602   Archangel of the Annunciation

c. 1393
Limestone, considerably weathered, hands lost and damage to head and draperies h. 1.67 m
The Warden and Scholars of Winchester College, on loan to Winchester City Museums

This statue of Gabriel, which comes from the north side of Middle Gate at Winchester College, must date between March 1387, when the foundation stone of the college was laid, and the formal entry into the buildings of March 1394. A date in 1393 seems likely, on the grounds that fittings were being installed that year. Just as William of Wynford's design for Winchester College depends on that of his earlier collegiate plan for Bishop William of Wykeham, New Col-

lege, Oxford, so does the conception of the two sculptural groups of the Annunciation and donor on Middle Gate depend on those at Oxford. The sculpture is clarified in a similar fashion to that of the architecture: whereas the New College Virgins are placed in a higher and architecturally emphasised niche, at Winchester all three niches are given equal weighting. The imagery is also of better quality, being much more fully three-dimensional, and the draperies possess a greater weightiness, volume and elegance. This must undermine the theory that John Sampson, who was probably the master sculptor at Oxford, was also the carver of the later figures. The suave pose of this angel, the elaborate cloak and spiralling coiffure are evident in spite of the considerable weathering. Still, for all its accomplishment, it hardly

602

prepares us for the magnificent *c.* 1395 image of the Virgin and Child on the outer gate of the college, which marks the highpoint of fourteenth-century sculpture in England.   PL

PROV. Winchester College.

LIT. Prior & Gardner 1912, p. 394; Chitty 1932; Harvey 1965, repr. pl. XXXVI, 2; Dow 1971. p. 33; Harvey 1982a, pp. 83–4.

603

603   Head of a queen

c. 1400
Limestone, considerable losses from bottom and sides of head: h. 22.5 cm, w. 26.5 cm, d. 21.5 cm
The Dean and Chapter of Winchester

Lawrence Stone first separated this and two other heads from Winchester (Cat. 604–5) from a large number of fragments assigned by T.D. Atkinson to the early fifteenth century. The three heads are evidently from internal statuary, as can be seen from their crispness of detail and by the fact that they are carved in the round (showing that they cannot be vaulting bosses or corbel sculptures). No fragment of the body of any of the images appears to survive. The dating of the three heads is extremely problematic. Stone rejected Atkinson's suggestion in favour of a later fifteenth-century date, and even argued that they might have come from the Great Screen. Such a late dating seems to be untenable on stylistic grounds, as this trio has nothing in common with the large quantity of extraordinarily realistic heads which almost certainly belonged to the screen. Their characteristics align them rather with early fourteenth-century models such as the alabaster effigy of Edward II at Gloucester Cathedral or the splendid queen's head from Cobham (Cat. 508) than with fifteenth-century sculpture. The highly stylised hair in wavy curls and the proportions and treatment of the head, however, are also found in late fourteenth-century models such as the gilt-bronze effigies of Richard II and Anne of Bohemia at Westminster Abbey, which show a rather conservative adherence to earlier models. This point and the fact that there is only one possible location for large-scale internal figure sculpture in Winchester Cathedral apart from the Great Screen, namely William of Wykeham's Chantry Chapel, suggest that they may have come from the image niches inside the latter, which was probably in course of construction *c.* 1399–1403. There are partial parallels for their style at Winchester in the nave corbel table, aisle vaulting bosses and in the corbel in the consistory court, though these works are all distinguished by an interest in physiognomic expression (see also the misericord sculptures at Winchester and New College; Cat. 539) which is not exhibited by the trio of detached heads. This is partly to be explained by the solemn, devotional nature of chantry chapel imagery, but it may also be because Bishop William of Wykeham ordered these sculptures from elsewhere, perhaps from London, as he had his alabaster effigy and the wooden rood-screen sculptures obtained for Winchester College in 1402.

The identity of the two queens is difficult to establish, although one or both might represent the Virgin or female royal saints such as St Catherine. PL

PROV. Winchester Cathedral.

LIT. Atkinson 1936, p. 165, repr. pl. LIII, fig. 5; Stone 1972, p. 226, p. 269 n. 61 (in n. 67, fig. 5 must be a misprint for fig. 3).

604

604 Head of a queen

c. 1400

Limestone, many breakages and damage to nose and hair: h. 34 cm, w. 24.5 cm, d. 23.5 cm

The Dean and Chapter of Winchester

That this head should be grouped together with another queen's head from Winchester Cathedral (Cat. 603) is clear from such similarities as the crown shape and beading decoration, the general proportions of the head and the handling of the hair which is centrally parted and swept back over the rim of the crown. The high, broad forehead, the

rounded eyebrows, the mouth and eye shape are also very similar. PL

PROV. Winchester Cathedral.

LIT. Atkinson 1936, p. 165, repr. pl. LIII, fig. 4; Stone 1972, pp. 226, p. 269 n. 61.

605 Head of Christ wearing the Crown of Thorns

c. 1400

Limestone, damage to forehead and nose: h. 32 cm, w. 27.5 cm, d. 25 cm

The Dean and Chapter of Winchester

This head shares many characteristics with the two queens' heads from Winchester (Cat.

605

603–4), the high forehead, eye shape and artificially stylised hair all being remarkably close. When Prior & Gardner first published this head they claimed that it had a treatment suggestive of a fourteenth-century date, 'though it may be quite late in the century', and compared it with the heads of kings on the Christchurch Priory reredos, a work of mid-century date and intimately linked to the sculptures of the west façade of Exeter Cathedral. Such a superficial comparison highlights the difficulty of adducing accurately dated material with which to compare *ex situ* fragments such as the Winchester heads. More interesting, perhaps, is the problem of envisaging to what kind of image this head originally belonged. All the niches inside William of Wykeham's Chantry Chapel are suited to standing rather than seated figures, though a seated image of the Risen Christ would be especially suitable for a chantry chapel, and can be paralleled in contemporary alabasters. PL

PROV. Winchester Cathedral.

LIT. Prior & Gardner 1912, p. 360, fig. 411; Atkinson 1936, p. 165, repr. pl. LIII, fig. 2; Stone 1972, pp. 226, 269 n. 61.

606

607

606–7 Mitre and case

Late 14th/early 15th century

Mitre, cloth-of-gold (mounted on modern backing) embroidered with pearls and trimmed with silver-gilt ornaments, imitation turquoises and pastes: 606 h. 26.5 cm, w. 29 cm, d. 10 cm; 607 h. 49 cm, w. 32 cm, d. 35 cm

The Warden and Fellows of New College, Oxford

William of Wykeham bequeathed the mitre to New College in his will, 24 July 1403. Its case is of sheet iron, covered with black leather stamped all over with small fleurs-de-lis and banded with iron hoops; lined with baize. Despite the protection afforded by the original leather case, the mitre fell to pieces in the course of the centuries and was reconstructed from fragments in 1929. DK

PROV. New College; beq. by Founder, Wykeham: will dated 24 July 1403.

LIT. Hope 1907.

608 Wykeham's crosier

c. 1367

Silver-gilt with enamel: l. 206 cm; diam. of crook 18.2 cm; h. of cast figures *c.* 2.5–5 cm

The Warden and Fellows of New College, Oxford

The crosier consists of three principal sections: shaft, the central architectural knop, and crosier head. The shaft is made up of three sections of tube, with a spike at the

608

bottom and three intermediate lobed bosses. Modern screws hold the tubes together. The whole shaft is decorated with bands of three panels, each stamped in relief with a lily stem. Each has been separately made and inserted into its frame; fragments of green and blue enamel (on alternating panels) indicate the original background.

The knop consists of four distinct parts. The lowest, immediately above the shaft, forms a sub-capital consisting of coving with projecting fleurons, and an abacus above, with a cast double rose attached to each face. From this rises a buttressed octagonal shaft, each side engraved. Above this is a cornice decorated with leaves supporting another shaft; the sides form triple-canopied niches, the backgrounds enamelled alternately in translucent green and blue. Each shelters a figure, cast and gilt: Christ with an orb, flanked by a veiled and nimbed kneeling woman, probably the Virgin, and a bearded nimbed man, probably John the Baptist (Hope 1907, p. 468); St Catherine crowned, trampling on Maximian; St Peter with key (partly broken); the Virgin holding an open book, crowned and with the Child; St John the Evangelist with cup; and St James of Compostella, with scallop shell. Above these niches rises a boldly-projecting cornice with clusters of foliage bosses as corbels which alternate with four standing angels. A balustrade of quatrefoils with battlemented edges rises above the coving, and from it a double tier of pinnacled and canopied niches, topped by another similar platform.

The niches are enamelled alternately blue and green and enclose twelve cast figures: Christ; the Virgin (both figures similar to but not identical with those below); St Peter with key; St Paul with sword and book; St Bartholomew with knife and book; an unidentifiable figure, emblem missing (St James [?]; Hope 1907, p. 469); St Andrew with cross; St Matthew with axe; two figures of St John the Baptist holding the Lamb; St Simon with saw and book; St John the Evangelist with cup (similar to figure below). The upper level of niches is similarly enamelled, but lacks figures; large blue enamelled finials embellish the pinnacles. Rising above the balustrading is a miniature six-sided house; from its roof the crosier head itself appears to spring. The six square-headed doorways to the house are obviously incomplete: only one now has a figure outside it, an angel musician.

The crosier head is crocketed, the crook apparently held up by a winged angel standing on a corbel formed as a bearded head. Ten plaques decorate each side of the crozier, enamelled in translucent green, blue, yellow, purple and brown, and show angels playing musical instruments. In the crook is a platform on which kneels a cast, bearded figure (similar to the figure of John the Baptist on the knop). Raised above him on a curved piece of metal is the Annunciation: a kneel-ing angel holding a scroll engraved in black letter *ave ma[ria]* and the Virgin.

This imposing piece, bequeathed by Wykeham to the college he founded, is the only remaining treasure which was incontrovertibly his (Lowth 1759, appendix, p. xxxix). The general form of the crosier is one produced in metal throughout Gothic Europe: fourteenth-century examples survive in Cologne, Haarlem (Paris 1982, nos 478–9), Spain (Valdovinos 1984, no. 2), and Italy (Sienna 1982, nos 70–1). Only two others survive from Britain – the Limerick crosier made in Ireland in 1416, and Bishop Fox's crosier of *c.* 1501, at Corpus Christi College, Oxford (Wilson 1980–1, pp. 8–27).

The history of repairs carried out on the crosier in the past has still to be unravelled; aspects of the piece remain puzzling. The presence of many duplicate figures: John the Baptist, the Virgin Mary, Peter, Paul, John the Evangelist, Christ, suggests that some are not original. The original scheme may have included the twelve Apostles in the niches (only eight are there now); some of the duplicated figures may be after-casts (Hope 1907). The present scene in the crook dates from before 1815 (cf. dated drawing Oxford, Bodleian Library, MS Top. Oxon d. 340, no. 356) but after 1785 (Carter engraving 1786), perhaps from 1810–15 (Hollis engraving of 1815: Bodleian Library, MS Top. Oxon a. 36 f. 24). The crosier certainly received attention in 1753: in March it was recorded as 'in many pieces' (New College archives, no. 3509 f. 169); in November a goldsmith, Wilkins, was paid £1.18s.0d for repairs (ibid. no. 4293). The Annunciation group may originally have been attached to the miniature house below the crosier head. The bearded figure of St John (mistaken for Wykeham by early writers) appears in the crook in the Carter engraving of 1786, but it seems reasonable to doubt whether the figure is either original, or in its original position. The proportions seem unduly small for the space. Moreover, Wykeham as Bishop of Winchester would more plausibly carry a crosier decorated with one of the patron saints of the Cathedral – St Peter and St Paul – as did Fox for example, or else decorated with an image venerated by himself. He is not recorded as having a particular devotion to John the Baptist, while his veneration for the Virgin Mary is celebrated – both Winchester and New College were dedicated to her. Hope suggested, on grounds of architectural style, that Wykeham might have inherited the crosier from his predecessor, William Edington – unlikely, since Edington's detailed will omits mention of it (Wood 1956, pp. 318–24). The double roses adorning the lower knop – apparently original – may be significant. Wykeham's arms included roses and he bequeathed silver bowls to the king decorated with double roses (Lowth 1759, appendix, p. xxxviii). It is possible that one of the figures of the Virgin, now in the knop, stood originally in the crook.

Although the crosier has occasionally been called Italian (Chamot 1930, no. 35) its battlemented cornices are distinctively English in style (Bony 1979, p. 21, pl. 120). Both the octagonal cross-section of the shaft and the cornice are exact parallels of the Waltham Cross (cf. Cat. 373) begun in 1291; another of the Eleanor crosses was at Cheapside just by the London goldsmiths' quarter, and it may possibly have served as a model (Hope 1907, p. 472; Cat. 375–6). But at what date? Although goldsmiths undoubtedly reused old models, such a crosier would have been an expensive commission, looking somewhat old-fashioned in 1367, the date Wykeham became bishop.

The stiffly-posed small figures seem closest in style to those on the wine-fountain fragment of c. 1350 in the Museum Mayer van den Bergh, Antwerp (Cleveland 1967, p. 250), while they are in type finer versions of the figures on the St George reliquary-casket (Cat. 88). The enamels are probably c. 1330.

It may seem less likely that the bishop of the richest see in England should have commissioned such a piece, than that he should have inherited it from his predecessor Edington, consecrated in 1346. Wykeham's contemporary, Grandisson, Bishop of Exeter, in 1369 bequeathed his best crosier of silver-gilt and enamel to his successors in office (Oliver 1861, p. 447). But conservatism of design caused by the use of old moulds is witnessed far more strikingly in the crosier of another Bishop of Winchester, that of Fox of c. 1501. Not even the richest of patrons cared always to be up-to-the-minute.   MLC

PROV. New College; beq. by Founder, Wykeham: will dated 24 July 1403.

LIT. Lowth 1759, appendix, p. xxxix; Carter 1786, I, p. 47, repr.; Manchester 1857, pp. 14, 148; London 1862, no. 3212; Moffat 1906, p. 60, pl. xxx; Hope 1907, pp. 465–72; Chamot 1930, no. 35; Oman 1979, pp. 293–4.

609   Girdle

c. 1350–1400
Silver-gilt, set with crystals, pearls, green and
   white glass, and enamels; total l. 130 cm;
   plaques h. approx. 8 mm, w. approx. 8 mm
The Warden and Fellows of New College, Oxford

Although many elements are missing and the whole is broken up into sections, the original design seems clear. This was based on the alternation of three types of plaque: (a) set with a green and white paste, (b) set with a crystal encircled by eight pearls, and (c) set with an enamel. The latter now number seventeen, their subjects in different poses, consisting of monkeys (3), hares (10), a dog (?) (1), a deer (1), monkeys blowing horns (2). The enamels used are translucent: green, blue, purple and yellow. The plaques

609

are linked by double hinges and may have been attached to a silk or leather backing.

It seems probable that the ensemble formed part of a girdle, as first suggested by Oman (in Evans 1970, p. 61), followed by Chamot (1930). Certainly it cannot be part of the Wykeham 'mitre' as thought by Way (1845), followed by Hope (1907), and there is no evidence, other than tradition, to link it with Wykeham. The girdle was detached from the mitre in 1929.

The enamel motifs have a general resemblance to contemporary manuscript marginalia, also to the enamels on the French table foundation at Cleveland (Paris 1981–2, no. 191), and closely resemble the plaques from the Victoria and Albert Museum (Cat. 610). Although several fourteenth-century European girdles survive (Fingerlin 1971, pp. 14, 66, 335, 419, 465) none exactly resembles this in its wholly hinged construction. Girdles were an essential part of dress, worn by both sexes at this date.   MLC

PROV. Not known; New College.

LIT. Way 1845c, pp. 205–6; Hope 1907, pp. 473–7; Chamot 1930, no. 26; London 1953, no. 5.

610   Four plaques

c. 1350
Silver, enamelled, parcel-gilt: h. 9 mm, w. 9 mm
The Board of Trustees of the Victoria and Albert
   Museum, London, 229m to 229p–1874

610

Each plaque depicts a sprig of oak and animals: (hare, fox [?], seated dog [?], and running dog [?]). The enamel colours are randomly applied irrespective of the composition. The plaques were originally enamelled all over in translucent green, yellow, purple and blue. The enamel is crazed and damaged; all the plaques have been slightly repaired. The borders are gilt, much worn. A short silver tang, soldered to the backs of two plaques, was the means of securing them.

Such enamels were probably made in large numbers to embellish girdles, book covers etc. Although these have been considered, on grounds of subject and size, to belong with 'Wykeham's girdle' (Cat. 609), there is no evidence for this.   MLC

PROV. John Webb; bt by V&A, 1874.

LIT. London 1874 no. 815; Chamot 1930, no. 27; London 1930, no. 821.

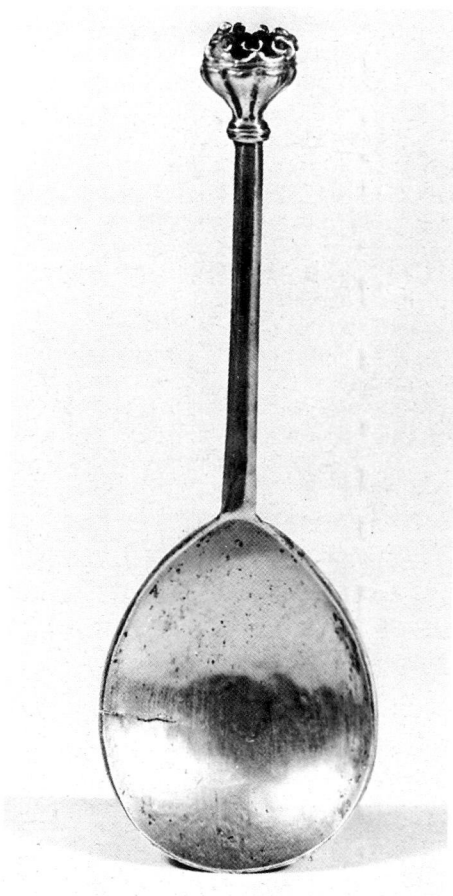

611

611   The Founder's spoon

c. 1400

Silver-gilt, unmarked: l. 16.5 cm

The Warden and Scholars of Winchester College

The fig-shaped bowl is slightly cracked; the hexagonal stem is topped by a finial composed of a coronet of fleurs-de-lis, bent inwards probably to hold a jewel, now lost. The shape of the spoon resembles the Whittington ones (Cat. 216).

It has traditionally been called the Founder's spoon at Winchester College, founded by Wykeham in 1382, although the earliest reference to it as such occurs only in 1672–3, when 6s.6d was spent in gilding and mending 'the ancient spoon called the Founder's' (College Bursar's accounts). There is, however, no reason why the tradition should not be true, and although no spoons were among the plate (a silver-gilt cup and cover, and a ewer) that Wykeham bequeathed to his college (Lowth 1759, p. xl), he may have given it before his death, as he did the basins enamelled with his arms, listed in a sixteenth-century college inventory (Gunner 1853, p. 235), which also includes spoons set with pearls and balas rubies.   MLC

PROV. Winchester College since at least 1672–3.

LIT. How 1952, I, p. 352; Oman 1962b, pp. 24–5.

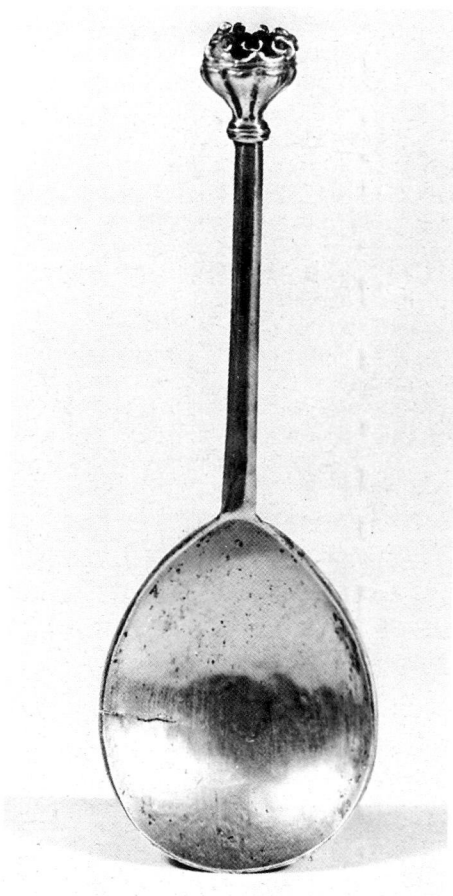

612

612   William of Wykeham and the Virgin and Child

c. 1393

Stained glass: h. 103 cm, w. 65.2 cm

The Warden and Scholars of Winchester College

The glazing of the chapel in William of Wykeham's foundation of Winchester College was in progress in 1393, when glass was taken from Oxford to Winchester. It appears to have been completed before the windows were repaired in 1396–7. The glass-painter was Thomas of Oxford, who also glazed the chapel of New College, Oxford (fig. 110),

another Wykeham foundation, and very probably the nave clerestory of Winchester Cathedral, which was carried out after Wykeham's death in 1404 and financed by a bequest of 500 marks in his will. Thomas Glazier was originally depicted below a Tree of Jesse in the east window of Winchester College chapel, in company with two other craftsmen, the clerk of works, Edward III, Richard II and William of Wykeham (twice). Much of this glass has been lost since its removal in 1821 and replacement by copies made by the firm of Betton and Evans. The majority of the surviving figures from the

Jesse, together with the votive panels depicting Richard II (Cat. 613) and William of Wykeham, were returned to the College and in 1951 were re-set in the west window of Thurbern's Chantry in the chapel. Seven more figures from the Jesse are in the east window of Fromond's Chantry.

Wykeham is shown kneeling before the Virgin and Child in an architectural framework and against a ruby 'seaweed' diapered ground. The bishop is mitred, wears a green chasuble over a white alb and holds a crosier. The enthroned Virgin is clad in a light-brown mantle; the child Jesus on her lap is robed in white. The faces, hair, haloes and architectectural details are in white glass with yellow stain touches. Wykeham's head is modern and his hands are from the second votive panel in which he was represented; other fragments from the side windows of the chapel have been used to patch the throne and part of Wykeham's figure. The centre of the Infant Jesus's body and parts of the Virgin's hands are fifteenth-century repairs. William of Wykeham was greatly devoted to the Virgin and dedicated both Winchester and New Colleges to her. This panel, with its sensitive modelling of faces and heavy swathes of drapery, is in the International Gothic style, of which Thomas Glazier of Oxford was one of the first exponents in England.   RM

LIT. Le Couteur 1920, pp. 62–98; Harvey & King 1971, *passim*.

613   King Richard II and St John the Baptist

c. 1393
Stained glass: h. 103 cm, w. 65.5 cm
Inscr. in black letter RIC(ARD' S)E(CUNDUS) REX ANGLI(E ET) FRANCI(E)
The Warden and Scholars of Winchester College

Richard II kneels before St John within an architectural framework and set against a blue ground diapered with a 'seaweed' pattern. The king wears a purple mantle lined with ermine, an ermine tippet and green robe. In common with his portrait in the Wilton Diptych, Richard is shown clean-shaven, whereas his tomb effigy and portrait in Westminster Abbey depict him with two small tufts of beard. St John the Baptist is clad in ruby robes over a camel-skin garment to which the beast's skull is still attached, an iconographical detail found on a number of representations of the saint in English glass. Richard II succeeded to the throne on the eve of the Vigil of St John the Baptist, who remained his patron saint. St John appears on the Wilton Diptych and is referred to in the inscription on the king's tomb (Wormald 1954, p. 200). In common with the panel depicting William of Wykeham and the Virgin (Cat. 612) this glass was painted in *c.* 1393 by Thomas Glazier of Oxford for the east window of Winchester College chapel. It

613

is now in the west window of Thurbern's Chantry in the chapel.   RM

LIT. Le Couteur 1920, pp. 80–1; Harvey & King 1971, *passim*.

Edward of Woodstock, the Black Prince (1330–76)

Edward, the eldest son of Edward III and Philippa of Hainault, was born at Woodstock in 1330. He was made Earl of Chester in 1333, Duke of Cornwall in 1337 and Prince of Wales in 1343. In 1361 he married Countess Joan, 'the fair maid of Kent', a marriage which according to Froissart was a love match; and in the following year the king granted his son all his dominions in southern France and the title of Prince of Aquitaine. Edward of Woodstock became known as the Black Prince probably because of his black armour. His glorious achievements in battle brought him fame as the oustanding figure of chivalric society. When only sixteen he played a prominent part in his father's campaign of 1346, commanding the right wing of the English forces at Crécy, and he was at the Siege of Calais in 1347. In 1355 he led an English army to Gascony, moving at first south as far as Narbonne, and then in 1356 as far as the Loire. In September he was confronted by the army of King John of France, and the hard-fought battle of Poitiers showed the superior military capacity and tactical skills of the English forces and their commander. The capture of King John, who was treated with ostentatious magnanimity and brought to London by sea from Bordeaux, was a high-point in the career of the Black Prince. In 1363 the Black Prince and his wife moved to Gascony and established their Court at Bordeaux and Angoulême. It was at Bordeaux in 1367 that his second son, the future Richard II, was born. Although his relations with the Gascon nobles were tense, the Black Prince kept peace in his principality for six years, and in 1367 he led an army into Spain over the Roncesvalles pass in support of the deposed King of Castile. In the last of the great victories which brought him renown he defeated Bertrand du Guesclin at Najera.

By 1369 the prince faced revolt in the whole of Aquitaine, and after capturing Limoges in the following year he was merciless in his slaughter of the people of the city. In declining health he returned to England in 1371 and soon abandoned military activities, resigning the principality of Aquitaine to the care of his brother, John of Gaunt, Duke of Lancaster. He died in the summer of 1376 and was buried in the east end of Canterbury Cathedral. His splendid tomb, erected in accordance with the detailed instructions of his will, shows on the tester the Trinity, to whom he was especially devoted (cf. Cat. 624, 625). His bequests included church plate, a jewelled reliquary of the True Cross, vestments and manuscripts to the cathedral, to his own religious foundation at Ashridge, and to the chapel of his castle at Wallingford. The will also specified magnificent gold embroidered textiles and bed furnishing left to his son, Richard, and to his wife. Many of these objects are described as decorated with his arms and emblem of ostrich plumes (cf. Cat. 70, 623).

The knights-errant of chivalric romance seem in some ways far removed from the realities of the thirteenth and fourteenth centuries. But the real world certainly had its chivalric heroes, and the Black Prince was the highest born and the most outstanding. Famous in tournaments as well as in battle, he was closely associated with the establishment of the Order of the Garter. Contemporaries held him in the highest respect, as the eulogies of both English and French chroniclers show (e.g. Cat. 623). He was, as Froissart wrote, 'the flower of chivalry of all the world'.

The coinage of Aquitaine in the fourteenth century

The Plantagenets had extensive minting rights in France through the inheritance of the duchy of Aquitaine. Until the fourteenth century their coinage there consisted of deniers and obols of a typical French feudal sort. Under Edward II larger silver coins appeared, copying the French *gros tournois*, but the great age of Gascon coinage began under Edward III, emerging as among the most splendid of the French feudal series. From the 1330s several great French vassals began to challenge the royal monopoly on gold coinage, among them Edward III.

The launching of the Gascon gold coinage followed soon on the appearance of the English gold issues. In March 1344 Edward wrote to his officers in Aquitaine announcing the English development and suggesting that a gold issue in the duchy would be useful. Apart from a lightweight and unpopular imitation of the Florentine florin, the main sequence of Gascon gold coins began and remained in the French style of coinage. Some of them may amount to a challenge as much as an imitation of style. By 1348, and probably earlier, Edward was issuing *écus* practically identical to the contemporary coins of Philip VI of France, even to the retention of the French arms on the shield. The main difference was the replacement of the sceptre by a sword in the king's hand.

From 1355 a distinctive new coin was issued, the *léopard d'or*, appearing first when the Black Prince was at Bordeaux preparing to invade the Languedoc. It may have been inspired by the French *mouton d'or*, but replacing the Paschal Lamb with the English leopard. Leopards replace *fleurs-de-lis* on the back also. In 1361 a new gold coinage was instituted as part of a mint reform, the French title being omitted as the Treaty of Brétigny was operative. The new *guyennois* displayed the king as a warrior with shield and sword. On its reverse a new text was adopted to replace the *Christus vincit* legend which had until then appeared on most of the Gascon gold coins in imitation of the French royal issues.

From 1362 to 1372 Aquitaine was under the rule of Edward the Black Prince, created Prince of Aquitaine on 19 July 1362. Lack of documentation makes it difficult to establish the sequence of his Gascon coinage. At some point new types were introduced: the *chaise d'or*, the only gold coin of the Black Prince to show him bearded and without a sword, and the *pavillon d'or*, the most magnificent of the Gascon issues. The last new type of the Black Prince was the *hardi d'or*, which may have appeared as part of a monetary reform in 1368 inspired by the financial strains of the expedition to Castile in 1367. Once established, the *hardi* remained the dominant gold coin of Aquitaine throughout the reigns of Edward III and Richard II. The latter's main contribution to the series was to issue the *demi-hardi d'or* for the first time, but this, like most of the half denominations, was always rare.

The silver and base coinages of Aquitaine in the fourteenth century were complicated and various, though generally remaining in the French feudal style. Under the Black Prince designs were changed on the *gros* and its half. Instead of the French *gros tournois* type, they bore a half-length figure of the bearded prince holding a sword. Even the smaller denominations took over this new design, the reverse of which copied the style of English silver coins.

614 Florin of Edward III as Duke of Aquitaine

614

?1352–4
Gold, obv. St John the Baptist between two crowns, rev. Florentine fleur-de-lis: wt 3.42 g (52.8 gr)
Inscr. obv. SIOHANNES B
rev. DVX ACITANIE
The Trustees of the British Museum, London, CM 1840, 7–14, 29

PROV. Coll. G.R. Ainslie; bt by British Museum, 1840.

LIT. Hewlett 1920, pp. 44–5; Elias 1984, p. 71 no. 36.

615 *Écu d'or* of Edward III

615

c. 1348–52
Gold, obv. king crowned and enthroned holding sword and shield with arms of France, rev. cross with each arm ending in quatrefoil from which spring three trefoils, quatrefoil in centre, all within large quatrefoil foliated at each angle with trefoil: wt 4.48 g (69.2 gr)
Inscr. obv. EDWARDVS DEI GRA AGL FRANCIE REX [pellet and saltire stops]
rev. XPC VINCIT XPC REGNAT XPC IMPERAT [pellet stops] ('Christ conquers, Christ reigns, Christ commands')
The Trustees of the British Museum, London, CM 1840, 4–3, 116

PROV. Collections of M. Young; bt by British Museum, 1840.

LIT. Hewlett 1920, pp. 45–6; Elias 1984, p. 69 no. 33.

616 *Léopard d'or* of Edward III, third issue

616

1357
Gold, obv. crowned leopard passant within tressure of ten arches, rev. foliated cross with each arm ending in trefoil and leopard in each quarter, all within ornamented quatrefoil: wt 3.59 g (55.4 gr)
Inscr. obv. EDWARDVS DEI GRA ANGLIE FRANCIE REX [pellet stops]
rev. XPC VINCIT XPC REGNAT XPC IMPERAT
The Trustees of the British Museum, London, CM E3620

PROV. Not known.

LIT. Hewlett 1920, p. 48; Elias 1984, p. 74 no. 39.

617 *Guyennois d'or* of Edward III, third type

617

Struck at La Rochelle, 1361–2
Gold, obv. king in armour marching to right under Gothic portico with leopard under each foot, letter R between his legs, rev. foliated cross with each arm ending in trefoil, fleurs-de-lis quartered with leopards: wt 3.81 g (58.8 gr)
Inscr. obv. ED D GRA REX AGLIE DO AQVITANIE [no stops]
rev. GLIA IN EXELCIS DEO ET IN TERRA PAX HOBVS [pellet in circle stops] ('Glory to God on high and on earth peace to men', *Luke* II, 14)
The Trustees of the British Museum, London, CM 1920, 8–16, 240

PROV. Coll. R. Carlyon-Britton; bt by Goldsmiths' Company and presented to British Museum, 1920.

LIT. Hewlett 1920, pp. 55–6; Elias 1984, p. 78 no. 49.

618 *Chaise d'or* of Edward the Black Prince

618

Mint of Bordeaux, 1362–72
Gold, obv. prince wearing fillet of roses, holding
sceptre and seated on throne ornamented with
Gothic arches, rev. floriated cross within
ornamented quatrefoil, leopards quartered with
fleurs-de-lis: wt 3.47 g (53.6 gr)
Inscr. obv. ED PO GNS REGIS ANGLIE PNS
ACITANIE [rosette stops]
rev. DEVS IVDEX IVSTVS FORTIS Z PACIENS
B [rosette stops] ('God is a righteous judge,
strong and patient', Psalm VII, 12)
The Trustees of the British Museum, London.
CM E3651

PROV. Not known.

LIT. Hewlett 1920, p. 106; Elias 1984, p. 167 no.
143.

619 *Pavillon d'or* of Edward the Black Prince, first issue

619

Struck at Poitiers, 1362–72
Gold, obv. prince standing beneath a Gothic
canopy wearing fillet of roses and holding
sword, two leopards at his feet and two ostrich
feathers at either side, rev. cross quernée within
ornamented quatrefoil, fleurs-de-lis quartered
with leopards: wt 5.30 g (81.8 gr)
Inscr. obv. ED PO GNS REG ANGL PNS AQVI
[quatrefoil stops]
rev. DNS AIVTO Z PTCETO ME Z IIPO
SPAVIT COR MEVM P [quatrefoil stops] ('The
Lord is my strength and my shield, and my
heart hath trusted in Him', Psalm XXVIII,
8)
The Trustees of the British Museum, London.
CM E3653

PROV. Not known.

LIT. Hewlett 1920, p. 111; Elias 1984, p. 170
no. 150.

620 *Hardi d'or* of Edward the Black Prince

620

Struck at Limoges, ?1368–72
Gold, obv. half-length figure of prince facing,
sword in right hand, left hand raised, plain fillet
in hair, all within tressure of twelve arches, rev.
cross quernée within tressure of sixteen arches,
fleurs-de-lis quartered with leopards: wt 4.01 g
(61.9 gr)
Inscr. obv. ED PO GNS REGIS ANGLIE PNS
ACITANI [rosette stops]
rev. AVXILIVM MEVM A DOMINO L [rosette
stops] ('My help cometh from the Lord',
Psalm CXXI, 2)
The Trustees of the British Museum, London,
CM 1915, 5–7, 489

PROV. Coll. Sir John Evans; bt by J.P. Morgan,
1908; bt by British Museum, 1915.

LIT. Hewlett 1920, p. 117; Elias 1984, p. 174
no. 162.

621 *Demi-gros* of Edward the Black Prince

621

Struck at Poitiers, 1362–72
Silver, obv. half-length figure of prince to right,
sword in right hand, left hand raised, rev. long
cross with three pellets in each angle: wt 2.24 g
(34.5 gr)
Inscr. obv. ED PO GNS REGIS ANGLIE [double
annulet stops]
rev. GLIA EXCE DE ET IN TERA PAX –
PRNCPS AQITAN [pellet stops]
The Trustees of the British Museum, London.
CM 1935, 4–1, 6578

PROV. Coll. T.B. Clarke-Thornhill; beq. to British
Museum, 1935.

LIT. Hewlett 1920, pp. 126–7; Elias 1984, p. 181
no. 179.

622 *Demi-hardi d'or* of Richard II

622

Struck at Bordeaux, 1377–99
Gold, obv. facing bust of king within tressure of
seven arches, rev. cross quernée, leopards
quartered with fleurs-de-lis: wt 1.85 g (28.6 gr)
Inscr. obv. RICARD RX ANGLIE FRACI [pellet
stops]
rev. AVXILIVM MEVM A DNO B [pellet
stops]
The Trustees of the British Museum, London.
CM 1922, 12–17, 13

PROV. Bt by Goldsmiths' Company and presented
to British Museum, 1922.

LIT. Hewlett 1920, p. 155; Elias 1984, p. 202
no. 225.

623 Chandos Herald, Life of the Black Prince

Late 14th century
Vellum, ff. 70: 23 × 14 cm
University of London Library, ULI MS 1

This metrical chronicle, in French, of the life
and deeds of the Black Prince was composed
by a poet who had been herald to Sir John
Chandos (d. 1369–70), the prince's friend
and companion in arms. It is a rare example

623

of a medieval French biography and an important source for certain episodes in the Hundred Years War. The author was a native of Hainault and thus a compatriot of Froissart, whom he may well have known. He was apparently writing about ten years after the prince's death in 1376.

The frontispiece (f. 3v.) shows the Black Prince, flanked by the ostrich feathers and motto of the Prince of Wales, kneeling before the Holy Trinity, to whom he had shown a lifelong devotion. The miniature and decoration are in a style found in a number of manuscripts probably produced in London during the 1390s. JB

PROV. John Shirley (d. 1456); William Cecil, 1st Lord Burghley (d. 1598); the Cecil family; the Earls of Elgin; bt by Sir Roger Mostyn, Bt, 1687; Mostyn sale, Sotheby's, 13 July 1920, lot 33; bt by London University for presentation to Edward, Prince of Wales, 1921, and deposited by him in the University Library.

LIT. Gollancz 1921; Tyson 1975; Alexander, 1983, p. 148, pl. 5; Sandler 1986, p. 177.

624   Pax

Late 14th century
Elephant ivory; upper border broken and trimmed for mend: h. 10.3 cm, w. (top) 7.8 cm, (bottom) 8.1 cm
The Board of Trustees of the Victoria and Albert Museum, London, 34–1867

624

The plaque is nearly rectangular, tapering towards the top, with a slot and pinholes on the back to secure a handle so that it could be stood on the altar and used as a pax. It was probably framed. England was precocious in introducing the pax, a tablet decorated with a sacred image, as an instrument for transferring the Kiss of Peace after the *Agnus Dei* from the celebrant to clergy and laity (Braun 1932, pp. 557–72; Jungmann 1962, II, pp. 408–9): a pax is already recorded in a

London church in 1251 (Sparrow Simpson 1895 miscellany, p. 6). By the late thirteenth century the pax (called variously *paxillum*, *tabula pacis*, *osculatorium*, etc.) had become indispensable to the liturgy, even in parish churches (cf. Powicke Cheney 1964, II, pp. 1006, 1128). Visitations of churches in the London and Exeter dioceses in the 1290s and in 1301 record numerous examples (Sparrow Simpson 1895; Hingeston-Randolph 1892, *passim*). Often simple images of painted wood or base metal (cf. Cat. 120), they could also be of precious metal, marble or ivory (the tell-tale slot survives on the back of several ivory plaques). The Crucifixion is the commonest of pax images, though here it acts as the central element of a traditional Trinity: within a border studded with rosettes against a diaper background, God the Father with cruciform nimbus is seated on a throne decorated with blank arcading, its ends issuing in foliate volutes; the dove of the Holy Spirit emanates from God's mouth, its beak touching the head of the crucified Christ; the ends of the Cross, now broken, are held by God; *sol* and *luna*, normal accompaniments to the Crucifixion, are shown in the top corners. The head of Christ on the Cross has been worn smooth by the kisses of the faithful. The plaque is similar in style to some of the later fourteenth-century English alabasters, although images of the Trinity so popular with the alabaster carvers do not normally follow the particular iconography of this plaque (Cheetham 1984, pp. 296–309). For the Trinity, see Cat. 519. NS

PROV. Bt from a Mr Willson, London, 1867.

LIT. Maskell 1872, pp. 75–6; Longhurst 1926, no. LXIII, pp. 48, 106, pl. 43; Longhurst 1929, p. 7, pl. II; Porter 1974, pp. 107–10, no. 40.

625   Trinity from a brass

Late 14th century
Latten: h. 31.1 cm, w. 13.9 cm
The Board of Trustees of the Victoria and Albert Museum, London, M39–1946

In this incomplete piece God the Father, nimbed, crowned and bearded, is seated and wearing a cloak over a close-fitting, belted robe. With His outstretched left hand He supports the corresponding arm of a tau crucifix between his knees, while the dove of the Holy Spirit descends from His mouth on to the head of Christ; His right hand, which is missing, would have been raised in benediction. The foot of the Cross rests on a sphere divided vertically into two halves (symbolising the Continents of Europe and Asia?), of which one contains a representation of a tree.

This is a standard late medieval representation of the Trinity from the canopy of a large brass: for example, the stylistically very similar one on the London 'Series B' brass of Sir Reginald Braybrook (engraved *c.* 1410),

625

at Cobham, Kent. It is possibly from the missing brass of Thomas of Woodstock, Duke of Gloucester (d. 1397), formerly in Westminster Abbey, of which the indent, at present inaccessible, still survives. CB

PROV. Anonymous, Sotheby's; Dr W. L. Hilburgh; V&A, 1946.

LIT. Evans 1963–8, p. 90, fig. 2; Norris 1978a, p. 54, fig. 20.

626–33   The Black Prince's funeral achievements

Before 1376
Dean and Chapter of Canterbury

Edward, Prince of Wales, popularly known as the Black Prince since the sixteenth century, was born in 1330 and died on 8 June 1376. In his will, written in French and dated the day before he died, he gave instructions that his funeral procession through Canterbury should be preceded by 'two destriers covered with our arms and two armed men in our arms and in our helms ... that is to say, one for war with our full quartered arms and the other for peace with our badges of ostrich plumes ...', together with various banners. His funeral was held on 29 September, and there can be little doubt that the present achievements, which were hung up in Canterbury Cathedral, formed part of the equipment of one or both of the two armed men. The shield bears the full arms, showing that it was for war. We do not know whether the arms for peace – that is for the tournament – were also suspended, though another shield, painted with scrollwork round a small central escutcheon of the full arms, is depicted on an anonymous drawing of the achievements of *c.* 1600 in the Library of the Society of Antiquaries (MS 62). The same drawing also shows a sword and dagger, of which the former is said to have been removed by Oliver Cromwell.

Whatever the origin of the practice of carrying a dead knight's crested helm and other armour at his funeral, and then hanging them over his tomb, the earliest clear evidence for it appears to be provided by mortuary bequests to churches contained in wills of the 1370s. There is also the achievement of Sir Richard Pembridge (d. 1375), once hung in Hereford Cathedral and of which the helm is now in the Royal Scottish Museum, Edinburgh (1905–489). St John Hope asserted that the Canterbury pieces are of a 'temporary character', unfitted for practical use and made especially for the funeral. In fact, as was established beyond question when they were conserved in the Tower of London Armouries in 1949–50, they are very much the real thing, and it would be surprising if this were not so at this early date: all the evidence points to the use of personal armour for achievements before the sixteenth century, when an enormously increased demand for heraldic funerals from the many non-military armigers created by the Tudors led to its being supplied by the heralds. Given that the Canterbury pieces are designed for practical use, there would obviously have been no reason for making them specially for the funeral when the prince's own armoury provided a readily available source of supply, especially in view of the instructions in his will that the armed men accompanying his body should wear 'our' helms. It can hardly be doubted, therefore, that the pieces did, in fact, belong to him personally: the Henry of Bolingbroke sword at Dublin (Cat. 730) and the Henry v achievements in Westminster Abbey are the only other surviving examples of the personal military equipment of a medieval English prince.

As indicated below in the comments on the individual pieces, the helm, gauntlets and gipon, except for its sleeves, provide characteristic, and almost unique, examples of the standard equipment of the period from *c.* 1370 to the early fifteenth century, depicted, *inter alia*, on countless effigies and brasses, including the Black Prince's own gilt-latten effigy at Canterbury (cf. also Cat. 140). Indeed, the crested helm under the head – described in his will as 'our leopard helm' – might almost have been modelled from the one in the achievement. CB

626 Helm

Iron or steel: h. 31 cm

This is made of three parts riveted together: a front and a back plate, forming a cylinder that curves down to a central point at front and rear, and a top piece formed as a truncated cone surmounted by a flattened cone; a medial ridge extends from front to rear. A section of the top of the front plate is

626–33

cut to form two horizontal vision slits with flanged lower edges, divided by a vertical tongue terminating in a fleur-de-lis, and the bottom edge has a narrow inward turn. On the right a series of small circular ventilation holes are pierced, arranged as a three-pointed coronet, while the front lower point is flanked by a pair of cruciform openings for guard-chain toggles. The rivets attaching the top plate are fitted with internal latten(?) washers holding a strap to which the missing lining was stitched: pairs of lace-holes above and below were probably for both additional attachments for the lining and for affixing a coronet or crest, though apparently not the present one, since it now shows no signs of corresponding fittings.

By the time of the prince's death the use of helms of this kind, designed to be worn over the visorless bacinet, was probably already becoming less frequent in battle, though it was to continue for many years in the tournament. The type is one that, together with the gauntlets and coat armour described below, is depicted frequently in art during the second half of the fourteenth century, especially on effigies and brasses – for example, on the prince's own effigy at Canterbury and Cat. 140 here. Two closely

similar helms are recorded, both with English associations, of which the best known is that of the Pembridge achievement in Hereford Cathedral (see above); the other is in the Royal Armouries at the Tower of London (no. IV.600). It is also related to two helms, apparently dating from the end of the century, in Cobham Church, Kent. The probability that all were produced in England is therefore very strong. CB

627 Crest

Moulded leather and canvas, covered with gesso on linen and painted: h. 74 cm

This is in the form of a lion (or leopard) statant guardant, originally crowned, standing on a cap of maintenance shaped to fit the top of the helm: a cadency label would originally have been fastened round the neck, as on the crest depicted on the prince's tomb, but no trace remains. The parts are stitched together and the long tail is fitted over a wooden dowel. The details are modelled in the gesso, the hair being produced with stamps on separate lozenge-shaped pieces of leather glued in position. The ears and the inside of the mouth, including the tongue, are missing. The lion was gilded, its eyes were painted red and black; the upper surfaces of the cap of maintenance were red, stencilled all over with gold rosettes, and the underside, including the upturned brim, white stencilled with conventional heraldic ermine tails in black.

This is one of only five surviving medieval crests, of which all the others are Continental. CB

628 Pair of gauntlets

Gilt copper or copper alloy (latten?) and leather: l. left 28 cm, right 15.5 cm

These are of 'hour-glass' form, the main part of each made from a single plate, wrapped round the hand behind the fingers, shaped to the bases of the thumbs, embossed slightly over the knuckles and metacarpal bones, and, after narrowing at the wrist, expanding into a short, bell-shaped cuff: the edge of the cuff has a narrow turn bordered by a row of domed rivets, of which alternate ones hold the cuff of the lining glove. The metacarpal plate overlaps a narrow riveted lame (missing from the left), which forms a prolongation of it over the bases of the fingers. Riveted inside are leather finger-strips to which are riveted small overlapping plates (many missing, including both thumbs). At the base of each thumb on the main plate is a circular stud cast with a leopard's head in relief, while the knuckles were originally set with gadlings in the form of small cast figures of leopards, of which only one, now detached, survives. The lining gauntlets of buff leather, originally stitched to the finger leathers, are embroidered in silk with zigzag patterns.

Only three other gauntlets of this type with English associations are known to survive, and only one other pair with its lining-gloves is recorded anywhere, at Churburg in the South Tyrol. They are often depicted on effigies and brasses (see the comments on the helm, above). CB

629 Coat armour or gipon

Linen base, padded with lamb's wool, covered with velvet, and embroidered with gold and silk thread, now enclosed in a nylon net: h. approx. 87.6 cm (originally approx. 91.4 cm)

This is the only surviving example of the close-fitting, waisted, hip-length type of coat armour that was almost standard all over Europe from c. 1360 until the early fifteenth century, and which is frequently depicted in the art of this period (see the comments on the helm, above). It was laced up the front through close-set eyelet holes, and is unusual in having elbow-length sleeves, rather than no sleeves at all, or wrist-length ones: it is possible, however, that lower halves are missing. It is quilted in straight lines, and bears on the front and back the English royal arms (France ancient quartering England), each quarter formed from a separate square of velvet with the charges embroidered in

gold on separate linen appliqués. Each sleeve bears a pair of similar quarters in reverse order. There are traces of the silver cadency label at the top of the front only, and one is depicted on each of the sleeves on the Society of Antiquaries drawing (MS 162) mentioned above.

The only other surviving fourteenth-century coat armour is one of slightly different type made for a child, probably Charles VI of France as Dauphin, in Chartres Cathedral. CB

630 Shield

Poplar wood, covered with canvas and faced with paper covered by leather, heraldic charges applied in moulded leather (filled with gesso?): h. 73 cm

This is heater-shaped and slightly concave towards the body. The front bears the same arms as the coat armour, painted and gilded, the quarters originally being marked off by applied twisted cords; the fields are punched all over with numerous tiny crosses, arranged diagonally on the French quarters and horizontally on the English ones. There is no trace of a cadency label, but one is illustrated on the Society of Antiquaries drawing mentioned above. The back is painted green, and contains various holes indicating where the brases for the arms and the guige for hanging it round the neck were attached. Two leather loops at the top probably served to suspend it over the tomb.

This is an example of a standard thirteenth- or fourteenth-century type of shield: apart from the Henry V shield in Westminster Abbey, it is the only one known to survive in Britain. In style and construction it relates closely to Continental examples, of which the largest collection is in the museum at Marburg. CB

631 Part of a scabbard

Leather, set with copper-alloy (latten?) studs: l. 68.5 cm

This is now broken into three pieces supported on a later wooden former. Straight and tapering, it has a stitched seam up the back and a corresponding row of studs, with square beaded heads set lozengewise, up the front. It was originally painted red. CB

632 Part of a belt with buckle

Tablet-woven linen, buckle, eyelets and band of gilt copper alloy (latten?): l. 12.5 cm, w. 3 cm

There survives a short section of a plain belt, originally dyed red, with three eyelets for the tongue of the buckle and a plain loop. The buckle is cast in the form of two dragon bodies which curve round to join a common head, into the open mouth of which the tongue fits; its plate is riveted to the belt. The parts have probably been reassembled after becoming detached, since the present rela-

tion between them does not seem to be practical.

This has always been regarded as part of a sword belt. It is possible, however, that it is actually part of the guige by means of which the shield was suspended round the neck in mounted use (cf. Cat. 235, 690). CB

633 Length of chain

Iron l. 51.5 cm

A section remains from a much longer piece, comprising five long oval links and a terminal ring. This was probably part of a guard chain for the helm of the kind illustrated, for example, on the brass of Sir Roger II de Trumpington, c. 1326, at Trumpington Church, Cambridge. CB

PROV. Suspended over tomb of the Black Prince in Canterbury Cathedral since his funeral in 1376; replaced with replicas and transferred to a showcase, 1954.

LIT. Stanley 1855, pp. 118–22, 132–44; Hewitt 1860, p. 227; Hope 1895; Laking 1920–2, I, pp. 152–6, 275–81, figs 185–9, 322–4; II, pp. 103–5, figs 450–1, 207–8; V, fig. 559, p. 193; Beard 1935, pp. 136–7, figs I–III; Cripps-Day & Dufty 1939, p. 151; Cripps-Day 1941, pp. 115–21, fig. 9; Mann 1941; Cripps-Day 1942; Mann 1950; Hamilton-King 1954; Mann 1954a; Nickel 1958, pp. 55–6, fig. 60; Wagner 1967, pp. 106–7, 110; Norman 1972, p. 13 no. 3; Harvey 1976, pp. 160–1.

Jewellery

634 Ring

Early 13th century
Gold set with a cabochon ruby pierced longitudinally, diam. 1.9 cm
The Dean and Chapter of Wells

634

At least three English bishops' rings set with rubies are known. As well as this example the rings of Archbishops Sewell (d. 1258) and Greenfield (d. 1315) at York are both set with rubies. The ruby, like the stone in the ring of Bishop Woodlock (Cat. 637), was pierced for a previous use. The stirrup-shaped ring provides a massive setting for the stone. JC

PROV. Described (1834) as having been found in the ground adjacent to Wells Cathedral about 30 years ago; more recent research (Colchester

1984) has suggested that it and a Limoges crosier head (Cat. 257) were probably found in the tomb of Bishop Jocelyn (d. 1242) in the eighteenth century.

LIT. Church, 1885–7, p. 407; Taylor & Scarisbrick, 1978, p. 47, no. 271; Colchester 1984, pp. 19–23.

635 Ring

Before 1255
Gold set with a cabochon sapphire surrounded by eight minute rubies and emeralds in small collets: diam. 2.5 cm
The Dean and Chapter of York

635

This is the only example of a 'pontifical' ring found in an English bishop's or archbishop's grave. The 'pontifical' was especially large and impressive, and was worn at major feasts and ceremonies. This ring is not only set with a fine sapphire in an octagonal bezel with incurved sides, but each of the eight sides has a tiny collet with either a ruby or an emerald set in it. Walter de Gray was consecrated archbishop in 1216. He held high political office under two kings. He was Chancellor under John from 1205 to 1214. He was also a favourite of Henry III, acting on occasion as his ambassador abroad and regent at home. He died in 1255.   JC

PROV. Found in grave of Archbishop Walter de Gray in York Minster, 1968.

LIT. Oman 1971, p. 126; Oman 1974, p. 95, pl. 19A.

636 Ring

Before 1269
Gold set with a cabochon sapphire: diam. 2.5 cm
The Dean and Chapter of York

636

The irregular hexagonal sapphire is held by four claws in a stirrup-shaped hoop which may be compared with that of Bishop Jocelyn (Cat. 634).   JC

PROV. Found in grave of Archbishop Godfrey de Ludham (d. 1269) in York Minster, 1969.

LIT. Oman 1971, p. 135; Oman 1974, p. 95.

637 Ring

13th century
Gold set with a sapphire: diam. 2.7 cm
The Dean and Chapter of Winchester

637

This ring was found in the grave of Bishop Henry Woodlock (d. 1316) who was buried at the entrance to the choir. The sapphire is particularly fine and has been longitudinally pierced for suspension. It is set in a deep bezel and held in place with claws in the form of tiny fleurs-de-lis. In size of stone and shape of setting this must rank as one of the finest Gothic episcopal rings.   JC

PROV. Found in grave of Bishop Henry Woodlock, 18th century.

LIT. Milner 1798, p. 113; London 1862, p. 636; Waterton 1863, p. 236, fig. 2; Oman 1974, p. 93 pl. 13 f.

638 Ring

Early 14th century
Gold with oval enamelled bezel, diam. 2 cm
Inscr. in Lombardic letters
    on back of bezel IH̅ C X P̅ C
    outside hoop AVE MARIA GRACIA PLENA
Dean and Chapter of Exeter

638

The remarkable aspect of this ring is the bezel engraved with the Virgin and Child against a blue-enamelled background. Grandisson was clearly devoted to the Virgin and Child as an image, for not only does it appear on the ivory (Cat. 596) but also on his signet seal (Birch 1887, p. 227 no. 1560). On this bezel there is a half-length figure of the Virgin holding the Child with her left hand. The Infant Jesus offers his mother an apple. The background is decorated with five four-pointed stars. The style of the engraving and

enamelling suggests a French origin. The inscription on the back of the bezel is the usual Greek abbreviation for Jesus Christ. That on the outside of the hoop, in a rectangular panel, is a type of inscription that often occurs on Italian rings. It is possible that this combination of Italian and French influence indicates that the ring was produced at Avignon, which Grandisson visited in 1327 and where he heard that he was appointed to the see of Exeter. This pictorial image may have led to the development of iconographic enamelled rings in the fifteenth century.   JC

PROV. Found in grave of Bishop Grandisson in early 1950s, when tomb was opened during restoration work in chapel outside west door of Exeter Cathedral, where bishop was buried.

LIT. Anon. 1957, pp. 23–5.

639 Ring

1360–74
Gold: diam. 2.4 cm
Inscr. in black letter *Willms Wytlesey*
The Board of Trustees of the Victoria and Albert Museum, London, M.191–1975

639

This impressive ring is set with a drilled octagonal sapphire set in a six-cusped setting. The hoop is stirrup-shaped and the shoulders are each decorated with two panels of foliage and flowers formerly enamelled. Together with the ring of Bishop Grandisson (Cat. 638) this ring provides an example of the change in episcopal rings from the thirteenth to the fourteenth century. It provides one of the finest and earliest examples in England of elaborate enamelled floral and foliage decoration. William Wytlesey died in 1374. The fact that his name is inscribed on the ring does not prove that it was found in his tomb. It is unusual for an owner to have his name inscribed inside a ring, but it may be that it was kept in the cathedral treasury rather than buried with Wytlesey. JC

PROV. Said to have been found in the tomb of William Wytlesey, Archbishop of Canterbury; Sir Arthur Evans Coll.; Joan Evans Coll.

LIT. Oman 1974, p. 94 pl. 18c; Cherry 1981, p. 71 no. 148; Bury 1982, p. 181.

640 Jewel

Late 14th century
Silver-gilt set with rubies, diamond, emerald and pearls: h. 5.7 cm, w. 4.9 cm
The Warden and Fellows of New College, Oxford

This jewel is in the form of a crowned Lombardic letter M with gold figures of the Archangel Gabriel and the Virgin framed in the double arch of the letter. On the central bar is a pot of lilies formed of a carved ruby. Above this are three pearls surmounted by a diamond, with a ruby on each side, below which is an emerald between two rubies. On each of the two sides of the letters were a large ruby and two emeralds (one ruby and one emerald are missing). The edges of the letters and the main compartments for the stones have beaded edges. Enamel is used sparingly. There is blue enamel on the back-

ground of the central bar. The lily has leaves of translucent green enamel and the three flowers are enamelled white. The wings of the archangel, made separately, are enamelled green with yellow bars.

The jewel, often mistakenly referred to as the jewel of William of Wykeham, was given to the college by Peter Hylle, a citizen of Winchester, Christina Hylle his wife and Master Thomas Hylle their son and a fellow of New College in 1455. The gift is recorded in the *Liber Albus* (New College Archive 9654, f. 15) and the jewel described as *preciosum et sumptuosum valde illud Jocale totaliter argenteum et deauratum continens gloriosum ymaginem eiusdem Matris domini atque ymaginem Archangeli Gabrielis cum olla cristallina in medio situata mirifice fabricata ex cuius ore exire videtur lilium ex toto argenteum* (this costly and sumptuous jewel all in silver and gilt bearing the glorious likeness of the very Mother of the Lord and the likeness of the Archangel Gabriel with a crystal vase set in the middle, wonderfully crafted, from whose opening may be seen to arise a lily all of silver).

The jewel is very similar to one which was in the Treasury of St-Denis, near Paris, until 1798. This is also in the form of a letter M with figures of the Archangel and Virgin within the letter. The framework of the letter is decorated with stones and pearls.

Although the St-Denis brooch contains niches with the figures of St Denis and a kneeling monk, the two brooches are so close that it has even been suggested that they are from the same atelier (Montesquiou Fezensac 1977, p. 47, pl. 29c). If so, it would suggest a French origin for the Hylle jewel. JC

PROV. Given by Hylle family to New College, 1455.

LIT. Way 1845c, pp. 206–7; Hope 1907, pp. 484–5; Evans 1970, p. 60.

641 Two brooches

Mid-13th century
Silver, (i) int. diam. 0.5 cm, ext. diam. 2.2 cm; (ii) int. diam. 7 cm, ext. diam. 1.8 cm
The Trustees of the British Museum, London, (i) MLA 1983, 1–3, 1; (ii) MLA 1983, 4–4, 2

641

These two brooches were apparently found together, and although they do not form a pair they are clearly of the same date and workmanship. They are both ring brooches, the ring formed of animals and figures. The first depicts a man fighting a dragon. The man has one hand on the dragon's neck and grasps the dragon's tail with the other. The second is formed of two dragons face to face with their tails intertwined. Both brooches are decorated with punching. The most famous example of a brooch where the ring is composed of dragons is the Kames brooch (Evans 1970, pl. 13a) usually dated to c. 1300. These two brooches with their winged dragons probably date to the mid-thirteenth century. JC

PROV. Said to have been found in Bennington, Herts, between 1960 and 1970.

642

642 Brooch

13th century
Gold set alternately with cabochon rubies and
sapphires, the pin set with a sapphire:
diam. 3.8 cm
Inscr. in Lombardic letters rev. IO SUI ICI EN LIU
[sic] DAMI : AMO
The Trustees of the British Museum, London,
MLA AF 2683

This is a fine example of a gem-set ring
brooch where the gems are used to provide
an alternation between red and blue. The
space between the stones is decorated with
punched crosses alternating with a series of
letters. The inscription engraved on the reverse ('I am here in place of a friend: love'),
indicates that like Cat. 646 it was a lover's
gift. JC

PROV. A. W. Franks Coll.

LIT. Evans 1970, pl. 8a; London 1976, p. 160
no. 264.

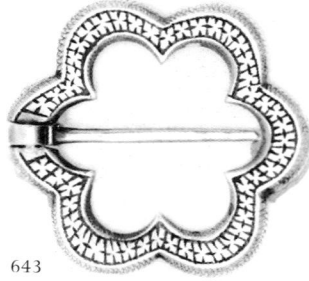

643

643 Brooch

13th century
Gold. diam. 2.5 cm
Inscr. in Lombardic letters + AVE MARIA
GRACIA PLENA DON
The Board of Trustees of the Victoria and Albert
Museum, London, M.245-1923

This brooch is in the shape of a sexfoil. The
front is decorated by a series of engraved
four-petalled flowers and the back is engraved in a florid Lombardic ('Hail Mary, full
of Grace'). JC

PROV. Rosenheim Coll.

LIT. Bury 1982, p. 59 no. 26.

644

644 Ring brooch

13th century
Gold: diam. 2 cm
Inscr. in Lombardic letters
obv. + IEO : SUI : FERMAIL : PUR :
GAP[sic] : DER : SEIN
rev. + KE : NU : SVILEIN : NIMETTE :
MEIN
The Trustees of the British Museum, London,
MLA 1929, 4-11, 1

This brooch provides a neat illustration of the
use of the ring brooch to close a garment at
the neck, since the inscription means 'I am a
brooch to guard the breast, that no rascal
may put his hand thereon.' JC

PROV. Found at Writtle, Essex, before 1847; F.A.
Harrison Coll.

LIT. Neale 1848, p. 125; Cuming 1862, p. 228;
Evans 1970, p. 46; London 1976, p. 160 no.
263.

645

645 Ring

13th century
Gold ring set with a green jasper intaglio:
diam. 2.2 cm
Inscr. in Lombardic letters + S'CRISTINE
ALMARICI
The Trustees of the British Museum, London,
MLA AF 552

The legend around the octagonal bezel indicates that it was used as the signet ring of
Christine Almaricus (possibly to be interpreted as Christine the Librarian). In the
centre of the bezel is an oval intaglio engraved with the bust of a man in profile
wearing a pointed pendent hood. The en-

graving is medieval and provides an interesting comparison with the Oxwich brooch
(Cat. 653). Although it was found in England
it is not certain that the ring is English, and
the shape of the ring and the engraving of the
stones may suggest an Italian origin. JC

PROV. Found in Canterbury; T. G. Faussett Coll.;
A. W. Franks Coll.

LIT. Dalton 1912, no. 220; Cherry 1981, p. 63
no. 123.

646

646 Ring

13th century
Gold set with a sapphire: diam. 2.3 cm
Inscr. in Lombardic letters + IE · SUI · DE · DRUE
· RIE · E · SI · NE · ME · DO · NEI · MIE
The Trustees of the British Museum, London,
MLA 1980, 12-2, 1

Although the triangular bezel and stirrup-
shaped hoop recall religious rings, this is a
secular ring. The bezel emerges from the
mouths of dragons on each shoulder. The
dragons' tails end in a pair of clasped hands
opposite the bezel – a symbol of love and
trust. The engraving in Lombardic letters on
the outer faces of the hoop (I am a love token,
do not give me away) indicates that the ring
was a gift between lovers. JC

PROV. Found in Hatfield Forest, Essex, 1980.

LIT. Cherry 1981, p. 64 no. 125.

647

647 Ring

13th century
Gold set with a wolf's tooth: diam. 2.2 cm
Inscr. in black letter + Buro + Berto +
Berneto + Consumatum e
The Board of Trustees of the Victoria and Albert
Museum, London, M. 816-1902

The shoulders of the ring are decorated in
stiff-leaf foliage moulded in high relief against
a cross-hatched background which suggests
both a thirteenth-century date and an English origin. On each side of the ring are
pierced pear-shaped holes within which
there are small openwork crowns. The heart-
shaped bezel is set with a wolf's tooth. Inside

the hoop there is a later fourteenth-century inscription. 'Consum(m)atum e(st)', the beginning of the last words of Christ on the Cross, was used as a charm to calm storms, while the three words beginning with B were a magical charm to appease toothache.   JC

PROV. Not known.

LIT. Oman 1930, p. 115, no. 757; Cherry 1981, no. 131; Bury 1982, p. 187.

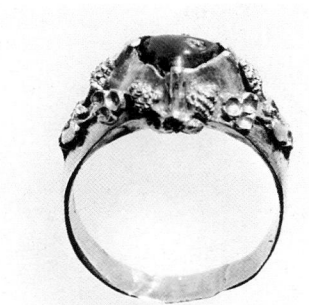

648

648   Ring

13th century
Gold set with an amethyst: diam. 2 cm
The Trustees of the British Museum, London,
    MLA AF 1887

This fine stirrup-shaped gold ring is decorated on each shoulder and on the sides of the bezel with symmetrical foliate designs in relief. This design may be compared with that on Cat. 647. The amethyst is held by four claws.   JC

PROV. Found at Wiston, near Pulborough, Sussex, before 1861; A.W. Franks Coll.

LIT. London 1861, p. 488; Dalton 1912, p. 262 no. 1852.

649

649   Ring

Late 13th century
Gold set with a sard intaglio: diam. 2 cm
Inscr. in Lombardic letters IOHANNES EST
    NOMEN EIUS
The Board of Trustees of the Victoria and Albert
    Museum, London, M. 290-1962

The inscription around the edge of the oval bezel is a quotation from Luke 1, 63. The gem, a sard, is engraved with a man's head in profile and is a medieval copy of a classical

original. It is unlikely that the gem was engraved in England and it was probably imported from France or Italy possibly by the first owner John. The setting of the gem and its inscription may be compared to Cat. 654 and Cat. 645.   JC

PROV. Not known.

LIT. Nelson 1934, p. 305; Oman 1974, p. 101, pl 36B; Bury 1982, p. 191 no. 4.

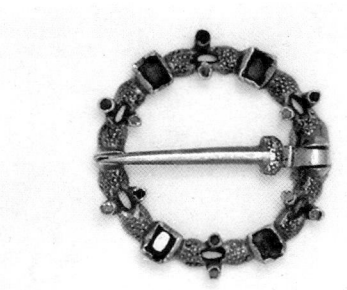

650

650   Brooch

Late 13th century
Gold set with rubies and sapphires: diam. 1.5 cm
The Board of Trustees of the Victoria and Albert
    Museum, London, 6808-1860

This is an example of a small gold ring brooch set with stones. Its delicacy and small size

may be compared with the ring brooch (Cat. 643). The four rubies are in rectangular settings alternating with two small collets each set with very small stones. The back is plain. The collar of the pin and the gold between the stones is decorated with punching, which is a common feature on late thirteenth-century English gold brooches.   JC

PROV. Found in London, before 1860.

LIT. Bury 1982, p. 58 no. 10.

651   Brooch

Late 13th/early 14th century
Gold set with garnets and sapphires: int. diam.
    2.5 cm, ext. diam. 3.7 cm
Manchester City Art Galleries, 1977.168

The brooch is formed in a ring with eight collets set alternately with garnets and sapphires divided by a raised boss. The bosses are each decorated with punching and surmounted by an open fruit pod. The present arrangement of stones is certainly not the original arrangement since only six of the stones have survived, and they have come out of their original settings. However, the present arrangement of colours is the most probable. It is this combination of two elements of decoration that gives the brooch its interest. The British Museum brooch (Cat. 642) has stones divided only by decoration

651

485

on the flat surface of the ring, although otherwise the alternation of colours and the presence of a stone in the pin may make comparison of the two brooches interesting. It has been suggested that the pod containing seeds and the remains of the flower beyond may represent the fruit of the broom, the badge of the Plantagenet kings of England. Whether or not this is so, the brooch certainly combines the setting of stones with a sculptural decoration in an unusual manner.

JC

PROV. Found in Victoria St, Manchester, May 1971.

LIT. Cherry 1983, pp. 77–9.

652

652 Ring brooch

c. 1270–1330
Silver oval (originally circular): h. 3.5 cm, w. 2.4 cm
Hereford City Museum, 1986–67

Constructed of circular-sectioned wire, this brooch has four knops each decorated with punched circles between which are four rosettes with eight petals alternately large and small. Silver brooches of wire decorated with knops and rosettes were common in northern England and southern Scotland at the end of the thirteenth and beginning of the fourteenth century. Examples have been found at Langhope, Borders; Canonbie and Middlebie Church, Dumfries and Galloway; Norham Castle, Northumberland; and Perth. This brooch is the first of its type to be found in southern England.

JC

PROV. Found during excavations at Berrington St, Hereford, *c.* 1976.

LIT. Shoesmith 1985, pp. 21–4.

653 The Oxwich brooch

English?: *c.* 1320–40 but cameos probably *c.* 1250
Gold set alternately with three chalcedony cameos and three cabochon rubies, one missing; pin also missing: diam. 4 cm
The National Museum of Wales, Cardiff, 76.39 H

This is the most remarkable ring brooch to be found in England or Wales. The base of the brooch was not cast in one piece but consists of twelve separate sections soldered together. Of the stones set around the ring the rubies fit their settings very well but the cameos do

653

not. The beaded edges of the settings of the stones have been compared to the settings of the elaborate brooch (D2) and three rings (EIO–EI2) found in the Colmar treasure deposited in 1348, now in the Musée de Cluny, Paris. Similar beaded settings also occur on the New College brooch (Cat. 640) and the Munich crown (Cat. 13). The place of manufacture of the brooch is uncertain: it could be Paris, the Rhineland or even London. The cameos show a man's head in profile with a coif. This headdress was fashionable in the middle of the thirteenth century. The art of cameo cutting was revived in the thirteenth century, notably in Paris, and busts in profile were one of the standard themes. It is not clear when or why the original stones (? sapphires) that filled these three settings were removed and the cameo replacements fitted.

JC

PROV. Found at Oxwich Castle, W. Glam., during clearance of undercroft of east block, May 1968.

LIT. Evans 1970, pp. 11–12, pl. 11a, b; Paris 1981–2, p. 243; Lewis 1982, pp. 126–9; Taburet 1984, pp. 89–101; Lewis 1987.

654 Ring

Late 13th/early 14th century
Gold: diam. 2.1 cm
Inscr. in Lombardic letters ∗ TECTA : LEGE : LECTA : TEGE
The Board of Trustees of the Victoria and Albert Museum, London, 89–1899

On the rim of the oval bezel of this ring is engraved in Lombardic letters, the inscription (Read what is held, hold what is read) indicating that the ring was used as a signet

to seal personal correspondence. Engraved gems, either classical or medieval, were often chosen for such private seals or rings. A similar inscription occurs on two seal matrices thought to be British (Tonnochy 1952, nos 705 and 706), and it was also used by Matthew Paris of St Albans (Cat. 437). The hoop of the ring is open at the back of the bezel so that the finger can touch the sapphire. The sapphire intaglio in the centre of the bezel is engraved with a head in profile of a lady in a veil. Engraving of sapphires is technically difficult and is usually thought to indicate a Parisian provenance. It may well be that the gem was engraved in Paris but set in England.

JC

PROV. Found in a well in Hereford, 1824; Waterton Coll.

LIT. Oman 1930, no. 534 p. 91; Oman 1974, p. 61 pl. 36c; Cherry 1981, no. 134 p. 66; Bury 1982, p. 191.

654

655

655 Ring

14th century
Gold set with an emerald: diam. 2 cm
Inscr. in black letter + *qui plus despent qua li nafiert*
sans colp ferir a mort se fiert
The Trustees of the British Museum, London,
MLA 99, 5–20, 2

The conical bezel rises from the hoop and is supported by two openwork scrolls which have nielloed stars on their sides. The hoop, of triangular section, is engraved with a proverb, meaning: 'He who spends more than belongs to him, kills himself without striking a blow'.

It is unusual to find such an elaborate inscription on a ring, but the rhyming proverb recalls the homely wisdom of the inscriptions on the Ashanti jug (Cat. 726). The use of French rather than English raises the possibility that this ring is a French import; but French was still widely used in England among the nobility. JC

PROV. Found on site of Queen's Head Tavern, Hornsey, London, 1898.

LIT. Dalton 1912, no. 929; Cherry 1981, p. 67 no. 136.

656

656 Ring

14th century
Gold set with an amethyst: diam. 2 cm
The Trustees of the British Museum, London,
MLA AF 1825

Although the faceting of the amethyst recalls that of twelfth-century rings such as that found in the tomb of William de St Barbara, Bishop of Durham (d. 1152), the setting and

hoop suggest that this ring probably dates from the fourteenth century. The stone with three longitudinal facets is set in a deep octagonal bezel. The hoop is faceted and each shoulder has an openwork square panel with a quatrefoil set in it. JC

PROV. Found at Wells; Soden Smith Coll.; A.W. Franks Coll.

LIT. London 1872, no. 901; Dalton 1912, p. 254 no. 1780.

657 The Thame ring

Late 14th century
Gold set with an amethyst in the form of a double-armed cross, and around the hoop seven amethysts: enamelled on back of bezel: bezel 2.5 cm × 1.6 cm, int. diam. 2.2 cm, ext. diam. 2.5 cm
Inscr. on bezel in Lombardic letters MEMANTO MEI DOMINE
The Visitors of the Ashmolean Museum, Oxford, 1940.224

657

This large and impressive gold ring (wt 23.50 g) is unusual since the amethysts are cut to fit the goldsmith's work. The oblong bezel is set with an amethyst in the form of a cross of Lorraine, and the outside of the hoop is set with seven amethysts curved to the shape of the hoop. Amethysts were used for abbots' rings, but not exclusively. The double-armed cross was a characteristic of Byzantine cross reliquaries, so it is likely that the relic contained in the Thame ring was a fragment of the cross. This is further confirmed by the back plate of the bezel which is engraved with the Crucifixion with the Virgin and St John, against a background of red enamel.

Although the hoard in which it was found was not deposited until after 1457 (the date of the latest silver coin), it appears that this ring and possibly the other four rings may have been some eighty years old when they were deposited. Although Joan Evans suggested a sixteenth-century date, the comparison by John Hunt with a silver and tortoiseshell casket in the Museum of Fine Arts, Boston, which has a similar style of inscription and tiny stones cut to fit the tracery decoration of the sides of the casket, led him to suggest a date at the end of the fourteenth century.

The place of manufacture of the casket and also of the Thame ring are uncertain. Both must have been produced at a place where there was a high quality of stone cutting, so Paris is most probable.

There is some evidence for such rings in the possession of English nobles at this time. Philippa, Countess of March, left to her son Edmond a gold ring containing a fragment of the True Cross and bearing the inscription *In nomine Patris et Filii et Spiritus Sancti* (Nichols 1780, p. 100). In Richard II's wardrobe accounts for 1397 is a payment of 12d to a goldsmith for repairs to a ring containing '*lignum dominicium*' (Pailey Baildon 1910, p. 499). We do not know where these rings were made. The Thame ring represents the type worn at the highest levels of English society in the late fourteenth century. JC

PROV. Found on River Thame about 1 mile north of town, together with coins and four other rings, 1940; acq. as treasure trove by Ashmolean Museum.

LIT. Evans 1941, pp. 197–202; Cherry 1973, p. 322; Hunt 1973, pp. 346–53; Hinton 1982, pp. 40–1.

658 Ring

Late 14th century
Gold: diam. 1.9 cm
Inscr. in black letter *nul si bien*
The Board of Trustees of the Victoria and Albert Museum, London M. 235–1962

658

This ring is inscribed on the shoulders in black letter with a phrase ('none so good') which also occurs on other rings found in England. This style of lettering suggests a date in the second half of the fourteenth century. The oval bezel has inset a relief of St George standing holding in both hands a lance that pierces the mouth of the dragon. Iconographic rings, or rings with engraved or relief figures of saints on the bezel, were an English type and St George is often depicted on them. JC

PROV. Found at King's Langley, Hertfordshire, 1866; Joan Evans Coll.

LIT. Bury 1982, p. 181.

659 The Dunstable Swan Jewel

c. 1400
Gold with white and black enamel: h. 3.2 cm, w. 2.5 cm, l. of chain 8.2 cm
The Trustees of the British Museum, London, MLA 1966, 7–3, 1

Opaque white enamel is used over gold, modelled to give the form of a swan. Traces of

659

black enamel remain on the legs and feet. Around the neck is a gold coronet to which is attached a chain ending in a ring. At the back there is the original pin and catch. The jewel is a fine example of opaque white enamel *en ronde bosse*. This rich technique was developed in Paris in the second half of the fourteenth century and was certainly used there in the early fifteenth century for larger reliquaries. It was certainly known in England in the 1390s since Henry of Lancaster, later Henry IV, gave his wife Mary a garter decorated with a golden hind enamelled in white with a collar around its neck in 1391. Eleanor de Bohun, in her will dated 1399, left a psalter with clasps enamelled with white swans to her son. She had inherited it from her father, so the white enamelling here may date from before 1373. This use of white enamel in the circle of Henry of Lancaster is particularly interesting, since the swan was worn by various notables who were proud of their descent from the Knight of the Swan, in England particularly through the families of Tony and de Bohun. Henry of Lancaster, son of John of Gaunt, married Mary de Bohun,

one of the two co-heiresses of Humphrey de Bohun, in 1380. He used the swan as a badge, and after he became king the swan badge was used as a livery badge of the Prince of Wales. The Dunstable Swan Jewel offers an excellent illustration of the type of jewel used as a livery badge by Richard II. On the Wilton Diptych (fig. 104) Richard and nine of the eleven angels surrounding the Virgin are depicted as wearing white harts with coronets and gold chains. The manner in which the harts are painted suggests that the badges are *en ronde bosse*. The jewels of the white hart worn in the circle of Richard II are very likely to have been produced in England. The Swan Jewel is therefore an illustration of that concern for genealogy combined with a love of display characteristic of the English Court at the end of the fourteenth and beginning of the fifteenth century.   JC

PROV. Found during excavations on site of Dominican Friary at Dunstable, 1965.

LIT. Cherry 1969, pp. 38–53; London 1976, p. 162 no. 268; London 1981b, p. 106 no. 8.

XVI Edward III (1327–77)

Edward of Windsor became king at the age of fifteen in 1327 and married Philippa of Hainault in 1328. She bore him the first of twelve children in 1330, Edward of Woodstock, later known as the Black Prince (p. 476). In the same year the young king secured full power following the execution of his mother's paramour, Roger Mortimer. Despite the inauspicious beginnings to the new reign it was soon apparent that Edward III was unusually gifted in two essential aspects of kingly power: leadership over the nobility and leadership in warfare.

A decline in the number of earls was reversed with the revival early in Edward's reign of the earldoms of Lancaster, Arundel, Devon and Pembroke, and then with the creation of many new ones, six being nominated together in one session of Parliament in 1337. By the fourteenth century newly created earldoms carried the limitation that succession could only be by male heirs, but royal policy ensured that earls were still quasi-territorial rulers, who were girded with the sword when they acceded to their earldoms and who were frequently enriched by grants from the Crown. In the same year the first duke was created when the Black Prince became Duke of Cornwall. This new – or recreated – title of Duke went mostly to royal princes. Especially notable was the creation of the Duchy of Lancaster: in 1351 Henry of Grosmont and then in 1362 John of Gaunt, third son of Edward III, were made dukes of Lancaster. The Duchy of Lancaster was to pass permanently to the Crown when the son of John of Gaunt became king as Henry IV in 1399.

The development of Parliament in the fourteenth century was important not only for the emergence of a politically influential House of Commons, but also because a new legal status was given to a section of the nobility through their summons to Parliament. Until about 1350 individual nobles were summoned irregularly; after that year the parliamentary peerage became a regular group of about fifty. For this group of nobles the inheritance of their patrimony had become linked to the right to sit in the House of Lords. England was ruled by its king and its aristocracy, and rarely more successfully than between the 1330s and the 1360s.

This age of the Black Death (1348–9) and rising social disorder was also an age of splendour in the courts of king and nobility. The earls and dukes of Lancaster spent lavishly on buildings: Thomas of Lancaster had created from nothing a new fortress in Northumbria, sited dramatically at Dunstanburgh; Henry of Grosmont rebuilt his palace at the Savoy, London; and John of Gaunt transformed the castle of Kenilworth into a splendid palace, retaining the twelfth-century keep and adding a vast range of apartments. Edward III undertook the hugely expensive rebuilding of Windsor Castle, whose function had much more to do with chivalric and kingly display than with defence.

The prestige of the English nobility was nourished by success in war. The so-called Hundred Years War began with the French offensive against Gascony in 1337 and Edward III's claim to the French Crown soon after. But the king's successes began with the naval victory of Sluys in 1340, when the large French fleet was almost completely destroyed. In the years which immediately followed, despite campaigns in Flanders, Brittany and Gascony, there was no direct engagement of the English and French armies. In 1346, however, Edward's superb skill as a soldier was fully revealed. Landing in Normandy and moving eastwards in August with the intention of meeting up with the Flemings, he was faced with certain engagement at Crécy. The French forces were larger and better provisioned; but Crécy was a resounding victory for the English army, with the king skilfully commanding a combination of archers and dismounted men-at-arms. Victory in France was followed by the defeat of David II, King of Scots, by the northern barons at Neville's Cross, near Durham. Then in the summer of 1347 Edward overcame Calais, which was to be held by English colonists for two hundred years.

Warfare had its direct effects at home. Tournaments were already popular in the thirteenth century, and closely associated with them were the legends of King Arthur which fed not only the world of romance literature but also the world of political aspirations. Edward I had sponsored and patronised 'Round Tables' which were times of tournament involving sworn brotherhood, feasting and theatrical spectacle. But it was Edward III, another enthusiastic jouster, who gave new significance to the idea of the 'Round Table'. At a magnificent banquet at Windsor in January 1344 he swore to found a 'Round Table' 'to the number of three hundred knights' (the same number as King Arthur's). Despite elaborate preparations this foundation had in fact to be abandoned because of the renewed war with France. Soon, however, new and rather different plans were afoot. Between 1348 and 1349, following Crécy and the conquest of Calais, and in order no doubt to glamorise the war, Edward founded the spectacularly successful Order of the Garter. It was one of the first and certainly the most prestigious of the European confraternities of knights of the late Middle Ages, and in organisation it was linked to the serious and ceremonious business of tourneying. Membership was not confined to the highest in rank, but the Order was none the less a new élite society of only twenty-five including the king, glorifying the virtues of knighthood and nobility (Cat. 678, 681). The motto of the Order of the Garter was in effect a challenge to anyone who opposed the English claim to the French throne: *Honi soit qui mal y pense* – 'Shame to him who thinks evil of it'.

Actually the king's victories in France proved difficult to build upon and there was a series of yearly truces. But the prestige of the English Crown was still in the ascendant, for the expedition of the Black Prince in 1355, first to Gascony and then further afield, culminated in another major victory at Poitiers in September 1356. King John of France was captured and escorted triumphantly to London. While Edward was unable to capitalise on these resounding successes in his campaign of 1359–60, the terms of the settlement of Brétigny and at Calais in 1360 were nevertheless heavily in his favour. The settlement secured for him sovereignty in Gascony and Calais and their surrounding areas.

Soon, however, Edward was facing problems on all sides, in Scotland, in Flanders and in Gascony. War was a protracted affair and success was often short-lived. During the last part of the fourteenth century many of his achievements were lost: while Calais was retained, the French regained control of Flanders and the Franco-Scottish alliance re-emerged. Harmony within the royal family was an outstanding feature of Edward's reign, for which Queen Philippa, much loved in England, was largely responsible; but after the queen's death in 1369 Edward's health rapidly deteriorated, and he came under the influence of unpopular courtiers and of his grasping mistress, Alice Perrers. The problems of the 1370s form a preface to the social and political disruptions of the next reign. Edward's long reign had, however, brought to the English and to the English Court the kind of glory which contemporaries prized highly. Soon after celebrating his jubilee the king died on 21 June 1377.

English coinage under Edward III

The reign of Edward III witnessed the transformation of the English currency, establishing its pattern for the rest of the Middle Ages. However, it was as usual some time into the reign before the coinage received very active attention. The revival of the currency was undertaken in 1344, when Edward began his attempt to create a viable gold coinage for England. By this time foreign gold coins were in regular use here, despite the constant hostility of English kings to the circulation of foreign coins in their realm. The question of a native gold coinage was definitely in the air,

with specific proposals made in the Parliament of 1343.

Financial and commercial considerations were always the dominant motives behind medieval monetary changes, but in this case the factor of royal prestige may not have been irrevelant. The kings of France maintained a gold coinage, and the dynastic rivalry which engendered the Hundred Years War may have affected Edward's monetary policy. Whether or not the political element was prominent in stimulating the new coinage, it certainly affected its appearance.

In January 1344 a royal proclamation authorised the currency of three new gold coins: the florin of six shillings; the half-florin or leopard and the quarter-florin or helm. Of these coins, the florin was the one with the most obvious model, as it clearly resembles the contemporary French issues. The enthroned king with sceptre was common to most French gold coins, though the orb was peculiar to English ones. Other features, like the leopards at the king's feet and the background of fleurs-de-lis, also appear on French coins. The designs on the smaller denominations were more innovative. The crowned leopard of the half-florin echoes the direct identification of the king with the English leopard which features in Edward's epitaph in Westminster Abbey. He is described there as *invictus pardus*, the unconquered leopard. The ornate helmet on the quarter-florin accurately portrays the heraldically decorated headgear of princes at that period. The legends on all three coins include the king's French title.

The backs of all the coins are on the French model, showing a cross almost transformed into pure ornament by the addition of decoration. As on French coins, the cross is enclosed within a large quatrefoil, except on the small helm which features a more simple foliated cross. On the two larger coins English leopards appear in the angles of the quatrefoil, displacing the crowns present there on French coins of 1338–9. A new element on the backs of English coins was the use of religious quotations, again a borrowing from French coins which all carried the Easter acclamation: 'Christ conquers, Christ reigns, Christ commands'. On the English coins a different text was applied to each denomination. That used on the florin was also common on amulets and charms and may have served as an invocation against clipping.

The year 1344 also began a revival of the silver coinage with a renewal in the issue of pennies though with slight modifications in design such as wide, realistic shoulders, large fleurs-de-lis on the crown and more ornate lettering. The weight of the penny was reduced in two stages to 20 grains by 1346.

The florin gold issues ran into trouble for not accurately reflecting the current price ratio of gold to silver, the perennial problem of bimetallic currencies. The coins were overvalued in relation to the price of silver so people were reluctant to accept them and their production was discontinued after a few months. They are now exceedingly rare. However, before the year was out Edward made a second attempt to launch an acceptable gold coinage, consisting of the noble with its half and quarter. The noble was valued at 6s.8d, one-third of a pound or half a mark in the two main English denominations of account. This time the coinage was somewhat undervalued against silver, and slight weight reductions in 1346 and 1351 were

needed to establish a satisfactory relationship with silver.

The elaborate design of the new coin was without medieval precedent and is said to commemorate the English naval victory over the French at Sluys in 1340, though the image of the king as captain of the ship of state was a well-established symbol. On the back the ornate cross, surrounded by French fleurs-de-lis and English leopards surmounted by crowns, was enclosed within a tressure of eight arches instead of the French-style quatrefoil. The small quarter-noble could not accommodate the ship design, and a simple shield bearing the arms of France and England took its place.

The year 1351 was a particular landmark in the history of English coinage as it also saw the expansion of the range of silver coins. Rises in prices and wages after the Black Death helped prepare for the reintroduction of the groat, and the first appearance of the half-groat of twopence. The silver coins retained in essentials the design established by Edward I for the penny but with a more carefully modelled royal bust which, on the groat and half-groat, was surrounded by a tressure of nine arches. A religious phrase was also added to the reverse legend of the new denominations.

The gold and silver coinages continued throughout the reigns of Edward III and Richard II in the form in which they had been established in 1351. Between 1351 and 1377 they are subdivided into three periods reflecting the royal titulature on the coins which followed the political developments of the Hundred Years War. While the Treaty of Brétigny was operative (1360–9), and Edward's claims to France were in abeyance, the title 'Duke of Aquitaine' replaced the French title. Coins of the Treaty period represent the highest level of workmanship of the whole reign. From 1363 a mint at Calais was open, issuing both gold and silver as part of the arrangements which set up a wool staple and channelled the wool trade through the town.   BC

660   Florin of Edward III

660

Struck at London, Jan.–Aug. 1344

Gold, obv. king enthroned holding sceptre and orb under canopy with leopard to either side against backdrop of fleurs-de-lis, rev. short cross with quatrefoiled and foliated ends and crown at each end all within large quatrefoil, leopard in each angle outside quatrefoil: wt 6.94 g (107.1 gr)

Inscr. obv. EDWR D GRA REX ANGL Z FRANC DNS HIB [annulet stops]
rev. IHC TRANSIENS PER MEDIVM ILLORVM IBAT [annulet stops] ('But Jesus, passing through the midst of them, went His way', *Luke* IV, 30)

The Trustees of the British Museum, London. CM 1915, 5–7, 572

PROV. Found in River Tyne at Newcastle, deposited 1344, found *c.* 1857; Coll. William Foster; bt by Sir John Evans, 1868, bt by J.P. Morgan, 1908; bt by British Museum, 1915.

LIT. Evans 1900, pp. 236–7; North 1980, p. 34 no. 1105.

661   Half-florin or leopard of Edward III

661

Struck at London, Jan.–Aug. 1344

Gold, obv. crowned leopard sejant with banner bearing arms of England and France attached to neck, rev. short cross with arms ending in quatrefoil surrounded by three trefoils all enclosed in large quatrefoil with leopard in each angle outside quatrefoil: wt 3.47 g (53.5 gr)

Inscr. obv. EDWAR D GRA REX ANGL Z FRANC DNS HIB [annulet stops]
rev. DOMINE NE IN FVRORE TVO ARGVAS ME [double annulet stops] ('Lord, rebuke me not in thy anger', *Psalm* VI, 1)

The Trustees of the British Museum, London, CM 1915, 5–7, 573

PROV. Coll. J. Brumell; bt by E. W. Wigan, 1850; bt by Sir John Evans, 1872; bt by J.P. Morgan 1908; bt by British Museum, 1915.

LIT. Evans 1900, pp. 337–8; North 1980, p. 34 no. 1106.

662 Quarter-florin or helm of Edward III

662

Struck at London, Jan.–Aug. 1344
Gold, obv. helmet surmounted by cap and
    crowned leopard against background of fleurs-
    de-lis, rev. short cross with foliated ends:
    wt 1.69 g (26.1 gr)
Inscr. obv. EDWR R ANGL Z FRANC D HIB
        rev. EXALTABITVR IN GLORIA [double
    annulet stops] ('He shall be exalted in
    glory', Psalm CXII, 9)
The Trustees of the British Museum, London.
    CM 1915, 5–7, 574
PROV. Coll. J. Brumell; bt by E. W. Wigan, 1850;
bt by Sir John Evans, 1872; bt by J. P. Morgan,
1908; bt by British Museum, 1915.

LIT. Evans 1900, p. 238–40; North 1980, p. 35,
no. 1107.

663 Penny of Edward III, third ('Florin') coinage

663

Struck at London, 1344–51
Silver, obv. crowned facing bust, rev. long cross
    with three pellets in each quarter: wt 1.32 g
    (20.3 gr)
Inscr. obv. EDW R ANGL DNS HYB [annulet stops]
    rev. CIVITAS LONDON
The Trustees of the British Museum, London.
    CM E4455
PROV. Not known.

LIT. North 1980, p. 35 no. 116.

664 Noble of Edward III, pre-Treaty coinage, Series B

664

Struck at London, 1351
Gold, obv. king in armour standing in a ship,
    sword in right hand and shield quartered with
    arms of England and France in left, rev. foliated
    cross with fleur-de-lis at end of each arm and
    letter E in a central compartment, lion under
    crown in each quarter, all contained in tressure
    of eight arches: wt 7.67 g (118.3 gr)
Inscr. obv. EDWARD DEI GRA REX ANGL Z FRANC
        D HYB [annulet stops]
        rev. IHC AVTEM TRANSIENS PER MEDIVM
        ILLORVM IBAT [annulet stops]
The Trustees of the British Museum, London.
    CM 1935, 1–1, 7
PROV. Coll. L. A. Lawrence; bt by British Museum,
1935.

LIT. Lawrence 1937, pp. 10–13; Potter 1963, pp.
115–19; North 1980, p. 37 no. 1138.

665 Half-noble of Edward III, Treaty period

665

Struck at Calais, 1363–9
Gold, obv. king in armour standing in ship, sword
    in right hand and shield quartered with arms of
    England and France in left, flag at stern of ship,
    rev. foliated cross with fleur-de-lis at the end of
    each arm and letter C in central compartment,
    lion under crown in each quarter, all contained
    in tressure of eight arches: wt 3.83 g (59.1 gr)
Inscr. obv. EDWARD DEI G REX ANGL D HYB Z
        AQT [double saltire stops]
        rev. DOMINE NE IN FVRORE TVO ARGVAS
        ME [double saltire stops]
The Trustees of the British Museum, London.
    CM E4376
PROV. Not known.

LIT. Lawrence 1937, pp. 196–201, 219–20;
Potter 1964, p. 313; North 1980, p. 43 no. 1241.

666 Quarter-noble of Edward III, Treaty period

666

Struck at London, 1363–9
Gold, obv. shield quartered with arms of England
    and France within tressure of eight arches, rev.
    foliated cross with fleur-de-lis at the end of each
    arm and in central compartment, a leopard in
    each quarter, all within tressure of eight
    arches: wt 1.96 g (30.3 gr)
Inscr. obv. EDWARD DEI GRA REX ANGL
    [double saltire stops]
    rev. EXALTABITVR IN GLORIA [double
    saltire stops]
The Trustees of the British Museum, London.
    CM 1935, 4–1, 2589
PROV. Coll. T. B. Clarke Thornhill; beq. to British
Museum, 1935.

LIT. Lawrence 1937, pp. 197–201; Potter 1964,
p. 313; North 1980, p. 43 no. 1243.

667 Groat of Edward III, pre-Treaty period, Series B

667

Struck at London, 1351
Silver, obv. crowned facing bust within tressure of
    nine arches, rev. long cross with three pellets in
    each quarter: wt 4.34 g (66.9 gr)
Inscr. obv. EDWAR D G REX ANGL Z FRANC D HYB
    [annulet stops]
    rev. POSVI DEVM ADIVTOREM MEVM –
    CIVITAS LONDON [annulet stops] ('I have
    made God my helper')
The Trustees of the British Museum, London.
    CM 1924, 5–7, 42
PROV. Bt by British Museum, 1924.

LIT. Lawrence 1937, pp. 26–7; Potter 1960, pp.
139–44; North 1980, p. 37 no. 1142.

668 Half-groat of Edward III, post-Treaty period

668

Struck at London, 1369–77

Silver, obv. crowned facing bust within tressure of nine arches, rev. long cross with three pellets in each quarter: wt 2.23 g. (34.4 gr)

Inscr. obv. EDWARD REX ANGL Z FRANC [saltire stops]

rev. POSVI DEVM ADIVTOREM MEV – CIVITAS LONDON [saltire stops]

The Trustees of the British Museum, London, CM 1896, 6–9, 147

PROV. Coll. H. Montagu; bt by British Museum, 1896.

LIT. Lawrence 1937, pp. 250–1; Potter 1962, pp. 221–2; North 1980, p. 45 no. 1289.

669 Coining dies from the reign of Edward III for striking pennies

Late fourteenth century

Iron: pile l. 15 cm, wt 626 g; trussel l. 8.3 cm, wt 486 g

The Trustees of the British Museum, London, CM, coin dies 313, 314

The manufacture of coins in the Middle Ages was done by hand. Metal of the correct fineness was made into blanks which were placed between two iron dies. The lower die or 'pile' was held in place by the spike on the bottom being driven into a wooden anvil. This die usually carried the more elaborate obverse or head side design. The upper die or 'trussel', which imprinted the reverse design, was placed on top of the blank by the moneyer and struck with a hammer to impress both sides of the coin simultaneously. The trussel bore the brunt of the impact and hence had a shorter working lifespan, so it was common practice to provide two reverse dies for each obverse one.

The dies were not engraved individually, as this was too time-consuming, but were mass-produced from a small set of iron punches which were used to build up the design, e.g. one punch for the face, one for the crown and a few with basic shapes to make up the letters. When gold coinage was introduced, much larger punches were needed to cope with the intricate designs and lettering.

Royal control of the English coinage was emphasised by the manufacture of dies, which were usually made centrally and then distributed to the mints. Occasionally, during a major recoinage, it was the iron punches rather than the finished dies which were distributed. The king strictly regulated the

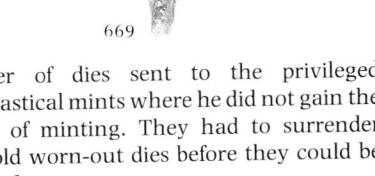

669

number of dies sent to the privileged ecclesiastical mints where he did not gain the profits of minting. They had to surrender their old worn-out dies before they could be replaced.

PROV. Found in Chapel of the Pyx, Westminster Abbey, 1911.

LIT. Fox & Fox 1909, pp. 201–5; Allen 1938, p. 31; Potter 1963, pp. 114–17; Sellwood 1963, pp. 57–65.

Seals of the mid-fourteenth century

The stylistic changes seen on seals from the period *c.* 1325–75 were initially both more varied and more far-reaching than on those from the mid-thirteenth century. In part this was because more elements were involved, such as the architectural canopy-work surrounding figures, the quantity of subsidiary figures represented and the employment of heraldry and other badges, but it also resulted from an atmosphere of greater experimentation in such fields as figure pose and proportion. It is once again the seals of bishops that demonstrate the changes most dramatically. Already in the late 1320s and early 1330s considerable variety is apparent. On some seals the bishop is shown enthroned (Cat. 95), but even when the more usual standing pose is adhered to there is striking diversity. The squat proportions and symmetrical pose of Bishop Northburgh of Lichfield (Cat. 673) are quite unlike the elegant *déhanchement* of Bishop Bury on his first seal (Cat. 674). An equivalent contrast is visible in their surrounding architectural frames. Northburgh's makes play with such quintessentially Decorated features as the ogee arch and sub-cusping, while Bury's has something of the rectilinear, panelled quality of the Perpendicular. With the benefit of hindsight we can see that the most significant and revolutionary changes occurred in 1335 on Bishop Bury's second seal (Cat. 675). Here we see a slender, swaying figure with a hint of three-quarter profile in his pose. The work is minutely detailed both in its representation of the eleven auxiliary figures and in the intricate housings in which they stand. Perhaps most significant, though, is the very sophisticated illusion of the third dimension created both by the half-octagonal plan to the niche behind the bishop and by the tracery in its back wall which implies a view through windows to the world beyond. In all these respects this seal is a portent of future taste. In 1340, Bishop Stratford of London (Cat. 676) adopted the spatial illusion of Bury's second seal, although retaining the pose of the first. But from the 1350s other prelates, for example the archbishops of York, John Thoresby and Alexander Neville (Cat. 677), accepted the whole aesthetic.

The succession of Great Seals is not rapid enough to permit us to trace the impact of the new ideas in chronological detail. None the less, from a starting-point in 1327, the seals of Edward III follow a similar development to that outlined above. The fifth and sixth seals (Cat. 671) closely resemble Bishop Stratford's of the same year in their creation of a three-dimensional cavity for the figure. But we have to wait until the 'Brétigny' seal of 1360 for a full assimilation of all the ideas promulgated in Bury's second seal (Cat. 672). TAH

493

670 Second Great Seal of Edward III

1327, before 3 Oct.
Wax: diam. 11 cm
Inscr. obv. EDWARDUS DEI GRACIA REX ANGLIE
DNS HYBERNIE DUX AQUITANIE
rev. same as obv.
The Dean and Chapter of Durham, 1.4. Reg. 2.

Edward began his reign in January 1327 using the Great Seal which his father and grandfather had used but with two fleur-de-lis added to it for purposes of differentiation and to refer to the French royal connection of his mother, Isabella, daughter of Philip IV.

pp. 166–7) supposed that this was the Great Seal made by John of Castle Acre, goldsmith of London, which was weighed at the Exchequer in February 1326 (London, Public Record Office, E159/102 m 107d). He must have inferred that the date was actually 1327, but in this he was mistaken. This seal, weighing £6.10s of silver at the rate of the London exchange, is an otherwise unrecorded Great Seal for use by Edward II's chancellor, and of its appearance we know nothing. This is unfortunate since it means we cannot assess the influence it may have had on the seal of mid-1327 here under discussion.

The architecture of the throne on the 1327

Edward's case the debt is certain: the disposition of the cloth under the king's right arm, the fact that he holds his left hand in front of him, even the type of ogee arch, all derive from the second seal of Louis X of France. It is hard to imagine a contract emanating from the king himself which would bother to specify such minutiae. Alternatively the goldsmith had independent access to Continental royal seals! Doubtless the king did stipulate that the fleurs-de-lis should be retained. Even at this stage he may have had thoughts about his claim to the French throne, which was to lead to the Hundred Years War.   TAH

LIT. Willis 1846; Wyon 1887, nos 53–4, pp. 29–30, 150–1; Birch 1887, I, nos 161–78; Greenwell & Blair 1919, XVI, no. DS 3745; Kingsford 1940, pp. 166–7.

670

671

671 Sixth Great Seal of Edward III

Mar.–June 1340
Wax: diam. 11.7 cm
Inscr. obv. + EDWARDUS DEI GRACIA REX
FRANCIE ET DOMINUS HIBERNIE
rev. same as obv.
British Library, Loose seal XXXVI.4

Under Edward III the royal administration used many different seals including seven Great Seals, one of which was re-engraved and so has two states (Cat. 672). As a result the literature is more than usually confusing.

From 1337 onward Edward occasionally styled himself King of France, but it seems that it was not until early 1340, and largely for the benefit of his Flemish allies, that he had a new Great Seal made which gave him this title. Such a seal, apparently of foreign manufacture, was brought by the king from Flanders on his return to England on 21 February of that year, but he did not use it for

During the year he had a new matrix made. On 3 October the king wrote from Nottingham to the sheriffs of London notifying them that a new seal was being adopted which differed in circumference and design from the old one. He added that an impression of it, in white wax, was being forwarded for exhibition in the city (Thomas 1924, pp. 32–3). Kingsford (1940,

seal, with its nodding ogee arch and wave parapets, shows a developed Decorated style; so too does the elegance of the king's pose with knees pushed to one side and a subtle bend in the waist. Such stylishness was part of the currency of European royal seals at the period. Haakon V Magnusson of Norway and Robert Bruce of Scotland had adopted the pose, probably under French influence. In

long. The matrices were broken on 20 June when the king was again about to leave the country. On the same day a new seal, of English workmanship but still claiming sovereignty over France, was delivered for the government of the kingdom during the king's absence. On 30 November Edward returned home with yet another seal which he had probably taken with him in June (Lyte 1926, p. 316). While the basic pattern they follow is the same, there are small, but no doubt deliberate, differences between the two English-made seals of 1340: for example the men-at-arms on the battlements of the 'fifth' seal are here replaced by hunched and bearded 'watchmen'.

The throne niche, with its vault, traceried back wall and projecting wings, clearly shows the influence of developments in monastic and ecclesiastical seal design (e.g. Cat. 674–5). The style is close to the Bishop of London's seal of the same year (Cat. 676), and makes a London origin for the matrices a virtual certainty.   TAH

LIT. Willis 1846, pp. 20–7, 37–8; Wyon 1887, nos 61–2, pp. 35–6, 152–4; Birch 1887, I, nos 186–209, Greenwell & Blair 1915, XIII, no. DS 3031; Lyte 1926; Jenkinson 1936, pp. 18–19.

672

672 Seventh Great Seal of Edward III (The 'Brétigny' seal)

May–Oct. 1360
Wax: diam. 11.5 cm
Inscr. obv. *Edwardus Dei Gracia Rex Anglie Dns Hibernie et Acquitannie*
rev. same as obv.
The Dean and Chapter of Durham, 1.3. Reg. 11

After the treaty of Brétigny in May 1360, Edward had a new seal made which omitted the title 'King of France'. It appears on a document of 24 October of that year and remained in use for a further nine years, but was then put to one side in favour of predecessors which included the French title (Cat. 671). Within two years the 'Brétigny' seal was back in service, and soon afterwards its legend was altered to bring it into line with the French claim. In this new form, with

appropriate reworkings of the king's name, it served English sovereigns intermittently for another hundred years.

The elaboration of the imagery, which includes the Virgin and Child, St George and angels flanking the king, is in line with changes that had occurred on episcopal seals (Cat. 675). Perhaps more surprising is the presence of God in the small niche above the king's head. His pose, particularly the way the orb is held on the knee, is very similar to the king's and no doubt was intended to convey, to anyone who could see it, that the king governed on earth as God did in Heaven.

The slender figures, with tightly tailored garments on their torsos, are typical of the second half of the century. The use of heraldic beasts, such as the greyhounds at the base of the shield-bearing trees, is also a recent development.   TAH

LIT. Willis 1846, pp. 22–4, 27–8, 38–9; Wyon 1887, nos 63–4, pp. 37–9, 154–5; Birch 1887, I, nos 210–23; Blair 1924, pp. 92–3. London 1959, esp. pp. 151–2.

673 Seal of Roger Northburgh, Bishop of Lichfield 1322–58

Before July 1323
Wax: h. 7.9 cm, w. 4.8 cm
Inscr. ROGERUS DEI GRACIA COVENTREN ET LICHFELDEN EPS
The Dean and Chapter of Durham, 1.13 Pont 3

An impression of this seal is on a charter in the Public Record Office (E 135/3/53) dated 4 Nones July 1323. The architecture of the canopy surrounding Bishop Roger is particularly elaborate for the 1320s. Certain monastic seals, for example that of Reading Abbey dated 1328 (Birch 1887, I, no. 3882), show something of the same complexity, but it is only in the 1330s that other episcopal

673

seals fully explore the repertoire of Decorated architectural forms. The seal of Robert Wyvil, Bishop of Salisbury (Birch 1887, I, no. 2199) is a case in point. The engraver who made Wyvil's seal may also be responsible for the *tour de force* in this mode: the third seal of Glastonbury Abbey (Ellis 1986, no. M 339). The taste for a full-blown, weighty, Decorated style was in the south and west of the country rather than the north and east. This assertion can be further supported by, for example, the seals of successive bishops of Worcester in the 1320s and 1330s. The exception which proves the rule is Simon Montacute, whose seal as Bishop of Ely is in the south-western manner; but he had just been translated to Ely from Worcester.

The figural counterpart of this style of canopy-work also tends towards heaviness. The human form is usually rendered as rather stocky and with a large head. The frontality and relative lack of Gothic 'sway' at the hips reinforce the sense of solidity.   TAH

LIT. Birch 1887, I, no. 1638; Greenwell & Blair 1916, XIV no. DS 3106.

674 First seal of Richard of Bury, Bishop of Durham 1334–45

Feb.–June 1334
Wax: h. 7.8 cm, w. 5 cm
Inscr. SIGILLUM RICARDI DEI GRA DUNELMENSIS EPI
The Dean and Chapter of Durham, 2.13 Pont 9

674

Bury was consecrated bishop on 6 February 1334 and was using this seal by 7 June, the date of the charter exhibited here. In design and workmanship it is very similar to that made for John of Kirkby, Bishop of Carlisle, and in use by October 1333. They are quite likely to be by the same maker who may, therefore, have been based in the north of

England. The elegant pose and proportions of the bishop are, however, reminiscent of such metropolitan works as the weepers on the tomb of Aymer de Valence in Westminster Abbey (Prior & Gardner 1912, fig. 433, right-hand figure). The architectural surround is made up of panels articulated by thin shafts and arch members. This is in complete contrast to the style used on Northburgh's seal (Cat. 673), and represents what may be regarded as the metalworking equivalent of proto-Perpendicular.   TAH

LIT. Birch 1887, I, no. 2462; Greenwell & Blair 1916, XIV, no. DS 3132; Blair 1922, p. 7; Heslop 1980, pp. 155–6, 159.

675   Second seal of Richard of Bury, Bishop of Durham 1334–45

June 1334–Jan. 1335
Wax: h. 8.7 cm, w. 5.6 cm
Inscr. S RICARDI DEI GRA DUNELMENSIS EPI
The Dean and Chapter of Durham, 3.9 Pont 6a

The earliest extant impression of this seal is on the charter exhibited here, dated 1 February 1335. Although an almost identical figure-style can be found slightly earlier on the seals of a Bishop of Langres and a Bishop of Arras, neither of those has the architectural complexity or the attendant figures. None the less, it seems likely that all three are by a single maker working on the Continent.

There is no evidence in Bury's well-documented career that he was out of England in the period when this seal was cut, so perhaps the matrix was a gift. Bury had been abroad on diplomatic missions for the king, and was well known at the Papal Court at Avignon. Common papal patronage may explain the widely dispersed œuvre in this style. However, an origin further north in Europe must also be a possibility since a comparable seal, though without the three-dimensional canopy-work, was made for Edward III's sister Eleanor, Countess of Guelders, probably in 1332 when she married Count Rainald (Cologne 1978, III, p. 158).

Whatever the nationality of the engraver, this particular seal's influence was felt most strongly in England, where it initiated a fashion that lasted for a century and a half. At first it was the minute and elaborate canopy-work with its tracery continuing behind the figure which was imitated. Subsequently both the diagonal projections and recessions of the niche, which help to convey a three-dimensional effect, and the population of small accompanying figures were also adopted.   TAH

LIT. Birch 1887, I, no. 2463; Greenwell & Blair 1916, XIV, no. DS 3133; Blair 1922, p. 7; Heslop 1980, pp. 156–60.

676

676   Seal of Ralph Stratford, Bishop of London 1340–54

Mar.–Oct. 1340
Wax: h. 8.4 cm, w. 5 cm
Inscr. SIGILLU RADULPHI DEI GRA
    LONDONIENSIS EPI
British Library, Cotton Charter v. 10

This seal is a fascinating compromise between the first and second seals of Richard of Bury. On the one hand the bishop's pose and the flat, panelled effect of the architectural surround are like those of Bury's first seal (Cat. 674). On the other, the tracery behind

675

the figure and the ribbed vault over his head are acknowledgements of the second (Cat. 675).

In many of its details the design is extremely close to the 1340 Great Seals of Edward III (e.g. Cat. 671). However, certain details, particularly of lettering, suggest that they are not by the same goldsmith. The fact that they are so very similar may be because they are exactly contemporary works by London-based artists who were acutely aware of what their local rivals were doing.

TAH

LIT. Birch 1887, I, no. 1919.

677

677 Seal of Alexander Neville, Archbishop of York 1374–88

Before Aug. 1382
Wax: h. 9.3 cm × 5.8 cm
Inscr. S Alexandri Di Gra Archiepi Eborac Anglie
    Primat & Aplice Sedis Legatus
The Dean and Chapter of Durham, 3.2. Archiep.
    8a

Like his predecessor Giffard (Cat. 280), Neville is shown accompanied by Sts Peter and Paul. Several other figures have joined them in the complex canopies that surround the archbishop. The Virgin and Child in the topmost niche had been a feature of Richard of Bury's second seal (Cat. 675), but angels bearing royal shields of England were a very recent invention. Neville was one of the last bishops to show himself full-length with smaller attendant saints. It was becoming normal at this date to place the prelate, half-length, in a pose of submission below a central niche which was occupied by a saintly patron or patrons.

The competitive spirit implied by the size of this seal is echoed by the title 'Legate of the Apostolic See'. This must mean 'Legatus natus' (a sort of sitting tenant's role as legate),

a rank apparently granted to archbishops of Canterbury by Pope Urban VI in 1378. Its appearance here implies a similar grant to York in right of the Northern Province. However, Neville alone before the mid-fifteenth century bothered to have the fact mentioned on a seal.

TAH

LIT. Birch 1887, I, no. 2322; Porter 1891, pp. 57–9; Greenwell & Blair 1916, XIV, no. DS. 3233.

678 Brass of Sir Hugh Hastings

c. 1347
Replica: l. of figure as it now exists 114 cm
Rough Leonine hexameter inscription on
    marginal fillet, missing, but recorded: *Hic iacet
    humatus Hastynges Hugo veneratus./Ymodum fari
    potuit, petijt tumulari/Luce ter x mense Julij mors
    hinc terit ense/Anno fertur in M. ter C quater x.
    quoque septem/Vos qui transitis Christum rogitare
    velitis./Hunc ut saluet a ve Finis sit cum pater Aue*
Parochial Church Council, St Mary's Church,
    Elsing, Norfolk (original in church)

Parts of the brass now missing have been reconstructed in the replica from eighteenth-century ink impressions. Sir Hugh is shown as a full-length knight, his bare hands in prayer, his feet supported on a lion and his head on a six-tasselled cushion held by two angels. He wears full armour, comprising: a rounded bacinet with a raised visor; a mail aventail, partly covered by a narrow plate bevor, and with a fringe – presumably attached to a lining – along its lower edge; sleeveless, close-fitting coat armour with a short, full, fringed skirt, split vertically over each thigh; underneath, a slightly shorter mail habergeon with wrist-length sleeves, the cuffs fringed – again indicating a lining(?) – and with the cuffs of the quilted hacketon visible beneath them; vambraces formed of gutter-shaped plates strapped to the upper and lower arms and with circular besagews at the elbows and armpits, cuisses studded with rivets, indicating that they were of textile lined with small plates, and carrying poleyns with small side wings, and a polygonal, conical central boss over each knee; lower legs in mail hosen with short-necked rowel spurs. Buckled slackly round his hips is a belt, decorated with lozenges and circles, carrying a cruciform sword with wheel pommel bearing his arms, long grip, and short, slightly-arched quillons. On the left arm is a small heater-shaped shield suspended from a narrow guige over the right shoulder. The coat armour, shield and sword pommel all bear Sir Hugh's arms, Or a maunche gules with a label of three points argent, with the maunche filled with a pattern of foliated scrollwork.

The elaborate canopy has side shafts, each originally surmounted by pinnacles and a tabernacle containing the figure of an angel, and comprising originally four oblong panels with weepers standing under a cusped and

678

crocketed gable canopy set against narrow tracery lights. Inside the top of the arch is a representation of Sir Hugh's soul borne aloft in a napkin by two angels against a ground of stars and scrolling lines. In the oculus of the gable is St George on a trappered horse, wearing armour similar to Sir Hugh's, but with a heart-shaped shield, laminated spaudlers – a very early representation – laminated plate gauntlets, a visor with an extension over the throat, no besagews, and, apparently, closed plate vambraces and greaves; the shield, coat armour and trapper bear St George's crosses. He is set against a background of stars and is spearing a prostrate devil. On the central pinnacle of the canopy is a helm with the Hastings bull's head crest, flanked by two panels mounted on brackets and together engraved with a Coronation of the Virgin, with Christ and Mary seated on canopied thrones, shown in rudimentary perspective, she crowned by an angel. Above are two censing angels.

The weepers represent distinguished companions in arms of Hastings. All are standing figures dressed in armour generally similar to that of St George. Their coat armours bear their arms, and some have shields, now blank. They are (in pairs from the top): (1). Edward III, holding a naked sword upright, his bare head crowned, the high collars of his habergeon and the hacketon beneath visible; Henry, Earl of Lancaster holding a crested helm similar to the Black Prince's (Cat. 626–7) and a lance with a pennon bearing a St George's cross; (2) Thomas Beauchamp, Earl of Warwick, holding a similar lance; Laurence de Hastings, 1st Earl of Pembroke; (3) Edward le Despenser (missing, but recorded as apparently similar to Lord St Amand, below); Ralph, Lord Stafford, carrying a lance similar to those of Lancaster and Warwick; (4) usually identified as Roger, Lord de Grey of Ruthin, but, since the arms are charged with a label, more probably his eldest son John, bare-headed and leaning on a long-handled axe, called a 'Galwaysparth' in the description of 1408 mentioned below; Almaric, Lord St Amand, wearing a very unusual basinet with a pronounced comb and broad brim, and a plate bevor as on the main figure; he holds a staff with a spiked end like an alpenstock (plançon á picot).

All the metal surfaces were originally gilt, the heraldry of the main figure was filled with colour (probably a wax composition rather than enamel), and the shields of the weepers were set with their arms, either in glass or in painted gesso covered with glass; the tracery of the canopy was also partly filled with coloured glass. The inscription incorporated a shield at each corner with the coloured arms respectively of Hastings and Foliot, and also figures of the Evangelists, while two pairs of glass or painted gesso shields with the same arms originally flanked the top of the canopy.

Sir Hugh de Hastings, the elder son of John, 2nd Baron Hastings by his second wife Isabel le Despenser, married Marjorie, daughter of Sir Jordan Foliot, and built Elsing church. He was a soldier who saw much service in the early campaigns of the Hundred Years War (he fought at Crécy), as did all the men represented as weepers, which must be the main reason for their selection, though some were also related to him. The three who are distinguished by lances bearing St George's pennons were, in addition to the king himself, founder members of the Order of the Garter, which was closely associated with the cult of St George, then gaining renewed popularity in England – and the saint is himself prominently represented on the brass. The Order was founded formally in 1349, but there is evidence that it was under consideration some time before, and the presence of these figures – the earliest known representations of Knights of the Garter as such – need not mean that the brass was produced in or after that year, though it must have been designed by someone with

679

up-to-date information about events at Court. The inclusion of the Coronation of the Virgin scene no doubt reflects Hastings's own devotional preference, like the dedication of his church.

This is one of the of the most magnificent brasses ever produced, and apparently unique in its use of glass as an enrichment. It is almost certainly of London origin, like the related Wautone brass at Wimbish, Essex, but it may have connections with the earlier Seymour workshop, which used comparable canopy shafts filled with weepers under gable canopies. A detailed description of the brass was made in 1408, when it was used as evidence in the case of Grey versus Hastings in the Court of Chivalry.   CB

LIT. Carter 1780–7, I, pp. 12–13; Hartshorne & Hope 1906; Wagner & Mann 1939; Norris 1978a, pp. 29, 39, 42, 69, 103, figs 103, 129, 130, 1978b, p. 18, figs 21–2; Vale 1982, pp. 76–91; Binski 1985; Binski 1987, pp. 119–25.

679 Inscription from Bisham Abbey

c. 1340(?)

Latten or other copper alloy: h. 13.2 cm, w. 44.2 cm

Inscr. Edward Roy Danglet[er]re qe fist le siege deuant la Cite de Be rewyk' & co[n]quyst la bataille illeoq[ue]s & la dite Cite la Veille sein te Margarete Ian de g[ra]ce M.CCC.xxxiii. mist ceste pere a la requeste Sire William de Mountagu foundour de ceste mesoun

Parochial Church Council of St James's, Denchworth, Oxfordshire

Thanks to being used on its reverse side in the 1560s, for a memorial inscription, this commemorative inscription survives as a record that 'Edward [III], King of England, who besieged the city of Berwick [on Tweed] and there won the battle and the same city on St Margaret's Eve [19 July] in the year of grace 1333, laid this stone at the request of Sir William de Montagu, founder of this house'. By his victory on 19 July 1333 at Halidon Hill Edward won control over the Scottish pretender Edward Balliol; the house named in the inscription must have been Bisham Priory (near Denchworth), whose foundation charter from William de Montagu, Earl

of Salisbury, is dated 1337 (VCH, Berks., ii, p. 82). The inscription was presumably cut a few years later, c. 1340.

It is in a mixture of letter forms, with a wide, round Gothic for most of the capital letters and a simple textura (often called black letter) for the lower case: it was in the course of the fourteenth century that the former style (often called Lombardic, ever since the term was coined by the French scholar Jean Mabillon [1632–1707] gave way to the more angular textura and the inscription may be seen as illustrating the transitional phase between one style and the other. The transition was lengthy: bells and painted lettering continue to show a mixture of Lombardic capitals and textura lower-case letters well into the fifteenth century (e.g. Nelson 1919, p. 140; Boughey 1919, p. 77).

NLR

PROV. Bisham Abbey; Denchworth Church, Berks., since 1560s.

LIT. Page-Phillips 1980, I, p. 58, repr. II, pl. 80.

680 St Stephen's Chapel, Westminster Palace, east end of north wall: scenes from the Book of Job

1350–63

Tempera and oil on stone; gilded gesso: seven fragments, max. h. 118 cm, min. h. 18.5 cm

Inscriptions in Latin

The Trustees of the British Museum, London.

MLA 14, 3–12, 2

Although begun by Edward I (see Cat. 324–5), the chapel did not receive its painted decoration until the reign of his grandson, Edward III (for the dating evidence see Cat. 324–5, 681). This decoration, the most magnificent programme of the century, was rediscovered and recorded, and some few fragments saved, in the period 1795–1800, before its final destruction in 1800 in Wyatt's remodelling of the chapel.

The scheme, which can be reasonably reconstructed from antiquarian material and from original royal accounts, included Infancy and patron subjects on the east wall (see Cat. 681), biblical narratives (some sur-

680

viving) and possibly scenes from the Lives of Saints (Smith 1807, pp. 153–4) arranged in two tiers of four scenes each below the five windows of each side wall; angels holding draperies behind the wall arcade; warrior saints on the window piers. In addition, all architectural elements were painted or gilded. Hugh of St Albans was master of the numerous painters impressed for the work, though records of equal payments suggest a sharing of the design role. The purchase of lavish quantities of expensive materials is recorded (see Colvin 1963, pp. 518–19): the elaborate technique has parallels in contemporary mural painting in England and Italy (see p. 130 above), as well as France (Avignon) and Bohemia (Karlstein).

Italian sources may be adduced for a number of elements including the handling of perspectival space, the use of Tuscan architectural vocabulary, iconographical motifs, consistent directional lighting, and facial types and modelling. However, the style of the various paintings is by no means uniform and presents, rather, a blending of features selected from English and Continental idioms (see p. 130 above). Such diversity and experimentation is only to be expected given the courtly ambience.　　DP

PROV. Removed from St Stephen's Chapel, 1800.

LIT. Topham 1795–1813, pp. 8–22; Smith 1807, pp. 147–8, 155–64, 174–223; Tristram 1955, pp. 48–54, 57–8, 206–19, repr. pls 1–6; Colvin 1963, pp. 518–19; Vale 1982, pp. 53–6; Simpson 1984, pp. 161–7, repr. pls 316–23, 326–7; Binski & Park 1986, pp. 37, 415; Lindley 1986b, pp. 87–90; Roberts 1986.

681　Copy by Richard Smirke of mural formerly at east end of St Stephen's Chapel, Westminster

c. 1800
Tempera and gold leaf on thick paper: h. 83 cm, w. 116 cm
Society of Antiquaries of London

Smirke's large-scale copy of this mural gives a clear impression of the rich oil-based coloration and lavishly gilt surface texturing of the murals formerly in St Stephen's Chapel (see also Cat. 680). The original was destroyed *c.* 1800. It lay immediately to the north of the high altar. In the upper register is the Adoration of the Magi. The young king to the left bears a pyx and a sceptre and is most fashionably arrayed, having slippers with a rose window design of the sort mentioned in Chaucer's Miller's Tale (see above, p. 49).

Another king bears a magnificent incense boat (cf. Cat. 122) before the Virgin, who is seated on an obliquely-placed throne. The motif of sword-bearing attendants to the left is derived from Trecento Italy.

In the lower register, beneath an elaborate arcade representing the chapel's interior, kneel the male members of the royal family led towards the high altar by St George; they regard the scene above. Behind St George are: King Edward III; Edward, Prince of Wales; Lionel, Duke of Clarence; John of Gaunt, Earl of Lancaster; Edmund, Duke of York; and (presumably) Thomas of Woodstock, Duke of Gloucester, the latter originally set at an angle at the junction of the north and east walls of the chapel (Smith 1807, pl. opp. p. 153). The composition was reflected on the south side of the altar by the females of the royal family headed by Queen Philippa, beneath pictures of the Nativity and Presentation. The nature of the altarpiece framed by these Gospel events is a matter of conjecture, but it should have been Marian in content. The stress on St George and the Virgin reflects the religious sentiments of the Order of the Garter, founded in the 1340s (see also Cat. 672).

Royal accounts show that the mural must

681

have been executed after 1350, and probably after 1355 (as Gloucester is included) but before 1363 – if our present understanding of the accounts is correct (Colvin 1963, I, pp. 518–19). The painted arcade is a variant of the lateral arcading of the chapel itself; fleurons and crenellations also figured in the design of the main elevation (see Cat. 325). The window tracery depicted on the female side must also have followed that of the chapel. The architecture has points of contact with Flemish painting (e.g. James 1933), and the format of kneeling patrons under such arcades can also be matched in Flemish glazing of c. 1350 (Helbig 1961, figs 7–8). The relationship of these murals to Italian and Flemish art is in need of scrutiny. PB

PROV. Executed for Society of Antiquaries by Richard Smirke (d. 1815); displayed in General Secretary's office at the Society.

LIT. Topham 1795–1813, pl. xvi; Smith 1807; Tristram 1955, pp. 48–58, 206–19, pls 2–6 (a); Colvin 1963, I, pp. 518–19.

682 Treatise of Walter of Milemete

1326–7
Parchment, ff. 82: 24 × 21 cm
The Governing Body of Christ Church, Oxford, MS 92

In 1326–7 Master Walter of Milemete, King's Clerk and later Fellow of King's Hall, Cambridge, composed this treatise, *De nobilitatibus, sapientiis, et prudentiis regum*, as a companion to a copy of the *Secreta Secretorum* attributed to Aristotle (London, British Library, Add. MS 47680). He intended, according to his introduction, to present the vol-

682

umes as a pair to the new king, Edward III. Whether Edward actually received them is uncertain, since the decoration of neither book is finished.

The texts are manuals of scientific, religious, moral, military and political instruction for a sovereign. The dimensions, format and decoration of the volumes are similar, but the Milemete treatise has a more elaborate programme of illustration, which includes frontispieces of St George presenting a shield to an English king (f. 3; cf. Cat. 151) and a double 'portrait' of Edward II and Isabella of France (f. 4v.), as well as nineteen other full-page miniatures, primarily of battles and sieges

(some unfinished). In addition, each division of the text is introduced by a large miniature showing a king with advisers or supplicants, or in religious devotion (f. 5). But the main decoration of the volume consists of broad rectilinear borders on each text page. They are divided into compartments crammed with heraldry, contorted hybrids, human monstrosities and combats.

The chief artist of the Milemete treatise worked in conjunction with four others, three of whom also participated in the illustration of the *Secreta Secretorum*. These Milemete artists seem to have formed a loose group, shifting in personnel and perhaps also in place of production. Milemete hands occur in numerous other manuscripts of the 1320s; among the most elaborate are the Sidney Sussex Psalter (MS 76), the DuBois Hours (New York, Pierpont Morgan Library, M. 700) and the Douce Hours (Cat. 683). Some Milemete-related artists were also active in the illustration of legal and theological texts as diverse in destination or provenance as Oxford (Oxford, Bodleian Library, MSS e Mus. 60 and Lat. Misc. b. 16) and Paris (Bibliothèque nationale, MSS lat. 3114[1] and 3114[2]). LFS

PROV. William Carpender, rector of Staunton super Vagam, Heref. & Worcs.; beq. to Christ Church, 1707.

LIT. James 1913; Sandler 1986, no. 84, II, pp. 91–3, repr. I, figs 217, 222; Michael 1987.

683 Psalter

c. 1325–35
Parchment, ff. 138: 23.3 × 15.5 cm
Oxford, Bodleian Library, MS. Douce 131

The historiation of the initial for Psalm CXIX, the first of the Gradual Psalms, may provide

683

some clue to the owner of a psalter, since an identifiable individual in prayer is sometimes the subject of the illustration. Here the person represented may be Edward III (f. 119). He wears the arms of Montreuil (of which he was Lord), the arms of England and France form a background behind the initial, and the bird-topped sceptre held by the Virgin before whom he kneels may reflect the sceptre of the English kings (cf. Cat. 14).

Although the calender and Litany are lost, it is clear that the manuscript belongs artistically to a group including the Douai (Douai, Bibliothèque publique, MS 171), St-Omer (London, British Library, MS 39810), and sections of the Luttrell (Cat. 575) and Ormesby (Cat. 573) Psalters, all books characterised by the introduction of contemporary Italian techniques of shading and rendering of surface textures. The chief artist of the Douce Psalter employed these techniques idiosyncratically, especially in his creation of brilliant architectural fantasies consisting of pile-ups of projecting dormers supported on obscene squatting male 'caryatids' (Cat. 502–5), devilish waterspouts and puffy foliage, all executed expertly in grisaille. LFS

PROV. Johannes Adams, 16th century; William Bendlowes, d. 1613; John Jackson, FSA; sale 28 April 1794, bt by Frances Douce; beq. to Bodleian Library, 1834.

LIT. Alexander 1983; Sandler 1986, no. 106, II, pp. 117–8, repr. I, figs 268–9.

684 Psalter

1337–45 and c. 1380
Parchment, ff. 160; 30 × 19.1 cm
The Master and Fellows of St John's College Cambridge, MS.D.30

The arms of Simon de Montacute, Bishop of Ely 1337–45, appear on the Beatus page of this psalter (f. 7), preceded by an Ely diocese calendar. Although Montacute was undoubtedly the intended owner, much of the decoration of the manuscript was finished only towards the end of the fourteenth century in a style comparable to that of the Litlyngton Missal of 1383–4 (Cat. 714). The original work is best seen on the Beatus page. David's heavily shaded facial features are in the tradition of the physiognomic types of the Luttrell Psalter (Cat. 575), but the drapery treatment is marked by the elaborate convoluted and cascading folds associated with the imported style of Jean Pucelle (cf. Cat. 569). The thin rectilinear border, with its corner knots of interlace and symmetrically placed curling sprigs tipped with small even-sized leaves and flowers, is in the new taste of the 1330s and 1340s. Similar decorative borders occur in the Astor Hours and Psalter (Ginge Manor, Viscount Astor), a psalter in Brescia (Biblioteca Queriniana, MS A. V. 17, also of Ely destination), and a psalter made for Queen Philippa between 1328 and 1340 (London, British Library, Harley MS 2899).

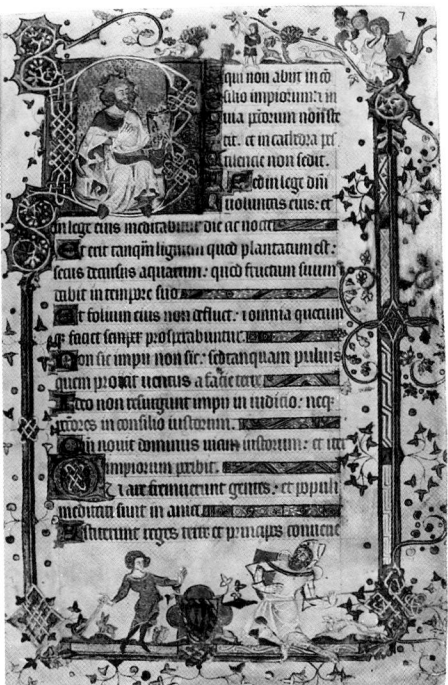

684

Around 1380 another artist completed the decoration of the manuscript, in part guided by drawings left by the first hand, especially for the borders (Psalms XXXVI, XXVIII, CIX). His own historiated initials, for Psalms LII, LXVIII, LXXX, XCVII and the Office of the Dead, contain large plump, softly-shaded figures typical of the Litlyngton style, and his borders employ the new vocabulary of foliate types – especially kite- and bell-and-clapper-shaped leaves – that appeared in the last two decades of the fourteenth century. LFS

PROV. Simon de Montacute (?); Thomas Moyle, Wakefield, 18th century; Revd Henry Zouche, Swillington, Yorks., end 18th century; Earls of Lonsdale, 19th–20th century; H.W.P. Gatty, Librarian of St John's College; given to St John's, 1948.

LIT. Sandler 1986, no. 113, II, pp. 125–6, repr. I, figs 291–3.

685 The Fitzwarin Psalter

c. 1350–60 and c. 1370
Parchment, ff. 230; 31.5 × 21 cm
Paris, Bibliothèque nationale, MS lat. 765

Except for the miniature of the female owner or donor kneeling piously in the presence of the young Virgin Mary and her parents (f. 7), the original cycle of scenes preceding the text of the Fitzwarin Psalter is devoted to thirteen episodes in the Passion of Christ. These events are presented in a grippingly theatrical fashion; the figures are large with exceptionally vehement gesticulations; the faces, particularly of the villains, are caricatures, hideously dark and forcefully shaded.

In an important study, Francis Wormald dated the psalter to the third quarter of the

fourteenth century and named the book after the Somerset families of Fitzwarin and Clevedon. Their arms appear on the Beatus page (f. 23). Wormald identified the artist of the Fitzwarin Psalter as the painter of another psalter, in the Bodleian Library (MS Liturg. 198). He also suggested that the facing

685

miniatures of Christ in Majesty and the Crucifixion (ff. 21–2) at the end of the Fitzwarin cycle – framed in architectural fantasies similar to those of the preceding Passion miniatures – were the work of the artist of the Egerton Genesis (London, British Library, MS Eger. 1894), the Psalter of Stephen of Derby (Oxford, Bodleian Library, MS Rawl. G. 185), and the M.R. James Psalter (London, British Library, Add. MS 44949). This artist figured in the 'Giottesque episode' in English art first defined by Otto Pächt. The delicate volumes and self-contained contours of his work are linked to the Italianate features of the Bohun manuscripts of c. 1360–80 (Cat. 686–91). Consequently, the two pages – not part of the gathering structure of the book – could be later in date than the rest. LFS

PROV. Fitzwarin or Clevedon families; Sir John Cockayne, d. 1429.

LIT. Wormald 1943, pp. 71–9, repr. pls 22a,c,d, 23, 25a, b; Dennison 1986, pp. 42–66, repr. figs 5, 8, 20; Sandler 1986, no. 120, II, pp. 133–5, repr. I, figs 314–7; Avril & Stirnemann 1987, no. 202, repr. pls N, O, lxxxiv–vi.

686 Psalter

Begun c. 1350–60
Parchment, ff. 160; 28.3 × 19.2 cm
Vienna, Oesterreichische Nationalbibliothek Cod. 1826*

From the evidence of about ten surviving manuscripts, the greatest patrons of English

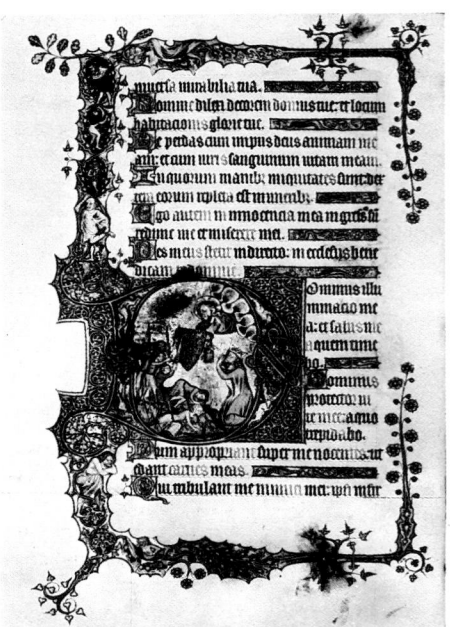

686

illumination during the fourteenth century were members of the Bohun family, Earls of Hereford, Essex and Northampton. The Vienna Psalter may have been made, or at least begun, for Humphrey de Bohun, sixth Earl of Hereford and Essex (1309–61) as we know from a number of prayers in his name (later erased) and a profusion of heraldic shields with his arms, those of his married sisters, and those of England.

The manuscript, a psalter with textual additions such as the Penitential Psalms, *memoriae* of saints, and Gospel sequences characteristic of Books of Hours, is decorated with large historiated initials with full borders at the main divisions and with hundreds of small historiated initials, primarily literal text illustrations, recalling the rare, ancient tradition of the ninth-century Utrecht Psalter. Some of the large initials follow the same principle, Psalm XXVI, for example, showing David praying as he is threatened by his enemies and receiving a lantern and a shield from the Lord, following the words, 'The Lord is my light and my salvation, whom shall I fear?' (f. 25v.).

Several artists worked on the Vienna Psalter. The page design and figure style of the first (ff. 7–47v.) almost duplicate the work of the Beatus page artist of the Psalter of Simon de Montacute (Cat. 684), begun between 1337 and 1345. This style characterised a number of mid-century English manuscripts and suggests a starting date for the Vienna Psalter of not much later than 1350, a decade before that suggested by earlier scholars.

The other artists of the Vienna Psalter, however, painted in a style typical of the Bohun manuscripts (Cat. 686–91). Their figures are large-headed but wasp-waisted, spindly-limbed and unstable; the faces have ovoid contours, and are notable for their half-lowered eyelids over dark disc-like pupils. The work of these artists could well have extended into the time of Humphrey de Bohun, seventh Earl of Hereford, Essex and Northampton (1342–73), nephew of the sixth Earl for whom the book had been begun. LFS

PROV. Johann Stanilaus Reznicki, 17th century; bt in Vienna in 1852.

LIT. Hermann 1936, pp. 17–38; James & Millar 1936, pp. 33–6, repr. pls XXXXIX–LVI; Brussels 1973, no. 69; Sandler 1985, pp. 364–72; Sandler 1986, no. 133, II, pp. 147–9, repr. I, figs 354–5; Dennison 1987.

687 Psalter

c. 1360–73 (?)
Parchment. ff. 127: 28.6 × 18.4 cm
Exeter College. Oxford (Rector and Fellows), MS 47

Only two of the ten or more large historiated initials in figured architectural borders that once subdivided the text of this Bohun Psalter survive to give a hint of the original magnificence of decoration of the volume (ff. 33v.–4, Psalms LI–LII). Together with hundreds of small historiated initials with thin rectilinear borders for the remaining psalms and canticles, they recount the Old

687

Testament narrative from Creation to Moses (*Genesis* I–*Numbers* XXXII) in a continuous cycle. At the end, the collects following the Litany, *memoriae* of saints, and Gospel sequences (cf. Cat. 686, 689) are also illustrated, with historiated initials of the saints invoked in the text.

A historical mode of illustration of the Psalms, represented in the first half of the fourteenth century by the Tickhill Psalter (Cat. 568), was also practised in other Bohun manuscripts (Cat. 689–90, and Oxford, Bodleian Library, MS Auct. D.4.4). At least one of the artists of the Exeter College Psalter painted the same subjects elsewhere among the Bohun manuscripts, without replicating the compositions, even when depicting the rarest of scenes.

The heraldic elements of the Exeter College Psalter – shields with the arms of England (before 1340) and Bohun in the borders – are more sparse than in other manuscripts of the Bohun group, but the text includes *memoriae* of the Apostles in the name of 'thy servant Humphrey', as in other Bohun books. This may refer to Humphrey, sixth Earl of Hereford and Essex (d. 1361) or Humphrey, seventh Earl (d. 1373). But the illustration of the manuscript might possibly have continued even past the lifetime of the seventh Earl, since the gentle, Italianate figure style and florid decoration of the second major artist (ff. 84 on) – inconceivable as early as the time of the sixth Earl – suggest a dating in the last two decades of the century.   LFS

PROV. Elizabeth of York, wife of Henry VII, d. 1503; Catherine of Aragon, wife of Henry VIII, d. 1536; given to Exeter College by Sir William Petre, c. 1556.

LIT. James & Millar 1936, pp. 1–22, repr. pls I–XXII; Sandler 1986, no. 134, II, pp. 149–51, repr. I, figs 356–8; Dennison 1987.

688 Fragmentary Book of Hours

1361–73
Parchment, ff. 15: 17 × 12.2 cm
Pommersfelden, Graf von Schönborn
   Schlossbibliothek, MS 348

All that remains of the original text are *memoriae* of the Apostles, Commemorations of the Deity and the Saints, and the Gospel sequences, material usually following the main offices of a Book of Hours. The saints are invoked in the name of Humphrey, and the selection of texts, the pictorial programme and the heraldry all make it probable that the Humphrey in question was Humphrey de Bohun, seventh Earl of Hereford, Essex and Northampton, who succeeded to the title in 1361.

The Bohun family employed artists who worked in a uniquely 'Bohun' style, not found in books made for other owners. The original appearance of the Pommersfelden fragment can be reconstructed from the

688

nearly identical psalter and Hours in the Bodleian Library (Oxford, MS Auct. D.4.4), probably made c. 1380 for Humphrey de Bohun's daughter Mary. Like the Bodleian manuscript, the Pommersfelden fragment includes a remarkable devotional image – not illustrating a text – of the Wounds of Christ, the Crucifixion and Resurrection, and the Instruments of the Passion (f. 9v.). Another full-page miniature shows standing saints (f. 10), and each text section has an historiated initial, some with narrative scenes, particularly of saints' martyrdoms.

The figure style is typical of the Bohun group: heads are large, shoulders narrow, bodies tubular, and limbs wobbly. The decoration is notable for bearded profiles and jaw-to-jaw monsters as initial frames, two motifs ubiquitous in the Bohun manuscripts.   LFS

PROV. Not known.

LIT. Sandler 1986, no. 137, II, pp. 155–7, repr. I, figs 364–5; Dennison 1987.

689   Psalter and Hours of the Virgin

1361–73(?)
Parchment, ff. 170: 39.5 × 23 cm
British Library, Egerton MS 3277

A volume of grand dimensions, formal script and magnificent decoration, this major manuscript of the Bohun group came to light after M. R. James's study of the Bohun manuscripts was published in 1936. Like other Bohun books (Cat. 686–91), its decorative programme consists of hundreds of historiated initials at the beginning of major and minor text divisions and a veritable encyclopedia of motifs incorporated into marginal extensions from the initial frames. The initials to the Psalms, Canticles, Litany and collects (ff. 7–110v.) contain a continuous cycle originally of at least 220 Old Testament

subjects from the life of David, from I *Kings* IX to II *Kings* XXII (five of the large historiated initials are lost). The initials in the Hours of the Virgin and the Office of the Dead (ff. 111–159v., again several are lost) form a long pictorial narrative of the Life of Christ.

Most of the decoration was done by an illuminator whose work is prominent in other Bohun manuscripts (e.g. Cat. 690), above all the small-format psalter and Hours in the Bodleian (MS Auct. D.4.4). There, as in the Egerton volume, he was teamed with a second master, whose luminous colour and delicately shaded figure style has been linked to contemporary Italian painting.

Textual supplications in the name of Humphrey, and heraldry, connect the manuscript to the Bohun family, most likely to Humphrey, seventh Earl of Hereford, Essex and Northampton. There are also a number of witty pictorial references to contemporary people and events, such as a figure of Elizabeth de Bohun, daughter of Edward I and grandmother of Humphrey (f. 131v.), identifiable by her heraldic garment and by the adjacent lion surmounted by a castle, recalling the arms of Castile and León used by her own mother, Eleanor of Castile. The most notable pictorial reference to recent events is the marginal vignette of Jean le Bon, King of France surrendering to Edward III after the Battle of Poitiers in 1356, while Charles le Mauvais of Navarre looks on, identifiable by his shield with the arms of England and his leonine mount (f. 68v.).   LFS

PROV. Lowther family, Earls of Lonsdale, c. 1800; Sotheby's, 6 Dec. 1937, bt by British Library.

LIT. Sandler 1985, pp. 364–72; Sandler 1986, no. 135, II, pp. 151–4, I, repr. figs 359–62; Dennison 1987.

689

690

690 Psalter

c. 1380
Parchment, ff. 243 : 16.8 × 11 cm
The Syndics of the Fitzwilliam Museum
Cambridge, MS 38–1950

The Fitzwilliam Psalter is one of a pair of devotional volumes made in all likelihood on the occasion of the betrothal or marriage in 1380 of Henry of Bolingbroke (the future Henry IV), son of John of Gaunt, Duke of Lancaster, and Mary de Bohun, daughter of Humphrey, seventh Earl of Hereford, Essex, and Northampton. The other volume, a psalter and Hours in the Bodleian Library, Oxford (MS Auct. D.4.4), contains a miniature showing Mary de Bohun adoring the Virgin (f. 181v.) and both are liberally ornamented with heraldic shields with the arms of the Bohuns and related families, of England, and of Lancaster. Since the Fitzwilliam Psalter includes a prayer on behalf of a male supplicant, perhaps it was intended for Henry while the Bodleian volume was for his bride.

The text is illustrated with half-page miniatures and historiated initials at the main divisions. The thirty-five subjects form a cycle from the life of David. Characteristic of Bohun iconography is the narrative detail and inventiveness. The compositions do not duplicate representations of the same subjects in other Bohun manuscripts, such as the Egerton Hours (Cat. 689), even though painted by the same artist.

The artist of the Fitzwilliam Psalter was the mainstay of the Bohun group. His work occurs not only in the Bodleian psalter and Hours but also in the Egerton Hours in the British Library (Cat. 689), and perhaps in the Vienna and Exeter College Psalters as well (Cat. 686–7). It is possible that he can be identified as John de Teye, an Augustinian

friar, who served as illuminator to Humphrey de Bohun, sixth Earl of Hereford and Essex (d. 1361), and was still active as an illuminator, probably in Bohun service, in 1384. LFS

PROV. Henry VI or Margaret of Anjou, 15th century; John Stafford, Lord Chancellor and Archbishop of Canterbury 1443–53; Barnaby family, 15th century; Walton family, 16th century; Emma, Lady Stafford, before 1884, bt by Henry Yates Thompson, 1907; Sotheby's, 23 March 1920, bt by T.H. Riches; beq. to Fitzwilliam Museum, 1935.

LIT. James & Millar 1936, pp. 51–9, pls LII–LIX; Brussels 1973, no. 70; Sandler 1985, pp. 364–72; Sandler 1986, no. 139, II, pp. 159–61, I, repr. figs 369–70; Dennison 1987.

691 Book of Hours

1380–94
Parchment, ff. 66 ; 17.9 × 12.9 cm
The Royal Library, Copenhagen, MS Thott 547, 4

Closely related in style and format to the Bohun Psalter and Hours in the Bodleian Library, Oxford (MS Auct. D.4.4), the Copenhagen Hours seems to have been made for Mary de Bohun, daughter of the seventh Earl of Hereford, Essex and Northampton, after her marriage to Henry of Bolingbroke (the future Henry IV), son of the Duke of Lancaster, in 1380. Bohun and Lancaster arms are prominent, and Mary de Bohun (d. 1394) is probably the praying woman represented on the Matins page of the Hours of the Virgin (f. 1).

The book is illustrated at the text divisions, mainly with historiated initials showing events from the lives of Christ and the Virgin and with *bas-de-page* scenes of Miracles of the Virgin. The artist worked to a small scale,

691

painting animated figures in typical Bohun proportions and crowding them together. His work is marked, however, by a unique technique of rendering the illusion of light and atmosphere, which dissolves the edges of forms, sometimes, as in the representation of Heaven (f. 32v.), in a spectacular radiance. This painterly technique heralds the developed qualities of light and surface found in the early fifteenth-century work of Hermann Scheerre in England and the Boucicaut Master on the Continent. LFS

PROV. Beq. by O. Thott, 1785.

LIT. James & Millar 1936, pp. 47–52, pls LVII–LXI; Sandler 1986, no. 140, II, pp. 161–2, repr. I, figs 366, 375; Dennison 1987.

XVII Richard II (1377–99)

During Edward III's last years the government lacked leadership; and little changed when Richard, son of Edward the Black Prince, became king in 1377, for he was only ten years old. The council which led the government faced problems because of continuing tension between the royal Court and the king's uncle, John of Gaunt, Duke of Lancaster (see Cat. 745), and because of mounting financial needs following the reopening of the French war. Severe lack of confidence in the government came to a dramatic head with the Peasants' Revolt in 1381. Social discontent erupted in both town and countryside especially, though not exclusively, in the south-east, including East Anglia. The occasion for revolt was an unusually high tax of 1s per head of population which was distributed unfairly and fell particularly heavily on the poor. Men from Essex and Kent, under the leadership of Wat Tyler and John Ball, converged on London. When John Ball preached at Blackheath he achieved fame with his 'When Adam delved and Eve span, Who was then the gentleman?' After Wat Tyler with his followers had taken London by assault, destroying Gaunt's palace of the Savoy, opening prisons, breaking into the Tower of London and murdering the king's Chancellor, Archbishop Sudbury, and others, the young Richard showed great courage and determination in negotiating with the rebels at Mile End and Smithfield, winning their confidence especially after Tyler's death. The revolts quickly ran their course; little that is measurable was achieved to satisfy the peasants' grievances, save an end to the poll-tax.

The king had come of age in the midst of the worst social disorder that England had ever known. Through it all, reverence for kingship did not wane, a reverence to which Richard responded; but, despite his efforts to enhance the splendour of sovereign rule, political stability proved difficult to secure. The spread of Wycliffite heresy was causing alarm, and tensions among the nobility were unresolved. No diplomatic advantage was gained, as had been hoped, by Richard's marriage to Anne of Bohemia, and failures abroad continued, notably with the disastrous 'crusade' led by the Bishop of Norwich to relieve Flanders of the French. Partly at the instigation of his favourite, Robert de Vere, the king's bitterness against John of Gaunt re-emerged. Gaunt was critical of the Court Circle and drew attention to misgovernment and to Richard's distaste for military leadership. While Gaunt had a reputation for prudence, the king and his courtiers were widely regarded as extravagant and irresponsible. A major crisis followed Gaunt's departure to lay claim to Castile in 1386. To the great humiliation of the king, Michael de la Pole, the principal minister, was tried in Parliament and dismissed from office, and in the 'Merciless' Parliament of 1388 the Court was purged by the conviction for treason of the king's friends. The Crown was in the grip of lords known as the 'appellants', and aristocratic rivalry was injected with new venom.

A short period of relative calm followed. The king broke free from the controls which the 'appellants' had put upon him, and John of Gaunt, benefiting from the fact that he was not associated with the events of 1388, returned to England and exercised an important moderating influence. Richard achieved some success in Ireland in 1395, reasserting English lordship there. His queen had died, childless, in 1394, and in 1396 he reinforced a truce with France by marrying Isabella, the six-year-old daughter of Charles VI of France. But the alliance with France in fact spelt deep trouble for Richard. It was far from popular in England, and Anglo-French enmity could not be dispelled. It is significant that when Henry Bolingbroke was driven into exile, he was to be welcomed at the French Court.

The French alliance had, however, freed Richard from the shackles of dependence upon Parliament for war finance. His greatly increased self-assurance led to an attempt to establish autocratic royal control, beginning with an attack upon the 'appellants' of 1388 and upon their policies. A dispute between two of the 'appellants',

Thomas Mowbray, Duke of Norfolk, and Henry Bolingbroke, Duke of Hereford and son of John of Gaunt, was settled by their banishment. When John of Gaunt died in February 1399, Richard took immediate steps to prevent Bolingbroke from succeeding to the Lancastrian inheritance and, soon after, left England with innocent self-confidence to deal with a pressing situation in Ireland. The banished Bolingbroke, finding crucial support among the northern magnates, especially the Percys, landed at Ravenspur in East Yorkshire. The king, returning through Wales, was quickly weakened by desertions and taken prisoner. On 29 September in the Tower of London Richard resigned his throne, and allegiance to him was renounced by the estates in Parliament on the next day. Whatever attempts were made to give legality to these acts of deposition, Henry Bolingbroke had supplanted Richard II by force. In mitigation, the new king could claim descent from Henry III. More important, since there was no defined law of succession, Bolingbroke had no obvious rival and Richard, during the previous two years at least, had abandoned attempts to rule according to the laws and customs of the kingdom; his policies had become foolhardy and dangerous. The political turmoils of his reign are to be contrasted with the brilliant achievements of his Court, among them the patronage of Chaucer (Cat. 719) and the building of the new Westminster Hall (Cat. 692). In the Wilton Diptych (fig. 104) and the king's portrait in Westminster Abbey (Cat. 713) we see portrayals of the cult of kingship in which Richard believed. Kingship itself was in no way threatened by his failures; but absolute kingship could not easily take root in England. Early in 1400 the former king, held captive in Pontefract Castle, was murdered, in all probability at the command of the new king, Henry IV.

The architecture of the later fourteenth century sees the French-inspired Perpendicular transformed into a national Gothic style. The Black Death hardly affected the progress of major building projects, though some of the leading master masons died from the plague. Perpendicular proved to be a highly adaptable style, using veneers of tracery to transform Romanesque structures into Gothic (e.g. Cat. 498), and responding to the architectural needs of a changing society with a variety of ingenious solutions. William of Wykeham's New College, Oxford (Cat. 599), established a lasting model for English university colleges. The friars' churches – simple, spacious and wooden-roofed – set the pattern for the larger parish churches of the fourteenth and fifteenth centuries. English carpentry emerged as the most sophisticated in Europe (see Cat. 692). And churches of all kinds, from cathedrals to parish churches, continued to crown their long horizontal roof lines with tall steeples. As symbols of local pride and as images of the Heavenly Jerusalem, the towers and spires of the fourteenth century transformed the English countryside into a sacred landscape.

The patronage of Edward III and Richard II included illuminated manuscripts, though on the surviving evidence their libraries were on nothing like the scale of those of their French royal contemporaries. The major patrons of surviving manuscripts were members of the Bohun family (Cat. 686–91), admittedly closely connected with the royal family. The royal inventories and accounts make clear how much was spent, particularly on textiles, plate and jewellery, but almost none of these objects survive. From Richard II's reign the names of two men with the title of King's Painter are known to us: Gilbert Prince and Thomas Litlyngton, although nothing securely attributable to either survives (cf. Cat. 713). Perhaps the most impressive evidence of English pictorial art of the fourteenth century to remain is in the stained-glass windows which form, therefore, a fitting final climax in the last room of the exhibition.

692   Westminster Hall, interior looking south-east

1394–1401
Photograph

At the time of its original building c. 1097–9 this was the largest hall in Europe. It was to be outdone in size by the halls in the Palais de la Cité in Paris (c. 1301–13), and the Palazzo della Ragione in Padua (c. 1306) but its remodelling under Richard II made it the most architecturally splendid of all medieval halls. Like Henry III's equally exceptional rebuilding of Westminster Abbey (Cat. 262 and pp. 75–8), Richard's refashioning of the secular ceremonial centre of the English Crown was part of an attempt to establish an absolute monarchy. The immediate stimulus to build may have been the completion c. 1391 of a magnificent hall at Kenilworth for Richard's over-mighty uncle, John of Gaunt.

The present hall is the same size as the Romanesque building, and its side walls are the Romanesque walls refaced – hence their comparative lowness and the smallness of their windows. Only the end walls gave the master mason Henry Yevele major opportunities. The south wall, now dominated by a nineteenth-century staircase, originally contained a large window above the marble throne occupied by the king at feasts and by the Lord Chancellor when the royal Courts were in session. Flanking the throne and window, standing figures of six English kings (Cat. 708–9) reinforced the authority of the royal presence.

The masonry of Westminster Hall is little more than an envelope and support for the contribution of Hugh Herland, chief royal carpenter from 1375 to 1404. The Romanesque hall must have been divided into three aisles by timber posts, but Herland was able to dispense with all internal supports and cover the hall in a single 20.3 m span. In width Herland's roof is admittedly less than that of the Palazzo della Ragione, but artistically and technically it ranks as the greatest creation of medieval timber architecture. Credit for this must go not only to Herland but to his predecessors who, during the century or so before 1394, had made English roof carpentry by far the most sophisticated in Europe. Hammer beam trusses had been gaining in popularity in the fourteenth century but their use here was the first in a building of the highest ambition. Possibly they were adopted because the arch braces linking them longitudinally echoed the Romanesque arcades or colonnades removed by Herland. The massive transverse arch

693

the pattern appears regular only because allowances have been made for the distortion caused by its application to curving vault webs.

The dominant element in the view east is the piers. These are totally unlike thirteenth-century English piers such as those at Lincoln, whose full thickness is used to carry deep arcade arches (Cat. 240). Here the arcade arches are made very thin, so that almost half the bulk of the piers can be continued up as massive responds to the high vault, quite unlike the slim, corbelled-out responds at Lincoln. The source of Canterbury's emphatic bay divisions and their arcade arches was almost certainly the largely destroyed choir of Glastonbury Abbey (complete by 1374). The source of the detailing of the piers was the main monument of early Perpendicular in London, the cloister of Old St Paul's Cathedral, where the vault responds had the same profile as here, including the prominent double-ogee mouldings between the shafts.

Circumstantial evidence suggests that the designer was Henry Yevele, chief architect in the employ of the Crown until his death in 1400, and the stylistic evidence is corroborative, for there are indications of close familiarity with both the royal and non-royal works of Yevele's predecessors. William Ramsey's cloister at St Paul's has already been mentioned, and there can be little doubt that the exterior of St Stephen's Chapel in Westminster Palace was the source of the traceried spandrels over the main arcades (Cat. 324). cw

LIT. Woodman 1981, pp. 151–64; Harvey 1985.

694 Lincoln Cathedral, towers looking north-east
Mid-12th to late 14th century

Photograph

Towered great churches are symbols of 'many-towered Sion', the New Jerusalem. They are also expressions of the self-esteem and competitiveness of their owners. Lincoln's towers, like those on most English cathedrals, were not conceived by one architect but were added piecemeal with little regard for overall coherence. The collapse of the recently completed crossing tower in 1237 or 1239 may explain the modest height of its replacement. By 1307 this was no longer regarded as adequate, and what had been a complete tower in itself became the podium for a gigantic bell stage and a spire of timber and lead, the latter destroyed in the sixteenth century. The total height was 160 m (524 ft), 1.2 m (4 ft) higher than its nearest rival, the steeple of Old St Paul's in London. In the late fourteenth century the Romanesque west towers were raised and given needle-like spires which survived until 1809. cw

braces, like the pierced Perpendicular tracery above them, derive from the hall roof at Windsor (c. 1362–5, destroyed) by William Herland, almost certainly Hugh's father. cw

LIT. Colvin 1963, pp. 527–33; Colvin 1966, pp. 33–6, 76–93, 99; Courtenay 1984.

693 Canterbury Cathedral, nave looking east

Begun by 1378, completed by 1405
Photograph

This was the earliest work of Perpendicular architecture in the south-east to rival in ambition the remodelling of the choir of Gloucester Cathedral, the fountainhead of the south-western branch of the style (Cat. 498). Some of the many differences between Canterbury and Gloucester are due to their differing relationships with the earlier parts of the churches to which they were added. Unlike Gloucester, Canterbury was a total rebuilding of a Romanesque structure, but the presence of earlier work is acknowledged by making the upper limits of the storeys correspond to those of the twelfth-century choir (Cat. 17). Since the choir is raised above a high crypt and the nave is not, the main arcades of the latter become very elongated. Obviously high arcades and a comparatively low clearstorey must have been liked for themselves as well as for their value in continuing the twelfth-century levels, and it can hardly be a coincidence that such proportions were by this time normal in major parish churches (e.g. Cat. 90) and friars' churches.

The lighting in the photograph differs from the original effect in that the very high aisle windows are shown partly blocked after wartime damage and the clearstorey is dimmed by exceptionally dark Victorian glass, unfortunately still in place. The high vault (Cat. 496) illustrates the new Perpendicular emphasis on total effect rather than on striking detail. Comparison with the Tewkesbury choir vault highlights both its sobriety and its superior organisation, for whereas at Tewkesbury the surface pattern looks best in plan and is disrupted by the three-dimensional form of the vault, at Canterbury

694

695 St Michael's Church, Coventry, west tower looking south-east

1373–94, spire begun 1432
Photograph

The tower of St Michael's is arguably the finest on any late medieval English parish church. Stylistically and typologically it represents a fresh start, for it is the earliest major work of Perpendicular in the city and its rich treatment owes less to the modest parish church towers of the locality than to crossing towers on great churches such as Lichfield Cathedral. The omission of set-offs from the corner buttresses and other variations of detail show that the fourth storey was an afterthought, possibly prompted by the decision to rebuild the nave higher than its thirteenth-century predecessor. Whether the original plans had included an octagonal top storey is impossible to say. In general, the late medieval vogue for such terminations – particularly strong in the Midlands – can be ascribed to the influence of the friars' churches. The octagonal Greyfriars steeple at Coventry (c.1350) is a rare surviving example of a once very common type derived from the modest timber bellcotes of thirteenth-century friars' churches.   CW

LIT. VCH, *Coventry*, pp. 346–55

695

696 Crucifixion (lost) with flanking saints

c.1390–5
Wall painting in Byward Tower, Tower of London
Photograph

Discovered in 1953, the paintings cover the south wall of the principal first-floor room of this gatehouse to the outer ward of the castle. The surviving figures of St John the Baptist, the Virgin, St John the Evangelist and St Michael weighing souls clearly flanked a central Crucifixion, destroyed by the insertion of a Tudor chimney-breast. They are set against a background of gilt popinjays, fleurs-de-lis and lions arranged in a diaper pattern on an emerald ground; a similar pattern covers a beam extending the length of the room. The paintings are executed in an oil medium.

The outstanding example of the International style in English wall painting, the facial types and soft draperies are similar to those of the angel musicians in the Westminster Abbey chapter house scheme (fig. 100), though the superb quality is more comparable to the Wilton Diptych (fig. 104). Stylistically the painting may be assigned to the 1390s, though no work on the Byward Tower is documented for that time. Tiles surviving in an adjoining room probably date from the same phase of renovation, though

696

the design of a standing stag which they include cannot be identified as the couchant and chained white hart emblem of Richard II.

The heraldic diaper ground of the painting is coeval with the paintings and reminiscent of royal heraldic schemes recorded in stained glass and wall painting elsewhere: e.g. the windows of the constable's lodgings of the Tower of London 'worked with fleurs-de-lys and borders of the king's arms' (1360s); and the white harts painted in the great chapel of the Old Manor at Windsor, for which Thomas Litlyngton was paid in 1397. Popinjays arranged in diapers were a popular motif in the fourteenth century, occurring, for example, in a painted tomb at Rochester Cathedral, while 'parrots in lozenges' appeared in enamelled decoration on French plate (Lightbown 1978a, p. 69). They also occur in brocades depicted in Italian Trecento altarpieces, and probably derive from such textile designs. DP

LIT. Tristram 1955, pp. 36–8, 193–4, pls 8b, 9, 10; Rickert 1965, p. 151, pl. 154c; Simpson 1984, pp. 174–5, pls 352–3.

697 Brass of Eleanor (de Bohun), Duchess of Gloucester

c. 1399

Rubbing: l. of figure 162 cm

Inscr. in Gothic letters on marginal fillet, a small portion missing, but recorded, probably inaccurately, by Weever: + *Cy gist Alianore de Bohun eisne fille & vn des heirs a lounrable seignour mons' Humfrey de Bohun Counte de Hereforde Dessex & de Norhamptoñ & Conestable Dengletre· ffemme a puissant & noble Prince Thomas de Wodestoke filz a tresexcellent & trepuissant seignour Edward Roy Dengletre puis le Conquest tierz· Duc de Gloucestre Counte Dessex & de Bukyngham & Conestable Dengletere Qe morrust le treiz jour Doctobr lan du (grace 1399. de gi aisme Dieux face mercy, Amen)*

Rubbing by Derrick A. Chivers (original in Westminster Abbey)

The brass, on a Purbeck altar-tomb, is a full-length figure under a triple canopy supported on buttressed shafts (bottom of right-hand one replaced). The Bohun badge, a swan, is shown in the central circular eye of the canopy, and as a corbel on each side of the arch. On each shaft are three shields, the two bottom ones held by female weepers, the others suspended, bearing respectively the arms of France and England quarterly with a border, Bohun, England and France quarterly impaling Bohun and quartering the Constableship of England, Bohun impaling Fitzalan and Warenne quarterly, and the Constableship; the replaced right-hand one is blank. The Duchess stands on a patch of flowery grass supported on a platform decorated with a row of blank shields in quatrefoils, her hands in prayer and her head supported on two tasselled cushions, the top one, which is set crosswise, decorated with a trellis and quatrefoil pattern, and the lower one with scrolls of broom (*planta genista*), the Plantagenet plant.

The inscription can be translated: 'Here lies Alianore de Bohun, eldest daughter and one of the heirs to the honourable Humfrey de Bohun, Earl of Hereford, Essex and Northampton, and Constable of England, wife of the puissant and noble Prince Thomas of Woodstock, son of the most excellent and most puissant lord, Edward, the third since the Conquest, King of England, Duke of Gloucester, Earl of Essex and of Buckingham, who died the third day of October, in the year of grace 1399, on whose soul may God have mercy, Amen.' The bottom of the inscription fillet, where there are no letters, is decorated with swans and sprigs of broom.

This London 'Series B' brass, one of the finest of any period in existence, demonstrates the extent to which this type of memorial had risen socially by the late fourteenth century. CB

PROV. Westminster Abbey.

LIT. Weever 1631, p. 638; Norris 1978a, pp. 54, 69, 103, figs 172–3; 1978b pp. 60, 66–8, 70.

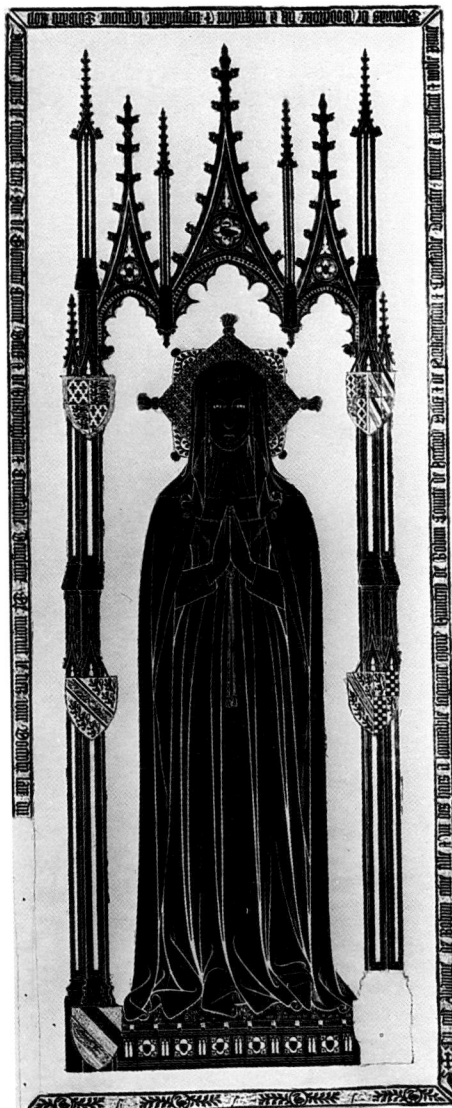

697

698 Altarpiece

Mid-14th century
Limestone (Caen stone), with slight traces of
    paint: w. 150 cm, h. of central panel 140.5 cm
The Board of Trustees of the Victoria and Albert
    Museum, London, A. 58–1921

The altarpiece was removed from Sutton Valence Church, Kent, when it was demolished in 1823, and presumably at this time underwent considerable restoration. In re-

698

cent conservation work it has been established that the altarpiece had been pieced together from many small fragments and that a number of newly-carved parts had been inserted. Some of these, such as the two corbels with grotesque heads in the central panel (repr. Bedford 1923) have been removed.

Originally comprising five panels, the Sutton Valence altarpiece now consists of three sections: that on the left is blank, the centre is taken up with a seated Virgin and Child with the remains of two flanking angels, floating in clouds and playing musical instruments, and the right panel shows the Ascension of Christ. By analogy with alabaster altarpieces of slightly later date, it seems likely that the Sutton Valence altarpiece illustrated the Five Joys of the Virgin: the Annunciation, the Adoration of the Magi, the Nativity (in this case simply the Virgin and Child), the Ascension of Christ, and the Assumption or Coronation of the Virgin. The medieval church at Sutton Valence was, and the present church still is, dedicated to St Mary. PW

PROV. Church of St Mary's, Sutton Valence, Kent, until 1823; moved to no. 7, High Street, Maidstone, until 1921; purchased by the V & A from William Day & Son, 1921.

LIT. Review 1921, p. 10, fig. 8; Bedford 1923; London 1930, no. 337; Williamson (forthcoming), no. 39.

699–701 The Flawford alabasters

c. 1340–80
Nottingham Castle Museum, 08–146, 147, 148

These figures, discovered in 1779 on the site of the altar of St Peter's Church, Flawford, are among the earliest English alabasters of their kind to survive. Formerly richly painted and gilded, they were designed to stand against a plane surface, secured by latten wires issuing from lead-plugged holes in their flat backs. The present arrangement, in which the figures are set upon large, rectangular bases, effectively turning them into free-standing statuettes, is not original. All three figures show the same silky, elegantly composed drapery treatment and would appear to be contemporary. Their attitudes, dimensions and common format suggest that they may have formed part of a symmetrical composition, possibly an altarpiece, in which the bishop was flanked on his right by the Virgin and St Peter, and on his left by other figures which have failed to survive. There is every likelihood that they were carved in Nottingham, five miles north of Flawford and the main centre for the production of alabaster altarpieces in England.

The Virgin has been compared in a general way to French work of the mid- and late fourteenth century (Stone 1955; Paris 1968; Cheetham 1973), although the immediate source for the style would appear to lie in a group of English sculpture dating from the second quarter of the century and associated with the master responsible for carving the bosses of the Percy tomb in Beverley Minster (Dawton [forthcoming]). Closely related to this group, and particularly close to the Flawford bishop in its drapery arrangement, is a statue of St Cuthbert holding the head of King Oswald in Durham Cathedral (Prior & Gardner 1912, fig. 369 p. 332).   ND

699   Virgin and Child

Alabaster: h. 81.3 cm, w. 24.7 cm, d. 10.2 cm

The Virgin is shown suckling the infant Christ who holds her exposed right breast with both hands. Crowned and dressed in a long robe, she sways to her left in a graceful *contrapposto* which is accentuated by the alternating rhythm of the folds falling across the front of the figure.   ND

700   St Peter

Alabaster: h. 82.5cm, w. 31.7 cm, d. 13.6 cm

St Peter, the saint to whom Flawford Church was dedicated, holds a model of a cruciform church in his left hand and carries the keys, his principal attribute, over his right arm. In accordance with his position as first Bishop of Rome, he wears the mitre, tiara and pall, the latter having been painted on the chasuble. He twists to his right in an attitude full of movement, his form emphasised by the depth of the cutting and the thin, figure-revealing drapery. At his feet is a small figure, probably the donor, who kneels in prayer and fomerly held a long scroll, traces of which remain on the saint's chasuble.   ND

701   Bishop

Alabaster: h. 92.3 cm, w. 28.5 cm, d. 12.1 cm

The precise identity of this figure is unknown, although the mitre and the ring worn above the lower joint of the middle finger are both indicative of episcopal rank. The possibility that the figure represents an archbishop cannot be discounted, for the pall could have been added in paint, as it was in

699

700

701

the case of St Peter. Dressed in Mass vestments, he raises his right hand in blessing and holds in his left the remains of a crosier. The facial features are modelled with great sensitivity and give the figure an appearance of solemnity which is enhanced by the frontal pose and regular drapery arrangement. ND

PROV. Found under the chancel floor of Flawford Church, 1779; in possession of John Throsby before 1790, held by favour of Mr Breedon, Ruddington; given by Francis Breedon, Ruddington, to Henry Percy, Nottingham, 1833; given to Colonel Wildman, Newstead Abbey, on whose death in 1859 acq. by Edmund Percy; given to City of Nottingham by the Misses Percy, 1908.

LIT. Prior & Gardner 1912, pp. 66, 358, 460, 472, 692, repr. fig. 60 p. 67, fig. 408 p. 359; London 1910, nos 74, 75, 80, repr. pl. XXVII; London 1930, nos 604, 605, 606, repr. pl. 82; Stone 1955, pp. 190–1, repr. pl. 145; Paris 1968, no. 187; Cheetham 1973, pp. 14, 18–20, 22, 24, repr. pls pp. 21, 23, 25; Cheetham 1984, pp. 41, 53, 158, 191–2, repr. fig. 21, p. 41; Dawton (forthcoming).

702   Virgin and Child

c. 1360s–1380s
Alabaster: h. 46.3 cm, w. 24.5 cm
The Burrell Collection, Glasgow Museums and Art
    Galleries, 1/19

Apart from a slight awkwardness in the carving of her hands and neck, this seated Virgin has been gracefully rendered; if the top of her head were not missing, her figure would appear better balanced. She has no crown – exceptionally among English alabaster images of the Virgin – but by way of

702

sovereignty she holds an orb (now lacking its cross); there are holes for a nimbus to be fitted to her veil. With one foot on the throne and the other on her right knee stands the Infant Christ, cradling a bird whose bill is closing on one of His fingers (as, for instance, in an alabaster Tree of Jesse in the Victoria and Albert Museum, A 36–1954); with His left hand He grasps the veil which frames the Virgin's face.

The carving has been compared with the figure of the Virgin and Child found at Flawford (Cat. 699; Pitman 1964, p. 87; followed by Marks 1983, p. 288 fig. 10), but while the carver of the Burrell Collection figure has an almost excessive love of folds (as at the Virgin's waist and in the way her veil and outer garment fall away before her), they are perhaps not rendered with quite the assurance of the Flawford standing figure's folds, which also has a gentle sense of movement that contrasts with the passivity of this Virgin and the boldness of her Child (emphasised by His rolled-up left sleeve). NLR

PROV. Bt by Sir William Burrell from John Hunt, 1938; also numbered 31.

LIT. York 1954, no. 96; Hildburgh 1955, p. 338, fig. 3 p. 339; Pitman 1964, p. 87, pl. 2a; Glasgow 1977, no. 160, repr.

703–5   Three alabaster carvings

c. 1370s(?)
Alabaster: (i) Annunciation h. 25 cm, w.
    24.8 cm; (ii) Assumption h. 18 cm, w. 29 cm;
    (iii) Coronation of the Virgin h. 24.5 cm, w.
    29.3 cm;
The Trustees of the British Museum, London,
    MLA 83, 8–6, 2, 3, 4

Fragmentary though they are, these three carvings are perhaps the finest of the early alabaster panels that (when complete) are of greater height than width. The figures' faces are missing, but their drapery has an elegance that combines with their carefully stylised disposition to surmount the impression of flatness that might result from such a linear emphasis, and leaves instead a sense of grace and simplicity.

Comparisons with work of around 1340, such as the weepers on John of Eltham's tomb in Westminster Abbey, are unconvincing; as Hildburgh argued (1950), the carvings are most easily related stylistically to other alabaster panels of about the 1370s. Their freshness and their novelty (for instance, in the Coronation of the Virgin, where she is portrayed as kneeling and stretching up to receive her crown) arise from the sculptor's treatment of the subjects. Certain of the carvings have been seen as by the same hand or workshop as other alabaster panels – the Coronation of the Virgin has been stated as being probably by the same artist as an Assumption now in the Victoria and Albert Museum (A. 147–1946; Stone

703

704

705

1972, p. 264 n. 46) and a Coronation table now in the Victoria and Albert Museum (A. 29–1950; Hildburgh 1950, pp. 8, 11), and the Annunciation has been seen as the model or inspiration of an Annunciation panel also now in the Victoria and Albert Museum (A. 28–1950; Hildburgh 1950, p. 11) – but, despite close sculptural parallels, these other panels lack the same sense of stylised elegance.

Hildburgh argued that these and other early alabasters were carved in Nottingham, partly on the evidence of such decorative details as the small clusters of white and red dots (symbolising flowers) on the green-painted ground (of which there are traces on each of these panels) and also the clusters of dots or small bosses applied to the panels' backgrounds (found on the Coronation of the Virgin in this set) which he attributed to Nottingham. Nottingham was certainly a centre of the alabaster industry from the mid-

706

fifteenth century onwards, and in the 1360s was the place of work of Peter the Mason, carver of a costly alabaster altarpiece for St George's Chapel, Windsor; but Hildburgh's arguments are mostly circular and his case is not proven.

The carvings were found (with a fragmentary fourth panel of God the Father and Christ Crucified, of later date) in Kettlebaston Church; the manor of Kettlebaston was held by Henry le Scrope (executed 1415; C.L. Kingsford, *Archaeologia*, LXX, 1920, pp. 74, 89) and it is just possible that he or his family gave these carvings to the church. NLR

PROV. Kettlebaston Church (Suffolk), found in the chancel wall, c. 1864 or 1870 (*Proc. Soc. Ants.*, 2nd ser., ix, p. 71; *Proc. Suffolk Inst. Arch.*, xxxi, 1967–9, p. 202); presented by Rector of Kettlebaston to James Beck, Rector of Bildeston, who presented them to British Museum, 1883.

LIT. Prior & Gardner 1912, p. 472, fig. 541; London 1910, p. 26; Hildburgh 1950, pp. 7–9, 11–12, 15–17, figs 12, 14; Pitman 1964, p. 83, repr. pp. 86, 87; Taylor 1964–6; Stone 1972, p. 190, pl. 146.

706 Passion altarpiece

late 14th century
Alabaster panels: (i) 39.8 × 37.2 cm; (ii) 45.3 × 37.3 cm; (iii) 54.6 × 37.4 cm; (iv) 37.7 × 37.5 cm; (v) 41 × 36.8 cm
The Board of Trustees of the Victoria and Albert Museum, London, A 48–1946, A 50–1946, A 49–1946, A 51–1946, A 52–1946

These five panels, of the Last Supper, the Crucifixion, the Deposition, the Three Marys at the Sepulchre, and the Incredulity of St Thomas, are the remnants of an altarpiece of the Passion of Christ. The altarpiece might originally have had terminal panels of single saints; it would almost certainly have had further main panels, allowing the Crucifixion to be at the centre, as in later Passion altarpieces. They are larger than panels of a later date, and finely carved, with chamfered edges (cf. Cat. 464), and, given the remarkable iconography of (iv) and (v), it is likely that they represent a very early phase in the history of such altarpieces.

Panels (i) and (iv) are the less successful in arrangement; in the former, the Last Supper, Christ (blessing a large, prism-shaped loaf; there is no chalice) is shown surrounded by the Apostles, but attention is deflected from Him by the prominence given to the slumped figure of John the Evangelist, while there is a certain repetitiveness in the treatment of the three Apostles in the foreground at left. Below John kneels Judas, holding what appears to be a fish. In (ii), the Crucifixion, the figures surrounding Christ have been arranged as two groups; at left, attention is focused on the swooning Virgin, looking away from Christ, while the right-hand group is dominated by the centurion who with one hand holds a dagger (echoed by the battle-axe held by the soldier at right) and with the other points up at Christ. The sole intact panel (iii) is of the Deposition: Christ is received from Nicodemus (standing on a ladder) by Joseph of Arimathaea (identified by the purse suspended from his belt). Christ's right arm is taken by the Virgin (now headless), who is supported by Mary Magdalene or Mary Cleophas. To the far right is a man (in padded clothing rather than armour; personal communication, Claude Blair) whose prominence has led to the suggestion (Evans 1949, p. 110) that he is the donor of the altarpiece – but this is not possible, as he can be paralleled on two other alabaster Depositions (Cheetham 1984, p. 259) and is not kneeling but standing, his legs positioned as though he faces the viewer, and his hands and lower arms (now broken away) originally held pliers to pull the nail out of Christ's feet. The lower ground has traces of green paint; the background was gilt, with an elaborate diamond-based pattern, each diamond containing a six-lobed boss. The closest parallel to this is on an early fifteenth-century embattled Crucifixion in the Metropolitan Museum of Art, New York (repr. Pitman 1954, p. 221, no. ix).

The Three Marys at the Sepulchre (iv) is the most severely damaged panel, only the left-hand Mary and the angel in the foreground being intact; the man at right is perhaps St John the Evangelist. Artistically, the panel is not wholly successful, lacking in balance between the angel and empty tomb at front and the four figures behind, but iconographically it is remarkable, being paralleled only on three other English alabasters, all of the fifteenth century (Cheetham 1984, p. 282). The Incredulity of St Thomas (v) is iconographically unique among English alabasters; the kneeling Thomas puts the first two fingers of his right hand into Christ's side, while eight Apostles (including Peter, with keys in his right hand and putting his left hand on Thomas's shoulders) are gathered around. NLR

PROV. Bt in Paris from a Bordeaux-based collector-dealer by W.L. Hildburgh, 1923; given by Hildburgh to the Victoria & Albert Museum, 1946.

LIT. Hildburgh 1925, pp. 307–15, pls I–II pp. 310–11; Hildburgh 1950, pp. 13, 18–19, figs 23–6; Pitman 1964, pp. 87–8, figs 5–9; Cheetham 1984, pp. 67, 222, 246, 259, 282, 286.

707 'Bosom of Abraham' Trinity

14th century
Alabaster: h. 88.9 cm, w. 33 cm
The Burrell Collection, Glasgow Museums and Art Galleries, 1/2

Carved on a scale that is large by the standards of other English alabaster figures, God the Father is shown seated, crowned, His regality emphasised by the smallness of the figure of Christ on the Cross, positioned between His knees. In His hands, God was carved as holding a napkin of souls, although these have mostly been broken away. God the Father is a figure of considerable presence, and the sculpture was praised by

707

subject not otherwise understood as being portrayed in medieval English art but one which undoubtedly was represented (*Reliquary* 1892; Sheingorn [forthcoming]). NLR

PROV. Bt by Sir William Burrell from John Hunt, 1938; also numbered 19.

LIT. Hildburgh 1933, pp. 50–6, pl. IV; London 1939, no. 131; York 1954, no. 76, repr. front cover; London 1972, no. 263, repr. p. 16; London 1975, p. 45, no. 366; Marks 1983, p. 92, repr.; Cheetham 1984, repr. p. 42; Sheingorn (forthcoming).

708–9 Two kings

c. 1385
Chilmark stone, treated with white gesso wash: each h. 2.03 m
Westminster Hall

The first attempt to modernise the decoration of William Rufus's Hall preceded the decision to rebuild it by eight years. In 1385, thirteen statues of kings were commissioned from Thomas Canon, one of a well-known family of Purbeck marblers – presumably as a iconographic programme running from Edward the Confessor to Richard II. These figures cost £2.6s.8d each. Six of them were

housed in tabernacles carved by Walter Walton and they were painted at a cost of £8.13s.4d by Nicholas Tryer. The rest of this batch of figures was put in store to await reconstruction of the Hall; they were added fifteen years later to the north front.

As evidence of London architectural sculpture at the end of the fourteenth century the six kings from the Hall's interior are of great importance. Comment on them is difficult because they have been heavily restored and the surfaces are clogged with the white gesso applied after they were taken out of their niches during the Second World War. Their stylistic crudity has been exaggerated: where the details are original they sometimes show the sweeping drapery folds drawn across the stomach and undulating hemlines that characterise the contemporary sculptures at Winchester College. The kings are accomplished works and their swaying poses, carefully modelled heads with rolling curly hair and beards, and tall crowns were to have considerable influence on sculpture in the next century. PL

PROV. Westminster Hall, London.

LIT. Carter 1838, pp. 89–90; Gardner 1951, pp. 229–31; Colvin 1963, pp. 528–32; Salzman 1967, p. 130; Stone 1972, p. 194.

Pevsner as 'a piece of the highest emotional qualities' (1939, p. 15), although that was before the recent revelation (*Burl. Mag.*, LXXV) that some substantial portions are modern restorations (notably the hands, right shoulder, ends of hair and beard, and finials of crown of God the Father, and the feet, arms and beard of Christ). Traces of polychromy include white and red dots at bottom right, the remnants of floral decoration of a sort found on many English alabasters.

Four other flat-backed figures and seven panels representing God the Father with both Christ and a napkin of souls are known, while the combination cannot be paralleled in Continental art. The belief that the souls of the dead are gathered to Abraham's bosom ceased to be theologically acceptable from about the early fourteenth century, and artists increasingly came to represent souls as being gathered instead to God the Father or to His Son. At about the same time, the Trinity was increasingly associated with all the Saints of Heaven, and it has recently been suggested that alabaster carvings such as this are representations not just of an assimilation of the traditional image of Abraham's bosom to the image of the Trinity, but also of God's rescue of both the blessed dead who died in the Lord and, more generally, of the souls that have been freed from Purgatory. And as a representation of the blessed dead, it has been proposed that such carvings would have been seen as representing All Saints, a

708–9

710

710 Part of chest front

c. 1410
Elm: h. 49 cm, w. 98.5 cm, d. 40 cm
Museum of London, 75.2

This is the right-hand section of the front panel from a very large chest, formerly lap-jointed to the left-hand part. Traces of original polychromy are visible in the interstices. It is sculpted with three scenes from Chaucer's 'Pardoner's Tale'. The youngest 'riotour' having 'borrowed hym large botels thre', on the left, is stabbed to death by the two older men, in the centre, who in turn 'fynde Death' by imbibing the poisoned wine, on the right. It has been suggested that the fox, in the lower right-hand corner, is an allusion to the Pardoner. The left-hand panel must have illustrated the earlier parts of the story – the tavern, the encounter with the old man, and finding the treasure.

The compositional treatment, with one scene above another set against a decorative background, recalls Netherlandish textiles such as the Devonshire Hunting Tapestries in the Victoria and Albert Museum, London. A useful stylistic analogy is the edition of Gaston Phébus's *Livre de Chasse* in the Bibliothèque nationale in Paris (MS fr. 616), dated by Panofsky to the first decade of the fifteenth century.

Elm wood, although commonly enough used in the Middle Ages particularly for table tops, or 'bordes' (Eames 1977) very rarely survives owing to its vulnerability to worm.

CT

PROV. Bt. by Museum of London, 1975.

LIT. Eames 1977, p. 64

711 The Despencer retable

1370–1406
Panel, framed with glass: h. 112.4 cm, w. 259 cm
The Dean and Chapter of Norwich

The Norwich retable was no doubt made as part of the new furnishings for the sanctuary, provided after the damage to the presbytery following the fall of the cathedral spire in 1362. It bears upon the original framing the arms of Bishop Despencer (1370–1406), and of six well-known Norfolk families: Hales, Morieux, Clifford (?), Kerdiston, Gernon and Howard. Seven more shields of arms were too fragmented for W.H. St John Hope to decipher. The thirteen arms on the top are modern. However, the heraldic evidence favours the earlier part of Bishop Despencer's episcopate. No doubt the heraldry commemorates not only those who contributed to the altarpiece itself, but those who had helped fund the reconstruction of the eastern arm of the church.

The length and importance of this altarpiece, plus the central nature of its iconography, are appropriate for a high altarpiece. The lack of a reference to its commission in the sacrist's rolls for 1364–1400, where the other furnishings for the restored choir are itemised, suggest that it was a lay gift. The iconography of the five scenes of the Passion and Resurrection presents no irregularities. The detail of Christ at the Resurrection stepping out of the coffin on to one of the sleeping soldiers is commonly found in alabasters, and was no doubt taken over from performances of the Mystery Plays. Note the Arabic lettering on the garments of St John in both the Crucifixion and the Ascension scenes.

Its closeness to the Betrayal and Crucifixion paintings from St Michael at Plea, Norwich, now in the cathedral, points to its having been executed by local craftsmen. The arms and head of the crucified Christ on the fifth (replaced) panel were copied in 1958 by Pauline Plummer from the St Michael at Plea Crucifix. That model fitted within dimensions based on the assumption that only a fifth plank, and the return of the frame along the top, were missing.

711

A similar mixture of Netherlandish and Italianate elements characterises the manuscripts associated with the Bohun family and the Litlyngton Missal (Cat. 686–91, 714). Compare the poses, facial types, hands and gestures with three alabasters in the Victoria and Albert Museum of the Annunciation (A146–1946, Cheetham 1984, no. 91), the Crucifixion (A106–1946, Cheetham 1984, no. 172 and the Ascension (A147–1946, Cheetham 1984 no. 216), probably from one late fourteenth-century altarpiece.

The disappearing Christ in the Norwich Ascension scene is contained in a mandorla. Unlike the summary medieval convention of two feet and stiffly arranged robes disappearing into a cloud, this figure must surely have been complete. The treatment here recalls the diminutive blessing Christ of the Ascension by the Master of St Lawrence in his early fifteenth-century altarpiece from the Church of St Lawrence, Cologne, now in the Wallraf-Richartz Museum (no. 737).   PT-C

PROV. Found just before Norwich meeting of Archaeological Institute in 1847, upside-down and forming top of table in upper part of one of the flanking apsidal chapels of the cathedral.

LIT. Hope 1898, pp. 293–314; London 1923, no. 32, pl. XIX; Borenius & Tristram 1927, pp. 39–40, pl. 71; Rickert 1954, pp. 176–7, pl. 159a; London 1956b; Norwich 1973, no. 51.

712   Entombment panel

1390–1400
Panel painting; h. 53 cm, w. 42.75 cm
Ipswich museums and galleries, R1936–41

This modest panel is presumably of East Anglian origin. A pair of panels from another Passion cycle in the Fitzwilliam Museum in Cambridge, of similar scale and rustic quality, dating from the beginning of the fifteenth century, was found in the panelling of a Norwich cottage. Another two panels, showing the Kiss of Judas and the Crucifixion, are in Norwich Cathedral. We have therefore parts of three altarpieces of Passion cycles, lesser counterparts of the Norwich retable itself, and a parochial alternative to an alabaster altarpiece. No fewer than ninety alabaster panels of the Entombment, once belonging to Passion sequences, survive. They testify to the literal devotion to the Corpus Christi which found expression in France and Germany in life-sized tableaux of the Entombment. The heavily embossed gesso ground is typical of the group. This composition is unusual in finding no place for Mary Magdalene, who usually kneels on our side of the chest, and is often shown kissing Christ's right hand. Joseph of Arimathea and Nicodemus are usually dressed, as here, in contemporary fashion, confirming the dating suggested by the sharply-pointed faces, heavily modelled features, blown hair and claw hands of the *Liber Regalis*. One of the

712

figures has a padded doublet with a high collar, tight waist and an ornamental design of floral sprays, fashions still worn *c.* 1400. By 1410, however, the tight wrist and sleeve over the hand which is the hallmark of the 'Bohemian' fashion had given way to a very full sleeve, gathered to a cuff at the wrist.

Unlike the majority of surviving medieval panel paintings, this panel has not been deliberately defaced.   PT-C

PROV. Acq. by Christchurch Mansions Museum, Ipswich, from coll. of G. Houghton Brown of Waresby Hall, Sandy, Beds., 1936.

LIT. Norwich 1973, p. 38, repr. p. 37 no. 53.

713   Portrait of Richard II

7 June 1394–15 December 1395
Panel: h. 213.5 cm, w. 110 cm
Dean and Chapter of Westminster

A Westminster inventory of 1388 mentions a canopy for the king's 'cage' by the great altar, which is taken to be the royal pew west of the sedilia. After the death of his first queen, Anne of Bohemia, on 7 June 1394, Richard II was closely involved in the creation of the three major works of art surviving from his reign: the joint monument to Anne and himself, the Wilton Diptych, and the portrait of him in the abbey. The issue roll for 15 December 1395 (E.403/554) records the payment under the privy seal of £20 to Master Peter Combe, sacrist, for the picture over the tomb of Anne, for moving a tomb to make room for the monument of Anne, for a painting for that tomb, and 'for the picture of an image in the likeness of a king in the choir of the church'. There is no mention of the artist, but Richard II's painter until 1395 was Gilbert Prince of London, who was succeeded before January 1397 by Thomas Litlyngton.

It would seem that Richard II commissioned this portrayal of himself to represent his perpetual presence in the choir of the abbey, where with his queen he had frequently worshipped with the monks. It may be presumed that this life-sized panel painting was placed at the back of the king's pew. The continuity of its presence there was broken at the Reformation. It was rediscovered 'fastened to the backside of a door of a base room' by John, Lord Lumley. Lumley brought the portrait to the attention of Elizabeth I, and it may well have been the basis for the portrait of Elizabeth in her coronation robes now in the National Portrait Gallery. Elizabeth's sense of identity with Richard II ('Know you not that I am Richard II?'), and her refusal to allow Shakespeare's *Henry IV Part I* to be performed after Essex's rebellion, are well known.

It would seem that the portrait was restored to its original position by Queen Elizabeth. Weever's *Funeral Monuments* of 1631 describes it at the upper end of the choir. Sandford's view of the coronation of James II (Abbott *et al.* 1972, p. 117) shows it at the back of the east stall on the south side of the choir. It was moved in 1775 to the Jerusalem Chamber, but returned the following century to its previous position. It has hung in the nave only in recent years.

When the painting was cleaned in 1866 by George Richmond and Henry Merritt, the face was changed, becoming plumper, and the gilt gesso background was largely lost.

Recent literature stresses comparison with the cycle of full-size images of kings painted for Charles IV, Anne of Bohemia's father, in the great hall of Karlstein, the Emperor's castle in Bohemia. Images of 'kings' in silver as votive offerings, in glass, or for the back of the king's seat, had been commissioned by Henry III; what is new is the element of undoubted portraiture. Richard II did not grow his little double-goatee beard until after the death of Anne. With the effigy of Edward III (d. 1377), these images are the first unmistakable likenesses of English monarchs.

PT-C

LIT. Weever 1631; Scharf 1867, p. 80, repr.; Rickert 1954, pp. 175–6, 191, nn. 40–3, pl. 162; Harvey 1961a, esp. p. 12, n. 2; Tudor-Craig in Wilson *et al.* 1986, pp. 109–11, repr.

714 The Litlyngton Missal

1383–4

Vellum, ff. 341 (bound in two vols, of which the first is shown): 52.5 × 36 cm

Dean and Chapter of Westminster, MS 37

This magnificent book was produced to the order of Nicholas Litlyngton, Abbot of Westminster 1362–86, for use in his abbey church. The text includes orders for the coronation of both a king and a queen and directions for a royal funeral, all of which customarily took place at Westminster. The left-hand exhibited page (f. 8v.) shows the calendar entries for December, with the name of St Thomas Becket and the title of the Pope erased in accordance with the decree of Henry VIII. On the right (f. 9) is the ceremony of the exorcism of salt and water, preceding the Mass for the first Sunday in Advent. Litlyngton's arms and monogram appear frequently here and throughout the manuscript and may be seen painted on the edges of the pages when the book is closed.

Very full details of the cost of the Missal are enrolled in Litlyngton's treasurer's accounts for 1383–4 (Cat. 715). Unfortunately, although the scribe is named as Thomas Preston, the names of the illuminators are

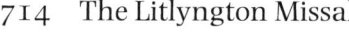

713

714

not recorded. The work on the exhibited pages was carried out by two distinct hands, one supplying the decoration and the other specialising in the painting of figures. Two further figure painters collaborated with the decorator elsewhere in the book. None of these is a major innovator, though their style is related to other English work of the end of the century. However, a fourth figure painter, who contributed to the manuscript only its large and extremely complex Crucifixion miniature, seems to have been directly influenced by Italian work.   JB

PROV. Westminster Abbey, from 1383–4 until the present.

LIT. Brussels 1973, no. 71; Simpson 1980, p. 144, repr. pl. 16; Sandler 1986, no. 150.

715 Nicholas Litlyngton's treasurer's account roll

1383–4
Vellum: 72 × 24 cm
Dean and Chapter of Westminster, W.A.M. 24265*

The cost of making the Litlyngton Missal (Cat. 714) is recorded in detail in this account roll covering the year between Michaelmas 1383 and Michaelmas 1384. It is very rare indeed for so much information about a single manuscript to be found. All aspects of the work, from the purchase of the vellum at a cost of £4.6s.8d to the embroidery of the original covers for 6s.8d, are specified. A layman, Thomas Preston, was housed and clothed by the abbey for two years while he wrote out the text, for which he was paid £4. The illumination cost £23.0s.3d and an extra 10s was paid to the painter of the Crucifixion miniature. In all, work on the manuscript totalled £34.14s.7d, about a tenth of the whole amount accounted for in the year covered by this document.   JB

PROV. Westminster Abbey, from 1383–4 until the present.

LIT. Robinson & James 1909, pp. 7–8; Sandler 1986, p. 173.

715

716

716 Charter of Richard II to Shrewsbury

1389
Vellum: 69.5 × 100.5 cm
Shrewsbury and Atcham Borough Council,
Guildhall, Shrewsbury, Muniments I.24

The charter, issued on 22 November 1389,
confirms to the citizens of Shrewsbury the
privileges granted to them by Edward III. It
opens with a particularly fine illuminated
initial enclosing the figure of Richard II,
crowned and robed, delivering the charter
into the hands of a kneeling queen, presumably Anne of Bohemia though the nature of
her implied personal connection with
Shrewsbury has not been explained.

Stylistically this initial is very close to the
work of the Dutch master of the Carmelite
Missal (London, British Library, Add. MSS
29704–5), which was illuminated in London
during the last decade of the fourteenth
century. The composition is very simple, like
that of the Crucifixion page in the Lapworth
Missal (Cat. 717), relying for effect upon the
superb execution of the painted draperies and
the striking realism of the faces of the king
and queen. The recipients of the charter are
likely to have commissioned the embellishments in London before the charter was
delivered to Shropshire.   JB

PROV. At Shrewsbury from about 1389 until the
present.
LIT. HMC 15th report, pt 10, 1899, p. 4, no. 23;
Whittingham 1971, pp. 15–6, repr. pl. 20.

717

717 The Lapworth Missal

1398
Vellum, ff. 257: 44.5 × 27.5 cm
President and Scholars of Corpus Christi College,
Oxford, MS 394

A number of large-scale and richly illuminated missals were produced in England
around 1400 for use in public worship. This
one is of particular interest because it is
specifically dated. It takes its name from

Lapworth in Warwickshire, to the parish
church of which it was given by Thomas
Asheby, who died in 1443.

The magnificent painting of the Crucifixion which introduces the Canon of the Mass
(ff. 102v.–103) is close in style to the work of
the main illuminator of another splendid
manuscript, the Carmelite Missal (London,
British Library, Add. MSS 29704–5) produced in London at the end of the fourteenth
century. He was probably a Dutchman, and

his work had a great impact upon the native English illumination of the period. The composition of this page is distinguished by the contrast between the simplicity of the picture and the complexity of its surrounding border. In the figure of Christ the artist has attempted to portray real suffering. JB

PROV. Given to parish church of Lapworth, War., by Thomas Asheby (d. 1443); given to Corpus Christi College by Henry Parry, 1618.

LIT. Brussels 1973, no. 72, repr. pl. 35; Watson 1984, no. 784; Alexander & Temple 1985, no. 333.

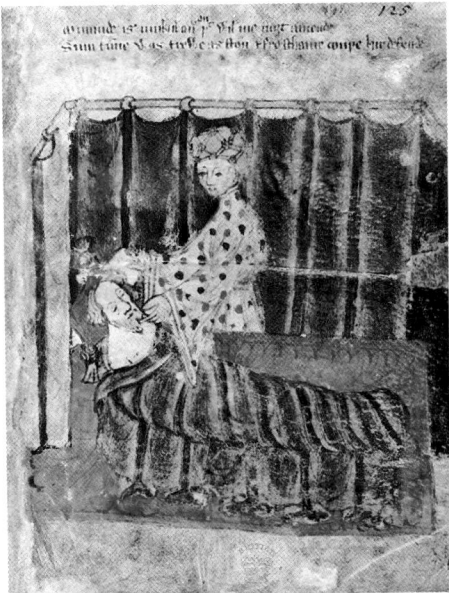

718

718 Sir Gawain and the Green Knight

c. 1400
Vellum, ff. 130: 17 × 12 cm
British Library, Cotton MS Nero A.x

An exceptionally important group of Middle English poems, including the famous Arthurian tale of Sir Gawain and the Green Knight, survives only in this modest and heavily-used copy, written and illustrated about 1400. The language of the poems, which are in rhymed and alliterative verse, suggests that they were composed in the north-west Midlands, possibly in Cheshire or south Lancashire.

The manuscript is of particular interest because, uniquely for an English literary work of the period, it includes a series of large illustrations. These are crudely executed and their detail is often at variance with the descriptions of events and objects given by the poet, but none the less they were deliberately designed to accompany these specific texts. Although they are only clumsily inserted into the structure of the book, being largely bunched together at the beginning and the end, the inclusion of several subjects within the main body of the manuscript makes it clear that they were always a part of the design. The exhibited picture (f. 129) shows the wife of the Green Knight, decked out in a fashionable gown of the period, tempting the virtuous Gawain by paying a secret visit to his bedside. JB

PROV. Sir Robert Bruce Cotton (d. 1631); acq. by the nation with his coll., 1702.

LIT. Gollancz 1923; Wright 1960, no. 15; Bennett 1986b, pp. 202–58, 482–3; Kelliher & Brown 1986, p. 9, repr. pl. 4.

719 Geoffrey Chaucer, The Canterbury Tales

c. 1410
Vellum, ff. 206: 35 × 24.5 cm
British Library, Harley MS 7334

The Canterbury Tales probably took shape in 1386–9 when Chaucer, temporarily out of favour at Court, was living in retirement in Kent, close to the Canterbury road. He had already enjoyed thirty years in the royal

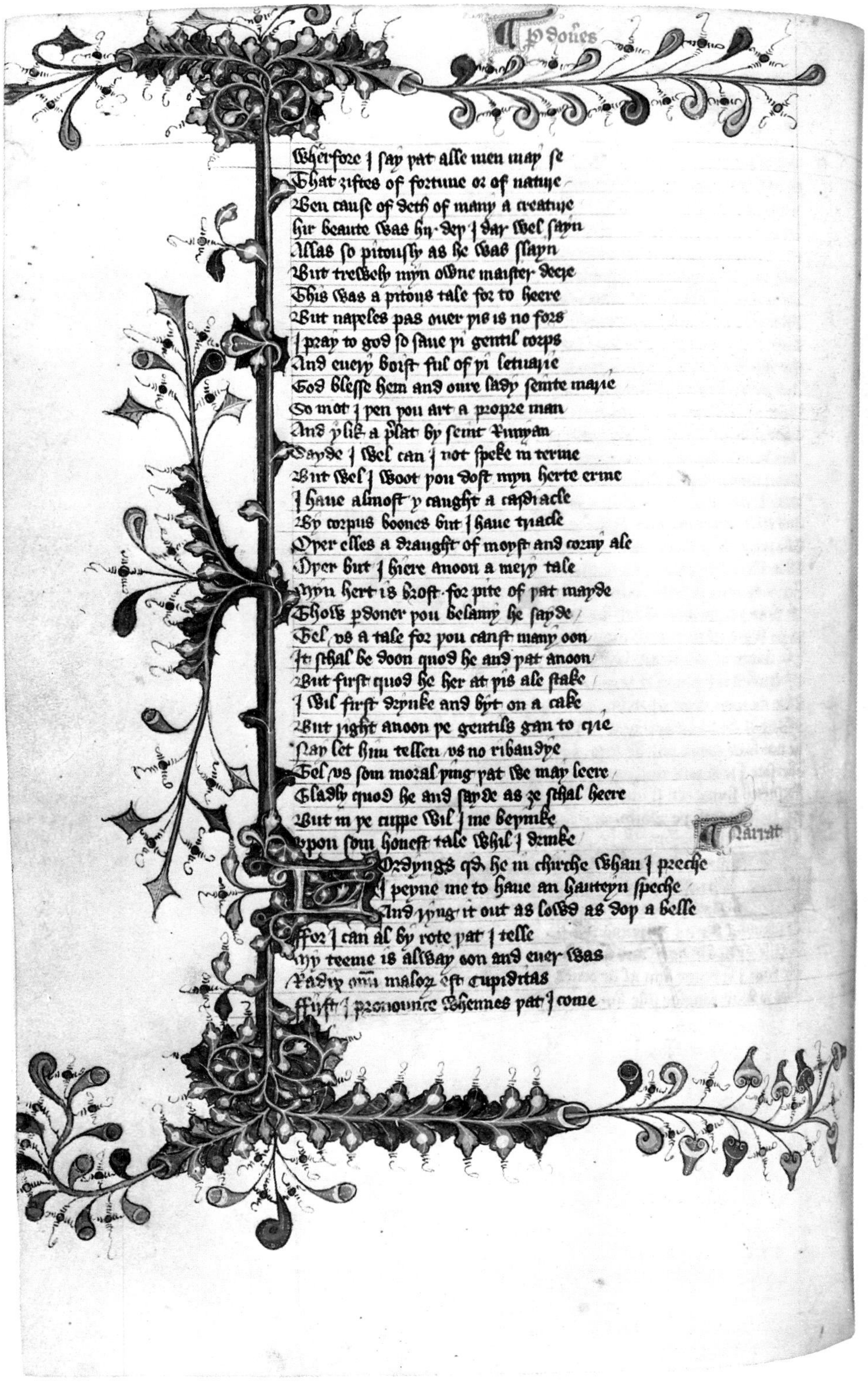

Wherfore I say þat alle men may se
That ȝiftes of fortune or of nature
Ben cause of deth of many a creature
hir beaute was hir deþ I dar wel sayn
Allas so pitously as she was slayn
But trewely myn owne maister dere
This was a pitous tale for to heere
But napeles pas ouer þis is no fors
I pray to god so saue þi gentil corps
And eueri boist ful of þi letuarie
God blesse hem and oure lady seinte marie
So mot I þen þou art a propre man
And ylik a prelat by seint Ronyan
Sayde I wel can I not speke in terme
But wel I woot þou doste myn herte erme
I haue almost y caught a cardiacle
By corpus boones but I haue triacle
Oþer elles a draught of moyst and corny ale
Oþer but I here anoon a mery tale
Myn hert is lost for pite of þat mayde
Thow pardoner þou belamy he sayde
Tel vs a tale for þou canst many oon
It shal be doon quod he and þat anoon
But first quod he her at þis ale stake
I wil first drynke and byt on a cake
But right anoon þe gentils gan to crie
Nay let him tellen vs no ribaudye
Tel vs som moral þing þat we may leere
Gladly quod he and sayde as ȝe shal heere
But in þe cuppe wil I me bebynke
Vpon som honest tale whil I drinke
Narrat
Lordyngs quod he in chirche whan I preche
I peyne me to haue an hauteyn speche
And ryng it out as lowd as doþ a belle
For I can al by rote þat I telle
My teeme is alway oon and euer was
Radix omnium malorum est cupiditas
First I pronounce whennes þat I come

719

service as page, esquire, ambassador and, most recently, Controller of the Customs. Between 1389 and 1391 he was to be Richard II's Clerk of the Works. He was also beyond question the outstanding literary figure of the day. His official career had brought him into contact with men and women in all walks of life and had required him to travel quite extensively, notably in France, Flanders and Italy, where he had become acquainted with the writings of such innovators as Dante and Boccaccio. The fruits of his wide experience are clear in the structure and content of his own masterpiece.

Despite its unfinished state at Chaucer's death in or about 1400, The Canterbury Tales achieved an instant popularity. More than eighty surviving manuscripts have been listed and the work was first printed by Caxton in 1478. This particular manuscript, one of the four earliest known copies, was written by a scribe whose hand appears in numerous literary volumes of the beginning of the fifteenth century, including the exhibited copy of Gower's *Confessio Amantis* (Cat. 720). Its decoration, seen on the opening pages of The Pardoner's Tale (ff. 185v.–186), is very typical of a grand literary manuscript of the day. In common with the great majority of such books, this volume is entirely without illustration.   JB

PROV. Brunston family, Preston by Faversham, late 15th century; Lady Anne Grey, 1556; Thomas Leuenthorpe, 1564; John Brograve the Elder (? Sir John Brograve, d. 1613), before 1602; John, 1st Baron Somers, c. 1701; Sir Joseph Jekyll, d. 1738; bt for Edward Harley, 2nd Earl of Oxford; bt for the nation with Harley Coll., 1753.

LIT. Manly & Rickert 1940, pp. 219–30; Doyle & Parkes 1978, pp. 177, 192–4; Kelliher & Brown 1986, p. 10, repr. pl. 5.

720 John Gower, *Confessio Amantis*

Early 15th century
Velum, ff. 209: 34 × 23 cm
President and Scholars of Corpus Christi College, Oxford, MS 67

John Gower's *Confessio Amantis*, like Boccaccio's Decameron and Chaucer's Canterbury Tales, is a collection of stories held together by a narrative framework. The penitent Lover confides his sins to a Confessor, who relates the tales to him as examples to drive home his failings against Love. According to the poet's preface, the work was written in 1390 at the request of Richard II. Its dedication was changed in favour of Henry of Lancaster in 1393.

Gower was a London lawyer, connected with the county of Kent. He was also a friend of Chaucer, whose power of attorney he held in 1378. The *Confessio* is his best-known work, surviving in numerous copies, several of which include versions of the miniature

720

seen in the exhibited manuscript (f. 9v.), showing the Lover making his confession. It is painted in the style associated with the name of Hermann Scheerre, a German or Netherlandish illuminator working in London.   JB

PROV. Thomas Crispe, early 16th century; William Rawson, 1580.

LIT. Macaulay 1900, p. cxlviii; Doyle & Parkes 1978, pp. 177, 194–5, repr. pl. 50; Alexander & Temple 1985, no. 391, repr. pl. xxvi.

721 Thomas Hoccleve, The Regimen of Princes

Early 15th century
Vellum, ff. 95: 26.5 × 18.5 cm
British Library, Harley MS 4866

Hoccleve's Regimen of Princes, offering advice on conduct to a potential ruler, was composed in 1411–12 and addressed to Henry, Prince of Wales, then less than two

721

years away from his accession to the throne as Henry V. The author, a Clerk of the Privy Seal and a professional scribe, had lived and worked in London for several decades and clearly enjoyed the social life of the city. Although his book is based on several earlier sources, principally the *De Regimine Principum* of Aegidius Romanus, it is overlaid with contemporary colour and comment.

Among Hoccleve's wide circle of acquaintance had been Geoffrey Chaucer, many years his senior, whom he greatly admired and whose literary style he strove to emulate. This particular manuscript of the Regimen is of special importance because it includes the famous portrait of Chaucer painted in accordance with Hoccleve's own memory of his appearance (f. 88). The accompanying verse tells us that '... the resemblaunce/Of him hath in me so fressh lyflynesse/That to putte othir men in remembraunce/Of his persone I have heere his lyknesse ...'. Most other depictions of Chaucer, including that in the celebrated Ellesmere copy of The Canterbury Tales (San Marino, California, Huntington Library, MS 26.C.9), seem to depend on the Hoccleve image. JB

PROV. Robert Harley, 1st Earl of Oxford (d. 1724); bt for the nation with Harley Coll., 1753.

LIT. Furnivall 1897; Spielmann 1900, pp. 5–10, repr. pl. 1; Rickert 1954, p. 185, repr. pl. 169b; Strong 1969, pp. 46–8, repr. pl. 83; Seymour 1982, pp. 618, 621, pl. 41; Kelliher & Brown 1986, p. 10, repr. cover & p. 9.

722 Mazer with cover

c. 1350–1400
Maple wood, gold, pearls and a ruby: h. 8.8 cm, diam. 14.8 cm
Warden and Fellows of All Souls College, Oxford

The shallow mazer bowl is mounted with a narrow gold lip-band; inside, instead of the customary print, is a miniature low square tower in gold, with crenellated walls and four round turrets enclosing an irregular-shaped grey stone (not precious). The low cover has traces of a rim mount, now missing, and an elegant knop made up of a gold stem entwined with four ivy leaves, above which project two pearls (and mounts for two more, now missing) and a polished ruby, uncut.

This is a very rare instance of a gold and gem-mounted mazer; no other survives with similar mounts. The mazer probably belonged to an individual of some substance.

An early college inventory, of 1448 (Hope 1894, p. 120) mentions only the Ballard mazer, still owned by the college. An entry of the time of Warden Stokes (1460–94) in the Vellum inventory describes what may be the mazer: *circulis aureis haben[s] in fu[n]do cornu unicornis cu[m] coperto haben[s] etiam margaritas in summitate eiús ex dono M. Wraby unius executorum fundatoris nostri.* The word for mazer is absent; if, as likely, *circulis* refers to

722

the bands on the mazer, the description is accurate, apart from describing the stone as unicorn horn (thought efficacious in detecting poison).

The inventory of King Charles V of France of 1380 records different types of table plate with poison-detecting stones attached (Evans 1922, p. 115); in 1414 the Duke of Burgundy owned a great gold cup given by the King of England, with unicorn horn and other things *contre venin* in its bottom (ibid., p. 116). The mazer has been thought French (Hope 1887) for no better reason than the lavishness of its mounts, which can however be paralleled in English records, such as the will of Richard, Earl of Arundel, 1392 (Nichols 1780, p. 142), but its style is too international to be localised. Little is known of the putative donor, Wraby, except as one of the executors of the founder, Henry Chichele (*c.* 1362–1443). MLC

PROV. Oxford, All Souls; given by M. Wraby (?), before 1466–94; appears in college inventories, 1488 (two pearls already missing), 1642.

LIT. London 1862, no. 3203; Cripps 1878, pp. 241–2; Hope 1887, p. 137; Moffatt 1906, pp. 92–3, repr.

723 Astrolabe

1326
Brass: diam. 13.2 cm
The Trustees of the British Museum, London, MLA 1909, 6–17, 1

This is the oldest dated European astrolabe, since it bears the date 1326 on the reverse. The astrolabe was developed by the Arabs, from whom the knowledge of using and making it was brought to Europe. In 1391 Chaucer wrote a treatise on the use of the astrolabe for his son Lewis. The instrument is

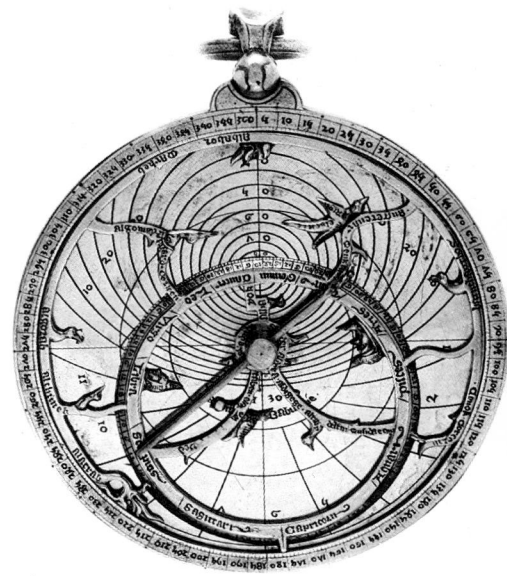

723

used chiefly for taking the altitude of sun or stars in order to determine the time. It has four basic parts. The mater (or mother) is a thick circular plate marked with a series of hours and degrees. On one side an alidade (arm) is used for sighting the sun or a star. On the other side there is a circular recess known as the womb into which are fitted plates engraved with various projections of the celestial sphere for use in different latitudes. Over this is the rete (net), a pierced plate joining a pattern of chosen fixed stars indicated by decorative cut pointers. The rete on this example has twenty-eight star points. JC

PROV. Not known.

LIT. Gunther 1932, no. 291; Ward 1981, pp. 112–13 no. 325.

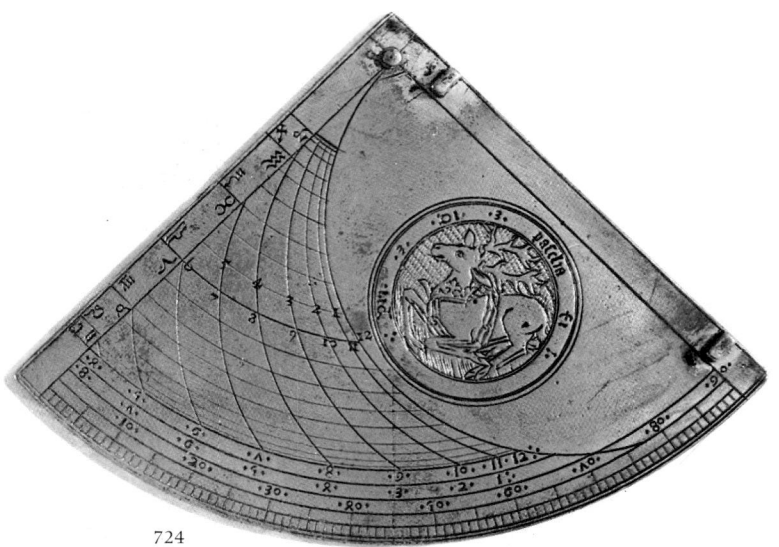

724

724 Horary quadrant

1399
Brass originally gilded, plumb line now missing:
  side l. 8.9 cm
Inscr. in black letter ·:Pri. .3. .Di. .3. Pascha fi·:
The Trustees of the British Museum, London,
  MLA 60, 5–19, 1

On the obverse is an horary quadrant show-ing equal hours, a date scale for setting the plumb line, marked with the signs of the zodiac, and a set of hour numerals. Both the zodiac signs and the hour numerals were added in about 1595, probably by Charles Whitwell. To the right is an engraved badge of Richard II – a white hart lodged, round its neck a crown-collar and chain – and around the badge is the inscription the meaning of which remains obscure. The reverse is en-graved with a table showing the sun's noon altitude for a selection of ninety-six days of the year. The maximum and minimum alti-tudes correspond to latitude 52 degrees north (approximately that of London). Above this scale is a circle of dominical letters for twenty-eight years beginning with the letter 'e' adjacent to the engraved date of 1399. The centre of this table is engraved with a spray of leaves and a rabbit surrounding the inscription *Tabula bisexti*. A similar quadrant dated 1398 is in the Dorchester Museum, Dorset (DORCM. 1973. 7).   JC

PROV. Revd Greville J. Chester Coll.

LIT. Ward 1981, p. 55 no. 146.

725 Badge of Richard II

c. 1377–99
Copper alloy, silver and enamel, gilt: diam. 3.5 cm
Musée des Beaux-Arts, Troyes, France, 871.6.1

The circular silver plaque decorated with a white hart lodged, coloured with opaque white and blue enamel, is set into a cast copper frame with projecting fleurons. Two roughly symmetrical holes pierce the frame, now of doubtful purpose. The closest paral-lels to this piece are three 'morses' of c. 1400 from Warden Abbey, in the British Museum (London 1978, no. 142), each with enamel-led centres and heavy rims, one (Chamot 1930, no. 21a) with a border of fleurons comparable with this, also enclosing an enamel badge. All four roundels are com-paratively heavy and robustly made, less appropriate for use as morses than, for example, as harness ornament. Numerous smaller horse pendants survive, usually her-aldically enamelled. (Cat. 157–64).

Richard II's French second wife Isabella returned to France after his death, perhaps taking some of his plate with her. Richard's

725

diplomatic relations with the Dukes of Bur-gundy included the exchange of gifts, per-haps the origin of the brooch owned by Philip the Good in 1435, like this: *a la devise du Roy Richart a la facon d'un cerf*, ornamented with twenty-two large pearls, two balas rubies, two sapphires, a ruby and a large square diamond the size of a hazelnut (London 1956, p. 4 n. 6).   MLC

PROV. Coffinet Coll., sold Paris 10–11 Aug. 1842, no. 110; beq. to Troyes Museum by Camusat de Vaugourdon, 1871.

LIT. Darcel & Le Clerc 1892, pp. 47–52.

726 Jug

1377–99
Copper alloy: h. 40.2 cm.
Inscr. in Lombardic letters HE THAT WYL NOT
  SPARE WHEN HE MAY
  HE SHAL NOT SPEND WHEN HE WOULD
  DEME THE BEST IN EVERY DOWT
  TIL THE TROWTHE BE TRYID OWTE
The Trustees of the British Museum, London,
  MLA 96, 7–27, 1

On the front of the jug are the royal arms of England as used in the period 1340 to 1405, with a crown above and two lion supporters. On each side of the neck of the jug are three roundels with a falcon spreading its wings, the two near the spout having the falcon looking to the front while on the others the falcon looks to the back. The heraldry and badges on the jug could apply to either Edward III or Richard II, but the badges on the lid indicate a date in the reign of Richard II. The lid is original and its survival, together with the jug, is quite astonishing. The lid is seven-sided. Each facet has a lion facing left and a stag couchant, without chain, facing right. On the lip are three lions facing left and a stag in a circle facing right. The presence of the stag indicates that the jug was made in Richard's reign, and probably between 1390 and 1400. Around the belly of the jug are three lines which form two mottoes; they begin on the bottom line. The jug was possibly the work of a London bell founder but his identity remains unknown. It is not known when or how it arrived in West Africa.   JC

PROV. Found in palace of Ashanti King Prempeh at Kumasi, Gold Coast (now Ghana), 1895.

LIT. Read 1898, pp. 82–7; Read 1921, no. XVII.

727 Jug

Late 14th century
Copper alloy, a heavily-leaded bronze with high antimony and arsenic levels: h. 38.5 cm
Inscr. in Lombardic letters
  + GODDIS GRACE BE IN THIS PLACE AMEN. +
  STOND UTTIR FROM THE FYRE
  AND LAT ON IUST COME NERE
The Board of Trustees of the Victoria and Albert Museum, London, 217–1879

This jug has the royal arms of England as used between 1340 and 1405 on the front, surmounted by a crown. This is repeated twice on each side of the neck of the jug. There are crowns also on the spout and the sides. The jug is cast in the same workshop as the jug found in Ashanti (Cat. 726) since there are close similarities in the spout, handle and lettering used in the inscription. The English inscription means 'God's grace be in this place, amen. Stand away from the fire and let just one come near'. The crosses at the beginning and in the middle of the inscription, the letter forms, and also the manner in which the words are placed not in their proper order to read consecutively, but

726

727

in sudden jumps, closely recall the Ashanti jug. Analysis (personal communication Dr R. Brownsword) has indicated a close similarity between the metals used in the two jugs. The British Museum jug has 70 per cent copper and 17 per cent lead, while the Victoria and Albert Museum jug has 77 per cent copper and 12 per cent lead. Both have high levels of antimony and arsenic. In view of this it is likely that this jug dates from the last ten years of the fourteenth century.   JC

PROV. Found in a manor house in Norfolk; Robinson Coll.

LIT. Romilly Allen 1896, pp. 103–6; Read 1898, pp. 82–7.

728   The Studley bowl

c. 1400
Silver, parcel gilt: h. 14.5 cm, diam. of bowl
    14.3 cm, wt 25½ troy oz
The Board of Trustees of the Victoria and Albert
    Museum, London, M. 1–1914

The bowl stands on a heavy foot-ring. The lid has a rim punched with pellets, and a knop engraved with a textura minuscule *a*. Both cover and bowl are gilt on the outside (except for the inscription), inside the lid and under the foot. Each is engraved with an identical inscription in textura minuscules in two rows, separated by leafy wreaths. The in-

728

scription begins with a cross, followed by the alphabet (lacking letters *j, w*), the symbol for *et*, the word *est*, a tittle (the line drawn over an abridged word), and the symbol for *con*.

The letter *x* is made like the *y* beside it, but although its form is close to that of the Anglo-Saxon runic letter thorn (p = th) still used at this date (Wright 1960, pp. xiv–v), its position in the letter sequence makes such an interpretation unlikely (personal communication, A.I. Doyle). The symbols following the alphabet are part of a set of common abbreviations which conclude alphabets in primers, which were for children to learn (Plimpton 1935, p. 18, pl. IX.I; Wolpe 1965, pp. 70–4, pls 18, 19, 23). Before starting the primer the child crossed itself, an act symbolised in the cross with which it, like the bowl, begins, giving rise to the name crisscross (Christ cross) row.

The bowl is both beautiful and unique. Its function is unclear, but it may have been made for a rich or noble child to eat from. A similar sounding vessel, 'a silver bowl with the ABC on the cover', was bequeathed by John Morton of York in 1431.   MLC

PROV. Lady Ripon (d. 1907), said to have been inherited; given to Aldfield cum Studley Church, near Ripon, for use as alms basin, *c.* 1872; sold by church, 1913; bt by C.J. Jackson; bt by Harvey Hadden as gift for V&A, 1914.

LIT. Fallow 1904, pp. 74–6, repr.; Watts 1920, no. 1; London 1930, no. 626; Vienna 1962, no. 450.

729   Prior Chillenden's ablution basins

c. 1400
Silver-gilt: each diam. *c.* 28.5 cm, h. 3.2 cm
Dean and Chapter of Canterbury

The only decoration to each is a central cusped sexfoil boss, and a rim punched with a repeating five-pellet motif. The gilding on each is worn, but possibly renewed; the weight is pounced in (?) nineteenth-century numerals underneath each one, respectively 19¾ and 20¾ oz.

The basins are listed in all inventories (see below) as the gift of Thomas Chillenden, Prior of Canterbury Cathedral 1391–1411, who rebuilt the nave and gave other plate and furnishings. Oman has convincingly argued that these basins were for liturgical use, since they appear among the chapel furnishings in pre-1534 inventories of Canterbury College, the Oxford foundation maintained by Christ Church Cathedral Priory, Canterbury. The basins must have come to the cathedral after the college ceased to exist (*c.* 1539?); otherwise only books from the college returned to Canterbury.

Ablution basins were used in pairs, the water being poured from one into another, to enable the priest celebrating Mass to wash after the Communion and before the Benediction (Rock 1905, IV, pp. 192–6). Silver

729

examples are found only in the inventories of important churches or episcopal chapels; only three other English pre-Reformation basins of this type are known to survive (Glanville 1983–4, p. 75). In form they were probably identical to their secular counterparts.   MLC

PROV. Prior Chillenden; probably given to Canterbury College, Oxford before 1411 and mentioned in inventories of 1459, 1501, 1510 (Oman 1980); Canterbury Cathedral, by 1563.

LIT. Oman 1980, pp. 49–52.

730   The great Dublin civic sword

c. 1390–9 (1395–6 ?); silver-gilt mounts probably by Herman van Cleve; scabbard, apart from one original mount, 17th-century and later
Blade steel, hilt iron and silver-gilt, scabbard mounts silver-gilt: l. 138.7 cm
Inscr. in engraved Gothic minuscules on hilt and original scabbard mount *souereyne souereyne*
Dublin Corporation

This is a hand-and-a-half sword. The tapering, straight, double-edged blade of flattened hollow-diamond section is struck with two maker's marks on each face, one a Gothic minuscule *o*. The cruciform hilt with plummet-shaped pommel and straight cross, tapering to downturned tips, is of iron encased in silver-gilt. The tapering grip and, in the centre of the cross, the double D-shaped 'chappe' are both of silver-gilt. The one original scabbard mount is in the form of a garter. The inscriptions appear on this last and on scrolls on the 'chappe'. The rest of the hilt and the garter are engraved with designs including scrolling stems with stylised forget-me-not (Germander speedwell) flowers and, on the pommel, ostrich feathers entwined with scrolls with traces of inscriptions.

Sovereyne – or, more usually, *Ma sovereyne* – and the forget-me-not were devices used by King Henry IV from before his accession to the throne in 1399, and both are represented, for instance, on the canopy of his tomb at

Canterbury. The badge of an ostrich feather entwined with a scroll inscribed *ma souereyne* was also used by him as Earl of Derby and Duke of Hereford, for example on his seals, but apparently not after his accession. This, coupled with the absence of any royal devices from the sword, indicates that it must have been made for Henry before 1399. His wardrobe accounts record many payments to his goldsmith, Herman van Cleve, for mounting swords and daggers, and this sword may be the subject of one such payment made during the year ending 1 February 1396. It would thus appear to be the only recorded piece of English secular goldsmith's work (excluding seals) which can be attributed even tentatively to a known maker.

In 1403 Henry granted the Mayor of Dublin and his successors the right to have a sword borne before them, and he must have supplied this one for the purpose from his personal armoury.   CB

LIT. Dublin 1895–6, pp. 9–12; Blair & Delamer (forthcoming).

730

Stained glass of all artistic media probably best epitomises for us today the art of the Gothic period. The major surviving ensembles of stained glass in England at Canterbury Cathedral and York Minster, both represented in the exhibition (Cat. 3, 4, 5, 27, 563, 741, 748), do not compare in scale with such French glazing schemes as those at Chartres and Bourges. Time, corrosion, neglect and religiously inspired destruction have resulted in immense losses in England. The present exhibition nevertheless serves to draw attention to the superlative quality of English medieval glass-painting, which is often to be found in widely scattered and remote parish churches. This is a rich inheritance still threatened and desperately in need of protection.

For medieval theologians light was a powerful symbol of God's presence in the world. St John in the Book of Revelation had described the Heavenly Jerusalem as a city of light and colourful radiance, which was constructed of precious materials, gold, jewels and glass. Stained-glass windows therefore helped to make the Church on earth a symbol of that heavenly vision. In the English Gothic churches of this period, as the windows grew in size in proportion to the wall space, stained glass became the principal and certainly the most costly form of monumental painting.

The two-hundred-year span of the exhibition saw notable changes in style and design, as a comparison between the two kings from Canterbury will demonstrate (Cat. 3, 748). The purpose in proclaiming the central messages of the Christian faith remained constant, however. The saints in particular were represented in the windows as intercessors between earth and Heaven, guaranteeing salvation for the faithful both living and dead (Cat. 731). 'Pierce the Plowman's Crede', a Middle English text of *c.* 1394, describes how in the 'wide windows... with gaie glittering glas glowing as ye sonne' Christ and his saints are shown. The text continues: 'Seynt Fraunces himself schall folden the in his cope, and presente the to the Trynitie and praie for thy synnes'.

We end as we began: with the image of a king from Canterbury (Cat. 3, 748), showing how the continuing alliance between the secular and the religious remained crucial throughout the period.

731 Effigy of Sir Robert du Bois

c. 1340
Oak, with pigment: l. 202 cm
The Parochial Church Council of Fersfield,
  Norfolk

The effigy was carved from a single piece of oak hollowed out in the centre and filled with burnt coals to absorb damp. The knight is wearing a close-fitting coat of mail with coif and hose, beneath a knee-length surcoat flaring from the hips. On his head is a conical headpiece, and his feet rest on a hart couchant. The belt, sword and spurs were formerly gilded and set with coloured glass in imitation of enamels. The figure itself still retains

731

much of of its medieval polychromy: the surcoat, helmet, gauntlets and hart are painted in the heraldic fur ermine.

The antiquary, Francis Blomefield, who was rector of Fersfield, Norfolk, from 1729 to 1752, discovered under the head of the effigy a board painted with the arms of Bois and Latimer, the latter with a label of three points indicating that an eldest son was represented. He suggested on this evidence that the figure was Sir Robert du Bois, lord of the manor of Fersfield from 1298 to 1311, and husband of Christiana Latimer. However, the details of the armour and the style of the figure itself, with its slender, curved torso, argues for a date approaching that of the tomb of John of Eltham in Westminster Abbey, or Sir Oliver de Ingham at Ingham, Norfolk, both c. 1340; so Blomefield concluded that it was made some time after Sir Robert's death and also after the death of his unmarried son and heir in 1333. It is perhaps more likely that the tomb represents the younger Sir Robert bearing the arms of his parents, and that it was commissioned by his sister Alice, whose husband Sir John Howard inherited the manor in her right upon his death. Blomefield noted the heraldry of Howard and Bois in the windows of the south aisle of the church, which was begun by the elder Sir Robert, and presumably therefore finished at Alice's instigation. The effigy may have been supplied from a major centre of production, perhaps in London.　　　vs

PROV. Church of St Andrew, Fersfield, Norfolk.

LIT. Blomefield 1805, vol. I, pp. 74–9, 102–5, repr. p. 105; Prior & Gardner 1912, pp. 661–71.

732　The Return of the Dove to the Ark

c. 1220–30

Stained glass: h. 59 cm, w. 59 cm

Dean and Chapter, Lincoln Cathedral, choir, sII 4c

As part of a late eighteenth-century tidying up of the surviving medieval glass this panel was inserted with miscellaneous other figure panels in the east window of the south aisle of the choir. The medallion depicts the dove returning to the ark (Genesis VIII, 11), a yellow ship with multicoloured architectural superstructure sailing on a stylised sea. Noah, bearded and wearing a purple robe, appears on the roof with hands outstretched to receive a white dove bearing an olive branch. A white tree on the right appears above the water. The medallion has a blue ground and ruby border and is placed on a grisaille background made up of miscellaneous fragments of mainly stiff-leaf foliage. In the borders are curling trails of white and yellow foliage placed on ruby and blue grounds. Apart from a few insertions and a little paint loss the medallion is well preserved. The Canterbury Cathedral glaziers restored the panel recently.

732

According to the thirteenth-century Metrical Life of St Hugh 'the top row of windows shines forth, bent down with a covering of flowers, signalling the manifold beauty of the world; the lower ones set forth the name of the holy fathers'. This suggests extensive use of grisaille in the clerestory at Lincoln, and traditional small-scale figure panels like the Noah medallion at lower level. Its exact original location is not known. It may have come from a window like those at Auxerre and Chartres depicting the life of Noah, but it might also, like its companion (Cat. 733), have originated in a typological window symbolically linking the Old Testament and the New, in which case Pentecost may have been the corresponding subject. The architectural elements in the ship accord with Augustine's interpretation of the ark as an image of the Church and 'a symbol of the City of God on pilgrimage in this world' (Knowles 1972, p. 643).

With so few firm architectural contexts for the Lincoln glass precise dating is a problem, though in broad terms the glazing belongs to the period c. 1201–35 and is contemporary with the architecture. The Noah medallion shares certain features with a panel depicting St Nicholas stilling the storm (Morgan 1983, pl. 4b), possibly associated with a chantry founded at an altar to the saint in 1223/4. The date proposed here would make the panel roughly contemporary with those of the choir aisles and Trinity Chapel at Canterbury (Cat. 27).　　　DO'C

LIT. Lafond 1946, p. 127, pl. XXII; Morgan 1983, p. 13, pl. 4a.

733　The Crossing of the Red Sea

c. 1220–30

Stained glass: h. 52 cm, w. 54 cm

Dean and Chapter, Lincoln Cathedral, choir, nII 4a

Like the previous panel (Cat. 732) this was inserted into a corresponding position on the north of the choir during the late eighteenth

733

734

century. The medallion is divided horizontally to show the Israelites on dry land and the Egyptians drowned (*Exodus* XIV). In the upper half, on a blue ground, the horned figure of Moses in purple and white garments and green nimbus leads a group of men, women and children to safety. One man carries a child on his back, another carries a scroll. Below, Pharaoh, identified by a gold crown, his horsemen, two horses and a wheeled chariot are shown beneath a blue and streaky ruby sea. There is a made-up grisaille background like that in the Noah panel, and the borders are of the same type. Apart from a few insertions the medallion is in good condition and the paint unusually well preserved. Recent conservation is again the work of the Canterbury Cathedral glaziers.

Lafond and Morgan have identified a number of Moses panels at Lincoln which may have belonged to a narrative window like those at Le Mans or the Ste-Chapelle in Paris. The rarity of certain scenes prompted Mor-

gan to postulate the existence of a theological window connected with the Epistle to the Hebrews which refers to them (Morgan 1983, pp. 29–30). Another possibility is that the present medallion, like Noah's Ark to which it is close in size and style, came from a typological window where a likely parallel would have been the Baptism of Christ. Both medallions exhibited could be seen as images of the safety afforded to God's people and the destruction wrought upon his enemies. DO'C

LIT. Lafond 1946, p. 127; Morgan 1983, p. 9.

734 Ornamental window

c. 1220–60
Stained glass: h. 78.8 cm, w. 30.5 cm
Collection Alfred Fisher, King's Langley

This panel has a pointed head indicating its original location in a lancet window. The ornamental pattern is formed entirely by the leading (which is almost all medieval) and consists of three roundels linked in overlap-

ping planes by a diamond-shaped strapwork and set within a plain border. The panel is in grisaille except for the fillings between the strapwork and the borders to the roundels. The upper and lower roundels contain plain streaked ruby and blue glass, the centre one blue and pot-metal yellow glass. The left-hand blue piece and the top ruby pieces of the upper roundel are post-medieval restorations. Several of the grisaille pieces are also restoration work.

Grisaille windows with the design formed entirely by the leading are a characteristic feature of Cistercian abbeys of the twelfth and thirteenth centuries on the Continent (Zakin 1979). Similar designs to the window exhibited here are known from the abbeys at Obazine, Pontigny and Marienstatt; they also occur in non-Cistercian glass, as in a chancel window at Hastingleigh, Kent. The closest comparison is one of the ornamental grisaille patterns from Salisbury Cathedral, datable to between 1220 and 1258 (Winston 1847, p. 121, pl. IV [2]). RM

PROV. James Powell & Sons, Whitefriars, Ltd.; Alfred Fisher, King's Langley, Herts., 1980.

735

Paris (1242–8); certainly the pointed quatrefoil and vesica shapes of the Westminster glass find close counterparts in the Ste-Chapelle glass, but there is no trace of the latter's broken-fold drapery style. RM

LIT. Lethaby 1906, pp. 299–304; Lethaby 1925, pp. 234–53; RCHM, *Westminster Abbey*, 1924, p. 87, pls 17–19; Eden 1927, pp. 81–8; Baker 1960, pl. 13; Eeles 1978–80, pp. 17–21, 47–53; Grodecki & Brisac 1985, pp. 187–8.

736 Scene from the legend of St Nicholas

c. 1246–59
Stained glass: h. 61 cm, w. 45.7 cm
Dean and Chapter of Westminster

The episode depicted in this vesica-shaped panel is from the story of the little boy and the golden cup: a nobleman prayed to St Nicholas, promising that should his wish for a son be granted, he would take him on a pilgrimage to the saint's shrine and leave a gold cup there as an offering. The boy was duly born and the father had the cup made, but liked it so much that he kept it for his own use and commissioned a replica for St Nicholas' shrine. Both cups were taken on the pilgrimage, but on the voyage the young boy fell overboard with the first cup and disappeared. Eventually he reappeared at the shrine with the cup, having been saved from drowning by St Nicholas. The Westminster panel shows the nobleman's son falling overboard from the ship, watched by his helpless father and the crew; on the extreme right is St Nicholas with mitre and crosier. The only original heads are those of the crew member on the extreme left and St Nicholas; the oar and part of the lowest section of the panel are also restored. The panel is in the same style as the St Stephen scene (Cat. 735). RM

LIT. See Cat. 735.

737 Figures in grisaille

After 1245, probably *c.* 1260–80
Stained glass: h. 320 cm, w. 55.6 cm
The Parochial Church Council, Chetwode, Buckingham, window s.II

This glass, which now fills the central lancet of the south chancel window, was originally in one of the two lancets flanking the central light in the east wall of the church. In 1842 it was replaced by the present glazing. The medieval glass consists of grisaille with stylised leaves and stems arranged in overlapping roundels and other shapes and enlivened by border strips, bosses and foliate fillings in coloured glass. The shield at the base of the light bears the royal arms of England; the vesica-shaped panel in the centre contains an archbishop in Mass vestments, his right hand raised in blessing, his left holding the archiepiscopal cross-staff. The head, hands and

735 The stoning of St Stephen

c. 1246–59
Stained glass: h. 63.5 cm, w. 45.7 cm
Dean and Chapter of Westminster

The almost total loss of the glazing of the eastern part of Westminster Abbey undertaken during Henry III's lavish rebuilding in 1246–72 is one of the great lacunae in the history of English medieval stained glass. All that survive of the figural glass are seven panels, six of which are in the Jerusalem Chamber and the seventh in the Muniment Room in the south transept; none is *in situ*. Glazing using white and coloured glass was in full progress by the time of the first surviving detailed building account in 1253. Between 1 February and 13 July of that year between thirteen and fifteen glaziers were employed weekly. Work on the windows was still under way in 1272 (Colvin 1971) and in Edward I's reign. If, as it seems likely, the panels depicting St Nicholas (Cat. 736) and

the death of St John the Baptist were originally located in the apsidal chapels dedicated to these saints, then they can be presumed to have been executed and in place before the completion of the transepts in June 1259.

In the St Stephen panel the poses of the three men carrying out the stoning curve in conformity with the pointed quatrefoil shape of the panel. Apart from the blue ground the predominant colours are yellow, ruby and white. In the reduction of the incidental landscape elements almost to shorthand, the St Stephen and the other Westminster panels conform to a trend apparent in English glass from the last phase of the Canterbury glazing onwards. There the loss of detail compared with the earlier Canterbury windows is counterbalanced by the dramatic silhouetting of the slender, elongated figures and their lively gestures against the plain ground. The Jerusalem Chamber panels have been compared with the glazing of the Ste-Chapelle,

736

pall are in white glass, the chasuble and slippers are ruby, the mitre, staff and tunicle pot-metal yellow and the dalmatic green. The figure is set on a blue ground enlivened with quatrefoil roundels and with a ruby border. The vesica near the apex of the lancet encloses a full-length figure of St John the Baptist. In his left hand he holds the *Agnus Dei*. Hands, legs and face are in pink glass, the mantle is pot-metal yellow and the nimbus ruby. The other two lights in this window (not exhibited) are almost certainly *in situ* and consist of thirteenth-century grisaille quarries (somewhat restored) with a repeated foliate motif and a medley of contemporary and early fourteenth-century figures in coloured glass.

The Augustinian priory of Chetwode was founded in 1245 and the glass appears to have been executed in the third quarter of the century. The presence of St John the Baptist may indicate that the window was executed during the priorate of John of Woodstock (1261–70). The priory was recognised as a royal foundation and received endowments from Henry III. The royal arms, shown contourné, are among the earliest examples of heraldic stained glass in England. The overlapping of the vesica-shaped panels into the circular grisaille motifs is a characteristic feature of English late thirteenth-century glazing, and the figure of St John is one of the first appearances, in this medium, of the angular broken-fold drapery style and associated s-shaped stance.　　　RM

LIT. Lysons 1813, p. 488, repr.; RCHM, *Buckinghamshire*, 1913, p. 86, colour frontispiece; Greening Lamborn 1949, pp. 60–1.

737

738

738 Henry de Mamesfeld

c. 1294

Stained glass: h. 89 cm, w. 63 cm

Inscr. MAGISTER : HENRIC' DE : MAMESFELD :
  ME : FECIT :

The Warden and Fellows of Merton College,
  Oxford, chancel sv 3a

This panel represents the kneeling figure of the donor, Henry de Mamesfeld, Doctor of Theology, wearing a blue robe, white hooded gown and purple pileus. He is placed against a blue maple *rinceau* ground beneath a canopy consisting of side shafts with two-light traceried windows and pinnacles, cusped arch, crocketed gable, and masonry superstructure with crenellation and domed roof, all in blue, green, white and pot-metal yellow glass. There is an inscription beneath

the figure and the borders contain white and yellow maple leaves on blue grounds. Skilful restoration by Powells in the nineteenth century and Caldwell in 1931 is difficult to spot from the ground. The head and hands look restored and there are replacements in other areas of the panel. The windows are currently being conserved by King & Sons.

The chapel glazing is a virtually complete band-window scheme with each of the fourteen lateral windows of the chancel filled with naturalistic foliage grisaille crossed by a single band of colour formed by a standing apostle flanked by representations of de Mamesfeld (fig. 109). Although replaced by ecclesiastical saints in the two windows above the sedilia, he still appears twenty-four times in an unparalleled example of personal

display. The chapel was constructed between 1289 and 1294 and there is documentation for the glazing towards the end of this period, when a gift of £4 from Mamesfeld is recorded. Newton apart, most previous writers have ignored the documents and proposed dates extending well into the fourteenth century for the glass. The donor was a fellow of the college between 1288 and 1296 when he took holy orders. He became Chancellor of Oxford University and Dean of Lincoln, but refused the bishopric to which he was elected in 1320 (Emden 1958, II, pp. 1211–12).

Like its architectural setting the Merton glass is a precocious example of the Court style of the 1290s. The refined and elegant figure-style owes much to manuscript illumination, and the architectural settings, which contain advanced features such as ogee arches, can be paralleled in Court works of the period. Apart from the absence of yellow stain the Merton glass anticipates the trends in English glass-painting of the first quarter of the fourteenth century.   DO'C

LIT. Garrod 1931; RCHM, *Oxford*, 1939, p. 80; Newton, 1961, I, pp. 5–10; Paris 1968, no. 204; Newton in Sherwood & Pevsner 1974, pp. 81–3; Grodecki & Brisac 1985, pp. 188, 264.

739 The Prophet Isaiah

1303–4

Stained glass: h. 175 cm, w. 70 cm

Inscr. in Lombardic letters
  EGREDIETVR : VIRGA : DE : RADICE : IESSE
Dean and Chapter of Exeter, east window

The confused history of the glazing of the great east window of Exeter Cathedral has recently been elucidated (Brooks [forthcoming]). The present contents of the window fall into three main groups of figures: (a) Sts Margaret, Catherine, Mary Magdalene, Peter, Paul and Andrew and the prophets Abraham, Moses and Isaiah; (b) Sts Sidwell, Helena, Edward the Confessor (Cat. 746) and Edmund; (c) Sts Barbara, Martin and Catherine, the Virgin and Child and two archangels. The last group is not *in situ* and appears to have been taken in 1751 from the fifteenth-century glazing of the chapter house. The second series was executed by Robert Lyen in 1391 when the east window was reconstructed (see Cat. 746). The figures comprising the first group are all that survive of the original glazing of the choir windows. They can be dated precisely by the Fabric Accounts. In the summer of 1304 Master Walter the glazier received £4.10s in wages *assident' vitrum summi gabuli et viij summarum fenestrarum et vj fenestrarum in alis novi operis*; 'for setting the glass of the high gable and 8 high windows and 6 windows in the aisles of the new work' (Erskine 1981, p. 35). This is the earliest instance so far discovered where existing English glass can be firmly attributed to a named glazier. Master Walter was still working on the Exeter choir glazing in

739

1310–11 (Erskine 1981, p. 57).

The varied iconography of the first group (three female saints, three apostles and three prophets) makes it improbable that all of the figures originally belonged to the east window; some may have been brought from the choir clerestory in 1751. The three prophets are the most likely to have formed part of the glazing scheme of 1303–4: the text on the scroll held by Isaiah (*Isaiah* XI, 1) refers to the stem of Jesse, and the Tree of Jesse was quite a common choice of subject for east windows of important churches in the first half of the fourteenth century (e.g. Wells, Bristol and Selby). The figure of Isaiah is one of the finest examples of English glass of the first decade of the fourteenth century, although the borders tiled base, canopy and side shafts (except for the foliate capitals) were executed by Frederick Drake in 1884–96. The rich purple robe with its pot-metal yellow bands, the green staff and edging to the white mantle and the deep blue foliate diapered ground and ruby nimbus are characteristic of the more varied range of colours introduced into glazing around 1300. The elegant stance of the slender figure, and the lack of modelling in facial features, are also typical of the period.

RM

LIT. Drake 1912; Brooks (forthcoming).

740   The Virgin Annunciate

c. 1330–50
Stained glass: h. 167 cm, w. 46 cm
The Stained Glass Museum, Ely, 76/4/2

One of the most exquisite panels in English fourteenth-century glass is the Virgin from an Annunciation formerly in Hadzor Parish Church, Worcestershire. The Virgin is shown full-length in an S-shaped swaying posture. She wears a green robe under a pot-metal yellow mantle; her hands and face are in white glass and her wavy hair is yellow-stained. The patterned nimbus is ruby. She is looking at the white dove of the Holy Spirit, and at her feet is the pot of lilies. The figure is set on a blue ground with coils of *rinceaux* delicately picked out against a matt wash and within an architectural framework comprising a cusped arch, pinnacles and side shafts with the superstructure tipped forward in 'bird's-eye' perspective. The border consists of roundels containing cinquefoil yellow stain flowers alternating with diamond-shaped pieces with foliage, animal masks, fleurs-de-lis and other heads in yellow stain, all on a ruby ground. Part of the canopy, the nimbus, most of the lower half of the figure and some of the border and side shafts were restored by Hardman & Co. in 1866. Almost all of the accompanying panel with the Archangel Gabriel (not exhibited here) is Hardman's work.

The style of the foliage sprays, the delicate modelling and sensitive shading, the impression of three-dimensionality given by the

740

placing of the Virgin in front of the right-hand side shaft and the perspective in the canopy are all features which indicate that this panel belongs with a considerable group of works influenced by French art of the 1320s and 1330s (see Cat. 741). The Hadzor glazier was also responsible for a heavily restored Coronation of the Virgin in the tracery of a nave south aisle window in Worcester Cathedral, and the figures of Sts Margaret, Catherine, Cuthbert and an unidentified archbishop in the chancel of Kempsey, also in Worcestershire.

RM

PROV. Parish Church of St John the Baptist, Hadzor, Worcestershire; presented by Diocese of Worcester to the Stained Glass Museum, Ely, 1976.

LIT. Green 1938, pp. 10–12; Harrison 1978, no. 4.

741   St John the Evangelist, St Peter and the Nativity

1339
Stained glass: each light h. 431 cm, w. 75 cm
The Dean and Chapter of York, nave west window, WI. 5c–9c, 5d–9d

The York west window is one of the great monuments of English glass-painting. Thanks to the seventeenth-century antiquarian James Torre, who copied the now lost contract, we know that the commission was given in 1338/9 to a glazier called Robert, probably Robert Kettlebarn, freeman of York in 1324. Archbishop William de Melton (Cat. 112) gave 100 marks to the work, for which the glaziers charged 6d a foot for white glass and 12d a foot for coloured. The huge eight-light window proclaims the power of the church of York. Eight of Melton's predecessors, regarded as saints, founders and benefactors, stand beneath the twelve Apostles with the Minster patron, St Peter, in their midst. Above are five Joys of the Virgin, the Annunciation, Nativity, Resurrection, Ascension and Coronation, spread over pairs of lights for greater monumentality. Grisaille foliage designs virtually fill the flowing tracery.

Standing at the bottom of the section exhibited are two Apostles, John in ruby robe and white mantle, holding his eagle and

741

741

palm, and Peter in white robe and blue mantle, holding a key and church. The lightly-coloured canopies have crocketed gables and horizontal decorative bands terminating in perspective battlements. In the Nativity, Mary, wearing ruby robe and pot-metal yellow mantle, is seated offering her breast to the Christ Child; facing them on the right is Joseph in yellow robe, blue mantle, and blue and green hat. An architectural crib unites the design and above it are the heads of the ox and the ass expressing their joy. The borders on the left are of white trefoils on blue and ruby grounds, and on the right, gold crowns on blue grounds. At a major restoration in 1757 William Peckitt painted the heads of Peter and Joseph, but generally the glass is in good condition.

Rich pot-metal and ruby colours create a sumptuous effect, but white is also prominent, allowing extensive use of yellow stain, sometimes on blue. Smear-shading is painted on both surfaces to create three-dimensional effects in the drapery, reinforcing the perspective elements in the architecture. By painting her hair on the outside the Virgin is given a transparent veil. Stickwork and scratching techniques are used for much of the ornament, notably for the finely-controlled *rinceaux* grounds behind the figures.

The large body of related material to be found in the north of England, in the Minster, the parish churches of York and major sites such as Beverley Minster, Selby Abbey and Carlisle Cathedral, points to the importance of the Master Robert workshop, which is well represented in the exhibition (Cat. 6, 562–3). The York work shares certain trends with contemporary work elsewhere in England, for example Ely (Cat. 230, 743), Hadzor (Cat. 740) and Tewkesbury (Cat. 742); it also anticipates Edward III's glazing of St Stephen's Chapel, Westminster of 1349 to 1352. One of the major influences on the York style was from French glass-painting, notably the great schemes of the 1320s and 1330s in Évreux and Rouen, as well as from Italian inspired Parisian manuscript illumination associated with Jean Pucelle. Despite the disparity in scale close comparisons can be made between the York glass and those contemporary English manuscripts showing most French influence, the Queen Mary Psalter group (Cat. 570) and the work of the Majesty Master in the Psalter of Robert de Lisle (Cat. 569)   DO'C

LIT. French 1975; O'Connor & Haselock 1977, pp. 358–64, repr. pl. 115; French & O'Connor 1987.

742

742   Hugh le Despenser the Younger

c. 1340–4
Stained glass: h. 136 cm, w. 65 cm
The Vicar, Churchwardens and the Parochial
   Church Council of Tewkesbury Abbey,
   Gloucestershire, choir clerestory NIV 2c–3c

The seven high windows at the east end of Tewkesbury form one of the most impressive glazing schemes of the mid-fourteenth century. Flanking the Last Judgement and Coronation of the Virgin in the east window are four windows containing Old Testament prophets and kings. The two westernmost windows contain figures of nobles who held the honour of Tewkesbury, Robert Fitz-hamon, Robert Fitzroy, four de Clare earls, a Despenser (the figure exhibited) and William Lord Zouche of Mortimer. The last two were the first and second husbands of the heiress Eleanor de Clare (d. 1337) who is probably

the naked donor kneeling in the Judgement window. Damaged armorials around the base of the windows contain royal heraldry and shields of families connected with the de Clares and Despensers. The great power of the Despensers was destroyed with the demise of Edward II and the execution of Hugh the Younger in 1326. Before this date Hugh was converting the east end of the abbey into a family mausoleum, and the glazing, which associates him with his illustrious predecessors, on almost equal footing with the saints, is a most effective piece of propaganda.

Hugh stands on a hillock, armed with sword and lance, and wearing plate armour, ailettes, spurs and a heraldic surcoat charged with the Despenser arms, Quarterly 1st and 4th argent, 2nd and 3rd gules fretty or, over all a bendlet sable. There is a green trefoil ground behind him, and the three-dimensional canopy (not exhibited) has side shafts and capitals in yellow stain. The borders consist of yellow oak leaves on ruby grounds. Technically the glass is very proficient, with yellow stain used extensively for details. Smear shading is used to give depth to the modelling and a backpainted quatrefoil diaper decorates the surcoat. Kempe & Co. restored the panels in 1923 and inserted a few plain pieces; recent repair work has been carried out by King & Sons.

Rushforth pointed out that the Despenser figure was more likely to be commemorative of Eleanor's husband Hugh the Younger, rather than their son Hugh, who was alive when the glass went up. The heraldry yields a date of *c.* 1340–4, confirmed by expert opinion on the armour (Kerr 1985, p. 127). The glass has much in common with other West Country schemes (e.g. Bristol, Wells, Gloucester). This figure typifies the secular spirit of so much Decorated glass and is a fitting memorial to a man who at one time was one of the most powerful, most wealthy, and most hated magnates in the kingdom.   DO'C

LIT. Rushforth 1924, pl. VIII, iii; Baker 1960 p. 113; Morris 1974.

NOTE

I wish to acknowledge the assistance of the conservators (see Acknowledgements) and also of Dr Peter Newton, Brian O'Callaghan, Hugh Murray, Penny Hedgin-Barnes and Kerry Folcard.

743   Canopy with niche figures

c. 1340–9
Stained glass: h. 176 cm, w. 86 cm
Dean and Chapter , Ely Cathedral, on loan to
   The Stained Glass Museum, Ely, 78/10/1

This panel comes from the head of a main light in the second window from the east on the south side of the Lady Chapel. It consists of the upper section of the crocketed main gable of the canopy and two rows of cusped niches containing small figures of soldiers wearing long surcoats over chainmail and standing in a variety of lively poses. Each of

743

the figures is surmounted by a steep crocketed gable. Most of the canopy is executed in white glass with yellow stain touches and some pot-metal yellow; green is used for the crockets to the main gable and the battlements of the turret in the apex. The canopy is set on a ruby ground and within a border of lions passant or, alternating with plain ruby glass (cf. Cat. 230).

The construction of the Lady Chapel (Cat. 491) began in 1321 and two windows on each side of it had been glazed by the time of the death in 1349 of John of Wisbech, the monk in charge of the work. The glazing was still in progress in 1356–9 when Simon de Lenne (King's Lynn) was paid for a window donated by John of Gaunt. If a normal east-to-west programme was followed for the glazing, the canopies in the two easternmost windows on each side were finished by 1349. A date in the 1340s is supported by stylistic comparisons. Small niche figures in canopies occur frequently in glass in York and also in manuscripts (e.g. the De Lisle Psalter of c. 1339, Cat. 569) and appear to be derived from glass in Normandy of the 1320s (French 1971; O'Connor & Haselock 1977); the Ely figures are comparable with the small figures in armour in the side shafts of the brass to Sir Hugh Hastings (d. 1347) at Elsing in Norfolk (Cat. 690). Niche figures are present in canopies in a window which can be dated 1348 in Buckland Church, Hert-

fordshire, and the canopies in St Stephen's Chapel, Westminster, glazed between c. 1349 and 1352, also included similar niche figures (Smith 1807, figs between pp. 232 and 233). Simon de Lenne was one of the glaziers employed there. The Ely canopy shows no traces of the use of perspective which is such a marked feature of contemporary glass at Wells, Tewkesbury and Gloucester (Marks 1982. Kerr 1985). RM

LIT. Norwich 1973, no. 33.

744   Sir James Berners

After 1361, probably c. 1380–90
Stained glass: h. 60.2 cm, w. 44.5 cm
Inscr. in black letter IACOBUS : BERNERS
   P(AT)R(O)NUS ISTIU(S) : ECCL[ES]IE
The Rector and Parochial Church Council of the
   Parish Church of St Mary's, West Horsley,
   Surrey, window n. IV

In this north-western chancel window, the figure of Berners kneels in prayer on a tiled floor against a background of quarries decorated with yellow stain flowers and edgings.

He wears plate armour and a tabard with the family arms Quarterly or and vert.

In 1361 James Berners, then a minor, succeeded his grandfather as lord of the manor and patron of the living of West Horsley. He was later knighted and became one of Richard II's favourites and chief confidants. Following the victory of the insurrection led by Thomas, Duke of Gloucester and the summoning of the 'Merciless' Parliament in 1388, Berners was tried and beheaded. Comparisons of the facial features with the Crucifixion page in the Litlyngton Missal of 1383–4 (Cat. 714) and Thomas Glazier of Oxford's earlier work at New College, Oxford (Woodforde 1951), indicate that the Berners panel was executed around 1380–90. The figures of Sir Thomas Hungerford at Farleigh Hungerford, Somerset, two members of the Ruyhale family at Birtsmorton, Worcestershire, and a military saint from Adderbury in the Bodleian Library are in similar style. RM

LIT. Eeles & Peatling 1930, pp. 52–3, colour pl. opp. p. 97; Baker 1960, pl. 40.

744

745

from Frederick Drake's restoration of 1884–96. The original canopies and bases were similar to those executed in *c.* 1380–6 by Thomas Glazier for the chapel windows of New College, Oxford (Woodforde 1951). The delineation of faces and the modelled treatment of the draperies are also comparable with Thomas Glazier's work at New College and Winchester College (Cat. 612–13, 747; fig. 110); also with the kings in the west window of Canterbury Cathedral (Cat. 748). All of these mark the introduction of the International Gothic style into English glass-painting. Although the canopy and borders are restored, the figure of St Edward is almost complete. The right foot is Drake's work, and there have been minor repairs using medieval glass to the blue tunic and ruby mantle. RM

LIT. Drake 1912; Brooks (forthcoming).

746

745   Arms of John of Gaunt

1372–*c.* 1393
Stained glass: h. 29.3 cm, w. 22.9 cm
The Board of Trustees of the Victoria and Albert
    Museum, London, 6911–1860

The shield bears the arms of England quartered with France ancient, differenced with a label of three points ermine – those of John of Gaunt (1340–99) – impaled with those of Castile and León. In 1369 he took as his second wife Constance, younger daughter and co-heiress of Peter I, King of Castile and León; in 1372 John himself assumed the title of King of Castile and León. The ermine label was replaced in *c.* 1393 by a label of France (Humphery-Smith & Heenan 1962–3, pp. 81–4). Above the shield is blue 'seaweed' pattern diapering. RM

PROV. Unknown before its acq. by V & A, 1860.

LIT. Rackham 1936, pp. 42–3; London 1978a, no. 28.

746   St Edward the Confessor

1391
Stained glass: h. 175 cm, w. 70 cm
Dean and Chapter of Exeter, east window (light
    A.12)

The figure of St Edward the Confessor holding his traditional attribute of a ring is one of a set of four (the others are St Sidwell, St Helena and St Edmund of East Anglia) which were executed by an Exeter glazier named Robert Lyen in 1391 for the reconstructed great east window of the cathedral. On 28 April Lyen was sworn in as cathedral glazier and on 7 May he and the chapter made an agreement for glazing the east window; for this he was to be paid 1s.8d for each square foot of new glass he provided and 3s.4d per week for setting the old glass. The latter comprised the figures executed by Master Walter in 1303–4 (see Cat. 739).

Lyen's four figures are set within an architectural framework and borders which date

747 Two Apostles and a prophet from Winchester College Chapel

c. 1393

Stained glass: h. 357 cm, w. 165 cm

Inscr. in black letter sc̄s IOHANNES;
SOPHONIAS; SC̄S IACOBUS

The Board of Trustees of the Victoria and Albert
Museum, London, 4237–1855

These three figures are the only substantial remains of the glazing of the eight side windows of Winchester College chapel to have been discovered since its removal in 1825–8. The medieval glass was replaced by copies made by Betton and Evans, from which the original iconography can be reconstructed, The eastern pair of windows on either side each contained three prophets above three Apostles, and the remaining four windows were glazed with various saints. The surviving figures of St John the Evangelist and St James the Less are from the second window on the south side, and the prophet Zephaniah (Sophonias) was originally in the second window on the north side. Each of them is set upon an arched base and tiled floor and below a tall rib-vaulted architectural canopy with gables, pinnacles and buttresses. The design of the canopy over Zephaniah differs slightly from that over the two Apostles. The 'seaweed' diapered grounds behind the latter are ruby, and that behind the prophet is blue. All three figures are clad in white mantles with yellow-stain hem patterns and have white faces and hands. St John wears a blue gown and has a blue nimbus; he holds a pot-metal yellow cup with a purple dragon emerging from it. Zephaniah holds a scroll, wears a ruby gown and has a murrey cap. St James has a pot-metal yellow scimitar (instead of his usual attribute of a fuller's bat), blue nimbus and pink robe. There is some restoration in the panels, but the heads are all genuine. The glass is in the international Gothic style, and is the work of Thomas Glazier of Oxford (see Cat. 612–13, 747; fig. 110).   RM

PROV. Winchester College chapel until 1825–8;
Revd W.G. Roland and installed by him in St
Mary's Church, Shrewsbury; beq. to P. Corbet of
Shrewsbury; acq. by V&A from Mr Corbet, 1855.

LIT. Le Couteur 1920, pp. 86, 91; Harvey & King
1971.

748 English king

1396–1411

Stained glass: h. 162.5 cm, w. 76 cm

Dean and Chapter of Canterbury, window nave w

This is one of a series of figures of English monarchs in the great west window of the nave. Canute, Edward the Confessor and William I are identified in a description made in 1777. Each one is standing full-length against a coloured foliate ground ornamented with beaded latticework and rosettes and set within an architectural framework. The

747

side shafts have niches, sometimes containing falcons and greyhounds, and the canopy consists of multiple small gables, pinnacles and buttresses organised around a central structure of varying design. The king exhibited here stands frontally with a sword in his left hand. He wears an ermine tippet with ermine cuff (mainly restored) to a green mantle with purple lining over a blue robe; the shoes are red and the ground under them is green. Apart from the tippet the panel has suffered only minor restoration.

The representation of kings at the west end of the building was a long-established practice in French and English cathedral sculpture (e.g. Wells, Exeter and Lincoln), and it seems likely that it was at this entrance that the prior and monks of Canterbury met the reigning monarch when he visited the cathedral. Moreover, the commemoration of the kings who had been crowned by the Archbishop of Canterbury was a natural choice of subject for a window. The west window can be dated on heraldic evidence to after March 1396, and it was probably completed before Richard II's deposition in September 1399; however, a lost inscription to Prior Chillenden (in office 1391–1411) may indicate that the glazing continued past 1400. The window is one of the most important monuments of the period around 1400. Although the rich latticework grounds are a motif borrowed from English glass of the first half of the fourteenth century (e.g. Peterborough Cathedral, Stanford on Avon, Northamptonshire, Eaton Bishop, Hereford and Worcestershire), in the massive, bulky proportions of the figures, the simplified drapery folds and the use of sensitive modelling the glass firmly belongs to the International style. The canopies and treatment of figures are similar to Thomas Glazier of Oxford's work in Winchester College chapel (Cat. 612–13, 747, fig. 110). RM

PROV. Canterbury Cathedral, west window.

LIT. Caviness 1981, pp. 231–8, colour pl. XVII, figs 380–432.

Glossary

abacus The horizontal slab forming the uppermost portion of the capital of a *column* or *pier*.

achievement A complete display of armorial bearings, i.e. shield, *crest*, mantling and helm, with *supporters*.

ailette An appendage, usually rectangular, sometimes depicted attached to the point of each shoulder on armour dating between the late 13th century and the mid 14th. It appears to have been purely heraldic or decorative.

alb A priest's linen vestment, like a long shirt, often worn under other vestments.

altar frontal A rectangular hanging covering the front face of an altar; it may also consist of a panel painting or precious metalwork.

ambulatory An aisle surrounding the east end of a church, enclosing an *apse* or a straight-ended *sanctuary*, to serve as a procession path.

amice The neckerchief of a priest's vestments, embroidered with a cross.

antependium See *altar frontal*.

Apocalypse An illustrated book of the Revelation of St John with a Latin or French text, sometimes with commentary, popular in 13th-century England.

apparel Ornamentation, usually embroidered, on some priestly vestments.

apse A vaulted semicircular or polygonal termination at the eastern end of a chapel or *sanctuary*.

aquamanile A metal ewer used for ablutions at altar or table.

arcade A row of arches supported on *columns* or *piers* either free standing or blind (i.e. attached to a wall).

arch brace See *brace*.

arch-façade A façade in the shape of a large screen hollowed out into a series of deep and monumental arches. In England the form appeared first in Romanesque architecture, and most dramatically in the west façades of Lincoln Cathedral and the abbey church of Bury St Edmunds.

argent Silver (heraldic).

armature Wrought-iron framework used to support panels of stained glass and establish the formal layout of early Gothic windows.

ashlar Hewn or squared stone used in building.

asperge To sprinkle holy water over an altar or congregation.

Atlas (pl. Atlantes) A male figure used as a support for an architectural feature; the female equivalents are called Caryatids.

aventail A mail tippet protecting the neck and tops of the shoulders, attached to the lower edge of the basnet. Sometimes called by its French name, *camail*.

azure Blue (heraldic).

badge A device not borne on a shield, usually employed as a mark of identification, ownership or allegiance.

ballflower A small ball-like ornament, its front surface often pierced with a trefoil shape to resemble a flower. Common in the first quarter of the fourteenth century, especially in the West Country.

banner A rectangular flag, mounted lengthways along a lance or staff, bearing the arms of the owner; it later became a square.

bar tracery See *tracery*.

baselard A civilian short sword taking its name from the city of Basle in Switzerland.

bacinet (bascinet/basinet) Form of helmet introduced in the 13th century most widely used in the 14th and 15th centuries. At first small and hemispherical, it was subsequently given a high conical form.

basse-taille A development of *champlevé* technique: translucent enamel used on a base of gold or silver, onto which a design in low relief was chased or engraved. Great tonal richness and subtlety in the modelling of forms could be achieved by variations in the depth of the engraving, and hence in the thickness of the enamel, through which light was reflected back from the metal base.

bay The vertical compartment of a building, marked outside by windows or buttresses, and inside by columns or *shafts* (on the walls) and transverse arches or beams (on the *vault* or ceiling).

bestiary A book with moralising descriptions of animals real, fantastic or mythological, often with illustrations.

bevor A chin-defence, usually of plate.

besagew A plate, usually circular, attached to armour at the elbow and over the front of the armpit; also a disc-shaped guard for the hand on a weapon.

bifolium Two pages (folios) made up of a single sheet of vellum.

black letter (textura) A form of Gothic lettering commonly used from the late 14th century; its name comes from its having been used by the earliest Gothic painters. Its main characteristic is angularity and verticality of form.

blazon The description of arms in heraldic language.

blind tracery Tracery decorating a solid wall.

bordure A narrow band around the edge of a shield of arms.

boss A carved decorative knob at the intersection of vault ribs.

brace Subsidiary timber inserted at an angle between two main members of a roof to stiffen them. *Arch brace*: a subsidiary timber, curved in shape, and running between a vertical and horizontal timber.

brase A strap securing a shield to the arm. Also a general term for the armour on an arm.

breviary A book containing all the offices for the daily hours of the public liturgy of the church.

burin A metal tool used for engraving coins or monumental brasses.

buttress A vertical mass projecting from a wall to give extra strength.

cabochon A round or oval convex polished stone or gem.

cadency label (label) A device in the form of a horizontal bar with three or more pendant bars or 'points', placed on the coat of arms borne by an eldest son during his father's lifetime.

cambered beam A *beam* in which one or more surfaces are curved upwards towards the centre.

canting arms Arms which allude in a punning way to the bearer's name.

capital The top part of a *pier*, *column* or colonette.

cartoon A full-scale design for stained glass.

Caryatid See *Atlas*.

censer A metal utensil for burning incense in church, usually swung from chains.

chamfer The slanting face of a piece of wood or stone, produced by cutting off its corner, usually at forty-five degrees to its other two surfaces.

champlevé A method of enamelling whereby the design was gouged out of the surface of the metal to be treated, leaving thin ridges of metal standing above the resulting troughs and channels. Powdered glass was then placed in the depressions and fired, and often several colours might be included in a single compartment. The process required a substantial thickness of metal, and was therefore used on base metals such as copper or bronze.

chancel Normally the whole area of the church containing both *choir* and *sanctuary*; usually all those parts of the church east of the *transepts*.

chantry An endowment for a priest to say masses for the soul of a founder or other individual; also applied to any chapel in which such masses were said.

chape A pointed metal mount at the end of a scabbard or belt.

chappe A French term, used in the absence of an English one, to denote a double flap of leather or metal in the centre of a sword-guard, designed originally to keep moisture out of the scabbard.

chapter house In a monastery, the room off the east side of a cloister used by monks for formal assemblies and for reading the chapters of the monastic rule; in cathedrals, often belonging to the secular canons, the cathedral chapter.

charge Anything depicted on a shield of arms.

châsse See *feretory*.

chasuble A sleeveless vestment worn by a priest for the celebration of Mass. Originally conical, it was later curtailed at the sides. It may have orphreys on back and front.

chevet In English Gothic churches, an east end of French type with semicircular or half-polygonal *ambulatory* and radiating chapels.

chevron An heraldic charge shaped like an inverted 'V'.

choir The part of the church containing the seats of the religious community or clergy.

chrismatory A utensil for holding chrism, a mixture of olive oil and balsam used in the Sacraments.

ciborium A vessel to contain the reserved consecrated eucharistic host; in architecture, a vault, canopy or dome over a relic, altar, image or tomb.

clerestory (clerestorey/clearstorey) The upper storey of the main walls of a church, pierced by windows.

cloisonné In enamelling of metalwork, thin strips of metal bent to form the outline of a design and soldered edge-on to the surface of the metal object. The resulting cells were then filled with enamel, often restricted to one colour per cell. This was sufficiently delicate work to warrant the use of silver or gold in the making of the cells.

coat armour Textile garment worn over armour, usually bearing a coat-of-arms.

coat-of-plates A 16th-century term for a particular form of textile body armour lined with plates. Now often applied to all body armour of this construction (cf. *plates*).

coif A hood.

collar beam (collar, collar piece) A horizontal member in a roof connecting a pair of inclined timbers, and placed about halfway between the roof's base and apex.

collar purlin   A member running horizontally the length of a roof immediately below the collar *rafters* and supported at the *bay* intervals by *crown posts*.

colossal order   See *giant order*.

column   A vertical support for a superstructure, usually made of superimposed circular blocks of stone, sometimes of a single monolithic *shaft*.

cope   A vestment worn by a priest for various church ceremonies. It is semicircular, with an orphrey along the front edge and a vestigial hood behind.

corbel   A projecting block of stone to support a statue or architectural member.

cornette   A female hairstyle popular in the mid-14th century whereby two plaits of hair were arranged vertically on either side of the face.

Coronation of the Virgin   An image of the Virgin Mary being crowned by, or in the presence of, Christ in Heaven; popular in the thirteenth and fourteenth century.

costrel   A bottle with one or more handles through which a cord may be passed so that it can be suspended from the waist, especially of a pilgrim.

cote-hardie   A female dress worn over a *kirtle* with elbow-length sleeves and lappets reaching down almost to the ground.

cowter   A plate elbow-defence.

crenellation   A parapet with alternating indentations or *embrasures*, and raised portions or merlons.

crest   In heraldry, a device fixed upon a helm; in spurs, the top edge of the spur above the junction of the neck and sides, often curled decoratively.

cresting   A pierced ornament on the uppermost edge of a screen, shrine, etc.

crocket   A projection used at regular intervals to decorate the sloping edges of spires, gables, pinnacles etc. Often foliate in form.

crosier   The pastoral staff of bishops, abbots and abbesses, taking its form from the shepherd's crook.

cross   In armour, a sword guard formed as a single horizontal bar.

crossing   The space at the intersection of nave, *transepts* and east end in a cross-plan church.

crown-post   A post standing centrally on a *tie beam* to support a *collar purlin* and *collar beam*.

crucks   Large heavy pairs of timbers rising from, or near, ground level to meet at, or near, the apex of the roof. Each individual cruck is called a blade.

cuirass   The breast and backplate of an armour together.

cuisse   A thigh defence.

cuir-bouilli (French: 'boiled leather')   Leather treated in various ways rendering it malleable and finally hard. Often used in armour.

cusp   A projecting point formed at the meeting of two curves, commonly used in Gothic *tracery* and as a means of decorating the underside of an arch.

cutline   A full-scale outline drawing of a window leading, used for the cutting of stained glass.

dado   The lowest part of a wall, often decorated.

dalmatic   A shin-length tunic worn by deacons assisting the priest at Mass.

Decorated   The phase of English Gothic architecture lasting from *c.* 1250 to *c.* 1360.

déhanchement   A term denoting the characteristic Gothic figure stance whereby the weight is shifted on to one leg, so pushing the hip out and giving the figure a graceful curve.

detached fillet   A fillet which is given emphasis by being cut back sharply on either side, usually

as a result of its position between two hollow mouldings.

dexter   The wearer's right side of a shield, i.e. to the observer's left.

diaper   All-over surface decoration composed of small repeated patterns carved in relief.

difference   Marks introduced to a coat of arms to distinguish different members of a family.

diptych   A representation consisting of two hinged tablets of equal size; often an altarpiece.

dogtooth   Characteristic ornament of the Early English style consisting of a row of pyramids undercut to resemble foliage.

donjon   See *keep*.

dorse   The back of an object.

dorter   The dormitory in a monastic establishment.

Early English   The phase of English Gothic architecture lasting from *c.* 1190 to *c.* 1250

Easter sepulchre   A temporary or permanent furnishing set up to the north of the high altar, and used in the Easter services to represent Christ's tomb.

Ecclesia   The personification of the Church as a crowned female figure holding a cross staff, and a chalice or small church; usually paired with *Synagogue*.

elbow   A hand rest projecting from the arm of a choir stall, or a division between two stalls, consisting of a carved knop.

elevation   A drawing made in projection on a vertical plane showing any one face of a building; the external or internal face of a building.

émail en ronde bosse   Technique of enamelling the irregular surface of figures, or of objects, in the round or in very high relief. These small-scale sculptural compositions were invariably of gold or silver, whose surface was roughened to hold the enamel coating in place.

embrasure   A small opening in the wall or parapet of a building, usually *splayed* inside.

en délit (French: 'against the bed')   Marble or stone shafts quarried from a horizontal stratum but set vertically (i.e. against their natural position in the quarry bed) in the building.

ermine   A conventional representation of fur (heraldic).

falchion   A sword with a broad, curved convex-edged blade.

false gallery   A middle storey comparable in height to a gallery but opening into the roof space over the aisles without external windows.

fan vault   See *vault*.

feretory   The part of a shrine, usually of precious metal, comprising the container for relics; usually placed upon a base.

field   The background of a shield of arms on which the *charges* are placed.

fillet   A narrow, flat band often placed between two mouldings or used to form a raised strip on the surface of a roll moulding.

finial   The terminating motif of an arch, gable or pinnacle.

flying buttress   A buttress in which a half-arch or flyer receives the outward and downward thrust of a vault, and transmits it to a buttress pier.

foil   A lobe-shaped curve of wood or stone formed by the *cusps* of an arch or circle. The number of foils is indicated by a prefix, e.g. quatrefoil.

four-centred arch   A pointed arch composed of four arcs, the upper two springing from centres

below the springing line, the two lower from centres on the springing line. Common in *Perpendicular* architecture, but known in the 13th century.

frater   The dining-hall or refectory of a monastic establishment.

frontlet   A band of embroidery running along the front edge of the top of an altar

gablet   A small gable.

gallery   A large upper storey carried on the aisles of a church, also called a tribune.

gambeson   See *hacketon*.

garderobe   A medieval privy.

gathering   Folded sections of vellum leaves sewn together in groups to form a book.

giant order   *Columns* or pilasters that run up through more than one storey of a façade or *elevation*.

gipon (**jupon**)   A tight-fitting doublet, also used sometimes as a *coat armour*.

gittern   A plucked musical instrument with gut strings.

gown   In armour, the term normally used for what is now called a *surcoat*.

Gnadenstuhl Trinity (German: *Gnadenstuhl*, 'Grace' or 'Mercy' seat)   A way of representing the Trinity whereby the First Person, God the Father, is shown seated and holding the arms of the Cross upon which the Second Person, the Son, is crucified, with the Dove of the Holy Spirit hovering over the Cross.

great basnet   A large form of *basnet* with a plate *bevor* and visor.

greave   Plate armour for the leg below the knee.

grisaille   Panels or windows of predominantly white glass leaded or painted to form geometric or foliage designs; monochromatic painting in grey or beige.

guardant   Of a beast with its head turned towards the observer.

guige   A strap for suspending a shield round the neck.

gules   Red (heraldic).

habergeon   A short form of *hauberk* without a coif.

hacketon (aketon)   A quilted garment worn under armour. *Gambeson* was the term for a similar, but apparently not identical, garment.

hall church   A church without a *clerestory*, and having aisles the same, or almost the same, height as the nave.

hammer beam   A short beam projecting horizontally into the roof space at *wall plate* level, supported by a curved or inclined *brace*, and carrying a *hammer post*.

hammer post   A straight post rising vertically, from the inner end of a *hammer beam* to meet the principal *rafter*.

hauberk   A long mail shirt.

head stop   The carved head at the end of a *hood mould* or label; sometimes called a label-stop.

heater-shaped   A modern term for a shield shaped like the bottom of a flat-iron.

historiated initial   An initial letter enclosing a figural representation.

hoarding   A timber gallery projecting from a castle tower or wall and supported on joists. It had openings in its floors through which to drop missiles. The same device in stone is called machicolation. See also *murder holes*.

hood mould   A projecting *moulding* to throw off the rain, placed above an arch, doorway or window. Also called a dripstone or a label.

hounskull A rare English version of the modern German term *Hundsgugel* (hound-hood), referring to the form of *basnet* with a pointed visor.

Hours A book containing the Hours of the Virgin Mary which became popular among the laity in the late 13th and 14th centuries, often including additional prayers, the Office of the Dead, the penitential psalms, the gradual psalms and certain special Hours (as of the Trinity). The Hours were eight: Matins, Lauds, Prime, Terce, Sext, None, Vespers and Compline.

impaled A method of setting two coats of arms side by side on a shield, e.g. for displaying the arms of a married woman.

intersecting tracery See *tracery*.

jamb The straight side of a window, door, or archway.

Jesse, Tree of An image from *Isaiah* XI, showing the ancestors of Christ in the form of a family tree ascending from Jesse, and commonly including prophets, King David and the Virgin Mary, with Christ at the top.

keel moulding A curved *moulding* with a nib or arris so that the profile resembles a ship's keel.

keep The principal tower of a castle, containing (often in times of siege) the residential quarters of the lord, garrison and household. Also called a donjon.

king-post An upright post rising from the centre of a *tie beam* to carry a ridge *purlin* or ridge.

kirtle A female dress with tight sleeves.

knot The central knob on a chalice stem.

label See *cadency label* and *hood mould*.

Lady Chapel A chapel dedicated to the Virgin Mary.

lancet A slender window with an acutely pointed arch at the top.

lantern tower A tower open to view from the ground and with an upper tier of windows admitting light to the interior; often over the *crossing* of a church.

latten Copper alloy resembling modern brass, but usually containing tin as well as zinc.

lectern A reading desk in a church on which the Bible is placed and from which lessons are read.

lierne See *vault*.

liripipe The long tubular extension of a hat, common in the mid-14th century.

Litany A series of petitionary prayers, including invocations of saints arranged in the order Apostles, Martyrs, Confessors and Virgins, usually followed by short prayers or Collects.

locket One of the metal mounts on a scabbard, excluding the *chape*.

Lombardic The term coined by Jean Mabillon (d. 1707) for the wide, round Gothic lettering, especially capitals, used in inscriptions in the 13th and 14th centuries before the emergence of *black letter*.

mail Armour made of interlinked metal rings. The term 'chain mail' is a modern pleonasm.

maniple A Mass vestment comprising a strip of cloth suspended from a priest's left arm.

martyrology A history of martyrs or a book containing anniversaries of martyrs and other saints.

maunche A type of lady's sleeve.

misericord (Latin: *misericordia*, 'pity') A hinged seat which gives support to standing clergy when tipped up; often carved on the underside.

missal A book containing masses for feast days and saints' days.

mitre A cap with two points or horns, worn by bishops and some abbots.

mouchette A curved, leaf-like tracery form.

moulding The contour given to projecting architectural members.

mullion A slender upright *shaft* or bar dividing windows into lights.

murder holes Holes in the floor of a space through which missiles can be thrown below.

necking A thin, annular moulding between a capital and its supporting member.

net vault See *vault*.

niello A black substance composed of sulphides of lead, silver and copper used as an inlay for incised decorations usually on silver or gold and fixed by the application of heat.

night stair A staircase, usually running down into the south *transept* of a monastic church, and connecting the dormitory on the first floor with the interior of the church. Used by the monks for the earliest offices in the morning.

nimbus A halo.

nodding ogee An *ogee arch*, the apex of which projects forward beyond the vertical plane of the wall or supporting members.

obverse The side of a coin or seal bearing the head or principal design; the opposite side is known as the *reverse*.

oculus A round window or opening.

ogee arch An arch composed of two double-curved lines meeting at the apex.

opus anglicanum (Latin: 'English work') Highly ornate English embroidery found especially on vestments.

or Gold (heraldic).

ordinary A roll of arms classified by *charges*, e.g. lions, griffins, etc.

oriel window An angular or curved projection on the upper floor of a house, and filled with windows. Known as a bay window at ground level.

orphrey A band of gold embroidery decorating chasubles, copes, etc. According to its shape it may be called a cross-orphrey or a pillar-orphrey.

pall (**pallium**) A woollen shoulder-band with long pendants in front and behind, worn over the *chasuble* by the Pope and archbishops.

parcel gilt Partially gilt.

parclose A screen which separates a chapel from the body of a church.

paten A shallow dish on which the bread is placed at the Offertory of the Mass and on which the consecrated Host is placed after the fraction. Invariably made of gold or silver, it was usually made to match a chalice.

patera (Latin: 'plate') A sculptural ornament in low relief, normally circular, set on a wall or ceiling.

pavise A rectangular form of shield invented in Pavia.

pax A tablet, often of ivory or precious metal, decorated with a sacred image, for transferring the Kiss of Peace from the celebrant at Mass to the clergy and laity.

penetration A fragmentary transverse tunnel vault cutting into or penetrating a higher longitudinal tunnel vault.

pennon A narrow pointed lance-flag charged with the arms or armorial device of the bearer.

Perpendicular The phase of English Gothic architecture lasting from *c.* 1330 to *c.* 1550.

pier A solid support which is not a column, usually for the main arcade, of varied section from square to compound (i.e. with attached *shafts*).

pinnacle A turret-like feature usually terminating in a pyramid or cone, crowning a buttress, parapet, canopy etc.

piscina (Latin: 'basin') A niche in a wall, usually on the south side of an altar, for washing the priest's hands, and the chalice and paten at Mass.

plate (tracery) See *tracery*.

plates (pair of plates) The medieval term for a form of body armour comprising a leather or textile garment lined with metal plates.

plinth A projecting base of a wall, pier or column.

poleyn Armour for the knee, usually of plate.

pommel The knob at the top of the hilt of a sword, designed to counterbalance the blade.

pontifical Of, or pertaining to, a bishop; a liturgical text containing the rites to be performed by a bishop.

pot-metal Window glass coloured throughout by the addition of metallic oxides to the molten glass during manufacture.

prayer niche A niche in the side of a shrine base for the use of pilgrims; also called a 'squeezing place'.

presbytery See *sanctuary*.

prick spur The earliest form of spur with a fixed goad of one point.

pricket An early form of candlestick with a projecting spike to hold the candle upright.

psalter A service book containing the psalms, a selection of prayers and other items like a calendar; a very popular book of private devotion, it was commonly lavishly decorated.

pulpitum A screen of solid construction, normally stone, dividing the *choir* from the nave, and forming a backing for the return choir stalls.

Purbeck marble A fossiliferous limestone quarried on the Dorset coast; not a marble, but employed as one on account of its being able to take a high polish and so much favoured in English architecture and tombs.

purlin A longitudinal timber giving support to the common *rafters* of a roof, and placed parallel to the *wall plate* and ridge beam some way up the slope of a roof.

pyx A small vessel in which the sacrament is reserved for later use, usually a round ivory or metal box.

quadripartite vault See *vault*.

quartering Dividing a shield into quarters with a coat of arms in each. Later used less strictly for 'quarterings' of six, eight, etc.

quatrefoil See *foil*.

quarry A diamond- or square-shaped piece of window glass.

quillon A 16th-century French term, commonly used by modern writers on swords, for the arms of the *cross*.

quire Sheets of paper or vellum folded ready for binding, but unsewn.

rafter An inclined member following the slope of the roof.

rampant Descriptive of a beast when in an erect position (heraldic).

Rayonnant The phase of French Gothic architecture from *c.* 1230 to *c.* 1350 named after the radiating arrangement of lights in rose windows. Its main characteristics are the extreme thinness of all members and the maximum extension of tracery and glazing.

reguardant Of a beast looking backwards over its shoulder (heraldic).

relieving arch An arch usually of rough construction placed in a wall, above the true arch of an opening, to relieve it of the weight above.

reredos A high screen, often with carved decoration, behind and above an altar, commonly a high altar.

respond A shaft or half-pier coursed into a wall to carry an arch from a free-standing pier.

retable A carved or painted panel placed above the back of an altar.

reticulated Patterned like a net.

retrochoir The space behind the high altar in a large church.

reverse See *obverse*.

rib An arch carrying a *vault*, or placed across the cells of a vault.

ridge-rib A rib running along the transverse or longitudinal ridge of a *vault*.

rinceaux A background design of flowering or curling foliage used in stained glass.

roll moulding A moulding of convex profile.

rood A cross or Crucifix, especially one placed on the screen at the entrance to the *choir*.

rowel A revolving disc goad of several points on a spur.

ruby A term used in stained glass for a flashed glass (a basic white glass with a thin coating of colour, in this case red).

sabaton Armour for the foot, usually of plate.

sable Black (heraldic).

sacrist In a monastery, the monk responsible for the upkeep of the church and its equipment.

sanctuary Part of the church which lies east of the *choir*, and where the high altar is placed.

saltire An heraldic term for a diagonal cross.

Sarum Use The calendar, liturgical texts and practices codified by Bishop Richard Poore (1217–28) of Salisbury (New Sarum). Used increasingly in the 13th and 14th centuries outside the Province of York.

schynbald A *greave* for the shin only.

screens passage The space at the service end of a medieval hall between the screen and the entrance to kitchen, buttery and pantry.

sedilia (Latin: 'seats') Seats for clergy (priest, deacon, sub-deacon) officiating at services, situated on the south side of the chancel or sanctuary and usually three in number.

set-off The sloping surface of a buttress by which its projection is reduced.

sexpartite vault See *vault*.

sgraffito (Italian: 'scratched') The technique of producing a design by scratching through a layer of paint or other material to reveal a ground of a different colour.

shaffron Armour for a horse's head. The common modern form *shanfron* derives from a misread document.

shaft A slender column, usually not weight-bearing.

sinister The bearer's left side of a shield, i.e. the observer's right.

smear shading Applications of thin washes of paint on glass.

socle A plinth or pedestal, especially for a statue.

soffit The underside of any architectural feature.

solar (Latin: solarium, 'sunny place') A private chamber in a residential suite, usually on the first floor, and adjoining the hall of a medieval house or castle.

span The maximum width between the *terminals* of a spur.

spandrel The triangular area between two arches or between an arch and the adjacent wall or vertical moulding.

spaudler Armour for the shoulder.

splay A *chamfered* edge at the side of a door or window.

springer The lowest stones of the arches of the vault-ribs; the level at which an arch or vault leaves its supporting members.

spur neck The rear projection which supports the goad of a spur.

staff-weapon Any weapon, like a spear, incorporating a wooden staff.

stick work The removal of paint from glass with a stick or needle before firing.

stiff leaf A many-lobed type of foliage decoration developed in the late twelfth century and used widely throughout the thirteenth century in England.

stipple shading Method of shading stained glass by dabbing paint with the end of the brush. It first appears around the middle of the 14th century.

stole A priestly vestment comprising a strip of cloth hung around the neck.

stoup A vessel containing holy water, often located near the door of a church.

string course A projecting moulding running horizontally along the face of a building, and usually dividing one register from another.

style Honoré A generic term for the style of manuscripts associated with Master Honoré, a late 13th-century Parisian illuminator.

supporters In heraldry, the human, natural or fabulous creatures on either side of a shield of arms: on *misericords*, subsidiary carvings on tendrils or in roundels emanating from either side of the seat ledge. Rare on Continental misericords.

surcoat A term now used for the gown worn over armour. In the Middle Ages it denoted a civilian over-garment.

Synagogue The personification of the Jewish Synagogue as a female figure; usually shown with a blindfold and holding a spear, often broken, and the tablets of the law. Generally paired with *Ecclesia*.

terminals In spurs, the front ends of the two sides of the spur.

textura See *black letter*.

tie beam A horizontal transverse beam, tying together the top of a timber-framed wall. In a roof, it connects the ends of blades or principle *rafters* and sometimes supports a *crown post*.

tierceron vault See *vault*.

tinctures The metals, colours and furs of heraldry.

tower-hoard See *hoarding*.

tracery Geometrical patterns of cut stone, found in windows, on walls or freestanding. *Bar tracery*: geometric patterns decorating heads of windows made up of thin bar-like pieces of stone. *Intersecting tracery*: tracery composed of a number of arches, all struck from the same base line, and intersecting in the window heads. *Plate tracery*: tracery in which the patterns are formed by piercing continuous surfaces of masonry.

transept The transverse arms of a cross-shaped church.

translation The moving of sacred relics from one resting place to another.

transom A horizontal bar of stone or wood across the opening of a window or across a panel.

trapper An ornamental cloth spread over a horse in ceremonies.

Trecento Italian term denoting the 14th century.

trefoil See *foil*.

triforium An arcaded wall passage facing on to the interior of a church, and placed above the *arcade* and below the *clerestory*. The word is often wrongly applied to a gallery or tribune.

triptych Like a *diptych*, but with three panels instead of two.

truss A timber frame in which the pieces are jointed and braced to retain their shape under load. A roof truss is composed of a series of timbers framed together and placed at bay intervals along a building to support *purlins* and *rafters*.

tunicle A fringed vestment slit at the sides, longer and less ample than the *dalmatic*, worn by sub-deacons; also part of *pontifical* vestments.

tympanum The field in the head of an arch.

under-side couching A technique of embroidery in which gold, silver or silk threads laid on the face of the ground material are fixed at intervals by linen threads which are on the back of the material.

vair One of the furs of heraldry, represented by a conventional variegated pattern of blue and white.

vambrace Plate armour for the arm.

vault An arched ceiling or roof of stone or brick, sometimes imitated in timber or plaster. *Barrel vault*: a continuous half cylinder of masonry, sometimes subdivided into bays by transverse arches (also called a tunnel vault). *Fan vault*: a vault composed of ribs of (usually) equal curvature and length, and with surfaces decorated with applied *tracery* panels bifurcating like the spokes of a rose window. At the top of the vault is a central *spandrel* panel, framed by the semicircular bounding ribs of each vault cone. *Lierne vault*: a vault decorated with lierne ribs, i.e. short intermediate ribs which do not spring from the main capitals, but connect the vault bosses and the intersections of ribs. *Net vault*: a vault composed of parallel ribs running diagonally across the vault surface, often across two or more bays, and crossing the other sets of parallel ribs to form a net pattern. *Quadripartite vault*: a rib vault, whose four diagonal ribs divide the vault surface into four compartments or cells. *Sexpartite vault*: one bay of *quadripartite* vaulting is divided transversely by a rib so that each bay has six compartments. *Tierceron vault*: a vault composed of tierceron ribs, i.e. secondary ribs which spring from the main capitals but end on a ridge rib, not in the centarl boss. *Tunnel vault*: see *barrel vault*.

vert Green (heraldic).

voussoir A wedge-shaped block of stone used in arch construction.

wall arcade A blind arcade decorating a wall.

wall plate A piece of timber running horizontally along the top of a wall to receive the ends of *rafters*.

wall-shaft A demi-shaft bonded to a wall.

web The stone or wooden surfaces between the *ribs* of a vault.

weepers Small images of mourners on tombs, usually set in arcading along the side of the tomb-chest.

yellow stain A technique developed in the early 14th century which colours white glass yellow, or blue glass green, by applying a solution of a silver compound to the exterior surface and firing it.

Bibliography

Abbot et al. 1972
E. Abbott et al., *Westminster Abbey*, 1972

Adams 1983
B. Adams, *London Illustrated 1604–1851*, 1983

Aldrich 1985
M. Aldrich, 'Gothic architecture illustrated: the drawings of Thomas Rickman in New York', *Antiq. J.*, LXV, 1985, pp. 427–33

Alexander 1978
J. J. G. Alexander, 'Scribes as artists: the arabesque initial in twelfth-century English manuscripts', *Medieval Scribes, Manuscripts & Libraries. Essays presented to N. R. Ker*, ed. M. B. Parkes & A. G. Watson, 1978, pp. 87–116

Alexander 1983
J. J. G. Alexander, 'Painting and manuscript illumination for royal patrons in the later Middle Ages', in Scattergood & Sherborne 1983, pp. 141–62

Alexander & Crossley 1976
J. J. G. Alexander & B. P. Crossley, *Medieval and Early Renaissance Treasures in the North-west*, Whitworth Art Gallery, University of Manchester, 1976

Alexander & Temple 1985
J. J. G. Alexander & E. Temple, *Illuminated Manuscripts in Oxford College Libraries, the University Archives and the Taylor Institution*, 1985

Allen 1896
J. R. Allen, 'Inscribed bronze flagon of the fourteenth century in the South Kensington Museum', *The Reliquary and Illustrated Archaeologist*, n.s., II, 1896, pp. 103–6

Allen 1938
D. F. Allen, 'Dies in the Public Record Office 1936', *Brit. Numismatic J.*, XXIII, 1938, pp. 31–50

Allison 1955–7
K. J. Allison, 'The lost villages of Norfolk', *Norfolk Archaeology*, XXXI, 1955–7, pp. 116–62

Altschul 1965
M. Altschul, *A Baronial Family in Medieval England: The Clares 1217–1314*, 1965

Ancrene Wisse 1962 edn
Ancrene Wisse (The English text of the Ancrene Riwle), ed. J. R. R. Tolkien, Early English Text Soc., 1962

Anderson 1935
M. D. Anderson, *The Medieval Carver*, 1935

Anderson 1938
M. D. Anderson, *Animal Carvings in British Churches*, 1938

Anderson 1954
M. D. Anderson, *Misericords: Medieval Life in English Woodcarving*, 1954

Anderson 1955
M. D. Anderson, *The Imagery of British Churches*, 1955

Anderson 1963
M. D. Anderson, *Drama and Imagery in English Medieval Churches*, 1963

Anderson 1967
M. D. Anderson, *The Choir Stalls of Lincoln Minster*, 1967

Andersson 1949, 1950
A. Andersson, *English Influence in Norwegian and Swedish Figure Sculpture in Wood 1220–70*, 1949, 1950 (reprint)

Andersson 1964, 1966, 1975, 1980
A. Andersson, *Gothic Wooden Sculpture in Sweden*: I *Attitudes to the Heritage*, 1964 (by B. Thordeman); II *Romanesque and Gothic Sculpture*, 1966; III *Late Medieval Sculpture*, 1980; IV *The Museum Collection Catalogue*, 1975 (by A. Andersson & M. Rydbeck); V *The Museum Collection Plates*, 1964

Andersson 1970
A. Andersson, 'The Holy Rood of Skokloster and the Scandinavian Early Gothic', *Burl. Mag.*, CXII, 1970, pp. 132–40

Andersson 1983
A. Andersson, *Medieval Drinking Bowls of Silver found in Sweden*, 1983

Annales Londonienses 1882 edn
'Annales Londonienses', *Chronicles of the reigns of Edward I and Edward II*, ed. W. Stubbs, I, Rolls series LXXVI, 1882

Anon. 1926
Anon., 'Bronze mould from Essex', *Antiq. J.*, VI, 1926, pp. 447–8

Anon. 1957
Anon., 'Two medieval bishops' tombs', *Friends of Exeter Cathedral, 27th Annual Report*, 1957, pp. 23–5

Anon. 1978
'A medieval cruet', *J. Pewter Soc.*, I, 3, 1978

Apokalypse 1982
Apokalypse, MS Douce 180 der Bodleian Library, Oxford, 1982

Arentzen 1984
J.-G. Arentzen, *Imago Mundi Cartographica*, 1984

Armitage, Pearce & Vince 1981
K. H. Armitage, J. E. Pearce & A. G. Vince, 'A late medieval "bronze" mould from Copthall Avenue, London', *Antiq. J.*, LXI, 1981, pp. 362–4, 369

Ashby 1980
J. E. Ashby, 'English Medieval Murals of the Doom: A Descriptive Catalogue and Introduction', M.Phil. Thesis, Centre for Medieval Studies, University of York, 1980

Ashdown 1948
C. H. Ashdown, *History of the Worshipful Company of Glaziers*, 1948

Aston 1984
M. Aston, *Lollards and Reformers: Images and Literacy in Late Medieval Religion*, 1984

Atkinson 1889
J. C. Atkinson (ed.), *Cartularium Abbathiae de Rievalle*, Surtees Society, LXXXIII, 1889

Atkinson 1936
T. D. Atkinson, 'Medieval figure sculpture in Winchester Cathedral', *Archaeologia*, LXXXV, 1936, pp. 159–67

Atkinson 1953
T. D. Atkinson, (Architectural description of Ely Cathedral and precincts), VCH, *Cambridge and the Isle of Ely*, IV, 1953, pp. 50–82

Avril 1978
F. Avril, *Manuscript Painting at the Court of France*, 1978

Avril & Stirnemann 1987
F. Avril & P. Stirnemann, *Manuscrits enluminés d'origine insulaire de la Bibliothèque nationale*, 1987

Aylmer & Cant 1977 (1979)
G. E. Aylmer & R. Cant (eds), *A History of York Minster*, 1977 (repr. with corrections 1979)

Ayloffe 1786
J. Ayloffe, 'An Account of the body of King Edward the First, as it appeared on opening his tomb in the year 1774', *Archaeologia*, III, 1786, pp. 376–413

Backhouse 1975
J. Backhouse, *The Madresfield Hours*, Roxburghe Club, 1975

Baddeley 1908
W. St Clair Baddeley, *A Cotteswold Shrine. Being a Contribution to the History of Hailes*, 1908

Badham 1985
S. Badham, (Report of lecture), *Monumental Brass Soc. Bull.*, XXXIX, 1985, pp. 140–2

Bagnall-Oakeley 1889
M. E. Bagnall-Oakeley, 'Sanctuary knockers', *Trans. Bristol & Glos. Archaeol. Soc.*, XIV, 1889–90, pp. 131–40

Baker 1836–41
G. Baker, *History and Antiquities of the County of Northampton*, 2 vols, 1836–41

Baker 1960, 1978
J. Baker, *English Stained Glass of the Medieval Period*, 1960, 1978

Baldock 1911 edn
'Registrum diversarum litterarum Radulphi Baldock, episcopi Londoniensis', *Registrum Radulphi Baldock, Gilberti Segrave, Ricardi Newport et Stephani Gravesend, episcoporum Londoniensium*, ed. R. C. Fowler, Canterbury and York Soc., VII, 1911

Barber 1904
E. Barber, 'St Werburgh and her shrine', *J. Archit., Archaeol. and Hist. Soc. of Chester and North Wales*, n.s., X, 1904, pp. 68–85

Barber 1981
R. W. Barber, *Edward, Prince of Wales and Aquitaine: A Biography of the Black Prince* (1978), repr. 1981

Barlow 1986
F. Barlow, *Thomas Becket*, 1986

Barnum 1976
P. H. Barnum (ed.), *Dives and Pauper*, Early English Text Soc., 1976

Baron 1968
F. Baron, 'Enlumineurs, peintres et sculpteurs parisiens des XIIIe et XIVe siècles d'après les rôles de la Taille', *Bull. Archéol. du Comité des Travaux Historiques et Scientifiques*, IV, 1968, pp. 37–121

Baron 1970
F. Baron, 'Enlumineurs, peintres et sculpteurs parisiens des XIVe et XVe siècles d'après les archives de l'Hôpital Saint-Jacques-aux-Pèlerins', *Bull. Archéol. du Comité des Travaux Historiques et Scientifiques*, VI, 1970, pp. 77–115

Baron 1975
F. Baron, 'Le décor sculpté et peint de l'Hôpital Saint-Jacques-aux-Pèlerins', *Bulletin Monumental*, CXXXIII, 1975, pp. 29–72

Barraud 1865
Abbé Barraud, 'Notice sur les instruments de paix', *Bulletin Monumental*, 4th ser., I, 31, 1865, pp. 249–93

Barrett 1981
G. N. Barrett, *Norwich Silver . . . The Goldsmiths of Norwich*, 1981

Barron 1969
C. M. Barron, 'Richard Whittington: the man behind the myth', *Studies in London History*, ed. A. Hollaender & W. Kellaway, 1969, pp. 197–250

Barton 1959
K. J. Barton, 'A group of medieval jugs from Bristol Castle Well', *Trans. Bristol and Glos. Archaeol. Soc.*, LXXVIII, 1959

Barton 1979
K. J. Barton, *Medieval Sussex Pottery*, 1979

Bassham & Gee 1974
C. J. Bassham & E. A. Gee, *York Minster Chapter House and Vestibule*, 1974

Bäuml 1980
F. H. Bäuml, 'Varieties and consequences of medieval literacy and illiteracy', *Speculum*, LV, 1980, pp. 237–65

Beard 1933
C. R. Beard, '"Westminster Bridge Sword" lent to the London Museum', *Connoisseur*, Feb. 1933, pp. 104–6

Beard 1935
C. R. Beard, 'The "Joseph Mayer Collections"', *Connoisseur*, Mar. 1935, pp. 135–204

Becksmann 1967
R. Becksmann, *Die architektonische Rahmung des hochgotischen Bildfensters. Untersuchungen zur oberrheinischen Glasmalerei von 1250 bis 1350*, 1967

Becksmann 1975
R. Becksmann, *Vitrea Dedicata: das Stifterbild in der deutschen Glasmalerei des Mittelalters*, 1975

Bedford 1923
R. P. Bedford, 'A fourteenth-century altarpiece from Sutton Valence', *Archaeologia Cantiana*, XXXVI, 1923, pp. 149–52

Bellamy 1973
J. G. Bellamy, *Crime and Public Order in England in the Later Middle Ages*, 1973

Bennett 1968
B. T. N. Bennett, *The Choir Stalls of Chester Cathedral*, 2nd edn, 1968

Bennett 1972
A. Bennett, 'Additions to the William of Devon group', *Art Bull.*, LIV, 1972, pp. 31–40

Bennett 1980
A. Bennett, 'The Windmill Psalter: the historiated letter E of Psalm One', *J. Warb. Court. Inst.*, XLIII, 1980, pp. 52–67

Bennett 1982
A. Bennett, 'Noah's Recalcitrant Wife in

the Ramsey Abbey Psalter', *Source*, II, 2, 1985, pp. 2–5

Bennett 1985
A. Bennett, 'A late thirteenth-century Psalter-Hours from London', in Ormrod 1985, pp. 15–30

Bennett 1986a
A. Bennett, 'Anthony Bek's copy of *Statuta Angliae*', in Ormrod 1986, pp. 1–27

Bennett 1986b
J. A. W. Bennett, *Middle English Literature*, Oxford History of English Literature, I, 2, 1986

Benson 1898
G. Benson, 'York bell founders', *Annual Report of the Yorkshire Philosophical Society*, 1898, pp. 17–35

Benson 1943–51
E. G. Benson, 'The Cantilupe Indent in Hereford Cathedral', *Trans. Monumental Brass Soc.*, VIII, 1943–51, pp. 322–30

Bentham 1771
J. Bentham, *The History and Antiquities of the Conventual and Cathedral Church of Ely from . . . 673 to the year 1771*, 1771

Beresford 1975
G. Beresford, *The Medieval Clay-Land Village: Excavations at Goltho and Barton Blount*, Soc. for Med. Archaeol. Monograph Ser., VI, 1975

Bergen 1978
Handbook to Bryggens Museum Bergen, 1978

Berling 1920
C. Berling, *Altes Zinn: ein Handbuch für Sammler und Liebhaber*, 1920

Bernardus Claraevallensis, III, 1963 edn
Sancti Bernardi Opera, III, Tractatus et Opuscula, ed. J. Leclercq & H. M. Rochais, 1963

Bernath 1925
M. H. Bernath, 'An English pewter pax', *Burl. Mag.*, XLVII, 1925, pp. 245–6

Bernheimer 1952
R. Bernheimer, *Wild Men in the Middle Ages*, 1952

Beryn 1887 edn
The Tale of Beryn, ed. F. J. Furnivall & W. G. Stone, Chaucer Soc., 2nd ser., XVII, 34, 1887

Betjeman 1970
John Betjeman's Collected Poems, 3rd edn, 1970

Bickerton-Hudson 1905
C. H. Bickerton-Hudson, 'Kewstoke reliquary', *Proc. Somersetshire Archaeol. and Nat. Hist. Soc.*, LI, 1905, pp. 28–31

Biddle 1961
M. Biddle, 'A thirteenth-century architectural sketch from the Hospital of St John the Evangelist, Cambridge', *Proc. Camb. Antiq. Soc.*, LIV, 1961, pp. 99–108

Biddle & Clayre 1983
M. Biddle & B. Clayre, *Winchester Castle and the Great Hall*, 1983

Biehn 1957
H. Biehn, *Die Kronen Europas und ihre Schicksale*, 1957

Binney 1972
M. Binney, 'Penshurst Place, Kent – 1', *Country Life*, 9 Mar. 1972, pp. 554–8

Binski 1980
P. Binski, 'Chartham, Kent and the Court', *Trans. Monumental Brass Soc.*, XIII, 1, 1980, pp. 73–9

Binski 1983
P. Binski, 'The Painted Chamber and painting at Westminster c. 1250 to 1350', Ph.D. Thesis, Cambridge University, 1983

Binski 1985
P. Binski, 'The Coronation of the Virgin on the Hastings Brass at Elsing, Norfolk', *Church Monuments. J. Church Monuments Soc.* I, 1, 1985, pp. 1–9

Binski 1986
P. Binski, *The Painted Chamber at Westminster*, Society of Antiquaries of London Occasional Paper, n.s. IX, 1986

Binski 1987
P. Binski, 'What was the Westminster Retable?', *J. Brit. Archaeol. Assoc.*, CXI, 1987

Binski 1987
P. Binski, 'The stylistic sequence of London figure brasses', in Coales 1987

Binski & Park 1986
P. Binski & D. Park, 'A Ducciesque episode at Ely: the mural decorations of Prior Crauden's Chapel', in Ormrod 1986, pp. 28–41

Birch 1878–1900
W. de G. Birch, *Catalogue of Seals in the Department of Manuscripts in the British Museum*, 6 vols, 1887, 1892, 1894, 1895, 1898, 1900

Bishop & Prideaux 1922
H. E. Bishop & E. K. Prideaux, *The Building of the Cathedral Church of St Peter in Exeter*, 1922

Blackett & de Cosson 1893
Sir E. W. Blackett, Baron C. A. de Cosson et al., (Notes on the Conyers Falchion), *Proc. Soc. Antiq. Newcastle-Upon-Tyne*, V, 1893, pp. 26–8, 42–4, 252–4

Blackley 1983
F. D. Blackley, 'The tomb of Isabella of France, wife of Edward II of England', *International Soc. for the Study of Church Monuments Bulletin*, VIII, 1984, pp. 161–4

Blair 1922
C. H. Hunter Blair, 'Medieval Seals of the Bishops of Durham', *Archaeologia*, LXXII, 1922, pp. 1–24

Blair 1924
C. H. Hunter Blair, 'Supplement to Durham Seals', *Archaeologia Aeliana*, XXI, 1924, pp. 92–3

Blair 1943
C. H. Hunter Blair, 'Armorials upon English Seals from the twelfth to the sixteenth centuries', *Archaeologia*, LXXXIX, 1943, pp. 1–26

Blair 1958
C. Blair, *European Armour circa 1066 to circa 1700*, 1958

Blair 1959
C. Blair, 'Medieval swords and spurs in Toledo Cathedral', *J. Arms and Armour Soc.*, III, 1959, pp. 41–52

Blair 1978
W. J. Blair, 'The Buslingthorpes and their monuments', *Trans. Monumental Brass Soc.*, XII, 4, 1978, pp. 265–70

Blair 1981
W. J. Blair, English Monumental Brasses before the Black Death', in *Collectanea Historica*, ed. A. P. Detsicas, Kent Archaeol. Soc., 1981, pp. 256–72

Blair 1984
C. Blair, 'The Word "Baselard"', *J. Arms & Armour Soc.*, XI, 4, 1984, pp. 193–206

Blair 1985
C. Blair, 'An early fifteenth-century London Latoner', *Monumental Brass Soc. Bull.*, XXXVIII, Feb. 1985, p. 129

Blair 1987
W. J. Blair, 'English Monumental Brasses before 1350: types, patterns and workshops', in Coales 1987

Blair & Blair (forthcoming)
C. & W. J. Blair, 'Copper alloys' in Blair & Ramsay (forthcoming)

Blair & Delamer (forthcoming)
C. Blair & I. Delamer, 'The Dublin Civic Swords'. In preparation probably for publication in *Proc. Royal Academy of Ireland*

Blair & Ramsay (forthcoming)
W. J. Blair & N. L. Ramsay (eds), *Medieval English Industries* (forthcoming)

Bland 1926
C. C. S. Bland (ed.), *Autobiography of Guibert de Nogent*, 1926

Blatchly 1975
J. M. Blatchly, 'The lost cross brasses of Suffolk 1320–1420', *Trans. Monumental Brass Soc.*, XII, 1, 1975, pp. 21–45

Blindheim 1952
M. Blindheim, *Main Trends of East-Norwegian Wooden Figure Sculpture in the second half of the Thirteenth Century*, 1952

Blindheim 1979
M. E. Blindheim, 'Fortiden Forteller, *Universitets Oldsaksamling 1829/1979*, 1979

Blindheim 1986
Fetskrift til Martin Blindheim ved 70-Årsdagen, Oslo Universitet Oldsaksamlings Skrifter, Ny Rekke 7, 1986

Blomefield 1805–10
F. Blomefield, *An Essay Towards a Topographical History of the County of Norfolk*, ed. C. Parkin, 11 vols, 1805–10

Bloxam 1859
M. H. Bloxam, 'On the sepulchral effigies in Bottesford Church, Leicestershire', *Assoc. Archit. Soc. Repts. & Papers*, X, 1, 1859, pp. 146–52

Blum 1969
P. Blum, 'The Middle English Romance "Jacob and Josep" and the Joseph Cycle of the Salisbury Chapter House', *Gesta* VIII, 1969, pp. 18–34

Blum 1978
P. Blum, *The Salisbury Chapter House and its Old Testament Cycle*, Ph.D. Thesis, Yale University, 1978

Blunt 1967
A. Blunt, 'The history of Thomas Gambier Parry's Collection', *Burl. Mag.*, CIX, 1967, pp. 112–16

Boccia 1980
L. G. Boccia, Francesco Rossi & Marco Morin, *Armi e Armature Lombarde*, 1980

Boccia & Coelho 1967
L. G. Boccia & E. T. Coelho, *L'Arte dell'Armatura in Italia*, 1967

Bock 1865
F. Bock, *Karls des Grossen Pfalzkapelle und ihre Kunstschätze*, 1865

Bock 1962
H. Bock, *Der Decorated Style. Untersuchungen zur englischen Kathedralarchitektur der ersten Hälfte des 14 Jahrhunderts*, 1962

Bolingbroke 1914
L. G. Bolingbroke, 'The Pilgrim's Chapel at Houghton', *Norfolk Archaeology*, XVIII, 1914, pp. xviii–xix

Bolton 1980
J. L. Bolton, *The Medieval English Economy, 1150–1500*, 1980

Bond 1910
F. Bond, *Wood Carvings in English Churches*, 2 vols, 1910

Bony 1979
J. Bony, *The English Decorated Style: Gothic Architecture Transformed 1250–1350*, 1979

Boon 1976
G. C. Boon, 'An early Tudor coiner's

**mould and the working of Borrowdale graphite', *Trans. Cumberland & Westmorland Antiq. & Archaeol. Soc.*, n.s. LXXVI, 1976, pp. 97–132

Bordier 1865
H. L. Bordier, 'Les statues de Saint-Jacques l'Hôpital au musée de Cluny', *Mémoires de la Société Impériale des Antiquaires de France*, XXVIII, 1865, pp. 111–32

Bordier & Brièle 1877
H. L. Bordier & L. Brièle, *Les Archives hospitalières de Paris*, 1877

Borenius 1929
T. Borenius, 'The iconography of St Thomas of Canterbury', *Archaeologia*, LXXIX, 1929, pp. 29–54

Borenius 1932a
T. Borenius, *St Thomas Becket in Art*, 1932

Borenius 1932b
T. Borenius, 'A destroyed cycle of wall paintings in a church in Wiltshire', *Antiq. J.*, XII, 1932, pp. 393–406

Borenius 1933
T. Borenius, 'Some further aspects of the iconography of St Thomas of Canterbury', *Archaeologia*, LXXXIII, 1933, pp. 171–86

Borenius 1936
T. Borenius, 'An English painted ceiling of the late fourteenth century', *Burl. Mag.*, LXVIII, 1936, pp. 268–76

Borenius 1943
T. Borenius, 'The cycle of images in the palaces and castles of Henry III', *J. Warb. Court. Inst.*, VI, 1943, pp. 40–50

Borenius & Tristram 1927
T. Borenius & E. W. Tristram, *English Medieval Painting*, 1927

Bossy 1973
J. Bossy, 'Blood and baptism: kinship, community and Christianity', *Studies in Church History*, X, 1973, pp. 129–43

Borg & Martindale 1981
A. Borg & A. Martindale (eds) *The Vanishing Past, Studies of Medieval Art, Liturgy and Metrology, Presented to Christopher Hohler*, Brit. Archaeol. Reports International Ser., III, 1981

Bossard 1934
G. Bossard, *Die Zinngiesser der Schweiz und ihr Werk*, II, 1934

Botfield 1841
B. Botfield, *Manners and Household Expenses of England*, ed. T. Hudson Turner, Roxburghe Club, 1841

Boucaud & Fregnac 1978
P. Boucaud & C. Fregnac, *Les Etains*, 1978

Boughey 1919
A. H. F. Boughey, 'Inscriptions upon medieval bells', *Archaeol. J.*, LXXVI, 1919, pp. 74–83

Bradfer-Lawrence 1922
H. L. Bradfer-Lawrence, 'King John's Cup', *Lynn Advertiser*, 17 Mar. 1922

Bradshaw & Wordsworth 1897
H. Bradshaw & C. Wordsworth (eds), *Statutes of Lincoln Cathedral*, 1897

Braikenridge n.d.
G. W. Braikenridge, unpubl. MS catalogue and notes, City of Bristol Museum and Art Gallery

Brakspear 1922
H. Brakspear, 'St Mary Redcliffe, Bristol', *Trans. Bristol and Glos. Archaeol. Soc.*, XLIV, 1922, pp. 271–92

Brand 1964
J. D. Brand, 'Some "Short Cross" questions', *Brit. Numismatic J.*, XXXIII, 1964, pp. 57–70

Brandon 1847
R. & J. A. Brandon, *An Analysis of Gothick Architecture*, 2 vols, 1847

Branner 1964
R. Branner, 'Westminster Abbey and the French Court style', *J. Soc. Archit. Historians*, XXIII, I, 1964, pp. 3–18

Branner 1965
R. Branner, *St Louis and the Court Style*, 1965

Branner 1968
R. Branner, 'The painted medallions in the Sainte-Chapelle in Paris', *Trans. American Philosophical Soc.*, n.s. LVIII, 1968, pp. 5–42

Brault 1972
G. J. Brault, *Early Blazon: Heraldic Terminology in the Twelfth and Thirteenth Centuries with special reference to Arthurian Literature*, 1972

Brault 1973
G. J. Brault, *Eight Thirteenth-Century Rolls of Arms in French and Anglo-Norman Blazon*, 1973

Braun 1932
J. Braun, *Das christliche Altargerät in seinem Sein und in seiner Entwicklung*, 1932

Braun 1940
J. Braun, *Die Reliquiare des christlichen Kultes*, 1940

Braunfels 1954
W. Braunfels, *Die Heilige Dreifaltigkeit*, 1954

Brett 1981
V. Brett, *Phaidon Guide to Pewter*, 1981

Bridbury 1962
A. R. Bridbury, *Economic Growth. England in the later Middle Ages*, 1962

Bridge 1905
C. Bridge, 'Horns', *J. Chester and N. Wales Archaeol. and Hist. Soc.*, n.s., XI, 1905, pp. 85–166

Brieger 1957, 1968
P. Brieger, *English Art 1216–1307*, Oxford History of English Art, IV, 1957, reprint 1968

Brieger 1967
P. Brieger, *The Trinity College Apocalypse*, 1967

Brighton 1985
C. R. Brighton, *Lincoln Cathedral Cloister Bosses*, 1985

Bristol 1984
Civic Treasures of Bristol, cat. by M. E. Williams, Bristol, City Museum and Art Gallery, 1984

British Archaeological Association 1844
Transactions: 1st Annual Congress, Canterbury, 1844

British Archaeological Association 1845
Transactions: 2nd Annual Congress, Winchester, 1845

British Museum 1958
Guide to the Antiquities of Roman Britain, 2nd edn, London, British Museum, 1958

Britton 1835
J. Britton, *A Chronological History and Graphic Illustrations of Christian Architecture in England*, 1835

Brook n.d.
W. Harvey Brook, *Inventory for a Catalogue of the Museum of Medieval Architecture*, unpubl. MS, Yorkshire Museum

Brooke 1974
C. N. L. Brooke, *The Monastic World, 1000–1300*, 1974

Brooke 1978
C. N. L. Brooke, '"Both Small and Great Beasts": an introductory study', *Medieval Women*, ed. Derek Baker, 1978, pp. 1–13

Brooks (forthcoming)
C. Brooks 'The Figure Glass of the Great East Window: a reinterpretation', *Medieval Art and Architecture at Exeter Cathedral*, Brit. Archaeol. Assoc. Conf. (forthcoming)

Broude & Garrard 1982
N. Broude & M. D. Garrard (eds), *Feminism and Art History*, 1982

Brown 1885
R. Brown, 'Remarks on the Gryphon, heraldic and mythological'. *Archaeologia*, XLVIII, 2, 1885, pp. 355–78

Brown 1954
T. J. Brown, 'Pictor in Carmine', *British Museum Quarterly*, XIX, 1954, pp. 73–5

Browne 1847
J. Browne, *The History of the Metropolitan Church of St Peter, York*, 2 vols, 1847

Browne 1915
J. Browne, *A Description of the Representation and Arms in the Glass in the Windows of York Minster, also the Arms on Stone*, 1915

Brownsword et al. 1984
R. Brownsword et al., 'X-ray fluorescence analysis of 13th–16th-century pewter flatware', *Archaeometry*, XXVI, 1984, pp. 237–43

Brownsword, Pitt & Symons (forthcoming)
R. Brownsword et al., 'The analysis of some metal objects from Weoley Castle', *Trans. Birmingham and Warwickshire Archaeol. Soc.* (forthcoming)

Bruce-Mitford 1976
R. L. S. Bruce-Mitford, 'The Chapter House Vestibule graves at Lincoln', *Tribute to an Antiquary: Essays presented to Mark Fitch*, ed. F. G. Emmison & R. Stephens, 1976, pp. 127–40

Brunner 1971
H. Brunner, *Kronen und Herrschaftszeichen in der Schatzkammer der Residenz, München*, 1971

Buckler 1843
J. C. & C. A. Buckler, *Remarks upon Wayside Chapels*, 1843

Burge 1843
W. Burge, *The Temple Church. An Account of its Restoration and Repairs*, 1843

Burrell 1930
H. J. L. Burrell, *The Church of the Holy Trinity, Balsham*, 1930

Bury 1982
S. Bury, *Jewellery Gallery Summary Catalogue*, 1982

Butler 1951
L. H. Butler, 'Archbishop Melton, his neighbours and his kinsmen 1317–40', *Journ. Eccles. Hist.*, II, 1951, pp. 54–68

Byrne 1971
M. Byrne, 'Instruments for the Goldsmiths Company', *Galpin Society Journal*, XXIV, 1971, pp. 63–8

Cabrol & Leclercq 1907–1953
F. Cabrol & H. Leclercq, *Dictionnaire d'Archéologie chrétienne et de liturgie*, 30 vols, 1907–1953

Calkins 1983
R. G. Calkins, *Illuminated Books of the Middle Ages*, 1983

Camber & Cherry 1977
R. Camber & J. Cherry, 'The Savernake Horn', *British Museum Yearbook*, II, 1977, pp. 201–11

Cameron 1979
H. K. Cameron, 'Fourteenth-century Flemish brasses at King's Lynn', *Archaeol. J.*, CXXXVI, 1979, pp. 151–72

Camille 1985a
M. Camille, 'Seeing and reading: some visual implications of medieval literacy and illiteracy', *Art History*, VIII, 1985, pp. 26–49

Camille 1985b
M. Camille, 'Illustrations in Harley MS 3487 and the perception of Aristotle's *Libri Naturales*', in Ormrod 1985, pp. 31–44

Camille 1985c
M. Camille, 'The Book of Signs: writing and visual difference in Gothic manuscript illumination', *Word and Image*, I, 1985, pp. 133–48

Camm 1910
B. Cam, *Forgotten Shrines*, 1910

Campbell 1980
M. L. Campbell, 'The Campion Hall triptych and its workshop', *Apollo*, CXI, June 1980, pp. 418–23

Campbell 1981–2
M. L. Campbell; 'Bishop Fox's gold chalice and paten', *Corpus Christi College 1981–2 Annual Report and The Pelican*, 1981–2, pp. 20–44

Campbell 1983
M. L. Campbell, *An Introduction to Medieval Enamels*, 1983

Campbell 1983–4
M. L. Campbell, 'Bishop Fox's salt', *Corpus Christi College 1983–4 Annual Report and The Pelican*, 1983–4, pp. 39–72

Campbell (forthcoming)
M. L. Campbell, 'L'oreficeria italiana nell' inghilterra medievale con una nota sugli smalti medievali Italiani del Victoria and Albert Museum', *Bollettino D' Arte* (supplement; forthcoming)

Cann Hughes 1895
T. Cann Hughes 'Misericords at Chester cathedral', *J. Chester Archaeol. Hist. Soc.*, n.s., V, 1895, pp. 46–57

Caröe 1911
W. D. Caröe, 'Canterbury Cathedral Choir during the Commonwealth and after, with special reference to two oil paintings', *Archaeologia*, LXII, 1911, pp. 353–66

Carpenter 1972
D. Carpenter, 'Westminster Abbey; some characteristics of its sculpture 1245–59: The workshop of the censing angels in the South Transept', *J. Brit. Archaeol. Assoc.*, 3rd ser., XXXV, 1972, pp. 1–14

Carpenter 1986
D. Carpenter 'The Gold Treasure of Henry III' in *Thirteenth-Century England I*, Proc. Newcastle-upon-Tyne Conference 1985, ed. P. Coss & S. Lloyd, 1986

Carpenter 1987
D. Carpenter, 'Gold and gold coins in England in the mid-thirteenth century', *Numismatic Chronicle*, CXLVII, 1987

Carré 1971
L. Carré, *A guide to old French plate* (reprint 1971)

Carter 1780–87, 1838
J. Carter, *Specimens of Ancient Sculpture and Painting*, 2 vols, 1780–87, 2nd edn 1838

Carus-Wilson 1937
E. M. Carus-Wilson, *The Overseas Trade of Bristol in the later Middle Ages*, 1937

Caudron 1975
S. Caudron, *Les Emaux champlevés meridionaux dans les cabinets d'Amateurs Britanniques des 17–18e Siècles*, Mémoire de maîtrise d'histoire de l'art et d'archéologie, University of Paris – Sorbonne, 1975 (London, Soc. Antiq. Library, MS 866)

Cave 1929
C. J. P. Cave, 'Roof bosses in the nave of Tewkesbury Abbey', *Archaeologia*, LXXIX, 1929, pp. 73–84

Cave & Borenius 1937
C. J. P. Cave & T. Borenius, 'The Painted Ceiling of the nave of Peterborough Cathedral', *Archaeologia*, LXXXVII (2nd ser., XXXVII), 1937, pp. 297–309

Caviness 1977
M. H. Caviness, *The Early Stained Glass of Canterbury Cathedral c. 1175–1220*,

Caviness 1979
M. H. Caviness, 'Conflicts between *Regnum* and *Sacerdotium* as reflected in a Canterbury Psalter of c. 1215', *Art Bull.*, LXI, 1979, pp. 38–58

Caviness 1981
M. H. Caviness, *The Windows of Christ Church Cathedral Canterbury*, Corpus Vitrearum Medii Aevi, Great Britain, vol. II, London 1981

Cescinsky & Gribble 1922
H. Cescinsky & E. R. Gribble, *Early English Furniture and Woodwork*, 2 vols, 1922

Chadour & Joppien 1985
Kunstgewerbemuseum der Stadt Köln: Schmuck, I, ed. A. B. Chadour & R. Joppien, 1985

Challis & O'Connor (forthcoming)
T. Challis & D. E. O'Connor, 'The Medieval Stained Glass of Beverley Minster', *Brit. Archaeol. Assoc. Conf.*, IX, L 1983 (forthcoming)

Chambers 1791
W. Chambers, *A Treatise on the Decorative Part of Civil Architecture*, 3rd edn, 1791 (reprint 1969)

Chamot 1930
M. Chamot, *English Medieval Enamels*, 1930

Chancellor 1927
E. B. Chancellor, 'Wren's restoration of Westminster Abbey: I. The drawings', *Connoisseur*, LXXVIII, 1927, pp. 145–51

Chanter 1932
J. F. Chanter, *The Bishop's Palace, Exeter*, 1932

Chaplais 1952
P. Chaplais, 'The Making of the Treaty of Paris (1259) and the Royal Style', *Engl. Hist. Rev.*, LXVII, 1952, pp. 235–53

Chapman 1859
G. Chapman, (Note on thirteenth-century casket exhibited Soc. of Antiq. 10 June 1858), *Proc. Soc. Antiq. London*, IV, 1859, p. 208

Chatwin 1934–5
P. Chatwin, 'Recent finds in Coventry', *Trans. Birmingham Archaeol. Soc.*, LVIII–LIX, 1934–5, pp. 56–8

Chaucer 1966 & 1985 edns
The Complete Works of Geoffrey Chaucer, ed. F. N. Robinson, 2nd edn 1966, 6th edn 1985

Chautard 1871
J. Chautard, *Imitations des Monnaies au type esterlin*, 1871

Cheetham 1973
F. W. Cheetham, *Medieval English Alabaster Carvings in the Castle Museum, Nottingham*, revised edn, 1973

Cheetham 1984
F. W. Cheetham, *English Medieval Alabasters: With a Catalogue of the Collection in the Victoria and Albert Museum*, 1984

Cheney 1951–2
C.R.Cheney, 'Church building in the Middle Ages', *Bull. John Rylands Library*, XXXIV, 1951–2, pp. 20–36

Cherry 1969
J.Cherry, 'The Dunstable Swan Jewel', *J. Brit. Archaeol. Assoc.*, 3rd ser., XXXII, 1969, pp. 38–53

Cherry 1973
J. Cherry, 'The medieval jewellery from the Fishpool, Nottinghamshire, hoard', *Archaeologia*, CIV, 1973, pp. 307–21

Cherry 1976
J.Cherry, 'A face on front jug from Worcester', *British Museum Yearbook*, I, 1976, pp. 236–8

Cherry 1981
J.Cherry, 'Medieval Rings' in A.Ward, J.Cherry, C.Gere & B.Cartlidge, *The Ring*, 1981

Cherry 1983
J.Cherry, 'A medieval gold brooch found in Manchester' in M.Morris, *Medieval Manchester*, 1983

Cherry (forthcoming)
J.Cherry, 'A copper alloy die found at Hartlepool' in J.Hinchcliffe, 'Excavations in Church Walk, Hartlepool, Cleveland', *Durham Archaeol. J.*, IV (forthcoming)

Chitty 1932
H.Chitty, *Medieval Sculptures at Winchester College*, 1932

Christie 1938
A.G.I.Christie, *English Medieval Embroidery*, 1938

Christine de Pisan 1983 edn
Christine de Pisan, *The Book of the City of Ladies*, ed. & trans. E.J.Richards, 1983

Church 1885–7
C.M.Church, 'Note on the head of a crosier, a pontifical ring, and an early episcopal ring from Wells', *Proc. Soc. Antiq. London*, 2nd ser., XI, 1885–7, p. 407

Church 1897
C.M.Church, 'The prebendal stalls and misericords in the Cathedral Church of Wells', *Archaeologia*, LV, 1897, pp. 319–42

Clanchy 1978
M.T.Clanchy, 'Highway robbery and trial by battle in the Hampshire eyre of 1249', in *Medieval legal records edited in memory of C.A.F.Meekings*, ed. R.F.Hunnisett & J.B.Post, 1978, pp. 26–61

Clanchy 1979
M.T.Clanchy, *From Memory to Written Record: England 1066–1307*, 1979

Clanchy 1983
M.T.Clanchy, *England and its Rulers 1066–1272*, 1983

Clapham 1930
A.W.Clapham, *English Romanesque Architecture, before the Conquest*, 1930 (reprints 1964, 1969)

Clapham & Godfrey 1913
A.W.Clapham & W.H.Godfrey, *Some famous Buildings and their Story*, 1913

Clark 1962
K.Clark, *The Gothic Revival: an Essay in the History of Taste*, 3rd edn, 1962

Clark 1956–7
E.Clark, 'Somerset Piscinas', *Proc. Somersetshire Archaeol. and Nat. Hist. Soc.*, CI, 1956–7, pp. 108–29

Clarke & Carter 1977
H.Clarke & A.Carter, *Excavations in King's Lynn, 1963–1970*, Soc. for Med. Archaeol. Monograph Ser., VII, 1977

Clay 1952
C.T.Clay, *Early Yorkshire Charters*, IX,

Yorkshire Record Soc., extra ser. VIII, 1952

Clay 1966
R.M.Clay, *The Medieval Hospitals of England*, 1966

Clifford Smith 1923
H.Clifford Smith, 'An English fourteenth-century bronze figure of Christ from a crucifix', *Antiq. J.*, III, 1923, pp. 226–7

Clift 1909
J.G.N.Clift, 'The Stoke D'Abernon Brasses', *J. Brit. Archaeol. Assoc.*, n.s. XV, 1909, pp. 77–111

Clinch 1910
G.Clinch, 'Armorial pendant found at Mitcham', *Surrey Archaeol. Coll.*, 1910, p. 212

Coad 1969, 1972
J.G.Coad, *Hailes Abbey, Gloucestershire*, Department of the Environment: Ancient Monuments and Historic Buildings, 1969, amended reprint, 1972

Coales 1987
J.Coales (ed.), *The Earliest English Brasses: Patronage, Style and Workshops 1270–1350*, Monumental Brass Society, 1987

Coates 1861
R.P.Coates, 'A discovery in Cobham Church, Kent', *Ecclesiologist*, XXII, 1861, pp. 110–11

Cobb 1980
G.Cobb, *English Cathedrals: The Forgotten Centuries. Restoration & Change from 1530 to the Present Day*, 1980

Cocke 1985
T.H.Cocke, 'The William Butterfield Font from Amesbury Church', *Wilts. Archaeol. and Nat. Hist. Mag.*, LXXIX, 1984–5, pp. 248–50

Cockerell 1907
S.C.Cockerell, *The Gorleston Psalter*, 1907

Cockerell 1930
S.C.Cockerell, *The Work of W. de Brailes*, Roxburghe Club, 1930

Cockerell & James 1926
S.C.Cockerell & M.R.James, *Two East Anglian Psalters at the Bodleian Library, Oxford*, Roxburghe Club, 1926

Colchester 1982
L.S.Colchester (ed.), *Wells Cathedral: A History*, 1982

Colchester 1984
L.S.Colchester, 'Dragons, serpents and St Michael', *Friends of Wells Cathedral Report*, 1984, pp. 18–23

Colchester & Harvey 1974
L.S.Colchester & J.H.Harvey, 'Wells Cathedral', *Archaeol. J.*, CXXXI, 1974, pp. 200–14

Coldstream 1972
N.Coldstream, 'York Chapter House', *J. Brit. Archaeol. Assoc.*, 3rd ser., XXXV, 1972, pp. 15–23

Coldstream 1976
N.Coldstream, 'English Decorated shrine bases', *J. Brit. Archaeol. Assoc.*, 3rd ser., XXXIX, 1976, pp. 15–34

Coldstream 1979
N.Coldstream, 'Ely Cathedral: the fourteenth-century work', *Brit. Archaeol. Assoc. Conf.*, 1976, II, 1979, pp. 28–46

Coldstream 1980
N.Coldstream, 'York Minster and the Decorated Style in Yorkshire', *Yorkshire Archaeol. J.*, LII, 1980, pp. 89–110

Coldstream 1985
N.Coldstream, 'The Lady Chapel at Ely:

Its place in the English Decorated Style', *East Anglian and other studies presented to Barbara Dodwell*, Reading Medieval Studies, XI, 1985, pp. 1–30

Coldstream 1987
N.Coldstream, 'The Decorated Style', *Bulletin Monumental*, CXLV, 1987

Cole n.d.
Manuscript Collections of William Cole, B.L. Add. MS 5481

Collin 1955
B.Collin, *The Riddle of a 13th-Century Sword-belt*, Heraldry Society, 1955

Collins 1896
F.Collins (ed.), *Register of the Freemen of ... York. I: 1272–1558*, Surtees Society XCVI, 1896

Collins 1955
A.J.Collins (ed.), *Jewels & Plate of Queen Elizabeth I: The Inventory of 1574*, 1955

Colvin 1963
H.M.Colvin (ed.), *The History of the King's Works: The Middle Ages*, 2 vols, continuously paginated, 1963

Colvin 1966
H.M.Colvin (ed.), 'Views of the Old Palace of Westminster', *Architectural History*, IX, 1966, pp. 23–184

Colvin 1968
H.M.Colvin, 'Aubrey's Chronologia Architectonica', in *Concerning Architecture*, ed. J.Summerson, 1968, pp. 1–12

Colvin 1971
H.M.Colvin (ed.), *The Building Accounts of King Henry III*, 1971

Colvin 1975
H.M.Colvin (ed.), *History of the King's Works*, III, pt I, 1975

Colvin 1978
H.M.Colvin, *A Biographical Dictionary of British Architects 1600–1840*, 1978

Commissioners 1852
'Commissioners appointed to inquire into the ... University and Colleges of Cambridge', *Documents relating to the University and Colleges of Cambridge*, 3 vols, 1852

Contamine 1984
P.Contamine, *War in the Middle Ages*, trans. M.Jones, 1984

Conway 1918–19
W.M.Conway, 'Portable reliquaries of the early medieval period', *Proc. Soc. Antiq. London*, 2nd ser., XXXI, 1918–19, 218–41

Cook 1958
J.M.Cook, 'An early medieval pen from the City of London', *Medieval Archaeology*, II, 1958, pp. 177–8

Cook 1963
G.H.Cook, *Medieval Chantries and Chantry Chapels*, revised edn, 1963

Cooper 1900
T.S.Cooper, 'The church plate of Surrey' (cont.), *Surrey Archaeol. Collections*, XV, 1900, pp. 137–57

Coppack 1986
G.Coppack, 'Some descriptions of Rievaulx Abbey in 1538–9: The disposition of a major Cistercian precinct in the early sixteenth century', *J. Brit. Archaeol. Assoc.*, CXXXIX, 1986, pp. 100–33

Cordingley 1963
R.A.Cordingley, 'Stokesay Castle, Shropshire: The chronology of its buildings', *Art Bull.*, XLV, 1963, pp. 91–107

Costume Society 1883
The Costume Society (annual), I, 1883

Coulton 1918
G.G.Coulton, *Social Life in Britain from

the Conquest to the Reformation*, 1918

Coulton 1967
G.G.Coulton, *Life in the Middle Ages*, 4 vols (1928–30), reissued 1967

Councer 1952
C.R.Councer, 'The ancient glass from Petham Church now in Canterbury Cathedral', *Archaeologia Cantiana*, LXV, 1952, pp. 167–70

Courtauld Wells and Lincoln
Courtauld Institute Illustration Archives, gen. ed. P.Lasko, I, *Cathedrals and Monastic Buildings in the British Isles*: pts 2, 4, 6 & 8 (Wells Cathedral); pts 1, 3, 5 & 7 (Lincoln Cathedral), 1976–8

Courtenay 1984
L.T.Courtenay, 'The Westminster Hall roof and its 14th-century sources', *J. Soc. Archit. Historians*, XLIII, 1984, pp. 295–309

Cox 1875, 1877
J.C.Cox, *Notes on the Churches of Derbyshire*, I, 1875; II, 1877

Cox 1913
J.C.Cox, *Churchwardens' Accounts From the Fourteenth Century to the close of the Seventeenth Century*, 1913

Cox 1915
J.C.Cox, *Pulpits, Lecterns and Organs in English Churches*, 1915

Cox 1923
J.C.Cox, *English Church Fittings, Furniture, and Accessories*, 1923

Cox 1959
M.D.Cox (née Anderson), 'The twelfth-century design sources of the Worcester Cathedral misericords', *Archaeologia*, XCVII, 1959, pp. 165–78

Cox & Harvey 1907
J.C.Cox & A.Harvey, *English Church Furniture*, 1907

Cripps 1878
W.J.Cripps, *Old English Plate*, 1878

Cripps-Day 1941
F.H.Cripps-Day (ed.), *Fragmenta Armamentaria, V: The Past is Never Dead, Part I. Order for a New Trial*, 1941

Cripps-Day 1942
F.H.Cripps-Day, 'The armour at Chartres', *Connoisseur*, Dec. 1942, pp. 91–5, 158

Cripps-Day & Dufty 1939
F.H.Cripps-Day & A.R.Dufty, *Fragmenta Armamentaria, IV: Church Armour*, 1939

Croft, Mynard & Kerr 1986
R.A.Croft, D.C.Mynard & J.Kerr, 'A late 13th-century grisaille window panel from Bradwell Abbey, Milton Keynes, Bucks.' *Medieval Archaeology*, XXX, 1986, pp. 106–12

Crone 1954
G.R.Crone, *The World Map by Richard of Haldingham in Hereford Cathedral*, 1954

Crone 1965
G.R.Crone, 'New light on the Hereford Map', *Geographical Journal*, CXXXI, 1965, pp. 447–62

Crook 1965
J.M.Crook, 'The restoration of the Temple Church: Ecclesiology & recrimination', *Architectural History*, VIII, 1965, pp. 39–51

Crook 1968
J.M.Crook, 'John Britton & the genesis of the Gothic Revival', in *Concerning Architecture*, ed. J.Summerson, 1968, pp. 98–119

Crook 1985
J.Crook, 'The thirteenth-century shrine and screen of St Swithun at Winchester', *J. Brit. Archaeol. Assoc.*, 3rd ser., CXXXVII, 1985, pp. 125–31

Crossley 1916
F.H.Crossley, 'Stallwork in Cheshire', *Trans. Lancs. and Cheshire Hist. Soc.*, LXVIII, 1916, pp. 86–106

Crossley 1918
F.H.Crossley, 'On the remains of medieval stallwork in Lancashire', *Trans. Lancs. and Cheshire Hist. Soc.*, LXX, 1918, pp. 1–42

Crossley 1921
F.H.Crossley, *English Church Monuments A.D. 1150–1550*, 1921

Crossley 1937
F.H.Crossley, 'On the constructional design of timber roofs in the churches of Cheshire', *Trans. Lancs. and Cheshire Antiq. Soc.*, LII, 1937, pp. 81–150

Crossley 1939
F.H.Crossley, 'Cheshire church furniture, II', *Trans. Lancs. and Cheshire Antiq. Soc.*, LIV, 1939, pp. 157–89

Crossley 1940
F. H. Crossley, 'The timber-framed churches of Cheshire', *Trans. Lancs. and Cheshire Hist. Soc.*, XCII, 1940, pp. 1–49

Crossley 1981
P.Crossley, 'Wells, the West Country and Central European Late Gothic', *Brit. Archaeol. Conf.*, 1978, IV, 1981, pp. 81–109

Cuming 1862
H.S.Cuming, 'On the Norman fermail', *J. Brit. Archaeol. Assoc.*, XVIII, 1862, pp. 227–31

Cuming 1865
H.S.Cuming, 'Sacred vessels and signacula recently found in London', *J. Brit. Archaeol. Assoc.*, XXI, 1865, pp. 193–6

Dale *et al.* 1917
W.Dale, *et al.*, *Proc. Soc. Antiq. London*, 2nd ser., XXIX, 1917, pp. 101–7

Dallaway 1834
J.Dallaway, *Antiquities of Bristow in the Middle Centuries*, 1834

Dalton 1909
O.M.Dalton, *Catalogue of the Ivory Carvings of the Christian Era . . . in the Department of British and Medieval Antiquities and Ethnography of the British Museum*, 1909

Dalton 1912
O.M.Dalton, *Franks Bequest. Catalogue of the Finger Rings . . . in the (British) Museum*, 1912

Dalton 1915
O.M.Dalton, *Catalogue of Engraved Gems of the Post-classical Period in the British Museum*, 1915

Dalton 1917
J.N.Dalton, *The Collegiate Church of Ottery St Mary*, 1917

Dalton 1926
O.M.Dalton, 'A fourteenth-century English ivory triptych', *Burl. Mag.*, XLIX, 1926, pp. 74–83

Darcel & Le Clert 1892
A.Darcel & L.Le Clert, 'Note sur un émail conservé au Musée de Troyes', *Bulletin Archéologique*, 1892, pp. 47–52

Davey & Hodges 1983
P.Davey & R.Hodges, *Ceramics and Trade*, 1983

Davis 1934
A.H.Davis (trans.), *William Thorne's Chronicle of St Augustine's Abbey, Canterbury*, 1934

Davis Weyer 1971
C.Davis Weyer, *Early Medieval Art, 300–1150, Sources and Documents*, 1971

Dawton (forthcoming)
N.Dawton, 'The Percy Tomb Workshop', *Brit. Archaeol. Assoc. Conf.*, IX, 1983 (forthcoming)

Day 1909
L.F.Day, *Windows: A Book about Stained & Painted Glass*, 3rd edn, 1909

Day 1963
J.Day, *Les Douanes de Gênes 1376–1377*, 2 vols, 1963

Dean 1929
B.Dean, *The Metropolitan Museum of Art: Catalogue of European Daggers*, 1929

Dean 1986
M. Dean, 'The Angel Choir and its local influence', *Brit. Archaeol. Assoc. Conf.*, 1982, VIII, 1986, pp. 90–101

Deans 1860–1
J.Deans, 'On some wall paintings discovered in Melbourne Church', *The Reliquary*, I, 1860–1, pp. 31–3

de Beaurepaire 1897–9
C. de Baurepaire, 'Notes sur les tablettes de cire', *Bulletin, Commission des Antiquités, Seine-Inférieure*, XI, 1897–9, pp. 579–85

de Beer 1948
E.S. de Beer, 'Gothic: origin and diffusion of the term; the idea of style in architecture', *J. Warb. Court. Inst.*, XI, 1948, pp. 143–62

Debruge-Duménil 1847
Description des Objets d'Art qui composent la collection Debruge-Duménil, 1847

Delaine 1972
M.N.Delaine, 'Les grilles romanes en France', *Revue d'histoire des Mines et de la Metallurgie* IV, 172, 1972, pp. 117–78

Delaine 1973
M. N. Delaine, 'Les grilles médiévales du centre de la France', *Revue d'Auvergne*, LXXXVII, 2, 1973, pp. 97–150

Delisle & Meyer 1900–1
L.Delisle & P.Meyer, *L'Apocalypse en français au XIIIe Siècle (Bibl. Nat. fr.403)*, 1900–1

Demay 1873
G.Demay, *Inventaire des sceaux de la Flandre*, I, 1873

Demus & Hirmer 1970
O.Demus & M.Hirmer, *Romanesque Mural Painting*, 1970

Denholm-Young 1965
N.Denholm-Young, *History and Heraldry, 1254 to 1310*, 1965

Dennison 1984
L.Dennison, '"Liber Horn", "Liber Custumarum" and other manuscripts of the Queen Mary Psalter Group', *Brit. Archaeol. Assoc. Conf.*, X, 1984 (forthcoming)

Dennison 1986
L.Dennison, '"The Fitzwarin Psalter" and its Allies: a reappraisal', in Ormrod 1986, pp. 42–66

Dennison 1987
L.Dennison, 'The Stylistic Sources, Dating and Development of the Bohun Workshop, c. 1340–1400'. Ph.D. Thesis, in preparation. Univ. of London. 1987

Deschamps & Thibout 1963
P.Deschamps & M.Thibout, *La peinture murale en France au début de l'époque gothique*, 1963

Destombes 1964
M.Destombes, *Mappemondes, A.D. 1200–1500*, 1964

Dickinson 1956
J.C.Dickinson, *The Shrine of Our Lady of Walsingham*, 1956

Digby 1822
K.H.Digby, *The Broad Stone of Honour: or, Rules for the Gentlemen of England*, 1822 (2nd edn, 2 vols, 1828–9)

Dillon & Hope 1897
H.A.Dillon & W.H.St J.Hope, 'Inventory of the goods and chattels belonging to Thomas, Duke of Gloucester, and seized in his Castle at Pleshy . . . (1397)', *Archaeol. J.*, LIV, 1897, pp. 275–310

Dobson 1983
R.B.Dobson (edn), *The Peasants' Revolt of 1381*, 1970 (reprint 1983)

Dodwell 1961
Theophilus, *De Diversis Artibus*, ed. C.R.Dodwell, 1961

Dodwell 1982
C.R.Dodwell, *Anglo-Saxon Art: A New Perspective*, 1982

Dolley 1972
M.Dolley, *Medieval Anglo-Irish Coins*, 1972

Dolley & Jones 1961
R.H.M.Dolley & F.E.Jones, 'A new suggestion concerning the so-called martlets in the azure of St Edward', *Anglo-Saxon Coins. Studies presented to F.M.Stenton*, ed. R.H.M.Dolley, 1961

Dow 1971
H.J.Dow, 'André Beauneveu and the sculpture of fourteenth-century England', *Peregrinatio*, I, 1971, pp. 19–38

Downes 1959
K. Downes, *Hawksmoor*, 1959 (2nd edn 1979)

Dowsing 1885 edn
The Journal of William Dowsing for Demolishing the Superstitious Pictures and Ornaments of Churches etc. within the county of Suffolk in the years 1663–65, ed. C.H.Evelyn White, 1885

Doyle 1984
A.I.Doyle, 'Medieval blind-stamped bindings associated with Durham Cathedral', *De Libris Compactis Miscellanea*, Brussels, Bibliotheca Wittockiana, 1984, pp. 31–42

Doyle & Parkes 1978
A.J.Doyle & M.B.Parkes, 'The production of copies of the Canterbury Tales and the Confessio Amantis in the early fifteenth century', *Medieval Scribes, Manuscripts and Libraries. Essays presented to N. R. Ker*, ed. M.B.Parkes & A.G.Watson, 1978

Drake 1736
F.Drake, *Eboracum: or, the History and Antiquities of the City of York*, 1736

Drake 1912
F.M.Drake, 'The fourteenth-century stained glass of Exeter Cathedral', *Transactions of the Devonshire Association*, XLIV, 1912, pp. 231–51

Draper 1981
P.Draper, 'The sequence and dating of the Decorated Work at Wells', *Brit. Archaeol. Assoc. Conf.*, IV, 1978, 1981, pp. 18–29

Druce 1914
G.C.Druce, 'Animals in English woodcarvings', *Walpole Society*, III. 1913–14, 1914, pp. 57–73

Druce 1915
G.C.Druce, 'Some abnormal and composite human forms in English church architecture', *Archaeol. J.*, LXXII, 1915, pp. 135–86

Druce 1917
G.C.Druce, 'The carvings of the stalls, St Katherine's Chapel, Regent's Park', *Trans. London and Middx Archaeol. Soc.*, III, 1917, pp. 3–27

Druce 1919
G.C.Druce, 'The medieval bestiaries and their influence on ecclesiastical decorative art', *J. Brit. Archaeol. Assoc.*, n.s., XXV, 1919, pp. 40–82

Druce 1931
G.C.Druce, 'Misericords: their form and decoration', *J. Brit. Archaeol. Assoc.*, n.s., XXXVI, 1931, pp. 244–64

Dryden 1893
H.Dryden, 'On two sculptures in Brixworth Church, Northamptonshire', *Associated Architectural Societies Reports and Papers*, XXII, 1893, pp. 77–82

Dufty 1968
A.R.Dufty, *European Armour in the Tower of London*, 1968

Dugdale 1655–73, 1817–30, 1846 edns
R.Dodsworth & W.Dugdale, *Monasticon Anglicanum*, 3 vols, 1655–73; ed. J.Caley and others, 6 vols 1817–30; 6 vols 1846

Dugdale 1656
W.Dugdale, *Antiquities of Warwickshire illustrated*, 1656

Dugdale 1658, 1716
W.Dugdale, *The History of St Paul's Cathedral*, 1658, 2nd edn 1716

Duncombe 1785
J.Duncombe, *The History and Antiquities of the three Archiepiscopal Hospitals at and near Canterbury*, 1785

Dunkin 1845
A Report of the Proceedings of the British Archaeological Association at the first General Meeting held at Canterbury, Sept. 1844, ed. A.J.Dunkin, 1845

Dunning 1933
G.C.Dunning, 'An inventory of medieval polychrome ware found in England and Scotland', *Archaeologia*, XXXIII, 1933, pp. 126–34

Dunning 1955
G.C.Dunning, 'The decorated jug from the Moot Hall at Nottingham', *Annual Report of the Peverel Archaeol. Group*, 1955, pp. 18–23

Dunning 1968
G.C. Dunning, 'The trade in medieval pottery around the North Sea'. *Rotterdam Papers*, 1968, pp. 35–58

Durham 1977
B.Durham, 'Archaeological investigations in St Aldates, Oxford', *Oxoniensia*, XLII, 1977, pp. 87–203

Dykes 1963
D.W.Dykes, 'The Irish coinage of Henry III', *Brit. Numismatic J.*, XXXII, 1963, pp. 99–116

Eadmer 1962 edn
Eadmer, *Life of St Anselm*, ed. R.W.Southern, 1962

Eames 1955
E.Eames, 'The products of a medieval tile kiln at Bawsey, Kings Lynn', *Antiq. J.*, XXXV, 1955, pp. 162–81

Eames 1965
E.Eames, 'The royal apartments at Clarendon Palace in the reign of Henry III', *J. Brit. Archaeol. Assoc.*, 3rd ser., XXVIII, 1965, pp. 57–85

Eames 1974
E.Eames, 'The tiles', M.McCarthy, 'The medieval kilns on Nash Hill, Lacock, Wiltshire', *Wilts. Archaeol. and Nat. Hist. Mag.*, LXIX, 1974, pp. 131–45

Eames 1977
P.Eames, *Furniture in England, France and the Netherlands from the twelfth to the fifteenth century*, Furniture History Society, XIII, 1977

Eames 1980
E.Eames, *Catalogue of Medieval Lead-*

glazed Earthenware Tiles in the Department of Medieval and Later British Antiquities, British Museum, 1980

Eastlake 1970 edn
C.L.Eastlake, *A History of the Gothic Revival*, 1872, reprint with intro. by J.M.Crook, 1970

Eden 1927
F.S.Eden, 'Ancient painted glass in the conventual buildings other than the church of Westminster Abbey', *Connoisseur*, LXXVII, 1927, pp. 81–8

Eden 1929–30
F.S.Eden, 'Ancient painted glass at Stanford-on-Avon', *J. British Society of Master Glass-Painters*, 3, 1929–30, pp. 156–65

Edwards 1943
J.G.Edwards, 'Confirmatio Cartarum and baronial grievances in 1297', *English Historical Review*, LVIII, pp. 147–71, 273–300

Edwards 1949
K.Edwards, *The English Secular Cathedrals in the Middle Ages*, 1949 (2nd edn 1967)

Edwards 1986
J.Edwards, *English Medieval Wall-painting: the Monica Barbwell Papers*, 1986, pp. 368–9

Edwards & Macquoid 1924–7
R.Edwards & P.Macquoid, *Dictionary of English Furniture*, 1924–7

Eeles 1978–80
F.C.Eeles, 'The ancient stained glass of Westminster Abbey, from a manuscript dated 1398', *J. British Society of Master Glass-Painters*, 17, 1978–9, pp. 17–30; pt 2, 16, 1979–80, pp. 47–53

Eeles & Peatling 1930
F.C.Eeles & A.V.Peatling, *Ancient stained and painted glass in the churches of Surrey*, Surrey Archaeol. Soc., 1930

Egan 1986a
G.Egan, 'A late medieval trumpet from Billingsgate', *London Archaeologist*, v, 6, 1986, p. 168

Egan 1986b
G.Egan, 'Finds recovered on riverside sites in the City of London', *Popular Archaeology*, VI, 14, 1986, pp. 42–9

Egbert 1940
D.D.Egbert, *The Tickhill Psalter and Related Manuscripts*, 1940

Ekwall 1960
E.Ekwall, *Concise Oxford Dictionary of English Place-Names*, 4th edn, 1960

Elias 1984
E.R.D.Elias, *The Anglo-Gallic Coins*, 1894

Elliott 1851
G.P.Elliot, Note on Hyde Abbey crosier exhibited Archaeol. Instit., 6 June 1851, *Archaeol. J.*, VIII, 1851, pp. 319–20

Ellis 1900
The Golden Legend or Lives of the Saints as Englished by William Caxton, ed. F.S.Ellis, 7 vols, 1900

Ellis 1978, 1981
R.H.Ellis, *Catalogue of Seals in the Public Record Office: Personal Seals*, I, 1978; II, 1981

Ellis 1986
R.H.Ellis, *Catalogue of Seals in the Public Record Office: Monastic Seals*, I, 1986

Emden 1957–9
A.B.Emden, *A Biographical Register of the University of Oxford to A.D. 1500*, 3 vols, 1957–9

Emden 1963
A.B.Emden, *A Biographical Register of the University of Cambridge to 1500*, 1963

Emerson 1906
O.F.Emerson, 'Legends of Cain, especially in Old and Middle English', *Publications of the Modern Language Association of America*, XXI, 1906, pp. 832–929

Emmerson 1980
R.Emmerson, 'St Thomas Cantilupe's Tomb and Brass of 1287', *International Soc. for the Study of Church Monuments Bulletin*, II, 1980, pp. 41–5

Emmerson 1981
R.K.Emmerson, *Antichrist in the Middle Ages: A Study of Medieval Apocalypticism, Art and Literature*, 1981

Enzler et al. 1876
L.Enzler, J.Stockbauer & F.Zettler, *Ausgewählte Kunstwerke aus der Königlicher Residenz zu München*, 1876

Erasmus 1849 edn
D. Erasmus, *Pilgrimages to Saint Mary of Walsingham and Saint Thomas of Canterbury*, trans. J.G. Nichols, 1849

Erasmus 1965 edn
D.Erasmus, *The Colloquies*, trans. C.R. Thompson, 1965

Erskine 1981–3
A.M.Erskine (ed.), *The Accounts of the Fabric of Exeter Cathedral, 1279–1353*, Devon & Cornwall Record Society, n.s., XXIV, XXVI, 1981–3

Esdaile 1933
K.A.Esdaile, *Temple Church Monuments*, 1933

Essex & Smirke 1845
W.R.H.Essex & S.Smirke, *Illustration of the Architectural Ornaments and Embellishments and Painted Glass of the Temple Church, London*, 1845

Etherton 1965
D.Etherton, 'The morphology of flowing tracery', *Architectural Review*, CXXXVIII, 1965, pp. 173–80

Evans 1900
J.Evans, 'The earliest gold coins of England', *Numismatic Chronicle*, XX, 1900, pp. 218–51

Evans 1921
J. Evans, *English Jewellery from the Fifth Century A.D. to 1800*, 1921

Evans 1922
J.Evans, *Magical Jewels of the Middle Ages and the Renaissance*, 1922

Evans 1938
J.Evans, *The Romanesque Architecture of the Order of Cluny*, 1938

Evans 1941
J.Evans, 'A hoard of gold rings and silver groats found near Thame, Oxfordshire', *Antiq. J.*, XXI, 1941, pp. 197–202

Evans 1949
J.Evans, *English Art 1307–1461*, Oxford History of English Art, V, 1949

Evans 1950
J.Evans, *Cluniac Art of the Romanesque Period*, 1950

Evans 1956
J.Evans, *A History of the Society of Antiquaries*, 1956

Evans 1963–8
H.F.Owen Evans, 'Two little-known Holy Trinities', *Trans. Monumental Brass Soc.*, X, 1963, pp. 90–2

Evans 1970
J.Evans, *A History of Jewellery, 1100–1870*, 2nd edn, 1970

Evans 1982
M.Evans, 'An illustrated fragment of Peraldus's *Summa* of Vice: Harleian MS 3244', *J. Warb. Court. Inst.*, XLV, 1982, pp. 14–46

Evans & Cook 1956
J.Evans & N.Cook, 'A statue from the Minories', *Archaeol. J.*, CXIII, 1956, pp. 102–7

Evans & Rhys 1893
The Text of the Book of Llan Dâv, ed. J.G.Evans & J.Rhys, 1893

Evelyn 1723
J.Evelyn, 'An Account of Architects and Architecture', appendix to Evelyn's trans. of Freart's *A Parallel of the Ancient Architecture with the Modern*, 3rd edn, 1723

Evelyn 1955 edn
J.Evelyn, *The Diary of John Evelyn*, ed. E.S.de Beer, 6 vols, 1955

Faksimile 1982
Faksimile Ausgabe der Handschrift MS Ashmole 1511, Bestiarium, aus dem Besitz der Bodleian Library, Oxford, 1982

Falke & Meyer 1935
O.von Falke & E.Meyer, *Bronzegeräte des Mittelalters*, 1935

Fallow 1904
T.M.Fallow, 'Yorkshire plate and gold-smiths', *Archaeol. J.*, LXI, 1904, pp. 74–6

Farley 1981
J.Farley, *The Misericords of Gloucester Cathedral*, 1981

Farmer 1979
P.G.Farmer, *An Introduction to Scarborough ware and a reassessment of Knight Jugs*, 1979

Faussett 1868
T.G.F[aussett], Note on a medieval pen, *Archaeologia Cantiana*, VII, 1868, p. 341

Favier 1974
J.Favier, *Nouvelle histoire de Paris: Paris au XVe siècle 1380–1500*, 1974

Fett 1908
H.P.Fett, *Billedhuggerkunsten i Norge under Sverreaetten*, 1908

Fett 1917
H.P.Fett, *Norges Malerkunst i Middelalderen*, 1917

ffoulkes 1916
C.J.ffoulkes, *The Armouries of the Tower of London*, 2 vols, 1916

Finucane 1977
R.C.Finucane, *Miracles and Pilgrims: Popular Beliefs in Medieval England*, 1977

Fingerlin 1971
I. Fingerlin, *Gürtel des hohen und späten Mittelalters*, 1971

Fischer 1965
G.Fischer, *Domkirken i Trondheim. Kirkebygget i Middelalderen*, 2 vols, 1965

Fitch 1858
R.Fitch, Note on mould 'lately exhumed near to the London Gate', Norwich, exhibited Brit. Archaeol. Assoc., 13 Jan. 1858, *J. Brit. Archaeol. Assoc.*, XIV, 1858, pp. 270–1

Fletcher 1930–2
J.M.J.Fletcher, 'The Stained Glass in Salisbury Cathedral', *Wilts Archaeol. and Nat. Hist. Soc. Mag.*, XLV, 1930–2, pp. 235–53

Folda 1976
J.Folda, *Crusader Manuscript Illumination at Saint-Jean d'Acre 1275–91*, 1976

Forsyth 1938
W.H.Forsyth, 'A French mediaeval writing tablet', *Bulletin of the Metropolitan Museum of Art*, XXXIII, 1938, pp. 259–60

Foster 1977
B. Foster (ed.), *The Anglo-Norman 'Alexander' by Thomas of Kent*, Anglo-Norman Text Society, XXII, XXIII, 1977

Fould 1861
A.Chabouillet, *Description des Antiquités et Objets d'Art composant le Cabinet de M.Louis Fould*, 1861

Fowler, 1898, 1899, 1901
J.T.Fowler (ed.), *Extracts from the Account Rolls of the Abbey of Durham*, 3 vols, Surtees Soc., XCIX, C, CIII, 1898, 1899, 1901

Fox 1984
M.E.Fox, 'The King John Cup', unpubl. M.Phil. Thesis, Univ. of London, 1984

Fox & Shirley Fox 1909–13
H.B.E.Fox & J.S.Shirley Fox, 'Numismatic history of the reigns of Edward I, II, and III', *Brit. Numismatic J.*, VI, 1909, pp. 197–213; VII, 1910, pp. 91–142; VIII, 1911, pp. 137–49; IX, 1912, pp. 181–207; X, 1913, pp. 95–125

Frankl 1960
P.Frankl, *The Gothic: Literary Sources & Interpretations through Eight Centuries*, 1960

Franks 1849
A.W.Franks, *A Book of Ornamental Glazing Quarries, Collected and Arranged from Ancient Examples*, 1849

Franks 1861
A.W.Franks ('. . . On two carvings in ivory'), *Proc. Soc. Antiq. London*, 2nd ser., I, 1861, pp. 376–8

Franks 1892
A.W.Franks ('. . . Notes on some ornamental cases of leather'), *Proc. Soc. Antiq. London*, 2nd ser., XIV, 1892, pp. 346–54

French 1971
T.W.French, 'Observations on some medieval glass in York Minster', *Antiq. J.*, LI, 1971, pp. 86–93

French 1975
T.W.French, 'The West Windows of York Minster', *Yorkshire Archaeol. J.*, XLVII, 1975, pp. 81–5

French & O'Connor 1987
T.W.French & D.O'Connor, *York Minster: A Catalogue of Medieval Stained Glass. 1: The West Windows of the Nave*, Corpus Vitrearum Medii Aevi, III/1, 1987

Frere 1898
W.H.Frere, *The Use of Sarum*, 1898–1901

Freyhan 1955
R.Freyhan, 'Joachism and the English Apocalypse', *J. Warb. Court. Inst.*, XVIII, 1955, pp. 211–44

Frisch 1971
T.G.Frisch, *Gothic Art, 1140–c.1450. Sources and Documents*, 1971

Fritz 1982
J.M.Fritz, *Goldschmiedekunst der Gotik in Mitteleuropa*, 1982

Frodl-Kraft 1970
E.Frodl-Kraft, *Die Glasmalerei: Entwicklung, Technik, Eigenart*, 1970

Fryde 1979
N.Fryde, *The Tyranny and Fall of Edward II*, 1979

Fryer 1924
A.C.Fryer, *Wooden Monumental Effigies in England and Wales*, 1924

Fuller 1662
T.Fuller, *The History of the Worthies of England*, 1662

Furnivall 1897
F.J.Furnivall (ed.), *Hoccleve's Works*, III, *The Regiment of Princes*, Early English Text Society, Extra Series, LXXII, 1897

Furnivall 1901
F.J.Furnivall (ed.), *Robert of Brunne's 'Handlyng Synne'*, Early English Text Soc., Orig. Series, CXIX, 1901

Gaborit-Chopin 1978
D. Gaborit-Chopin, *Ivoires du Moyen Age*, 1878

Galli 1940–1
R. Galli, 'Un prezioso salterio della Biblioteca Comunale d'Imola' *Accademie e Biblioteche d'Italia*, XV, 1940–1, pp. 325–38

Gardner 1927
A. Gardner, *English Gothic Foliage Sculpture*, 1927

Gardner 1927
J. S. Gardner, *Ironwork*, 4th edn, revised by W. W. Watts, 1927

Gardner 1951
A. Gardner, *English Medieval Sculpture*, revised edn, 1951

Gardner 1952
A. Gardner, *The Lincoln Angels*, Lincoln Minster Pamphlets, VI, 1952

Gardner 1956
A. Gardner, *Wells Capitals*, 1956

Gardner 1958
A. Gardner, *Minor English Wood Sculpture*, 1400–1550, 1958

Gardner & Eames 1954
J. S. Gardner & E. Eames, 'A tile kiln at Chertsey Abbey', *J. Brit. Archaeol. Assoc.*, 3rd ser., XVII, 1954, pp. 24–42

Garrod 1931
H. W. Garrod, *Ancient Painted Glass in Merton College Oxford*, 1931

Garstin 1898
J. R. Garstin, *Irish State and Civic Maces, Swords and Other Insignia of Office: Chiefly those in the Exhibition of the Arts and Crafts Society of Ireland at Dublin, 1895–6*, reprinted with additions and corrections from *The Journal of the Arts and Crafts Society of Ireland*, 1, 2, 1898

Gauthier 1972
M. M. Gauthier, *Émaux du Moyen Age occidental*, 1972

Gawthorp 1926
W. E. Gawthorp, 'Ancient and modern methods of engraving brasses', *Transactions of the St Paul's Ecclesiological Society*, IX, pts ii–iv, 1926, pp. 15–24

Gawthorp 1934–42
W. E. Gawthorp, 'The brasses at Stoke D'Abernon', *Trans. Monumental Brass Soc.*, VII, 1934–42, pp. 84–5

Gay 1883
V. Gay, *Glossaire archéologique du Moyen Age et de la Renaissance*, I, 1883

GEC
G. E. Cokayne, *The Complete Peerage*, ed. Lord Howard de Walden, G. H. White, R. S. Lea, 13 vols, 1910–59

Geddes 1978
J. Geddes, 'English Decorative Ironwork 1100–1350', unpubl. Ph.D Thesis, Courtauld Institute, London University, 1978

Geddes (forthcoming)
J. Geddes 'The Medieval Iron Industry', in Blair & Ramsay (forthcoming)

Geddes & Sherlock (forthcoming)
J. Geddes & D. Sherlock, 'The Church Chests at Icklingham, Suffolk and Church Brampton, Northamptonshire', *Proc. Suffolk Instit. Archaeol. and Hist.*, XXXVI, 3 (forthcoming)

Gee 1979
L. L. Gee, '"Ciborium" tombs in England 1290–1330', *J. Brit. Archaeol. Assoc.*, CXXXII, 1979, pp. 29–41

Gent 1733
T. Gent, *The Antient and Modern History of . . . Rippon . . . with Particular Accounts . . . of several Archbishops*, 1733

Géraud 1837
H. Géraud, *Paris sous Philippe-le-Bel d'après . . . le Rôle de la Taille imposée . . . 1292*, 1837

Gesta Abbatum 1867 edn
Gesta Abbatum Monasterii Sancti Albani, ed. H. T. Riley, 3 vols, Rolls series XXVIII, 1867–9

Gibbons 1888
A. Gibbons, *Early Lincoln Wills*, 1888

Gibson 1806
W. Gibson, 'Observations on the remains of the dormitory and refectory which stood on the south side of the cloister of the Cathedral Church of Norwich', *Archaeologia*, XV, 1806, pp. 326–32

Giles 1847
J. A. Giles (trans.), *William of Malmesbury's Chronicle of the Kings of England*, 1847

Gilissen 1969
L. Gilissen, 'Un élément codicologique trop peu exploité: la reglure', *Scriptorium*, XXIII, 1969, pp. 150–62

Giraud 1876
F. F. Giraud, 'Expenses of the Corporation of Faversham, temp. Hen. VIII', *Archaeologia Cantiana*, X, 1876, pp. 233–41

Giraud 1897
F. F. Giraud, *On the Insignia of the Corporation . . . of Faversham in Kent*, 1897

Given-Wilson 1986
C. Given-Wilson, *The Royal Household and the King's Affinity: Service, Politics and Finance in England, 1360–1413*, 1986

Gjerlöw 1971
L. Gjerlöw, 'Le culte de Saint Michel en Norvège', *Millénaire Monastique du Mont-Saint-Michel* (4 vols, 1966–71), III, 1971, pp. 489–93

Glanville 1983–4
P. G. Glanville, 'Bishop Fox's ablution basins', *Pelican and Annual Report of Corpus Christi College, Oxford*, 1983–4, pp. 73–86

Glanville-Richards 1882
W. U. S. Glanville-Richards, *Records of the Anglo-Norman House of Glanville*, 1882

Glasgow 1962
Glasgow Art Gallery and Museum, *Stained and Painted Heraldic Glass: Burrell Collection*, 1962

Glasscoe & Swanton 1978
M. Glasscoe & M. Swanton, *Medieval Woodwork in Exeter Cathedral*, 1978

Glenn 1986
V. Glenn, 'The sculpture of the Angel Choir at Lincoln', *Brit. Archaeol. Assoc. Conf.*, VIII, 1982, 1986, pp. 102–8

Gnudi 1975
C. Gnudi, 'I rilievi esterni del coro di Notre Dame e la Vergine Annunciata del Metropolitan Museum', *Études de l'art français offertes à Charles Sterling*, ed. A. Chatelet & N. Reynaud, 1975, pp. 41–6

Goldberg 1984
P. J. P. Goldberg, 'The Percy Tomb in Beverley Minster', *Yorkshire Archaeol. J.*, LVI, 1984, pp. 65–74

Golden Legend 1941 edn
The Golden Legend of Jacobus de Voragine, trans. G. Ryan & H. Ripperger, 1941 (reprint 1969)

Goldschmidt 1902
A. Goldschmidt, 'Drei Elfenbein-Madonnen', *Das Hamburgische Museum für Kunst und Gewerbe. Dargestellt zur Feier des 25 jährigen Bestehens von Freunden und Schülern Justus Brinckmanns*, 1902, pp. 277–81

Goldschmidt 1923, 1926
A. Goldschmidt, *Die Elfenbeinskulpturen XI–XIII Jahrhundert*, III, IV, 1923, 1926

Goldschmidt 1928
E. P. Goldschmidt, *Gothic & Renaissance Bookbindings*, 2 vols, 1928

Gollancz 1921
I. Gollancz, *Ich Dene: Some Observations on a Manuscript of the Life and Feats of Arms of Edward Prince of Wales*, 1921

Gollancz 1923
I. Gollancz (ed.), *Pearl, Cleanness, Patience and Sir Gawain*, Early English Text Society, CLXII, 1923

Good & Tabraham 1981
G. L. Good & C. J. Tabraham, 'Excavations at Threave Castle, Galloway, 1974–78', *Medieval Archaeology*, XXV, 1981, pp. 90–140

Goodall 1959
J. A. Goodall, 'The use of armorial bearings by London aldermen in the middle ages', *Trans. London and Middx Archaeol. Soc.*, XX, 1, 1959, pp. 1–5

Goodall 1981
I. H. Goodall, 'The medieval blacksmith and his products', D. W. Crossley (ed.), *Medieval Industry*, C.B.A. Res. Rep., 1981, pp. 51–62

Goodman 1927
A. W. Goodman, 'The Choir Stalls, Winchester Cathedral', *Archaeol. J.*, LXXXIV, 1927, pp. 125–6

Gosselin 1880 edn
J. Gosselin, *Historia Collegii Corpus Christi*, ed. J. W. Clark, Cambridge Antiquarian Society, XVII, 1880

Gough 1786–96
R. Gough, *Sepulchral Monuments in Great Britain*, 2 vols, 1786–96

Gransden 1974
A. Gransden, *Historical Writing in England c. 550 to c. 1307*, 1974

Gransden 1982
A. Gransden, *Historical Writing in England II: c. 1307 to the Early Sixteenth Century*, 1982

Gras 1918
N. S. B. Gras, *The Early English Customs System*, 1918

Gray 1935 edn
T. Gray, *Correspondence of Thomas Gray*, ed. P. Toynbee & L. Whibley, 3 vols, 1935, 1957 (reprint 1971)

Green 1937
M. A. Green, 'Old Painted Glass in Worcestershire, Part IV', *Trans. Worcestershire Archaeol. Soc. 1936*, XIII, 1937, pp. 1–10

Green 1938
M. A. Green, 'Old painted glass in Worcestershire, Part V', *Trans. Worcestershire Archaeol. Soc.*, XV, 1938, pp. 10–26

Green 1942
M. A. Green, 'Old painted glass in Worcestershire, Part VII', *Trans. Worcestershire Archaeol. Soc.*, XIX, 1942, pp. 42–4

Green 1947
M. A. Green, 'Old painted glass in Worcestershire, Part X', *Trans. Worcestershire Archaeol. Soc. 1946*, XXIV, 1947, pp. 1–26

Green 1951
D. B. Green, *Blenheim Palace*, 1951

Green 1968
R. B. Green, 'Virtues and Vices in the Chapter House Vestibule in Salisbury', *J. Warb. Court. Inst.*, XXXI, 1968, pp. 148–58

Greenhill 1958
F. A. Greenhill, *The Incised Slabs of Leicestershire and Rutland*, 1958

Greenhill 1976
F. A. Greenhill, *Incised Effigial Slabs: A Study of Engraved Stone Memorials in Latin Christendom, c. 1100 to c. 1700*, 1976

Greening Lamborn 1949
E. A. Greening Lamborn, *The Armorial Glass of the Oxford Diocese 1250–1850*, 1949

Greenwell & Blair 1910–20
W. Greenwell & C. H. Hunter Blair, 'Durham Seals: catalogue made by the Rev. W. Greenwell and annotated by C. H. Blair', *Archaeologia Aeliana*, 3rd ser., VII, 1911, pp. 268–360; VIII, 1912, pp. 46–136; IX, 1913, pp. 281–336; XI, 1914, pp. 177–277; XII, 1915, pp. 287–332; XIII, 1916, pp. 117–56; XIV, 1917, pp. 221–91; XV, 1918, pp. 115–204; XVI, 1919, pp. 155–206; XVII, 1920, pp. 244–313 (introduction and notes)

Greygoose 1979
F. Greygoose, *Chessman*, 1979

Grieg 1933
S. Grieg, *Middelalderske Byfund fra Bergen og Oslo*, 1933

Griffiths 1986a
N. Griffiths, 'Horse Harness Pendants', *Finds Research Group 700–1700 Datasheet no. 5*, pp. 1–4

Griffiths 1986b
N. Griffiths, 'Medieval pendants from Edington and Sharcott', *Wiltshire Archaeological Magazine*, LXXX, 1986, pp. 221–3

Grimme 1972
E. Grimme, 'Der Aachener Domschatz', *Aachener Kunstblätter*, XLII, 1972

Grodecki 1949
L. Grodecki, 'Le vitrail et l'architecture au XIIe et XIIIe siècles', *Gazette des Beaux-Arts*, XXXVI, 1949, pp. 5–24

Grodecki & Brisac 1985
L. Grodecki & C. Brisac, *Gothic Stained Glass 1200–1300*, 1985

Grose 1786
F. Grose, *A Treatise on Ancient Armour and Weapons*, 1786

Grosseteste 1890 edn
R. Grosseteste, 'Les Reules Seynt Roberd', *Walter of Henley's Husbandry*, ed. & trans. E. Lamond, 1890, pp. 122–50

Grössinger 1975
C. Grössinger, 'English Misericords of the thirteenth and fourteenth centuries and their relationship to manuscript illuminations', *J. Warb. Court. Inst.*, XXXVIII, 1975, pp. 97–108

Guildhall Museum 1903, 1908
Catalogue of the Collection of London Antiquities in the Guildhall Museum, intro. by C. Welch, 1903, 2nd edn, 1908

Gunner 1853
W. H. Gunner, 'Inventories of plate given to the College of Winchester . . . by William of Wykeham . . . and subsequent benefactors', *Archaeol. J.*, 1853, pp. 235–9

Gunther 1932
R. T. Gunther, *Astrolabes of the World*, 1932

Guth-Dreyfus 1954
K. R. Guth-Dreyfus, *Transluzides Email in der ersten Hälfte des 14 Jahrhunderts am Ober-, Mittel- und Niederrhein*, 1954

Gwynn 1977–9
R. T. Gwynn, 'A recently discovered

painting of arms and armour in the collection of Baron C.A.de Cosson', *J. Arms & Armour Soc.*, IX, 1977–9, pp. 1–5

Haedeke 1963
H.U.Haedeke, *Zinn*, 1963

Haines 1861
H.Haines, *A Manual of Monumental Brasses*, 1861

Halfpenny 1795
J.Halfpenny, *Gothic Ornaments in the Cathedral Church of York*, 1795

Hall 1973
I. & E.Hall, *Historic Beverley*, 1973

Hallam 1981
H.E.Hallam, *Rural England 1066–1348*, 1981

Hallam 1982
E.M.Hallam, 'Royal burial and the cult of kingship in France and England, 1066–1330', *J. Medieval History*, VIII, 1982, pp. 359–80

Hamann 1927
R.Hamann, 'Die Salzwedeler Madonna', *Marburger Jahrbuch für Kunstwissenschaft*, III, 1927, pp. 77–146

Hamburg Museum 1980
Museum für Kunst und Gewerbe Hamburg, *Handbuch*, 1981

Hamilton 1986
B.Hamilton, *Religion in the Medieval West*, 1986

Hamilton-King 1954
Mrs Hamilton-King, 'Replica of surcoat of the Black Prince made by the Royal School of Needlework', *Canterbury Papers*, VIII, 1954, pp. 23–4; *cf.* also *Canterbury Cathedral Chronicle*, Sept. 1954, p. 15

Hamilton Thompson 1925
A.Hamilton Thompson, *Cathedral Churches of England*, 1925

Hampshire 1907a
Hampshire Chronicle, 31 Aug. 1907

Hampshire 1907b
Hampshire Independent, 31 Aug. 1907

Handlyng Synne 1901, 1903 edns
Robert of Brunne's 'Handlyng Synne', ed. F.J.Furnivall, Early English Text Soc., orig. ser. vols CXIX, 1901, and CXXIII, 1903

Hansen 1939
C.Hansen, *Die Wandmalereien des Kapitelhauses der Westminsterabtei in London*, 1939

Harding 1930
N.Dermott Harding (ed.), *Bristol Charters 1155–1373*, Bristol Record Society, I, 1930

Hardy 1976
R.Hardy, *Longbow: A Social and Military History*, 1976

Harrison 1896
W.Harrison, 'Ancient fords, ferries and bridges in Cheshire', *Trans. Lancs. and Cheshire Antiq. Soc.*, XIV, 1896, pp. 67–94

Harrison 1927
F.Harrison, *The Painted Glass of York*, 1927

Harrison n.d.
F.Harrison, *Stained Glass of York Minster* (1937)

Harrison 1978
M.Harrison, *Glass/Light: an international exhibition of stained glass at the Royal Exchange*, 1978

Harriss 1975
G.L.Harriss, *King, Parliament and Public Finance in Medieval England to 1369*, 1975

Harrod 1874
H.Harrod, *Report on the Deeds & Records of the Borough of King's Lynn*, 1874

Hart 1894
C.J.Hart, 'Old Chests', *Trans. Birmingham and Midlands Inst.*, XX, 1894, pp. 60–94

Hartshorne 1876
A.Hartshorne, *The Recumbent Monumental Effigies in Northamptonshire*, 1876

Hartshorne & Hope 1906
A.Hartshorne, 'On the brass of Sir Hugh Hastings in Elsing Church, Norfolk . . . with a note by W.H. St John Hope', *Archaeologia*, LX, 1906, pp. 25–42

Harvey 1947a, 1948
J.H.Harvey, *Gothic England: A Survey of National Culture 1300–1550*, 1947, 2nd edn, 1948

Harvey 1947b
J.H.Harvey, 'Some London painters of the 14th and 15th centuries', *Burl. Mag.*, LXXXIX, 1947, pp. 303–9

Harvey 1961a
J.H.Harvey, 'The Wilton Diptych: A re-examination', *Archaeologia*, XCVII, 1961, pp. 1–28

Harvey 1961b
J.H.Harvey, 'The origin of the Perpendicular Style', *Studies in Building History: Essays in recognition of the work of B.H. St J.O'Neil*, ed. E.M.Jope, 1961, pp. 134–65

Harvey 1965
J.H.Harvey, 'Winchester College', *J. Brit. Archaeol. Assoc.*, 3rd ser., XXVIII, 1965, pp. 107–28

Harvey 1969a
J.H.Harvey, 'The tracing floor in York Minster', *Friends of York Minster Annual Report for 1968*, 1969

Harvey 1969b
J.H.Harvey, *William Worcestre: Itineraries*, 1969

Harvey 1975
J.H.Harvey, *Mediaeval Craftsmen*, 1975

Harvey 1976
J.H.Harvey, *The Black Prince and his Age*, 1976

Harvey 1982a
J.H.Harvey, 'The buildings of Winchester College', *Winchester College Sixth-Centenary Essays*, ed. R.Custance, 1982, pp. 77–127

Harvey 1982b
J.H.Harvey, 'The building of Wells Cathedral, II: 1307–1508', in Colchester 1982

Harvey 1984
J.H.Harvey, *English Mediaeval Architects. A Biographical Dictionary down to 1550*, revised edn, 1984

Harvey 1985
J.H.Harvey, 'Henry Yeveley and the nave of Canterbury Cathedral', *Canterbury Cathedral Chronicle*, LXXIX, 1985, pp. 20–30

Harvey 1987
J.H.Harvey, *English Medieval Architects: A Biographical Dictionary down to 1550. Supplement to the revised edition of 1984*, 1987

Harvey & King 1971
J.H.Harvey & D.G.King, 'Winchester College stained glass', *Archaeologia*, CIII, 1971, pp. 149–77

Hassall 1954
W.O.Hassall, *The Holkham Bible Picture Book*, 1954

Hassall & Hassall 1961
A.G. & W.O.Hassall (eds), *The Douce Apocalypse*, 1961

Hastings 1955
J.M.Hastings, *St Stephen's Chapel*, 1955

Hatcher & Barker 1974
J.Hatcher & T.C.Barker, *A History of British Pewter*, 1974

Hatcher & Miller 1978
J.Hatcher & E. Miller, *Medieval England: Rural Society and Economic Change, 1086–1348*, 1978

Havergal 1884
F.T.Havergal, *Description of the Ancient Glass in Credenhill Church, Herefordshire: Representing Archbishop Thomas à Becket and St Thomas de Cantelupe, Bishop of Hereford*, 1884

Hawkins 1846
W.Hawkins, 'Ancient Sword discovered in the bed of the Thames' (exhibited Soc. of Antiq. of London), *Archaeologia*, XXXI, 1846, p. 477

Hawkins 1851
E.Hawkins, 'Note on Ramsey Abbey censer and boat' (exhibited Archaeol. Instit., 7 Mar. 1851), *Archaeol. J.*, VIII, 1851, pp. 195–6

Hawthorne & Smith 1963, 1979 edns
J.G.Hawthorne & C.S.Smith (ed.), *Theophilus, On Divers Arts*, 1963, 1979 edns

Heales 1869
A.Heales, 'Easter sepulchres: their object, nature and history', *Archaeologia*, XLI, 1869, pp. 263–308

Helbig 1961
J.Helbig, *Corpus Vitrearum Medii Aevi, Belgique I, 1200–1500*, 1961

Hemming 1929
A.G.Hemming, 'Dated English bell-metal mortars', *Connoisseur*, LXXXIII, 1929, pp. 158–66

Henderson 1961
G.D.S.Henderson, 'Giraldus Cambrensis: a note on his account of a painting in the King's Chamber at Winchester', *Archaeol. J.*, CXVIII, 1961, pp. 175–9

Henderson 1967
G.D.S.Henderson, 'Studies in English Manuscript Illumination, I–II', *J. Warb. Court. Inst.*, XXX, 1967, pp. 71–104 and 104–37 (reprint Henderson 1985a)

Henderson 1968
G.D.S.Henderson, 'Studies in English Manuscript Illumination, III', *J. Warb. Court. Inst.*, XXXI, 1968, pp. 103–47 (reprint Henderson 1985a)

Henderson 1970
G.D.S.Henderson, 'An Apocalypse manuscript in Paris: B.N. MS lat. 10474', *Art Bull.*, LII, 1970, pp. 22–31

Henderson 1978
G.D.S.Henderson, 'Romance and politics on some medieval English seals', *Art History*, I, 1978, pp. 26–42

Henderson 1985a
G.D.S.Henderson, *Studies in English Bible Illustration*, II, 1985

Henderson 1985b
G.D.S.Henderson, 'The imagery of St Guthlac of Crowland', in Ormrod 1985, pp. 76–94

Henig 1976
M.Henig, 'The small finds', in G.Lambrick & H.Woods, 'Excavations on the Second Site of the Dominican Priory, Oxford', *Oxoniensia*, XLI, 1976, pp. 213–20

Henig & Heslop 1986
M.Henig & T.A.Heslop, 'Three thirteenth-century seal matrices with intaglio stones in the Castle Museum, Norwich', *Norfolk Archaeology*, XXXIX, 3, 1986, pp. 305–9

Hermann 1936
H.J.Hermann, *Beschreibendes Verzeichnis der illuminierten Handscriften in Oesterreich. N.F. Die illuminierten Handschriften und Inkunabeln der Nationalbibliothek in Wien. Die westeuropäischen Handschriften und Inkunabeln det Gotik und der Renaissance*, VII, 2, 1936

Herteig 1969
A.E.Herteig, *Kongers havn og handels sete: fra de arkeologiske undersøkelser på Bryggen i Bergen 1955–68*, 1969

Heseltine 1981
J.Heseltine, *Catalogue of the Drawings Collection of the RIBA: the Scott Family*, 1981

Heslop 1980
T.A.Heslop, 'The Episcopal Seals of Richard of Bury', *Brit. Archaeol. Assoc. Conf.* III, 1977, 1980, pp. 154–62

Heslop 1982
T.A.Heslop, 'The conventual seals of Christ Church, Canterbury', *Brit. Archaeol. Assoc. Conf.*, V, 1979, 1982, pp. 94–100

Heslop 1986a
T.A.Heslop, 'Seals as evidence for metalworking in England in the later twelfth century', in *Art and Patronage in the English Romanesque*, ed. S.Macready & F.H.Thompson, 1986, pp. 50–60

Heslop 1986b
T.A.Heslop, 'English Cistercian seals' in Norton & Park, 1986, pp. 266–83

Hewitt 1855–60
J.Hewitt, *Ancient Armour and Weapons in Europe*, 3 vols, 1855–60 (reprint 1967)

Hewlett 1920
L.M.Hewlett, *Anglo-Gallic Coins*, 1920

Heyd 1885–6
W. von Heyd, *Histoire du Commerce du Levant au Moyen-Age*, 2 vols, 1885–6

Heyman & Wade 1985
J.Heyman & E.C. Wade, 'The timber octagon of Ely Cathedral', *Proc. Institution of Civil Engineers*, LXXVIII, 1985, pp. 1421–36

Higgs 1964
J.W.Y.Higgs, *The Land*, 1964

Highfield 1964
J.R.L.Highfield (ed.), *Early Rolls of Merton College, Oxford*, Oxford Historical Society, 1964

Hildburgh 1925
W.L.Hildburgh, 'A group of panels of English alabaster.' *Burl. Mag.*, XLVI, 1925, pp. 307–15

Hildburgh 1933
W.L.Hildburgh, 'Iconographical peculiarities in English medieval alabaster carvings', *Folk-Lore*, XLIV, 1933, pp. 32–56, 123–50

Hildburgh 1937
W.L.Hildburgh, 'Notes on medieval English representations of the Resurrection of Our Lord', *Folk-Lore*, XLVIII, 1937, pp. 95–8

Hildburgh 1942
W.L.Hildburgh, 'A gilt-bronze cross of the early thirteenth century', *Antiq. J.*, XXII, 1942, pp. 144–6

Hildburgh 1949
W.L.Hildburgh, 'English alabaster carvings as records of the medieval religious drama', *Archaeologia*, XCIII, 1949, pp. 51–101

Hildburgh 1950
W.L.Hildburgh, 'English alabaster tables of about the third quarter of the fourteenth century', *Art Bull.*, XXXII, 1950, pp. 1–23

Hildburgh 1955
W.L.Hildburgh, 'Some further medieval English alabaster images of the Virgin and Child', *Burl. Mag.*, XCVII, 1955, pp. 338–42

Hill 1950
J.W.F.Hill, *The City of Lincoln Insignia*, 1950

Hilton 1973
R.H.Hilton, *Bond Men Made Free*, 1973 (2nd edn, 1980)

Hilton 1975
R.H.Hilton, *The English Peasantry in the Later Middle Ages*, 1975

Hingeston-Randolph 1892
F.C.Hingeston-Randolph (ed.), *The Episcopal Registers of the Diocese of Exeter: The Register of Walter de Stapleton, Bishop of Exeter, 1307–1326*, 1892

Hingeston-Randolph 1894–9
F.C.Hingeston-Randolph (ed.), *The Episcopal Registers of the Diocese of Exeter: The Register of John de Grandisson, Bishop of Exeter, A.D. 1327–1369*, 1894–9

Hinton 1973
D.A.Hinton, *Medieval Pottery of the Oxford Region*, 1973

Hinton 1982
D.A.Hinton, *Medieval Jewellery*, 1982

Hirschhorn 1977
R.E.Hirschhorn, *The Chapter-Room Doorway at Rochester Cathedral*, MA report, Courtauld Institute, University of London, 1977

Hobson 1903
R.L.Hobson, *Catalogue of the collection of English Pottery in the British Museum*, 1903

Hobson 1929
G.D.Hobson, *English Binding before 1500*, 1929

Hobson 1934–5
G.D.Hobson, 'Further notes on Romanesque bindings', *The Library*, 4th ser., XV, 1934–5, pp. 161–211

Hobson 1938–9
G.D.Hobson, 'Some early bindings and binders' tools', *The Library*, 4th ser., XIX, 1938–9, pp. 202–49

Hodges 1892
C.C.Hodges, 'The Conyers Falchion', *Archaeologia Aeliana*, n.s. XV, 1892, pp. 214–17

Hodgkinson 1976
T.W.I.Hodgkinson, *English Medieval Alabasters*, Victoria & Albert Museum, Small Colour Book 7, 1976

Hoffmeyer 1952–4
A.B.Hoffmeyer, 'To riddersvaerd: en dansk privatsamling', *Vaabenhistoriske Aarbøger*, VII, Vaabenhistorisk Selokab, Copenhagen, 1952–4, pp. 21–39

Hoffmeyer 1954
A.B.Hoffmeyer, *Middelalderens Tveaegedde Svaerde*, 2 vols, 1954

Holcot 1510 edn
Robert Holcot, *In Proverbia Salomonis*, 1510

Hollaender 1943
A.Hollaender, 'The Sarum Illuminator and his school', *Wilts. Archaeol. and Nat. Hist. Mag.*, L, 1943, pp. 230–62

Hollaender 1944
A.Hollaender, 'The pictorial work in the "Flores Historiarum" of the so-called Matthew of Westminster', *Bull. John Rylands Library*, XXVIII, 1944, pp. 361–81

Holles 1911 edn
Lincolnshire Church Notes by Gervase Holles A.D. 1634 to A.D. 1642, ed.

R.E.G.Cole, Lincoln Record Society, I, 1911

Holmes 1953
U.T.Holmes, *Daily Living in the Twelfth Century*, 1953

Holt 1965
J.C.Holt, *Magna Carta*, 1965

Homer 1973
R.F.Homer, 'Unique mediaeval pewter spoon', *Connoisseur*, Apr. 1973, pp. 263–4

Homer 1975
R.F.Homer, *Five Centuries of Base-metal Spoons*, Pewterers' Hall, 1975

Homer 1985
R.F.Homer, 'The origins of the craft in London', *J. Pewter Soc.*, V, 2, 1985, pp. 54–7

Hope 1887a
W.H. St J.Hope, 'On the English medieval drinking bowls called Mazers', *Archaeologia*, L, 1887, pp. 129–93

Hope 1887b
W.H. St J.Hope, 'The seals of English bishops', *Proc. Soc. Antiq. London.*, 2nd ser., XI, 1887, pp. 271–306

Hope 1889
R.C.Hope, (Remarks on the Scarborough spoon exhibited Soc. of Antiq., 14 Feb. 1889), *Proc. Soc. Antiq. London.* 2nd ser., XII, 1889, pp. 308–10

Hope 1893
W.H. St J.Hope, 'Silver-gilt chalice & paten found at Dolgelly', *Archaeologia*, LIII, 1893, pp. 575–6

Hope 1894
W.H. St J.Hope, 'Inventory of jewels and plate at All Souls College, Oxford, 1448', *Archaeol. J.*, LI, 1894, pp. 120–2

Hope 1895a
W.H. St J.Hope, 'The Atchievements of Edward, Prince of Wales (the "Black Prince") in the Cathedral Church of Canterbury', *Vetusta Monumenta*, VII, 2, 1895, pp. 13–22

Hope 1895b
W.H. St J.Hope, 'The municipal seals of England and Wales', *Proc. Soc. Antiq. London.*, 2nd ser., XV, 1895, pp. 434–55

Hope 1897a
W.H. St J.Hope, (Description of possible pix-canopy in Wells Cathedral exhibited Soc. of Antiq., 4 Feb. 1897), *Proc. Soc. Antiq. London.*, 2nd ser., XVI, 1897, pp. 287–9

Hope 1897b
W.H. St J.Hope, 'The seals of English bishops', *Proc. Soc. Antiq. London.*, 2nd ser., XI, 1887, pp. 271–306

Hope 1898
W.H. St J.Hope, 'On a painted table or reredos of the fourteenth century, in the Cathedral Church of Norwich', *Norfolk Archaeology*, XIII, 1898, pp. 293–314

Hope 1907
W.H. St J.Hope, 'The episcopal ornaments of William of Wykeham and William of Waynfleet', *Archaeologia*, LX, 1907, pp. 465–92

Hope 1913a
W.H. St J.Hope, *Windsor Castle*, 2 pts, 1913

Hope 1913b
W.H. St J.Hope, *Heraldry for Craftsmen and Designers*, 1913

Hope 1915
W.H. St J.Hope, (The seal of John de Warenne, Earl of Surrey and Stratherne exhibited Soc. Antiq., 26 Nov. 1914), *Proc. Soc. Antiq. London.*, 2nd ser., XXVII, 1915, pp. 4–5

Hope 1929
W.H. St J.Hope, *Heraldry for Craftsmen and Designers*, 1929

Hope & Fallow 1886
W.H. St J.Hope and T.M.Fallow, 'English medieval chalices and patens', *Archaeol. J.*, XLIII, 1886, pp. 137–61, 364–402

Hope & Lethaby 1905
W.H. St J.Hope & W.R.Lethaby, 'The imagery and sculptures on the West Front of Wells Cathedral', *Archaeologia*, LIX, 1905, pp. 143–206

Horlbeck 1962
F.R.Horlbeck, 'The vault paintings of Salisbury Cathedral', *Archaeol. J.*, CXVII, 1960, pp. 116–30

Horn 1958
W.Horn, 'On the origins of the medieval bay system', *J. Soc. Archit. Historians*, XVII, 2, 1958, pp. 2–23

Horn & Born 1965
W.Horn & E.Born, *The Barns of the Abbey of Beaulieu at its Granges of Great Coxwell and Beaulieu-St Leonards*, 1965

Horn & Born 1979
W.Horn & E.Born, *The Plan of St Gall*, 3 vols, 1979

How 1946
G.E.P. & J.How (Letter to the Editor), 'A correspondence on the King's Lynn Cup', *Connoisseur*, CXVII–CXVIII, 1946, p. 120

How 1952–7
G.E.P. & J.How, *English and Scottish Silver Spoons . . . and pre-Elizabethan Hallmarks on English Plate*, 3 vols, 1952–7

Howard & Crossley 1917, 1927
F.E.Howard & F.H.Crossley, *English Church Woodwork 1250–1550*, 1917, 2nd edn, 1927

Howe 1983
M.D.Howe, 'A medieval knife-handle from Crowland, Lincolnshire', *Medieval Archaeology*, XXVII, 1983, pp. 146–50

Hudleston 1951
F.C.R.Hudleston, 'Medieval glass in Penrith Church', *Trans. Cumberland and Westmorland Antiquarian and Archaeological Soc.*, n.s., LI, 1951, pp. 96–102

Hudson 1853
F.Hudson, *The Brasses of Northamptonshire*, 1853

Hudson 1978
A.Hudson (ed.), *Selections from English Wycliffite Writings*, 1978

Hughes 1895
T.Cann Hughes, 'The Misericords in Chester Cathedral', *J. Chester Archaeol. and Hist. Soc.*, n.s., V, 1895, pp. 46–57

Hughes 1897
T.McK. Hughes, 'On some waxed tablets said to have been found at Cambridge', *Archaeologia*, LV, 1897, pt ii, pp. 257–82

Hughes 1913
H.Hughes, 'Harlech Castle', *Archaeologia Cambrensis*, 6th ser., XIII, 1913, pp. 275–316

Hull 1902
Hull Museum Publications, 3, Aug. 1902

Hume 1863
A.Hume, *Ancient Meols: or . . . Antiquities found near Dove Point, on the Sea-Coast of Cheshire*, 1863

Humphery-Smith & Heenan 1962–3
C.R.Humphery-Smith & M.G.Heenan, 'The Royal Arms of England', *The Coat of Arms*, VII, 1962–3, pp. 18–24, 80–4, 122–7, 164–9

Hunt 1884
R.Hunt, *British Mining. A Treatise on the History . . . of metalliferous Mines in the United Kingdom*, 1884

Hunt 1973
J.Hunt, 'A silver-gilt casket, and the Thame ring', *Intuition und Kunstwissenschaft, Festschrift für Hanns Swarzenski*, 1973

Hunt 1984
R.W.Hunt, *The Schools and the Cloister. The Life and Writings of Alexander Nequam (1157–1217)*, ed. N. Gibson, 1984

Hunter 1842
J.Hunter, 'On the death of Eleanor of Castile, Consort of Edward I, and the honours paid to her memory', *Archaeologia*, XXIX, 1842, pp. 167–91

Hurd 1911 edn
R.Hurd, *Letters on Chivalry & Romance (1762)*, ed. E.J.Morley, 1911

Husband 1980
T. Husband, *The Wild Man: Medieval Myth and Symbolism*, 1980

Husenbeth 1882
F.C.Husenbeth, *Emblems of Saints: in which they are distinguished in Works of Art*, 3rd edn, 1882

Hussey 1848
R.C.Hussey, (Note on a brass writing implement), *Archaeol. J.*, V, 1848, pp. 161–2

Hussey 1944
C.Hussey, 'Cobham, Kent: III', *Country Life*, 4 Feb. 1944, pp. 200–3; IV, 11 Feb. 1944, pp. 244–7

Huws 1987
D.Huws, 'The making of *Liber landavensis*', *National Library of Wales Journal*, XXV, 2, 1987

Ingamells 1972
J.Ingamells, 'Joseph Halfpenny of York', *Country Life*, 3 Aug. 1972, pp. 285–6

Instrumenta Ecclesiastica
'Instrumenta Ecclesiastica', MS album of 18th & 19th century illustrations in Library of Society of Antiquaries of London (shelf 195H)

Jackson 1862
J.E.Jackson, *Wiltshire, The Topographical Collections of John Aubrey, A.D. 1659–70*, 1862

Jackson 1893
C.J.Jackson, 'The spoon and its history . . . more particularly in England', *Archaeologia*, LIII, 1893, pp. 107–46

Jackson 1911
C.J.Jackson, *An Illustrated History of English Plate*, 2 vols, 1911

Jackson 1921
C.J.Jackson, *English Goldsmiths and their Marks*, 2nd edn, revised and enlarged, 1921

Jackson-Stops 1979
G.Jackson-Stops, 'The architecture of the College: the buildings of the late medieval College', *New College, Oxford, 1379–1979*, ed. J.Buxton & P.Williams, 1979

James 1895a
M.R.James, *On the Abbey of S. Edmund at Bury (I. The Library. II. The Church)*, 1895

James 1895b
M.R.James, *The Sculptures in the Lady Chapel at Ely*, 1895

James 1901
M.R.James, 'On two Series of Paintings formerly at Worcester Priory', *Proc. Cambridge Antiquarian Soc.*, X, 1900–1, p. 99, 1901

James 1909
M.R.James, *The Trinity College Apocalypse*, Roxburghe Club, 1909

James 1911–12
M.R.James, 'The earliest inventory of

Corpus Christi College', *Proc. Cambridge Antiquarian Soc.*, XVI, 1911–12, pp. 88–114

James 1913
M. R. James, *The Treatise of Walter de Milemete*, Roxburghe Club, 1913

James 1920
M. R. James, *La Estoire de Seint Aedward Le Rei*, Roxburghe Club, 1920

James 1922
M. R. James, *The Apocalypse in Latin and French (Bodleian MS Douce 180)*, Roxburghe Club, 1922

James 1923a
M. R. James, 'An English bible-picture book of the fourteenth century (Holkham MS 666)', *Walpole Society*, XI, 1922–3, 1923, pp. 1–27

James 1923b
M. R. James, 'Rare medieval tiles and their story', *Burl. Mag.*, XLII, 1923, pp. 32–7

James 1924–5
M. R. James, 'An English medieval sketch-book, No. 1916 in the Pepysian Library, Magdalene College, Cambridge', *Walpole Society*, XIII, 1924–5, pp. 1–17

James 1925–6
M. R. James, 'The drawings of Matthew Paris', *Walpole Society*, XIV, 1925–6, 1926, pp. 1–26

James 1926
William Horman, *Vulgaria*, ed. M. R. James, Roxburghe Club, 1926

James 1928
M. R. James, *The Bestiary (Cambridge, Univ. Lib. MS Ii. 4.46)*, Roxburghe Club, 1928

James 1933
M. R. James, *The Romance of Alexander*, 1933

James 1951
M. R. James, 'Pictor in Carmine', *Archaeologia*, XCIV, 1951, pp. 141–66

James & Millar 1936
M. R. James & E. G. Millar, *The Bohun Manuscripts*, Roxburghe Club, 1936

Jansen 1979
V. Jansen, 'Superposed wall passages and the triforium elevation of St Werburg's, Chester', *J. Soc. Archit. Historians*, XXXVIII, 1979, pp. 223–43

Jarrett 1926
B. Jarrett, *Social Theories of the Middle Ages*, 1926

Jenkinson 1915
H. Jenkinson, 'Mary de Sancto Paulo, Foundress of Pembroke College, Cambridge' *Archaeologia*, LXVI, 1915, pp. 401–46

Jenkinson 1936
H. Jenkinson, 'The Great Seal of England: some notes and suggestions', *Antiq. J.*, XVI, 1936, pp. 8–28

Jenni 1976
U. Jenni, *Das Skizzenbuch der internazionalen Gotik in den Uffizien. Der Übergang von Musterbuch zum Skizzenbuch*, 1976

Jewitt & Hope 1895
L. F. W. Jewitt & W. H. St J. Hope (eds), *The Corporation Plate and Insignia of Office of the Cities and Towns of England and Wales*. 2 vols, 1895

Johns 1978
C. N. Johns, *Caerphilly Castle*, 1978

Johnston 1907a
P. M. Johnston, 'Stoke D'Abernon Church', *Surrey Archaeol. Coll.*, XX, 1907, pp. 1–89

Johnston 1907b
P. M. Johnston, 'Church chests of the twelfth and thirteenth centuries', *Archaeol. J.*, LXIV, 1907, pp. 243–306

Jones 1907
E. A. Jones, *Old English Gold Plate*, 1907

Jones 1910
E. A. Jones, *The Old Plate of the Cambridge Colleges*, 1910

Jones 1938
E. A. Jones, *Catalogue of the Plate of the Queen's College Oxford*, 1938

Jones 1945–6
E. D. Jones, 'The Book of Llandaff', *National Library of Wales J.*, IV, 1945–6, pp. 123–57

Jones 1977
W. R. Jones, 'Art and Christian piety: iconoclasm in medieval Europe' in *The Image and the Word: Confrontations in Judaism, Christianity and Islam*, ed. J. Gutmann, 1977, pp. 75–105

Jungmann 1962
J. A. Jungmann, *Missarum Sollemnia. Eine genetische Erklärung der römischen Messe*, 5th edn, 1962 (trans. *The Mass of the Roman Rite: Its Origins and Development*, new edn, 1959)

Katzenellenbogen 1968
A. Katzenellenbogen, *Allegories of the Virtues and Vices in Mediaeval Art*, reprint 1968

Kauffmann 1975
C. M. Kauffmann, *Romanesque Manuscripts 1066–1190*, A Survey of Manuscripts Illuminated in the British Isles, III, 1975

Keen 1973
M. H. Keen, *England in the Later Middle Ages*, 1973

Keen 1984
M. H. Keen, *Chivalry*, 1984

Keene 1985
D. Keene, *Survey of Medieval Winchester*, 2 vols, 1985

Keepe 1683
H. Keepe, *Monumenta Westmonasteriensia*, 1683

Kelliher & Brown 1986
H. Kelliher & S. Brown, *English Literary Manuscripts*, 1986

Kempe 1834
A. J. Kempe, 'Description of the sepulchral effigy of John de Sheppy [sic], Bishop of Rochester, discovered in Rochester Cathedral A.D. 1825', *Archaeologia*, XXV, 1834, p. 122–6

Kent 1949
J. P. C. Kent, 'Monumental brasses: a new classification of military effigies c. 1360–c. 1485', *J. Brit. Archaeol. Assoc.*, 3rd ser., XII, 1949, pp. 70–97

Ker 1957
N. R. Ker, *Catalogue of Manuscripts containing Anglo-Saxon*, 1957

Ker 1960
N. R. Ker, *English Manuscripts in the Century after the Norman Conquest*, 1960

Kerr 1985
J. Kerr, 'The East Window of Gloucester Cathedral', *Brit. Archaeol. Assoc. Conf.* VII, 1981, 1985, pp. 116–29

Kerrich 1812
T. Kerrich, 'Some observations on the Gothic buildings abroad, particularly those in Italy', *Archaeologia* XVI, 1812, pp. 292–325

Ketteringham 1976
L. L. Ketteringham, *Alsted: Excavations of a Thirteenth-Fourteenth Century Sub-Manor House with its Ironworks in Netherne Wood, Merstham, Surrey*, Surrey Archaeological Society, Research volume 2, 1976

Keyser 1912
C. E. Keyser, 'Notes on a Sanctuary Knocker, at St Nicholas' Church, Gloucester', *J. Brit. Archaeol. Assoc.*, n.s., XVIII, 1912, p. 161; also *Berks., Bucks. and Oxon Archaeol. J.*, XVIII, 1912, pp. 70, 96

Kielland 1926
T. B. Kielland, *Guldsmedkunst, Norsk Guldsmedkunst I Middelalderen*, 1926

King 1672
D. King, *The Cathedrall and Conventuall Churches of England and Wales*, 1656 (2nd edn, 1672; repr. 1969)

King 1864
C. W. King, 'Medieval gem engraving', *Archaeol. J.*, XXI, 1864, p. 335

King 1955
A. A. King, *Liturgies of the Religious Orders*, 1955

King 1963
D. King, *Opus Anglicanum: English Medieval Embroidery*, Great Britain, Arts Council: London, Victoria and Albert Museum, 1963

King 1979
E. King, *England 1175–1425*, 1979

Kingsford 1924
H. S. Kingsford, 'Seal matrices with screw-out centres', *Antiq. J.*, IV, 1924, pp. 249–56

Kingsford 1940
H. S. Kingsford, 'Some English medieval seal engravers', *Archaeol. J.*, XCVII, 1940, pp. 155–79

Kingsley Porter 1909
A. Kingsley Porter, *Medieval Architecture: Its Origins and Development*, 2 vols, 1909

Kite 1860
E. Kite, *The Monumental Brasses of Wiltshire*, 1860 (repr. 1969)

Klein 1983
P. Klein, *Endzeiterwartung und Ritterideologie. Die Englischen Bilderapokalypsen der Frühgotik und MS Douce 180*, 1983

Klingender 1971
F. Klingender, *Animals in Art and Thought*, 1971

Klukas 1981
A. W. Klukas, 'The *Liber Ruber* and the rebuilding of the east end at Wells', *Brit. Archaeol. Assoc. Conf.*, IV, 1978, 1981, pp. 30–5

Knoop 1934
D. Knoop, 'Some notes on three early documents relating to masons', *Ars Quatuor Coronatorum*, XLIV, 1934, pp. 223–35

Knoop & Jones 1933
D. Knoop & G. P. Jones, *The Medieval Mason*, 1933

Knowles 1927a
J. A. Knowles, 'Mediaeval Cartoons for Stained Glass: how made and how used', *J. of the American Inst. of Architects*, XV, 1927, pp. 8–22

Knowles 1927b
J. A. Knowles, 'Medieval Stained Glass Designers', *Architects J.*, LXVI, 1927, pp. 94–6

Knowles 1936
J. A. Knowles, *Essays in the History of the York School of Glass-Painting*, 1936

Knowles 1941, 1963
D. Knowles, *The Monastic Order in England, 940–1216*, 1940, 2nd edn, 1963

Knowles 1972
D. Knowles (ed.), *St Augustine, Concerning the City of God against the Pagans*, trans. H. Battenson, 1972

Knowles 1976
D. Knowles, *Bare Ruined Choirs*, 1976

Koechlin 1911
R. Koechlin, 'Quelques ivoires gothiques français connus antérieurement au XIXe siècle', *Revue de l'art chrétien*, 1911, p. 291

Koechlin 1924
R. Koechlin, *Les Ivoires gothiques français*, 3 vols, 1924

Kolve 1984
V. A. Kolve, *Chaucer and the Imagery of Narrative*, 1984

Krasa 1972
J. Krasa, 'The English Psalter in the Library of Křivoklát Castle', *Umĕni*, XX, 1972, pp. 211–26

Kraus 1967
H. Kraus, *The Living Theatre of Medieval Art*, 1967

Labarge 1986
M. Wade Labarge, *Women in Medieval Life*, 1986

Labib 1965
S. Y. Labib, *Handelsgeschichte Ägypters im Spätmittelalter, 1171–1517*, 1965

Laclotte & Thiébaut 1983
M. Laclotte & D. Thiébaut, *L'École d'Avignon*, 1983

Ladner 1979
G. B. Ladner 1979, 'Medieval and modern understanding of symbolism: a comparison', *Speculum*, LIV, 1979, pp. 223–56

Lafond 1946
J. Lafond, 'The stained glass decoration of Lincoln Cathedral in the thirteenth century', *Archaeol. J.*, CIII, 1946, pp. 119–56

Lafond 1954
J. Lafond, 'Le Vitrail du XIVe siècle en France', in L. Lefrançois-Pillion, *L'Art du XIVe siècle en France*, Paris, 1954, pp. 187–238

Laking 1920–2
G. F. Laking, *A Record of European Armour and Arms through Seven Centuries*, 5 vols, 1920–2

Lancaster 1948
J. C. Lancaster, *Official Guide to St Mary's Hall, Coventry*, 1948

Lancaster 1972
R. Kent Lancaster, 'Artists, suppliers and clerks: the human factors in the art patronage of King Henry III', *J. Warb. Court. Inst.*, XXXV, 1972, pp. 81–107

Lane 1985
R. Lane, *The Mercers' Company Plate*, Mercers' Company, 1985

Lange 1953–6
B. C. Lange, 'St Peter fra Faaberg', *Maihaugen*, 1953–6, pp. 189–96

Lange 1973
B. Lange, *Vern og Virke*, 1972, 1973

Langfors 1914
A. Langfors, *L'Histoire de Fauvain*, 1914

Lasko & Morgan 1973
P. Lasko & N. Morgan (eds), *Medieval Art in East Anglia 1300–1520*, Norwich Castle Museum, 1973

La Tour Landry 1868 edn
The Book of the Knight of La Tour Landry, ed. Thomas Wright, Early English Text Society, 1868

Lavillegille et al. 1840
de Lavillegille, Longperier & Gilbert, 'Rapport sur les statues du moyen-Age découvertes à Paris, rue de la Santé, en décembre 1839', *Mémoires et. Dissertations sur les Antiquités Nationales et Étrangères*, Société Royale des Antiquaires de France, V, 1840, pp. 370–3

Law 1986
A.S.Law, 'The Tonbridge Octagonal Flagon', *J. Pewter Soc.*, V, no. 3, spring 1986

Lawrence 1912–14
L.A.Lawrence, 'The Long Cross coinage', *Brit. Numismatic J.*, IX, 1912, pp. 145–81; X, 1913, pp. 71–95; XI, 1914, pp. 101–23

Lawrence 1914a
L.A.Lawrence, 'The Short Cross Coinage', *Brit. Numismatic J.*, XI, 1914, pp. 59–101

Lawrence 1937
L.A.Lawrence, *The Coinage of Edward III from 1351*, 1937

Lawson 1987
G.Lawson, 'Musical instruments from medieval London: the Billingsgate trumpet', *Early Music*, 1987

Lawson & Smith 1958
P.H.Lawson & J.T.Smith, 'The Rows of Chester: two interpretations', *J. Chester and North Wales Archit., Archaeol. and Hist. Soc.*, XLV, 1958, pp. 1–42

Layard 1904
N.F.Layard, 'Notes on Some English Paxes', *Archaeol. J.*, LXI, 1904, pp. 120–30

Le Couteur 1920
J.D.Le Couteur, *Ancient Glass in Winchester*, 1920

Le Couteur 1926
J.D.Le Couteur, *English Mediaeval Painted Glass*, 1926

Le Couteur & Carter 1924
J.D.Le Couteur & D.H.M.Carter, 'Notes on the Shrine of St Swithun, formerly in Winchester Cathedral', *Antiq. J.*, IV, 1924, pp. 25–70

Leedy 1980
W.C.Leedy, *Fan Vaulting: A Study of Form, Technology, and Meaning*, 1980

Leeuwenberg 1969
J.Leeuwenberg, 'Early nineteenth-century Gothic ivories', *Aachener Kunstblätter*, XXIX, 1969, pp. 111–48

Legg 1900
J.W.Legg, *Three Coronation Orders*, Henry Bradshaw Society, XIX, 1900

Legg 1901
L.G.W.Legg (ed.), *English Coronation Records*, 1901

Legg 1916
J.W.Legg (ed.), *The Sarum Missal edited from Three Early Manuscripts*, 1916

Legge 1931–2
T.Legge, 'Trade Guild Windows', *J. Brit. Soc. Master Glass-Painters*, 1931–2, pp. 51–64

Lehmann-Brockhaus 1955–60
O.Lehmann-Brockhaus, *Lateinische Schriftquellen zur Kunst in England, Wales und Schottland vom Jahre 901 bis zum Jahre 1307*, 5 vols, 1955–60

Le Patourel 1968
H.E.J.Le Patourel, 'Documentary evidence and the medieval pottery industry', *Medieval Archaeology*, XII, 1968, pp. 101–27

Lespinasse & Bonnardot 1879
R. de Lespinasse & F.Bonnardot, ed., *Histoire Générale de Paris. Les Métiers et Corporations de la ville de Paris. XIIIe siècle. Le Livre des Métiers d'Etienne Boileau*, 1879

L'Estrange 1874
J.L'Estrange, *The Church Bells of Norfolk*, 1874

Lethaby 1906
W.R.Lethaby, *Westminster Abbey and the King's Craftsmen*, 1906

Lethaby 1917
W.R.Lethaby, 'English primitives, V', *Burl. Mag.*, XXXI, 1917, pp. 45–52

Lethaby 1925
W.R.Lethaby, *Westminster Abbey Re-examined*, 1925

Lethaby 1935
W.R.Lethaby, *Philip Webb and his Work*, 1935

Lethaby 1949
W.R.Lethaby, *Medieval Art from the Peace of the Church to the Eve of the Renaissance 312–1350*, rev. edn by D.Talbot Rice, 1949

Lewis 1877
D.Lewis (trans) & N.Sander, *Rise and growth of the Anglican schism*, 1877

Lewis 1958
C.S.Lewis, *The Allegory of Love: A Study in Medieval Tradition* (1936), reprint 1958

Lewis 1964
C.S.Lewis, *The Discarded Image: An Introduction to Medieval and Renaissance Literature*, 1964 (reprint 1967)

Lewis 1965–9
J.M.Lewis, 'Two pewter vessels from White Castle', *The Monmouthshire Antiquary*, II, pt III, 1965–9, pp. 127–30

Lewis 1968
J.M.Lewis, 'Medieval church cruets in pottery', *Medieval Archaeology*, XII, 1968, pp. 147–9

Lewis 1982
J.M.Lewis, 'A medieval ring-brooch from Oxwich Castle, West Glamorgan', *Antiq. J.*, LXII, 1982, pp. 126–9

Lewis 1985
F.Lewis, 'The Veronica: Image, Legend and Viewer', in Ormrod 1985, pp. 100–6

Lewis 1986
S.Lewis, '*Tractatus adversus Judaeos* in the Gulbenkian Apocalypse', *Art Bull.*, LXVIII, 1986, pp. 543–66

Lewis 1987
J.M.Lewis, 'The Oxwich brooch', *Jewellery Studies*, II, 1987

Lewis 1987
S.Lewis, *The Illustrations of the Chronicles of Matthew Paris*, 1987

Liebgott 1985
N.-K.Liebgott, *Elfenben – fra Danmarks Middelalder*, Copenhagen Nationalmuseet, 1985

Lightbown 1978a
R.W.Lightbown, *Secular Goldsmiths' Work in Medieval France: A History*, 1978

Lightbown 1978b
R.W.Lightbown, 'An English Gothic base-metal censer from the Victoria and Albert Museum' *Antiq. J.*, LVIII, 1978, pp. 377–9

Lightbown 1978c
R.W.Lightbown (ed.), *Victoria and Albert Museum Catalogue: French silver*, 1978

Lightbown (forthcoming)
R.W.Lightbown, *Medieval Jewellery* (forthcoming)

Lillich 1970
M.P.Lillich, 'The band-window: a theory of origin and development', *Gesta*, IX, no. 1, 1970, pp. 26–33

Lillich 1973
M.P.Lillich, 'Three essays on French thirteenth-century grisaille glass', *J. Glass Studies*, XV, 1973, pp. 69–78

Lillich 1978
M.P.Lillich, *The Stained Glass of Saint-Père de Chartres*, 1978

Lillie 1933a
W.W.Lillie, 'A medieval retable at

Thornham Parva', *Burl. Mag.*, LXIII, 1933, pp. 99–100

Lillie 1933b
W.W.Lillie, 'The retable at Thornham Parva', *Proc. Suffolk Inst. of Archaeology*, XXI, 1933, pp. 153–65

Lindblom 1916
A.A.F.Lindblom, *La Peinture Gothique en Suède et en Norvège*, 1916

Lindley 1984
P.Lindley, 'The tomb of Bishop William de Luda: an architectural model at Ely Cathedral', *Proc. Cambridge Antiquarian Soc.*, LXXIII, 1984, pp. 75–87

Lindley 1985
P.Lindley, 'The Monastic Cathedral at Ely, circa 1320 to circa 1350: Art and Patronage in Medieval East Anglia', unpubl. PhD Thesis, Cambridge University, 1985

Lindley 1986a
P.Lindley, 'The fourteenth-century architectural programme at Ely Cathedral', in Ormrod 1986, pp. 119–29

Lindley 1986b
P.Lindley, 'The imagery of the Octagon at Ely', *J. Brit. Archaeol. Assoc.*, 3rd ser., CXXXIX, 1986, pp. 75–99

Lindley (forthcoming)
P.Lindley, '"Carpenter's Gothic" and gothic carpentry: contrasting attitudes to the restoration and removal of the choir at Ely Cathedral', *Architectural History* (forthcoming)

Little 1908
A.G.Little (ed.), *Liber Exemplorum ad usum Praedicantium, saeculo XIII*, British Society of Franciscan Studies, I, 1908

Little 1937
A.G.Little, *Franciscan History and Legend in English Medieval Art*, 1937

Lodge & Somerville 1937
E.C.Lodge & R.Somerville, 'John of Gaunt's Register 1379–1383', *Camden Society*, 3rd ser., LVI & LVII, 1937

London 1956
H.S.London, *Royal Beasts*, Heraldry Society, 1956

London 1959
H.S.London, 'The greyhound as a royal beast', *Archaeologia*, XCVII, 1959, pp. 139–63

London Museum 1937
London Museum, *Twenty-five years of the London Museum*, 1937

London, London Museum, 1940
London Museum Catalogues No. 7: Medieval Catalogue, 1940

London, Museum of London, 1983
The Museum of London 1981–1982: The Fourth Report, 1983

London, Museum of London, 1985
The Museum of London (souvenir guide), 1985

London, Pewterers' Hall, 1974
London, Pewterers' Hall, *Pewterware with Royal Associations*, 1974

Longhurst 1926
M.H.Longhurst, *English Ivories*, 1926

Longhurst 1929
M.H.Longhurst, *Catalogue of Carvings in Ivory ... Victoria and Albert Museum*, II, 1929

Longstaffe 1876
W.D.D.Longstaffe, 'The Stained Glass of Durham Cathedral', *Archaeologia Aeliana*, n.s., VII, 1876, pp. 125–41

Loomis 1915
R.S.Loomis, '*Richard Coeur de Lion* and the *Pas Saladin* in Medieval Art', *Publication of the Modern Language Assoc.*, XXX, 1915, pp. 509–28

Loomis 1916
R.S.Loomis, *Illustrations of Medieval Romance on Tiles from Chertsey Abbey*, 1916

Loomis 1918
R.S.Loomis, 'Alexander the Great's Celestial Journey', *Burl. Mag.*, XXXII, 1918, pp. 136–40, 177–85

Loomis 1924, 1963
L.H.Loomis, *Medieval Romance in England*, 1924; 2nd edn, 1963

Loomis 1938
R.S.Loomis, *Arthurian Legends in Medieval Art*, 1938

Lovell 1892
W.Lovell, 'Queen Eleanor's crosses', *Archaeol. J.*, XLIX, 1892, pp. 17–43

Lowe, Jacob & James 1924
W.R.L.Lowe, E.F.Jacob & M.R.James, *Illustrations to the Life of St Alban in Trin. Coll. Dublin MS E. I. 40*, 1924

Lowth 1759
R.Lowth, *The Life of William of Wykeham*, 2nd edn, 1759

Luard 1859
H.R.Luard (ed.), *Bartholomaei de Cotton Liber de Archiepiscopis et Episcopis Angliae*, Rolls series XVI, 1859

Luard 1865, 1869
H.R.Luard (ed.), *Annales Monastici*, II, IV, Rolls series XXXVI, 1865, 1869

Luard 1876
H.R.Luard, 'A list of documents in the University Registry from the year 1266 to the year 1544', *Cambridge Antiquarian Communications*, III, 1876, pp. 385–403

Ludke 1983
D.Ludke, *Die Statuetten der gotischen Goldschmiede. Studien zu den 'autonomen' und vollrunden Bildwerken der Goldschmiede-plastik und den Statuettenreliquiaren in Europa zwischen 1230 und 1530*, 2 vols, 1983

Lysons 1810
D. & S.Lysons, *Magna Britannia*. II, *Cambridgeshire*, 1810

Lysons 1813
D. & S. Lysons, *Magna Britannia*. I, 3, *Buckinghamshire*, 1813

Lyte 1926
H.C.Maxwell Lyte, *Historical Notes on the Use of the Great Seal of England*, 1926

Macaulay 1900
G.C.Macaulay, *The English Works of John Gower*, Early English Text Society, Extra Series, LXXXI, 1900

McCarthy 1974
M.McCarthy, 'The medieval kilns on Nash Hill, Lacock, Wiltshire', *Wilts. Archaeol. and Nat. Hist. Mag.*, LXIX, 1974, pp. 97–160

MacColl 1905–6
D.S.MacColl, 'Grania in Church: or the Clever Daughter', *Burl. Mag.*, VIII, 1905–6, pp. 80–6

McCulloch 1960
F.McCulloch, *Medieval Latin and French Bestiaries*, 1960

McCulloch 1981
F.McCulloch, 'Saints Alban and Amphibalus in the works of Matthew Paris: Dublin, Trinity College MS 177', *Speculum*, LVI, 1981, pp. 761–85

McFarlane 1973
K.B.McFarlane, *The Nobility of Later Medieval England*, 1973

Macek 1986
P.M.Macek, 'The Westminster Retable: A Study in English Gothic Panel Painting', unpubl. PhD Thesis, University of Michigan, 1986

MacGregor 1983
A. MacGregor (ed.), *Tradescant's Rarities: Essays on the Foundation of the Ashmolean Museum, 1683, with a catalogue of the surviving early collections*, 1983

MacGregor 1985
A. MacGregor, *Bone, Antler, Ivory & Horn. The Technology of Skeletal Materials since the Roman Period*, 1985

Mackenzie 1844
F. Mackenzie, *The Architectural Antiquities of the Collegiate Chapel of St Stephen, Westminster*, 1844

Mackerell 1738
B. Mackerell, *The History and Antiquities of ... King's Lynn*, 1738

McKinney & Bober 1960
L. C. McKinney & H. Bober, 'A thirteenth-century medical case history in miniatures', *Speculum*, XXXV, 1960, pp. 251–9

McKisack 1959
M. McKisack, *The Fourteenth Century 1307–1399*, 1959

Macquoid & Edwards 1924–7, 1954
P. Macquoid & R. Edwards, *The Dictionary of English Furniture*, 3 vols, I & II, 1924; III, 1927, 1954

Macray 1898
W. D. Macray, *Catalogus codicum Ricardi Rawlinson (MSS. Rawl. A, B, C, D)*, Bodleian Library, IV, 1898

Madden 1831
F. Madden, 'A Description of the Matrix of the Seal of Southwick Priory ...', *Archaeologia*, XXIII, 1831, pp. 374–9

Maddison 1984
J. Maddison, 'St Werburgh's shrine', *Annual Report of the Friends of Chester Cathedral*, 1984, pp. 11–17

Magrath 1921
J. R. Magrath, *The Queen's College, Oxford*, 1921

Majendie 1924
S. Majendie, *The Ancient Hospital of St Katherine*, 1934

Major 1946
K. Major, 'The Thornton Abbey Chronicle', *Archaeol. J.*, CIII, 1946

Manchester 1965
Catalogue of silver from the Assheton Bennett Collection, Manchester City Art Gallery, 1965

Mango 1972
C. Mango, *The Art of the Byzantine Empire, 312–1453. Sources and Documents*, 1972

Manly & Rickert 1940
J. M. Manly & E. Rickert, *The Text of the Canterbury Tales*, I, 1940

Mann 1935–6
J. G. Mann, 'Die alten Rüstkammer bestände auf Warwick Castle', *Zeitschrift für Historische Waffen- und Kostümkunde*, XIV, 1835–6, pp. 157–60

Mann 1936
J. G. Mann, 'The visor of a fourteenth-century bascinet found at Pevensey Castle', *Antiq. J.*, XVI, 1936, pp. 412–19

Mann 1941
J. G. Mann, 'Fourteenth-century gauntlets', *Connoisseur*, Aug. 1941, pp. 69–73

Mann 1942
J. G. Mann, 'Two fourteenth-century gauntlets from Ripon Cathedral', *Antiq. J.*, XXII, 1942, pp. 113–22

Mann 1950
J. G. Mann, *The Funeral Achievements of Edward the Black Prince*, Tower of London, 1950 (rev. edn, 1951)

Mann 1954a
J. G. Mann, 'The Black Prince's Achievements in Canterbury Cathedral', *Canterbury Cathedral Chronicle*, Sept. 1954, pp. 12–14

Mann 1954b
J. G. Mann, 'Replicas of the Achievements of the Black Prince', *Canterbury Papers*, VIII, 1954, pp. 9–23

Manning 1884
C. R. Manning, 'Moulds for casting pilgrims' signs: found at Walsingham and Lynn', *Norfolk Archaeology*, IX, 1884, pp. 20–4

Mansell-Sympson 1895–6
E. Mansell-Sympson, 'Notes on Easter sepulchres in Lincolnshire and Nottinghamshire', *Assoc. Archit. Soc. Repts and Papers*, XXVIII, 1924, pp. 290–6

Margeson 1985
S. Margeson, '14th century seal-dies from Norfolk', *Norfolk Archaeology*, XXXIX, pt II, 1985, pp. 218–19

Marks 1981
R. Marks, 'An English stonemason in stained glass', in Borg & Martindale 1981, pp. 105–7

Marks 1982
R. Marks, 'The mediaeval stained glass of Wells Cathedral', *Wells Cathedral: A History*, ed. L. S. Colchester 1982, pp. 132–47

Marks 1983
R. Marks, *et al.*, *The Burrell Collection*, 1983

Marks 1986
R. Marks, 'Cistercian window glass in England and Wales' in Norton & Park 1986, pp. 211–27

Marks & Morgan 1981
R. Marks & N. Morgan, *The Golden Age of English Manuscript Painting 1200–1500*, 1981

Marks & Payne 1978
British Heraldry from its origins to c. 1800, ed. R. Marks & A. Payne, 1978

Marquet de Vasselot 1936
J. J. Marquet de Vasselot, 'La Crosse de Wells', *Bulletin Monumental*, XCV, 1936, pp. 145f.

Marquet de Vasselot 1941
J. J. Marquet de Vasselot, *Les Crosses Limousines du XIIIe siècle*, 1941

Martin 1896
T. A. Martin, 'Misericords in the Church of All Saints, Wellingborough', *Northants, Notes and Queries*, VI, 1896, pp. 33–5

Martindale 1972
A. Martindale, *The Rise of the Artist*, 1972

Martindale 1973
A. Martindale, *Medieval Art in East Anglia, 1300–1500*, 1973 (contrib.)

Martindale 1981
A. Martindale, 'Painting for pleasure – some lost fifteenth-century secular decorations of northern Italy' in Borg & Martindale 1981, pp. 109–31

Maryon 1953
H. Maryon, 'The King John Cup at King's Lynn', *Connoisseur*, CXXXI, 1953, p. 88

Maskell 1872
A Description of the Ivories ancient and mediaeval in the South Kensington Museum, preface by W. Maskell, 1872

Maskell 1875
W. Maskell, *Ivories ancient and mediaeval*, 1875

Massé 1910
H. J. L. J. Massé, *Pewter Plate*, 1910

Mate 1978
M. Mate, 'The role of gold coinage in the English economy, 1338–1400', *Numismatic Chronicle*, CXXXVIII, 1978, pp. 126–41

Mayhew 1977
N. J. Mayhew (ed.), *Edwardian Monetary Affairs (1279–1344)*. British Archaeological Reports, XXXVI, 1977

Mayhew 1983
N. J. Mayhew, *Sterling Imitations of Edwardian Types*, 1983

Maynard 1986
S. T. J. Maynard, *A Study of the Wall Paintings of St Mary's, Chalgrove*, M.A. diss., Centre for Medieval Studies, University of York, 1986

Meaux 1868 edn
Chronica Monasterii de Melsa, ed. E. A. Bond, vol. III, Rolls series XLIII, 1868

Medcalf 1981
S. Medcalf, *The Later Middle Ages*, Context of English Literature, I, 1981

Meiss 1967
M. Meiss, *French Painting in the Time of Jean de Berry: The late XIV century and the patronage of the Duke*, 2 vols, 1967

Mende 1981
U. Mende, *Die Türzieher des Mittelalters*, 1981

Merrifield 1849
M. P. Merrifield, *Original Treatises ... on the Arts of Painting*, 1849

Meyer 1885
P. M. Meyer (ed.), *Fragments d'une Vie de Saint Thomas de Cantorbéry*, 1885

Meyrick 1836
S. R. Meyrick, 'The Doucean Museum', *Gent. Mag.*, n.s., V, 1836, pp. 245–53, 378–84, 585–90; VI, 1836, pp. 158–60, 378–84, 492–4, 598–601

Michael 1982
M. A. Michael, 'Some early fourteenth century English drawings at Christ's College, Cambridge', *Burl. Mag.*, CXXIV, 1982, pp. 230–2

Michael 1985
M. A. Michael, 'A manuscript wedding gift from Philippa of Hainault to Edward III', *Burl. Mag.*, CXXVII, 1985, pp. 582–98

Michael 1987
M. A. Michael, 'The Artists of the Walter de Milemete Treatise', PhD Thesis, University of London, 1987

Micklethwaite 1872
J. T. Micklethwaite, 'The Shrine of St Alban', *Archaeol. J.*, XXIX, 1872, pp. 201–11

Micklethwaite 1883
J. T. Micklethwaite, '... On rubbings from chalice cases', *Proc. Soc. Antiq. London*, 2nd ser., IX, 1883, pp. 328–9

Midgley 1942–5
L. M. Midgley (ed.), *Ministers' Accounts of the Earldom of Cornwall, 1296–1297*, 2 vols, Camden Third Series, LXVI, LXVIII, 1942–5

Migne 1862
J.-P. Migne, *Patrologia Latina*, LXXVII, 1862

Millar 1932
E. G. Millar, *The Luttrell Psalter*, 1932

Millar 1953
E. G. Millar, *La Somme le Roy*, Roxburghe Club, 1953

Millar 1959
E. G. Millar, *The Parisian Miniaturist Honoré*, 1959

Millar 1963
O. Millar, *The Tudor, Stuart & Early Georgian Pictures in the Collection of Her Majesty the Queen*, 2 vols, 1963

Millers 1807
G. Millers, *A Description of the Cathedral Church of Ely*, 1807

Milner 1798–1801, 1809
J. Milner, *The History of Civil and Ecclesiastical ... of Winchester*, 2 vols, 1798–1801, 2nd edn, 2 vols, 1809

Milner-White 1952
E. Milner-White, 'The resurrection of a fourteenth-century window', *Burl. Mag.*, XCIV, 1952, pp. 108–12

Minns 1918
G. W. W. Minns, (Notes on the Godsfield Pyx, exhibited at the Soc. of Antiq. 12 Dec. 1918), *Proc. Soc. Antiq. London*, 2nd ser., XXXI, 1918, pp. 63–5

Miracles of the Virgin 1928 edn
Miracles of the Blessed Virgin Mary by John Herolt, trans. C. C. S. Bland, 1928

Mirk 1905 edn
J. Mirk, *Mirk's Festial: a Collection of Homilies*, ed., T. Erbe, Early English Text Soc., extra ser. XCVI, 1905

Mitford 1809
W. Mitford, *Principles of Design in Architecture, traced in Observations on Buildings*, 1809 (2nd edn, 1824)

Moffat 1906
H. C. Moffatt, *Old Oxford Plate*, 1906

Molinier 1896
E. Molinier, *Catalogue des ivoires*, Musée National du Louvre, 1896

Montefusco 1970
F. B. Montefusco, *Il piviale di San Domenico*, 1970

Montesquio-Fezensac 1973–7
Comte B. de Montesquio-Fezensac, *Le Trésor de Saint-Denis. Inventaire de 1634*, 3 vols, 1973–7

Moor 1923
C. Moor, 'The Seal of Chichester Cathedral Church', *Antiq. J.*, III, 1923, p. 267

Moorman 1955
J. R. H. Moorman, *Church Life in England in the Thirteenth Century*, 1955

Mora, Mora & Philippot 1984
P. Mora, L. Mora & P. Philippot, *Conservation of Wall Paintings*, 1984

Morand 1962
K. Morand, *Jean Pucelle*, 1962

Morgan 1966
F. C. Morgan, *Hereford Cathedral Misericords*, 1966

Morgan 1973
N. J. Morgan, *Medieval Art in East Anglia, 1300–1520*, 1973 (contrib.)

Morgan 1982
N. J. Morgan, *Early Gothic Manuscripts 1190–1250*, A Survey of Manuscripts Illuminated in the British Isles, IV, vol. I, 1982

Morgan 1983
N. J. Morgan, *The Medieval Painted Glass of Lincoln Cathedral*, Corpus Vitrearum Medii Aevi Great Britain – Occasional Paper, III, 1983

Morgan 1984
F. C. Morgan, *A Short Account of the Church of Abbey Dore*, 1984

Morgan 1987
N. J. Morgan, *Early Gothic Manuscripts 1250–85*, A Survey of Manuscripts Illuminated in the British Isles, IV, vol. 2, 1987

Morgan & Morgan 1966
F. C. Morgan & P. Morgan, *A Concise List of Seals belonging to the Dean and Chapter of Hereford Cathedral*, Woolhope Naturalists' Field Club, 1966

Morris 1910–15
W. Morris, *The Collected Works*, ed. M. Morris, 24 vols, 1910–15

Morris 1936
H. Morris, *William Morris, Artist, Writer,*

Socialist, 2 vols, 1936

Morris 1972
R.K.Morris, 'Decorated Architecture in Herefordshire: Sources, Workshops and Influence', unpubl. PhD Thesis, University of London, 1972

Morris 1974
R.K.Morris, 'Tewkesbury Abbey: the Despenser Mausoleum', *Trans. Bristol and Glos. Archaeol. Soc.*, XCIII, 1974, pp.142–55

Morris 1978
R.K.Morris, 'The development of later Gothic mouldings in England c.1250–c.1400', *Architectural History*, XXI, 1978, pp.18–57

Morris 1979
R.Morris, *Cathedrals and Abbeys of England and Wales*, 1979

Morris 1985
R.K.Morris, 'Early Gothic Architecture at Tewkesbury', *Brit. Archaeol. Assoc. Conf.* VII, 1981, 1985, pp.93–115

Munch 1864
P.A.Munch, *Porvelige Nuntiers Regnskabsog Dagböger ... 1282–1334*, 1864

Muratova 1978
X.Muratova, 'Les miniatures du manuscrit fr. 14969 de la Bibliothèque Nationale de Paris et la tradition iconographique franciscaine', *Marche Romane*, XXVIII, 1978, pp.142–8

Muratova 1986
X.Muratova, 'Bestiaries: an aspect of medieval patronage', *Art and Patronage in the English Romanesque*, ed. S.Macready & F.H.Thompson, 1986, pp.118–44

Murray 1913
H.J.R.Murray, *A History of Chess*, 1913

Murray 1935
K.M.E.Murray, 'Faversham and the Cinque Ports', *Trans. Royal Historical Soc.*, 4th ser., XVIII, 1935, pp.53–84

Musée Sauvageot 1861
Catalogue du Musée Sauvageot, by A.Sauzay, 1861

Musty, Algar & Ewence 1969
J.Musty, D.J.Algar & P.F.Ewence, 'The medieval potter kilns at Laverstock, near Salisbury, Wiltshire', *Archaeologia*, CII, 1969, pp.83–150

Natanson 1951
J.Natanson, *Gothic Ivories of the 13th and 14th Centuries*, 1951

NACF 1971
National Art-Collections Fund, *68th Annual Report*, 1971

Neal 1977
D.S.Neal, 'Excavations at the Palace of King's Langley, Hertfordshire, 1974–1976', *Medieval Archaeology*, XXI, 1977, pp.124–65

Neale 1848
Mr Neale, of Chelmsford, re '... a circular gold brooch of the fourteenth century, found at Writtle', *J. Brit. Archaeol. Assoc.*, III, 1848, p.125

Nelson 1913
P.Nelson, *Ancient Painted Glass in England 1170–1500*, 1913

Nelson 1918
P.Nelson, 'English alabasters of the embattled type', *Archaeol. J.*, LXXV, 1918, pp.310–34

Nelson 1919
P.Nelson, 'The earliest type of English alabaster panel carvings', *Archaeol. J.*, LXXVI, 1919, pp.84–95

Nelson 1934
P.Nelson, 'A thirteenth-century signet ring', *Antiq. J.*, XIV, 1934, pp.305–6

Newman 1976
J.Newman, *The Buildings of England, North East and East Kent*, 2nd edn, 1976

Newton 1961
P.A.Newton, 'Schools of Glass Painting in the Midlands 1275–1430', unpubl. PhD Thesis, University of London, 3 vols, 1961

Newton 1962
P.A.Newton, 'Three panels of heraldic glass in the Burrell Collection', *Scottish Art Review*, VIII, 4, 1962, pp.13–16

Newton 1979
P.A.Newton, *The County of Oxford: A Catalogue of Medieval Stained Glass, Corpus Vitrearum Medii Aevi Great Britain*, I, 1979

Newton 1980
S.M.Newton, *Fashion in the Age of the Black Prince: A Study of the Years 1340–1365*, 1980

Nichols 1780
J.Nichols, *A Collection of all the Wills ... of the Kings & Queens of England ... and the Blood Royal*, 1780

Nichols 1812–15
J.Nichols (ed.), *Literary Anecdotes of the Eighteenth Century*, 9 vols, 1812–15

Nichols 1842
J.G.Nichols, 'Observations on the heraldic devices discovered on the effigies of Richard the Second and his Queen ...', *Archaeologia*, XXIX, 1842, pp.32–59

Nickel 1958
H.Nickel, *Der mittelalterliche Reiterschild des Abendlandes*, 1958

Nickel 1969
H.Nickel, 'Sir Gawayne and the Three White Knights', *Metropolitan Museum of Art Bulletin*, Dec. 1969, pp.174–82

Nicolas 1826
N.H.Nicolas, *Testamenta Vetusta*, 2 vols, 1826

Nicolas 1832
N.H.Nicolas, *The Scrope and Grosvenor Controversy 1385–1390*, II, 1832

Nicolas 1846a
N.H.Nicolas, 'Observations on the Institution of the most Noble Order of the Garter', *Archaeologia*, XXXI, 1846, pp.1–163

Nicolas 1846b
N.H.Nicolas, 'Observations on ... the origin and history of the Badge ... of Edward Prince of Wales', *Archaeologia*, XXXI, 1846, pp.350–84

Noppen 1931
J.G.Noppen, 'The Westminster Apocalypse and its source', *Burl. Mag.*, LXI, 1931, pp.146–59

Nordenfalk 1976
C.Nordenfalk, 'Les Cinq Sens dans l'art du Moyen Age', *Revue de l'Art*, XXXIV, 1976, pp.17–28

Nordenfalk 1985
C.Nordenfalk, 'The Five Senses in late medieval and renaissance art', *J. Warb. Court. Inst.*, XLVIII, 1985, pp.1–22

Norgate 1912
K.Norgate, *The Minority of Henry III*, 1912

Norman 1971
A.V.B.Norman, *The Medieval Soldiers*, 1971

Norman 1972
A.V.B.Norman, *Arms and Armour in the Royal Scottish Museum*, 1972

Norman 1974–6
A.V.B.Norman, 'Notes on a newly discovered piece of fourteenth-century armour', *J. Arms and Armour Soc.*, VIII, 1974–6, pp.229–33

Norman 1976
A.V.B.Norman, 'An early illustration of a body armour', *Waffen- und Kostümkunde*, XVIII, 1976, pp.38–9

Norris 1978a
M.Norris, *Monumental Brasses: The Craft*, 1978

Norris 1978b
M.Norris, *Monumental Brasses: The Memorials*, 2 vols, 1978

North 1968
J.J.North, *The Coinages of Edward I and Edward II*, 1968

North 1980
J.J.North, *English Hammered Coinage*, 2 vols, 1980

Norton 1981
E.C.Norton, 'Review Article – The British Museum collection of medieval tiles', *J. Brit. Archaeol. Assoc.*, 3rd ser., CXXXIV, 1981, pp.107–19

Norton & Park 1986
E.C.Norton & D.Park (eds), *Cistercian Art and Architecture in the British Isles*, 1986

Norton, Park & Binski 1987
E.C.Norton, D.Park & P.Binski, *Dominican Painting in East Anglia: the Thornham Parva Retable and the Musée de Cluny Frontal*, 1987

Nyborg 1977
E.Nyborg, 'Mikaels-altre', *Hikuis*, III, 1977, pp.157–82, 335

Nyborg 1981
E.Nyborg, 'Det store krucifiks', *Skalk*, V, 1981, pp.3–8

Oakeshott 1959
W.F.Oakeshott, *Classical Inspiration in Medieval Art*, 1959

Oakeshott 1960
R.E.Oakeshott, *The Archaeology of Weapons*, 1960

Oakeshott 1964
R.E.Oakeshott, *The Sword in the Age of Chivalry*, 1964

Oakeshott 1972
W.Oakeshott, *Sigena: Romanesque Paintings in Spain and the Winchester Bible Artists*, 1972

O'Connor 1980
D.E.O'Connor, 'Fourteenth-century glass design in the York area and its relationship to tile design', *Synopses of Contributions presented to the York Tile Seminar*, ed. P.J.Drury, 1980

O'Connor & Haselock 1977
D.E.O'Connor & J.Haselock, 'The stained and painted glass', in Aylmer & Cant 1977, pp.313–93

Ogilvie 1959
R.M.Ogilvie, 'The Longthorpe murals', *J. Warb. Court. Inst.*, XXII, 1959, pp.361–2

Oliver 1861
G.Oliver, *Lives of the Bishops of Exeter, and a History of the Cathedral*, 1861

Olrik 1909
J.Olrik, *Drikkehorn og sølvtøj*, 1909

Oman 1930
C.Oman, *Catalogue of Rings in the Victoria and Albert Museum*, 1930

Oman 1932
C.Oman, 'The goldsmiths at St Albans Abbey during the 12th and 13th centuries', *St Albans and Herts. Archit. and Archaeol. Soc. Trans.*, 1932, pp.215–36

Oman 1944
C.Oman, 'English medieval drinking horns', *Connoisseur*, CXIII, 1944, pp.20–3

Oman 1950
C.Oman, 'The Swinburne Pyx', *Burl. Mag.*, XCII, 1950, pp.337–41

Oman 1952
C.Oman, 'The Bermondsey Dish', *Burl. Mag.*, XCIV, 1952, pp.23–4

Oman 1957
C.Oman, *English Church Plate 597–1830*, 1957

Oman 1959
C.Oman, *English Domestic Silver*, 4th edn, 1959

Oman 1962a
C.Oman, 'The Winchester College Plate', *Connoisseur*, CXLIX, 1962, pp.24–33

Oman 1962b
C.Oman, 'English medieval base metal church plate', *Archaeol. J.*, CXIX, 1962, pp.195–207 (pub. 1964)

Oman 1971
C.Oman, 'The ring, chalice, and paten' in H.G.Ramm et al., 'The Tombs of Archbishops Walter de Gray and Godfrey de Ludham in York Minster', *Archaeologia*, CIII, 1971, pp.126–7, 135

Oman 1972
C.Oman, 'Cambridge and Cornelimünster', *Aachener Kunstblätter*, XLIII, 1972, pp.305–7

Oman 1973
C.Oman, 'Insignia and civic plate of the City of Bristol, I', *Connoisseur*, Mar. 1973, pp.170–4

Oman 1974
C.Oman, *British Rings 800–1914*, 1974

Oman 1979
C.Oman, 'College Plate', *New College, Oxford, 1379–1979*, ed. J.Buxton & P.Williams, 1979, pp.293–305

Oman 1980
C.Oman, 'Plate from a lost Oxford College', *Archaeologia Cantiana*, XCV, 1980, pp.49–52

Ord 1792
Craven Ord, 'Inventory of Crown Jewels, 3 Edw. III', *Archaeologia*, X, 1792, pp.241–60

Ó Ríordáin 1975
B.Ó Ríordáin, 'Excavations at High Street and Winetavern Street, Dublin', *Medieval Archaeology*, XV, 1971, pp.73–85

Orme 1986
N.Orme, *Exeter Cathedral as it was 1050–1550*, 1986

Ormrod 1985
W.M.Ormrod (ed.), *England in the Thirteenth Century. Proceedings of the 1984 Harlaxton Symposium*, 1985

Ormrod 1986
W.M.Ormrod (ed.), *England in the Fourteenth Century. Proceedings of the 1985 Harlaxton Symposium*, 1986

Oswald 1962
A.Oswald, 'Excavations at Weoley Castle 1955–60', *Essays in honour of Philip B.Chatwin*, Birmingham Archaeological Society, 1962

Otaka & Fukui 1977
Y.Otaka & H.Fukui, *Apocalypse Anglo-Normande (Cambridge, Trinity College MS R.16.2)*, 1977

Otaka & Fukui 1981
Y.Otaka & H.Fukui, *Apocalypse (Bibliothèque Nationale Fonds Français 403)*, 1981

Otavsky 1985
K.Otavsky, 'Deux plaques d'argent portant le nom, les armes et la devise de Guillaume de Grandson (+ 1389)', *Rencontres de Fribourg (14–16 septembre 1984): Activités artistiques et pouvoirs dans les Etats des ducs de Bourgogne et des*

Habsbourg et les régions voisines, 1985, pp. 7–14

Ovid 1916 edn
Ovid, *Metamorphoses*, ed. F.J.Miller, Loeb Classical Library, 1916 (reprint 1964)

Ovid 1969 edn
Ovid: The Art of Love and Other Poems, ed. J.H.Mozley, 1969

Owen 1953–6
H.J.Owen, 'The Romance of the chalice and paten of Cymer Abbey', *Journal of the Merioneth Historical Society*, II, 1953–6, pp. 181–90

Owst 1926
G.R.Owst, *Preaching in Medieval England*, 1926

Owst 1933, 1961
G.R.Owst, *Literature and Pulpit in Medieval England*, 1933, 1961

Oxford 1656
Oxford, Ashmolean Museum, 'Museum Tradescantianum', MS catalogue, 1656

Oxford 1685
Oxford, Ashmolean Museum, MS catalogue, c.1685

Oxford 1952
Oxford, Bodleian Library, *English Rural Life in the Middle Ages*, Bodleian Picture Book, no. 14, 1952, 1965 (reprint 1977)

Oxford 1983
Tradescant's Rarities: Essays on the Foundation of the Ashmolean Museum 1683 with a Catalogue of the Surviving Early Collection, ed. A.MacGregor, 1983

Pächt 1943
O.Pächt, 'A Giottesque Episode in English Mediaeval Art', *J. Warb. Court. Inst.*, VI, 1943, pp. 51–70

Pächt 1950
O.Pächt, 'Early Italian Nature Studies and the early Calendar Landscape', *J. Warb. Court. Inst.*, XIII, 1950, pp. 13–47

Pächt 1961
O.Pächt, 'A cycle of English frescoes in Spain', *Burl. Mag.*, CIII, 1961, pp. 166–75

Pächt & Alexander 1973
O.Pächt & J.J.G.Alexander, *Illuminated Manuscripts in the Bodleian Library, Oxford*, III, British School, 1973

Page-Phillips 1980
J.C.Page-Phillips, *Palimpsests: The Backs of Monumental Brasses*, 2 vols, 1980

Palgrave 1836
F.Palgrave, *Antient Kalendars and Inventories, of the Treasure of His Majesty's Exchequer*, 3 vols, 1836

Palmer 1897
G.H.Palmer, *The Cathedral Church of Rochester*, Bell's Cathedral Ser., 1897

Pantin 1955
W.A.Pantin, *The English Church in the Fourteenth Century*, 1955 (reprint 1962)

Park 1983
D.Park, 'The wall paintings of the Holy Sepulchre Chapel', *Brit. Archaeol. Assoc. Conf.*, VI, 1980, 1983, pp. 38–62

Park 1986a
D.Park, 'The creation, marginalia and ornament in the refectory paintings of Bushmead Priory', *Bedfordshire Archaeology*, XVII, 1986, pp. 72–6

Park 1986b
D.Park, 'The medieval painted decoration of Lincoln Cathedral', *Brit. Archaeol. Assoc. Conf.*, VIII, 1982, 1986, pp. 75–82

Park & Cather (forthcoming)
D.Park & S.Cather (eds), *Horsham St Faith Priory and its Wall Paintings*

Parker 1932
A.Parker, 'Nottingham Pottery', *Trans. of the Thoroton Society*, XXXVI, 1932, pp. 90f.

Parker 1984
R.Parker, *The Subversive Stitch*, 1984

Parkes & Salter 1978
Troilus and Criseyde: Geoffrey Chaucer (a facsimile of Corpus Christi College Cambridge MS 61), intro. M.B.Parkes & E.Salter, 1978

Parks 1954
G.B.Parks, *The English Traveller to Italy*, 1954

Parry 1986–7
E.G.Parry, 'Helmdon Stone', *Northamptonshire Past and Present*, VII, 4, 1986–7, pp. 258–69

Parsons 1977
J.C.Parsons, *The Court and Household of Eleanor of Castile in 1290*, 1977

Parsons 1980–1
D.Parsons, 'Brixworth and the Boniface connexion', *Northamptonshire Past and Present*, VI, 4, 1980–1, pp. 179–82

Parsons 1983
D.Parsons, *The Mystery of the Brixworth Relic*, 1983

Pastoureau 1979
M.Pastoureau, *Traité d'héraldique*, 1979

Paul 1904
R.Paul, 'The church and monastery of Abbey Dore, Herefordshire', *Trans. Bristol and Glos. Archaeol. Soc.*, XXVII, 1904, pp. 117–26

Paul 1927
R.Paul, 'Abbey Dore Church, Herefordshire', *Archaeologia Cambrensis*, LXXXII, 1927, pp. 269–75

Pearce, Vince & Jenner 1985
J.E.Pearce, A.G.Vince & M.A.Jenner, *Medieval Pottery, London Type Ware*, London and Middx. Archaeol. Soc. Special Paper, VI, 1985

Pearce, Vince & White 1982
J.E.Pearce, A.G.Vince & R.White, 'A dated type series of London Medieval Pottery. Part one: Mill Green Ware', *Trans. London and Middx. Archaeol. Soc.*, XXXIII, 1982, pp. 266–98

Pearl 1978 edn
Poems of the Pearl Manuscript, ed. M.Andrew & R.Waldron, 1978

Pedrick 1902
G.Pedrick, *Monastic Seals of the XIIIth Century*, 1902

Pedrick 1904
G.Pedrick, *Borough Seals of the Gothic Period*, 1904

Peek & Hall 1962
H.E.Peek & C.P.Hall, *The Archives of the University of Cambridge*, 1962

Peers 1922
C.R.Peers, 'Harlech Castle', *Trans. of the Hon. Soc. of Cymmrodorion*, 1921–2, pp. 63–82

Peers & Tanner 1949
C.Peers & L.E.Tanner, 'On some recent discoveries in Westminster Abbey', *Archaeologia*, XCIII, 1949, pp. 151–63

Pegge 1801
S.Pegge, *An Historical Account of Beauchief Abbey...*, 1801

Pegolotti 1936 edn
Francesco Balducci Pegolotti. La Pratica della Mescatura, ed. A.Evans, 1936

Penzer 1946
N.M.Penzer, 'The King's Lynn Cup', *Connoisseur*, CXVIII, 1946, pp. 12–16, 64, 79–84, 120

Pérté 1911
A.Pératé, *Collections Georges Hoertschel*, 1911

Percival 1871
C.S.Percival, 'Some account of the family of Abernon of Albury and Stoke D'Abernon', *Surrey Archaeol. Coll.*, V, 1871, pp. 53–74

Perkins 1938–52
J.Perkins, *Westminster Abbey, Its Worship and Ornaments*, Alcuin Club Collections, 3 vols, 1938–52

Perrot 1972
F.Perrot, *Le Vitrail à Rouen*, 1972

Pevsner 1945
N.Pevsner, *The Leaves of Southwell*, 1945

Pevsner 1958
N.Pevsner, *The Buildings of England: North Somerset and Bristol*, 1958

Pevsner 1962
N.Pevsner, *The Buildings of England: North-east Norfolk and Norwich*, 1962

Pevsner 1963
N.Pevsner, *The Buildings of England: Herefordshire*, 1963

Pevsner 1966a
N.Pevsner, *The Buildings of England: Yorkshire; The North Riding*, 1966

Pevsner 1966b
N.Pevsner, *The Buildings of England: Warwickshire*, 1966

Pevsner 1967
N.Pevsner, *The Buildings of England: Yorkshire; The West Riding*, 2nd edn, rev. E.Radcliffe, 1967

Pevsner 1970
N.Pevsner, *The Buildings of England: Cambridgeshire*, 2nd edn, 1970

Pevsner 1972
N.Pevsner, *Some Architectural Writers of the 19th Century*, 1972

Pevsner 1973a
N.Pevsner, *The Buildings of England: North-West and South Norfolk*, 1973

Pevsner 1973b
N.Pevsner, *The Buildings of England: London I. The Cities of London and Westminster*, 3rd edn, rev. B.Cherry, 1973

Pevsner 1976
N.Pevsner, 'Scrape and Anti-scrape', *The Future of the Past*, ed. J.Fawcett, 1976, pp. 34–53

Pevsner (rev. Cherry) 1973
N.Pevsner, *The Buildings of England: Northamptonshire*, rev. B.Cherry, 1973

Pevsner & Harris 1964
N.Pevsner & J.Harris, *The Buildings of England: Lincolnshire*, 1964

Pevsner & Metcalf 1985a
N.Pevsner, P.Metcalf et. al., *The Cathedrals of England: Southern England*, 1985

Pevsner & Metcalf 1985b
N.Pevsner, P.Metcalf et al., *The Cathedrals of England: Midland, Eastern and Northern England*, 1985

Pewterers' Company 1979
The Worshipful Company of Pewterers of London, *Supplementary Catalogue of Pewterware*, 1979

Philippowich 1961
E.V.Philippowich, *Elfenbein*, 1961

Phillips 1973
J.Phillips, *The Reformation of Images: Destruction of Art in England 1535–1660*, 1973

Philobiblon 1970 edn
Philobiblon Ricardi de Bury, ed. & transl. E.C.Thomas, foreword by M.MacLagan, 1970

Phipson 1896
E.Phipson, *Choir Stalls and their Carvings*, 1896

Pickering 1971
F.P.Pickering (ed.), *The Anglo-Norman Text of the Holkham Bible Picture Book*,

Anglo-Norman Text Society, XXIII, 1971

Piers Plowman 1959 edn
W.Langland, *Piers the Plowman*, trans. J.F.Goodridge, 1959

Piers Plowman 1978 edn
W.Langland, *The Vision of Piers Plowman*, ed. A.V.C.Schmidt, 1978

Piggot 1985
S.Piggott, *William Stukeley: An 18th Century Antiquary*, 1950 (revised edn, 1985)

Pinto 1969
E.H.Pinto, *Treen & other Wooden Bygones: an Encyclopedia and Social History*, 1969

Pitman 1954
C.F.Pitman, 'Reflections on Nottingham Alabaster Carving...', *Connoisseur*, CXXX, 1954, pp. 217–28

Pitman 1964
C.F.Pitman, 'Speculations on fourteenth-century English alabaster work', *Connoisseur*, CLV, 1964, pp. 82–9

Platt 1981
C.Platt, *The Parish Churches of Medieval England*, 1981

Platt & Coleman-Smith 1975
C.Platt & R.Coleman-Smith, *Excavations in Medieval Southampton 1953–1969*, 2 vols, 1975

Plenderleith & Maryon 1959
H.J.Plenderleith & H.Maryon, 'The royal bronze effigies in Westminster Abbey', *Antiq. J.*, XXXIX, 1959, pp. 87–90

Plimpton 1935
G.Plimpton, *The Education of Chaucer*, 1935

Pollard 1956
G.Pollard, 'William de Brailes', *Bodleian Library Record*, V, 1956, pp. 202–9

Pollard 1962
G.Pollard, 'The construction of English twelfth-century bindings', *The Library*, 5th ser., XVII, 1962, pp. 1–22

Pollard 1964
G.Pollard, 'The University and the book trade in medieval Oxford', in *Miscellanea Mediaevalia: Veröffentlichen des Thomas-Instituts an der Universität Köln*, III, 1964, pp. 336–44

Pollard 1976
G.Pollard, 'Describing medieval bindings', *Medieval Learning and Literature: Essays presented to Richard William Hunt*, ed. J.J.G.Alexander & M.T.Gibson, 1976, pp. 50–65

Pollard 1983
H.B.C.Pollard, *Pollard's History of Firearms*, ed. C.Blair, 1983

Poole 1857
G.A.Poole, 'The architectural history of Lincoln Minster', *Assoc. Archit. Soc. Repts & Papers*, IV, I, 1857, pp. 8–48

Poole & Hugall 1850
G.A.Poole & J.W.Hugall, *An Historical & Descriptive Guide to York Cathedral and its Antiquities*, 1850

Pope 1751
A.Pope, *The Works of Alexander Pope Esq.... together with the Commentaries & Notes of Mr Warburton*, 9 vols, 1751

Pope & Lodge 1910
M.K.Pope & E.C.Lodge, *Life of the Black Prince by the Herald of Sir John Chandos*, 1910

Porter 1891
A.S.Porter, 'The seals of the Archbishops of York', *Proc. Soc. Antiq. London*, 2nd ser., XIII, 1891, pp. 45–64

Porter 1974
D.Porter, *Ivory Carving in Later Medieval England, 1200–1400*, 2 vols, Ph.D.

1974, State University of New York at Binghamton, pub. University Microfilms International, 1977

Posse 1909
O.Posse, *Die Siegel der deutschen Kaiser und Könige*, I, 1909

Postan 1972
M.M.Postan, *The Medieval Economy and Society*, 1972

Potter 1960, 1962
W.J.W.Potter, 'The silver coinage of Edward III from 1351', *Numismatic Chronicle*, CXXIII, 1960, pp. 137–87; CXXV, 1962, pp. 203–24

Potter 1963–4
W.J.W.Potter, 'The gold coinage of Edward III', *Numismatic Chronicle*, CXXVI, 1963, pp. 107–28; CXXVII, 1964, pp. 305–18

Power 1922
E.Power, *Medieval English Nunneries*, 1922 (1984)

Power 1926
E.Power, 'The position of women', *The Legacy of the Middle Ages*, ed. C.G.Crump & E.F.Jacob, 1926, pp. 401–33

Power 1975
E.Power, *Medieval Women*, ed. M.M.Postan, 1975

Powicke 1908
F.M.Powicke, 'The Chancery during the minority of Henry III', *Engl. Hist. Rev.*, XXIII, 1908, pp. 220–35

Powicke 1947
F.M.Powicke, *King Henry III and the Lord Edward*, 2 vols, 1947

Powicke 1953
F.M.Powicke, *The Thirteenth Century*, 1953 (1962)

Powicke & Cheney 1964
F.M.Powicke & C.R.Cheney (eds), *Councils and Synods with other documents relating to the English Church*. II, AD. 1205–1313, 2 vols, 1964

Preston 1936
A.E.Preston, 'The fourteenth century painted ceiling at St Helen's Church, Abingdon', *Berkshire Archaeol. J.*, XL, 1936, pp. 115–45

Prestwich 1980
M.Prestwich, *The Three Edwards: Law and State in England, 1272–1377*, 1980

Prestwich 1985
M.Prestwich, 'The piety of Edward I', in Ormrod 1985, pp. 120–8

Price 1753
F.Price, *A Series of particular and useful Observations . . . upon . . . the Cathedral Church of Salisbury*, 1753

Prideaux & Holt Shafto 1910
E.K.Prideaux & G.R.Holt Shafto, *Bosses and Corbels of Exeter Cathedral*, 1910

Prior & Gardner 1912
E.S.Prior & A.Gardner, *An Account of Medieval Figure-Sculpture in England*, 1912

Pritchard n.d.
R.E.Pritchard, *The Choir and Misericords of St Mary's Nantwich*, n.d.

Purcell 1974
D.Purcell, 'The priory of Horsham St Faith and its wallpaintings', *Norfolk Archaeology*, XXXV, 1974, pp. 469–73

Quinn & Ruddock 1937–8
D.B.Quinn & A.A.Ruddock (ed.), *The Port Books or local Customs Accounts of Southampton for the reign of Edward IV*, 2 vols, 1937–8

RCHM, *Bucks*, 1913
Royal Commission on Historical Monuments, *Buckinghamshire*, II, North, 1913

RCHM, *Cambridge* 1959, 1968–72
Royal Commission on Historical Monuments, *City of Cambridge*, 2 pts, 1959, and 2 vols, 1968–72

RCHM, *Essex*, 1916, 1922
Royal Commission on Historical Monuments, *Essex*, I, 1916; III, 1922

RCHM, *Herefordshire*, 1931–4
Royal Commission on Historical Monuments, *Herefordshire*, 3 vols, 1931–4

RCHM, *Huntingdon*, 1926, 1936
Royal Commission on Historical Monuments, *Huntingdon*, 1926, 1936

RCHM, *London*, 1924
Royal Commission on Historical Monuments, *London*, I, *Westminster Abbey*, 1924

RCHM, *Oxford*, 1939
Royal Commission on Historical Monuments, *City of Oxford*, 1939

RCHM, *Salisbury*, 1980 and forthcoming
Royal Commission on Historical Monuments, *Ancient and Historical Monuments in the City of Salisbury*, I, 1980; II (forthcoming)

RCHM, *Stamford*, 1977
Royal Commission on Historical Monuments, *The Town of Stamford*, 1977

RCHM, *York*, 1975
Royal Commission on Historical Monuments, *City of York*, IV, *Outside the City Walls and East of the Ouse*, 1975

RCHM, *York*, 1981
Royal Commission on Historical Monuments, *City of York*, V, *The Central Area*, 1981

RUSI
Official Catalogue of the Royal United Service Museum, Whitehall, 8th edn, n.d. (c.1930)

Rackham 1936
B.Rackham, *Victoria and Albert Museum, Department of Ceramics: A Guide to the Collections of Stained Glass*, 1936

Rackham 1948, 1972
B.Rackham, *Medieval English Pottery*, 1948 & 1972 edns

Ragusa & Green 1961
I.Ragusa & R.B.Green (ed.), *Meditations on the Life of Christ*, 1961

Raimes 1951–6
A.L.Raimes, 'The Swinburne Pyx', *Proc. Soc. Antiq. Newcastle-upon-Tyne*, 5th ser., I, 1951–6, pp. 66–8

Raine 1842
J.Raine (ed.), *Description . . . of all the Ancient Monuments, Rites . . . of Durham'*, Surtees Society, XV, 1842

Randall 1957
L.M.C.Randall, '*Exempla* as a Source of Gothic marginal illumination', *Art Bull.*, XXXIX, 1957, pp. 97–107

Randall 1966a
L.M.C.Randall, *Images in the Margins of Gothic Manuscripts*, 1966

Randall 1966b
R.H.Randall, 'The medieval artist and industrialized art', *Apollo*, LXXXIV, July–Dec. 1966, pp. 434–41

Randall 1974
R.H.Randall, 'A fourteenth-century altar-frontal', *Apollo*, Nov. 1974, pp. 368–71

Randall 1985
R.H.Randall, *Masterpieces of Ivory from the Walters Art Gallery*, 1985

Read 1898
C.H.Read, 'Bronze Jug', *Proc. Soc. Antiq. London*, 2nd ser., XVII, 1898, pp. 82–7

Read 1915
H.Read (Note on a sword from the River Ouse at Cowood Castle exhibited to the Society of Antiquaries by Col. J.W.R.Parker, 8 Feb. 1915), *Proc. Soc. Antiq. London*, 2nd ser., XXVII, 1914–15, pp. 111–14

Read 1921
C.H.Read, a Tribute and a Record 1896–1921, Trustees of the British Museum, London, 1921

Reddaway & Walker 1975
T.F.Reddaway & L.E.M.Walker, *The Early History of the Goldsmiths Company 1327–1509*, 1975

Rees 1840
W.J.Rees, *The Liber Landavensis*, Society for the Publication of Ancient Welsh Manuscripts, 1840

Rees 1974
W.Rees, *Caerphilly Castle and its place in the Annals of Glamorgan*, 1974

Reitzenstein 1972
A. von Reitzenstein, *Rittertum und Ritterschaft*, 1972

Reliquary 1892
'The Image of All Saints', *The Reliquary*, n.s., VI, 1892, pp. 169–71

Remnant 1969
G.L.Remnant, *A Catalogue of Misericords in Great Britain*, 1969

Remnant 1978
M.Remnant, *Musical Instruments of the West*, 1978

Remnant & Marks 1980
M.Remnant & R.Marks, 'A medieval "gittern"', *British Museum Yearbook*, IV, 1980, pp. 83–134

Repton 1806
J.A.Repton, 'Description of the ancient building at Norwich which is the subject of the preceding paper' [Gibson 1806], *Archaeologia*, XV, 1806, pp. 333 ff.

Review 1912–39
Victoria and Albert Museum, Review of the Principal Acquisitions during the years 1911–38, 1912–39 (annual)

Reynolds 1977
S.Reynolds, *An Introduction to the History of English Medieval Towns*, 1977

Richard de Bury 1902 edn
R.d'Aungerville, *The Love of Books. The Philobiblon of Richard de Bury*, trans. E.C.Thomas, 1902

Richardson 1951
L.Richardson, 'The Stone of the Canopy of Edward II's Tomb in Gloucester Cathedral', *Trans. Bristol and Glos. Archaeol. Soc.*, LXX, 1951, pp. 144–5

Richardson 1976
M.Richardson (ed.), *Catalogue of the Drawings Collection of the Royal Institute of British Architects*, V, 1976

Richardson 1980
R.D.Richardson, 'Boyton: the church, the Giffards, and their successors'. *Hatcher Review*, IX, 1980, pp. 26–33 (also a corrected version, typescript, n.d.)

Rickert 1954, 1965
M.Rickert, *Painting in Britain: the Middle Ages*, 1954 (2nd edn, 1965)

Rickman 1817
T.Rickman, *An Attempt to Discriminate the Styles of English Architecture, from the Conquest to the Reformation*, 1817

Ridgway 1968
M.Ridgway, *Chester Goldsmiths from early times to 1726*, 1968

Rigg 1965
A.G.Rigg, *An edition of a Fifteenth-century Commonplace Book*, PhD Thesis, Oxford, 1965

Rigold 1977
S.E.Rigold, 'Two Common species of medieval seal matrix', *Antiq. J.*, LVII, 1977, pp. 324–9

Riley 1863–4
H.T.Riley (ed.), *Thomae Walsingham, Historia Anglicana*, 2 vols, Rolls series, XXVIII, 1863–4

Riley 1867
H.T.Riley (ed.), *Gesta abbatum monasterii Sancti Albani*, 3 vols, Rolls series XXVIII.4, 1867–9

Riley 1868
H.T.Riley, *Memorials of London and London Life, in the 13th, 14th & 15th Centuries*, 1868

Rites of Durham 1903 edn
Rites of Durham, being a description or brief declaration of all the ancient monuments, rites and customs belonging or being within the monastical church of Durham before the Suppression written 1593, ed. J.T.Fowler, Surtees Soc., CVII, 1903

Roach Smith 1854
C.Roach Smith, *Catalogue of the Museum of London Antiquities*, 1854

Robbins 1960
R.H.Robbins (ed.), *Secular Lyrics of the XIV and XV Centuries*, 1960

Roberts 1973
M.E.Roberts, 'Towards a literary source for the scenes of the Passion in Queen Mary's Psalter', *J. Warb. Court. Inst.*, XXXVI, 1973, pp. 361–5

Roberts 1985
M.E.Roberts, 'The Relic of the Holy Blood and the iconography of the thirteenth-century north transept portal of Westminster Abbey', in Ormrod 1985, pp. 129–42

Roberts 1986
M.E.Roberts, 'John Carter at St Stephen's Chapel: a Romantic turns archaeologist', in Ormrod 1986, pp. 202–12

Robinson 1916–17
J.A.Robinson, 'King Ina's reputed burial place in Wells Cathedral', *Somerset & Dorset Notes & Queries*, XV, 1916–17, pp. 153–5

Robinson 1931
J.A.Robinson, 'The fourteenth-century glass at Wells', *Archaeologia*, LXXXI, 1931, pp. 85–118

Robinson & James 1909
J.A.Robinson & M.R.James, *The Manuscripts of Westminster Abbey*, 1909

Rock 1905
D.Rock, *The Church of Our Fathers*, 2nd edn, 4 vols, 1905

Rodwell 1979
W.Rodwell, *Wells Cathedral Excavations and Discoveries*, 1979

Roe 1929
F.Roe, *Ancient Church Chests and Chairs in the Home Counties*, 1929

Rogers 1986
N.J.Rogers, 'The Old Proctor's Book: A Cambridge manuscript of c.1390', in Ormrod 1986, pp. 213–26

Rogers 1987
N.J.Rogers, 'English Episcopal Monuments. 1270–1350', in Coales 1987

Rokewode 1885
J.G.Rokewode, 'A memoir on the Painted Chamber in the Palace of Westminster', *Vetusta Monumenta*, VI, 1885, pls XXVI–XXXIX

Romilly Allen 1896
J. Romilly Allen, 'Inscribed bronze flagon of the fourteenth century in the South Kensington Museum', *Reliquary and Illustrated*

Archaeologist, II 1896, pp. 103–6

Roosen-Runge 1961
H. Roosen-Runge, 'Ein Werk englischer Grossplastik des 13. Jahrhunderts und die Antike', *Festschrift Hans R. Hahnloser zum 60. Geburtstag 1959*, 1961, pp. 103–12

Roper 1931
I. M. Roper, *The Monumental Effigies of Gloucestershire and Bristol*, 1931

Rosenberg 1924–5
M. Rosenberg, *Niello*, 1924–5

Rosenthal 1976
J. T. Rosenthal, *Nobles and the Noble Life 1250–1500*, 1976

Rose-Troup 1928
F. Rose-Troup, 'Bishop Grandisson: student and art lover', *Trans. Devonshire Assoc.*, LXI, 1928, pp. 239–75

Ross 1953
D. J. A. Ross, 'A lost painting in Henry III's palace at Westminster', *J. Warb. Court. Inst.*, XVI, 1953, p. 160

Ross 1963
D. J. A. Ross, *Alexander Historiatus*, 1963

Ross 1969
D. J. A. Ross, 'A thirteenth-century Anglo-Norman workshop illustrating secular literary manuscripts', *Mélanges offerts à Rita Lejeune*, 1969, pp. 690–4

Rossi Manaresi 1986
R. Rossi Manaresi, *Restauria Bologna e Ferrara: Conservation Works in Bologna and Ferrara*, 1986

Rouse 1935
E. C. Rouse, 'Wall paintings in the church of All Saints, Chalgrove, Beds.', *Archaeol. J.*, XCII, 1935, pp. 81–97

Rouse 1951
E. C. Rouse, 'Wall paintings and other discoveries in St Andrew's Church, Pickworth, Lincolnshire and a wall painting at Great Sturton', *Lincolnshire Archit. and Archaeol. Soc. Reports and Papers*, n.s., IV, I, 1951, pp. 57–67

Rouse 1953
E. C. Rouse, 'Wall paintings in the church of St Pega, Peakirk, Northamptonshire', *Archaeol. J.*, CX, 1953, pp. 135–49

Rouse 1964
E. C. Rouse, *Longthorpe Tower, Peterborough*, 1964

Rouse & Baker 1955
E. C. Rouse & A. Baker, 'The wall paintings at Longthorpe Tower, near Peterborough, Northants', *Archaeologia*, XCVI, 1955, pp. 1–57

Rowe 1876
R. R. Rowe, 'The Octagon and Lantern of Ely Cathedral', *RIBA Sessional Papers, 1875–6*, 1876, pp. 69–85

Rowe 1880
R. R. Rowe, 'Walter Gifford, Archbishop of York, 1266–79', *Assoc. Archit. Soc. Repts & Papers*, XV, 1880, pp. 216–19

Rupin 1890
E. Rupin, *L'Oeuvre de Limoges*, 1890

Rushforth 1919
G. M. Rushforth, 'Magister Gregorius, *De Mirabilibus Urbis Romae*: a new description of Rome in the twelfth century', *Journal of Roman Studies*, IX, 1919, pp. 14–58

Rushforth 1924
G. M. Rushforth, 'The Glass in the Quire Clerestory of Tewkesbury Abbey', *Trans. Bristol and Glos. Archaeol. Soc.*, XLVI, 1924, pp. 289–324

Rushforth 1926
G. M. Rushforth, 'The Baptism of St Christopher', *Antiq. J.*, VI, 1926, pp. 152–8

Rushforth 1936
G. M. Rushforth, *Medieval Christian Imagery*, 1936

Ruskin 1903–12
J. Ruskin, *Collected Works*, ed. E. T. Cook & A. Wedderburn, 39 vols, 1903–12

Russell 1939
J. Russell, 'English Medieval Leatherwork', *Archaeol. J.*, XCVI, 1939, pp. 132–41

Rutter 1961
J. G. Rutter, *Medieval Pottery in the Scarborough Museum*, 1961

Ryan & Ripperger 1969
G. Ryan & H. Ripperger (ed. & trans.), *The Golden Legend of Jacobus de Voragine*, 1969

Rydbeck 1964
M. Rydbeck, 'Thomas Becket's Ampuller', *Fornvännen*, V–VI, 1964, pp. 236–48

Ryder 1985
P. F. Ryder, *The Medieval Cross Slab Grave Covers in County Durham*, 1985

Rymer 1739–45
T. Rymer (ed.), *Foedera . . .*, 10 vols, 1739–45

Sabin 1957
A. Sabin, 'The Fourteenth-century Heraldic Glass in the Eastern Lady Chapel of Bristol Cathedral', *Antiq. J.*, XXXVII, 1957, pp. 54–70

Salaman 1975
R. A. Salaman, *Dictionary of Tools used in the Woodworking and Allied Trades, c.1700–1970*, 1975

Salaman 1986
R. A. Salaman, *Dictionary of Leather-Working Tools, c.1700–1950*, 1986

Salter 1907–8
H. E. Salter (ed.), *Eynsham Cartulary*, 2 vols, Oxford Historical Society, XLIX, LI, 1907–8

Salter 1983
E. Salter, 'Conditions and status', *Fourteenth-Century English Poetry*, 1983

Salzman 1923
L. F. Salzman, *Medieval English Industries*, 2nd edn, 1923

Salzman 1926–7
L. F. Salzman, 'The Glazing of St Stephen's Chapel, Westminster, 1351–2', *J. Brit. Soc. Master Glass-Painters*, I, 1926–7, pp. 14–16, 31–5, 38–41

Salzman 1927–28, 1929–30
L. F. Salzman, 'Medieval Glazing Accounts', *J. Brit. Soc. of Master Glass-Painters*, 2, 1927–28, pp. 116–20, 188–92; 3, 1929–30, pp. 25–30

Salzman 1952, 1967
L. F. Salzman, *Building in England down to 1540*, 1952; reprints 1967, with additions 1979

Sandford & Stebbing 1707
F. Sandford & S. Stebbing (ed.), *A Genealogical History of the Kings & Queens of England . . . from the conquest, Anno 1066 to the Year 1707*, 1707

Sandler 1970
L. F. Sandler, 'A Follower of Jean Pucelle in England', *Art Bull.*, LII, 1970, pp. 363–72

Sandler 1974
L. F. Sandler, *The Peterborough Psalter in Brussels and other Fenland Manuscripts*, 1974

Sandler 1983
L. F. Sandler, *The Psalter of Robert de Lisle in the British Library*, 1983

Sandler 1985a
L. F. Sandler, 'A bawdy betrothal in the

Ormesby Psalter', *A Tribute to Lotte Brand Philip*, ed. W. Clark, C. Eisler, W. Heckscher & B. Laine, 1985, pp. 154–9

Sandler 1985b
L. F. Sandler, 'A note on the illuminators of the Bohun manuscripts', *Speculum*, LX, 1985, pp. 364–72

Sandler 1986
L. F. Sandler, *Gothic Manuscripts 1285–1385, A Survey of Manuscripts Illuminated in the British Isles*, V, 2 vols, 1986

Sauerländer 1965
W. Sauerländer, 'Über einen Reimser Bildhauer in Cluny', *Gedenkschrift Ernst Gall*, ed. M. Kuehn & L. Grodecki, 1965, pp. 255–68

Sauerländer 1971
W. Sauerländer, 'The Year 1200' (exhib. review), *Art Bull.*, LIII, 1971, pp. 506–16

Sauerländer 1972
W. Sauerländer, *Gothic Sculpture in France 1140–1270*, 1972

Saxl 1954
F. Saxl, *English Sculptures of the Twelfth Century*, 1954

Saxl & Wittkower 1969
F. Saxl & R. Wittkower, *British Art and the Mediterranean*, 1948, reprint 1969

Sayer 1972
M. J. Sayer, *Reepham's Three Churches*, 1972

Sayers 1806
F. Sayers, 'Notices concerning the dormitory of the Cathedral Monastery of Norwich', *Archaeologia*, XV, 1806, pp. 311–14

Sayles 1974
G. O. Sayles, *The King's Parliament of England*, 1974

Scarisbrick 1984
J. J. Scarisbrick, *The Reformation and the English People*, 1984

Scattergood & Sherborne 1983
V. J. Scattergood & J. W. Sherborne (eds), *English Court Culture in the Later Middle Ages*, 1983

Schapiro 1960
M. Schapiro, 'An illuminated English psalter of the early thirteenth century', *J. Warb. Court. Inst.*, XXIII, 1960, pp. 179–89

Scharf 1867
G. Scharf, 'Westminster Portrait of Richard II', *Fine Arts Quarterly*, Jan. 1867, p. 80

Schaube 1906
A. Schaube, *Handelsgeschichte der romanischen Volker des Mittelmeergebiets bis zum Ende der Kreuzzuge*, 1906

Scheler 1867
A. Scheler (ed.), *Lexicographie latine du XIIe et du XIIIe siècle*, 1867

Scheller 1963
R. W. Scheller, *A Survey of Medieval Model Books*, 1963

Schiller 1966–80, 1971–2
G. Schiller, *Ikonographie der christlichen Kunst*, 4 vols, 1966–80; Engl. trans. J. Seligman (*The Iconography of Christian Art*), 1971–2

Schlosser 1899
J. von Schlosser, 'Die Werkstatt der Embriachi in Venedig', *Jahrbuch der Kunsthistorischen Sammlungen des allerhöchsten Kaiserhauses*, 1899, pp. 220–82

Schuermans 1866
H. Schuermans, 'Des styles à écrire', *Académie d'Archéologie de Belgique*, XXII, 1866, pp. 577–9

Scott n.d. (1851)
W. B. Scott, *Antiquarian Gleanings in the North of England*, n.d. (1851)

Scott 1857
G. G. Scott, *Remarks on Secular and Domestic Architecture, Present and Future*, 1857

Scott 1863
G. G. Scott, *Gleanings from Westminster Abbey*, 2nd enlarged edn, 1863

Scott 1885
G. G. Scott, 'On the architectural history of Chester Cathedral as developed during the present work of restoration', *J. Archit., Archaeol. and Hist. Soc. of Chester and North Wales*, III, 1885, pp. 159–82

Scott 1986
M. Scott, *A Visual History of Costume: The Fourteenth and Fifteenth Centuries*, 1986

Scott-Moncrieff 1909
C. E. Scott-Moncrieff, 'Mattersey Priory', *Trans. Thoroton Soc.*, XIII, 1909, pp. 2–5

Sears 1986
E. Sears, *The Ages of Man: Medieval Interpretations of the Life Cycle*, 1986

Secomska 1975
K. Secomska, 'The miniature cycle in the Sandomierz *Pantheon* and the medieval iconography of Alexander's Indian Campaign', *J. Warb. Court. Inst.*, XXXVIII, 1975, pp. 53–71

Sekules 1981
V. Sekules, 'A Lost Tomb from Sawley' in Borg & Martindale 1981, pp. 173–7

Sekules 1983
V. Sekules, 'A group of masons in early fourteenth-century Lincolnshire: research in progress', in Thompson 1983, pp. 151–64

Sekules 1986
V. Sekules, 'The tomb of Christ at Lincoln and the development of the sacrament shrine: Eastern Sepulchres reconsidered', *Brit. Archaeol. Assoc. Conf. VIII, 1982*, 1986, pp. 118–31

Sellers 1912
M. Sellers (ed.) *York Memorandum book . . . A/Y*, Surtees Society, CXX, 1912

Sellwood 1963
D. Sellwood, 'Medieval minting techniques', *Brit. Numismatic J.*, XXXI, 1963, pp. 57–65

Serbat 1913
L. Serbat, 'Tablettes à écrire, du XIVe siècle', *Mémoires, Société Nationale des Antiquaires de France*, LXXIII, 1913, pp. 301–13

Seymour 1982
M. Seymour, 'Manuscript Portraits of Chaucer and Hoccleve', *Burl. Mag.*, CXXXIV, 1982, pp. 618–23

Shahar 1983
S. Shahar, *The Fourth Estate. A History of Women in the Middle Ages*, 1983

Sharpe 1889
R. R. Sharpe (ed.), *Calendar of Wills proved and enrolled in the Court of Husting, London A.D. 1258–A.D. 1688. Part I: A.D. 1258–A.D. 1358*, 1889

Sharpe 1899 etc.
R. R. Sharpe (ed.), *Calendar of Letter-Books . . . of the City of London. Letter-Book A* (etc.), 1899, etc.

Sharpe 1904
R. R. Sharpe (ed.), *Calendar of Letter-Books . . . of the City of London: Letter-Book F*, 1904

Sharpe 1907
R. R. Sharpe (ed.), *Calendar of Letter-Books . . . of the City of London: Letter-Book H, c.1375–99*, 1907

Shaw 1836
H.Shaw & S.R.Meyrick, *Specimens of Ancient Furniture*, 1836

Sheingorn (forthcoming)
P.Sheingorn, 'The Bosom of Abraham Trinity: a late Medieval All Saints Image', *England in the Fifteenth Century. Proceedings of the 1986 Harlaxton Conference*, ed. D.Williams (forthcoming)

Shelby 1964
L.R.Shelby, 'The role of the Master Mason in Medieval English Building', *Speculum*, XXXIX, 1964, pp. 387–403

Shemmell 1978
S.Shemmell, 'More Pewter from Tong Castle', *J. Pewter Soc.*, I, 4, autumn 1978, p. 2

Sheppard 1901
T.Sheppard, *Local Antiquities, etc. in the Hull Museum*, Hull Museum Publications, 3 Sept. 1901 (2nd edn Aug. 1902)

Sherlock 1976
D.Sherlock, 'Discoveries at Horsham St Faith Priory, 1970–1973', *Norfolk Archaeology*, XXXVI, 1976, pp. 202–23

Sherwood & Pevsner 1974
J.Sherwood & N.Pevsner, *The Buildings of England: Oxfordshire*, 1974

Shoesmith 1985
R.Shoesmith, *Hereford City Excavations* III, *The Finds*, 1985

Shortt 1951
H. de S.Shortt, 'An enamelled roundel from Wiltshire', *Antiq. J.*, XXXI, 1951, pp. 72–4

Shurlock 1885
M.Shurlock, *Tiles from Chertsey Abbey, Surrey, representing early Romance Subjects*, 1885

Shuttleworth
C.B.Shuttleworth, *The Cathedral Misericords* (MS in Worcester Cathedral Library)

Simms 1983
R.S.Simms, 'Pewter vessel from Ashby de la Zouche Castle', *Antiq. J.*, XVIII, 1938, pp. 178–80

Simpson 1938
W.D.Simpson, 'Warkworth, castle of livery and maintenance', *Archaeologia Aeliana*, 4th ser., XV, 1938, pp. 115–36

Simpson, 1941
W.D.Simpson, 'The Warkworth donjon and its architect', *Archaeologia Aeliana*, 4th ser., XIX, 1941, pp. 93–103

Simpson 1978
A.Simpson, 'The Connections between English and Bohemian Painting during the Second Half of the Fourteenth Century', Ph.D. Thesis, Courtauld Institute of Art, 1978

Simpson 1980
A.Simpson, 'English art during the second half of the fourteenth century', *Die Parler und der Schöne Stil 1350–1400*, extra vol. 1980, pp. 137–59

Simpson 1984
A.Simpson, *The Connections between English and Bohemian Painting during the Second Half of the Fourteenth Century*, 1984

Sinclair 1984
K.V.Sinclair, 'The manuscript evidence for the *Dedicatio ecclesie* of Ramsey Abbey', *Scriptorium*, XXXVIII, 2, 1984, pp. 305–9

Singer, Holmyard, Hall & Williams 1954–78
C.Singer, E.J.Holmyard, A.R.Hall & T.I.Williams (ed.), *A History of Technology*, 7 vols, 1954–78

Skeat 1873
W.W.Skeat, *The Vision of William concerning Piers the Plowman*, Early English Text Society, IV, 1873

Skelton 1823
J.Skelton, *Oxonia Antiqua restaurata*, 1823

Sledmere 1914
E.Sledmere, *Abbey Dore, Herefordshire, its Building and Restoration*, 1914

Sleigh 1952
B.L.Sleigh, *St Etheldreda's and Ely Place*, 1952

Smith 1792
G.Smith, (Note on holy-water stoup belonging to wife of George Smith, now in Wreay Church, Cumbria), *Archaeologia*, X, 1792, p. 472, pl. XXXVIII

Smith 1807
J.T.Smith, *Antiquities of Westminster*, 1807

Smith 1852, 1857
C.R.Smith, *Collectanea Antiqua*, 7 vols, 1848–80; II, 1852; IV, 1857

Smith 1956
J.T.Smith, 'Stokesay Castle', *Archaeol. J.*, CXIII, 1956, pp. 211–14

Smith 1969
J.C.D.Smith, *Church Woodcarvings: A West Country Study*, 1969

Smith 1975
A Picture Book of the Misericords of Wells Cathedral (photographed by J.C.D.Smith), Friends of Wells Cathedral, 1975 (reprint 1981)

Smith 1983
M.Q.Smith, *The Stained Glass of Bristol Cathedral*, 1983

Sneyd 1847
C.A.Sneyd (ed.), *A Relation ... of the Island of England about the year 1500*, Camden Society, XXXVII, 1847

Soltykoff 1861
Catalogue des Objets d'Art (et de ... Haute Curiosité) composant la célèbre Collection du Prince Soltykoff, sale catalogue, 1861

Southern 1962
R.W.Southern (ed.), *Eadmer, Life of St Anselm*, 1962

Sparrow Simpson 1895a
Visitations of Churches belonging to St Paul's Cathedral 1249–1252, ed. W.Sparrow Simpson, Camden Society, n.s. 53, 1895

Sparrow Simpson 1895b
Visitations of Churches belonging to St Paul's Cathedral in 1297 and in 1458, ed. W.Sparrow Simpson, Camden Society, n.s. 55, 1895

Spencer 1968
B.Spencer, 'Medieval pilgrim badges', *Rotterdam Papers: a Contribution to Medieval Archaeology*, ed. J.G.N.Renaud, 1968, pp. 137–53

Spencer 1969
B.Spencer, 'London – St Albans Return', *London Archaeologist*, spring 1969, pp. 34–5, 45

Spencer 1972
B.Spencer, *Chaucer's London*, London Museum, 1972

Spencer 1975
B.Spencer, 'The ampullae from Cuckoo Lane', *Excavations in Medieval Southampton 1953–1969*, ed. C.Platt & R.Coleman-Smith, II, 1975, pp. 242–9

Spencer 1980
B.Spencer, *Medieval Pilgrim Badges from Norfolk*, Norfolk Museums Service, 1980

Spencer 1982
B.Spencer, 'Pilgrim souvenirs from the medieval waterfront excavations at Trig Lane, London 1974–76', *Trans. London & Middx Archaeol. Soc.*, XXXIII, 1982, pp. 304–20

Spencer 1984
B.Spencer, 'Medieval seal-dies recently found at London', *Antiq. J.*, LXIV, 1984, pp. 376–82

Spencer 1987
B.Spencer, 'Catalogue of the medieval pilgrim badges in the Salisbury Museum' in Salisbury & S.Wilts. Museum, *Medieval Catalogue*, I, 1987

Spielmann 1900
M.H.Spielmann, *The Portraits of Geoffrey Chaucer*, 1900

Spitzer 1890
La collection Spitzer. Antiquité–Moyen-Age-Renaissance (6 vols, 1890–2), I, *Les Ivoires*, 1890

Spitzer 1893
Catalogue des Objets d'Art et de Haute Curiosité, Antiques, du Moyen Age et de la Renaissance, composent l'importante et precieuse Collection Spitzer, Paris sale catalogue, 1893

Squilbeck 1938
J.Squilbeck, 'Quelques sculptures anglaises d'albâtre conservées en Belgique', *Antiq. J.*, XVIII, 1938, pp. 58–67

Stahlschmidt 1884
J.Stahlschmidt, *Surrey Bells and London Bell-founders*, 1884

Stahlschmidt 1887
J.Stahlschmidt, *The Church Bells of Kent*, 1887

Staniland 1986
K.Staniland, 'Court style, painters and the Great Wardrobe', in Ormrod 1986, pp. 236–46

Stanley 1855
A.P.Stanley, *Historical Memorials of Canterbury*, 1855

Stapleton 1836
T.Stapleton, 'A brief summary of the wardrobe accounts of ... Edward the Second', *Archaeologia*, XXVI, 1836, pp. 318–45

Statutes 1810–28
Statutes of the Realm, 10 vols, 1810–28

Steer 1961
F.W.Steer, *Misericords in Chichester Cathedral*, 1961

Steer 1973
F.W.Steer, *Misericords at New College, Oxford*, 1973

Steinberg 1938
S.H.S.Steinberg, 'A Portrait of Beatrix of Falkenburg', *Antiq. J.*, XVIII, 1938, pp. 142–5

Stephenson 1921
M.Stephenson, *A List of Monumental Brasses in Surrey*, 1921 (reprint 1970)

Stephenson 1934
M.Stephenson, (Note on 'Incised slab from the site of the church of St Christopher-le-Stocks, Threadneedle Street'), *Antiq. J.*, XIV, 1934, p. 297

Stevenson 1817
W.Stevenson, *A Supplement to the First Edition of Mr Bentham's History and Antiquities of the Cathedral and Conventual Church of Ely*, 1817

Stevenson 1839
Chronicon de Lanercost, ed. J.Stevenson, 1839

Stevenson & Wood 1940
J.M.Stevenson & M.Wood, *Scottish Heraldic Seals*, III, 1940

Stewart 1868
D.J.Stewart, *On the Architectural History of Ely Cathedral*, 1868

Stewart 1875
D.J.Stewart, 'Notes on Norwich Cathedral', *Archaeol. J.*, XXXII, pp. 155–87

Stewart-Brown 1933
R.Stewart-Brown, 'The Old Dee Bridge at Chester', *J. Chester and N. Wales Archit., Archaeol., and Hist. Soc.*, XXX, n.s., 2, 1933, pp. 63–78

Stoddard 1983
S.Stoddard, *George Weare Braikenridge (1775–1856): A Bristol Antiquarian and his Collections*, M.Litt. Thesis, 1983, University of Bristol

Stone 1964
B.Stone (ed.), *Medieval English Verse*, 1964

Stone 1955, 1972
L.Stone, *Sculpture in Britain: the Middle Ages*, 1955, reprint 1972

Storer 1822
J. & H.S.Storer, *The Oxford Visitor*, 1822

Stothard 1817
C.A.Stothard, *The Monumental Effigies of Great Britain*, 1817

Stow 1908 edn
J.Stow, *A survey of London, reprinted from the text of 1603*, with intro. and notes by C.L.Kingsford, 2 vols, 1908

Stow 1977
G.B.Stow (ed.), *Historia Vitae et Regni Ricardi Secundi*, 1977

Stratford 1983
N.Stratford, 'Glastonbury and two Gothic ivories in the United States', in Thompson 1983, pp. 208–16

Stratford 1986
N.Stratford, 'Niello in England in the 12th century', in *Art and Patronage in the English Romanesque*, ed. S.Macready & F.H.Thompson, 1986, pp. 28–49

Strong 1969
R.Strong, *Tudor and Jacobean Portraits*, National Portrait Gallery, 1969

Strutt 1903 edn
J.Strutt, *Glig-Gamena Angel Deod, or the Sports and Pastimes of the People of England* (1801), new edn revised by J.C.Cox (1903)

Stubbs 1879–80
W.Stubbs (ed.), *Historical Works of Gervase of Canterbury*, 2 vols, Rolls series, LXXIII, 1879–80

Stukeley 1776
W.Stukeley, *Itinerarium Curiosum*, 2nd edn, 1776, 2 pts in 1 vol. (reprint 1969)

Sudhoff 1914
K.Sudhoff, 'Beiträge zur Geschichte der Chirurgie im Mittelalter', *Studien zur Geschichte der Medizin*, X, 1914, pp. 33–42

Summerly 1843
F.Summerly, *Handbook for the City of Canterbury*, 1843

Swanson 1980–1
H.C.Swanson, *Craftsmen and Industry in late Medieval York*, unpubl. PhD Thesis, Univ. of York, 1980–1

Swartout 1932
R.E.Swartout, *The Monastic Craftsman*, 1932

Taburet 1984
E.Taburet, 'Le Trésor de Colmar', *La revue du Louvre*, II, 1984, pp. 89–101

Tait 1936
J.Tait, *The Medieval English Borough*, 1936

Tait 1955
H.Tait, 'Pilgrim-signs and Thomas, Earl of Lancaster', *British Museum Quarterly*, XX, 1955, pp. 39–46

Tartarkiewicz 1970
W.Tartarkiewicz, *History of Aesthetics*, II, *The Middle Ages*, 1970

Tatton-Brown 1974
T. Tatton-Brown, 'Excavations at the Custom House site, City of London, 1973', *Trans. London and Middx. Archaeol. Soc.*, XXV, 1974, pp. 117–219

Taylor 1808
J. Taylor (ed.), *Essays on Gothic Architecture*, 3rd edn, 1808

Taylor 1904
C. S. Taylor, 'The Old Church of St Thomas the Martyr, Bristol', *Trans. Bristol and Glos. Archaeol. Soc.*, XXVII, 1904, pp. 340–51

Taylor 1952
A. J. Taylor, 'Building at Caerphilly in 1326', *Bulletin of the Board of Celtic Studies*, XIV, 4, 1952, pp. 299–300

Taylor 1964–6
M. R. Taylor, 'The Kettlebaston Alabasters', *Proc., Suffolk Inst. Archaeol.*, XXX, 1964–6, pp. 252–4

Taylor 1977
A. J. Taylor, 'A fragment of a Dona account of 1284', *Bulletin of the Board of Celtic Studies*, XXVII, 1977, pp. 258–62

Taylor & Scarisbrick 1978
G. Taylor & D. Scarisbrick, *Finger Rings from Ancient Egypt to the Present Day*, 1978

Testamenta Eboracensia 1836–1902
Testamenta Eboracensia; or wills registered at York illustrative of the history, manners, language, statistics, etc., of the province of York, from the year 1300 downwards, Surtees Society, pt 1, vol. 4 (1836); pt 2, vol. 30 (1855); pt. 3, vol. 45 (1865); pt 4, vol. 53 (1869); pt 5, vol. 79 (1884); pt 6, vol. 106

Thiébaux 1967
M. Thiébaux, 'The Medieval Chase', *Speculum*, XLII, 1967, pp. 260–74

Thiébaux 1974
M. Thiébaux, *The Stag of Love. The Chase in Medieval Literature*, 1974

Thomas 1924
A. H. Thomas, *Calendar of Plea and Memoranda Rolls 1323–64*, 1924

Thompson 1925
A. H. Thompson, *The Cathedral Churches of England*, 1925

Thompson 1925
F. Thompson, *The First Century of Magna Carta*, 1925

Thompson 1935
D. V. Thompson, 'Trial Index to some unpublished sources for the history of medieval craftsmanship', *Speculum*, X, 1935, pp. 410–30

Thompson 1948
F. Thompson, *Magna Carta: its role in the making of the English constitution, 1300–1629*, 1948

Thompson 1983
F. H. Thompson (ed.), *Studies in Medieval Sculpture*, Society of Antiquaries, Occasional Paper, n.s., III, 1983

Thordemann 1939
B. J. N. Thordemann, *Armour from the Battle of Wisby, 1361*, 2 vols, 1939–40

Thoroton 1797
R. Thoroton, *History of Nottinghamshire*, 3 vols, 1790

Toke 1935
N. E. Toke, 'The medieval stained glass windows at Upper Hardres', *Archaeologia Cantiana*, XLVII, 1935, pp. 153–65

Tonnochy 1952
A. B. Tonnochy, *Catalogue of British Seal-dies in the British Museum*, 1952

Topham 1795–1813
J. Topham, 'Some Account of the Collegiate Chapel of St Stephen, at Westminster', issued with: *Plans,*

elevations, sections, and specimens of the architecture . . . engraved . . . from drawings . . . by J. Carter, Society of Antiq., 1795–1813

Torr 1963–8
V. J. Torr, 'Re-dating and other notes', *Trans. Monumental Brass Soc.*, X, 1963–8, pp. 9–12

Tracy 1986a
C. Tracy, 'The early fourteenth-century choir-stalls at Exeter Cathedral', *Burl. Mag.*, CXXVIII, 1986, pp. 99–103

Tracy 1986b
C. Tracy, 'The choir furniture of St Katharine's-by-the-Tower and its position in the stylistic development of English choir-stalls during the second half of the fourteenth century', *Archaeol. J.*, CXLIII, 1986, pp. 322–30

Tracy 1987a
C. Tracy, *English Gothic Choir-Stalls, 1200–1400*, 1987

Tracy 1987b
C. Tracy, *Catalogue of English Medieval Furniture and Woodwork*, Victoria and Albert Museum, 1987

Tremlett & London 1967
T. D. Tremlett & M. S. London, *Aspilogia, II, Rolls of Arms; Henry III*, 1967

Treue et al. 1965
W. Treue et al. (eds), *Das Hausbuch der Mendelschen Zwölfbrüderstiftung zu Nürnberg*, 1965

Tristram 1926
E. W. Tristram, 'The wall painting at Horsham St Faiths', *Norfolk Archaeology*, XXII, 1926, pp. 257–9

Tristram 1943
E. W. Tristram, 'An English mid-fourteenth century picture', *Burl. Mag.*, LXXXIII, 1943, pp. 160–5

Tristram 1944
E. W. Tristram, *English Medieval Wall Painting: The Twelfth Century*, 1944

Tristram 1950
E. W. Tristram, *English Medieval Wall Painting: The Thirteenth Century*, 2 vols, 1950

Tristram 1955
E. W. Tristram, *English Wall Painting of the Fourteenth Century*, 1955

Tristram & James 1927
M. R. James & E. W. Tristram, 'Wall-paintings in Croughton Church, Northamptonshire', *Archaeologia*, LXXVI, 1927, pp. 179–204

Trollope 1857
E. Trollope, 'The captivity of John, King of France at Somerton Castle, Lincolnshire', *Assoc. Archit. Soc. Repts and Papers*, IV, 1, 1857, pp. 49–68

Trusted 1985
M. Trusted, *Catalogue of European Ambers in the Victoria & Albert Museum*, 1985

Tuck 1973
A. Tuck, *Richard II and the English Nobility*, 1973

Tuck 1985
A. Tuck, *Crown and Nobility 1272–1461*, 1985

Tucker 1846
C. Tucker, 'Notes on the Bishop's Palace, Exeter', *Archaeol. J.*, V, 1848, pp. 224–5

Tudor-Craig 1957
P. Tudor-Craig, 'The Painted Chamber at Westminster', *Archaeol. J.*, CXIV, 1957, pp. 92–105

Tudor-Craig 1973
P. Tudor-Craig, *Richard III*, National Portrait Gallery, 1973

Tudor-Craig 1982
P. Tudor-Craig, 'Wells Sculpture', in

Colchester 1982, pp. 102–31

Tudor-Craig & Keen 1983
P. Tudor-Craig & L. Keen, 'A recently discovered Purbeck marble sculpture screen of the thirteenth century and the shrine of St Swithun', *Brit. Archaeol. Assoc. Conf.* VI, 1980, 1983, pp. 63–72

Tummers 1980
H. A. Tummers, *Early Secular Effigies in England: The Thirteenth Century*, 1980

Turner 1841
T. H. Turner (ed.), *Manners and Household Expenses of England . . .*, Roxburghe Club, 1841

Turner 1845
T. H. Turner, 'Usages of domestic life in the Middle Ages', *Archaeol. J.*, II, 1845, pp. 258–66

Turner 1847
D. Turner, 'Second letter . . . upon . . . the Crucifix . . .', *Norfolk Archaeology*, I, 1847, pp. 300–4

Turner 1968
D. H. Turner, 'The Development of Maître Honoré', *The Eric George Millar Bequest of Manuscripts and Drawings, 1967, A Commemorative Volume*, 1968, pp. 53–65

Turner 1969
D. H. Turner, 'Two rediscovered miniatures of the Oscott Psalter', *British Museum Quarterly*, XXXIV, 1969, pp. 10–19

Turner 1985
B. Turner, 'The patronage of John of Northampton', *J. Brit. Archaeol. Assoc.*, CXXXVIII, 1985, pp. 89–100

Turner & Turner 1978
V. Turner & E. Turner, *Image and Pilgrimage in Christian Culture*, 1978

Tweddle 1986
D. Tweddle, *The Archaeology of York: The Scroll Finds. XVII, 4, Finds from Parliament Street & other Sites in the City Centre*, 1986

Twining 1960
E. F. Twining, *A history of the Crown Jewels of Europe*, 1960

Twining 1967
E. F. Twining, *European Regalia*, 1967

Twopeny 1859
W. Twopeny, *Specimens of Ancient Wood-Work*, 1859

Tylecote 1986
R. F. Tylecote, *A History of Metallurgy*, revised edn, 1986

Tyson 1786
Rev. M. Tyson, 'Account of the horn belonging to Corpus Christi College Cambridge', *Archaeologia*, III, 1786, p. 19

Tyson 1975
D. B. Tyson, *La Vie du Prince Noir by Chandos Herald*, Beihefte zur Zeitschrift für Romanische Philologie, CXLVII, 1975

Uhler 1975
S. Uhler, 'English Customs Ports 1275–1343', unpubl. PhD Thesis, St Andrews University, 1975

Ullmann 1961
W. Ullmann (ed.), *Liber Regie Capelle*, Henry Bradshaw Society, XCII, 1961

Untracht 1968
O. Untracht, *Enamelling on Metal*, 1968

Unwin 1925, 1938
G. Unwin, *The Gilds and Companies of London*, 2nd edn, 1925; 3rd edn, 1938

Urry 1967
W. G. Urry, *Canterbury under the Angevin Kings*, 1967

VCH, *Berkshire*, 1907
The Victoria History of the Counties of

England: Berkshire, ed. P. H. Ditchfield & W. Page, 4 vols (1906–24), II, 1907

VCH, *Cambridge and the Isle of Ely*, 1938–78
The Victoria History of the Counties of England: Cambridge and the Isle of Ely, ed. L. F. Salzman, R. B. Pugh & C. R. Elrington, 7 vols, 1938–78

VCH, *Coventry*, 1969
The Victoria History of the Counties of England: Warwick, VIII, *City of Coventry and Borough of Warwick*, ed. W. B. Stephens, 1969

VCH, *Hertfordshire*, 1908
The Victoria History of the Counties of England: Hertfordshire, ed. W. Page, II, 1908

VCH, *Lincoln*, 1906
The Victoria History of the Counties of England: Lincoln, ed. W. Page, 1906

VCH, *Northants*, 1906
The Victoria History of the Counties of England: Northamptonshire, II, 1906

VCH, *Oxfordshire*, 1907
The Victoria History of the Counties of England: Oxfordshire, II, ed. W. Page, 1907

VCH, *Yorkshire, East Riding*, 1969
The Victoria History of the Counties of England: Yorkshire, East Riding: the City of Kingston upon Hull, ed. K. J. Allison, 1969

Vaivre 1974
J.-B. de Vaivre, 'Orientations pour l'étude et l'utilisation des armoriaux du moyen âge', *Cahiers d'héraldique*, I, 1974, pp. I–XXXIV

Valdovinos 1984
J. Valdovinos, *Catalogo de la Plateria: Museo Arqueologico*, Madrid, 1984

Vale 1982
J. Vale, *Edward III and Chivalry: Chivalric Society and its context 1270–1350*, 1982

Vallance 1920
W. H. A. Vallance, *Old Crosses and Lychgates*, (1920)

Vallance 1931
W. H. A. Vallance, 'Cobham Collegiate Church', *Archaeologia Cantiana*, XLIII, 1931, pp. 133–60

Vallance 1947
W. H. A. Vallance, *Greater English Church Screens*, 1947

Vallet de Viriville 1866
A. Vallet de Viriville, '. . . Note sur les crayons employés à régler les manuscrits', *Bulletin, Société Impériale des Antiquaires de France*, 1866, pp. 72–7

Van Dijk 1956
S. J. P. Van Dijk, 'An advertisement sheet of an early fourteenth-century writing master at Oxford', *Scriptorium*, X, 1956, pp. 47–64

Van Geersdaele & Goldsworthy 1978
P. C. Van Geersdaele & L. J. Goldsworthy, 'The restoration of wallpainting fragments from St Stephen's Chapel, Westminster', *The Conservator*, II, 1978, pp. 9–12

Varty 1963
E. K. C. Varty, 'Reynard the Fox and the Smithfield Decretals', *J. Warb. Court. Inst.*, XXVI, 1963, pp. 347–54

Varty 1967
E. K. C. Varty, *Reynard the Fox. A Study of the Fox in Medieval English Art*, 1967

Vasari 1966 edn
G. Vasari, *Le Vite' Più Eccellenti Pittori Scultori e Architettori*, ed. R. Beltarini, P. Barocchi, 8 vols, 1966

Vasselot 1941
J. J. Marquet de Vasselot, *Les crosses limousines du XIIIe siècle*, 1941

Vauchez 1981
A. Vauchez, *La Sainteté en Occident aux derniers siècles du Moyen Age*, 1981
Vaughan 1958
R. Vaughan, *Matthew Paris*, 1958
Vaughan 1970
R. Vaughan, *Philip the Good*, 1970
Vaughan 1984
Chronicles of Matthew Paris: Monastic Life in the Thirteenth Century, ed., trans. & intro. R. Vaughan, 1984
Verdier 1980
P. Verdier, *Le Couronnement de la Vièrge. Les Origines et les Premiers Développements d'un Thème Iconographique*, 1980
Verey 1970
D. Verey, *Buildings of England: Gloucestershire, The Vale and Forest of Dean*, 1970
Verster 1954
A. J. G. Verster, *Tin door de Eeuwen*, 1954
Verster 1957
A. J. G. Verster, *Das Buch vom Zinn*, 1957
Vertue 1770
G. Vertue, 'A Dissertation on the Monument of Edward the Confessor . . . 1736', *Archaeologia*, I, 1770, pp. 32–9
Vézin 1982
J. Vézin, 'Une reliure en cuir souple estampé du XIIIe siècle (Paris, Bibliothèque nationale lat. 6637 A)', *Revue Française d'Histoire du Livre*, XXXVI, 1982, pp. 243–9
Victoria and Albert Museum 1883
Inventory of Reproductions in metal . . . Electrotypes made . . . for the use of the South Kensington Museum, 1883
Victoria and Albert Museum 1912–39
Victoria and Albert Museum, Review of the Principal Acquisitions during the years 1911–38, 1912–39
Victoria and Albert Museum 1938
London, Victoria and Albert Museum, *Review of the Principal Acquisitions during the year 1937*, 1938
Victoria and Albert Museum 1960
British Pewter, Victoria and Albert Museum Small Picture Book, LIV, 1960
Victoria and Albert Museum 1978
Victoria and Albert Museum Catalogue: French silver, ed. R. Lightbown, 1978
Victoria and Albert Museum 1986a
London, Victoria and Albert Museum, *The Medieval Treasury. The Art of the Middle Ages in the Victoria and Albert Museum*, ed. P. Williamson, 1986
Victoria and Albert Museum 1986b
Victoria and Albert Museum Album, V, 1986
Vidler 1933
L. Vidler, 'Medieval Pottery and Kilns found at Rye', *Sussex Archaeol. Coll.*, LXXIV, 1933, pp. 45–64
Vila-Grau 1985
J. Vila-Grau, 'El Vitrall Gòtic a Catalunya Descoberta de la taula de vitraller de Girona', *Reial Acadèmia Catalana de Belles Arts de Sant Jordi*, 1985
Vince 1985
A. G. Vince, 'Saxon and medieval pottery in London: a review', *Medieval Archaeology*, XXIX, 1985, pp. 25–93
Viollet-le-Duc 1854–68
E. E. Viollet-le-Duc, *Dictionnaire raisonné de l' Architecture française*, 10 vols, 1854–68
Viollet-le-Duc 1871
E. E. Viollet-le-Duc, *Dictionnaire Raisonné du mobilier français* (6 vols, 1858–75), II, 1871

Wagner 1950
A. R. Wagner (ed.), *Aspilogia I: A Catalogue of English Mediaeval Rolls of Arms*, Harleian Society, c. 1950
Wagner 1956
A. R. Wagner, *Heralds and Heraldry in the Middle Ages*, 2nd edn, 1956
Wagner 1967
A. R. Wagner, *Heralds of England. A History of the Office and College of Arms*, 1967
Wagner 1978
A. R. Wagner, *Heralds and Ancestors*, 1978
Wagner & Mann 1939
A. R. Wagner & J. G. Mann, 'A Fifteenth-century description of the brass of Sir Hugh Hastings at Elsing, Norfolk', *Antiq. J.*, XIX, 1939, pp. 421–8
Walford 1856
W. S. Walford, 'Some remarks on a casket at Goodrich Court', *Archaeol. J.*, XIII, 1856, pp. 134–8
Walker 1890
J. W. Walker, *St Mary's Chapel on Wakefield Bridge*, 1890
Wall 1905
J. C. Wall, *Shrines of British Saints*, 1905
Waller 1877
J. G. Waller, 'The Lords of Cobham, their monuments and the church', *Archaeologia Cantiana*, XI, 1877, pp. 49–112
Waller 1975 edn
J. G. & L. A. B. Waller, *A Series of Monumental Brasses from the Thirteenth to the Sixteenth Century* (1842–64), reprint with corrections and additions by J. A. Goodall, 1975
Ward 1963–8
J. C. Ward, 'Sir Robert de Bures', *Trans. Monumental Brass Soc.*, X, 1963–8, pp. 144–50
Ward 1981
F. A. B. Ward, *A Catalogue of European Scientific Instruments in the . . . British Museum*, 1981
Ward Perkins 1940
London Museum Medieval Catalogue, by J. B. Ward Perkins et al., London Museum Catalogues, VII, 1940
Ward Perkins 1941a
J. B. Ward Perkins, 'A late 13th-century tile pavement at Cleeve Abbey', *Proc. Somerset Archaeol. and Nat. Hist. Soc.*, LXXXVII, 1941, pp. 39–55
Ward Perkins 1941b
J. B. Ward Perkins, 'Persistence of Viking types of sword', *Antiq. J.*, XXI, 1941, pp. 158–61
Warner 1912
G. F. Warner, *Queen Mary's Psalter*, 1912
Warner 1928
The Guthlac Roll. Scenes from the Life of St Guthlac by a Twelfth Century Artist, reproduced from Harley Roll Y. 6 in the British Museum, intro. Sir George Warner, Roxburghe Club, 1928
Warner 1978
M. Warner, *Alone of All Her Sex*, 1978
Warner 1985
M. Warner, *Monuments and Maidens. The Allegory of the Female Form*, 1985
Waterer 1968
J. W. Waterer, *Leather Craftsmanship*, 1968
Waterman 1959
D. M. Waterman, 'Late Saxon, Viking, and early medieval finds from York', *Archaeologia*, XCVII, 1959, pp. 59–105
Waterton 1863
E. Waterton, 'On Episcopal Rings', *Archaeol. J.*, XX, 1863, pp. 224–38

Watson 1879–81
C. K. Watson, (Remarks on the Granborough and Canterbury chrismatories exhibited Soc. of Antiq. 16 Dec. 1880), *Proc. Soc. of Antiq. London*, 2nd ser., VIII, 1879–81, pp. 430–2
Watson 1967
A. M. Watson, 'Back to Gold – and silver', *Economic History Review*, 2nd ser., XX, I, 1967, pp. 1–34
Watson 1970
B. Watson, 'The place of the Cuerden Psalter in English illumination', *Gesta*, IX, I, 1970, pp. 34–41
Watson 1984
A. G. Watson, *Catalogue of Dated and Datable Manuscripts c.435–1600 in Oxford Libraries*, 1984
Watts 1920
W. W. Watts, *Victoria & Albert Museum: Catalogue of English Silversmiths' Work Civil and Domestic*, 1920
Watts 1924
W. W. Watts, *Catalogue of Pastoral Staves*, Victoria and Albert Museum, 1924
Way 1845a
A. Way, 'Decorative processes connected with the arts during the Middle Ages: Enamel', *Archaeol. J.*, II, 1845, pp. 155–72
Way 1845b
A. Way, 'Notices of ancient ornaments, vestments and appliances of sacred use . . . the pax', *Archaeol. J.*, II, 1845, pp. 145–51
Way 1845c
A. Way, (Drawings of jewelled ornaments and mitre at New College, Oxford, exhibited Archaeol. Instit., 28 May 1845), *Archaeol. J.*, II, 1845, pp. 205–7
Way 1846
A. Way, 'Ancient chess-men, with some remarks on their value as illustrations of medieval costume', *Archaeol. J.*, III, 1846, pp. 239–45
Way 1850
A. Way, 'Notices of foreign sepulchral brasses', *Archaeol. J.*, VII, 1850, pp. 283–91
Webb 1965
G. Webb, *Architecture in Britain: the Middle Ages*, 2nd edn, 1965
Webster 1938
J. C. Webster, *The Labors of the Months in Antique and Medieval Art*, 1938
Webster & Dunning 1960
G. Webster & G. C. Dunning, 'A medieval pottery kiln at Audlern, Cheshire', *Medieval Archaeology*, IV, 1960, pp. 109–25
Wedgwood 1977
A. Wedgwood, *Catalogue of the Drawings Collection of the RIBA: The Pugin Family*, 1977
Wedgwood 1985
A. Wedgwood, *Catalogue of Architectural Drawings in the Victoria and Albert Museum: A. W. N. Pugin and the Pugin Family*, 1985
Weever 1631
J. Weever, *Ancient Funerall Monuments*, 1631
Wellbeloved 1829
C. Wellbeloved, *Account of the Ancient and Present State of the Abbey of St Mary, York, and the Discoveries made in the Recent Excavation*, 1829
Wellbeloved 1858, 1891
C. Wellbeloved, *A Descriptive Account of the Antiquities in the Grounds and*

Museum of the Yorkshire Philosophical Society, 3rd edn, 1858; 8th edn, 1891
Wells 1966
W. Wells, 'The Richard de Bury Chest', *Scottish Art Review*, 196, X, 4, 1966, pp. 14–18, 31–2
Welter 1914 edn
J. H. Welter (ed.), *Le Speculum Laicorum. Edition d'une collection d'exempla composée en Angleterre à la fin du XIII siècle. Thesaurus Exemplorum*, V, 1914
Weoley Castle 1965
A Guide to Weoley Castle, Birmingham, 1965
Westlake 1882
N. H. J. Westlake, *A History of Design in Painted Glass*, II, 1882
Westlake 1919
H. F. Westlake, *The Parish Gilds of Medieval England*, 1919
Westwood 1876
J. O. Westwood, *A descriptive Catalogue of the Fictile Ivories in the South Kensington Museum*, 1876
Whalley 1791
P. Whalley, *The History and Antiquities of Northamptonshire*, 1791
Wharton 1691
H. Wharton, *Anglia Sacra*, 2 pts, 1691
Whewell 1835
W. Whewell, *Architectural Notes on German Churches. A New Edition* [with] *. . . Notes written . . . in Picardy and Normandy*, 1835
White 1896
G. White (ed.), *The Cathedral Church of Canterbury*, 1896
White & Lea 1959
G. H. White & R. S. Lea (eds), *The Complete Peerage*, XII, 2, 1959
Whiting 1982
R. Whiting, 'Abominable images: image and image-breaking under Henry VIII', *J. Ecclesiastical History*, XXXIII, 1982, pp. 30–47
Whittingham 1949
A. B. Whittingham, 'The monastic buildings of Norwich Cathedral', *Archaeol. J.*, CVI, 1949, pp. 86–7
Whittingham 1970
S. Whittingham, *A Thirteenth-Century Portrait Gallery at Salisbury Cathedral*, 1970
Whittingham 1971
S. Whittingham, 'The chronology of the portraits of Richard II', *Burl. Mag.*, CXIII, 1971, pp. 12–21
Whittingham, Rouse & Baker 1980
A. B. Whittingham, C. Rouse & A. Baker, 'Horsham St Faith's priory', *Archaeol. J.*, CXXXVII, 1980, pp. 323–6
Wichmann 1960
H. & S. Wichmann, *Schach. Ursprung und Wandlung der Spielfigur in zwölf Jahrhunderten*, 1960 (English edn, *Chess*, 1964)
Wichstrom 1981
A. Wichstrom, 'Maleriet i høymiddelalderen', in *Norges kunsthistorie*, II, 1981, pp. 252–314
Wildridge 1899
T. Wildridge, *The Grotesque in Church Art*, 1899
Wilkins 1737
D. Wilkins, *Concilia Magnae Britanniae et Hiberniae*, 4 vols, 1737
Wilkins 1808
W. Wilkins jr, 'An account of the Prior's Chapel at Ely', *Archaeologia*, XIV, 1808, pp. 105–12
William of Malmesbury 1870 edn
William of Malmesbury, *De Gestis Pontificum Anglorum libri quinque*, ed.

W.E.S.A.Hamilton, Rolls series, LII, 1870

William of Malmesbury 1887 edn
Willelmi Malmesburiensis Monachi, De Gestis Regum Anglorum, ed. W.Stubbs, 2 vols. Rolls series, XC,(1887, 1889)

Williams 1963
G.A.Williams, *Medieval London. From Commerce to Capital*, 1963

Williams 1967
C.H.Williams (ed.), *English Historical Documents*, V, (1485–1558), 1967

Williams 1977
F.Williams, *Pleshey Castle, Essex (XII–XVI Century): Excavations in the Bailey, 1959–1963*, British Archaeological Reports, XLII, 1977

Williams 1979
J.H.Williams, *St Peter's Street, Northampton. Excavations 1973–1976*, 1979

Williams 1984
M.E.Williams, *Civic Treasures of Bristol*, 1984

Williamson 1982
P.Williamson, *An Introduction to Medieval Ivory Carvings*, 1982

Williamson 1986
P.Williamson (ed.), *The Medieval Treasury. The Art of the Middle Ages in the Victoria and Albert Museum*, Victoria and Albert Museum, 1986

Williamson 1987
P.Williamson, *The Thyssen-Bornemisza Collection: Medieval Sculpture and Works of Art*, 1987

Williamson (forthcoming)
P.Williamson, *Northern Gothic Sculpture 1200–1400*, Victoria and Albert Museum (forthcoming)

Willis 1845
R.Willis, *Architectural History of Canterbury Cathedral*, 1845

Willis 1846
R.Willis, 'On the great seals of England, especially those of Edward III', *Archaeol. J.*, II, 1846, pp. 14–41

Willis 1863
R.Willis, 'The architectural history of the cathedral and monastery at Worcester', *Archaeol. J.*, XX, 1863, pp. 83–132, 254–72, 301–18

Wilson 1943
R.M.Wilson, 'English and French in England 1100–1300', *History*, n.s., XXVIII, 1943, pp. 37–60

Wilson 1977
C.Wilson, *The Shrines of St William of York*, 1977

Wilson 1980a
C.Wilson, 'The Origins of the Perpendicular Style and its Development to circa 1360', unpubl. PhD Thesis, Univ. of London, 1980

Wilson 1980b
C.Wilson, 'The Neville Screen', *Brit. Archaeol. Assoc. Conf.*, III, 1977, 1980, pp.90–104

Wilson 1980–1
T.Wilson, 'Bishop Fox's Crozier', *Corpus Christi College 1980–1 Annual Report and The Pelican*, 1981, pp. 9–27

Wilson 1981
C.Wilson, review of Leedy 1980, *J. Brit. Archaeol. Assoc.*, 3rd ser., CXXXIV, 1981, pp. 137–9

Wilson, Tudor-Craig, Physick & Gem 1986
C.Wilson, P.Tudor-Craig, J.Physick & R.Gem, *Westminster Abbey*, New Bell's Cathedral Guides, 1986

Winston 1847
C.Winston, *An Enquiry into the Differences of Style Observable in Ancient Glass Painting*, 1847

Winston 1849
C.Winston, in *Architectural Notices of the Churches of the Archdeaconry of Northampton*, 1849, pp. 218–28

Winston 1865
C.Winston, *Memoirs Illustrative of the Art of Glass Painting*, 1865

Winston & Walford 1860
C.Winston & W.S.Walford, 'On an heraldic window in the north aisle of the nave of York Cathedral', *Archaeol. J.*, XVII, 1860, pp. 22–34, 132–48

Withers 1896
H.Withers (ed.), *The Cathedral Church of Canterbury*, 1896

Wixom 1980
W.D.Wixom, in *Notable Acquisitions 1979–80*, Metropolitan Museum of Art, New York, 1980

Wolfgang 1911
A.Wolfgang, 'Misericords in Lancashire and Cheshire Churches', *Trans. Lancs. and Cheshire Hist. Soc.*, LXIII, 1911, pp. 79–87

Wolpe 1965
B.Wolpe, 'Florilegium Alphabeticum' in *Calligraphy & Palaeography: Essays presented by Alfred Fairbank*, ed. A.Osley, 1965

Wood 1786
A.à Wood, *The History and Antiquities of the Colleges and Halls of the University of Oxford*, 3 vols, 1786

Wood 1890
A.Wood, *Survey of the Antiquities of the City of Oxford*, II, Oxford Historical Society, XVII, 1890

Wood 1941
G.B.Wood, 'The bridge chapel at Wakefield and its restoration', *Country Life*, LXXXIX, 1941, p. 39

Wood 1956
A.C.Wood (trans. and ed.) *Registrum Simonis Langham*, Canterbury & York Society, LIII, 1956

Wood 1965
M.Wood, *The English Mediaeval House*, 1965

Woodfield 1981
C.Woodfield, 'Finds from the Free Grammar School at the Whitefriars, Coventry, c.1545–c.1557/8. With special reports by J.M.Holmes and S.E.Rigold', *Post-Medieval Archaeology*, XV, 1981, pp. 81–159

Woodforde 1933
C.Woodforde, 'Ancient glass in Lincolnshire I – Haydor', *Lincolnshire Mag.*, I, 3, 1933, pp. 93–7

Woodforde 1935–7
C.Woodforde, 'Glass-painters in England before the Reformation', *J. Brit. Soc. Master Glass Painters*, VI, 1935–7, pp. 62–9, 121–8

Woodforde 1946
C.Woodforde, *Stained Glass in Somerset 1250–1830*, 1946

Woodforde 1951
C.Woodforde, *The Stained Glass of New College, Oxford*, 1951

Woodforde 1954
C.Woodforde, *English Stained and Painted Glass*, 1954

Woodman 1981
F.Woodman, *The Architectural History of Canterbury Cathedral*, 1981

Woodman 1984
F.Woodman, 'The vault of the Ely Lady chapel: fourteenth or fifteenth century?', *Gesta*, XXIII, 2, 1984, pp. 137–44

Woodruff & Danks 1912
C.E.Woodruff & W.Danks, *Memorials of Canterbury Cathedral*, 1912

Woolley 1924
E.Woolley, 'Some Nottinghamshire and Lincolnshire Easter Sepulchres', *Trans. Thoroton Soc.*, XXVIII, 1924, pp. 67–72

Wordsworth 1901
C.Wordsworth, *Ceremonies and Processions of the Cathedral Church of Salisbury*, 1901

Wordsworth & Macleane 1915
C.Wordsworth & D.Macleane, *Statutes and Customs of the Cathedral Church of the Blessed Virgin Mary, Salisbury*, 1915

Wormald 1942–3
F.Wormald, 'More Matthew Paris drawings', *Walpole Society*, XXXI (1942–3), 1946, pp. 109–12

Wormald 1943
F.Wormald, 'The Fitzwarin Psalter and its allies', *J. Warb. Court. Inst.*, VI, 1943, pp. 71–9

Wormald 1949
F.Wormald, 'Paintings in Westminster Abbey and contemporary paintings', *Proc. Brit. Acad.*, XXXV, 1949, pp. 161–76

Wormald 1954
F.Wormald, 'The Wilton Diptych', *J. Warb. Court. Inst.*, XVII, 1954, pp. 191–203

Wormald 1960
F.Wormald, 'A Note on the Glazier Psalter', *J. Warb. Court. Inst.*, XXIII, 1960, pp. 307–8

Wormald 1961
F.Wormald, 'The Throne of Solomon and St Edward's Chair', in *De Artibus Opuscula; essays in honour of Erwin Panofsky*, ed. M.Meiss, 1961, pp. 532–9

Wormald 1968
F.Wormald, 'Some Pictures of the Mass in an English XIVth-Century Manuscript', *Walpole Society*, XLI (1966–8), 1968, pp. 39–45

Wormald & Giles 1982
F.Wormald & P.M.Giles, *A Descriptive Catalogue of the Additional Illuminated Manuscripts in the Fitzwilliam Museum*, 2 vols, 1982

Worshipful Company of Pewterers 1968
Catalogue of Pewterware, Worshipful Company of Pewterers of London, 1968

Worshipful Company of Pewterers 1979
Supplementary Catalogue of Pewterware, The Worshipful Company of Pewterers of London, 1979

Wren 1750
S.Wren (ed.), *Parentalia: or, Memoirs of the Family of the Wrens*, 1750 (repr. 1965)

Wright 1844
T.Wright, *Early Mysteries and other Latin Poems of the 12th and 13th centuries*, 1844

Wright 1865 (1968)
T.Wright, *A History of Caricature and Grotesque in Literature and Art*, 1865 (ed. F.K.Barasch, 1968)

Wright 1887
W.A.Wright (ed.), *The Metrical Chronicle of Robert of Gloucester*, Rolls series, LXXXVI, 1887

Wright 1960
C.E.Wright, *English Vernacular Hands from the 12th to the 15th centuries*, 1960

Wright 1973
C.E.Wright, *English Heraldic Manuscripts in the British Museum*, 1973

Wylson 1845
J.Wylson, 'York Minster; its fires and restorations', *The Builder*, III, 1845, pp. 158–9, 175–7

Wyon 1883
A.B.Wyon, 'On the Great Seals of Henry IV, Henry V, and Henry VI', *J. Brit. Archaeol. Assoc.*, XXXIX, 1883, pp. 139–67

Wyon 1887
A.B. & A.Wyon, *The Great Seals of England*, 1887

Yapp 1978
W.B.Yapp, 'The birds and other animals of Longthorpe Tower', *Antiq. J.*, LVIII, 1978, pp. 355–8

Yapp 1981
W.B.Yapp, *Birds in Medieval Manuscripts*, 1981

Yapp 1983
W.B.Yapp, 'Birds in some medieval manuscripts in Aberdeen', *Aberdeen University Review*, CLXX, 1983, pp. 134–9

Yates 1974
W.N.Yates, 'The authorship of the Hereford Mappa Mundi and the career of Richard de Bello', *Trans. Woolhope Naturalists' Field Club*, XLI, 1974, pp. 165–72

Yorks. Phil. Soc. 1858
A Descriptive Account of the Antiquities in the Grounds and in the Museum of the Yorkshire Philosophical Society, 1858

Young 1947
N.D.Young, *Richard of Cornwall*, 1947

Young 1977
P.A.Young, 'The origin of the Herlufsholm ivory crucifix figure', *Burl. Mag.*, CXIX, 1977, pp. 12–19

Zakin 1979
H.J.Zakin, *French Cistercian Grisaille Glass*, 1979

Zettler, Enzler & Stockbauer 1876
F.X.Zettler, L.Enzler & J.Stockbauer, *Ansgewählte Kunstwerke aus dem Schatze der Reichen Capelle in der Königlichen Residenz zu München*, 1876

Zupko 1985
R.E.Zupko, *Dictionary of Weights and Measures for the British Isles*, 1985

Exhibition catalogues

Amsterdam 1979
Amsterdam, Museum Willet Holthuysen, *Keur van tin uit de havensteden Amsterdam*, Antwerpen en Rotterdam, 1979

Baltimore 1949
Baltimore, Walters Art Gallery, *Illuminated Books of the Middle Ages and Renaissance*, 1949

Birmingham 1948
Birmingham, City Museum and Art Gallery, *Church Plate from the Midlands*, 1948

Bristol 1938
Bristol, *Guide to the Church Congress and Exhibition*, 1938

Brunswick 1985
Braunschweig, Landesmuseum, *Stadt im Wandel. Kunst und Kultur des*

Bürgertums in Norddeutschland,
1150–1650, ed. C.Meckseper, 4 vols,
1985
Brussels 1967
Brussels, Musées royaux d'Art et
d'Histoire, *Exposition de Sculptures*
anglaises et malinoises d'Albâtre,
catalogue by G.Derveaux-Van Ussel,
1967
Brussels 1973
Brussels, Bibliothèque royale Albert Ier,
English Illuminated Manuscripts
700–1500, catalogue by J.J.G.Alex-
ander & C.M.Kauffmann, 1973

Cambridge 1896
Cambridge, Fitzwilliam Museum, *An*
Illustrated Catalogue of the Collection of
Plate exhibited in the Fitzwilliam 1895,
by J.E.Foster & T.D.Atkinson, 1896
Cambridge 1966
Cambridge, Fitzwilliam Museum,
Illuminated Manuscripts in the
Fitzwilliam Museum, 1966
Cambridge 1975
Cambridge, Fitzwilliam Museum,
Cambridge Plate, 1975
Cambridge 1984
Cambridge, Fitzwilliam Museum, *The*
Ingenious Mr Essex, Architect; a
Bicentenary Exhibition, 1984
Cambridge, Mass., 1975
Cambridge, Mass., Busch-Reisinger
Museum, *Eucharistic Vessels of the*
Middle Ages, 1975
Cardiff, 1981
Cardiff, National Museum of Wales, *The*
Strange Genius of William Burges, 'Art-
Architect', 1827–1881, 1981
Chicago 1970
Chicago, Loyola University, Martin
D'Arcy Gallery of Art, *Enamels XII to XVI*
Century, 1970
Cleveland 1967
Cleveland, Museum of Art, *Treasures*
from Medieval France, catalogue by
W.D.Wixom, 1967
Cologne 1972
Cologne, Kunsthalle, *Rhein und Maas:*
Kunst und Kultur, 800–1400, 1972
Cologne 1978
Cologne, Kunsthalle, *Die Parler und der*
schöne Stil: 1350–1400, 3 vols, 1978

Detroit 1928
Detroit, Institute of Arts, *Catalogue of a*
Loan Exhibition of French Gothic Art,
1928
Dublin 1895–6
Dublin, *Irish State and Civic Maces,*
Swords and other insignia of office . . .
1895–6, 1898

Edinburgh 1856
Edinburgh, Archaeological Institute
Museum, *Catalogue of Antiquities, Works*
of Art and Historical Scottish Relics
exhibited in the Museum of the
Archaeological Institute of Great Britain
and Ireland . . . Edinburgh, July 1856, ed.
A.Way, 1859

Glasgow 1977
Great Britain, Arts Council: Glasgow,
The Burrell Collection, 1977

Leeds 1868
Leeds, *National Exhibition of Works of Art*
at Leeds, 1868. Official Catalogue, 1869
Lincoln 1850
Lincoln, Archaeological Institute,
Memoirs illustrative of the History and
Antiquities of the County and City of

Lincoln, 1850
London 1850
London, Royal Society of Arts, *Catalogue*
of Antient and Medieval Art, 1850
London 1861
London, Ironmongers' Hall, *A Catalogue*
of the Antiquities and Works of Art
exhibited . . . May, 1861, 2 vols, 1869
London 1862 (1863)
London, South Kensington Museum,
Catalogue of the Special Exhibition of
Works of Art of the Medieval, Renaissance,
and More Recent Periods . . . June 1862,
revised edn, 1863
London 1872
London, South Kensington Museum, *A*
Loan Exhibition of Jewellery at South
Kensington, ed. R.H.Sodem Smith
London 1874
London, South Kensington Museum,
Catalogue of Special Loan Exhibition of
Enamels on Metal, 1874
London 1880
London, Royal Archaeological Institute,
Ancient Helmets and Examples of Mail.
A Catalogue of the Objects exhibited . . . .
June 3rd–16th, 1880, ed. Baron de
Cosson & W.Burges, reprinted from
Archaeol. J., 1881
London 1897
London, Burlington Fine Arts Club,
Catalogue of a Collection of European
Enamels, 1897
London 1901
London, Burlington Fine Arts Club, *A*
Collection of Silversmiths' Work of
European Origin, 1901
London 1908
London, Burlington Fine Arts Club,
Exhibition of Illuminated Manuscripts,
1908
London 1910
London, Society of Antiquaries,
Illustrated Catalogue of the Exhibition of
English Medieval Alabaster Work held in
. . . 1910, 1913
London 1923
London, Burlington Fine Arts Club,
Catalogue of an exhibition of Carvings in
Ivory, 1923
London 1923
London, Royal Academy of Arts,
Exhibition of British Primitive Paintings,
1923
London 1930
London, Victoria and Albert Museum,
Exhibition of English Medieval Art,
c. 700–1500, 2 vols, 1930
London 1934
London, Royal Academy of Arts,
Exhibition of British Art c. 1000–1860,
1934
London 1936
London, Burlington Fine Arts Club,
Catalogue of an Exhibition of Gothic Art in
Europe (c. 1200–c. 1500), 1936
London 1939
London, Burlington Fine Arts Club,
Catalogue of an Exhibition of British
Medieval Art, 1939
London 1945
London, Victoria and Albert Museum,
The Royal Effigies, Sculpture & other
Works of Art from Westminster Abbey,
1945
London 1951
London, Goldsmiths' Hall, *Catalogue of*
the Exhibition of the Historic Plate of the
City of London, 1951
London 1952
London. Goldsmiths' Hall, *Corporation*
Plate of England and Wales: Catalogue of
the Exhibits, 1952

London 1953
London, Goldsmiths' Hall, *Treasures of*
Oxford, 1953
London 1955
London, Christie's, *Catalogue of Silver*
Treasures from English Churches: an
Exhibition of Ecclesiastical Plate of
Domestic Origin, 1955
London 1956
London, Victoria and Albert Museum,
Exhibition of Medieval Paintings from
Norwich St. Michael at Plea, catalogue by
P.Tudor-Craig, 1956
London 1957
London, Goldsmiths' Hall, *Treasures of*
Cambridge, 1957
London 1963
Great Britain, Arts Council: London,
Victoria and Albert Museum, *Opus*
Anglicanum: English Medieval
Embroidery, 1963
London 1964
London, Council for British
Archaeology Medieval Research
Committee, *Exhibition of Medieval*
Pottery, 1964
London 1972
London, Museum of London, *Chaucer's*
London, 1972
London 1974
London, Royal Academy of Arts, *Turner*
1775–1851, Tate Gallery, 1974
London 1975
Great Britain, Arts Council: London,
Hayward Gallery, *Treasures from the*
Burrell Collection, 1975
London 1976
London, British Museum, *Jewellery*
through 7,000 years, 1976
London 1978a
London, British Museum, *British*
Heraldry from its origins to c. 1800,
catalogue by R.Marks & A.Payne,
1978
London 1978b
London, Tate Gallery, *William Blake,*
1978
London 1978c
London, Goldsmiths' Hall, *Touching Gold*
and Silver: 500 years of Hallmarks, 1978
London 1980
London, British Library, *The Benedictines*
in Britain, 1980
London 1981a
London, Victoria and Albert Museum,
Splendours of the Gonzaga, 1981
London 1981b
London, Royal Institution of Chartered
Surveyors, *Royal Westminster:*
Centenary Exhibition, 1981
London 1981c
London, British Museum, *Medieval*
Enamels: Masterpieces from the Keir
Collection, exhibition catalogue by
M.M.Gauthier, 1981
London 1984a
Great Britain, Arts Council: London,
Hayward Gallery, *English Romanesque*
Art 1066–1200, 1984
London 1984b
London, British Museum, *The Golden*
Age of Anglo-Saxon Art 966–1066,
1984

Manchester 1867
Manchester, Art Treasures Exhibition,
Catalogue of the Art Treasures of the
United Kingdom, 1857
Manchester 1959
Manchester, City Art Gallery,
Romanesque Art c. 1050–1200 from
Collections in Great Britain and Eire,
catalogue by C.M.Kauffmann, 1959

Manchester 1976
Manchester, Whitworth Art Gallery,
Medieval and Early Renaissance Treasures
in the North-west, ed. J.J.G.Alexander &
B.P.Crossley, 1976
Munich 1980
Munich, Residenz, *Wittelsbach und*
Bayern, 1980

New York 1970
New York, Metropolitan Museum of
Art, *The Year 1200: I, The Exhibition,* ed.
K.Hoffman; II, *A Background Survey,* ed.
F.Deuchler, 1970
Norwich 1973
Norwich, Castle Museum, *Medieval Art*
in East Anglia 1300–1520, eds P.Lasko
and N.J.Morgan, 1973
Norwich 1983
Norwich, University of East Anglia:
Sainsbury Centre for the Visual Arts,
Treasures from Norfolk Churches, 1983

Oslo 1972
Oslo, Universitets Oldsaksamling, *Norge*
872–1972: Medieval Art Abroad, 1972
Ottawa 1972
Ottawa, National Gallery of Canada, *Art*
and the Courts, France and England from
1259 to 1328, I, Exhibition guide; II,
Essays and Catalogue, 1972
Oxford 1980
Oxford, Bodleian Library, *The*
Benedictines and the Book, 1980
Oxford 1984
Oxford, Bodleian Library, *The Douce*
Legacy, 1984

Paris 1968
Paris, Musée du Louvre, 12th Council of
Europe Exhibition, *L'Europe Gothique*
XIIe–XIVe Siècles, 1968
Paris 1970–1
Paris, Salle des Gens d'Armes du Palais,
La France de Saint Louis, 1970–1
Paris 1979
Paris, Hôtel de Sully, *Le Gothique*
retrouvé avant Viollet-le-Duc, 1979
Paris 1981–2
Paris, Galeries nationales du Grand
Palais, *Les Fastes du Gothique: le siècle de*
Charles V, 1981–2

Rome 1954
Rome, Palazzo di Venezia, *Mostra*
Storica Nazionale della Miniatura, 1954

St Albans 1905
St Albans, Town Hall, *English Church*
History Exhibition, 1905
Sienna 1982
Sienna, Palazzo Pubblico, *Il Gotico a*
Sienna, 1982
Stuttgart 1977–9
Stuttgart, Württembergisches
Landesmuseum, *Die Zeit der Staufer,*
Geschichte-Kunst-Kultur, catalogue pts
I–IV, 1977; V, 1979

Vienna 1962
8th Council of Europe Exhibition,
Europäische Kunst um 1400 (L'art
Européen vers 1400), Kunsthistorisches
Museum, Vienna, 1962

York 1954
York, Festival Exhibition, City Art
Gallery, *English Medieval Alabaster*
Carvings, 1954
York 1972
York, City Art Gallery & Minster
Library, *The Beautifullest Church, York*
Minster 1472–1972, 1972

Index

Royal Academy Trust

Friends of the Royal Academy